Modernization Science

Chuanqi He

Modernization Science

The Principles and Methods of National Advancement

Springer

Chuanqi He
China Center for Modernization Research
Chinese Academy of Sciences
Room 726, No.33
Beisihuanxilu, Zhongguancun
Beijing 100190
P.R. China

MSC 2010: 91- 01, 91F10, 91D10, 91B76 , 91B44

ISBN 978-3-642-25458-1 e-ISBN 978-3-642-25459-8
DOI 10.1007/978-3-642-25459-8
Springer Heidelberg Dordrecht London New York

Library of Congress Control Number: 2012932063

Printed on acid-free paper

Springer is part of Springer Science+Business Media (www.springer.com)

Preface

From the perspective of the world frontier of human development, some scholars hold that human beings originated in Africa, initiated agricultural civilization in Asia and industrial civilization in Europe, and fostered knowledge civilization in America approximately. In its about 5,500 years of history, the center and frontier of human civilization has been moving, with different performance in different countries and nations. There is universality as well as diversity in the changes of national and human civilization.

Modernization, a worldwide phenomenon since about eighteenth century, refers to the frontier changes and international competition of human civilization generally. It is the frontier process of the formation, development, transformation, and international interaction of modern civilization; the composite process of the innovation, selection, diffusion, and withdrawal of civilization elements in an alternating way; and also the process of international competition for catching up with, reaching, and maintaining the world's advanced level as well as international differentiation. Countries that reached and maintained the world's advanced level are advanced ones, while the rest are developing ones. A country may change from a developing one to an advanced one, or vice versa. There is a certain probability that the international status of a country changes in some term.

In the eighteenth century, the Industrial Revolution took placed, and modernization began when British political economist Adam Smith finished his magnum opus *An Inquiry into the Nature and Causes of the Wealth of Nations* (1776). According to the book, the annual supply of a nation depends on two circumstances: the productivity of labor and the proportion between the number of those who are employed in useful labor and that of those who are not so employed.

The nineteenth century saw the expansion of the Industrial Revolution and the diffusion of modernization. In this century, British political economist David Ricardo (1817) put forward that "possessing utility, commodities derive their exchangeable value from two sources: from their scarcity and from the quantity of labor required to obtain them." German philosopher Carl Marx (1867) argued that "a country should and can learn from other countries" and "what industrially developed countries show to industrially undeveloped countries is just the future of the latter."

The twentieth century witnessed the outbreak of the information and knowledge revolution as well as the transition of modernization. In this century, Austrian economist Joseph Schumpeter (1912) proposed his "innovation theory" where innovation of businesses is used to explain economic development; American scholars came up with the classical modernization theory, which explains the shift from a traditional agricultural to a modern industrial society in 1950s to 1960s. Around the 1960s, advanced countries finished their classical modernization. Since the 1970s, information and ecological revolutions have swept across the globe, modernization studies have been enriched again gradually, and advanced countries have started the historical transition from industrial to knowledge society, from industrial to knowledge economy, from material to ecological culture, etc.

Over the past 300 years, human civilization has undergone revolutionary changes. An outstanding change in the international system is international differentiation and national stratification. According to the research by economist Angus Maddison (2001), the ratio of average GDP (PPP) per capita of Western European countries to that of African countries was about 2.6 in 1700, about 2.9 in 1820, about 5.9 in 1913, and up to 13.1 in 1998. Ever since the beginning of the nineteenth century, international differentiation has accelerated. Countries are divided into advanced and developing ones, and developing countries are divided into moderately developed, preliminarily developed, and underdeveloped ones.

In the twenty-first century, modernization, international competition, and differentiation will go on.

The second modernization theory holds that the national advancement is an objective phenomenon and the result of national modernization, international competition, and differentiation. Generally, the national level in the world is in direct proportion to its percentage of innovation value, effective and efficient labor, effective investment and advanced assets, advanced technology, as well as capital and skills per capita.

The modernization science is an interdisciplinary one which deals with modernization phenomena. It has two basic tasks: (1) describing and explaining the frontier changes and international competition of modern civilizations and (2) explaining and providing principles and methods on national advance. As the first monograph on modernization science in English language, this book includes three parts with eight chapters: the basic concepts and research methods; the general theories and brief histories of the modernization; the stage-specific, level-specific, field-specific, and sector-specific modernization; as well as modernization policies.

There were a lot of excellent scholars in the last 50 years who had made the remarkable contributions to the modernization studies, such as Talcott Parsons, Daniel Lerner, Walt W. Rostow, Cyril E. Black, Samuel Huntington, and Alex Inkeless, etc., to the *classical modernization theory*; Andre G. Frank, etc., to the *dependence theory*; Immanuel Wallerstein, etc., to the *world system theory*; Daniel Bell, Jean-Francois Lyotard, Ronald Inglehart, and Stephen Crook, etc., to the *postmodernization theory*; Joseph Huber, Martin Janicke, and Arthur P. J. Mol, etc., to *ecological modernization theory*; Ulrich Beck, Anthony Giddens, and Scott Lash, etc., to the *reflexive modernization theory*; Edward A. Tiryakian and Wolfgang Zapf to the *new or continual modernization theory*; David Herd, etc., to the *globalization theory*; Shmuel N. Eisenstadt, etc., to the *multiple modernities theory*; and Chuanqi He, etc., to the *second modernization theory* and *integrated modernization theory*.

In the People's Republic of China, eight monographs on the *second modernization* since 1999 and more than 12 books on the *China Modernization Report* since 2001 have been published. I am grateful to the experts who have provided valuable comments to above work, including Ioan Bolovan (Romania), Geoffrey Hodgson (UK), Joseph Huber (Germany), Andras Inotai (Hungary), Nikolay Lapin (Russia), Alberto Martinelli (Italy), Arthur Mol (Netherlands), Witold Morawski (Poland), Edward A. Tiryakian (USA), Hellmut Wollmann (Germany), etc.

So many people have contributed to the successful completion of this book in China. I extend my heartfelt thanks to the Peking University Press for its support on the *China Modernization Reports* since 2001, which provides the most positive studies in the different fields on the modernization science; special thanks to the Science Press for its support on the Chinese edition of *Modernization Science* (He 2010a), which is the member of *Second Modernization* series and provides the important thoughts and strong foundation to this book, and to my colleagues at the China Center for Modernization Research and the Research Group for China Modernization Strategies, Chinese Academy of Sciences, and to all the friends and scholars who have given great attention and support to the publishing of the *Second Modernization* and *China Modernization Report* series.

I wish to express my sincere appreciation to the Springer-Verlag GmbH and her editors including Lisa Fan, Leana Li, Esther Otten, Niels Peter Thomas, and Lu Ye for their kindness and help on the publishing of this book.

I would also like to particularly thank my parents Mr. Hanshan He and Ms. Shaozhen Yan and my wife Ms. Feng Zhang.

The modernization science is much more than a new science. It represents a new hope.

P.R. China Chuanqi He

Abstract

Modernization, a worldwide phenomenon since about eighteenth century, is a sort of frontier changes and international competition of human civilization and includes the formation, development, transformation, and international interaction of modern civilization, the innovation, selection, diffusion, and withdrawal of civilization elements, as well as the international competition for catching up with, reaching, and maintaining the world's advanced level and international differentiation. Countries that reached and kept the world's advanced level are advanced ones, while the rest are developing ones. Over the past 300 years, the proportion of advanced countries has been below 20% and that of developing ones has been over 80%. In the past 50 years, the probability that an advanced country descends to a developing one is about 10%, and the probability that a developing country ascends to an advanced one is about 5%.

The modernization science is an interdisciplinary one that deals with modernization phenomena. This book, the first one on the modernization science in English language, interprets the basic concepts, research methods, and general theories and histories of the modernization, stage-specific (first and second) modernization, level-related (world, international, national, regional, organizational, and individual) modernization, field-specific (economic, social, political, cultural, ecological, and human) modernization, sector-relative modernization, modernization evaluation, modernization strategies and policies, and introduces the principles and methods on national advancement.

This interdisciplinary monograph is designed to provide a clear, systematic, and up-to-date knowledge of the theoretical, empirical, analytical, and policy study on the modernization science, and it includes 438 figures and tables, covers 97% of world population, and involves multidisciplines such as the social science, global politics, civilization, history, modernization, and development study.

About the Author

Chuanqi He, research professor, was born in 1962 in Wuhan city, Hubei Province. Graduated from the Department of Biology, Wuhan University, in 1983, he currently serves as director of the China Center for Modernization Research, CAS, and head of the research group for China modernization strategies. He is the author or coauthor of over 20 books on the study of modernization and innovation and over 100 articles in academic journals. He advanced the second modernization theory in 1998 and has headed the completion of the *Second Modernization* series (eight books) since 1999, covering second modernization, national innovation system, modernization of public awareness, modernization of business management, knowledge innovation, distribution according to contribution, Oriental Renaissance (three roads to modernization), and the modernization science. Since 2000, he has taken charge of the research on China modernization strategies and guided the completion of the *China Modernization Report* each year from 2001 to 2011. Contents of such reports include modernization theories, world, international, national, regional, economic, social, cultural, and ecological modernization, as well as modernization evaluation. In 2002, he established the China Center for Modernization Research, CAS, and has since served as the director of the center.

Contents

List of Figures

List of Tables

List of Examples

Introduction 1

Human fingers differ in their length (Chinese proverb), while countries differ in their level. According to national level of income, development, and modernization, all countries in the world can be categorized into advanced and developing ones generally (Example 1.1). Studies on why advanced ones get advanced, how they maintain their level, and how developing ones enter into the advanced club are interdisciplinary and fall into the scope of the modernization science or modernizations. This chapter briefly introduces the definition and nature of the modernization science and its methodology in general sense.

Example 1.1 Grouping of Countries
Countries can be categorized in different ways and compared no matter how they are classified. The World Bank divided countries into three groups according to the national income per capita, namely, high-income, middle-income, and low income countries (World Bank 2008); the United Nations Development Program (UNDP) categorizes countries into three groups with high, middle, and low human development indexes, respectively (UNDP 2009); the United Nations Statistics Division classifies countries into more-developed and less-developed countries, or developed and developing countries, for the statistical purpose (UN 2008). *China Modernization Report* divided countries into advanced and developing countries based on their second modernization indexes. Developing countries are further divided into moderately developed, preliminarily developed, and underdeveloped ones (RGCMS 2008). Advanced countries are not advanced in all aspects, and developing counties may take the lead in some fields.

(continued)

C. He, *Modernization Science*,
DOI 10.1007/978-3-642-25459-8_1, © Springer-Verlag Berlin Heidelberg 2012

Classification of countries in 2005

World Bank		UNDP		United Nations Statistics Division		China Modernization Report	
Category	Number	Category	Number	Category	Number	Category	Number
High income	57	High human development	73	More developed	56	Advanced countries	20
		Very high	*31*				
Middle income	97	*General high*	*42*	Less developed	173	Developing countries	111
Upper middle	*40*	Medium human development	76	*Other less developed*	*123*	*Moderately developed*	*25*
Lower middle	*57*					*Preliminarily developed*	*39*
Low income	56	Low human development	21	*Least developed*	*50*	*Underdeveloped*	*47*
Total	210	Total	170	Total	229	Total	131

Note: (1) Grouping samples from the World Bank, UNDP, and United Nations Statistics Division, including qualified countries and regions; (2) according to the classification of the World Bank, middle-income and low-income countries are all developing countries; (3) UNDP considers 31 countries or regions with very high human development are advanced ones and another 149 countries (or regions) are developing ones; (4) according to the United Nations Statistics Division, developed countries (more-developed countries) include European countries, North American countries, Australia, New Zealand, and Japan, and others are developing countries (less-developed countries) including 50 least-developed countries and other developing ones; (5) in *China Modernization Report*, the 131 sample countries have a population of over one million in 2000 and with complete data; the average value of high-income countries' second modernization index is 100; the second modernization index of an advanced country should be higher than or equal to 80 and that of a developing country should be lower than 80; among developing countries, moderately developed countries have their indexes lower than 80 but higher than the world average; preliminarily developed countries have their indexes lower than the world average but higher than that of underdeveloped countries whose indexes should be less than 30 (or 60% of the world average)

Source: World Bank (2008), UNDP (2009), UN (2008), RGCMS (2008), He (2010a)

1.1 Definition of Modernization Science

Necessity is the mother of invention is an English proverb, and the appearance of modernization science may be taken as an example for it. Generally, modernization, a worldwide phenomenon and conception since about eighteenth century, refers to the frontier change of modern civilization and the international competition around the world (Fig. 1.1). It not only expedites the civilization progress and international differentiation and heightens the social productivity and quality of life, but also causes some side effects, etc. As an interdisciplinary one, modernization science deals with modernization phenomena, including modernization studies and modernization theories, etc. (Fig. 1.1).

1.1.1 What Is Modernization?

The English word "modernization" appeared approximately in the eighteenth century and was translated into Chinese in the early twentieth century. Modernization was widely used between the eighteenth and the nineteenth centuries and gradually became an academic term in the twentieth century. So far, modernization has been explained from three perspectives: the basic meaning, the theoretical meaning, and the policy implication.

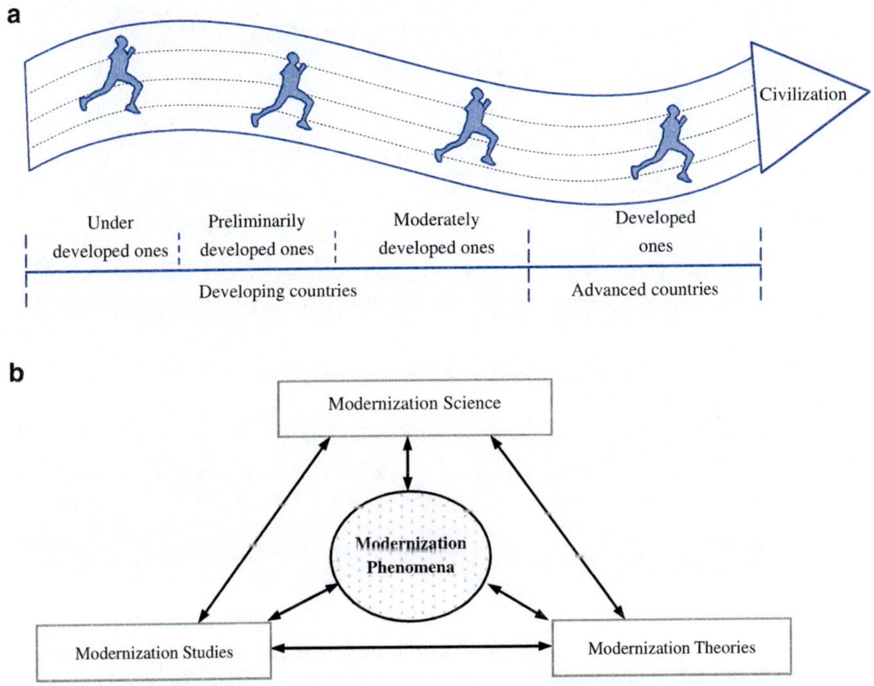

Fig. 1.1 Interaction between the modernization science and modernization phenomena. (**a**) Modernization movement is just like an international marathon in some content figuratively. (**b**) The relation among modernization science, modernization phenomena, modernization study and theories. Note: Modernization movement is just like an international marathon from the perspective of the national level (such as the level of the labor productivity, national development, and human development index) and international competition, figuratively, in which the countries running ahead become advanced or developed ones, while the rest become developing ones, and the developing ones may be divided into the three groups: moderately, preliminarily, and underdeveloped ones according to their status or level. There is some mobility among them. Hereinafter, the national level refers to the relative level of the development and transformation of national civilization in the world, international competition stands for the competition for catching up, reaching, or maintaining the world's advanced level of national development and transformation around the world.
Source: He (2010a, 2011)

1.1.1.1 Origin of the Concept of Modernization

According to Merriam-Webster Dictionary, "modernization" derives from "modern" which appeared in about the sixteenth century. These two words share similar basic meanings (Example 1.2).

Example 1.2 Origin of the Word "Modernization"

During the 185 years since the English adjective "modern" was created in about 1585, the "modernize" and finally its noun form "modernization" came into being in 1748 and 1770, respectively. There are two kinds of the basic meanings of the "modern"; one was the nature relating to present (or newest) and the other the time period since AD 1500. Based on them, it can be concluded that modernization refers to the act of becoming modern and meeting the modern needs and the states with that act finished.

Basic meaning of "Modernization" in English

Item	Modern	Modernize	Modernization
Basic meaning	Adj. Date: 1585 1. Relating to or characteristic of the present or the immediate past 2. Of or relating to the period from approx. AD 1500 to the present	Verb. Date: 1748 1. To make or become modern 2. Make suitable for present-day needs	Noun. Date: 1770 1. The act of modernizing: the state of being modernized 2. Something modernized: a modernized version
Remark	Nature: latest (newest) in whatever field Time: have initiated point but no end	Being modernized (or becoming modern), satisfying the present needs	A kind of act (a process) A kind of state

Source: Merriam-Webster Online Dictionary (2009a, b, c)

Compared to the Middle Ages featuring the control of the church and feudalism, the sixteenth century witnessed great changes in the mind and life of European people, as the Renaissance was about to end. People at that time believed that a new "modern"[1] era had begun.

Profound changes in Europe had convinced people in the mid- and late eighteenth century that "having modern characteristics and satisfying modern demands" represented the new trend of social development, after a cluster of major movements

[1] When referring to time, modern is related to the division of historical stages. In European and American countries, historians divide the history into the ancient times (before AD 500), the Middle Age (AD 500–1500), and the modern times (after AD 1500) approximately, while the divided time has some change in different references. The mid-twentieth century saw a surge of "postmodernism" in these counties; therefore, the mid- and late-twentieth century is called by some the "postmodern" era. Some Chinese scholars divide the history into the ancient times (before 1840), the modern times (1840–1919), and the contemporary times (after 1919).

in Europe, including the Scientific Revolution from the sixteenth to the seventeenth century, the English Revolution in seventeenth century, the Enlightenment between the seventeenth and the eighteenth centuries, and the Industrial Revolution in Britain in the eighteenth century. Against such a background did the verb "modernize" come into being, and soon the noun "modernization."

1.1.1.2 The Conceptual Evolution of Modernization

Between the eighteenth and nineteenth centuries, the word "modernization" was a common word to describe a social phenomenon. Integrating the meaning of "modernize" and "modern," "modernization" has the following two basic meanings: (1) a kind of act, the behavior and process to satisfy the present needs or to be characterized by the present features; and (2) a kind of state, a state or version when present characteristics and needs have been met.

Chinese scholars began to explore China's modernization in the 1930s. A total of 26 articles published on Shanghai-based *Shenbao Monthly* in 1933 discussed China's modernization and proposed some basic concepts of modernization; for example, modernization meant industrialization, scientific progress, rationalization, professionalization, standardization, progress, democracy, better productivity and modern ideas, etc.

During the Cold War in the 1950s and the 1960s, the USA and Soviet Union tried to affect the development of the third world and new independent countries which had to choose the route of development. Under the support of the US Government and some foundations, American scholars began their research on modernization. The word "modernization" gradually became an academic term in social sciences.

And its meanings have been constantly changing and developing. In the 1960s, some American scholars regarded modernization a shift from traditional to modern society and another revolutionary transformation after the agricultural revolution in human affairs (Fig. 1.2), which includes the changes in knowledge, politics, economics, society, and psychology (Black 1966). But some early arguments about modernization have been criticized since the 1970s, which constantly enriched the connotation of modernization and yielded mushrooming new modernization theories.

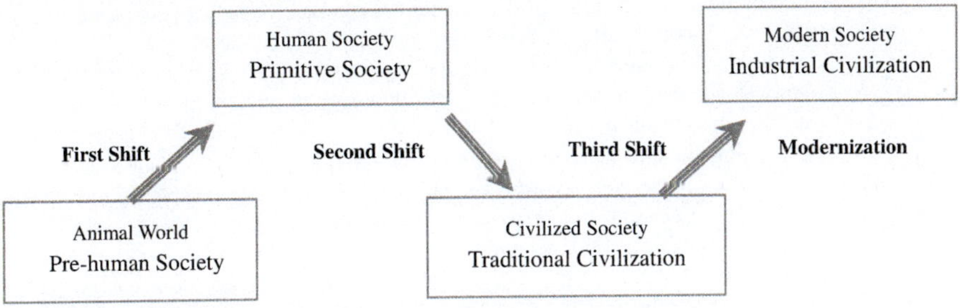

Fig. 1.2 Three revolutionary shifts in human affairs.
Note: Based on Professor Black's ideas on the three great transformations of human affairs (Black 1966)

1.1.1.3 Three Explanations of Modernization

So far, modernization has been researched for over 50 years, but no agreement on its definition has been reached yet (Pandey 1988), as people's understandings in this regard vary. Generally, modernization is interpreted in three ways (Table 1.1), just like a box, you can see different views from different perspectives.

(1) The Basic Meaning of Modernization

It refers to the definition of the "modernization" in different dictionary. As defined in the English dictionary, modernization means a kind of act (process) or a state:

Table 1.1 Three explanations of modernization

Perspectives	Meanings
Basic meaning	As defined in the English dictionary, "modernization" has two basic meanings: (1) an act or process of becoming modern or meeting modern demands; (2) a state with modern characteristics or having met modern demands. Modern characteristics refers to new changes emerged from AD 1500 to date
Theoretical meaning	American scholar Bendix regards modernization as a type of social change which started from the British Industrial Revolution and the French Revolution; it exists in the economic and political progress of several pioneer societies and the change of the follow-up societies (Bendix 1967)
	Eisenstadt, an Israeli scholar, regards modernization as process of transforming to modern social, economic, and political systems, which started from Western Europe and North America between the seventeenth and nineteenth centuries and spread to other European countries and finally to South America, Asia, and Africa in the nineteenth and twentieth centuries (Eisenstadt 1966)
	According to Prof. Luo, modernization, as a worldwide historical process, is a rapid change undergone by the human society since the Industrial Revolution in the broad sense. Driven by industrialization, it is a great transformation from traditional agricultural society to modern industrial society, during which industrialism has spread to spheres of economy, politics, culture, and ideology and caused profound changes. In the narrow sense, modernization means a process in which laggard countries catch up with industrial ones and adapt to the modern world (Luo 1993)
	In Prof. He's view, modernization is a frontier change of modern civilization and international competition since the Industrial Revolution in the eighteenth century; and from the eighteenth century to the end of twenty-first centuries, modernization process can be divided into two stages: The first modernization means the transformation and great changes from agricultural to industrial society, economy, politics, culture, and civilization; and the second modernization refers to the transformation and great changes from industrial to knowledge-based society, economy, politics, culture, and civilization. New changes will occur in the twenty-second century (He 1998a, b, 1999)
Policy implication	It is the application of modernization theory in policy sphere, including the strategies, policies, and measures to promote the modernization. There are different implications of modernization theories in different countries, stages, and fields. For example, in developing countries in 1960s, the modernization theory was reflected in economic policies such as driving industrialization, standardization, production of scale, and modernization of agriculture, industry, science and technology and management, and in social policies such as promoting urbanization, enhancing social welfare and facilitating education modernization

Source: He (2003)

Generally, the former means the behavior (process) of becoming the latest, the best, and the most advanced, and the latter means the state with the behavior (process) completed. The word modernization is widely used in its different forms, for example, a modernized hospital (the adjective form), modernize the agriculture (the verb form), and the modernization of education (the noun form).

(2) The Theoretical Meaning of Modernization

It refers to the definition of "modernization" in different modernization theories. Generally, different theories interpret modernization in different ways. For example, sociologies view modernization as a social change which refers to the transformation from traditional to modern society[2]; historians regard it as a historical process; some scholars focus on interpreting the modernity or the state of having been modernized; and others think modernization is the change of civilization. That is quite like an allegory saying several blind people taking part of an elephant for the whole. Scholars often define modernization to enhance the operability of their research (Table 1.1).

(3) The Policy Implication of Modernization

It refers to the application of modernization theories in the policy domain and also the policy explanation of "modernization" in different nations. Different policies may reflect different theories, and one modernization theory may have different explanation in policy sphere in different countries, stages, and spheres (Table 1.1). As advanced countries and developing ones are in different stages and there is a wide gap between them (Example 1.3), their modernization policies are in quite different ways, which should be specially studied.

Example 1.3 Gap Between Advanced and Developing Countries

Since the eighteenth century, the gap between advanced and developing countries has changed in different aspects and stages. For example, it has been constantly widened in terms of per capita national income, widened first and then narrowed in terms of the urbanization level in last 300 years, and been gradually narrowed in terms of the proportion of agriculture, and

(continued)

[2] According to classic modernization theory, modernization refers to the transformation from traditional society to modern society, which may confuse people in two ways. The first is the relationship between "modernization" and "social modernization." Generally, the former refers to the modernization of whole human society, while the latter refers to the modernization of the social sphere. The "human society" is a macro concept, and the "social field" is a micro one, but they are usually simplified as "society" without clear explanation in some papers. The second is the relationship between the two meanings of time and nature of the word "modern." In terms of the time period, the modern means the time about since AD 1500, so 1960 is a modern time, and the societies in 1960 are all the "modern society." It is not so, however, if the modern is interpreted from its nature: only the society featuring the characteristic of industrial civilization can be regarded as a modern society; without industrial civilization, the society is only a traditional one; so the societies in the year 1960 are not all the modern society. In the modernization science, "modern" refers to nature related to the characteristic of industrial civilization in general.

disappeared in terms of adult literacy in the twentieth century. This gap changes differently among developing countries and among advanced ones.

Such a gap between advanced and developing countries is wide as indicated in the comparison of some indicators. For example, it was particularly obvious in 2005, as on average, the per capita national income of high-income countries was 60 times that of low-income countries; the popularization rate of Internet of the former was over 10 times that of the latter; and the average life expectancy of the former (79) was 19 years longer than that of the latter (60).

Comparison between advanced and developing countries in 2005

Field, indicator, and unit		Advanced countries (examples)			Developing countries (examples)				Difference
		HIC	USA	UK	MIC	LIC	China	India	
Economy	National income per capita (USD)	35,014	43,210	38,140	2,646	583	1,740	730	60.1
	Proportion of agricultural added value (%)	1.5	1.2	0.9	9	22	13	18	0.1
Society	Average life expectancy (year)	79	78	79	70	60	72	64	1.3
	Proportion of urban population (%)	77	81	90	54	30	40	29	2.6
Politics	Proportion of government income (%)	26	18	37	18	13	10	13	2.0
	Proportion of government expenditure (%)	18	16	22	15	11	14	11	1.6
Culture	Adult literacy (%)	99	99	99	90	61	91	61	1.6
	Popularization rate of Internet (%)	56	67	53	11	4	9	5	14.0
Humans	Gross enrollment rate of tertiary education (%)	67	82	59	27	9	22	11	7.4
	Popularization rate of private cars (%)	47	46	46	5	0.8	1.5	0.8	58.8
Environment	Per capita energy consumption (kg oil equivalent)	5,498	7,893	3,884	1,486	486	1,316	490	11.3
	Per capita international trade (USD)	17,783	11,207	21,049	1,881	319	1,187	321	55.8

Note: (1) HIC, MIC, and LIC refer to high-income, middle-income, and low-income countries, respectively; (2) the proportion of agricultural added value is an inverse indicator, and lower value indicates more advanced, while others are positive indicators; (3) not all high-income countries are advanced ones, but the average value of these countries can reflect the level of advanced countries; (4) difference = average value of high-income countries ÷ average value of low-income countries; and (5) income from grant is not included in government income. The data of this table comes from the World Bank (2008)

(4) The Relationship Between the Three Explanations

The basic meaning remains unchanged, its policy implication change to keep pace with time, and theoretical meanings vary in different schools. Generally, policies are the embodiment of the theoretical meaning which is closely related to the basic meaning but has quite different implications.

For example, according to the second modernization theory, modernization has six theoretical meanings (Table 1.2), which are obviously related to the basic meaning, despite the remarkable differences in the connotation (Fig. 1.3).

The meaning of modernization has undergone five changes from its basic meaning to the theoretical meanings.

The first is the change of start time from the sixteenth century to the eighteenth century.

The second is the difference in the attribute from "latest and present" to "advanced and frontier." The latest and the present may not have to be the advanced and the frontier in the world (Fig. 1.4).

Third, the state changes from "having met the modern needs" (state with modern characteristics and modern needs met) to the "world frontier of human civilization" (the state with advanced level in the world), the latter of which is defined more clearly. Besides, some modern features and needs do not necessarily represent the world frontier and direction of human civilization.

Fourth, the act of "becoming modern" (becoming modern and meeting modern needs) evolves to the act of "reaching the world frontier" (reaching the world's advanced level), with the latter better defined. The latter can be divided into three groups: catching up with, reaching, and maintaining the world's advanced level, which is not only independent but also an international competition.

Fifth, the process of "becoming modern" (becoming modern and meeting the modern needs) is changed to "reaching the world frontier" (reaching the world's advanced level), and the latter is clearer. There are two paths to reach the world frontier: from the old to the new frontier and from the nonfrontier to the new frontier (Fig. 1.5). Two transformations of civilization are involved during this process: from agricultural to industrial civilization and from industrial to knowledge civilization.

From the perspective of civilization change and transition, all countries will make progress in and may succeed in modernization, but some may be fast and

Table 1.2 Theoretical meanings of modernization

Aspect	Basic meaning
Change	Modernization is the frontier change of human civilization since the Industrial Revolution in the eighteenth century, including the formation, development, transformation, and international interaction of modern civilization, as well as the innovation, selection, diffusion, and withdrawal of civilization elements, and so on
Competition	It also involves the international competition through which countries have tried to catch up with, reach, and maintain the world's advanced level since the eighteenth century. Those successfully reaching and maintaining the world's advanced level become advanced countries, while others, developing ones
State	It means the world frontier of human civilization since the eighteenth century (the world's advanced level)
Act	It is a kind of act to reach or keep the world frontier of human civilization since the eighteenth century
Process	It is a historical process to reach or keep the world frontier of human civilization since the eighteenth century. Between the eighteenth and twenty-first centuries, modernization process has undergone two stages with the first featuring industrialization, urbanization, and democratization and the second featuring the increasing role of knowledge and information and the enhancing awareness of environmental protection
Transformation	It is the transformation of civilization. The first modernization is the transformation from agricultural civilization to industrial one, including from agricultural economy to the industrial one, agricultural society to industrial one, agricultural politics to industrial one, and agricultural culture to industrial one. The second modernization is transformation from industrial civilization to knowledge one and from material civilization to eco-civilization, including from industrial economy to knowledge one, industrial society to knowledge one, industrial politics to knowledge one, industrial culture to knowledge one, and material culture to eco-culture
Formula	Modernization $\approx$ civilization development $\times$ civilization transformation $\times$ international competition and differentiation. Modernization's connotation: the change of civilization and the international competition since the Industrial Revolution in the eighteenth century, including a frontier process of formation, development and transformation and international interaction of modern civilization, a composite process of innovation, selection, diffusion and withdrawal of civilization elements, and the international competition in which countries have tried to catch up with, reach, and maintain the world's advanced level and international differentiation. Modernization's denotation: It involves the modernizations in different stages, at different levels, in all fields, sectors, aspects, and types, including the modern changes of civilization behavior, structure, system, and ideas

Note: (1) There is no agreed definition about civilization. From the perspective of this operation, civilization is regarded as the achievements aggregate of human development since 3500 BC. (2) There is no unified classification of civilization either. According to the productivity level and the structure of civilization, civilization can be divided into agricultural civilization which is based on the agricultural economy, society, politics, and culture; industrial civilization based on the industrial economy, society, politics, and culture; knowledge civilization which features with knowledge-based economy, society, politics, and culture. The ecological civilization, which features ecological rationality and environmentally friendliness and constitutes a component or is an embodiment of knowledge civilization, includes eco-economy, eco-society, eco-politics, and eco-culture. (3) Changes of civilization include the frontier changes of human civilization and the civilizations of different countries and nations. The frontier changes of developed countries' civilization intersect with those of the human civilization, while those for developing countries are more of catching up with developed countries. While civilization changes also include the development and transformation of civilizations, world' advanced level of the development and transformation of national civilizations can be shortened as world's advanced level hereinafter. (4) Modern civilization may be interpreted differently. Some hold that the modern civilization means industrial civilization, while traditional civilization means agricultural civilization; both agricultural and industrial civilizations are material civilization; some others argue that modern civilization includes the primary modern and the hypermodern civilizations, the former refers to industrial civilization and the latter knowledge civilization. (5) The civilization transformation may be interpreted differently. First, transformation of modern civilization means to turn from industrial civilization to knowledge one and from material civilization to eco-civilization. Second, modern civilization has taken shape through transformation from agricultural civilization to industrial one

Source: RGCMS (2010), He (2010a)

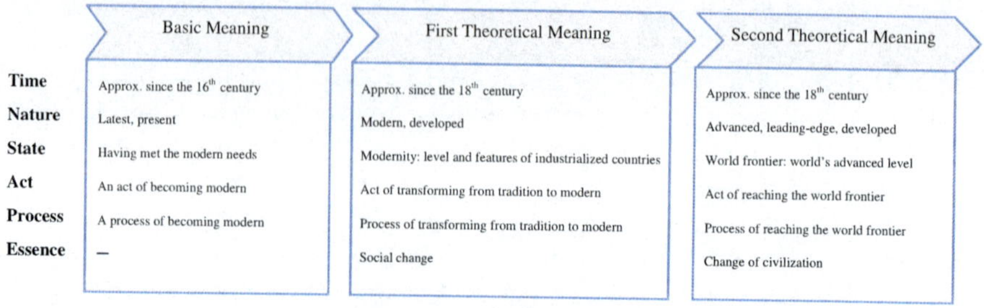

Fig. 1.3 From basic to theoretical meanings of modernization.
Note: The first theoretical meaning is the interpretation of the classic modernization theory, while the second one is the explanation of the second modernization theory

Fig. 1.4 The set of "advanced and frontier" included in the set of "latest and present"

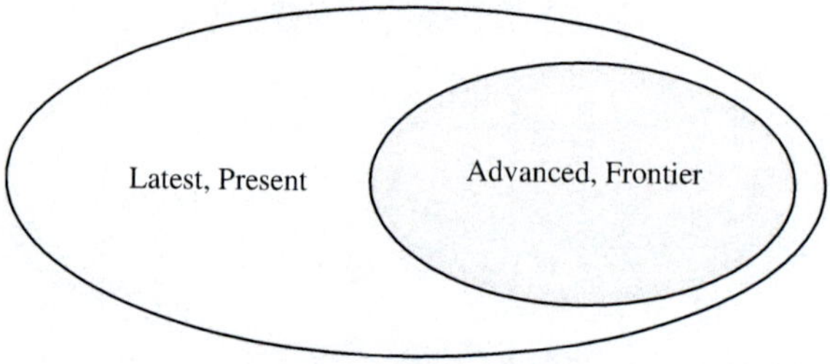

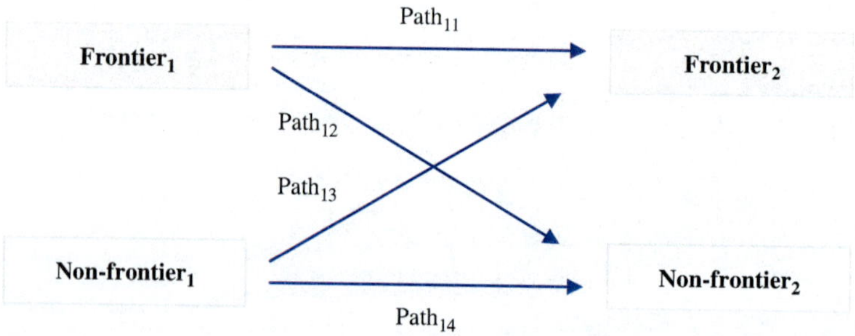

Fig. 1.5 Two paths to reach the world frontier. Note: $Frontier_1$ refers to the start of the world frontier (old). $Frontier_2$ means the terminal of the world frontier (new). $Path_{11}$ means the way from the old frontier to the new. $Path_{12}$ is the way from the old frontier to the nonfrontier. $Path_{13}$ represents the way from the nonfrontier to the new frontier. $Path_{14}$ refers to the way from the nonfrontier to the nonfrontier. $Path_{11}$ and $Path_{13}$ are the ways to maintain the world frontier and the catch up with the world frontier, respectively

other may be slow. In the past 300 years, modernization in different countries has been asynchronous.

From the perspective of world frontier and international competition, only some countries can reach and maintain the world frontier. In the past 300 years, advanced counties have accounted for less than 20%, while the percentage of developing countries has been more than 80%; in a span of about 50 years, the probability that a developing country is upgraded to an advanced one is approximately 5%, and the probability that an advanced country maintains its status is about 90%.

From the theoretical perspectives, modernization is a type of civilization change and international competition since eighteenth century, and from the perspective of national level, modernization refers to the world's advanced level and the process to reach or keep this advanced level. The national level stands for the relative level of the development and transformation of national civilization in the international system. Generally, absolute level reflects the inner and vertical level of national development and transformation, while relative level is the level based on the international and horizontal comparison of the absolute level.

1.1.2 What Is Modernization Science?

As a new interdisciplinary one, the modernization science follows the rules for all sciences.

1.1.2.1 The General Concept of Science

The word "science" in the Western language appeared in about the fourteenth century and was translated into Chinese from English at the end of the nineteenth century. So far, there is no agreed definition of this word.

Example 1.4 What Is Science?

What is science? Many people expect an answer as simply as the question itself. However, the answer we need is quite complicated. In the human society, the seed of science is planted in human beings' inherent and ceaseless attempt to understand and control the world they are in through rational thinking and behaviors. Essentially, science is a social activity and rational thinking and behaviors, rather than loose corroborant knowledge, or a series of logics to acquire such knowledge (Barber 1952). In this point of view, science is a highly integrated concept which is closely related to corroborant and systematic knowledge and behaviors and ways to acquire this knowledge.

What kind of knowledge is within the scope of science? *According to Overton, an American judge, a scientific theory shall have five features: in compliance with natural law; the capability of explaining phenomena according to the natural law; capability of being tested in the empirical world; conclusion is temporary, rather than final; and allowing falsification. That can be used as a standard to judge science* (Bird 1998).

(continued)

Basic meanings of the English words "Science" and "Knowledge"

	Science	Knowledge
Basic meaning	Noun Date: fourteenth century 1. The state of knowing: knowledge as distinguished from ignorance or misunderstanding 2. (a) Knowledge or a system of knowledge covering general truths or the operation of general laws especially as obtained and tested through scientific method; (b) such knowledge or such a system of knowledge concerned with the physical world and its phenomena: natural science 3. The investigation of natural phenomena through observation, theoretical explanation, and experimentation, or the knowledge produced by such investigation	Noun Date: fourteenth century 1. The fact or condition of knowing something with familiarity gained through experience or association, acquaintance with or understanding of a science, art, or technique 2. The sum of what is known: the body of truth, information, and principles acquired by humankind 3. The state or fact of knowing, it applies to facts or ideas acquired by study, investigation, observation, or experience
Note	A knowledge system or a discipline about the world, which can be professional and be studied and learned; research activities to acquire professional knowledge	Aggregate knowledge of human beings about the world, especially that acquired by research, investigation, observation, experience, and reflection

Source: Merriam-Webster Online Dictionary (2009d, e)

(1) The Basic Meaning of Science

According to scientific philosopher's definition of science, science has three meanings.

First, it is a knowledge system about nature and society and has been tested and corroborated.

Second, it is about research activities to acquire the above-mentioned knowledge and knowledge system.

Third, it is a kind of thinking and methodology to acquire the above-mentioned knowledge system.

To put it simple, science is a knowledge system about nature and society and the research activity to acquire such knowledge, and the aggregation of scientific knowledge, research, thinking, and methodology. Neither nature nor society falls into the scope of science; only rational research and corroborant knowledge about them is science.

(2) The Disciplinary Structure of Science

Science is composed of a range of disciplines. But there is no unified way to divide these disciplines. For example, they can be divided into basic and applied science; natural and social sciences; and natural science, technological science, social science, humanities, and interdisciplinary science. In some countries, mathematics, system science, logistics, statistics, and computing science are incorporated into formal sciences.

First, natural science deals with natural phenomena, such as material science, geosciences, and life science.

Second, technological science is the study of engineering techniques, like material science, engineering science, and the science of architecture.

Third, social science is about the study of human society, including economics, sociology, politics, psychology, and so on.

Fourth, humanities is about study of the state of human beings, such as history, linguistics, literature, and anthropology.

Fifth, interdisciplinary science refers to research on complex phenomena which involves many disciplines, such as system science, cognitive science, and environmental science. It does not mean the intersection inside natural, technological, social science, or humanities, but means to involve two or more of them, for example, the interdisciplinary science involving natural science and social science.

(3) Methods of Scientific Research

Basic methods of scientific research include observation, investigation, experiment, theoretical explanation, etc.

Scientific research usually includes a series of steps, the following four of which are universally followed.

First, collect true information and data by careful observation or investigation.

Second, propose preliminary theoretical concepts or assumptions by logic analysis and summary.

Third, test and correct theoretical assumptions by further experiment or observation.

Fourth, only the theoretical assumptions that have passed all the tests can be accepted as a scientific theory.

Scientific attitude is the soul of scientific activities, with emphasis upon the justice of rationality, accuracy, and no bias.

1.1.2.2 Definition of the Modernization Science

The modernization science is a branch of science that deals with the modernization phenomenon, and a new member of the interdisciplinary science. The modernization phenomenon is a world movement including the frontier changes of modern civilization and international competition since eighteenth century; it involves two aspects: the world frontier and frontier changes of modern civilization, the process and act to catch up with or reach the world frontiers.

According to the definition of science, the modernization science has the following three meanings:

First, modernization science, as a knowledge system, is about the facts, features, and principles of the modernization phenomenon.

Second, modernization science, as a social activity, refers to the scientific researches on the modernization phenomenon.

Third, modernization science, as a thinking and approach, refers to the rational thinking and approach applied to the modernization research.

To put it in simple words, the modernization science refers to the knowledge system and scientific research concerning the modernization phenomenon, including modernization researches and modernization theories.

Figuratively, the modernization science is an interdisciplinary one that deals with the world frontier and national advancement since the eighteenth century, which includes the frontier change of modern civilization and international competition, the principles and methods of national advance.

The modernization science could be shortened as modernizations.

1.1.2.3 The Significance of the Modernization Science

The modernization science is a strategic science, which helps us to understand the world frontier of modern civilization and international competition as well as the principles of and approaches to national advancement, and fosters the awareness of an overall picture and strategic thinking. Its important role is embodied at three aspects: the theoretical, the practical, and the social aspect.

First, at the theoretical aspect, it helps understand and explain the modernization phenomenon, specifically speaking, including understanding the world frontier of modern civilization, revealing the laws of world frontier change, and explaining the general principles of national advancement.

Second, at the practical aspect, it provides principles of and approaches to national advancement, specifically speaking, including the knowledge, principles, approaches, and countermeasures required for national advancement; the theoretical basis and historical experience for national strategy and planning; and the all-round talent to meet strategic needs for modernization.

Third, at the social aspect, it satisfies people's curiosity about the modernization phenomenon. It provides answers to the questions people are asking, such as why some countries are advanced while others are not? How do advanced countries stay advanced? And how can developing countries become advanced?

The emergence of modernization science is not only the natural result of the modernization study through about 50 years but also fit to the need of the world modernization and the international competition in the twenty-first century.

1.1.3 Natures of Modernization Science

The modernization science is a new member of the big family of sciences. It is an interdisciplinary one and also an applied one. It not only explains the world frontier of human civilization and its changes but also analyzes national advancement and international competition; it not only crosses with all the other sciences but also involves the integrated application of them. It is a highly interdisciplinary and integrated big science. Here address its structure and characteristics briefly.

1.1.3.1 Structure

Modernization involves the profound changes occurring in all the aspects of human life since the eighteenth century, but it does not mean that modernization science excludes nothing. In fact, only the knowledge acquired from the study of modernization, tested and systematized, belongs to the modernization science; the knowledge of modernization and the modernization study constitute two pillars of the modernization science (Fig. 1.6).

(1) The Basic Structure

Generally, the modernization science includes modernization research and modernization knowledge (Fig. 1.6), and the latter involves experienced and theoretical knowledge. The experienced knowledge refers to the general understanding about the facts and features of modernization coming from historic and present practices and studies, while the theoretic knowledge refers to the basic definitions and principles of modernization and is a collection of all kinds of modernization theories.

The modernization theory provides theoretical abstraction and explanation of the modernization phenomenon. Modernization involves the all-round changes of human civilization, but the modernization study often begins with a certain aspect. The knowledge derived from researches conducted from different perspectives varies, and thus, different theories of modernization are formed. That is why the modernization theory does not stand alone but is a cluster of theories.

As far as the modernization science is concerned, modernization research and modernization theory are closely related. The modernization theory is not only the fruit of modernization research but also provides an analytical framework for it; the two of them support and evolve with each other. Meanwhile, though the modernization research and the modernization theory have their own structures, they are connected.

(2) The Research Structure

According to the objects and natures of the study, the modernization study can be classified into three clusters: the basic, applied, and development research (Fig. 1.7). However, the division is not fixed and absolute; sometimes the three clusters can overlap with each other. The modernization study can be integrated and serve multiple purposes on some occasions.

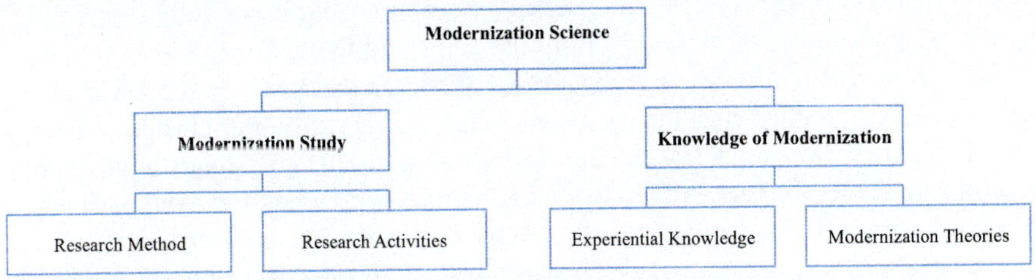

Fig. 1.6 Basic structure of the modernization science.
Note: The method employed in modernization research is also a kind of modernization knowledge

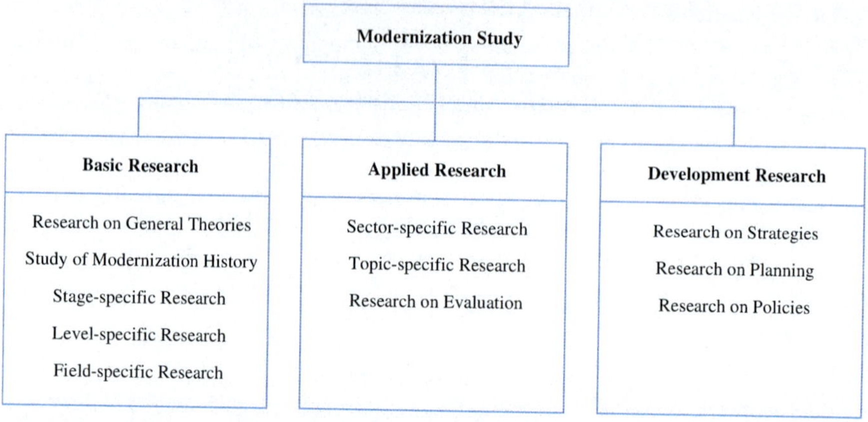

Fig. 1.7 Internal structure of the modernization research.
Note: The division is not fixed and absolute; the three clusters may overlap with each other. Some topic research such as the modernity study also belongs to basic research, and some topic research such as the urbanization study belongs to the applied research. Evaluation is a research method and can be regarded as part of the basic, applied, and development research

Basic research studies on general nature and principles of modernization, identifies the world frontier of human civilization, explains the laws of change of the civilization frontier, and provides general principles of national advancement.

Applied research studies on general way and approaches of modernization, identifies the world frontier in a certain aspect, and illustrates the ways and approaches to maintain or reach the world frontier and to realize national advancement.

Development research (or policy research) studies and provides the strategies, planning, polices and measures, etc., concerning modernization.

(3) The Theoretical Structure

As a scientific theory, the modernization theory needs to respect the scientific standards. Generally, a scientific theory has the following three features: the ability to describe and explain objective phenomena precisely and accurately, the ability to forecast and be testable, and beautiful and simple forms. The modernization theory generally includes the systematic illustration of the definition, process, result, dynamics, and models of modernization that can stand the test.

According to the illustrated objects and natures of theories, the modernization theory can be classified into three clusters (Fig. 1.8), namely, the cluster of basic theories, applied theories, and relevant theories. However, the division is not fixed or absolute; the three clusters can overlap with each other sometimes. For example, some relevant theories may belong to the cluster of basic theories or that of applied theories.

The modernization study has so far had a history of over 50 years, producing a range of modernization theories, which can be sorted and categorized according to the internal structure (Fig. 1.9) and constitute a key basis for the modernization science.

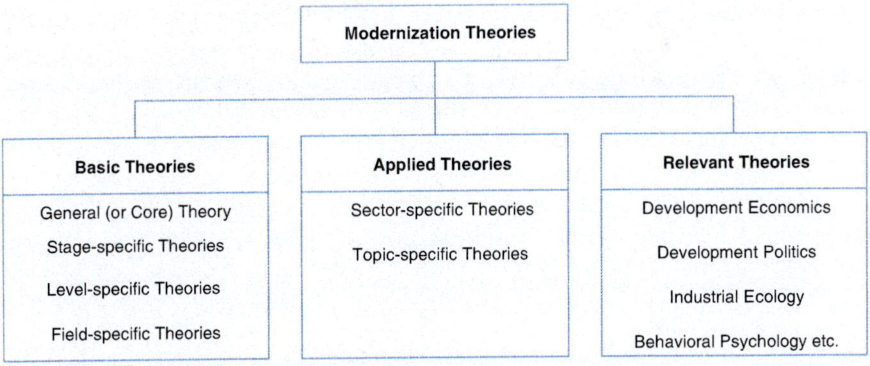

Fig. 1.8 Internal structure of modernization theories.
Note: Some theories regarding specific topics such as the modernity belong to the cluster of basic theories, and some such as the urbanization theory belong to the cluster of applied theories. Relevant theories refer to the existing theories in natural science, technical science, social science, humanities, and other interdisciplinary sciences, which can be used to illustrate and explain certain phenomena of modernization and can also be directly borrowed by the modernization science to avoid redundant research

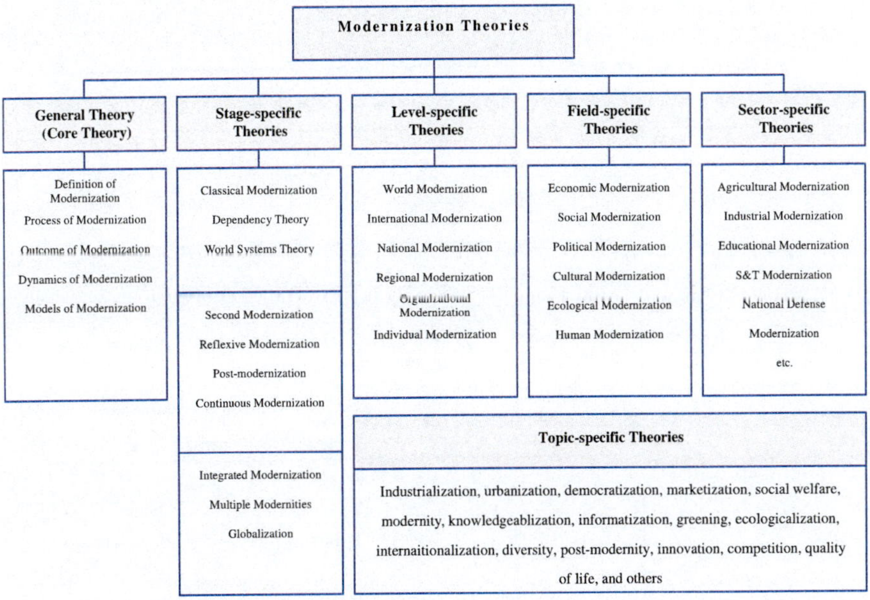

Fig. 1.9 System of modernization theories.
Note: The division is not fixed or absolute. Integrated modernization does not happen in the third stage of modernization, but a path paralleling the second stage of modernization, specifically referring to the modernization of developing countries. Generally speaking, when advanced countries are in the second stage of modernization, developing countries might still be in the first stage or adopt the model of coordinated development of twice modernization. That model is the path of integrated modernization of developing countries, which coexists with the second stage of modernization of advanced countries.
Source: He (2010a, 2011)

(4) The Disciplinary Structure

According to the definition of science, systematic modernization research and theories are the basic components of the modernization science. The disciplinary structure of the modernization science can be extracted by integrating the structure of modernization research and modernization theories (Fig. 1.10), which includes the following seven parts: the general theory (modernization theory), the history of modernization, stage-specific modernization, level-specific modernization, field-specific modernization, sector-specific modernization and modernization policies, etc.

1.1.3.2 Characteristics

The modernization science involves the civilization frontier and national advance, can be and needs to be analyzed from multiple perspectives.

(1) Modernization Science as an Interdisciplinary Science

The modernization science is one about the world frontier of human civilization and its changes. The change of civilization involves the development and application of all the sciences. It has both abundant internal and external crossover.

First, the internal crossover. The internal disciplinary crossover, such as the crossover between modernization at different stages and the modernization on

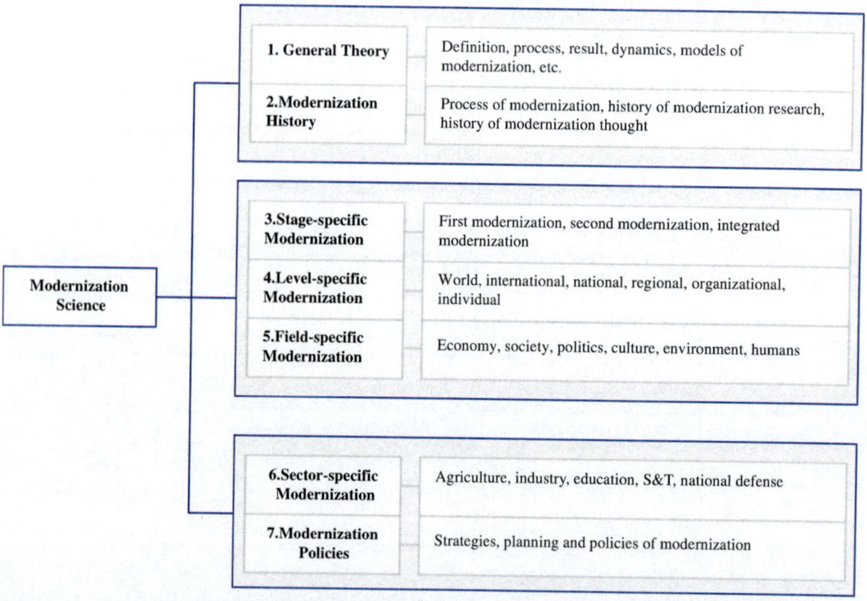

Fig. 1.10 Disciplinary structure of the modernization science.
Note: The general theory of modernization can be shortened as modernization theory or core theory. The environment refers to the natural environment here. The process of modernization refers to the frontier trajectory of human and national civilization since the eighteenth century.
Source: He (2010a, 2011)

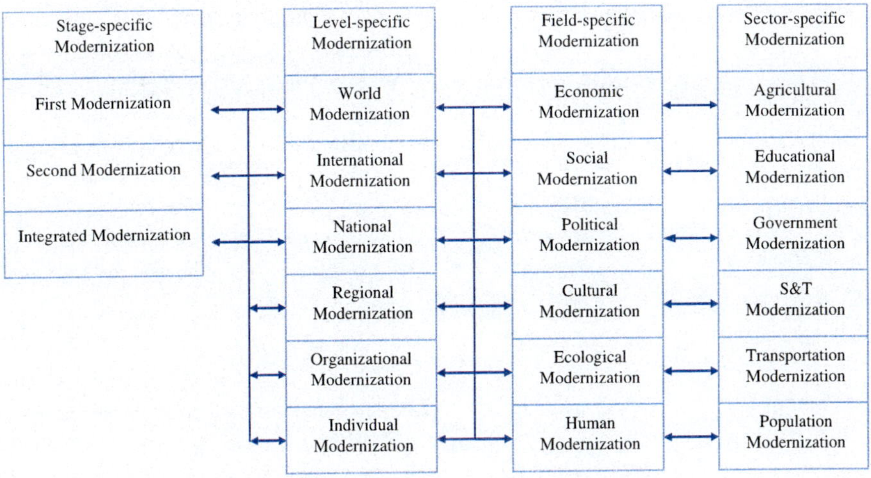

Fig. 1.11 Internal crossover of modernization science (schematic diagram).
Note: The world modernization has crossover with economic, social, political, cultural, ecological, and human modernization and other crossover can be deduced in the similar way

different layers and in different fields and sectors, overlaps between stratified modernization and modernization in different fields and sectors and overlaps between field-specific modernization and sector-specific modernization (Fig. 1.11).

The crossover of the different researches, such as the crossover between the basic and applied research in the modernization science and that between applied and development research.

The crossover of the different theories, such as the crossover between the general theory, stage-specific theories, level-specific theories, field-specific theories, and sector-specific theories.

The interaction between research and theories. The modernization research is the source of modernization theories, and the latter is the product of the former and provides research framework or guidance for former. They promote each other in a mutual way.

The interaction between theory and practice. Modernization theories provide theoretical guidance for modernization practice, and the latter provides the former with research objects. They interact with and promote each other.

Second, the external crossover of the modernization science. The modernization science is one about the world frontier. Generally, different disciplines have different world frontiers (those of research subjects and contents). The crossover between the modernization science and other sciences involves the frontier as well as the contents.

The crossover between the modernization science and natural and technical sciences. The world frontier of modern science and technology and that of human civilization are closely related. Scientific and technological progress is the driving force and intellectual source of modernization. There are a lot of crossovers between the modernization science and modern science and technology, such as the crossovers between economic modernization and high technology, ecological modernization and ecology, and agricultural modernization and agricultural science and technology (Fig. 1.12).

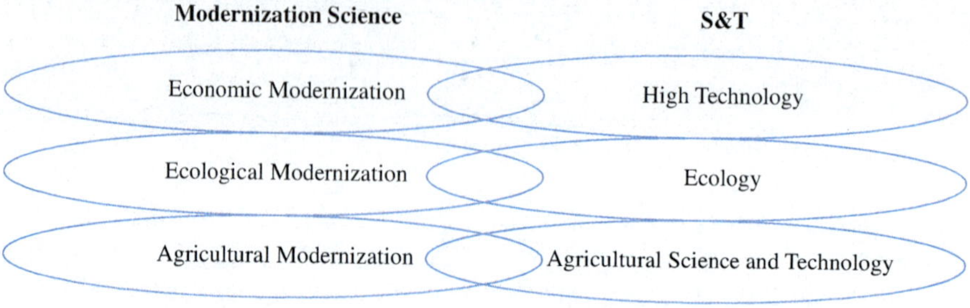

Fig. 1.12 Crossover between the modernization science and natural and technical sciences (schematic diagram)

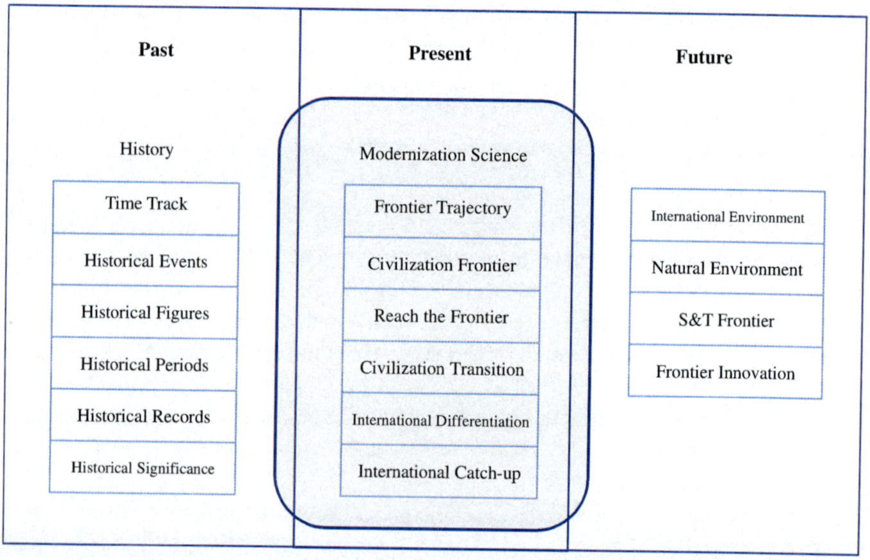

Fig. 1.13 Crossover and difference between modernization science and history (schematic diagram). Note: Relatively, history (Merriam-Webster Online Dictionary 2009f) focuses on the time track and significance of history, while modernization science focuses on the frontier trajectory of history and principles of national advancement

The crossover between the modernization science and humanities and social sciences. The world frontier of humanities and social sciences involves that of their research objects and contents and is closely related to that of human civilization. There are a lot of crossovers between the modernization science and humanities and social sciences, such as that between modernization science and history (Fig. 1.13), economic modernization and economics (Fig. 1.14), political modernization and politics, cultural modernization and culture study, and human modernization and psychology.

Third, the crossover between the modernization science and other interdisciplinary sciences, such as the crossover between regional modernization and economic geography, ecological modernization and environmental science, science and

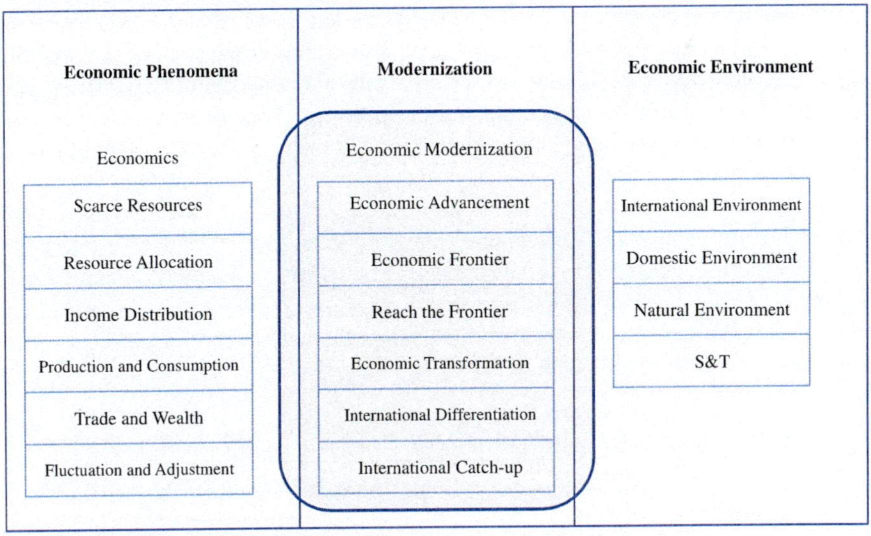

Fig. 1.14 Crossover and difference between economic modernization study and economics (schematic diagram).
Note: Relatively, economics (Samuelson and Nordhaus 1992; Merriam-Webster Online Dictionary 2009g) focuses on the allocation of scarce resources, while the research on economic modernization is interested in the principles of economic advancement

technology modernization and the science of sciences, and management modernization and system science.

(2) Modernization Science as an Applied Science

The science of modernization is one about national advancement and international competition and closely related to national construction and international stratification and differentiation.

First, the practical value of modernization science. Before the 1970s, the modernization study paid more attention to the developing countries, especially those newly liberated from colonization, as the objects. These countries found classical modernization theory either practical value or useful as a reference source. However, for advanced countries, the classical modernization theory was of value only in the field of international policy, not in domestic policy, for by that time, they had completed classical modernization, whose historical experience helped develop concepts of classical modernization theory.

Since the 1970s, there have emerged new theories of modernization, including the postmodernization theory, ecological modernization theory, reflexive modernization theory, multiple modernities theory, second modernization theory, etc. They are of practical value and useful as a reference source to both advanced and developing countries for they represent the world trend and direction.

In fact, these new theories on modernization are of plain practical value to advanced countries for the following two main reasons. For one thing, advanced countries, having completed classical modernization, need new theories to guide them or to refer to. For another, most of the advanced countries are democratic countries, whose periodic democratic elections provide opportunities for the application of new modernization theories. For example, the Green Party in Europe once adopted the theory of ecological modernization as their policy guideline during the election campaign.

Second, the differences between modernization science and development study. Modernization science and development study differ in a lot of aspects (Table 1.3). Simply speaking, the former studies phenomenon of national advancement, focusing on the world frontier of human civilization and principles of national advancement, while the latter is about developing countries, about the development and policies of the third world. They are overlapped with certain differences.

Table 1.3 Comparison between the modernization science and development study

Aspect	Modernization science	Development study
Category	A discipline of interdisciplinary science	A interdisciplinary discipline of social science
Features	Advancement study	Development study
	Science of advancement	Science of development
	Study of the civilization frontier	Study of the third world
	Combination of the past, the present, and the future	Focus on present and future, applied study
	Pay attention to the world frontier and international differentiation of human civilization	Pay attention to the national development and international relations of developing countries
Objects	The frontier changes of human civilization and international competition since the eighteenth century	Changes of developing countries since the twentieth century
	The formation, development, transformation, and international interaction of modern civilization	Development issues of developing countries
	International competition to catch up with, reach, and maintain the world's advanced level	Economic, social, and political development of developing countries
Priorities	Principles and methods of the national advancement	Development and policies of the third world
	World frontier and long-term trend of human civilization	Application of western social science in the third world
	Why are advanced countries advanced?	Economic and political development and modernization of developing countries
	How do advanced ones maintain the advanced level?	Theories, management, and policies of development
	How can developing ones become advanced?	Area study, etc.
Methods	Multi-, cross-disciplinary, and interdisciplinary study	Multi-, cross-disciplinary, and interdisciplinary study
	Integration of natural science and social science	Integration of social science and humanities

(continued)

Table 1.3 (continued)

Aspect	Modernization science	Development study
	Research that varies in stages, at levels, or in fields	Research that varies in countries, regions, and fields
	Logic: international comparison, competition, relative	Logic: Historic comparison, progress, absolute
	International comparison based on civilization time and advanced level or world frontier	Historic comparison based on physical time
Theories	Classical modernization theory, postmodernization theory, ecological modernization theory, reflexive modernization theory, multiple modernities theory, second modernization theory, etc.	Classical modernization theory, dependency theory, world systems theory, state theory, development theory, imbalanced development theory, balanced development theory, development economics, etc.
Scope	Advanced countries and developing countries	Developing countries and the third world

Note: There is no single definition on the development (Merriam-Webster Online Dictionary 2009h) study. Civilization time is one marked by the frontier trajectory of human civilization
Source: He (2010a, 2011)

If development study is a science about the development of developing countries, then modernization science is one about national advancement. The former focuses on the changes of developing countries and the development of the third world, while the latter focuses on issues such as why some countries were advanced and others were not, how advanced countries stay advanced, how developing countries become advanced, and the world frontier and its changes of human civilization.

(3) Modernization Science as an Integrated Science

Modernization science is an integrated science or complex science about civilization frontier and national advancement. Like any other integrated science, it is highly interdisciplinary and integrated, large-scaled, theoretically, and strategically grand (Table 1.4).

First, features of modernization science from the perspective of modernization phenomenon. As a complex phenomenon, modernization involves the world frontier of human civilization and the process to reach it and the international competition to catch up with, reach, and maintain the world's advanced level. Science, innovation, competition, and exchange play vital roles in the modernization process. From the perspective of modernization phenomenon, the modernization science is complex, forward, international, interdisciplinary, and integrated.

Second, features of modernization science from the perspective of modernization research. Modernization research is the research activity of modernization science. The features of the former affect and constitute the features of the latter, such as being empirical, interpretive, descriptive, practical, international, interdisciplinary, and openness. Generally, modernization research did not spring up

Table 1.4 16 Features of the modernization science

No.	Feature	Explanation
1	Highly interdisciplinary	Modernization science is highly interdisciplinary involving all the other sciences
2	Highly integrated	Modernization science is highly integrated involving the application of all the other sciences
3	Large-scaled	Many modernization study is conducted on a large scale, covering a large span of time or space
4	Theoretically grand	Modernization theory is a grand theory, explaining the grand transformation of human civilization
5	Strategically grand	Modernization science explains the great trend of human civilization and provides strategic options for national advancement
6	Complex	Modernization is a complex phenomenon and modernization science is a complex science
7	Forward	Modernization involves the world frontier and the process to reach it
8	Practical	Modernization is a practical issue, modernization theories have a lot of implication of policy
9	International	Modernization is a world phenomenon, involving the international interaction, differentiation, stratification, and international catch up since the eighteenth century
10	Openness	Modernization is a dynamic process since the eighteenth century; the modernization study is not limited to certain disciplines but open to all of them
11	Empirical	Some modernization study is empirical, such as quantitative study and case study
12	Interpretive	Some modernization study is interpretive, lack of empirical basis
13	Descriptive	Some modernization study is descriptive, lack of theoretical basis
14	Diversified	There are multiple theories on modernization without a universally agreed theory so far
15	Stratified	The theory of modernization is stratified with country as the basic unit
16	Experiential	Some theories of modernization are summarized based on historical experience

Source: He (2010a, 2011)

until the 1950s. Early modernization research was marked with humanities and social sciences. But since the 1970s, with the development of environmental protection, information revolution, and knowledge economy, the connotation of modernization has undergone profound changes, and modernization science has become an interdisciplinary science with various flourishing schools of modernization research.

Third, features of modernization science from the perspective of modernization theory. Modernization research and modernization theories are two independent and interactive parts of modernization science. The former, as the main body of the knowledge of modernization science, will inevitably affect and constitute the features of modernization science, such as being macro, integrated, strategic, diversified, stratified, experiential, and practical. The theory of modernization does not stand alone but a collection of theoretical achievements of various schools of modernization research.

1.2 Methodology of Modernization Science

An ancient Chinese had said "A thousand kilometer journey begins with the first step." This section will discuss the methodology of the modernization study in a general sense, and which is the foundation of the following chapters on their research methods.

1.2.1 Paradigm of Modernization Study

In the twentieth century, modernization study fell into the category of social science or humanities, and the research paradigm of social science or comparative history was usually adopted. In the twenty-first century, as a cross-disciplinary study, it can make the form of its own paradigm and analysis structure (Fig. 1.15).

1.2.1.1 Objective

All countries used to be agricultural until the eighteenth century, and the emerging industrial civilization began to change the world structure. With only a few exceptions, agricultural civilizations have declined since then, while industrial

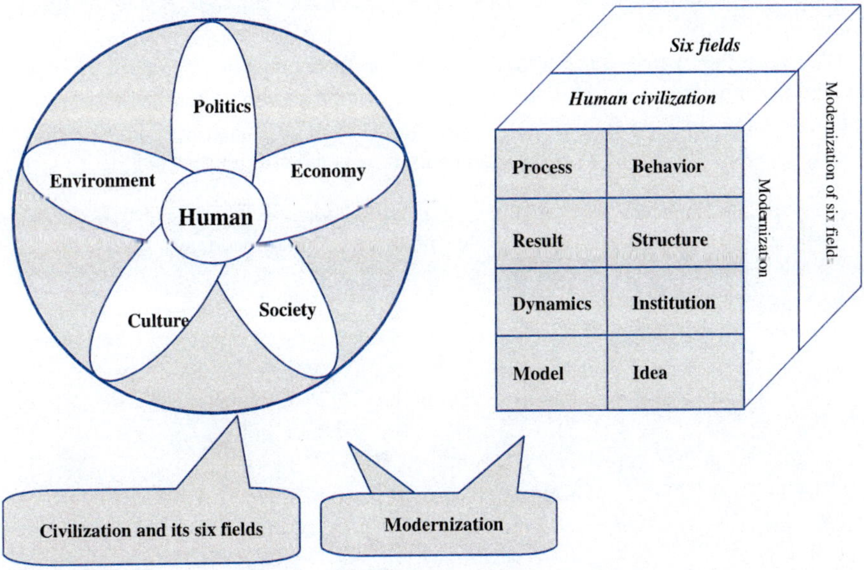

Fig. 1.15 Analysis structure of human civilization and modernization study (schematic diagram). Note: Human civilization is an organic whole and also a collection of the civilizations of all nations. The study on human civilization and modernization can be conducted by field or by country. The six major fields, including economy, society, politics, culture, environment, and human, are parallel, both independent and overlapping. The analysis structure abovementioned is for operational purpose; incomplete though, it is useful as an analysis framework.
Source: RGCMS (2005, 2006, 2010)

Table 1.5 Purpose of modernization study

Item	Scientific meaning	Academic purpose	Applied purpose
Modernization science	An interdisciplinary science that explores and explains modernization phenomena	To study the rules of frontier change of human civilization, the principles and method of modernization	To supply the approaches of modernization, the knowledge about modernization
Basic research	Studying modernization principles and establishing modernization theories	Finding out general attributes and rules of modernization	Accumulating modernization knowledge and solving related problems
Applied research	Studying modernization methods and explaining its approaches	Elaborating general approaches and methods of modernization	Offering approaches and methods of modernization
Policy research	Testing modernization theories and methods	Testing modernization theories and methods	To offer modernization strategies, plans, policies, suggestions, etc.

Note: The research activities of modernization science are divided into basic research, applied research, and policy research in a relative way, and comprehensive research in many cases

countries continue to prosper (Example 1.5). In the twentieth century, most industrial nations were developed countries, while all agricultural countries were developing ones. Why and what are the principles and methods underlying national prosperity in the twenty-first century? To answer these questions in a scientific way is the main purpose of modernization research. The research activities of modernization science (modernization study) can be divided into basic research, applied research, and policy research, depending on their varying purposes (Table 1.5).

Example 1.5 International Differentiation of the Countries

Modernization is a profound change of human civilization since the Industrial Revolution. During the 150 years (1763–1913) of the Industrial Revolution, the world underwent fundamental structural changes; some emerging industrial countries became developed and imperialist nations, while some traditional agricultural empires became developing countries (regions) or colonies (semicolonies), and America rose from a colony to become a developed country and an industrial power. From 1700 to 1913, international ranking and disparity in terms of GDP (PPP) per capita was significantly changed, for example, in 1700 China's GDP (PPP) per capita came after Britain, but before India and America, while in 1913 the ranking changed to America, Britain, India, and China; also during this period, GDP (PPP) per capita increased by 2.5 times in industrial countries (12 Western European countries), tripled in Britain, and grew ninefold in America; many agricultural countries underwent little or negative growth; for example, the GDP (PPP) per capita increased by 22% in India but dropped by 8% in China. All these led to a much widened rich–poor gap in the world.

1700–1970 Comparison between four countries

Item	GDP (PPP) per capita/at 1990 international dollar price					Rank in terms of GDP (PPP) per capita				
Year	1700	1820	1870	1913	1970	1700	1820	1870	1913	1970
America	527	1,257	2,445	5,301	15,030	51	6	4	1	3
Britain	1,250	1,707	3,191	4,921	10,767	2	2	1	5	12
India	550	533	533	673	868	50	73	72	72	90
China	600	600	530	552	783	18	48	73	104	92

Note: A total of 104 countries and regions are ranked, and in some cases, a regional average is used for a country's GDP (PPP) per capita in given years. In 1700, America was a colony of Britain (it became independent in 1776), and Britain, India, and China were all agricultural countries; Britain was the power in Europe, while India and China were the powers in Asia. In 1913, America and Britain became developed countries and major industrial powers in the world and in Europe, respectively, while India, colonized by Britain, and China, a semicolony, were developing nations (or regions). The data of this table comes from Maddison (2001)

(1) Academic Purpose

Modernization studies may fall into different categories and serve different purposes.

First, generally, modernization studies attempt to acquire modernization knowledge, both experimental and theoretical, and to establish the framework and paradigm of modernization science. Experimental knowledge includes the facts, features, and experiences of modernization; and theoretical knowledge covers all kinds of modernization theories about the universals, rules, and principles underlying modernization phenomena.

Second, to produce professional researchers is one of academic purposes of modernization research.

Third, specific research programs may have different academic purposes.

(2) Practical Purposes

The modernization studies, of practical use, allow various purposes for different researches.

First, generally, it attempts to provide modernization knowledge, methods, and solutions. Among them, the first one includes experimental and theoretical knowledge, for example, basic theories and historical experiences and lessons; the other two refer to approaches, strategies, plans, and policy recommendations for modernization.

Second, for developed countries, the major practical purpose is to grasp the knowledge and tools to maintain their advanced level.

Third, for developing countries, the major practical purpose is to obtain the knowledge and tools to become developed countries.

Modernization study also tries to satisfy people's curiosity about modernization phenomena and answer their questions, for example, which countries are developed ones? Why are they developed countries? What is the level of our own country? Can developed countries maintain their advanced level, or be degraded to developing countries? Can developing countries become developed ones? And so on.

1.2.1.2 Scope

No consensus has been reached on the scope of the modernization study. Generally, it involved the object, content, and the relation between each other, and the division of the two is relative.

(1) Object

Apparently, modernization phenomenon is the object of modernization study. Modernization usually has three explains, namely, basic literal meaning, theoretical implication, and policy meaning. Theoretical implications are different in various theories. The second modernization theory holds that modernization reflects a change of not only civilization but also the international competition. Civilization is the sum of human's achievements since 3500 BC in general sense, and its changes involve all aspects of people's life; therefore, it is impossible and irrational to make all changes in human civilization since the eighteenth century the objects of modernization research. As a matter of fact, the frontier of civilization since the eighteenth century and how to reach this frontier is the major object of modernization research.

First, the limits of modernization. In line with the basic literal meaning and theoretical implication, modernization has two limits in time and nature, respectively.

The first is the time limit: Modernization refers to changes of civilization since the eighteenth century, not those that had occurred before.

The other limit is about the nature: Modernization must be about new and cutting-edge changes; those other than the civilization frontier are not modernization.

Accordingly, it can be inferred that not all changes of human civilization are the objects of modernization research, but only the frontiers and frontier changes of the civilization in the world since the eighteenth century and the process and behaviors to reach the frontier are (Fig. 1.16).

Second, the category of the objects. The modernizations refer to the changes in different time period, fields and aspects, and at various levels (Fig. 1.17); therefore, the research objects can be further classified (Table 1.6).

Third, the content. Modernization means the world frontiers of human civilization since the eighteenth century and the process and efforts to reach this frontier in short word. The connotation, features, and rules of modernization are the major contents of modernization research.

The world frontiers of human civilization are dynamic, and the process and efforts to reach it are complex, so research can and should be done from various perspectives. The research contents can be classified according to the purpose and nature of the research (Table 1.7).

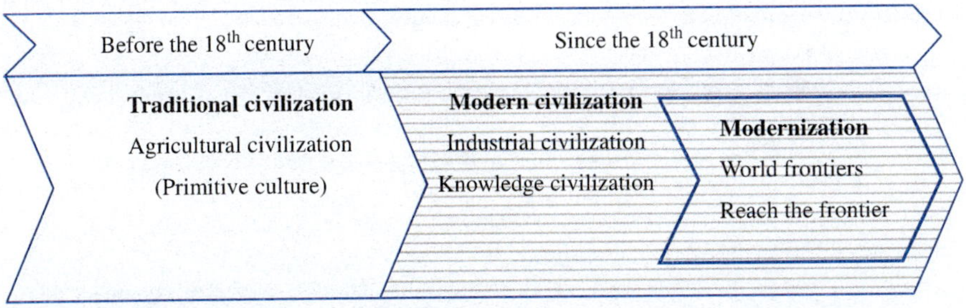

Fig. 1.16 Relationship between civilization and modernization (schematic diagram).
Note: On the international level, some countries that reached or are keeping the world's advanced level of human civilization become developed countries, while others become developing countries. Nationally, the cutting edge of the civilization of developed countries may represent not only the most advanced level of their own but also that of the whole human civilization; but that is not true for developing countries which are trying to catch up with developed countries. Of course, that is not absolute; developed countries may be laggard in some aspects, while developing one may be advanced in particular fields

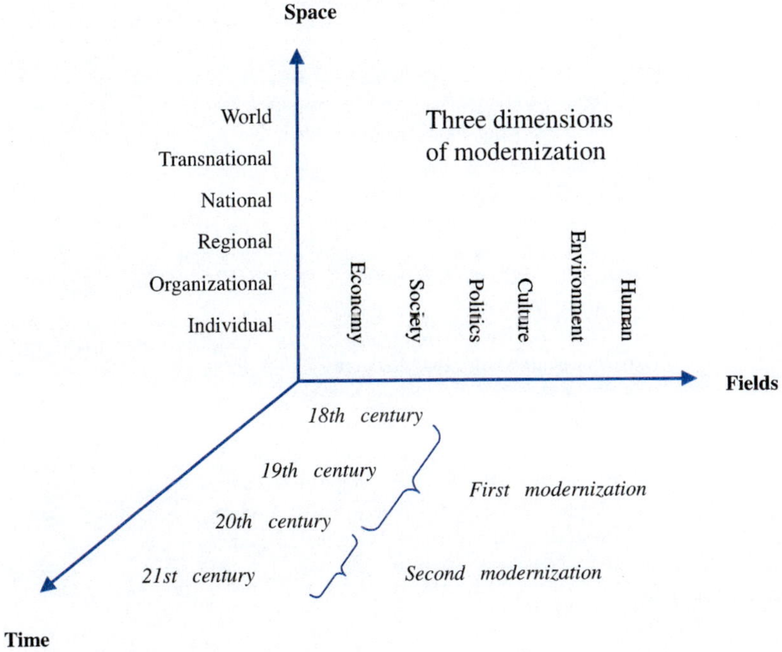

Fig. 1.17 Three dimensions of modernization.
Source: RGCMS (2010)

Fourth, the research matrix. There are three matrixes generally. One is the matrix of research scale and unit (Table 1.8), the other is the matrix of research objects and contents (Table 1.9), and the last is the matrix of fields and sectors (Table 1.10).

Table 1.6 Category of objects for modernization study

Dimension	Description
Time	Modernization, the first modernization, the second modernization, and the integrative modernization
Space	Six levels: world, transnational, national, regional, organizational, and individual modernization
Field	Six fields: modernization of economy, society, politics, culture, environment, and human
	Sectors: modernization of agriculture, industry, education, science, communication and finance, etc.
	Themes: industrialization, urbanization, informatization, competitiveness, innovation, quality of life, and so on

Source: RGCMS (2010)

Table 1.7 Category of research contents

Basis	Description
Concept research	The formation, development, transformation, and international interaction of modern civilization frontier
	Innovation, selection, diffusion, and withdrawal of modern civilization factors
Process and behaviors research	Four aspects: the process, results, driving forces, and mode of modernization
	Four elements: modernization of behavior, structure, institution, and ideas
	Interaction: interaction between different fields and factors
Research of results	Four results: modernity, characteristics, diversity, and side effect
	Four structures: geographic structure, international structure (horizontal structure and tiers of countries), demographic structure, and field structure, etc.
Research topics	Theoretical: world frontiers, long-term trend, civilization transformation, international differentiation, etc.
	Applied: international competition, experience, catching up with advanced level, frontier innovation, etc.
Nature of the research	Basic research: features and rules of world frontiers and its changes, and scientific principles underlying national advance, etc.
	Applied research: methods and tools to reach and maintain world frontiers, and basic devices for national advance, etc.
	Policy research: modernization strategies, plans and policies, etc.

Source: RGCMS (2010)

Usually, modernization research can be done in six fields, each involving or incorporating several sectors. The fields and sectors research matrix reflects the cross-disciplinary nature of modernization research.

1.2.1.3 Academic Pattern

Like other sciences, modernization science should establish its own academic norms.

Table 1.8 Matrix of research scale and unit

Unit	Scale		
	Global	National	Regional
World	Modernization at the world level	–	–
Country	Modernization at the national level across the globe	Modernization of a country	–
Region	Modernization at regional level around the globe	Regional modernization of a country	Modernization of a locality

Source: RGCMS (2010)

Table 1.9 Matrix of research object and content

Content		Object		
		Civilization	Economy, society, politics, culture, and human	Environment (natural and international environment)
		Modernization	Modernization of five fields	Ecological modernization, international modernization
Element	Behavior Structure Institution Idea	Modernization of behavior, structure, institution, and idea	Modernization of behavior, structure, institution, and idea in five fields	Modernization of behavior, structure, institution, and idea of ecological and international interaction
Aspect	Process Result Dynamics Model	Process, result, dynamics, and model of modernization	Process, result, dynamics, and model of modernization in five fields	Process, result, dynamics, and model of ecological and international modernization

Note: Generally, ecological modernization is the interaction between the modernization of a country and its natural environment (ecological interaction) and the ecologically friendly transformation of the country's modernization; and the international modernization is the interaction between the modernization of a country and its international environment (international interaction)
Source: RGCMS (2010)

(1) Main Steps of Modernization Research

Modernization research can be done through seven steps in general sense (Table 1.11), which can be followed in an orderly, cyclic, overlap, or selective way.

First, to pose problems. Scientific research starts from posing problems, which includes three aspects as follows in general. (1) Recognizing: whether it is a problem; why is it important? (2) Assessing: What is the nature of the problem? Is there any suitable research method? (3) Identifying: the problem that must be and can be solved and that can be the object of research.

Second, conceptualization. Conceptualization means the selection, deliberation, and definition of concepts and the establishment of basic concepts for scientific research. It mainly includes three aspects also. (1) Selection: Choose proper concepts and try to extract a new one. (2) Appraisal: Compare and deliberate concepts. (3) Standardization: Define concepts in a scientific way.

Third, operationalization. Operationalization means to make detailed plans and establish basic procedures for scientific research. It mainly includes plan preparation

Table 1.10 Matrix of fields and sectors on modernization study

Sector	Field						
	Politics	Economy	Society	Culture	Human	Ecological modernization	International modernization
Government	*						
Defense	*						*
Diplomacy	*						*
Legislation	*						
Justice	*						
Agriculture		*				*	
Industry		*				*	
Service		*				*	
Population			*		*	*	*
Health			*		*		
Social security			*				
Energy		*	*			*	
Transportation		*	*			*	
Information		*	*	*			
Trade		*		*			*
Finance		*					
Tourism		*	*	*	*	*	*
Technology		*		*		*	*
Education			*	*	*		
Culture industries				*	*		*
Sports			*	*	*		*
Environment						*	*

Note: * means the overlap between modernization in this field and modernization in a major sector. The international modernization falls into the "transnational" category
Source: RGCMS (2010)

Table 1.11 Seven steps of modernization study

No.	Steps	Content
1	Posing problems	Recognize, assess, and identify problems
2	Conceptualization	Select, appraise, and standardize concepts
3	Operationalization	Prepare plans, select methods, and choose indicators
4	Collecting materials	Collect, sort, and standardize materials by studies, etc.
5	Analyzing objectively	Analyze materials, assess results, and falsifiability test
6	Presenting results	Results statement, theoretical model, statistical tables and diagrams
7	Offering recommendations	Brief comment, academic suggestions, and policy recommendations

Notes: The methods of data analysis are diverse and have different features, such as empirical analysis, interpretive analysis, realist analysis, and coordinate analysis
Source: He (2010a)

and methods and indicators selection. (1) Plan preparation: Make scientific and rational research plans, including the research subject, object, purpose, target, content, principles, schedule, and so on. (2) Methods selection: Choose a scientific and rational research method. (3) Indicator choosing: Select key analysis indicators and parameters to explain and measure the concepts.

Fourth, to collect materials. Material collection is an important job in scientific research, mainly including three steps as follows. (1) Collecting: Acquire reliable materials and data through experiment, observation, and gathering. (2) Sorting: Eliminate unqualified, vague, and redundant materials through primary examination, observation, and assessment. (3) Standardizing: Verify, classify, standardize, and systematize materials and make up the deficiency.

Fifth, analyzing objectively. Objective analysis is a significant part of scientific analysis, consisting of three aspects. (1) Material analysis: unbiased qualitative and quantitative research. (2) Result assessment: result examination (cross-checking, logical check, and value check) and result analysis (correlation analysis, and analysis of theoretical and practical value). (3) Falsifiability test: negative verification of key conclusions, including reverse check, negative check, and marginal check.

Analysis approaches are diverse, including empirical analysis, interpretive analysis, realist analysis, coordinate analysis, and so on. Generally, empirical analysis would identify the causality without any bias; interpretive analysis would explain the significance of phenomena, respect the rules and the interests of the mankind, and reduce and avoid biases; and realist analysis would respect laws and objective conditions. The coordinate analysis will be discussed later.

Sixth, presenting results. Results presentation is an important component of scientific research, mainly including result statement, theoretical model, statistical tables, and diagrams. (1) Result statement: neutral and unbiased result report. (2) Theoretical model: theoretical abstraction or interpretation based on facts. (3) Statistical tables and diagrams: Present theoretical model, facts, or other evidences in a statistical or digital format.

Seventh, offering recommendations. Recommendation is usually the last part of scientific research, which is composed of brief comment, academic suggestions, and policy recommendations. (1) Brief comment: Make objective and brief comment on the method, result, significance, and defects of the research. (2) Academic suggestions: Identify problems to be further studied or needing attention. (3) Policy recommendations: presenting policy implications of the research findings.

(2) Main Requirements for Modernization Research

There are six requirements for modernization research generally (Table 1.12).

First, specifying the purpose. It is crucially important for scientific research to clarify its purpose, meaning, and nature. Generally, the basic research of modernization study mainly has academic purposes, the applied research serves both academic and practical ends, and the policy research is for useful purposes (Table 1.17).

Second, defining the object. Modernization research has myriads of objects to explore. A specific object and related materials should be carefully chosen when the modernization research is conducted. The object, once selected, should be further defined, mainly in terms of time, place, and actor (Table 1.13).

Table 1.12 Six requirements for modernization study

No.	Requirement	Content
1	Specifying the purpose	Making clear the purpose, meaning, and nature of the research
2	Defining the object	Selecting and defining the object, including defining time, place, and the actor
3	Establishing the content	Selecting and defining the research content, focusing on civilization frontier and international division, and catching up with other countries
4	Scientific approaches	Conducting experiment and observation, collecting and sorting materials, and analyzing materials and results through scientific methods
5	Objective and unbiased	Holding an unbiased attitude in selecting the object and the content, collecting materials, and analyzing materials and results
6	Sound citation	Introducing and citing previous literature in an objective, systematic, and comprehensive way

Source: RGCMS (2006)

Table 1.13 Define the research object

Item	Content
1. Time	Time period: a year, several decades, or centuries
2. Place	Geographical boundary: a region, a country, countries in a specific category, or the whole world
3. Actor	Actor: the world, a country, a region, a sector, an enterprise, a household, individuals, etc.

Third, establishing the content. The content of modernization studies is diverse (Table 1.7). After the selection and definition of object of modernization research, research content also needs to be selected and defined.

Fourth, adopting scientific approaches. Scientific research approaches should be adopted, which are embodied in three aspects as follows. (1) Previous research should be objectively treated. Literature related to the research subject and content shall be reviewed, so as to understand studies that have been done, their findings and arguments, as well as deficiencies and thus to avoid repetition. (2) Rational research principles should be adopted. The research principle must be logical, serve the research purpose, and cater to the research object and content. (3) Likewise, reasonable research approaches are also significant. They must be scientific, serve the research purpose, and cater to the research object and content.

Fifth, being objective and unbiased. One needs to be objective in establishing the purpose and selecting the object and content. The research principle and approach should be selected in an unbiased way. Research materials and results should be analyzed and presented objectively. The scientific significance of research finding should be presented as it is, instead of exaggerated or overstated. It is acceptable to make reasonable inferences based on research findings, but preconditions for the inference should be clarified, while undue "amplification" is prohibited.

Sixth, sound citation. Sound citation is the basis for scientists to assess the scientific and academic value of others' research work and also an honor and credit mechanism recognized by the research community and the society. Without sound citation, it is hard to tell which part in a modernization research has been actually done by previous researchers and which part is new.

The modernization research should be in conformity with scientific norms and be conducted in a rational, systematic, objective, and unbiased way.

1.2.2 General Methods of Modernization Study

Since modernization science is an interdisciplinary one, modernization research involves multiple disciplines. Country is usually taken as a basic unit in the research, but research can also be extended to other levels such as world and region.

1.2.2.1 Methodologies

Modernization research can be done from different perspectives which may require different methodologies (Table 1.14). From the perspective of science, positive methods can be used in the research to reveal objective facts and basic laws about

Table 1.14 Three methodologies in modernization research

Aspects	Positivism	Interpretivism	Realism
Core ideas	The world is an objective being and can be observed objectively. There are no deep structures that cannot be observed	The world is not an independent being; it is made up of societies or discourses. It is impossible to do an objective analysis	The world is an independent being. Any observation is subject to the influence of theory. There are deep structures that cannot be observed
Purpose of research	Statements of causality and objective facts. Establishment of cause-and-effect relations and explanation of the laws	Statements of correlations and interpretation of significance. Significance and expressions of and motives behind phenomena	Causality and the key role of deep structures that cannot be observed directly in the results
Subject of research	Empirical question about "what is it"	Normative question (significance and belief) about "what should it be"	Realist question about what to do and how to do; separation of phenomena and facts
Research results	Causality, explanation, and forecast models; objective and neutral	Subjective judgment; establishment of belief, ideas, and discourses; development of significance and interpretation	Causality and the influence of interpretation and understanding on the results, structure, and behaviors
Academic value	Scientific value: understanding the world	Humanistic value: interpreting the world	Realist value: discovering and changing the world
Applied disciplines	Natural and social sciences	Social sciences and humanities	Social sciences, policy research, etc.

Note: It is based on the ideas of Marsh and Stocker (2002)
Source: RGCMS (2010)

modernization so as to establish an objective and unbiased cause-and-effect model. From a humanistic perspective, interpretive methods can be adopted to describe the significance of and correlations in modernization so as to develop the discourse and concepts about the phenomenon of modernization. From a policy perspective, realist approaches can be taken to summarize the causality and value orientation in modernization so as to offer a model to explain modernization and relevant policy recommendations. Despite having some mutual criticisms among them, the three methodologies are actually complementary to each other.

(1) Positivism

Positive study is a basic style of natural sciences, but it is also getting increasingly popular in social sciences. As an English proverb *Seek the truth from facts*.

First, modernization phenomena are objective and independent beings.

Second, knowledge about modernization can be acquired through objective observations.

Third, the study is about observing modernization, proposing a hypothesis and testing, and revising the hypothesis.

Fourth, the purpose is to identify the causality and laws in modernization.

Fifth, modernization theory can explain modernization phenomena and make forecast which can be tested.

Sixth, the study addresses questions as to "what is it?" and "why is it?"

(2) Interpretivism

Normative study is a basic style of social sciences, particularly humanities.

First, modernization phenomena are not independent beings but made up of societies or discourses.

Second, it is impossible to make an objective analysis of modernization, and the understanding of modernization will influence its results.

Third, the belief, ideas, or discourses about modernization are studied to explain the relations between belief, ideas, and behaviors.

Fourth, the relations between modernization phenomena are interpreted to find the correlations.

Fifth, the interpretation theory can well explain the significance and expressions of and motives behind modernization.

Sixth, the study addresses questions as to "what should it be?" and "what significance does it take?"

(3) Realism

Realist study is a basic style of social sciences and policy research.

First, modernization phenomena are objective and independent beings.

Second, only part of modernization phenomena and their relations can be observed directly.

Third, facts and phenomena can be separated sometimes. The understanding of modernization affects modern behaviors and structure.

Fourth, the purpose is to identify the causality and laws in modernization.

Fifth, modernization behaviors are usually affected by laws and significance.

Sixth, the study addresses questions as to what to do and how to do.

In the science of modernization, the differences between positive, interpretive, and realist studies are relative, and sometimes, the three approaches are used alternatively or simultaneously. In general, a positive study offers the facts and principles about modernization; an interpretive one offers the significance of and correlations between modernization phenomena; a realist one offers the choices and suggestions about modernization.

Modernization research and theory are also greatly influenced by critical theory and futurology.

1.2.2.2 Interdisciplinary Approaches

There are a variety of methods to do modernization research. A basic principle is that the method should fit the purpose and object of the research. In general terms, modernization refers to world frontiers as well as the behaviors and process to reach the frontiers. Therefore, the two focuses in modernization research are the analysis of world frontiers and that of the process to reach the frontiers where different research models are adopted.

(1) General Measures

Since modernization is an interdisciplinary science, many research methods in natural and social sciences can also be applied in modernization research such as observation, survey, simulation, hypothesis, psychological, statistical, quantitative and qualitative analysis, model, theoretical, comparative, historical, literature, process, and scenario analysis, as well as case study.

There are many types of modernization research where different research methods are adopted (Table 1.15). Specifically, it can be ex post, ex ante, or systematic analysis in terms of the timing of the research, and one-dimensional, cross-disciplinary, or comprehensive studies in terms of the research dimensions. Cross-disciplinary and comprehensive studies are both multidimensional. In addition, different methods are needed for the research about the past, present, and future of modernization.

(2) Frontier Analysis of Modernization

Frontier analysis includes the identification, comparison, and change analysis of global modernization frontiers. By analyzing the characteristics, levels, and changes of world frontiers, we can find out the laws governing the evolution of civilizations and the basic principles about the development of a country.

First, the identification of world frontiers. How to identify world frontiers is a key question in modernization research. Modernization involves the change in every aspect of human civilization, which makes it necessary to ask the following questions. Where are the frontiers in the changes of those different aspects? Where is the general frontier in the evolution of human civilization as a whole?

- The identification of world frontiers in one aspect or by one indicator (Table 1.16).

  (1) The changes in some aspects can be analyzed on a quantitative basis, and relevant

Table 1.15 Main types of modernization study

No.	Type	Features and methods
1	Ex post analysis	Research done after the occurrence of modernization phenomena, such as the studies of the process and results of modernization
2	Ex ante analysis	Research done before the occurrence of modernization phenomena, such as the studies of the prospects and strategies of modernization
3	Systematic analysis	Cross-disciplinary and systematic research about the entire process of modernization from its origin, innovation, to the end, modernity
4	One-dimensional study	One-dimensional and one-disciplinary research about modernization phenomena
5	Cross-disciplinary study	Two- or multidimensional and cross-disciplinary research about modernization phenomena
6	Comprehensive study	Multidimensional and interdisciplinary research about modernization phenomena
7	Research on the past	Research about the past of modernization including studies about the timing, sections, process, frontiers, and paradigm, as well as literature and historical analysis
8	Research on the present	Research about the present of modernization including hierarchy, section, statistical, and comparative analysis, as well as frontier analysis, social surveys, and case studies
9	Analysis of the future	Research about the future of modernization including regression and trend analysis, linear and nonlinear extrapolation, as well as analysis of approaching objectives and scenarios

statistics are available. The world frontiers of such changes can be identified through international comparison of the statistics. (2) The changes in some aspects can be analyzed on a quantitative basis, but relevant statistics are not available. The world frontiers of such changes can be identified through case studies and comparison between nations in the world. Since it is hard to acquire relevant information and data, such comparison is not easy. (3) The changes in some aspects are hard to be analyzed on a quantitative basis. Identifying the world frontiers of such qualitative changes requires comprehensive analysis including positive and interpretive studies. (4) The changes in some aspects have just occurred so it requires rational analysis and takes time to see whether such changes represent world frontiers.

- The identification of world frontiers in a specific field. It can be done by comparing the key indicators in the field or setting a composite index which includes quantitative and qualitative indicators. Both approaches may give rise to controversy. In a single field, the level and characteristics of developed countries usually represent world frontiers.
- The identification of world frontiers in the development of human civilization as a whole. It can be done by setting a composite index which includes quantitative and qualitative indicators to make assessment, comparison, and judgment. The model and method of the composite index may give rise to controversy. The level and characteristics of developed countries usually represent world frontiers.
- Is there just one frontier or multiple global frontiers? The answers may differ in different fields and aspects. There is only a single frontier in some aspects like

Table 1.16 Identification of world modernization frontiers

No.	Indicators	Frontiers or the methods to identify the frontiers	Indicator examples
	Quantitative indicators		
1	Increasing variables	Global maximum value, average value of high-income countries, average value of developed countries	GNI per capita
2	Decreasing variables	Global minimum value, average value of high-income countries, average value of developed countries	Infant mortality rate
3	Transitional variables	Average value of high-income countries, average value of developed countries	Ratio of industrial value-added in GDP
4	Fluctuating variables	There are frontiers to talk about only for some variables (average value of developed countries)	Growth rate of GDP per capita
5	Random variables	There are differences between different nations but usually no world frontiers	Losses caused by natural disasters
6	Regional variables	There are differences between different nations but usually no world frontiers	Water resource per capita
7	Stable variables	There are differences between different nations but, usually, no world frontiers	Land resource per capita
	Qualitative indicators		
8	Institutional variables	Case studies are required. Sometimes, institutions of developed countries represent the frontiers, while sometimes, there are diversified frontiers	Welfare system
9	Conceptual variables	Case studies are required. Sometimes, ideas of developed countries represent the frontier, while sometimes, there are diversified frontiers	Cultural concepts
10	Characteristic variables	Case studies are required. Sometimes, characteristics of developed countries represent the frontier, while sometimes, there are diversified frontiers	Educational pattern

Notes: Developed countries refer to the group of some 20 countries categorized as developed nations according to the second modernization index

university education penetration but multiple frontiers in other aspects such as cultural concepts.

- The research reports of OECD contain substantial data about world frontiers.

Second, the comparison between world frontiers. (1) Comparison and analysis should cover the qualitative characteristics, quantitative levels, and categories of world frontiers. (2) Qualitative characteristics: In many cases, the qualitative characteristics of developed countries represent those of world frontiers. (3) Quantitative levels: In many cases, the quantitative levels of developed countries represent those of world frontiers. (4) Categories: single frontier, multiple frontiers, or no frontiers.

Third, changes in world frontiers. (1) Analysis of the changes in world frontiers may include trend and time-series analysis, and the comparison of multiple sections. (2) Quantitative changes in frontiers include regression, trend and time-series analysis, and the comparison of multiple sections. (3) Qualitative changes in frontiers include case study, comparative and interpretive analysis, and the comparison of multiple sections.

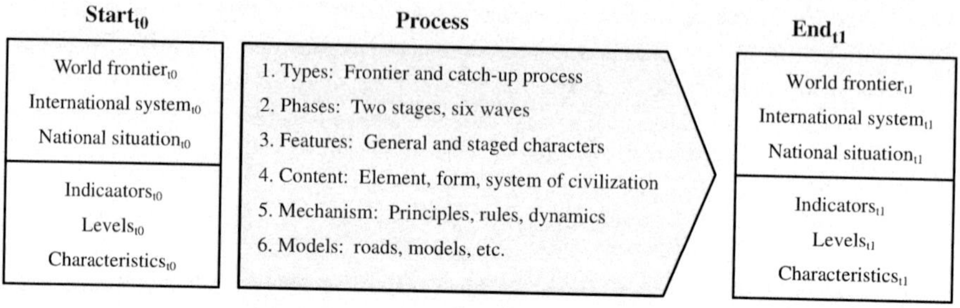

Fig. 1.18 Analysis of the processes of modernization.
Note: The elements of civilization include the behavior, structure, institution, and ideas of civilization

(3) Process Analysis of Modernization

Process analysis covers the types, phases, characteristics, contents, principles, dynamics, roads, models and results concerning the process, and so on (Fig. 1.18), and the analysis of the frontier process and catch-up process is different in some content.

First, the analysis of phases and characteristics. The analysis of the process of modernization is to identify and describe the main phases during the process and the characteristics of each phase. The analysis can be either qualitative or quantitative. The phasing of the process of modernization should be in line with that of the development of human civilization.

In qualitative terms, the phasing of modernization can be either theoretical or practical. Theoretical phasing, widely seen in various modernization theories, is based on the track of frontiers in the process of modernization. Practical phasing refers to the fact different countries have different phasing of the process of modernization. For instance, the second modernization theory suggests that the period between the eighteenth century and the end of the twenty-first century is divided into the two stages: the first modernization and the second modernization. Each stage includes four phases, that is, start phase, development phase, mature phase, and transition phase, and three waves. Such phasing is made based on the frontier track in the process of modernization.

The quantitative phasing of modernization requires the defining of standards. Generally, such phasing can be made according to the quantitative indicators for the frontier track in the process of modernization. For example, the phasing standards for the first and second modernization are set based on the indicators for industrial and employment structures (Tables 1.17 and 1.18).

The qualitative phasing is usually made based on the frontier track and major historical events in the process of modernization. Quantitative phasing is usually made according to the statistical indicators. Every statistical indicator has a value which represents the average level of a country by that indicator, so it reflects the average level of a country. Apparently, the two types of phasing are different in some ways.

To put it simple, qualitative phasing is based on frontier track while quantitative phasing is based on average level. The analysis of the characteristics of the process of modernization is usually qualitative and about theoretical generalization.

Table 1.17 Phasing standards for the first modernization

Phases	Ratio of agriculture value-added in GDP	Agriculture value-added/ industry value-added	Assigned value	Annotation
Transition	<5%	<0.2	4	One standard for the completion of the first modernization is that the ratio of agriculture value-added to GDP takes up less than 15%. It is set based on the 200-year history of economic development of industrialized countries
Mature	<15%, ≥5%	<0.8, ≥0.2	3	
Developing	<30%, ≥15%	<2.0, ≥0.8	2	
Start	<50%, ≥30%	<5.0, ≥2.0	1	
Traditional societies	≥50%	≥5.0	0	

Phases	Ratio of agricultural labor in total labor force	Agricultural labor/ industrial labor	Assigned value	Annotation
Transition	<10%	<0.2	4	One standard for the completion of the first modernization is that ratio of agricultural labor to total labor makes up less than 30%. It is set based on the 200-year history of economic development of industrialized countries
Mature	<30%, ≥10%	<0.8, ≥0.2	3	
Developing	<50%, ≥30%	<2.0, ≥0.8	2	
Start	<80%, ≥50%	<5.0, ≥2.0	1	
Traditional societies	≥80%	≥5.0	0	

Notes: The values of the phases of the first modernization equal the average of the assigned values of the four indicators in the four phases
Source: RGCMS (2010), He (2010a, b)

Table 1.18 Phasing standards for the second modernization

Phases	Ratio of material industries value-added in GDP	Ratio of material industries labor in total labor	Assigned value	Precondition
Mature	<20%	<20%	3	Only countries at the transition phase of the first modernization are eligible for identifying which phase of the second modernization they are in
Developing	<30%, ≥20%	<30%, ≥20%	2	
Start	<40%, ≥30%	<40%, ≥30%	1	
Preparatory	<50%, ≥40%	<50%, ≥40%	0	

Notes: The values of the phases of the second modernization equal the average of the assigned values of the two indicators in the four phases. Material industries refer to agriculture and industry
Source: RGCMS (2010), He (2010a, b)

Second, the analysis of contents and principles. (1) The content analysis can be either positive or interpretive such as time-series, cross-sectional, hierarchy, structural, historical, and qualitative analysis and case study. (2) The analysis of the principles, mechanism, and dynamism in the process of modernization can be kinetic, element, competitiveness, interpretive, model, regression, and random process analysis and case study. (3) The analysis of the path and model of modernization can be case study and comparative analysis. (4) There are close relations between the contents, principles, and results of modernization, particularly between the contents and principles, contents and results. Such correlations can be analyzed.

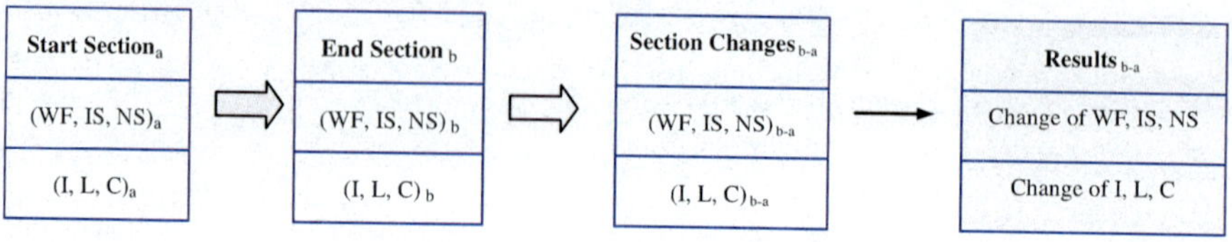

Fig. 1.19 Analysis of the results of modernization.
Notes: WF refers to the world frontier, IS refers to the international system, and NS refers to the national situation. I represents the indicators, L represents the levels, and C represents the characteristics. From the start section$_a$ to the end section$_b$, the results of modernization mainly include the macrochanges, such as the changes of world frontier, international system, and national situation, and also microchanges, such as the changes of indicators (new/canceled ones), levels of original and new indicators as well as characteristics (new/lost ones). Such results contain modernity, individuality (particularity), diversity and side effect, etc. During the process of modernization, some changes may disappear and thus are not reflected in the results

Third, the analysis of results. The results of modernization process relate closely to the span of the process, or in other words, the start and end sections (analysis sections) (Fig. 1.19). By comparing the world frontier, international system and national situation in the macroperspective and the indicators, levels, and characteristics in the microperspective that modernization takes on at two different historical sections, we can find out the results of modernization produced between the two sections. The comparative analysis of sections can be either quantitative or qualitative. In general terms, the results of modernization are represented as a function of time. So is modernity.

Between the start section$_a$ and the end section$_b$, the results of modernization = section$_b$ − section$_a$.

Simplified mathematical expression: $f_{b-a} = f_b - f_a$.

In the expression, f represents the function of the status of modernization and f_{b-a} represents the change of the status. f_b and f_a represent the status of section$_b$ and section$_a$, respectively.

(4) Analysis or Interpretation of the Modernity

Modernity study is an interdisciplinary one with diversity of the approach. Definitely, modernity is one part of the results of modernization, but there is not yet a consensus on the modernity at all. There are more than 3,800 papers by the "modernity" key word search from 2001 to 2010 in the database of "Web of Science." The researches can be divided mainly into two categories.

One is by interpretive methods. Some scholars interpret the modernity with individual value or social ideology. This method was widely adopted in the field of culture study and postmodernity study, etc.

The other is by positive methods. Some researchers state the modernity with the collection of the characteristics of modern industrial society based on the historical and objective facts. This method was widely applied in the study of second modernization, *China Modernization Report* and this book.

The former approach is the way of normative study, sometimes the theoretical analysis, and the later is the way of scientific study especially natural science. Both of them are applied to modernization science.

The modernity study and modernization study overlap with each other. In the developed countries, more scholars pay more attention to the modernity study, and it is more relative to the necessity and future of themselves. In the developing countries, more scholars focus more on modernization study especially the process and frontier analysis, which is more necessary for their countries and the policy-making.

(5) Analysis of the Particularity and Diversity

The particularity is the individual features of a single country, which is affected by its history, customs, tradition, environment, relative level, and status, including the individuality of process and result, etc.

The diversity is mainly based on the collection of the particularities of different countries generally. The process diversity and result diversity are related to the aggregates of the particularities of processes and results of different countries separately. The vertical diversity is relative to the gathering of the particularity of country with different level, while the horizontal diversity is almost based on the sum of the particularity of country in the same level, such as the diversity of the developed countries and the developing countries, the diversity of moderately, preliminarily and underdeveloped countries separately.

The diversity of the developed countries is related to the multiple modernities.

1.2.2.3 Challenges

Modernization research is faced with a series of internal and external challenges.

(1) Challenges on Positive Study

Positive research about modernization is faced with many challenges. For example, comparative analysis is a basic method in modernization research. But there are several key questions to address before making such analysis. Who are going to be compared? What is the comparison about and based on? How is the comparison going to be done?

First, if country is taken as a basic research unit, comparison can be done both vertically and horizontally. However, given that countries differ a lot in terms of size, development level, and culture, and that the geographical scope and environment of the same country are different in different historical periods, the comparison of modernity between different countries is often questioned and challenged.

Second, if the world was taken as a research unit, it would be rather hard to do the comparative analysis. The researcher will run into a good number of questions that are difficult to address. Who is the world? Who is going to be compared with the world? What is the comparison about and based on? How is the comparison going to be done? It is relatively easy to do a vertical comparison between the world at present and that in the past. But it is hard to make horizontal comparison because many questions cannot be addressed. For example, who is going to be compared with the world today? How to compare and define the world's development level as a whole?

(2) Challenges on Interpretive Study

Interpretive studies are often seen in modernization research. Such studies are conducted based on the researcher's value judgment which is often challenged by people because it may be subject to subjective bias, social implications, the limit of knowledge, and other negative factors.

Interpretive studies are to find out the essence, significance, characteristics, motive, and belief pertaining to the subject of the research. If the subject is simple, it is easy to do the interpretation. But if the subject is very complicated, it will be completely the other way around.

For instance, world modernization at global level includes the world as a whole, global behavior, structure, institution, and six fields such as economy. Suppose that every aspect has its own characteristics, then how can we interpret the integrated characteristics the world modernization at global level takes on? Do integrated characteristics equal the sum of each aspect's characteristics?

Interpretive modernization is usually qualitative. But without quantitative analysis, the academic value of modernization research will be questioned because qualitative interpretation is usually based on the researcher's value judgment which is faced with challenges in three aspects, namely, the conformity of personal judgment to objective phenomena, the recognition of the academic community, and the acceptance by the general public.

(3) Challenges on Interdisciplinary Science

Modernization research is also challenged as an interdisciplinary science.

First, very few people master interdisciplinary knowledge. Second, interdisciplinary research is usually very difficult to carry out. Third, very few experts can give an objective evaluation of an interdisciplinary science. Fourth, interdisciplinary researchers are usually marginalized in their own original field, without getting due attention. Fifth, people are giving more attention to interdisciplinary sciences, but it is still hard to obtain the funds for interdisciplinary research.

Despite all the difficulties, interdisciplinary sciences have witnessed marked development in recent years. Since 1998, interdisciplinary research and education have received growing attention in American universities. Statistics of the National Center for Education Statistics (NCES) of the United States in 2005 show that the number of university graduates with bachelor's degree in interdisciplinary sciences grew from 7,000 in 1973 to 30,000 in 2005.

1.2.3 Coordinate Analysis of Modernization Study

The science of modernization is a newly emerging discipline, which can and needs to seek for useful tools from the research tool kit of natural and social sciences and establish scientific methodology of its own. The second modernization theory lays out an approach to study and mark the development of modernization by using the "coordinates of modernization," which is called the "coordinate analysis of the modernization research" for short.

1.2.3.1 Three Steps

The coordinate analysis approach of the modernization research mainly includes three steps and six parts (Table 1.19), with the major characteristics as follows: the combination of time-series analysis and cross-sectional analysis, the combination of quantitative analysis and qualitative analysis, modeling, graphical and quantitative representation of the analysis approach and results, and of systematic, empirical, and scientific nature. The three steps and the six parts relate to and support each other and form the continuous and serial-time coordinate graph and cross-sectional distribution chart, so as to mark the development and distribution of modernization in a relatively straightforward and systematic way. The approach can be applied to all the research areas of the modernization science.

(1) Setting Up the Coordinate System of Modernization

As the core component of the coordinate analysis, the coordinate system of modernization includes the timetable, the periodic table, the coordinates, and the road map of civilization and modernization. Here we are going to discuss the coordinates of civilization and modernization, leaving the rest for Chap. 3.

First, the coordinates of civilization and modernization. It consists of the horizontal and vertical coordinates. The former may refer to the historical time and the "civilization time" while the latter may refer to the level of civilization, modernization, and modernization indicators. The "civilization time" is a timescale marked according to the "frontier track" of human civilization (Table 1.20).

All the countries in the world use the same historical time; however, during the same historical period, the "civilization time" in different countries may vary. The historical time is like the biological age of human body, while the civilization time is the physiological age. For those countries which are advanced in terms of human civilization, the civilization time might be in coincidence with the historical time, but for those which are underdeveloped in terms of human civilization, their civilization time is not in coincidence with the historical time. For example, in 2000, the United States was in the stage of knowledge civilization while some African countries were still in the stage of agricultural civilization.

Table 1.19 Coordinate analysis approach of the modernization study

No.	Main steps	Six parts	Notes
1	Setting up the coordinates	Coordinate system of modernization	Defining the horizontal and vertical coordinates
2	Variable analysis	Paradigm analysis, quantitative analysis, time-series analysis, and cross-sectional analysis	Analyzing the variables of modernization
3	Result statement	Coordinate map and road map of modernization	Marking the analysis results on the coordinates

Source: RGCMS (2006)

Table 1.20 Civilization time and historical time

Civilization time	Historical time (approx.)	Civilization time	Historical time (approx.)
Primitive culture	2.5 million years ago to 3500 BC	Industrial civilization	1763–1970
Start period	2.5 million years ago to 200 thousand years ago	Start period	1770–1870
Developing period	200,000 to 40,000 years ago	Developing period	1870–1913
Mature period	40,000 to 10,000 years ago	Mature period	1914–1945
Transition period	10,000 years ago to 3500 BC	Transition period	1946–1970
Agricultural civilization	3500 BC–AD 1763	Knowledge civilization	1970–2100
Start period	3500 BC–500 BC	Start period age	1970–1992
Developing period	500 BC–AD 618	Developing period	1992–2020
Mature period	618–1500	Mature period	2020–2050
Transition period	1500–1763	Transition period	2050–approx. 2100

Note: Time period refers to the physical time, while the "civilization time" refers to a timescale marked according to the "frontier track" of human civilization
Source: He (1999)

Table 1.21 The coordinate system of the modernization study

Item	The basic coordinate system	The coordinate system of specific fields
The vertical coordinate	The level of civilization or modernization	The level of economic, social, political, and cultural modernization and the level of a certain indicator
The horizontal coordinate	The historical time and the civilization time	The historical time, the civilization time, the time of economic development, the time of social development, and the productivity

Note: The time of economic development refers to a timescale marked according to the "frontier track" of the world economic development. The other similar terms can be analogized likewise
Source: RGCMS (2010)

Second, the coordinate types. The coordinates of civilization and modernization can be divided into several categories: basic coordinates, coordinates of different stages, levels, fields, sectors, themes, and single indicators (Table 1.21). They are all important part of the coordinate system of modernization.

(2) The Variable Analysis in the Coordinate Analysis

First, the paradigm analysis, which is a qualitative analysis approach. The modernization paradigms include fundamental paradigms (the modernization and the forms of civilization, etc.) and the paradigms of all the fields of human civilization (such as the economic formation, the social formation, the political formation, and the cultural formation). The result of the analysis of modernity, the formation of civilization, and the paradigms of all areas of human civilization can serve as the basic variable of the coordinate system of modernization.

Second, the quantitative assessment, which includes the general assessment and the measure of different stages, levels, fields, sections, themes, and single indicators. Sometimes the quantitative and the qualitative evaluation can be combined together to form a comprehensive one.

Third, the time-series analysis includes the analysis of civilization, modernity, different stages, levels, fields, sector, themes, and single indicators.

Fourth, the cross-sectional analysis includes the analysis of civilization, modernity, different stages, levels, fields, sections, themes, and single indicators.

(3) Result Statement of the Coordinate Analysis

If the results of the assessment of modernization process, the time-series analysis, the cross-sectional analysis, the paradigm analysis, and the general process analysis are marked in the coordinates of modernization, then we will have the coordinate graph and the road map of modernization. The general graphs and the decomposition graphs of different stages, levels, fields, sections, themes, and indicators form a system of coordinate graph and road map of modernization, to present a comprehensive view of the development and distribution of modernization.

1.2.3.2 Four Approaches

(1) The Paradigm Analysis

Generally, the modernization research consists of not only the analysis of single elements but also the analysis of overall picture, to avoid missing the forest for the trees. The overall analysis of the modernization research is to analyze the overall change of modernization, but so far, there is no general way of doing it. One alternative is to analyze the change of modernization "paradigm" in the light of the concept of "paradigm" of the philosophy of science and form the paradigm analysis of modernization research. It is an approach with the combination of positivism and interpretivism.

The paradigm analysis of modernization research can be used to analyze not only the paradigm shift of human civilization but also that of economic, social, political, cultural, and ecological modernization. The paradigm analysis of human civilization is used here as an example to illustrate its analysis approach. The paradigm of human civilization[3] is based on the basic types of human civilization (civilization paradigm) to analyze its development mode (Example 1.6) and establish an overall analysis framework of the development of human civilization.

[3] The approach of paradigm analysis of human civilization is controversial because simply attributing the development mode of human civilization to the evolution and shift of some basic "civilization paradigms" is considered to oversimplify the problem, and there is yet no universal understanding of "civilization paradigm." However, the paradigm analysis can be still used as a valuable analysis approach in the modernization research.

Example 1.6 The Development Mode of Human Civilization

The human civilization has a history of about 5,500 years, yet without a unified definition of civilization. From the practicality perspective, civilization refers to all the achievements of human development since about 3500 BC. The human achievements can be measured by a series of indicators, with the development level of one indicator showing that of one civilization element and the comprehensive development level of all indicators showing that of civilization. One question has to be answered before the research on the development mode of human civilization begins: Is the human civilization a whole or a set? There is yet no universal answer to this question. Therefore, we can discuss it in two ways.

1. The Human Civilization as a Whole

Suppose that the human civilization is an organic whole. The research on the overall development of human civilization requires the measurement of the general development level of civilization. But there is no universal way of measuring it. In 2006, with over 6.5 billion world population and over 190 countries, there was great lack of balance in the development of different countries: Some had entered into the stage of knowledge civilization, some were still in the stage of industrial civilization or agricultural civilization, and the primitive culture was still pervasive in a few ethnic tribes. So, which country is to represent the overall development level of the human civilization?

A group of indicators are used in *China's Modernization Report* to represent the "overall development level of human civilization," which are the average level, the advanced level, and the bottom level of the development of human civilization. The average level is represented by "the world average level," the advanced level by "the average level of developed countries," and the bottom level by "the average level of underdeveloped countries" (Research Group for China Modernization Strategies et al. 2010).

The approach of analyzing the overall development of human civilization by comparing the changes of "the overall development level of human civilization" might be subject to debates, because there is no universally recognized way of measuring "the overall development level of human civilization." Therefore, it is controversial to adopt a group of indicators to represent the level.

2. The Human Civilization as a Set

Suppose that the human civilization is a set of national and ethnic civilizations, then the research on the development of the civilization set requires the analysis of the structure and changes of the set. Though the civilization set consists of different civilizations, there is no universal rule of categorizing civilizations yet. For instance, each language has its own civilization, so does each people, each country, each region, each religion, and also each kind of social productivity. According to different kinds of social productivity, civilizations can be categorized as the primitive culture, the agrarian civilization, the industrial civilization, and the knowledge civilization (He 1999).

The structure of human civilization system (civilization set)

Basis of civilization category	Examples of different types of civilizations	Annotation
World civilization	Relatively speaking, it normally refers to the civilization formation with "the world as the unit of analysis"	
According to different levels of civilization	The advanced level, middle level, and the bottom level of the development of the human civilization	It changes any time
According to different levels of productivity	The primitive culture, the agricultural civilization, the industrial civilization, and the knowledge civilization	In the order of time sequence
According to different historical periods	The ancient civilization, the classic civilization, the Middle-Ages civilization, the near modern civilization, and the modern civilization	In the order of time sequence
According to the characteristics of civilization	The terrestrial civilization, the maritime civilization, and the cosmic civilization	In the order of time sequence
According to the natures of civilization	The material civilization, the spiritual civilization, and the ecological civilization	It changes any time
Regional and national civilization	Relatively speaking, it normally refers to the civilization formation with "the nonworld as the unit of analysis"	
According to different regions	The Asian civilization, the African civilization, the American civilization, and the European civilization	With multiple categories
According to different countries	Chinese civilization, Indian civilization, Egyptian civilization, American civilization, and German civilization	Categorized according to different levels and characteristics of countries
	The civilization of developed countries and the civilization of underdeveloped countries	
	Countries of agricultural civilization, countries of industrial civilization, and countries of knowledge civilization	
According to different ethnic groups	Chinese civilization, Japanese civilization, Arabic civilization, Mexican civilization, and Spanish civilization	It may be cross-national
According to different religion	Buddhist civilization, Taoist civilization, Hindu civilization, and Christian civilization	It may be cross-national
According to different languages	Chinese civilization, Arabic civilization, English civilization, French civilization, and Russian civilization	It may be cross-national

Note: The structural change of the civilization system includes the changes of type structure, proportion structure, level structure, and the structure characteristics

Source: RGCMS (2010)

(continued)

The structural change of the human civilization set is a form of representing the civilization development. The mode of evolution and shift of civilization types of the set may represent the development mode of human civilization. With various types of human civilization, the structure of "civilization set" becomes very complex.

If the research focuses on the "subset of national civilizations" inside the "civilization set," it will be simplified, such as, using the evolution and shift of national civilization types (the unit of the research) to reflect the development mode of human civilization.

Furthermore, if the research narrows down to the "civilization types of developed countries" (types representing the world leading productivity) inside the "subset of national civilization," then the focus will be shifted to the research of "the advanced level of human civilization," that is, to study the changes of "the advanced level of human civilization" by analyzing the evolution and shift of "civilization types of developed countries" in different periods. Such changes, to some extent, indicate the development trend of the human civilization.

As a way of studying the development mode of human civilization, it is simple and easy, but it also has its own weakness. For example, using the national civilization as the unit to study the development of human civilization cannot show the changes of the overall development level and international gap of human civilization, for it uses the national civilization instead of the human civilization as the unit and focuses on the advanced civilization instead of the general civilization. However, without any other more reasonable approaches, this one is still of significance.

First, the basic concept of paradigm. The philosopher of science, Kuhn, proposes the concept of "paradigm" in his book *The Structure of Scientific Revolution.* According to him, the development mode of mature science can be represented as "Paradigm I–Scientific Revolution–Paradigm II." To put it in a simple way, the paradigm refers to the examples universally recognized by all the communities of science, including theorems, theories, and practices. In the history of scientific development, one paradigm represents one common science (which is mature), and the shift from one paradigm to another one represents the Scientific Revolution. In the field of science philosophy, though there are still some debates over it, the paradigm and Scientific Revolution theory is regarded as a powerful theory to explain the scientific advancement.

Second, the basic types of human civilizations. There are different ways of categorizing human civilizations (Table 1.22). They can be categorized into four types according to different levels of social productivity: the primitive culture, the agricultural civilization, the industrial civilization, and the knowledge civilization.

Third, the paradigm analysis of human civilization. According to Kuhn's "paradigm" concept, the "type of civilization" which is closely related to the distinct characteristics of economic, social, political, cultural, and environmental management and individual behaviors can be regarded as a kind of "civilization paradigm" (Table 1.23). Based on this assumption, the development of civilization can be

Table 1.22 Types of civilization and society

Ways of categorization	Examples of types of society	Examples of types of civilization
Dividing into three types	Traditional society, modern society, postmodern society	Traditional civilization, modern civilization, postmodern civilization
Dividing into four types	Primitive society, agricultural society, industrial society, knowledge society	Primitive culture, agricultural civilization, industrial civilization, knowledge civilization
	Primitive society, agricultural society, industrial society, information society	Primitive culture, agricultural civilization, industrial civilization, information civilization
	Primitive society, agricultural society, industrial society, ecological society	Primitive culture, agricultural civilization, industrial civilization, ecological civilization
Dividing into five types	Primitive society, slave society, feudal society, capitalist society, socialist society	Primitive culture, slave civilization, feudal civilization, capitalist civilization, socialist civilization
Dividing into six types	Hunting and gathering society, gardening society, nomadic society, agrarian society, industrial society, postindustrial society	Hunting and gathering culture, gardening culture, nomadic civilization, agrarian civilization, industrial civilization, postindustrial civilization

Note: The information society and the ecological society are two components of the knowledge society; likewise, the information civilization and the ecological civilization are two components of knowledge civilization
Source: RGCMS (2010)

Table 1.23 Civilization paradigms and their representative characteristics

Item	Primitive culture	Agricultural civilization	Industrial civilization	Knowledge civilization
Historical period	From the birth of human beings to 3500 BC	From 3500 BC to AD 1763	From 1763 to 1970	From 1970 to approx. 2100
Economy	Hunting and gathering	Agricultural economy	Industrial economy	Knowledge economy
Society	Primitive society	Agricultural society	Industrial society	Knowledge society
Politics	Primitive democracy	Autocracy	Democracy	Pluralism of politics
Culture	Primitive culture	Agricultural culture	Industrial culture	Networking culture
Individual	Tribal lifestyle	Rural lifestyle	Urban lifestyle	Cyberspace lifestyle
Environmental characteristics	Worship of nature	Adaptation to nature	Conquering nature	Win–win game for man and nature
	Tribal interaction	International relationship, etc.	International war, etc.	International dependency, etc.

Note: The four civilization paradigms listed in this table represent only one way of categorizing civilization paradigms
Source: RGCMS (2010)

represented as "civilization paradigm I–civilization revolution (civilization transformation)–civilization paradigm II," or "civilization type I–civilization revolution (civilization transformation)–civilization type II." Hence, the development of civilization is represented by the evolution and shift of civilization paradigm in an abstract way, and modernization by the formation and transformation of modern civilization paradigm. In other words, we can use the civilization paradigm and paradigm shift as the framework for the discussion of the qualitative changes of the characteristics of civilization and modernization.

The civilization paradigm is a three-dimensional concept. (1) It is limited to a certain historical period. Every fundamental civilization paradigm corresponds to a certain civilization period. The time of civilization is marked according to the "frontier track" of human civilization with the state as the unit. (2) It is structured. Every civilization paradigm has its own basic structure, such as the structure of knowledge, technology, production, institution, or conception. (3) It is clearly characterized. Every civilization paradigm has its own basic characteristics, such as economic, social, political, cultural, individual, and environmental characteristics.

The categories of and relationship between civilization paradigm and civilization form. As far as the human civilization is concerned, its paradigm can be divided into the fundamental paradigm and the transitional one and its form, the fundamental form, and the transitional one. As to the national civilization, its paradigm can be divided into the main paradigm and the subparadigm and its form, the main form and the subform.

The fundamental paradigm of human civilization. It refers to the relatively mature and stable form of national civilization which represented the highest level of social productivity in the world in its own historical period. From the birth of human beings to the end of the twenty-first century, the human civilization has gone through four basic forms, which are the primitive culture (precivilization), the agricultural civilization, the industrial civilization, and the knowledge civilization. There are essentially different from each other in terms of the economic, social, political, cultural, environmental, and individual characteristics.

The transitional paradigm of human civilization. It refers to the transitional civilization form existing between two kinds of fundamental civilization forms. Since the formation of a new fundamental civilization form cannot take place overnight and has to go through several phases and it also takes a long time for one fundamental civilization form to transform into another fundamental form, therefore, it is implied that besides the fundamental civilization form, there are also some transitional forms. For example, the garden culture and the nomadic culture in the late primitive cultural period, the nomadic civilization and mixed civilization of hunting and farming in the early agricultural civilization period, the half agricultural and half industrial civilization in the early industrial civilization, and the half industrial and half knowledge civilization, ecological civilization, information civilization, and networking civilization in the early knowledge civilization.

The main paradigm (civilization) of the national or ethnic civilization. It is a relative concept, mainly referring to the civilization form corresponding to the average production capacity of a country/people. It can be some kind of fundamental civilization form or transitional civilization form, such as the primitive culture, the agricultural civilization, the industrial civilization, the knowledge civilization, or some transitional form.

The subparadigm (subcivilization) of the national or ethnic civilization. It is a relative concept, mainly referring to the civilization form which coexists with the main civilization form inside a country and whose social productivity is greatly different from that of the main civilization form, or whose characteristics in the six fields such as economy are greatly different from those of the main civilization form.

Generally, the development of human civilizations does not synchronize and the domestic development is not balanced either. When a country is dominated by a main civilization form, there may exist other civilization forms which are inferior or superior to the main civilization form in terms of social productivity. Because of their relative small size, they are called the subcivilization form. The main and the subcivilization forms are relative, not absolute, and one form can transform into the other.

(2) The Quantitative Assessment

Modernization is a kind of civilization change, including the qualitative change and quantitative change. The latter can be evaluated quantitatively. For example, *China Modernization Report* proposes a batch of quantitative assess models to be applied in the modernization process, including approaches of the first modernization, the second modernization, the comprehensive modernization, the local modernization, the economic modernization, the social modernization, the modernization of cultural life, the ecological modernization, and the international modernization; it also completes the quantitative assessment of the modernization of 131 countries since 1950.

(3) The Time-Series Analysis

The time-series analysis of the modernization research is an important component of the coordinate analysis of modernization. It aims to reveal the long-term trend and law of change of modernization by analyzing and comparing the data, characteristics, materials, and variations of the time series of modernization. It is mainly practiced in the studies of the historical development of modernization and can be used as a kind of trend analysis.

First, selecting the indicators, generally the key indicators for the analysis. The selection can be made from the following three aspects: the comprehensive indicators of modernization; the modernization of behavior, structure, institution, and ideas; and the modernization in six fields such as economy. The indicators of behavior and structure are mostly quantitative while those of institution and ideas are mostly qualitative indicators.

Second, selecting sample countries. Currently, there are more than 190 countries in the world. If possible, the time-series analysis can be conducted for every country; otherwise, a number of countries can be selected for the time-series analysis according to the purpose of the studies.

Third, selecting the time term, generally with the time span of about 300 years (from 1700 to present).

Fourth, collecting the time-series data and materials of the indicators. Generally, for quantitative indicators, statistical data of authorities and related data of well-known academic institutes are used, while for qualitative indicators, relatively scientific and objective research materials should be used.

Fifth, systematically analyzing the variation and long-term trend of the quantitative indicators of modernization.

Sixth, systematically analyzing the long-term trend and characteristics of the qualitative indicators of modernization.

(4) The Cross-Sectional Analysis

The cross-sectional analysis of modernization is an important component of the coordinate analysis of modernization. It aims to reveal or illustrate the structural characteristics and pattern of modernization by analyzing and comparing the data, characteristics, materials, and changes of different time sections. The cross-sectional analysis is mainly used in the studies of the status quo and the historical development of modernization with three major functions: (1) analyzing and illustrating the characteristics of a section of modernization, including the structure, level, and nature; (2) revealing and summarizing the development trend and pattern of modernization; and (3) cross-examining the result of time-series analysis.

There is an assumption behind the cross-sectional analysis. The development of human civilization does not synchronize. The civilization structure of a certain historical section can be regarded as the "historical representation" of the process of human civilization and it transforms the "time sequence structure" of human civilization into the "spatial structure." It is similar to the phenomenon that the embryonic development of animals is the representation of their evolution process. Of course, this kind of representation is not a repetition; it might leave out some information. The characteristics and laws of the human civilization and modernization can be revealed through the cross-sectional analysis.

Generally, the result of the cross-sectional analysis and that of the time-series analysis can cross-check each other. If the two results are in line with each other, then they are reliable; if they are in conflict with each other, then in-depth thematic studies are needed.

First, selecting the variables. Key indicators are selected from three aspects which is similar to the time-series analysis.

Second, selecting the sample countries and dividing them into groups. The universal cross-sectional analysis of modernization research may cover all the countries in the world (countries whose data is available). For the convenience of representing the sectional characteristics, the countries can be divided into groups to calculate the eigenvalue of each group.

The countries can be categorized according to their level of modernization and civilization as well as that of economic development. In *China Modernization Report*, the countries are divided into nine groups according to their GNI per capita, which of four groups are higher than the world average GNI per capita while which of the rest groups are lower than the world average.

Third, selecting the section according to the purpose and needs of the studies. There are eight sections chosen in *China Modernization Report*: the year 2001, 1980, 1960, 1900, 1870, 1820, 1750, and 1700.

Fourth, collecting the sectional data and materials of indicators. Generally, for quantitative indicators, the statistical data of authorities and related data of well-known academic institutes are used, while for qualitative indicators, relatively scientific and objective research materials should be used.

Fifth, for each group of countries, the "eigenvalue" of a certain variable needs to be calculated for the quantitative analysis method. There are mainly three ways of calculation: the median method, the method of arithmetical average, and the regression analysis. The second one—the method of arithmetical average is adopted in *China Modernization Report*.

Sixth, the systematic analysis of one single section mainly covers the characteristics of the structure, level, and nature of the section, such as the sectional characteristic relationship and statistical relationship between the national economic level and the modernization variable, and the sectional characteristics of institution and conception. The analysis of sectional characteristics can be qualitative, quantitative, or comprehensive.

Seventh, the comparative analysis of two or more sections, including the comparison of structures, levels, characteristics, and natures. And the change rate of the indicators can also be calculated.

1.2.3.3 Variables

Variables or indicators should be selected appropriately for the modernization research.

(1) The Principle of Selecting Variables

Since the subject of the modernization science is very complex, it is impossible to analyze all the aspects and the whole process in one single research. The more reasonable and efficient way is to select a limited number of key variables for analysis. The selection should be made in consideration of the following three factors: The variable should be of academic or policy significance; it should be easy to be compared and analyzed internationally; the data and materials are available and continuous (OECD 2001).

First, policy related and of practical value. (1) Key indicators reflecting the level, structure, or characteristics of modernization. (2) Key indicators reflecting human behaviors. (3) Simple and straightforward, easy to be expressed, able to show temporal trend. (4) Laying the foundation for international comparison, internationally comparable. (5) Reflecting the development issues at the national or regional level. (6) Having marginal or quotation value, and users can make comments on its significance (OECD 2001).

Second, easy to be analyzed. (1) With the solid theoretical foundation of science and technology. (2) With the international agreement on the legitimacy of international standards and indicators. (3) Related to the economic model, forecasting model, and statistical information system (OECD 2001).

Third, measurable. (1) The data is available and at reasonable costs. (2) With enough documents (data records) and trustworthy data. (3) With reliable data which is updated regularly (OECD 2001).

(2) The Nature of Variables

The variables of the modernization research include quantitative and qualitative variables, universal and individual indicators (Table 1.24). Sometimes, by means of social survey, qualitative variables can transform into quantitative variables. For example, the world values survey studies the change of world values by analyzing the result of the questionnaire survey. Generally, conception variation is a qualitative variable.

Table 1.24 Main types of variables in the modernization study

Type	Explanation	Example
Quantitative		
Comprehensive	The comprehensive indicator is the result of the model calculation of several single-item indicators	Human development index
Aggregate	The value of the indicator will reflect the aggregate	Population and GDP
Per capita	The value of the indicator will reflect the per capital amount	GDP per capita
Structure	The value of the indicator will reflect the structural proportion	The proportion of agricultural labor
Efficiency	The value of the indicator will reflect the output of every unit	Productivity
Growth rate	The value of the indicator will reflect the yearly variation rate	The growth rate of GDP per capita
Frontier	The value of the indicator will reflect the advanced level of the world	GNI per capita of developed countries
Average	The value of the indicator will reflect the world average level	The world average of GNI per capita
Bottom	The value of the indicator will reflect the bottom level of the world	GNI per capita of underdeveloped countries
Gap	The value of the indicator will reflect the international gap	The largest gap of GDP per capita
Qualitative		
Institution	Characteristics and variation of institutions	The pension system
Conception	Characteristics and variation of conceptions	The conception of environment protection
Two types		
Universal	Universal indicators related to the common of modernization	GNI per capita
Individual	Individual indicators related to the diversity of modernization	Water resource per capita

Source: RGCMS (2010)

(3) Types of Variables

Based on their varying long-term trends and variation characteristics, the variables in the modernization research can be divided into seven categories (Table 1.25). (1) The increasing variable: As time goes by, the value of some variables will increase

Table 1.25 The categorization of the trends of quantitative variables in the modernization study (based on the long-term trend and variation characteristics)

Type	Long-term trend and variation characteristics	Example	Variation mode
Increasing variable	The value is open and increasing for a long term. It will fluctuate within the short term and is related to the national level	Income per capita	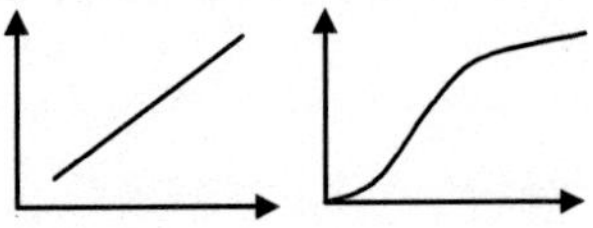
	The value is of limits and increasing for a long term. It will fluctuate within the short term and is related to the national conditions	The literacy rate of adults	
Decreasing variable	The value is open and decreasing for a long term. It will fluctuate within the short term and is related to the national level	Mortality rate	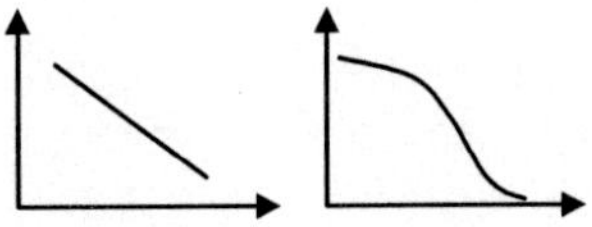
	The value is decreasing for a long term and approaching toward the limit. It will fluctuate within the short term and is related to the national level	The proportion of agriculture	
Transitional variable	Increasing and then decreasing It is related to the national level	The proportion of industry	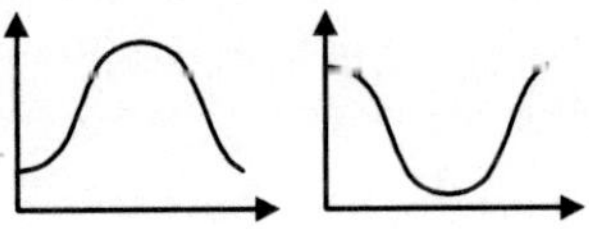
	Decreasing and then increasing It is related to the national level	Labor safety	
Fluctuating variable	It will fluctuate for a long term with a stable trend. It is related to the national level and conditions	Unemployment rate	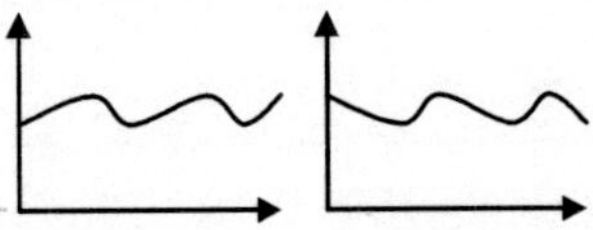
	It will fluctuate in cycles with a stable trend. It is related to the nature of variables	The growth rate of GDP	
Random variable	It happens occasionally and changes randomly. It is related to the national level and conditions	Scientific discoveries and natural disasters	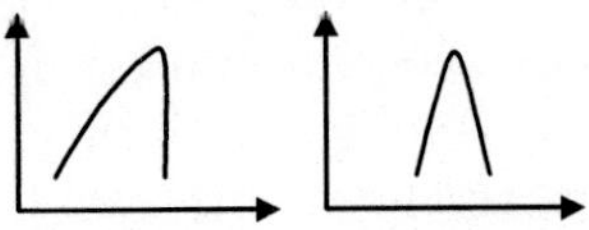

(continued)

Table 1.25 (continued)

Type	Long-term trend and variation characteristics	Example	Variation mode
Regional variable	The global trend varies greatly in different regions and countries and takes various kinds of forms such as increasing and decreasing	Mineral resources	↓ ↑ 
Stable variable	The variable whose value is relatively stable	Land resources	

Source: RGCMS (2006, 2010)

and fluctuate within a short term. The value of some variables is open while that of other variables is of limits. (2) The decreasing variable: As time goes by, the value of some variables will decrease and fluctuate within a short term. The value of some variables is of limits while that of other variables is open. (3) The transitional variable: The value of some variables will go through two stages of increasing and then decreasing (or decreasing and then increasing). (4) The long-term fluctuating variable: Some variables will fluctuate within a certain range in the long term, whose variation trend is stable, without obvious movement direction. (5) The random variable: The variation of some variables is random, without distinct trend. (6) The regional variable: For the variation trend of some variables, there are obvious regional differences and multiple forms, without a unified trend. (7) The stable variable: Some variables of some countries change to a limited extent or hardly change, such as the land resources.

If some of the increasing and decreasing variables reach or are close to the saturation number (reach or are close to its limits), then there will be the eighth variable: the saturation number variable. The saturation number variable indicates an ever narrowing international gap and ultimately the indicators of different countries will approach to the limits. Therefore, it is inappropriate to use it as one of the indicators of international comparison.

Obviously, the fluctuating and random variables are less internationally comparable than the increasing and decreasing variables. And the transitional, regional, and saturation number variables are of more policy significance.

Summary

Modernization is an objective phenomenon since about eighteenth century in the world, the modernization science is a newly emerging interdisciplinary one which deals with the modernization phenomenon, and the modernization study is an interdisciplinary or multidisciplinary one. The word modernization first appeared in the eighteenth century (1748–1770). It was commonly used between the eighteenth and the nineteenth centuries and gradually became an academic term in the twentieth century. The modernization science came into being in the twenty-first century.

What's Modernization?

There is no unified definition for modernization, which can be interpreted in mainly three ways.

First, the word modernization has two basic meanings: For one thing, it is an action—an action and process to be modern and adapt to the modern needs (the action and process of realizing modernization); for another, it is a state—a state which has modern features and meets the modern needs (the modernization state). Modern features refer to the new features and changes (normally progressive changes) since about AD 1500

We have the verb "modernize," the noun "modernization," and the adjective "modernized." To put it in a popular way, the modernized refers to the newest, the best, and the most advanced.

Second, the theoretical meaning of modernization. It refers to the definition of modernization in different modernization theories. And different theories have different explanations, as well as sociologists and historians have different thoughts.

Third, the policy meaning of modernization. It refers to the practical application of the modernization theory, and different theories have different policy implication in different nations and stages. From the perspective of national level in policy sphere, modernization refers to the world's advance level at present and the process of reaching or maintaining this advanced level.

Generally, modernization consists of about six layers of theoretical meaning according to the second modernization theory.

First, modernization is a change of civilization, a frontier change of human civilization since the Industrial Revolution in the eighteenth century, including the formation, development, transformation and international interaction of modern civilization, and the innovation, selection, dissemination and withdrawal of civilization elements.

Second, modernization is the international competition to catch up with, reach, and maintain the world's advanced level since the eighteenth century; those countries which reach and maintain the world's advanced level are advanced countries while the rest are developing countries. The two kinds of countries can change their status, and the division is not fixed.

Third, modernization is the world frontier of human civilization since the eighteenth century.

Fourth, modernization is the action to reach or keep the world frontier of human civilization since the eighteenth century.

Fifth, modernization is the historical process to reach or keep the world frontier of human civilization since the eighteenth century. From the eighteenth to the twentieth centuries, the process of modernization can be divided into two stages: the first modernization and the second modernization, with the former characterized by industrialization, urbanization, and democratization and the latter by knowledge-based, information intensive, and greening. The process of modernization can also be divided into two categories: the frontier process and that of catch up.

Sixth, modernization is a transformation of civilization. The first modernization realized the transformation from agricultural to industrial civilization while the second modernization means the transformation from industrial to knowledge civilization and from material to ecological civilization.

The connotation of modernization: Modernization is the civilization change and international competition since the Industrial Revolution in the eighteenth century, and includes the frontier process of the formation, development, transformation, and international interaction of modern civilization; the compound process of the alternative occurring of innovation, selection, dissemination, and withdrawal of civilization elements; and the international competition and international differentiation to catch up with, reach, and maintain the world's advanced level The countries that reached and kept the world's advanced level are advanced ones while others are not; two kinds of countries can change the status of each other in some possibility.

The denotation of modernization: Modernization happens in different periods, at different levels, in different fields, sectors, and aspects, covering the modern changes of behavior, content, structure, organization, institution, and ideas of the civilization.

The duality of modernization: For one thing, seen from the perspective of civilization change, every country will progress and has the chance to succeed one after another; for another, seen from the perspective of international competition, only a few countries are able to reach and maintain the world's advanced level. In the past 300 years, the number of advanced countries accounted for less than 20% of the total of all the countries in the world while that of developing countries exceeded 80%. In the past 50 years, about 5% of the developing countries have been upgraded to advanced countries while about 10% of the advanced countries have been downgraded to developing countries.

What's Modernization Science?

Modernization science is about the modernization phenomenon, with roughly three meanings:

First, the modernization science is the knowledge system concerning the facts, features, and principles of the modernization phenomenon.

Second, the modernization science is the scientific research activity studying the modernization phenomenon.

Third, the modernization science is the rational thought and method applied to the modernization research.

Generally, the modernization science is a knowledge system and scientific activity concerning the modernization phenomenon.

Figuratively, the modernization science or modernizations is an interdisciplinary science that deals with modernization phenomenon including the world frontier and national advancement since the eighteenth century, which involves the frontier change of modern civilization and international competition, the principles and methods of national advance.

Structure of Modernization Science

The modernization science includes the modernization knowledge and modernization studies. The modernization knowledge includes all kinds of theories and experience concerning modernization, and the modernization studies involve the research activities and methods of modernization science. The knowledge acquired from modernization research does not belong to the modernization science before it is tested and systematized. The modernization studies can be classified into the basic, applied, and development research (policy research). The modernization theories include the basic, applied, and other relevant theories.

Normally, the modernization science consists of seven parts: the general theory (the core theory), the history of modernization, stage-specific modernization, level-specific modernization, field-specific modernization, sector-specific modernization, and modernization policies.

Characteristics of Modernization Science

The modernization science is a new member of the big family of sciences.

The modernization science is not only a cross-disciplinary, applied science but also an integrated science.

The modernization science does not only cross with other sciences but also involves the integrated application of them.

So far, there have been 16 key features of modernization science, such as being cross-disciplinary, highly integrated, large-scaled, and strategically grand.

If the development study is a science about developing countries, then the modernization science is a science about national advancement. Modernization science focuses on how the advanced countries stay advanced, and how the developing countries become advanced, and explains the world frontier of human civilization, the process to reach it, and the principles and methods of national advance.

Paradigm of the Modernization Study

Purpose: to reveal the law of change in the frontiers of modern civilization and the law of national advance, explain and provide approaches to reach the world frontier and realize national prosperity, and satisfy people's curiosity for modernization.

Object: the phenomenon of modernization. The science of modernization focuses on and mainly studies the world frontiers of human civilization and the process and behavior needed to reach the frontier since the eighteenth century and the phenomena of national advance and international differentiation.

Content: the meaning, characteristics, and law of modernization, the principles and approaches for national advance; and so on. It normally covers the process, result, driving force and mode of modernization and the variation of behaviors, structures, institutions and ideas at the frontier of civilization.

Steps: There are seven steps: posing questions, conceptualizing, operationalization, collecting materials, analyzing objectively, presenting results, and offering recommendations, which can be followed in an orderly, cyclic, cross-cutting, or selective way.

Requirements: specifying the purpose, defining the object and the content, adopting scientific approaches, being objective and unbiased, and making complete citations.

General Approaches of the Modernization Study

The methodology of the modernization research: positivism, interpretivism, and realism. Generally, positive studies focus on the facts and principles of the modernization phenomenon, the interpretive studies focus on the meaning of and relationship between phenomena of modernization, while the realist studies provide the choice and suggestions of the modernization phenomenon. Criticism and futurism have great influence upon the studies.

Research approaches of natural and social sciences can be selectively adopted, such as observation, survey, simulation, assumption, psychological analysis, statistical analysis, quantitative analysis, qualitative analysis, model approach, theoretical analysis, comparative analysis, historical analysis, literature analysis, process analysis, scenario analysis, and case studies.

Frontier analysis includes the identification, comparison, and variation analysis of the world frontiers.

Process analysis includes the analysis on the stages, characteristics, contents, principles, and results of the modernization process.

The Coordinate Analysis of the Modernization Study

The second modernization theory forms an approach to study and mark the development of modernization by using the "modernization coordinates," which is called the "the coordinate analysis approach of modernization research" for short.

The coordinate system of modernization includes the timetable, the periodic table, the coordinates, and the road map of civilization and modernization. The coordinate system of civilization and modernization consists of horizontal and vertical coordinates. The former may refer to the historical time or the time of civilization, while the latter may refer to the level of civilization, modernization, or the indicators of modernization.

The "civilization time" is a timescale marked according to the "frontier track" of human civilization.

The variable analysis in the coordinate analysis: paradigm analysis, quantitative analysis, time-series analysis, and cross-sectional analysis.

The result statement of the coordinate analysis: marking the quantitative measure, the time-series analysis, the cross-sectional analysis, the paradigm analysis, and the result of general process analysis in the coordinates of modernization, so as to form the coordinate map and road map of modernization.

The selection of variables: Three factors should be taken into consideration: the variable should be of academic or policy significance, it should be easy to be compared and analyzed internationally, and the data and materials are available and continuous.

Variable types: qualitative and quantitative indicators, the increasing variable, the decreasing variable, the transitional variable, the long-term fluctuating variable, the random variable, the regional variable, the stable variable, and the saturation variable.

Further Reading

Babbie E (1999) The basics of social research. Wadsworth, Belmont, CA (Trans. Qiu Z. Beijing: Huaxia Publishing House, 2002)

Bird A (1998) Philosophy of science. Routledge, London (Trans. Jia Y, Rong X. Beijing: China People's University Press, 2008)

Black CE (ed) (1976) Comparative modernization: a reader. Free, New York (Trans. Yang Y, Chen Z. Shanghai: Shanghai Translation Publishing House, 1996)

He C (1999) The second modernization: inspiration of human civilization process. Higher Education, Beijing

He C (2003) Oriental renaissance: three roads to the modernization. Commercial, Beijing

Kuhn T (1962) The structure of scientific revolutions. University of Chicago Press, Chicago, IL (Trans. Jin W, Hu X. Beijing: Peking University Press, 2004)

Luo R (1993) New approach on modernization: the world and China's modernization process. Peking University Press, Beijing

Marsh D, Stocker G (eds) (2002) Theory and methods in political science. Palgrave Macmillan, Basingstoke (Trans. Jing Y, Zhang X, Ouyang J. Beijing: China People's University Press, 2006)

Martinelli A (2005) Global modernization: rethinking the project of modernity. Sage, London

Pieterse JN (2009) Development theory, 2nd edn. Sage, London

RGCMS (Research Group for China Modernization Strategies et al) (2010) China Modernization Report 2010–world modernization outline 1700–2100. Peking University Press, Beijing

Sayer A (1992) Method in social science: a realist approach. Routledge, London

2 General Theory

No rule, no success (Chinese proverb). There are both universals and diversity in the modernization process, and here, we focus on its generality including general rules, principles, features, and so on (Fig. 2.1).

2.1 Core Theory of General Modernization

Generally, world change occurs constantly and follows certain laws, while the cognition of these laws is deepened gradually. Modernization is a type of change, and the cognition of modernization laws also is deepened gradually. Currently, there are different schools of modernization theories, which have different understandings and explanations of modernization laws. This section deals with the core theory of general modernization (Fig. 2.2). As so far, the consensus on the general modernization has not been achieved; hereinafter, the general theory of the second modernization theory has been taken as a replacement of the core theory of general modernization (Table 2.1), and some contents of which come from other theories.

2.1.1 Operational Definitions

In the modernization science, there is no universal definition of modernization, but there is a variety of operational definitions. These operational definitions each have distinctive features and reflect some particular connotation and characteristics of modernization and meet the needs of modernization research. Modernization involves changes in all aspects of human civilization, while modernization research is carried out step by step.

2.1.1.1 Basic Concepts of Modernization

Chapter 1 has discussed the three explanations (Table 1.1) and six theoretical meanings (Table 1.2) of modernization in general. Operational definitions of modernization can be raised according to the theoretical meanings and research

C. He, *Modernization Science*,
DOI 10.1007/978-3-642-25459-8_2, © Springer-Verlag Berlin Heidelberg 2012

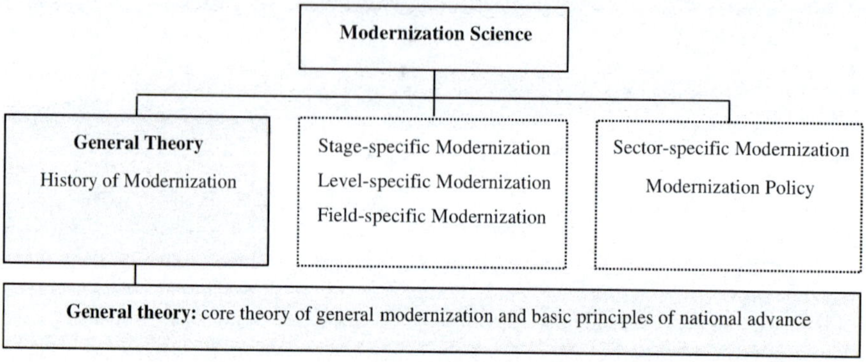

Fig. 2.1 Positioning and structure of the general theory. Note: The general modernization refers to the modernization in the world in general sense and not to any special one

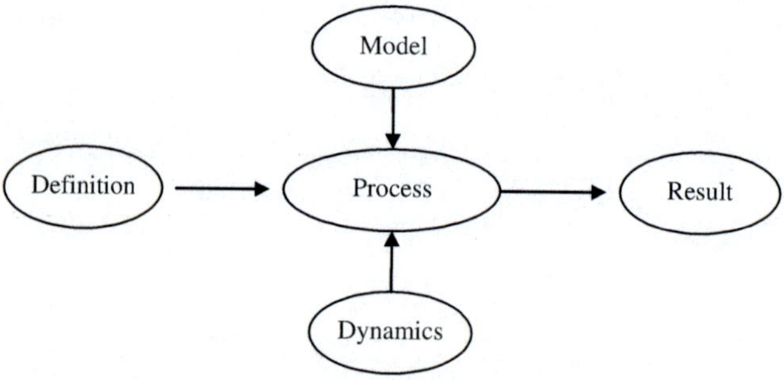

Fig. 2.2 Core theory of general modernization (structural diagram). Source: RGCMS (2009, 2010), He (2010a, 2011)

needs. Because of such rich theoretical meanings and the various research needs, the operational definitions are diversified.

(1) Operational Definitions of Modernization

Modernization may have a variety of operational definitions. Here are three of them, which are closely correlated (Table 2.2). We may have an understanding of their structures and interrelations through the general models of modernization (structural model, conceptual model, and logical model).

There are more definitions to be introduced based on above three definitions. For example, based on the definition 3 above, we can say that from the perspective of national level, modernization refers to the world's advanced level at present and the process to reach or maintain this advanced level.

(2) General Models of Modernization

First, the structural model of modernization. In essence, modernization is a type of civilization change which occurs at multiple levels such as contents and forms of civilization, and international competition is also its main content (Fig. 2.3).

Table 2.1 Core theory of general modernization (general theory of second modernization theory)

Aspect	Basic contents
Definition	Modernization is an objective phenomenon since the Industrial Revolution in the eighteenth century. First of all, it is a type of frontier change of human civilization, a frontier process of the formation, development, and transition and international interaction of modern civilization, and a composite process of alternate innovation, selection, diffusion, and withdrawal of civilization elements. Second, it is an international competition for catching up with, reaching, and maintaining the world's advanced level and international differentiation; while countries that reached and maintained the world's advanced level are advanced ones, and others are developing ones; there is mobility from one type of country to another
Process	Modernization is a historical process. Between the eighteenth century and the twenty-first century, it could be divided into two stages: the first modernization, the transformation from agricultural to industrial civilization and from traditional to modern civilization; and the second modernization, the transformation from industrial to knowledge civilization and from material to ecological civilization. The second modernization is not the end of history, and there will still be new changes in the future. The typical characteristics of the first modernization include industrialization, urbanization, democratization, and rationalization, and the typical characteristics of the second modernization include knowledgeablization, informatization, greening, and globalization, at present. The first modernization is the foundation of the second modernization, and the latter is partly the continuity and conversion of the former; the coordinated development of the first and second modernization is the integrated modernization. The modernization process has not only generality but also diversity and follows ten basic principles
Result	The outcomes of modernization include the formation of modernity, particularity, and diversity; improved labor productivity and quality of life, social progress, political democracy, cultural diversity, ecological change, and all-round human development; international differentiation, national stratification, and side effects; and the change in world frontier, international system, and national state. The main outcomes of the first modernization are the formation of the first modernity, particularity, and diversity, and its main features include industrialization, urbanization, democratization, social welfare, and universal compulsory education; the side effects include environmental pollution and so on. The main outcome of the second modernization is the formation of the second modernity, particularity, and diversity, and its current features include knowledge intensiveness, information intensiveness, innovation, environmental friendliness, and universal higher education; the side effects include cybercrime
Dynamics	Driving forces of modernization include innovation, competition, adaptation, exchange, national interests, market demand, etc. The driving mechanisms include innovation drive, triple-innovation drive, two-wheel drive, associative action, four-step hypercycle, composite interaction of three civilizations, innovation diffusion, innovation spillover, competition drive, productivity function, etc. For different stages, levels, fields, sectors, countries, paths, and models, the driving forces of modernization differ in some content
Models	Modernization has path diversity, model diversity, and path dependency, roughly including three basic paths and over 50 models of element mix

Note: As no consensus on the general modernization has been achieved up to now, this book take the general theory of the second modernization theory as a replacement of the core theory of general modernization. Some ideas and contents of the general theory of second modernization come from other theories such as the features and results of first (or classical) modernization
Source: RGCMS (2010), He (2010a, 2011)

Table 2.2 Operational definitions of modernization

Item	Operational definition	Application
Definition 1	Modernization is a type of frontier change and international competition of human civilization since the Industrial Revolution in the eighteenth century. It is the frontier process of the formation, development, and transition and international interaction of modern civilization; the composite process of alternate innovation, selection, diffusion, and withdrawal of modernization elements; and the international competition to catch up with, reach, and maintain the world's advanced level and the international differentiation thereof; in which, countries that reached and maintained the world's advanced level are advanced countries, and others are developing countries; there is mobility between the two groups of countries	Theoretical analysis
Definition 2	Modernization is the intersection of civilization development, civilization transition, and international interaction since the eighteenth century	Quantitative assessment
Definition 3	Modernization is the world frontier of modern civilization and the process and act of reaching the world frontiers	Policy analysis

Source: He (2010a, 2011)

The change in content of civilization includes the innovation, selection, diffusion, and withdrawal of civilization elements that includes the behaviors, structures, institutions, and ideas of civilization. The change in forms of civilization includes the formation, development and transition, and international interaction of modern civilization. The change of content occurs at microlevel and that of forms at macrolevel, with the former being the foundation of the latter.

Second, conceptual model of modernization. The theoretical meanings of modernization involve a great many basic concepts, such as civilization development, progress, adaptation and transition, and international interaction. There are no standard definitions of them. Models of their relations can be established according to their operational definitions (Table 2.3; Fig. 2.4).

Third, logical model of modernization. Modernization includes civilization change and international competition; world frontier of human civilization and the process and act of reaching the frontier; civilization development, civilization transition, and international interaction; and the innovation, selection, diffusion, and withdrawal of civilization elements. Logical relations exist among them (Fig. 2.5).

(3) Generality of Modernization

In the eighteenth to the twenty-first centuries, modernization involves multiple aspects. Generally, it has a starting point, early or late; it has the frontier which is dynamic and diverse; it has a process which is nonlinear and involves multiple paths; and it has outcomes which have both generality and diversity. As long as the world is diversified, modernization will continue for a long time. Now, it is impossible to figure out when it will end.

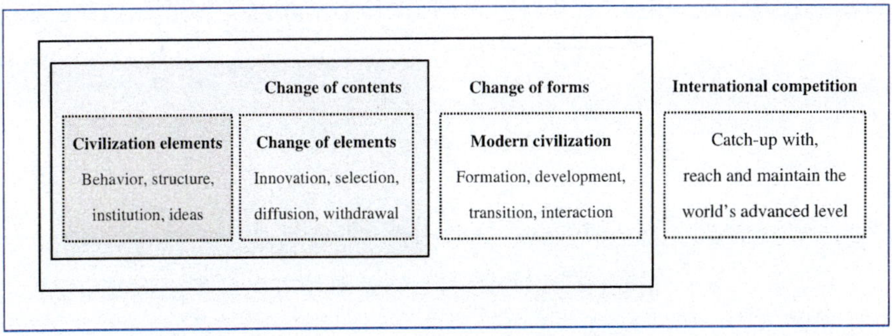

Fig. 2.3 Structural model of modernization: changes at two levels and international competition. Source: He (2011)

Table 2.3 Conceptual model of modernization

Item	Main contents
Hypothesis 1	Civilization progress means the change of civilization conducive to the emancipation and improvement of productivity, social equity and justice, and human liberation and development
Hypothesis 2	Positive adaptation of civilization means the adjustment of civilization that has no adverse effects on the improvement of productivity, social progress, and all-round human development
Hypothesis 3	Civilization transition means the transformation from agricultural to industrial civilization, from industrial to knowledge civilization, and from material to ecological civilization
Hypothesis 4	International interaction includes international cooperation, exchange, competition, and conflicts, excluding international wars
Inferences 1	Civilization development ≈ civilization progress + positive adaptation of civilization (improved quality and level + expanded scale and scope)
Inferences 2	Modernization ≈ civilization development × civilization transition × international interaction (change of international system and national status)

Source: RGCMS (2010)

According to the theoretical meanings and multifaceted examination of modernization, modernization roughly has the following generalities:

First of all, modernization is not only a sort of civilization change but also the civilization's competition. From the perspective of human civilization, modernization is a sort of civilization change and is driven by human interests and the advancement of science and technology. From the perspective of international relations, modernization is the international competition between different civilizations which are affected by national interests and the international environment. The two types of interests are sometimes consistent and sometimes in contradiction.

Second, modernization is not only a world trend but also a social option. To human civilization, modernization is historically inevitable and stands for the basic direction of human civilization process, while to individuals and ethnic groups, it is

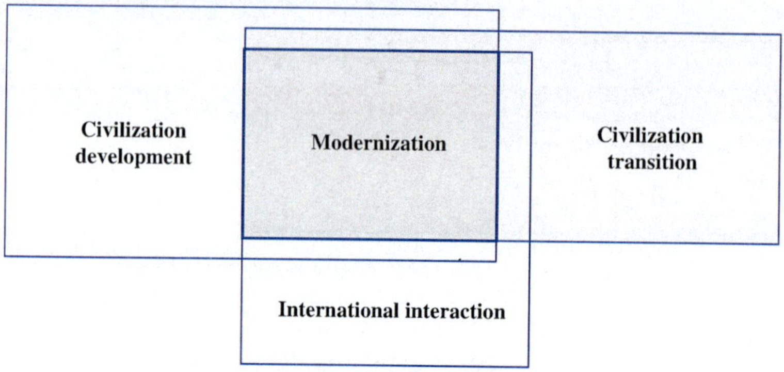

Fig. 2.4 Conceptual model of modernization. Note: Modernization is the intersection of civilization development, civilization transition, and international interaction. Source: RGCMS (2010)

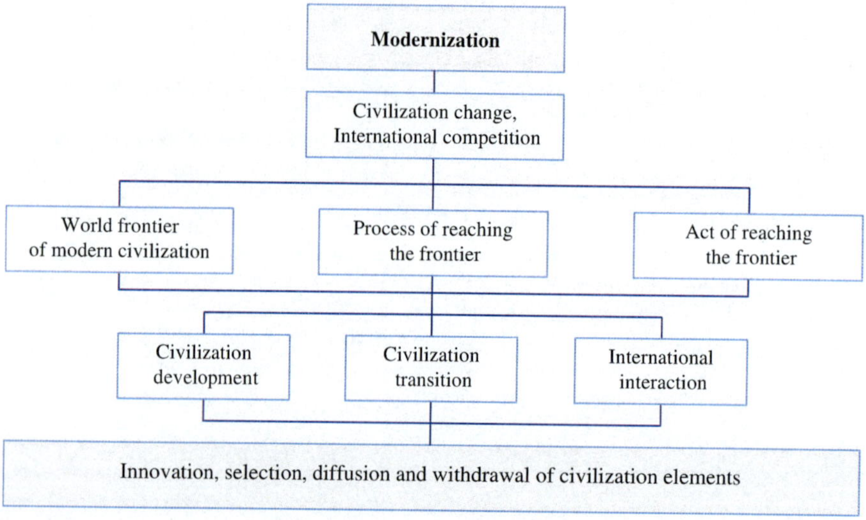

Fig. 2.5 Logical model of modernization. Source: RGCMS (2010)

a rational option which can be either accepted or rejected (Example 2.1). Choosing modernization entails the participation in the international competition for modernization, and rejecting it means to be left far behind the frontier of human civilization.

Example 2.1 The Choice of the Amish in the United States
The United States is an advanced country. In 2000, there were some 200,000 Amish in the United States, living in more than 20 states. A small number of Amish people also live in Canada. They are the descendants of immigrants from Europe, they have maintained the traditions of agricultural society; they neither use phones, nor watch TV, and take buses, but use buggies instead.

Third, modernization involves multiple dimensions which highly overlap with each other. It occurs at all levels of civilization and in all fields and aspects, entailing analysis of such dimensions as time, space, field, and content; different dimensions have different features, adding diversity to modernization. At the same time, different dimensions of modernization are independent while overlapping and interacting with each other.

Fourth, modernization should be analyzed at both national and international level. At national level, modernization includes the development and transition of national civilization. From the perspective of development and transition, each country's modernization is likely to advance and succeed, early or late. At international level, modernization includes international interaction and the change of international status. From the perspective of international interaction and competition, only a number of countries can reach and remain at the world frontier, suggesting that the probability of national success is limited.

Fifth, modernization gives rise to not only civilization progress but also side effects. On the one hand, modernization brings about the improvement of productivity and quality of life, social progress, and human development; on the other, it gives rise to many side effects which differ from stage to stage. For example, the side effects of the first modernization include environmental pollution, ecological degradation, gaps between the rich and poor, recurrent economic crisis, etc., while those of the second modernization include information divide, cybercrime and international risk, and so on.

Sixth, modernization has both generality and diversity. They are the collections of the general and individual features, respectively, and reflected at all levels and in all fields of modernization, ranging from the process, outcome, and dynamics to models of modernization and from the behavior, structure, and institution to ideas of civilization (Fig. 2.6). They do not exclude each other, but emerge as two objective laws.

Seventh, there is not only international convergence but also international differentiation in modernization. International convergence includes the convergence in terms of industrial structure, employment structure, educational structure, government structure, infrastructure, and urbanization. International differentiation

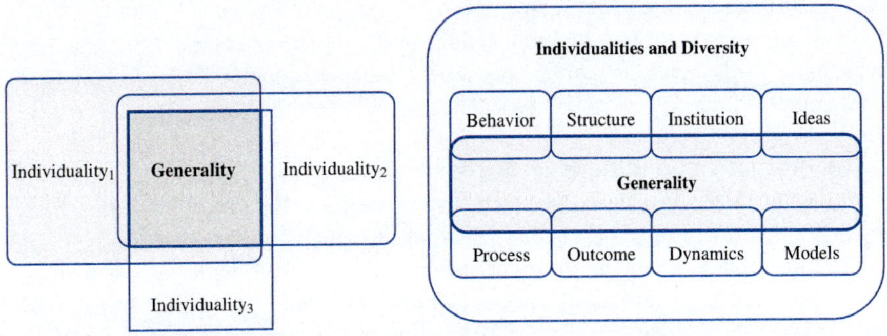

Fig. 2.6 Generality and diversity of modernization. Source: RGCMS (2006, 2010)

includes widening international gaps in economic efficiency and national income per capita, international division of labor, and the diversification of social pattern and cultural values, and so on. Differentiation and convergence arise in different aspects.

Eighth, modernization cannot be done once and for all; not to advance is to go back. An advanced country may be downgraded to a developing one, falling from the world frontier, and a developing country may be upgraded to an advanced one, rising to the world frontier (Example 2.2). In the process of modernization, both stagnation and slow advancement lead to a downgraded status.

Example 2.2 Rise and Fall of the National Level and Status in the International System

Between 1700 and 2005, Portugal was downgraded to a developing country from an advanced one; Argentina was upgraded to an advanced country from a developing one and then downgraded again to a developing country; both the United States and Japan were upgraded to advanced countries. The ranking is based on the GDP per capita (at PPP-based prices) (Maddison 2001).

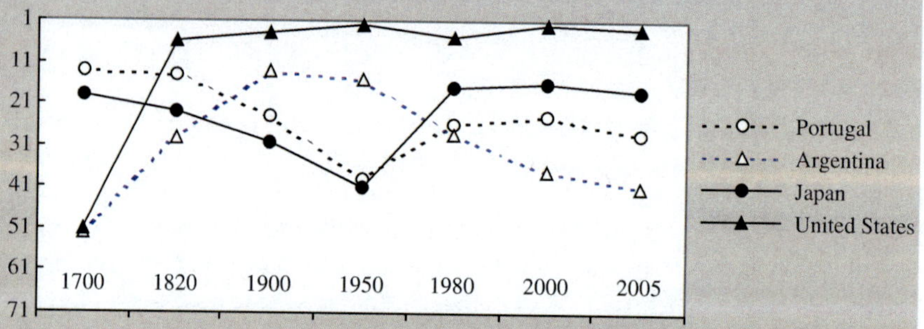

Change of countries' rankings between 1700 and 2005

2.1.1.2 Basic Scope of Modernization

Modernization is a sort of civilization change and international competition, but not all changes of civilizations can be counted as modernization and also the international competition.

(1) The Restrictive Conditions of Modernization

Generally, modernization has two restrictive conditions. First of all, it is the time, which is since the eighteenth century. Second, it is the nature, which is advanced and frontier. Only changes of civilization which accord with the restrictive conditions can be regarded as modernization. In brief, the world frontier of human civilization since the eighteenth century, the act and process of reaching the frontier, and related civilization changes belong to modernization (Fig. 2.2).

(2) The Criteria of Modernization

The second modernization theory holds that the ultimate goal of human civilization and modernization is to improve the quality of life (including people's material and cultural life) and help human beings liberate themselves and achieve all-round development. Based on this goal, three criteria of modernization can be laid down, i.e., productivity, social progress, and human development (Table 2.4).

The three criteria of modernization are qualitative and are fairly ambiguous because there is no standard understanding of social equity and all-round human development. For example, social equity is a vague concept. It includes the equity in opportunity, process, outcome, etc. But it is very hard, or impossible, to achieve equity in process and outcome at the same time. Since individuals differ considerably in abilities, process equity will lead to outcome inequity and result equity to process inequity. That is the so-called "equity paradox." Different nations or cultural models differ substantively from each other in the understanding of social equity and all-round human development.

(3) The Basic Scope of Modernization

According to the theoretical meanings, two restrictive conditions and three criteria of modernization, we can identify what belong to and what do not belong to modernization and therefore define the basic scope of modernization (Table 2.5).

2.1.1.3 Basic Types of Modernization

There are many methods for defining the basic types of modernization. For example, classification can be made according to the main denotation of modernization (Fig. 2.7) or to the key elements and denotation of modernization (Table 2.6). Types of modernization in different stages are different; for example, the four types of the first modernization are innovative, follow-up, grafting, and learning modernization, and the types of the second modernization are taking shape.

Table 2.4 Three criteria of modernization

Criteria	Content	Remark
Criterion 1	Conducive to the emancipation and improvement of productivity, without damaging the natural environment	Criterion of productivity
Criterion 2	Conducive to social equity and progress, without hindering economic development	Criterion of social progress
Criterion 3	Conducive to the liberation and all-round development of human beings, without undermining social harmony	Criterion of human development

Note: This table provides the criteria of the second modernization. Because there was absence of ecological awareness before the 1960s, the three criteria of the first modernization are being conducive to the emancipation and improvement of productivity, to social equity and progress, and to the liberation and development of human beings

Source: RGCMS (2010)

Table 2.5 Basic scope of modernization

No.	Civilization changes in the scope of modernization	Civilization changes not in the scope of modernization
1	World frontier and the process of reaching it since the eighteenth century	Civilization changes prior to the eighteenth century
2	Transition from agricultural to industrial civilization since the eighteenth century	Traditional changes in traditional agricultural civilization since the eighteenth century
3	Transition from industrial to knowledge civilization since the twentieth century	Traditional changes in hunting and gathering culture since the eighteenth century
4	Civilization developments during the above process	Civilization degeneration since the eighteenth century
5	Forward civilization adaptation during the above process	Backward civilization adaptation (adverse to human development) since the eighteenth century
6	International interaction during the above process	Antimodernization since the eighteenth century

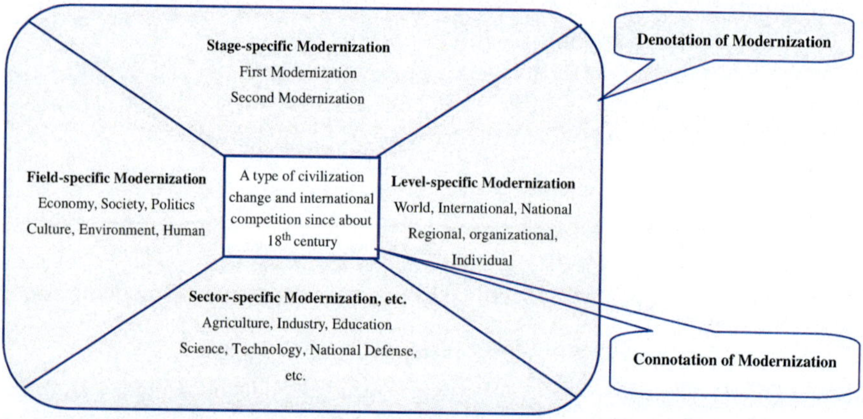

Fig. 2.7 Connotation and denotation of modernization. Note: By connotation, modernization is a type of civilization change and international competition. Its denotation includes modernization of different stages, levels, fields, sectors, and aspects, as well as of civilization behavior, structure, institution, and ideas

2.1.2 General Process

The general process refers to the process of the modernization in the world, which is based on the national modernization around the world, but not refers to any special country at all. The analysis of modernization process includes that of the types, phases, characteristics, contents, and principles concerning the process (Fig. 1.18), and result, dynamics, and models of the process could be discussed separately.

Generally, the process of modernization can be roughly divided into two types according to the theoretical meanings and practical experience of modernization. One type is the frontier trajectory of modernization process, which can be called the

Table 2.6 Basic types of modernization

No.	Classified by	Type of modernization
1	Starting time	First-initiated modernization, later-coming modernization
2	Source of knowledge	Endogenous or exogenous modernization, innovative or learning modernization, follow-up modernization, etc.
3	Main feature	Active or reactive modernization, market-oriented or planning-commanded modernization, leading or catch-up modernization, etc.
4	Geographic region	Modernization of East Asia, Middle East, Eastern Europe, Latin America, Africa, etc.
5	Civilization element	Modernization of civilization behavior, structure, institution, idea, etc.
6	Object of study	Stage-specific modernization, level-specific modernization, field-specific modernization, sector-specific modernization, special modernization, etc.

Source: RGCMS (2010)

frontier process of modernization. Another type is the process of catching up with the world frontier, which can be called the catch-up process of modernization. The two types of processes are not only interconnected but also different from each other and, what is more, they interact with each other. The two processes may promote each other in the context of fair trade but may conflict with or even restrain each other in the case of unfair trade.

2.1.2.1 Main Stages of Modernization Process

Modernization is one type of changes of human civilization since about eighteenth century, and the stage division of the modernization and civilization should be coordinated with each other. The main stages of the frontier process and the catch-up process of modernization are different from each other.

(1) Main Stages of the Frontier Process of Human Civilization

According to the second modernization theory (He 1999), the stages of the frontier trajectories of human civilization include four ages (tool-making, agricultural, industrial, and knowledge age) from the origin of human beings to the end of twenty-first century, and each age includes four phases (the start, developing, mature, and transition phase). The frontier process of human civilization includes the four eras and 16 phases (Table 2.7), and each age and phase has different structure of social productivity (Table 2.8).

Countries differ from each other in the process of human civilization. Taking the four ages of civilization as horizontal axis and the level of social development as the vertical axis, we can get the coordinates of the frontier trajectories of human civilization and modernization (Fig. 2.8). Every country or region can find its position in the coordinates according to their level and phase of developing, and some countries will see that the different regions in the different position (phase), such as the situation of People's Republic of China (Example 2.3).

Table 2.7 Periodic table of the frontier trajectories of human civilization and modernization process

Stages	Chronology[a]	Time span	Main characteristics	Annotation
Tool-making age	ca. 2.5 m–5,500 years ago	2.5m years	Primitive culture, economy, society	Emergence of human beings, socialization
Start phase	ca. 2.5m–0.2m years ago	2.3m years	Early of Paleolithic Age, hunting, and gathering	
Developing phase	ca. 0.2m–0.04m years ago	0.16m years	Middle of Paleolithic Age, consanguineous clans	
Mature phase	ca. 0.04m–0.01m years ago	0.03m years	Late of Paleolithic Age, matrilineal society	
Transition phase	ca. 0.01m–5,500 years ago	5,000 years	Neolithic Age, horticulture, patrilineal society	
Agricultural age	ca. 3500 BCE–AD 1763	5,260 years	Agricultural civilization, economy, society	Birth of civilization, agriculturalization
Start phase	ca. 3500 BCE–500 BCE	3,000 years	Ancient civilization, planting and breeding, slave system	
Developing phase	ca. 500 BCE–AD 618	1,100 years	Classical civilization, feudal system	
Mature phase	ca. AD 618–1500	900 years	Thriving of oriental civilization, European Middle Ages	
Transition phase	ca. 1500–1763	260 years	Rise of European civilization, spread of renaissance	
Industrial age	ca. 1763–1970	210 years	Industrial civilization, economy, society	
Start phase	ca. 1763–1870	110 years	First Industrial Revolution, mechanization	First modernization, industrialization, urbanization, democratization, deagriculturalization
Developing phase	ca. 1870–1913	40 years	Second Industrial Revolution, electrification	
Mature phase	ca. 1914–1945	30 years	Family mechanization and electrification, mixed economy	
Transition phase	ca. 1946–1970	20 years	Third Industrial Revolution, automation, electronic computer	
Knowledge age	ca. 1970–2100	130 years	Knowledge civilization, economy, society	Second modernization, knowledge intensive, ecologization, suburbanization, deindustrialization

(continued)

Table 2.7 (continued)

Stages	Chronology[a]	Time span	Main characteristics	Annotation
Start phase	ca. 1970–1992	20 years	First Information Revolution, personal computer, knowledge based	
Developing phase	ca. 1992–2020	30 years	Second Information Revolution, networking, greenization	
Mature phase	ca. 2020–2050	30 years	Biological design and cloning, new biological revolution	
Transition phase	ca. 2050–2100	50 years	New carrier vehicles, new physical revolution	

[a]The stages are defined based on the level and characteristics of the frontier trajectory of human civilization and modernization process; nations and countries do not develop on a synchronous basis
Source: He (1999)

Example 2.3 Yangtze River Model of Human Civilization and Modernization Process

Many historians compare human history to a long river. The Yangtze River is the third longest river in the world. It flows for about 6,300 km from the glaciers on the Tibetan Plateau in the west and empties into the East China Sea at Shanghai. The Yangtze drains an area of some 1.81 million square kilometers, and its river basin which includes 12 regions is home to about 517 million Chinese people (figure of 2006). Based on the studies we have made since 2000 about the civilization and the spatial distribution of modernization in the Yangtze River Valley, we have found the temporal and spatial convergence between civilization and modernization process (He 2003).

In the upper reaches of the Yangtze River, agriculture covers most regions, and some regions still have the characteristics of primitive societies. For example, about 40,000 Moso people lived in the border areas of Yunnan and Sichuan provinces; they preserved the lifestyle of a "matriarchal society" which is close to that in late Paleolithic period some 10,000 years ago. Besides, some ethnic minorities living in the mountainous areas in southern Yunnan such as Bulang, Jino, Lahu, and Hani still had a slash-and-burn lifestyle which is close to people's life in the Neolithic period about 6,000 years ago.

The middle reaches of the Yangtze River are mostly rural areas where peasant economy, agricultural society, and agricultural civilization are dominant. For example, in 2006, 61% of the population of Hunan province lived in rural areas, and 54% of the labor force engaged in agricultural production.

In the lower reaches of the Yangtze River, there are many cities in southern Jiangsu province which have the features of industrial societies; industrial civilization is dominant there. In 2006, the proportion of agricultural labor fell to 28%, and urbanization rate reached 52% in Jiangsu.

(continued)

Table 2.8 Stages in the frontier trajectory of human civilization and estimated structures of productivity

Stages in the frontier trajectory of human civilization		Labor distribution in frontier countries and regions (%)				
Stages	Period of time (approximately)	Hunting and gathering	Agriculture	Industries	General services	Knowledge industries
Tool Age	Birth of humans–3500 BC					
Start stage	2.5 million BC–200000 BC	100	–	–	–	–
Developing stage	200000 BC–40000 BC	100	–	–	–	–
Mature stage	40000 BC–10000 BC	98	–	–	1	1
Transition stage	10000 BC–3500 BC	95	2	1	1	1
Agricultural Age	3500 BC–AD 1763					
Start stage	3500 BC–500 BC	90	6	1	2	1
Developing stage	500 BC–AD 618	45	50	1	2	2
Mature stage	AD 618–1500	5	88	2	3	2
Transition stage	AD 1500–1763	–	90	2	6	2
Industrial Age	1763–1970					
Start stage	1763–1870	–	80	10	8	2
Developing stage	1870–1913	–	50	30	16	4
Mature stage	1914–1945	–	30	40	20	10
Transition stage	1946–1970	–	10	50	20	20
Knowledge Age	1970–2100					
Start stage	1970–1992	–	8	32	30	30
Developing stage	1992–2020	–	5	25	25	45
Mature stage	2020–2050	–	2	18	20	60
Transition stage	2050–2100	–	1	16	18	65

Note: Labor distribution in frontier countries and regions, roughly the employment structure at the starting of different stages, indicates the world's advanced level of development at that time. Agriculture includes crop farming and animal husbandry. Knowledge industries refer to knowledge-intensive industries including the production and dissemination of knowledge and knowledge-based services. The data on labor distribution in the Tool Age are estimates; those on labor distribution in the late period of Knowledge Age are forecasts; those on labor distribution in the initial periods of the Agricultural Age, the Industrial Age, and the Knowledge Age are simulated figures of countries at different development stages. The symbol "–" indicates "zero" or "approximately zero"

Source: He (2003), RGCMS (2006)

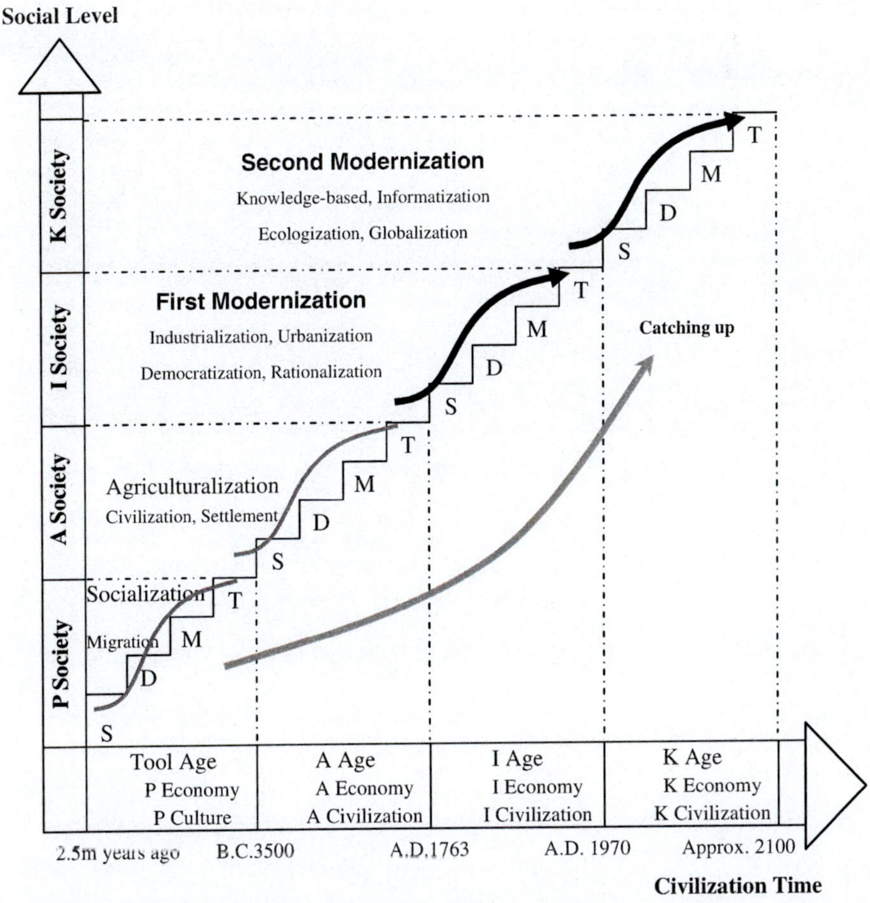

Fig. 2.8 Coordinates of the frontier trajectories of human civilization and modernization process. Note: P, A, I, and K refer to primitive, agricultural, industrial, and knowledge, respectively. S, D, M, and T refer to the start, developing, mature, and transition phase, respectively. The time of civilization is based on the frontier trajectory of human civilization; time span is just a relative criterion. Civilization development is asynchronous among different countries and regions. Source: He (2003)

In the Yangtze River estuary, Shanghai is developing a knowledge-based economy and walking toward a knowledge society. Since 1990, the city has seen the decline in the proportion of industrial labor and the increase in the percentage of labor for the service sector. The proportion of service labor reached 54% in 2006. Now, Shanghai is going through the changes from modernization to postmodernization just as advanced countries have experienced since 1970.

The Yangtze River Valley has its cultural diversity. According to *China Statistical Yearbook*, 35 ethnic minorities of the 56 ethnic groups in China live in the 12 regions in the Yangtze River Basin; every ethnic group has its own culture, so there are diverse cultures in the areas. Development is uneven in different sections of the Yangtze River. For instance, in the middle reaches,

(continued)

there are both rural areas and large- and medium-sized cities, so such areas have the characteristics of agricultural and industrial civilization, displaying the diversity of civilization.

To conclude, in 2006, the upper, middle, and lower reaches and estuary of the Yangtze River respectively showed the typical features of the four stages in the evolution of human society; they are primitive, agricultural, industrial, and knowledge societies. It is just like the history flows along the river. Such a phenomenon can be regarded as a case of "river of human history" or a microcosm of social evolution; briefly, it is called the Yangtze River model of human civilization and modernization process (Fig. 3.12). The model turns the temporal structure of the frontier trajectories of civilization and modernization process into a spatial structure, leading to the temporal and spatial convergence of civilization development and modernization process.

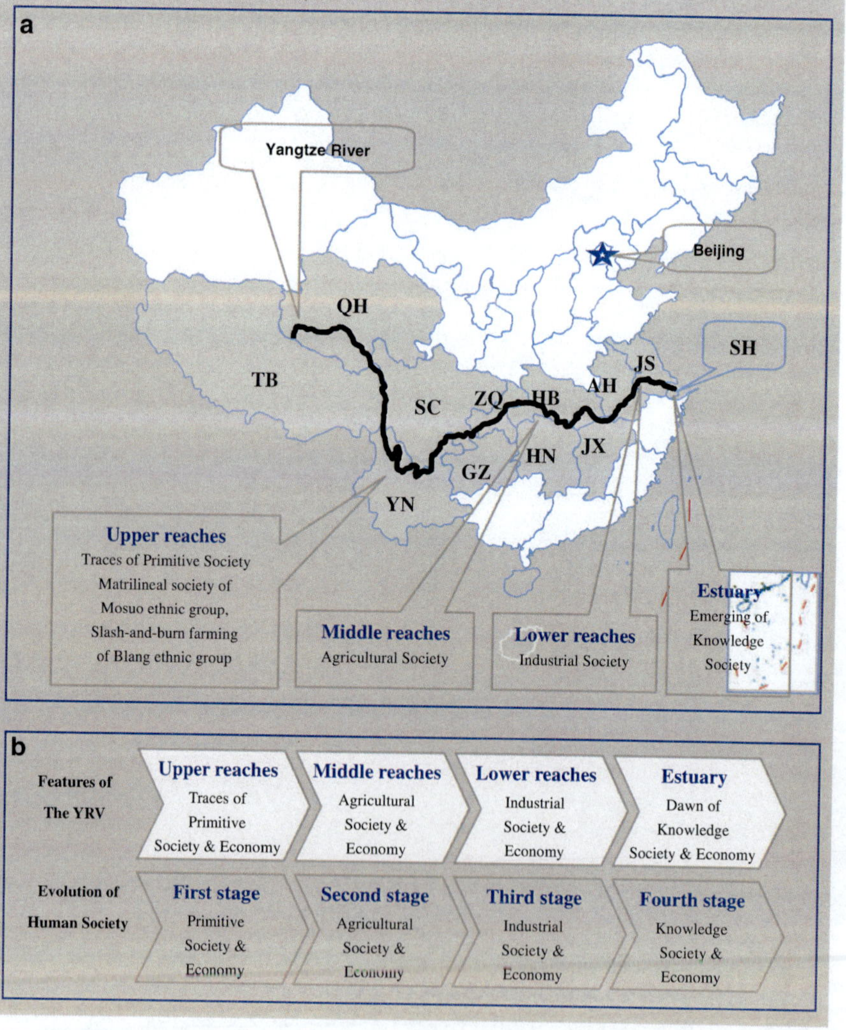

Yangtze River model of human civilization and modernization process. **(a)** The regional features of the Yangtze River Valley in 2006. **(b)** The Yangtze River model of the human civilization process. Note: The upper reaches of YRV include the six regions of Qinghai (QH), Tibet (TB), Yunnan (YN), Sichuan (SC), Chongqing (CQ), and Guizhou (GZ); its middle reaches comprise the four regions of Hubei (HB), Hunan (HN), Jiangxi (JX), and Anhui (AH) (partial), while its lower reaches include the two regions of Jiangsu (JS) and Shanghai (SH). The most parts of Anhui belong to the lower reaches. Shanghai lies near the estuary of the river. The first modernization refers to the shift from agricultural to industrial society; the second modernization refers to the shift from industrial to knowledge society.
Source: He (2003, 2010)

The frontier process of civilization is not linear. Although productivity has been increasing during the process, several shifts have occurred in the direction and productivity structure. Thus, civilization process has been on an upward spiral. Taking productivity structure as the horizontal axis, productivity level as the vertical axis, and the frontier trajectories of human civilization and modernization process as variables, we can draw a road map of such frontier trajectories (Fig. 2.9). Every country and region can find its position in the road map.

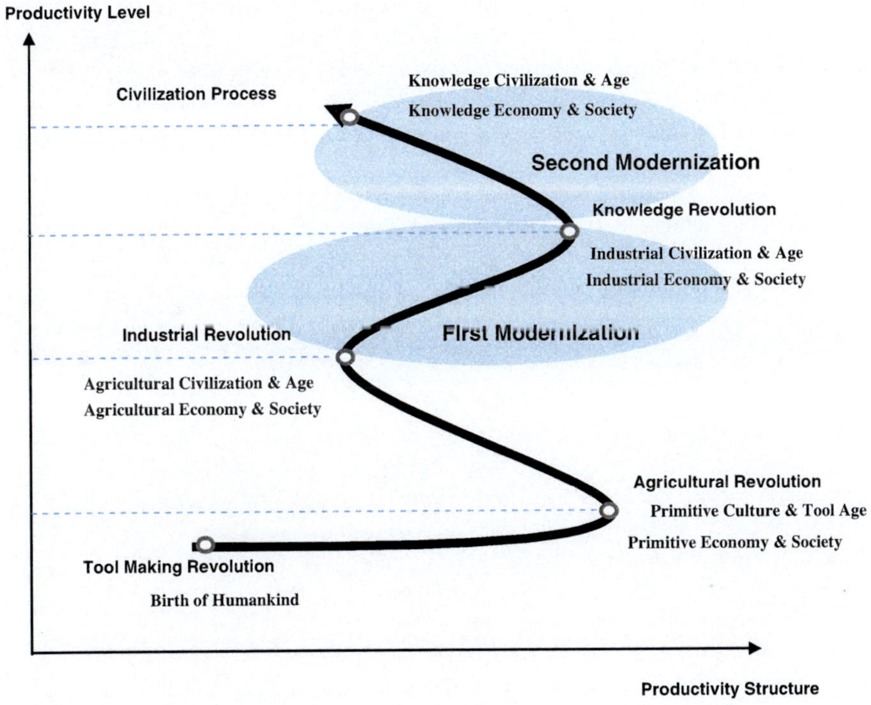

Fig. 2.9 Road map of the frontier trajectories of human civilization and modernization process. Note: The central axis of human civilization has experienced three shifts, giving rise to four ages which have distinctive structures of civilization. The *vertical axis* represents productivity level, and the horizontal one represents productivity structure. The *horizontal scale* is the ratio of labor in agriculture to that in hunting and gathering in the Tool Age, the ratio of labor in hunting and

Table 2.9 Stages of the frontier process of modernization

Item	First modernization	Second modernization
Duration	Approximately 1763–1970	Approximately 1970–2100
Content	Transition from agricultural to industrial civilization and from traditional to modern civilization	Transition from industrial to knowledge civilization and from material to ecological civilization
	Transition from agricultural to industrial society, from agricultural to industrial economy, from agricultural to industrial politics, and from agricultural to industrial culture	Transition from industrial to knowledge society, from industrial to knowledge economy, from industrial to knowledge politics, from industrial to knowledge culture, and from material to ecological culture
Period	Start, development, mature, and transition	Start, development, mature, and transition
Wave	Mechanization, electrification, and automation	Informatization, bionics, and experiencing

Source: RGCMS (2010)

(2) Main Stages of the Frontier Process of Modernization

The frontier process of modernization is just the frontier trajectory of the modernization process. We have discussed the main stages of the frontier trajectory of the civilization process (Table 2.7). Summarily, the frontier process of modernization includes two major stages, eight phases, and six waves (Table 2.9).

First, two major stages of the frontier process. During the eighteenth to twenty-first centuries, the frontier process of modernization includes the first modernization and the second modernization.

Second, eight phases of the frontier process. Divided according to industrial and employment structures, both the first modernization and the second modernization include four phases, namely, start, developing, mature, and transition (Example 2.4).

Example 2.4 Stages of National Modernization in 2005

In 2005, among 131 countries, 28 countries were in the second modernization; of them, eight countries including the USA were in the development phase of the second modernization, and 20 countries including Japan were in the start phase. Ninety countries were in the first modernization; of them, 12 countries including Czech were in the transition phase of the first modernization, 31 countries including China were in the mature phase, 28 countries including India were in the development phase, 19 countries including Laos were in the start phase, and 13 countries including Burundi remained traditional agricultural societies, with some ethnic groups still living in a primitive

Fig. 2.9 (Continued) gathering to that in agriculture in the Agriculture Age, the ratio of labor in industries to that in agriculture in the Industrial Age, and the ratio of labor in material industries to that in knowledge-based industries in the Knowledge Age. The *circles* represent tool-making revolution, agricultural revolution, industrial revolution, and knowledge revolution (including information and ecological revolutions), respectively. Source: He (2003) society. The features of 2005 reflected the historical footsteps of the frontier process of modernization.

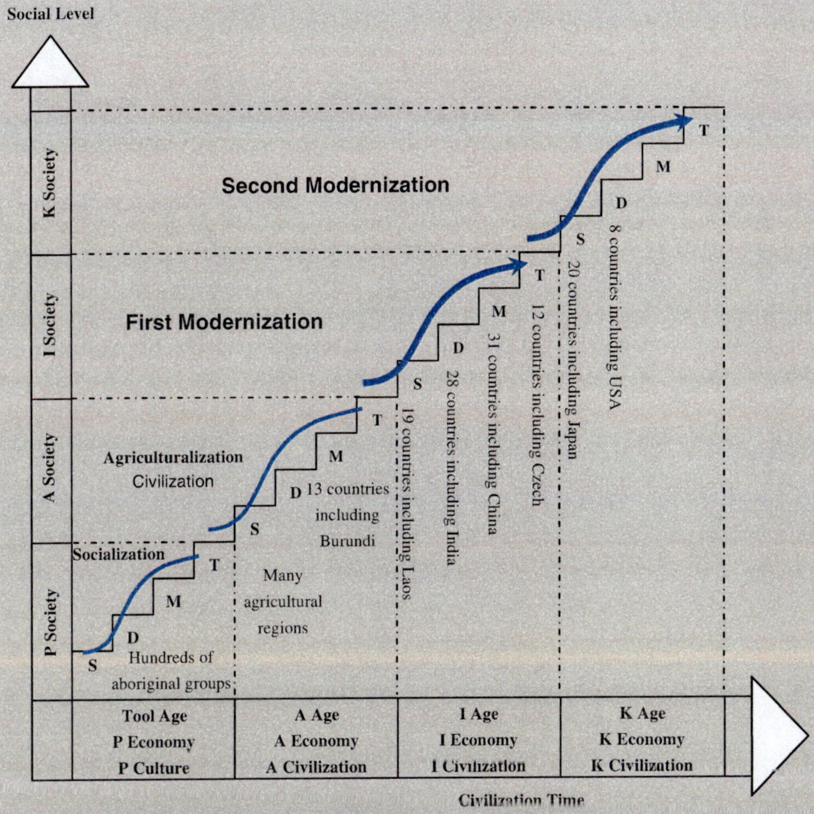

Stages of national modernization in 2005. Note: P, A, I, and K refer to primitive, agricultural, industrial, and knowledge, respectively. S, D, M, and T refer to the start, developing, mature, and transition phase, respectively. The civilization time was the time based on the track of the forerunner of the civilization process. Source: RGCMS 2008)

Third, six waves of the frontier process. According to the contents of economic and social modernization, the frontier process of modernization includes six waves (Table 2.9 and Table 3.6); the first four waves are the frontier trajectory of the modernization process, and the last two waves (the fifth and sixth waves) are just forecasts. The first modernization includes three waves, and the second modernization is expected to experience three waves as well.

(3) Main Stages of the Catch-Up Process of Modernization

The catch-up process of modernization is the process where developing countries catch up with the world frontier. The stages of the catch-up process in different

Table 2.10 Paths of the catch-up process of modernization

Path	Main stage	Annotation
Follow-up path	First modernization and second modernization	First and second modernization take place one after another
Catch-up path	First modernization and integrated modernization	Integrated modernization is coordinated development of the first and second modernization
Restricted catch-up path	First modernization, integrated modernization, and second modernization	Integrated modernization is inserted between the first and second modernization
Restricted catch-up path	Integrated modernization and second modernization	Appropriate for countries which started modernization after 1980

countries may overlap or differ to some degree. They are closely related to the starting time and level of national modernization and with the time span of the frontier process.

First, main stages of the catch-up process. The main stages basically accord with the frontier process, but there are roughly four catch-up paths. The first is the follow-up path; the second is the catch-up path; the third and fourth are restricted catch-up paths (Table 2.10).

Second, eight phases of the catch-up process. The eight phases of the frontier process are defined according to industrial and employment structures. The change of industrial and employment structures is gradual, generally without progress by leaps and bounds. These phases also apply to the catch-up process. The major stages of the catch-up process may be different from the frontier process, but the eight phases are essentially consistent.

Third, the waves of the catch-up process are, sometimes, unnoticeable. The six waves of the frontier process are noticeable. In the catch-up process, the contents of the six waves are essential, which can be advanced one after another or at the same time in a mixed way. For example, countries which started modernization in 1960 need not achieve mechanization first and then electrification, but instead advance mechanization, electrification, and automation at the same time; when the three waves are fused, the manifestation will be unnoticeable. Other waves can be advanced in the same way.

Fusion of two waves: Mechanization and electrification, or automation and informatization, go hand in hand.

Fusion of three waves: Mechanization, electrification, and automation or electrification, automation, and informatization go hand in hand.

Fusion of four waves: Mechanization, electrification, automation, and informatization go hand in hand.

The fusion of waves is related to the start time, progress, and world frontier of national modernization (Fig. 2.10) and to the stages of national modernization. For example, the fusion of four waves is equal to the coordinated development of the first and second modernization, namely, integrated modernization.

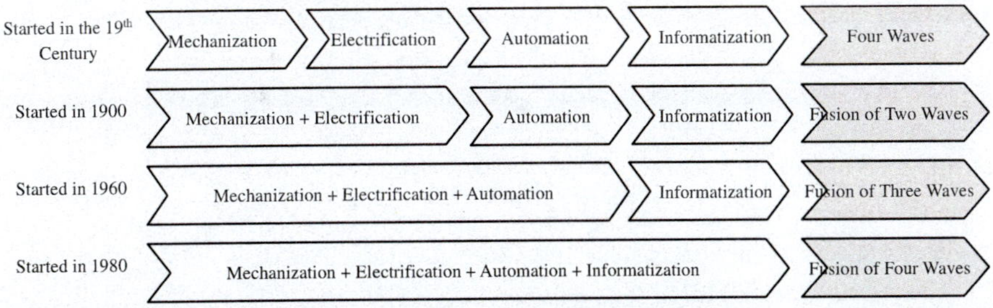

Fig. 2.10 Fusion of waves in the catch-up process of modernization. Note: Fusion of waves means that two or more than two waves advance at the same time instead of occurring one after another in an orderly manner

2.1.2.2 Main Characteristics of Modernization Process

Features of modernization process can be understood from different perspectives and at different levels.

(1) General Features of the Frontier Process

The world frontier in the process of modernization is, in some fields and aspects, unitary, while in other fields and aspects, diversified. The frontier process of modernization has not only generality but also diversity. *China Modernization Report 2010* summarizes its about 22 features (Table 2.11). Sometimes, features of the frontier process may represent those of the modernization process.

(2) General Features of the Catch-Up Process

First of all, generally, the features of the frontier process also apply to the catch-up process.

Second, there are differences between the catch-up process and the frontier process in time, technology, level, etc., and the two processes interact with each other. The catch-up process has about 12 features of its own (Table 2.12).

Third, features of the catch-up process in relation to the frontier process. For example, it cannot leap over a historical stage; it may choose a development path and fuse the contents of different stages; it may skip a technological stage, fuse technological waves, and choose technology; and it may reduce the time, social, ecological, and opportunity costs, but can hardly reduce the economic cost (Table 2.13).

(3) Main Features of Two Major Stages

Between the eighteenth and twenty-first centuries, the frontier process of modernization can be divided into two major stages: the first and second modernization. They differ from each other in main contents, main features, and features of different fields (Table 2.14).

First, the main features of the first modernization (*until 1970*). They include, for example, industrialization, urbanization, democratization, bureaucratization, institutionalization, rationalization, secularization, mechanization, electrification, automation,

Table 2.11 Characteristics of the frontier process of modernization

No.	Feature	Exemplary phenomena or explanation
1	Long-term	A long-term process. Modernization has continued to the twenty-first century from the eighteenth century, and there will be new changes in the twenty-second century
2	Stage-specific	A process with stages. Modernization in the eighteenth to twenty-first centuries is divided into two stages, first and second modernization
3	Asynchronous	A process of asynchrony. Modernization in different countries and fields is asynchronous
4	Unbalanced	An unbalanced process. Different countries and fields differ in the level of modernization
5	Predictable	A predictable process. The process of modernization follows certain patterns and is partly predictable
6	Optional	An optional process. Some world frontiers are diversified, frontiers and paths of which are optional
7	Multipath	A multipath process. Paths to world frontiers are sometimes unitary and sometimes diversified
8	Path dependency	A process of path dependency. The selection of paths for modernization is subject to national objective conditions and international environment
9	Global	A global process. It originated in Western Europe and gradually spread to other parts of the world
10	Interactive	An internationally interactive process. Different countries' modernization, frontier process, and catch-up process interact with each other
11	Competitive	A process of international competition. It includes international competition for reaching and maintaining the world's advanced level of development and transformation
12	Risky	A process involving risks. For example, an advanced country may be downgraded to a developing one
13	Reversible	A process that may suspend or reverse. It may suspend, discontinue, or reverse for a short period
14	Systematic	A systematic process. Modernization in different fields and aspects interacts with each other
15	Composite	A composite process. It includes the innovation, selection, diffusion, and withdrawal in six fields such as economy
16	Two-sided	A process with not only general but also individual characteristics. It has general and diverse characteristics in stage, content, and feature
17	Revolutionary	A revolutionary change. It compares to the transition from primitive culture to agricultural civilization
18	Innovative	A process comprising innovation. Innovation is the source and powerhouse of modernization
19	Progressive	A process comprising progress. It includes the improvement of productivity and quality of life, all-round human development, etc.
20	Adaptable	A process comprising adaptation. It has not only progress but also adaptable changes such as the change of family size
21	Conflicting	A process comprising multiple conflicts, such as the conflict between tradition and modernity and conflict of interests
22	Side effects	A process with side effects. There are different side effects in different stages, such as environmental pollution and widening gaps between the rich and poor

Source: RGCMS (2010)

Table 2.12 Characteristics of the catch-up process of modernization

No.	Feature	Exemplary phenomena or explanation
1	Unequal	An internationally unequal process. Advanced countries are at an advantage and powerful position, while developing ones are at a disadvantage weak one
2	Unstable	An unstable process. Fast transition of civilization may evoke varieties of social and economic conflicts
3	Contradictory	A process full of contradictions. There is the need to constantly make a choice between catching up with frontiers and social stability
4	Diversified	A process that is more diversified still. The catch-up process surpasses the frontier process in diversity
5	Goal-oriented	A goal-oriented process, usually targeted at world frontiers and the world's advanced level
6	Passive	A process comprising passive changes, for example, passively accepting international rules made by advanced countries
7	Initiative	A process comprising initiative choice. A country may choose a path, model, and technology according to its own features
8	Pioneering	A process comprising local innovation. A country may make path innovation according to its own features
9	Learning	A process of borrowing international experience. Experience of foregoers can be used as reference
10	Integrative	A process comprising content integration and stage fusion. A country may experience several waves at the same time
11	Leaping	A process in which it is possible to skip a technological stage, for example, entering the era of combustion engine age by leaping over the era of steam engine
12	Challenging	A process with restricted potentials for upgrading. There is an approximately 5% probability that a developing country catches up with the world frontier

Source: RGCMS (2010)

Table 2.13 A comparison of features between the catch-up process and the frontier process

Item	Features of the frontier process	Features of the catch-up process
Historical stage	May not leap over, two major stages and eight phases	May not leap over, paths may be chosen and stages fused
Technological stage	May not leap over, six technological waves	May leap over, technological waves may be fused and technology chosen
Time cost	Differ from one country to another	May be lowered, time taken may be shortened
Economic cost	Cost for economic transition, economic cycle, and innovation	Can hardly be lowered, technology can be imported, cost for purchasing intellectual property
Social cost	Cost for social transition and social mobilization	May be lowered, substantive mistakes may be avoided or reduced
Ecological cost	Environmental pollution and ecological degradation	May be lowered, an environmentally friendly path may be chosen
Opportunity cost	Differ from one country to another, cost for path choice	May be lowered, international experience may be used as reference to reduce policy cost

Note: The fusion of stages refers to the phenomenon that the contents of two stages are fused into one stage
Source: RGCMS (2010)

Table 2.14 Main features of the first and second modernization

Item	First modernization	Second modernization
Time span	Approximately 1763–1970	Approximately 1970–2100
Comprehensive	Industrialization, urbanization, democratization, and social welfare	Knowledgeablization, informatization, greening, and globalization
Economy	Industrialization, marketization, standardization, and deagriculturalization	Knowledgeablization, ecologicalization, globalization, and deindustrialization
Society	Urbanization, social welfare, mobilization, and universal compulsory education	Informatization, suburbanization, greening, and universal higher education
Politics	Democratization, rule of law, bureaucratization, centralization, and institutionalization	Knowledgeablization, internationalization, decentralization, and individuation
Culture	Secularization, rationalization, popularization, and material value	Diversification, networking, industrialization, and the quality of life
Environment	Economism, conquest of nature, and, ecological damage	Environmental protection, mutualism, and economic growth while ensuring environmental protection
Human	Opening, equalization, sense of achievement, and personal values	Lifelong learning, individuation, sense of happiness, and self-realization
Side effects	Environmental pollution, differentiation between the rich and poor, etc.	Cybercrime, information divide, etc.
Other	Some traditional values continue to exist and function	Some traditional values continue to exist and function

Note: The environment refers to the natural environment here. The features of the second modernization are ones that appeared in and before 2005; there will be new development in the future
Source: RGCMS (2010)

standardization, specialization, marketization, centralization, social differentiation and integration, mobilization, social welfare, high efficiency, deagriculturalization (lowered percentage of agriculture), modern science and energy, public communication, and universal compulsory education, with side effects including environmental pollution and differentiation between the rich and poor, etc.

Second, the main features of the second modernization (*until 2005*). They include, for example, knowledgeablization (knowledge intensive), informatization (information intensive), service orientation, networking, digitalization, intelligentization, globalization, innovation, individuation, diversification, decentralization, greening, ecologicalization, dematerialization (lowered material and energy intensity), deindustrialization (lowered percentage of industry), suburbanization, urban–rural balance, lifelong learning, and universal higher education, with side effects including cybercrime and information divide, etc.

Third, the relation between two modernizations. The first modernization is the foundation of the second modernization. The second modernization is the continuity and development of the first modernization in some aspects such as democratization, rationalization, and scientific and technological advance; in some aspects, it is the "reversion" or transition of the first modernization, for example, from industrialization to deindustrialization, from centralization to decentralization, and from ecological destruction to environmental protection; and in some aspects, it is innovation, for example, knowledgeablization, informatization, and networking.

2.1.2.3 Contents and Principles of Modernization Process

Modernization is a sort of civilization change and international competition, including the changes of civilization contents, civilization forms, and international systems. The process of modernization includes the modernization of civilization's contents and forms and the change of international systems. Relatively speaking, civilization contents are at microlevel, while civilization forms and international systems are at macrolevel; the microprocess is the important foundation of the macroprocess, while the latter is the concentrated reflection of the former.

The basic principles of the modernization process include not only the main mechanisms and fundamental principles for changes in civilization's contents, forms, and international systems but also their driving forces and models. The analysis of driving forces and models will be discussed later. The civilization change and international competition involve the change of civilization in all fields, including economic, social, political, cultural, ecological, and human fields. The change in different fields will be specially treated in Chap. 6.

(1) Main Mechanism of the Modernization of Civilization Contents

The modernization of civilization contents is an essential part of the modernization process. Civilization contents include all sorts of civilization elements, such as behavior, structure, institutions, and ideas. Generally, the modernization of civilization contents is a composite process of the alternate innovation, selection, diffusion, and withdrawal of civilization elements; it includes the two-way circulation of the innovation, selection, and diffusion of civilization elements and the reversible withdrawal of civilization elements, which together form a hypercycle (Fig. 2.11). The prominent feature of these processes is diversity.

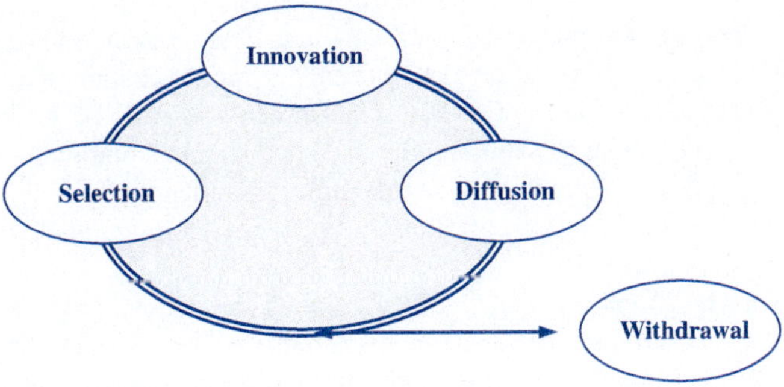

Fig. 2.11 Hypercycle model of civilization content modernization (four-step hypercycle). Source: RGCMS (2010)

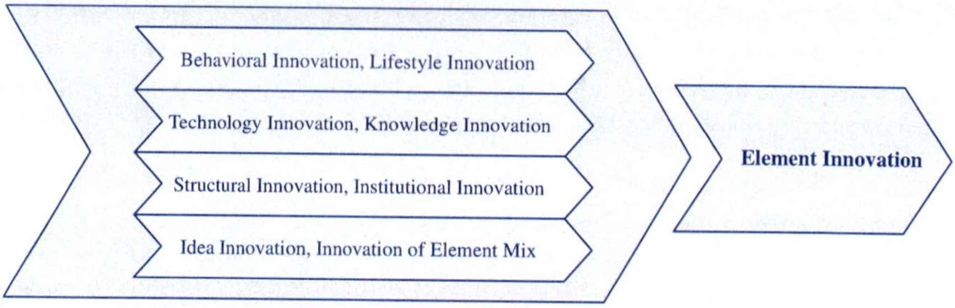

Fig. 2.12 Main paths of civilization element innovation. Source: RGCMS (2010)

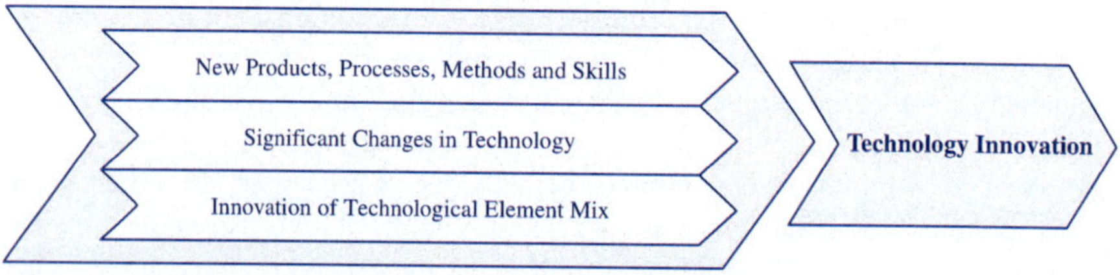

Fig. 2.13 Main paths of technology innovation. Source: RGCMS (2010)

First of all, innovation of civilization elements is of diversity (Fig. 2.12). The innovation of civilization elements is a form and path of the modernization of civilization contents. It has a diversity of forms and paths, for example, behavioral innovation, lifestyle innovation, component innovation, structural innovation, institutional innovation, idea innovation, and innovation of civilization element mix. Component innovation, where the word "component" refers to a structural unit corresponding to a structure, including objects and knowledge, embraces object innovation (technology innovation), knowledge innovation, etc. On element innovation, the technology innovation, knowledge innovation, institutional innovation, and conceptual innovation play a very prominent role, entailing an intensive discussion.

Paths of technology innovation (Fig. 2.13). Technology innovation is a form and path of the innovation of civilization elements and the modernization of civilization contents. Generally, technology innovation is a process in which a technological invention is first successfully commercially used and acquires commercial profits. There are many types of technologies, for example, solidified technology, independent methods, and know-how. Different types of technology innovation have different characters.

Paths of knowledge innovation (Fig. 2.14). Knowledge innovation is a form and path of the innovation of civilization elements and the modernization of civilization contents. Generally, knowledge innovation is the discovery, invention, creation, or application of some new knowledge for the first time in the world (He and Zhang 2001). There are many types of knowledge, for example, scientific knowledge,

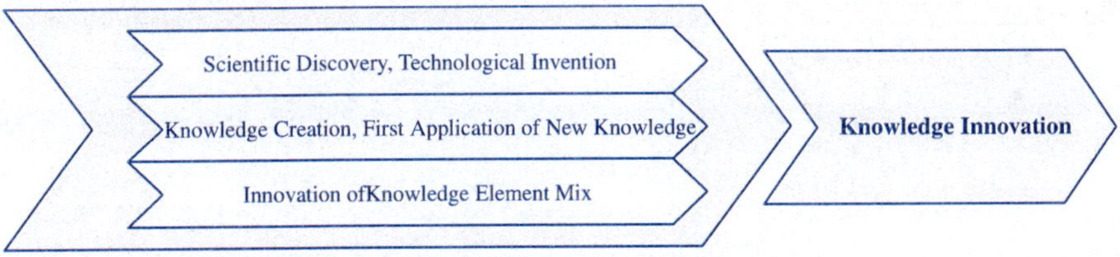

Fig. 2.14 Main paths of knowledge innovation. Source: RGCMS (2010)

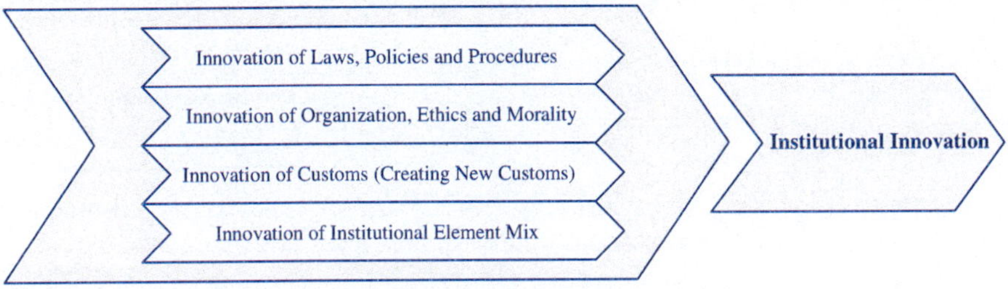

Fig. 2.15 Main paths of institutional innovation. Source: RGCMS (2010)

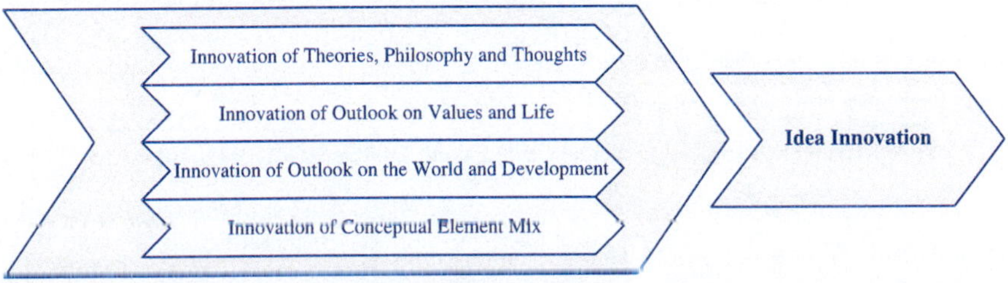

Fig. 2.16 Main paths of idea innovation. Source: RGCMS (2010)

technical knowledge, social knowledge, cultural knowledge, integrated knowledge, coded knowledge, and noncoded knowledge (implied knowledge); innovation in different types of knowledge has different features.

Paths of institutional innovation (Fig. 2.15). Institutional innovation is a form and path of the innovation of civilization elements and the modernization of civilization contents. Generally, institutional innovation is to establish a new institution which appears in the world for the first time. There are many types of institutions, for example, political, economic, social, cultural, and environmental institutions; innovation in different types of innovation has different features.

Paths of idea innovation (Fig. 2.16). Idea innovation is a form and path of the innovation of civilization elements and the modernization of civilization contents. Generally, idea innovation is to raise a new concept which appears in the world for

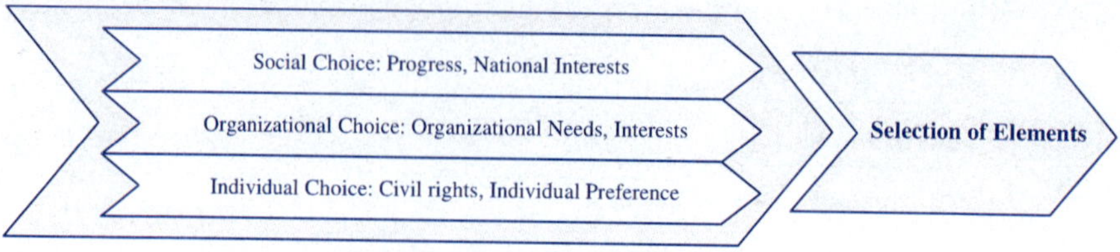

Fig. 2.17 Main paths of civilization element selection. Source: RGCMS (2010)

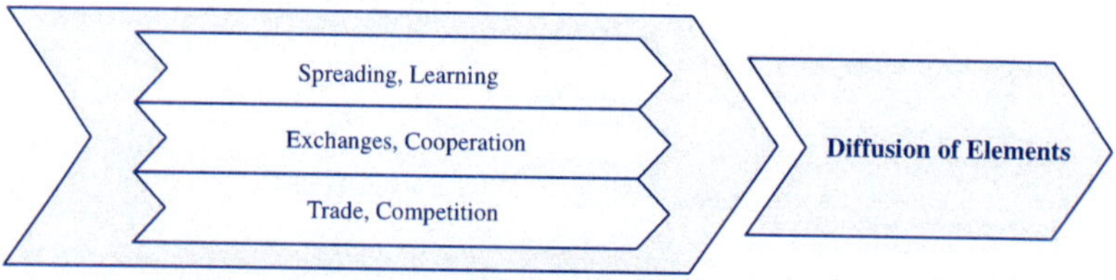

Fig. 2.18 Main paths of civilization element diffusion. Source: RGCMS (2010)

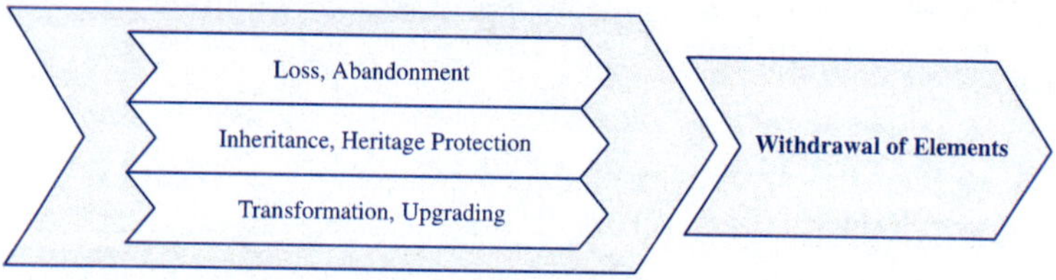

Fig. 2.19 Main paths of civilization element withdrawal. Source: RGCMS (2010)

the first time. There are many types of ideas, for example, political, economic, social, cultural, environment, and life concepts; innovation in different types of concepts has different features.

Second, the selection of elements is of diversity (Fig. 2.17). The selection of elements is an important part and form of the modernization of civilization contents.

Third, the diffusion of elements is of diversity (Fig. 2.18). The diffusion of elements is a form and path of the modernization of civilization contents.

Fourth, the withdrawal of elements is of diversity (Fig. 2.19). The withdrawal of elements is a form and path of the modernization of civilization contents.

(2) Main Mechanisms of the Modernization of Civilization Forms

Modernization of civilization forms is an essential part of the modernization process. Generally, it is a composite process of the formation, development, transition, and international interaction of modern civilization, with each aspect having a diversity of paths, contents, or forms.

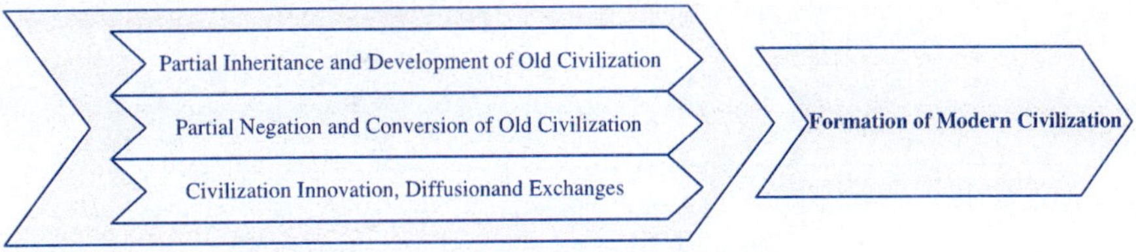

Fig. 2.20 Three sources of modern civilization. Source: RGCMS (2010)

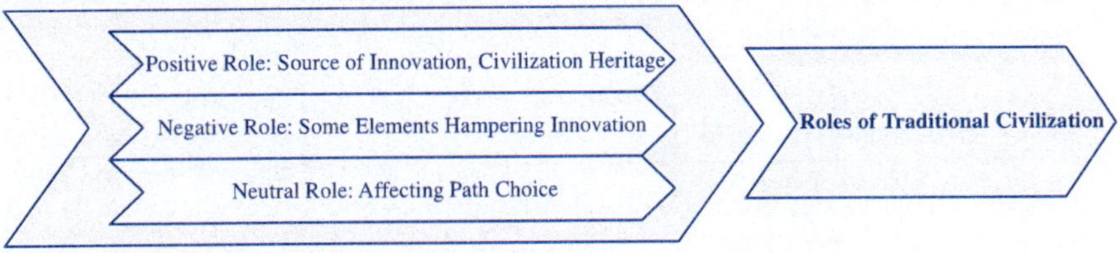

Fig. 2.21 Three roles of traditional civilization. Source: RGCMS (2010)

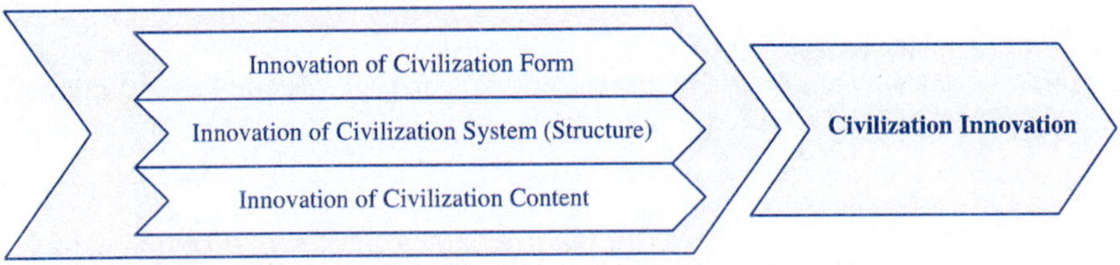

Fig. 2.22 Main paths of civilization innovation. Source: RGCMS (2010)

First of all, there are three paths in the formation of modern civilization (Fig. 2.20). The formation of modern civilization is an important part of the modernization of civilization forms and is closely related to traditional civilization, civilization innovation, civilization diffusion, and exchange.

Traditional civilization roughly has three types of functions (Fig. 2.21). During the process of modernization, traditional civilization did not disappear, but has long existed and continued to play three roles (a) a positive role: some elements of traditional civilization serve as the source of innovation, while some—for example, civilization heritage—may add diversity to civilization; (b) a negative role: some elements of traditional civilization hinder innovation of civilization; and/or (c) a neutral role: for example, affecting the path choice for modernization and the choice of direction for civilization innovation.

Civilization innovation is of diversity (Fig. 2.22). Civilization innovation is a path in the formation and development of modern civilization and involves a diversity of forms and paths. Content innovation is at microlevel, while the form and system innovation is at macrolevel; content innovation is the important foundation, while the form and system innovation is the concentrated reflection of content innovation.

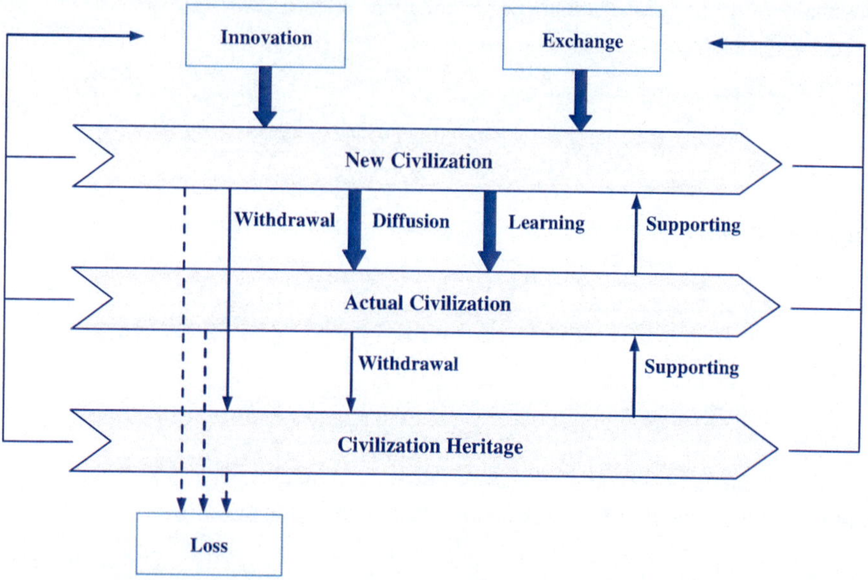

Fig. 2.23 Composite interaction in civilization system innovation (composite interaction among three types of civilization). Note: Civilization heritage is roughly equal to cultural heritage, including general cultural heritage, endangered intangible cultural heritage, and invalid traditional knowledge. Source: RGCMS (2010)

The principle of civilization system innovation (Fig. 2.23). Civilization system innovation is an expressive form of modernization and a process of interaction among civilization heritage, actual civilization, and new civilization. It involves a variety of paths of action, such as civilization innovation, exchange, diffusion, learning, withdrawal, and loss. The macroexpression is mainly the structural change of actual civilization, including falling percentage of traditional civilization, first rising then falling percentage of modern civilization, and increasing percentage of postmodern civilization.

Second, the development of civilization is a sort of civilization change, including civilization advancement and adaptation. In the process of the first modernization, a civilization change falls into civilization development if it is conducive to (a) the emancipation and improvement of productivity, (b) social equity and progress, and (c) human liberation and development (Fig. 2.24). In the process of the second modernization, the three conditions need to be complemented by the harmonious relationship between the economy and the natural environment.

Third, civilization transition is of diversity (Fig. 2.25). Civilization transition is an important part of the modernization of civilization forms. It is a long-term and progressive process, in which different civilization forms change in terms of their percentages; when a new civilization form overtakes an old one, civilization transition is basically completed (Fig. 2.26).

Fourth, international interaction is of diversity (Fig. 2.27). International interaction is an important part of the modernization of civilization forms. If it is carried

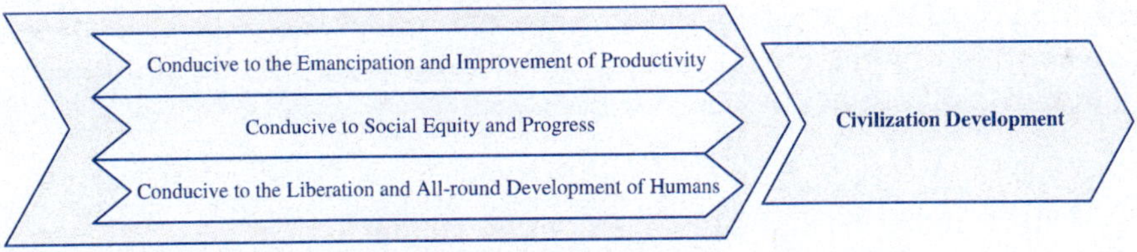

Fig. 2.24 Three criteria of civilization development. Source: RGCMS (2010)

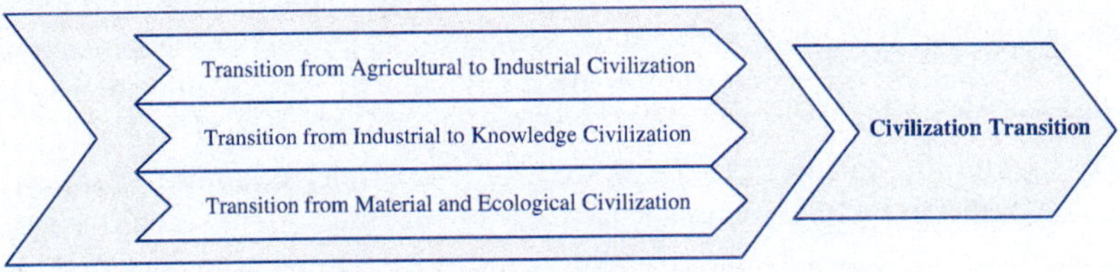

Fig. 2.25 Main paths of civilization transition. Source: RGCMS (2010)

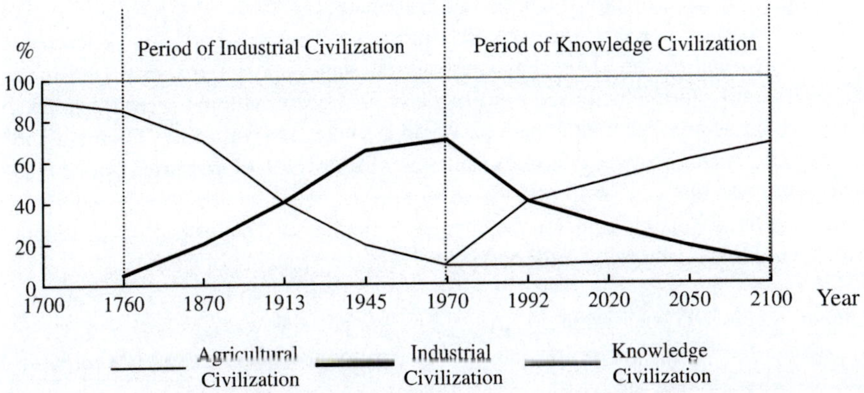

Fig. 2.26 Transition of civilization forms. Note: The *curves* in the diagram represent the percentages of three civilization forms in national civilization. When the percentage of industrial civilization exceeds that of agricultural civilization, the transition from agricultural to industrial civilization is basically completed; when the percentage of knowledge civilization exceeds that of industrial civilization, the transition from industrial to knowledge civilization is basically completed. Source: He (2010a)

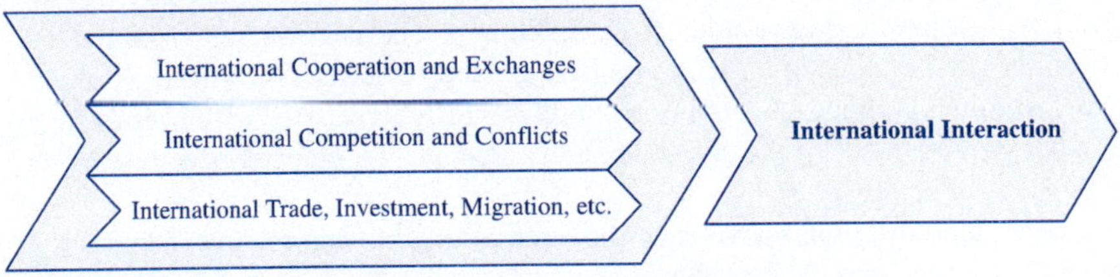

Fig. 2.27 Main paths of international interaction. Source: RGCMS (2010)

out on an equal basis, countries promote each other; if not, in the short run, some countries profit, while some countries suffer; in the long run, countries might restrain each other.

(3) Main Mechanisms of the Change of International System

There has been no unified definition of international system. Generally, the international system means the maximum aggregation of numerous units that interact with and depend on each other; currently, this system includes all countries in the world (Buzan and Little 2000). The international system in the process of modernization is one that "sees national modernization as the structural unit," or modernization system for short.

The change of the international system is a multiple, composite process of international differentiation, national stratification, national mobility, and structural changes, occurring at two levels: structural units and the international system, with the former being the foundation for the latter. The change in the international system generally follows four basic principles: asynchronous process, unbalanced distribution, structural stability, and changeable status.

International differentiation generally means international gaps and differences widening as well as the change in international status and international divisions. National stratification chiefly refers to the stratification of national levels; countries which have reached and maintained the world's advanced level of development and transformation are advanced countries, and others are developing countries that include moderately developed, preliminarily developed, and underdeveloped countries. National mobility mainly refers to the change in international status based on national levels, including changes in world rankings and in the grouping of countries.

First of all, the change in levels of structural units mainly includes the change of national levels and international status.

The change in national levels. The level of national modernization is a function of time, which changes over time.

The change in world rankings. The change of a country in world rankings is in positive correlation with the country's initial level and relative speed that is the difference between the modernization speeds of two countries.

The change in the grouping of countries. The change in the grouping of countries is random, changing only among several states, which can be analyzed through a Markov chain (Fig. 2.28). There is certain probability of such change, which is related to time spans. For example, for a span of 50 years, the probability that an advanced country is downgraded to a developing one is about 10%, while the probability that a developing country is upgraded to an advanced one is about 5%; the probability that moderately and preliminarily developed countries change in status is about 40%; and the probability that an underdeveloped country is upgraded is about 10%.

Second, the change in the level of the international system mainly includes the change of system level and structure.

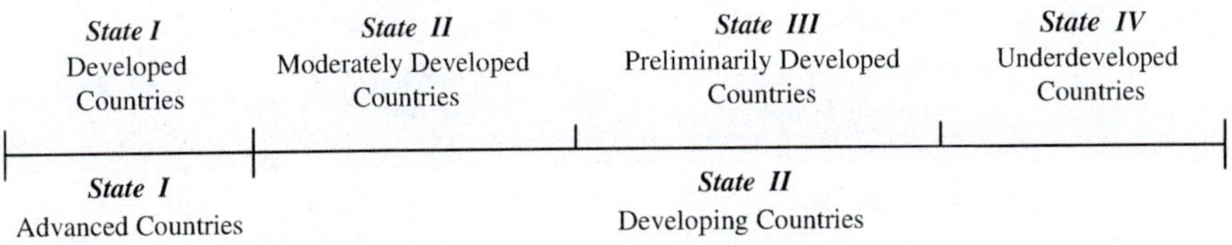

Fig. 2.28 Several international statuses in terms of national level (Markov Chain). Note: Random process I: There are two states for the international status of a national level: advanced and developing countries; one country can only be in either of the states at a particular time, and it may enter from one to another state randomly. Random process II: There are four states for the international status of a national level: developed, moderately developed, preliminarily developed, and underdeveloped countries; one country can only be in one of the four states at a particular time, and it may enter from one to another state randomly. Source: He (2010a)

The change in system level. The level of the international system is a function of time and improves over time. The level of the international level is in positive correlation with the modernization levels and stages of its structural units.

The change in system structure. The structure of the international system is relatively stable. Generally, the percentage of advanced countries is around 15% and that of developing countries is around 85%; in a period of 50 years, the probability that an advanced country remains an advanced one is about 90%, and the probability that a developing country remains a developing one is about 95%.

(4) Basic Principles of the Modernization Process

The process of modernization generally follows ten basic principles (Table 2.15), involving the change in civilization contents, civilization forms, and international systems, as well as the process, distribution, structure, level, path, demand, effectiveness, behavior, state, axis, etc., of modernization.

Principle 1: Asynchronous process. Asynchronous in space: One country differs from another in the start and pace of modernization. Asynchronous in fields: Modernization of different fields is asynchronous. Asynchronous in elements: Modernization of civilization elements is asynchronous.

Principle 2: Unbalanced distribution. Unbalanced in spatial distribution: The vertical and lateral distribution of modernization in a country or region is unbalanced. Unbalanced in field distribution: The vertical and lateral distribution of modernization in different fields is unbalanced. Unbalanced in element distribution: The vertical and lateral distribution of modernization of civilization elements is unbalanced.

Principle 3: Structural stability. The vertical and lateral distribution structures of modernization in countries and regions, in different fields, and of civilization elements are relatively stable.

Generally, the percentage of advanced countries is below 20% and that of developing countries is above 80%; in a period of 50–100 years, there is an approximately 90% probability that an advanced country maintains its status and an approximately 95% probability that a developing country maintains its status.

Table 2.15 Basic principles of the second modernization theory

Principle	Content or explanation	Annotation
Asynchronous process	The process of modernization is asynchronous; the process of modernization in different countries, fields, and elements are all asynchronous	International system
Unbalanced distribution	The distribution of modernization is unbalanced; both the lateral and vertical distribution of modernization in space, fields, and elements are unbalanced	
Structural stability	The distribution structure of modernization is relatively stable; the percentage of advanced countries is below 20% and that of developing countries is above 80%	
Changeable status	The international status of modernization is changeable, with an approximately 10% probability that an advanced countries descends and an approximately 5% that a developing country ascends	
Predictable behavior	The behavior of modernization is partly predicable, decisions of which have limited rationality (bounded rationality principle)	Civilization contents
Optional path	Modernization paths are optional; the choice of a path is subject to a country's own history and condition (path dependency)	
Increasing needs	Social needs for modernization increases; need I—satisfaction—and need II (Maslow's need hierarchy theory)	
Diminishing returns	The effectiveness of modernization policy decreases; innovation I—change in effectiveness—and innovation II; effectiveness cycle and solidification	
Unrepeatable state	The state of modernization changes in an unrepeatable way; state I—change—and state II	Civilization forms
Changing axis	The axis of modernization changes, and different fields have different axes (Bell's axis theory)	

Source: RGCMS (2006, 2010)

The international structure of modernization roughly follows the 20/80 rule that people usually speak of.

Principle 4: Changeable status. The relative modernization level, status, and gap of countries and regions, various fields, and civilization elements are changeable. There is certain probability for transfer of status. In a period of 50–100 years, there is an approximately 10% probability that an advanced country is downgraded to a developing one and an approximately 5% probability that a developing country is upgraded to an advanced one.

Principle 5: Optional path. Modernization paths are optional; patch choice has certain path dependency; which path to choose is relative and conditional, and there are path-locking phenomena; path choice is closely connected with social achievement and involves very high opportunity cost.

All roads lead to Rome is a worldwide proverb. Every person may take his own path, but not all can arrive at Rome at a prescribed time. As a matter of fact, some cannot reach Rome all their life in a predictable time. The stability of advanced and developing countries in terms of international status may be closely linked to path dependency and path locking.

Principle 6: Predictable behavior. The behavior of modernization is partly predictable; the behavioral predictability is relative and conditional; the behavioral predictability is closely related to social achievement; the predictability of behavior will increase, because the development of information technology will improve access to information.

According to the "bounded rationality" theory of the recipient of the Nobel Prize for Economics, due to the presence of risk, uncertainty, and information incompleteness, behavioral decisions of humans are usually "the choice of seeking satisfaction" rather than "the choice of seeking the best" (Simon 1982). The behavioral rationality of humans is limited. That is the behavioral basis for the principle of behavioral predictability.

Principle 7: Increasing needs. Social needs in the process of modernization increase gradually. The satisfaction of a need does not mean the termination of social advance, but the emergence of a new need. The circular advancement of need I—satisfaction—need II is one of the major mechanisms in the process of modernization.

According to American psychologist Maslow's need hierarchy theory (Gobble 1970), human behavior is dominated by five types of needs: physiological needs, safety needs, social needs (needs for belonging and love), needs for respect, and needs for self-realization, and the five types of needs go from lower to higher levels. That is the psychological foundation for the increasing needs principle.

Principle 8: Diminishing returns. In the process of modernization, there will be three types of change in effectiveness of social policies and innovations. The first change is decreasing effectiveness. The effectiveness of social policies and innovations decreases over time and finally tends to be ineffective. This does not mean that a social policy is ineffective but that it has fulfilled its historical mission. The second change is effectiveness cycle. The effectiveness of some social policies and innovations has a life cycle, during which it undergoes rises and falls and finally tends to be ineffective. The third change is effectiveness solidification. The effectiveness of some social policies and innovations undergoes rises and saturates and finally becomes part of the social institution and functions stably in a long run. The principle of decreasing effectiveness explains the features of decreasing effectiveness and of the downward trend of an effectiveness cycle.

The circular advancement of policy innovation I—change in effectiveness—policy innovation II is an important mechanism of modernization.

Principle 9: Unrepeatable state. The process of modernization is the aggregation of a series of civilization states, while each civilization state is an aggregation of a group of civilization changes. During this process, no two civilization states are completely the same. The circular advancement of civilization state I—change—civilization state II is an important mechanism of modernization. Therefore, the significance of historical experience is relative.

Principle 10: Changing axis. The process of modernization is a sort of axis change. American sociologist Bell (1973) holds that different societies have different axis principles and structures; the axis principle is the dynamic principle, the most important of all logic, and the axis structure is the sort of organizational structure surrounded by other structures; for each aspect of society, there is a dominating axis principle, and the transition from the preindustrial to industrial society and to postindustrial society embraced the change of social axes. Generally, the axis principle is the core rule and process of a society, and the axis structure is the core structure of a society; the process of modernization is a transition process of not only the axis principle but also the axis structure.

(5) Applicability of Principles of Modernization Process

The abovementioned main principles of the modernization process generally apply to the frontier process and to the catch-up process on the whole; their applicability may differ slightly in different fields and stages and greatly in different levels, which needs to be specially dealt with.

2.1.3 General Result

The general result refers to the result of the modernization in the world, which is based on the national modernization around the world, but not refers to special country at all. By comparing the macro- and the microfacts at the start and end sections of the modernization process, we can identify the result (Fig. 1.19).

According to the theoretical meanings and empirical studies of modernization, the outcomes of modernization include the formation of modernity, particularity, and diversity; the improvement of labor productivity and quality of life, social progress, political democracy, cultural diversity, ecological changes, and all-round human development; the international differentiation, national stratification, and side effects; and the changes in world frontiers, international system, and national state.

Generally, outcomes in the process of modernization are a function of time, changing over time, which include the changes of indicators, levels, and characteristics (Fig. 1.19), and can be analyzed at three levels: world frontier, international system, and national state. Modernization outcomes are closely related to not only the time span of the modernization process but also its starting section, finishing section (end point for analysis), and geographic coverage, as well as modernization goals.

2.1.3.1 Change of World Frontier

In the process of modernization, the world frontier of human civilization is the frontier of modernization, which is closely connected with modernity. So far, there has been no uniform definition of modernity. Roughly before 1970, modernity (first modernity) was a theoretical summarization of the structures and characteristics of industrialized countries. Roughly from 1970 onward, postmodernity or second modernity was raised, which was a general theoretical summarization of the structures and characteristics of the world frontier. There are roughly two ways of research into modernity: interpretivist analysis and positivist induction. If there are no definite time boundaries and geographic coverage, the discussion about modernity is more of dialectic. Generally, the change of world frontier may be understood from theoretical and practical perspectives, which support each other rather than being isolated from each other.

(1) Theoretical Analysis of the Change of World Frontier

First, the frontier trajectory of the modernization process. According to the second modernization theory, between the eighteenth and the twenty-first centuries, the frontier trajectory of the modernization process can be divided into two stages: the first and second modernization, each with different contents and features (Table 2.16). The contents and features of the world frontier are different on different historical sections.

Second, the change of the world frontier of the modernization process. Generally, the change of the world frontier may be understood by comparing the differences in the world frontiers between the starting and finishing sections of the modernization process. Before 1970, the world frontier of the modernization process was in the first modernization stage, and the change of the world frontier was mainly that of first modernity. From 1970 onward, the world frontier of the modernization process entered the second modernization stage, and the change of the world frontier was mainly that of second modernity.

Table 2.16 World frontiers of human civilization and modernization (exemplary contents and features)

Item	Civilization universals	Tradition	World frontier of first modernization Formation of first modernity	World frontier of second modernization Formation of second modernity
Time	From 3500 BC	3500 BC–1763 AD	Approximately 1763–1970	Approximately 1970–2100
Civilization	–	Agricultural civilization	Industrial civilization	Knowledge civilization
Economy	Division of labor, exchange, currency	Agricultural economy, handmade	Industrial economy, industrialization	Knowledge economy, knowledgeablization
Society	Family, education, crime	Agricultural society, familial	Industrial society, urbanization	Knowledge society, informatization
Politics	Government, diplomacy, power	Agricultural politics, feudal	Industrial politics, democratization	Knowledge politics, internationalization
Culture	Language, literature, art	Agricultural culture, fatalism	Industrial culture, rationalization	Knowledge culture, networking
Environment	Change or adapt to the environment	Develop or adapt to the nature	Economism, conquer the nature	Environmental protection, mutualism
Humans	Gender role; etiquette	Conservative, hierarchical	Openness, equality	Lifelong learning, sense of happiness

Note: Civilization universals refer to the elements of civilization that always exist in the course of human civilization, but the connotations or features of which might change. Generally, the contents and outcomes of the modernization process are closely connected. Not only is modernity a theoretical summarization of the outcomes of the modernization process, but it also reflects the contents and features of the frontier process of modernization. Rather than being totally opposed to each other, tradition and modernity are relative and represent features of different stages. The environment refers to natural environment here

Source: He (2003), North (1981), Brown (1991)

Table 2.17 Positivist approach to the world frontier of the modernization process

No.	Basic requirements	Attention
1	Define the start, end, and coverage of the modernization process	Avoid shooting randomly and interpreting without real understanding
2	Compare the starting and finishing sections of modernization	Avoid confusing one thing with another and taking imaginations as facts
3	Have an appropriate induction method and moderate theoretical abstraction	Avoid excessive abstraction
4	Pay attention to not only general outcomes but also diversity and side effects	Avoid manmade bias and major omissions

Source: RGCMS (2010)

(2) Positivist Analysis of the Change of the World Frontier

First, identification of the world frontier. Chapter 1 has discussed the methods of identifying the world frontier, including the identification of the world frontier of a single indicator, a single field, or human civilization. A positivist analysis of the world frontier generally should pay attention to four points (Table 2.17). Generally, advanced countries are those with the world's advanced level of development and transformation of human civilization, and the aggregation of their frontiers is the world frontier.

Second, the change of the world frontier is an aggregation of the frontier changes of advanced countries. The change of the world frontier may be understood by comparing the frontier differences of advanced countries between the starting and finishing sections (analysis sections) of the modernization process. For example, advanced countries in 1970 were the countries that had completed the first modernization, their frontiers together represented the world frontier of the year, and its differences from the world frontier in 1763 (first modernity) reflected the change of the world frontier during the period; advanced countries in 2005 were countries that entered the second modernization, their frontiers together represented the world frontier of the year, and its differences from the world frontier in 1970 (second modernity) represented the change of the world frontier during the period (Table 2.18).

Third, the result of modernization process from the perspective of the change of the world frontier. The main outcomes of the modernization process include the formation of modernity, particularity, diversity, and side effects, the improvement of labor productivity and quality of life, social progress, political democracy, cultural diversity, ecological changes, and all-round human development.

The main outcome of the first modernization process was the formation of first modernity, particularity, diversity, and side effects. The main features of the first modernity in 1970 included industrialized, urbanized, democracy, rule of law, rational, secular, centralized, mobility, marketed, social welfare, specialized, high efficiency, openness, liberty, equality, modern science and energy, mass communication, and universal compulsory education. The side effects of the first modernization included environmental pollution, differentiation between the rich and poor, economic crisis cycle, and weakening human relationship.

Table 2.18 World frontiers at three historical sections of the modernization process (exemplary contents and features)

Item	Tradition	First modernity	Second modernity
Time	About 1763	About 1970	About 2005
Scope	Worldwide	Countries which completed the first modernization	Countries which were in the second modernization
Economy	Handmade, decentralized, self-sufficient	Industrialized, market-based, efficient, scientific	Knowledge-intensive, information-intensive, green, global
Society	Rural, familial, education not universal	Urbanized, social welfare, universal compulsory education	Networked, knowledge-intensive, universal higher education
Politics	Autocratic, feudal, religious	Democratic, rule of law, professional, centralized	Knowledge-intensive, international, individualized, decentralized
Culture	Religious, superstitious, fatalism	Secular, rational, mass communication, materialism	Diversity, networking, cultural industries, quality of life
Environment	Develop and adapt to the nature, differ from one region to another	Economism, environmental pollution, ecological damage	Environmentally friendly, symbiotic, healthy development of both economy and the environment
Humans	Conservative, hierarchical, familial values	Open, equal, mobile, individual values	Lifelong learning, innovative, individualized, self-realization

Note: Second modernity is a picture that has not yet unfolded totally. The two types of modernity both reflect some contents and features of the first and second modernization. The environment refers to natural environment here
Source: He (2003)

The main outcome of the second modernization process was the formation of second modernity, particularity, diversity, and side effects. The main features of the second modernity in 2005 included knowledge intensiveness, information intensiveness, networking, intellectualized, internationalized, global, innovation, individuation, diversification, decentralized, community, greening, ecological, organic, risk, suburbanized, urban–rural balance, environmental friendliness, life-long learning, and universal higher education. Currently, the side effects of the second modernization include cybercrime, information divide, international risk, and widening inequality.

Four, relationships between the two types of modernity. In some aspects, the second modernity is the continuity and development of the first modernity, for example, democracy, individuation, and science; at the same time, some features of the first modernity, such as rationality and secularity, continue to exist. In some aspects, the second modernization is the "reversion" of the first modernity, for example, decentralization vs. centralization, deindustrialization vs. industrialization, suburbanization vs. urbanization, and environmental friendliness vs. ecological destruction. In some aspects, the second modernity appears as new features, such as knowledge and information intensiveness, networking, intellectualization, and universal higher education. And in some aspects, the second modernity is the "return" to tradition, for example, community, decentralization, and being natural and organic. Of course, such "return" does not mean going back to tradition, but based on the modern information and transportation networks, and due to that, the decreasing influence of geographic distance has made the world an "information-based global village."

2.1.3.2 Change of the International System

The change of the international system may be understood by comparing the differences in the international system between the starting and finishing sections (analysis sections) of the modernization process. The change of the international system includes the change of system composition, structure, level, and characters, which can be analyzed qualitatively and quantitatively.

(1) Qualitative Analysis of the Change of the International System

First, change of composition and structure of the international system. For example, in the international system in the modernization process, civilization universals exist all the time, while the percentages of tradition, first modernity, and second modernity change over time (Fig. 2.29).

In the first modernization process, the first modernity gradually came into being and spread; in the civilization structure of the international system, the percentage of the first modernity increased, the percentage of tradition declined, and civilization universals continued to exist.

In the second modernization process, the second modernity gradually came into being and spread; in the civilization structure of the international system, the percentage of the second modernity increased, the percentage of the first modernity declined, the percentage of tradition was very small, and civilization universals continued to exist.

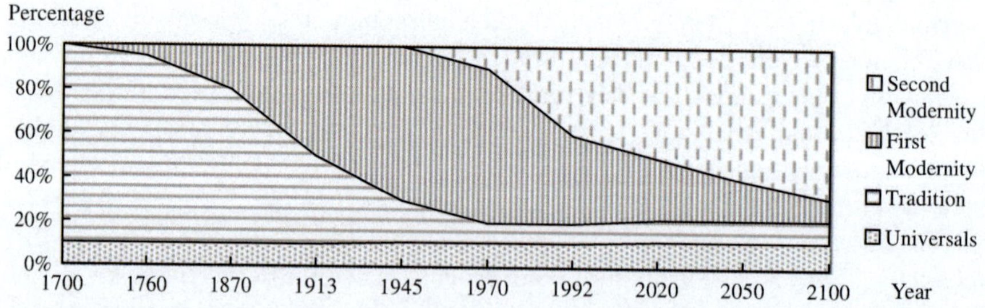

Fig. 2.29 Civilization structure of the international system in the modernization process between 1700 and 2100. Note: Civilization includes civilization universals, tradition (agricultural civilization), first modernity (industrial civilization), and second modernity (knowledge civilization). Source: RGCMS (2010)

Second, change in the level of the international system. In the international system, from 1763 to 1970, the number of countries that entered and/or completed the first modernization gradually increased; from 1970 onward, countries that entered second modernization and/or completed the first modernization increased in both number and percentage, while those remaining a traditional agricultural society decreased in both number and percentage.

(2) Quantitative Analysis of the Change of the International System

First, stage structure of the international system. From 1700 to 1970, the number of countries that entered the first modernization increased; from 1970 onward, the number of countries that entered the second modernization increased (Fig. 2.30). The stage structure of the international system changed over time.

Second, level structure of the international system. For example, from 1700 to 2005, the percentage of advanced countries was below 20% and that of developing countries was above 80%. The level structure of the international system is of relative stability (Fig. 2.31).

Third, population structure of the international system. For example, from 1960 to 2005, the population percentage of advanced countries declined and that of developing countries increased; population that entered the second modernization

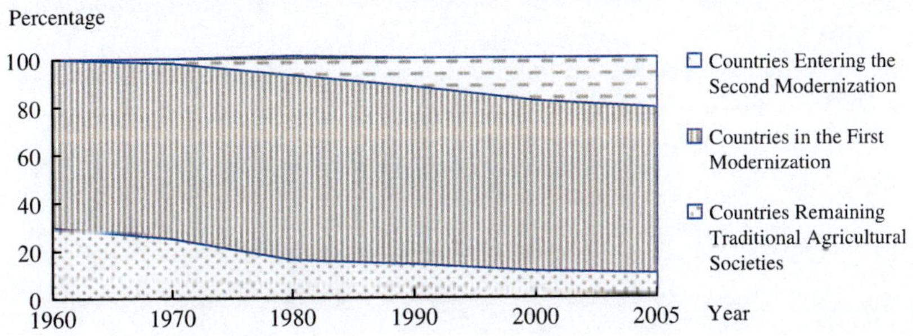

Fig. 2.30 Stage structure of the international system in the modernization process between 1960 and 2005. Source: RGCMS (2010)

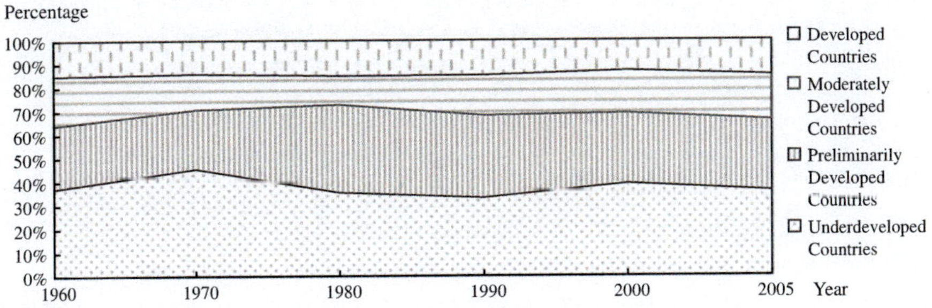

Fig. 2.31 Level structure of the international system in the modernization process between 1960 and 2005. Source: RGCMS (2010)

increased in both quantity and percentage, and those that were still in a traditional agricultural society decreased in both quantity and percentage. The population structure of the international system changed constantly.

Fourth, international gaps in the international system. From 1700 to 2005, the international gaps of some indicators such as per capital national income and economic efficiency continued to widen; some indicators, such as elementary school popularization and adult literacy, saw their international gaps widening and then narrowing.

2.1.3.3 Change of National States

The state of a country in the process of modernization refers to the country's modernization state, including its stage, frontier, level, and international status (Example 2.5). The change in national states can be analyzed qualitatively and quantitatively, by comparing the differences in national states between the starting and finishing sections (analysis sections) of the national modernization process.

Example 2.5 Types of Changes in International Status

Between 1700 and 2005, the types of changes in international status of countries mainly included: from rising to stabilizing, from rising to falling, from falling to rising, from falling to stabilizing, continuously falling and steady fluctuation, etc. Steady fluctuation included high-level fluctuation (fluctuation of advanced countries), middle-level fluctuation (fluctuation of moderately and preliminarily developed countries), and low-level fluctuation (fluctuation of underdeveloped countries).

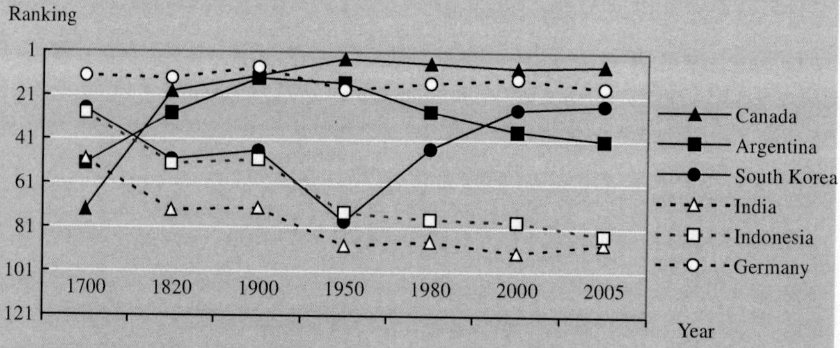

Changes in the international status of countries between 1700 and 2005.
Note: The ranking is based on the GDP per capita (at PPP-based prices in 1990) (Maddison 2001)

(1) Qualitative Analysis of the Change of National State

First, a comparison of starting and finishing sections. It can be used to analyze the change of national modernization in stage, frontier, level, and international status. Generally, the stage and frontier of national modernization change over time; from the national perspective, the absolute level of a country may continue to improve; from the international perspective, the relative level of a country may rise or fall, leading to the change in the country's international status.

Second, analyzed from the perspective of national frontier change. The main outcomes of the modernization process include the formation of modernity, particularity, and side effects and the improvement of labor productivity and quality of life, social advances, political democracy, cultural diversity, ecological changes, and all-round human development.

The main outcome in the process of a country's first modernization is the formation of first modernity, particularity and, possibly, side effects which may differ from one country to another. The main outcome in the process of a country's second modernization is the formation of second modernity, particularity and, possibly, side effects which may differ from one country to another. The main outcomes of a developing country's integrated modernization include the formation of first modernity, second modernity, and particularity; a rising and then falling percentage of first modernity; an increasing percentage of second modernity; and, possibly, side effects which may differ from one country to another.

Third, analyzed from the perspective of international status change. The outcomes of the modernization process include international differentiation and international mobility, for example, change of international gaps in economic efficiency and national income per capita, relative pauperization of underdeveloped countries, change of international divisions, widening international gaps, and the change of national rankings and stratification.

(2) Quantitative Analysis of the Change of National State

The stage, level, and international status of national modernization may be analyzed quantitatively.

First, stage analysis of national modernization. China Modernization Report evaluates and defines the stages of national modernization according to industrial and employment structures (Tables 1.17 and 1.18).

Second, level analysis of national modernization. China Modernization Report raised the models for evaluating the first modernization, the second modernization, and the integrated modernization. The four groups of countries differed obviously in their levels in 2005 (Table 2.19).

Third, international status analysis of national modernization. China Modernization Report raised the criteria for classifying countries into advanced and developing countries: developed, moderately developed, preliminarily developed, and underdeveloped countries. For example, in a span of 50 years, the probability that an advanced country is downgraded is about 10%, while the probability that an underdeveloped country is upgraded is about 10%.

Fourth, gap analysis of national modernization. The change of national modernization in international and regional gaps may be analyzed by comparing its international and regional gaps at the starting and finishing points.

Table 2.19 Modernization levels of four groups of countries in 2005

Country	FMI	SMI	IMI	GNI-PC	Country	FMI	SMI	IMI	GNI-PC
DC					PDC				
USA	100	109	96	43,560	Brazil	95	47	52	3,550
Japan	100	102	94	38,950	South Africa	87	40	42	4,770
Germany	100	93	93	34,870	China	86	40	38	1,740
France	100	92	90	34,600	Thailand	81	36	35	2,720
UK	100	91	90	37,740	Egypt	85	35	34	1,260
MDC					UDC				
Greece	100	70	71	19,840	India	65	26	28	730
Portugal	100	68	69	17,190	Kenya	54	25	24	540
Czech	100	68	63	11,220	Nigeria	55	25	23	560
Poland	100	60	60	7,160	Nepal	47	20	22	270
Chile	98	57	58	5,870	Burundi	38	15	17	100

Note: DC refers to developed countries, MDC refers to moderately developed countries, PDC refers to preliminarily developed countries, and UDC refers to underdeveloped countries. FMI refers to first modernization index, SMI refers to second modernization index, IMI refers to integrated modernization index, and GNI-PC refers to GNI per capita measured with the US dollar
Source: RGCMS (2008)

(3) Main Outcomes of Worldwide National Modernization

From the perspective of worldwide national modernization, outcomes of national modernization mainly include the formation of modernity, particularity, and diversity and the change of national levels and international status, as well as side effects. At any historical sections, no two countries have completely the same modernization outcomes, and different countries have different characteristics, with an international gap of different sizes. The universality of different national modernization outcomes makes up modernity, and different countries' particularity, existing tradition, and side effects form the diversity of modernization outcomes in terms of the form of expression (Fig. 2.32). Relatively, if we say that modernity reflects the nature of modernization, particularity chiefly reflects the diversity in form and environmental adaptability of modernization.

2.1.3.4 National Objectives in the Modernization Process

Generally, countries are the primary behavioral agents of modernization. The relationships between modernization outcomes and objectives are gradually formed at national layer.

(1) Analyzing National Objectives from the Theoretical Perspective

Theoretically, national modernization has three main objectives.

The first objective: to complete the first modernization and effect the transition from agricultural to industrial civilization.

The second objective: to complete the second modernization and effect the transition from industrial to knowledge civilization.

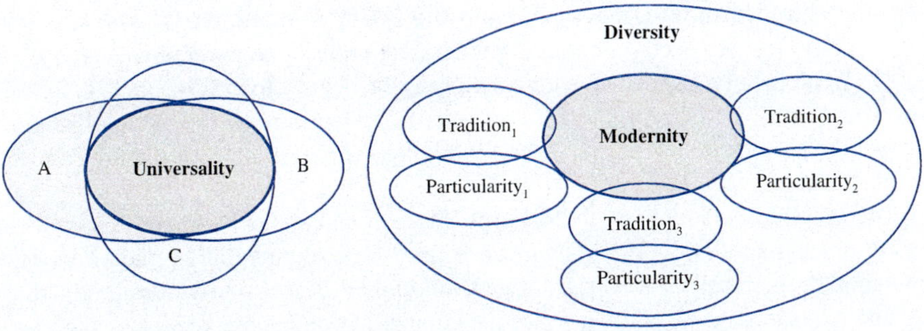

Fig. 2.32 Main outcomes of worldwide national modernization. Note: A, B, and C stand for the outcomes of modernization in different countries, respectively. Intersection of them stands for the universality or modernity, and the parts without intersection stand for particularity or individuality. Modernity is the universality of national modernization, and particularity belongs to the individuality. Different countries have different particularity and tradition. There has been no final conclusion about the boundaries between modernity and particularity, now that the boundaries are sometimes vague. Modernity can be divided into first modernity (modernity of industrial civilization) and second modernity (modernity of knowledge civilization). The outcomes in this diagram include no change of national level and status as well as side effects. Source: RGCMS (2010)

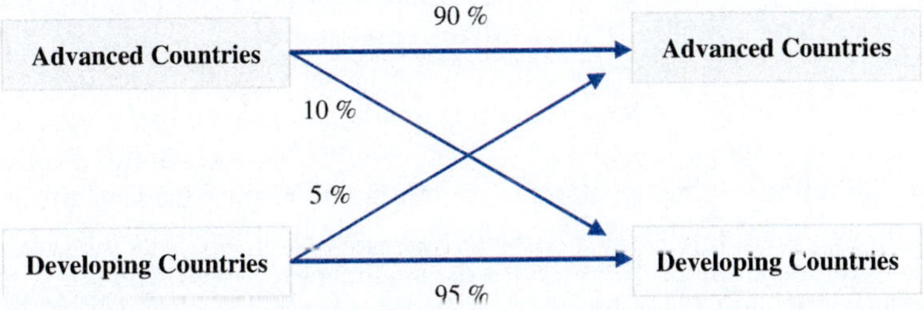

Fig. 2.33 Probability of transition between advanced and developing countries in 50 years

The third objective: a dynamic objective to catch up with, reach, or maintain the world's advanced level of development and transformation of human civilization.

Generally, the realization of the first and second objectives is a "matter of time"; different countries could complete both the first and second modernizations, though not at the same time. The realization of the third objective is a "matter of percentage and probability" since only a portion of countries could reach and maintain the world's advanced level; over the past 300 years, the percentage of advanced countries was below 20%, and in some 50 years, the probability that advanced countries maintained the world's advanced level was about 90%, and the probability that developing countries reached the world's advanced level was about 5% (Fig. 2.33).

(2) Analyzing National Objectives from the Policy Perspective

From the policy perspective, national modernization has two main objectives.

The first objective, which concerns national advances, is to improve productivity and the quality of life, promote social equity and progress, promote all-round human development, and promote the mutual symbiosis of man and nature. It can be made further specific.

The second objective, which concerns international status, is to catch up with, reach, or maintain the world's advanced level of development and transformation of national civilization. Advanced countries' policy objective is to maintain the world's advanced level, while developing countries' policy objective is to catch up with and reach the world's advanced level.

(3) Relationship Between Modernization Objectives and Outcomes

First of all, before 1950, there was generally no relationship between the outcomes and objectives of the national modernization process. There were neither modernization theories nor the spreading of modernization knowledge at that time.

Second, from 1960 onward, the relationship appeared in many developing countries. Modernization theories produced a major influence on their development objectives and modernization process, and modernization outcomes and objectives were closely related in some developing countries.

Third, from 1970 onward, the relationship occurred both in advanced and developing countries. Since 1970s, modernization research gave birth to a group of new theories, such as postmodernization theory, ecological modernization theory, reflexive modernization theory, multiple modernities theory, and second modernization theory. Closely linked with national policy objectives, these theories not only had an influence on developing countries but also influenced the policy agendas of advanced countries. For example, ecological modernization became the primary campaigning creed of the European Greens; coupled with other things, the knowledge economy, knowledge society, and related second modernization theory influenced the world agenda.

Fourth, the modernization science is an applied science. Modernization research and theories can not only help governments make policies but also provide policy options for political campaigning. The relationship between modernization outcomes and objectives will become increasingly close.

2.1.4 General Dynamics

The general dynamics refers to the result of the modernization in the world, which is based on the national modernization around the world, but not to special country at all. The driving force analysis on the process of modernization can be conducted at micro- and macrolevels, involving dynamic factors and mechanisms. The dynamics in the process of modernization represent a basic principle on modernization.

2.1.4.1 Dynamic Factors of the Modernization Process

Modernization is a complex process and is inevitably subject to many factors. Different factors have different functions. Some factors function as promoters while some as inhibitors. Influencing factors playing a greater promoting role can be called dynamic factors of the modernization process.

(1) Influencing Factors at Microlevel

Generally, microfactors include individual psychological factors and social factors.

Psychological factors. Modernization is carried out by human beings, and human behavior is affected by psychological factors such as curiosity, emulation, vanity, aspiration, enterprise, greed, and sense of fear, honor, achievement, responsibility, and nationality. *Human go forward to higher and water flows to lower* (Chinese proverb). These factors inevitably influence human behavior and modernization.

Social factors. Modernization is a sort of social behavior and is influenced by social factors such as knowledge, institutions, concepts, structure, history, tradition, family, organization, interests, power, status, scarcity, capital, resources, market, innovation, adaptation, exchange, cooperation, conflict, and competition. These factors have an influence on social choice and behavior and on modernization.

(2) Influencing Factors at Macrolevel

Generally, macrofactors include internal and international factors.

Internal influencing factors include economy, society, politics, culture, science and technology, education, natural environment, etc.

International influencing factors include international system, international status, international geography, international interaction, globalization, etc.

(3) Main Dynamic Factors of Modernization

Dynamic factors. They include innovation, competition, adaptation, exchange, national interests, market demand, etc. Innovation is the essential source of modernization; competition is the incentive mechanism for modernization; adaptation is the self-adjusting mechanism for modernization; exchange is the promoting factor of modernization; national interest is the leading factor of international competition; and market demand is the leading factor of product innovation.

National differences. In advanced countries, innovation is prominent; in developing countries, exchange is prominent.

2.1.4.2 Dynamic Models of the Modernization Process

How do the dynamic factors of modernization function? There is the need to build dynamic models by which to explain dynamic mechanisms of modernization (Table 2.20).

(1) Dynamic Models at Microlevel

Model of innovation-driven in modernization process (Fig. 2.34). Innovation is the fundamental source of modernization. It gives rise to new ideas, new institutions,

Table 2.20 Dynamic models of modernization process

No.	Dynamic model	Annotation
1	Innovation-drive model: Innovation gives birth to new ideas, new institutions, new knowledge, and new products and promotes the modernization	Models at microlevel
2	Triple-innovation-drive model: Joint action of knowledge innovation, institutional innovation, and technological innovation promotes modernization	
3	Two-wheel-drive model: joint action of national interests and market demands	
4	Associative action model: associative action of innovation, competition, adaptation, and exchange	
5	Hypercycle model: hypercycle of civilization elements: innovation—choice—diffusion—withdrawal (Fig. 2.11)	
6	Innovation diffusion model: Internal and international diffusion of major innovations promotes modernization	Models at macrolevel
7	Innovation spillover model: External effects of major innovations (effects on other fields) promote modernization	
8	Competition-drive model: Action of international competition, market competition, and democratic election promotes modernization	
9	Composite interaction model: the composite interaction process of new civilization, actual civilization, and civilization heritage (Fig. 2.23)	
10	Productivity function: Productivity is in positive proportion to technical progress, per capita skills, and per capita capital	Quantitative models

Source: RGCMS (2010)

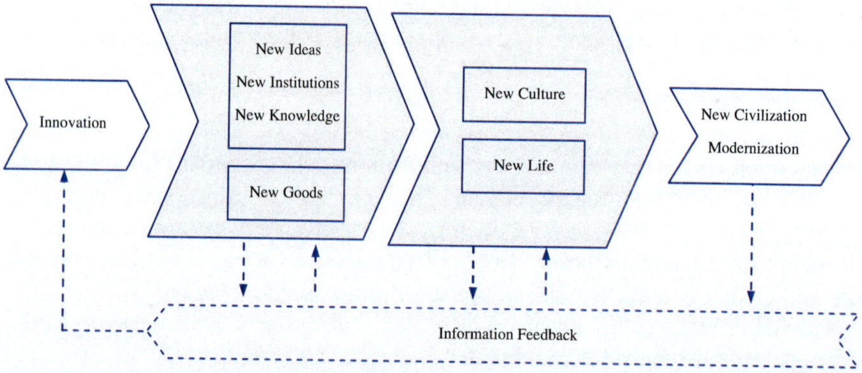

Fig. 2.34 Model of innovation-driven in modernization process. Note: Innovation means the introduction for the first time in the world of a new thing, a new idea, or a new change, where "new" concerns intellectual property rights rather than geography or time. Innovation involves numerous types or forms of expression. In the diagram, the *dotted lines* refer to information feedback, and the solid lines refer to the routes of action; the same below. Source: RGCMS (2010)

new knowledge, and new products which form new culture and new life and thus advance new civilization and modernization. In every stage, there is information feedback, which forms a cycle of positive feedback from innovation to modernization.

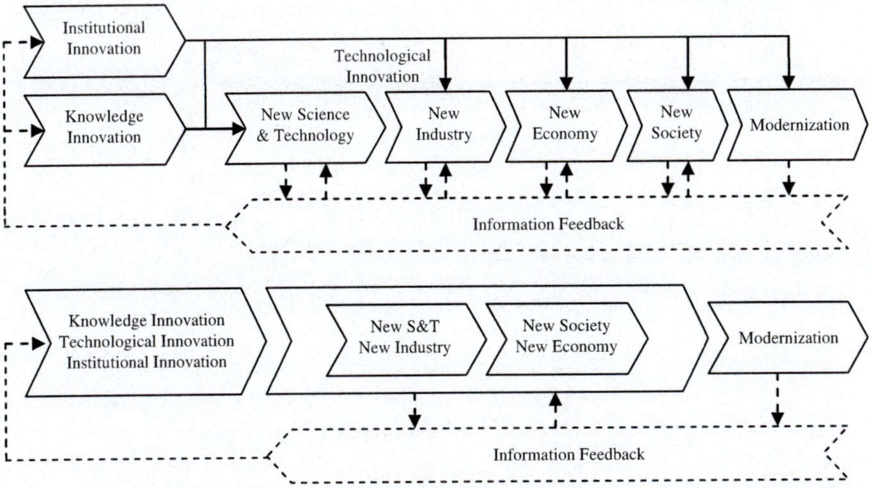

Fig. 2.35 Model of triple-drive in modernization process. Note: Knowledge innovation includes scientific discovery, technical invention, knowledge creation, and the first application of new knowledge (He and Zhang 2001). Institutional innovation is the founding of new institutions. They happen at each step of the model. Technological innovation means the first successful commercial application of technical inventions, mainly happening in the process from new sciences and technologies to new industries. Source: RGCMS (2010)

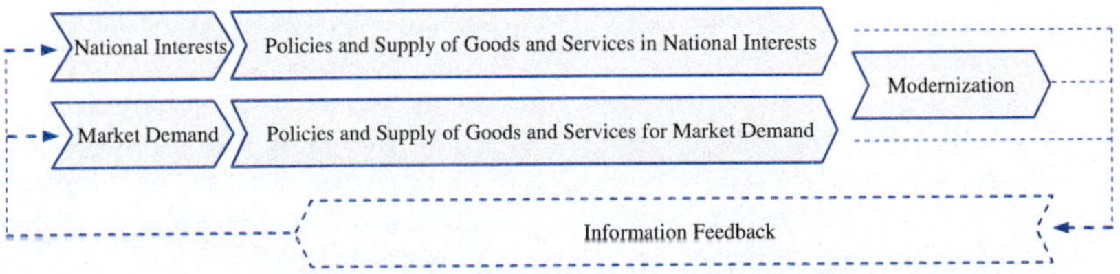

Fig. 2.36 Model of two-drive in modernization process. Source: RGCMS (2010)

Model of triple-innovation-drive in modernization process (Fig. 2.35). The associative action of knowledge innovation and institutional innovation gives rise to new sciences and technologies; technological innovation and new sciences and technologies give birth to new industries (products) that lead to new economy; new economy promotes new society that drives modernization; modernization advances knowledge innovation, technological innovation, and institutional innovation. At each step of the model, there is information feedback which forms a cycle of positive feedback from the three types of innovation to modernization.

Model of two-drive in modernization process (Fig. 2.36). The modernization process is codriven by national interests and market demand. National interests drives the policies and supply of goods and service used to maintain national interests, and market demand drives the policies and commodity and service supplies geared to the needs of internal and international markets; they together drive the process of modernization, in each step of which there is information feedback that forms a cycle of positive feedback.

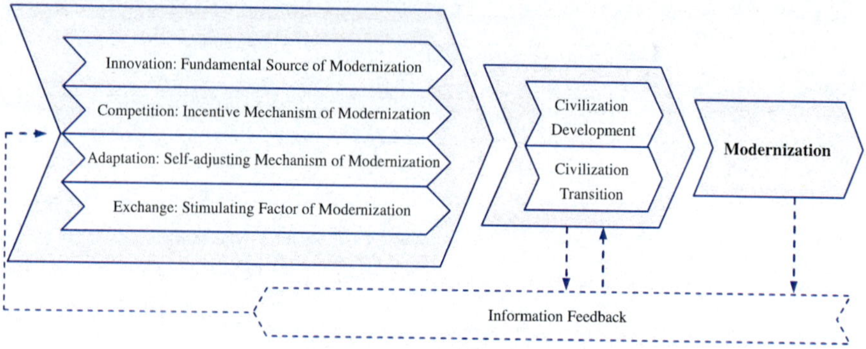

Fig. 2.37 Model of associative action in the modernization process. Source: RGCMS (2010)

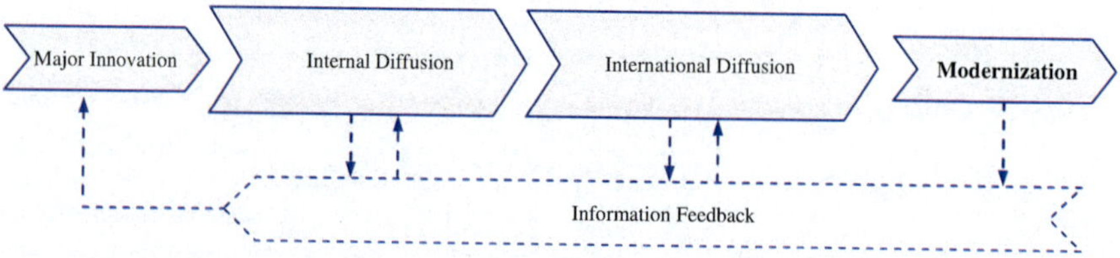

Fig. 2.38 Model of innovation diffusion in the modernization process. Source: RGCMS (2010)

Model of associative action in the modernization process (Fig. 2.37). The modernization process is a composite process; it is the result of the associative action of multiple dynamic factors including innovation, competition, adaptation, and exchange. The associative action of these factors promotes the development and transition of civilization and thus drives modernization; in each process, there is information feedback that forms a cycle of positive feedbacks.

For modernization of a particular country, perhaps multiple factors and models act jointly, or perhaps, a particular model dominates. Dynamic mechanisms of the modernization process differ in advanced countries and developing ones and in different stages and fields of modernization. The above-described dynamic models are only part of the dynamic principles of the modernization process.

(2) Dynamic Models at Macrolevel

Model of innovation diffusion in the modernization process (Fig. 2.38). The process of modernization is an aggregation of considerable innovations. It is impossible that all innovations are completed by one country; after completed, a major innovation is bound to spread domestically and internationally and thus promotes civilization development and transition and drives modernization. In each stage, there is information feedback that forms a cycle of positive feedback from innovation to modernization.

Model of innovation spillover in the modernization process (Fig. 2.39). Different fields of modernization have different innovations. Major innovations in one field

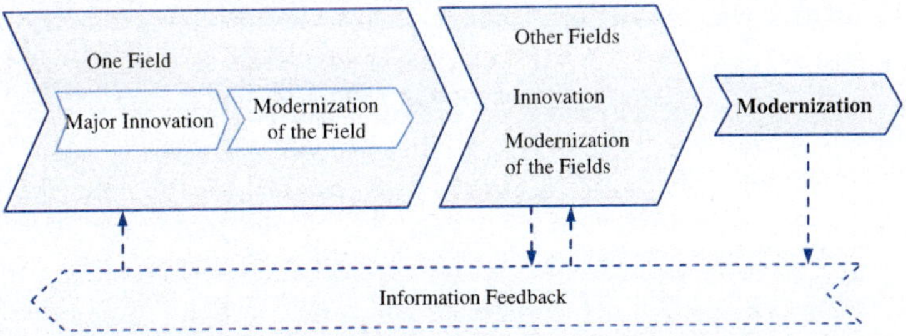

Fig. 2.39 Model of innovation spillover in the modernization process. Source: RGCMS (2010)

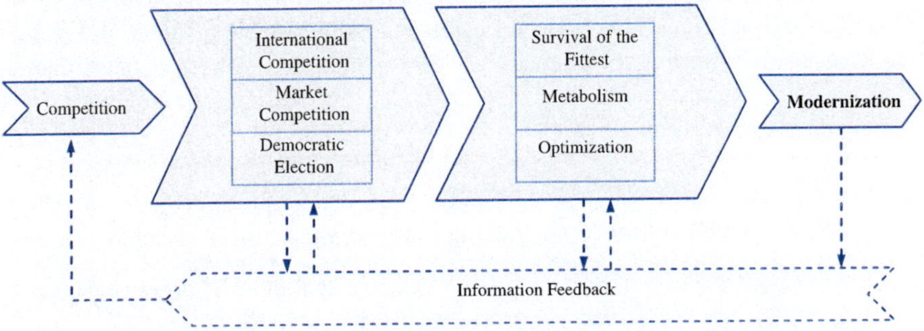

Fig. 2.40 Model of competition-driven in modernization process. Source: RGCMS (2010)

are bound to advance modernization of the field. Major innovations and modernization in one field may give rise to the spillover effect that influences or fuels the innovation and modernization in other fields and thus promotes civilization development and transition and accelerates modernization. In each stage, there is information feedback that forms a cycle of positive feedback from innovation to modernization.

Model of competition-driven in modernization process (Fig. 2.40). The process of modernization is a process of competition, including international competition, market competition, and democratic election, which gives rise to survival of the fittest, metabolism, and optimized allocation of resources and therefore promotes civilization development and transition and drives modernization. In each stage, there is information feedback that forms a cycle of positive feedback from competition to modernization.

(3) Quantitative Model of Modernization Dynamics

There are three criteria of modernization: conducive to the emancipation and improvement of productivity, to social equity and progress, and to the liberation and all-round development of human beings. The first criterion can be quantified, and a mathematical model can be established accordingly.

The Cobb–Douglas production function:

$$Y = A \times K^a \times L^{1-a} \quad (1)$$

where "*Y*" is output, "*K*" is capital, "*L*" is labor, "*a*" is the share of capital output, "(1 − *a*)" is the share of labor output, and "*A*" is the multiplier of technical advancement.

The productivity function (He 2009):

$$P = A \times (K/N)^a \times S^{1-a} \quad (2)$$

where "*P*" is productivity (per capita output of the labor force), "*A*" is the multiplier of technical advancement, "*K*/*N*" is per capita capital of the labor force, "*N*" is the number of people forming the labor force, "*S*" is per capita skill of the labor force, "*a*" is the share of capital output, and "(1 − *a*)" is the share of labor output.

According to the productivity function, labor productivity is in positive proportion to technical advancement, to per capita capital of the labor force, and to per capita skill of the labor force.

The dynamic factors of modernization include technical advancement, per capita capital, and per capita skill.

2.1.5 General Models

Modernization is a historical process involving a time span and development paths. Different countries have their own development paths and phase models of modernization. A development path means the road between the start and end of modernization process, which has direction, stages, and structural features. A modernization model is a historical period of the development path of modernization process; it is a mix (formula) of key elements of modernization, which is time dependent and targeted. Generally, a model is an alternative term for the practical experience of modernization.

The paths and models of modernization represent the basic principles of modernization.

2.1.5.1 Modernization Paths

History has proved that both processes of civilization and modernization take multiple paths. Paths can be grouped into three types according to nature. The first type is the basic paths, namely, the main paths of modernization, each with a unique direction and structural features. The second type is the subdivided paths, also known as subpaths, which are a group of paths, out of the basic paths, that have a consistent direction but different structural features. The third type is the forked paths, which are paths that seem to lead to modernization objectives but virtually cannot reach them.

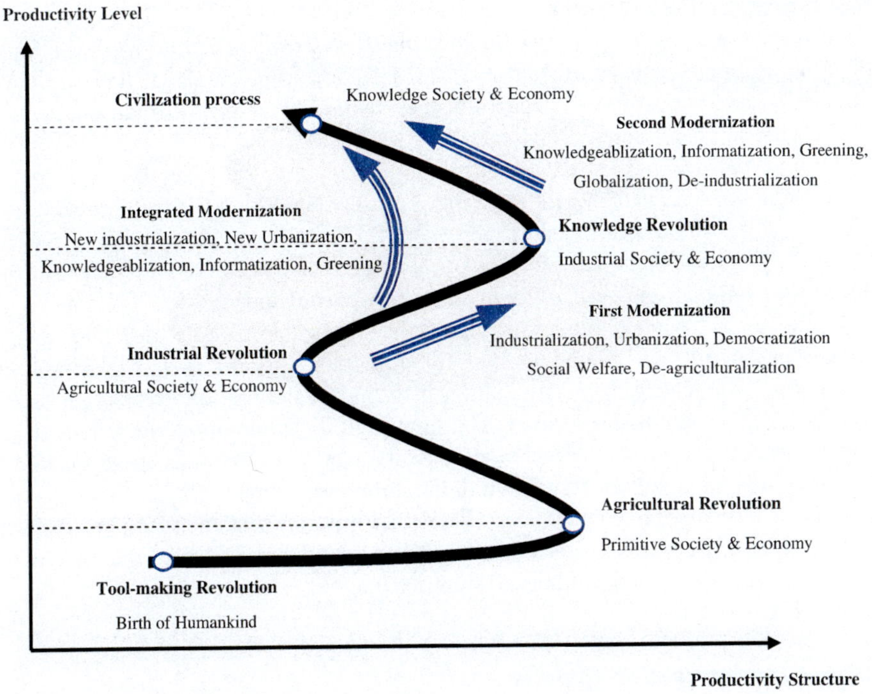

Fig. 2.41 Three basic paths of modernization in the twenty-first century. Note: In the twenty-first century, the first modernization path will be affected by the second modernization and has, more or less, features of the integrated modernization. The integrated modernization path is of great variety and closely related to the choice of start and objectives. Source: RGCMS (2010), He (2010a)

(1) Basic Modernization Paths in the Twenty-First Century

There are three basic paths for modernization in the twenty-first century (Fig. 2.41), and they are the path of the second modernization, the first modernization, and the integrated modernization. The integrated modernization path is the coordinated development of the first and second modernization and the transition toward the second modernization. Every field- and sector-specific modernization has its own paths, so does the modernization of civilization contents and forms. And the three basic paths are the "envelope curve" of these paths for fields, sectors, and civilization contents and forms.

(2) No Best Path for Modernization

According to the historical experience in modernization, there are no best but only appropriate paths for modernization. Both basic paths and subdivided paths are optional. One subdivided path is different from another in applicability, and the same path is not applicable to different countries equally.

Modernization Path Options

First, there are a number of factors influencing the selection of a path. The selection of an appropriate path is affected by modernization principles and international interaction and is restricted by such objective factors as countries' tradition, basic conditions, and external environment.

Second, the selection of a modernization path is relative and conditional. Path selection has certain path dependency and is closely connected with modernization achievements. The risk and opportunity cost of path selection is fairly high.

Third, from the perspective of modernization policies, there are three path options for national modernization in the twenty-first century.

Option 1: the second modernization path. Applicable to countries that have already or basically completed the first modernization.

Option 2: the catch-up modernization path. Finish the first modernization first and then the second modernization. The first stage is the first modernization path, and the second stage is the second modernization path. This option is appropriate to countries that have not yet completed the first modernization.

Option 3: the integrated modernization path. Finish the first and second modernization in a coordinated way and continue the transition toward the second modernization. This option is appropriate to countries that have not yet completed the first modernization.

2.1.5.2 Modernization Models

A modernization model is an abstract expression of the typical features of a particular historical period in the process of national modernization or the "name" of a historical period of the national modernization path. Modernization encompasses a great many basic elements, such as economy, society, politics, culture, ecology, life, structure, institution, and concept. A modernization model is just a particular mix of these modernization elements. In different historical periods, different countries need different mixes of modernization elements for they have different conditions and environments. If there has been remarkable success or failure in a particular period of national modernization, people would summarize the path for the stage and its features as "a model." Some successful modernization models of pioneer countries are usually used as reference by backward countries.

First, there are a wide variety of modernization models (Table 2.21). Different countries and different stages may have different success or failure models, and these models are closely related to historical phases and objective conditions.

Second, modernization models are relative, and there are no obvious boundaries between related models.

Third, different models may be applied alternately, and several models may be combined into a composite one.

Fourth, there are no best but only appropriate models. A country may choose or make innovation in a model. For example, none of the three mix models of industrialization and democratization is superior or inferior (Fig. 2.42). Roughly speaking, in the eighteenth to nineteenth centuries, the USA and UK adopted the coordinated development of industrialization and democratization, France gave

Table 2.21 56 element mix models for national modernization (excluding repeated ones)

No.	Mix models for the first modernization		Mix models for the second modernization		Mix models for the integrated modernization	
	Element mix	Model	Element mix	Model	Element mix	Model
1	Industrialization and democratization	Industrialization first	Knowledgeablization and informatization	Knowledgeablization first	Knowledgeablization and industrialization	Knowledgeablization first
2		Democratization first		Informatization first		Industrialization
3		Coordinated development		Coordinated development		Coordinated development
4	Industrialization and urbanization	Industrialization first	Knowledgeablization and ecologicalization	Knowledgeablization first	Informatization and industrialization	Informatization first
5		Urbanization first		Ecologicalization first		Industrialization first
6		Coordinated development		Coordinated development		Coordinated development
7	Economy and education	Economy first	Informatization and ecologicalization	Informatization first	Industrialization and ecologicalization	Industrialization first
8		Education first		Ecologicalization first		Ecologicalization first
9		Coordinated development		Coordinated development		Coordinated development
10	Market and planning	Free market economy	Economy and ecology	Economy first	Urbanization and informatization	Urbanization first
11		Planned economy		Ecology first		Informatization first
12		Mixed economy		Coordinated development		Coordinated development
13	Catch-up modernization	Import substitution	Society and ecology	Society first	Urbanization and ecologicalization	Urbanization first
14		Export orientation		Ecology first		Ecologicalization first
15		Coordinated development		Coordinated development		Coordinated development
16	International interaction	National industry protection	Economy and society	Economy first	Economy and society	Economy first
17		Free trade		Society first		Society first

(continued)

Table 2.21 (continued)

No.	Mix models for the first modernization Element mix	Mix models for the first modernization Model	Mix models for the second modernization Element mix	Mix models for the second modernization Model	Mix models for the integrated modernization Element mix	Mix models for the integrated modernization Model
18		Colonial empire		Coordinated development		Coordinated development
19		Dependency development	International interaction	High trade and high investment	International interaction	High trade and high investment
20	–	–		Moderate trade and moderate investment		Moderate trade and moderate investment
21	–	–		Low trade and low investment		Low trade and low investment
22	–	–	Economy, society, and ecology	Coordinated development	Economy, society, and ecology	Coordinated development

Note: The gray section means these models repeat those of the second modernization. See Chap. 6 for the subject of ecologicalization
Source: RGCMS (2010)

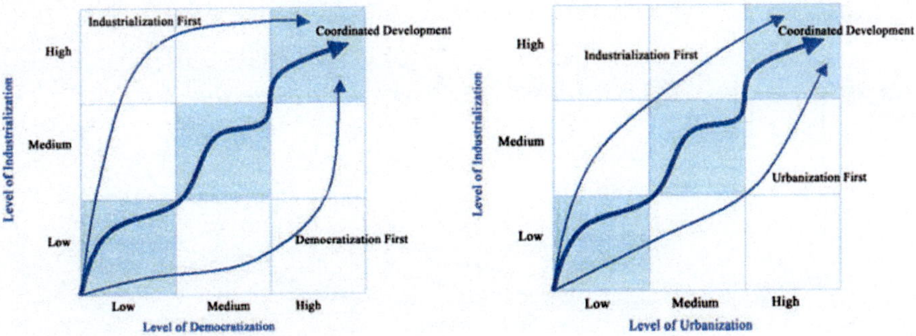

Fig. 2.42 Mix models of industrialization and democratization as well as industrialization and urbanization. Source: RGCMS (2010)

priority to democratization, and Germany gave priority to industrialization. In the twentieth century, Japan and Germany gave priority to industrialization, while India adopted the model of democratization first. In the same way, there are cases of both success and failure in the three mix models of industrialization and urbanization.

Fifth, there are also a variety of modernization models in the economic, social, political, cultural, human, and ecological fields. For example, in the economic field, advanced countries' economic governance models include mixed market economy, welfare-oriented market economy, and social market economy; in the social field, advanced countries have a diversity of national educational systems, public health systems, and social welfare models; in the political field, advanced countries' political systems include constitutional monarchy, parliamentary republicanism, and presidential republicanism.

2.2 Basic Principles of National Advance

Since about eighteenth century, some countries have reached or maintained the world's advanced level and became advanced ones; while others have failed to do so and became developing ones; a country may change from an advanced one to a developing one or vice versa with some probability in some term. Such a phenomena can be referred to as "national advancement" or "national advance" in short words.

This phenomenon is also an attendant one to the modernization process, and there have been already some theoretical explanations—modernization science could provide a new approach on it.

2.2.1 Modernization and National Advance

Generally, national advance is closely related to the classification of countries, national stratification, and international differentiation, and this classification is

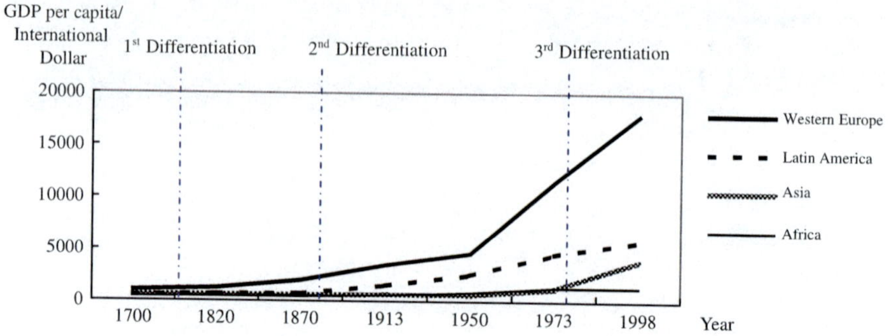

Fig. 2.43 International differentiation in per capita GDP between 1700 and 1998. Note: Japan is not included in the data of Asia. The unit of per capita GDP is international dollar at PPP-based prices in 1990. Differentiation refers to the widening gap between countries in per capita GDP, a phenomenon caused by the shift from agricultural to industrial civilization. The first differentiation occurred among Western countries in the eighteenth century; the second one happened among Latin American countries in the nineteenth century; and the third one took place among Asian countries in the twentieth century. It is based on the data coming from Maddison (2001). Source: He (2011)

mainly based on the level of national modernization. There are three times of international differentiation, and the gap in wealth between advanced and developing ones has been growing since eighteenth century (Fig. 2.43).

2.2.1.1 Modernization and National Classification

Before the eighteenth century, all the countries in the world were agricultural civilizations despite the differences in their states and levels. With the advancing and spreading of modernization since the eighteenth century, more and more countries have been involved in this process. Countries initiated modernization at different time and with some different outcomes. As a result, the international poverty gap has been widening, and international differentiation has become increasingly outstanding.

(1) Classification of Countries in the Modernization Process

There is no standard method of classifying countries. The classification of countries in the modernization process can be based on development level, development stage, and national strength or according to the level of modernization in a specific field or indicator. *China Modernization Report* adopts modernization evaluation and classifies countries according to modernization level, stage, and national strength (Table 2.22).

First, the classification of countries based on development level. No consensus has been reached on the definition of the level of national development. Generally, the level of national development refers to a country's relative level of development in the process of modernization; many indicators can be used to describe the development level such as modernization index, civilization index, economic, and

Table 2.22 Classification of countries based on development level and stage

No.	Classification of countries	Classified by	Annotation
1	Advanced countries and developing countries (moderately developed, preliminarily developed, and underdeveloped countries)	Modernization index	Level
2	High, middle, and low human development countries	HDI	
3	High-income, middle-income (upper-middle and lower-middle income), and low-income countries	Per capita national income	
4	Developed and developing countries (more and less developed countries)	Statistical criterion[a]	
5	Knowledge, industrial, and agricultural civilization countries	Level of civilization	
6	Second modernization, first modernization, traditional agricultural countries	Modernization stage	Stage
7	Frontier (early starter), catch-up (late coming) countries	Start time	
8	Large, medium-sized, small, and microcountries	Population, territory, and scale of economy	Strength
9	World powers, medium powers, primary powers, weak nations	Strength, competitiveness, influence	

Note: UNDP classifies countries according to the Human Development Index (HDI). The World Bank classifies countries according to the national income per capita

Source: UNDP (2000), World Bank (2000), RGCMS (2008)

[a]According to the Population Division, Department of Economic and Social Affairs, United Nations, developed countries include European countries, North American countries, Australia, New Zealand, and Japan, while other countries are developing ones; developed countries refer to industrialized countries, and developing countries include 50 least developed countries and other less developed countries (UN 2004)

social indicators. According to *China Modernization Report*, based on the national modernization level, countries can be classified into advanced and developing ones; developing countries include moderately developed, preliminarily developed, and underdeveloped ones (Example 2.6). Such a classification of countries applies to modernization studies of all kinds.

Example 2.6 Classification of Countries Based on National Modernization Level

According to national modernization level and world ranking, *China Modernization Report* classifies countries into developed, moderately developed, preliminarily developed, and underdeveloped ones; while developed countries are advanced countries, developing countries include moderately developed, preliminarily developed, and underdeveloped countries.

The modernization-level-based classification goes like this in general: Countries whose modernization level exceeds 80% of the average level of high-income countries are classified as advanced or developed ones; countries whose modernization level is below that of advanced countries

(continued)

are developing ones; countries below that of advanced countries but above the world's average level are moderately developed ones; countries below the world's average level but above that of underdeveloped countries are preliminarily developed ones; and countries below 60% of the world's average level are underdeveloped ones.

The world-ranking-based classification goes like this: Countries ranking among the world's top 20 in terms of modernization level are classified as advanced ones; countries ranking between the 21st and the 45th places are moderately developed ones; countries ranking between the 46th and the 80th places are preliminarily developed ones; and countries ranking the 81st place and below that are underdeveloped ones. It is how the 131 countries are classified according to their rankings in 2005.

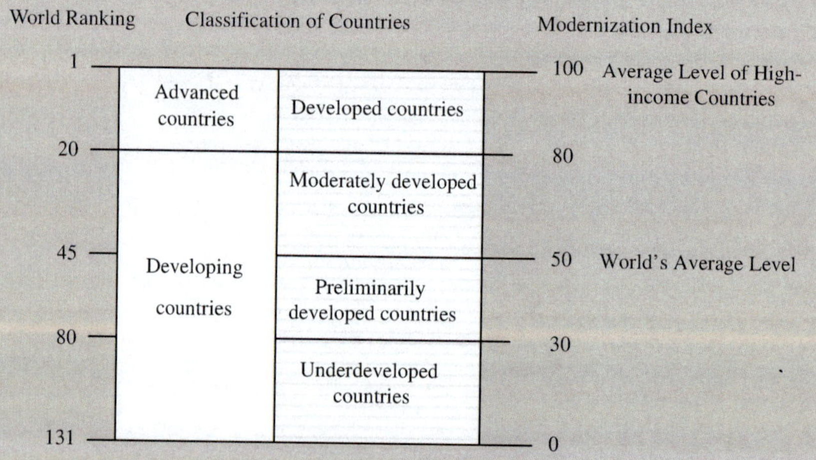

Classification of 131 countries in 2005 based on modernization level and world ranking.
Note: The 131 countries are the ones whose population exceeded 1 million in 2000, and statistics are relatively complete here and after. The world's average second modernization index (SMI) and integrated modernization index (IMI) may fluctuate around 50, and the numbers of the four groups of countries may change slightly.
Source: RGCMS (2010)

Second, the classification of countries based on development stage. There is no standard method of defining a country's development stage. *China Modernization Report* defines the development stages of countries according to their industrial structure and employment structure (Tables 1.17 and 1.18). Although the classification of countries by development stage is different from that by modernization level, they are greatly correlated with each other, and it is worth making a comparison between them (Fig. 2.44).

Third, the classification of countries based on national strength. Generally, national strength refers to the sum of assets and capacities a country has to survive

Classification of Countries	Modernization Level	Modernization Stage	Civilization Level
Advanced countries	Developed Countries	Second modernization countries	Knowledge civilization countries
Developing countries	Moderately developed countries Preliminarily developed countries Underdeveloped countries	First modernization countries Traditional agricultural countries	Industrial civilization Agricultural civilization countries

Fig. 2.44 Comparison between the classifications of countries in 2000 based on level and stage (schematic diagram). Note: Of countries that were in second modernization as knowledge civilization in 2000, some were advanced ones, and some were moderately developed ones

and develop. Many indicators can be used to reflect a country's strength such as comprehensive national strength, objective national strength, economic strength, scale of economy, population, and territory. National strength is in positive correlation with the size and development level of a country. For indicators whose international structures are different, the criteria for classifying countries can be different.

China Modernization Report 2008 introduced the classifications of countries based on such indicators as objective national strength, economic strength, objective competitiveness, objective influence, population, territory, and scale of economy.

(2) Methods of National Classification Based on the Level

National advancement is an objective phenomenon and is closely related to the level of national modernization and the criteria for classifying countries.

First, the classification based on the level of national modernization. (1) The classification based on the index of national modernization (Example 3.2), such as second modernization index (SMI) or integrated modernization index (IMI). The averages of world and high-income countries are the key criteria for this classification. (2) The classification based on the ranking of the national modernization level in the world (Example 3.2), such as the world ranking of SMI or IMI.

Second, the classification based on the level of field- and indicator-specific modernization. (1) In the fields where quantitative evaluation is allowed, the classification can borrow or copy those based on modernization level. (2) In the fields where it is hard to do quantitative evaluation, special research needs to be done. (3) The classification based on the level of modernization indicators may change one to one. (4) In the case of qualitative indicators, special research should be done.

There are mainly seven types of quantitative indicators (Tables 1.16 and 1.25). For upward and downward variables, the classification can borrow or copy those based on modernization level; for shifting variables (up and then down or down and then up), random, geological, and stable variables, special research should be done.

The level of national modernization can be consistent with or different from that of field or indicator specific modernization. Advanced countries may have not reached the world's advanced level in the modernization in some fields or indicators; developing countries may have reached the world's advanced level in terms of modernization in some fields or indicators.

2.2.1.2 Modernization and National Stratification

The Charter of the United Nations holds that all countries in the world are equal in sovereignty terms. Countries may have equal legal status, but they are very different in terms of development level and strength. National stratification based on development level and strength is an objective phenomenon. Modernization research focuses on the national stratification based on modernization level which is closely related to the criteria for defining national advancement.

(1) National Stratification in the Modernization Process

Generally, national stratification refers to countries' positions in the international system and the changes thereof. It is an objective phenomenon in the modernization process and a manifestation of international differentiation.

First, the national stratification based on the level of national modernization. Based on the level of national modernization, countries can be stratified into four groups: developed ones, moderately developed ones, preliminarily developed ones, and underdeveloped ones. Between 1960 and 2005, the proportion of developed countries was 13–15%; that of moderately developed ones, 12–21%; that of preliminarily developed ones, 25–35%; and that of underdeveloped ones, 33–45% (Fig. 2.45).

Second, the national stratification based on the level-of-field- and indicator-specific modernization. Based on the level of field or indicator-specific modernization, countries can also be stratified into four groups: developed ones, moderately developed one, preliminarily developed ones, and underdeveloped ones in specific fields or indicators. According to the analysis of *China Modernization Report 2010*, between 1700 and 2005, the proportion of economically developed countries was 12–20%; that of moderately developed ones, 12–36%; that of preliminarily developed ones, 17–43%; and that of underdeveloped ones, 30–55% (Fig. 2.46).

(2) National Mobility in the Modernization Process

National mobility is an objective phenomenon in the modernization process and a manifestation of national stratification. Generally, national mobility refers to the change of a country's status in the international system including the changes in its level (or classification) and world ranking. Countries' world rankings change

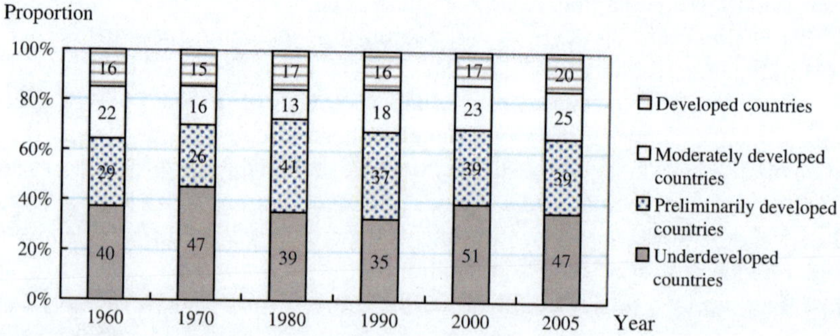

Fig. 2.45 National stratification based on modernization level between 1960 and 2005 (number and proportion of countries). Source: RGCMS (2010)

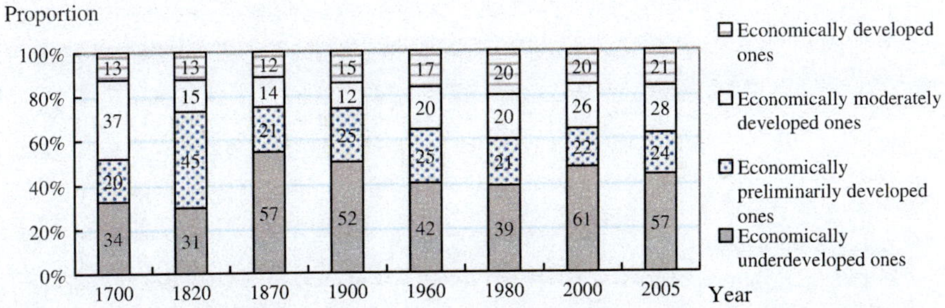

Fig. 2.46 National stratification based on economic level between 1700 and 2005 (number and proportion of countries). Note: The total number of countries is 104–130. There are no data on some countries between 1700 and 1900, so their development levels are represented by the average levels of the regions where they are (Maddison 2001). For example, the development level of African countries is the average level of Africa. Countries are classified according to per capita GDP (PPP) at 1990 price. The classification goes like this: Countries whose development level exceeds 80% of the average level of high-income countries are classified as economically developed ones; countries below that of advanced countries but above the world's average level are moderately developed ones; countries below the world's average level but above that of underdeveloped countries are preliminarily developed ones; and countries below 50% of the world's average level are underdeveloped ones. Source: RGCMS (2010)

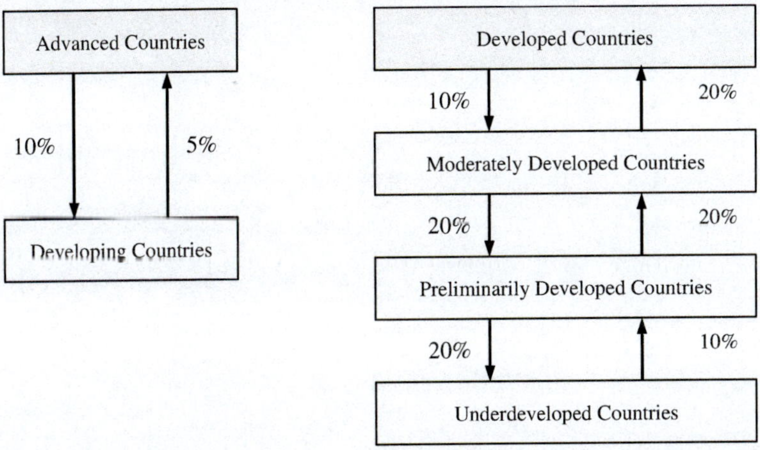

Fig. 2.47 Probabilities of transferring status among two and four types of countries in a span of 50 to 100 years. Source: RGCMS (2010)

frequently; there is a probability that a country changes its level, which is called status transfer probability in short and can be analyzed with a Markov chain model.

First, the probability of transferring status between two types of countries. If countries are divided into advanced and developing ones, we can work out the probability of transferring status between the two types of countries during different periods of time (Example 2.7). In a time span of 50–100 years, the average probability from advanced to a developing one is about 10% (6–23%) and that from developing to advanced one is about 5% (1–9%) (Fig. 2.47).

Example 2.7 Probability of Transferring Status Between Advanced and Developing Countries

According to the economic data of the World Bank (2008) and Maddison (2001), *China Modernization Report 2010* does a Markov chain analysis and works out the probabilities of transferring status between advanced and developing countries between 1700 and 2005. In the eighteenth century, the United Stated was upgraded to an advanced country, while Portugal was downgraded to a developing one. In the nineteenth century, Canada, Australia, New Zealand, Ireland, and Argentina were upgraded to advanced countries, while Spain, Italy, and Norway were downgraded to developing ones. In the twentieth century, Finland, Japan, Singapore, and South Korea were upgraded to advanced countries, while the Soviet Union (Russia) and Argentina were downgraded to developing ones.

Probabilities of transferring status between advanced and developing countries between 1700 and 2005

Group[a]		A	D	A	D	Upgraded countries	Downgraded countries
Number of countries in 1700		Number of countries in 1820		Transfer probability in the 120 years (%)			
A	13	12	1	92	8	–	Portugal
D	91	1	90	1	99	United States	–
Number of countries in 1820		Number of countries in 1900		Transfer probability in the 80 years (%)			
A	13	10	3	77	23	–	Spain, Italy, Norway
D	91	5	86	5	95	Canada, Argentina, Australia, New Zealand, Ireland	–
Number of countries in 1900		Number of countries in 2005		Transfer probability in the 105 years (%)			
A	15	13	2	87	13	–	Argentina, New Zealand
D	88	8	80	9	91	Finland, Spain, Italy, Norway, Japan, Singapore, Greece[c], Kuwait[c]	–
Number of countries in 1960[b]		Number of countries in 2005[b]		Transfer probability in the 45 years (%)			
A	16	15	1	94	6	–	Russia
D	91	5	86	5	95	Finland, Ireland, Japan, Singapore, South Korea	–

Note: "A" represents advanced countries; "D" represents developing countries
[a]The grouping is based on per capita GDP (PPP) index
[b]The grouping is based on modernization index
[c]Greece and Kuwait are high-income countries according to their per capita GDP (PPP) index and are moderately developed countries according to their modernization index. The international statuses of Norway, Spain, Italy, and Ireland were shifting between advanced and developing countries
Source: RGCMS (2010)

Second, the probability of transferring status among four types of countries. If countries are divided into developed, moderately developed, preliminarily developed, and underdeveloped ones, we can work out the probability of transferring status among the four types of countries during different periods of time. In a time span of 50–100 years, the average probability of a developed country downgraded to a moderately developed one is about 10% (6–23%), that of a moderately developed country upgraded to an advanced one is around 20% (0–42%), that of a preliminarily developed country upgraded to a moderately developed one is about 20% (14–24%), and that of an underdeveloped country upgraded to a preliminarily developed one is about 10% (5–14%). The probability of preliminarily developed and underdeveloped countries getting upgraded by more than one level is about 5%.

2.2.1.3 Modernization and International Differentiation

International differentiation is an objective phenomenon in the modernization process. Generally, it refers to the increasing differences and gaps between countries as international divisions and the change of international status. International status and its changes are phenomena of national stratification and have already been discussed previously.

(1) Modernization and International Differences

Both international convergence and differentiation occur in the process of modernization. International convergence is reflected in many aspects such as industrial, employment, government structure, social, and education structures, as well as infrastructure. International differentiation is also reflected in many aspects such as the diversity of civilizations, economies and societies, development stages, and cultures (Table 2.23). The causes of such diversity are complicated such as asynchronous processes of modernization and multiple development models.

(2) Modernization and International Gaps

In the process of modernization, the international gaps in some indicators widen and then narrow down such as the proportion of urban population, while the international gaps in some indicators keep growing such as per capita national income and economic efficiency. For example, between 1700 and 1998, per capita GDP (PPP at 1990 price) rose from 1,024 to 17,921 international dollars in Western Europe and from 400 to 1,368 international dollars in Africa; the absolute gap

Table 2.23 Expanding international differences and diversity between 1760 and 2005

Item	Features of 1760	Diversity of 1970	Diversity of 2005
Civilization	Agricultural civilization	Agricultural and industrial civilization	Agricultural, industrial, and knowledge civilization
Economy	Agricultural economy	Agricultural and industrial economy	Agricultural, industrial, and knowledge economy
Society	Agricultural society	Agricultural, semi-industrial, and industrial society	Agricultural, industrial, and knowledge society
Culture	Traditional culture	Traditional and modern culture	Traditional and modern culture, cultural diversity
Stage	Traditional society	Traditional society, first modernization	Traditional society, first and second modernization

Source: RGCMS (2010)

Table 2.24 Gaps between Western Europe and Africa in per capita GDP between 1700 and 1998

Item	1700	1820	1870	1913	1950	1973	1998	1998/1700
Western Europe	1,024	1,232	1,974	3,473	4,594	11,534	17,921	17.5
Africa	400	418	444	585	852	1,365	1,368	3.4
Absolute gap	624	814	1,530	2,888	3,742	10,169	16,553	26.5
Relative gap	2.6	2.9	4.4	5.9	5.4	8.4	13.1	5.1

Note: The unit of GDP is international dollar at PPP-based prices in 1990. The data comes from Maddison (2001)

between Western Europe and Africa increased from 624 to 16,553 international dollars, and the relative gap grew from about twice to 12 times (Table 2.24). In the modernization process, the international income gap keeps widening.

(3) Modernization and International Divisions

International divisions have been changing in the modernization process. There are international divisions of knowledge, labor, and market, which are different in the eras of industrial and knowledge economy (Table 2.25). Generally, advanced counties are at the high end of international divisions and engage in knowledge- and capital-intensive and high-value production; developing countries are at the low end and engage in resource- and labor-intensive and low-value production. But such divisions are not absolute; developing countries can also participate in the international competition in the high-end and knowledge markets which requires rational competition strategies and national policies.

To conclude, national advancement is an objective phenomenon that some countries reach and maintain the world's advanced level and stand in the frontier of human civilization and modernization process, thus becoming advanced ones, while others become developing ones; there is mobility between the two types of countries. From the perspective of national classification, advanced countries are defined according to the national level of modernization. From the perspective of national stratification, advanced countries are those which reach the world's

Table 2.25 International divisions in the modernization process

Item	Developing countries	Advanced countries
Division of knowledge	Knowledge users, knowledge importers	Knowledge creators, producers, and consumers
Division of labor	Primary production, simple labor	High-value production, production of knowledge, knowledge-intensive work
Division of market	Primary market, raw material market, primary products, low-value-added manufactured goods	High-value market, knowledge market, financial market, high-value-added manufactured goods, knowledge products, service products, design products
Era of industrial economy	Manufacturing of primary products, import of industrial products	Manufacturing and export of industrial products, purchase of raw materials
Era of knowledge economy	Primary products, mid- and low-end products "trunk countries"	High-end products, knowledge-based products, and services "brain countries"

Note: International divisions are relative. Developing countries can participate in the international competition in the high-end and knowledge markets. There are also international divisions within the circle of advanced countries and that of developing countries
Source: RGCMS (2010), He (2010a, 2011)

advanced level. From the perspective of international differentiation, advanced countries are those which are at the high end of international divisions.

2.2.2 Theoretical Explanation of National Advance

National advancement is a complex phenomenon, which can and do need to be analyzed from different perspectives. According to the discussion before, national advancement is also an attendant phenomenon to the modernization process, and it can be interpreted based on the modernization theory (He 2011).

In the process of modernization, national advancement involves the national progress and the formation and change of advanced countries; the former is fundamental and the latter is essential. Generally, advanced countries are those which have reached world's advanced level in the modernization process, and also, they have reached the world's advanced level in the six fields of modernization, i.e., economic, social, political, cultural, ecological, and human modernization, and especially maintained the world's advanced level in the aspects of the advanced productivity, social progress, and all over human development.

2.2.2.1 Three Hypotheses on National Advance

First of all, national advancement is a historical phenomenon and the outcome of national modernization, international competition, and international differentiation. In the process of modernization, advanced countries are those that have reached and maintained the world's advanced level of national modernization, and other

Table 2.26 Logical relationship between national level and key elements

Element	In direct proportion to national level	In inverse proportion to national level
Value	Percentage of innovation value	Percentage of labor value
Labor	Percentages of materialized labor, effective labor, and high-efficiency labor	Percentages of living labor, ineffective labor, and low-efficiency labor
Capital	Percentages of effective investment, high-efficiency investment, and advanced assets	Percentages of ineffective investment, low-efficiency investment, and primary assets
Technology	Percentage of advanced technologies	Percentage of backward technologies

Note: A country's level of development in the world is related to many elements, such as industrial structure, employment structure, key institutions, quality of life, and level of human development.
Source: He (2010a, 2011)

countries are developing ones; the percentage of advanced countries is generally below 20% and that of developing countries is generally above 80%; there is mobility between the two types of countries. The transformation includes the transition from agricultural to industrial civilization and then the transition from industrial to knowledge and ecological civilization.

Second, national advancement is in positive correlation with the national level. In general, the level of a country in the modernization process is in direct ratio to the country's percentage of innovation value, and in inverse proportion to its percentage of labor value; is in positive proportion to its percentage of materialized labor and effective labor, and in reverse proportion to that of living labor and ineffective labor; is in direct proportion to its percentage of effective investment and advanced assets, and in reverse proportion to that of ineffective investment and primary assets; and is in positive proportion to its percentage of advanced technologies, and in reverse proportion to that of backward technologies (Table 2.26). The percentages of value and interrelationships between them will be discussed later.

Third, national advancement has its duality. On the one hand, it has relative stability; for example, in a span of about 50 years, the probability that advanced countries maintain the advanced level is approximately 90%. On the other hand, it has mobility; for example, advanced countries may be downgraded to developing ones, with an approximately 10% of probability, and developing countries may be upgraded to advanced ones, with an approximately 5% of probability in a span of some 50 years.

2.2.2.2 Main Dimensions of National Advance

National advancement is a multidimensionally composite phenomenon. Theoretically, countries that have achieved the world's advanced level in economic, social, political, cultural, ecological, and human modernization are defined as advanced countries. From the policy perspective, countries whose productivity, social progress, and level of human development are at the world's advanced level fall into the category of advanced countries. The advanced productivity, social progress, and human development are the three dimensions of national advancement. The fourth dimension of that is environmental friendliness.

The first dimension: advanced productivity. Generally, productivity means the value created by labor in a unit time.

Table 2.27 Sources and types of scarcity

Type	Explanation	Example	Annotation
Natural	Scarcity created by nature and history	Cultural relics, special resources, etc.	Restricted amount and very small percentage
Managerial	Scarcity created by artificial monopoly, etc.	Market monopoly by monopoly enterprise	Restricted by antimonopoly law, with various minus effects
Technical	Scarcity created by patents for invention	Patented products, new drugs, etc.	Valid during the period of patent protection; able to produce innovation value

Note: Both patents for invention and leading technologies can lead to scarcity to some degree. The period of patent protection is generally about 18 years
Source: He (2010a, 2011)

British scholar David Ricardo (1817) thought that "... the exchange value of utility commodities comes from their scarcity and/or the amount of labor needed to acquire them. The value of some commodities is determined only by the scarcity of them, and this type of commodities is only an extremely very small part of the commodity volumes exchanged every day on the market" (Ricardo 1821). Austrian economist Schumpeter (1912) raised his "innovation theory" and explained economic development by means of enterprise innovation. He holds that "upon the emergence of a new product, the producer has no rivals, and the price of the product is thoroughly, or within certain limits, decided by the principle of monopoly price."

Currently, there are roughly three types of scarcity (Table 2.27): natural scarcity, involving restricted numbers or amounts; "managerial scarcity," usually illegal; and technical scarcity, chiefly as a result of patents and innovations. In and before the nineteenth century, technical scarcity was less; since the twentieth century, technical scarcity has increased considerably in both number and percentage. Generally, the value determined by technical scarcity could be called innovation value for short, and it includes innovation value added produced by creative labor (He 2001) (Example 2.8).

Example 2.8 Innovation Value and Excess Profits

From being developed to going on market and finally exiting from the market, an innovated product roughly undergoes five stages (He 2001): the innovation stage, in which the new product is developed without profits; the monopoly stage, in which the technological and product monopoly as a result of patent protection produces innovation value and gains excess monopoly profits; the diffusion stage, in which a number of enterprises monopolize the new product and gain high profits; the imitation stage, in which a large number of imitators emerge and share average profits, the term of patent protection ends; and the exit stage, in which the product produces no profits and exits from the market, in the case of that the supply exceeds need or new replaceable product markets.

(continued)

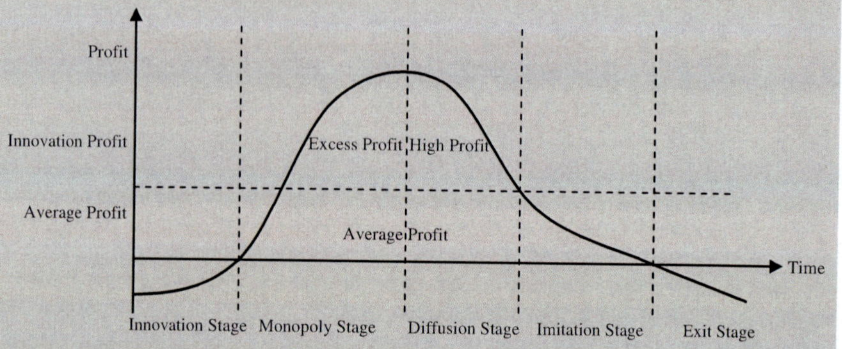

Market cycle and innovation profit of a new product. Source: He (2001)

Table 2.28 Aggregate value created by social labor (fourfold value theory)

Value	Meaning	Explanation	Annotation
Labor value	Value created by common labor	Value created by common living labor and materialized labor	A country's labor force and investment capital are restricted
Innovation value	Value created by creative labor	Value created by knowledge, technological, and institutional innovations	Innovation value, able to increase in an unlimited way
Resource value	Value of resource costs	Use and wastage of natural resources	Increase GDP and lower national net savings
Environmental value	Value of environmental change	Value of environmental damage and improvement	Environmental damage produces a negative value; environmental improvement produces a positive value

Note: Living labor means work done by a laborer, including common living labor and creative labor. Materialized labor means the labor solidified in investment capital. Common labor includes common living labor and materialized labor. Knowledge and technological innovations include new intellectual property rights, new commodities, and new services. Institutional innovations include institutional and conceptual innovations here, for example, new institutions, new models, and new concepts. Resource value includes the use of resources (transfer of value) and the wastage of resources (loss of value)
Source: He (2010a, 2011)

In the unit labor time, the aggregate value created by aggregate social labor mainly includes four types of value (Table 2.28); of these types, the labor value and the innovation value are the main value, and the resource value and the environmental value are the secondary value and are of duality.

If the resource and environmental value is not considered, the value created by social labor includes labor value and innovation value, where labor value is created by common labor and innovation value by creative labor (related to the economic

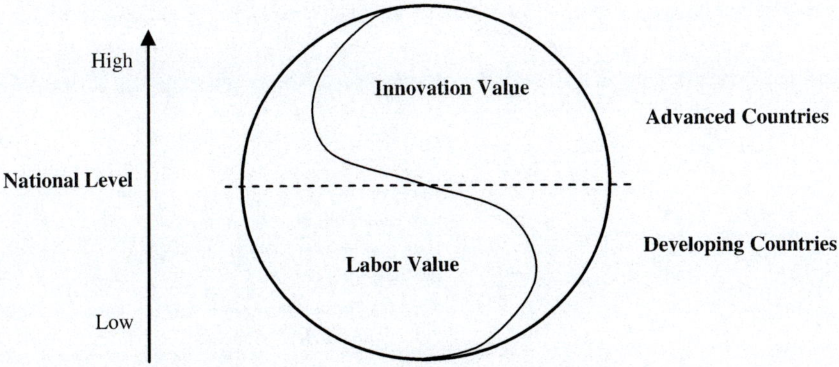

Fig. 2.48 Taiji diagram of value percentage. Source: He (2010a, 2011)

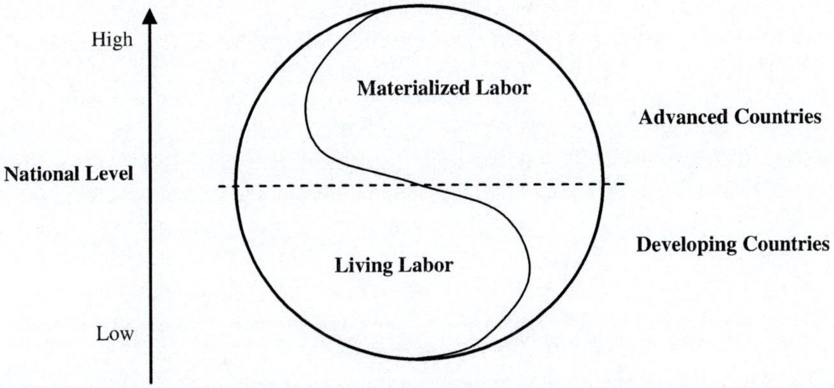

Fig. 2.49 Taiji diagram of labor percentage. Source: He (2010a, 2011)

system). Generally, advanced countries have a higher percentage of innovation value, while developing countries have a higher percentage of labor value in GDP; the national level is in positive correlation with the proportion of innovation value and in negative correlation with that of labor value (Fig. 2.48); advanced countries have a higher percentage of materialized labor, while developing ones have a higher percentage of living labor; the national level is in positive correlation with the proportion of materialized labor and in negative correlation with that of living labor (Fig. 2.49).

The second dimension: social progress. Social progress includes the development of public services and the improvement of the quality of life. It entails promotion and realization of social equity which includes opportunity equity, process equity, and result equity (Table 2.29). Because of inborn difference in individuals, the three types of equity can hardly be realized at the same time. Distribution according to contribution promotes process equity, and adjustment according to need promotes result equity.

Table 2.29 Model of social equity

Equity	Field	Explanation
Opportunity equity	Opportunity of education, employment, public service, etc.	Equity in compulsory education, full employment, universal suffrage, etc.
Process equity	Income distribution: according to contribution	Both investment capital and knowledge capital (labor, knowledge, and management) participate in net income distribution
Result equity	Income adjustment: according to need	Personal income adjustment: income tax, excise, property tax, etc.
		Social income adjustment: social insurance, social aid, social welfare, transfer payment, etc.

Note: There are four models of distribution according to contribution: contribution-based joint-stock system, contribution-based sharing system, contribution-based system of coalition, and contribution-based remuneration system
Source: He (2001, 2010a, 2011)

The third dimension: all-round human development. UNDP thinks that all-round human development includes advances in four aspects, i.e., democracy and participation, economy and equity, health and education, and peace and personal safety (UNDP 2002). Inglehart and Welzel think that human development may be divided into three dimensions: the socioeconomic dimension, the cultural dimension, and the institutional dimension and that the essential outcome of human development is the expansion of human choice and autonomy (Inglehart and Welzel 2005). Generally, all-round human development requires the liberation of humans which entails equality for all, the elimination of fear, the increase of options, the maintenance of equal rights of humans, the improvement of universal education and social security, and the respect for diversity in professions and lives.

The fourth dimension: environmental friendliness since about 1970s. Ecological modernization needs the benign interaction among economy, society, and the environment; the complete disconnection of economic growth from environmental degeneration; the healthy development of both economy and the environment; and the mutual symbiosis (mutualism) between human and nature.

2.2.2.3 Main Driving Forces of National Advance

The driving factors of modernization include innovation, competition, adaptation, exchange, national interests, and market demand, which also drive national advancement. In material and technical aspects, innovation and learning (communication) are critical driving factors; in institutional and conceptual aspects, competition and market are critical driving factors. Innovation, learning, and competition are the fundamental driving forces of national advancement (Table 2.30).

For countries at different development levels, the three driving forces work in considerably different ways. In the technological aspect, advanced countries stress both innovation and learning, while developing countries put more emphasis on learning. For example, high-income countries outperform other countries in the percentages of spending on R&D and technology import in GDP (Table 2.31).

Table 2.30 Three driving forces of national advancement

Driving force	Example of policy measure	Application scope
Innovation	Knowledge innovation, institutional innovation, technological innovation, etc.	In technological, institutional, and conceptual aspects
Learning	International exchange, cooperation, technology import, foreign direct investment, etc.	In technological and institutional aspects
Competition	Fair competition, antimonopoly, anti-infringement, antifraud, antidumping, rational regulation, etc.	In institutional and conceptual aspects

Source: He (2010a, 2011)

Table 2.31 Percentages of spending on R&D and technology import in GDP

Item	R&D spending/GDP (%)				Technology import spending/GDP (%)			
Year	1980	1990	2000	2005	1980	1990	2000	2005
High-income countries	2.2	2.3	2.5	2.4	0.10	0.13	0.29	0.34
Middle-income countries	0.5	0.6	0.7	0.9	0.03	0.04	0.17	0.23
Low-income countries	0.3	0.3	0.7	0.6	0.02	0.01	0.05	0.07
World	1.9	2.1	2.2	2.1	0.08	0.11	0.26	0.31

Note: Spending on technology import refers to the royalty and license fees in international technology transfer and licensing. The figures in the table are obtained through calculation based on the data in the *World Development Indicators 2008* (World Bank 2008) and in *China Modernization Reports* (RGCMS 2006, 2007, 2008)

Table 2.32 Percentages of transfer payments and government revenue in GDP

Item	Transfer payments/GDP (%)				Government revenue/GDP (%)			
Year	1990	1995	2000	2005	1990	1995	2000	2005
Developed countries	17.8	19.6	19.2	19.2	31.8	31.8	32.0	31.1
Moderately developed countries	16.2	17.1	16.5	16.5	31.3	30.4	30.5	30.0
Preliminarily developed countries	9.5	9.0	10.2	12.0	26.3	26.0	25.8	27.2
Underdeveloped countries	3.5	2.9	4.3	6.0	17.6	17.1	16.0	17.2

Note: Transfer payments include all kinds of subsidies and other transfers, calculated based on the data in *World Development Indicators 2008* (World Bank 2008). In 2005, in Finland, Norway, the Netherlands, France, and Belgium, the percentage of government revenue (excluding grants) in GDP registered 39%, 40%, 40%, 43%, and 42%, respectively and that of transfer payments in GDP stood at around 26%, 23%, 31%, and 33%, respectively. In 2008, Norway saw the percentage of government revenue (excluding grants) in GDP registering some 51%, and that of transfer payments in GDP about 21%

In the institutional aspect, advanced countries emphasize both competition and the rational regulation of market competition and income distribution, while developing countries impose less regulation on market and income. For example, advanced countries have a higher percentage of transfer payments in GDP than developing ones (Table 2.32).

2.2.3 General Criteria of National Advance

National advancement is both a process and an outcome. At national level, it is the development process of a country through which it reaches and maintains the world's advanced level. At the level of the international system, it is the process of international differentiation through which some countries become advanced ones while others become developing ones. Advanced countries enjoy the world's advanced level and lead the frontier of the world. National advancement is closely related to the national level and the criteria for the classification of the national level.

2.2.3.1 Criteria Based on National Modernization Level

First, advanced countries are those which lead the world's frontier in the process of modernization. Now, there is no standard definition on world frontier, but generally it can be defined according to the world rankings on modernization level. For example, the world's top 20 countries in 2005 were advanced countries among the 131 countries whose populations were over one million in 2000.

Second, advanced countries are those with the world's advanced level. There is no standard definition of the world's advanced level; generally, it can be defined according to the modernization level. For example, countries whose SMI and IMI reach or exceed 80 (80% of high-income countries' average level) are advanced countries.

Third, qualitative criteria on advanced countries. Advance countries are those which enjoy the world's advanced levels in modernization process. Generally, advanced countries are, first and foremost, those with advanced productivity; only the countries whose productivity, social progress, and human development have all reached the world's advanced level are advanced countries.

2.2.3.2 Criteria Based on Levels of Field- and Indicator-Specific Modernization

First, in the fields where quantitative evaluation is allowed such as economic, social, cultural, ecological, and human modernization, the criteria for defining advanced countries can borrow or copy those based on national modernization level.

Second, in the fields where it is hard to do quantitative evaluation such as political, institutional, and conceptual modernization, special research needs to be done on the criteria for defining advanced countries. The criteria can be established based on case studies about advanced countries and international comparison and should keep up with the times.

Third, the criteria for defining advanced countries may vary with the indicators of modernization which can be divided into quantitative and qualitative ones (Table 2.33). There are roughly eight categories of quantitative indicators. For increasing and decreasing variables, the criteria for defining advanced countries can borrow or copy those based on national modernization level; for transitional variables, the criteria can be established based on case studies about advanced countries and international comparison; for random, regional, and stable variables, there are international differences, but there are usually no criteria for defining the

Table 2.33 Criteria or methods for defining advanced countries according to modernization indicators

Type of indicator	Criteria/method	Sample indicator
Increasing variables	Approximately among the world's top 20, with values above 80% of the average level of high-income countries	Per capital national income
Decreasing variables	Approximately among the world's top 20, with values below 80% of the average level of high-income countries	Infant mortality
Transitional variables	Developing criteria through case studies about and international comparison between given advanced countries	Percentage of industrial labor force
Fluctuating variables	Varying from country to country, generally no criteria of world frontier and national advancement	Annual growth rate of GDP
Random variables		Natural disasters
Regional variables		Mineral resources
Stable variables		Territory area
Saturation variables	The values are already saturated in many countries, so they are generally not used as indicators for classifying countries	Enrollment of elementary school
Qualitative variables	Developing criteria through case studies about and international comparison between given advanced countries	Social security system and environment awareness

Note: World rankings refer to the rankings in 131 countries with a population of more than one million in 2000 and with fairly complete statistical data; the same below
Source: He (2010a, 2011)

world frontier and national advancement. Regarding qualitative indicators, special research should be done on the criteria for defining advanced countries. Generally, the criteria can be established based on case studies about advanced countries and international comparison and should keep up with the times.

Fourth, if there is only one world frontier, the criteria of national advancement can be articulated clearly; if there are multiple frontiers, their types and states can be described, but it is hard to set the criteria of national advancement.

Fifth, modernization changes, and the criteria of national advancement thus need to keep up with the times.

Sixth, the level of national modernization and the levels of field- and indicator-specific modernization may be consistent with or different from each other. Advanced countries might have not yet reached the world's advanced levels in some fields or by some indicators, while developing countries might have already reached the world's advanced levels in some fields or by some indicators.

The basic criteria of advanced countries in 2005 are given in Table 2.34: the level of national modernization and the level of modernization in major fields are among the world's top 20; the SMI, IMI, and modernization indexes in major fields

Table 2.34 General criteria of national advancement in 2005

Country	Level of indicators (common indicators)	Indicator ranking (among 131 countries)
Developed countries	Modernization index and 80% of the modernization indicators are greater than 80% of high-income countries' average level	The world's top 1–20
Moderately developed countries	Modernization index and 80% of the modernization indicators are higher than or equal to the world's average level but lower than that of advanced countries	The world's top 21–45
Preliminarily developed countries	Modernization index and 80% of the modernization indicators are higher than or equal to 60% of the world's average level in general but lower than the world's average level	The world's top 46–80
Underdeveloped countries	Modernization index and 80% of the modernization indicators are lower than 60% of the world's average level (30% of high-income countries' average level) in general	The world's top 81–131

Source: He (2010a, 2011)

exceed 80 (80% of high-income countries' average level); the modernization level by some 80% of the evaluation indicators reaches the world's advanced level (approximately among the world's top 20 or above 80% of high-income countries' average level). In the requirement that the world's advanced level is reached by 80% of the indicators, the figure 80% is just an estimate.

2.2.4 General Methods of National Advance

Generally, the method of achieving national advancement is to follow the basic principles of modernization and national advancement and choose the right modernization path, strategies, and measures based on national conditions and the international environment (Table 2.35). Because advanced countries and developing ones differ in national condition and international environment, there are not only similarities but also differences when it comes to what methods to choose (Table 2.36). Different paths, models, and priorities may be chosen in different periods in the different fields. From the theoretical perspective, advanced countries do need to reach and maintain the world's advanced level in the six fields, i.e., economic, social, political, cultural, ecological, and human fields; from the policy perspective, advanced countries should keep the world's advanced level in three aspects such as the advanced productivity, social progress, and human development.

Table 2.35 Principles and methods on national advancement

Element	Principles of national advancement	Methods of national advancement
Value	National level is in direct ratio to its percentage of innovation value and in inverse proportion to that of labor value	Improve national innovation capacity, increase the percentage of per capita innovation value, reduce the percentage of per capita labor value, etc.
Labor	National level is in positive proportion to its percentage of material labor and of effective and high-efficiency labor and is in reverse proportion to that of living labor and of ineffective and low-efficiency labor	Increase per capita investment, increase the percentage of per capita material labor and of per capita effective and high-efficiency labor, decrease the percentage of per capita living labor and of per capita ineffective and low-efficiency labor, etc.
Capital	National level is in direct proportion to its percentage of effective investment and of high-efficiency investment and is in inverse proportion to that of ineffective investment and of low-efficiency investment	Increase investment efficiency, increase the percentage of per capita effective investment, high-efficiency investment and advanced assets, reduce the percentage of per capita ineffective investment, low-efficiency investment and primary assets, etc.
Technology	National level is in positive proportion to its percentage of advanced technologies and in reverse proportion to that of backward technologies	Accelerate technological advancement and the withdrawal of backward technologies, increase the percentage of per capita advanced technologies, reduce the percentage of per capita backward technologies, etc.
Productivity	National level is in direct proportion to labor productivity	Increase the levels of per capita capital, skills, and management
Society	National level is in direct proportion to social progress	Distribution according to contribution, adjustment as needed, making money perfectly, and fair and mutual help
Humans	National level is in direct proportion to the all-round development of people	Promotion according to achievement, selection according to public opinion, everyone doing his best, equality, and mutual benefit

Source: He (2010a, 2011)

Table 2.36 Choosing the methods for national advancement

Element	Advanced countries	Developing countries
Value	Improve innovation capacity, increase per capita innovation value, etc.	Improve innovation capacity, increase per capita innovation value and per capita labor value, etc.
Labor	Increase per capita living labor (international employment) and per capita high-efficiency labor, etc.	Increase per capita investment, increase per capita effective and high-efficiency labor, reduce ineffective and low-efficiency labor, etc.
Capital	Increase investment efficiency, per capita high-efficiency investment, per capita advanced assets, etc.	Increase investment efficiency, increase per capita effective investment, high-efficiency investment and advanced assets, reduce ineffective and low-efficiency investment, etc.

(continued)

Table 2.36 (continued)

Element	Advanced countries	Developing countries
Technology	Accelerate technological advancement and the withdrawal of backward technologies	Increase advanced technologies, reduce backward technologies, etc.
Productivity	Increase per capita capital and per capita skills, etc.	Raise levels of per capita capital, skills, management
Society	Distribution according to contribution, adjustment as needed, etc.	Selection according to national conditions
Humans	Promotion according to performance, selection according to public opinion, etc.	Selection according to national conditions

Source: He (2010a, 2011)

Summary

Modernization is a complex phenomenon with both universality and diversity. This chapter deals with the universality.

Core Theory of General Modernization

Modernization is a sort of civilization change, and it follows regular patterns which can only be understood step by step. There are different schools of modernization theories, which have different understandings about modernization laws. This chapter mainly deals with the core theory of general modernization, which includes the basic contents of five aspects of modernization—definition, process, result, dynamics, and models. The general modernization refers to the modernization in general sense and not to special one.

(1) Operational Definition

In the modernization science, there is no unified definition of modernization, but there is a variety of operational definitions. Chapter 1 has discussed the three explanations and six theoretical meanings of modernization. Operational definitions of modernization can be raised as per theoretical meanings and research needs.

Definition 1: Modernization is a type of frontier change of human civilization and international competition since the Industrial Revolution in the eighteenth century. It is the frontier process of the formation, development, transformation, and international interaction of modern civilization; the composite process of alternate innovation, selection, diffusion, and withdrawal of modernization elements; and the international competition for catching up with, reaching, and maintaining the world's advanced level and the international differentiation thereof. Countries which have reached and maintained the world's advanced level are advanced countries, and others are developing countries; there is mobility between the two groups of countries.

Definition 2: Modernization is the intersection of civilization development, civilization transition, and international interaction since the eighteenth century.

Definition 3: Modernization is the world frontier of modern civilization and the process and act of reaching the world frontier.

There are more definitions that can be introduced based on over three definitions. For example, based on the definition 3 above, it can be introduced: from the perspective of policy and national level, modernization refers to the world's advanced level at present and the process to reach or maintain this advanced level.

Eight characteristics of modernization. Modernization is a sort of not only civilization change but also civilization competition; it is not only a world trend but also a social choice; it involves multiple dimensions that intersect to a very high degree; it needs to be treated from both internal and international perspectives; it has not only civilization progresses but also side effects; it has not only generality but also diversity; it involves not only international convergence but also international differentiation; and it cannot be done once and for all. Much controversy now still exists over the scopes and boundaries of the generality and individuality, modernity (universals) and particularity (diversity) of modernization.

Three criteria of modernization. Modernization is a sort of frontier change of modern civilization and must meet three conditions. In the second modernization process, it must be conducive to the emancipation and improvement of productivity without prejudice to the natural environment, be conducive to social equity and progress without hindering economic development, and be conducive to human liberation and all-round development without damaging social harmony.

(2) General Process

Generally, there are roughly two types of modernization process, the frontier process and the catch-up process, both of which are connected, differ, and interact with each other. The frontier process roughly has about over 20 features, which are the general manifestations of the modernization process. The catch-up process has some 12 features. Generally, historical stages cannot be leaped over, but some technical stages can be skipped.

Between the eighteenth century and the twenty-first century, the frontier process of modernization can be divided into two major stages.

The main features of the first modernization include industrialization, urbanization, and democratization; different fields have different features.

The main features of the second modernization include knowledgeablization, informatization, and greening; different fields have different features.

The first modernization is the foundation for the second modernization. The second modernization is the continuity and development of the first modernization in some aspects such as democratization, rationalization, and scientific and technological advance; in some aspects, it is the "reversion" or transition of the first modernization, for example, from industrialization to deindustrialization, from centralization to decentralization, and from ecological destruction to environmental protection; and in some aspects, it is innovation, for example, knowledgeablization, informatization, and networking. The coordinated development of the first and second modernization and the transition toward the second modernization mark the integrated modernization.

If we say that modern civilization can be divided into two stages, primary modern civilization and advanced modern civilization, then industrial civilization is the primary modern civilization, and knowledge civilization and ecological civilization are the advanced modern civilization. If we say that the first modernization is the transition from traditional to primary modern civilization, then the second modernization is the transition from primary modern to advanced modern civilization; the integrated modernization is the coordinated development of the first and second modernization and the continuous transition toward advanced modern civilization.

Modernization of civilization contents is an essential part of the modernization process. Generally, it is a composite process of the alternate innovation, selection, diffusion, and withdrawal of civilization elements, with the prominent feature being the diversified paths and forms.

Modernization of civilization forms is an essential part of the modernization process. Generally, it is a composite process of the formation, development, transition, and international interaction of modern civilizations, each aspect of which has a diversity of paths and forms.

The change of the international system is an essential part of the modernization process, including changes in its structure and level.

Modernization follows ten basic principles: asynchronous process, unbalanced distribution, structural stability, changeable status, predictable behavior, optional path, increasing needs, decreasing effectiveness, unrepeatable state, and changing axis (Table 2.15).

(3) General Result

According to the theoretical meanings and empirical study of modernization, the outcomes of modernization include the formation of modernity, particularity, and diversity; the improvement of labor productivity and quality of life, social progress, political democracy, cultural diversity, ecological change, and all-round human development; the international differentiation, national stratification, and side effects; and the changes in the world frontier, international system, and national state.

Modernization outcomes are closely related to not only the time span of the modernization process but also its start, end (end point for analysis), and geographic coverage, as well as modernization goals.

The main outcome of the first modernization process is the formation of first modernity, particularity, diversity, and side effects. The main features of the first modernity include industrialized, urbanized, democracy, rule of law, rational, secular, centralization, mobility, marketed, social welfare, special, high efficiency, opening, liberty, equality, modern science and energy, mass communication, and universal compulsory education. The side effects of the first modernization include, among other things, environmental pollution, differentiation between the rich and poor, economic crisis cycle, and weakening human relationship.

The main outcome of the second modernization process is the formation of second modernity, particularity, diversity, and side effects. The main features of the second modernity in 2005 included knowledge intensiveness, information intensiveness, networking, intellectualized, global, innovation, individual, diversified, greening, ecological awareness, risk, urban–rural balance, environmental friendliness, lifelong learning, and universal higher education. Currently, the side effects of the second modernization include cybercrime, information divide, international risk, and widening inequality.

From the theoretical perspective, national modernization has three main objectives: completing the first modernization, effecting the transition from agricultural to industrial civilization; completing the second modernization, effecting the transition from industrial to knowledge civilization; and catching up with, reaching, or maintaining the world's advanced level. The realization of the first two objectives is a "matter of time," and all countries may complete them early or late; the realization of the third objective is a "matter of percentage and probability," and only a portion of countries could reach and maintain the world's advanced level. Advanced country is of the minority, while developing country is of the majority in the world.

From the policy perspective, national modernization has two main objectives: internal goal is improving productivity and the quality of life, promoting social equity and progress, promoting all-round human development, and promoting the symbiosis of man and nature; international goal is about the status that advanced countries' policy objective is to maintain the world's advanced level, while developing countries' policy objective is to catch up with and reach the world's advanced level.

The connection between objectives and outcomes of national modernization was reinforced gradually. Before 1950, there was generally no relationship between the outcomes and objectives of the national modernization process. From 1960 onward, the modernization outcomes and objectives of developing countries were closely connected. Since 1970, modernization theories have begun influencing advanced countries' policy objectives. The relationship between modernization outcomes and objectives will become increasingly close.

(4) General Dynamics

The analysis of the driving forces in the process of modernization can be conducted at micro- and macrolevels, involving dynamic factors and mechanisms.

Dynamic factors of modernization include innovation, competition, adaptation, exchange, national interests, market demand, etc.

Dynamic mechanism of modernization include innovation drive, triple-innovation drive, two-wheel drive, associative action, four-step hypercycle, complete interaction of three types of civilization, innovation diffusion, innovation spillover, competition drive, and productivity function (Table 2.20).

(5) General Models

Both civilization and modernization involve multiple paths. Modernization has path diversity, model diversity, and path dependency.

The modernization process roughly has three basic paths, many subdivided paths, forked paths, and more than 50 element mix models.

The three basic paths are the first modernization path, the second modernization path, and the integrated modernization path from theoretical perspective, each having a unique direction and structural features; they are the "envelope curves" of these paths for fields, sectors, and civilization contents and forms.

Subdivided paths, also known as subpaths, are a group of paths, out of the basic paths, that have a consistent direction but different structural features.

Forked paths are paths that seem to lead to modernization objectives but virtually cannot reach them.

Countries in the twenty-first century can choose one of the three basic paths. If a country choose to finish the first modernization first and then the second modernization, then the first stage is the first modernization path and the second stage is the second modernization path. The practice may also be named as the catch-up modernization path for short.

There are three paths from policy perspective: second modernization path, integrated modernization path, and catch-up modernization path. The former one is applicable to the countries that have completed first modernization or entered second modernization, while the latter two are applicable to the countries that have not yet finished the first modernization.

Modernization and National Advance

Countries are the basic units of modernization movement. In the process of modernization, the grouping and stratification of countries and the international differentiation exist as objective phenomena. Countries are grouped into advanced countries and developing ones according to their levels of national modernization.

First of all, on national advancement. The national advancement is an objective phenomenon that in the process of modernization. A portion of countries that have reached and maintained the world's advanced level and become advanced countries, and other countries became developing ones, and there is mobility between the two groups of countries in the modernization process. On national level, it is a process of national development by which to reach and maintain the world's advanced level, along with the change of national status. On international level, it is a process of international differentiation, in which a group of countries become advanced countries and other countries became developing ones.

Second, on classification of advanced countries. Generally, countries can be divided into different groups based on their levels of modernization at national, field, and indicator layers. The criteria in 2005 included the level of national modernization and the level of modernization in major fields standing at the world's top 20 and the SMI, IMI, and modernization indexes in major fields reaching or exceeding 80 (80% of the average level of high-income countries). Not every field and every index of advanced countries are advanced; developing countries may also have reached the world's advanced level in some fields or in terms of some indexes.

Third, on the percentage of advanced countries. Over the past 300 years, the percentage of advanced countries has been below 20% and that of developing ones has been above 80%.

Fourth, on the change in the status of advanced countries. In a span of 50–100 years, the probability that an advanced country is downgraded to a developing one is about 10%, and the probability that a developing country is upgraded to an advanced one is about 5%.

General Principles of National Advance

The phenomenon of national advancement is both a complex one which needs analysis from different perspectives and also an attendant one to the modernization process, so it can be interpreted based on the modernization theory.

First, national advancement is an objective phenomenon and the result of national modernization, international competition, and international differentiation. In the process of modernization, advanced countries are those that have reached and maintained the world's advanced level of national modernization, and others are developing countries; the percentage of advanced countries is generally below 20% and that of developing countries is above 80%; there is mobility between the two groups of countries.

Second, national advancement is in positive correlation with the national level. In general, the level of a country is in direct ratio to the country's percentage of innovation value, and in reverse proportion to its percentage of labor value; is in positive proportion to its percentage of materialized labor and effective labor, and in inverse proportion to that of living labor and ineffective labor; is in direct proportion to its percentage of effective investment and advanced assets, and in reverse proportion to that of ineffective investment and primary assets; and is in positive proportion to its percentage of advanced technologies, and in reverse proportion to that of backward technologies.

Third, national advancement is of duality: relative stability and mobility. For example, the probability that in a span of 50 years advanced countries maintain an advanced level is about 90%. Advanced countries may be downgraded to developing ones, with a probability of approximately 10% in a span of 50 years; developing countries may be upgraded to developed ones, with a probability of approximately 5% in a span of 50 years.

Fourth, national advancement has three criteria: advanced productivity, social progress, and all-round human development. National advancement is first manifested as having advanced productivity; only those with the world's advanced levels of productivity, social progress, and human development are advanced countries. The fourth criterion is environmental friendliness, which requires the healthy development of both economy and the environment, as well as the mutualism between man and nature.

Fifth, national advancement involves three driving forces: innovation, learning, and competition. In technological aspects, advanced countries emphasize both innovation and learning, with the latter playing a more prominent role in developing countries. In institutional aspects, advanced countries stress both fair competition and rational regulation, and developing countries should ensure moderate and progressive regulation on market competition and income distribution.

Sixth, general methods of national advance. Generally, the method of achieving national advancement is to follow the basic principles of modernization and national advancement and choose the right modernization path, strategies, and measures based on national conditions and the international environment. There are not only similarities but also differences for the methods to the advanced and developing countries. Different paths, models, and priorities may be chosen in different periods in different fields. From the theoretical perspective, advanced countries do need to reach and maintain the world's advanced level in the six fields, i.e., economic, social, political, cultural, ecological, and human modernization; from the policy perspective, advanced countries should keep the world's advanced level in three aspects such as the advanced productivity, social progress, and human development.

Further Reading

Beck U, Giddens A, Lash S (1994) Reflexive modernization: politics, tradition and aesthetics in the modern social order. Stanford University Press, Stanford, CA

Bell D (1973) The coming of postindustrial society. Penguin, New York

Black CE (ed) (1976) Comparative modernization: a reader. Free, New York (Trans. Yang Y, Chen Z, Shanghai: Shanghai Translation Publishing House, 1996)

Brown DE (1991) Human universals. McGraw-Hill, New York

Crook S, Pakulski J, Waters M (1992) Post-modernization: change in advanced society. Sage, London

Harrison D (1988) The sociology of modernization and development. Unwin Hyman, London

He C (1999) The second modernization: inspiration for human civilization process. Higher Education, Beijing

He C (2003) Oriental renaissance: three roads to the modernization. Commercial, Beijing

He C (ed) (2010) China modernization report outlook: 2001–2010. Peking University Press, Beijing

Inglehart R, Welzel C (2005) Modernization, cultural change, and democracy: the human development sequence. Cambridge University Press, New York

Maddison A (2001) The world economy: a millennial perspective. OECD, Paris (Trans. Wu X, et al. Beijing: Peking University Press, 2003)

Martinelli A (2005) Global modernization: rethinking the project of modernity. Sage, London

Ralph PL et al (1991) World civilizations: their history and their culture. W. W. Norton, New York (Trans. Zhao F, Beijing: The Commercial Press, 1998/1999)

RGCMS (Research Group for China Modernization Strategies et al) (2005) China modernization report 2005: a study of economic modernization. Peking University Press, Beijing

RGCMS (Research Group for China Modernization Strategies et al) (2006) China modernization report 2006: a study of social modernization. Peking University Press, Beijing

RGCMS (Research Group for China Modernization Strategies et al) (2010) China modernization report 2010: world modernization outline 1700–2100. Peking University Press, Beijing

Rostow WW (1960) The stages of economic growth: a non-communist manifesto. Cambridge University Press, Cambridge (Trans. Guo X, Wang S, Beijing: China Social Sciences Press, 2001)

Stavrianos LS (1982) The world since 1500: a global history. Prentice-Hall, Englewood Cliffs, NJ (Trans. Wu X, Liang C, Shanghai: Shanghai Academy of Social Sciences Press, 1992)

3 History of Modernization

"A fact is more power than many words" (Chinese proverb). There are about 300 years of history of world modernization and over 50 years of history of modernization study. Here, we focus on its general and brief historic facts of modernization process, study, and thoughts (Fig. 3.1). Generally, modernization is the new phase of human civilization process, and the interaction between them took place naturally (Fig. 3.2).

3.1 Historical Process of Modernization

Definitely, the modernization process is part of the history of human civilization. We will address the process of modernization and civilization together. So far, scientists have estimated that *Homo sapiens* appeared about 2.5 million years ago, civilization emerged about in 3500 BC, and modernization started in about eighteenth century. There are so many interactions between them since about eighteenth century.

3.1.1 Main Stages of Modernization

Generally, the process of civilization and of modernization overlaps with each other, and modernization research overlaps with the civilization study. Here, we mainly address their frontier processes in general.

3.1.1.1 Main Stages of Human Civilization

Human civilization is an organic whole and also an aggregation of the civilizations of different countries and nations whose process is not on a synchronous basis. The frontier trajectory of human civilization can be divided into different stages by the level and characteristics of civilization, but historians and sociologists have different ways of doing so.

C. He, *Modernization Science*,
DOI 10.1007/978-3-642-25459-8_3, © Springer-Verlag Berlin Heidelberg 2012

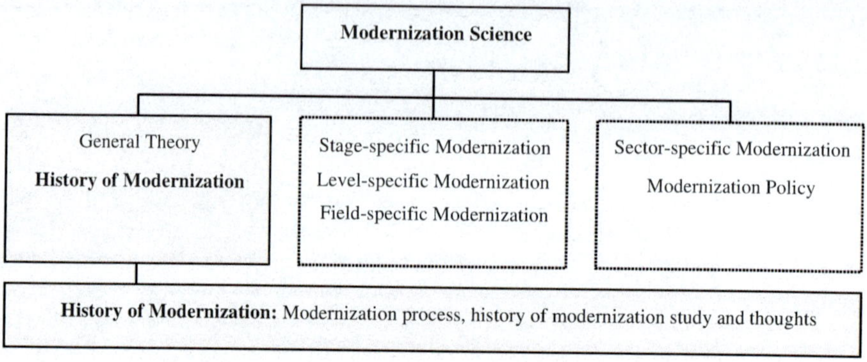

Fig. 3.1 Positioning and structure of the history of modernization

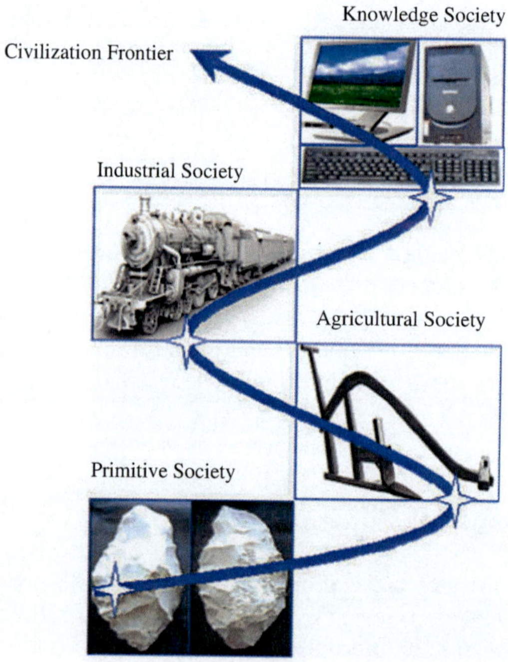

Fig. 3.2 Four forms, three shifts, and two modernizations in the frontier process of human civilization.
Note: Ever since the birth of humankind, the frontier of human civilization has undergone three shifts. The first one is from primitive society and culture to agricultural society and civilization, the second one from agricultural to industrial society and civilization, and the third one from industrial to knowledge-based society and civilization. The second shift is the first modernization; the third one, the second modernization. The four images above represent stone tool, plow, steam engine, and computer, respectively.
Source: He (2010a, b)

(1) Stage Division of Frontier Process of Human Civilization

There are various views on the historical stages of human civilization, among which five are closely related to modernization study. They see the process of human civilization consisting of three to seven historical stages, respectively (Fig. 3.3). The second modernization theory and *China Modernization Report* hold that human civilization has witnessed the process of four stages according to the level and structure of the civilization's productivity, namely, the Tool Age, the Agricultural Age, the Industrial Age, and the Knowledge Age.

The views on the social stages of human civilization are also diversified, and four of them, which are closely related to modernization research, see the process of human civilization consisting of three to six social stages, respectively (Fig. 3.4). The second modernization theory and *China Modernization Report* hold that human civilization has witnessed the process of four stages according to the level and structure of social productivity, namely, primitive society, agricultural society, industrial society, and knowledge society.

(2) Main Features of Frontier Process of Human Civilization

First of all, different periods took place in the frontier process of human civilization. There are many periods in the frontier process of human civilization, and here are three examples:

- The periods of civilization elements. Human civilization is composed of many elements. Some of them follow the evolution theory and change from a lower to

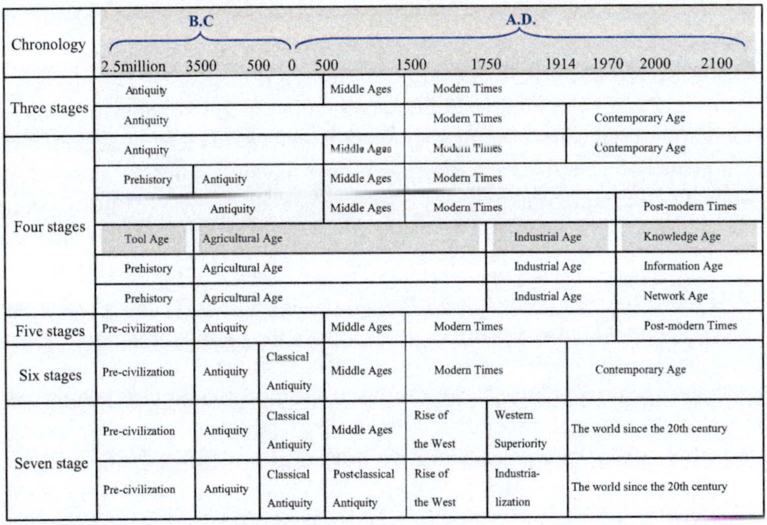

Fig. 3.3 Historical stages of human civilization.
Note: The process of human civilization can be divided into stages according to the level and characteristics of civilization frontier; time span is just a relative criterion. The frontier and average level of civilization vary greatly from stage to stage; countries and regions do not develop on a synchronous basis. It is based on the ideas of Thorndike (1926), Lyotard (1984), Stavrianos (1982), Ralph et al. (1991), Stearns et al. (1992), Wu et al. (1994), He (1999), and Palmer et al. (2002).
Source: RGCMS (2010)

	B.C.					A.D.						
Chronology	2.5million	8000	3500	500	0	500	1500	1750	1914	1970	2000	2100

Stages						
Three stages	Traditional Society				Modern Society	Postmodern Society
	Pre-industrial Society				Industrial Society	Postindustrial Society
Four stages	Primitive Society		Agricultural Society		Industrial Society	Knowledge Society
	Primitive Society		Agricultural Society		Industrial Society	Information Society
	Primitive Society		Agricultural Society		Industrial Society	Network Society
	Primitive Society		Agricultural Society		Industrial Society	Ecological Society
	Primitive Society		Agricultural Society		Industrial Society	Risk Society
Five stages	G & H Society	Horticultural Society	Agrarian Society	Agricultural Society	Industrial Society	
	G & H Society	Horticultural Society	Pastoral Society	Agricultural Society	Industrial Society	
	G & H Society	Pastoral Society	Agrarian Society	Traditional Civilization Society	Industrial Society	
	Primitive Society		Slavery Society	Feudalism Society	Capitalism Society	Socialist Society (Communist Society)
Six stages	G & H Society	Horticultural Society	Pastoral Society	Agricultural Society	Capitalism Society	Postcapitalism Society
	G & H Society	Horticultural Society	Pastoral Society	Agricultural Society	Industrial Society	Postindustrial Society

Fig. 3.4 Social stages in the history of human civilization.
Note: G&H Society refers to Gathering and Hunting Society. The division of social stages is based on the frontier characteristics of human civilization; time span is just a relative criterion. Countries and regions do not develop on a synchronous basis. It is based on the ideas of Marx (1954), Black (1966), Bell (1973), Beck (1992 [1986]), Ralph et al. (1991), Crook et al. (1992), Leakey (1994), Inglehart (1997), He (1999), Castells (1996), UNESCO (2005), and Servaes and Carpentier (2006). *Source*: RGCMS (2010)

a higher level and from being simple to being complex, like the development of knowledge and education. Some elements change in cycles. They start from a point and finally return to the starting point; the two points may be slightly different. For example, the division of powers develops from primitive democracy to feudal autocracy and then to democratic election. Individual rights develop from primitive equality to hierarchy and then to modern equality.

- The periods of national civilization. In the Agricultural Age, the civilizations of many countries and nations develop in the cycles of rise, development, maturity, and fall, such as the feudal dynasties in ancient China.
- The periods of human civilization. From the birth of mankind to the end of the twenty-first century, the process of human civilization goes through four ages, namely, the Tool (the age of primitive culture), Agricultural, Industrial, and Knowledge Age. In every age, four stages constitute a cycle including the start, development, mature, and transition stage (Table 3.1). Thus, there are four cycles in the entire development process of human civilization.

If there are "small periods" in each country and nation and a "midperiod" in each age, there should be a "big period" of the four ages in the process of human civilization as a whole. In such a "big period," the Tool Age is the incubation stage; the Agricultural Age, the start stage; the Industrial Age, the development stage; and the Knowledge Age, the mature stage (Table 3.1). When a period ends,

Table 3.1 "Big periods" in the frontier process of human civilization

Item	Incubation stage	Start stage	Development stage	Mature stage
Four ages	Tool Age	Agricultural Age	Industrial Age	Knowledge Age
Four forms	Primitive culture	Agricultural civilization	Industrial civilization	Knowledge civilization
Direction	Hunting and gathering	Farming and animal husbandry	Industries and services	Knowledge and information
Goals	Establishing a human society	Meeting survival needs	Meeting material needs	Meeting spiritual needs
Major innovation	Stone tool	Plow	Steam engine	Computer
Frontiers	Socialization, food gathering, personalization	Agriculturalization, food production, rise of civilization	Industrialization, deagriculturalization, first modernization	Knowledgeablization, deindustrialization, second modernization

Note: Meeting survival needs means meeting such basic needs as clothing, food, housing, and transportation, mainly the needs for food
Source: He (2003)

human civilization enters a new transition stage (incubation stage of a new civilization) and then a new "big period" starts.

Second, there are periodic shifts in the frontier process of human civilization. Periodic shifts can be seen in many aspects of civilization process, and here are three examples:

- The periodic shifts of civilization direction. In the history of human civilization, three shifts have taken place in the direction of civilization process (Fig. 3.2). The main orientation and goals of civilization development are gathering, hunting, and socialization in the Tool Age; crop farming, animal husbandry, and meeting survival needs in the Agricultural Age; industries, services, and meeting material needs in the Industrial Age; and knowledge, information, and meeting spiritual needs in the Knowledge Age. As the direction of human civilization changes cyclically, the frontier and state of civilization also go through periodic shifts (Table 3.1) and so do the connotation and characteristics of civilization (Table 1.23).
- The periodic shifts of civilization axis. In the history of human civilization, there are three shifts of civilization axis (Table 3.1). The first one is from primitive culture to agricultural civilization, leaving the former marginalized (decreased importance and percentage); the second one is from agricultural to industrial civilization, leaving the former marginalized; the third one is from industrial to knowledge civilization, leaving the former marginalized. During such a process, economic and social axes have also changed (Table 3.2).
- The periodic shifts of civilization center. Based on available information, in the Tool Age, Africa is the cradle of human beings; in the Agricultural Age, Asia (Middle East) is a major cradle of agricultural civilization; in the Industrial Age, Europe is the birthplace of industrial civilization; in the Knowledge Age, North America is a major cradle of knowledge civilization. Thus, the geographic center of human civilization has been changing on a cyclical basis (Table 3.2).

Table 3.2 Periodic shifts of axis and center in the frontier process of human civilization

Item	Primitive culture	Agricultural civilization	Industrial civilization	Knowledge civilization (2005)
Civilization axis	Hunting and gathering	Farming and animal husbandry	Industries and services	Knowledge and information
Economic axis	Food	Land	Capital	Innovation
Social axis	Kinship	Power	City	Internet
Civilization center	Africa	Multiple centers	Europe	America (North America)
Cradle of civilization	Africa	Asia (middle east)	Europe (Western Europe)	America (North America)
Center of science	–	Multiple centers	Europe (Italy, France, UK, Germany)	America (North America) (USA)

Note: American scholar Daniel Bell believes that in the process of social development, there is an organizational structure that stands at the center and is surrounded by other structures, some social logic is primary while others are secondary, and there is always an axis principle that rules in every society (Bell 1973). The age of primitive culture is before the birth of civilization, so the civilization axis here actually refers to its cultural axis. The center of agricultural civilization changes with time, so there are multiple centers. For example, there were four great ancient civilizations including ancient Babylon, ancient Egypt, ancient India, and ancient China, as well as four classical civilizations including ancient Greece, ancient Rome, India, and China. The characteristics of knowledge civilization are limited to the civilization by 2005

Source: Bell (1973) and He (1999, 2003)

Table 3.3 Accelerations in the periods and stages of frontier process of human civilization

Item	Tool Age	Agricultural Age	Industrial Age	Knowledge Age
Time spans	2.5 million years	5,260 years	Approx. 210 years	Approx. 130 years
Start stage	2.3 million years	3,000 years	110 years	20 years
Development stage	160,000 years	1,100 years	40 years	30 years
Mature stage	30,000 years	900 years	30 years	30 years
Transition stage	3,500 years	260 years	20 years	50 years

Note: The time spans of different periods and stages are rough figures. Those of the Knowledge Age are estimated figures

Source: He (2003)

Third, there are accelerations in the frontier process of human civilization. Acceleration is embodied in many aspects of civilization process, and here are three examples (He 2003):

- The acceleration in the periods of civilization process. The time span of a period becomes shorter and shorter in the four stages of human civilization. The Tool Age spans nearly 2.5 million years; the Agricultural Age, over 5,000 years; the Industrial Age, more than 200 years; and the Knowledge Age is expected to span some 100 years (Table 3.3).
- The acceleration in the stages of civilization process. In the three periods of the Tool Age, the Agricultural Age, and the Industrial Age, the time span of a stage gets shorter and shorter from the start stage to the development, mature, and then transition stages; it is the same in the first 12 stages of civilization development (Table 3.3).

Table 3.4 Acceleration in the growth of productivity

Item	Agricultural Age		Industrial Age		Knowledge Age	
Year	1000	1700	1700	1950	1973	1998
World's average per capita GDP	435	615	615	2,114	4,104	5,709
Average annual growth rate	0.05%		0.50%		1.33%	
Growth rate 1	0.26 International dollar per year		6.00 International dollars per year		64.20 International dollars per year	
Growth rate 2	26 International dollars per 100 years		60 International dollars per 10 years		64 International dollars per year	

Note: The unit of per capita GDP is the international dollar at PPP-based prices in 1990. It is based on the data coming from Maddison (2001)
Source: RGCMS (2010) and He (2010a)

- The acceleration in the elements of civilization such as productivity and knowledge. If productivity grows every 10,000 years in the Tool Age, every 100 years in the Agricultural Age, and every 10 years in the Industrial Age, the pace should be in yearly terms in the Knowledge Age. Per capita GDP grows faster in the Knowledge Age than in the Industrial Age where the growth rate is higher than in the Agricultural Age based on the increased value per year (Table 3.4).

3.1.1.2 Main Stages of General Modernization

Modernization is both a world trend and a collection of modernization in different countries and fields. The modernization processes in different countries and fields are not on a synchronous basis. Here, we focus on the frontier process of general modernization. The stages of modernization's frontier trajectory are closely related to the start of modernization and criteria to define the stages. There has been no consensus on the start of modernization, but a common view is that modernization started in the 1760s (Example 3.1).

Example 3.1 Start of Modernization

Currently, there are mainly three views on the start of modernization. The first one holds that modernization started from the revolution of science in the sixteenth and seventeenth centuries; the second one suggests that it is the Enlightenment in the seventeenth and eighteenth centuries; the third one indicates that it is the British Industrial Revolution and the French Revolution in the eighteenth century. Of the three views, the third one is the most popular. In China Modernization Report, *the British Industrial Revolution in the eighteenth century is taken as the start of modernization. Modernization research may start with the beginning of the eighteenth century, but the idea of modernization can be traced back earlier.*

If modernization started from the British Industrial Revolution in the eighteenth century, then in which year did it start? There is no consensus on this issue either. There are several options like 1750, 1760, 1763, and 1770. In 1763, Scottish inventor James Watt improved the steam engine, which was later patented in 1769. The invention and application of the steam engine is a typical representative of the Industrial Revolution.

(continued)

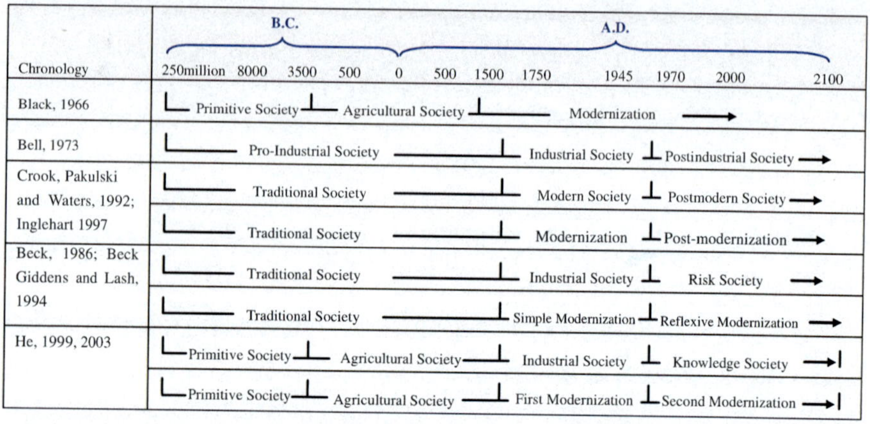

Fig. 3.5 Stages in the frontier process of modernization and civilization.
Note: The stage divisions are defined based on the level and characteristics of frontier trajectory of modernization and civilization; time span is just a relative criterion. Modernization processes in different countries are not on a synchronous basis.
Source: He (2010a, b)

Generally, the 1760s (1760 or 1763) can be taken as the start of modernization. If so, modernization starts along with the advent of the Industrial Age, industrial societies, and modern societies.

No consensus has been reached on how to define the stages in modernization's frontier trajectory (Fig. 3.5). Now there are five views on defining the stages according to the characteristics (qualitative criterion) of the modernization frontier (Table 3.5). The fifth view agree that the modernization process consists of two major stages (though their names and contents may be different), and the dividing time is around 1970 (knowledge and information revolution).

Based on the characteristics (qualitative criterion) and level (quantitative criterion) of modernization's frontier, modernization between the eighteenth and the twenty-first centuries consists of two major stages, namely, the first modernization and the second modernization; each stage is composed of four phases including the start, development, mature, and transition phases. The quantitative criteria for defining the phases of each modernization stage are addressed in Chap. 1 (Table 1.17, Table 1.18).

3.1.1.3 Relationship Between Modern Civilization and General Modernization

There is no single definition of modern civilization. In general sense, modern civilization refers to modern industrial civilization; in broad sense, it also includes knowledge civilization and ecological civilization. Modern civilization can be traced back to the Renaissance, the religion Reformation, and the scientific revolution in Europe. They represent origin of modern civilization and the preparatory stage of

Table 3.5 Defining the stages of the modernization process

Stages	Contents	Annotation
Three waves	First wave (1780–1860), second wave (late nineteenth century–early twentieth century), and third wave (second half of the twentieth century) (Luo 1993)	Stages of classical modernization
Four stages	Challenges posed by modernity, stabilization of modern leadership, economic and social transformation, and social integration (Black 1966)	
Five stages	Five stages of economic growth: traditional society, the stage to create preconditions for the take-off, the take-off stage, the maturation stage, and the stage of massive consumer spending (Rostow 1960); a sixth stage was later added: the quality of life stage	
Four periods	Preparatory period, transformation period, advanced modernization period, and international integration period (Black 1976)	
Two major stages	Classical and post modernization (modern and postmodern society) (Crook et al. 1992; Inglehart 1997)	Two kinds of modernizations
	Simple and reflexive modernization (industrial society and risk society) (Beck 1986; Beck et al. 1994)	
	First and second modernization (industrial and knowledge society) (He 1998a, b, 1999, 2003)	

Source: RGCMS (2010)

modernization. The development of modern civilization has witnessed a series of major historical events which are closely related to the stages of modernization (Fig. 3.6). Generally, the frontier trajectory of modernization consists of the preparatory stage, the first modernization, and the second modernization; the first modernization comprises of three waves, and the second modernization includes three waves.

3.1.2 Main Waves of Modernization

There are different ideas on the waves of modernization process at present.

According to the connotation and characteristics of the frontier, the two stages of the modernization process can be divided into several waves. *China Modernization Report 2005* introduced the six waves of economic modernization, while *China Modernization Report 2006* brought up the six waves of social modernization (Table 3.6). But the fifth and the sixth waves are just forecasts.

3.1.3 Options on Modernization Paths

Modernization is the world frontier of modern civilization as well as the act and process of reaching that frontier since the eighteenth century. The act and process of reaching the frontier is closely related to the path of modernization and the characteristics of civilization frontier. From the perspective of the universality of

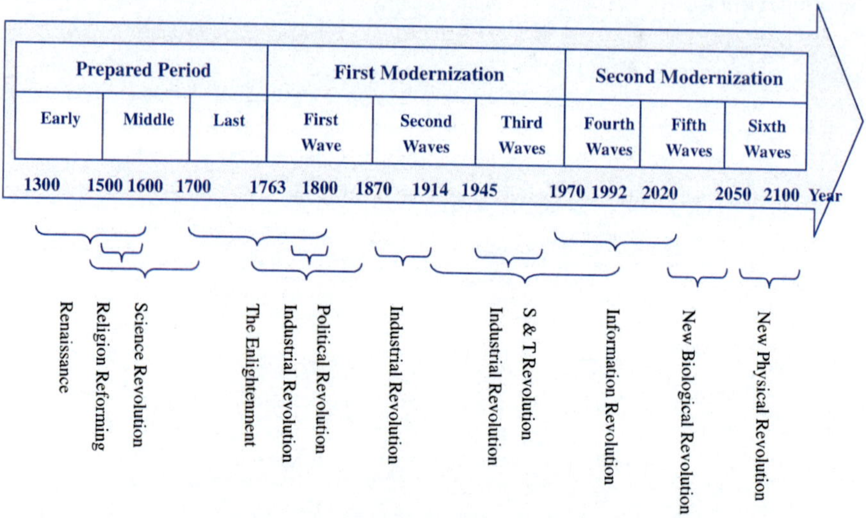

Fig. 3.6 Major events in modern civilization and the stages of modernization's frontier trajectory. *Note*: The typical feature of the first industrial revolution is mechanization; that of the second one is electrification; and that of the third one is automation. The fifth and sixth waves are just forecasts. Modernization processes in different countries are not on a synchronous basis. *Source*: RGCMS (2010) and He (2010a, b)

Table 3.6 Six waves of economic and social modernization

Wave	Chronology	Economic modernization	Social modernization	Annotation
First	ca. 1763–1870	First industrial revolution	Urbanization, mechanization	*First modernization* Industrialization, urbanization, democratization, rationalization
Second	ca. 1870–1945	Second industrial revolution	Electrification, compulsory education	
Third	ca. 1946–1970	Third industrial revolution	Social welfare, automation	
Fourth	ca. 1970–2020	Information revolution	Network, knowledge-based	*First modernization* Knowledge-intensive, networking Globalization, greenization
Fifth	ca. 2020–2050	New biological revolution	Biological economic society	
Sixth	ca. 2050–2100	New physical revolution	Cultural economic society	

Note: The waves are defined based on the connotation and characteristics of modernization's frontier trajectory. The fifth and sixth waves are just forecasts. Modernization processes in different countries are not on a synchronous basis, and the stages may also be different. For advanced countries, the six waves may occur one after another. But for those left behind, two or more waves may happen at the same time, which means that the changes of several waves may take place during the same period of time
Source: RGCMS (2005, 2006)

modernization, there is usually a single frontier, but there can be multiple frontiers from the perspective of the diversity of modernization. There are many optional modernization paths. In choosing the path, the general law of modernization should be followed and the objective conditions should be met.

3.1.3.1 The Path Options for Advanced Countries (Frontier Paths)

First, suppose there is a single frontier of civilization. If there is one old frontier of civilization and one new frontier, there can be a single path or multiple paths for advanced countries to move from the old frontier to the new one (Fig. 3.7).

Second, suppose there are multiple frontiers of civilization. If there are both multiple old frontiers of civilization and multiple new frontiers, there will be multiple paths for advanced countries to move from an old frontier to a new one (Fig. 3.8). If there are either multiple old frontiers or multiple new frontiers, there will also be multiple paths.

3.1.3.2 The Path Options for Developing Countries (Catch-up Paths)

First, suppose there is a single frontier of civilization. If there is one old frontier of civilization and one new frontier, there can be a single path or multiple paths for developing countries to move from the nonfrontier to the old frontier and then to the new one; there may be a path or no path for developing countries to move directly from a nonfrontier to a new frontier (Fig. 3.9). If such a path does exist, it might be different from that for advanced countries.

Second, suppose there are multiple frontiers of civilization. If there are multiple frontiers of civilization, there will be multiple paths for developing countries to move from nonfrontier to old frontier and multiple paths from the old frontier to a new one; there may be a path from nonfrontier to a new frontier.

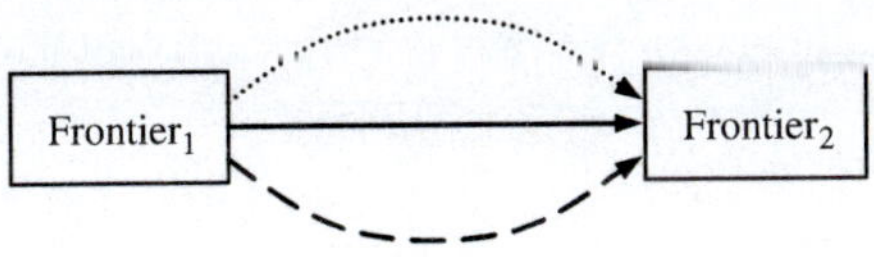

Fig. 3.7 Modernization paths of advanced countries (one frontier).
Note: The *solid line* indicates a single path; the *dotted lines* represent optional paths.
Source: He (2010a)

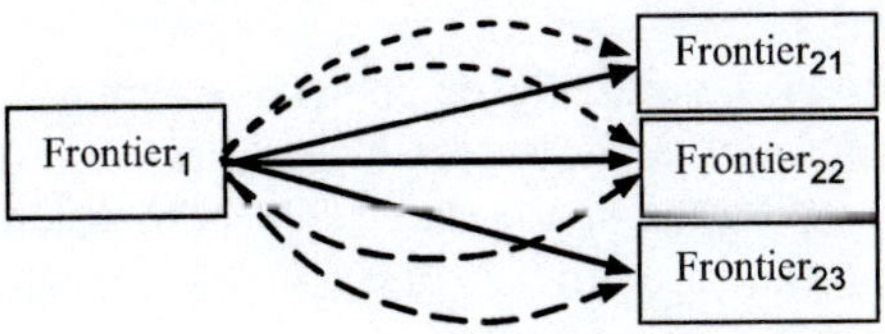

Fig. 3.8 Modernization paths of advanced countries (multiple frontiers).
Note: The *solid lines* indicate a single path; the *dotted lines* represent optional paths.
Source: He (2010a)

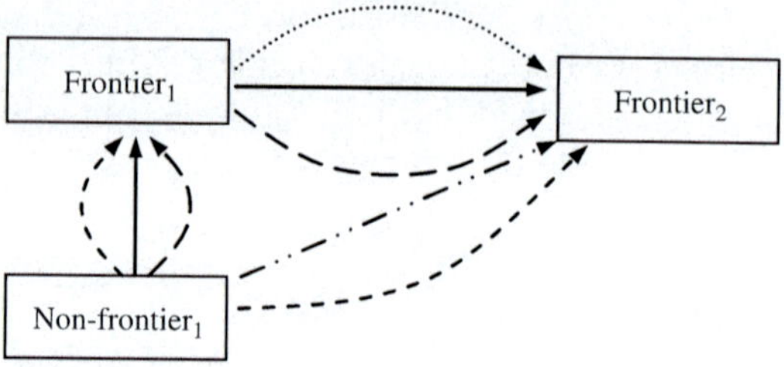

Fig. 3.9 Modernization paths of developing countries (one frontier).
Note: The *solid line* indicates a single path; the *dotted lines* represent optional or possible paths.
Source: He (2010a)

Table 3.7 Options of modernization path in developing countries

Unskippable	Annotation	Skippable	Annotation
1. Urbanization	A major stage that cannot be skipped, but "semiurbanization" is possible	Steam engine	Not necessary. Internal combustion engine is an alternative
2. Industrialization	A major stage that cannot be skipped, but "semi-industrialization" is possible	Telegraph	Not necessary. Internet is an alternative
3. Knowledgeablization	The stage of education popularization cannot be skipped	Phonograph	Not necessary. CD play is an alternative
4. Informatization	A major stage that cannot be skipped, but some technology stages can be skipped	Pager	Not necessary. Cell phone is an alternative

Note: The major stages in historical development cannot be skipped, but the paths are optional; some technology stages can be skipped
Source: RGCMS (2010) and He (2010a)

Third, if modernization process is the ordered arrangement of a series of states, does it mean that developing countries have to experience all the states? The answer is no from the perspective of technological progress. Some technological states are necessary, but some are not; developing countries may skip some technological states (Table 3.7).

3.2 History of Modernization Study

Modernization has become a world phenomenon since about eighteenth century. It was common in the eighteenth and nineteenth centuries but did not attract special attention from scholars and was not a research subject of academic studies. In the early twentieth century, the term "modernization" first appeared in the academic literature. Since the 1950s, the research on modernization has witnessed several climaxes with continuous theoretical innovations (Fig. 3.10). There were two main tracks in the early development of modernization science: modernization research and modernization theories that promoted each other.

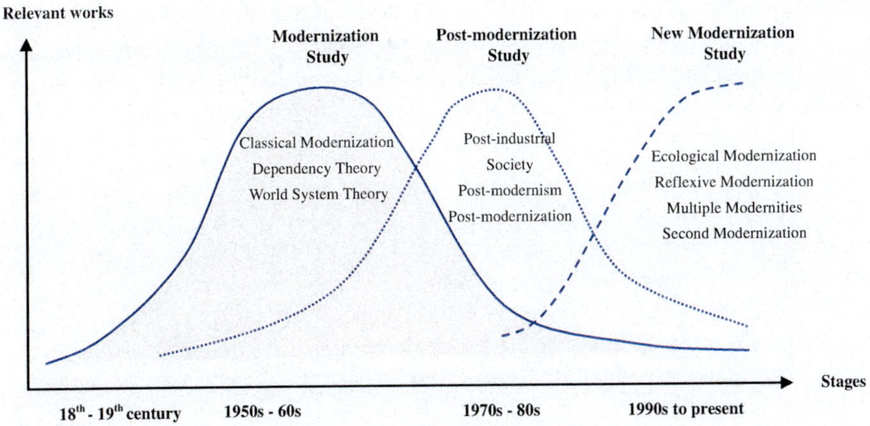

Fig. 3.10 Three waves of modernization research in the twentieth century.
Source: He (2003)

Table 3.8 Origin of modernization research

Stage	Approx. period	Subjects
Breeding	Third century BC to 1950	Research of early development: research of the world history and human development and research in the four fields such as economy
Exploring	1950–1960	Multidisciplinary research: research of developing countries and in various fields
Maturing	1960–1970	Multidimensional research: theoretical research, empirical research, and research in various fields

Source: RGCMS (2010)

3.2.1 Origin of Modernization Study

It is almost impossible to identify the exact origin of modernization research at present. If we do not take into consideration the early research done by Chinese scholars, modernization research in the West has a history of at least over 50 years. However, there is no consensus on the division of modernization research stages yet.

Generally, modernization research began in the twentieth century. Chinese scholars began the research in the 1930s, while their American counterparts, in the 1950s. If we categorize modernization research as a research on human development, the history of which can be traced back to years before Christ, then the history of modernization research can be roughly divided into the following three stages (Table 3.8).

3.2.1.1 Breeding Stage: Early Development Research

Modernization is a profound change of human civilization since the eighteenth century, which is inevitably integrated with the human civilization history and the world history. The early research on the world history, human civilization history, and human development can be regarded as the "prehistoric" predecessor of modernization research. Though it is not modernization research itself, it provides historical background and academic basis for the birth of the latter. In addition, some early academic literature and thoughts are still of practical value and of lasting influence upon modernization research (Example 3.2).

Example 3.2 Early Research of Human Development
The research on human development can be traced back to years before Christ. After thousands of years of effort spent in exploring the pattern for human development and civilization progress, a large quantity of academic literature has been accumulated. Some early literature is more or less related to the modernization research whose academic impact is still alive today.

First, research literature on the human civilization history and the world history is represented by The Republic *(Plato, third century BC)*, New Science *(Vico 1725)*, Essay on the Mores and the Spirit of Nations *(Voltaire 1756)*, Sketch for a Historical Picture of the Progress of the Human Mind *(Condorcet 1795)*, The Decline of the West *(Spengler 1918)*, A Study of History *(Toynbee 1934–1961), and* World Civilizations: Their History and Their Culture *(Burns et al. 1955)*.

Second, research literature in the four fields of human civilization is represented by Politics *(Aristotle, third century BC)*, Two Treatises of Government *(Locke 1690)*, Social Contract, or Principles of Political Right *(Rousseau 1762)*, An Inquiry into the Nature and Causes of the Wealth of Nations *(Smith 1776)*, Course of Positive Philosophy *(Comte 1830–1841)*, Social Statics *(Spencer 1850)*, Capital *(Marx 1867)*, Primitive Culture *(Taylor 1871)*, Ancient Society *(Morgan 1877)*, Gemeinschaft and Gesellschaft *(Tönnies 1887)*, Division of Labor *(Durkheim 1893)*, The Protestant Ethic and the Spirit of Capitalism *(Weber 1904)*, The Theory of Economic Development *(Schumpeter 1912), and* The Structure of Social Action *(Parsons 1937)*.

In the research on world history, civilization history, and human development, there is abundant literature of the early research in this aspect, including some literature and thoughts closely tied to modernization research (Example 1.5). Ideas about the ideal society (Plato, third century BC), the recurring cycle and spiral evolution of historical development (Vico 1725), the common pattern of the development of nations (Voltaire 1756), the advancement of science and technology (Condorcet 1795), and the recurring cycle of civilization development (Spengler 1918) have great impact upon the modernization research.

Second, in the research in the four fields of economy, society, politics, and culture. Some early literature and thoughts in these fields are to some extent related to the modernization research (Example 3.2). Ideas about equality and freedom (Rousseau 1762), labor productivity (Smith 1776), positivism (Comte 1830–1842), social evolution (Spencer 1850), class conflicts (Marx 1867), division of labor (Durkheim 1893), rationality (Weber 1904), and structural functionalism (Parsons 1937) have profound and long-lasting influence upon modernization research.

3.2.1.2 Exploring Stage: Multidisciplinary Research

The 1950s marked the exploring stage of modernization research. Supported by the American government and some private foundations, a group of young political scientists, economists, sociologists, psychologists, anthropologists, and demographers conducted study of modernization (So 1990), the results of which were published on journals such as *Economic Development and Cultural Change*.

First, the study on developing countries. In the representative works, *The Passing of Traditional Society: Modernizing the Middle East* (Lerner 1958), Lerner analyzes the modernization process of seven countries in the Middle East and believes that modernization refers to the transformation from traditional society to modern society.

Second, the research in fields such as economy. The representative works include *Social System* (Parsons 1951), *The Stages of Economic Growth: A Non-Communist Manifesto* (Rostow 1960), and *The Politics of the Developing Areas* (Almond and Coleman 1960). Parsons proposes five sets of model variants of social system, while Rostow divides the economic growth into five stages.

3.2.1.3 Maturing Stage: Multidimensional Research

The 1960s marked the maturity stage of modernization research in which a number of works on modernization research with long-lasting influence were published.

First, theoretical research. The representative works include *The Dynamics of Modernization: A Study in Comparative History* (Black 1966), *Modernization, Protest, and Change* (Eisenstadt 1966), *Modernization: the Dynamics of Growth* (Weiner 1966), "*Tradition and Modernity Reconsidered*" (Bendix 1967), and so on.

Second, the research in fields such as economy. The representative works include *The Achieving Society* (McClelland 1961), *Political Modernization in Japan and Turkey* (Ward and Rustow 1964), *The Politics of Modernization* (Apter 1965), *Modernization and the Structure of Societies* (Levy 1966), and *Political Order in Changing Societies* (Huntington 1968), as well as some works published in the 1970s, such as *Becoming Modern: Individual Change in Six Developing Countries* (Inkeles and Smith 1974).

3.2.2 Three Waves of Modernization Study

In the second half of the twentieth century, there were three worldwide climaxes of modernization research (Fig. 1.15), namely, the modernization research in the 1950–1960s period, the postmodernization research in the 1970–1980s period, and the new modernization research since the 1980s. Of course, these three waves are not completely separated from each other but highly integrated and need to refer to each other while being discussed.

3.2.2.1 The First Wave: Classical Modernization Research

The period from the 1950s to the 1960s was the golden age for modernization research when it became a hot topic of humanities and social science and was conducted in a multidisciplinary and multidimensional way. However, the period from the 1970s to 1980s marked the lowest point of the first wave of modernization research, where the classical modernization study was widely criticized, while new theories such as the dependency theory and the world systems theory were gaining ground (Martinelli 2005). The period from the 1980s to 1990s was the adjustment period of the first wave, when the modernization theory was valued once more thanks to the success of modernization in East Asia and the modernization-oriented transformation in East Europe and Latin America, but its methods were adjusted and viewpoints corrected. Some scholars regard the modernization research in the 1950s to 1960s as classical modernization research and, since the end of the 1970s, as new modernization research (So 1990), the latter being distinguishable with the adjustment of research methods and the change of some viewpoints.

3.2.2.2 The Second Wave: Postmodernization Research

The period from the 1970s to 1980s marked the climax of postmodernization research which included three parts: the postindustrial society, postmodernism, and postmodernization research. Though postmodernism can be traced back to the nineteenth century, the research did not reach the climax until the 1970–1980s and lasted through the 1990s.

In the 1970s, there were mainly three branches of modernization research: one continued with the study of modernization theories (including the modernization history, public policies, and the relationship between economy and democracy of developed countries), which enriched the modernization theories; one studied the modernization in developing countries, making corrections of the classical modernization theory; and another studied the future development of advanced countries (futurology), bringing about various new theories, including the postindustrial society, postmodernism, postmodernization, new modernization, continuous modernization, information society, knowledge society, and so on. The postmodernization research was part of the study of the third branch.

3.2.2.3 The Third Wave: New Modernization Research

The period from the 1980s to 1990s marked the climax for new modernization research, which mainly included the research on ecological modernization, the reflexive modernization research, the multiple modernities research, and the second modernization research.

Besides inheriting the social science paradigm of the classical modernization research, new modernization research introduced the methodology of natural science and borrowed useful concepts from it. Researches on ecological modernization, reflexive modernization, and second modernization pay more attention to the social impact of natural science and high technology and the duality of science and technology, namely, their positive effects and side effects.

3.2.3 Criticism on Modernization Study

Especially in the 1970s and 1980s, modernization research was widely criticized by people from many aspects of the society, including both mainstream and radical sociologists (So 1990).

First of all, it was criticized for its own flaws. For example, the concept of modernization did not have a clear span; the connotation of the concept was too general and preferential (favorable to some countries and the rich); the concepts of modernity and tradition were obscure, subjective, and did not echo with each other; and the modernization theories were too general and lagging behind. Second, there was not merely one direction of development but many of them, and there was not merely one path of development either. Third, modernization was not linear, partially reversible, and with occasional discontinuity. Fourth, the significance of traditional value could not be totally denied. Fifth, we could not be too optimistic or ignore the external factors. In some developing countries, the policies and measures adopted based on the classical modernization theory did not achieve the expected results.

Of course, the research on modernization and the practice of it are two different issues which need to be dealt with in different ways.

The criticism of modernization research reveals its problems, creating more room for theoretical development and in-depth research.

Problems arising in the practice of modernization might be an attendant phenomenon or side effect (by-product) of modernization or mistakes in the practice. If we can foresee the problems beforehand, then we might probably prevent them from happening. Problems of countries which have practiced modernization earlier provide historical experience and lessons for those which come after. These problems, called modern diseases by some, include environmental pollution, ecological degradation, indifference of social relationships, international conflicts, gap between the rich and the poor, economic crisis, and so on. The problems of practice have something to do with people's ideas and thoughts. The side effect is not inevitable, but it is indeed difficult to prevent it completely.

There is an antimodernization trend while modernization is sweeping the whole world (Alitto 1991), which will not be discussed here.

3.3 History of Modernization Thoughts

Despite over 50 years of modernization research, there is no universally agreed theory on modernization yet. Some hold that the theory of modernization misses not only systematic theoretical structure but also agreed basic definition. To a large extent, the theory of modernization is a collection of academic thoughts on modernization research, of research results, and ideas of scholars in different fields.

3.3.1 Origin of Modernization Theory

Throughout the history of human civilization, the development of thought does not always synchronize social practices; some thoughts go ahead of the society, while some summarize social practices. In the field of modernization research, there are some thoughts preceding social practices. Modernization began around the eighteenth century, and the research on it in the twentieth century, but some core concepts of modernization can be traced back much earlier.

3.3.1.1 Origin of Modernization Thoughts

Generally, different thoughts of modernization have different origins. The Enlightenment in the eighteenth century witnessed the burst of Western modernization thoughts, many of which can be traced back to the literature in this period. Of course, there are also several other sources which can be dated back to much earlier days, such as the Renaissance from the fourteenth to the sixteenth centuries, the Protestant Reform in the sixteenth century, the scientific revolution and bourgeois revolution from the sixteenth century to the seventeenth century, the Industrial Revolution in England in the eighteenth century, and the French Revolution.

The Renaissance was a period when the mind was emancipated; the feudal autocracy and religious tyranny gradually collapsed; secularism, individualism, and humanitarianism spread across the Europe; and a society which did not belong to the church with metropolises as its center appeared in Europe. At the same time, capitalism also rose in Europe thanks to commercial revolution. The subsequent scientific revolution introduced to Europe scientific knowledge, scientific thoughts, scientific spirit, and scientific methods, providing intellectual support for the modernization movement.

In the Enlightenment period, thinkers collected, sorted out, and spread philosophical and scientific knowledge and analyzed the history from a rational perspective. Many of their ideas became part of the classical modernization theory, such as forgiveness, justice, rationality, freedom, equality, democracy, and rule by law. The term "modernization" was coined in this period (1748–1770). The modernization in Europe would be impossible without the Enlightenment.

In the Industrial Revolution period, Smith proposed economic liberalism, Saint Simon described the picture of industrial society, Comte brought forward sociology, Spencer developed the theory of social evolution, Marx introduced the theory of scientific socialism, Durkheim published Division of Labor in Society, and Weber illustrated the concepts of legitimacy and bureaucracy. The political revolution promoted the spread and practice of nationalism, liberalism, democracy, rule by law, and socialism.

In the early twentieth century, some scholars began to study modernization. For example, in 1933, there was a special issue of *Shenbao Monthly* on modernization problems in China, including 26 articles discussing the difficulties and paths of modernization in China. In 1937, American scholar Parsons published *The Structure of Social Action*, and structural functionalism later became an important theoretical framework of classical modernization research.

The modernization research in the first half of the twentieth century was scarce, and there was no theory formed yet.

3.3.1.2 Establishment of Modernization Theory

Generally, the establishment of modernization theory refers to that of classical modernization theory, which was the first, but not only, member of the big family of modernization theories. Here, we will briefly introduce the establishment and evolution of classical modernization theory.

(1) Origin of Classical Modernization Theory

According to British scholar Harrison (1988), the classical modernization theory was established in the 1950–1960s, and its theoretical sources included evolutionism, the diffusion theory, structural functionalism, the systems theory, and the theory of interaction (Fig. 3.11). Political science, anthropology, psychology, economics, and geography also made their contributions. The classical modernization theory did not stand alone but was a cluster of different thoughts; its origin can be traced back to the classical evolution theory in the nineteenth century (Harrison 1988).

Based on Harrison's point (Harrison 1988), there are over 30 Western scholars who have contributed to the formation of classical modernization theory, including classical evolutionists, new evolutionists, and scholars on the diffusion theory, the social system theory, structural functionalism, and so on.

(2) Academic Challenges Against the Classical Modernization Theory

In the late 1960s, the classical modernization theory began to be criticized widely not only by the outsiders but also by the scholars engaged in the modernization research. New theories began to catch eyes, including the dependency theory, the world system theory, and postmodernism, which were all critical about or against the classical modernization theory.

(3) Academic Evolution of the Classical Modernization Theory

Since the 1970s, the classical modernization research has undergone dramatic changes, with part of the theory corrected. Based on abundant case studies and empirical studies, scholars found and corrected some one-sided views of classical modernization theory (Black 1976; Harrison 1988; So 1990; Inglehart 1997; Inglehart and Welzel 2005; Martinelli 2005). For instance, secularism is a complex social process, but religion will always exist and play a role in it; modernization is not linear, and there are multiple paths; tradition and modernity do not totally contradict with each other, and the traditional value will exist for a long time and play a role; the relationship between democracy and economy is not linear and is complicated; and the new modernization, Confucian culture, and export-oriented industrialization in East Asia have a positive role, as well as the new modernization in East Europe and the transformation from planning-commanded modernization to market-oriented modernization.

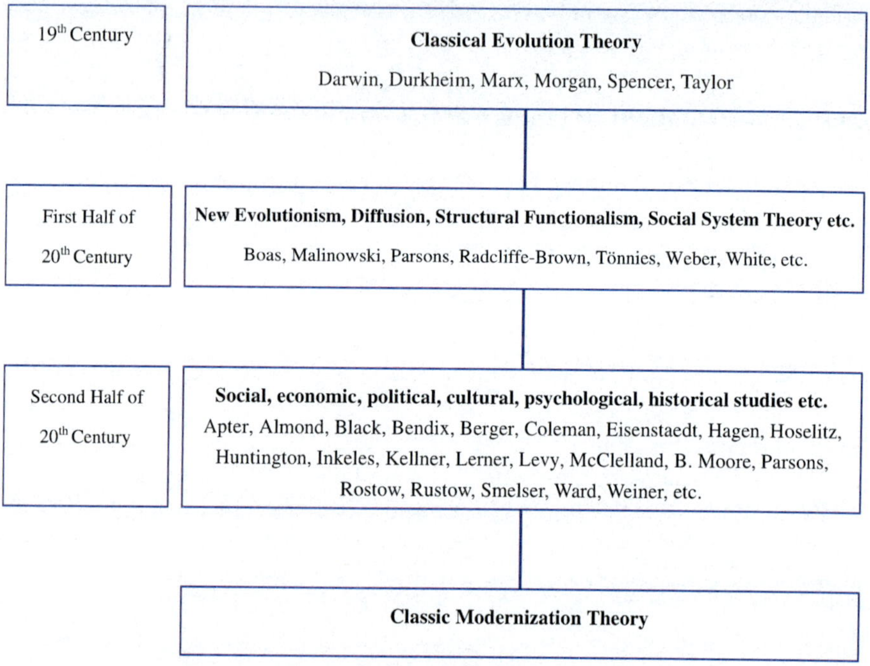

Fig. 3.11 Establishment of classical modernization theory.
Note: It is based on the thoughts of Harrison (1988)

3.3.2 Evolution of Modernization Theory

The evolution of the modernization theory roughly refers to two things: the evolution of the classical modernization theory and the establishment and evolution of other modernization theories. The former having been discussed above, we are going to discuss the latter here. On the whole, the classical modernization theory is the basis of modernization theory, and other theories were derived from it later (Fig. 3.12).

3.3.2.1 (1) Formation and Evolution of Postmodernization Theory

In the 1970s, the future development of advanced countries caught people's attention, and a lot of new thoughts such as postmodernism and postindustrial society emerged. There were various schools of postmodernism, and in the 1990s, the postmodernization theory was formed.

3.3.2.2 (2) Formation and Evolution of New Modernization Theory

From the 1980s to the early 1990s, some scholars continued the research on modernization and brought forward some new ideas such as new modernization, continuous modernization, ecological modernization, reflexive modernization, multiple modernities, and globalization, which will be discussed later in this book.

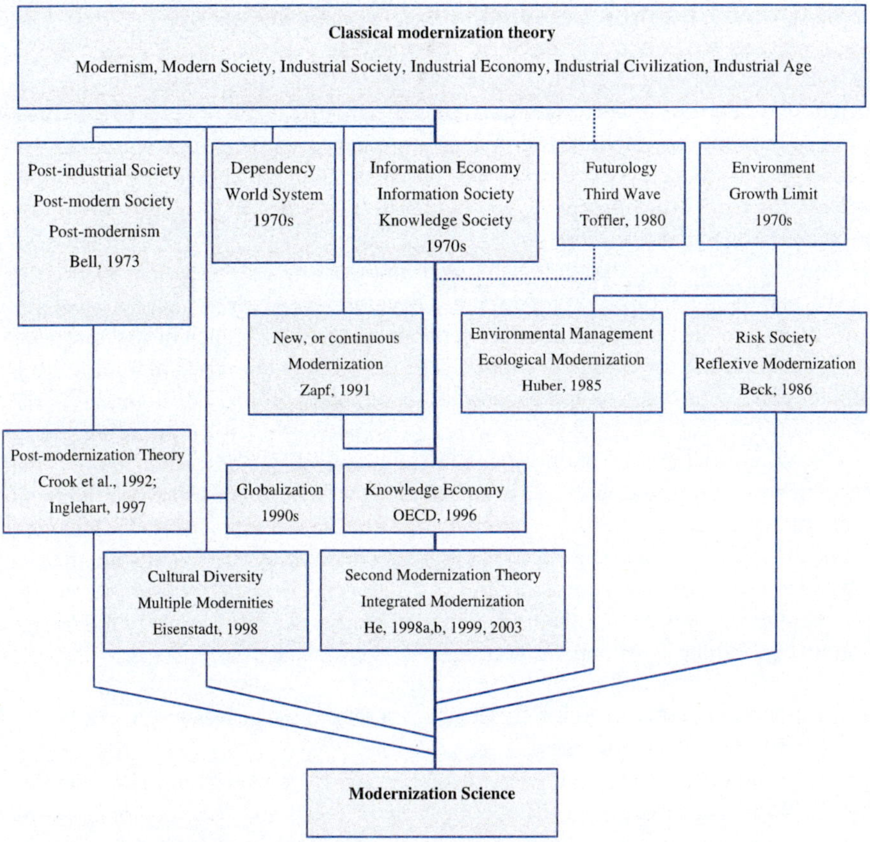

Fig. 3.12 Evolution of modernization theory (*Theory Tree*)
Source: RGCMS (2006) and He (2010a, 2011)

3.3.2.3 (3) Formation and Evolution of the Second Modernization Theory

At the end of the 1990s, with the rising of knowledge economy and knowledge society, the second modernization theory came into being. In the early twenty-first century, it gradually developed into a general theory of modernization, including the first and second modernization, as well as integrated modernization.

3.3.3 Emergence of Modernization Science

As the definition shows, science is a systematic, confirmed kind of knowledge. For a long time, the modernization research and the modernization theory were not systematic or regulated and thus could not be called a science. Now, the systematic modernization research, knowledge, and theory are qualified to constitute a science known as the modernization science.

3.3.3.1 Modernization Research in the Twentieth Century Was Not an Independent Science Yet

In the twentieth century, the modernization research was scattered in different disciplines of social science and humanities in a marginal and unfavorable position most of the time; the modernization theory was not systematic in structure, and its knowledge is loosely developed. The situation falls far behind the conditions needed for a science. Therefore, the "modernization science" was only a science-to-be in the twentieth century, not a new science.

Some scholars hold that the modernization theory is a development theory (So 1990), and the modernization research is a development study, which emerged as a new science in the second half of the twentieth century as a branch of social science and addressed the development problems of developing countries in a multidisciplinary way, with focus on the economic, social, and political development in the third world.

Development theories mainly include the classical modernization theory, the dependency theory, the world systems theory, the state theory, the development economics, etc. In the development study, the social development study generally adopts the classical modernization theory, the economic development study generally adopts the development economics, the dependency theory, and the world systems theory, and the political development study uses the classical modernization theory and the development politics.

3.3.3.2 Modernization Science Gradually Becomes a New Science in the Twenty-First Century

Science is an open system, with new disciplines and knowledge emerging successively. With the expansion of modernization research and the accumulation of modernization knowledge, the modernization science will come to the surface and become a new member of the big family of sciences.

(1) Abundant Accumulation

Starting from the 1950s, the modernization research has a history of over 50 years, with three climax researches, respectively, on classical modernization, the postmodernization, and the new modernization. The modernization theory has developed into a big family, including the classical modernization theory, the postmodernization theory, the ecological modernization theory, the reflexive modernization theory, the multiple modernities theory, the second modernization theory, and so on. There is rich knowledge on modernization too. For instance, in the National Library of China, there are over 1,000 kinds of Chinese books and about 400 English books themed on modernization (according to the search result on Dec. 12, 2009).

(2) Adapting to the General Trend of Interdisciplines and Integration of Sciences

The new division and integration of sciences have become a world trend, and the interdisciplinary science has been widely valued. The modernization science is a highly interdisciplinary science, involving multiple disciplines of natural sciences and social sciences, and also a highly integrated science for explaining modernization phenomena requires the cooperation of multiple disciplines.

(3) Meeting the Needs of Globalization and International Competition

Economic globalization and greening have become a world trend too, and the international cooperation and competition have been unprecedentedly intense. The international community has been increasingly concerned about how the advanced countries can stay advanced and how developing countries can become advanced in the process of international interaction. The research subjects of the modernization science include: why are advanced countries advanced while others are not? How can advanced countries stay advanced? And how can developing countries become advanced? The appearance of modernization science meets the needs of international competition in the twenty-first century.

3.3.3.3 Contributions from Chinese Scholars

Chinese scholars' research on modernization began early and has reached three climaxes (Table 3.9). As early as in the 1930s, Chinese scholars began academic discussions on China's modernization which was interrupted and stopped later. Since the reform and opening up of the Chinese mainland in 1978, there has been a climax of research on the classical modernization, with a batch of high-quality works published. Since the 1990s, Chinese scholars in the field of natural science have partaken in the modernization research, and China's modernization study has entered the stage of multidisciplinary research, where Professor Chuanqi He proposed the second modernization theory, the integrated modernization theory, the international modernization theory, the modernization science (He 2010a, 2011), and so on.

Table 3.9 Three climaxes of Chinese scholars' research on modernization

Item	Early discussions on modernization	Classical modernization research	Multidisciplinary research on modernization
Approx. period	1930s	End of 1970s to mid-1990s	Since the 1990s
Research subjects	Discussions on the problems of China's modernization	Classical modernization research Research on China's modernization	New modernization research Discussions on modernity and postmodernity
Works	Symposium on China's Modernization (1933) *Modernization* (semimonthly) (1937)	*A New Approach on Modernization* (1993) *Study of the World Modernization Process*	*Series of Second Modernization* (1999–2010) *Modernization Science (2010)* *China Modernization Report* (2001–2011)
Literature translation	–	Translation of classical modernization works	Translation of works on modernity, postmodernity, and new modernization

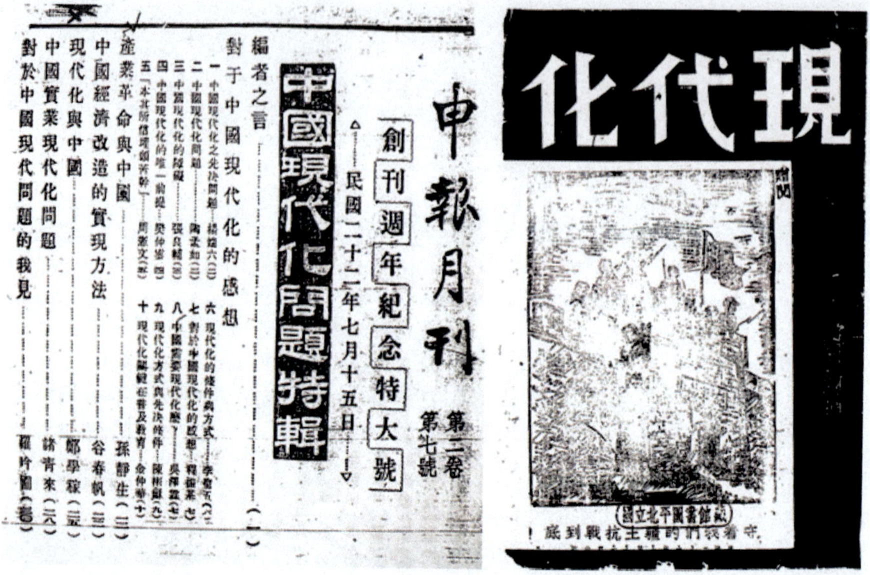

Fig. 3.13 Symposium on modernization and the modernization magazine published in the 1930s in China.
Note: *Left*, the symposium on the problem of China's modernization published by *Shenbao Monthly* in 1933 in Shanghai; *right*, the semimonthly magazine *Modernization* published in 1937 in Taiyuan, Shanxi Province

(1) Discussions on China's Modernization in the First Half of the Twentieth Century

Chinese scholars began to discuss problems concerning China's modernization as early as in the 1930s (Fig. 1.18). In 1933, there was a special issue of *Shenbao Monthly* dedicated to the problems of China's modernization, including 10 short comments and 16 long essays. It was probably the first symposium on modernization published in China. In 1948, *Chinese Culture and the Modernization Process* was published by Shanghai Observation Press (Wu 1948). Around the 1930s, a group of modern periodicals were published in China, such as *Modern Weekly* (1931), *Modern Society* (1932), *Modern Politics* (1932), *Modern Economy* (1933), and *Modernization* (1937); the latter was a semimonthly based in Taiyuan and probably the first periodical named as modernization in China.

(2) Classical Modernization Research in the Second Half of the Twentieth Century

From the 1950s to the 1970s, the modernization study in the Chinese mainland was at the low point, with rare literature on this issue. However, since 1978, the number of literature on modernization research has increased. In the period from 1979 to 1998, the China Association of Science and Technology founded and ran the *Modernization* magazine. And in 1981, the Science Press founded *Study on Agricultural Modernization*. In 1989, Tianjin Social Science Association founded *Theory and Modernization*. Chinese scholars have completed a lot of high-quality researches and published a lot of high-level works, such as *From Tradition to*

Modern (Jin 1979), *The Road toward a Modern Country* (Qian and Chen 1987), *Social Modernization* (Sun 1988), and *A New Approach on Modernization* (Luo 1993).

(3) Multidisciplinary Research on Modernization Since the End of the 1990s

Since the late 1990s, there have emerged various schools of Chinese scholars dedicated to the modernization study, with the theory of classical modernization and its application continuing to be promoted, the research on modernity and postmodernity attracting more and more attention, and several new modernization theories being introduced. In 1998, Chinese scholar Chuanqi He proposed the second modernization theory (He 1998a, b); since 1999, eight books of the *Second Modernization series* have been published, which include the *Modernization Science: the Principles of National Advance (He 2010a)*; since 2001, there have been 11 *China Modernization Reports* published, which cover the topics such as modernization and evaluation, knowledge economy and modernization, the modernization theory and the prospects, regional modernization, economic modernization, social modernization, ecological modernization, cultural modernization, international modernization, world modernization, and modernization science. The second modernization theory adopts the research method combining natural sciences and social sciences, with the stress on the empirical research and quantitative analysis.

Summary

Modernization is an objective phenomenon since about eighteenth century in the world, and the modernization science is a newly emerging interdisciplinary science which deals with the modernization phenomenon.

Historical Process of Modernization

Modernization is not only a sort of change of civilization but also the competition among different civilizations. Human civilization is not only an organic whole but also an aggregation of civilizations of different countries and nations. Both modernization and civilization development are asynchronous.

First, frontier and stages of human civilization. According to the level and characteristics of civilization, the frontier trajectory of human civilization can be divided into different stages. Historians and sociologists split over the stage division of human civilization.

There are mainly three theories on civilization development: cyclical theory, evolution theory, and periodic theory.

The second modernization theory holds that from the emergence of humankind to the end of the twenty-first century, when the productivity level and structure is used as the main basis of stage division, the frontier trajectory of human civilization may be divided into 16 stages and 4 ages and that civilization process has such features as periodicity, nonlinearity (periodic shifts), and acceleration, termed "periodic shift theory" of civilization development, for short.

Second, frontier and stages of general modernization. There has been no consensus on the division of stages of modernization process in general sense.

The frontier trajectory of modernization process from the eighteenth century to the twenty-first century could be divided, according to the features and level of modernization frontier, into two major stages: first and second modernization, both of which can be further divided into four phases—start, developing, mature, and transition. *China Modernization Report* proposed the six waves of modernization frontier according to its connotation and features.

Third, the relationship between modernization and civilization frontiers. Modernization and the world frontier of human civilization are coupled in terms of stage, progress, path, and time–space structure, as shown in the periodic table, coordinates system, and roadmap concerning the frontier trajectories of human civilization and modernization.

Brief History of Modernization Science

"Rome was not built in a day" is a world proverb and suitable to modernization science. There are two main threads throughout the development of modernization science: the modernization study and modernization theory, which complement each other.

The modernization study in the West began in the 1950s, and the research on human development can be traced back to years before Christ.

There are three waves of modernization research: the classical modernization research in the 1950–1960s, the postmodernization research in the 1970–1980s, and the new modernization research since the 1980s. The modernization study was criticized in the 1970–1980s and valued again in the 1990s.

The classical modernization theory was formed in the 1950–1960s, whose ideas can be traced back to the Enlightenment or even the Renaissance and whose origin can be traced back to the classical evolutionism in the nineteenth century. It is related to evolutionism, the theory of diffusion, the structural functionalism, and the theory of social system.

Since the 1960s, there have emerged about ten theories on modernization and relevant theories, which are the classical modernization theory, the dependency theory, the world systems theory, the postmodernization theory, the ecological modernization theory, the reflexive modernization theory, the continuous modernization theory, the globalization theory, the multiple modernities theory, and the second modernization theory.

In the twentieth century, the research on and the theory of modernization belonged to different disciplines and did not constitute a science yet.

In the twenty-first century, modernization science will come to be a new one which is interdisciplinary and highly integrated.

There are three waves of Chinese scholars' modernization research: the research on China's modernization problems in the 1930s, the classical modernization research in the 1970–1990s, and the multidisciplinary research on modernization since the end of the 1990s. The classical modernization research has produced a batch of high-level works, and the multidisciplinary research on modernization has led to many innovations, such as the second modernization theory and the modernization science.

Further Reading

Beck U, Giddens A, Lash S (1994) Reflexive modernization: politics, tradition and aesthetics in the modern social order. Stanford University Press, Stanford, CA

Bell D (1973) The coming of postindustrial society. Penguin, New York

Black CE (ed) (1976) Comparative modernization: a reader. Free, New York (Trans. Yang Y, Chen Z, Shanghai: Shanghai Translation Publishing House, 1996)

Crook S, Pakulski J, Waters M (1992) Post-modernization: change in advanced society. Sage, London

Gilman N (2007) Mandarins of the future: modernization theory in Cold War America. The Johns Hopkins University Press, Baltimore

Grasso J, Cornin J, Kort M (2009) Modernization and revolution in China: from the opium wars to the olympics, 4 Revisedth edn. M.E. Sharpe, New York

Harrison D (1988) The sociology of modernization and development. Unwin Hyman, London

He C (1999) The second modernization: inspiration for human civilization process. Higher Education, Beijing

He C (2003) Oriental renaissance: three roads to the modernization. Commercial, Beijing

He C (ed) (2010) China modernization report outlook: 2001–2010. Peking University Press, Beijing

Inglehart R (1997) Modernization and postmodernization: cultural, economic and political change in 43 societies. Princeton University Press, Princeton

Inglehart R, Welzel C (2005) Modernization, cultural change, and democracy: the human development sequence. Cambridge University Press, New York

Luo R (1993) New approach on modernization: the world and China's modernization process. Peking University Press, Beijing

Martinelli A (2005) Global modernization: rethinking the project of modernity. Sage, London

Ralph PL (1991) World civilizations: their history and their culture. W. W. Norton, New York, Trans. Zhao F, Beijing: The Commercial Press, 1998/1999

RGCMS (Research Group for China Modernization Strategies et al) (2010) China modernization report 2010: World modernization outline 1700–2100. Peking University Press, Beijing

Ritzer G, Goodman DJ (2004) Modern sociology theory. McGraw-Hill, New York

Rostow WW (1960) The stages of economic growth: a non-communist manifesto. Cambridge University Press, Cambridge, Trans. Guo X, Wang S, Beijing: China Social Sciences Press, 2001

Shah H (2011) The production of modernization: Daniel Lerner, mass media, and the passing of traditional society. Temple University Press, Philadelphia

So AY (1990) Social change and development. Sage, Newbury Park

Stavrianos LS (1982) The world since 1500: a global history. Prentice-Hall, Englewood Cliffs, NJ (Trans. Wu X, Liang C, Shanghai: Shanghai Academy of Social Sciences Press, 1992)

Vago S (1999) Social change, 4th edn. Prentice Hall, Upper Saddle River, NJ

4 Stage-Specific Modernization

The Greek philosopher Heraclitus said: *one cannot step twice into the same river*. There are different features in different stages of the process of human civilization and world modernization. In general, modernization in different phases has both generality and diversity, and the core theory of general modernization has somewhat different applicability in different phases.

From the eighteenth century to the close of the twenty-first century, the frontier process of modernization can be divided into two stages: the first and second modernization according to its main structure and characteristics. Since the 1980s, some developing countries have started pursuing the path of integrated modernization to achieve the coordinated development of the first and second modernization. As an important part of modernization science (Fig. 4.1), stage-specific modernization overlaps with level-related and field-relative modernization.

4.1 First Stage of Modernization

As the world frontier of human civilization, the first stage of modernization, or the first modernization for short, is the transition from an agricultural civilization to an industrial one, a process which spans about 210 years (approximately 1763–1970 AD) and includes the transformation from agricultural to industrial economy, society, politics, and culture (Fig. 4.2). In 2005, all advanced countries and a number of developing ones finished the first modernization while the majority of developing countries did not. There are mainly eight relevant theories about the first modernization, but in this section, only three of them are to be discussed (Table 4.1).

4.1.1 Classical Modernization Theory

Classical modernization theory, which emerged in the 1950s–1960s, explains the process of modernization since the industrial revolution in the eighteenth century. It is not a single theory but a collection of different ideas. As indicated

C. He, *Modernization Science*,
DOI 10.1007/978-3-642-25459-8_4, © Springer-Verlag Berlin Heidelberg 2012

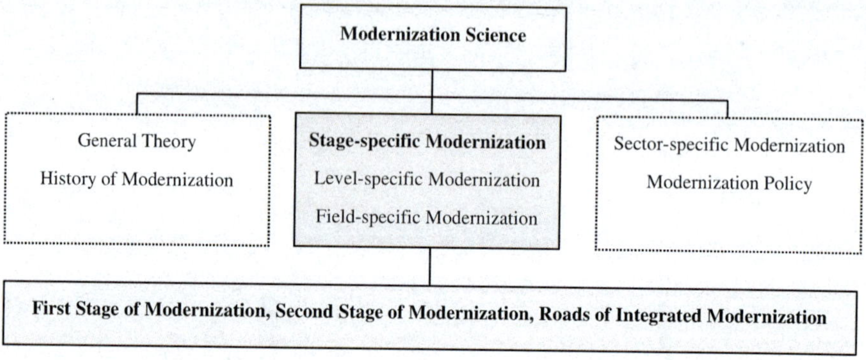

Fig. 4.1 Positioning and structure of stage-specific modernization

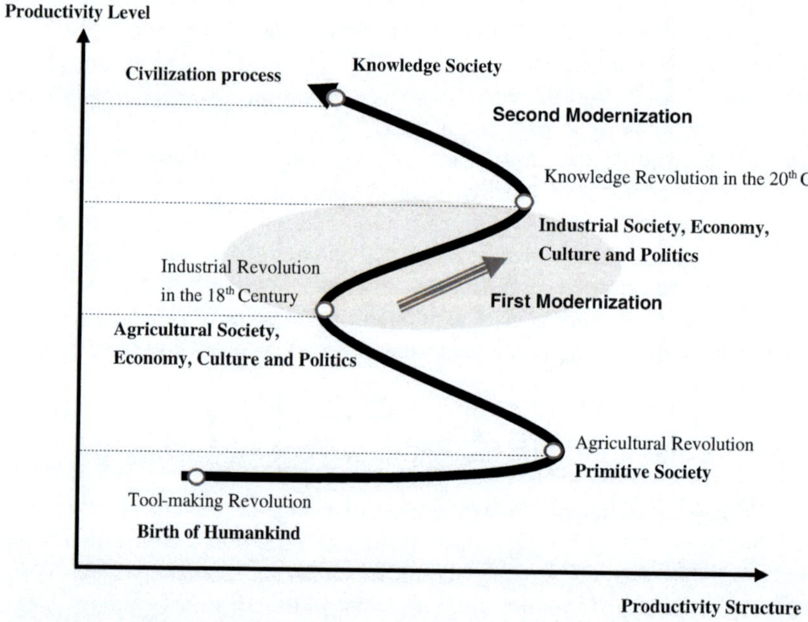

Fig. 4.2 Positioning of the first modernization.
Note: Affected by the second modernization, some changes may occur in the contents of the first modernization of developing countries in the twenty-first century. Source: He (2003)

in *China Modernization Report 2010: World Modernization Outline 1700–2100* (RGCMS 2010), it consists of general and branch theories and has different schools of ideas (Fig. 4.3). In this part, its general theory, major schools of ideas, limitations, and the corrections to it are to be analyzed.

Table 4.1 Three relevant theories on the first modernization

Item	Classical modernization theory	Dependency theory	World-system theory
Research content	Transition from an agricultural society to an industrial one, modernization policies of underdeveloped countries	Causes of and countermeasures against underdevelopment in the process of modernization	Evolution of the world-system since the sixteenth century and the law of such evolution
Research subject	Changes in a country	International dependency	Changes of the world-system
Research level	National level	Transnational level	World-system level
Research unit	Country, society	A group of countries	World-system
Main features	Characteristics and the law of a country's modernization. Implications of modernization on the policy of underdeveloped countries. Focus on the role of internal factors	Influences of international relations on classical modernization. Impact of dependency on underdeveloped countries. Stress on the role of external factors	Implications of the world-system on classical modernization. Influences of the world-system on developed and underdeveloped countries. Focus on the role of the world-system

Note: Relevant theories about the first modernization include classical modernization theory, dependency theory, world-system theory, postmodernization theory, reflexive modernization theory, second modernization theory, multiple modernities theory, and globalization theory. In this section, only three of them are discussed; the rest will be discussed in the following two sections
Source: RGCMS (2008)

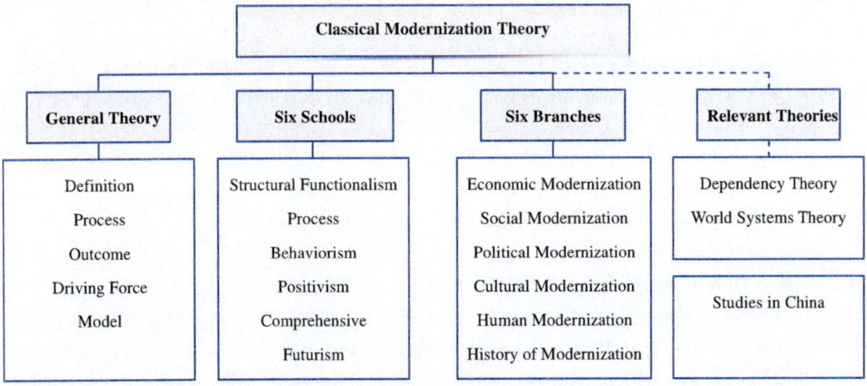

Fig. 4.3 Structure of classical modernization theory. Note: The six branch theories involve five fields, and multifields of modernization will be discussed in Chap. 6. Source: He (2003)

4.1.1.1 General Theory on Classical Modernization

In the 1950s–1960s, modernization and modernization study were hot-spot topics in the international scientific community. A great number of books and papers on modernization were published, giving birth to the modernization theory. During the 1970s and 1980s, modernization theory was questioned and criticized, leading to a downturn in modernization research. In the 1990s, such research was given weight again, and scholars began to call the modernization study in the 1960s "classical modernization study" and the modernization theory in the 1960s "classical modernization theory" (So 1990). But at that time, the theory was not actually expressed in a systematic manner. Thus, we would like to analyze the theory in five dimensions, namely, the definition, process, outcome, driving force, and models of modernization, and such analysis can be regarded as the general theory about classical modernization (He 2003).

(1) Definition of Classical Modernization

In classical modernization theory, different schools and scholars in different fields may have differing conceptions of what modernization is (Pandey 1988). For instance, sociologists and historians differ a lot on the understanding and interpretation of modernization (Table 1.1). Despite that, two basic views about modernization are widely accepted among scholars. One is that modernization refers to the profound changes that have taken place since the industrial revolution in the developed countries; the other is that modernization refers to the process of developing countries' catching up with the world's advanced countries.

According to American historian C.E. Black, human affairs have undergone three revolutionary transformations. The first one is from prehuman to human society; the second one is from primitive to civilized society; the third one is from traditional civilized to modern society, namely, the process of modernization (Black 1966).

The general consensus is that modernization is a profound change that human society has experienced since the industrial revolution in the eighteenth century and a transition from traditional to modern society. It happens to advanced countries and in the process of less-advanced countries' catching up with the world's advanced ones.

Professor Luo holds that it may be appropriate to take the formation of a highly developed industrial society, a specific process in recent human history, as a main mark of realizing modernization (Luo 1993).

(2) Process of Classical Modernization

On the process of the classical modernization, some believe that it consists of three phases, some think that there are four phases, and others insist on five phases (Table 4.2). The modernization process entails changes in many aspects including knowledge, politics, economy, society, and psychology (Black 1966). The changes in different fields will be addressed in the dedicated section in Chap. 6.

There is no consensus on the characteristics of the classical modernization process. Some think that modernization is nonlinear (Inglehart 1997), while others have proposed a linear model of modernization (Fig. 4.4). American scholar S.P. Huntington believes that the modernization process takes on nine characteristics (Table 4.3).

Table 4.2 Phasing of the classical modernization process

Phasing	Contents	Note
Three phases	*Three phases*. The first one is led by the northwest corner of Europe (UK, France, the Netherlands) and represented by UK's industrial revolution and France's political revolution. The second one is represented by the fast industrialization of the northeast corner of Europe (Germany) where political democratization lags behind industrialization, resulting in the disastrous Nazi fascism. The third one is led by the USA after the Second World War which did well in combing the democratic revolution and the industrial one (Parsons 1951)	World history
	Three waves. The first one is the early industrialization starting with the industrial revolution in the UK and spreading to western Europe, spanning from the late eighteenth century to the mid-nineteenth century. The second one is the process that industrialization swept the entire Europe and spread to North America, spanning from the late nineteenth century to the early twentieth century. The third one is the process that developed industrialized countries stepped forward to a higher level of industrialization, and a good number of underdeveloped countries began to industrialize, spanning the second half of the twentieth century (Luo 1993)	World history
Four phases	*Four phases*. First, challenges posed by modernity. The emergence of modern ideas and institutions as well as the advocates of modernization posed initial challenges to the traditional knowledge of society. Second, stabilization of modern leadership. The transfer of power from traditional to modern leadership usually means fierce revolutionary struggles of several generations. Third, economic and social transformation. Economic growth and social changes reach a level that the focus of lifestyle shifts from rural areas and agriculture to urban areas and industry. Fourth, social integration. Economic and social transformation results in the reorganization of the entire society's basic structure (Black 1966)	Economic and social development
	Four periods. Preparatory period, transformation period, advanced modernization period, and international integration period (Black 1976)	World history
	Four phases. Start phase, developing phase, mature phase, and transition phase (He 1999)	Progress of civilization
Five phases	*Five phases*. First, the traditional society phase. Second, the phase to create preconditions for the take-off when agricultural productivity increases rapidly, social infrastructure is established more efficiently, new ideas are growing in society, and a new class of entrepreneurs emerges. Third, the take-off phase. It takes quite a long time to remove all the obstacles in economic development so as to realize industrialization and establish the industrial sectors. Fourth, the mature phase. When technology is disseminated out of the industrial sectors, economy and society are getting mature. Fifth, the phase of massive consumer spending (Rostow 1960). A sixth phase of quality of life was added later on	Economic development

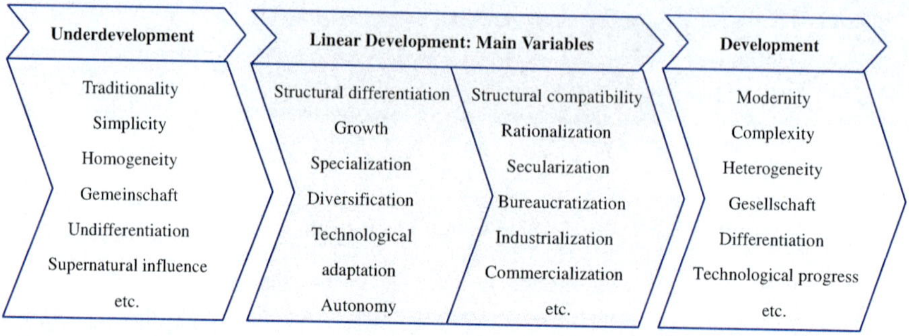

Fig. 4.4 Linear model of the classical modernization process. Note: It is based on the thoughts of Coetzee et al. (2001)

Table 4.3 Nine characteristics of the classical modernization process

Characteristics	Interpretation
Revolutionary process	The transition from traditional to modern society can only be comparable to the origin of mankind and the transition from primitive to civilized society
Complex process	It actually contains the changes in all the fields concerning human thoughts and behavior
Holistic process	The change of one factor is associated with and affects the changes of other factors
Global process	Modernization started in Europe but is now a global phenomenon
Long-term process	It takes a long time to address the all-round changes that modernization brings about
Phased process	The modernization process of any society may include different levels or phases
Convergent process	There are many types of traditional society, but modern societies are basically similar
Irreversible process	Despite some temporary and occasional setbacks, modernization is a trend in the long run
Progressive process	During the transformation, modernization incurs great costs and pain. But in the long run, it increases the cultural and material well-being of human beings

Note: It is based on the thoughts of Huntington (Black 1976)

The classical modernization process takes on different characteristics in different fields. For instance, in the economic field, it brings industrialization, market-based operation, mass production, and specialization. In the social field, it introduces urbanization, social welfare, mobility, social mobilization, social differentiation, social integration, and universal compulsory education. In the political field, it entails democratization, rule of law, centralization, institutionalization, and bureaucratization. In the cultural field, it highlights rationalization, secularization, and mass communication. In the personal field, it is represented as openness, equality, liberalization, and achievement motivation.

As Marx believed, *what industrially developed countries show to industrially undeveloped countries is just the future of the latter . . . A country should and can learn from other countries. Even if having found out the law of its own development, a society can neither skip nor cancel with a decree any natural stage of its development. But it can shorten the process and alleviate the pain of delivery* (Marx 1967). That is a very important idea for understanding the process and outcome of modernization.

(3) Outcome of Classical Modernization

Generally, the outcome of modernization is closely related to the content, characteristics, as well as the starting and finishing points of the modernization process. Modernity embodies the main outcome and to some extent the main content and characteristic of the modernization process. Scholars summarize the feature of traditional agricultural society as tradition and that of modern industrial society which has finished the modernization process as modernity. Tradition and modernity is relative and asymmetrical.

Scholars may have different understanding of modernity, but its basic characteristics are distinct. Modernity is represented differently in different fields (Table 4.4). The dispute on modernity has continued for over 50 years; some views are actually a mixture of facts and concepts.

(4) Driving Force of Classical Modernization

There is an extensive literature on the driving force of classical modernization. One example is the three views on the subject summarized by Professor Ronald Inglehart at the University of Michigan (Inglehart 1997). The first one is "economic determinism" which holds that economic development determines the change of politics and culture and that industrialization drives modernization. The view is mainly influenced by Marx's idea that the economic base determines the superstructure and class conflict. The second one is "cultural determinism" which holds that culture affects people's economic and political life and that democratization drives modernization. The view is mainly influenced by German scholar Max

Table 4.4 Modernity of classical modernization (first modernity)

Field	Tradition	Modernity (first modernity)
Economy	Peasant economy, self-sufficient, decentralized	Industrialized, market-based, specialized, highly efficient, scientific
Society	Rural, family, stability, undeveloped education	Urbanized, social welfare, social mobility, universal compulsory education
Politics	Autocratic, feudal, religious	Democracy, the rule of law, centralized, bureaucratic (bureaucratization)
Culture	Religious, superstitious, fatalism, natural, closed	Rational, secular, utilitarianism, modernism, mass communication
Individual	Conservative, passive, dependent, emotional, hierarchy, community values, family motivation	Openness, participation, independence, equality, personal interests orientation, achievement motivation

Note: First modernity is a theoretical expression of the outcome of the first modernization and closely related to the content and characteristics of the first modernization process
Source: He (2003)

Weber's thought of "the Protestant ethic and rationalization." The third one is integrated determinism which holds that modernization is the outcome of the interaction between politics, economy, and culture.

Marx put forward the well-known "base-superstructure" concept in the book *A Critique of Political Economy* (Storey 1993). *The "base" comprehends the productivity and the relations of production while the "superstructure" includes all the institutions and "various forms of social consciousness" thereof. The base determines (conditions) the content and form of the superstructure while the* ***superstructure reflects and confirms the base. Technological progress and eco-*** *nomic development may lead to political and cultural changes.* Such thought is regarded as the source of "economic determinism." And the idea that modernization is industrialization is also an extension of the thought.

(5) Models of Classical Modernization

Many scholars believe that the development model of classical modernization features diversity and path dependence and is affected by history, culture, and geographical conditions. According to European scholars, modernization of the UK and the USA is driven by democratization and industrialization; in the case of France, democratization goes before industrialization; in the case of Germany, industrialization goes before democratization. Black categorizes the modernization of over 170 countries and regions in the world into seven patterns (Black 1966), while Professor He puts classical modernization into four categories, namely, innovating, tracking, grafting, and learning (He 1999).

Classical modernization mainly includes the following types: forerunner and latecomer, endogenous and exogenous, active and passive, and market-based and planned modernizations. Latin America, East Asia, East Europe, and Middle East all have their respective characteristics of modernization.

4.1.1.2 Major Schools of Classical Modernization Theory

There is an extensive literature on classical modernization and a considerable number of articles overlap with or validate each other. Except the general theory, classical modernization theory has six branches by the field of research (Fig. 4.2). The multifields of modernization will be discussed in Chap. 6. By research method and characteristic, classical modernization theory can be divided into six schools of ideas (Table 4.5). Such artificial division may seem arbitrary to some extent because the ideas of some scholars like Parsons, Black, and Huntington may cross several schools.

(1) Structural Functionalism

Scholars of this school are characterized by the structural-functionalistic approach to modernization (Black 1976). They believe in social Darwinism and start with Durkheim's classification of binary opposition. They hold that modernization is the transition from traditional to modern society and that the fundamental differences between modern and traditional societies are structural differentiation, functional specialization, and social integration. More attention is given to the comparison

Table 4.5 Six schools of classical modernization research

School	Main views or characteristics	Representative
Structural functionalism	Modernization is the transition from traditional to modern society. The focus of research is on the comparison between modernity and tradition and the transformation from latter to the former	T. Parsons
Process	Modernization is the process of the transition from agricultural to industrial society which includes a series of profound changes at different phases. The focus of research is on the characteristics and law of the process	W. Rostow
Behaviorism	Modernization involves the changes in personal psychology and behavior. The focus is on the modernization of the people	A. Inkels
Positivism	The modernization of different countries takes on different characteristics. Empirical research on modernization is carried out	S.P. Huntington
Comprehensive	Modernization involves profound changes in every aspect of people's life. Comparative studies, studies on development model, and research based on quantitative indicators are carried out	C.E. Black
Futurism	The research is about the future development trend. The focus is on the development trend of developed countries	D. Bell

Source: He (1999)

between modernity and tradition and the transformation from one to the other. In other words, the focus is on the outcome instead of the process of the transformation. Scholars attempt to categorize and interpret the different types or models of society from social, economic, political, cultural, knowledge, and other perspectives.

(2) Process School

The main characteristic of this school of modernization theory is the focus on the process rather than the outcome of modernization. They believe that modernization is the process of the transition from agricultural to industrial society which consists of a series of development phases and that modernization theory is the representation of the process. The focus of research is on the development phases of modernization, the characteristics of each phase, and the development law of modernization.

(3) Behaviorism

Modernization involves the changes in personal psychology and behavior. Without the transformation from traditional to modern values, psychology, and behavior, people will find it hard to adapt to changes brought by modernization, and it will be impossible to realize modernization. Psychologists stress the importance of psychological and behavioral changes in modernization.

(4) Positivism

Modernization is a historical process. The positivist modernization theory is based on the empirical research on the modernization processes of countries around the world. Representative examples include Huntington's theory on political order and Gerschenkron's theory on the model of industrialization.

(5) Comprehensive School

Modernization is a process which involves profound changes in every aspect of people's life. There is no doubt that it is important to study modernization from different perspectives like sociology, economics, political science, and psychology, but such studies are always one dimensional. It may be risky to take a holistic approach to modernization research, but it is necessary to do so, and the key is to find the suitable research method (Example 4.2). In this regard, Black provided a solution which is comparative modernization research. Since many historians conducted such research, the comprehensive school is also called comparative history school. Representative theories of this school include the theory of endogenous and exogenous modernization and that on spontaneity and stress.

Example 4.1 Evaluation of a Country's Modernization Level

In 1965, American scholar Hadley Cantril designed a composite index with 11 structural variables to measure the modernization levels of 14 countries. The values of the 11 indicator indexes and the composite index range between 0 and 1.

Modernization levels of 14 countries

Country	Modernization level	Country	Modernization level	Country	Modernization level
USA	1.00	Cuba	0.35	Brazil	0.16
W. Germany	0.71	Panama	0.31	Egypt	0.14
Israel	0.67	Yugoslavia	0.19	Nigeria	0.02
Japan	0.60	Philippines	0.17	India	0.00
Poland	0.45	Dominican Republic	0.16		

Note: The data comes from Black (1976)

(6) Futurism

Modernization is not only the past of developed countries but also the present and future of developing countries. Besides, the future of developed countries should also draw the attention of researchers. On the development of developed countries, futurists proposed such ideas as information society, knowledge society, postindustrial society, postmodern society, and postmodernization, which Professor Black calls "postindustrial society" or "highly modernized society."

4.1.1.3 Criticisms and Revision on Classical Modernization Theory

(1) Criticisms on the Classical Modernization Studies

In the 1970s–1980s, criticism on the classical modernization study prevailed in the academic community (Table 4.6); critics came from that internal and outside of modernization studies. New and classical modernization studies are related and different (So 1990).

Similarities *(1) Research focuses the development of the Third World. (2) Level of analysis is on the national level. (3) Key variables are about the internal factors, such as cultural values and social institution. (4) Key concepts are the issues of tradition and modernity. (5) Policy implication is of modernization and generally* ***beneficial issues*** (So 1990).

Table 4.6 Criticisms on the classical modernization study

Subject	Views or characteristics of classical modernization study	Questions and criticisms
Direction of development	One-directional development. Western countries are modern societies while countries in the Third World are traditional societies. Western countries represent the future of the Third World, and the latter should adopt the Western model of development	Why are Western countries modern but those in the Third World traditional? Why cannot countries in the Third World have their own path of development?
Form of development	Some believe that modernization is linear and irreversible	Modernization is nonlinear and partially reversible
Prospect of development	Optimism. It is believed that Western countries will succeed and so will the Third World if the Western model is adopted	Overoptimism. Uncertainties of development are overlooked. Some countries in the Third World have stagnated and even suffered setbacks
Traditional values	Tradition and modernity confronts each other. Tradition is the barrier to development; modernization is the transition from traditional to modernity	What is real tradition? Is tradition and modernity mutually exclusive? Is tradition always the barrier to modernization? Can modernization eliminate traditional values completely?
Research method	Highly abstract, typology, key factors, dichotomy, transnational research	Unclear time and scope. Is the dichotomy of tradition and modernity rational?
Ideology	Countries in the Third World can become developed countries only by copying the Western model of development instead of the Soviet model	Radicals hold that modernization theory is the academic representation of the "cold-war ideology" and serves the interest of the USA
External factors	Focus more on internal factors of a country like tradition and investment but little on external factors	External factors, colonial history, multinationals' control, unfair trade, and international system are overlooked
Theoretical factor	There are no uniform definitions of modernization, tradition, and modernity	Ambiguous concepts of modernization and modernity. Asymmetry between tradition and modernity. Prejudices from modernity

Sources: Black (1976), Harrison (1988), Pandey (1988), So (1990), Inglehart (1997), and He (1999)

The Third World refers to countries at relatively low levels of development such as the least developed countries. There are a total of 50 least developed countries in the world (UN 2008). New modernization research is different from the classical one and falls into two categories.

Differences *(1) According to the classical modernization studies, tradition is an obstacle to development; methodology is of typology construction, highly level abstraction; direction of development is of unidirectional path, toward the U.S. model; relative neglect of external factors and conflicts. (2) According to new modernization studies, tradition is an additive factor to development; methodology pay more attention to concrete case studies, historical analysis; direction of development is the multidirectional paths of development; and greater attention to external factors and conflicts* (So 1990).

(2) Revision on Classical Modernization Theory

Revision on classical modernization theory mainly comes from three aspects: criticisms against the theory and the responses to such critiques, new findings from historical and case studies, as well as the new progress of classical modernization. Some earlier ideas about modernization are corrected such as the idea that modernization is Westernization, Europeanization, or Americanization (Table 4.7).

First, criticisms against the theory and the responses to such critiques. There are multiple paths to realize modernization, and diversity can be seen in the "Western model" of modernization. Tradition and modernity are not completely exclusive to each other; partial coexistence is possible. The dependency theory and world-systems theory can be regarded as both the criticisms against and complements to classical modernization theory.

Second, new findings from historical and case studies. *The direction of modernization can be expected but the process is uncertain. In the process of modernization,*

Table 4.7 Revision on classical modernization theory

Earlier ideas of classical modernization theory	Corrections to classical modernization theory
Modernization is a historical necessity	Although the direction of social and economic development can be expected, the process is uncertain
Tradition is the barrier to modernization	Religion and other traditional cultural heritage are always there and play their due role
Modernization is irreversible	Cultural modernization is reversible; modernization is partially reversible
Modernization is linear	None of economic, social, and cultural modernization is linear; modernization is nonlinear
Modernization is Westernization or Americanization	The idea is wrong. The modernization of East Asia takes on new characteristics. The USA does not lead the world's cultural changes
Modernization is the end of historical development	Classical modernization is a stage of historical development. The postindustrialization stage will see the development and liberation of mankind

Note: It is a collection of the thoughts of Inglehart (1997) and Inglehart and Welzel (2005) *religion and other traditional cultural heritage are always there and play their due role. Modernization is partially reversible. Cultural modernization is nonlinear. The idea that modernization is Westernization or Americanization does not hold water* (Inglehart and Welzel 2005). The relation between democracy and economy is not linear but complicated.

Third, new progress of classical modernization. Since the 1960s, the new modernization of East Asia has undergone industrialization first and then democratization. It is the Confucian culture rather than the Protestant culture that is working (Borrego 1995). Another example is the modernization of East Europe. After the incidents in the late twentieth century, Eastern European countries began to transform from planned to market economy and from planned to market modernization. The process is somewhat different from that of the developed European countries and the USA.

(3) Limitations of Classical Modernization Theory

Classical modernization theory is quite successful in explaining the development of developed industrialized countries between the 1760s and the 1960s and can also explain the process of developing countries' catching up with developed ones. But it fails to explain the development process of developed countries since the 1970s. There are two major challenges in this regard. First, since the 1970s, developed industrialized countries have started to shift to a deindustrialization track. Second, a shift has also occurred in the urbanization of such countries. Urban residents have started to move to suburbs and towns in a broad scale. The two shifts have shaken the economic and social foundation of the classical modernization theory which is characterized by industrialization and urbanization.

4.1.1.4 Classical Modernization Studies in China

Since the 1980s, Chinese scholars have published a good number of papers and books on classical modernization research (Table 4.8) including those on classical modernization theory, world history of modernization, Chinese history of modernization, field-specific modernization, and sector-specific modernization (Example 4.2).

Table 4.8 Chinese books and papers on modernization research

Book search by	Chinese books of the National Library of China	Paper search by	Chinese journal papers from Weipu database	Core journal papers from CNKI	Journal papers from CNKI
Title	2,491	Title	32,092	10,184	59,461
Keywords	1,747	Keywords	73,691	1,960	9,110
Title + Keywords	1,181	Title + Keywords	24,908	1,241	5,887

Note: Searching all the Chinese books about modernization by entering book title, keywords, and title + keywords. Searching all the Chinese papers about modernization by entering paper title, keywords, and title + keywords. Search time: July 7, 2009

Example 4.2 Classical Modernization Studies in China
Since the 1980s, Chinese scholars have achieved a lot in classical modernization studies.

On classical modernization theory, there are books including *The Road to Modern State* (Qian and Chen 1987), *New Theory of Modernization* (Luo 1993), *Social Theory on Modernity* (Liu 1998), *Global Perspective: Lost Modernization* (Qian and Liu 1999), *What is Modernization* (Yin 2001), and so on.

On the world history of modernization, there are studies about world modernization (Qian et al. 1997; Dong 2009a, b), the modernization of Latin America (Zeng 2000; Su 2006), Asian modernization (Luo and Dong 1997; Zhang 2001), the modernization of the Middle East (Ha 2006), the modernization of developed countries (Ding 1999), the modernization of the USA (Zhang 1996), the modernization of the UK (Qian 1988), the modernization of India (Lin 2001), the modernization of Brazil (Wu 2001a, b; Dong 2009a, b), and the modernization of Mexico (Zeng 1996).

On the Chinese history of modernization, there are studies by Luo (1990), Zhang (1992), Luo and Niu (1992), Zhang and Luo (1993), Hu (1994), Xu and Chen (1995), Zhou (1996), Wu (2001a, b), and Yu (2002).

On field-specific modernization, there are studies about social modernization (Sun 1988; Zhu and Wu 2001), economic modernization (Ding 2000; Wang 2002), political modernization (Yan 2006; Xu 2007), cultural modernization (Liu 1997; Xin 2007), and human modernization (Ye 1998; Zheng 2003).

On sector-specific modernization, there are studies about agricultural modernization (Qiu 1980; Huang and Lin 2003; Liu 2006), industrial modernization (Chen et al. 2004), and urban modernization (Zhu 2002).

4.1.2 Dependency Theory

Dependency theory is an international political economy theory that arose in the 1960s. It seeks to use the relation of dependence between core and periphery countries to explain the underdevelopment of periphery countries and attributes such underdevelopment to external factors (Fig. 4.5). There is an extensive literature about dependency theory, and there are many schools of dependency theorists. But to date, there has been no systematic theoretical expressions and complete

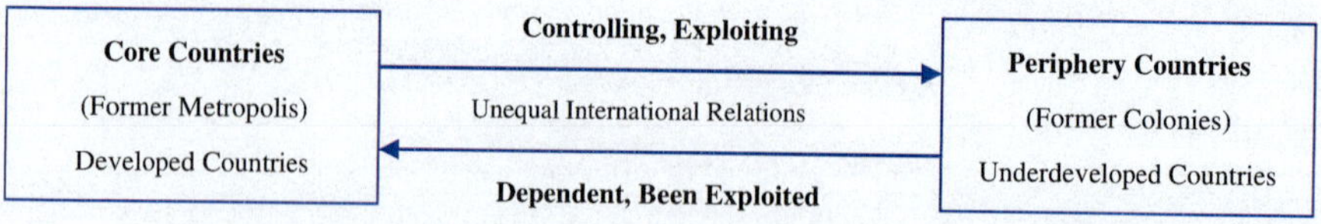

Fig. 4.5 Schematic diagram of dependency theory. Source: RGCMS (2010)

theoretical structure. Besides, in the system of modernization theories, the position and role of dependency theory have been disputed. History shows that it is impossible for all countries to progress at the same pace, and thus, the modernization process is bound to come along with development and underdevelopment. Developed countries are modern ones, while underdeveloped are not. Given that underdevelopment is a hard fact about modernization, the theory to explain the phenomenon of underdevelopment should be recognized as a branch of classical modernization theory.

4.1.2.1 Rise of Dependency Theory

Underdevelopment has been a widespread phenomenon over the past 300 years. Despite the lack of an established definition, underdevelopment usually refers to a state where a country's development level is far below that of developed countries. The causes of underdevelopment are multifold including external and internal factors. How to explain underdevelopment is a subject for development economics and international political economy and also a question that is overlooked by classical modernization theory. Economic liberalism, Marxism, and the theory of underdevelopment have different explanations for underdevelopment. In late 1960s and the 1970s, dependency theory replaced structuralism to be the most important explanation for the underdevelopment of the Third World (Gilpin 1987).

4.1.2.2 Propositions of Dependency Theory

The dependency theory that arose in mid-1960s is a mixture of classical Marxism and economic nationalism. It includes the analysis of (1) the nature and evolution of the capitalist world-system; (2) the relation or association between developed capitalist countries and underdeveloped ones; (3) the internal characteristics of dependent countries. According to Theotonio dos Santos, "dependence is a situation in which the economy of certain countries is conditioned by the development and expansion of another economy to which the former is subjected" (Gilpin 1987).

Dependency theory holds that due to its own development law and economic ***conflicts, capitalism has to expand to the underdeveloped periphery of the world economy; given the insufficient consumer spending and low profitability in parent*** *countries, capitalist countries have to control and exploit underdeveloped countries; that leads to the structured hierarchy between industrial centers and the dependent peripheries. Despite the various versions of dependency theories, there is a consensus that the underdevelopment of underdeveloped countries is mainly caused by external forces in the world capitalist system rather than the policies of such countries. Both the underdevelopment of underdeveloped countries and the development of capitalist countries are the outcome of the international capitalist expansion. The situation has not changed radically. International balances of economic and political power continue to tilt in the interests of developed capitalist countries. Dependent underdeveloped countries are also progressing in absolute terms, but they have been lagging behind in relative terms. On the cause of underdevelopment, there are different explanations including the exploitation, the neglect of imperialism and dependent development but the* *prevailing view is that capitalism and dependence causes underdevelopment* (Gilpin 1987).

The dependent development represents the new development of dependency theory. *It recognizes the economic achievements of such underdeveloped countries as Brazil and South Korea and believes that under certain conditions dependence may lead to rapid economic growth. But such growth is not development in real terms because it does not bring national independence. In addition, international capitalist centers cooperate with the existing capitalist aristocrats in the Third World countries to integrate them into the world economic system, which turns out to prevent such countries achieve economic development, social welfare and political independence. The aristocrats resist the loss of their privileges and depend on external forces to maintain the regime* (Gilpin 1987).

Neocolonialism holds that colonialism is just replaced by a slier but still effective way of exploitation. The newly independent countries are still dependent on their former metropolis and other industrialized countries in technology, finance, market, industry, and other aspects.

Professor Baoyun Yin of Peking University believes (2001) that there are three types of dependency theory. ***The first type is structuralist dependency theory.*** *Such dependency theorists represented by Raul Prebisch believe that the relationship between developed and developing countries is an unequal "core–periphery" dependency relation. The international trade between them is also unequal so developing countries should adopt the strategy of Import-Substitution Industrialization (ISI). The second one is radical dependency theory which is regarded as the* ***reflection of new Marxism in Western development theory. Such dependency*** *theorists represented by Gunder Frank and Samir Amin believe that capitalism results in underdevelopment and advocates that periphery countries should be decoupled from core countries and pursue development on their own. The third one is dependent development theory. Such dependency theorists represented by F. H. Cardoso, Raúl A. Fernández and Peter Evans stress the role of countries and hold that developing countries can achieve development under the condition of dependence.*

4.1.2.3 Limitations of Dependency Theory

According to the dependency theory, historically developed core countries put periphery countries in a subordinate position by exploiting and extracting their human resources and raw materials; currently, the governments and multinationals of industrialized countries manage to control the political and economic institutions of developing countries by bribing their ruling elites and collaborating with local capitalists, which has extended the historical dependency relationship; it is such an exploitation relationship that has helped developed countries become wealthier and more modernized and caused the poverty and backwardness of less developed countries and their dependence on developed countries for capital and technology (Pearson and Payaslian 1999). The phenomenon described here is indeed a fact, but the theory also has its obvious limitations.

First, dependency theory is mainly based on the unsuccessful modernization experience of Latin American countries. It is too focused on the experience of Latin American countries without looking at the differences between developing countries. Second, it is inconsistent with the development experience of the emerging industrialized countries in East Asia. For instance, countries like South Korea, Singapore, and Malaysia were members of the Third World only decades ago but are now emerging industrialized countries. A portion of East Asian and Latin American countries used to be colonies (Example 4.3). Third, it is too focused on the external factors of development without looking at the internal causes of backwardness. It is somewhat radical to attribute underdevelopment completely to capitalism and external factors. Fourth, the negative effects of dependency are exaggerated, but its positive effects like international assistance and dissemination of technology are overlooked. Fifth, it is not recognized that capitalist expansion comes with the spreading of industrial civilization, which is actually a historical progress. Sixth, it does not have a well-established theoretical system.

Example 4.3 European Colonies
In the eighteenth century, some parts of the Americas, Africa, and Asia became European colonies. In the nineteenth century, a prime period of colonial empires, some parts of Africa, Asia, and Oceania were turned into European colonies. By then, the area of European colonies and the population of such colonies had far exceeded that of the mother countries. In 1914, the area of British colonies was 99 times that of the UK, and the population of such colonies was eight times that of the UK (Stavrianos 1982).

4.1.3 World-System Theory

The world-system theory arose in the 1970s and has produced extensive implications since then. It attempts to use such variables as the dependency

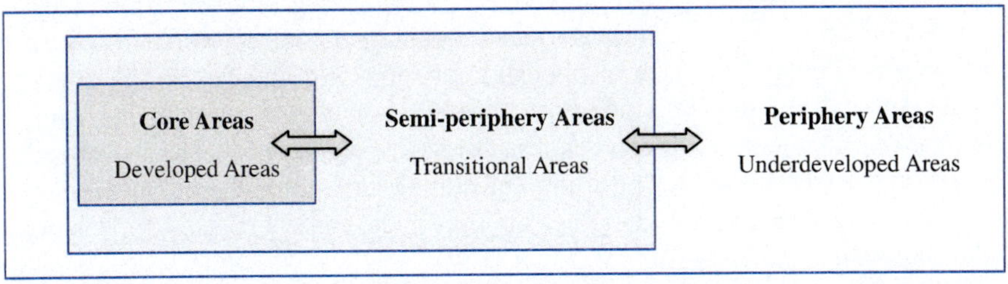

Fig. 4.6 Schematic diagram of world-system theory. Note: Economic system: a single system, unequal exchange; status of a country: changeable, up or down; trend of change: polarization, widening gap. Political system: coexistence of multiple systems; status of a country: in the periphery or in the core; trend of change: hegemony cycle, changes in materials, trade, and finance. Source: RGCMS (2010)

relationship among core, semiperiphery and periphery areas, international division of labor, and class conflict to analyze the historical revolution of the world-system and thus explain the world history of development since the sixteenth century (Fig. 4.6). Representative world-system theorists include Immanuel Wallerstein, Terence K. Hopkins, etc.

Currently, there is no consensus on the relationship between the world-system theory and the modernization theory. As a representative of the world-systems theory, Immanuel Wallerstein criticized the modernization theory (Wallerstein 1976). The two theories both tried to explain the 300 years of world history in the past. Classical modernization theory did that on a national level, while world-systems theory, on a world-system level. From the perspective of modernization study, the two theories are different in research content and method, but they are complementary to each other to some extent. Modernization is a global movement which is bound to cause the change of the world-system. The change of the world-system will definitely influence the modernization of any country. But classical modernization theory failed to do analysis on the world-system level. Given that the modernization process is bound to change the world-system, it is acceptable to establish a theory about the world-system in the process of modernization as a branch of the classical modernization theory. Besides, like dependency theory, the world-system theory is an independent and developing academic thought.

4.1.3.1 Rise of World-System Theory

The rise of the world-system theory is closely related to the criticisms against classical modernization study and theory. In the 1950s–1960s, modernization theory contended that developing countries would catch up with developed countries and realize modernization if they follow the development pattern of modernization. In late 1960s, some scholars found that developing countries which had followed the pattern did not succeed as expected. For example, Latin American countries had started to seek modernization in the nineteenth century but still did not succeed in the 1960s. And it was much harder for African countries to modernize. Therefore, they began to question the rationality and feasibility of modernization as a universal model of development. In the 1970s, the Western academic community came to be very active in criticizing modernization theory and westernization. Besides, the emergence of international environment movement helped to spread the idea of opposing modernization theory. In the 1960s, Wallerstein realized the limitations of modernization theory through the study about the development of African countries like Ghana and thus began to criticize the theory. In early 1970s, he began to publish the multivolume book *The Modern World-System* and studying developing countries in the context of the world history of development.

The world-systems theory is to a large extent the development of dependency theory (Pearson and Payaslian 1999). It adds the concept of semiperiphery areas to the core–periphery analysis of dependency theory and holds that the relationship between core countries and peripheries is dependency which is fundamentally exploitation relationship. Western scholars regard the world-system theory as a branch of Marxism (Pearson and Payaslian 1999). Indeed, the theory contains many Marxist concepts like exploitation, class conflict, and so on. In Wallerstein's view, "the political reality of the world economy is class conflict in different forms: open class awareness confronting the race-state awareness or domestic classes confronting multinational classes."

4.1.3.2 Propositions of World-System Theory

The world-systems theory covers many issues. Wallerstein divides them into ten aspects including cycle and trend, commodity chain, hegemony and competition, regional and semiperiphery, integration and periphery, antisystem movement, family, racism and sex, science and knowledge as well as geo-culture, and civilization. These aspects can be addressed at three levels, namely, world economic system, world political system, and world civilization (Wang 2006).

(1) World Economic System

Wallerstein analyzed the world-system and world economic system in the first three volumes of *The Modern World-System.* In his view, "the world-system is a social system which has its scope, structure, member groups, rational rules and cohesion. The vitality of the world-system consists of various conflicts." The world economic system has the following features.

First, the world-system has a single world economic foundation. It is an entity of extensive division of labor; the international division of labor covers functional tasks at all levels; the emergence and role of classes and status groups are elements of the world-system.

Second, division of labor divides the world into three zones, core areas, semiperiphery areas, and periphery areas. Core areas are economically developed; periphery areas are economically underdeveloped; and semiperiphery areas are midway between the core and periphery.

Third, the global expansion of capitalism involves the periphery areas into the world economic system and puts them in a peripheral position; the unequal exchange between the core and periphery guarantees capitalist development and capital accumulation.

Fourth, the development of capitalism experiences a long-term cycle of stagnation and expansion. In the expansion period, economic growth expands from the core to the periphery while, in the stagnation period, the interest of periphery areas are undermined in the first place.

Fifth, national economic status changes, so does the geological distribution of the status. The core and periphery status is not fixed, periphery areas may become core areas and vice versa. In the stagnation period, semiperiphery countries undergo the greatest changes in their status.

Sixth, the development of the world economic system tends to widen the economic and social gaps between different areas, showing the trend of polarization.

(2) World Political Systems

Wallerstein believes that there are multiple political systems in the world economy which guarantees the prosperity of capitalism in the long run. The world political systems mainly take on the following features.

First, modern states and the state system are the unique outcomes of capitalist economy. The form, strength, and boundary of states have been changing, and the state system has been expanding. There are multiple state systems in the world-system.

Second, the evolution of state systems includes two processes, namely, the process of becoming core countries and the process of becoming periphery countries. During the former process, core areas use state apparatus to monopolize commodities and seek maximum profits in the world economy and finally become core countries. In the latter process, periphery areas use less advanced technology and unequal exchange to become periphery countries gradually (Wang 2006).

Third, the development of state systems is cyclical, which is called the hegemony cycle. The capitalist world-system has experienced three hegemony cycles and produced three hegemony countries including the Netherlands in the seventeenth century, the UK in the nineteenth century, and the USA in the twentieth century.

Fourth, hegemony in the state systems is a mechanism which has three material bases. The hegemony mechanism is that in the competition among major countries, one country can impose its political, economic, military, diplomatic, and cultural principles and will on the states system. The material base of hegemony is more efficient industrial and agricultural production, commerce, and finance. Its rise and fall is closely related to the efficiency of the three economic sectors. Hegemony countries gain advantage first in the industrial and agricultural sector, then in international trade, and at last in the financial sector. With the dominance in the three fields, a country is given the transitory hegemony status.

Fifth, state systems are temporarily stable during the rule of hegemony countries. Like the economic pursuit of maximum profits, the political pursuit of hegemony is also the driving force behind the development of the capitalist world-system. Pursuing hegemony status is a shared goal among capitalist countries.

Sixth, hegemony countries can use their state apparatus to seek maximum profits for their own capital in the world market so as to facilitate their political hegemony. But the political function of hegemony is restricted by the state system and competing countries.

(3) World Civilization

In Wallerstein's view, when discussing the relations between various civilizations which we regard as different habits, structures, and cultures, we should do the analysis in the context of world history. Ever since the creation of Newtonian mechanics, the pursuit of science has been a symbol of civilization and has evolved into a universal civilization along with the outbreak of the British industrial revolution and the global expansion of capitalism. That is the manifestation of the capitalist world-system in civilization. Facing the scientific civilization created by core countries, periphery countries are put in a dilemma and find it hard to make any effective response (Wang 2006).

(4) Three Points of View

According to the analysis of American scholar Robert Gilpin, the world-systems theory is based on but also different from the Marxist views on social realities (Gilpin 1987). *First, as the determinants of human behavior, economic activities and class struggles are more important than political and group conflicts. More focus is put on ruling at the international level as well as the struggles between different countries and classes. Second, a unified world economic system consists of class-based ruling countries at various levels. These countries come together with great economic strength which leads to the underdevelopment of the peripheries. Third, modern world economy is characterized by its inherent conflicts and compliance with the law of fatalism. The law governs its historical development, the inevitable crisis and the final demise. The world economy is actually an international structure composed of many countries with unequal status. The structure maintains the international division of labor, helps advanced capitalist countries to accumulate capital and perpetuates the backwardness and underdevelopment of other countries* (Gilpin 1987).

(5) Six Variables

Hopkins and Wallerstein (1996) contended that the world-system is at a transitional stage of its development between 1945 and 2025. They put forward six variables in the revolution of the modern world-system which they believe are interrelated. The six variables include interstate systems, world production structure, world labor structure, human welfare model, as well as social cohesion and knowledge structure of all countries. The two scholars used such variables to analyze the evolution of the world-system between 1945 and 1990 and made predictions about its future development.

4.1.3.3 Limitations of World-System Theory

The world-system theory is significant in the sense that it analyzes the world history of development at the world-system level which is an important complement to classical modernization theory. But it also has four limitations. First, there are no quantitative criteria for the classification of core and periphery countries. Second, too much focus is on the world-system in analyzing world development but not enough on the role of productive forces and technological progress. Third, many concepts of the theory are confusing and even contradictory. Fourth, the world-systems analysis fails to reflect the full picture of world development and modernization.

4.2 Second Stage of Modernization

As the world frontier of human civilization, the second stage of modernization, or the second modernization for short, is the transition from an industrial civilization to a knowledge one and from a material civilization to an ecological one, a process which spans over about 130 years (approximately 1970–2100 AD) and includes the

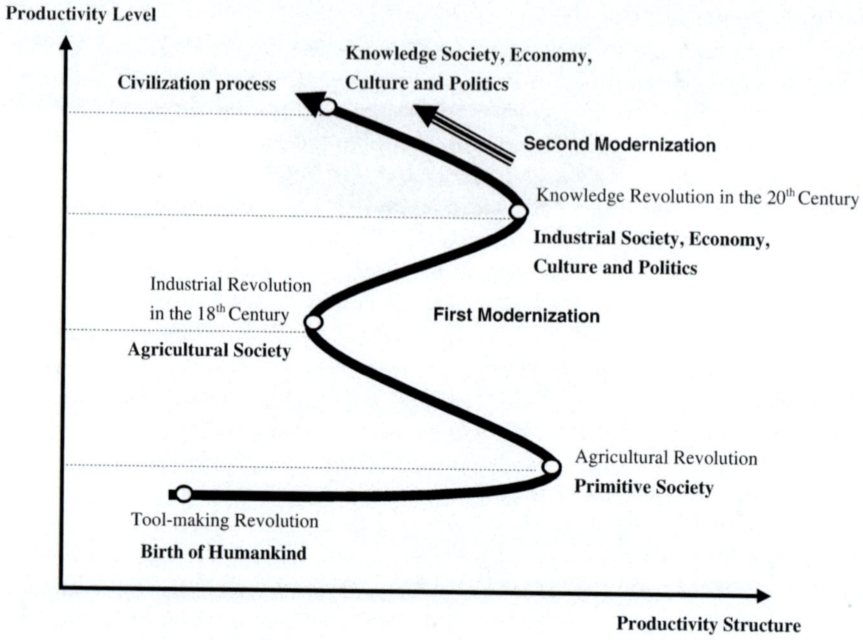

Fig. 4.7 Positioning of the second modernization. Source: He (2003)

transformation from industrial to a knowledge society, economy, politics, and culture and from material culture to ecological culture (Fig. 4.7). In 2005, about 28 countries started the second modernization while others were either in the process of the first modernization or at the stage of a traditional agricultural society. There are mainly seven relevant theories about the second modernization, but in this section, only three of them are to be discussed (Table 4.9), in addition to a brief introduction to the continuous modernization theory.

4.2.1 Second Modernization Theory

Such new concepts as knowledge economy, knowledge society, and national innovation system drew worldwide attention in the 1990s, which influenced for sure the process of modernization in the world. Chinese scholar Chuanqi He devised the second modernization theory (He 1998a, b, 1999). The theory divides the frontier of modernization process between the eighteenth and twenty-first centuries into two stages, the first modernization and the second modernization; if we say that the first modernization is classical modernization featuring industrial economy and society, the second modernization is new modernization characterized by knowledge economy and society. Chapter 2 has dealt with the general theory about the second modernization. Here, we mainly focus on its theoretical structure and the stage theory. Its level theory will be discussed in Chap. 5, and the field theory addressed in Chap. 6.

Table 4.9 Three theories on the second modernization

Item	Second modernization	Reflexive modernization	Postmodernization
Stages	First modernization and second modernization	Simple modernization and reflexive modernization	Modernization and postmodernization
Definition	Transition from industrial to knowledge society	Transition from industrial to risk society	Transition from industrial to postindustrial society
Features	A composite process of the innovation, selection, diffusion, and recession of civilization elements	A process of creative destruction, elimination of simple modernization, and re-creation	A process of change in survival strategy and fundamental change in and partial continuation of direction of modernization
Driving forces	Knowledge innovation, institutional innovation, and specialized talents	Knowledge, side effects, and individualization	Synergy of economy, culture, and politics
Duration	Approx. 1970–2100	The later stage of developed industrial society	Since 1970
Problem	The second modernization has not yet developed thoroughly	Risk society is an aspect of society	The period of postmodernization is self-inconsistent in time

Note: Theories on the second modernization include second modernization theory, reflexive modernization theory, postmodernization theory, continuous modernization theory, ecological modernization theory, multiple modernities theory, and globalization theory. Only three of them are compared here in the table; the rest will be discussed in dedicated sections later
Source: He (2003)

4.2.1.1 Structure of Second Modernization Theory

Second modernization theory is both a modernization theory in broad sense and a theory of civilization development (Fig. 4.8). It holds that modernization is a profound change of human civilization, the frontier of human civilization, and the behavior and process to reaching the frontier. It establishes an organic connection between the modernization theory and the civilization development theory, including the periodical chart, coordinate system, and road map of the frontier process of civilization and modernization processes.

(1) A Theory of Civilization Development: Civilization Periodic Transfer Theory

The second modernization theory, as a civilization development theory, can be called civilization periodic transfer theory. Chapter 3 discusses the periodicity, acceleration, and periodical shifts of civilization development. According to this theory, human civilization is both an organic whole and an aggregation of the civilizations of different nationalities and countries; civilization development involves accelerated periods with different themes; the periodical shifts include the shifts of civilization in direction, axis, and center. In the process of human civilization, the socioeconomic development, productivity, and quality of life increased continuously, but the direction of development had three transitions, namely, from primitive culture to

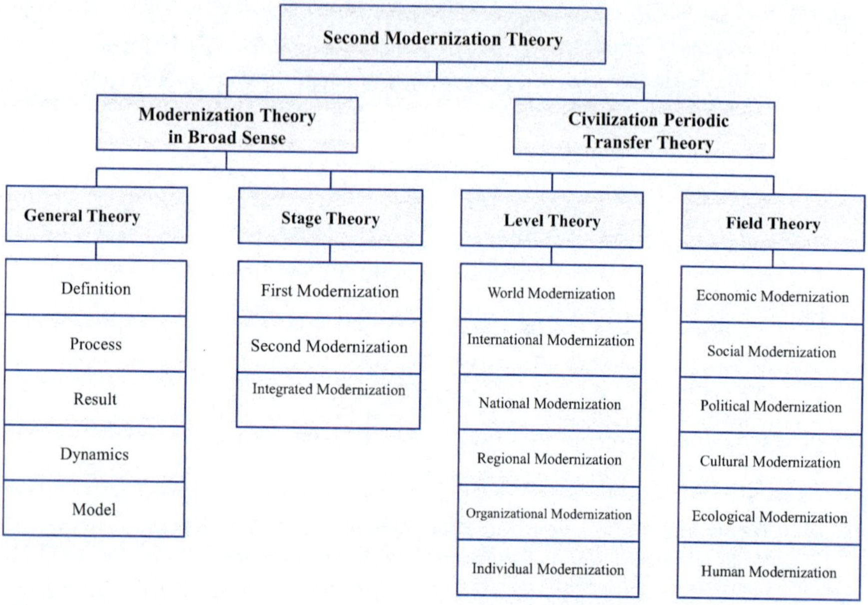

Fig. 4.8 Structure of second modernization theory. Source: He (1999, 2003)

agricultural civilization, from agricultural to industrial civilization, and from industrial to knowledge civilization; human civilization development in different ages and stages had different characteristics, in different countries and nationalities behaved in different ways, and in different aspects of human civilization development had different regular patterns and features.

(2) A Modernization Theory in Broad Sense: Twice Modernization Theory

The second modernization theory, as a modernization theory in broad sense, can be called twice modernization theory or multiplex modernization theory for short. It includes general theory, stage theory, level theory, field theory, sector theory, and so on. The general theory is a generalized version of stage, level, and field theories, and the latter are the specific reflection of the former at/in different stages, levels, and fields; they together form the theoretical framework of the modernization theory in broad sense (Table 4.10).

Chapter 2 has discussed the general theory of the second modernization theory (Table 2.1). Here, we focus more on the relationships and differences between the first and second modernization.

(a) Domestic relationship between the first and second modernization. In the same country, the first modernization lays the material and social foundation for the second modernization. The second modernization, in many aspects, is the elimination or "reversion" (or "regression" to traditions) of the first modernization; in some aspects, it is the inheritance and development of the first modernization or new (knowledge and institutional innovation).

Table 4.10 Structure of modernization theory in broad sense

Category	Theory	Main contents
General theory	Core theory	Definition, process, results, dynamics, and models of modernization
Branch theories	Stage theory	First modernization, second modernization, and integrated modernization
	Level theory	World, international, national, regional, organizational, and individual modernization
	Field theory	Economic, social, political, cultural, ecological, and human modernization
	Sector theory	Modernization of the sectors such as agriculture, industry, education, science and technology, finance, national defense, and transportation
Relevant theories	Other modernization theories	Classical modernization, postmodernization, ecological modernization, reflexive modernization, etc.
	Social sciences	Development economics, development sociology, development politics, international relations, etc.
	Humanities	Cultural changes, cultural anthropology, modern history, philosophy of science, civilization theory, etc.
	Natural sciences	Psychology, ecology, environmental science, geoscience, life sciences, etc.
	Engineering sciences	Organic agriculture, clean energy, cleaner production, green manufacturing, green chemistry, high technology, etc.
	Interdisciplinary science	Systems science, management science, development study, area study, complexity study, information science, etc.

Note: Relevant theories refer to modernization-related theories which expound the features and principle of a specific aspect of the modernization process, and they had existed in other science for a long time

Source: RGCMS (2010)

The coordinated development of the first and second modernization and toward second modernization in the last is the integrated modernization.

(b) International relationship between the first and second modernization. Between different countries, the first modernization and the second modernization influence and compete with each other. They promote each other under fair trade conditions and restrict each other under unfair trade conditions.

(c) The difference in model between the first and second modernization. In the process of the first modernization, economic development takes the first place, where material production expands the space of material life to satisfy human beings' material pursuit and economic security. In the process of the second modernization, the quality of life is the most important, where knowledge and information production expands the space of spiritual life to satisfy human beings' pursuit of happiness as well as self-expression and self-realization; the quality of material life may converge, but the spiritual and cultural life will be highly diverse.

(d) The difference in driving force between the first and second modernization. In the process of the first modernization, the interaction between industrialization, urbanization, and democratization leads to the change in the economic, social, political, and cultural structures, thereby boosting modernization. In the process of the second modernization, knowledge and institutional innovation lead to new science and technology, and new science and technology leads to new economy and society which give rise to new modernization; the institutional and knowledge innovation also lead to new politics and culture which promote new modernization; new modernization promotes new institutional and knowledge innovation whose interaction boosts modernization.

4.2.1.2 Stage Theory of Second Modernization Theory in Broad Sense

Stage theory on second modernization theory in broad sense includes first modernization theory on the first stage of modernization, second modernization theory in narrow sense on the second stage of modernization, and integrated modernization theory on some developing countries and regions. The last theory will be dealt with in a dedicated chapter later.

(1) First Modernization Theory

The first modernization and the classical modernization are synonyms, and their theories are roughly the same. First modernization theory includes general theory, branch theories, and relevant theories (Table 4.11); the general theory is a systematic interpretation of the process of the first modernization (Table 4.12).

(2) Second Modernization Theory in Narrow Sense

Second modernization theory in narrow sense is a theory on the second stage of the modernization, including the general theory, branch theories, and related theories (Table 4.13). The general theory is a systematic exposition of the process of the second modernization in narrow sense (Table 4.14).

Table 4.11 Structure of first modernization theory

Category	Theory	Main contents
General theory	Core theory	Definition, process, result, dynamics, and model of the first modernization
Branch theories	Level theory	The first modernization of the world, countries, regions, organizations, individuals, and international interactions (first international modernization)
	Field theory	The first modernization in economic, social, political, cultural, and human fields
	Sector theory	The first modernization in the sectors such as agriculture, industry, education, national defense, and transportation
Relevant theories	Other modernization theories	Classical modernization theory, dependency theory, world-system theory, multiple modernities theory, etc.
	Other relevant theories	Development theory, transition theory, evolution theory, conflict theory, modernism, etc.

Source: RGCMS (2010)

Table 4.12 General theory of the first modernization theory

Aspects	Main contents
Definition	The first modernization, an objective phenomenon since the industrial revolution of the eighteenth century, is the frontier process of the formation, development, and international interaction of industrial civilization; the composite process of the alternate innovation, selection, diffusion, and recession of industrial civilization elements; and the international competition for catching up with and reaching the advanced level of industrial civilization. Countries which have reached the advanced level of industrial civilization (the average level of industrialized countries in 1960 or so) are the countries that have completed the first modernization, and those which have failed to do so are ones that have not yet completed the first modernization
Process	The first modernization is a transformational process from agricultural civilization to industrial civilization and from traditional civilization to modern civilization, including the transition from agricultural society to industrial society, from agricultural economy to industrial economy, from agricultural politics to industrial politics, from agricultural culture to industrial culture, and from traditional culture to modern culture, and its typical characteristics include industrialization, urbanization, democratization, rationalization, market orientation, social welfare, etc. It follows ten principles of modernization (Table 2.15)
Result	The formation of the first modernity, particularity, diversities, and side effects, and the change in world forefront, international system, and state conditions. Features of the first modernity involves industrialized, urbanized, democracy, rationality, social welfare, modern science and energy, popularization of compulsory education, etc.; side effects include environmental pollution, polarization between the rich and the poor, periodic economic crisis, weakening of human relationship, etc.; a portion of traditional values continue to exist and work
Dynamics	Driving force includes innovation, competition, adaptation, exchange, technology, capital, state interest, market demand, etc. Motivational models include innovation drive, two-wheel drive, combined action, four-step supercycle, composite interaction of the three civilizations, innovation diffusion, competition drive (Table 2.20), etc. There are three views: economic development determinism, cultural development determinism, and combined action of politics, economy, and culture
Model	Path and model diversity, starting point dependence, and path dependence. About 19 types of element mix (Table 2.21). Developed countries differ from developing countries in path and pattern, and developed countries also differ from each other

Source: RGCMS (2004, 2010)

4.2.1.3 Main Features of the Second Modernization Process

Because the second modernization started not too long ago, it is apparently difficult to summarize the features of the second modernization now. Nevertheless, features of the second modernization have been revealed in different fields, some noticeable and some not. If we sum up its features in different fields, main features of the second modernization for the present are at least reflected in the following ten aspects (He 2003).

Table 4.13 Structure of second modernization theory in narrow sense

Category	Theory	Main contents
General theory	Core theory	Definition, process, outcome, driving force, and models of the second modernization in narrow sense
Branch theories	Level theory	The second modernization of the world, countries, regions, organizations, individuals, and international interactions (second international modernization)
	Field theory	The second modernization in economic, social, political, cultural, natural environment, and human fields
	Sector theory	The second modernization of the sectors such as agriculture, industry, education, national defense, and transportation
Relevant theories	Other modernization theories	Postmodernization theory, ecological modernization theory, reflexive modernization theory, multiple modernities theory, globalization theory, etc.
	Other relevant theories	Civilization theory, transition theory, postmodernism, human ecology, informatization theory, etc.

Source: RGCMS (2010)

Table 4.14 General theory of the second modernization theory in narrow sense

Aspects	Main contents
Definition	The second modernization, an objective phenomenon since the knowledge revolution of the twentieth century, is the frontier process of the formation, development, and international interaction of knowledge civilization (including ecological civilization and cyberspace civilization); the composite process of the alternate innovation, selection, diffusion, and recession of knowledge civilization elements; and the international competition for pursuing, reaching, and keeping the advanced level of world. Countries which have reached and kept the advanced level of the world are the developed countries, and other countries are developing countries; the two types of countries may change to each other
Process	The second modernization is a transformational process from industrial to knowledge civilization and from material to ecological civilization, including the transition from industrial to knowledge society, from industrial to knowledge economy, from industrial to knowledge politics, from industrial to knowledge culture, and from material to ecological culture, and its typical characteristics include knowledgeablization (knowledge-intensive), informatization (information-intensive), greening, globalization, individualization, etc. It follows ten principles of modernization (Table 2.15)
Result	The formation of the second modernity, particularity, diversities, and side effects, and the change in world frontier, international system, and state conditions. Features of the second modernity currently include being knowledge-intensive, information-intensive, global, innovative, environmentally friendly, and popularization of higher education, etc.; side effects include cyberspace crime, information gap, and international risk; a portion of traditional values continue to exist and work
Dynamics	Driving forces include innovation, competition, adaptation, exchange, knowledge, system, state interest, market demand, etc. Motivational modes include innovation drive, two-wheel drive, combined action, four-step supercycle, composite interaction of the three civilizations, innovation diffusion, innovation overflow, competition drive, etc. (Table 2.20)
Model	Path and model diversity and path dependence; about more than 20 types of element mix (Table 2.21)

Source: He (2003), RGCMS (2010)

(1) Knowledgeablization Is the Fundamental Driving Force of the Second Modernization

Knowledgeablization (or knowledgization or intellectualization) refers to the phenomenon that knowledge intensity and knowledge value increase in economic and social activities. The production, dissemination, and application of new knowledge quicken the transformation of economy and society. Knowledge progress contributes more than 50% to economic growth, the knowledge-related workers account for over 50% of the whole workforce, and the knowledge industry (knowledge economy) takes a share of more than 50% of GDP (OECD 1996). In economy, the knowledge content and the knowledge value-added have increased considerably, the spreading of scientific knowledge has been enhanced constantly, knowledge management has been widely emphasized, and knowledge has become the core of social progress and the primary foundation of social power. The knowledge society has been gradually formed along with the rapid rise of knowledge economy and the fall of industrial economy. The knowledge society is a harmonious society, where knowledge rules over capital, cooperation promotes development, and knowledge and innovation boost economic development and social progress; it is featured by everyone doing his best, equality of opportunity, distribution according to contribution, and adjustment according to requirement. Simply say: do your best, enjoy your chance, share you did, and pay you should.

(2) Informatization Is the Typical Feature of the Second Modernization

Informatization refers to economic and social changes arising from the development and application of modern information technology. Changes brought about by the information revolution since the 1970s are so immense that people have to try to adapt themselves to a new life space, the cyberspace. People will travel between the physical space and the cyberspace. We have seen the waves of informatization, digitalization, and networking (or netization) sweep across the globe; the Internet grows explosively; and the e-commerce and e-government make inroads into our life, and in the future, we will experience the digital integration of computer networks, communications networks, and media networks; every aspect of our work and life is influenced by digital networks. Thus, knowledge society in the twenty-first century is also a network society and an information society.

(3) Greening Is the Basic Requirement of the Second Modernization

Greening (or greenization) refers to the phenomenon that ecological awareness and green elements increase in economic and social life. Green elements are conducive to environment and health, involving all aspects of people's work and life. Contrary to "artificialization," greening, ecologicalization, and naturalization have become the general trends of the second modernization. People are paying increasing attention to the protection of nature; environmental protection and the pattern of green development are being increasingly widely supported. Natural lifestyle and living environment, natural working style and environment, and green food and green technologies are favored by people. People are not simply taking things from nature or trying to conquer it. They have gradually "learned" to get along with it in a harmonious way, to promote it, and to embrace it. Man is part of nature rather than the master of it. Knowledge society is not only an ecologically balanced society but also an environmentally friendly society.

(4) Innovation Is the Powerhouse of the Second Modernization

Innovation is the fountain of civilization progress and the powerhouse of knowledgeablization, informatization, and greening. Knowledge production (research and development input) of society has gradually surpassed grain production (agricultural output), with innovation activities being socialized. Although research and development activities are still the source of new knowledge, innovation activities have gradually been society-wide. Innovation has become the decisive factor of corporate competition, economic development, and social progress. In agricultural society, innovation was mostly the behavior of individuals; in the industrial society, it became the behavior of organizations and enterprises; in the knowledge industry, it has become the national behavior, and increasing the national capacity for innovation has become a national policy. A national innovation system is a national system which promotes and conducts innovation and the powerhouse of the second modernization. Thus, knowledge society is also an innovative society.

(5) Globalization Is a Widespread Phenomenon in the Second Modernization

Globalization refers to the phenomenon that worldwide connections and interdependences are increasing. The advanced information and transport networks make the world into a whole, leading to the decrease of difficulties and estrangements caused by geography, languages, etc. People found that we are all inhabitants of the global village; we supply each other's needs and learn from each other. Accepting each other, respecting each other, living in harmony, and developing side by side has become the direction toward which international political and economic relations strive to move. The economic globalization, political internationalization, cross-border working and living, and the rapid development of international nongovernmental organizations (NGOs) and nonprofit organizations (NPOs) have already been undisputed facts and generally accepted. Thus, knowledge society is also a cosmopolitan society.

(6) Decentralization Is the Spatial Feature of the Second Modernization

Contrary to the centralization of the first modernization, decentralization is reflected by many aspects of the second modernization. The decentralized, flexible, and diverse modes of production are replacing the centralized large-sized industrial production; medium and small-sized enterprises are playing a growing role in economy and employment; various types of organizations are upholding their say and interests; and economic and political powers are becoming more and more decentralized. The populations in metropolises are moving into suburbs and small cities, and communities with distinctive features are thriving. Human beings have the tendency to live in compact communities and exchange; the information technology (IT) and means of transportation have partly eliminated the geographic separation, and "virtual communities" have partly satisfied this nature of human beings, making distance no longer a problem and thereby driving the decentralization of society. If we say that human beings lived in tribes based on blood lineage in the primitive society, in villages based on family relation in the agricultural society, and in cities based on economic relations in the industrial society, then in the knowledge society, they would live in communities based on cultural relations. Conflicts based on classes have decreased, while those based on cultures and individual values have increased. The development of globalization will lead to the global diffusion of such conflicts and risks, along with widespread ecological and technical risks. Knowledge society, therefore, is also a risk society, just like what Beck had mentioned (Beck 1992).

(7) Diversity Is the Cultural Feature of the Second Modernization

Contrary to the industrial convergence of the fist modernization, the second modernization will be a process of cultural diversification. In this process, the families, organizations, means of production, and lifestyles will be diverse, and cultural diversification will determine that the knowledge era is an era featuring the convergence of material civilization and the diversity of nonmaterial civilization (culture). Although material civilization has a great influence on cultural change, culture depends mainly on the languages, religions, arts, customs, habits, morals, values, laws, standards, etc., of nationalities. The material life of people will gradually converge, but their spiritual and cultural life will remain diverse. In the twenty-first century, mankind will protect the diversity of human culture like they protect biodiversity. Thus, knowledge society is a diversified democratic society.

(8) Individualization Is the Behavioral Feature of the Second Modernization

Contrary to the "rigidity" and "mechanical orientation" of the first modernization, the second modernization has revealed in many fields the features of "flexibility" and "individuality." There is increasing flexibility and respect for humanity, for example, in organizational structure, management thought and approach, and the mode and environment of production. Man is the creator and user of knowledge, and innovation is the creative activity of man; without man, there is no innovation and knowledge. The flexible and individualized organization and management is crucial for enhancing the capacity for knowledge and innovation and is the key to success. Among other things, flexible organizations, virtual enterprises, flextime, and distribution according to contribution all reflect the features of individualization. These new phenomena now are in vogue worldwide. Thus, knowledge society is a humane, rational society.

(9) Intelligentization Is the Technical Feature of the Second Modernization

The development and application of artificial intelligence technology constantly changes the things we use for work and life and environments in which we work and live. More and more labors have been replaced by intelligent robots. What are active in numerous jobs will be intelligent robots, making it inevitable that ordinary workers will lose their jobs. In the meanwhile, the intelligent levels of housing, transportation, technology, production, management, and many products will rise increasingly; working and life will become more and more prompt, convenient, and comfortable; the number of people engaged in physical labor and in repeated mental labor will be on constant decrease; and more people will put more time into creative work. This will further increase the level of intelligentization of society, thereby forming a positive feedback cycle conducive to intelligentization. Therefore, knowledge society is also an intelligent society.

(10) Lifelong Learning Is the Lifestyle Favored in the Second Modernization
In the twenty-first century, knowledge is being updated at a pace of doubling every 5 years, and the aging of knowledge is faster than its updating. And knowledge is the decisive factor of economic growth and success. All these determine the importance of learning. Higher education has been gradually generalized, and lifelong learning has become the generally accepted law of success. Successful governments, enterprises, and organizations will be learning organizations. Learning no longer means receiving education at school, but has become a part of daily work and life of everyone. The popularization of lifelong learning and the position of knowledge as a daily necessity and consumable will boost the upgrading of knowledge and further increase the pressure of continuous learning. Therefore, knowledge society is also a learning society.

The process of the second modernization is the process of establishing knowledge society as well as the development process of knowledge economy. Knowledge society is a new society, and knowledge economy is a new type of economy. Both knowledge society and economy are a polyhedron. When we look at them from different angles, we will have different views as well as different understandings and descriptions of them. For example, when we look at society from an economic perspective, a new society is a knowledge society, information society, or innovation society; when we look at economy from a technical point of view, a new economy is a knowledge economy, information economy, digital economy or network economy, and so on. This reveals the complexity of social and economic development.

Different aspects of both knowledge society and economy develop constantly, with different features in different development stages as well as great differences in the prominent features of different development stages. For example, the prominent feature of the current stage is IT and its influence, making many believe they are information society and economy. Knowledge economy is a new form of economy in relation to the primitive economy, agricultural economy, and industrial economy (Table 4.15). There is substantial literature on research of knowledge economy, including analysis about the origin and features of knowledge economy. Similarly, knowledge society is a new form of society, about which there are also numerous research papers (Example 4.4).

Table 4.15 Comparison between knowledge and industrial economy

Item	Knowledge economy	Industrial economy
Production	Knowledge production outpaces grain production	Industrial production outpaces grain production
	Knowledge industry surpasses material industry	Industry surpasses agriculture
	Knowledge and information production dominate	Large-sized industrial production dominates
Circulation	Market globalization (global market)	Market nationalization (national market)
	E-commerce, virtual market trade	Tangible market trade
	Fast market change	Slower market change
	Higher degree of securitization (credit card)	Lower degree of securitization (currency)
Distribution	Distribution according to contribution; adjust as necessary	Distribution according to capital; "to each according to his work"
	Knowledge capital and investment capital participate in distribution of net income	Investment capital participates in distribution of net income; "no pains, no gains"

Source: Research Group for China Modernization Strategies (2002)

Example 4.4 Towards Knowledge Societies
The United Nations held the "World Summit on the Information Society" (WSIS) in 2003 and 2005. The summit held that currently the fundamental change is happening from the industrial to the information society. This information revolution is influencing people's styles of life, study, and work, as well as the interaction between governments of countries and civil societies. Unless the vast majority of people in the world could adequately participate in the emerging knowledge society, they would not benefit from this revolution. In 2005, the UNESCO published the report "Towards Knowledge Societies," advocating the sharing of knowledge and the building of knowledge societies together (UNESCO 2005).

4.2.1.4 Limitations of Second Modernization Theory

In second modernization theory, the first modernization is described as the classical modernization, and the second modernization as the ongoing new modernization. Second modernization theory is in fact the theory on the twice modernization. The second modernization has just undergone a 30-year course of history, whose regular pattern and features are still in development. Therefore, the current understanding of the second modernization is rather limited. Second modernization theory fails to explain development after the second modernization, leaving a question to us that what the world will be like in the twenty-second century.

4.2.2 Reflexive Modernization Theory

In April 1986, a devastating nuclear accident occurred at the Chernobyl Nuclear Power Plant in the former Soviet Union, drawing worldwide attention to the massive risk of modern technology. The same year, *Risk Society: Towards a New Modernity* in the German language, a book by German scholar Ulrich Beck, was published; in the book, he raised two concepts which would later produce a widespread influence: risk society and reflexive modernization. It has been noticed that the dual character of technology drives social progress on the one hand and produces the side effect—technical and ecological risk—on the other. Risk has become a common social character.

4.2.2.1 Risk Society Theory

Beck holds that our modern world is in change, from the industrial society to the risk society. The emergency of the risk society represents the advent of a new era (Beck et al. 1994).

The industrial society is one in which modern science and rationality superseded religions and classes as social principles. The bureaucratic, technical and scientific elite began occupying the positions of knowledge and authority of society, whose decisions and technical innovation led to substantial consequences of organization and life (Beck 1992; Beck et al. 1994).

The risk society depicts a development stage of modern society. At this stage, the social, political, economic and individual risk increasingly tends to evade the risk prevention and supervision mechanisms established in the industrial society. The formation of the risk society consists of two stages. At the first stage, risk emerges systematically but has not yet become the focus of public agenda and political conflict, and the industrial society keeps its own features. At the second stage, the risk of the industrial society becomes a prominent topic of public, political and individual conflicts and arguments, the organs of the industrial society become the makers and legislators of risk, and social and political problems become a prominent feature (Beck 1992; Beck et al. 1994).

4.2.2.2 Reflexive Modernization Theory

Beck raised the concept of reflexive modernization in 1986 (Beck 1992) and made a detailed exposition of the theory of reflexive modernization in 1994 (Beck et al. 1994). Below is an introduction to the main points of the theory from five aspects.

(1) Definition

Beck holds that *the reflexive modernization is an era during which an industrial society makes creative destruction, and that the behavioral agent of creative destruction is the triumph of Western modernization rather than revolution and crisis* (Beck et al. 1994). *The simple modernization is the transition from a traditional society to an industrial society, and the reflexive modernization is the transition from an industrial society to a risk society. In a new period, progress*

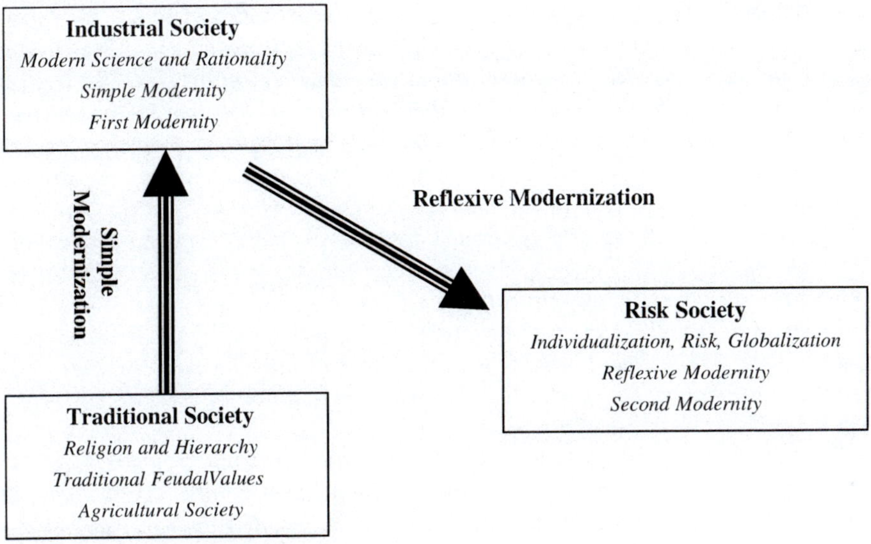

Fig. 4.9 Reflexive modernization is the modernization of modernization. Note: It is one representation of the thoughts of Beck et al. (1994)

becomes self-deconstruction, and one form of modernization destroys another; that ***is reflexive modernization*** (Fig. 4.9).

(2) Process

According to Beck, *world modernization consists of two stages, i.e. simple* ***(or orthodox) modernization and reflexive modernization. In the nineteenth century,*** *simple modernization broke down the structure of agricultural society, leading to* ***industrial society. Similarly, today's reflexive modernization is breaking down*** *industrial society and leading to another type of modernity, and this new emerging modernity is risk society. Simple modernization forms modern industrial society,* ***while reflexive modernization disintegrates it.***

If simple modernization is the disintegration and reconstruction of traditional ***society by industrial society, then reflexive modernization is the disintegration and*** *reconstruction of industrial society by another type of modernity. Modern society now is eliminating the structures of its own classes, stratums, careers, gender roles, neutral families, factories and commercial sectors, as well as the persistent state and premise of natural technological and economic progress. The higher degree of modernization the modern society has, the more the foundation of industrial society is eliminated, consumed, changed and impacted.*

The behavioral agents of reflexive modernization are: individuals and groups; *scientists and average people; organs and organizations.*

(3) Outcome

According to Beck, *industrial society is the result of simple modernization, and risk society the result of reflexive modernization. The modernity of industrial society is simple (or industrial) modernity, while the modernity of risk society is reflexive modernity. Simple modernity is the first modernity, and reflexive modernity is the second modernity.*

Simple modernity refers to the characteristics of industrial society between 1800 and 1950. It is a state of semimodernization, containing the factors of antimodernization that hinder further modernization. Simple modernization is only half of the course of modernization.

Reflexive modernity refers to the characteristics of risk society, such as individualization of social inequality, uncertainty, risk globalization, democratic dialogue, structural unemployment, partial employment, degradation of job security, etc. (Beck 1992).

Reflexive modernity is the automatic self-relief and self-doubt of general modernity. It is the nonplanned and invisible elimination by one type of modernization of another. It deals with the side effects and dangers stemming from general modernity, frees people from the current structure or defines a new structure and, even more radically, re-creates society and politics.

(4) Driving Force

There is a variety of views about dynamics of reflexive modernization. For example, Beck holds that the dynamics of reflexive modernization is side effects and reflexivity, while Lash thinks it is individualization (Beck et al. 1994).

Reflexivity is a process of transformation from industrial to risk society in an independent, undesired and invisible way. The automatic, unexpected and invisible transformation from industrial society to risk society is reflexivity. Reflexive modernization is the self-opposition of the effect of risk society. This effect cannot be solved and absorbed by industrial society. Reflexive modernization is the self-supervision of modern risk (Beck et al. 1994).

There is cognitive, esthetics, expository, structural, institutional, and self-reflexivity.

(5) Models

Reflexive modernization can be understood as the inevitable disintegration of industrial society, the being forced to find and invent new inevitability, new interdependence and even global interdependence. Individualization and globalization are the two aspects of reflexive modernization.

The occurrence of reflexive modernization is a quiet, unplanned change of industrial society, which is the end of normal, automatic modernization. Nevertheless, the political and economic order remains unchanged and complete. The radicalization of modernity smashes the structure and beliefs of industrial society and opens the door into another type of modernity.

The transition from one to another epoch of society can be realized through undersigned and nonpolitical promotion as well as promotion by various forums; new society is not always born out of suffering (Beck et al. 1994).

In 2000, *Liberty and Capitalism* (Beck and Willms 2000) was published. With the central subject of "the second modernization," the book discusses a number of relevant concepts, for example, globalization, uncertainty, "side effect," global risk society, second enlightenment, and the difference between the first modernization and the second modernization.

Beck says that *the purpose of the wordings "second modernization" or "**reflexive** modernization" **is, first of all, letting the Western modernization theory and modern** sociology make thorough self-criticism so that the room is made for cosmopolitan discussion about different goals, values, premises, relations and paths of modernization.*

The transition from the first to the second modernization cannot be completed at *one blow. It is not a revolution, but on the contrary, it proceeds in a nonpolitical way, bypassing the parliament, government and public opinion, like a mutation triggered off by side effects, whose total profundity and extensity appear gradually along with the emergence of opposite opinion and exposition.*

The transition from the first to the second modernization manifests itself in *various aspects. The basic concepts of labor organization and labor supervision, as well as the economy, businesses, technology and market, are disintegrating quietly; in the meanwhile, some things are coming into being. Currently no one* ***knows clearly what structural forms they will finally take.***

So far there has been no established arguments on the second modernization. My observation is that, the nation-state "container" will collapse of its own accord, and gain another nature whereby we form new notions about cross-border circulation, lifestyle and exchange relationship and whereby various mechanisms emerge within nation-states, regions and organizations, i.e. at all levels of society and in ***economic field, labor fields, social networks and political organizations.***

Beck's description of the second modernization (reflexive modernization) can come down to several aspects (a) globalization, including economic, political, social, and cultural globalization; (b) individualization, that is, some institutionalized individualism; (c) world risk society; (d) erosion of the foundation of labor society, with labor being no longer the sole significance; (e) diversity, manifested in various aspects; and (f) political diversification, subpoliticization, cosmopolitan democracy, and democratic authoritarianism.

In Beck's view, the second modernization (reflexive modernization) is the transition from labor (industrial society) to global risk society, and the future is a cosmopolitan society totally open to the world. Cosmopolitanism accepts true diversity, but globalism negates it.

4.2.2.3 Limitations of Reflexive Modernization Theory

The theory of reflexive modernization considers risk society as the second modernity and sees the formation of risk society as the purpose of reflexive modernization. This view reflects a portion of, but not all, features of the new changes in developed countries. Knowledge economy and knowledge society have become a world trend in the twenty-first century, and risk is a side feature of this world trend.

4.2.3 Postmodernization Theory

The postmodernization theory emerged in the 1970s–1980s. As early as the 1960s, three new phenomena appeared in developed countries. First, the economic development shifted from industrialization to deindustrialization, with industrial economy proportionally decreasing continuously and service economy rising continuously. Second, the social development changed from urbanization to deurbanization (or counterurbanization), with urban population moving into suburbs and towns. Third, the environmental movement arose, along with the spreading of postmodern culture. Apparently, classical modernization theory is unable to explain these new changes. From the 1970s onward, scholars began looking into the future development of advanced industrial countries, drawing widespread attention to futurology and postmodernization.

The theory of postmodernization is not a complete theoretical system but a collection of thoughts about postindustrial society, postmodernism, and postmodernization. The theory of postmodernization originated mainly from the following: the criticism of classical modernization and modernity, the futurological look into postindustrial society, and empirical research of postmaterialism and postmodernization.

4.2.3.1 Main Propositions of Postindustrial Society Theory

American scholar Daniel Bell is the representative postindustrial society theorist, who divided the process of social development in his book *The Coming of Post-Industrial Society* into three stages, preindustrial society, industrial society, and postindustrial society. Bell depicted postindustrial society from five aspects (a) economic aspect: the transition from product economy to service economy; (b) occupational distribution: technicians and professionals are the "pre-eminent" social groups; (c) axial principle: theoretical knowledge is at the core and the prime source of social reform and policymaking; (d) future direction: control over technological development and appraisal of technology; and (e) decision making: creation of new "intelligent technology" (Bell 1973).

4.2.3.2 Main Propositions of Postmodernism

Postmodernism originated in Western developed countries. According to Merriam-Webster's Dictionary, the world "postmodern" is of, relating to, or being any of various movements in Western art, philosophy, architecture, literature, etc., in the middle of the twentieth century that react against the philosophy and practice of modern movements and advocate a return to traditional elements and technology. German philosophers Nietzsche and Heidegger are regarded as the precursors of postmodernism, and representative theorists include Jean Francois Lyotard, Gilles Deleuze, Jacques Derrida, Michel Foucault, Fredric Jameson, David Harvey,

Richard Rorty, Jacques Lacan, and Jean Baudrillard. Postmodernism has neither a uniform definition nor a systematic theory, but has a distinctive feature, that is, posing challenges to all-inclusive modernity (Rosenau 1992).

French scholar Lyotard's book, *The Postmodern Condition*, promoted the rise of postmodernism. According to Lyotard, *the status of knowledge is altered as societies enter what is known as the postindustrial age and cultures enter what is known as the postmodern age. Knowledge has become the principal force of production over the last few decades, and this has already had a noticeable effect on the composition of the work force of the most highly developed countries and constitutes the major bottleneck for the developing countries. The relationships of the suppliers and users of knowledge to the knowledge they supply and use is now tending, and will increasingly tend, to assume the form already taken by the relationship of commodity producers and consumers to the commodities they produce and consume. Knowledge is and will be produced in order to be sold, and it is and will be consumed in order to create more value in a new production: in both cases, the goal is exchange* (Lyotard 1984).

German scholar Peter Koslowski made a comparison in differences between modern cultures and postmodern cultures. According to Koslowski, *modernization is necessary, but this is not to force people to react to modernization in a solely technology-oriented way. A postmodern culture is nothing but a social culture which realizes modernization in a way that is humane and accords with the wishes of people, while maintaining a balance in relation to the past and tradition. A postmodern period is more determined by various new and culture-oriented forms of social and economic modernization. The feature of a postmodern culture lies in its new relationship with more criticism of scientism, a culture-oriented economy, and nonfantasy, sensible relationship with progress and modernization. As far as a postmodern culture is concerned, modernization doesn't take only a form, but involves a variety of steps; these steps must bring actual benefits to people* (Koslowski 1987).

Generally, postmodernism is a trend of thought in relation to modernism and is built on the reflection and criticism of the problems and limitations of modernism, modernity, and modernization movement. As the product of classical modernization, modernity has brought not only the enormous material wealth but also "modern diseases" which people can increasingly hardly tolerate, such as rational autocracy, machine ruling, weakened humanity, spiritual vacuity, and ecological disasters. By disclosing, criticizing, and negating these "modern diseases," postmodernism broadened the horizons of people and provided new hints for future development. Postmodernism is the change of cultural paradigm and the cultural turn (Chaney 1994). American scholar David Harvey (2003) analyzed the transition of the contemporary culture from modernity to postmodernity and from modernism to postmodernism (Table 4.16). The changes brought by the shift from a modern to a postmodern culture are profound.

Table 4.16 Differences between modernism and postmodernism

Modernism	Postmodernism
Production capital, material capital, scale economy	Virtual capital, symbolic capital, regional economy
Mass production, operation management	Small-scale production, strategic management
Industry, industrialization, mechanical reproduction	Service, nonindustrialization, electronic reproduction
Specialized labor, blue collar	Flexible worker, white collar
Metropolis, urban renaissance, integration	Counterurbanization, urban regeneration, deconstruction
Goal, design, centralization, tangibility	Games, opportunity, decentralization, intangibility
State strength, class politics, trade union	Financial strength, social movement, individualism
Homogeneity, universalism, technology–science rationality	Diversity, localism, pluralism
Materiality, protestant ethic, epistemology	Immateriality, provisional contract, ontology
State interventionism, authority, internationalism	Noninterventionism, eclecticism, geopolitics

Note: This table is the collection of the ideas of Hassan (1987) and Harvey (1989)

4.2.3.3 Main Propositions of Postmodernization Theory

One of the representative works about the theory of postmodernization is *Postmodernization: Change in Advanced Society*, a book coauthored by British scholars Stephen Crook, Jan Pakulski, and Malcolm Waters (Crook et al. 1992). The book discusses the transition of developed countries from modernization to postmodernization and gives an analysis of six aspects, namely, culture, the state, inequality, politics, work organization, and science and technology (Table 4.17). In their opinion, *advanced societies are now undergoing a long-term and multidimensional process of postmodernization; postmodernization is best understood as a continuation of the process of modernization, but it erodes the stability of modernity; the transformation of postmodernization includes disorganization, hyperdifferentiation and dedifferentiation, hyperrationalization and hypercommercialization; the transformation from modernization to postmodernization involves the combination of hyperdifferentiation and monocentric organization; postmodernizing change becomes multidirectional and unpredictable*.

American scholar Inglehart is one representative postmodernization theorist. After analyzing the massive data and outcomes obtained from the World Values Survey, he wrote the book *Modernization and Postmodernization: Cultural, Economic, and Political Change in 43 Societies* (Inglehart 1997), one of representative works on the theory of postmodernization.

In Inglehart's opinion, *historical development is not linear, the transformation from traditional society to modern society is modernization, and that from modern society to postmodern society is postmodernization* (Fig. 4.10); *the change which occurred in industrialized countries from 1970 onwards is postmodernization, and that in developing countries is modernization; the transformation from modernization to postmodernization includes the profound changes in politics, economy,*

Table 4.17 Differences between modernization and postmodernization

Aspect	Modernization	Postmodernization
Culture	Cultural modernization is a process of transition from traditional to modern culture, including cultural differentiation, rationalization, and commercialization; cultural modernity is the product of cultural modernization and produces a series of tensions, between differentiation and dedifferentiation, rationalization and nonrational moment in art, and commercialization and its denial	Postmodernization of culture is multidirectional and unforeseeable process, which is a mixture of the expansion and reversion of cultural modernization, including hypercommercialization, hyperrationalization, hyperdifferentiation, and dedifferentiation, cultural postmodernity is the result of cultural postmodernization, which is also a mixture
State	Modernization produces the state as a container of rationalized power, the creator and protector of citizenship rights. The modern state gradually becomes a corporate manager, and its functions include stabilization, economic regulation, infrastructure development, the amelioration of social issues, and political legitimatization	Postmodernization shakes some concepts of corporatist state power, including the transformation from centralization to decentralization and from authoritative to manipulative forms of control; it challenges the idea that the state automatically enjoys privileges in political and public fields
Inequality	Liberal capitalism believes that the class and gender inequalities are determined by production, accumulation, and social reproduction, there are three inequalities: the male capitalists, male workers, and women. Organized capitalism has changed the situation: the service classes superseded the capitalist class, the working class was fragmented, and women became reproducers of the public domain	Inequalities of organized capitalism in the later stages are more determined by consumption pattern rather than production pattern. In postmodernity, mass media play a key role, which promotes identity diversity. Equal multiple communities are based on shared interest, choice, and responsibility and are floating and crossed
Politics	Modern politics is organized, formalized, and instrumentalized, which is centralized at state level and concerns formalized citizenship and orderly interest representation; politics in the first half of the twentieth century was more organized and bureaucratized	New politics is decoupled from the class structure and antibureaucratic; the change of postmodern politics includes the change from class structural bases to diverse groups, from economic topics to social and cultural topics, and from interest-focused politics to universal care

(continued)

Table 4.17 (continued)

Aspect	Modernization	Postmodernization
Work organization	Modern enterprises are highly rationalized and alienated. Modern organization with fordist production lines is characterized by standardization, continuity and constraint, and task-simplicity; due to market saturation, the fordist production strategy is challenged; the alliances of enterprises and organizations emerge	Postindustrialism promotes the development of professional, collegial forms of work organization; the petty entrepreneurialism promotes self-employment, and flexible specialization promotes the diversity of jobs. Flexible specialization, computer-controlled production, decentralized and dehierarchized management systems, flexible labor market, etc.
Science and technology	Modern organized science is the outcome of the institutionalization and professionalization, which is fit for the "grand design" that human control of nature; organized science is an autonomous system and produces new useful knowledge in exchange for the political and financial support from governments and industry	Modern sciences faces many pressures, for example, posed by finance and public understanding of science; postmodern science must ultimately eliminate the boundaries between science and other domains and needs to face public interests and hypercommercialization

Note: This table is a collection of the thoughts of Crook et al. (1992)

gender and family, religion and notion, etc., for example, from materialism to postmaterialism, from modern values to postmodern values and from survival values to happiness values; the central goal of modernization is economic growth, expanding tangible products through industrialization and the systematic application of technology; the central goal of postmodernization is the maximization of personal happiness, emphasizing on quality of life and life experience; On specialization, secularization and individualization, postmodernization is the continuity of modernization. Cultural change is of path dependence, and that of postmodernization includes the rise of postmodernism. Postmodernism may be divided into three broad schools (a) postmodernism that rejects modernity, i.e. rejecting rationality, authority, technology and science; (b) postmodernism that is the ***revalorization of tradition, thinking that tradition has positive significance;*** *(c) postmodernism that is the rise of new values and lifestyles, with greater tolerance for ethnic, cultural, sexual diversity and individual choice concerning the kind of life on wants to lead.*

In the book *Modernization, Cultural Change, and Democracy: The Human Development Sequence*, Inglehart and Welzel (2005) give a detailed discussion of cultural change in the process of modernization. In their opinion, *the direction of*

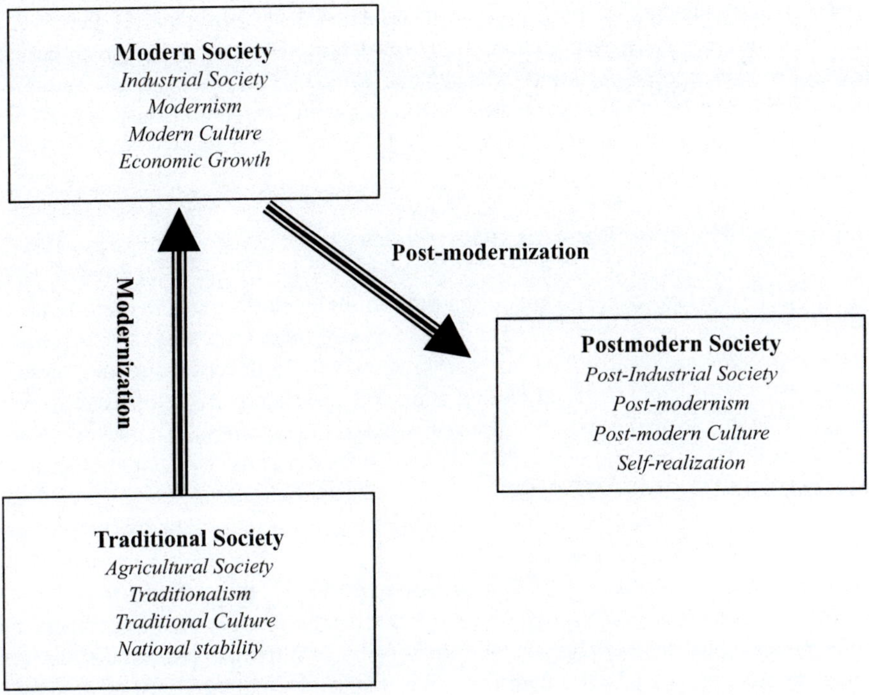

Fig. 4.10 From modernization and modern society to postmodernization and postmodern society. Note: It is based on the thoughts of Inglehart (1997), Crook et al. (1992), and Bell (1973)

modernization is expectable, but the process is uncertain; the role of religion and traditional cultural heritance didn't disappear, global cultures didn't converge, cultural change is not linear, cultural conversion occurred over and over again, and cultural modernization is not irreversible; industrialization brought rationality, bureaucratization and secularization, and postindustrialization led to values of self-discipline and self-expression; modernization is not Westernization, and the United States is not the leader of the world's cultural change; the development and emancipation of human has already become the feature of modernization in the era of postindustrialization.

4.2.3.4 Limitations of Postmodernization Theory

To a great degree, the theory of postmodernization is blamed as much as praised. Here is a brief discussion of its limitations, leaving aside criticisms against it. First, it is suspected to be "self-inconsistent in time." If we say that "postmodern" is a concept of time, "modern" and "postmodern" are time-overlapped. From a time point of view, "postmodern" is a "self-inconsistent" vague concept. Second, it contains no new developments such as knowledge economy and network society, as well as new changes in the future. Third, it has a limited ability of expression. It holds that modernization is not the end of history nor is postmodernization, and what is beyond postmodernization is "post-post-modernization." If this is the case, then what is beyond "post-post-modernization?" In industrialized countries, the time self-inconsistence of postmodernization leads to the confusion of thoughts. In developing countries, the contradiction between modernization and postmodernization makes people not know what course to take. The theory of postmodernization has restricted its own development because of defects in itself.

4.2.4 Continuous Modernization Theory

Since the 1970s, new concepts regarding the future development of modern industrial society have emerged one after another. Some of them are about society, some are about economy, and others are comprehensive. While reflecting the social reality, they transcend the social reality, and some are characteristic of futurology. In the 1980s, German scholars raised the theory of ecological modernization (discussed in Chap. 6), and in the 1990s, they put forward the theory of continuous modernization.

4.2.4.1 Main Propositions of Continuous Modernization Theory

German scholar Zapf (1999) thinks that none of such concepts as postmaterialist society, postindustrial society, postmodern society, information society, risk society, and perceptual society is semantically more dynamic than the concept "modern society."

Zapf agrees with American scholar Talcott Parsons' view that development (modernization and change) is a synthesis of tolerance, generalization of values, differentiation, and status improvement. Professor Zapf holds that the modernization theory, "quenched" by conflict theory and innovation theory, is a theoretical pattern appropriate to explain the present and future development of the world and that modern society needs continuous modernization.

Continuous modernization includes technological and social innovation; social change mechanisms about tolerance, generalization of values, differentiation, and status improvement; and the dual meaning of directional invariableness and structural improvement (Zapf 1999). Based on Zapf's view, Professor Tiryakian (1991) at Duke University calls this modernization "a second type of modernization" or "neomodernism."

4.2.4.2 Limitation of Continuous Modernization Theory

Professor Zapf stressed the continuity of modernization, but ignored major turns in the direction of modernization. With advent of information revolution and rise of knowledge economy, both the direction and the implication of modernization have changed fundamentally, for example, from industrialization to deindustrialization, from material to service economy, and from materialism to environmentalism.

4.3 Roads of Integrated Modernization

Since the 1970s, while more and more advanced countries have entered the stage of a second modernization, developing countries that have not yet completed the first one are now facing the doubled pressures from twice modernization tasks. In the twenty-first century, it is quite likely that more developing countries will adopt the model of the coordinated development of the twice modernization, that is, an integrated modernization path (Fig. 4.11). There are six theories concerning the integrated modernization, of which integrated modernization theory, multiple modernities theory, and globalization theory will be the focus of discussion in this section (Table 4.18).

4.3.1 Integrated Modernization Theory

Integrated modernization theory, first put forward by Chinese scholar Chuanqi He, is a path theory for the second modernization theory. The book *Oriental Revitalization: Three Roads of Modernization* (He 2003) gives a systematic elaboration of the integrated modernization theory, which incorporates general theories, branch theories, and relevant theories (Table 4.19). Among them, the general theories

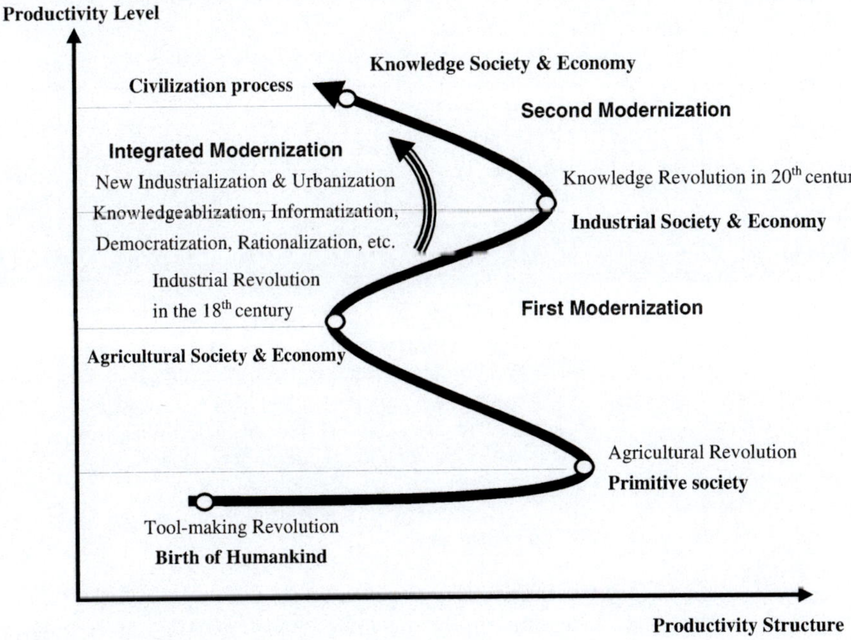

Fig. 4.11 Positioning of the integrated modernization. Note: The integrated modernization path is a basic route appropriate for developing nations who have not yet completed the first modernization. Some, while still stuck in the first modernization, are confronted with the challenge of the second one, to which the solution might be an integrated modernization path. Different nations might have different starting points, finishing points, as well as different trajectories. For instance, the earliest starting point can be traced back to the 1980s. Source: He (2003)

Table 4.18 Three relevant theories on integrated modernization

Item	Integrated modernization theory	Multiple modernities theory	Globalization theory
Research content	A coordinated development of twice modernization	Diversity of culture and modernity	Growing international relations and dependency
Research subject	Integrated modernization phenomena in developing countries	A solution of modernity in all countries	A globalization process and its impacts that involve all countries
Research level	National level	National level	A system incorporated levels of multinational companies, nations, and international entities
Research scope	Developing countries	All countries	All countries
Characteristics	A path theory	A topic theory	A topic theory

Note: Theories concerning the integrated modernization include integrated modernization theory, multiple modernities theory, globalization theory, classical modernization theory, ecological modernization theory, and secondary modernization theory. Developing countries, who have adopted a comprehensive modernization path, are confronted with the challenges of multiple modernities and globalization. The multiple modernities theory and globalization theory are topic-relative theories on modernization as much as theories that are closely related with integrated modernization

Source: RGCMS (2010)

Table 4.19 Structure of integrated modernization theory

Category	Theory	Main contents
General theory	Core theory	Definition, process, result, dynamics, and models of integrated modernization
Branch theories	Level theory	Integrated modernization of nations, regions, organizations, and individuals
	Field theory	Integrated modernization in economical, social, political, cultural, and natural environment and human fields
	Sector theory	Integrated modernization in the sectors such as agriculture, industry, education, science and technology, national defense, and transportation
Relevant theories	Other modernization theories	Classic modernization theory, multiple modernities theory, globalization theory, second modernization theory, etc.
	Other relevant theories	Development theory, transition theory, dependency theory, world-system theory, etc.

Source: RGCMS (2010)

represent the systematic discussion of the integrated modernization. It is quite possible that through a coordinated development of the twice modernizations, these countries can catch up with the developed ones and successfully reach the advanced level of second modernization. The comprehensive modernization path of the developing countries parallels the second modernization path of the developed countries.

4.3.1.1 General Theory of Integrated Modernization

The general theory on integrated modernization include five basic aspects concerning its definition, process, result, dynamics, and model (Table 4.20), which will be discussed separately later.

(1) Definition of Integrated Modernization

Integrated modernization (or comprehensive modernization), a specific phenomenon in developing countries, is the coordinated development of the twice

Table 4.20 General theory of integrated modernization

Aspect	Main contents
Definition	Integrated modernization, a specific phenomenon in developing countries, is the process of the coordinated development of twice modernizations and continuous transition to the second modernization; a process of the formation, development, transformation, and international interaction of the modern civilization; a compound process of the innovation, selection, diffusion, and recession of civilization elements; and an international competition for developing nations to catch up with the developed ones and reach world advanced levels
Process	Integrated modernization is a double-transition process that involves the transition from agricultural to industrial civilization and from industrial to knowledge civilization, as well as the coordination of the twice transformations and a continuous change toward knowledge civilization, and includes many contents such as the new type of the industrialization and urbanization, knowledgeablization, informatization, democratization, social welfare, greening, ecologization, and globalization; the dropping of the proportion of agricultural civilization; the first rising then declining of the proportion of industrial civilization; and the growing of the proportion of knowledge civilization and ecological civilization. It follows the ten principles of modernization (Table 2.15)
Result	From domestic perspective, the national level rises, and civilization structure changes; the proportion of first modernity first surging and then falling and that of second modernity climbing up with parts of traditional values continues to exist and function; the ultimate outcome will be the formation of the second modernity, particularity, and side effects. From the global perspective, the nation involved will be able to catch up and reach the world advanced level of the second modernization
Dynamics	The driving forces of comprehensive modernization include innovation, competition, adaptation, exchange, technology, systems, national interests, market demands, etc., among which national interests and urge to catch up will play the major roles. The models of dynamics are as follows: three-element model, innovation drive, three-innovation drive, two-wheel drive, united action of two transitions, combinative action, four-step supercycle, composite interaction of three civilizations, innovation diffusion, innovation overflow, competition drive, etc. (Table 2.20)
Model	It is featured with the diversification in path and pattern and has around 30 types of element mix (Table 2.21). More features include path dependency, susceptible to traditional, objective conditions as well as international environment, and origin dependency, susceptible to timetable and level of the nation's modernization. Different nations with different timings of integrated modernization "start-up" call for different trajectories and patterns

Source: He (2003), RGCMS (2010)

modernizations, a composite process that features continuous transition to the second modernization; a process of the formation, development, transformation, and international interaction of modern civilization; a compound process of innovation, selection, diffusion, and recession of civilization elements; and a competitive instrument for developing nations to catch up with developed nations and reach world advanced levels.

Integrated modernization, aiming at catching up to the advanced level of the second modernization, is to coordinate the developments of twice modernizations, let the second modernization take the lead on the process, let the first one follow and push forward the second one, and ultimately accomplish the second modernization.

In integrated modernization process, the first modernization is not required to be completed first, but instead the twice modernizations can be carried out in parallel. In areas without conflicts of the two modernizations, we should comply with the inherent logics of development, advance step by step, reduce the occurrence of mistakes, and accelerate growth. In areas where conflicts emerge, we should adopt three principles of precedence, that is, always give priority to compliance of the inherent logics of development, adherence of the basic principles of the second modernization, and satisfaction of the development needs of the second modernization.

(2) Process of Integrated Modernization

Integrated modernization aims at a knowledge-based civilization through twice successful transitions, first from agricultural to industrial civilization and then from industrial to knowledge civilization. This process can be elaborated using the "united action of two transitions model" (He 2003) and follows the ten principles of modernization (Table 2.15).

Firstly, the stages of the process of integrated modernization.

Generally, the process of integrated modernization can be divided into three stages (Fig. 4.12).

The first stage puts the first modernization in the first place and the twice modernizations in coordinated development. For a country still in the initial stage or developing stage of the first modernization when its proportion of agricultural civilization exceeds that of industrial civilization, it can enter the first stage of comprehensive modernization with the first one as the main task, which is referred to as industrialization-dominated stage.

In the first stage, the first modernization always remains as the main task, including industrialization, urbanization, democratization and rationalization, etc., while at the same time, the basic elements of second modernization can be involved, like knowledgeablization, informatization, and greening. Then, a developing mode featured with quaternary structure and successive transitions is formed. The main contents include coexistence of knowledge economy, ecological economy, industrial economy, and agricultural economy; successive transitions to industrial economy, to eco-economy, and at last to knowledge economy; coexistence of knowledge society, ecological society, industrial society, and agricultural

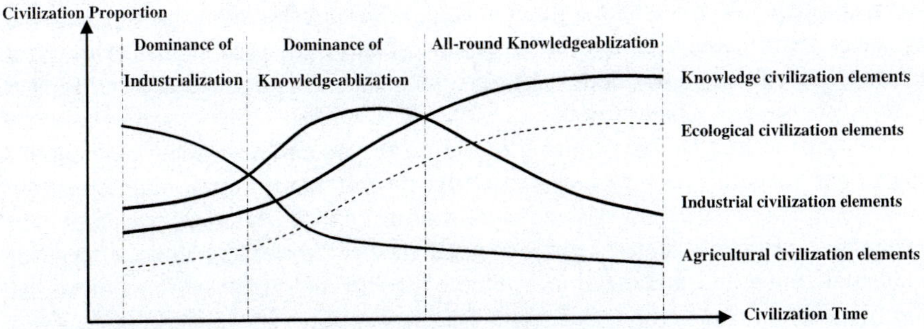

Fig. 4.12 Three stages and civilization structure of comprehensive modernization process. Note: Different countries with different starting points in comprehensive modernizations have different stage divisions. For a country still in the start stage or developing stage of the first modernization when its proportion of agricultural civilization exceeds that of industrial civilization, it will go through three stages after entering the comprehensive modernization process. For a country in the mature stage of the first modernization when the proportion of agricultural civilization is far lower than the industrial civilization, it will then go through two stages. To some extent, ecological civilization can be regarded as part, or one aspect, of knowledge civilization; in similar way, the eco-economy and eco-society may well be regarded as part, or one aspect, of knowledge economy and knowledge society. Source: He (2003), RGCMS (2010)

society; and successive transitions to industrial society, to eco-society, and at last to knowledge society.

The second stage will take the second modernization as priority and also has the twice modernizations in coordinated development. For a country in the mature stage or transitional stage of the first modernization, or reaching the point where its industrial civilization proportion exceeds the agricultural civilization proportion, it can straightly enter the stage two with the second modernization as the priority, which is referred to as knowledge-dominated stage.

In the second stage, the nation shall have the second modernization in the dominant role and speed up the process of knowledgeablization, informatization, and greening, while at the same time finish the trailing work for the first one and complete the process of industrialization, urbanization, and democratization, shaping a developing mode of duel structure and successive transitions. The main elements in this stage will be as follows: coexistence of knowledge economy, ecological economy, and industrial economy; successive transitions to eco-economy and to knowledge economy; coexistence of knowledge society, ecological society, and industrial society; and successive transitions to eco-society and to knowledge society. In this process, the proportion of agricultural civilization will continue dropping but remain throughout this stage.

The third stage is entirely dedicated to advancing the second modernization. For a country whose share of knowledge civilization has already surpassed share of industrial civilization, or who has already completed the first modernization, developed its industrial civilization to its acme, and seen the share of industrial civilization in a downward trend, it shall dedicate all its efforts on boosting the second modernization, referred to as the all-round knowledgeablization stage.

In this stage, the main tasks of modernization for developing nations include the all-round developments of knowledge economy, knowledge society, and ecological civilization; catching up with developed nations; and achieving the world advanced level of the second modernization.

Both in the first and second stages, due to the adoption of many elements of the second modernization such as knowledgeablization, informatization, greening, and globalization, the nation's industrialization and urbanization processes will experience profound changes that are distinguished from the traditional type of industrialization and urbanization in the eighteenth and nineteenth centuries and the first half of the twentieth century. This new pattern of industrialization is a quintuple interactive process that involves industrialization, deindustrialization, informatization, greening, and globalization. As for new type of urbanization, it is a quintuple interactive process that involves urbanization, suburbanization, informatization, greening, and internationalization.

Secondly, the characteristics of integrated modernization process.

Integrated modernization is a new path, whose practical characteristics are still taking shape. There are five basic features of comprehensive modernization process (a) diversity, for instance, of starting point, of path, and of finishing point (the time point of reaching the level of developed countries); (b) comprehensiveness, from the coordinated development mode of twice modernizations; (c) complication, including the contents and transitions of two modernizations; (d) risks, successive transitions of two modernizations are risky; and (e) innovativeness, it is a new route different from that of developed countries.

Thirdly, the "canal model" of the integrated modernization process.

Human history is very similar to a long river, which can be divided into four "reaches": primitive society, agricultural society, industrial society, and knowledge society. The voyage that the ark of civilization takes from agricultural to industrial society is called the first modernization and that from industrial society to knowledge society is the second modernization. In the modernization process of developed countries, the ark of civilization has navigated along the main channel of the river of human civilization, sailing from the first modernization to the second, which is a natural progression with the twice modernizations taking place one after another. In the modernization process of developing countries, "a man-made canal (canal of modernization)" is dug between the reach of industrial society and reach of knowledge society, and the ark of civilization will navigate along the canal to the knowledge society, making possible the conjunction of the first and second modernizations and the coordinated developments of twice modernizations (Fig. 4.11).

Fourthly, the "united action of two transitions" of integrated modernization process.

Integrated modernization requires the coordinated developments of twice modernizations and two successful transitions from agricultural to industrial society and from industrial to knowledge society. Generally speaking, there are three origins for the generation of knowledge society.

To some extent, the knowledge society is inherited and developed from industrial society, such as democratization, secularization, and popularization of compulsory education.

Meantime, the knowledge society will eliminate or "reverse" part of industrial society, for instance, decentralization vs. centralization, deindustrialization vs. industrialization, suburbanization vs. urbanization, community vs. noncommunity, organic vs. mechanic, cultural diversification vs. industrial convergence, environment friendly vs. environment damages, etc. Some parts of the knowledge society are a spiral "reversion" of traditions, like community, decentralization, and naturalism.

At last, the knowledge society incorporates large amounts of innovations, including knowledge and institutional innovation, etc., and features with knowledgeablization, informatization, networking, intellectualization and popularization of high education.

In the process of establishing an industrial society, we can selectively eliminate and "reverse" or inherit and develop its already-established parts to generate required elements for a knowledge society, while at the same time conduct the knowledge and institutional innovations that are essential for the knowledge society. The formation of the industrial society and the knowledge society will be a coherent process. Comprehensive modernization resembles a "reactor," which, on one hand, decomposes the agricultural society and creates the industrial society and, on the other hand, decomposes the industrial society and gives birth to the knowledge society, with these two transitions closely linked together (Fig. 4.13). This "reactor" can by no means function automatically, but instead is controlled by men, whose ultimate goal is to establish the knowledge society.

Fifthly, the favorable factors for the integrated modernization process.

(a) Borrow international practices. Draw lessons from the experiences of developed countries in building up the industrial society and knowledge society, avoid the mistakes that once made by developed countries, save time costs in groping and probing, cut down the construction costs that are cuttable, reduce

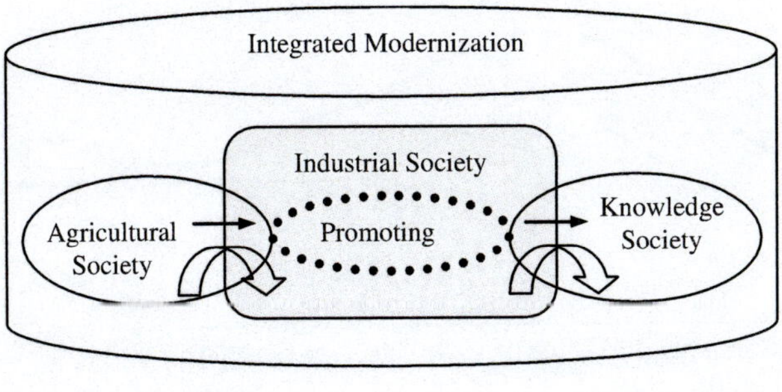

Fig. 4.13 United action of two transitions in the formation of the industrial and knowledge societies. Note: United action of two transitions: one involves the dissolution of agricultural society and the generation of industrial society, and the other is the dissolution of industrial society and the generation of knowledge society. Source: He (2003)

the cost of social transitions, and take control of the development pace in self-eliminating and "reversing" the components of industrial society.

(b) Make full use of regional imbalance. If a country is undergoing the developing stage of the first modernization in the national level, it is quite possible that some regions have already entered the mature stage or transitional stage while other regions are still in developing stage or initial stage. The former can straightly employ the elements of knowledge society, while the latter should promote the self-elimination and "reversion" of parts of industrial society and convert them into components of the knowledge society. In some countries, some regions in the first modernization and others in the second modernization process.

(c) Take advantage of field imbalance. The development paces of different fields are not synchronized. Those with faster pace can make the transition first, and those with slower pace may follow. The timings of transition for different fields may also be different, with some making the transition in advance, for example, the economic field can enter the deindustrialization phase before the industrialization process reaches its "peak" (Fig. 4.14).

(d) Draw on the compatibility of two societies. The formation processes of knowledge society and industrial society are partly compatible, thus the innovations needed by the two societies can be conducted at the same time. For example, while in the process of industrialization and urbanization, strategies like knowledgeablization, informatization, intellectualization, greening, and globalization can be carried out at the same time instead of after the completion of industrialization and urbanization.

(e) Advance the timing of the ecological transition. Developed countries enter the second modernization after completion of the first, who suffered from severe environment pollutions, growing environment pressures, and surging ecological cost in the first modernization, and then employ ecological modernization

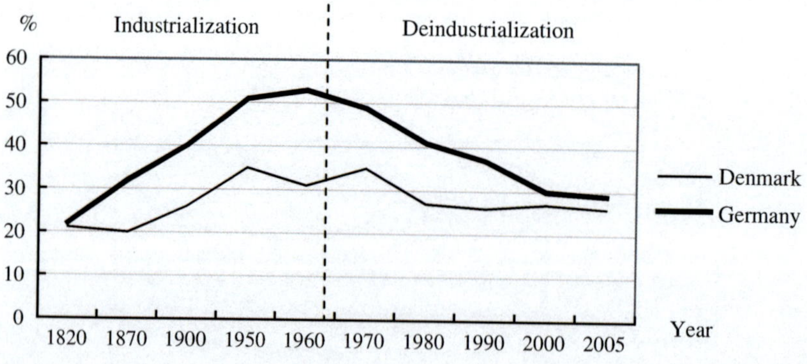

Fig. 4.14 Changing percentage of industrial added value in GDP (industrialization and deindustrialization). Note: The percentage of industrial added value in GDP in Denmark began to fall before reaching 40%, indicating the country is entering the deindustrialization phase. Source: RGCMS (2010), He (2010a, 2011)

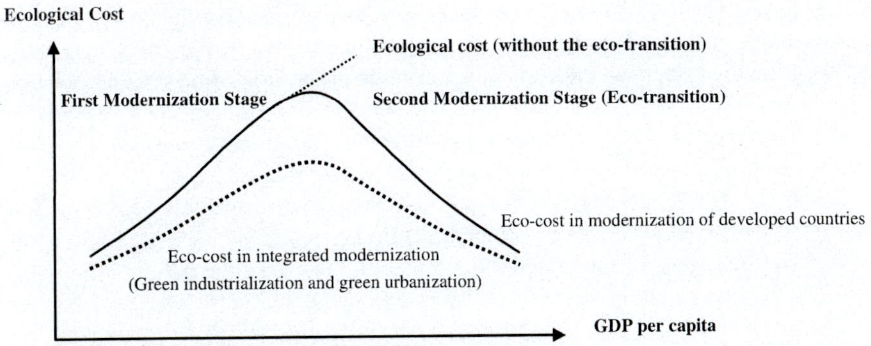

Fig. 4.15 Ecological cost in integrated modernization of developing countries (RGCMS 2007)

theories, dedicate great efforts to ecological modernization transition, adopt an environment-friendly development mode, and reduce the environment pressures as well as ecological costs in the second modernization. So we can see that in the modernization process, developed countries adopted an "abatement after pollution is done" tactic and saw a "first rising and then falling" trend in the environmental pressures and ecological costs. However, in the integrated modernization process, developing countries can introduce the ecological modernization theories and the environment-friendly development mode to start a path of green industrialization and green urbanization so as to reduce the environmental pressures and ecological costs during the modernization process (Fig. 4.15). Although developing countries will also experience a "first rising and then falling" trend in the environmental pressures and ecological costs, their overall figures may be smaller than those of developed peers.

Sixthly, the risks in the integrated modernization process.

Integrated modernization is still an exploration, which will naturally encounter ups and downs, and has many potential risks. In contrast, risks in comprehensive modernization will be higher than those in the first and second modernizations because the former is a man-made selection while the latter two are natural evolutions of the society. Some of those risks are a result of cognition problems, and some are caused by practice mistakes. So it is important to enhance the risk management, sharpen recognitions of risks, augment the psychological enduring ability, and reduce the side effects of risks within a socially acceptable level. For those developing countries who hope to catch up with the developed countries in an expected period, comprehensive modernization will be a key to the success, if not the only one.

(3) Results of Integrated Modernization

The outcome of the integrated modernization can be analyzed from two perspectives.

From the domestic perspective, the national level rises and civilization structure changes; for instance, the share of agricultural civilization drops, share of industrial civilization first increases and then declines, and share of knowledge civilization and ecological civilization sees continuous expansion (Fig. 4.12), but the agricultural civilization does not entirely fade away; the proportion of first modernity first raising and then falling and that of second modernity climbing up with parts of traditional values continues to exist and function; the ultimate result will be the formation of the second modernity, particularity, and side effects.

From the global perspective, the nation involved will be able to catch up and reach the world advanced level of modernization.

The national goal of integrated modernization is to raise the nation's modernization level and catch up to the world advanced level.

(4) Dynamics of Integrated Modernization

The analysis of driving force in general modernization theory discussed in Chap. 2 also applies to the integrated modernization. It includes innovation, competition, adaptation, exchange, technology, systems, national interests, market demands, etc., among which national interests and urge to catch up will play the major roles.

The dynamic models are as follows: three-element model, innovation drive, three-innovation drive, two-wheel drive, united action of two transitions, combinative action, four-step supercycle, composite interaction of three civilizations, innovation diffusion, innovation overflow, competition drive, etc.

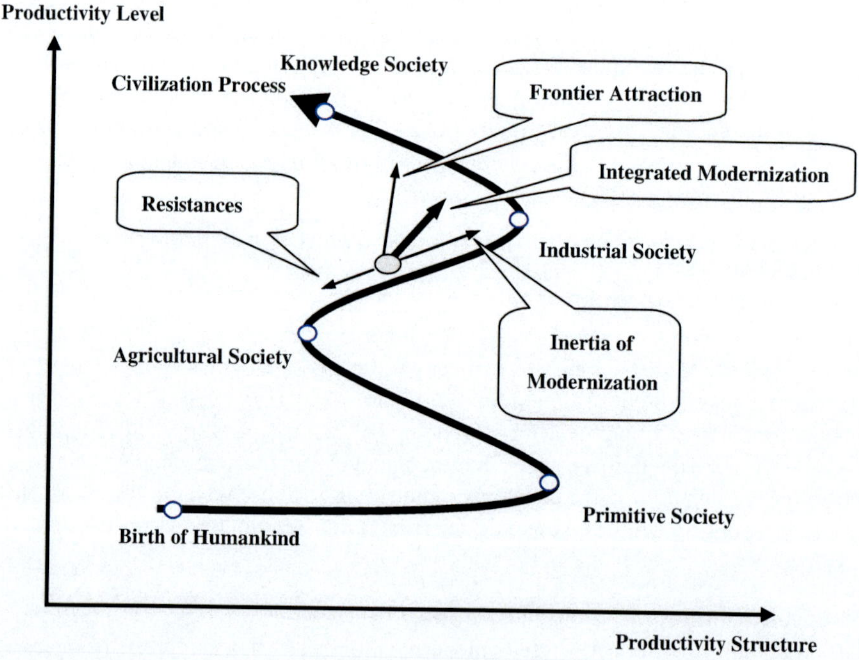

Fig. 4.16 Three-factor model of integrated modernization. Note: Factors like the country's current modernization stage, level and conditions, and international environment will all influence the route of the integrated modernization. Source: He (2010a, 2011)

Generally speaking, the integrated modernization is susceptible to three factors: resistances to modernization, which are various obstacles standing in the way of modernization; modernization inertia, which is the inertial effect of the first modernization; and frontier attraction, which refers to the attraction coming from the frontier of the second modernization. The interaction of these factors determines the trajectory and content of integrated modernization, which is called "three-factor model (Fig. 4.16)." In brief, the combined influence of these three factors will decide what kind of orbit the integrated modernization takes and affect the content and growing pace of integrated modernization as well as its results and probability of success.

It is expected that the twenty-first century will see enhancing frontier attraction of the second modernization, ever existing inertia of the first modernization, different expressions of resistances in different countries and different times, increasing developing countries that embark on the road of integrated modernization, and diversity in integrated modernization routes. At some point of this century, all those that have not completed the first modernization may enter the phase of integrated modernization. If that happens, then all nations will be either in the stage of second modernization or in the phase of integrated modernization.

(5) Models of Integrated Modernization

Integrated modernization is featured with diversity in paths and models, which has about over 20 types of element mix (Table 2.21). It is path-dependent, susceptible to traditional, objective conditions as well as international environment and origin-dependent, and susceptible to current stage and level of the nation's modernization. The route choice for modernization is a result of combined effect of modernization resistance, inertia, and frontier attraction (Fig. 4.16). Different nations with different timings of integrated modernization "start-up" call for different paths and models.

First, the innovation of development path. The "canal model" requires that countries should adhere to fundamental principles of the first and second modernizations and build upon the existing modernization level and economic as well as geographical conditions, to open up a new modernization canal that fits developing countries and catch up with developed countries. Different nations and regions should have their own distinguished canals.

Second, the innovation of development models. The "united action of two transitions" requests different countries and regions in different modernization stages to find and establish a new development model that is compatible with their integrated modernization path and, moreover, make constant adjustments to the model so as to keep up with the rising modernization level and ever changing environments at home and abroad; to break the shackles of old pattern and establish new one; to quicken the metabolism process of development pattern; and to gradually approach the second modernization level that developed nations have achieved.

Third, deliver strategic management. The level of second modernization in developed countries keeps changing, so should the strategic objective of integrated modernization. Therefore, the development path, model, and strategic goal of integrated modernization must change with the times, and to that purpose, governments should implement dynamic management over their own development strategies.

4.3.1.2 Strategic Focuses in the Process of Integrated Modernization

Different stages of integrated modernization may have distinguished strategic focuses. It is also true for different countries. Integrated modernization is the coordinated development of twice modernizations, so we can fix the strategic focus from these two aspects.

1. Strategic Focuses for the First Modernization
   (a) New type industrialization. With both progressions and regressions of the industrialization to attach equal importance to industrialization and industrial transfer; to select sectors to be developed and those to be transferred or eliminated; and to boost high-tech industries, push forward service industry, and enhance productivity.
   (b) New type urbanization. With the ins and outs of urbanization, simultaneous developments of urbanization and suburbanization, facilitating migrants from rural to urban areas, encouraging urban population to move to suburbs, and enhancing construction of communities, transportations, and commercial infrastructures. Meantime, new urbanization also incorporates coordinated developments of urbanization, informatization and ecologicalization, popularization of high education, as well as establishment of a society with balanced rural and urban areas.
   (c) Advance democratization. To improve democratic election, legislation, and supervision system; respect individual choices; and build a democratic society.
   (d) Construct welfare system. To establish a new type welfare society and a social welfare system that covers the whole population.
   (e) Encourage rationalization. To promote the professionalization and commercialization of culture, develop culture industry and mass culture, and melt down the feudalism culture.
2. Strategic Focuses for the Second Modernization
   (a) To promote knowledgeablization and establish a knowledge society. Develop knowledge industries including knowledge production, communication, and services; construct infrastructures for knowledge society; enlarge the knowledge density in agriculture, industry, and service sector; and raise productivity.
   (b) To accelerate informatization and build up an information society. Develop information technology industry, build infrastructures for information society, establish an Internet network among all people and all enterprises, and realize e-government and e-commerce.
   (c) To engage in economic globalization and lift international competitiveness. Establish international economic corporation zone and free-trade zone.

(d) To expand high education and build up a learning society. Strive to develop vocational education, remote education, and formal high education.

(e) To improve national innovation system and build up an innovative nation. Establish an innovation network, optimize innovation policies, cultivate innovative culture, strengthen national innovation capability, and enhance knowledge innovation, technology innovation, and institution innovation.

(f) To carry out the ecological modernization strategy and build up an environment-friendly society. Facilitate the breakage of the linkage between economic growth and environment deterioration, reinforce the risk management, and achieve the win–win result of economic growth and environment protection.

(g) To implement a distribution system based on contribution and build up a society of equality. Implement the distribution by contribution and adjustment by requirement; include intellectual capital and investment capital into the distribution of the net income; narrow the gaps between the rich and poor, among industries and among regions; and create a harmonious society.

4.3.1.3 Limitations of Integrated Modernization Theory

Integrated modernization theory only applies to developing countries that have adopted it.

Integrated modernization is distinguished from both the first and second modernization, but takes these twice modernizations as a base or reference. Every nation has its own unique characteristics in terms of integrated modernization route and pattern, so it is hardly possible to succeed by simply copying other nations' practice. Without long time, arduous, and persistent efforts and innovations, the success of integrated modernization will be impossible.

Integrated modernization is a rapidly changing process; it will have its ups and downs, bring pains, incur frustrations, require sacrifices, and generate by-products that are unwelcome. Integrated modernization rejects romanticism, utopianism, and idealism but welcomes deep thinking and hardworking. The inevitable results of integrated modernization are drastic changes of social structure and redistribution of powers, from which some will gain and some will lose. Thus, in this process, it is necessary to show understanding and respect as well as make compensations for those who sacrifice and rewards to those who contribute.

4.3.2 Multiple Modernities Theory

Since 1990s, cultural diversity and cultural pluralism have aroused a broad range of attentions. This idea also finds echoes in the modernization study area. "Multiple modernities" gradually becomes a new academic buzzword in the time of globalization, but no agreed definition is given.

Israel scholar Eisernstadt believes that *multiple modernities is a specific viewpoint over the history and characteristics of modern era, different from the elaboration of classical modernization theory in 1950s. Classical Modernization Theory deems Europe as the birthplace of modernity, which was then proliferated to all corners of the world and wholly accepted by followers. Indeed, modernity managed to reach the majority of countries and regions, but failed to generate a unified civilization, or an institutional pattern, Instead, it gave birth to and grew several modern civilizations or at least, several civilization patterns* (Eisenstadt 2003).

4.3.2.1 Basic Points of Multiple Modernities Theory

Basic contentions of the multiple modernities theory are as follows (Eisenstadt 2000, 2003):

1. *Modernity should be deemed as a unique civilization with distinct institutional and cultural characteristics. The core of modernity is the formation and development of one or more ways for interpreting the world, which is a kind of ontology prospect featured by formation and development of a unique culture blueprint combined with the development of one or more sets of new institutional patterns. The center of this core is unprecedented openness and uncertainties.*
2. *The continuous variability of institutional patterns and ideological models for modernity has well proven that it is better to regard the history of modernity as a story of constant developing, shaping, building and reconstructing the plural culture scheme of modernity, the unique modern institution patterns and diverse self-conceptions of modern society—a story of multiple modernities.*
3. *"Multiple Modernities" have several implications. First, modernity is totally different from westernization and the western model or modernity model is not the only, "true" modernity, although in comparison with other kinds of modernity, western model appeared much earlier, is and will continue to be the critical reference model for other modernity models. Second, the shaping of the multiple modernities has not only been branded in the international conflicts, but also in different national levels and multinational scopes. Third, multiple modernities is constantly changing rather than staying "immobile."*
4. *The diverse cultural schemes and institutional patterns of modernity are the results from the on-going interactions of several factors. The first factor is the cosmic views and social structure shaped by the whole history of these societies; the second is historical experience and institutional patterns in these civilizations; the third is the new culture of modernity and international interaction of various political regimes in the modernization process; the fourth factor is internal tensions and conflicts concerning population structure, economic and political changes.*
5. *The essential core of modernity culture scheme involves the individual subjective activity and independence, highlights the expansion of personal freedom and institution freedom, and broadening of spaces for individual activities, creativity and independence.*
6. *The analysis of cultural diversity does not deny that the initial convergence theories of modernization and industrial society embody highly true elements—the majority of modern societies do experience convergence in some of the most basic element of their institutional aspect. For instance, in terms of social organizations, there are convergent industrial relations and modern urban*

issues; in terms of ideology, there are convergent subjects like equality and political participation, but there is a lot of difference in the treatment models of the deal and solution of these issues in the different modern societies.

4.3.2.2 Limitations of Multiple Modernities Theory

Modern societies and societies in the process of modernization are featured with far deeper diversity and pluralism than it was ever recognized before. Modernity is represented in diverse cultural schemes and institutional models. Diversity and pluralism are two major determinants for the unique features of various modern societies (Eisenstadt 2001, 2003).

Multiple modernities theory is closely related to culture and institutions that are the most important areas but not the whole of modernization.

If there are multiple modernities, then two questions will arise. First, assuming there are several kinds of modernity coexisting, then which one is the true modernity or whether there is so-called true modernity? Second, are these kinds of modernity totally heterogeneous or partially heterogeneous? If the answer is the former, then the definition of modernity is problematic; if the answer is the latter, then is it possible to extract the homogeneous elements from these kinds of modernity and constitute the true modernity.

Generally, the world frontier of modernization has its unitary aspects as well as plural aspects. From the unitary perspective, modernity is homogeneous; from the plural perspective, modernity is partially heterogeneous. It depends on at what levels and from what perspective the observation is made.

4.3.3 Globalization

Globalization theory stirred intensive attentions in the 1990s. So far, there is still no agreed definition of globalization. In a narrow sense, globalization is the global linking network of economic activities and extension of interdependence. In a broad

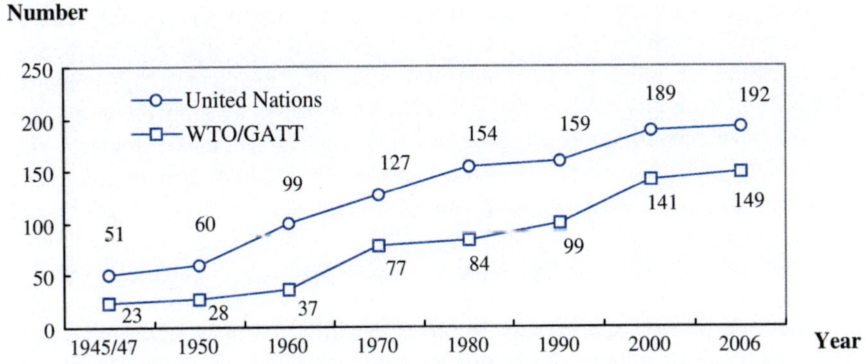

Fig. 4.17 Member number of United Nations and WTO/GATT. Source: RGCMS (2008)

Table 4.21 One theoretical interpretation of globalization

Item	Main contents
Definition	Generally, globalization refers to a highly differentiated historic process that is taking place in all areas of human activities such as economic, political, cultural, social, military, and ecological areas. It is a complex process of increasing social and economical integration and broadening, deepening, and accelerating global interrelations in all aspects of human activities. There is no unified definition of globalization
Causes	Many believe that it is a result of combined influence of many factors, including economic, technological, social, cultural, and political revolutions. For instance, decreasing transportation cost, lowering tariff barriers, rapid communication of ideas, expanding capital flows, multinational companies, increasing migrant pressures, and global issues.
Stages	Some maintain that it started after 1970s, while others think it was a process in the nineteenth century or the twentieth century. It can be divided into three stages: initial stage of globalization (1500–1850), industrial globalization stage (1850–1970), and new emerging globalization (after 1970)
Influences	Globalization has immense impact on international system, national behave, as well as all aspects of human life. The national power, international system structure, international labor division, culture, and environment will be changed; some will gain from it, and some will lose; global inequality will be enlarged, and some nations will be marginalized
Trajectory	The route of globalization, to a large extent, remains uncertain. It is a complicated historic process with civilization and democratization within globalization, the global network, and interdependence enhancing and expanding. But the ultimate state is uncertain

Note: Globalization is a prevailing phenomenon. Since 1970, it has been found in developed countries in process of the second modernization, as well as in developing countries in process of the first modernization. Globalization theory is a topic theory that could be regarded as one theory for integrated modernization

Source: RGCMS (2008)

sense, globalization is a complicated internationalization process that takes place in economic, political, cultural, social, and environmental fields. When the internationalization reaches a certain level, say, over 50% involvement rate of nations in this process, it is globalization in its true sense (Fig. 4.17). Globalization is a historical process with growing international connections. The globalization theory is a collection of all theoretical interpretations of globalization phenomena (Table 4.21). Given that modernization is a global process and globalization is an associated phenomenon of modernization, so it is acceptable to make globalization theory a topic theory of modernization theories. In fact, the two theories are separately developed, with no direct relations.

4.3.3.1 Origin and Development of Globalization

Globalization is a complicated process and also an ancient phenomenon. Far back in ancient civilization and Roman Empire Era when people were engaged in commodity and slave trade, internationalization appeared; in the sixteenth to the eighteenth century, the advancement of marine technology and expansion of colonization activities and international trade boosted the internationalization of economic activities; in the late twentieth century, especially since 1970s, the international trade and finance have experienced unprecedented changes both in quantity and quality, the global interrelations among public and private economic activities have been growing closer, and interdependence in international relations has been increasing, which all together make the new globalization (Pearson and Payaslian 1999).

As to the exact year when globalization first emerged and the development stages of globalization, there are different opinions. British scholar Herd (1999) believes that globalization can be traced back to the initial stage of human civilization, from about 10,000 years ago up till now, which can be divided into four stages: premodern globalization (from 10,000 years ago to 1500 AD), initial modern globalization (1500–1850 AD), modern globalization (1850–1945), and contemporary globalization (from 1945 up till now). Contemporary globalization is a historical confluence and concentration of globalization phenomena in all areas and all aspects. Experts from the World Bank (Collier 2002) maintained that the globalization since 1870 has experienced three climaxes: the first globalization wave (1870–1914), retrogression to nationalism (1914–1945), the second globalization wave (1945–1980), and the third globalization wave (from 1980 to now).

4.3.3.2 Main Propositions of Globalization Theory

Globalization theory is not a unitary theory, but rather an aggregation of various related ideas. Herd et al. (1999) suggested that the globalization theory should clarify five issues, that is, the definition, causes, stages, influences, and track of globalization. More specifically, it must provide a consistent conceptualization, reasonable explanations of causal logics, clear standpoint of historical stage division, definite analysis of globalization impacts, and proper thinking over development track of the process itself.

Some insisted that globalization is the ascension of globalism (Keohane and Nye 2000). *Globalization is a buzzword in 1990s, which refers to undergoing fundamental changes worldwide. By globalization and deglobalization, we mean the ascending and descending of globalism, while globalism refers to a state of the world consisting of interdependent networks among several continents. These interdependent networks can be formed through linking mediums including capitals and commodities, information and ideas, human resource and violence, and mediums concerning environment and ecology. Both interdependency and globalism are multiple-dimension phenomena: economic globalism involves remote flowing of goods, services, capitals and accompanying information and ideas in the market exchange activities; military globalism refers to the remote interdependent network that consists of using violence, threatening to use violence or likelihood to use violence; environmental globalism means the long-distance transmission of substances in the air or sea, or of suspected bacteria or genetic matters that might have adverse impacts on human health and living standard; social and cultural globalism refers to movements of ideas, information, images and people, among which the movement of people will always bring along the free flow of ideas and information; political globalism mainly involves the globalization of ideas and information about power and governance; and there are also globalism in law, science, entertainment, fashion and language. The governance of globalism is taking place in supranational, national and subnational levels, in which government divisions, private divisions and nonprofit organizations (the third division) will all play a role.*

Based on the range, intensity, speed, and influence span of globalization, Herd et al. (1999) sorted it into four types:

Type 1: Intensive globalization, featured with on-going expansion of global network in all areas and aspects from economy to culture, and high intensity, high growing pace and deep influence. The global empire in the end of nineteenth century approximates this type.

Type 2: Diffused globalization, a global network featured with broad range, high intensity, high speed, but much smaller influence. Many key aspects of contemporary economic globalization manifest this formation.

Type 3: Expansive globalization, global interrelation networks with low intensity, low speed but broad range and deep influences. The expansion of modern western imperialism is most similar to this type.

Type 4: Discrete globalization, global networks with broad range and a low level of intensity, speed and influence. The initial trade between Europe and China and the Oriental world resembles this type.

According to Herd et al. (1999), globalization has five characteristics:

1. *Globalization is regarded as a process or a set of processes rather than a static state, which reflects neither simple linear development logic, nor a world society or world community. Instead, it reflects interregional contact and exchange networks and systems. In this sense, the interweaving of national systems and social systems in a broader ranged globalization process is no equal of global integration.*
2. *Globalization can be interpreted as a structuralized and stratified process. The globalization with broad spatial span and intensity, together with the close multinational interrelations, has weaved the relationships among Communities, nations, international institutions, nongovernment organizations, and multinational companies into a compound network and ultimately shaped global orders.*
3. *Globalization is better understood as a multidimensional or differentiated social phenomenon, or a multidimensional, differentiated process. Almost all areas in social life cannot be free of the impacts from globalization processes that will be found in all areas of human society, from cultural to economic fields, from political, legal, military to environmental fields.*
4. *Globalization process is a process that crosses national boundaries, so it is inevitable that it will involve the deterritorilization and reterritorilization of social, economic and political spaces. In the context of globalization, political, social and economical spaces in local, national and continental levels will be restructured, which will not necessarily be consistent with the established legal and sovereign boundaries. Besides, as the globalization picks up strength, it'll press forward the reterritorilization of social–economical activities, and enhance the localization and nationalization of societies.*

5. *Globalization also involves the on-going expansion of power organizations and implementation scales, which means the expansion of Internet and power circulation spaces. In fact, power is the ultimate symbol of globalization with power relationships deeply rooted in its process. Globalization will see the building and rebuilding of long distance power relationships, and the location and exertion of power getting further and further from the targets who experience the power and their sites.*

4.3.3.3 Main Debates Over Globalization

The era of globalization as a concept has dawned. Vague outlines of globalization concept were found in French and American works as early as 1960s, and now this ***term has presence in major languages of the world. However, explicit definition is*** *still absent. As matter of fact, there is chance that it will degrade to a lousy cliché of this era. Globalization is a mirror of a prevailing recognition that driven by economic and technological forces, the world is being shaped into a shared social space and that developments of one region can have profound impacts upon the living chances of an individual or group in another region* (Herd et al. 1999).

Debates over globalization have touched upon the concept, reasons, dynamics, stage division, influences, and trajectory of globalization, with someone even insisting that globalization is a fairy tale rather than economic reality (Rugman 2000).

Apart from debates, there are also concerns about globalization, for instance, the worsening of global inequality, global warming, and cross-nation coordination of government, labor, and capital elements. Developed and developing nations have different concerns (Collier 2002).

Concerns of developing countries include continuous marginalization of economy, loss of government power and capacity, market exclusion, susceptibility to the changes of interests of foreign investors, lack of competitiveness, unfavorable factors for improvement of working conditions, enlarging inequality, deterioration of environment, social transfer, and imbalance of international powers. Concerns of developed countries include terrorism, inequality among the rich nations, transfer of job opportunities in manufacturing sector to low-wage countries, homogenization and convergence of developing patterns among developed nations, and so on.

Globalization is not a new phenomenon, but globalization after the1970s is unprecedented in terms of range, scale, and content as well as intensity, depth, and speed. It is not only a time sequential process but also a series of sectional states each with unique features; it is a complicated process with different nations getting involved one after another. For different nations in different levels and strengths, the process, status, and profits of their own globalization are never the same. It is natural and understandable that various views and debates over the origin of globalization emerged. Globalization has different implications for different nations and individuals. How to deal with globalization is an inevitable task for every country. For developed nations and their multinational companies, globalization is a feast; for developing nations and their domestic enterprises, it is a challenge; for ambitious countries, it is an opportunity. Definitely, developed nations and their multinational companies are the largest beneficiaries of globalization. It requires sober mind and sense of rationality to deal with globalization.

Summary

In the period from the eighteenth to the twenty-first century, modernization process can be divided into two stages, the first and second modernization, and the coordinated development of the twice modernization is integrated modernization. Different stages have different theories.

First Stage of Modernization, Also the First Modernization: Focus on Three Schools

Classical modernization theory (So 1990), born in the period between 1950s and 1960s, viewed modernization as a historical transition process from traditional agricultural society to modern industrial society. Modernity is a theoretical epitome of modernization outcome. There are nine characteristics and multiple models in modernization process. Classical modernization process took place both in pioneering societies and latecomers, with typical features including industrialization, urbanization, democratization, rationalization, social welfare, and popularization of compulsory education. Classical modernization theory has six branch theories and six schools of ideas.

Dependency theory (Seers 1981) emerged in 1960s, which attempted to illustrate the underdevelopment phenomena in periphery countries by dependent relationship between the core nations and periphery nations, and blame external causes for this underdevelopment. History has repeatedly proven that it is unlikely for different nations to advance ahead side by side, and both development and underdevelopment are inevitable in the course of modernization. Developed nations will be the modern countries and underdeveloped nations are not. Underdevelopment is an objective phenomenon in modernization process, and it is tenable to regard the theoretical explanations of underdevelopment as a branch theory of classical modernization theory.

World-systems theory (Wallerstein 1976) was a very influential development theory that emerged in 1970s. It attempted to dissect historical evolution of the world-system using variables such as dependence relations among core–semiperiphery–periphery areas, international division of labor, and class conflicts and aimed to decipher the world development history since sixteenth century. Modernization is a world movement, which will definitely stir changes in the world-system, and in turn, these changes will surely affect modernization of a nation. However, classical modernization theory itself lacks a systematic analysis at the world-system level. Considering that modernization will inevitably lead to changes in the world-system, it is acceptable to regard theoretical illustrations of the world-system in modernization process as a branch theory of classical modernization theory.

Second Stage of Modernization, Also the Second Modernization: Focus on Four Schools

Chinese scholar Chuanqi He (1998a, b, 1999) proposed the second modernization theory in the 1990s. It is not only a modernization theory in broad sense but also a civilization development theory, which has established effective relationships between modernization theory and civilization development theory. The general theory on the second modernization theory is discussed in Chap. 2 and its theoretical structure and stage theories in this chapter.

Second modernization theory as a civilization development theory is called civilization periodic transfer theory, according to which human civilization is an organic whole as well as an aggregation of the civilizations of the different nationalities and countries. Development of civilization follows a cyclical route, with accelerating development cycles and distinguished themes in each cycle. Periodic transfer includes the shifts of civilization direction, axis, and center (He 1999).

Second modernization theory as a modernization theory in broad sense is called twice modernization theory, according to which modernization is a kind of civilization changes and international competition since the industrial revolution in the eighteenth century; the frontier process of formation, development, transformation, and international interaction of modern civilization; a compound process of the innovation, selection, diffusion, and recession of civilization elements; and an international competition to catch up with, reach, and keep the world advanced level. Developed nations succeeded in achieving and keeping the world frontier while others remained as developing nations, but the two categories of nations are mobile. From the eighteenth century to the end of the twenty-first century, modernization process can be divided into two stages: the first and second modernization; moreover, there are new changes in the twenty-first century. This theory incorporates general theory, stage theories, level theories, and field theories, among which the first category is abstraction of the latter three categories, and the latter three are specific expressions of the general theory in/at different stages, levels, and fields. Together, these theories make up the theoretical edifice of general modernization theory.

Stage theory on modernization in broad sense includes first modernization theory, second modernization theory in narrow sense, and integrated modernization theory. Each stage theory incorporates general theory, level theories, field theories, and sector theories. First modernization theory is much the same as the classical modernization theory. The second modernization process has ten features: knowledgeablization, informatization, greening, innovation, globalization, decentralization, diversity, individualization, intelligentization, and lifelong learning.

Reflexive modernization theory was put forward in the 1980s by German scholar Beck (1986) who believed that modernization includes two phases: simple and reflexive modernization. Simple modernization is the transition from traditional agricultural to industrial society, while reflexive modernization refers to the transition from industrial to risk society, also the modernization of "modernization" or "remodernization." The modernity of industrial society is general in nature, called the first modernity, while the modernity of risk society is reflexive, also referred to as the second modernity, with characteristics like riskiness, globalization, individualization, diversity, and diversification.

Postmodernization theory emerged in the 1970s–1980s, but it is a collection of ideas about postindustrial society, postmodernism, and postmodernization research rather than a complete theoretical system. American scholar Bell (1973) divides human social development into three phases: preindustrial society, industrial society, and postindustrial society. French scholar Lyotard (1984) believed that as the human society enters the so-called postindustrial era and culture enters the so-called postmodern era, knowledge will change the status. British scholar Crook et al. (1992) insisted that developed nations were going through a long and multidimensional postmodernization process. American scholar Inglehart (1997) maintained that the track of history was never linear and that the transition from traditional society to modern society is modernization while the transition from modern society to postmodern society is postmodernization. To be more specific, the changes occurred in industrial nations since 1970 represent postmodernization while those in developing nations stand for modernization. The transition from modernization to postmodernization involves penetrating changes in politics, economy, perceptions on sex and family, and religion, for example, shifts from materialism to postmaterialism, from modern value to postmodern value, and from survival value to happiness value.

Continuous modernization theory is an academic idea put forward by German sociologists in 1990s. German scholar Zapf (1999) believed that from semantic perspective, the concept of "modern society" shows more vitality than any concepts like postmaterial society, postindustrial society, information society, risk society, and perceptual society and that the modernization theories, after being "quenched" by conflict theories and innovation theories, is the appropriate theoretical model to illustrate the current and future developments of the world. The continuous modernization of modern society involves technological and social innovations, accommodation, generalization and differentiation of values, social change mechanism with high social status, as well as double messages of directions constancy and structure improvement.

Integrated Modernization Is a Path for Developing Nations. Focus Is on the Discussion of Three Relevant Theories

The integrated modernization theory, first put forward by Chinese scholar Chuanqi He (2003), is a path theory for the second modernization theory, which incorporates general theories, level theories, field theories, and sector theories. This theory is fit for developing nations who has not yet completed their first modernization process. It is quite possible that through a coordinated development of twice modernizations, these countries can catch up with the advanced level of second modernization that the developed nations have already achieved. The integrated modernization path parallels the second modernization route and at same time is a new one different from that of developed countries.

Integrated modernization is a double-transition process that involves the transition from agricultural to industrial civilization and from industrial to knowledge civilization, as well as the united action of two transitions and a continuous marching toward knowledge civilization. Integrated modernization includes elements such as new industrialization, new urbanization, knowledgeablization, informatization, democratization, social welfare, greening, ecologicalization, and globalization; the dropping proportion of agricultural civilization; the first rising then declining proportion of industrial civilization; and the growing proportion of knowledge civilization and ecological civilization. It consists of three stages: industrialization-dominated stage, knowledge-dominated stage, and stage of all-round knowledgeablization; the major features include diversity, comprehensiveness, complication, riskiness, and innovativeness.

In integrated modernization process, the first modernization is not required to be completed first, but instead the twice modernizations can be carried out in parallel. In areas without conflicts of the two modernizations, we should comply with the inherent logics of development, advance step by step, reduce the occurrence of mistakes, and accelerate growth. In areas where conflicts emerge, we should adopt three principles of precedence, that is, always give priority to adherence of the inherent logics of development, compliance of the basic principles of the second modernization, and satisfaction of the development needs of the second modernization.

Multiple modernities theory is a topic theory emerged in 1990s, which is a theoretical elaboration on diversity of modern cultures and institutions as well as the multiple-linear changes of culture. According to Israel scholar Eisenstadt (2003), first, modernity should be deemed as a unique civilization with distinct institutional and cultural characteristics; second, it is better to regard the history of modernity as a story of constant developing, shaping, building, and reconstructing the plural culture scheme of modernity, the unique modern institution patterns, and diverse self-conceptions of modern society—a story of multiple modernities; third, the diverse cultural schemes and institutional patterns of modernity are the results from the ongoing interactions of several factors; fourth, the essential core of modernity culture scheme involves the individual subjective activity and independence and highlights the expansion of personal freedom and institution freedom and broadening of spaces for individual activities, creativity, and independence; and fifth, the analysis of cultural diversity does not deny that the initial convergence theories of modernization and industrial society embody highly genuine elements. Multiple modernities are closely related to the route choice of integrated modernization made by developing countries.

Globalization theory stirred intensive attentions in the 1990s. So far, there is still no agreed definition of globalization. In a narrow sense, globalization is the global linking network of economic activities and extension of interdependence. In a broad sense, globalization is a complicated internationalization process that takes place in economic, political, cultural, social, and environmental domains. When the internationalization reaches a certain level, say, over 50% involvement rate of nations in this process, it is globalization in its true sense. Globalization is a historical process with growing international connections. The globalization theory is an aggregation of all theoretical interpretations of globalization phenomena. Given that modernization is a global process and globalization is an associated phenomenon of modernization, so it is acceptable to make globalization theory a topic-specific theory of modernization theories. In fact, the two theories are separately developed, with no direct relations.

Further Reading

Beck U, Giddens A, Rush S (1994) Reflexive modernization: politics, tradition and aesthetics in the modern social order. Stanford University Press, Stanford, CA (Trans. Zhao S. Beijing: Commercial Press, 2001)

Bell D (1973) The coming of postindustrial society: a venture in social forecasting. Penguin, New York (Trans. Gao T, Wang H, Wei Z. Beijing: Xinhua Publishing House, 1997)

Bendix R (1967) Tradition and modernity reconsidered. Comp Stud Soc Hist IX 3:292–346

Black CE (ed) (1976) Comparative modernization: a reader. Free, New York (Trans. Yang Y, Chen Z. Shanghai: Shanghai Translation Publishing House, 1996)

Crook S, Pakulski J, Waters M (1992) Post modernization: change in advanced society. Sage, London

Eisenstadt SN (2003) Comparative civilizations and multiple modernities. Reflection on modernity. Brill, Leiden (Trans. Kuang X, Wang A. Beijing: SDX Joint Publishing Company, 2006)

Frank AG (1978) Dependent accumulation and underdevelopment. Monthly Review, New York, NY (Trans. Gao T, Gao G. Nanjing: Yilin Publishing House, 1999)

He C (1999) The second modernization: revelations for human civilization process. Higher Education, Beijing

He C (2003) Oriental revitalization: three roads of modernization. Commercial, Beijing

He C (2010) China modernization report outlook: 2001–2010. Peking University Press, Beijing

Herd D et al (1999) Global transformations: politics, economics and culture. Stanford University Press, Palo Alto, CA (Trans. Yang X et al. Beijing: Social Sciences Academic Press, 2001)

Inglehart R (1997) Modernization and postmodernization. Princeton University Press, Princeton, NJ
Luo R (1993) New approach to modernization. Peking University Press, Beijing
Lyotard J-F (1984) The postmodern condition: a report on knowledge. University of Minnesota, Minneapolis [1979]
OECD (1996) Science, technology and industry outlook. OECD, Paris
RGCMS (Research Group for China Modernization Strategies et al) (2010) China modernization report 2010: World modernization outline 1700–2100. Peking University Press, Beijing
Wallerstein IM (1974) The modern world-system I: capitalist agriculture and the origins of the European world-economy in the sixteenth century. Academic, New York (Trans. You L et al. Beijing: Higher Education Press, 1998)
Yin B (2001) What is modernization: a study on concepts and paradigms. People's Publishing House, Beijing
Zapf W (1999) Modernisierung, Wohlfahrtsentwicklung und Transformation (Modernization and Social Transformation), 2nd edn. Sigma, Berlin (Trans. Chen L, Lu C. Beijing: Social Sciences Academic Press, 2000)

Level-Specific Modernization 5

So many countries, so many customs (American proverb); while so many layers, so many features. Modernization takes place in almost all countries and at all layers of human civilization including the world, international, national, regional, organizational, and individual layers. As the important part of modernization science (Fig. 5.1), level-specific, stage-related, and field-relative modernization overlaps with each other. There are both similarities and differences among all level-specific modernizations. The adaptability of the core theory of general modernization varies at different levels. Country is the basic unit of modernization, so modernization at every layer is closely related to national modernization.

5.1 World Modernization

World modernization may refer to either modernization at the world level or modernization in the world (Fig. 5.2). In this section, it is the first case. In other words, world modernization here means a way how the modernization phenomenon is presented to us and a level at which we analyze the phenomenon.

5.1.1 Studies

World modernization, which started in the 1760s, is believed to last 340 years until the end of the twenty-first century, and new changes are expected in the twenty-second century. The research into world modernization can begin with early eighteenth century and be approached from three perspectives including its past, present, and future. Since world modernization is a very complex phenomenon, a multidisciplinary, multidimensional, and gradual approach should be taken so as to take advantage of the complementarities and cross-examination of multiple disciplines.

C. He, *Modernization Science*,
DOI 10.1007/978-3-642-25459-8_5,

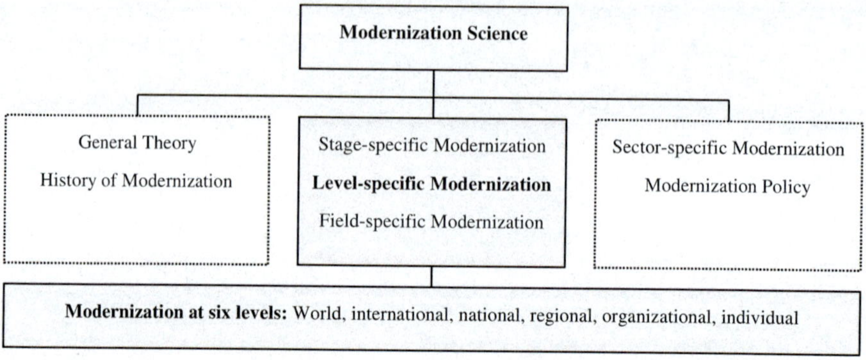

Fig. 5.1 Positioning and structure of level-specific modernization

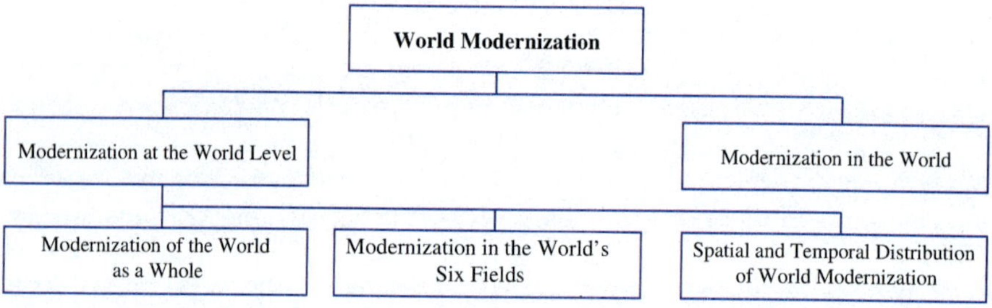

Fig. 5.2 Analytical structure of world modernization. Note: there are many explanations about world modernization. Modernization in the world includes the national and regional modernization across the world. National modernization across the world will be discussed in the third section of this chapter, while regional modernization will be addressed in the fourth section

5.1.1.1 Research Paradigm

World modernization research is the study of modernization at the world level.

(1) Research Matrix

The research objects in world modernization research include modernization of the world as a whole, modernization in the world's six fields, as well as the spatial and temporal distribution of world modernization; the research contents include the modernization of world behaviors, structures, institutions, and concepts, as well as the process, results, dynamics, and models of world modernization. All these factors can constitute a research matrix (Table 5.1).

(2) Research Method

Since world modernization study is a type of modernization study, the methodologies of modernization study can also be adopted here such as the positivist approach in sciences, the interpretivist approach in humanities, and the realist approach in policy studies. In addition, world modernization research

Table 5.1 Matrix of the world modernization study

Content		Object		
		Human civilization	Economies, societies, politics, cultures, environment, and humans of the world	Spatial and temporal distribution of human civilization
		World modernization as a whole	Modernization in the world's six fields	Spatial and temporal distribution of world modernization
Element	Behavior	Modernization of world's behaviors, structures, institutions, and ideas	Behavioral, structural, institutional, idea's modernization in the world's six fields	–
	Structure			
	Institution			
	Idea			
Aspect	Process	Process, result, dynamics, model of the world modernization	Processes, result, dynamics, model of modernization in the world's six fields	Geographical, population and level's distribution, international system of the world modernization
	Result			
	Dynamics			
	Model			

Note: the world's six fields are where human civilization is distributed (Fig. 2.1), and environment refers to natural environment only here. World modernization research also covers other contents such as analysis of human civilization frontiers, trend analysis, frontier process analysis, catch-up process analysis, international competition analysis, as well as the interaction between the elements and fields of world modernization. The modernization studies in the world's six fields will be addressed in Chap. 6

requires the use of multidimensional, multidisciplinary, and comprehensive analysis such as the coordinate analysis in modernization research.

(3) Research Purpose

World modernization study is conducted for both academic and policy purposes.

In academic terms, as an important part of modernization study at large, world modernization study is to reveal the basic facts, principles, and history of modernization at the world level and to improve and enrich the understanding of modernization and modernization theory.

In policy terms, world modernization is the international environment for national modernization so world modernization study is also to provide the theoretical base, historical experience, and policy recommendations for national and international modernization strategies.

5.1.1.2 Facts About World Modernization

China Modernization Report 2010: World Modernization Outline 1700–2100 (RGCMS 2010) gives a systematic analysis of the 300 years of history of world modernization as follows:

(1) Modernization of the World as a Whole

First, process of world modernization involves the start and stages of world modernization.

Table 5.2 Outcome of modernization of the world as a whole between 1760 and 1970 (Example)

Cross section: year 1760	Cross section: year 1970	Outcome of modernization between 1760 and 1970
The world was characterized by agriculture. Differentiation was low; gaps between nations were narrow; the international system was quite simple. Agricultural civilization was dominant; some regions were primitive societies; Industrialization and urbanization emerged in Europe. The world's average life expectancy was relatively short	The world was mixed. Differentiation was very high; gaps between nations were very wide; the international system was quite complicated. Industrial civilization was dominant but most countries were agricultural societies; some regions were primitive societies. The world's average productivity and standard of living was obviously higher over 1760; life expectancy far exceeded that of 1760. Environmental pollution was very serious	Differentiation was increased; gaps between nations were widened; the international system was more complicated. Industrial civilization was dominant; the world's average productivity and standard of living was improved; life expectancy was increased. Industrial civilization was mainly characterized by industrialization, urbanization, market orientation, democratization, secularization, rationalization, welfare society, and universal compulsory education

Source: RGCMS (2010)

No consensus has been reached on the start of world modernization yet. Currently, there are three main arguments in this regard, the third of which is most supported. The first one holds that the Scientific Revolution of the sixteenth and seventeenth centuries represents the start of world modernization; the second one believes it is the enlightenment of the seventeenth and eighteenth centuries; the third one believes it is the Industrial Revolution in England and the French Revolution of the eighteenth century. In *China Modernization Report,* the Industrial Revolution of the eighteenth century is regarded as the start of world modernization.

The next step is to identify the exact year when world modernization started. In regard, there is no consensus, either. The optional years include 1750, 1760, 1763, and 1770. Considering that James Watt began to improve the steam engine in 1763 and patented his steam engine in 1769 and that the invention and application of the steam engine is the most representative feature of the Industrial Revolution, it is desirable to take the 1760s as the starting years of world modernization.

There is still a lack of consensus on the stages of world modernization. The phasing of modernization's frontier process, discussed in Chap. 2, is actually in line with that of world modernization. Generally, world modernization consists of the preparatory stage, the first modernization, and the second modernization. The year 1970 marks the division of latter two stages.

Second, outcome of world modernization is related to the start cross section, end cross section, and time span of the process.

For example, by comparing the cross sections of years 1760 and 1970, we can find the major differences between the two sections, namely, the outcome of world modernization during the 210 years (Table 5.2). Likewise, by comparing the cross sections of years 1970 and 2005, we can find the major differences between the two

Table 5.3 Outcome of modernization of the world as a whole between 1970 and 2005 (Example)

Cross section: year 1970	Cross section: year 2005	Outcome of modernization between 1970 and 2005
The world was mixed. Differentiation was very high; gaps between nations were very wide; the international system was quite complicated. Industrial civilization was dominant, but most countries were agricultural societies; some regions were primitive societies. The world's average productivity and standard of living were obviously higher over 1760; life expectancy far exceeded that of 1760. Environmental pollution was very serious	The world was mixed. Differentiation was very high; gaps between nations were very wide; the international system became more complicated. Knowledge civilization was dominant; most countries are industrial societies; some countries are agricultural societies; some regions are primitive societies. The world's average productivity and quality of life were obviously higher over 1970; life expectancy far exceeded that of 1970. Information gap and cybercrime emerged	Differentiation was increased; gaps between nations were widened; the international system was changed. Knowledge civilization prevailed; the role of industrial civilization was weakened. The world's average productivity and quality of life were improved; life expectancy was increased. Knowledge civilization was mainly characterized by knowledge-intensity, information-intensity, globalization, greening, individualism, diversity, humanity, and universal higher education

Source: RGCMS (2010)

sections, namely, the outcome of world modernization during the 35 years (Table 5.3).

Third, driving force of world modernization is of diversity. Generally, innovation is the fundamental driving force of modernization. Other factors such as the dissemination of innovations, market competition, power competition, class competition, international competition, and capital accumulation also have considerable influence on world modernization.

Fourth, models and paths of world modernization are of diversity. Generally, between 1760 and 1970, the basic path of world modernization is the first modernization where industrialization, urbanization, and democratization progressed hand in hand. Between 1970 and 2100, world modernization takes multiple paths including the second modernization path where knowledgeablization, informatization, and greening went hand in hand; the catch-up modernization path (first modernization and then second modernization); and the integrated modernization path.

(2) Modernization in the World's Six Fields

(a) *Process of Modernization in the World's Six Fields*. Like modernization of the world as a whole, modernization in the economical, social, political, cultural, and individual fields consists of the preparatory stage, the first modernization, and the second modernization. In the ecological field, the relationship between national modernization and natural environment is a form of commensalism in the process of the first modernization where economic development causes environmental pollution but a form of mutualism in the process of the second modernization which is called "ecological modernization."

Table 5.4 Main features of the historical process of modernization in the world's six fields

Feature	Implication
Stage-based	Modernization in every one of the world's six fields is a stage-based historical process, and the modernization in most fields includes the first and second modernization
Asynchronous	Modernization in the six fields is not going simultaneously. For example, ecological modernization did not emerge until late twentieth century
Nonlinear	Modernization in economic, social, political, and cultural fields is nonlinear including the transformation from tradition to modernism and from modernism to postmodernism
Reversible	Modernization in economic, social, political, and cultural fields is partially reversible. Setbacks, interruptions, regression, and repetition may happen
Diverse	The processes and models of modernization in the world's six fields are different. It is impossible to find the same models of modernization in two different fields
Complex	The implications of the modernization in the six fields are very complicated, involving the changes in life, structure, institutions, and concepts
Prolonged	Modernization in the world's six fields is bound to be a long-term process. It is impossible to complete the process in a short period of time
Interactive	There are interactions between modernization in the six fields such as between economic and social modernization, political and cultural modernization, cultural and individual modernization, political, ecological modernization, etc.
Synergy-based	There are some synergistic effects in the modernization of the world's six fields, such as the synergies between economic, social, political, and cultural modernization
Global	Modernization in the world's six fields is a global phenomenon

Source: RGCMS (2010)

There are different views on the features of modernization in the world's six fields. The general consensus is that modernization in the six fields is stage based, asynchronous, nonlinear, reversible, diverse, complex, prolonged, interactive, synergy based, and global (Table 5.4).

(b) *Outcome of Modernization in the World's Six Fields*. At different cross sections of history, modernization in the world's six fields has different standards, levels, and characteristics. By comparing these standards, levels, and characteristics, we can find out the main outcomes of the modernization process in the six fields between the two cross sections.

(c) *Driving Force of Modernization in the World's Six Field*. The driving force varies from field to field, and the modernization in the six fields may affect each other. If the modernization in one field goes ahead of the rest, it may drive or facilitate the modernization in other fields.

(d) *Paths and Models of Modernization in the World's Six Fields*. Generally, between 1760 and 1970, the basic path of modernization in the world's five fields (excluding ecological modernization) is the first modernization; between 1970 and 2100, modernization in the six fields takes multiple paths including the second modernization path, the catch-up modernization path, and the integrated modernization path.

Table 5.5 Geographical distribution of world modernization (regions covered by modernization)

Stage		Time (year)	Europe	America	Oceania	Asia	Africa
First modernization	Preparatory stage	1300–1763	Western Europe				
	First wave	1763–1870	Western Europe	North America	Australia, New Zealand		
	Second wave	1870–1945	Europe	America	Australia, New Zealand	Part of Asia	Part of Africa
	Third wave	1946–1970	Europe	America	Oceania	Asia	Africa
Second modernization	Preparatory stage	1905–1970	Western Europe	North America			
	Fourth wave	1970–2020	Europe	America	Oceania	Asia	Africa

Note: the first modernization spread gradually; the second modernization spreads rapidly although most regions in the world have not finished the first modernization. If the beginning of the fourteenth century Renaissance is taken as the start of the first modernization, its preparatory stage lasted about 400 years. If the introduction of relativity (revolution in physics) in the twentieth century is taken as the start of the second modernization, its preparatory lasted some 60 years
Source: RGCMS (2010)

(3) Spatial and Temporal Distribution of World Modernization

(a) *The Geographical Distribution of World Modernization* (Table 5.5). In the eighteenth century, world modernization started in a small number of Western European countries. In the first half of the century, it spread to other parts of Western Europe, North America, Australia, and New Zealand. In the second half of the nineteenth century, it spread further to Eastern Europe, Southern Europe, Latin America as well as some Asian and African countries. In the first half of the twentieth century, it had covered most regions and countries in the world. In the second half of the twentieth century, the first modernization spread across the globe; the second modernization started and spread all over the world.

Where modernization started early kept a relative high level. In the past 300 years, Western Europe, the United States, Canada, Australia, and New Zealand which have maintained relatively high economic levels constitute the first cluster; Southern European countries which have lower economic levels than Western Europe but higher than other regions constitute the second cluster; Eastern Europe, Latin America, and Asia whose economic levels are very close constitute the third cluster; African countries whose economic levels are quite low constitute the fourth cluster. Asia was degraded to the fourth cluster in the first half of the twentieth century but rebounded to the third cluster again in late twentieth century.

Geographically, between 1950 and 2005, Europe had a quite high level of modernization; America and Asia had similar levels of modernization (lower than Europe but higher than Africa); Africa's modernization level was quite low.

(b) *The International System of World Modernization*. The international system has a quite stable horizontal structure in the term of the level of modernization. Between 1960 and 2005, by modernization index, the proportions of developed, moderately developed, preliminarily developed, and underdeveloped countries are 13–15%, 12–21%, 25–35%, and 33–45%, respectively (RGCMS 2010). The structure of international system in the process of modernization kept changing. Between 1960 and 2005, the number of countries completing the first modernization rose from 2 to 34, and the proportion of such countries in the international system increased from 2% to 26%; the number of countries entering the second modernization stage rose from 0 to 28, and the share of such countries increased from 0% to 21%; the number and proportion of countries as traditional agricultural societies fell (RGCMS 2010).

(c) *Population Distribution of World Modernization*. Between 1960 and 2005, the proportion of the population of advanced countries fell from about 20% to 14%; that of the population of moderately developed countries dropped from about 13% to 9%; that of the population of preliminarily developed countries grew from about 12% to 39%; that of the population of underdeveloped countries decreased from about 55% to 42%. Since 1960, the population of advanced countries has been growing at a decreasing rate; some developed countries have even witnessed negative population growth (RGCMS 2010).

Between 1960 and 2005, the population of countries completing the first modernization grew from about 200 million to some 1.1 billion, and the proportion of such population rose from around 7% to some 18%; the population of countries entering the second modernization stage increased from some 230 million to 950 million, and the proportion of such population grew from about 7% to some 15%; the population of countries still at the first modernization stage ran up from about 1.85 billion to 5.06 billion, and the share of such population rose from some 67% to 87%; the population of countries as traditional agricultural societies fell from about 920 million to 230 million, and the proportion of such population dropped from about 33% to 4% (RGCMS 2010).

5.1.1.3 Future of World Modernization

China Modernization Report 2010 also gives a systematic analysis of the 100 years of future of world modernization as follows. The linear analysis gives estimation based on the average annual growth rates in the past 25 or 15 years of 131 countries whose population combined accounts for 97% of the world's total. The twenty-first century is full of uncertainties. Due to the influence of many factors, the change of some factors may not be linear. The linear analysis of future prospects reveals some possibilities about the future.

(1) Modernization of the World as a Whole in the Twenty-First Century

Major factors that affect the modernization of the world as a whole in the twenty-first century include the development path of civilization, major scientific and technological breakthroughs, and the strategic needs of international interaction. Based on the experience in the last 300 years as well as the development trend of science and technology in the twenty-first century, we can take a look into the future of modernization of the world as a whole in the twenty-first century.

(a) *Path of World Modernization*. Unless major global crises happen, the path of world modernization in the twenty-first century will be the continuation of the twentieth century. It will be a mix path or a collection of several paths. The main paths include the second modernization path, the catch-up modernization path, and the integrated modernization path.
(b) *Level of World Modernization*. Main factors that will affect the level of modernization of the world as a whole in the twenty-first century include major scientific and technological breakthroughs, the dissemination speed of major innovations, value orientation of world cultures, and the rationality of international competition.

If the frequency of scientific and technological breakthroughs, the dissemination speed of innovations, as well as the rationality of world cultures and international competition, are not worse than those in the second half of the twentieth century and if no major crises that will change the destiny of mankind-like nuclear crisis, energy crisis, or crisis of the universe happen, we can extrapolate the modernization level of the world as a whole in the twenty-first century based on the modernization level and speed of the world in late twentieth century. But the twenty-first century is full of uncertainties, so extrapolation analysis can only provide a possibility rather than necessity or certainty.

The most advanced level of world modernization (Table 5.6) can be represented by the average level of advanced countries (high-income countries). The rough estimate is that the second modernization index of 2050 will be twice that of 2005 and that the index of 2100 will be about 2.5 times that of 2050 and about five times that of 2005.

A rough estimate is also done about the average level of world modernization. The world's average value of the level of the first modernization will reach 100 in 2020, which means that the world will have completed the first modernization in average terms (although many countries have not yet); the world's average second modernization index will stand between 85 and 103 in 2050, roughly equivalent to the level of advanced countries in 2005; the world's average second modernization index will stand between 159 and 235 in 2100, roughly equivalent to the level of advanced countries in 2050. The average level of world modernization is about 50 years behind the world's advanced level (RGCMS 2010).

Table 5.6 Most advanced level of modernization of the world as a whole (second modernization index)

Growth rate	2005	2010	2020	2030	2040	2050	2060	2070	2080	2090	2100
1.67	100	109	128	151	179	211	249	293	346	408	482
1.73	100	109	129	154	182	217	257	305	363	430	511

Note: the growth rates of the second modernization index are the average annual growth rates between 1980 and 2005 as well as between 1990 and 2005, respectively
Source: RGCMS (2010)

(2) Modernization in the World's Six Fields in the Twenty-First Century

(a) Paths of Modernization in the World's Six Fields. The paths will be consistent with the modernization path of the world as a whole. The modernization in economic, social, political, cultural, and individual fields will take mixed paths including the second modernization path, the catch-up modernization path, and the integrated modernization path. In the ecological field, the paths of interaction between national modernization and natural environment include all-round ecological modernization, integrated ecological modernization, and the ecological corrections to modernization.

(b) *Levels of Modernization in the World's Six Fields*. The frontier level of modernization in the six fields can be represented by the average level of high-income countries, and the bottom level can be represented by the average level of low-income ones. *China Modernization Report 2010* analyzes the frontier and bottom levels of modernization in the world's six fields. In the twenty-first century, international gaps may widen in about 44% of the analysis indicators and may narrow down in about 42% of the analysis indicators.

(3) Spatial and Temporal Distribution of World Modernization in the Twenty-First Century

(a) *Geographical Distribution of World Modernization*. In the twenty-first century, the modernization levels of Europe, America, and Asia are expected to remain higher than that of Africa. More countries and regions will enter the second modernization stage; fewer countries and regions will stay in the first modernization; there will be the smallest number of agricultural and primitive societies.

(b) *The International System of World Modernization*. In the second half of the twentieth century, the proportional relation between the 130 countries was roughly 15:20:28:37 or 20:25:35:50 (developed ones/moderately developed ones/preliminarily developed ones/underdeveloped ones). Thus, unless radical changes or major crises happen, the international system will maintain such a proportional structure in the twenty-first century almost, and the proportion of advance countries may be increased a little (RGCMS 2010).

The number and proportion of countries entering the second modernization stage will increase; those of countries at the first modernization stage will fall; there will be almost no countries which are still traditional agricultural societies.

(c) *Population Distribution of World Modernization*. In the twenty-first century, the population of countries completing the first modernization will grow from 1.1 billion in 2005 to about 6.9 billion in 2050 and then to 7.2–7.8 billion in 2100; the proportion of such population will increase from the 17% in 2005 to 75% in 2050 and then to 79–86% in 2100 (RGCMS 2010).

The population of countries entering the second modernization stage will grow from the 1.1 billion in 2005 to 4–4.7 billion in 2050 and then to 6.4–6.7 billion in 2010; the proportion of such population will increase from the 17% in 2005 to 44–51% in 2050 and then to 70–74% in 2100. Not considering the change in the grouping of countries, the population of advanced countries will reach

820–1,510 million, and the share of such population will stand around 11–17% (RGCMS 2010).

The population enjoying a modernized life was about one billion in 2000 and will reach 1.2–1.5 billion in 2050 and 1.2–1.7 billion in 2100. Among the 700 million of increased population enjoying a modernized life in the twenty-first century, around 500 million people may come from developing countries (RGCMS 2010).

For countries at different levels of modernization, the proportion of people enjoying a modernized life varies from country to country. Generally, the proportion is 90–95% in advanced countries and about 5% in developing countries (10–20% in moderately developed ones, 2.5–5% in preliminarily developed ones, and 0% in underdeveloped ones). If a developing country becomes a developed one, the proportion of population enjoying a modernized life will rise (RGCMS 2010).

5.1.2 Theories

World modernization theory is a type of theoretical explanation of the world's modernization phenomena and a level theory of the Second Modernization Theory and modernization science. World modernization is modernization at the world level; it has the general features of modernization and also its specific characteristics. The core theory on general modernization (Table 2.1) basically applies to world modernization.

Generally, world modernization theory includes general theory, branch theories, and relevant theories (Table 5.7). What is going to be introduced here is the general theory which covers five aspects, namely, its definition, process, results, dynamics, and models (Table 5.8).

Table 5.7 Structure of world modernization theory

Category	Theory	Main contents
General theory	Core theory	Definition, process, result, dynamics, and model of world modernization
Branch theories	Stage theory	First modernization of the world, second modernization of the world
	Field-related study	World modernization in the fields such as economy, society, politics, culture, natural environment, and humans
	Sector-related study	World modernization in the sectors such as agriculture, industry, education, science and technology, national defense, and transportation
Relevant theories	Other modernization theories	Classical modernization theory, world-system theory, second modernization theory, etc.
	Other relevant theories	Theory of civilization, theory of development, theory of evolution, theory of transformation, international study, etc.

Table 5.8 General theory on world modernization

Aspect	Main contents
Definition	World modernization, modernization at the world level, refers to the frontier changes and international differentiation of human civilization since the Industrial Revolution of the eighteenth century including the formation, development, transformation, and international interaction of modern civilization; the innovation, selection, diffusion, and exit of the elements of modern civilization; as well as the international competition, differentiation, and change of the international system in the process of catching up with, reaching, and maintain the world's advanced level
Process	World modernization is a complex which involves the change of human civilization and international differentiation, the change of the international system, and the change of world behavior, structure, institution, ideas, etc. Between the eighteenth century and the twenty-first century, the frontier process of world modernization consists of the first and the second modernization. During the process, ten principles are followed, namely, asynchronous process, uneven distribution, structural stability, early bird effect, fast–fast effect, power effect, adaptation effect, latecomer effect, creator effect, and Matthew effect
Result	The formation and spreading of modernity, diversity, and side effects including the improvement of productivity and quality of life, social progress, political democracy, cultural diversity, ecological changes, overall development of mankind, widening income gap worldwide, international differentiation, and changing international system. The horizontal structure of the international system is basically stable; the proportion of advanced countries is about 20%, the rest being about 80%. Some traditional values continue to exist and play their roles
Dynamics	Driving forces include innovation, competition, adaptability, communication, etc., at microlevel as well as national modernization, international competition, etc., at macrolevel. International competition is the asymmetric competition among four groups of countries. The competitiveness of a country is closely related to its history, current conditions, innovation, learning and game capacities, path selection, and the international system. The motivation model may be seen in Table 2.20
Model	World modernization takes different models in different periods of history. Before 1970, it was the first modernization model. Since 1970, it has taken a mixed model consisting of the first and second modernization. There is no standard model of international competition but path dependence. The international system changes but has structural stability

Note: there are many explanations about world modernization. The "world modernization" in world modernization theory refers to modernization at the world level
Source: RGCMS (2010)

5.1.2.1 Definition

World modernization, a way how modernization is presented, is modernization at the world level.

The Intension. World modernization is a sort of change of human civilization and international differentiation. It is a frontier process of the formation, development, transformation, and international interaction of modern civilization; a complex process of the innovation, selection, diffusion, and exit of the elements of modern civilization; as well as the international competition, differentiation, and

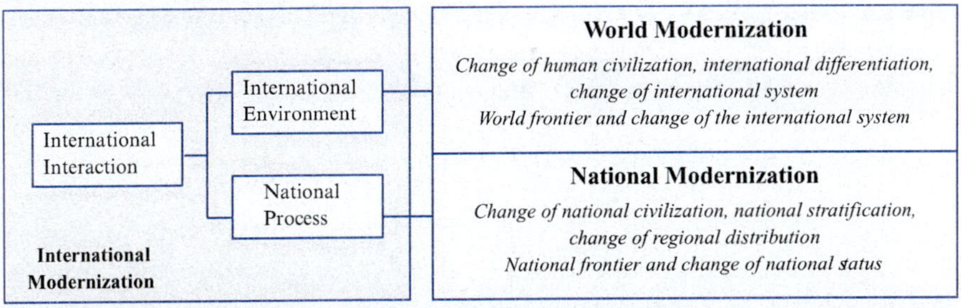

Fig. 5.3 Relations among world modernization, international modernization, and national modernization. Note: national process refers to the process of national modernization. International interaction includes international exchange, cooperation, competition, conflicts, etc. Source: RGCMS (2008)

changing international system in the process of catching up with, reaching, and maintaining the world advanced level.

The Extension. World modernization includes the modernization of the world as a whole, modernization in the world's six fields, the spatial and temporal distribution of world modernization, as well as the modernization of world's behavior, structure, institution, and ideas.

Generally, world modernization refers to the world frontiers of human civilization and the process and action to reach these frontiers. Country is the basic unit of world modernization. Modernization at the world level is just a concept for study rather than an operable unit in the development of modernization. So far, there has been not a "world government" which assumes the functions of a national government. The United Nations seems to be one like that, but it still has only some elements of a "world government."

Modernization at the world level is not an "independent unit" of modernization but just a unit of the level analysis. World modernization is related to national and international modernization. Generally, world modernization is the international environment of national modernization; national modernization is an important basis for world modernization; the interaction between national modernization and international environment is international modernization (Fig. 5.3).

5.1.2.2 Process

World modernization is a complex and long-term process. Between the eighteenth century and twenty-first century, the frontier process of world modernization consists of the first and the second modernization. The first modernization is the transformation from agricultural to industrial civilization; the second modernization is the transformation from industrial to knowledge civilization and from material to ecological civilization. Ten principles are followed in the process (Table 5.9).

Table 5.9 General principles of world modernization

No.	Principle	Content
1	Asynchronous process	World modernization in different regions and fields is asynchronous
2	Uneven distribution	World modernization is distributed unevenly in different regions and fields
3	Structural stability	The horizontal structure of the international system in world modernization is relatively stable
4	Early bird effect	Whoever goes earlier goes always ahead of others and gets more opportunities to succeed
5	Fast–fast effect	Whoever goes faster at first goes always faster and gets more opportunities to succeed
6	Power effect	Whoever is stronger at first is always more powerful and gets better right to speak
7	Adaptation effect	Countries adaptive to international competition benefit and those which cannot adapt have to pay the price
8	Latecomer effect	Latecomers can learn from and draw upon forerunners' experience and expertise and thus save the cost of time
9	Creator effect	Creators of knowledge and institutions will get due intellectual property or substantial relevant benefits
10	Matthew effect	Advanced countries become increasingly rich; underdeveloped countries get relatively more impoverished. The international income per capita gap is widened

Source: RGCMS (2010)

5.1.2.3 Result

The outcome of world modernization includes the formation and spreading of modernity, diversity, and side effects (Table 5.8).

Between 1760 and 1970, the outcome of world modernization is the formation and spreading of the first modernity and diversity. Countries are categorized into traditional and industrialized ones and developing and developed ones. There are side effects like environmental pollution and so on. Some traditional values continue to exist and play their roles.

Since 1970, the outcome of world modernization has been the formation and spreading of the first modernity, the second modernity, and diversity. Countries are categorized into traditional, industrialized, and knowledge-based ones and developing and advanced ones. There are side effects like cybercrime and so on. Some traditional values continue to exist and play their roles.

The development level of the international system keeps growing. Since 1760, the number of countries starting and completing the first modernization has been on the rise. Since 1970, the number of countries starting the second modernization and completing the first modernization has been increasing, while the number of traditional countries has been falling.

The horizontal structure of the international system is basically stable. Over the past 300 years, advanced countries make up about 20%, while developing countries, about 80%. In the last 100 years, about 90% of advanced countries have maintained their status as being developed, and some 10% of them have been degraded; about 5% of developing countries have become developed ones.

5.1.2.4 Dynamics

The driving forces of world modernization include those at micro- and macrolevels (Table 5.8).

International competition is mostly not fair in the first modernization and asymmetric in the second modernization. The competition among the four groups of countries in the twenty-first century is asymmetric international competition. The driving models may be seen on Table 2.20.

5.1.2.5 Model

World modernization takes different models in different periods of history.

Between 1760 and 1970, it took the first modernization model.

Since 1970, more and more countries have entered the second modernization stage and fewer are still at the first modernization stage. Thus, world modernization takes a mixed model involving two stages of modernization.

Since countries entering the second modernization stage are independent from those still at the first modernization stage and there is no coordination mechanism between them, it is not fair to say that world modernization is a type of comprehensive modernization which requires the coordinated development of the two stages of modernization.

There is no standard or best model for international competition. It calls for rational selection and has path dependence.

The changing international system is structurally stable. The proportions of developed and developing countries are relatively stable.

5.2 International Modernization

Generally, the survival and development of a country is restricted by two environmental factors, namely, natural environment and international environment, which overlap. If the interaction between and reciprocal coupling of national modernization and natural environment means ecological modernization, then the interaction between national modernization and international environment can be called international modernization for short (Figs. 5.3 and 5.4). International modernization is modernization at transnational level, which is a manifestation and analysis level of modernization phenomena.

5.2.1 Studies

The United Nations (UN) currently has 192 memberships. The success or failure of national modernization is determined jointly by self-endeavor and international environment. International modernization research is intended to unveil the

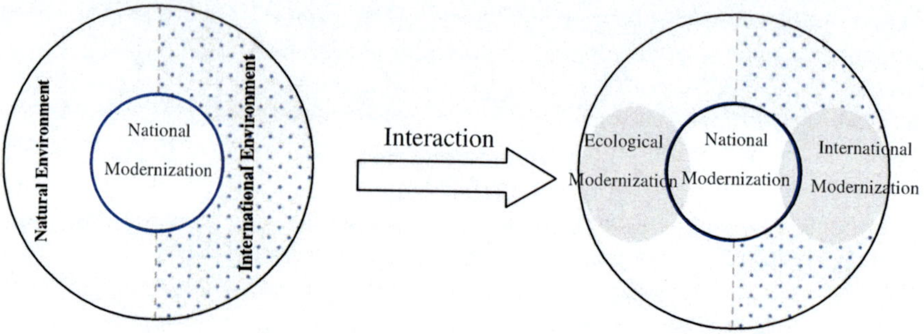

Fig. 5.4 Relationship between national modernization and international environment. Note: international modernization is the interaction between national modernization and international environment, while ecological modernization is the interaction between national modernization and natural environment. The international environment includes the international natural environment and human environment and focuses on international human environment here, while natural environment includes the internal and international natural environment and focuses on internal natural environment here. Source: RGCMS (2007)

characteristics and laws of the interaction between national modernization and international environment and provide a theoretical basis and international reference for making international strategies supporting national modernization, and it can be regarded as a branch of international relations or international politics.

5.2.1.1 Research Paradigm

International modernization study is the modernization study at transnational level.

(1) Research Matrix

The research object of international modernization study is the interaction between national modernization and international environment ("international interaction" for short), which includes international interaction at different levels and in different fields. Research contents include the modernization of international behavior, structures, institutions, and concepts, as well as the process, results, dynamics, and models of international modernization, which make up a research matrix (Table 5.10).

International environment refers to a summation of external factors for national modernization, which is generally divided into international natural environment and international human environment. The international natural environment, the part of the natural environment, is further divided into the geographic environment and ecological environment. International human environment is further divided into international economic, social, political, cultural, and individual environments. International environment can be also divided into world environment, transnational regional environment, and neighboring environment by scope; into general environment and the environment in different fields by content; and into historical environment, present environment, and future environment by time.

Table 5.10 Matrix of the international modernization study

Content		Object		
		International interaction	International interaction at different levels	International interaction in different fields
		International modernization	World, transnational region, neighbor, country	Economy, society, politics, culture, natural environment, humans
Element	Behavior Structure Institution Idea	Modernization of international behavior, structure, institution, and idea	Modernization of international behavior, structure, institution, idea at four levels	Modernization of international behavior, structure, institution, idea in six fields
Aspect	Process Result Dynamic Model	Process, result, dynamics, model of the international modernization	Processes, result, dynamics, model of international modernization at four levels	Process, result, dynamics, model of international modernization in six fields

Note: research on field-relative international interaction also includes the studies on geographic influence

International interaction refers to the interaction between national modernization and international environment. According to different interaction objects, international interaction can be divided into level-specific and field-specific international interaction. Level-specific international interaction includes the interaction a country has with the world, transnational regions, neighboring countries, and other countries. Field-specific international interaction occurs in six fields including economy, society, politics, culture, ecology, and individuals, which also includes geographic influence.

Many international relations scholars think that the real world is an anarchic international system which is quite similar to the self organization system defined in the systems theory and can be researched according to the principles of the self-organization theory. Most modern countries open up to the outside world; they are open systems exchanging materials and energy with the external environment. The interaction between national modernization and international environment includes the exchange of materials and energy or specifically the flows of population, capital, commodities, pollution, information, and knowledge. Such interaction determines the change in the international system structure and in the model of national behavior. From the perspective of the systems theory, the material flow, energy flow, system structure, and the change of national behavior are also research contents of international modernization (Fig. 5.5).

(2) Research Method

International modernization research is a type of modernization study, where the methodology of modernization study can be employed.

International modernization research requires multidimensional analysis, hierarchy analysis, case studies, interdisciplinary research, and comprehensive research, including the coordinate analysis of modernization study. The focus of

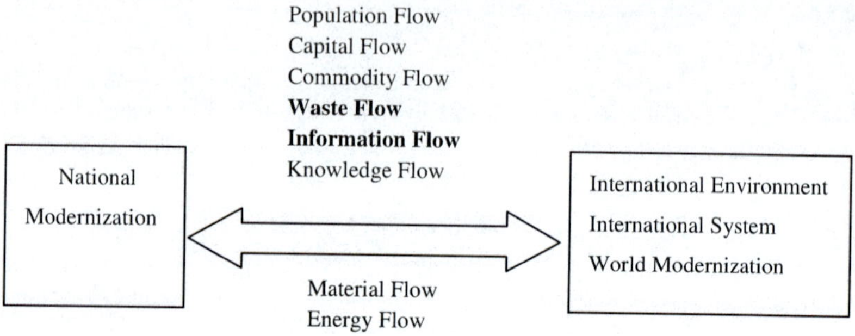

Fig. 5.5 Six flows between national modernization and international environment. Note: commodity flow includes the flows of goods and services. Other flows include the flows of ideas, species, pathogens, air, water, etc. Source: RGCMS (2007)

hierarchy analysis is placed on international system, transnational, and national layers.

The international system in international modernization study is different from that in international relations and international politics. The latter is an international system based on national strength and power distribution, while international institutions and cultures also have an influence, more exactly increasing influence, on national behavior. The international system in international modernization study is one based on national level of development and the distribution thereof, while national strength and power distribution also play an important part. The relationship between national level of development and national strength is complex and nonlinear. The international system based on national strength and the international system based on national level of development represent two analysis perspectives or two dimensions of the international system. International modernization research focuses on the international system based on national level of development while analyzing the role and influence of the international system based on national strength.

(3) Research Purpose

International modernization research is for both academic and policy purposes.

International modernization research is an important aspect of modernization study, with the aim of discovering the basic facts, characteristics, and principles of international modernization and enriching the modernization theory through systematic and overall research into the interaction between national modernization and international environment. International modernization research serves as an integral part of international relations research.

The success or failure of national modernization is determined by internal and external causes. Countries that hope to achieve and maintain success in modernization undoubtedly need appropriate international strategies to direct and effect their interaction with international environment. The facts and principles unveiled by international modernization research can provide a theoretical basis and references for countries to make international strategies.

5.2.1.2 Facts About International Modernization

China Modernization Report 2008: International Modernization Study (RGCMS 2008) gives the time series analysis, cross-sectional analysis, and country-relative analysis of the 300-year (1700–2005) historical process of international modernization, covering five fields (economy, society, politics, culture, and ecology) and four elements (international interaction, structure, system, and concepts). The time series analysis is at international system and national levels, and the cross-sectional analysis covers two dimensions (national level and national strength) and eight cross sections. Below is a brief introduction to the international interaction and historical experience in four fields. The followings came from this report:

(1) International Interaction in the Economic Field

The international interaction in the economic field was continuous and active, occurring in different sectors such as agriculture, industry, and service sector, and in diverse aspects, like raw material, production, market, capital, technology, information, and labor service, in a variety of types or manifestations (Fig. 5.6). Generally, the international interaction is of diversity in terms of form, type, and degree. For example, it can be divided into cooperation, exchange, competition, and conflict according to its nature, and into low, intermediate, and high-level interaction according to its intensity. Here, the focus is placed on the analysis of international trade, investment, and debts.

From the eighteenth century onward, the proportion of international trade in GDP increased, with a changing trade structure; the proportion of international investment in GDP rose, but differed considerably from country to country. From the nineteenth century, international debts rose, with developing countries being debt-ridden. In the twentieth century, the number of multinational companies grew, and tariffs declined on average; the proportion of international trade in GDP was not obviously related to national level and strength, but had positive correlation with national influence and competitiveness; developed countries contributed to about 80% of the international investment, while the rest contributed 20%.

Intensity \ Nature	Cooperation	Exchange	Conflict
High	Economic union, debt exemption or reduction, FTZ or FTA	Globalization, liberalization	Trade war, financial war
Intermediate	Investment, economic aid, training, preferential duty	Trade, negotiation	Trade transaction, threat, tariff increase
Low	Multinational corporation, economic cooperation	Personnel exchange, information exchange	Dumping, monopoly, infringement

Fig. 5.6 Type and intensity of international interaction in the economic field

(2) International Interaction in the Social Field

The international interaction in the social field occurred in different social sectors such as population, education, health, social security, transportation and communications, and tourism, as well as in different aspects like movement of population, educational exchange, health cooperation, information exchange, and international crime, involving a variety of types or manifestations (Fig. 5.7). Here, the focus is placed on the analysis of international migration, international tourism, and international organization.

From the eighteenth century on, international migration increased at fluctuating rates. In the twentieth century, international migration changed in the direction of flow, with developed countries becoming countries of net immigration. In the late twentieth century, the percentages of aliens, as well as alien students, in developed countries rose, and the size of international tourism continued to expand. International organizations have increased in quantity since the eighteenth century. Currently, the number of NGOs (nongovernmental organizations) is about ten times that of IGOs (intergovernmental organizations).

(3) International Interaction in the Political Field

Generally, the political sphere involves such aspects as national territory, sovereignty, government, distribution of powers, national interests, national security, military affairs, diplomacy, and so on. International interaction in the political field involves political elements of actors, the process of international interaction, international politics, international political system, and so on; interactive forms include international recognition, respect for sovereignty, respect for territorial integrity, international security, international war, international blockade, international threat, international sanction, trade in arms, international assistance, diplomacy, intelligence, intergovernmental organizations, international exchange, and international cooperation (Fig. 5.8). Below is a discussion of international war, trade in arms, and international assistance.

The number of modern states and intergovernmental organizations increased from the eighteenth century onward, and in the second half of the twentieth century, the number of established diplomatic relations and international interdependence grew. From the eighteenth century, the frequency of international war did not fall, but differed greatly from country to country; the distribution of international wars

Intensity	Cooperation	Exchange	Conflict
High	Education recognition, criminal repatriation, international aid	International migration, international labor service	Migrant repatriation, alien persecution, port blockage
Intermediate	Education cooperation, international police, refugee accepting	International tourism, educational exchange	Alien withdrawal, navigation interruption, refugee refusal
Low	Disease control, international communications	Health exchange, information exchange	International crime, entry discrimination

Nature

Fig. 5.7 Type and intensity of international interaction in the social field

Intensity	Cooperation	Exchange	Conflict
High	Allying, stationing troops, national civic treatment	Information sharing, trade in arms	War, interference, blockade, containment
Intermediate	Establishing diplomatic relations, assistance, training, joint military exercise	Visits, dialogues, negotiations	Breaking off diplomatic relations, sanction, retaliation, threat
Low	International peacekeeping, cooperation statement, declaration	Personnel exchange, information exchange	International warning, presenting a note, attention

Nature

Fig. 5.8 Type and intensity of international interaction in the political field

Intensity	Cooperation	Exchange	Conflict
High	Cultural investment, intellectual property protection	Free trade in culture	Cultural and religious conflict
Intermediate	Cooperation in science and technology, cultural heritage protection	Exchange in literature and art and publication	Conflict over intellectual property, hostile publicity
Low	Cooperation in sports, biodiversity protection	Exchange in science and technology and sports	Cultural smuggling, cultural discrimination

Nature

Fig. 5.9 Type and intensity of international interaction in the cultural field

and the structure of belligerent countries changed. In the late twentieth century, the international trade in arms fluctuated. In the last 40 years of the twentieth century, the total foreign assistance that developing countries received as well as per capita international aid increased, while there was a decrease in its proportion in the GDPs of developed countries and of recipient countries.

(4) International Interaction in the Cultural Field

International interaction in the field of culture, with a variety of types or manifestations, occurred in different cultural sectors such as press, publication, literature and art, sports, science and technology, as well as in diverse aspects like cultural trade, cultural exchange, athletics, intellectual property, and cooperation in science and technology (Fig. 5.9). Below is an analysis of cultural trade, technology trade, and international sports.

In the late twentieth century, international trade in information and culture developed rapidly, and the export of high technologies saw fast growth, with technology trade growing faster than economic growth; technology trade of developed countries accounted for over 90% of the world's total, while that of low-income countries was <1%. In the twentieth century, international exchange in sports developed rapidly, and that in science and technology as well as international conferences saw fast growth.

The analysis of international interaction at national level covers the international interaction at different levels and in different fields.

5.2.1.3 Historical Experience of International Modernization

China Modernization Report 2008 gives an analysis and summary of the historical experience of international modernization in the past 300 years as follows:

(1) General Experience of International Modernization

First, we cannot act blindly for international modernization. The structure of the international system is of relative stability. Without an adequate material basis and an appropriate international environment, attempts to change the international structure and world order unilaterally can hardly lead to success. Though the theory of hegemony cycle transfer is much criticized, the hegemony cycle is closely linked to the stability of the international system.

Second, we need patience for international modernization. A country may change its international status, but this is not probable in a short or medium term. For example, only a few countries successfully shifted from economically developing countries to developed ones (classified by GDP per capital); among them were the United States in the eighteenth century, Australia, New Zealand, and Argentina in the nineteenth century, as well as Finland, Japan, and Singapore in the twentieth century.

Third, the role of international modernization cannot be overestimated. Success or failure of modernization of a country is determined by the country's endeavor and its international environment. International modernization cannot determine success or failure of countries, but it can exert an influence on their success or failure and accelerate their differentiation. Generally, international dependence may be used as a short-term strategy, but not a long-term one.

Fourth, internal causes cannot be overlooked in international modernization. In the process of international modernization, in most cases, failure of developing countries is attributed largely to internal factors. Among internal causes which may lead to failure, the roles of geographic conditions, social systems, cultural beliefs, and the role of people cannot be underestimated. In the process of international interaction, some people may betray their countries or compatriots for personal benefit or seek private gains at public expense. Though the number of people of this kind is quite small, harm caused can be devastating.

Fifth, international modernization is not something of wishful thinking. The international interaction of international modernization is two-way behavior, and wishful thinking does not work. In the process of international modernization, pursuing international cooperation and communication unilaterally is likely to draw a blank at great cost, as if a person is lovesick. According to the interest interaction rule, interests are the decisive factor of international interaction, and the international interaction built on mutual benefit is likely to be lasting and trustworthy.

Sixth, we cannot put the cart before the horse when it comes to international modernization. National modernization is the ultimate goal, while international modernization is a measure. International modernization is a way of increasing the national level of development, rather than the goal. International modernization is not the goal, nor is the level of internationalization a performance indicator. The level of internationalization is only an indicator for analysis and reference. We cannot seek internationalization and globalization in a one-sided way. And internationalization and globalization must be geared to the strategic needs of national modernization as well as to national interests.

Seventh, we cannot expect perfection in terms of international modernization. In many ways, international modernization is an international game featuring information imperfection, status asymmetry, and rapid environment changes. It may be a zero-sum game or a non-zero-sum one. In some cases, a seemingly desirable international interaction is likely an international trap. International misleading and fraud happen from time to time. There is no best model, but only rational choice, for international interaction.

Eighth, lagging behind may be vulnerable, and agricultural civilization is powerless against industrial civilization. A backward small country may draw no attention, but a backward big country is frequently the target others nibble away at. An underdeveloped big country cannot be a major player in the world stage and, often, the object of division by developed countries. What was divided were political interests including land and right that in the eighteenth and nineteenth centuries, economic interests including resources and markets in the twentieth century will be strategic interests including values and knowledge in the twenty-first century. In a knowledge era, someone believe that developed countries are likely to become brain countries and underdeveloped countries the trunk ones and agricultural civilization is powerless to compete with industrial civilization, while the latter can hardly rival knowledge civilization.

Ninth, we should look at international trade and investment in a rational way. The percentages of international trade and international investment in GDP are not the higher the better, but require rational analysis. According to statistics in 2004, there is no obvious relationship between the percentage of international trade and the national income per capital and between the percentage of foreign investment stock and the national income per capita, and that there is significantly positive correlation between the percentage of overseas investment stock and the national income per capita and between the percentages of foreign and overseas investment stock and the national income per capital. Countries may be put into three categories according to the percentages of international trade and international investment in GDP, namely, countries with high levels of trade and investment (both above 80%), countries with moderate levels of trade and investment (both at about 60%), and countries with low levels of trade and investment (both generally below 40%). The distribution of countries in terms of international trade and investment is unbalanced, and there is no simple linear relationship between trade and investment models and the development levels of countries.

Finally, we must be on full alert to international wars. According to statistical analysis on international war, if differences in the size of wars are not considered, the frequency of international wars in the past two centuries has never fallen. International competition in the twenty-first century, some scholars believe, will continue to be fierce; the competitions for strategic resources, space resources, and cyberspace are likely to escalate, and the risk of international wars still exists.

Therefore, peace-loving countries need to be prepared for promoting peaceful development on the one hand and for keeping high alert to and making preparations for international wars on the other.

(2) Country-Relative Experience of International Modernization

In the past 300 years, some countries have succeeded, while others have not. Country-specific experience of international modernization is worthy of attention. There are four pieces of experience that are common among the United Kingdom (UK), the United States (USA), Japan, and Latin American countries.

(a) *Be Adept at Grasping International Opportunities.* The UK, the USA, Germany, and Japan are all adept at grasping international opportunities. The UK seized the historical occasion of Industrial Revolution in the eighteenth and nineteenth centuries to become the world's superpower. After becoming a European power through the second industrial revolution in the nineteenth century, Germany took advantage of two industrial revolutions in the twentieth century to become a developed country. Japan realized its economic takeoff in the nineteenth century by taking advantage of the diffusion of the second industrial revolution and the postwar recovery in the twentieth century by seizing the opportunities of the third industrial revolution and cold war, thereby becoming an economic power and developed country. By grasping the opportunities of the cold war and second industrial revolution, South Korea approached the level of developed countries in the end of twentieth century. In the fourth industrial revolution in the twentieth century, Finland and Ireland became developed countries with the world's top competitiveness.

(b) *Cooperation with Developed Counties is Conducive to Development.* "Keep good men company and you shall be of the number" is an English proverb which applies to the international modernization. Cooperation between developed countries and between developing and developed countries can improve national levels of development. Such examples include Japan, South Korea, and Singapore. The case of Japan provides some food for thought. Both the time and origin of modernization in Japan and China were roughly the same. In the 1860s or so, both countries were opened up by Western powers by force, but they chose different paths which turned out to bring considerably different results. Japan actively promoted overall modernization, gave equal emphasis on institutional and industrial modernization, and learned from the systems, cultures, and technologies of the West. China launched the Westernization Movement, adopted the pattern of industrial modernization, learned from Western modern technology and military, but overlooked institutional modernization. Thirty years later, Japan became an industrial power in the East by seizing the opportunity of the diffusion of industrial revolution, while China became a semifeudal and semicolonial country. In the second half of the twentieth century, Japan, South Korea, and Singapore saw rapid growth in technology and economy in partnership with developed countries and approached or reached the levels of developed countries one after another.

(c) *Attaching Importance to Science, Technology, and Education.* The USA, Germany, and Japan are countries giving top priority to education. Developed national education and higher education have helped to improve the competence of their people, which is an important condition for the pursuit of modernization. The UK, the USA, Germany, and Japan all attach importance to the roles of science and technology. Though these countries have distinctive science and technology systems, for example, the basic research system of the UK, the knowledge and technology innovation systems of the USA and Germany, and the technology innovation system of Japan, the roles that science and technology play in ensuring the success of these countries and maintaining their leading positions in the world are almost alike.

(d) *The Synergy of Internal and External Factors.* The success of the UK, the USA, Germany, and Japan is all dependent on the synergy of internal and external factors. External factors include historical opportunities in world development as well as favorable changes in international environment; internal factors include rational policies and measures adopted to promote modernization across the board. Latin American countries started modernization early, but there has been no case of complete success so far. The Dependency Theory alleges that the underdevelopment of Latin America was the inevitable result of Western capitalism. This view is reasonable in some way, but it is improper to attribute the underdevelopment of Latin America totally to external factors. Within Latin American countries, political corruption and turmoil, gap between rich and poor and social split, stressing economy while overlooking society are common phenomena, which also play a part in causing the underdevelopment there.

5.2.2 Theories

The international modernization theory gives theoretical explanation for international modernization phenomena and is a level theory in the second modernization theory and modernization science. Part of the core theory of the general modernization (Table 2.1) also applies to international modernization.

Generally, the international modernization theory includes the general theory, branch theories, and relevant theories (Table 5.11). Here, the focus is on the discussion of the general theory which covers five aspects including the definition, process, results, dynamics, and models of international modernization (Table 5.12). Raised by Chinese scholar Chuanqi He, the international modernization theory is built on the analysis and systematic theoretical summarization of the 300-year process of international modernization. It is an alternative theoretical explanation of the interaction between national modernization and international environment between the eighteenth and the twentieth centuries and can be a supplement to the international relations theory.

Table 5.11 Structure of international modernization theory

Category	Theory	Main contents
General theory	Core theory	The definition, process, result, dynamics, and model of international modernization
Branch theories	Stage theory	International interaction in the process of the first modernization, dependence theory, and world systems theory; international interaction in the process of the second modernization, globalization theory, etc.
	Field-related study	International interaction in the fields such as economy, society, politics, culture, humans, and natural environment
	Sector-related study	International interaction in the sectors such as agriculture, industry, education, science and technology, national defense, and transportation
Relevant theories	Other modernization theories	Ecological modernization theory, reflexive modernization theory, second modernization theory, etc.
	Other relevant theories	International relations theory, social interaction theory, conflict theory, game theory, regional cooperation, international study, etc.

Note: generally, international relations study is the study of the international environment and interaction based on national strength (from the perspective of international politics or politics), and international modernization study is the study of the international environment and interaction based on national level of development (from the perspective of modernizations). They both have their own emphasis and can be tested and supplemented by each other
Source: RGCMS (2008)

5.2.2.1 Definition

International modernization, a manifestation of modernization, is modernization at transnational level.

The Connotation. International modernization is an interaction between national modernization and international environment, as well as an international interaction in the process of modernization. International modernization is a complex process and transnational behavior, occurring at multiple levels and in many fields.

The Denotation. International modernization includes international interaction in the process of modernization at different levels and in different fields and the modernization of international behavior, structure, institution, and ideas. It involves three aspects: national modernization, international environment, and international interaction (Table 5.13; Fig. 5.10).

There are different types of international environment, for example, level-specific environment, field-specific environment, and time environment (Fig. 5.11). There are different types of international interaction, such as level-relative interaction (interaction with level-relative environment), field-relative interaction (interaction with field-relative environment), and geographic influence. There are also different ways of international interaction, such as international cooperation, international exchange, international conflict, and international competition (Fig. 5.11).

Table 5.12 General theory on international modernization

Aspect	Main contents
Definition	International modernization is transnational modernization, an interaction between national modernization and international environment, and an international interaction in the process of modernization
Process	International modernization is a historical process, including the changes of the behavior, structure, institution, and ideas of international interaction; in the terms of eighteenth to twenty-first century, international modernization can be divided into two stages, namely, international modernization in the age of industry (1760–1970) and that in the age of knowledge (1970–2100). There are four principles (synergy, interest-driven interaction, path selection, and quadrant interaction) as well as eight rules (acting and reacting force, different effects, like attracts like, good infection, goal orientation, national interests, maxmini, and bounded rationality) on the process
Result	The outcome of international modernization includes three types of change: national changes, for example, in national behavior, international status, and ideology; changes of the international environment, for example, in international structure, institutions, and ideology; and changes of international interaction, such as international behavior
Dynamics	Driving forces of international modernization include human nature, national interests, capital accumulation, international competition, epoch-making innovation, informatization, globalization, strategic resources, environmental pressure, etc. International interaction in different periods and of different types is different in the structure of driving forces
Model	There are diverse paths and models for international modernization, which have starting-point dependence and path dependence and are subject to the historical, geographic, level, strength, position, institutional, and ideological factors. Four basic paths: international cooperation, exchange, competition, and conflict. Four basic models: comprehensive interaction, lateral interaction, upward interaction, and downward interaction (vertical interaction)

Source: RGCMS (2008)

There can be many types of international interaction according to nature and purpose (Table 5.14). Sometimes, the nature and purpose of interaction does not completely match the outcome of interaction. The classification of interaction purpose and nature has only relative meanings.

If mutualism and synergy are regarded as the basic concepts of international interaction, the implications of international modernization will be enriched. In such an ideal scenario, international modernization refers to the interaction and mutualism between national modernization and international environment.

5.2.2.2 Process

The process of international modernization may be divided into two major stages. Theoretically, they are international modernization in the first modernization and that in the second modernization (Table 5.15). From the perspective of policy, they are international modernization in the age of industry and that in the age of knowledge (Table 5.16). The two stages are different in contents and features.

The process of international modernization roughly has 12 features: universality, diversity, stage-relative, complexity, evolution, nondetermination, differentiation between countries, effect of national level, effect of national strength, continual

Table 5.13 Main concepts of international modernization

Concept	Main contents
National modernization	Modernization at national layer, including modernization in a country as a whole, modernization in the six fields of the country, and the change in spatial and temporal distribution of national modernization, etc.
International environment	The sum of external factors of national modernization, including systems and concepts regarding world modernization, international system, and international interaction. It has a variety of forms of classification, for example, level-specific environment, field-specific environment, historical environment, present environment, and future environment
International interaction	In the process of modernization, the action a country takes toward other country and international environment in an alternate or exchange way, or its response to the action or change of other country and international environment. It is an important aspect of national modernization
International status	A country's position generally accepted in the international system, which can be defined according to the country's relative level or strength
Status quadrant	International status determined by national level and strength can be shown in a diagram with four quadrants: the first quadrant (high level and high strength), represented by the USA; the second quadrant (high level and low strength), represented by Luxemburg; the third quadrant (low level and high strength), represented by India; and the fourth quadrant (low level and low strength), represented by Burundi
International differentiation	The change of a country in international division of labor, international status, and international gap, including the country's role in international division of labor and market, international status division, and the widening of international gap and difference, as well as national stratification and mobility
National stratification	A country's grade, level, and change thereof in the hierarchy of the international system, including national mobility
National mobility	The change of a country's status in international system. It is the change from one international grade to another, or in international rankings, with certain probability
International structure	Way of association of various factors (e.g., countries) of the international system, with relative stability
	Development level: developed, moderately developed, preliminarily developed, and underdeveloped countries
	National strength: world powers, moderate powers, elementary powers, and weak countries
	National scale: large, medium-sized, small-sized, and mini countries

Source: RGCMS (2008)

existence of international war, gradually enhanced international cooperation, and effect of industrial civilization (Table 5.17). The age of industry is different from the age of knowledge in terms of the features of international modernization.

There are four principles on the process of international modernization, namely, synergy, interest-driven interaction, path choice, and quadrant interaction (Table 5.18). And they are theoretical explanations for the meaning, process, selection, and quadrant interaction.

A comparison of international status between two countries in the international status quadrants roughly leads to three results: they have roughly the same

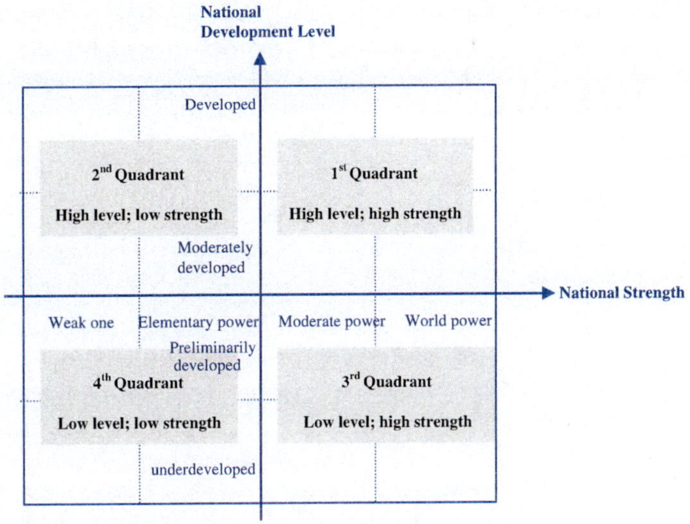

Fig. 5.10 Quadrants of international status. Source: RGCMS (2008)

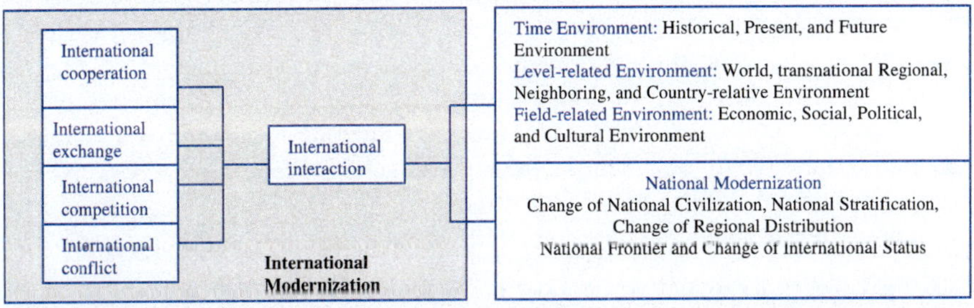

Fig. 5.11 Environments and paths of international modernization. Source: RGCMS (2008)

Table 5.14 Main types of international interaction

Classification by	Types of international interaction	Classification by	Types of international interaction
Motive	Goodwill, neutral, hostile interaction	Nature	Equal, unequal interaction
Outcome	Mutual-benefit, biased, mutually harmful interaction	Norm	Institutional, noninstitutional interaction
Meaning	Strategic, tactic, conventional interaction	Scope	All-round, partial interaction
Level	High-level, moderate, low-level interaction	Attitude	Active, passive interaction

Source: RGCMS (2008)

Table 5.15 Two stages of international modernization in theory

Item	International modernization in the process of the first modernization	International modernization in the process of the second modernization
Approximate time	1763–1970	1970–2100
Competition focus	Power, markets, resources, religion, territory, colonies, etc.	Knowledge, information, markets, strategic resources, outstanding talents, etc.
Main features	Hegemony competition, competition for existence, less international cooperation, etc.	Competition in cooperation, development competition, more international cooperation, etc.
International wars	Frequent	Less frequent between countries in the second modernization stage
Relevant theories	Dependency theory, world systems theory, realism, etc.	International modernization theory, interdependence theory, etc.

Source: RGCMS (2008)

international status, the international status of one country is higher than that of another, or the international status of one country is lower than that of another. Corresponding to its relative international status, a country's international interaction may have three forms: lateral interaction happens when its international status is roughly the same as another country's, downward vertical interaction happens when its international status is higher than another country's, and upward vertical interaction occurs when its international status is lower than another country's (Fig. 5.12). Policy for downward interaction is not thoroughly the same as policy for upward interaction. A country with downward interaction generally has superiority in psychology, development level, and strength, as well as greater initiative and option, while a country with upward interaction is generally disadvantaged in psychology, development level, and strength, as well as relative option and dependence possibility.

As a matter of fact, the correlation between national development level and national strength may form multiple combinations, making national behavior in the international status quadrants rather complex. Notwithstanding, there are two basic types of international interaction in the international status quadrants: lateral interaction and vertical interaction. For a specific country, vertical interaction can be either upward or downward.

There are eight rules on the process of international modernization: acting and reacting force, different effects, like attracts like, good spreading, goal orientation, national interests, maxmini, and bounded rationality (Table 5.19). These rules are relative and have many exceptions such as activities by international humanitarian organizations.

5.2.2.3 Result

The direct outcome of international modernization is reflected in three aspects: change of national modernization, including in national development level, international status, and international concepts; change of international environment,

Table 5.16 Two stages of international modernization in reality

Item	Industry age	Knowledge age
Rough time	1763–1970	1970–2100
Competition focus	Similar to international modernization in the process of the first modernization	Between countries in the second modernization stage: Knowledge, information, culture, markets, strategic resources, outstanding talents, etc.
		Between countries in the first modernization stage: power, capital, markets, resources, territory, religion, etc.
		Between countries in different stages: national independence, resources, markets, human rights, strategic interests, etc.
Main features		Between countries in the second modernization stage: development competition, mutualism, frequent war, etc.
		Between countries in different stages: hegemony competition, development competition, international cooperation, frequent war, etc.
International wars		Between countries in the second modernization stage: generally, no war or less frequent war
		Between countries in different stages: widespread international wars; no decrease in frequency
Relevant theories		International modernization theory, globalization theory, etc.

Note: countries in different stages refer to countries in the first and second modernization, respectively
Source: RGCMS (2008)

including in international structures, institutions, and concepts; and change of international interaction, including in the process, features, nature, and scale of international interaction.

The role of international modernization is manifested at three levels: change at national level, for example, in national behavior, national development level, international status, and concepts; change at international system level, for example, in national stratification and the structure, institutions, and concepts of international system; and change at transnational level, for example, in international differentiation and international interaction.

International modernization has three national objectives: lifting the national development level and international status, which is the ultimate goal; improving international environment to maintain a favorable international environment for itself; and increasing the ability of international interaction to ensure fulfillment of the previous two objectives.

Table 5.17 Twelve features of international modernization

Feature	Explanation
Universality	International interaction in modernization is a universal phenomenon as well as objective reality
Diversity	International interaction occurs at all levels and in all fields and aspects of modernization
Stage-relative	The process of international modernization can be divided into two major stages, with different contents and features in different stages
Complexity	International interaction depends on multiple factors, rather than some single factor. Among others, geographic locations, competence of the people, science and technology, national awareness, international structure, international systems, and international concepts all have an important influence on international interaction
Evolution	International modernization is a process of continual evolution, and international interaction shifts gradually from competition for existence to that for development and from strength competition to that in development level, with the ideal of mutualism and synergic development
Nondetermination	International modernization is an important influencing factor, rather than a decisive factor, that makes or breaks a country
Differentiation between countries	Differences in international modernization exist widely between developed and developing countries, between big and small countries, as well as among developed countries, developing countries, big countries, and small countries
Effect of national level	National development level has a great influence on the international interaction and national interests in national modernization
Effect of national strength	National strength has a great influence on the international interaction and national interests in national modernization
Existence of international wars	International war exists widely and in a long-standing way. But in the last 30 years of the twentieth century, there was no war fought between developed countries, but between developed and developing countries as well as between developing ones
Enhanced international cooperation	International cooperation and interdependence tends to gain momentum
Effect of industrial civilization	Traditional agricultural civilization is powerless against industrial civilization

Source: RGCMS (2008)

5.2.2.4 Dynamics

International modernization is the synergy of diverse factors, including humanity, interests, competition, science and technology, etc. First, international interaction is a kind of human behavior, while all human behavior is governed by humanity and values (biological instinct and socialization). Second, international behavior is a kind of national behavior, while all national behavior is driven by interests which may be national interests, government interests, group interests, or the interests of a group of people. Third, competition is a basic form of international interaction and also the driver of international interaction; because strategic

Table 5.18 Four principles of international modernization

Principle	Main contents	Remark
Synergy	Performance of national modernization is determined by national modernization and international environment. International interaction of national modernization does not decide the rise or fall of a country, but affects its success or failure and accelerate its differentiation	Meaning of interaction
Interest-driven interaction	Interests are the decisive factor of international interaction. National awareness, international concept, international system, and structure are influencing factors of international modernization, while interest maximization and loss minimization are basic principles	Process of interaction
Path selection	The interaction between national modernization and international environment is similar—to a certain extent—to that within biological species. International interaction can be seen as a composite manifestation at transnational level of a country's biological instincts and humanity and explained in part by biological species interaction for its selectability and variability	Selection of interaction
Quadrant interaction	International interaction of national modernization is closely related to a country's international status. Interaction between countries within the same international status quadrant is generally lateral interaction, while that between countries within different international status quadrants is generally vertical interaction; lateral interaction and vertical interaction have different features	Characteristics of interaction

Source: RGCMS (2008)

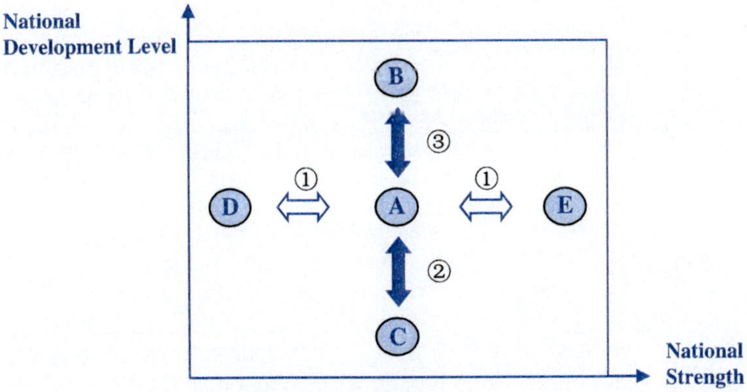

Fig. 5.12 Relative international status and behavioral choice. Note: country A's international behavior: (1) lateral interaction, (2) downward interaction (vertical interaction), and (3) upward interaction (vertical interaction). Source: RGCMS (2008)

resources and foundational interests are limited, rational competition for resources and interests become the strong motive of international interaction. Fourth, both the process and means of international interaction are subject to

Table 5.19 Eight rules of international modernization

Rule	Main contents
Acting and reacting force	International interaction in the process of modernization is a two-way process. One country exerts an acting force on another country and is inevitably subject to the reacting force from this country. Newtonian mechanics' acting and reacting force theorem applies roughly to international interaction analysis
Different effects	In the process of international interaction, if one country's acting force on another country is equal to the reacting force from this country and both countries differ in development level and strength, then the equal acting and reacting force have different effects of action on each other. International interaction with different countries has different effects of action
Like attracts like	"Birds of a feather flock together" is an English proverb which fit to the international modernization. The frequency of international interaction between countries with the same international status is higher, while that between countries with different international status is lower except the international union. Developed countries have more international interaction with developed countries. Like attracts like—a phenomenon widely existing in the process of international interaction of modernization
Good spreading	International interaction with high-level countries does much to improve national development level, while that with low-level countries helps little. Going with success will experience the success, while going with failure maybe share sadness
Goal orientation	Generally, international interaction is a kind of behavior with definite purpose and goal and is guided by its goal. Nevertheless, international interaction is complex, international change is rapid, and the purpose and goal may also change
National interests	National interests and humanitarianism are two root causes of international interaction. More often, the effect of national interests is more outstanding and even has a decisive influence
Maxmini	International interaction is an international game. The maxmini principle applies to international interaction alike. Maximization of gains and the minimization of cost and loss are principles for decision making in international interaction
Bounded rationality	International environment changes rapidly, and decisions on international interaction are a choice based on limited amounts of information. Limited by incomplete information, state rationality is only bounded rationality; there is neither best option nor optimal international interaction

Source: RGCMS (2008)

the influence of the science and technology development, while scientific and technological advances promote international interaction.

International interaction in international modernization has a variety of forms. The most basic forms are international exchange, cooperation, conflict, and international competition, whose driving forces are different. Main driving forces of international exchange are humanity, interests, informatization, globalization, etc. Main driving forces of international cooperation include humanity, interests, scientific and technological progress, and environmental pressure. International conflict has such driving forces as humanity, interests, capital accumulation, and strategic resources, and interests, resources, innovation, and market are the main driving forces of international competition.

In the process of international modernization in the age of industry, competition for powers and existence was the powerhouse of international interaction, while in the process of international modernization in the age of knowledge, cooperative competition and development competition serve as the boosters of international interaction. Competition in the age of industry was for national strength, with the aim of maintaining the right of national existence and contending for world hegemony; it was the powerhouse of international interaction. Competition in the age of knowledge is for improvement of national development level, necessary to maintain leading positions and catching up with advanced levels in the world; it is the powerhouse of international interaction.

5.2.2.5 Model

International modernization has four paths: international cooperation, exchange, competition, and conflict generally.

International modernization has four models, namely, comprehensive interaction, lateral interaction, downward interaction, and upward interaction. Downward interaction and upward interaction can be called lateral interaction collectively.

What path and model to take for international interaction is related to interactive counterparts, stakeholders, and the international system. A country generally chooses an interaction strategy through comparison with the counterpart country.

There are two strategies for international modernization: international interaction between countries in the same international status quadrant is generally equal and symmetrical lateral interaction, while that between countries in different international status quadrants is generally unequal and dissymmetrical vertical interaction.

There are four strategies for international modernization: for international interaction between countries in the same international status quadrant, lateral interaction is generally selected; interaction of one country with higher status with another with lower status is generally downward; interaction of one country with lower status with another with higher status is generally upward; if two countries have overlapping yet not the same international status, lateral and vertical interaction, or comprehensive interaction, may happen at the same time.

International interaction in the process of modernization generally includes the following six steps:

(a) *Acting according to actual circumstances*. Choose the interaction path and model appropriate for the needs of the country according to its international status, the counterpart's international status, and the international environment.
(b) *Rational assessment*. Assess the process, risk, cost, benefit, and effect of the chosen interaction path and model by using the cost-effectiveness analysis method.
(c) *Correlation analysis*. The assessment of the interaction path and model, which is conducted mainly through analysis on benefit and cost of the interactive parties, may not overlook the response from the third party, the fourth party, and

so on (if any) as stakeholders, as well as international influence and hierarchy. Correlation analysis helps correct or improve the results of a rational assessment.

(d) *Rational anticipation*. International interaction is an international game, with results subject to game rules, the development level, and strength of game parties, decision making in the process of the game, game environment, and condition and often hardly to be predicted precisely. Such extremities as idealism, pessimism, heroism, capitulationism, arrogance, and self-underestimation are harmful to international interaction.

(e) *Dynamic monitoring*. The international climate is unpredictable, and international interaction just takes place in such uncertain international environment. Moreover, national interests change too. The dynamic monitoring of the process of interaction is an important measure to increase the probability of success and gains.

(f) *Timely adjustment*. In most cases, international interaction proceeds according to international arrangement and established policy. But timely adjustment is necessary when major interests change, international changes or behavioral changes have happened or are happening, and these changes will affect for sure the achievement of the anticipated goals of international interaction.

International interaction involves a great many stakeholders and influencing factors. In some sense, international interaction strategies are different combinations of these factors. Choosing a strategy, in essence, is choosing an advantageous combination.

5.3 National Modernization

National modernization generally has two meanings, i.e., modernization at national layer and modernization of a single country. In modernization study, national modernization generally refers to that at national layer, including worldwide national modernization and national modernization of individual countries (Fig. 5.13); it is a form of manifestation and a level of analysis of modernization phenomena. Generally, country is the basic unit of modernization study and development. The process of national modernization is not only a relatively independent process but also a process of international interaction. National

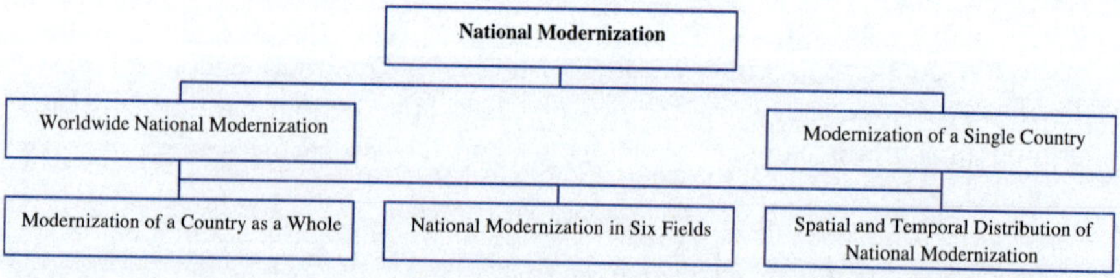

Fig. 5.13 Analytical structure of national modernization. Source: RGCMS (2010)

modernization serves as an important foundation for world modernization and international modernization; it is the domestic environment of regional, institutional, and individual modernization.

5.3.1 Studies

National modernization is the basic unit of modernization. National modernization study may be conducted from three perspectives, i.e., the past, present, and future. Relatively speaking, national modernization study and modernization policy are closely related.

5.3.1.1 Research Paradigm

National modernization study is the modernization study at national layer.

(1) Research Matrix

The research object of national modernization study includes modernization of a country as a whole, modernization of the country in six fields as well as the spatial and temporal distribution of national modernization. Research contents include modernization of national behavior, structures, institutions, and concepts, as well as the process, results, dynamics, and models of national modernization. They all together constitute a research matrix (Table 5.20).

Table 5.20 National modernization research matrix

Content		Object		
		National civilization	Economy, society, politics, culture, natural environment, and humans of the state	Spatial and temporal distribution of national civilization
		National modernization as a whole	Modernization in the national six fields	Spatial and temporal distribution of national modernization
Element	Behavior	Modernization of national behaviors, structures, institutions, and ideas	Behavioral, structural, institutional, idea's modernization in the national six fields	
	Structure			
	Institution			–
	Idea			
Aspect	Process	Process, result, dynamics, model of the national modernization	Processes, result, dynamics, model of modernization in the national six fields	Geographical, population, level's, and regional distribution of the national modernization
	Result			
	Dynamics			
	Model			

Note: national modernization study also includes many other contents, for example, the frontier, frontier process, and catch-up process analysis on national civilization, international competition analysis, international gap analysis, domestic gap analysis, elements of national modernization, and interaction between different fields

(2) Research Method

National modernization study is a level-relative modernization study and may use the methodology of modernization study. The research scope can be a particular country or countries throughout the world. The time span can be the total process or some particular stage.

National modernization is a complex multidimensional and multilevel analysis, requiring multidimensional analysis, hierarchy analysis, case study, and interdisciplinary and comprehensive studies, including the coordinate analysis method in modernization study.

The process study of national modernization generally adopts the research methods of positivism and interpretivism. The reality study of national modernization generally adopts the research methods of positivism, interpretivism, and realism. The prospect study of national modernization generally adopts the research methods of positivism, interpretivism, and futurology.

(3) Research Purpose

National modernization study is mainly for academic and policy purposes.

From the academic point of view, national modernization study is an important part of modernization study, with the aim to discover the basic facts, fundamental principles, and historical experience of national modernization and to enrich the implications of the modernization theory.

From the policy point of view, national modernization is the basic unit of modernization practice, and the purpose of national modernization study is to provide the theoretical basis, historical reference, and policy options for the practice of national modernization.

5.3.1.2 Facts About National Modernization

China Modernization Report 2010: World Modernization Outline 1700–2100 (RGCMS 2010) provides a systematic analysis of national modernization worldwide which involves 131 countries whose population was over one million in 2000 and statistic data was available as follows:

(1) Process of National Modernization

First, on the starting years of national modernization. American scholar Black (1966) found that different countries differed greatly in the start of modernization, the time required for the consolidation of modernization leadership, the time required for social and economic transition, etc. (Table 5.21). The process of modernization that Black (1966) described is in fact the process of the first modernization typical of industrialization, urbanization, and democratization.

According to research by Professor Black (1966), the 18 modernization foregoers (today's developed countries) took about 50–180 years (about 80 years on average) for the consolidation of the first modernization leadership and about 40–100 years (about 70 years on average) for the completion of economic and social transition; the starting time of the first modernization in developing countries

Table 5.21 Comparison between countries in starting and transition years

Type and country	Consolidation of modernization leadership	Economic and social transition	Social integration	Starting time difference	Years for consolidation	Years for transition
Type I						
UK	1649–1832	1832–1945	1945–	–	183	113
France	1789–1848	1848–1945	1945–	29	59	97
Type II						
USA	1776–1865	1865–1933	1933–	16	89	68
Canada	1797–1867	1867–1947	1947–	37	70	80
Australia	1801–1901	1901–1941	1941–	41	100	40
Type III						
Germany	1803–1871	1871–1933	1933–	43	68	62
Italy	1805–1871	1871–	–	45	66	–
Type IV						
Brazil	1850–1930	1930–	–	90	80	–
Mexico	1867–1910	1910–	–	107	43	–
Type V						
Russia	1861–1917	1917–	–	101	56	–
Japan	1868–1945	1945–	–	108	77	–
China	1905–1949	1949–	–	145	44	–
Type VI						
India	1919–1947	1947–	–	159	28	–
Indonesia	1922–1949	1949–	–	162	27	–
Type VII						
Nigeria	1960–	–	–	200	–	–

Note: (1) the years in this table are what were given in the original book (Black 1966), and some of them might be inaccurate. For example, the starting year of modernization in China, according to some Chinese scholars, is 1840 or 1860, while it is 1905 in this table, decades earlier. (2) This table reveals the view of the author of the original book published in 1966. From 1966 onward, the world saw great changes and modernization study led to many new results. (3) "Starting time difference" is the difference between the "starting year for consolidation of national modernization leadership" and the "starting year of world modernization" (approximately 1760). (4) "Years for consolidation" are the years which consolidation of modernization leadership took. (5) "Years for transition" are the years which economic and social transition took. The data of this table comes from Black (1966)

was about 60–200 years later than that of world modernization. Therefore, the task of modernization in developing countries is still formidable.

Second, on the stages of national modernization. The process of worldwide national modernization mainly includes the preparatory stage, the first modernization, and the second modernization. Different countries differ in the phasing and time of modernization.

Professor Black held that the process of modernization (classical modernization) could be divided into four stages: challenge of modernity, consolidation of modernization leadership bloc, social and economic transition, and social integration (Black 1966).

Third, on the common features of the process of national modernization. From the national perspective, national modernization roughly has ten features, i.e., predictable, multistages, long-term, revolutionary, progressive, adaptable, nonlinear, reversible, complex, and side effects. From the perspective of the international system, it roughly has ten main features, i.e., predictable, multistages, long-term, reversible, asynchronous, allometric, competitive, interactive, diverse, and stable. On the whole, the process of national modernization roughly has 16 features (Table 5.22), which overlap in part with the features of the frontier process of modernization (Table 2.11).

Fourth, on the diversity in the process of national modernization. The process of worldwide national modernization has not only generalities but also many

Table 5.22 Features of worldwide national modernization

Feature	Description
Basic features at national layer	
Predictable	A partly predictable process, with changes in one field affecting those in other fields
Multistages	A historical process consisting of several stages, roughly including the first and second modernization
Long-term	A long-term historical process, impossible to finish in a short term
Revolutionary	A revolutionary process, including far-reaching changes in politics, culture, etc.
Progressive	A progressive process, including improvement of productivity and of quality of life
Adaptable	An adaptable process, including adaptable changes in new science and technology and in new environment
Nonlinear	A process of transition (nonlinear process), including from tradition to modernity and from modernity to postmodernity
Reversible	A reversible process, including reversibility of political and cultural changes, frustration and repeat of modernization, etc.
Complex	A complex process, including changes in the six fields of a country—which may be at a different pace
Side effects	A process with side effects such as polarization between the rich and the poor and environmental pollution
Main features at international system level	
Asynchronous	Countries differ from each other in the start of modernization; they may be in different stages of modernization on some particular historical cross section
Allometric	Countries differ from each other in the pace and level of modernization
Interactive	National modernization is affected by international environment, and international interaction affects the performance of national modernization
Competitive	Countries compete with each other in terms of modernization; modernization is an international contest
Diverse	No two countries have completely the same features of modernization
Stable	The international system structure of world modernization is of relative stability; though positions of countries may change, advanced countries are likely to maintain their positions, while underdeveloped ones are more likely to be "locked" in the state of underdevelopment

Source: RGCMS (2010)

Table 5.23 Diversity in worldwide national modernization

Feature	Description
Different starts	One country is different from another in the start of modernization, either early or late
Different initial time	One country is different from another in the initial time of modernization; they have historical and traditional differences
Different paths	One country is different from another in the path of modernization; they have path dependence
Different models	One country is different from another in the model of modernization, which is diverse
Different dynamics	One country is different from another in the driving forces of modernization
Different policies	One country is different from another in the polices for modernization, which are different in different stages
Different paces	One country is different from another in the pace of modernization, which is different in a different stage or period
Different levels	One country is different from another in the level of modernization, which is also different in gap to the world's advanced level
Different outcomes	One country is different from another in the outcome of modernization, which is influenced by their history and path
Different features	One country is different from another in the features of modernization
Different challenges	One country is different from another in the challenges to modernization; countries differ in major problems
Different environments	One country is different from another in the environment of modernization; different countries have different international and internal environments

Source: RGCMS (2010)

differences. For example, a great many international differences exist in the start, initial time, path, model, driving force, policy, pace, level, outcome, feature, challenge, and environment with regard to the process of modernization (Table 5.23).

Fifth, on the complexity of the process of national modernization. It took developed countries about 160 years on average to complete the first modernization; some developed countries suffered setbacks and repetition in the first modernization, for example, the repetition in the process of establishing democracy in France and Spain. Many developing countries gained independence in the twentieth century, and their efforts to pursue the first modernization so far have been <100 years. If they borrow the experience of developed countries, it will still take some time for them to complete the first modernization. Around the 1960s, some developing countries saw setbacks and repetition in their fast modernization. This has led some scholars to question the practicability of the modernization theory. But if we negate the modernization theory just because of some setbacks and repetition, we might lose the chance of success for fear of failure.

(2) Main Outcomes of National Modernization

Generally, we may analyze the main outcomes of worldwide national modernization both on a national layer and on an international system level.

First of all, on a national layer, worldwide national modernization will lead to two outcomes: common outcomes and diversity of national modernization (Fig. 3.49). In analyzing the outcomes of national modernization, the following three points require particular attention:

(a) *There is the need to conduct a stage-relative analysis and make cross-sectional comparison.* At different historical cross sections, national modernization has different indicators, levels, and features. By comparing two cross sections in indicators, levels, and features, we can analyze the main outcomes of national modernization between the two cross sections. The main outcomes of the first modernization of a country are totally different from those of its second modernization.

(b) *There is a need to sum up the common outcomes and also recognize the diversity.* The United Nations (UN) currently has 192 member countries, and the outcomes of worldwide national modernization involve national modernization in all these countries. How to sum up the common outcomes of national modernization? Is that the collection of all national modernization outcomes? Apparently not. A general method is identifying the generality and diversity in the main outcomes of national modernization.

(c) *There is a need to find an appropriate analysis method.* National modernization covers modernization in the fields of economy, society, politics, culture, individuals, and natural environment, and the outcomes of national modernization include modernization outcomes in the six fields. This entails an appropriate method used to extract the outcomes of national modernization from the modernization outcomes in the six fields.

Second, on an international system level, worldwide national modernization will lead to two outcomes: the change of the international status of countries and structural change of the international system. In general, the structure of the international system is relatively stable, and the change in international status has its laws (RGCMS 2010).

Transition probabilities of four groups of countries over the last 100 years: there is an approximately 8–23% probability that developed countries go down; an approximately 0–42% probability that moderately developed countries go up; an approximately 0–24% probability that preliminarily developed countries go up to moderately developed countries and approximately 2–5% directly to advanced countries; and an approximately 0–14% probability that underdeveloped countries go up to preliminarily developed countries, approximately 0–12% directly to moderately developed countries, and approximately 0–4% directly to advanced countries (RGCMS 2010).

Transition probabilities of four groups of countries over the last 45 years: there is an approximately 6–12% probability that developed countries go down and an approximately 18–25% probability that moderately developed countries go up; an approximately 14–20% probability that preliminarily developed countries go

Table 5.24 Rise and fall of status in national modernization

Time	Upgraded from developing to advanced country	Downgraded from advanced to developing country
Eighteenth century	USA	Portugal
Nineteenth century	Canada, Argentina, Ireland, Australia, New Zealand	Spain, Italy, and Norway
Twentieth century	Finland, Japan, Singapore, South Korea, Israel, etc. (Italy, Spain, and Norway)	Argentina and Russia (USSR) (New Zealand and Venezuela)

Note: between the nineteenth century and the twentieth century, such countries as Italy, Spain, Norway, Ireland, New Zealand, and Venezuela saw fluctuations in their international status
Source: RGCMS (2010)

up to moderately developed ones and approximately 3–4% directly to developed ones; and an approximately 4–10% probability that less-developed countries go up to elementarily developed ones, approximately 3–5% directly to moderately developed ones, and approximately 0% directly to developed ones (RGCMS 2010).

Transition probabilities of two groups of countries over the last 100 years: there is an approximately 8–23% probability that advanced countries go down and an approximately 1–8% probability that developing countries go up to advanced ones. Aside from three countries with fluctuating status, the probability that developing countries go up is about 1–5% (RGCMS 2010).

Transition probabilities of two groups of countries over the last 45 years: there is an approximately 6–12% probability that advanced countries go down and an approximately 5–7% probability that developing countries go up to advanced ones. Aside from two countries with fluctuating status, the probability that developing countries go up is approximately 5% (RGCMS 2010).

Historical data show that over a span of 100 years, there was an approximately 5% probability that developing countries went up to advanced ones and an approximately 10% probability that advanced countries went down to developing ones and that there was mobility between developing and advanced countries (Table 5.24).

(3) Driving Force of National Modernization

The dynamics of worldwide national modernization has been dealt with in Chap. 2. Generally, innovation is the fundamental powerhouse of modernization. The first modernization and the second modernization, modernization foregoers and latecomers, and different models, all differ in driving forces.

(4) Paths and Models of National Modernization

Generally, between 1763 and 1970, the basic path of national modernization was the first modernization; in between 1970 and 2100, the basic paths of national modernization are diverse, including the second modernization of advanced countries, and the first modernization, second modernization, and integrated modernization of developing countries.

There has been substantial research on main models of national modernization.

Three Models of European Modernization. European scholars thought that modernization had different models, for example, the British model (industrialization is the leading factor; it promotes democratization and then bureaucratization), the French model (bureaucratization and democratization are the leading factors, while industrialization is a latecomer), and the German model (the combination of bureaucratization and democratization brings modernization, and democratization is always absent).

Seven Models of Political Modernization. Divided according to the political challenge to and starting years of modernization, they are the British–French model, the West-derived country model, model of other European countries, the Latin American model, the independent country model, the former colonial country model, and the Africa country model (Black 1966).

Main Types of the First Modernization. According to the different source of knowledge, institution, thought of modernization, and the industrialization, the first modernization can be divided into innovative modernization, follow-up modernization, grafting modernization, and learning modernization (Table 5.25). According to different factors, the first modernization can also be divided into many types, such as early bird and latecomer modernization, endogenous and exogenous modernization, active and passive modernization, and market-oriented and planned modernization; Latin America, East Asia, Eastern Europe, and Middle East have their distinctive features in modernization.

Element Mix Models of the First Modernization. The first modernization includes many elements, such as industrialization, urbanization, democratization, and international interaction. Different countries adopted different strategies in different periods and gave priority to developing a particular element in a particular period, thereby forming different models (Table 5.26) such as dependent development, catch-up industrialization, import substitution, and export-oriented industrialization.

Table 5.25 Four types of first modernization

Type	Source of knowledge	Source of thought	Source of institution	Occurrence of industrialization	Representative countries
Innovative	Mostly independent innovation	Mostly independent innovation	Mostly independent innovation	Spontaneous and endogenous	UK and France
Follow-up	Innovation and learning	Learning and innovation	Learning and innovation	External diffusion and conscious development	USA, Canada, Southern Europe, and Japan
Grafting	Passive learning	External input	External imposition	Externally input and exogenous	Former colonial countries
Learning	Active learning	Learning	Active imitation	Reactively introduced and exogenous	Latin American countries, South Korea, and Thailand

Source: He (1999)

Table 5.26 Element mix models in the first modernization

Element mix	Model	Representative countries
Industrialization and democratization	Giving priority to industrialization, or democratization, or developing in a coordinated way	Germany, France, UK, etc.
Industrialization and urbanization	Giving priority to industrialization, or urbanization, or developing in a coordinated way	Finland, Australia, UK, etc.
Economy and education	Giving priority to economy, or education, or developing in a coordinated way	UK, Germany, Italy, etc.
Market and planning	Free market economy, planned commanded economy, or mixed economy	UK in the nineteenth century, USSR and USA in the twentieth century, etc.
Catch-up industrialization	Import substitution, export orientation, or coordinated development	Latin American countries and East Asian countries in the 1960s, etc.
International interaction	Protectionism, free trade, colonization, or dependent development	Germany, UK, and Latin American countries in the nineteenth century, etc.

Note: industrialization is represented by the percentage of industrial value added in GDP, democracy by universal suffrage, urbanization by the percentage of urban population in total population, economy by the percentage of industrial value added in GDP, and education by adult literacy and popularization rate of primary education
Source: RGCMS (2010)

Element Mix Models of the Second Modernization. The second modernization includes many elements, such as knowledgeablization, informatization, ecologicalization, and international interaction. Different countries adopted different strategies in different periods and gave priority to developing a particular element in a particular period, thereby forming different models (Table 5.27), for example, giving priority to knowledgeablization, informatization, or ecologicalization and developing in a coordinated way.

Element Mix Models of Integrated Modernization. Integrated modernization is the coordinated development of the first and second modernization and the transition toward the second modernization, including many elements of the first and second modernization, such as industrialization, urbanization, democratization, knowledgeablization, informatization, ecologicalization, and international interaction. Different countries adopted different strategies in different periods and gave priority to developing a particular element in a particular period, thereby forming different models (Table 5.28), for example, giving priority to industrialization, knowledgeablization, and informatization, and coordinated development between knowledgeablization and industrialization, between informatization and industrialization, or between industrialization and ecologicalization. Because integrated modernization is the coordinated development of the first and second modernization, several models of the first and second modernization, such as giving priority to education, economy, society, or ecology and the coordinated development of economy, society and ecology also apply to comprehensive modernization.

Table 5.27 Element mix models in the second modernization

Element mix	Model	Representative countries
Knowledgeablization and informatization	Giving priority to knowledgeablization (or intellectualization), or informatization, or developing in a coordinated way	USA, Japan, UK, etc.
Knowledgeablization and ecologicalization	Giving priority to knowledgeablization, or ecologicalization, or developing in a coordinated way	Finland, UK, Japan, etc.
Informatization and ecologicalization	Giving priority to informatization, or ecologicalization, or developing in a coordinated way	Norway, Germany, Canada, etc.
International interaction	High-level trade and investment, moderate-level trade and investment, low-level trade and investment	Ireland, Germany, USA, etc.
Economy and society	Giving priority to economy, or society, or developing in a coordinated way	Japan, Sweden, Netherlands, etc.
Economy and ecology	Giving priority to economy, or ecology, or developing in a coordinated way	USA, Switzerland, Germany, etc.
Society and ecology	Giving priority to society, or ecology, or developing in a coordinated way	USA, Switzerland, and Denmark
Economy, society, and ecology	Developing in a coordinated way	France, Denmark, UK, etc.

Note: knowledgeablization is represented by the rate of popularization of higher education, informatization by the rate of diffusion of the Internet, and ecologicalization by the rate of treatment of domestic sewage. High-level trade and investment: international trade and investment accounting for $\geq$100% in GDP. Moderate-level trade and investment: international trade and investment accounting for $\geq$50% and <100% in GDP. Low-level trade and investment: international trade and investment accounting for <50% in GDP. Economy, society, and ecology are represented by their indexes of modernization, respectively
Source: RGCMS (2010)

5.3.1.3 Future of National Modernization

China Modernization Report 2010 provides an analysis of the prospects of worldwide national modernization in the twenty-first century as follows:

(1) Path Analysis on National Modernization

National modernization has path dependence, and what path to choose is subject to historical tradition, level of start, and international environment.

According to the second modernization, worldwide modernization in the twenty-first century has three basic paths: second modernization, catch-up modernization (from the first to second modernization), and integrated modernization (coordinated development of the first and second modernization).

On an international system level, the number of countries choosing either the path of second modernization or the path of integrated modernization will increase, while that of countries choosing the path of catch-up modernization will gradually decrease; developed countries will all choose the path of second modernization,

Table 5.28 Element mix models in comprehensive modernization

Element mix	Model	Representative countries
Knowledgeablization and industrialization	Giving priority to knowledgeablization, or industrialization, or developing in a coordinated way	Greece, Mexico, Chile, etc.
Informatization and industrialization	Giving priority to informatization, or industrialization, or developing in a coordinated way	Malaysia, Indonesia, Thailand, etc.
Industrialization and ecologicalization	Giving priority to industrialization, or ecologicalization, or developing in a coordinated way	Malaysia, Costa Rica, Chile, etc.
Urbanization and ecologicalization	Giving priority to urbanization, or ecologicalization, or developing in a coordinated way	–
Urbanization and Informatization	Giving priority to urbanization, or informatization, or developing in a coordinated way	–
International interaction	High-level trade and investment, moderate-level trade and investment, low-level trade and investment	Malaysia, China, India, etc.
Economy and education	Giving priority to economy, or education, or developing in a coordinated way	–
Economy and society	Giving priority to economy and society, and developing in a coordinated way	–
Economy and ecology	Giving priority to economy, or ecology, or developing in a coordinated way	–
Society and ecology	Giving priority to society, or ecology, or developing in a coordinated way	–
Economy, society and ecology	Developing in a coordinated way	–

Source: RGCMS (2010)

while developing countries have three path options, namely, second modernization, catch-up modernization, and integrated modernization.

On a national layer, the path selection in national modernization is closely connected with what stage of modernization a country is in.

First, countries that have completed the first modernization and entered the second modernization will choose the path of second modernization.

Second, countries that have not yet completed the first modernization have three options: catch-up modernization, integrated modernization, and second modernization. It is generally inappropriate for them to take the path of second modernization.

Third, countries as traditional agricultural societies generally choose the path of catch-up or integrated modernization.

(2) Scenario Analysis on National Modernization

A scenario analysis on national modernization in the twenty-first century involves a great many elements. Below is a discussion of the timeline and national layer.

First, time to complete the first modernization. The time a country completes the first modernization is the time it reaches the criteria of the first modernization. So far, there has been no agreement over the criteria of completion for the first modernization. Generally, typical features of the first modernization include industrialization, urbanization, and democratization. Whether or not to have completed industrialization, urbanization, and democratization may be used as the basic criteria of completion for the first modernization. Modernization is also a sort of international competition and change in international status, and the relative level of a country's modernization is closely connected with its international status. For example, by 1960, most of industrialized countries had completed industrialization, urbanization, and democratization, and they stood for the world's advanced level of modernization in 1960; they completed the first modernization in 1960.

Considering above-mentioned elements, *China Modernization Report* uses industrialization, urbanization, and democratization as the basic criteria of completion for the first modernization, with the average development level of high-income countries (industrialized countries) in 1960 being regarded as the primary criterion of completion for the first modernization.

On an international system level, by 2005, about 34 countries, including all developed countries and a number of developing ones, had completed their first modernization. About 86 countries will complete their first modernization by 2050, and 99–107 will complete their first modernization by 2100 (Table 5.29).

On a national layer, by 2005, 34 countries had completed their first modernization, while others had not. For these 34 countries, the average time spent to complete the first modernization was about 150 years. When estimated according to the average growth rates in the term of 1980–2005 and 1990–2005, countries which have not yet completed their first modernization will differ in the time spent to complete their first modernization. Here, we take 15 countries as an example (Table 5.30).

Second, time to complete the second modernization. The time a country completes the second modernization is the time it reaches the criteria of the second modernization. Currently, the frontier of world modernization has already arrived at the development stage of the second modernization; no country has completed the

Table 5.29 Predictions about national modernization in the twenty-first century

Item	2005	2010	2020	2030	2040	2050	2060	2070	2080	2090	2100
Prediction S1	28	33	37	54	59	64	71	79	81	83	84
Prediction S2	28	36	44	58	65	74	76	79	83	87	89
Prediction F1	34	38	60	69	79	86	90	96	104	106	107
Prediction F2	34	39	61	69	80	86	89	93	97	98	99

Note: predictions S1 and S2 refer to the number of the countries entering the second modernization. Predictions F1 and F2 refer to the number of the countries completing the first modernization. This analysis covers 131 countries whose population was over one million in 2000. The number of countries entering their second modernization is predicted according to the average annual growth rate of second modernization indexes in 1980–2005 and 1990–2005: when a country's second modernization index reaches or exceeds 70, it enters its second modernization. The number of countries that have completed their first modernization is predicted according to the average annual growth rate of first modernization levels in 1980–2005 and 1990–2005: when a country's first modernization level reaches 100, it has completed its first modernization
Source: RGCMS (2010)

Table 5.30 Time spent for the first modernization in 15 countries (Year)

Country	Starting year	Actual year of completion	Actual years spent	Predicted year of completion	Years already spent	Years still needed	Total years spent
USA	1776	1960	184				184
Canada	1797	1960	163				163
Japan	1868	1970	102				102
Germany	1803	1970	167				167
UK	1649	1970	321				321
France	1789	1970	181				181
Australia	1801	1970	169				169
Italy	1805	1970	165				165
Mexico	1867	2005	138				138
Russia	1861			2020	149	10	159
Brazil	1850			2020	160	10	170
China	1840			2020	170	10	180
Indonesia	1922			2020	88	10	98
India	1919			2040	91	30	121
Nigeria	1960			2070	50	60	110

Note: "Starting year" is based on the views of Black (1966). "Year of completion" refers to the year when the level of first modernization reaches "the average level in 1960 of high-income countries." "Years already spent" refer to the span of years from "starting year" to 2010. "Years still needed" refer to the span of years from 2010 to "predicted year of completion." "Total years spent" refer to the actual or predicted years needed to complete the first modernization
Source: RGCMS (2010)

second modernization; the criteria of completion for the second modernization are not yet to be determined.

According to the second modernization theory, the time span of knowledge civilization is about 130 years, and currently, the second modernization has such features as knowledgeablization, informatization, and ecologicalization. There are many methods to make predications about the second modernization. For example, based on the history between 1970 and 2005, it is estimated that about six countries will join the ranks of the second modernization drive every 10 years from 2001 to 2100.

On an international system level, by 2005, all advanced countries and a number of developing countries, about 28 together, had entered the second modernization. The number of countries which enter the second modernization will reach 64–74 by 2050 and 84–89 by 2100 (Table 5.29), and in the meanwhile, advanced countries will have completed the second modernization.

On a national layer, by 2005, 28 countries had entered their second modernization, while others had not. In the twenty-first century, countries will differ for sure in their time to enter and complete the second modernization, which entails special research.

Third, national modernization level. According to an analysis in which one developed country respectively from Europe, America, and Asia as well as one

Table 5.31 Predictions about national modernization levels in the twenty-first century (second modernization index)

Nation	Growth rate	2005	2010	2020	2030	2040	2050	2080	2100	2100/2005
Germany	1.55	89	97	113	131	153	179	283	385	4.33
	1.39	89	96	110	126	145	167	253	333	3.74
USA	1.60	111	121	141	166	194	227	366	503	4.53
	1.69	111	121	143	169	200	237	391	547	4.93
Japan	1.66	102	111	131	154	182	214	351	489	4.79
	1.27	102	109	123	140	159	180	263	338	3.31
Brazil	2.25	47	53	66	83	103	129	251	392	8.34
	1.74	47	52	61	73	87	103	173	244	5.19
India	1.82	24	26	32	38	45	54	93	134	5.58
	2.29	24	27	34	42	53	67	132	208	8.67
Nigeria	0.96	16	17	19	21	23	25	34	41	2.56
	1.35	16	17	20	23	26	30	45	59	3.69

Note: growth rate is the average annual growth rate in 1980–2005 and 1990–2005, respectively
Source: RGCMS (2010)

developing country respectively from America, Asia, and Africa (Brazil, India, and Nigeria) (Table 5.31) are chosen to be the object, the modernization level of developed countries is likely to increase 2.3–3.9-fold, and the level of developing countries is likely to increase 1.6–7.7-fold; some developing countries is likely to reach the level of developed countries, while some will see a widening gap to developed countries (RGCMS 2010).

(3) International Status in National Modernization

According to the historical experience over the past 300 years, in 100 years to come, the probability that a developed country descends into a developing one is about 8–23%, and the probability that a developing country ascends to a developed one is about 1–5%. If the historical experience works, in the twenty-first century, about 2–4 developed countries are likely to descend into developing ones, and about 1–5 developing countries are likely to ascend to developing ones. There are of course great uncertainties in the twenty-first century, which will make it impossible to predict accurately the future based on history (RGCMS 2010).

If the above predictions are proved to be true, international competition will remain fierce in the twenty-first century. Developed countries have to strive to maintain their international status, while developing countries will strive for ascension to the club of developed countries as soon as possible. For the over 100 developing countries, there are only about five "tickets" to the club of developed countries (Modernized Countries Club) in the twenty-first century.

5.3.1.4 Inspiration from the History of National Modernization

First of all, modernization needs both vertical and horizontal comparison. The vertical comparison of modernization reflects the progress in civilization and analyzes the increases in absolute levels of countries, while the horizontal comparison of modernization reflects the international difference and geographic distribution of civilization development and analyzes the changes in relative levels of countries and their international status. If the growth rate of the absolute level of a country is lower than other countries, this country's relative level and international status decline; on the contrary, they rise. An international comparison of modernization must be scientific and rational; some indicators, for example, language, are unsuitable for an international comparison of development levels.

Second, a latecomer may learn from the experience of a foregoer whereby it sees the epitome of its future civilization structure and quality of life in the developed country. But different countries differ in both lifestyle and culture to which new changes will happen with scientific and technological progress. The cross-sectional structure of world modernization is the epitome of its historical structure, while that of human civilization is the epitome of human civilization's historical structure. For example, the cross-sectional structure of 2,000-year human civilization is the epitome of the process of human history from the origin of human beings to the year 2000 and that 2,000-year world modernization is the epitome of the process of modernization from its' start to the year 2000, with the world's average level about 50 years behind the world's advanced level.

Third, there is no best model of modernization but only rational choice. Over the past 300 years, some countries have maintained their status as developed countries, some have successfully ascended, and some have descended. A comparison between their development models leads to no results of obvious orientation (Table 5.32). In the process of the first modernization, those ascending countries gave priority to industrialization, democratization, or urbanization, or to economy or education, or developed in a coordinated way; in the process of the second modernization, they gave priority to knowledgeablization, informatization, or ecologicalization or developed in a coordinated way. Therefore, countries need to research and find models appropriate to them, rather than simply copying the practices of other countries.

Fourth, modernization is subject to the Matthew Effect, with the international gap in per capita income widening constantly. In the international system, though most countries have seen an increase in per capita income, rich countries have become richer and poor countries have become poorer, with low-income countries tending to be impoverished. If the GDP per capita calculated based on prices in 2000 is used as the analytical index, from 1960 to 2000, the absolute difference between high-income and low-income countries widened from approximately 8,584 to 25,767 USD, and the relative difference increased from 42-fold to 66-fold. If the GDP (PPP) per capita calculated based on prices in 1990 is used as the analytical index, from 1960 to 2000, the absolute difference between high-income and low-income countries widened from approximately 6,577 to 21,163 international dollars, and the relative difference increased from 6-fold to 21-fold.

If both developed and developing countries take measures to control and narrow international income differences, a win–win situation is likely to happen. But international gaps between rich and poor countries continue to widen, and international conflicts are likely to intensify and lead to a situation harmful to both sides.

Table 5.32 Element mix models of different types of countries

Country and type	Element mix of the first modernization: Industrialization and democratization	Industrialization and urbanization	Economy and education	Element mix of the second modernization: Knowledgeablization and informatization	Knowledgeablization and ecologicalization	Informatization and ecologicalization
Ascending						
USA	Coordinately	Industrialization first	Education first	Knowledgeablization first	Knowledgeablization first	Coordinately
Canada	Industrialization first	Industrialization first	–	Coordinately	Coordinately	Coordinately
Australia	Democratization first	Urbanization first	–	Coordinately	–	–
Finland	Democratization first	Industrialization first	Economy first	Knowledgeablization first	Knowledgeablization first	Ecologicalization first
Greece	Coordinately	Coordinately	Coordinately	Knowledgeablization first	Knowledgeablization first	Ecologicalization first
Japan	Industrialization first	Industrialization first	Education first	Informatization first	Coordinately	Informatization first
South Korea	Industrialization first	Coordinately	Education first	Knowledgeablization first	Knowledgeablization first	Coordinately
Singapore	Industrialization first	–	Coordinately	–	–	–
Kuwait	Industrialization first	–	Economy first	–	–	–
Fluctuating						
New Zealand	Democratization first	Urbanization first	Education first	Coordinately	Coordinately	Coordinately
Ireland	Democratization first	Urbanization first	Education first	Knowledgeablization first	Coordinately	Ecologicalization first
Descending first and ascending later						
Italy	Industrialization first	Urbanization first	Coordinately	Knowledgeablization first	Coordinately	Ecologicalization first
Norway	Democratization first	Industrialization first	Education first	Informatization first	Coordinately	Informatization first
Spain	Industrialization first	–	Economy first	Knowledgeablization first	Ecologicalization first	Ecologicalization first
Ascending first and descending later						
Argentina	Industrialization first	Urbanization first	Coordinately	Knowledgeablization first	–	–
Russia	–	–	–	Knowledgeablization first	–	–
Venezuela	–	Coordinately	Economy first	Knowledgeablization first	–	–
Descending						
Portugal	Industrialization first	Industrialization first	Economy first	Knowledgeablization first	Coordinately	Ecologicalization first

Note: Industrialization first refers to giving the priority to industrialization, democratization first refers to giving the priority to democratization, coordinately refers to developing in a coordinated way, and so on
Source: RGCMS (2010)

Fifth, in the twenty-first century, developing countries still have prospects of success but have few possibilities of ascending to developed ones. According to the historical experience over the past 300 years, in the twenty-first century, there will be some 20 developed countries and more than 100 developing countries (based on samples of 131 countries), and about 1–5 of these developing countries are likely to ascend to developed ones, implying a fierce contest for the tickets to the club of developed countries. And in this century, some 700 million more people may possibly enjoy a modern life, about 500 million of whom are likely to come from developing countries; the population of developing countries is likely to reach 8–10 billion. That means some 10 billion people in developing countries will compete for 500 million tickets to a modern life. The international competition in the twenty-first century, therefore, will still be intense yet rational.

5.3.2 Theories

The national modernization theory is a theoretical explanation for national modernization phenomena; it is a level theory in the second modernization theory and modernization science. National modernization is modernization at national layer, which has not only generalities of modernization but also particularities. The core theory (Table 2.1) on the general modernization applies to national modernization on the whole. National modernization is the basic unit of modernization, and to a certain extent, the modernization theory is a theory on national modernization and a national-level theory.

Generally, the national modernization theory includes the general theory, branch theories, and relevant theories (Table 5.33). Below is a discussion of its general theory, including the definition, process, result, dynamics, and models of national modernization (Table 5.34). Because of the high consistency of the national modernization theory with the general theory on modernization, the discussion of the national modernization theory is greatly simplified.

Table 5.33 Structure of national modernization theory

Category	Theory	Main contents
General theory	Core theory	The definition, process, result, dynamics, and model of national modernization
Branch theories	Stage theory	National first modernization, second modernization, or integrated modernization
	Field-related study	National modernization in the fields such as economy, society, politics, culture, natural environment, and humans
	Sector-related study	National modernization in the sectors such as agriculture, industry, education, science and technology, national defense, and transportation
Relevant theories	Other modernization theories	Classical modernization theory, reflexive modernization theory, second modernization theory, etc.
	Other relevant theories	Civilization theory, state theory, development theory, transformation theory, area study, etc.

Table 5.34 General theory on national modernization

Aspect	Main contents
Definition	National modernization, i.e., modernization at national layer, is a sort of frontier change and international competition of national civilization since the Industrial Revolution in the eighteenth century. It includes the formation, development, transformation, and international interaction of national modern civilization; the innovation, selection, diffusion, and recession of the elements of national modern civilization; the international competition for catching up with, reaching, and maintaining the world advanced level; and the change in national stratification and civilization distribution
Process	National modernization is a complex process, including the change of national civilization, stratification, and civilization distribution and the change of national behavior, structure, institution, and ideas. The frontier process of national modernization in the eighteenth to twenty-first century may be divided into two stages: the first modernization, transformation from agricultural to industrial civilization, and the second modernization, transformation from industrial to knowledge civilization and from material to ecological civilization. It follows ten principles (Table 2.15): asynchronous process, uneven distribution, structural stability, status changeability, behavioral predictability, incremental demand, diminishing utility, optional paths, no repeated state, and axis transition
Result	The formation of modernity, particularity, diversity, and side effects, including the following: the improvement of labor productivity and quality of life, social progress, political democracy, cultural diversity, ecological change, and overall development of human; the change of national level, international status, and civilization distribution; and the persistent existence and functioning of a portion of traditional values. The main outcome of the first modernization includes the formation of first modernity, particularity, and diversity, with side effects including environmental pollution and periodic economic crises. The main outcome of the second modernization at present includes the formation of second modernity, particularity, and diversity, with side effects including information divide and cybercrime
Dynamics	Driving forces of national modernization include innovation, competition, adaptation, exchange, national interest, and market demand. Dynamic theories include innovation drive, three-innovation drive, two-wheel drive, associative action, four-step super cycle, composite interaction of three types of civilization, innovation diffusion, innovation spillovers, and competition drive (Table 2.20). Driving forces in different countries and stages are different, and different paths and models differ in their driving forces
Model	National modernization has path diversity, model diversity, and path dependence. There are roughly three basic paths and over 50 models (Table 2.21)

Source: He (2003)

5.3.2.1 Definition

National modernization is a manifestation of modernization at national layer.

The Intension. National modernization is a sort of change of national civilization and international competition; it is the frontier process of the formation, development, transformation, and international interaction of national modern civilization, as well as a composite process of alternate innovation, selection, diffusion, and recession of the elements of national modern civilization; it is also the change in international competition, national stratification, and civilization distribution with the aim of catching up with, reaching, and maintaining the world advanced level.

The Extension. National modernization includes modernization of a country as a whole, modernization in six fields, and the change in the spatial and temporal distribution of national modernization, as well as the modernization of national behavior, structure, institution, and ideas.

Generally, national modernization refers to the world frontiers of national civilization and the process and action to reach these frontiers. It is the basic unit of modernization study and practice. In the process of modernization study and practice, national modernization is at the core. In the system of modernization theories, the national modernization theory and the general theory on modernization have the highest degree of consistency with each other.

Modernization in the six fields including national economy will be dealt with in Chap. 6.

5.3.2.2 Process

National modernization is a complex, long-term process (Table 5.34). Between the eighteenth century and the twenty-first century, the frontier process of national modernization is divided into two stages, the first modernization and the second modernization, each having different features (Table 2.13).

The process of national modernization has not only common features (Table 5.22) but also diversity (Table 5.23).

National modernization follows ten fundamental principles of modernization (Table 2.15).

5.3.2.3 Result

Since the 1950s, there has been a correlation between the outcome and objective of national modernization, and this correlation has been gradually formed and enhanced.

The outcome of national modernization includes, among other things, the formation of modernity, particularity, diversity, and side effects (Table 5.34). Different countries have both common features and differences in this regard, along with changes in national levels and international status (Example 5.1).

Example 5.1 Change of National Modernization Level

The changes from 1700 to 2005 in national modernization level mainly include ascending, descending, ascending first and descending later, descending first and ascending later of international status; rise first and decline later, decline first and rise later, continuous decline, and sharp fluctuation and smooth fluctuation of national level. Status ascending refers to the transition from developing to developed countries, and status descending refers to the change from developed to developing countries. Smooth fluctuation includes high-level fluctuation (among developed countries) and

(continued)

medium-level fluctuation (among moderately and preliminarily developed countries). During the period, developed countries converged in the level of development, and gaps between developed and developing countries widened.

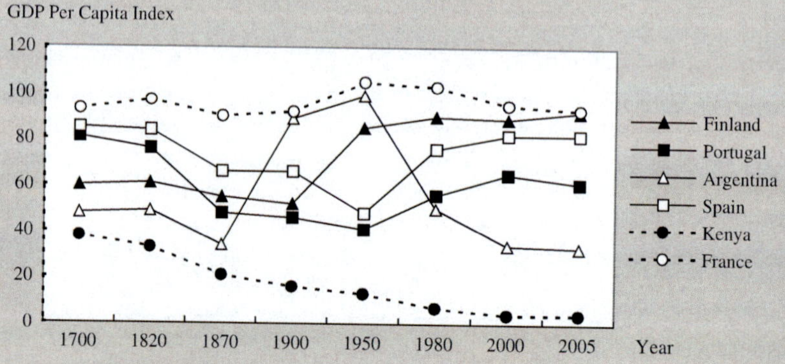

Change of national modernization level from 1700 to 2005. Note: according to the change of GDP (PPP) index calculated based on constant prices in 1990, the average modernization level of high-income countries (Western European countries) is 100.

Between 1760 and 1970, the outcome of national modernization included the formation of first modernity, particularity and diversity, and side effects such as environmental pollution, with a portion of traditional values continuing to exist and function.

From 1970 onward, the outcome of national modernization included the formation of first modernity, second modernity, particularity and diversity, as well as side effects such as cybercrime, with a portion of traditional values continuing to exist and function.

Theoretically, the goal of national modernization includes completing the first and second modernization, catching up with, reaching, and maintaining the world's advanced level of development.

From the policy perspective, the goal of national modernization includes improving productivity and quality of life and promoting social equity and progress, overall development of human, and the mutualism of humanity and the nature; the policy goal of developed countries is to maintain the world's advanced level of development and that of developing countries is to catch up with and reach that level.

5.3.2.4 Dynamics

Analysis on dynamics of national modernization covers dynamic factors and models (Table 5.34).

The driving forces of modernization may differ from country to country, stage to stage, path to path, and model to model. The motivation models may be seen on Table 2.20.

5.3.2.5 Model

Between 1760 and 1970, national modernization adopted the path of first modernization with some 19 element mix models (Table 5.26) and four types (Table 5.25).

From 1970 on, some countries adopted the path of second modernization with approximately 22 element mix models (Table 5.27); some adopted the path of integrated modernization with approximately 31 element mix models (Table 5.28); others adopted the path of first modernization but were affected by the second modernization. There are three basic paths in the twenty-first century: second modernization, catch-up modernization, and integrated modernization.

The choice of stage-related goal, path, and model of national modernization is strategically at the core of national modernization policy.

5.4 Regional Modernization

Regions can be understood—as the case may be—as transnational regions, the different areas in the world, or domestic regions, the different areas within a country. Here, regional modernization refers to modernization of domestic regions, including worldwide regional modernization, nationwide regional modernization, and regional modernization of individual region (Fig. 5.14). Regional modernization is a manifestation and analysis level of modernization phenomena and an integral part of national modernization; it is not only relatively independent but also governed by national modernization.

5.4.1 Studies

Regional modernization study may be conducted from three perspectives, i.e., history, reality, and future, and research can be conducted on worldwide, nationwide, or individual regional modernization.

5.4.1.1 Research Paradigm

Regional modernization study is an integral part of modernization study at regional level.

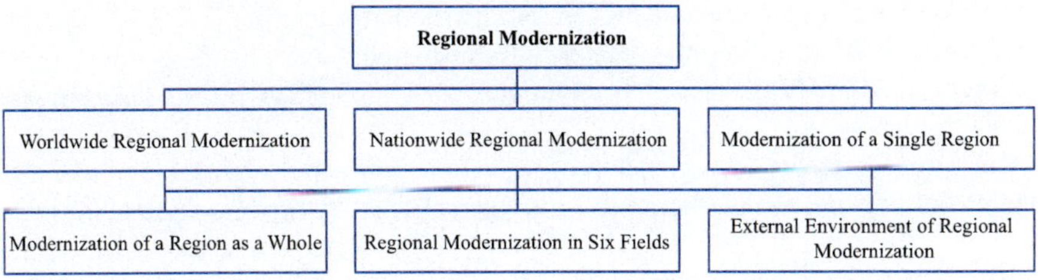

Fig. 5.14 Analytical structure of regional modernization. Note: worldwide regional modernization refers to regional modernization indifferent countries throughout the world

Table 5.35 Matrix of regional modernization study

Content		Object		
		Regional civilization	Regional economy, society, politics, culture, natural environment, and humans	Regional interaction
		Regional modernization as a whole	Modernization in the regional six fields	Interaction in regional modernization
Element	Behavior Structure Institution Idea	Modernization of regional behaviors, structures, institutions, and ideas	Behavioral, structural, institutional, idea's modernization in the regional six fields	–
Aspect	Process Result Dynamics Model	Process, result, dynamics, model of the regional modernization	Processes, result, dynamics, model of modernization in the regional six fields	International and internal environment and interaction of the regional modernization

Note: regional modernization study also includes many other contents, for example, the frontier, frontier process, and catch-up process analysis on regional civilization, regional competition analysis, regional gap analysis, elements of regional modernization, and interaction between different fields

(1) Research Matrix

The research object of regional modernization study includes modernization of a region as a whole, modernization in regional six fields, and interaction of regional modernization. Research contents include regional behavioral, structural, institutional, and ideal modernization, as well as the process, result, dynamics, and model of regional modernization, which constitute a research matrix (Table 5.35).

(2) Research Method

Regional modernization study is a level-relative study of modernization study and may use the methodology of modernization study.

The scope of regional modernization study can be one or more regions, worldwide or nationwide regions, or regions inside developed or developing countries. The time span can be the whole process or a particular stage.

Regional modernization may adopt multidimensional analysis, case study, and comprehensive study, such as the coordinate analysis method in modernization study.

The process study of regional modernization generally adopts the research methods of positivism and interpretivism. The reality study of regional modernization generally adopts the research methods of positivism, interpretivism, and realism. The prospect study of regional modernization generally adopts the research methods of positivism, interpretivism, and futurology.

(3) Research Purpose

Regional modernization study is mainly for academic and policy purposes.

From the academic perspective, regional modernization study is an important part of modernization study, with the aim to discover the basic facts, fundamental principles, and historical experience of regional modernization and thus enrich the implications of the modernization theory.

From the policy perspective, regional modernization is a unit of modernization practice, and the purpose of regional modernization study is to provide the theoretical basis, historical reference, and policy options for the practice of regional modernization.

5.4.1.2 Facts About Regional Modernization

China Modernization Report 2004: Regional Modernization Study (RGCMS 2004) analyzes the historical statistics on the development in the twentieth century of more than 170 regions in 18 countries, quotes extensive analysis results from scientists, and summarizes some basic facts and field-relative facts about regional modernization as follows:

(1) Basic Facts About Regional Modernization

First of all, regional modernization exists objectively. During the development of 171 regions in 18 countries, universal phenomena includes, among others, narrowing and widening of regional economic gaps, convergence and divergence of regional development levels, and catch-up and regress of relative regional levels. The changes in relative regional levels include the advanced becoming more advanced, the advanced keeping advanced, the backward one catching up with the advanced, the advanced becoming backward one, and the backward one remaining backward one. These roughly accord with the phenomena of national modernization (RGCMS 2004).

Second, regional modernization follows the general laws of modernization. In the process of regional modernization of the 18 countries, the basic laws of modernization such as the industrialization and urbanization in the first modernization and the knowledgeablization and informatization in the second modernization have all been verified by regional historical statistics and by scholars' analysis. Regional modernization includes political modernization whose subjects are countries. Although a region can also introduce innovation in the political system, its political modernization is determined by the politics of its country. Apparently, without political modernization, there will be no all-round national modernization and regional modernization.

Third, regional modernization is not simply a mini version of the modernization of the country to which the region belongs. A region is part of a country, and its modernization is part of the country's modernization. The average level of regional modernization is roughly equal to the country's level of modernization. But there is a variety of models and paths for regional modernization inside a country. For example, the modernization of 195 counties in 50 US states is greatly different from the country's national modernization in such aspects as industrialization and urbanization (RGCMS 2004).

Fourth, regional interaction and interdependence exist in the process of regional modernization. Regions not only compete with and depend on each other. Under the condition of free competition, a region with a higher level of modernization may diffuse its modernization outcome into a region with a lower level of modernization; meanwhile, it may also absorb important resources for modernization (including human capital, financial capital, and material resources) from the latter and is likely to transfer to the latter some adverse factors (e.g., polluting industries), thereby leading to a widening gap between the regions. Economic and population flows between regions, and state intervention [e.g., by means of financial and policy levers (transfer payment, preferential policy, etc.)] may promote the coordinated development of the regions.

Fifth, modernization of a region is closely connected with the region's basic capacity. For example, successful EU regions in the process of modernization all have the following features (Cuadrado-Roura 2001):

- A region's city system plays an important role in economic growth and production activity. Medium-sized cities as well as small cities with a population of 40,000–150,000 have obvious advantages, and big cities are particularly suitable for attracting and developing new industries. Urban competitiveness reflects regional competitiveness.
- Be easy to acquire human capital, have stable supply of qualified labor forces, and give publicity to the local high-level education via media.
- Accessibility. Have a high degree of openness which makes it easy to enter international markets, and be able to participate in national politics and the formulation of economic policies and to carry out innovation and technological development quickly. Relevant infrastructure such as information centers, research institutes, and technology centers may serve as channels and networks conducive to the capacity. Of course, it is also necessary to be able to accept these factors from outside.
- Be easy to acquire advanced production services, for example, regarding strategic planning, technical consultancy, commercialization and export, research and development, and professional financial services.
- The regional organization system is very important. Competitive local governments' ability to form a network of cooperation with the central government, other authorities, and nongovernmental organizations and to apply for and develop new programs.
- Have the "appeal" to external investment, or be able to take part in the cooperative development in the Pacific region.
- For regional development, having large-sized enterprises in declining and struggling industries is an adverse factor; to the contrary, having advantageous small-sized enterprises engaging in different production activities is a positive factor.

Sixth, regional modernization is unbalanced. Based on the development levels and stages of regional modernization in the 18 countries, countries differ greatly in regional modernization. Advanced countries have smaller regional gaps than developing countries, and countries which have entered their second modernization have smaller gaps than those which are in their first modernization.

The regional modernization of advanced countries has undergone two stages, i.e., first and second modernization. In the process of first regional modernization, basic contents are industrialization, urbanization, "deagriculturalization," and universal free compulsory education. In the USA, the relative gaps between regional economies shift from widening to narrowing, with widening absolute gaps; the income distribution inequality shift from widening to narrowing. In the process of second regional modernization, basic contents are knowledgeablization, informatization, deindustrialization, "deurbanization" (suburbanization and so on), and universal higher education. During this process, the narrowing trend of relative gaps between US regional economies and of income distribution inequality ends, while the trend of fluctuation and widening appears. The regional modernization of developing countries, which now is in the process of first modernization, still highlights industrialization and urbanization and, meanwhile, is affected by informatization.

(2) Economic Facts About Regional Modernization

In the economic sphere, regional modernization roughly has the same laws as national modernization, but they have some different features. Moreover, the regions at province level (equivalent to provincial regions in China) differ from the regions at county level (equivalent to counties in China) in the contents and features of economic modernization, which needs to be treated differentially.

First, as with national economic modernization, the basic characteristic of regional economic modernization is the improvement of productivity level, along with the steady increase of regional GDP per capital and regional labor productivity (GDP per work hour).

Second, if the decrease in the percentage of agriculture in GDP is described as "deagriculturalization," then "deagriculturalization" is the basic characteristic of economic modernization in a country and its province-level regions, and it is not absolute in the county-level regions.

In the province-level regions of developed countries, the percentages of value added of agriculture and agricultural labor force have decreased to about 2%; in the county-level regions of developed countries such as the USA, the percentages of value added of agriculture and agricultural labor force tend to decrease, but the percentage of value added of agriculture is not apparently relevant to the level of modernization (in fact, it is closely related to countries' agricultural policy), and the percentage of agricultural labor force still have a negative correlation with the level of modernization (RGCMS 2004).

The USA's county-level regions differ considerably in their percentages of agriculture. In 2000, for example, of the 195 counties in three states, six counties had a percentage of agricultural labor force below 1% (one of them was 0%), 19 counties exceeded 90%, 42 counties had a percentage of value added of agriculture below 1% (two of them were 0%, and 16 were negative), and 10 exceeded 20% (RGCMS 2004).

Third, the regional industry, which had a percentage increasing and then decreasing, experienced two stages, i.e., industrialization and deindustrialization;

some regions had already entered the stage of deindustrialization when they did not complete industrialization.

The developed countries did not enter the stage of deindustrialization until they had completed industrialization. From the 1980s onward, some developing countries saw the decrease in the percentage of industrial value added in GDP as well as fluctuation and even decrease in the percentage of industrial labor force when they had not complete industrialization, showing some features of deindustrialization. This suggested that developed countries' transition toward deindustrialization had already a massive influence on developing countries (RGCMS 2004).

Among province-level regions (50 states) in the USA, some regions experienced two typical stages, i.e., industrialization and deindustrialization; some began transition to deindustrialization in the medium stage of industrialization (proportion of industry in economy reaches 30%), and others began transition to deindustrialization at "the early stage of industrialization" (proportion of industries in economy <20%). But they all completed the "deagriculturalization" (RGCMS 2004).

In county-level regions in the USA, the transition from industrialization to deindustrialization is the trend of development, but they differ greatly from each other. In 2000, for example, of 195 the counties in 3 US states, 13 counties had a percentage of industrial labor force below 10% (2 counties were 0), 8 counties were over 40%, 9 counties had a percentage of industrial value added in GDP below 10% (2 counties were 0), and 12 counties were over 50% (RGCMS 2004).

Fourth, if the great increase in the percentage of service industries is described as service-oriented economy, then regional service-oriented economy is inevitable. For countries and their province-level regions, the percentages of service industries have increased and converged. In county-level regions of the USA, the percentages of service industries have increased and converged, but the regions differ greatly from each other. In 2000, of the 195 counties in three US states, 19 counties had a percentage of labor force in service industries above 80% (2 of them were over 90%), 9 counties were below 50%, 26 counties had a percentage of value added of service industries in GDP above 80% (4 of them were over 90%), and 24 counties were below 50% (3 of them were below 40%).

(3) Social Facts About Regional Modernization

In the social sphere, regional modernization roughly accords with national modernization. But because the development of different regions inside a country is not at the same pace, the regional social modernization is diverse as compared with the country's national modernization.

First, as with the social modernization of a country, the basic characteristic of the social modernization of a region is the improvement of residents' standard of living. It includes the following: raised up the level of medical services, prolonged life expectancy, increased survival rate of infants, improved quality of living environment, increased disposable income per capita, decrease of Engel's coefficient (decreased percentage of food consumption to total spending), reasonable increase in protein intake (increase within a reasonable range), increased coverage of social security system, improved the quality, and increased popularization of domestic consumer durables (such as home appliances and cars).

Second, if the massive concentration of population in cities is defined as "urbanization" and the massive dispersal of urban population into suburbs and towns as "deurbanization," then for a country and its province-level regions, social modernization experiences two stages, i.e., urbanization and deurbanization. In essence, "deurbanization" is the diffusion of urban civilization into suburbs and towns. For this reason, *China Modernization Report 2002* described "deurbanization" as "urban diffusion." In the stage of "deurbanization," urban population diffuses gradually; in the meanwhile, some old cities are expanding and new cities are emerging. The main features are, among others, rapid growth in suburban population of the central city (suburbanization), rapid growth in population of the metropolis (the central city and its suburbs), and decrease of urban and metropolitan population density.

In the process of social modernization of a country, urbanization and deurbanization are two natural stages. In province-level regions, both urbanization and deurbanization are diverse. For example, in the second half of the twentieth century, 3 out of the 50 US states saw a decrease in the percentage of urban population when they did not complete urbanization (with the percentage of urban population below 60%), and four saw a decline in their metropolitan population. Since the 1970s, seven metropolitan counties in the UK have seen a drop in their total populations (RGCMS 2004).

The evolution of cities in developed countries since the 1960s has been obviously different from the urbanization in the period of their industrialization. In the academic community, there are such concepts as "metropolitanization," "suburbanization," "counterurbanization," and "reurbanization." "Reurbanization," also known as "urban renaissance," means the flow of suburban and town population back into cities, thereby gross urban population and its percentage increase. The percentages of urban population in developed countries increased at the end of the twentieth century, which was much attributed to international migration rather than the mere concentration of domestic population into cities. In the late twentieth century, the majority of rural residents in developed countries were already no longer farmers.

Third, regional modernization includes the modernization of social infrastructure which experiences two development stages, i.e., "material life infrastructure" and "knowledge information infrastructure." A region's "material life infrastructure" includes its public utilities (supply of water, electricity, and gap), public traffic infrastructure (railways, civil aviation, expressways, etc.), logistics infrastructure, public health infrastructure, communications infrastructure typical of the age of industry (telephone, TV, etc.), and so forth. A region's "knowledge information infrastructure" includes "information network infrastructure" (information superhighway, etc.), satellite and mobile communications infrastructure, databases and knowledge bases, and innovation infrastructure (institutions of higher learning, scientific research institutions, etc.). In developed countries, the two stages of regional infrastructure development happened one after another; in developing countries and regions, the ongoing regional modernization includes the contents of the two stages concurrently.

(4) Knowledge Facts About Regional Modernization

In the knowledge sphere, regional modernization, for the most part, accords with national modernization. Because knowledge has such characteristics as free flow and interest overflow, a country and its province-level and county-level regions differ in strategy choice and manifestation of modernization in the sphere of knowledge.

First, as with national modernization in the sphere of knowledge, the basic characteristic of regional modernization in the sphere of knowledge is the improvement of production capacity and popularization of scientific knowledge and information. It includes the following: increased adult literacy, increased popularization of compulsory education and higher education, continuous development of vocational education, adult reeducation and lifelong learning, increased the proportion of labors with high education degree, increased capacity for knowledge production and innovation (intensity of investment in science and technology, fund, and manpower), increased popularization of telephone and TV (including telephone, mobile phone, fax, radio, TV, etc.), and increased popularization of computers and the Internet and so forth.

Second, developed countries' regional modernization in the sphere of knowledge experienced two stages, i.e., "popularization of compulsory education, telephone, and TV" and "knowledgeablization and informatization." Around the 1970s, regions of developed countries already completed the popularization of 12-year free compulsory education, telephone, and TV, as well as the dissemination of knowledge and information necessary for industrialization. Since the 1970s, the knowledgeablization and informatization, which was technically based on personal computers, the Internet, and mobile communications and featured mainly by universal higher education and lifelong learning, has become the theme of the second knowledge modernization.

Third, developing countries differ from developed ones in development models for regional modernization in the sphere of knowledge. The two stages of developed countries' regional modernization in the field of knowledge happened one after another, having the feature of "natural evolution." Developing countries' regional modernization in the sphere of knowledge has two models: copying in a follow-up way the two-stage model of developed countries, and advancing knowledgeablization and informatization while popularizing free compulsory education, telephone, and TV.

The above-mentioned facts of regional modernization are only a part of the basic facts.

5.4.1.3 Inspirations from the History of Regional Modernization

China Modernization Report 2004 analyzes the important inspirations from 18 countries in regional modernization as follows:

First, in province-level regions, regional modernization is highly consistent with national modernization. As seen by the historical statistics and research findings on modernization of province-level regions in the 18 countries, this region's modernization is consistent with modernization of their countries. Though they differ from their countries in such aspects as industrialization and urbanization, their modernization is similar to worldwide national modernization. The modernization of province-level regions inside a country not only follows the general laws of national modernization, but also has a variety of manifestations.

Second, in county-level regions, the relationship between regional and national modernization is diverse. From the historical statistics and research findings on modernization of 195 counties in three US states, the modernization of county-level regions is basically consistent with national modernization, but the correlation of regional modernization with national modernization vary from field to field. For example, on the economic front, the correlation of the economic and employment structures in county-level regions with their levels of modernization and productivity is weaker than the country; on the social front, the modernization of county-level regions is more correlated with national modernization; on the knowledge front, county-level regions' modernization differs considerably from national modernization in terms of development models (for instance, not every county-level region has a university of the world's advanced level, but the country must have a university system of the world's advanced level).

Third, the phenomenon that the processes of regional modernization are not at the same pace and are unbalanced is widespread. The historical truth about the modernization of 171 regions in the 18 countries is that in the same year in history (e.g., in 2000), different countries differ in the development stage and level of regional modernization, and different regions inside the same country differ from each other in the development stage and level of modernization. The historical truth about the US regional modernization is that, in the nineteenth and twentieth centuries, differences between US province-level regions in the development stage and level of modernization existed all the way. The degree of regional differences changes with ages, but regional differences do exist.

Fourth, the widening and narrowing of per capital income gaps between regions is widespread. If regional gaps linger on, the widening and narrowing of them is bound to exist objectively. Is there a natural law that governs such widening and narrowing? The neoclassical growth theory and the new growth theory have different explanations for this. This issue can be analyzed at two levels, namely, worldwide regional gaps and those inside countries.

In the 1960s, American economist Williamson raised an inverted U-shape curve model for regional economic gaps, holding that in the process of economic development, the change of regional economic gaps from widening to narrowing follows an inverted-U-shaped track (Williamson 1964). However, the inverted U model is not totally consistent with the actual changes in regional gaps in the USA. According to existing research papers and historical data, in the process of regional modernization, the widening and narrowing of regional gaps seems rather complex and has no simple model (Table 5.36).

Table 5.36 Per capita GDP gaps between tier-one administrative regions in four countries

Item	India		Mexico	UK		USA		
Year	1990/1991	1999/2000	2000	1990	1999	1980	1990	2000
Maximum GDP per capita ($)	634	824	13,870	19,423	27,280	37,331	45,044	46,767
Minimum GDP per capita ($)	165	146	2,273	11,190	16,220	8,541	15,214	23,380
Average ($)	317	381	5,210	14,618	20,147	12,170	22,108	33,663
Standard deviation	115	163	2,465	2,140	3,270	4,241	5,009	5,723
Absolute gap ($)	469	678	11,598	8,233	11,060	28,790	29,830	23,387
Relative gap	3.8	5.6	6.1	1.74	1.68	4.4	2.96	2.00
Coefficient of variation	0.364	0.427	0.473	0.146	0.162	0.348	0.227	0.17

Note: Absolute gap = Maximum–Minimum, Relative gap = Maximum/Minimum, Coefficient of variation = Standard deviation/Average
Source: RGCMS (2004)

Some scholars found that gaps in per capita income between countries throughout the world were widening from the nineteenth century into the twentieth century (Clark and Feenstra 2001). But some held that in the last 40 years of the twentieth century, the gaps between countries in per capita income based on PPP narrowed (Melchior et al. 2000), and the gaps in the standard of living (including life expectancy, survival rate of infants, composite enrollment rate, adult literacy, and popularization of telephone and TV) narrowed (Neumayer 2003). If national gaps widen, worldwide regional gaps are bound to widen. If national gaps narrow, there is the need for further research into worldwide regional gaps.

In both developed and developing countries, the widening and narrowing of regional gaps is a widespread phenomenon. The change of both absolute and relative gaps between regions is different. In the 1990s, absolute gaps between regions inside developed countries were greater than those inside developing countries, while relative gaps between regions inside developing countries were greater than those inside developed countries (Table 5.36).

An interesting phenomenon can be observed when the relative gaps between regions inside the USA and EU: during their process of industrialization (from the nineteenth century to around 1960s), the curve of change in the regional relative gap experienced the upward and downward stages; the downward trend was over as industrialization was completed. Around the 1970s, the curve of change fluctuated; from the 1980s onward, the curve took on an upward trend, but the gap was not greater than the past. Of course, this curve is not smooth, but wavy. The widening of the regional relative gap since the 1980s was undoubtedly related to the new industrial revolutions (information revolution and knowledge revolution). During the twentieth century, the absolute regional gap (standard deviation) was widening.

Given this situation, the curve of change in the regional relative gap is more like a declining curve of fluctuation. This phenomenon could be observed in the US change of regional relative gap in per capital income between 1840 and 2000, in the fluctuation in regional gap in GDP per capita between 1977 and 2000 in 50 US states, in the change of regional relative gap in GDP per capita in West Germany (Federal Republic of Germany), the UK, France, Italy, Spain, and Portugal in the 1960s–1990s, and even in the change of regional relative gap in GDP per capita and labor productivity (GDP per worker) in Mexico between 1940 and 2000.

Perhaps this is right the form of evolution of regional gap convergence and divergence in the process of regional modernization. Its basic characteristic is that the curve of change in regional relative gap is a declining curve of fluctuation and, in the meanwhile, the curve of change in regional absolute gap is likely an expanding curve of fluctuation (Fig. 5.15). Further research is required as to when the expanding curve of absolute gap will decline.

In the process of regional modernization, the curve of fluctuation in the change of regional relative gap is not absolute. It might be one form of change in regional relative gap. We can find examples different from such curve of change. For example, between 1911 and 1993, the regional relative gap in per capita income between all 24 counties in Sweden converged all the way (Persson 1997). Therefore, there is supposed to have other forms of change in regional relative gap, for example, the conditional convergence in regional economic gap.

Fifth, the fluctuation and narrowing of urban–rural gap is widespread. In the process of industrialization, urbanization is inevitable, thereby forming the dualistic urban–rural structure. Generally, the urban–rural gap is existent objectively. Currently, the economic gap between urban and rural areas inside developed countries is already very small, while, because countryside has better natural environment, urban residents are moving into suburbs and rural areas, and the majority of rural residents are nonfarmers. In developing countries, the urban–rural gap is still very large, and because rural infrastructure is backward relatively, rural population continues to flock to cities and the level of urban modernization is apparently higher than rural modernization.

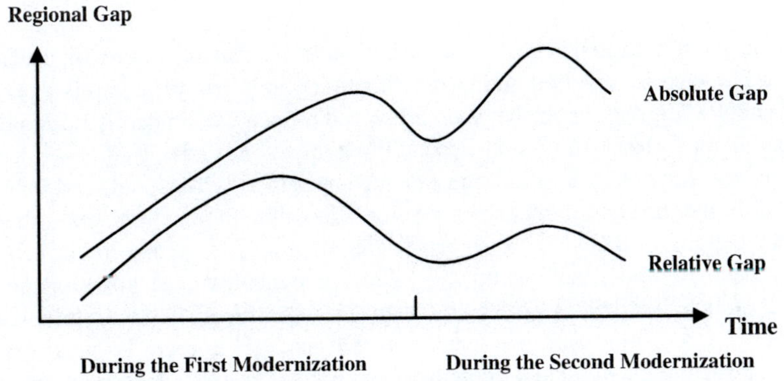

Fig. 5.15 Change of absolute and relative gaps in regional per capita income. Note: absolute gap is an expanding curve of fluctuation, and relative gap is a declining curve of fluctuation

In developed countries, for example the USA, there was a process of evolvement in the gap between urban and rural areas. When industrialization began, the urban–rural economic gap widened; when industrialization ended, the urban–rural economic gap narrowed; when informatization began, the urban–rural economic gap fluctuated. The urban–rural difference in natural environment always existed. From the 1820s, the US urban areas had higher labor productivity and wages than rural areas, but health conditions in rural areas were better than those in urban areas. Because of the poor sanitary conditions and high popularity density in cities, the life expectancy of the US urban population shortened. In 1900, the life expectancy of the urban population was averagely 10 years shorter than that of the rural population, along with higher urban adult and infant mortality rates than rural areas. The US urban–rural health gap began narrowing at the turn of the twentieth century until around 1940 when urban health conditions caught up with those in rural areas (Kim and Margo 2003). In the middle of the twentieth century, the USA completed its urbanization, with the narrowed economic gap between urban and rural areas. Because of traffic and environmental problems, urban residents' quality of life and economic efficiency were affected, and high-income urban residents began moving to suburbs and rural areas, leading to a drop in urban population density. In the meantime, the US rural population decreased, agriculture saw an improved efficiency, and the government's agricultural subsidy policy compensated in part for the natural risk and loss of agriculture; the urban–rural gap in per capital income narrowed. In the US Pacific coastal areas in 1975, the ratio of metropolitan to nonmetropolitan (urban to rural) per capital income was 1.1:1. In the late twentieth century, with knowledgeablization and informatization developing, the importance of geographic distance declined, but there was a certain gap between urban and rural areas in capability of acquiring and applying new knowledge and information for it took time for diffusion of knowledge and technology, leading to fluctuations in the economic gap between urban and rural areas.

The change of the urban–rural gap inside developing countries did not accord with that in developed countries. In the early and middle stages of industrialization, the economic gap was large between urban and rural areas. Currently, the urban–rural gap inside developing countries is somewhat obvious. The urban–rural economic gap is expected to narrow in the late stage of industrialization. In the early stage of knowledgeablization and informatization, the urban–rural gap is likely to widen and the "digital divide" between urban and rural areas can hardly be avoided. This gap is likely to narrow as the second modernization is advanced.

Sixth, the widening and narrowing of income gap is widespread, and income distribution requires government intervention. Undoubtedly, modernization should increase welfare for the whole of society, rather than only for a minority of people. In the process of modernization, however, income inequality exists for a long term. Without policy intervention by government, income inequality will follow the "Matthew Effect"—the rich get richer and the poor get poorer. To what extent policy intervention is applied by countries and regions results in different changes in income inequality.

In 1955, American economist Kuznets raised an "inverted U" model for income inequality, suggesting that income inequality increases during early industrialization, stabilizes during mid-industrialization, and decreases during late industrialization (Kuznets 1955). Though many still have questions over this, the "inverted U" model for income inequality during industrialization has been supported by massive facts (Chen 1994).

From the 1970s onward, however, massive changes happened in developed countries in trends of income inequality. In the 1970s, income inequality stopped narrowing and began widening in the USA (USCB 2002); income inequality has widened in the UK since the mid-1970s, and it was widening in Belgium, Sweden, Netherlands, Finland, Italy, and Germany from the mid-1980s to the mid-1990s (Förster and Pearson 2002).

According to economists (Piketty and Saez 2001) at the National Bureau of Economic Research, the widening of income inequality in developed countries since the 1970s poses no challenge to Kuznets' "inverted U" model. The fact is that new situations have happened to it because of new industrial revolutions and innovations, and this inequality will begin narrowing at some point.

If the above notion is tenable, the "inverted U" model for income inequality should be extended. And the new feature of income inequality in developed countries since the 1970s should be included.

In fact, the "inverted U" model is a visualized metaphor: the track of income inequality in the USA during industrialization is not a smooth curve, but a wavy curve typical of an inverted U shape. Coupled with the widening of income inequality since the 1970s and its possible future narrowing, the curve of change in income inequality can be imagined to be a fluctuating curve of periodic decline with the amplitude of knowledgeablization smaller than that of industrialization.

Seventh, the changing distribution of population and economic activities can be divided into two stages: concentration and decentralization. During its regional modernization, the US spatial distribution of population and production factors experienced the stages of concentration and dispersion. During the industrialization, the regional population, production factors, and industrial and economic activity converged into cities, leading to the increase of economic efficiency. During the late industrialization, or from the 1940s onward, the suburbanization of US population was very obvious. By 1960, the percentages of population in central cities and suburbs had been basically in balance, the density of urban population had declined rapidly, and the spatial distribution of population has entered a stage of relative divergence. American scholars attribute the dispersion of urban population mainly to the income increase of urban residents and the development of vehicles. Undoubtedly, the process of informatization will drive the dispersion of urban population. In 2000, 50% of Americans lived in suburbs, 30% lived in central cities, and 20% lived in the countryside (Hobbs and Stoops 2002).

If we say that the concentration of US population and economic activity was basically in a step with each other, then the dispersion of its urban population and economic activity happened step by step. The first wave was the suburbanization of urban population, and the second one was the suburbanization of urban economic activities (Glaeser and Kahn 2001). The US urban population began moving into suburbs at the end of the nineteenth century, and by 1960, 63% of jobs concentrated in central cities and 51% of urban residents lived in suburbs. People lived in suburbs, yet they worked in central cities. As urban population moved out of cities, jobs also flowed into suburbs. At the end of the twentieth century, for 150 cities in the USA, averagely 18% of population and 26% of jobs concentrated in central urban areas (three miles from city center) and 65% of population and 27% of jobs scattered in areas five miles farther from central business districts of cities (Glaeser and Kahn 2001). American scholars also found that in a relative sense, commercial services such as banking concentrated, manufacturing dispersed, and knowledge information-intensive industries concentrated (Glaeser and Kahn 2001).

Eighth, developed countries' regional modernization involves two stages and a variety of development models. As with national modernization, regional modernization is a long-term historical process, which is bound to have some development stages. The division of development stages is both artificial and objective because criteria for division are made by people based on objective facts. In different stages of regional modernization, a region is different from another in development concept and strategy as well as in model and path. For example, the US regional modernization can be divided into two development stages: first modernization and second modernization, which differ essentially in development model (RGCMS 2004).

Generally, modernization stages of countries and their province-level regions can be divided according to development levels of their industrial and employment structures, i.e., making reference to their levels of productivity. The division of modernization stages for county-level regions currently has no rational division methods available because of the decreased correlation between their industrial structures and modernization levels, and the method of reference is dividing according to employment structure and productivity level.

Ninth, the transfer probability of the relative position of regional development has some regularity. During regional modernization, regional gaps and phenomena of their widening and narrowing exist all the way. Among advanced regions, some maintained their leading positions, while some fell behind; among intermediate regions, some ascended to higher levels, while some not; among backward regions, some caught up with advanced regions, while some remained backward. So, is there some law about the transfer probability of the relative position of a region?

The answer is YES. Generally, the probability that a region remains its relative position is about 70%, while the probability that a region's relative position ascends or descends is some 30%. This can be demonstrated by research results by European scholars (Table 5.37). For 109 EU regions, among those whose GDP per capita was lowest in 1977, about 77% of them remained lowest in 1994 and about 30% ascended to a higher level; among those whose GDP per capita was highest in 1977, about 48% of them remained highest in 1994 and about 52% descended to a lower level. For 117 EU regions, about 94% of those whose per capita income was lowest in 1988 remained their lowest level in 1998, and about

Table 5.37 Transfer probability of national and regional levels in groups

Indicator	Sample	Period	Transfer probability of lowest level group (%)		Transfer probability of highest level group (%)	
			Unchanged	Upward	Downward	Unchanged
GDP per capita	107 EU regions	1977–1994	70	30	52	48
Per capita income	117 EU regions	1988–1998	94	6	32	68
Labor productivity	117 EU regions	1988–1998	93	7	24	76
Life expectancy	164 countries	1960–1999	78	22	30	71
Infant survival rate	161 countries	1960–1999	71	29	20	80
Composite enrollment rate	74 countries	1965–1999	74	26	28	72
Adult literacy	133 countries	1970–1999	88	12	3	97
Popularization rate of telephone	107 countries	1960–1999	82	18	19	81
Popularization rate of TV	109 countries	1965–1999	71	29	15	85

Source: Cuadrado-Roura (2001), Basile et al. (2001), and Neumayer (2003)

Table 5.38 Structure of regional modernization theory

Category	Theory	Main contents
General theory	Core theory	The definition, process, result, dynamics, and model of regional modernization
Branch theories	Stage theory	Regional first modernization, second modernization, or integrated modernization
	Field-related study	Regional modernization in the fields such as economy, society, politics, culture, natural environment, and humans
	Sector-related study	Regional modernization in the sectors such as agriculture, industry, education, science and technology, national defense, and transportation
	Subregion theory	Modernization in urban and rural areas, suburbs, mountainous areas, plains, hilly area, etc.
Relevant theories	Other modernization theories	Classical modernization theory, postmodernization theory, second modernization theory, etc.
	Other relevant theories	Economic geography, development theory, regional planning, space development theory, area study, etc.

Source: RGCMS (2004)

76% of those whose per capita income was highest in 1988 remained their highest level in 1998. The transfer probability of relative levels of countries is similar during national modernization.

An advanced region is likely to fall behind if it does not work hard, while a backward region is likely to go up if it works hard. Although it is possible for a backward region to catch up with those with higher levels of development, it is not an easy thing to do and requires much more endeavor.

5.4.2 Theories

The regional modernization theory is a theoretical explanation for phenomena of regional modernization; it is a level theory under the second modernization theory and modernization science. A region means one inside a country here. Regional modernization is modernization at regional level, which has not only generalities of modernization but also some particularities. The core theory (Table 2.1) on the general modernization basically applies to regional modernization. Regional modernization is an integral part of national modernization, it is not simply a mini version of national modernization, but also has greater diversity and structural flexibility.

According to Chinese scholar Chuanqi He, the regional modernization theory includes the general theory, branch theories, and relevant theories (Table 5.38), where the general theory includes five aspects of regional modernization: definition, process, result, dynamics, and model (Table 5.39).

5.4.2.1 Definition of Regional Modernization

Regional modernization is a manifestation of modernization at regional level and an integral part of national modernization here.

(1) The Connotation and Denotation of Regional Modernization

The Connotation. Regional modernization is a sort of change of regional civilization and regional competition; it is the frontier process of the formation, development, transformation, international, and interregional interaction of regional modern civilization, as well as a composite process of alternate innovation, selection, diffusion, and recession of the elements of regional modern civilization; it is also the change in regional competition, regional differentiation, and stratification, with aim of catching up with, reaching, and maintaining the world's advanced level of development.

The Denotation. Regional modernization includes modernization of a region as a whole, modernization in regional six fields, interaction of regional modernization, the modernization of regional behavior, structure, institution, and ideas, as well as regional sectoral modernization and the modernization in urban and rural areas, mountainous and plain areas, etc.

Generally, regional modernization refers to the world frontiers of regional civilization and the process and action to reach these frontiers. Regional

Table 5.39 General theory on regional modernization

Aspect	Main contents
Definition	Regional modernization, i.e., modernization at regional level, is a sort of frontier change and regional competition in regional civilization since the Industrial Revolution in the eighteenth century. It includes the formation, development, transformation, and interaction of regional modern civilization; the innovation, selection, exchange, and recession of the elements of regional modern civilization; and the regional competition, differentiation, and stratification for catching up with, reaching, and maintaining the world advanced level
Process	Regional modernization is a complex process, including regional civilization change, regional competition, regional polarization, and stratification, the changes of regional behavior, structure, institution, and ideas. The process of regional modernization between the eighteenth century and the twenty-first century may be divided into two stages: the first modernization, transition from agricultural to industrial civilization, and the second modernization, transition from industrial to knowledge civilization and from material to ecological civilization. The change of economic and social structures during regional modernization is flexible. It follows ten principles (Table 2.15)
Result	The formation of modernity, particularity, diversity, and side effects, including the improvement of labor productivity and quality of life, social progress, political democracy, cultural diversification, ecological change, and overall development of human, and the change of regional level, status, and civilization gap. Overall development of human is the essence of regional modernization. The main outcome of the first modernization includes the formation of first modernity, particularity, and diversity, with side effects including environmental pollution and periodic economic crises. The main outcome of the second modernization includes the formation of second modernity, particularity, and diversity, with side effects including information divide and cyber crime. The two types of regional modernity have great flexibility and regional diversity rather than being absolute; side effects differ from one region to another; and some traditional values continue to exist and function
Dynamics	Main driving forces of the regional first modernization are investment, technological progress, industrialization, and urbanization. Main driving forces of the regional second modernization are knowledge innovation, institutional innovation, and human capital. Main driving forces of regional integrated modernization are education and investment, industrialization and informatization, urbanization and suburbanization, technological and institutional innovation, and so on. Dynamic models include innovation drive, three-innovation drive, two-wheel drive, associative action, four-step super cycle, composite interaction of three types of civilization, innovation diffusion, innovation spillovers, competition drive, and productivity function (Table 2.20). Driving forces in different regions and stages are different, and different paths and models differ in their driving forces
Model	Regional modernization has a variety of paths and models and is influenced by regional geographic conditions, infrastructure, and external environment. Models of regional first modernization are diverse combinations of industrialization, urbanization, etc.; models of regional second modernization are diverse combinations of knowledgeablization, informatization, ecologicalization, suburbanization, etc.; models of regional integrated modernization are diverse combinations of industrialization, informatization, ecologicalization, urbanization, etc.

Note: regions can be divided into advanced regions and developing regions according to the classification of advanced and developing countries as well as the level of regional modernization. Advanced regions are those which have reached the world's advanced level of development, and the rest are developing ones. For the purpose of convenience, we see the words "region" and "area" as synonym and call "regional modernization" and "area modernization" regional modernization collectively

Source: RGCMS (2004)

modernization is a process that advanced regions reach and maintain the world advanced level, and developing regions catch up with the world advanced level.

Regional modernization is also an objective that advanced regions maintain the world advanced level—a level which is a function of continuously changing state, and developing regions catch up with and reach the world advanced level—a level which is a changing objective function.

(2) Relationship Between Regional and National Modernization

First of all, regional modernization is an organic part and the foundation of national modernization. National modernization is the objective environment and condition for regional modernization. Regional modernization must be subordinate to national modernization.

Second, regional modernization follows the general laws of modernization. Regional modernization is not simply a mini version of national modernization. For province-level regions, regional modernization is consistent with national modernization for the most part; for county-level regions, the relationship between regional modernization and national modernization is diverse.

Third, regional modernization is regional behavior and also needs to be subject to national regulation. Because competition and cooperation coexist between regions inside a country, regional modernization needs to be regulated by the country by giving consideration to the overall optimization of national modernization.

Fourth, regional modernization includes political modernization. Countries are basic units of political modernization. When we look at modernization from the political perspective, national modernization is a whole, and regional political modernization is subject to national politics. Generally, without national political modernization, regional political modernization is impossible, though a region may also introduce political innovation. Different regions differ in the level of political modernization. Without political modernization, there is no complete national modernization; without national political modernization, there is no complete regional modernization.

Fifth, regional modernization and national modernization interact with each other, and to what extent they interact is different in different fields. On the economic front, the economic restructuring of regional modernization is elastic, but that of national modernization is a must. On the social front, the urbanization and suburbanization during regional modernization is elastic, but to national modernization is a must.

(3) Relationship Between Regional Modernization and Regional Development

There is no uniform definition of development. French economist François Perroux raised in his book, *A New Concept of Development*, "the concept of global, integrated and endogenous development," exerting widespread social influence. According to him, development is different from both growth and progress. Growth is the expansion of scale, progress is the general expansion of income, and development involves optimization of structure. Development, or economic development, needs to be understood on three levels: the connection between integral parts of the whole, the action of and interaction between various sectors, and opportunities for human resources in various forms to obtain efficiency and capability. The optimization at the three levels is the basic requirement of development (Perroux 1983).

In general, development is unequal to modernization; modernization is based on development and aims to reach and maintain the world's advanced level of development. The relationship between regional modernization and regional development is complex, and advanced regions differ from developing ones in this regard (Table 5.40).

Table 5.40 Relationship between regional modernization and regional development

Region	Development	Modernization	Type
Advanced regions	Development level rises, maintaining the world's advanced level	Both absolute and relative levels of modernization rise	Modernization
	Development level rises, not maintaining the world's advanced level	Absolute level of modernization rises, while relative level of it declines	Semimodernization[a]
	Development level remains unchanged, not maintaining the world's advanced level	Absolute level of modernization remains unchanged, while relative level of it declines	Stagnation
	Development level declines, with negative development (regression)	Both absolute and relative levels of modernization decline	Regression
Developing regions	Development level rises, with a narrowing gap to the world's advanced level	Both absolute and relative levels of modernization rise	Modernization
	Development level rises, with an unchanged gap to the world's advanced level	Absolute level of modernization rises, while relative level of it remains unchanged	Semimodernization[a]
	Development level rises, with a widening gap to the world's advanced level	Absolute level of modernization rises, while relative level of it declines	Semimodernization[a]
	Development level remains unchanged, with stagnant development	Absolute level of modernization remains unchanged, while relative level of it declines	Stagnation
	Development level declines, with negative development (regression)	Both absolute and relative levels of modernization decline	Regression

[a]"Semimodernization" means that the absolute levels of modernization rise while its relative levels remains unchanged or declines

5.4.2.2 Process of Regional Modernization

(1) Two Stages

The process of regional modernization between the eighteenth century and the twenty-first century is generally divided into two stages. The first stage, called the regional first modernization, refers to the transition from agricultural to industrial civilization, including the transformation from agricultural to industrial economy, from agricultural to industrial society and from agricultural to industrial culture. The second stage, called the regional second modernization, refers to the transition from industrial to knowledge civilization and from material to ecological civilization, including the transformation from industrial to knowledge economy, from industrial to knowledge society, from industrial to knowledge culture, and from material and ecological culture. The regional second modernization is not the end, and there will be new changes in the future.

During regional modernization, the change of economic structure, as well as urbanization and suburbanization, is not absolute but elastic. And the change of society and civilization is bound to happen.

(2) Main Features

First, general features. Regional modernization is nonlinear, accelerated, out-of-step, long-term, progressive, and global and has multiple paths as well as path dependence and involves risk and side effects.

Regional modernization is a process involving a chain of economic and social transitions. Social costs need to be paid for every economic and social transition, along with enormous risks. Failure of such transition will lead to the break of modernization and even regression.

Second, development models. During the regional first modernization, economic development is primary, with material production aimed to expand the space of material life necessary to satisfy the material pursuit and economic security of humankind. In the process of the regional second modernization, quality of life is primary, with knowledge and information production aimed to expand the space of spiritual life necessary to satisfy humankind's pursuit of happiness and self-expression; the quality of material life might converge, but the spiritual and cultural life will be highly diversified.

Third, change of income inequality. A relative common change model for income inequality is: during the first modernization of a region, the phenomenon described by Kuznets' "inverted U" model happens, with income inequality changing from widening to narrowing; when the region enters its second modernization, income inequality stops narrowing and is likely to widen and fluctuate.

Fourth, change of regional income gap. A relative common change model for regional gap is: during the first modernization of a region, the phenomenon described by Williamson's "inverted U" model happens, with the region's relative economic gap changing from widening to narrowing, but its absolute economic gap widens; when the region enters its second modernization, its relative economic gap is likely to widen and fluctuate, and its absolute economic gap will continue to widen and fluctuate.

Fifth, change of urban–rural income gap. A relative common change model for a region's urban–rural economic gap is: during its first modernization, the urban–rural economic gap changes from widening to narrowing; when it enters its second modernization, the urban–rural gap is likely to expand and fluctuate.

Sixth, concentration and dispersion of population and economic activities. A commonly seen change model for the distribution of a region's population and economic activities is: during its first modernization, the population and economic activities converge toward cities; when it enters its second modernization, the population and economic activities tend to disperse.

Seventh, industrialization and deindustrialization. If industrialization is seen as the transition from agricultural to industrial civilization, then regional industrialization is a must. If industrialization is defined as the change of industrial and employment structures from agriculture to industry, regional modernization is of great elasticity rather than being absolute. Deindustrialization is a new stage of economic and civilization development and is fairly elastic in county-level regions.

Eighth, urbanization and suburbanization. If urbanization is understood as a form of transition from agricultural to urban civilization, then regional urbanization is a must. If urbanization is defined as the increase in the percentage of urban population, regional urbanization is of great elasticity. People living in countryside can also have access to urban civilization. Suburbanization is not only the diffusion of urban civilization but also the new development of it, which is fairly elastic.

(3) Differences Between Advanced and Developing Regions

The process of modernization in advanced regions generally undergoes two stages in succession, first modernization and second modernization. Following completion of the first modernization, strategic transitions must be done, including from industrialization to deindustrialization, from urbanization to suburbanization and metropolitanization and from relative concentration to relative dispersion, while popularizing higher education and accelerating knowledgeablization and informatization.

The process of modernization in developing regions can be either catch-up modernization by following and learning the experience of developed regions and engaging in the first and second modernization, or integrated modernization by accelerating the coordinated development of the first and second modernization.

The basic characteristic of catch-up modernization is following and imitating the modernization paths and models of developed countries and regions, and engaging in industrialization and urbanization first and then deindustrialization, informatization, etc. The basic characteristic of integrated modernization is developing in a coordinated way the first and second modernization and continuing the transition to the second modernization, implementing the "canal strategy" for modernization; advancing the innovation of the path, model, and strategy; and walking a new path of modernization featuring the coordinated development of industrialization, shift of industries, and informatization as well as of urbanization, suburbanization, and urban expansion, thereby catching up with the advanced level of developed regions.

(4) Regional Modernization at Different Levels

The modernization of province-level region generally has the apparent features of the first and second modernization. The two stages of modernization occur in succession, particularly in developed regions. Developing regions' first and second modernization may occur in succession or develop in a coordinated way.

The modernization of county-level region has the feature of diversity. Some have the features of the two stages, while some have no obvious features of the two stages. They differ greatly in industrialization and urbanization, with "deagriculturalization" and "deindustrialization" having great elasticity. Nevertheless, knowledgeablization and informatization are inevitable.

(5) Nationwide Regional Modernization

Nationwide regional modernization can be included in or seen as part of national modernization. Involving the spatial distribution of national modernization, it includes the regional distribution of national modernization, as well as cross-regional exchange and cooperation.

First, balanced development of nationwide regional modernization. When a country is small and developed enough, nationwide regional modernization can choose the modernization process of balanced development among its regions. If regional modernization is already unbalanced, measures for balanced development can be adopted to promote the balanced development of regional modernization. If regional modernization is already balanced, the country can promote the modernization process of balanced development.

Second, unbalanced development of nationwide regional modernization. When a country is big and backward one, nationwide regional modernization is generally unbalanced among its regions. Such imbalance will expand given the free market economy. In the case of mixed economy subject to national intervention, there can be two possibilities: pushing the balanced development of regional modernization and pushing the unbalanced development of regional modernization. The latter is just the process of unbalanced development of regional modernization.

Third, the process of nationwide regional modernization is dynamic. When we look at regional modernization on a national layer, there will be leaders, pursuers, innovators, learners, etc., of regional modernization. If nationwide regional modernization is in a process of unbalanced development, a center–periphery structure of regional modernization will appear. In countries with higher levels of modernization, regional relative gaps are smaller, while in those with lower levels of modernization, regional gaps are bigger.

Ten Principles of Regional Modernization

Generally, regional modernization follows ten principles of modernization, and they are asynchronous process, uneven distribution, structural stability, status changeability, behavioral predictability, optional paths, incremental demand, diminishing utility, no repeated state, and axis transition (Table 2.15).

5.4.2.3 Result of Regional Modernization

Since the 1950s, the correlation between the outcome and objective of regional modernization has increased gradually.

(1) Outcome of Regional Modernization

The outcome of regional modernization includes, among others, the formation of modernity, particularity, diversity and side effects (Table 5.40). Overall development of human beings is the essence of regional modernization. The outcome of the first and second modernization is different, and some traditional values continue to exist and function.

Province-level and county-level regions differ in manifestation of the two types of modernity. On the economic and social fronts particularly, province-level regions differ from county-level ones in the two types of modernity, and county-level regions will have greater diversity.

(2) Objectives of Regional Modernization in the Twenty-First Century

Generally, regional modernization has three objectives in the Twenty-first century.

The first objective is to complete the first modernization. Apparently, it is a static objective, roughly reaching the average level of developed industrialized countries (they entered the period of deindustrialization in the 1970s) in the 1960s.

The second objective is to complete the second modernization. In the first 50 years of the twenty-first century or so, it is a dynamic objective, with few countries and regions able to complete the objective; in the second half of the century, some countries and regions will complete the second modernization in succession, entering a mature knowledge society. By then, completion of the second modernization will become a static objective too.

The third objective is to reach and maintain the world's advanced level of development. Apparently, the world's advanced level of development ever changes. Therefore, this objective is a dynamic one.

(3) Realization of Regional Modernization Objectives

The first objective is realizable, but the time for regions to complete it is different.

The second objective is realizable, but the time for regions to complete it is different.

As to the third objective, only a portion of regions can realize it (Example 5.2). Advanced regions aim to maintain the world's advanced level of development, while developing ones aim to catch up with the world's advanced level of development.

Example 5.2 Transfer Probability of Regional Modernization

According to the experience of 50 states of the USA in the past 20 years, there was approximately 20% probability that high level regions descended to medium-level ones, a 20% probability that medium-level regions ascended to high-level ones, a 20% probability that preliminary-level regions ascended to medium-level ones, and a 20% probability that low-level regions ascended to preliminary-level ones.

(continued)

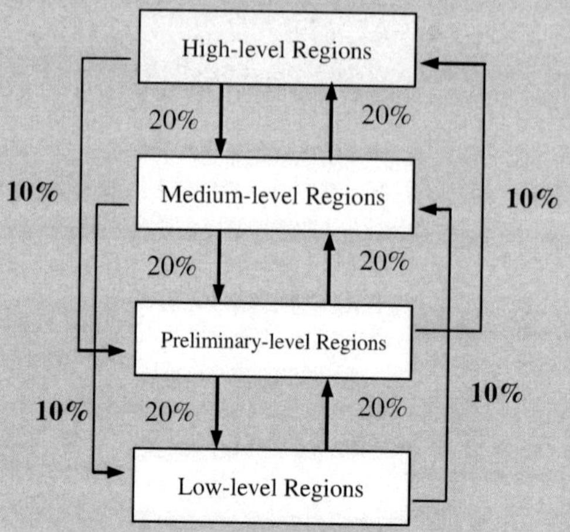

Reference transfer probabilities of tier one regions in 20 years

The third objective of regional modernization in the twenty-first century is to reach and maintain the world's advanced level of development, which generally has the following four features:

Feature 1. Only a portion of regions in the world can realize the third objective. Only a portion of regions in the world can reach the world's advanced level of development, and regions in developing countries cannot reach the world's advanced level at one time.

Feature 2. The third objective cannot be realized once and for all. A region which has already realized the third objective in a year is not necessarily able to realize this goal in the next year. That a region reached the world's advanced level of development in 2000 would not necessarily remain at the level in 2001.

Feature 3. Regions with different levels of development differ considerably in probability of realizing the third objective. For example, according to experience of the USA and EU, in a period of 20 years, the probability that province-level regions realized the third objective was about 70% for developed regions, about 20% for moderately developed regions, about 10% for minimally developed regions, and 0% for low-level regions.

Feature 4. Minimally developed and less-developed regions need to realize the third objective step by step. Generally, there is little probability that a minimally developed region will "skip" into the ranks of developed regions; it needs to go up to a moderately developed region first and then ascend to a developed one. It is generally impossible for a less-developed region to kip directly to a developed one; to change from a less-developed region to a developed one, it needs to go up to a minimally developed region first, then to a moderately developed region and finally to a developed one.

5.4.2.4 Dynamics of Regional Modernization

(1) Main Driving Forces of First Regional Modernization

The basic contents of the regional first modernization are industrialization, urbanization, democratization, etc. During this process, conditions differ considerably from one country to another. For example, during the regional first modernization in European countries, main driving forces were likely capital accumulation, technological progress, industrialization, urbanization, overseas immigration, etc. For the process of the regional first modernization in the USA, main driving forces were likely investment, land development, technological progress, industrialization, urbanization, receiving immigrants, etc. Main driving forces during the regional first modernization in developing countries were likely domestic and foreign investment, technology import and innovation, industrialization, urbanization, etc.

In general, the economic development during the regional first modernization can be explained by classical economic theory and neoclassical economic theory.

(2) Main Driving Forces of Second Regional Modernization

The basic contents of the regional second modernization are knowledgeablization, informatization, greening, globalization, etc. During this process, main driving forces are knowledge innovation, institutional innovation, human capital, and globalization. People's pursuit of the quality of life and sound environment becomes the driving force of regional development, and regional innovation system becomes the powerhouse of the regional second modernization.

A regional innovation system is an innovation cooperation network consisting of institutions and organizations relating to knowledge and technology innovation, including innovation-oriented enterprises, universities, and scientific research institutions, as well as policy makers and intermediary service agencies that promote innovation activities. The regional innovation policy is software of the innovation system, while the regional innovation culture is the soul of the innovation system.

The economic development during the regional second modernization is, for the most part, explained by using the new growth theory, regional new development theory, etc.

(3) Main Driving Forces of Regional Integrated Modernization

Main driving forces of regional comprehensive modernization are likely education and investment, urbanization and suburbanization, industrialization and informatization, technology import and innovation, knowledge innovation and institutional innovation, and so on. The regional innovation system and its innovation activity are the major powerhouse of regional comprehensive modernization of new type.

5.4.2.5 Models of Regional Modernization

There are three paths of regional modernization in the twenty-first century: second modernization, catch-up modernization, and integrated modernization. Regional modernization has a number of path and model options. There is no best model but only rational choice.

(1) Models of Regional First Modernization

Development models for the regional first modernization are a variety of combinations of industrialization, urbanization, etc. Some regions give priority to industrialization, some give priority to urbanization, and others push industrialization and urbanization in a coordinated way.

For province-level regions, the improvement of productivity and living standard is essential, and things that must be done include deagriculturalization, industrialization, and urbanization; popularization of free compulsory primary education, telephone, and TV; and establishment of social security systems as well as public infrastructure necessary for industrialization. But it is not that every region must increase the percentage of industrial sector to over 40%; industrialization has great elasticity as well as multiple models. Urbanization can also be elastic to some degree.

For example, in some states of USA with higher levels of modernization, industrialization is not adequate, but deagriculturalization is quite adequate with high levels of productivity. Their percentage of industry is not over 30%; what is more is that it is on the decline. They are now in a stage of deindustrialization. In these states, tourism and service industries are generally quite developed; their development relies on their own endeavor, and depends more on the increase of nationwide productivity.

For county-level regions, the improvement of productivity and living standard is crucial, and things that must be done include urbanization; popularization of free compulsory primary education, telephone, and TV; establishment of social security systems; as well as public infrastructure necessary for industrialization. But industrialization and deagriculturalization are elastic, and the percentages of industrial and agricultural sectors—rather than being fixed—are more the result of market mechanism regulation and of national economic division of work and are subject to international economic division of work. Though the percentages of industrial and agricultural sectors fluctuate, the industrial and agricultural productivity should reach the average level of national labor productivity.

(2) Models of Regional Second Modernization

Development models of the regional second modernization are a variety of combinations of knowledgeablization, informatization, greening, globalization, suburbanization, innovation system, etc. Some regions give priority to informatization and globalization, and some give priority to knowledgeablization and suburbanization, and regional innovation system is a choice for many regions. Currently, there is little research into models of the regional second modernization.

For province-level regions, the improvement of productivity, quality of life, and production capacity for and popularization of knowledge and information is crucial; things that must be promoted include knowledgeablization, informatization, globalization, suburbanization, and innovation system; popularization of higher education and lifelong learning, as well as computers and the Internet; establishment of knowledge and information infrastructure; and protection of ecological environment and cultural diversity. Deindustrialization and deurbanization are elastic, and ecological modernization is optional.

For county-level regions, the improvement of productivity, quality of life, and popularization of knowledge and information is crucial. Things that must be promoted are knowledgeablization, informatization, globalization, and suburbanization; popularization of higher education and lifelong learning, as well as computers and the Internet; establishment of knowledge and information infrastructure; and protection of ecological environment and cultural diversity. Deindustrialization and deurbanization are elastic, and innovation system is optional.

(3) Models of Regional Integrated Modernization

Models of regional comprehensive modernization are a variety of combinations of industrialization, informatization, greening, urbanization, suburbanization, etc. In his book, *Renaissance of the East: The Third Path of Modernization*, Chuanqi He (2003) raised the "canal strategy" for comprehensive modernization which requires path innovation, model innovation, and strategy innovation.

For province-level regions, the key to new comprehensive modernization is improving productivity, living standard, production capacity for and popularization of knowledge and information, and giving equal importance to industrialization and shift of industries, urbanization and urban expansion, informatization and knowledgeablization, material infrastructure and knowledge and information infrastructure, and popularization of free compulsory primary education and higher education. A regional innovation system and deagriculturalization must be promoted; ecological modernization is optional.

For county-level regions, the key to new comprehensive modernization is improving productivity, living standard, and popularization of knowledge and information; giving equal importance to informatization and knowledgeablization, material infrastructure, and knowledge and information infrastructure; popularizing free compulsory primary education; establishing a regional innovation system; boosting on a selective basis the industrialization and shift of industries, urbanization, and city modernization; and developing on a selective basis sci-tech industrial parks, eco-industry parks, and eco-agriculture parks.

5.5 Organizational Modernization

Generally, organizations include government agencies, nonprofit organizations, and profit organizations. Organizational modernization means modernization at organizational level, including modernization of global, national, regional, and sector's organizations as well as individual organizations. It is a manifestation and analysis level of modernization phenomena. Modernization of different types of organizations has different features, showing great diversity.

5.5.1 Studies

Organizational modernization study may be approached from three perspectives, i.e., its history, reality, and future, and research can be done about the organizational modernization of global, national, regional, and sector's organization as well as individual organizations.

5.5.1.1 Research Paradigm

Organizational modernization study is a part of modernization study at organization level.

Research Matrix

The research object of organizational modernization study includes modernization of government agencies, nonprofit organizations, and for-profit organizations, and interaction between organizations and environments. Research contents include modernization of organizational behavior, structures, institutions, and ideas, as well as the process, outcome, driving force, and models of organizational modernization, which make up a research matrix (Table 5.41).

Research Method

Organizational modernization study is a part of modernization study at organizational level and may use the methodology of modernization study. The scope of research can be global, national, regional, or sector's or individual organizations. This study may adopt case study, interdisciplinary research, comprehensive research, etc.

Table 5.41 Matrix of organizational modernization study

Content		Object		
		Organization	Government agencies, nonprofit organizations, and profit organizations	Interaction between organizations and environment
		Organizational modernization	Modernization of three types of organizations	Interaction between organizations and environment
Element	Behavior	Modernization of organizational behaviors, structures, systems, and ideas	Behavioral, structural, systematic, idea's modernization in the three types of organizations	–
	Structure			
	System			
	Idea			
Aspect	Process	Process, result, dynamics, model of the organizational modernization	Processes, result, dynamics, model of modernization in the three types of organizations	International and internal environment and interaction of the organizational modernization
	Result			
	Dynamics			
	Model			

Note: organizational modernization research also includes many other contents, for example, the frontier, frontier process, and catch-up process analysis on organizational modernization, international competition analysis, management modernization, and interaction between elements of organizational modernization

Research Purpose

Organizational modernization study is mainly for academic and policy purposes.

From the academic perspective, it is to discover the facts and principles of organizational modernization and enrich the modernization theory.

From the policy perspective, it is to provide the theoretical basis and policy options for the practice of organizational modernization.

5.5.1.2 Facts About Organizational Modernization

Currently, organizational modernization study is a bottleneck of modernization study here. For example, below is a brief discussion about management modernization of the organizations.

Management modernization is an important part of organizational modernization. Management in government agencies generally belongs to public management, and that in profit organizations generally belongs to business management. Public management modernization has different features from business management modernization, which requires separate research.

In the twentieth century, enormous changes happened to business management, with surging management thoughts. Chinese scholar Chuanqi He has concluded nine grades and nine models about the development of business management (Table 5.42), which can be used as a simplified model of business management (He 2000a). According to him, the development of business management is a process of change from elementary to intermediate and then to senior management; management in different grades has different features, which when put together are the basic track and nine models of management modernization, called nine-grades management for short. Generally, empirical management is a business' start of management; the efficiency, cost, and quality management is basic management. The flexible, knowledge, and innovation management is intermediate management (modern management), and the cultural and strategic management is senior management. Business management modernization may progress step by step or with several steps going hand in hand.

Grade 1: *Empirical Management*. A newly founded business generally starts from empirical management. Management of a business depends largely on the owner's personal interest and experience, and it can be random. As the business grows, it will gradually establish simple rules, regulations, and organizational structure, and finally set objectives to direct its development.

***Grade 2*: *EfficiencyManagement*.** Efficiency is the foundation for the success of a business. After entering the stage of development, it generally pays attention to the improvement of management, with a view of increasing its business efficiency. Efficiency management aims to increase business efficiency. Management methods include scientific management, administrative management, management by objectives, operations, etc.

Grade 3: Cost Management. Cost is the competitive advantage of a business. A business which has entered the stage of development needs not only to increase efficiency but also to endeavor to lower cost while guaranteeing quality, so as to improve competitiveness of its products. Cost management is management

Table 5.42 Nine grades of business management

Grades	Name	Feature	Basic contents			
Grade 1	Empirical management	Experience is start	Random management	Disciplinary management	Management organization	Management objective
Grade 2	Efficiency management	Efficiency is foundation	Planned management	Standardized management	Time control	Customer satisfaction
Grade 3	Cost management	Cost is advantage	Cost planning	Cost center	Profit center	Benefit first
Grade 4	Quality management	Quality is essence	Quality standard	Quality certification	Quality culture	Prestige uppermost
Grade 5	Flexible management	Flexibility is magic weapon	Featured products	Flexible production	Flexible organization	Humanity foremost
Grade 6	Knowledge management	Knowledge is wealth	Knowledge sharing	Organizational learning	Knowledge capital	Knowledge distribution
Grade 7	Innovation management	Innovation is soul	Technology innovation	Knowledge innovation	Innovation culture	Strategy innovation
Grade 8	Cultural management	Culture is value	Culture fostering	Culture shaping	Cultural products	Cultural strategy
Grade 9	Strategic management	Strategy is commander	Business strategy	Featured strategy	Development strategy	Art of strategy

Source: He (2000a)

whereby business cost is controlled. Management methods include cost accounting, value engineering, cost planning, cost effectiveness analysis, environment cost control, etc.

Grade 4: Quality Management. Quality is the essence of a business. Quality management of a business includes officially announcing the general quality principle and direction of the business; defining the quality management objective and responsibility; and fulfilling the quality principle, direction, objective, and responsibility prescribed by the business through systematic activities regarding quality planning, quality control, quality assurance, and quality improvement. Management methods include total quality management, quality control group, lean production, quality certification, etc.

Grade 5: Flexible Management. Flexibility is a magic weapon for a business to gain the upper hand. Flexible management is a humane, soft, and flexible management mode for modern businesses. It requires that the organizational structure of a business is flat and flexible; the business' product development, production, marketing, and services are market-oriented and responsive; information communication is smooth and fast; people's initiative is maximally aroused; and the business is able to react and adjust to market changes. Management methods include agile and smart manufacturing, flexible and intelligent manufacturing, flexible work, contingency management, etc.

Grade 6: Knowledge Management. Knowledge is the fundamental resource and biggest wealth of a business. Knowledge management is maximally satisfying—by means of knowledge creation, identification, sharing, and use—customer needs, thereby improving competitiveness and increasing market value. Management methods include knowledge agenda, knowledge bank, knowledge alliance, knowledge capital evaluation, etc.

Grade 7: Innovation Management. Innovation is the soul of progress for a business. There is innovation in different development stages of a business, but in different stages, the emphasis of innovation is different and the business gives importance to innovation to a different degree. Innovation management, a process of managing a business' innovation activities and capabilities, involves innovation resources, mechanisms and benefits and sees innovation capabilities as the core competitiveness of the business. Management methods include R&D management, innovation network, innovation timing, innovation group, etc.

Grade 8: Cultural Management. Culture means values. Corporate culture, a concentrated manifestation of corporate values, has such carriers as management philosophy, business philosophy, behavior norm, paragon, team spirit, and social image. Managing corporate culture is part, but not all, of what cultural management is about. Cultural management includes culture fostering, culture shaping, and cultural strategy. Management methods include corporate identity, corporate etiquette, cultural product development, cultural diagnosis, etc.

Grade 9: Strategic Management. Strategy is the commander in chief. The corporate strategy of a business represents its direction of development. Strategic management aims to realize the strategic objectives of a business through strategy making, implementation, and routine management. Management methods include strategic analysis, competitiveness analysis, strategic positioning, corporate reengineering, strategic reorganization, etc.

5.5.2 Theories

The organizational modernization theory is a theoretical explanation for the phenomena of organizational modernization; it is a level theory under the second modernization theory and modernization science. Organizational modernization is modernization at organizational level, which has not only generalities of modernization but also some particularities. The core theory (Table 2.1) on the general modernization basically applies to organizational modernization.

The organizational modernization theory includes the general theory, branch theories, and relevant theories (Table 5.43), where the general theory includes five aspects of organizational modernization: definition, process, result, dynamics, and model (Table 5.44). Government agencies, nonprofit organizations, and profit organizations differ in features of modernization, which should be explained by different theories. The organizational modernization theory is yet to be fully developed.

Table 5.43 Structure of organizational modernization theory

Category	Theory	Main contents
General theory	Core theory	The definition, process, result, dynamics, and model of organizational modernization
Branch theories	Stage theory	First organizational modernization, second organizational modernization
	Field-related study	Organizational modernization in the field such as economy, society, politics, culture, and natural environment
	Type-related study	Modernization of government agencies, nonprofit organizations, and profit organizations
	Crossover study	Organizational management modernization, etc.
Relevant theories	Other modernization theories	Classical modernization theory, postmodernization theory, second modernization theory, etc.
	Other relevant theories	Science of organizational behavior, management science, system theory, control theory, informatization, etc.

Table 5.44 General theory on organizational modernization

Aspect	Main contents
Definition	Organizational modernization is modernization at organizational level; it is the frontier change of organizations in the process of modernization, and a process of the formation, development, reorganization, and interaction of modern organizations; the innovation, selection, diffusion, and regression of the elements of modern organizations; and the organizational competition for catching up with, reaching, and maintaining the world advanced level
Process	Organizational modernization includes the change of organizational behavior, structure, system, and ideas, as well as modernization of organizational management, the world frontiers of organization change, and the process to reach these frontiers. The organizational modernization during the first modernization, called the first

(continued)

Table 5.44 (continued)

Aspect	Main contents
	organizational modernization for short, mainly includes rule by law, bureaucratization, large-scale operation, standardization, systematization, efficiency orientation, and management modernization (the first modernization of organizational management). The organizational modernization during the second modernization, called the second organizational modernization for short, mainly includes knowledgeablization, informatization, networking, flattening, flexibility orientation, learning, humanization, diversification, greening, internationalization, and management modernization (the second modernization of organizational management)
Result	The main outcome of the first organizational modernization is the formation of modern organizations fit for industrial civilization, with features including rule by law, stratification, standardization, mechanization, rigidity, and high efficiency. The main outcome of the second organizational modernization is the formation of organizations fit for knowledge and ecological civilization, with features including agility, smart, flexibility, flatness, organification, humanization, informatization, greening, learning, and innovation at present
Dynamics	Driving forces at microlevel includes innovation, competition, adaptation, exchange, organizational interest, and professionalism; driving forces at macrolevel includes national modernization, world modernization, informatization, and globalization. Driving forces differ in different types of institutions in different periods
Model	Organizational modernization has no standard path and model; it has starting-point dependence and path dependence and is influenced by personal qualities, historical traditions, cultural notions, national level, and international environment

Source: RGCMS (2010)

5.6 Individual Modernization

Generally, individuals are the smallest structural units of modernization which are different in different fields. For example, the smallest structural units are the enterprises and individuals in the economic field, the families and individuals in the social domain, the party and individuals in the political realm, and the groups of people in the cultural sphere.

Individual modernization means modernization at individual level, including modernization of global, national, and regional individuals as well as of single individuals. It is a manifestation and analysis level of modernization phenomena. Individual modernization in different fields has different features, showing great diversity. Individual modernization overlaps with human modernization, organizational modernization, cultural modernization, etc.

5.6.1 Studies

Individual modernization study is an integral part of modernization study. It can be approached from three perspectives, i.e., its history, reality, and future, and research can be done about the modernization of global, national, or regional individuals or single individuals. Currently, individual modernization study is a bottleneck in modernization research.

5.6.1.1 Research Matrix

The research object of individual modernization study includes modernization of individuals, families, groups of people, and enterprises, as well as interaction between individuals and environments. Research contents include modernization of individual behaviors, structures, institutions, and ideas, as well as the process, result, dynamics, and model of individual modernization, which make up a research matrix (Table 5.45).

5.6.1.2 Research Method

Individual modernization is a level-relative modernization study and may use the methodology of modernization study. The scope of research can be global, national, regional or industrial individual, or single individuals. It may adopt case study, interdisciplinary study, comprehensive research, etc.

5.6.1.3 Research Purpose

Individual modernization study is mainly for academic and policy purposes.

From the academic perspective, it is to discover the facts and principles of individual modernization and enrich the modernization theory.

From the policy perspective, it is to provide the theoretical basis and policy options for the practice of individual modernization.

Table 5.45 Matrix of individual modernization study

Content		Object		
		Individuals	Individuals, families, groups of people, enterprises, etc.	Interaction between individual and environment
		Individual modernization	Modernization of four types of individuals	Interaction between individual and environment
Element	Behavior	Modernization of individual behaviors, structures, systems, and ideas	Behavioral, structural, systematic, idea's modernization in the four types of individuals	–
	Structure			
	System			
	Idea			
Aspect	Process	Process, result, dynamics, model of the individual modernization	Processes, result, dynamics, model of modernization in the four types of individuals	International and internal environment and interaction of the individual modernization
	Result			
	Dynamics			
	Model			

Note: institutional modernization study also includes many other contents, for example, the frontier, frontier process, and catch-up process analysis on individual modernization, international competition analysis, and interaction between elements of individual modernization

5.6.2 Theories

The individual modernization theory is a theoretical explanation for the phenomena of individual modernization; it is a level theory under the second modernization theory and modernization science. Individual modernization is modernization at individual level, which has not only generalities of modernization but also some particularities. The core theory (Table 2.1) on the general modernization basically applies to individual modernization.

The individual modernization theory includes the general theory, branch theories, and relevant theories (Table 5.46), where the general theory includes five aspects of individual modernization: definition, process, result, dynamics, and model (Table 5.47). Individual modernization overlaps much with human modernization discussed in Chap. 6. The individual modernization theory is yet to be developed.

Table 5.46 Structure of individual modernization theory

Category	Theory	Main contents
General theory	Core theory	The definition, process, outcome, driving force, and models of individual modernization
Branch theories	Stage theory	First individual modernization, second individual modernization
	Field-related study	Individual modernization in the fields such as economy, society, politics, culture, and natural environment
	Type-related study	Modernization of individuals, families, groups of people, enterprises, etc.
Relevant theories	Other modernization theories	Classical modernization theory, postmodernization theory, multiple modernity theory, second modernization theory, etc.
	Other relevant theories	Ethology, behavioral psychology, social psychology, developmental psychology, etc.

Table 5.47 General theory on individual modernization

Aspect	Main contents
Definition	Individual modernization is modernization at individual level; it is the frontier change of individuals in behavior, qualities, ability, and ideas in the process of modernization; a composite process of innovation, selection, diffusion, and regression of individual elements; and the individual competition for catching up with, reaching, and maintaining the world advanced level
Process	Individual modernization is modernization of individual behavior, literacy, ability, and ideas, as well as the world frontiers of individual change and the process and action to reach these frontiers. The individual modernization during the first modernization, called the first individual modernization for short, mainly includes rule by law, efficiency orientation, equalization, rationalization, independence, initiative, and mobility. The individual modernization during the second modernization, called the second individual modernization for short, mainly includes knowledgeablization, informatization, greening, individuation, autonomy, learning, and internationalism at present

(continued)

Table 5.47 (continued)

Aspect	Main contents
Result	The main outcome of the first individual modernization is the formation of individual behavior, qualities, ability, and ideas fit for industrial civilization, with features including incorporation, high efficiency, equality, independence, initiative, and mobility. The main outcome of the second individual modernization is the formation of individual behavior, qualities, ability, and ideas fit for knowledge and ecological civilization, with features currently including knowledgeablization, informatization, environmental-friendliness, individuation, lifelong learning, and internationalization
Dynamics	Driving forces at microlevel include innovation, competition, adaptation, exchange, personal interest, and hobbies; driving forces at macrolevel include national modernization, world modernization, and globalization. Driving forces differ in different types of individuals and in individuals in different periods
Model	Individual modernization has no standard path and model; it has starting-point dependence and path dependence and is influenced by historical traditions, cultural notions, social opinion, educational level, national level, and international environment. Individual modernization in different fields has different models

Source: RGCMS (2010)

Summary

Modernization takes place at different levels such as world, international, national, regional, organizational, and individual level. Different levels of modernization have both similarities and differences. Country is the basic unit of modernization, and each level of modernization is closely related to national modernization.

World Modernization

World modernization is a form of manifestation of modernization at world level.

Generally, world modernization is the change of human civilization and international differentiation; the frontier process of the formation, development, transformation, and international interaction of human modern civilization; the composite process of alternate innovation, selection, diffusion, and regression of the elements of human modern civilization; and the change of international system, international differentiation, and international competition for catching up with, reaching, and maintaining the world's advanced level of development. It includes modernization of the world as a whole, world modernization in six fields, and the spatial and temporal distribution of world modernization, as well as the modernization of world behavior, structure, institution, and ideas.

Modern civilization can be divided into two stages, namely, preliminary modern civilization and advanced modern civilization. Preliminary modern civilization means industrial civilization, and advanced modern civilization means knowledge, while ecological civilization is a manifestation or an aspect of knowledge civilization.

Modernization at world level is not an "independent unit" of modernization, but an analysis level. World modernization is connected with national and international modernization. Generally, world modernization is the international environment of national modernization, national modernization is the important foundation for world modernization, and the interaction between national modernization and international environment is international modernization.

World modernization follows ten basic principles. They are asynchronous process, uneven distribution, structural stability, early bird effect, fast–fast effect, power effect, adaptation effect, latecomer effect, creator effect, and Matthew effect.

International Modernization

International modernization is a manifestation of modernization at transnational level.

Generally, international modernization is an interaction between national modernization and international environment. It is international interaction in the process of modernization, including international interactions at different levels and in different fields during modernization, as well as the modernization of international behavior, structure, institution, and ideas. It involves three aspects: national modernization, international environment, and international interaction.

The process of international modernization roughly has 12 features: universality, diversity, stage-relative, complexity, evolution, nondetermination, differentiation between countries, effect of national level, effect of national strength, continual existence of international war, gradually enhanced international cooperation, and effect of industrial civilization. The age of industry is different from the age of knowledge in features of international modernization.

The process of international modernization follows four principles, namely, synergy, interest-driven interaction, path selection, and quadrant interaction, as well as eight rules: acting and reacting force, different action effects, like attracts like, good spreading, goal orientation, national interests, maxmini, and bounded rationality. These rules are relative, and there are many exceptions such as activities by international humanitarian organizations.

National Modernization

National modernization is a form of manifestation of modernization at national layer.

Generally, national modernization is a sort of national civilization change and international competition; it is the frontier process of the formation, development, transformation, and international interaction of national modern civilization, as well as a composite process of alternate innovation, selection, diffusion, and recession of the elements of national modern civilization. It is also the change in international competition, national stratification, and civilization distribution with the aim of catching up with, reaching, and maintaining the world's advanced level of development. It includes modernization of a country as a whole, modernization in six fields, and the spatial and temporal distribution of national modernization, as well as the modernization of national behavior, structure, institution, and ideas.

National modernization is the basic unit of modernization study and practice. In the process of modernization study and practice, national modernization is at the core. In the system of modernization theories, the national modernization theory and the general theory on modernization have the highest degree of consistency with each other.

National modernization follows ten principles: asynchronous process, uneven distribution, structural stability, status changeability, behavioral predictability, incremental demand, diminishing utility, optional paths, no repeated state, and axis transition.

Dynamic models include innovation drive, three-innovation drive, two-wheel drive, associative action, four-step super cycle, composite interaction of three types of civilization, innovation diffusion, innovation spillovers, and competition drive.

National modernization has three basic paths in the twenty-first century: second modernization, catch-up modernization, and integrated modernization in the term of policy, and first modernization, second modernization, and integrated modernization in the term of theory.

Regional Modernization

If we define regions as domestic regions, then regional modernization is the important foundation and organic part of national modernization. National modernization is the objective environment and condition for regional modernization. Regional modernization interaction is generally subordinate to national modernization. Regional modernization is a manifestation of modernization at regional level.

Generally, regional modernization is a sort of regional civilization change and regional competition; it is the frontier process of the formation, development, transformation, international, and interregional interaction of regional modern civilization, as well as a composite process of alternate innovation, selection, diffusion, and recession of the elements of regional modern civilization. It is also the change in regional competition, regional differentiation, and stratification, with the aim of catching up with, reaching, and maintaining the world's advanced level of development. It includes modernization of a region as a whole, modernization in six fields, interaction of regional modernization, the modernization of subregions such as urban and rural areas, mountainous and plain areas, as well as the modernization of regional behavior, structure, institution, and ideas.

During regional modernization, the change of economic structure (industrialization and deindustrialization), as well as urbanization and suburbanization, is not absolute but elastic, and the change of society and civilization is bound to happen.

Regional modernization is not simply a mini version of national modernization. For province-level regions (at provincial level), regional modernization is highly consistent with national modernization; for county-level regions (at county level), the relationship between regional modernization and national modernization is diverse.

Organizational Modernization

Organizational modernization, namely, modernization at organizational level, is a manifestation and analysis level of modernization phenomena.

Generally, organizational modernization is a process of the formation, development, reorganization, and interaction of modern organization; the innovation, choice, diffusion, and exit of the elements of modern organizations; and the organizational competition for catching up with, reaching, and maintaining the world's advanced level of development. It includes the modernization of global, national, regional, and sector's organizations as well as individual institutions and that of government agencies, nonprofit organizations, and profit organizations, as well as the modernization of organizational behavior, structure, institution, and ideas.

Modernization of different types of organizations has different features, showing great diversity.

Management modernization is an important part of organizational modernization. Business management is a process of evolution from elementary to intermediate and then to senior management; management in different stages has different features, which when put together are the basic track and nine models of management modernization, called nine-grade management for short. They are empirical management, efficiency management, cost management, quality management, flexible management, knowledge management, innovation management, cultural management, and strategic management.

Individual Modernization

Individuals are the smallest structural units which are different in different fields.

Individual modernization is modernization at individual level; it is the change of individuals in behavior, qualities, ability, and ideas, as well as a composite process of alternate innovation, choice, diffusion, and recession of individual modern elements. It includes the modernization of global, national, and regional individuals as well as of single individuals, as well as the modernization of individual behavior, structure, system, and ideas. It is a manifestation and analysis level of modernization phenomena. Individual modernization in different fields has different features, showing great diversity. Individual modernization overlaps with human modernization, institutional modernization, cultural modernization, etc.

Further Reading

Buzan B, Little R (2000) International system in world history—remaking the study of international relations. Oxford University Press, London (Trans: Liu D et al. (2004). Higher Education, Beijing)

He C (2000) K management: modernization of business management. Economic Science, Beijing

Kennedy P (1987) The rise and fall of the great powers: economic change and military conflict from 1500 to 2000. Vintage Books, New York (Trans: Chen J et al. (2006). China International Culture Press Limited, Beijing)

Landes DS (1998) Wealth and poverty of nations: why some are rich and some so poor. W.W. Norton, New York (Trans: Men H et al. (2001). Xinhua Publishing House, Beijing)

Palmer RR, Colton J, Kramer L (2002) A history of the modern world, 9th edn. McGraw-Hill, New York

Smith A (1977) [1776] In: Cannan E (ed) Inquiry into the nature and causes of the wealth of nations. University of Chicago Press, Chicago (Trans: Guo D et al. (1997) The Commercial Press, Beijing)

RGCMS (Research Group for China Modernization Strategies et al) (2004) China Modernization Report 2004: regional modernization research. Peking University Press, Beijing

RGCMS (Research Group for China Modernization Strategies et al) (2008) China Modernization Report 2008: international modernization research. Peking University Press, Beijing

RGCMS (Research Group for China Modernization Strategies et al) (2010) China Modernization Report 2010: world modernization research. Peking University Press, Beijing

Inglehart R, Welzel C (2005) Modernization, cultural change, and democracy: the human development sequence. Cambridge University Press, New York

Martinelli A (2005) Global modernization: rethinking the project of modernity. Sage, London

Field-Specific Modernization 6

Every country has its customs (English proverb), and every field has its speciality. Modernization happens in all fields of human civilization, such as the spheres of economy, society, politics, culture, natural environment, and human self. Field-specific modernization is an important part of modernization science (Fig. 6.1) and interweaves with staged and stratified modernization. In general, modernization in different spheres has both commonality and difference, and the core theory of general modernization has somewhat different applicability in different spheres. Country is the basic unit for modernization, and modernization of each sphere is closely related with national modernization.

6.1 Economic Modernization

Economic modernization means the modernization of the economic sphere. It is a form of expression of the modernization phenomenon in the economic field. It comprises staged and stratified economic modernization, modernization of economic subspheres and sectors (Fig. 6.2). In developing countries, economic modernization plays prominent roles. It is both an important basis for modernization and also a main impetus for modernization.

6.1.1 Studies

Economic modernization study is a study on the modernization in the economic sphere and also a component of modernization study. Economic modernization study, which began in the early eighteenth century, can be analyzed from three perspectives: the past, the present, and the future.

There are no unified definitions about economy and economic sphere. In general, economy means the activities relating to the production, distribution, and consumption of goods and services. Its extension includes stratified economy, economic process, economic system, and economic environment (Fig. 6.3). Economic sphere

C. He, *Modernization Science*,
DOI 10.1007/978-3-642-25459-8_6, © Springer-Verlag Berlin Heidelberg 2012

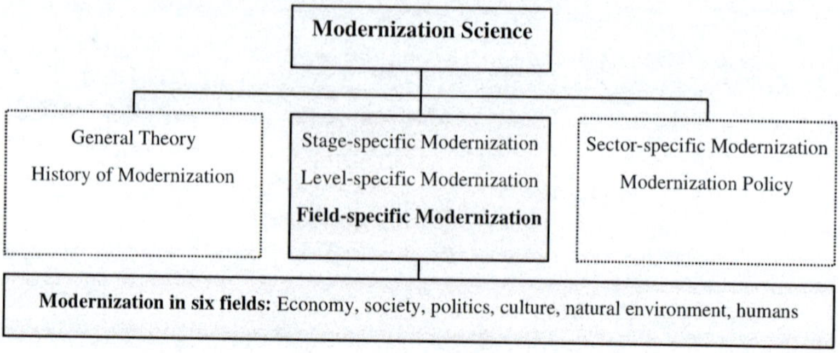

Fig. 6.1 Positioning and structure of field-specific modernization

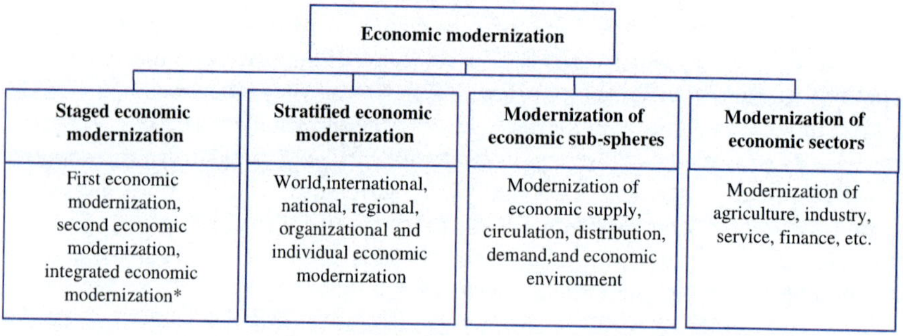

Fig. 6.2 Objects of economic modernization study. Note: (*Asterisk*) Integrated economic modernization means a coordinated development of twice economic modernizations, which is a basic path of economic modernization in developing countries

is a sphere of human civilization, and also a sphere in which scarce or limited resources are used to produce valuable goods and services, carry out distribution, and meet people's consumer demand. Economic modernization is a short term for modernization of economic sphere.

6.1.1.1 Research Paradigm

The object of economic modernization research is the modernization of the economic sphere, including the modernization of economic supply, circulation, distribution, demand, and environment and the modernization of the world, national, and regional economies. The contents of economic modernization research include the modernization of economic behavior, structure, system, and ideas and also the process, result, dynamics, and model of economic modernization. They can form a research matrix (Table 6.1). The objects of economic modernization research also include staged economic modernization, modernization of economic sectors, interaction between economy and modernization, etc.

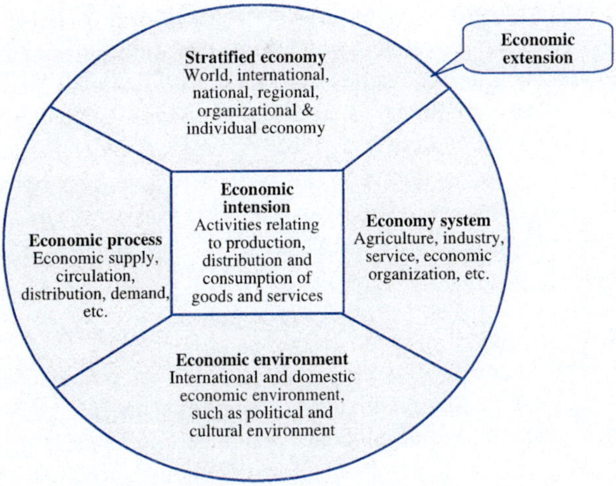

Fig. 6.3 Operational definitions of economic intension and extension

Table 6.1 Matrix of economic modernization study

Content		Object		
		Economic sphere	Economic supply, circulation, distribution, demand, and environment	World, national, and regional economies
		Economic modernization	Modernization of five economic subspheres	Economic modernization on the three levels
Element	Behavior	Modernization of economic behavior, structure, institution, and ideas	Modernization of economic behavior, structure, institution, and ideas in the five economic subspheres	Modernization of economic behavior, structure, institution, and ideas on the three levels
	Structure			
	Institution			
	Idea			
Aspect	Process	Process, result, dynamics, and model of the economic modernization	Process, result, dynamics, and model of economic modernization in the five economic subspheres	Process, result, dynamics, and model of economic modernization on the three levels
	Result			
	Dynamics			
	Model			

Note: economic supply involves input, output, production, cost, effectiveness, technology, system, etc. Economic circulation involves market, trade, logistics, finance, and so on. Economic distribution involves income distribution, taxation, transfer payment, etc. Economic demand involves consumption, investment, savings, government spending, net export, etc. Economic environment involves domestic economic environment (political, social, cultural, and ecological environment) and international economic environment. Economic modernization study also covers many other contents, such as staged economic modernization, modernization of economic sectors, analysis of economic frontiers, economic trend, economic frontier process, economic catch-up process, international competition, international economic gap, and interaction between economic modernization factors and between different spheres

Source: RGCMS (2005)

Economic modernization study is a part of modernization study in economic sphere and can use the methodology of modernization study. It uses diverse analytic methods, such as time-series analysis, cross-sectional analysis, process analysis, case analysis, qualitative analysis, quantitative evaluation, and coordinate analysis. Time span can cover a whole process or a specific period of time, and the scope can be the world, a country, or a region. The purposes include academic and policy ones. Research for different purposes can have different unique features.

6.1.1.2 Historical Facts

Over the past three centuries, economic modernization has been like a surging tide, wave upon wave. Specifically, the first three waves of economic modernization led to a transition from agricultural economy to industrial economy, and the fourth wave is promoting a transition from industrial economy to knowledge economy. Each wave has been driven by important inventions and technological innovations, and each system innovation has caused a change in economic form. The twenty-first century is expected to experience two economic waves. Each of the six economic modernization waves has had unique features (Table 6.2). *The China Modernization Report 2005: Economic Modernization Study* (RGCMS 2005) contains systematic analysis of economic modernization process, facts, and enlightenments as follows.

Table 6.2 Two major stages and six waves of economic modernization

Wave	Approx. time	Core content	Main feature	Annotation
First	1763–1870	First industrial revolution	Mechanization, steam engine, and colonial effect	*First economic modernization* Industrialization, marketization, deagriculturalization, nationwide market
Second	1870–1945	Second industrial revolution	Electrification, internal combustion engine, and trade effect	
Third	1946–1970	Third industrial revolution	Automation, computer, and Cold War effect	
Fourth	1970–2020	Knowledge revolution	Informatization, greening, and knowledge effect	*Second economic modernization* Intellectualization, informatization, de-industrialization, market globalization
Fifth	2020–2050	New biological revolution	Life engineering, nanotechnology, and new biological effect	
Sixth	2050–2100	New physical revolution	Super-transport, culture and experience, new physical effect	

Note: the time span of the second wave included the economic crisis and adjustment during the 1914–1945 period; the knowledge effect included the high-tech revolution; the fifth and sixth waves are forecasts, which will be determined by the future development of science and technology and that of culture. Knowledge revolution includes the information and ecological revolution
Source: RGCMS (2005)

(1) Process Analysis

First, the first wave of economic modernization. It mainly included the first industrial revolution, the European agricultural revolution, and the transport revolution. The main expressions were sustained economic growth, lower agricultural proportion, higher industrial proportion, integration of nationwide markets, and spread of industrial technologies and systems to other economic sectors. The main impetus was technological invention and innovation, colonial effect, overseas trade, and capital accumulation. During the 1763–1825 period, industrial revolution occurred mainly in Britain, even though some other European countries and the United States were "learning quietly." In 1825, Britain revoked the law banning the export of machinery, and hence, industrial revolution began to spread to other parts of Europe. Belgium, France, Germany, and other continental countries were the first to benefit. They were followed by the United States and the overseas colonies of Europe, and then by Russia and Japan. In 1870, about five countries were industrialized countries or countries with a fairly high level of industrialization. They were Britain, France, Belgium, and Germany in Europe and the United States in America. Britain became the target copied and chased by many countries.

Next, the second wave of economic modernization. It included both the spread of the first industrial revolution and the surging of the second industrial revolution. And the second industrial revolution represented the nucleus and frontier of the second wave. The two industrial revolutions had both commonality and difference. The commonality was that they were all driven by technological inventions and technological and system innovations. The difference was that the center of the second industrial revolution had shifted from Britain to the European continent and North America. While the first industrial revolution was based on technology and featured coal, steam engine, and mechanization, the second industrial revolution was based on science and featured electricity, internal combustion engine, and electrification. With the advance of the second wave, the world economic order underwent changes. Germany overtook Britain to become the largest industrial country in Europe, and the United States became the strongest industrial power in the world. Japan in Asia also scored marked progress in industrialization. In the early years of the twentieth century, roughly six countries already completed industrial revolution. They were Britain, the United States, Germany, France, Belgium, and the Netherlands. Many other countries, such as the Scandinavian countries, Japan, and Russia, were in the initial stage of industrialization (Habakkuk and Postan 1965). Industrial revolution spread mainly to Europe, America, Australia, New Zealand, and Japan.

The huge success of the second wave of economic modernization led to a reshuffle of the world order. The ensuing three decades (1914–1945) constituted a special period of human history, which experienced two World Wars and one global economic crisis, the adjustment and formation of modern political system, economic system, economic structure, science and technology, and modern lifestyle and the shift of the center of industrial civilization from Europe to North America. While free market economy moved to failure, planned economy and mixed market economy embarked upon the historical stage. Economic modernization was basically achieved in industrial countries in the course of wars, depression, and reform and continued to spread to other parts of the world.

Third, the third wave of economic modernization. It included the third industrial revolution and the economic modernization in agricultural countries. The former was the nucleus and frontier of the third wave of economic modernization, while the latter represented the beginning of the first wave of economic modernization in agricultural countries. The overlapping of the two produced many new changes and spread economic modernization to the whole globe. Economist Angus Maddison (1995) held that the 1946–1970 period represented the golden time of the economic history. While the global economy entered a fastest-growing period, the development of industrial economy reached its climax. This economic development can be attributed to many reasons. In particular, the efficient system of industrial economy, the thriving international trade, and the third industrial revolution played important roles. Of course, the postwar economic recovery, the expansion of investment scale, and the spread of industrialization also played inestimable roles.

The technological innovations in the third industrial revolution covered artificial synthesis, electronic industry, industrial automation, new materials, new energies, and aerospace industry. During this period, western Europe and Japan outpaced the United States in economic growth, with their labor productivity and GDP per capita being close to that of the United States. The economies of industrial countries demonstrated a phenomenon of convergence. The changes in economic structure were equally evident, with the proportion of agriculture in GDP continuing to fall, the proportion of industry beginning to fall, and the proportion of service industry rising rapidly.

The 1946–1970 period was a Cold War period, featuring confrontation between the Soviet Union and the United States. Economic modernization also carried the mark of Cold War. During this period, the outperforming countries and regions included industrialized countries such as Japan, Italy, and Finland and emergent industrialized countries and regions such as South Korea, Chinese Taiwan, Chinese Hong Kong, the Philippines, Malaysia, Singapore, and Greece. They were all in the "forward positions" of Cold War. Except countries in South America and South Europe, all other emergent industrialized countries and regions were in the "forward belts" of Cold War.

Fourth, the fourth wave of economic modernization. It included the knowledge revolution on economic frontiers, and the economic modernization in late-coming countries. While the first three waves were all driven by industrial revolution, the fourth was driven by knowledge revolution. Industrial revolution led to a rising proportion of industry and a falling proportion of agriculture in GDP, but knowledge revolution led to a falling proportion of industry and a rising proportion of knowledge industry. For this reason, this wave was an economic revolution in nature and affected the whole world.

Knowledge revolution at least included science revolution, high-tech revolution, information revolution, learning revolution, ecological revolution, and national innovation systems. Knowledge revolution and knowledge economy originated from the United States and spread rapidly to Europe and other parts of the world.

Because of knowledge penetration and attraction, the rise of knowledge economy was far faster than that of industrial economy. People began to realize the significance of industrial revolution a century later, but recognized and forecast the future of knowledge revolution almost immediately after it occurred. Based on the development cycle of information technology, the fourth wave in developed countries is expected to come to an end around 2020.

Fifth, the fifth and sixth waves of economic modernization. If the first four waves of economic modernization have become universally recognized reality, the fifth and sixth waves are merely a hypothesis. The fifth wave is expected to occur during the 2020–2050 period. Based on a new biological revolution, this wave should include the popularization of biotechnology and the application of nanotechnology and new energies. By then, biological plants will replace most of the physical plants, and biological production will replace most of physical manufacturing in some fields. Biotechnology, which concerns the treatment, transplant, repair, and improvement of human bodies and other organisms, will become the leading industry. The sixth wave is expected to occur during the 2050–2100 period. Based on a new physical revolution, this wave should include the overall thriving of cultural economy and experience economy. Super-manufacturing will replace most of human labor, and super-transport will bring human beings to where they want to go. Cultural life and spiritual experience will become the leading industry.

(2) Economic Modernization and Technological Change

Technological and institutional changes will be two key factors for economic modernization. All the six waves of economic modernization have been driven by technological innovation, and major inventions and innovations are closely linked with economic cycles (Table 6.3).

First, the technological innovations in the first wave. These innovations were mainly in six spheres: textile industry, coal industry, metallurgical industry, machine-building industry, transport industry, and communications industry. In particular, the invention and wide application of steam engines provided industries with power and brought an end to human dependence on animal, wind, and hydraulic powers. They also made the rapid development of many industries possible. This revolution featured light and textile industries and machine-building industry.

Next, the technological innovations in the second wave. These innovations were mainly in six industries: power industry, iron and steel industry, energy and petrochemical industry, coal chemical industry, transport industry, and telecommunications industry. This revolution featured iron and steel industry, petrochemical and heavy industry, and transport industry. The Americans invented standardized production technology, auto production and assembly line and "scientific management" method, which greatly raised the labor productivity of workers. Some major technological innovations also occurred in the adjustment period of economic modernization, such as agricultural technology, mining technology, modern transport industry, home appliance industry, chemical industry, and power industry.

Table 6.3 Major inventions, innovations and Kondratieff economic cycle

Cycle	Ascending and descending periods	Major inventions	Major innovations	Development stages
First	1790–1815 1815–1845	Electric motor, generator, steel, telegraph, and railway	Mechanization, textile, iron, steam engine, and railway	First industrial revolution
Second	1845–1873 1873–1890	Internal combustion engine, automobile, telephone, washing machine, refrigerator, aspirin, and man-made silk	Electrification, electric motor, generator-plant, chemicals, steel, and railway	Second industrial revolution
Third	1890–1929 1929–1948	Aircraft, production line, sulfa drug, semiconductor, computer, color television, and atomic bomb	Electricity, automobile, aircraft, and home appliance	Two World Wars
Fourth	1948–1973 1973–1992	Communications satellite, laser, microprocessor, contraceptive drug, space flight, DNA recombination, video recorder, and Internet	Automation, electronic computer, atomic energy, personal computer, and space flight	Third industrial revolution and first information revolution
Fifth	1992–2020 2020–2040	Gene mapping, nanotechnology, quantum computer, and biological chip	Internet, e-business, biotechnology, and software	Second information revolution and new biological revolution

Note: It is mainly based on the thoughts of Duijn (1983). Different countries and different scholars differ slightly in dividing the time of cycle. The first industrial revolution corresponds to the first wave of economic modernization, the second industrial revolution corresponds to the second wave of economic modernization, the third industrial revolution corresponds to the third wave of economic modernization, and the first and second information revolutions correspond to the fourth wave of economic modernization

Third, the technological innovations in the third wave. These innovations were mainly in six spheres: artificial synthesis technology, electronic industry, industrial automation, new materials, energy industry, and transport industry such as express-way, automobile, and aerospace industry.

Fourth, the technological innovations in the fourth wave. These innovations were mainly in three spheres. In the sphere of information technology, the innovations included microcomputer, Internet, mobile communications, e-business and e-government, new computing technology, and human–computer interaction technology. In the sphere of biotechnology, the innovations included DNA recombination, cloning technology, cell engineering, enzyme engineering, protein engineering, and gene engineering. In the sphere of other high technologies, the innovations included material technology, advanced manufacturing, advanced energy, space technology, automation technology, environmental technology, photoelectricity, marine technology, etc.

Fifth, the technological innovations in the fifth and sixth waves. The main innovations in the fifth wave would be in three spheres: life engineering, nanotechnology, and new energy. The main innovations in the sixth wave would also be in three spheres: super-manufacturing, super-transport, and cultural and spiritual experience. Naturally, these are only a forecast.

(3) Economic Modernization and Institutional Change

The change of economic institutions is an important content of economic modernization. In general, institutions are a collection of rules, procedures, ethics, and customs that govern human behavior (North 1981). Basic economic institution is the core institution governing economic activities and the ownership and allocation of production factors and the distribution of production fruits. In the age of primitive economy, the basic economic institution was primitive public ownership, under which production factors were publicly owned and production fruits were equally distributed. Private ownership appeared in the transitional period of the age of primitive economy, but the economic institution still carried the flavor of public ownership. In the age of agricultural economy, the basic economic institution was agricultural economy and agrarian institution, including slavery, manorialism, nomadism, tenancy, etc. The production factors were privately owned, and the slave owners (manor owners or landowners) determined the allocation of production factors and the distribution of production fruits. In the age of industrial economy, the basic economic institution is market economy, in which market determines the allocation of production factors and the distribution of incomes. The basic economic institution in the age of knowledge economy is knowledge economy, which is still in the process of formation (Table 6.4).

The basic economic institution changes from time to time and, generally, has several subinstitutions, such as nomadism in the age of agricultural economy and planned economy, mixed economy, welfare economy, and socialist market economy in the age of industrial economy. From the perspective of institutional change, the transition from agricultural economy to industrial economy represented first economic modernization, and the transition from industrial economy to knowledge economy represents second economic modernization.

(4) Economic Modernization and Change of Economic Form

The change of economic form is a macroform of expression for economic modernization. From the birth of mankind to the end of the twenty-first century, different "economic times" have different economic activities, the economic activities representing the then advanced level of productive forces have different features, and their core technologies, core industries, basic modes of production, structures, institutions, and concepts are essentially different. The economic activities in the four economic ages reflecting the advanced level of productive forces can be classified into different economic forms, or basic economic forms for short (Table 6.5). Different economic forms have way different industrial structures

Table 6.4 Basic economic institutions in economic history

Economic time	Age of primitive economy	Age of agricultural economy	Age of industrial economy	Age of knowledge economy
Historical time	Birth of mankind ~3500 BC	3500 BC–AD 1763	1763–1970	1970 to approx. 2100
Economic form	Primitive economy	Agricultural economy	Industrial economy	Knowledge economy
Basic institution	Primitive public ownership	Land institution	Market institution	Knowledge institution (still in process of formation)
Production	Collective labor	Agricultural production	Industrial production	Flexible work and knowledge production
Circulation	Exchange in kind	Regional trade and tariff	National market	Globalization and low tariff
Distribution	Equal distribution	Distribution according to power and land ownership	Distribution according to capital or labor	Distribution according to contribution and regulation according to demand
Consumption	Real-time consumption	Voluntary consumption	Taxed consumption and high consumption	Green consumption and reasonable consumption
Environment	Nature worship	Nature adaptation	Nature transition	Ecological–economic coordination

Source: RGCMS (2005)

and employment structures (Fig. 6.4). The transitions from agricultural economy to industry and that from industrial economy to knowledge economy represent two stages of economic modernizations.

(5) Basic Facts of Economic Modernization

First, the facts of economic supply. In the past three centuries, productivity has been continuously rising, but the sustainability of productivity growth has varied in different countries. In the meantime, the international gap in productivity has been widening, the world frontier of productivity has been shifting, and the shift in the world status of national economy has followed certain probability. After the nineteenth century, the unemployment rate was long fluctuating, and the economic cycle was long in existence. In the latter half of the twentieth century, the amplitude of vibration of the economic cycle became smaller. In the late years of the twentieth century, the effectiveness of resource use became higher, the contribution of knowledge economy to economic growth in developed countries became higher, and the contribution of capital and labor to economic growth became lower. Meanwhile, labor quality and infrastructure were in positive correlation with productivity.

Next, the facts of economic structure. After the eighteenth century, the ratio of agricultural economy to national economy dropped (deagriculturalization), and the

Table 6.5 Basic economic forms in economic history

Economic time	Age of primitive economy	Age of agricultural economy	Age of industrial economy	Age of knowledge economy
Historical time	Birth of mankind ~3500 BC	3500 BC–AD 1763	1763–1970	1970 to around 2100
Mode of production	Collective hunting and gathering	Family-based small-scale production	Industrial large-scale production	Knowledge-based global production
Core technology	Food-gathering technology	Food-producing technology	Material-producing technology	Production and application of knowledge and information
Leading industry	Natural food acquisition	Food production	Material production and service	Knowledge production and service
Basic structure	Over 95% for hunting and gathering	Over 90% for agriculture and animal husbandry	Over 50% for industry	Over 50% for knowledge industry
Basic institution	Primitive public ownership	Slavery and feudalism	Market economy	In process of formation
Basic concept	Equal distribution	Distribution according to power and land ownership	Distribution according to capital or labor	Distribution according to contribution
Economic form	Primitive economy	Agricultural economy	Industrial economy	Knowledge economy

Source: RGCMS (2005)

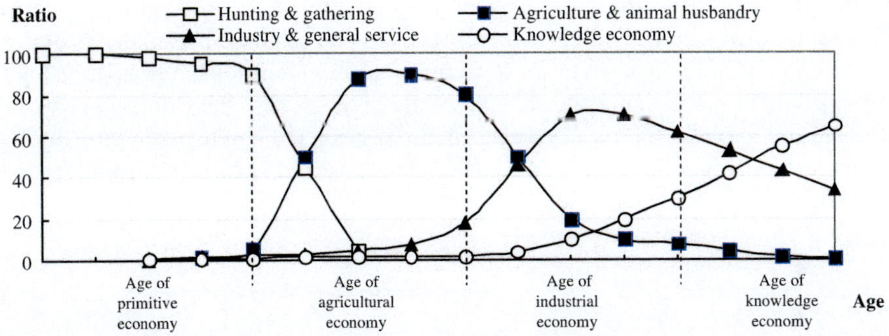

Fig. 6.4 Change and replacement of economic forms (using labor structure change as example). Source: He (2003)

ratio of industrial economy to national economy in developed countries experienced rising and falling periods (industrialization and de-industrialization). After the twentieth century, the ratio of service economy to national economy became higher (servicization or dematerialization), and the ratio of knowledge economy became higher in developed countries.

Third, the facts of economic circulation. After the eighteenth century, economy became growingly marketized and commercialized and international trade increased. After the twentieth century, the average tariff rate became lower. In the late years of the twentieth century, the ratio of money supply (M2) to GDP and the ratio of domestic credit were in positive correlation with national income per capita, and the ratio of international trade was not in tangible positive correlation with per capita national income.

Fourth, the facts of economic distribution. After the nineteenth century, the inequality in the income distribution rose first and dropped afterward in developed countries and then fluctuated in some countries (Fig. 6.5). After the twentieth century, the ratios of government taxation and transfer payment became higher. In the late years of the twentieth century, the equity in income distribution, the ratio of government revenue, the ratio of tax revenue, and the ratio of transfer payment were in positive correlation with per capita national income.

Fifth, the facts of economic demand. In the twentieth century, the ratio of consumption to the GDP became lower. In the late years of the twentieth century, the ratio of family consumption was in negative correlation with per capita national income, while the ratio of government consumption and the ratio of knowledge capital investment were in positive correlation with per capita national income.

Over the past three centuries, the economic behaviors, structure, institutions, and concepts and the key technologies, modes of production, and leading industries have undergone profound changes. And these changes were uneven. As the international gap in the income per capita widened, underdeveloped countries are in a state of relative poverty.

(6) Historical Enlightenments

First, economic modernization is relatively orderly and can be expected. In general, the world economic changes in the twentieth century were relatively continuous and regular. In particular, both economic effectiveness and the effectiveness of resource use were on the rise, and both the industrial and employment structures became deagriculturalized, servicized, and dematerialized and moved from industrialization to de-industrialization.

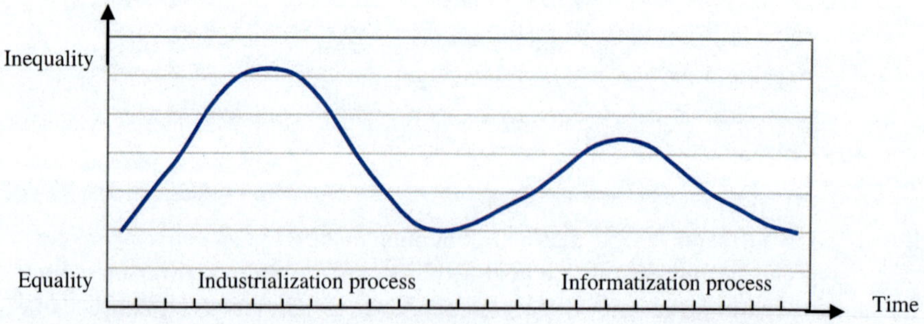

Fig. 6.5 One form of change in income inequality in course of economic modernization (one model). Source: RGCMS (2005)

Next, economic modernization is a process that can be stopped, interrupted, or retrograded. Economic modernization across the world is a continuous and irreversible process. But economic modernization in a specific country or region can have diverse forms of expression, can be continuous or discontinuous, and can stop or interrupt. It can have a temporary or long-term retrogression.

Third, economic modernization is a process in which the international gap in economic effectiveness widens (polarization of economic effectiveness). During the 1700–2001 period, the relative gap in per capita GDP (at 1990 price of PPP international dollar) widened from 15-folds to 73-folds, and the absolute gap widened about 15-folds from $1,700 to over $26,700, and the compound gap widened at an average annual rate of 0.92%. The huge gap in per capita income appeared in the past three centuries will continue to widen instead of narrowing in the next century.

Fourth, economic modernization is a process featuring an international convergency of economic structures. Over the past three centuries, the ratio of agriculture continued to fall, the ratio of service industry continued to rise, the ratio of industry experienced both rising and falling periods (Table 6.6), and the ratio of knowledge industry continued to rise. As different industries have a limit value for their ratios, industrial and employment structures tended to gradually converge. Naturally, convergency does not mean complete identity. Diversity still exists and convergency is relative.

Fifth, economic modernization is a process of progress. Over the past three centuries, economic modernization was both a process with growing labor productivity and growing effectiveness of resource use. Meanwhile, it was also a process with growing economic welfare and economic equity. We have no reason to suspect that this trend will interrupt or reverse in the next century. So economic modernization is progressive through the process of progress may have all sorts of problems and even catastrophic problems.

Sixth, economic modernization is a process full of risks. Economic modernization is not free; it requires costs and prices. In the course of economic modernization, old technologies and old industries will lose their original economic values and statuses, and some industries and population groups will suffer losses because of the replacement of core technologies and leading industries. And the accelerated technological aging and industrial transfer will increase the numbers of sufferers and beneficiaries and in turn sharpen economic and social contradictions. In the meantime, as Earth has limited economic resources, the rivalry for economic resources can also sharpen international and domestic contradictions. On the

Table 6.6 Industrialization and de-industrialization of American economy

Indicator	1900	1910	1920	1930	1940	1950	1960	1970	1980	1990	2000
Ratio of industrial added value (%)	26	27	29	33	35	39	37	33	32	27	24
Ratio of industrial labor force (%)	30	32	34	34	33	37	34	31	27	22	20

Source: RGCMS (2005)

other hand, science and technology is a double-edged sword. Technological risks always exist and may expand. The process of economic modernization requires risk control and crisis management.

Seventh, economic modernization is not a completely spontaneous process. Economic system is a self-organizing system and can operate under certain marginal conditions. However, economic modernization is a process of global competition. Both developed and developing countries inevitably seek favorable positions in fierce international competition and strive for more strategic resources and market spaces if they want to realize economic modernization and reach and maintain their advanced levels in the world economy. This competition is an uphill struggle. Economic modernization is a human-controlled open system, instead of a completely spontaneous process.

Eighth, the section structure of economic modernization is correlated to the structure of history. The result of time-series analysis of economic variables is largely consistent with that of section analysis. In a sense, the section structure of an economy can be used as a "time epitome" of the time-series changes of the economy. In other words, the "time structure" of economic changes can be converted into the "section structure" of economic changes for analysis. It also indicates that combining time-series analysis with cross-sectional analysis is an effective method for economic modernization research.

6.1.1.3 Present State and Prospect of Economic Modernization

(1) Present State

First, the level of economic modernization. In 2002, about 24, or 18%, of 131 countries had completed their first economic modernization. Another 18 countries or 14% of all had entered the process of second economic modernization. If classified according to second economic modernization index, 18 countries including the United States were developed countries, nine countries including Spain were moderately developed countries, 24 countries including Brazil were preliminarily developed countries, and 79 countries including China were underdeveloped countries (RGCMS 2005).

Next, the stage of economic modernization. In 2002, six countries including the United States had entered the developing stage of second economic modernization, 12 countries including Sweden were in the starting stage of second economic modernization, 11 countries including South Korea were in the transitional stage of first economic modernization, 22 countries including Greece were in the maturing stage of first economic modernization, 29 countries including China were in the developing stage, 26 countries including India were in the starting stage, and 14 countries including Mali remained traditional agricultural economies (Fig. 6.6).

Third, the world frontier of economic modernization. In 2002, the world top ten countries in terms of second economic modernization index were respectively the United States, Switzerland, Norway, Demark, Sweden, the Netherlands, Japan, France, Britain, and Belgium. Also in the year, six countries had entered the developing stage of second economic modernization. They were the United States, Demark, the Netherlands, France, Britain, and Australia.

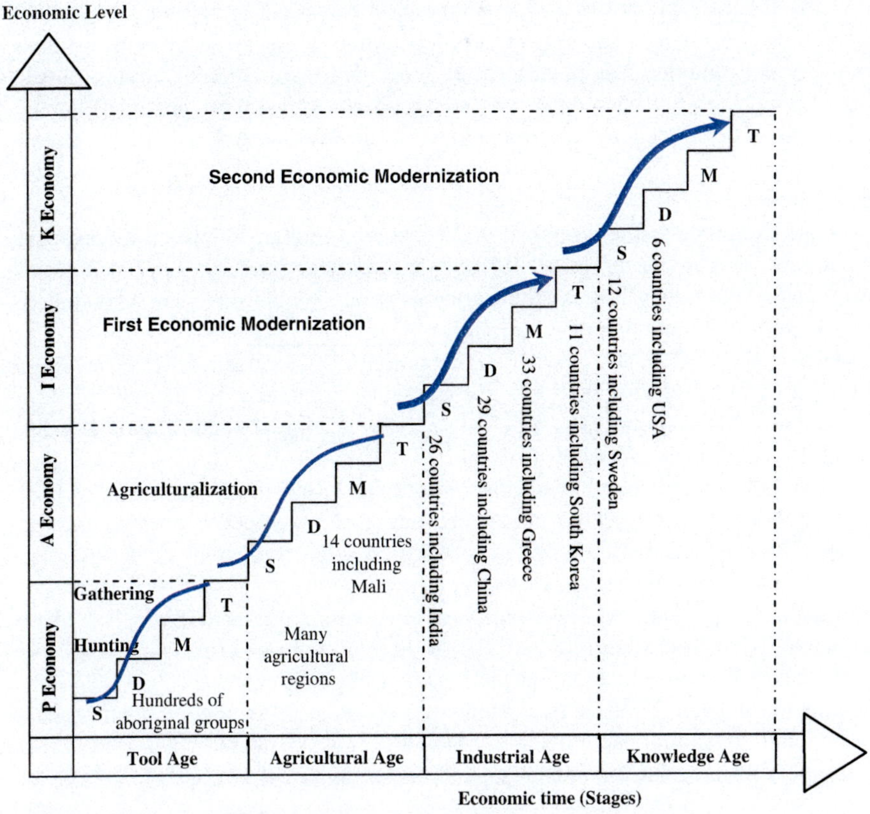

Fig. 6.6 Coordinates of world economic modernization in 2002. Note: P, A, I, and K refer to primitive, agricultural, industrial, and knowledge, respectively. S, D, M, and T refer to the start, developing, mature, and transition stage, respectively. Economic time refers to the time based on the frontier track of economic development. Source: RGCMS (2005)

Fourth, the achievement of economic modernization. In the latter half of the twentieth century, the number of countries that had completed first economic modernization rose from 1 to 24, and the number of the countries that had entered second economic modernization rose from 0 to 18. The direction of world economic modernization underwent a major change, with economic modernization in developed countries moving from the stage of industrialization to that of de-industrialization.

Fifth, the status change of economic modernization. During the 1950–2002 period, 21 countries including Japan saw their economic status upgraded, and six countries including Venezuela saw their economic status downgraded. In the four decades from 1960 to 2002, 15 countries saw their economic status upgraded, and five saw their economic status downgraded. In particular, Japan, Singapore, and South Korea saw their economic status jumped two grades straight.

Sixth, the international gap of economic modernization. During the 1970–2002 period, 36 countries including Argentina posted a negative growth in their first economic modernization index, and ten countries including Zambia posted a negative growth in their second economic modernization index. The international gap between developed and underdeveloped countries widened.

(2) Prospect

First, the time required to complete first economic modernization. At the average annual growth rate during the 1970–2002 period, moderately developed countries on average require 85 years, and the world on average requires 53 years to complete first economic modernization.

Second, the world's advanced level of economic modernization. At the average annual growth rate during the 1970–2002 period, second economic modernization index of developed countries in 2050 will be twice as high as in 2002, and the index in 2100 will be twice as high as in 2050.

Third, the world average level of economic modernization. The world average level is about 50 years behind the average level of developed countries, and the average level of the world economy in 2050 will be equivalent to the average level of developed countries in 2000.

Fourth, the national level distribution of economic modernization. At the average annual growth rate during the 1970–2002 period, 46 countries will complete first economic modernization, and 43 countries will enter second economic modernization by 2050. Sixty-two countries will complete first economic modernization, and 58 countries will enter second economic modernization by 2100 (Table 6.7). If the growth rate change, and the situation will change.

6.1.2 Theories

Economic modernization theories are those explaining the phenomenon of economic modernization and constitute a branch of modernization theories. Currently, there are two collections of theories, namely, classic economic modernization theory and broad-sense economic modernization theory.

6.1.2.1 Classic Economic Modernization Theory

As an important branch of classic modernization theory, classic economic modernization theory was formed in the 1950s and 1960s. The publication of *The Stages of*

Table 6.7 Estimated level of world economic modernization in twenty-first century

Item	2002	2010	2020	2030	2040	2050	2060	2080	2100
Number of countries entering second economic modernization	18	20	25	31	36	43	44	51	58
Number of countries completing first economic modernization	24	29	35	42	44	46	49	54	62

Source: RGCMS (2005)

Table 6.8 Structure of classic economic modernization theory

Category	Theory	Main content	Representative
General theory	Core theory	Basic law and features of classic economic modernization	
Branch theories	Economic stage theory	Five stages of economic growth	W. W. Rostow
	Industrialization theory	Definition, process, structure, impetus, and model of industrialization	A. Gerschenkron
	Sector economic modernization	Agricultural modernization, industrial modernization, financial modernization, etc.	
Related theories	Economic growth theory	Classical economic growth, neoclassifical growth, modern growth, etc.	S. S. Kuznets
	Economic development theory	Classical and neoclassical development, innovation, dependent development, etc.	A. Lewis and J. Schumpeter
	Economic structure theory	Dualist economic development model, development models, etc.	A. Lewis and H. Chenery
	Developmental economics	Economic growth and economic development in developing countries	
	Other related theories	Institutional economics, technological economics, comparative economic history, etc.	

Source: RGCMS (2005)

Economic Growth published in 1960 by American economist Walt Whitman Rostow was an important mark for the birth of classic economic modernization theory. So far, classic economic modernization theory has not had a universally recognized and complete theoretic system. Besides, this theory has diverse and inseparable links with the economic theories of grand magnitude and long history. In fact, classic economic modernization theory is a collection of academic thoughts about classic economic modernization (Table 6.8).

(1) General Theories of Classic Economic Modernization

The China Modernization Report 2005 analyzed the thoughts and theories regarding classic economic modernization and summarized the general theory of classic economic modernization (Table 6.9), including the definition, process, outcome, drive force, and model of classic economic modernization.

Classic economic modernization is not in isolation. It is subject to the influence of politics and culture and interacts with classic social modernization. At the same time, it is constrained by the level of science and technology and by international relations. It is both a global economic revolution and a world economic competition. It takes a country as the basic unit and the world as the competition arena.

Economic growth does not equal to economic development, economic development does not equal to economic modernization, and industrialization does not equal to economic modernization. Economic modernization covers not only economic growth and industrialization but also the changes in the world economic frontier and in the international economic gap.

Table 6.9 General theories of classic economic modernization

Aspect	Basic content
Definition	Classic economic modernization refers to the revolutionary change that occurred in the economic sphere since the eighteenth century, which included the comprehensive industrialization of the national economy, the sustained growth of labor productivity, and the continuous intensification of international economic competition
Process	Class economic modernization is a historical process, which is both a process of industrialization of production model, production technology, economic structure, economic system, and economic concept and also a process of sustained growth of labor productivity and national income. It is also a process of international competition to catch up, reach, and maintain the world's economic advanced levels. The process of classic economic modernization generally comprises four stages (starting, developing, maturing, and transitional). And the process of industrialization generally comprises three stages (early stage, middle stage, and late stage)
Outcome	The result of classic economic modernization comprises the transition from agricultural economy to industrial economy; the formation and popularization of the market economy concept; the mass application of modern science and technology and energy; the industrialization, diversification, and specialization of economic activities; the mechanization, electrification, and automation of production model; the rising ratio of industry and service; the falling ratio of agriculture; the formation and development of national market; the sustained growth of economy and productivity; the improvement of economic welfare and social equity; and the transfer of economic center. The key indicator for a country to complete classic economic modernization is the completion of industrialization and for its labor productivity to reach the world's advanced level in the 1960s
Drive force	The impetus of classic economic modernization comprises knowledge growth, capital accumulation, division of labor, international trade, population growth, political and cultural roles, etc.
Model	Classic economic modernization has diverse models, which are path dependent and are subject to the influence of historical, geographic, and objective conditions

Note: Developed countries completed industrialization in the 1960s and entered postindustrialization in the 1970s. Accordingly, the level of developed countries in the 1960s is taken as the then world's advanced level and as a standard to measure whether a country has completed classic economic modernization
Source: RGCMS (2005)

(2) Theories of Economic Growth Stages

In his *The Stages of Economic Growth* published in 1960, American economist Rostow divided economic growth into five stages (Rostow 1960). In his *Politics and the Stages of Growth* published in 1971, he added the sixth stage. Of all these stages, the second, third, fourth, and fifth stages belong to the process of classic economic modernization.

The first stage: traditional society. It was based on the science and technology and the material outlook before the Newton Age. Due to the constraint of productivity, traditional society used most resources for agricultural production and gave birth to a stratified social structure from this agricultural system.

The second stage: pretakeoff conditions. This stage, existing in all societies in transition, was first developed in western Europe at the end of the seventeenth century and the beginning of the eighteenth century, when modern scientific knowledge began to become a new production function in agriculture and industry.

The third stage: the takeoff stage. It was a stage during which the barriers and resistances to steady growth were eventually overcome. The forces promoting economic progress expanded and began to control the whole society. Growth became normality. During the takeoff stage, the ratio of effective investment rate and the savings rage to national income rose to over 10%. New industries developed rapidly and invested most of their profits in new factories. The class of new entrepreneurs expanded, agriculture became commercialized, and the revolutionary change in agricultural productivity became an indispensable condition for successful takeoff. After one or two decades, both the basic economic structure and the social and political structures underwent changes.

The fourth stage: moving toward maturity. The takeoff was followed by long and sustained growth (even with fluctuations). A society took about 60 years to go from takeoff to maturity. This was as long as two generations, but not an accurate length. With technological advance, accelerated development of new industries and the withering of old industries, economic structure continued to change, and national economy began to find a place in international economy.

The fifth stage: mass consumption. During this stage, the leading sector switched to consumer durables and services. When per capita real income rose to a high level, most people could acquire consumption beyond basic food, housing, and clothing. The labor structure underwent changes, urbanization was realized, and society began to use more resources for social welfare and social security. The emergence of welfare countries was an expression that society had surpassed technological maturity. Cheap mass automobiles produced revolutionary impacts on the people's life.

The sixth stage: pursuing life quality. The leading sector switched from consumer durables to services, especially to the service sectors that were closely related to the improvement of the quality of the people's life, such as education, health, culture, entertainment, and tourism.

Rostow's theory of economic development stages is the most representative one, although some other economic development theories and modernization theories also covered the stages of economic development. While different stages were classified, the stages of development were an objective reality.

(3) Theories of Industrialization

Industrialization is a core process of economic modernization. There has been no unified definition of industrialization (Table 6.10). In general, industrialization in the narrow sense refers to the continuous rise of the ratio of industry in the structures of national income and employment, while industrialization in the broad sense refers to a comprehensive industrialization of the national economy, including the continuous rise of the ratio of industries to the structures of national income and employment, the continuous fall of the ratio of agriculture, and the penetration of the mode and concept of industrial production into all economic

Table 6.10 Contents of industrialization

No.	Definition	Author
1.	Industrialization refers to the process of continuous changes of a host of strategic production functions in the national economy	P. Zhang
2.	Industrialization refers to a structural change from agriculture, namely, a fall of the share of agriculture in national income and employment and a rise of the share of manufacturing and service industries	G. Sak
3.	Industrialization refers to the process of continuous rise of the share of industry in national income and working population	Popular view
4.	Industrialization refers to the process of the growth of the share of manufacturing output value	H. Chenery
5.	Industrialization is a long process of economic restructuring. In this process, the industrial sector continued to expand, and in particular, the manufacturing industry grew rapidly, which led to a continuous fall in the ratio of the agricultural sector in net output value and labor force, a continuous rise in the ratio of the industrial sector and especially the manufacturing sector, and not much change in the ratio of the service sector. In the end, the industrial sector gradually got the upper hand in the national economy, and this meant the realization of industrialization of a country's economy	C. Tan, X. Guo

Note: It is based on the ideas of Tan (2001)

sectors. There have been large amounts of academic documents discussing the types and models of industrialization.

(4) Dual Sector Model

In the 1950s, Lewis introduced the dual sector model (Lewis 1955). He hypothesized that the economic of a developing country consisted of two sectors. One sector was the traditional agricultural sector, which had large numbers of rural people, could maintain a basic living, and had zero marginal labor productivity. The other was the modern industrial sector in urban areas, which had very high labor productivity and could absorb surplus rural labor. Wage gap existed between the agricultural and industrial sectors, and economic mechanisms could attract agricultural labor to the industrial sector. As the ratio between rural labor and land fell, the marginal labor productivity and wage of rural labor would rise. As the transfer of economic activities from traditional agriculture to modern industry would reach certain equilibrium, economic restructuring would complete (Lewis 1955).

6.1.2.2 Economic Modernization Theory in Broad Sense

The economic modernization theory in the broad sense is a theoretical interpretation of the phenomenon of economic modernization in the eighteenth to twenty-first centuries. Being an application of the second modernization theory in the economic sphere, it was introduced by Chinese scholar Chuanqi He. The economic modernization theory in the broad sense generally comprises general theories, branch theories, and related theories (Table 6.11). The general theories discussed here (Table 6.12) have five contents: the definition, process, result, dynamics, and model of economic modernization. Currently, there has been very limited cognition of

Table 6.11 Structure of economic modernization theory in broad sense

Category	Theory	Main contents
General theory	Core theory	Definition, process, result, dynamics, and model of economic modernization
Branch theories	Stage theory	First, second, or integrated economic modernization
	Stratified study	Modernization of world, national, and regional economies
	Subsphere study	Modernization of economic supply, circulation, distribution, demand, and environment
	Sector theory	Modernization of agricultural, industrial, service, information, financial and trade sectors, etc.
Related theories	Other modernization theories	Classic modernization theory, classic economic modernization theory, second modernization theory, etc.
	Related economic theories	Industrialization theory, economic development theory, evolutional economics, technological economics, industrial economy, knowledge economy, etc.

Source: RGCMS (2005)

second economic modernization and integrated economic modernization. The economic modernization theory in the broad sense is expected to have more research and development.

(1) Definition

Economic modernization is a form of expression for modernization in the economic sphere.

The intension: economic modernization is a sort of frontier change and international competition in the economic sphere since the industrial revolution in the eighteenth century. It comprises the formation, development, transformation, and international interaction of modern economy; the innovation, selection, diffusion, and withdrawal of economic factors; and the international competition, differentiation, and stratification of catching up, reaching, and maintaining the advanced level of the world economy.

The extension: economic modernization comprises the modernization of world, national, and regional economies; the modernization of economic behavior, structure, institution, and ideas; the modernization of economic supply, circulation, distribution, demand, and economic environment; and the modernization of agricultural and other economic sectors and the change of the temporal–spatial distribution of economic modernization.

In general, economic modernization refers to the world frontiers of economic change and the process and action to reach these frontiers, and includes the transition from agricultural to industry economy and the transition from industrial to knowledge economy, the continuous growth of economic efficiency and income per capita, and the change of economic welfare and equity, national economic status, and international economy system. Country is the basic unit for the research and practice of economic modernization, the world is the international arena for them, and regional economic modernization is a component of the modernization of

Table 6.12 General theory of economic modernization in broad sense

Aspect	Basic content
Definition	Economic modernization means the modernization of the economic sphere. It is also a form of economic change and international competition since the industrial revolution in the eighteenth century; a frontier process of the formation, development, transformation, and international interaction of modern economy; a compound process of the innovation, choice, diffusion, and withdrawal of economic factors; and a form of international competition and international differentiation to catch up, reach, and maintain the world's advanced level of the economic development
Process	Economic modernization is a complex process, comprising economic development, transformation, international economic competition, differentiation and national economic stratification, the changes of economic behavior, structure, institution, and ideas, and the world frontiers of economic change and the process of reaching the world frontier. During the eighteenth to twenty-first centuries, the frontier track of economic modernization process could be divided into two major stages. Specifically, first economic modernization was a transition and profound change from agricultural to industrial economy and from self-supporting to market economy, whose main features included industrialization, marketization, deagriculturalization, etc. Second economic modernization was a transition and profound change from industrial to knowledge economy and from material to ecological economy. Currently, its main features include intellectualization, greenization, de-industrialization, etc. The coordinated development of the two economic modernizations constitutes integrated economic modernization. Economic modernization in the twenty-second century will comprise new changes. It observes the ten basic principles governing modernization (Table 2.15)
Result	Formation of economic modernity, particularity, diversity, and side effects. They include the growth of economic efficiency and per capita income, the improvement of economic welfare and economic equity, and the change in national economic level, status, and international economic system. The results of first economic modernization were the formation of first economic modernity, particularity, and diversity, the side effects such as environmental pollution and cyclic economic crises, and so on. The main marks for the completion of first economic modernization were the finish of industrialization and marketization and the reaching of economic efficiency and per capita income to the advanced level of industrial economy (the average level of industrial countries in the 1960s). The results of second economic modernization were the formation of second economic modernity, particularity, and diversity and the side effects such as network crimes and international risks. The main marks for the completion of second economic modernization were the completion of intellectualization and ecologization, and the reaching of labor productivity and per capita national income to the advanced level of knowledge economy (sometime in the future). The basic standards for the realization of economic modernization include the reaching of economic effectiveness, per capita income, economic structure, and economic system to the world's advanced level at the time
Dynamics	The factors driving economic modernization include innovation, exchange, competition, adaptation, national interests, and market demand; include economic growth, demand change, globalization, and reasonable expectation; and include the growth of knowledge capital, social capital, material capital, human capital, ecological awareness, and knowledge consumption, the change of economic structure and the entrepreneurship. The impetus models include innovation driving, three-innovation driving, two-wheel driving, four-step supercycle, associative action, innovation dissemination, innovation spillover, competition driving, and productivity function (Table 2.20). Different countries have somewhat different impetuses for economic modernization in different stages

(continued)

Table 6.12 (continued)

Aspect	Basic content
Model	Economic modernization has diverse paths and models, is path dependent, and is subject to the influence of historical, geographic, and objective conditions. It has three basic paths in the twenty-first century: the path of first economic modernization, the path of second economic modernization, and the path of integrated economic modernization. The corresponding basic models are the model of industrialization, the model of paralleled intellectualization and informatization, the model of information economy, the model of ecological economy, the model of biological economy, the model of experience economy, the model of paralleled industrialization and informatization, the model of new industrialization, the model of green industrialization, etc.

Note: There has been no unified definition of modern economy. In general, modern economy comprises industrial economy (preliminary modern economy) and knowledge economy (advanced modern economy). Preliminary modern economy pursues the maximization of material interests, while advanced modern economy pursues both economic and environmental efficiencies
Source: RGCMS (2005, 2010)

Table 6.13 Conceptual models of economic modernization

Item	Content
Hypothesis 1	Economic growth refers to the expansion of economic aggregate and economic scale
Hypothesis 2	Economic progress refers to the improvement of economic quality, efficiency, and equity
Hypothesis 3	Economic transformation refers to the change and replacement between new and old economic forms (including two economic transitions)
Hypothesis 4	Change of international economic status refers to the change of the international status of national economy in world economy
Inference 1	Economic development = economic growth + economic progress + economic growth × economic progress
Inference 2	Economic modernization = economic development × economic transition × change of international economic competition and international economic status

Source: RGCMS (2005)

national economy and is subject to the constraint of the modernization of national economy.

Economic modernization is a change in the economic sphere. Apparently, not all economic changes belong to economic modernization. In general, only the economic changes that help improve productivity, social progress, and human development belong to economic modernization.

In general, economic development comprises economic growth and economic progress, and economic modernization is a collection of economic development, economic transformation, international economic competition, and international status change (Table 6.13). The change of international economic status has four scenarios: maintaining the advanced level of the world economy, narrowing the gap with the advanced level of the world economy, keeping the same gap with the advanced level of the world economy, and widening the gap with the advanced level of the world economy.

(2) Process

Economic modernization is a long and complex global process, which includes the change of production model, core technology, leading industry, economic behavior, structure, system, concept, etc. The process of economic modernization can be divided into two types: frontier process and catch-up process with both common and different features. During the eighteenth to twenty-first centuries, its frontier process experiences two stages: first and second economic modernizations (Table 6.14). First economic modernization comprises three waves, and second economic modernization comprises three waves (Table 6.2). The two economic modernizations have different contents and features (Table 6.15).

First economic modernization refers to the transitions and profound changes from agricultural to industrial economy and from self-supporting to market economy. It comprises the transitions from small-scale agricultural to commodity economy, from land to capital economy, from natural to technological economy, from scattered to central economy, and from regional to national economy. Its unique features include industrialization, mechanization, electrification, automation, specialization, standardization, centralization, scale operation, marketization, deagriculturalization, etc.

Second economic modernization is the transitions and profound changes from industrial to knowledge economy and from material to ecological economy. It comprises the transitions from product to service economy, from capital to information economy, from real to virtual economy, from scale to innovation economy, from efficiency to effectiveness economy, from national to global economy, etc. Currently, its unique features include intellectualization, informatization, servicization, intelligentization, decentralization, ecologization, greenization, dematerialization, globalization, de-industrialization, etc.

If first economic modernization is a preliminary economic modernization and a transition from traditional to primary modern economy, second economic modernization is an advanced economic modernization and a transition from primary modern to hypermodern economy. The coordinated development of the two economic modernizations is an integrated economic modernization.

The process of economic modernization has 12 unique features: it is revolutionary, long, complex, uneven, partial reversible, dynamic, global, progressive, risky, not completely spontaneous, economic efficiency popularization, and economic structure convergence.

Economic modernization is a sort of modernization and follows the ten basic principles (Table 2.15).

(3) Result

The outcome of economic modernization comprises the formation of economic modernity, particularity, diversity, and side effects. The result of economic

Table 6.14 Periodic table of economic modernization in broad sense—change of economic form

Stage (approx. starting year)	Features of economic form and structure	Economic modernization
Age of knowledge economy	*Knowledge, global, and ecological economy*	
Transition stage (2050)	Mature knowledge economy: knowledge industry and material and service industries	*Second economic modernization* Knowledge economic revolution Intellectualization and de-industrialization
Mature stage (2020)	Mixed knowledge economy: ratio of knowledge economy surpassing that of material industries	
Developing stage (1992)	Mixed knowledge economy: ratio of knowledge economy surpassing that of industry	
Start stage (1970)	Starting of knowledge economy and falling ratio of industry	
Age of industrial economy	*Industrial, market, and material economy*	
Transition stage (1946)	Mature industry economy: industry, service, and agriculture	*First economic modernization* Industrial economic revolution Industrialization and deagriculturalization
Mature stage (1914)	Mixed industrial economy: ratio of industry surpassing that of agriculture	
Developing stage (1870)	Mixed industrial economy: ratio of industry lagging that of agriculture	
Start stage (1763)	Initiation of modern industrial economy and falling that of agriculture	
Age of agricultural economy	*Agricultural, self-supporting, and material economy*	
Transition stage (AD 1500)	Mature agricultural economy: small-scale agricultural economy and handicraft industry	(Agricultural economic revolution) (Agriculturalization and hunting reduction)
Mature stage (AD 618)	Mixed agricultural economy: ratio of planting and animal husbandry surpassing that of hunting and gathering	
Developing stage (500 BC)	Mixed agricultural economy: ratio of planting and animal husbandry equaling that of hunting and gathering	
Start stage (3500 BC)	Starting of agricultural economy and falling of hunting and gathering	
Age of primitive economy	*Primitive, simple, and natural economy*	
Transition stage (10,000 years ago)	Primitive economy, and invention of planting and breeding	(Primitive agricultural revolution, and slash-and-burn farming)

(continued)

Table 6.14 (continued)

Stage (approx. starting year)	Features of economic form and structure	Economic modernization
Mature stage (40,000 years ago)	Hunting and gathering, and division of labor	
Developing stage (200,000 years ago)	Hunting and gathering	
Start stage (2,500,000 years ago)	Hunting and gathering	

Note: The time of chronology and the features were based on the frontier track of the development of world economy
Source: RGCMS (2005)

Table 6.15 Two stages of economic modernization in broad sense

Item	First economic modernization	Second economic modernization
Time	Roughly 1763–1970	Approx. 1970–2100
Content	Transition from agricultural to industrial economy	Transition from industrial to knowledge economy and from material to ecological economy
Feature	Industrialization, marketization, standardization, and deagriculturalization	Intellectualization, greenization, globalization, de-industrialization, and dematerialization
Concept	Economic growth, economic efficiency, and materialism	Economic quality, ecological awareness, and win–win of economy and environment
Technology	Mechanization, electrification, and automation	Informatization, digitization, intelligentization, intellectualization, and greenization
Production	Industrialized mass production, with industry being leading industry	Intellectualized, greenized, and globalized production, with knowledge industry being leading industry
Circulation	Marketization, commercialization, and monetization	Networking, internationalization, securitization, FTA, e-business
Dynamics	Technology, capital, population, and international competition	Knowledge, information, innovation, ecological awareness, and international competition
Objective	Production of material products to meet demand of material life	Production of material and intellectual products to meet demand of material and spiritual life
Modernity	First economic modernity: industrial, market, material, capital, and national economy	Second economic modernity: knowledge, information, ecological, cultural, biological, service, and global economy
Side effect	Environmental pollution and cyclic economic crises	Network economic crimes and international economic risks

Source: RGCMS (2005)

modernization in different countries has commonality and difference. And the results of the two economic modernizations are different (Table 6.15).

On the level of world economy, the result of economic modernization is manifested in six areas: the completion of twice economic revolutions and twice economic transitions; the growth of economic efficiency and per capita income; the improvement of economic welfare and equity; the widening of the gap in international economic efficiency and the narrowing of the gap in economic structure; the shift of the world economic center; and the change of the international economic system. The first three are applicable to the modernization of national and regional economies, and the latter also involves change in international economic status.

In the course of economic modernization, some countries reach and maintain the advanced level of the world economy and become advanced countries while others are developing countries. The two types of countries can change their places between them. In general, about 20% are advanced countries, and about 80% are developing countries. In a time span of 50 years, about 10% advanced country may degrade into developing countries, and about 5% developing countries may upgrade into advanced countries. The two types of countries are in a state of dynamic equilibrium.

The objectives of national economic modernization include completing first economic modernization, completing the second economic modernization, catching up, reaching, and maintaining the advanced level of the world economy, and becoming an advanced country or narrowing the international economic gap.

Since the 1950s, the result of economic modernization has been in correlation with its objective, and this correlation has been gradually formed and strengthened with the growth of modernization study.

(4) Dynamics

The drive force of economic modernization should be analyzed from two perspectives: impetus factors and impetus mechanisms (Table 6.12). In general, economic modernization has somewhat different drive force on different levels, in different countries, and during different stages. The dynamic models of the general modernization theories are basically applicable to economic modernization (Table 2.20).

(5) Model

In the twenty-first century, economic modernization has roughly three basic paths (Fig. 6.7) in the term of theory. The path of first economic modernization corresponds to the model of industrialization; the path of second economic modernization corresponds to the model of information economy, ecological economy, biological economy, and experience economy; and the path of integrated economic modernization corresponds to the model of new industrialization, including the coordinated development of industrialization, de-industrialization, intellectualization, informatization, and ecologization. Different models have many submodels.

In general, the process, result, dynamics, and model of economic modernization can be analyzed from the world, national, and regional perspectives, and the analysis from different perspectives can have somewhat different contents and unique features.

The *China Modernization Report 2005* introduced the economic timetable, periodical table, coordinates, and paths for economic modernization in the broad sense, and the conceptual model, quantitative model, objective model, and

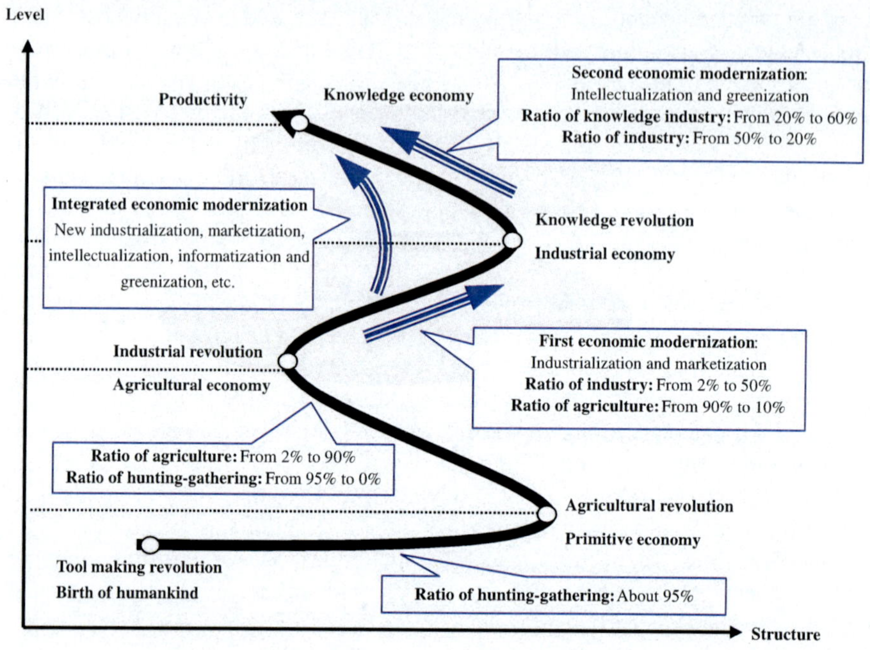

Fig. 6.7 Three paths for economic modernization in twenty-first century. Note: the horizontal coordinate represents the output structure of productivity. The structural graduation is the output ratio between agriculture and hunting–gathering (estimated) in the age of primitive economy, the output ratio between hunting–gathering and agriculture in the age of agricultural economy, the output ratio between industry and agriculture in the age of industrial economy, and the output ratio between industry and agriculture and knowledge industry in the age of knowledge economy. Source: RGCMS (2005)

dynamics model of economic modernization. It also discussed the stage theories of the economic modernization theory in the broad sense, and the methods for the modernization of the national economy.

(6) Second Economic Modernization

Second economic modernization is a form of expression for economic modernization and represents a frontier change occurring in the economic sphere since the 1970s. It comprises the transitions from industrial to knowledge economy and from material to ecological economy; the growth of economic efficiency and per capita income; the improvement of economic quality, welfare, and equity; the international economic differentiation; and the change of the international economic system.

Second economic modernization is a complex historical process, which includes economic development, economic transformation, international economic competition, and the change of national economic status and also includes the intellectualization and greenization of production model, core technology, leading industry, basic structure, basic system, and basic concept. In relation to industrial economy, knowledge economy is a new economic form and has many new features (Table 6.16).

Table 6.16 Main features of knowledge economy

Item	Main features
Production factor	Core production factors: knowledge (information), intangible assets, and intellectual workers
Production model	Informatization, networking, real-time production, clean production, agile production, smart and intelligent production
Corporation	Network structure, partnership, flexibility, innovativeness, environment-friendliness, and knowledge production
Management	Informatization, networking, personalization, elastic management, knowledge management, innovative management, cultural management, and strategy management
Technology	Digitization, intelligentization, intellectualization, greenization, visualization, and elastic manufacturing
Product	Intelligent, specialized, personalized, artistic, green, dematerialization, and short market cycle
Market	Globalized, no national boundary, fast changing, green, networking, and e-business
Industry	Three new major industries: knowledge industry plays leading roles and material industries (industry and agriculture) and traditional service industry play secondary roles
Distribution	Distribution according to contribution and regulation according to demand, with knowledge capital and investment capital participating in net income distribution
Employment	High employment rate for mental workers, high unemployment rate for physical workers, and wide unemployment insurance coverage
Corporate culture	Innovation, cooperation, learning, ecological awareness, and emphasis on knowledge capital and investment capital
Growth dynamics	Production and application of knowledge and information, innovation, knowledge workers, and environmental awareness

Source: He (1999)

(7) Integrated Economic Modernization

Integrated economic modernization is a basic path for economic modernization in the twenty-first century. It comprises the chain reaction between twice economic transitions (from agricultural to industry economy and from industrial to knowledge economy) and the continuous movement toward knowledge economy; comprises the coordinated development of the industrialization, deindustrialization, intellectualization, informatization, greenization, and globalization of national economy and the continuous movement toward intellectualization and greenization; and comprises the growth of economic efficiency and per capita income, the improvement economic quality, welfare, and equity, the international economic competition, and the change of international economic status (RGCMS 2005).

Integrated economic modernization is a historical process, which features the coordinated development of twice economic modernizations and the continuous transition to second economic modernization (Fig. 6.8). It comprises the change of

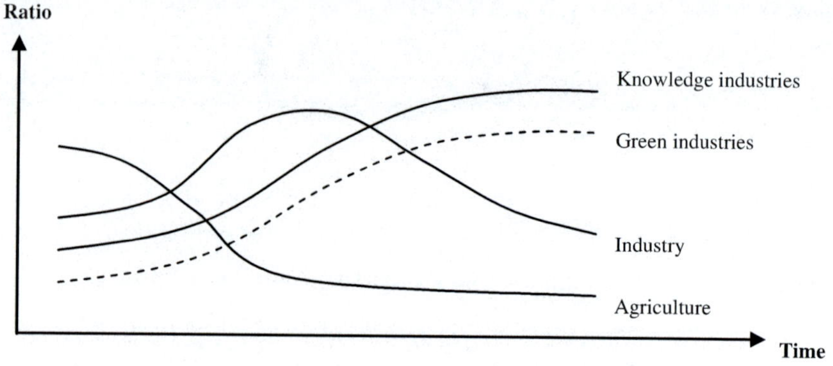

Fig. 6.8 Industrial structure of integrated economic modernization. Note: green industry refers to the industry that is unharmful to human beings and nature and is friendly to ecology and environment. Source: RGCMS (2005)

production model, core technology, leading industry, economic structure, system, and concept, and the international competition to catch up and reach the advanced level of the world economy. Integrated economic modernization comprises three equally important stages: new industrialization and informatization, deindustrialization and intellectualization, and intellectualization and greenization. Its objective is to catch up and reach the world's advanced level of economic modernization. The mark for the realization of integrated economic modernization is for economic efficiency, welfare, and system to reach the world's advanced levels at the time.

6.2 Social Modernization

Social modernization means the modernization of the social sphere and is a form of expression of the modernization phenomenon in social field. It comprises staged and stratified social modernization, the modernization of social subspheres and sectors (Fig. 6.9). In the documentation on classic modernization, social modernization and modernization often are not clearly distinguished, and sometimes they are regarded as being synonymous.

6.2.1 Studies

The social modernization study, a component of the modernization study, refers to the modernization study of the social sphere. This study, which dates back to the early years of the eighteenth century, can be analyzed from three perspectives: historical process, objective reality, and future prospect.

There is no unified definition of society and social sphere. In general, society refers to human community that shares a common culture and territory and interacts

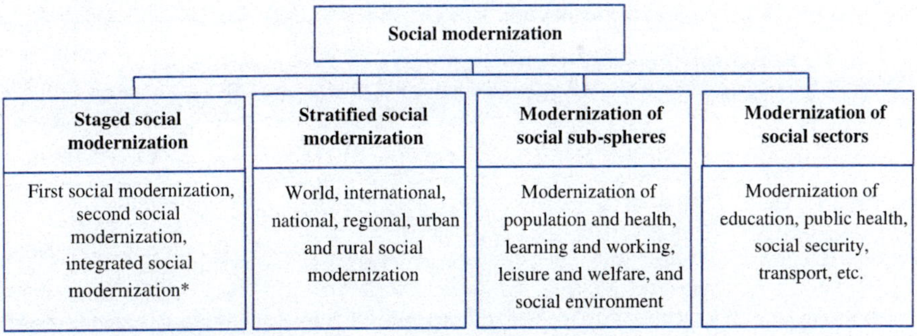

Fig. 6.9 Objects of social modernization study. Note: (*Asterisk*) Integrated social modernization means the coordinated development of twice social modernizations and is a basic path for social modernization in developing countries

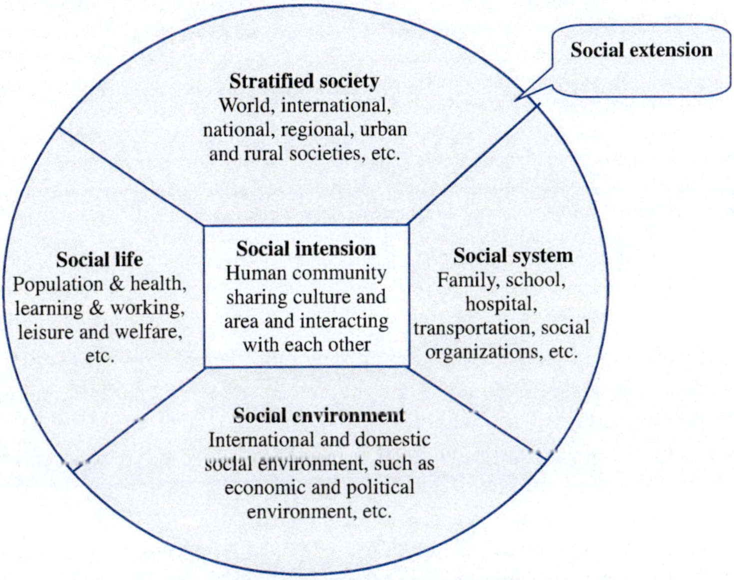

Fig. 6.10 Operational definitions of social intension and extension

with each other. Its extension includes stratified society, social life, social system, and social environment (Fig. 6.10). Social sphere refers to a sphere of human civilization and a sphere related to social behavior, structure, system, and change. Social modernization is a short term for the modernization of social sphere.

6.2.1.1 Research Paradigm

The objects of social modernization study are the modernization of social sphere, covering the modernization of population and health, learning and working, leisure and welfare, and social environment, as well as the world, national, and regional

Table 6.17 Matrix of social modernization study

Content		Object		
		Social sphere	Population and health, learning and working, leisure and welfare, and social environment	World, national, regional, urban, and rural societies
		Social modernization	Modernization of four social subspheres	Social modernization on five levels
Element	Behavior Structure Institution Idea	Modernization of social behavior, structure, institution, and ideas	Modernization of social behavior, structure, institution, and ideas in the four social subspheres	Modernization of social behavior, structure, institution, and ideas on the five levels
Aspect	Process Result Dynamics Model	Process, result, dynamics, and model of the social modernization	Process, result, dynamics, and model of social modernization in the four social subspheres	Process, result, dynamics, and model of social modernization on the five levels

Note: Population and health cover population, family, residence, medical care and health, etc. Learning and working cover education, employment, income, poverty, etc. Leisure and welfare cover leisure, entertainment, transportation, communication, social security, public security, etc. Social environment covers domestic social environment (political, economic, cultural, and cultural environment) and international social environment. The contents of social modernization study also cover staged social modernization, modernization of social sectors, analysis of social frontier, analysis of social trend, analysis of social frontier process, analysis of social catch-up process, and interaction between social modernization factors and different spheres. The social modernizations of urban and rural are two subregional social modernizations
Source: RGCMS (2006)

social modernization. The research contents include the modernization of social behavior, structure, system, and ideas and the process, result, dynamics, and model of social modernization. They can form a structural matrix (Table 6.17). The objects of social modernization study also include staged social modernization, the modernization of social sectors, etc.

Social modernization study is a branch of modernization study and can use the methodology of modernization study. It has diverse analytic methods, such as time-series analysis, cross-sectional analysis, process analysis, case analysis, social investigation, quantitative evaluation, and coordinates analysis. The research time span can be a whole process or a time period. The research scope can be the world, a country, or a region. The research objective includes academic and policy objectives. Different types of research have different features.

6.2.1.2 Historical Facts

Social modernization, which began in the middle of the eighteenth century, is a form of social change. In general, social modernization is closely linked with economic modernization. Social modernization surges when economic modernization surges (Table 6.18), but they were asynchronous. In relation to the six waves of economic modernization, the division of the six waves of social modernization is

Table 6.18 Two major stages and six waves of social modernization

Wave	Approx. time	Content	Annotation
First	1763–1870	Urbanization, mechanization, urban health, social relief, and primary education development	*First social modernization* Urbanization, social welfare, mobility, and compulsory education
Second	1870–1945	Urbanization, electrification, public health, social insurance, and universal compulsory education	
Third	1946–1970	Social welfare, automation, technologization, automobile popularization, and universal secondary education	
Fourth	1970–2020	Intellectualization, networking, greening, suburbanization, globalization, and universal higher education	*Second social modernization* Intellectualization, suburbanization, greening, and higher education
Fifth	2020–2050	Biological economy, urban–rural balance, barrier-free knowledge and information acquisition, leisure popularization, and intelligent transport	
Sixth	2050–2100	Experience economy, life engineering, leisure-working integration, and super-transport experience	

Note: The fifth and sixth waves are merely forecasts. Some scholars believe that developed countries enter "deurbanization" after completing urbanization, which includes migration of urban population to suburbs and townships before an urban–rural balance is reached. This migration is called suburbanization here
Source: RGCMS (2006)

not quite clear. The *China Modernization Report 2006: Social Modernization Study* (RGCMS 2006) systematically analyzed the process, facts, and enlightenments of social modernization as follows.

(1) Process Analysis

First, the first wave of social modernization. Corresponding to the first industrial revolution, this wave experienced a long process of preparation and mainly occurred in European countries. The essence was industrialization-induced urbanization, mechanization, rationalization, social differentiation, social mobility, development of primary education, establishment of public health and relief establishment, and the improvement of social productivity and living standards.

Second, the second wave of social modernization. It comprises two parts: the social change during the second industrial revolution and that during the two World Wars. Over the 60 years, the wave of social modernization spread to the vast areas of Europe, America, and Asia. The features were urbanization, electrification, mechanization, specialization, social mobility, social movement, social differentiation, social transition and integration, universal primary education, development of public health, establishment of social insurance system, formation of urban society, and improvement of living standard and social productivity. During the two World

Wars, the features were universal primary education, social movement, social differentiation, mechanization and electrification of family, improvement of living standards, and development of social security system.

Third, the third wave of social modernization. It comprises social modernization in industrial countries and that in developing countries. The former represented the core and frontier of the third wave of social modernization, while the latter represented the first wave of social modernization in developing countries. The main contents include urbanization, suburbanization, social welfare, social differentiation and integration, bureaucratization, technologization, automation, mass communication, establishment of welfare state, universal secondary education, and development of higher education.

Fourth, the fourth wave of social modernization. It was driven by knowledge and information revolutions. While industrial revolution led to a higher ratio of industrial labor force and a lower ratio of agricultural labor force, knowledge revolution led to a lower ratio of industrial labor force and a higher ratio of intellectual labor force (Knowledge labor force). Like the first wave, the fourth wave is a social revolution in nature. The fourth wave also has a process of preparation, and this process is not yet completed. So far, the main contents of the fourth wave include informatization, networking, intellectualization, innovatization, suburbanization, urban–rural balance, internationalization, greening, diversification, universal higher education, and lifetime learning.

Fifth, the fifth wave of social modernization. This wave is a forecast, featuring the new biological effects and formation of biological economy and society. The development of new biological revolution and high technologies will lead to the integration of biological technology, information technology, and nanotechnology and the formation of life-engineering technology that will transform and manipulate life functions. The life of organisms will become controllable, the biological economy will become the leading industry, and social concept will undergo revolutionary changes. The information converter will realize information conversion between human brains and computers, and barrier-free acquisition of knowledge and information will become a social reality.

Sixth, the sixth wave of social modernization. This is also a forecast, featuring the new physical effects and the formation of cultural economy and society. On the basis of new physical revolution and in conjunction with the development of high technologies and new energies, both manufacturing and transport technologies and temporal–spatial concepts will undergo revolutionary changes. Super-manufacturing systems will replace most of human physical and mental work, super-transport systems will make it possible for human beings to go where they want, and cultural life and sentimental experience will become the dominant form of social economy.

(2) Modernization of Three Subsocial Spheres

The social sphere comprises some subspheres or branch spheres, and different subspheres have different contents and features (Table 6.19).

Table 6.19 Modernization of three subsocial spheres

Approx. time	Sphere of population and health	Sphere of learning and working	Sphere of leisure and welfare
1763–1870	Social mobility, differentiation, urbanization, and urban health	Primary education development, 10-h working system, and lower ratio of agricultural labor force	Railway, shipping, highway, telegraph, and social relief
1870–1945	Accelerated urbanization, lower ratio of birth, mortality, fertility and marriage, expanded public health and middle class	Universal primary education, 8-h working system, lower ratio of agricultural labor force, strike movement	Social insurance, social security system, electrification, mechanization, automobile, telephone
1946–1970	Urbanization, suburbanization, higher divorce rate, small family, public health	Universal secondary education, 40-h working system, lower ratio of agricultural labor force	Welfare state, technologization, automation, expressway, air transport
1970–2020	Suburbanization, aging, family diversification, public health	Universal higher education, flexible working system, lower ratio of industrial labor force	Welfare reform, diversification, greening, globalization, informatization, cyberspace
2020–2050	Urban–rural dynamic balance, birth diversification, life engineering	Information conversion, barrier-free knowledge acquisition, higher ratio of intellectual jobs	Leisurization, entertainment diversification, intelligent transport
2050–2100	Dynamic balance of population spatial structure, birth diversification, life engineering	Cultural experience, flexible working system, higher ratio of intellectual jobs	Leisure–work integration, super-transport

Source: RGCMS (2006)

(3) Social Modernization and Change of Social Systems

The change of social system is an important component of social modernization. In general, the basic social system is a system that governs the ownership, allocation, and distribution of social resources. In the age of primitive society, the basic social system was primitive public ownership. Social resources were publicly owned and were distributed equally or according to needs. Private ownership came into being in the transitional period of the age of primitive society, but the social system still carried the color of public ownership. In the age of agricultural society, the basic social system is agrarian ownership, including slavery, manorialism, nomadism or tenancy, etc. Social resources were privately owned, and the kings, bureaucrats, and slave owners (manor or land owners) determined the allocation and distribution of social resources. In the age of industrial society, the basic social system was market economy and social welfare system. The state and the market determined the allocation and distribution of social sources. In the age of knowledge society, the

Table 6.20 Typical features of basic social systems in social history (examples)

Social time	Age of primitive society	Age of agricultural society	Age of industrial society	Age of knowledge society
Historical time	Birth of mankind ~3500 BC	3500 BC–AD 1763	1763–1970	1970 to approx. 2100
Social form	Primitive society	Agricultural society	Industrial society	Knowledge society
Basic system	Primitive public ownership	Agrarian system	Social welfare system	Information and knowledge system
Population	Natural birth	Encouraged birth	Controlled birth	Independently selected birth
Family	Matrilineal and patrilineal families	Big family, moral marriage	Small family, legal marriage	Family and marriage diversification
Education	Teaching by precept and example	Nonstandard education	Universal primary education	Universal higher education
Working	Male hunting and female gathering	Family-based natural working system	Industrialized standard working system	Diverse and flexible working systems
Distribution	Equal distribution	Distribution according to power and land ownership	Distribution according to capital or labor	Distribution according to contribution and regulation according to demand
Security	Clan self-security	Family self-security	Social security and welfare	Social security and welfare

Source: RGCMS (2006)

basic social system will be information networking and knowledge system, and the systems on the production, allocation, and distribution of knowledge resources are still in the process of formation (Table 6.20). From the perspective of social system change, the transition from agricultural social system to industrial social system constitutes first social modernization, and the transition from industrial social system to knowledge social system represents second social modernization.

The formation of a new social system is a historical process. From preparation, introduction, development, maturity, and elimination, each stage has its own features. Accordingly, there must be an intermediate form of social systems between one basic social system and another system. They can be called transitional social systems or subsocial systems. In the age of primitive society, the subsocial systems included the systems of matrilineal, tribal, fishing, horticultural, and pastoral society. In the age of agricultural society, the subsocial systems included systems of hunter–gatherer, pastoral, horticultural, feudal society, etc. In the age of industrial society, the subsocial systems included systems of various primitive and agricultural societies. In the age of knowledge society, the subsocial systems included systems of agricultural, industrial, information, virtual and service society, etc.

Table 6.21 Basic social forms and their typical features in social history

Type of society	Primitive society	Agricultural society	Industrial society	Knowledge society
Historical time	Birth of mankind ~3500 BC	3500 BC–AD 1763	1763–1970	1970 to approx. 2100
Production mode	Collective hunting and gathering	Agricultural manual production	Industrialized mass production	Intellectualized global production
Production technology	High-efficient hunting technology	Food production technology	Material production technology	Production and application of knowledge and information
Social life	Hunting, gathering, and migration	Farming and nomadic life	Urbanization and electrification	Networking, suburbanization and globalization
Social structure	Over 95% for hunting and gathering	Over 90% for agriculture and animal husbandry	Over 50% for industrial labor	Over 50% for knowledge labor
Social system	Primitive public ownership	Agrarian system	Social welfare system	Information society system
Social concept	Equal distribution	Distribution according to power and land ownership	Distribution according to capital or labor	Distribution according to contribution and regulation according to need

Source: RGCMS (2006)

(4) Social Modernization and Change of Social Forms

From the birth of mankind to the end of the twenty-first century, human society has had four basic social forms: primitive society, agricultural society, industrial society, and knowledge society. Each social form has its own basic structures, including the structures of population, family, residence, health, education, labor, income, leisure, transport, communications, and social system. Each social form also has its own basic features, including the features of social productivity, life, structure, system, and concept (Table 6.21).

(5) Basic Facts of Social Modernization

First, the facts of the population and health sphere. Since the eighteenth century, life expectancy and healthy life became longer, the rate of population natural growth rose first and fell later, and social mobility and differentiation continued, from urbanization to suburbanization and to urban–rural balance. Since the nineteenth century, the rates of population and infant mortalities fell steadily, population aging became increasingly visible, families became smaller and diversified, and public health and home facilities continued to improve. Since the twentieth century, public health spending and per capita health spending became higher.

Second, the facts of the learning and working sphere. Since the eighteenth century, the structures of labor force and employment continued to change, the social productivity and per capita income became higher, the equity of income distribution changed, and the equity of income distribution in developed countries fell first and rose later (fluctuations occurred in some countries). Since the nineteenth century, primary education was universalized, labor time became shorter, and the unemployment rate continued to fluctuate. Since the twentieth century, secondary and higher education was universalized, public education spending and per capita education spending rose, and the ratio of population living in absolute poverty became lower.

Third, the facts of the leisure and welfare sphere. Since the eighteenth century, transport continued to develop, and the development of the social security system experienced four stages: social relief, social insurance, social welfare, and welfare reform. Since the nineteenth century, leisure time became longer, and communications technology continued to develop. Since the twentieth century, entertainment and leisure were diversified and networked, the use of computers and Internet became higher, the information spending and per capita information spending became higher, and the spending on social security and welfare went up. In the twentieth century, crimes and suicides became rampant and long fluctuated. At the end of the twentieth century, 170 countries and regions established social security system.

Over the past three centuries, social life, structure, system, and concept continued to change, social change was highly uneven and asynchronous, and the international gap in per capita national income became wider.

(6) Historical Enlightenments of Social Modernization

First, social modernization is both a historical necessity and a social choice. To human civilization, social modernization is a historical necessity, which represents a direction of the advance of human civilization. To different countries and nations, social modernization is a social choice. The countries and nations that have chosen social modernization must bear the responsibility and result of social modernization. Of course, the countries and nations that have failed to choose social modernization must also bear the result of its choice. This result is roughly to stay in traditional agricultural society or primitive society (Table 6.22), and lag increasingly behind the frontier of human civilization.

Second, social modernization advances like waves, instead of a smooth sailing. Social modernization is independent of man's will and observes objective laws. Wave-like advance, one of the important laws, is determined by three factors: the fluctuation of knowledge and technological innovation, the fluctuation of economic performance, and the fluctuation of human idea and cognition (confrontation between innovation and conservativeness).

Third, major progress in social modernization depends on major innovation and its spreading. On the frontier of human civilization, social modernization is more of a natural evolution. But natural development is not a windfall, but a result of innovation and its spreading. In fact, each revolutionary advance in social modernization is a result of major innovation and its spreading.

Fourth, social modernization has three sources. First, it is a partial inheritance and development of traditional society, such as scientific and technological

Table 6.22 Roughly estimated world population distribution 1700–2001

Year	Population (10,000)	Estimated population (10,000)				Estimated population ratio (%)			
		Primitive society	Agricultural society	Industrial society	Knowledge society	Primitive society	Agricultural society	Industrial society	Knowledge society
1700	60,341	520	59,821	–	–	0.86	99	–	–
1820	104,109	520	102,152	1,437	–	0.50	98	1	–
1900	156,400	520	138,290	17,590	–	0.33	88	11	–
1960	302,040	520	210,957	90,563	–	0.17	70	30	–
1981	450,660	520	148,264	276,959	25,437	0.12	33	61	6
2001	612,770	520	109,026	413,744	90,000	0.08	18	68	15

Note: Primitive society refers to the society featuring hunting and gathering, and the 2001 data are used for the hunting and gathering population between 1700 and 2001

Source: RGCMS (2006)

knowledge and social morality. Second, it is a partial negation and conversion of traditional society, such as urbanization and suburbanization. Third, it is an innovation of knowledge and system, such as industrial revolution and knowledge revolution. The three sources have somewhat different importance in different stages of social modernization in different nations.

Fifth, social modernization is not only a social progress but also a social adaptation. Social modernization contains social progress, such as the improvement of life quality, social efficiency, national literacy, social welfare, and social equity. It also contains positive social adaptation, such as the positive changes in lifestyle, living environment, and social environment. Some social adaptations, such as informatization and leisurization, also represent a social progress. But some social adaptations, such as small families and lower birth rates, only reflect some social changes in conformity with social progress.

Sixth, social modernization has a "late-comer effect." The historical experience over the past three centuries indicates that social modernization can be divided into two types: "early-comer" and "later-comer." An "early-comer" country enjoys "competitive advantages" because it can lead the world trend, utilize world resources, and set world rules. A "late-comer" country can have "later-comer effect," because it can draw on and utilize the successful experience and advanced technologies of the "early-comer" countries, reduce miscalculations, and cut down time–cost of the process. But in the competition of the international community, the "later-comer effect" should not be overestimated, because technology attraction is a market behavior and is subject to the influence of many factors. The "late-comer" countries need to enhance their international competitiveness and their ability to differentiate and avoid falling into international traps of "being utilized, manipulated, and misled."

Seventh, social modernization has no best model, but rational choice and path dependency. Social modernization is same in nature but can have diverse forms. While social modernization can have the same direction, it can have diverse paths. For example, different developed countries in the West have different education systems, social security systems, and public health systems.

Eighth, social modernization is not once-and-for-all endeavor. It is in the relative, and its status is changeable. Social modernization is noted for structural stability and status changeability. The history of the past three centuries indicates that the world structure of social modernization has been basically stable, with about 20% countries being advanced countries and about 80% countries being developing countries in social modernization. The international social status of specific countries can change, and this change observes certain regularity. For example, in the 43 years from 1960 to 2003, about 88% advanced countries and over 90% developing countries saw no change in their international status. While about 12% advanced countries downgraded into developing countries, about 6% developing countries upgraded into advanced countries. Developing countries include moderately developed countries, preliminarily developed countries, and underdeveloped countries.

6.2.1.3 Present State and Prospect of Social Modernization

(1) Present State

First, the level of social modernization. Of the 131 countries in 2003, about 31 countries or 24% of all had completed first social modernization, and 23 countries or 18% of all had entered second social modernization. Classified according to the second social modernization index, 20 countries including Norway were developed countries, 33 countries including Spain were moderately developed countries, 17 countries including Thailand were preliminarily developed countries, and 61 countries including China were underdeveloped countries.

Second, the stage of social modernization. In 2003, eight countries including Norway entered the developing stage of second social modernization, 15 countries including France were in the start stage of second social modernization, 17 countries including Brazil were in the transition stage of first social modernization, 31 countries including Poland were in the mature stage of first social modernization, 28 countries including China were in the developing stage of first social modernization, 13 countries including India were in the start stage of first social modernization, and ten countries including Chad were still in traditional agricultural society (Fig. 6.11).

Third, the world frontier of social modernization. In 2003, the world top ten countries in terms of the second social modernization index were respectively Norway, Sweden, the United States, Denmark, Britain, Finland, Japan, the Netherlands, Switzerland, and Australia.

Fourth, the status change of social modernization. During the 1950–2003 period, 114 countries saw their social status changed, with 58 upgrades and 56 downgrades. During the 1960–2003 period, 20 countries saw their status upgraded, and 20 saw their status downgraded.

Fifth, the population distribution of social modernization. In 2001, about 15% people (900 million) in the world lived in knowledge society, 68% people (4.1 billion) lived in industrial society, and 18% people (1.1 billion) lived in agricultural society. In the 122 countries with complete evaluation data, 18% countries (22) entered knowledge society, 74% countries (90) were in industrial society, and 8% countries (10) and many regions were in agricultural society. Meanwhile, about 188 aboriginal groups lived in primitive society (Table 6.23).

(2) Prospect

First, the time of completing first social modernization. Estimated at the average annual growth rate during the 1980–2003 period, the low-income countries on average require 81 years, and the world on average requires 13 years to complete first social modernization.

Second, the world's advanced level of social modernization. Calculated at the average annual growth rate during the 1980–2003 period, developed countries will see their second social modernization index rising about twofold in 2050 over their 2003 level.

Third, the world average level of social modernization. The world average level is roughly 50 years behind the average level of socially developed countries, and the

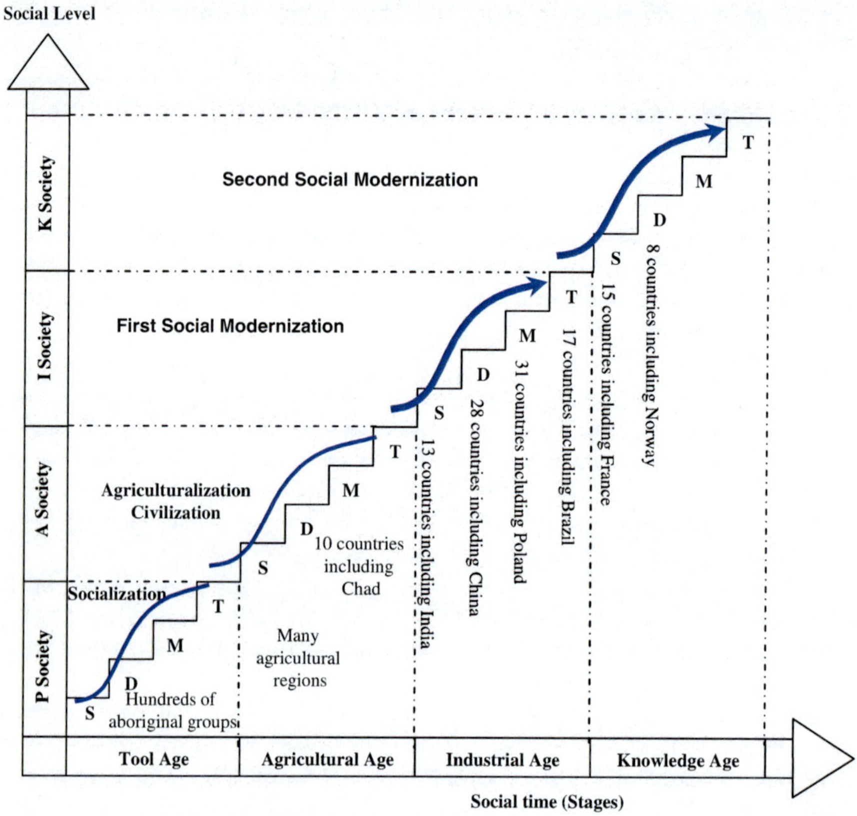

Fig. 6.11 Coordinates of world social modernization in 2003. Note: P, A, I, and K refer to primitive, agricultural, industrial, and knowledge, respectively. S, D, M, and T refer to the start, developing, mature, and transition stage, respectively. Social time refers to the time based on the frontier track of social development. Source: RGCMS (2005)

Table 6.23 Estimated world population distribution in 2001

Item	Classification standard and population distribution			Country distribution	
Classification	Classification standard	Population (10,000)	Ratio (%)	Number of countries	Ratio (%)
Knowledge society	Entered second social modernization	90,000	14.7	22	18.0
Industrial society	World population—population of agricultural and knowledge societies	413,744	67.5	90	73.8
Agricultural society	Living at less than one international dollar per day	109,026	17.8	10	8.2
Primitive society	Living on (or once) hunting and gathering	520	0.08	(188 Tribes)	–
World total		612,770	100	122	100

Source: RGCMS (2006)

Table 6.24 Estimated levels of social modernization in twenty-first century

Item	2002	2010	2020	2030	2040	2050	2060	2080	2100
Number of countries entering second social modernization	23	26	32	42	48	54	59	62	65
Number of countries completing first social modernization	31	53	63	76	81	84	84	87	90

Source: RGCMS (2006)

world average level in 2050 will be roughly equivalent to the 2000 average level of socially developed countries.

Fourth, the national level distribution of social modernization. Calculated at the average annual growth rate during the 1970–2003 period, about 84 countries will complete first social modernization, and about 54 countries will enter second social modernization in 2050; about 90 countries will complete first social modernization, and 65 countries will enter second social modernization in 2100 (Table 6.24).

6.2.2 Theories

Social modernization theory is a theory explaining the phenomenon of social modernization. It is a branch of modernization theory. Currently, there are roughly two theoretical collections: classic social modernization theory and social modernization theory in the broad sense.

6.2.2.1 Classic Social Modernization Theory

The classic social modernization theory began to form in the 1950s, but its ideological sources date back much earlier. In fact, the birth of human society meant the sprout of social ideas, and the change of human society was inevitably accompanied by the evolution of social ideas. Before the birth of Christ, ancient Greek thinker Plato introduced the concept of *the Republic*, and ancient Chinese thinkers introduced the concepts of "society of great harmony" and "society of great peace." In the twentieth century, "modernized society" became the pursuit of many countries and scholars. Ideal society has been the object thought and pursued by thinkers all the time, and social ideas date back long ago. However, the social ideas that had produced direct impacts on social modernization are the social ideas of Renaissance and Enlightenment. Sociology came into being in the middle of the nineteenth century. Although each social theory is more or less related to social modernization, the theories on social changes, such as social evolution theory, social transformation theory, and social development theory, are more closely related to social modernization.

As an important branch of classic modernization theory, classic social modernization theory was formed in the 1950s and 1960s. The publication of three works by American sociologists marked the birth of classic social modernization theory. They were the *Social System* (Parsons 1951), the *Passing of Traditional Society: Modernizing the Middle East* (Lerner 1958), and the *Modernization and the*

Table 6.25 Structure of classic social modernization theory

Category	Theory	Main contents	Representatives
General theory	Core theory	Basic rules and features of classic social modernization	
Branch theories	Modern society theory	Modern society theory, industrial society theory, etc.	T. Parsons, M. J. Levy
	Urbanization theory	Definition, process, structure, dynamics, model of urbanization, etc.	American Chicago School
	Social differentiation theory	Social polarization theory, rationalization theory, etc.	N. Smelser, M. Weber
	Sector theory	Education modernization, health modernization, social security modernization, etc.	
Related theories	Structural functionalism	Structure, function, differentiation, adaptation, and change of social system	T. Parsons, R. K. Merton
	Social system theory	Type, differentiation, integration, balance, control, and evolution of social system	T. Parsons, N. Luhmann
	Social evolution theory	Social evolution from low level to high level	
	Social development theory	Theory of development and dependency of underdeveloped countries, etc.	
	Other related theories	Circulation theory, conflict theory, interaction theory, transformation theory, diffusion theory, etc.	

Source: RGCMS (2006)

Structure of Societies (Levy 1966). So far, there has been no systematic and universally recognized general theoretic explanation about classic social modernization theory. Classic social modernization theory is a collection of academic ideas about classic social modernization (Table 6.25).

The *China Modernization Report 2006* analyzed the ideas and principles of classic social modernization theory and summarized the general theory of classic social modernization (Table 6.26), including the definition, process, result, dynamics, and model of classic social modernization.

(1) Definition

In general, classic social modernization is a social change since the eighteenth century. It is both a transition from traditional society to modern society, from agricultural society to industrial society, and from preindustrial society to industrial society and a process of underdeveloped societies to catch up and reach the advanced level of developed societies.

Table 6.26 General theory of classic social modernization

Aspect	Basic contents
Definition	Classic social modernization is a revolutionary social change since the eighteenth century. It includes the process and profound changes of the transition from traditional society to modern society, and also the process and change of underdeveloped societies catching up and reaching the advanced level of developed societies
Process	Classic social modernization is a historical process, which comprises social mobility, differentiation and integration, the mass application of nonbiological energies and modern science and technology, the change of population and family structures, and the change of social life, structure, and ideas. It has nine unique features
Result	The outcome of classic social modernization is the completion of the transition from agricultural society to industrial society. The features of industrial society have been summarized as the classic social modernity, which includes urbanization, social welfare, mobility, specialization, rationalization, universal primary education, mass communication, etc.
Dynamics	Classic social modernization is subject to the influence of many factors, including the economic, political, cultural, scientific and technological, population, environmental, and social factors
Model	Classic social modernization has diverse paths and models and path dependency and is subject to the influence of historical, geographic, and objective conditions. It is manifested in the diversity of urbanization model, national education system, public medical system, and social security system

Source: RGCMS (2006)

(2) Process

Classic social modernization is both a long and complex historical process. It mainly includes social mobilization, mobility, stratification, differentiation, and integration, the change of social structure, population and family structures, the urbanization of residential structure, the mass application of nonbiological energies and science and technology the change of public health and human health, the development of national education, the universalization of primary education, occupational division and specialization, the growth of social productivity and per capita income, the shortening of labor time and the extension of leisure time, family mechanization and electrification, the development of transport and communications, the establishment of social security system, and the change of social system and ideas.

The features of the classic social modernization process are basically similar to those of classic modernization. American scholar Samuel Huntington believes: modernization is a revolutionary, complex, systematic, global, long, staged, converging, irreversible, and a progressive process (Table 4.3). There have been many arguments over convergence and irreversibility, because somewhat different from social reality.

(3) Result

The outcome of classic social modernization is the completion of the transition from agricultural society to industrial society and becomes an industrial society. American scholar Frank Sutton compared the typical features of agricultural society and industrial society (Huntington 1971). A mature industrialized society has many common features, which can be called classic social modernity. It mainly includes social mobility, stratification, differentiation and integration, small family, urbanization, rationalization, specialization, family mechanization, electrification, automation, social welfare, universal primary education, and mass communication. At the same time, it also has some negative effects, such as the rich–poor gap and the environmental, family, and moral problems.

Industrialized society is also modernized society. American scholar Levy compared the features of modernized society and nonmodernized society and came up with eight features of modern society (Levy 1966). All organizations in modernized society are highly specialized; because of high specialization, various organizations are mutually dependent, and their functions are not self-supporting; morality is of a universalistic nature, instead of the individuality determined by family and relative relations; state power is centralized but not totalitarian; social relations are rationalist and universalistic with limited functions and neutral feelings; it has developed exchange media and markets; it has highly developed bureaucratic organizations; families are small and have less functions.

(4) Dynamics

Classic social modernization is a complex process, and its dynamic mechanism is also complex. Currently, there is no unified cognition over the issue. There are roughly five schools. The first school is that economic development and industrialization are the main driving force of the modernization process (Popenoe 2000). The second school is that cultural change is the main impetus to modernization (Weber 1958). The third view is that the interaction between politics, economy, and culture promotes modernization (Inglehart 1997). The fourth view is that the promoters of innovation, diffusion, and change are the key factors for modernization (Harrison 1988). The fifth view is that diverse factors, including economic, political, cultural, environmental, social, scientific and technological and social factors and social planning, impact social modernization.

(5) Model

Classic social modernization has diverse paths and models, such as the international disparities in the model of population and family changes, the urbanization model, the public health system, the national education system, and the social security system.

Classic social modernization is not in isolation. It is subject to the influence of politics and culture and interacts with classic economic modernization. At the same time, it is subject to the constraint of the level of science and technology. Therefore, the analysis of the relations between classic social modernization and the national modernization and modernization in other spheres should become the content of the classic social modernization theory. Classic social modernization theory takes countries as the basic units. In the regions at the different administrative levels within a country, regional social modernization can be somewhat different from national social modernization, such as the difference in urbanization models.

Regional social modernization should be included into the research scope of the classic social modernization theory.

6.2.2.2 Social Modernization Theory in Broader Term

The social modernization theory in the broad sense is a theoretical interpretation of the phenomenon of social modernization during the eighteenth to twenty-first century. It is an application of the second modernization theory in the social sphere and has been introduced by Chinese scholar Chuanqi He. The social modernization theory in the broad sense comprises the general theory, branch theories, and related theories (Table 6.27). Here our discussions focus on the general theory, including the definition, process, result, dynamics, and model of social modernization (Table 6.28). So far, there has been very limited cognition of second social modernization and integrated social modernization, and the social modernization theory in the broad sense still has vast room for development.

(1) Definition

Social modernization is a form of expression for modernization in the social sphere.

The intension: social modernization is a frontier change and international competition in the social sphere since the industrial revolution in the eighteenth century. It comprises the formation, development, transformation, and international interaction of modern society; the innovation, selection, diffusion, and withdrawal of social factors; and the international competition, international differentiation, and stratification to catch up, reach, and maintain the advanced level of world society.

The extension: social modernization comprises world, national, and regional social modernization; comprises the modernization of social behavior, structure,

Table 6.27 Structure of social modernization theory in broad sense

Category	Theory	Main contents
General theory	Core theory	Definition, process, result, dynamics, and model of social modernization
Branch theories	Stage theory	First, second, or integrated social modernization
	Stratified study	Modernization of global, national, and regional society
	Subsphere study	Modernization in the subfields of population and health, learning and working, leisure and welfare, social environment, etc.
	Sector theory	Modernization in education, health, social security, energy, transport, communications, and other social sectors
Related theories	Other modernization theories	Classic modernization theory, postmodernization theory, reflective modernization theory, second modernization theory, etc.
	Related sociology theories	Urbanization, social change, social evolution, social development, social system theory, industrial society, knowledge society, etc.
	Other related theories	Informatization, quality of life, ecological sociology, modernism, postmodernism, etc.

Source: RGCMS (2006)

Table 6.28 General theory of social modernization in broad sense

Aspect	Basic contents
Definition	Social modernization, a modernization of the social sphere, is a social change and international competition since the industrial revolution in the eighteenth century. It is the frontier process of the formation, development, transformation, and international interaction of modern society; a compound process of the innovation, selection, diffusion, and withdrawal of social factors; and also an international differentiation and competition to catch up, reach, and maintain the world's advanced level of social development
Process	Social modernization is a historical process, which comprises social development, social transformation, international social competition, international social differentiation, and national social stratification; comprises change of social behavior, structure, system, and ideas; and comprises the world frontier of social change and the process of reaching the world frontier. During eighteenth to twenty-first centuries, the frontier track of social modernization can be divided into two major stages. Specifically, first social modernization is a transformation and profound change from agricultural to industrial society and from feudal to civic society, and its main features include urbanization, mobility, social welfare and universal primary education, etc.; second social modernization is a transformation and profound change from industrial to knowledge society and from material to ecological society, and currently, its main features include intellectualization, informatization, greening, universal higher education, etc. The coordinated development of the twice social modernizations is integrated social modernization. Social modernization will have new changes in the twenty-second century. It follows the ten basic principles of modernization (Table 2.15)
Result	The formation of social modernity, particularity, diversity, and side effects, the improvement of social efficiency and quality of life, the improvement of social welfare and equity, and the change of lifestyle, living ideas, and international social status. The result of first social modernization is the formation of first social modernity, particularity, and diversity, and its side effects include a widening rich–poor gap; the main marks for completing first social modernization are the competition of urbanization, social welfare system and the reaching of social efficiency and life standard to the advanced level of industrial society (the average level of industrial countries in the 1960s). The result of second social modernization is the formation of second social modernity, particularity, and diversity, and its side effects include information divide; the main marks for completing second social modernization are the completion of intellectualization, greening, and the reaching of social effectiveness and quality of life to the world's advanced level of knowledge society (some time in the future). The basic standard for realizing social modernization is for social effectiveness, quality of life, social structure, and system to reach the world's advanced levels at the time
Dynamics	The drive factors for social modernization include innovation, exchange, competition, adaptation, national interests, and social demand, include social driving forces (economic growth, scientific advance, and education development), social pooling forces (political development, cultural change, and globalization), and social pressures (population and environmental changes). The dynamic models include innovation driving, three-innovation driving, associated action, four-step super circulation, social compound interaction, innovation diffusion, innovation spillover, and competition driving (Table 2.20). Different countries have somewhat different dynamics for their social modernization in different stages

(continued)

Table 6.28 (continued)

Aspect	Basic contents
Model	Social modernization has diverse paths and models, is path dependent, and is subject to the influence of historical, geographic, and traditional factors. It has three basic paths in the twenty-first century: first social modernization path, second social modernization path, and integrated social modernization path. The corresponding basic models are the model of urbanization, the model of paralleled intellectualization and greening, and the model of paralleled new urbanization, greening, informatization, etc.

Note: There has been no unified definition of modern society. In general, modern society includes industrial society (preliminarily modern society) and knowledge society (advanced modern society). Industrial society is based on industry, and knowledge society is based on knowledge and is sometimes called postmodern society

Source: RGCMS (2006, 2010)

system, and ideas; comprises the modernization of population and health, learning and working, leisure and welfare, and social environment; and comprises the modernization of education and other social sectors and the change of the temporal–spatial distribution of social modernization.

In general, social modernization refers to the world frontiers of social change and the process to reach these frontiers, and includes the transition from agricultural to industrial society and the transition from industrial to knowledge society, the improvement of social effectiveness and quality of life, the change of lifestyle and living concept, the improvement of people's literacy and health quality, and the change of social welfare, equity, and international social status. Countries are the basic units for social modernization study and practice, and regional social modernization is a component of national social modernization.

Social modernization is a change in the social sphere. Apparently, not all social changes belong to the scope of social modernization. In general, only the social changes that help promote productivity, social progress, and human development belong to the scope of social modernization.

In general sense, social development should include social progress and social adaptation, and social modernization is a collection of social development, social transition, international social competition, and the change of international social status (Table 6.29). The international social status can change in four ways: maintaining the advanced level of world society, narrowing the gap with the advanced level of world society, maintaining the same gap with the advanced level of world society, or widening the gap with the advanced level of world society.

Social modernization has three sources. The first is the partial inheritance and development of traditional society; the second is the partial negation and reversion (decomposition and turning) of traditional society; and the third is knowledge innovation, technological innovation, system innovation, and innovation diffusion. The traditional society here is a relative and dynamic concept. The traditional society in the course of first social modernization refers to agricultural society, while the traditional society in the course of second social modernization refers to industrial society.

Table 6.29 Conceptual model of social modernization

Item	Content
Hypothesis 1	Social progress refers to improvement of quality of life, social welfare, social effectiveness, and social equity
Hypothesis 2	Positive social adaptation refers to the positive change of lifestyle and living and social environment (higher rationality)
Hypothesis 3	Social transition refers to two transformations respectively from agricultural to industrial society and from industrial to knowledge society
Hypothesis 4	Change of international social status refers to the change of the international status of national social productivity and people's life quality
Deduction 1	Social development = social progress + positive social adaptation + social progress × positive social adaptation
Deduction 2	Social modernization = social development × social transition × international social competition and change of international social status

Source: RGCMS (2006)

(2) Process

Social modernization is a complex, multilevel, and multipath process, which includes the change of social behavior, structure, system, concept, etc. The process of social modernization can be divided into two types: frontier process and catch-up process with both common and different features. During the eighteenth to twenty-first centuries, its frontier process comprises two stages: first and second social modernizations (Table 6.30). First social modernization has three waves, and second social modernization will have three waves. The two social modernizations have different contents and features (Table 6.31).

First social modernization is a transformation and profound change from agricultural to industrial society and from feudal to civic society. It includes the transitions from rural to urban society, from clan to welfare society, from autocracy to democratic society, from closed to open society, from natural to technological society, and from stable to mobile society. Its features include urbanization, social welfare, mobility, generalization, specialization, secularization, rationalization, mechanization, electrification, automation, technologization, high effectiveness, openness, equity, social differentiation and integration, universal primary education, etc.

Second social modernization is a transformation and profound change from industrial to knowledge society and from material to ecological society. It includes the transitions from urban to urban–rural balanced society, from physical to virtual society, from educational to learning society, from tense to leisure society, from mechanic to humanity society, and from national to world society. Currently, its features include intellectualization, informatization, intelligentization, suburbanization, urban–rural balance, greening, ecologization, naturalization, innovation, internationalization, diversification, individualization, leisure, rights of women and children, universal higher education, lifetime learning, etc.

If first social modernization is a preliminary social modernization and a transition from traditional to primary modern society, second social modernization is an advanced social modernization and a transition from primary modern to hypermodern

Table 6.30 Periodic table of social modernization in broad sense—change in social form

Stage (approx. starting year)	Social form and features	Social modernization
Age of knowledge society	*Knowledge, ecological, and global society*	
Transition stage (2050)	Advanced knowledge society: cultural experience and super-transport	
Mature stage (2020)	Moderate knowledge society: life engineering and barrier-free knowledge and information acquisition	*Second social modernization*
Developing stage (1992)	Preliminary knowledge society: higher education, networking, and learning	Knowledge revolution
Start stage (1970)	Initiation of knowledge society: knowledge, information, suburbanization, and greening	Intellectualization and greening
Age of industrial society	*Industrial, material, and welfare society*	
Transition stage (1946)	Advanced industrial society: industrial society, welfare, and automation	
Mature stage (1914)	Moderate industrial society: social insurance, technologization, and electrification	*First social modernization*
Developing stage (1870)	Preliminary industrial society: compulsory education, electrification, and specialization	Industrial revolution
Start stage (1763)	Initiation of industrial society: modern industry, urbanization, and mobility	Urbanization and welfare
Age of agricultural society	*Agricultural, material, and familial society*	
Transition stage (AD 1500)	Advanced agricultural society: agricultural society, commercialization, and scientific revolution	
Mature stage (AD 618)	Moderate agricultural society: agricultural society, systematization, and feudal society	
Developing stage (500 BC)	Preliminary agricultural society: farming, pastoral, civilization, and settlement	(Agricultural revolution)
Start stage (3500 BC)	Initiation of agricultural society: farming, nomadic, agriculturalization, and civilization	(Agriculturalization and civilization)
Age of primitive society	*Primitive, tribal, and hunter–gatherer society*	
Transition stage (10,000 years ago)	Horticulture, nomadic, patrilineal society, and new stone age	(Primitive agricultural revolution)
Mature stage (40,000 years ago)	Hunter–gatherer, matrilineal society, Chiefdoms society, socialization, and last of old stone age	(Socialization, Tool-making revolution)
Developing stage (200,000 years ago)	Hunter–gatherer, clan society, structuralization, and middle of old stone age	
Start stage (2,500,000 years ago)	Hunter–gatherer, bands, migration, and early stage of old stone age	

Note: The time of chronology and the features were based on the frontier track of the development of human societies
Source: RGCMS (2006)

Table 6.31 Two stages of social modernization in broad sense

Item	First social modernization	Second social modernization
Approx. time	1763–1970	1970–2100
Population and health	Urbanization, mobility, mechanization, electrification, automation, small family, legal marriage, differentiation, stratification, integration, public health, etc.	Intellectualization, suburbanization, urban–rural balance, informatization, intelligentization, greening, family diversification, population aging, longer life expectancy, rights of women and children, etc.
Learning and working	Specialization, technologization, rationalization, universal primary education, etc.	Individualization, innovation, diversification, ecologization, universal higher education, lifetime learning, etc.
Leisure and welfare	Social welfare, equity, public transport, etc.	Naturalization, informatization, leisurization, new features in future, etc.
Modernity	First social modernity, including industrial, urban, welfare, rational, technological, open, and democratic society, living standard, etc.	Second social modernity, including knowledge, information, ecological, learning, world, innovative, leisure and plural society, quality of life, etc.
Side effect	Rich–poor polarization, and side effects of machinery and organization, etc.	Information divide and side effects of networking, etc.

Source: RGCMS (2006)

society. The coordinated development of the twice social modernizations is integrated social modernization. Social modernization will have new changes in the twenty-second century.

The process of social modernization has 12 features: it is relatively predictable, global, long-term, staged, progressive, positive, adaptable, transitional, systematic, uneven, complex international competition, and an irreversible trend.

Social modernization is a sort of modernization and follows the ten basic principles (Table 2.15).

(3) Result

The outcome of social modernization includes the formation of social modernity, particularity, diversity, and side effects. The results of social modernization in different countries are both common and different. And the results of the two social modernizations are different (Table 6.31).

The result of social modernization comprises changes in six areas: the completion of the two social form transitions, the improvement of social efficiency and quality of life, the positive change of lifestyle and living concept, the improvement of human cultural and health quality, the drastic improvement of social welfare and equity, and the widening of the international gap in life quality and the narrowing of the international gap in social structure.

In the course of social modernization, some countries reach and maintain the advanced level of world society and become socially advanced countries, while other countries are socially developing countries. The two types of countries can interchange. In general, about 20% countries reach and maintain the world's advanced level and belong to socially advanced countries, while about 80% countries fail to reach the world's advanced levels and belong to socially developing countries. Within a time span of 50 years, about 10% socially advanced countries can downgrade into developing countries, while about 5% socially developing countries can upgrade into advanced countries. The status change of the two types of countries is in a dynamic balance.

The goal of national social modernization is to complete first social modernization and transit from agricultural to industrial society; to complete second social modernization and transit from industrial to knowledge society; and to catch up, reach, and maintain the advanced level of world society and become socially advanced countries (socially modernized countries) or narrow its gap with international society.

Since the 1950s, the result of social modernization is correlative to its goal, and this correlation is gradually formed and reinforced while the modernization study growth.

(4) Dynamics

The drive force of social modernization comprises dynamic factor and principles (Table 6.28). Social modernization has different dynamics on different levels, in different countries, and in different stages. The dynamic model of the general theory of modernization can be used for social modernization (Table 2.20).

(5) Model

Social modernization has roughly three basic paths in the twenty-first century (Fig. 6.12). The path for first social modernization corresponds to the model of urbanization and social welfare, the path for second social modernization corresponds to the model of intellectualization and greening, and the path for integrated social modernization corresponds to the model of new urbanization, including the coordinated development of urbanization, suburbanization, social welfare, intellectualization, informatization, and greening.

In general, the process, result, dynamics, and model of social modernization can all be analyzed from the world, national, and regional perspectives. The contents and features analyzed from different perspectives are somewhat different.

The *China Modernization Report 2006* introduced the social timetable, periodical table, coordinates, and paths for social modernization in the broad sense and the conceptual model, quantitative model, objective model, and dynamic model of social modernization; discussed the staged theories of the social modernization theory in the broad sense, including second social modernization and integrated social modernization; and also discussed the methods for social modernization.

(6) Second Social Modernization

Second social modernization is a form of expression for social modernization and reflects the frontier change in the social sphere since the 1970s, which includes the

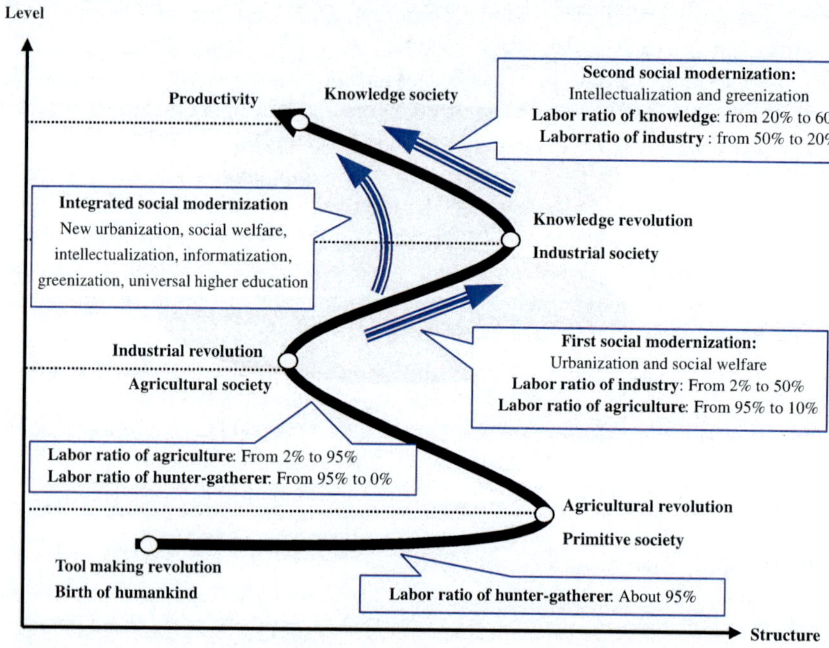

Fig. 6.12 Three paths for social modernization in twenty-first century. Note: the horizontal coordinate represents the labor structure of productivity. The structural graduation is the labor ratio between agriculture and hunter–gatherer (estimated) in the age of primitive economy, the labor ratio between hunter–gatherer and agriculture in the age of agricultural economy, the labor ratio between industry and agriculture in the age of industrial economy, and the labor ratio between material sector (including agriculture and industry) and knowledge sector in the age of knowledge economy. Source: RGCMS (2006)

transition from industrial to knowledge society and from material to ecological society and includes the improvement of social effectiveness and quality of life, the improvement of social welfare and equity, international social competition, and the change of international social system.

Second social modernization is a complex historical process, which includes social development, social transition, international social competition, and the change of national social status and includes the change of social life, behavior, structure, system, and ideas. In relation to industrial society, knowledge society is a new social form, which has many new features (Table 6.32).

(7) Integrated Social Modernization

Integrated social modernization is a basic path for social modernization in the broad sense in the twenty-first century. It comprises the interaction between two social transitions (from agricultural to industrial society and from industrial to knowledge society) and the continuous transition to knowledge society; comprises

Table 6.32 Main features of knowledge society

Item	Main features
Social intellectualization	Knowledge becomes the basis and axial of society. Social structure is intellectualized, and intellectual workers outnumber the total sum of all other workers. Consumption structure is intellectualized, and universal higher education and lifetime learning are realized. Knowledge innovation becomes an important source of social wealth and rights
Informatization and networking	Cyberspace becomes the second space, with Internet being popularized and cyberspace being formed. People travel between cyberspace and physical space, and lifestyle is digitized and internationalized
Innovation socialization	Innovation becomes national behavior. While technological innovation is popularized, knowledge innovation becomes the focus of international competition, system innovation becomes the key to social progress, and national innovation system becomes the policy tool to drive innovation
Intelligentization	Artificial intelligence is popularized, and working and living environments gradually become intelligent
Management personalization	With knowledge capital as its core and information network as its basis, management moves from mechanization to personalization
Suburbanization and community revives	People flow two-way between cities, suburbs, and rural areas, and urban–rural dynamic balance is gradually reached
Greening and ecologization	Green and eco-friendly lifestyle and ideas gradually occupy leading positions, and man and nature exist in harmony
Pluralization and diversification	Plural and diverse social life and concept, and equal status for women, children and minority groups, etc.

Source: He (1999)

the coordinated development of urbanization, suburbanization, social welfare, intellectualization, informatization, and greening and the continuous transition to intellectualization and greening; and comprises the improvement of social effectiveness and quality of life, the improvement of social welfare and equity, international social competition, and the change of international social status.

Integrated social modernization is a historical process, which features the coordinated development of two social modernizations and the continuous transition to second social modernization. It comprises the change of social behavior, structure, system, and ideas and the international competition to catch up and reach the advanced level of world society. Integrated social modernization comprises three stages: new urbanization and informatization, suburbanization and intellectualization, and intellectualization and greening. Its goal is to catch up with the world's advanced level of social modernization. The mark for realizing integrated social modernization is for social effectiveness, quality of life, social welfare, and social system to reach the world's advanced levels at the time.

6.3 Political Modernization

Political modernization refers to the modernization of the political sphere, and it is a manifestation of modernization phenomena in the political field. It includes staged and stratified political modernization, the modernization of political subfields and political sectors (Fig. 6.13). Political modernization occurs mainly at national level and may extend to the world, international, regional, organizational, and individual levels.

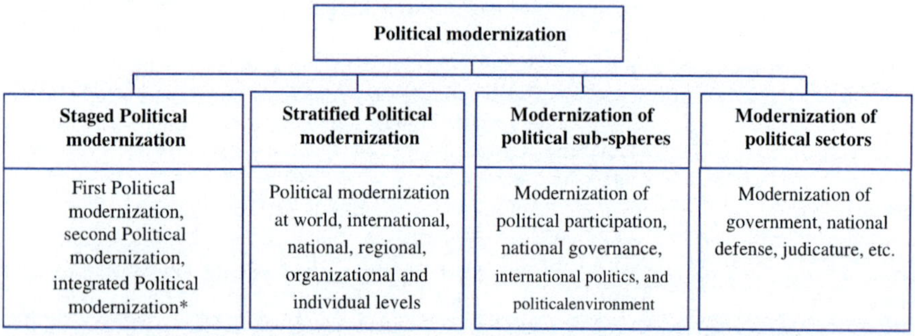

Fig. 6.13 Objects of political modernization study. Note: (*Asterisk*) Integrated political modernization means the coordinated development of twice political modernizations and is a basic path for political modernization in developing countries

6.3.1 Studies

Political modernization research is the research on the modernization of the political sphere, and it is a part of modernization research. The research may date back to the eighteenth century and may be approached from three perspectives including the historical process, objective reality, and future prospects.

There is no unified definition of politics and political sphere as well. In general, politics refers to the activity of defining, distributing, and managing public resources, interests, and power; its extension embraces stratified politics, political process, political system, and political environment (Fig. 6.14). The political sphere is the field where public affairs are defined, participated in, and managed. The modernization of the political sphere is called political modernization for short.

6.3.1.1 Research Paradigm

The objects of political modernization study are the modernization of political sphere, including the modernization of political participation, national governance, international politics, and political environment, as well as political modernization

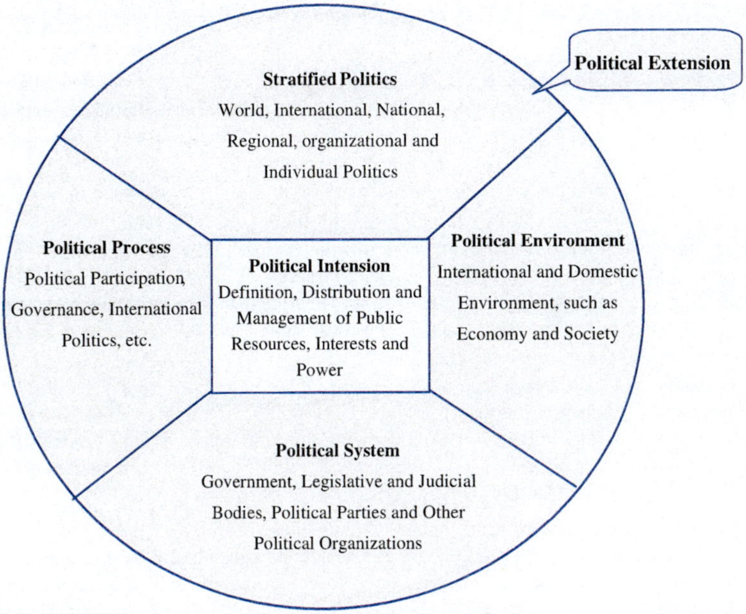

Fig. 6.14 Operational definitions of political intension and extension

at world, national, regional, organizational, and individual levels. The research contents include the modernization of political behavior, structure, institutions, and ideas, as well as the process, outcomes, dynamics, and models of political modernization, all of which constitute a research matrix (Table 6.33). Other objects such as stage-specific political modernization and the modernization of political sectors are also included in the research.

Political modernization research is a type of field-specific modernization research where the methodology of modernization study can be adopted. There are plentiful analysis methods, for example, time-series analysis, cross-sectional analysis, process analysis, case study, quantitative evaluation, and coordinates analysis. The research may target the whole process or a particular stage of the process, or the world, a country, or a region, and can be done for academic or policy purposes. Different types of research have different features.

6.3.1.2 Historical Facts

Political modernization started in the second half of the eighteenth century as a form of political change. Generally, political and economic modernizations are closely related with each other in a complex manner. Similar to the economic modernization, the frontier trajectory of political modernization consists roughly of the first and second modernization as well as six waves (Table 6.34). *The Second*

Table 6.33 The matrix of political modernization study

Content		Object		
		Political sphere	Political participation, national governance, international politics, and political environment	Politics at world, national, regional, organizational, and individual levels
		Political modernization	Modernization in four political subspheres	Political modernization at five levels
Element	Behavior Structure Institution Idea	Modernization of political behavior, structure, institution, and ideas	Modernization of political behavior, structure, institution, and ideas in the four political subspheres	Modernization of political behavior, structure, institution, and ideas at the five levels
Aspect	Process Result Dynamics Model	Process, result, dynamics, and model of the political modernization	Process, result, dynamics, and model of political modernization in the four political subspheres	Process, result, dynamics, and model of political modernization at the five levels

Note: Political participation involves civil rights and obligations, news media, political organizations and activities, etc. National governance involves legislation, judicature, administration, national defense, diplomacy, civil servants, etc. International politics involves international relations, systems and institutions, etc., and international political modernization intersects with international modernization and latter has been discussed in Chap. 5. Political environment involves domestic political environment (economic, social, cultural, and ecological environment) and international political environment. The research contents of political modernization also include stage-specific political modernization, the modernization of political sectors, political frontier and trend analysis, and interactions between the elements of political modernization and different fields

Modernization: Inspiration of Human Civilization Process (He 1999) provides a systematic analysis of the process of and facts about political modernization.

(1) Process Analysis

First of all, the first wave of political modernization emerged roughly during the First Industrial Revolution (1763–1870), mainly in such countries as the UK, USA, and France, which included—among other things—political revolutions and democratic reforms as well as male adults' gradually obtaining voting right (Table 6.35). The democratization of political participation included the recognition of men's voting right in 1790 in the aftermath of the French Revolution in 1789, the expansion of men's suffrage in the UK from 1832 onward, and the US and France's promulgation of civil rights acts. The institutionalization of national governance included the UK's introduction of limited monarchy and cabinet system; the US's founding of the presidential government with the separation of the legislative, judicial, and executive powers; and France's enforcement of secularized powers and founding of a republic. During this period, countries that gained independence included the USA (1776), Argentina (1816), Brazil (1822), Mexico (1822), Greece (1829), and Belgium (1831).

Table 6.34 Main stages of political modernization

Wave	Approx. time	Content	Annotation
First	1763–1870	Constitutional democracy, elite politics, the first wave of democratization	*First political modernization* Democratization, secularization, institutionalization, centralization, modern politics, industrial politics
Second	1870–1945	Mass democracy, class politics, the second wave of democratization	
Third	1946–1970	Social democracy, public politics, the third wave of democratization	
Fourth	1970–2020	Cyber democracy, consultative democracy, the fourth wave of democratization	*Second political modernization* Service orientation, networking, ecologicalization, decentralization, postmodern politics, knowledge politics
Fifth	2020–2050	Global democracy, green politics, the fifth wave of democratization	
Sixth	2050–2100	Cosmopolitan politics, universal politics, etc.	

Note: The fifth and sixth waves are merely forecasts

Second, the second wave of political modernization happened roughly during the Second Industrial Revolution (1870–1913) and between World Wars I and II (1914–1945). It mainly included the deepening and spreading of democratization, female adults' gradually obtaining suffrage, and the initial establishment of such modern political systems as political party system, parliamentary system, universal suffrage, constitutionalism and cabinet government system, etc. The development of nationalism expedited the rise of national independence movements. Fascist and socialist movements happened mainly in industrialized European countries and produced a considerable influence on European policies. The success of the Russian socialist revolutions changed the process of world history.

Modern political institutions stood the test of the two World Wars (Table 6.36). Modern democratic system continued to exist in the UK, France, USA, Switzerland, the Netherlands, Belgium, Scandinavian countries, Latin American republics, and Dominions of the British Commonwealth and played an important role in wartime. The Great Depression produced massive impact on politics, but US President Franklin D. Roosevelt's New Deal saved capitalism as some scholar believed. Modern political institutions saw great development and improvement during the wars and depression. This marked, to a certain degree, the maturity of political modernization in industrialized countries. In 1945, the United Nations was founded, bringing political modernization into a stage of globalization.

Third, the third wave of political modernization happened roughly during the Third Industrial Revolution (1946–1970). It mainly included the deepening of democratization, the spreading of universal suffrage, the development of civil rights, the rise of public political and environmental movements, and colonies' independence movements and democratization waves, etc. The development of domestic politics included the progress in democracy and the decentralization of powers, the increased, say, from varied social classes, and women's and ethnic

Table 6.35 Historical process of political democratization

Country	Starting year					Time span
	Freedom of speech	Long-standing parliamentary system	Men's suffrage	Women's suffrage	Universal suffrage	
UK	1795	1830	1910/1918	1918/1928	1928	133
France	1791	1870	1790/1840	1944	1948	157
USA	1795	–	1776	1920	1970	180
Belgium	–	1830	1890/1919	1919/1948	1948	–
Switzerland	1803	1840	1840/1848	1971	1971	168
Germany	1871	1870	1840/1870	1918	1949	78
Greece	–	1920	1840	1927/1952	1952	–
Spain	–	1860	1860	1931	1933	–
Austria	1867	1890	1880/1918	1918	1955	88
New Zealand	–	–	1893/1907	1893	1907	–
Finland	–	1900	1900/1906	1906	1906	–
Norway	–	1810	1898/1900	1907/1913	1913	–
Denmark	1849	1840	1901/1910	1915	1950	101
Netherlands	1581	1840	1887/1910	1919	1922	341
Italy	–	1840	1910/1919	1919/1945	1945	–
Australia	–	–	1902/1903	1902/1962	1962	–
Sweden	1776	1860	1909/1910	1861/1921	1918	142
Portugal	–	1910	1910	1931/1976	1976	–
Ireland	–	1920	1910/1919	1918/1928	–	–
Argentina	–	1853	1912	1947	1951	–

Note: Views vary in when suffrage was introduced in some countries, and the first option is probably the year when only some people obtained suffrage. Time span refers to the years between recognizing the freedom of speech and introducing universal suffrage. The democratization process in some countries, for example, France, Spain, and Italy, suffered setbacks and reversals. In Germany, universal suffrage was introduced in 1919 and 1933, respectively, but discontinued until its resumption in 1949. Tilly argues that there are four waves of democratization, which occurred in the 1940s, after World War I, after World War II, and after 1989 (Tilly 2003)
Source: Tilly (2003), Janoski (1998), UNDP (2002)

Table 6.36 Democratization in the twentieth century

Year	1900	1922	1942	1962	1973	1990	2001
Number of democratic countries	0	29	12	36	30	58	121
Number of nondemocratic countries	55	35	49	75	92	71	71
Total number of countries	55	64	61	111	122	129	192
Percentage of democratic countries/%	0	45	20	32	25	45	63

Note: Democratic countries refer to the countries whose civilian governments were formed through competitive elections by voting of all adults. In 1900, no countries were up to the democratic country standard, and there were about only more than ten countries where male adults were granted suffrage. The numbers of countries from 1922 to 1990 exclude countries with a population below one million
Source: Huntington (1991), Tilly (2003)

minorities' obtaining equal status. The students' movement in the late 1960s expressed the calls for peace, humanism, and justice. The change in international politics was quite remarkable. For example, more and more countries joined the United Nations, the Cold War was waged between the USA and the Soviet Union and their respective allies, Europe moved to revitalization from decline, and the Third World emerged in the world political arena, etc.

Fourth, the fourth wave of political modernization happened roughly during the Knowledge and Information Revolution (1970–2020). It mainly included the diversification of democracy (consultative democracy, cyber democracy, participating democracy, etc.), the diversification, decentralization, individuation and internationalization of politics, the rise of environmental politics and human rights politics, new public administration and e-governance as well as the democratization waves in eastern European countries.

Political modernization includes the modernization of civil rights and obligations. The developmental sequence of civil rights varies from country to country; though different in contents, civil rights and civil obligations should be in equilibrium (Janoski 1998). In some countries, civil rights develop gradually, from legal rights, political rights, social rights to participation rights. According to the average value of advanced countries (Table 6.37), legal rights (excluding property rights for married women which were introduced in the twentieth century) emerged in the eighteenth and nineteenth centuries, political rights in the nineteenth and twentieth centuries, social rights in the first half of the twentieth century, and participation rights in the second half of the twentieth century.

Fifth, the fifth and sixth waves of political modernization are "conjectures" about the future. The fifth wave is expected to happen between 2020 and 2050,

Table 6.37 Structure and time sequence of civil rights

Legal rights	Years	Political rights	Years	Social rights	Years	Participation rights	Years
Men's property right	222	Men's suffrage	107	First right	92	First right	22
Freedom of speech	176	Men's universal suffrage	91	Second right	80	Second right	9
Freedom of belief	158	Women's universal suffrage	70	Third right	68	Third right	3
Married women's property right	54	Universal suffrage	61	Fourth right	58		
				Fifth right	36		

Note: In this table, years mean the average value of the aggregate years from its beginning year of the rights to 1995. Sample countries for legal rights were 10 advanced countries, and those for other rights were 18 advanced countries. Social rights consist of five rights, to compensation for industrial injury, to retirement benefit, to health care, to unemployment insurance, and to subsidy for families with financial difficulties, respectively. Participation rights include the rights to labor and capital joint meeting, codetermination, and labor market policy protection, respectively. Different countries had different sequences of enforcing different social and participation rights. It is based on the data of Janoski (1998) likely to be characterized by green politics, bionic politics, global democracy, etc. The sixth wave is expected to happen between 2050 and 2100, likely to be characterized by cosmopolitan politics, universal politics, etc.

(2) Basic Facts About Political Modernization

First, facts about political participation. From the eighteenth century onward, civil rights were gradually expanded and deepened, the suffrage was gradually extended to the entire adult population, trade unions and strikes in some advanced countries were on the decline, and the political influence of news media expanded. The nineteenth century saw the rise of party politics and the gradual advancement in multiple ways of democratization. From the twentieth century onward, democratization fluctuated (Table 6.36), and human rights began drawing attention; in the late twentieth century, cyber democracy, consultative democracy, environmental politics, etc., emerged.

Second, facts about national governance. Since the eighteenth century, we saw the complication and secularization of the political system, the improvement of government capacity, the swelling of government, and the constant flux of state policies, and the nineteenth century witnessed the democratization and professionalization of national governance and the rise and then fall of political corruption in some advanced countries. From the twentieth century onward, some advanced countries saw the declining support of their governments, and from late twentieth century onward, the trends of government informatization, transparency, marketization, and service orientation became increasingly noticeable. The eighteenth century saw the standardization and nationalization of the military and fluctuation in its scale, the growth of defense expenditure, the professionalization and standardization of diplomacy, and the gradual increase in the number of diplomatic personnel; from the nineteenth century onward, the military became mechanized and professionalized. The twentieth century witnessed military professionalization and informatization as well as diplomatic diversification and service orientation.

Third, facts about international politics. From the eighteenth century, the frequency of international wars did not fall, but the situations varied greatly from country to country; there were great changes in the distribution of international wars and in the structure of countries engaged in the wars; and intergovernmental international organizations saw growth both in quantity and in membership. From the nineteenth century onward, international trade and investment continued to grow, and international contacts were enhanced. The twentieth century saw the increase in the number of diplomatic relations and in the degree of interdependence between countries, the fluctuant international trade in weapons, the growth of the aggregate foreign aid that developing countries received and of the per capita international aid, the decline in the percentage of advanced countries' foreign aid in their GDP and of foreign aid in recipient countries' GDP, the rapid change of international politics, the increasing numbers of international conventions and signatory countries, and the growing numbers of international migrants.

Fourth, facts about political environment. Over the past 300 years, the international political environment changed dramatically, and domestic political

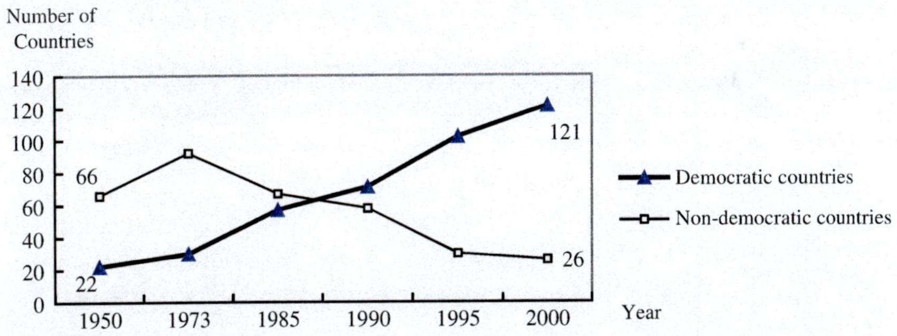

Fig. 6.15 Numbers of democratic countries in the second half of the twentieth century. Note: the number of democratic countries between 1985 and 2000 includes partly and completely democratic countries. It is based on the data of the UNDP (2000, 2002) and Huntington (1991)

environment differed greatly from country to country. From the eighteenth century onward, modernization gradually became the trend, and more and more countries started modernization; the century also witnessed the growth in world population, per capita wealth and per capita consumption, and the decline in per capita some natural resource. From the nineteenth century, nationalism saw climaxes once and again, the number of independent countries increased, and the international system changed time and again. From the 1950s onward, democracies increased both in number and percentage (Fig. 6.15), interdependence between countries increased, but international conflicts continued to exist.

Fifth, comprehensive facts about political modernization. Since the eighteenth century, political life, structure, institutions, and concepts have been changing, in nonlinear and multiple ways, and a portion of traditional political elements continue to exist and function.

(3) Inspirations from the History of Political Modernization

First of all, political modernization is nonlinear. Advanced countries' political modernization experienced two shifts, that is, from traditional to modern politics, including from feudal, autocratic, and religious politics to public, democratic, and secular politics, and from modern to postmodern politics, including from centralized, physical, and bureaucratic politics to decentralized, ecological, and self-government politics (Fig. 6.16).

Second, political modernization is reversible. The discontinuity or reversal of political modernization is common in both advanced and developing countries. When an economic or social crisis occurs, political modernization is likely to face challenges.

Third, there is not only a single-plank bridge but rather a variety of path options to political modernization. It might be a revolution, like the French Revolution, or a reform, as in the UK in 18th century. It may give priority to democratization, to coordinated development of democratization and industrialization, or to industrialization first and then democratization. In the twentieth century, Finland gave

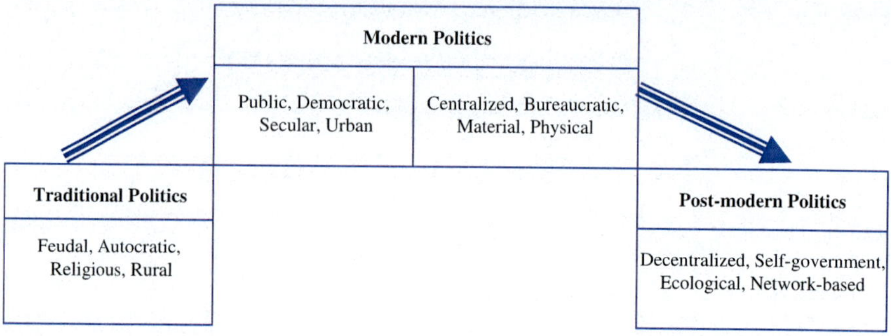

Fig. 6.16 Two shifts in the political modernization of advanced countries

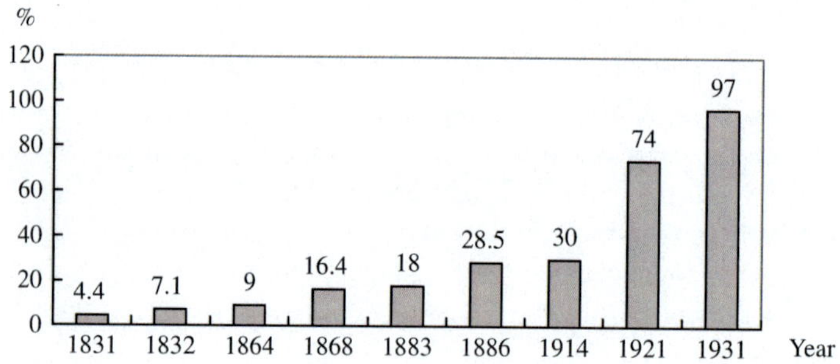

Fig. 6.17 Percentage of voters in the total population of adults in the UK. Note: it is based on the data of Dahl (1998)

priority to democratization while Japan and South Korea to industrialization, but all of them successfully turned into advanced countries from developing ones.

Fourth, political modernization is of path dependency. Different countries' political modernization is influenced by their own political and cultural traditions, their respective development levels, and the international environment.

Fifth, political modernization is partly predicable. The relationship between democratization and economic development is complex. Generally, economic development promotes and consolidates democratization, but there are some exceptions; educational development and informatization help to expand democracy.

Sixth, political modernization is of not only international convergence but also diversity. In the twentieth century, democratization was the world trend, and the structure of government had the feature of international convergence, as in the arrangement of government departments which was largely similar; political institutions vary greatly among advanced countries, for example, constitutional monarchy, parliamentary republicanism, and presidential republicanism.

Seventh, political modernization is a long-standing process (Fig. 6.17). Between the eighteenth and nineteenth centuries, no countries were up to the standard of democracy. According to the experience of nine advanced countries, it took them about 150 years to move from recognizing the freedom of speech to introducing universal suffrage

(Table 6.35). Some countries that gained independence in the twentieth century adopted the "one-step" democracy, whose outcome remains to be seen.

Finally, political modernization is a global process. In 2000, multiparty elections were practiced in about 140 countries in the world; of these countries, 82 were completely democracies, and their populations accounted for 57% of the world's total (UNDP 2002).

6.3.2 Theories

Political modernization theory is about the phenomenon of political modernization and represents a field-specific modernization theory. It is actually a collection of three theories: classical modernization theory, political modernization theory in broad sense, and the expositions on politics in different modernization theories, the last part of which can be found in Chap. 4.

6.3.2.1 Classical Political Modernization Theory

The classical political modernization theory, an important branch of the classical modernization theory, was established in the 1950s and 1960s. The publishing of the works by American political scientists, including *The Political System* (Easton 1953), *The Politics of the Developing Areas* (Almond and Coleman 1960), *Political Modernization in Japan and Turkey* (Ward and Rustow 1964), *The Politics of Modernization* (Apter 1965), *Social Origins of Democracy and Autocracy* (Moore 1966), and *Political Order in Changing Societies* (Huntington 1968), marked the birth of the classical political modernization theory. Though there is abundant academic literature on political modernization, the classical political modernization theory has so far had no systematic, acknowledged general theoretical expositions.

There are generally two sources of the classical political modernization theory: studies and explanations about political modernization by political scientists as well as those by modernization scholars in nonpolitical areas (e.g., history and sociology). By putting together their subjects of study and relevant thoughts, the structure of the classical political modernization theory (Table 6.38) can be formed, and its general theory—including definition, process, outcomes, driving forces, and models (Table 6.39)—summarized.

(1) Definition

There is no standard definition of classical political modernization. Generally, it is the political change in the process of classical modernization, and the transition from traditional to modern politics, from autocratic to democratic politics, and from religious to secular politics.

Indian scholar Desai holds that the political change of modernization embraces four features: *the legitimacy of sovereignty was not god-given but secularly recognized by and based on responsibility for the people; political rights were gradually extended to the entire adult population and fused into a generally accepted order of morality; the scope of politics was continuously expanded and*

Table 6.38 Structure of classical political modernization theory

Classification	Theories	Main contents
General theory	Core theory	The definition, process, outcomes, driving forces, models, etc., of the classical political modernization
Branch theories	Democratization theory	The definition, process, models, etc., of democratization
	Modernization of civil rights	Modernization of civil rights and obligations
	Modernization of public administration	Modernization of public administration
	Modernization of political sectors	Modernization of government, national defense, laws, etc.
Relevant theories	Politics	Development politics, comparative politics, political system, history of politics, history of political ideology, etc.
	Other relevant theories	Classical modernization theory, dependency theory, world systems theory, etc.

Table 6.39 General theory of classical political modernization

Aspect	Basic contents
Definition	Classical political modernization is the political change in the process of classical modernization, and the transition from traditional to modern politics and from autocratic to democratic politics
Process	Classical political modernization is a historical process, including the rationalization and secularization of political authority, the differentiation and specialization of political structure, the democratization and institutionalization of political participation, national governance becoming highly efficient and rational, etc.
Outcomes	The main outcome of classical political modernization is the formation and diffusion of classical political modernity. The characteristics of modern politics are summarized as classical political modernity, including being democratic, polarized, highly efficient, rule of law, bureaucratic, specialized, secular, rational and popular, etc.
Driving forces	Classical political modernization has a great many influencing factors, including economy, society, culture, science and technology, international relations, etc.
Models	Classical political modernization embraces a diversity of paths and models, is of path dependency, and is subject to historical, geographical, and objective conditions. These are manifested in such aspects as the diversity of political modernization paths, political systems, democratic models, etc.

the authority of political agencies enhanced; the political ruling took the people as ***its policy subject, beneficiary and legal person*** (Black 1976).

There are three views as to the relationship between political development and political modernization: political development is just political modernization, political development is a constituent part of political modernization, and political modernization is a form of manifestation of political development in modern societies.

(2) Process

American political scientist Huntington holds that political modernization embraces three aspects (Huntington 1968):

(a) *Rationalization of political authority. The singular, secularized and nationwide political authority supersedes all kinds of traditional, religious, family or ethnic political authority. Government is a product of mankind, rather than a product of the nature or god. The nation state is entitled to external sovereignty without interference by other countries; the central government is entitled to internal sovereignty, not influenced by any local or regional power. The state is integral, and the state power is centralized to the nationally accepted nationwide legislature.*

(b) *Political structural differentiation and functional specialization. Various specialized functional departments, such as legislative, military, administrative and scientific departments, should be all operated by specialized organs with decision-making power. Administrative institutions at all levels should become more sophisticated, complex and disciplined. The distribution of positions and powers should be based more on personal achievements and abilities.*

(c) *Increased level of political participation. All of the groups and classes of the whole society participate extensively in politics. In modern countries, citizens directly participate in and are influenced by government affairs. The people participate in politics beyond rural and urban levels, and there is the need to establish political institutions like parties that are intended to organize such participation.*

(3) Outcomes

The main outcome of classical political modernization is the formation of classical political modernity and diversity (Table 6.39).

Ward and Rustow summed up eight features of modern politics (Ward and Rustow 1964): *a highly different and functionally specialized government organization institution; highly integrated internal government structure; rational and secular political decision-making procedure; large numbers, wide coverage and high efficiency of political and administrative decisions; the people's extensive, effective identity with the country's history, territory and nationality; the people's broad interest and enthusiastic participation in political institutions, though not necessarily participating in decision making; distribution of political roles based on personal achievements rather than attribution; judicature and administration based mainly on a secular, not-a-particular-person-targeted legal system.*

(4) Driving Forces

There has been no consensus on the driving forces of classical political modernization.

Marx thinks that *economy is the base and political institutions are superstructure, and that the economic base determines and constrains superstructure which in turn reflects and acknowledges the economic base* (Storey 1993). According to this thought, economic development is the driving force of political modernization. History shows that the relationship between economic development and democratization is complex, rather than being simply linear.

The Protestant ethic, Weber says, is the spiritual base of modern economic life and the important root cause of European capitalism and modernization (Weber 1904). This argument is considered to be a kind of "cultural determinism." Weber's ideas about rationalization and bureaucratization have a far-reaching influence on modernization research. Rationalization and bureaucratization represent two important features of political modernization.

According to Huntington, *a political institution must, above all, enable policy innovation, to successfully address problems facing modernization; it must be able **to successfully assimilate all kinds of new social influences created by moderniza**tion; institutionalization is crucial for political modernization, and adaptation, complexity, self-determination and cohesion are the indicators for measuring the level of institutionalization* (Huntington 1968).

(5) Models of Classical Political Modernization

Huntington holds that the UK, France, and the USA took a different path of political modernization each (Huntington 1968). The UK practices constitutional monarchy, adopting the democratization road of parliamentary reform; France follows republicanism, whose political change was revolutionary and had several reversals; the USA adopts the presidential system, whose democratization was progressive.

Moore thinks, ***Political modernization has three models: the first is the progres****sive model of "violent revolution + reformism," as in the UK, US and France; the second is the zigzag model of "reformism + fascism + reformism," as in Germany and Japan; and the third is the model of "farmers' violent revolution + totalitarianism (or centralism)," as in Russia* (Moore 1966).

Lijphart argues that the model of "consensus democracy" has a better effect than that of "majority democracy" (Lijphart 1999).

6.3.2.2 Political Modernization Theory in Broad Sense

Raised by Chinese scholar Chuanqi He, the political modernization theory in broad sense serves as a theoretical explanation about the phenomenon of political modernization between the eighteenth century and the twenty-first century, and it is the application of the second modernization theory in the sphere of politics. It includes the general theory, branch theories, and relevant theories (Table 6.40). Below is a discussion of its general theory (Table 6.41), including five aspects of political modernization: definition, process, outcomes, dynamics, and models. Currently, there is a very limited knowledge of the second political modernization and integrated political modernization. The political modernization theory in broad sense is yet to develop.

(1) Definition

Political modernization is a manifestation of modernization in the sphere of politics.

The intension: political modernization is a sort of frontier change and international competition in the sphere of politics since the industrial revolution in the eighteenth century; it includes the formation, development, transition, and

Table 6.40 Structure of political modernization theory in broad sense

Classification	Theories	Main contents
General theory	Core theory	The definition, process, result, dynamics, models, etc., of political modernization
Branch theories	Stage theory	First and second political modernization, integrated political modernization
	Stratified study	Modernization of world, international, national, regional, etc.
	Subsphere study	Modernization in the subfields of political participation, national governance, political environment, political life, structure, institutions, and concepts
	Sector theory	Modernization of government, legislation, justice, national defense, diplomacy, public administration, etc.
Relevant theories	Other modernization theories	Classical modernization theory, postmodernization theory, ecological modernization theory, reflexive modernization theory, second modernization theory, dependency theory, world systems theory, globalization theory, etc.
	Politics-related studies	Development politics, comparative politics, international relations theory, political economy, etc.

international interaction of modern politics, the innovation, selection, diffusion, and withdrawal of political elements, and the international political competition for and national stratification as a result of catching up with, reaching, and maintaining the world's advanced level.

The extension: political modernization includes the modernization of political behavior, structure, institutions, and concepts; the modernization of political life, system, and culture; the modernization of political participation, national governance, international politics and political environment, and stage-, level-, and sector-specific political modernization; the interaction between politics and modernization in other fields; and the change in the temporal and spatial distribution of political modernization.

Generally, political modernization refers to the world frontiers of political change and the process and action to reach these frontiers and includes the transitions from traditional to modern politics and from modern to postmodern politics, includes the rationalization and democratization of political power, the legalization and equalization of political participation, the institutionalization and specialization of political system, and the rationalization and increased efficiency of political behavior.

Political modernization is an intersection of political changes and modernization. Obviously, not all political changes can be defined as part of political modernization. Generally, only those conducive to the rationalization and equalization of political participation, to the democratization and increasing efficiency of national governance, and to human liberty and overall development are truly political modernization (Table 6.42).

In general, political modernization roughly has three sources (Table 6.43): succession, transition, and innovation. Political modernization in different periods and subfields has different requirements (Table 6.44). Broadly, the basic

Table 6.41 General theory of political modernization in broad sense

Aspect	Basic contents
Definition	Political modernization is modernization in the sphere of politics. It is the political change and international competition since the industrial revolution of the eighteenth century; the frontier process of the formation, development, transformation, and international interaction of modern politics; the composite process of the alternate innovation, selection, diffusion, and withdrawal of political elements; as well as the international political competition for and national stratification as a result of catching up with, reaching, and maintaining the world's advanced level, etc.
Process	Political modernization is a long-standing historical process, including, among others, political development, political transition, international political interaction, and the change of international political status; the change of political behavior, structure, institutions, and concepts; and the democratization and rationalization of political culture, political participation and governance, world frontier of political change, and the process to reach these frontiers. In the eighteenth to twenty-first centuries, the frontier trajectory of political modernization could be divided into two major stages: first political modernization, the transition and profound change from agricultural to political politics, from autocratic to democratic politics, and from familiar to civil politics, featuring mainly democratization, rationalization, institutionalization, bureaucratization, and becoming highly efficient; and second political modernization, the transition and profound change from industrial to knowledge politics, from power politics to service politics, and from physical to ecological politics, currently characterized mainly by knowledgeablization, networking, greening, individuation, diversification, internationalization, etc. The coordinated development of the first and second political modernization is integrated political modernization. There will be new changes in the political modernization in the twenty-second century. Political modernization follows the ten basic principles of modernization (Table 2.15)
Results	The outcomes of political modernization include, among other things, the formation of political modernity, particularity, diversity, and side effects and the profound changes in political participation, national governance, international politics, political environment, etc. The result of the first political modernization is the formation of the first political modernity, particularity, and diversity, with side effects including political corruption, etc.; the main sign of the completion of the first political modernization is the formation of democratic, free, equal, and highly efficient modern politics. The outcome of the second political modernization is the formation of the second political modernity, particularity, and diversity, with side effects including declined political credibility, etc. Currently, the second political modernization is a picture scroll to be thoroughly unfolded
Dynamics	The influencing factors of political modernization include innovation, electioneering, adaptation, conflict, distribution of powers, public participation, international interaction, etc. Dynamic models include innovation drive, two-wheel drive, associative action, four-step hypercycle, composite interaction of three types of politics, innovation diffusion, innovation spillover, competition drive (Table 2.20), etc. Driving forces differ in different countries and at different stages, and driving forces in advanced countries are different from those in developing ones
Models	Political modernization has a diversity of paths and models, which are of starting dependency and path dependency and are subject to traditional politics, national level, and international system. In the twenty-first century, the basic paths are first political modernization, second political modernization, and integrated political modernization, each having a great number of subdivided paths and development models; and there are a variety of democratic models

Note: There has been no unified definition of modern politics. Generally, modern politics includes politics of industrial society (primary modern politics) and politics of knowledge society (advanced modern politics), sometime known as postmodern politics
Source: RGCMS (2010)

Table 6.42 Basic criteria of political modernization

Item	Political change as part of political modernization	Political change not as part of political modernization
Time	From the eighteenth century onward (meeting the criterion of nature at the same time)	Before the eighteenth century
Nature	(Political progress and positive adaptation)	(Political setback and reactive adaptation)
Criterion 1	Conducive to the equalization and rationalization of political participation	Adverse to the equalization and rationalization of political participation
Criterion 2	Conducive to the democratization and increasing efficiency of national governance	Adverse to the democratization and increasing efficiency of state governance
Criterion 3	Conducive to human liberty and overall development	Adverse to human liberty and all-round development

Table 6.43 Three sources of political modernization

Item	Source	Sample
Source 1	Partial succession and development of traditional politics	Territory, sovereignty, international relations, etc.
Source 2	Partial negation and transition of traditional politics	Selective development, transition, etc., of traditional political institutions and concepts
Source 3	Political innovation and exchange	Innovation in political institutions, concepts, process, etc.

Table 6.44 Basic requirements of political modernization

Item	Requirements of the first political modernization	Requirements of the second political modernization
Time	Approx. 1760–1970	Approx. 1970–2100
Political participation	Equalization, legalization, rationalization	Diversification, individuation, internationalization
National governance	Democratization, specialization, increasing efficiency	Service orientation, networking, increasing transparency
International politics	Institutionalization, rationalization, professionalization	Democratization, diversification, ecologicalization
Political environment	Economic and social development, etc.	All-round human development, etc.

requirements of the first political modernization include political democratization, power rationalization, organizational bureaucratization, and facilitation of economic and social development; those of the second political modernization include political diversification, power knowledgeablization, organizational networking, and promotion of all-round human development.

Political development involves political progress and positive adaptation, and political modernization is the intersection of political development, political transition, international political interaction, and the change of international status (Table 6.45).

Table 6.45 Conceptual model of political modernization

Item	Main contents
Hypothesis 1	Political progress means political changes conducive to political participation equalization, national governance democratization, and all-round human development
Hypothesis 2	Political positive adaptation means political adjustment conducive to political participation equalization, national governance democratization, and all-round human development
Hypothesis 3	Political transition means the transition from agricultural to industrial politics and from industrial to knowledge politics
Inference 1	Political development = political progress + political positive adaptation + political progress × political positive adaptation
Inference 2	Political modernization = political development × political transition × international political interaction and the change of international status

(2) Process

Political modernization is a long-standing complex historical process (Table 6.41). The process of political modernization can be divided into two types: frontier process and catch-up process with both common and different features. In the eighteenth to twenty-first centuries, its frontier process can be divided into two stages (Table 6.46), which have different connotations (Fig. 6.18; Table 6.47).

The first political modernization is the transition and profound change from traditional to modern politics and from autocratic to democratic politics, including the transition from feudalism to republic politics, from religionism to secular politics, from familiar politics to civilian politics, from aristocratism to class politics, from autocratic politics to legitimate politics, from agricultural to industrial politics, etc. Its features include political differentiation, democratization, rationalization, bureaucratization, legalization, secularization, institutionalization, systematization, professionalization, popularization, rationality, equalization, liberalization, specialization, division of classes, establishment of political parties, citizenship, emergence of organizations, etc.

The second political modernization is the transition and profound change from modern to postmodern politics and from power politics to service politics, including the transition from national to international politics, from centralized to decentralized politics, from class to public politics, from elite to civilian politics, from material to ecological politics, from physical to networking politics, from simple democracy to consultative democracy, from information control to information disclosure, from industrial to knowledge politics, etc. Currently, its features include knowledgeablization (knowledge-based), diversification, informatization, networking, individuation, greening, ecologicalization, decentralization, growth of political agendas, internationalization, service orientation, marketization, openness, transparency, and self-determination; there will be new developments in the future.

If the first political modernization is said to be the primary political modernization—the transition from traditional to primary modern politics—then the second political modernization is the advanced political modernization, the transition from

Table 6.46 Periodical table of political modernization in broad sense—change of political form

Stage (approx. starting year)	Political change and form (key elements)	Political modernization
Knowledge age	*Politics of knowledge society (knowledge politics)*	
Transition stage (2050)	Global politics, universal politics	
Mature stage (2020)	Global democracy, greening politics	*Second political modernization* Diversification, networking, individuation, postmodern politics, knowledge politics
Developing stage (1992)	Consultative democracy, networking, diversification, individuation	
Start stage (1970)	Postmodern politics, ecological politics, new public administration	
Industrial age	*Politics of industrial society (industrial politics)*	
Transition stage (1946)	Public politics, welfare state, social democracy	
Mature stage (1914)	Democracy state, socialism, fascism	*First political modernization*
Developing stage (1870)	Democratization, rationalization, civilian government	Democratization, institutionalization, specialization
Start stage (1763)	The Enlightenment, political revolution (USA and France)	Modern politics, industrial politics
Agricultural age	*Politics of agricultural society (agricultural politics)*	
Transition stage (AD 1500)	Renaissance, religion reformation, parliamentarism	
Mature stage (AD 618)	Caesarism, religionism, aristocratism	
Developing stage (500 BC)	Feudalism, bureaucracy, republicanism	(Agricultural revolution, agricultural politics)
Start stage (3500 BC)	Slavery, autocracy, familiar politics	
Primitive age	*Politics of primitive society (primitive politics)*	
Transition stage (10,000 years ago)	Farming, private ownership, union of tribes	(Primitive agricultural revolution, slash-and-burn cultivation)
Mature stage (40,000 years ago)	Primitive public ownership, democracy, tribal politics	(Tool-making revolution, primitive politics)
Developing stage (200,000 years ago)	Tool making, division of labor, clanship	
Start stage (2,500,000 years ago)	Stone tool making, colony, colonial politics	

Note: The time of civilization as well as political changes and forms are all based on the description of the temporal trajectory of human civilization frontiers

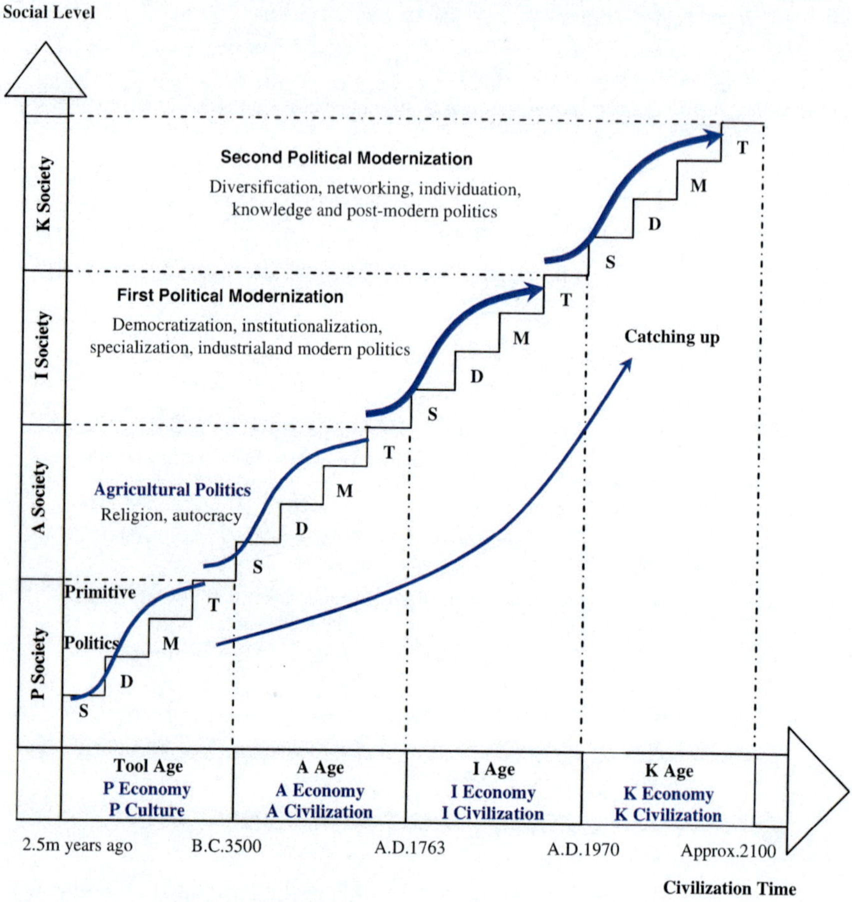

Fig. 6.18 Coordinates of political modernization. Note: P, A, I, and K refer to primitive, agricultural, industrial, and knowledge, respectively. S, D, M, and T refer to the start, developing, mature, and transition phase, respectively. The civilization time was the time based on the track of the forerunner of the civilization

primary to advanced modern politics; the coordinated development of the first and second political modernization is the integrated political modernization. There will be new changes in political modernization in the twenty-second century.

Political modernization has different features in different subfields and political sectors (Table 6.48).

The process of political modernization roughly has 12 features including non-linearity, reversibility, diversity, predictability, path dependency, path diversity, conflict, and being systematic, stage-specific, global, complex, and long-standing.

Political modernization is a manifestation of modernization and follows the ten basic principles of modernization (Table 2.15).

Table 6.47 Two major stages of political modernization in broad sense

Item	First political modernization	Second political modernization
Time	Approx. 1763–1970	About 1970–2100
Political democracy	Parliamentary democracy, mass democracy, social democracy, centralization of power	Decentralization of power, diversification, dialogue-style democracy, tolerance democracy, direct democracy, cyber democracy, consultative democracy
Political conflicts	Conflicts, strikes based on classes and powers, and conflicts between labor and capital	Reduced conflicts based on classes and wealth distribution, and increased conflicts based on ecological and technological risk
Political agendas	Economy, classes, wealth, rights, war, political parties and state	Increased agendas on life, ecology, risk, safety, sexual concepts, civil rights and globe
Form of participation	Political parties, voting, social movements, political organizations	Voters are not concerned with general ballots but with issues they are interested in, networking
Political power	Secular authority, state authority, constitutional power, institutional power	Reduced government authority, decentralization of power, individuation, human liberty
Political nature	National sovereignty, power politics, class politics	Political internationalization, service politics, civilian politics
Political form	Collective, antagonistic, centralized, class-based, violent	Individualized, nonantagonistic, decentralized, nonclass, peaceful

Table 6.48 Characteristics of subfields and sectors of political modernization in broad sense

Item	First political modernization	Second political modernization
Political participation	Democratization, secularization, division of classes, popularization, institutionalization, equalization, liberalization, rationalization	Diversification, consultative democracy, networking, individuation, internationalization, growth of political agendas, decentralization, knowledgeablization
National governance	Democratization, secularization, legalization, centralization, institutionalization, bureaucratization, specialization, standardization, procedure orientation, systematization	Knowledgeablization, informatization, service orientation, internationalization, greening, marketization, decentralization, diversification, increasing openness and transparency
National defense	Military mechanization, standardization, and nationalization	Military informatization, professionalization, and diversification
Diplomacy	Institutionalization, professionalization, normalization	Service orientation, multiplicity, diversification
Political parties	Legalization, normalization, classes-based	Popularization, particularization, multiplicity
Political organizations	Division of classes, specialization, standardization	Growth of political agendas, internationalization, diversification
International politics	Institutionalization, standardization, complication, international wars	Diversification, democratization, equalization, international aid
Political environment	Industrialization, urbanization, marketization, rationalization	Knowledgeablization, informatization, ecologicalization, globalization

Table 6.49 Modernity and side effects of political modernization

Item	First political modernization	Second political modernization
Modernity	First political modernity: democratic, rational, polarized, specialized, professional, organized, secular, liberal, equal, bureaucratic, popular, centralized, systematic, institutional, class-based, political party-based	Second political modernity: politically diverse, knowledge intensive, information intensive, individual, autonomous, networked, decentralized, green, agenda-focused, marketization, service-oriented, international, open, transparent (there still will be new features in the future)
Side effects	Political corruption, class conflict, etc.	Reduced support of government, international political risk, etc.

(3) Results

The outcomes of political modernization have been increasingly relevant to its goals since the 1950s.

They generally include the formation of political modernity, particularity, diversity, and side effects (Table 6.49).

The outcome of the first political modernization is the formation of the first political modernity, particularity, and diversity. It is characteristically democratic, rational, bureaucratic, rule-of-law-based, centralized, secular, specialized, and efficient, and side effects include political corruption, etc.

The outcome of the second political modernization is the formation of the second political modernity, particularity, and diversity. Currently, it is characteristically diverse, individual, green, networked, decentralized, knowledge intensive, information intensive, international, service-oriented, and transparent, and side effects include declined political credibility, etc.

The outcomes of political modernization include six aspects of profound changes such as the completion of two political transitions, the legalization and equalization of political participation, the rationalization and institutionalization of political system and structure, the democratization and rationalization of political institutions and concepts, government administration and public policy becoming increasing scientific and efficient, and the institutionalization and democratization of international politics and international relations. These changes can be seen in the fields of political participation, national governance, and international politics.

From the theoretical perspective, political modernization has mainly three goals: completing the first political modernization, completing the second political modernization, and improving the national capacity for international political interaction.

From the policy perspective, political modernization also has mainly three goals: legalization and equalization of political participation, democratization and increasing efficiency of national governance, and civil rights protection and all-round human development. These goals may also be further specified, and they have very rich connotation.

(4) Dynamics

The analysis of the driving forces of political modernization may be conducted in two dimensions: driving factors and driving mechanisms (Table 6.41).

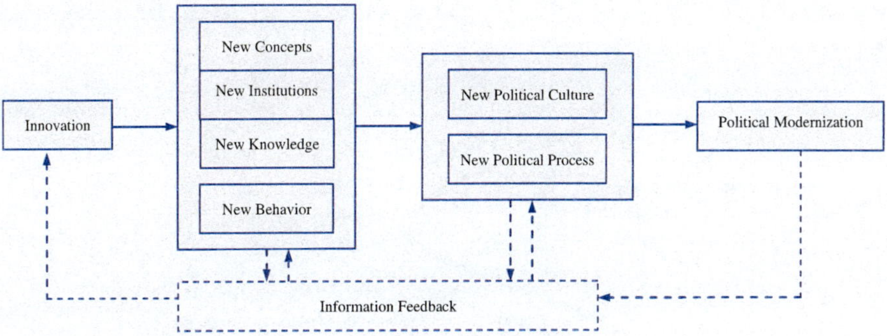

Fig. 6.19 Model of innovation-driven political modernization

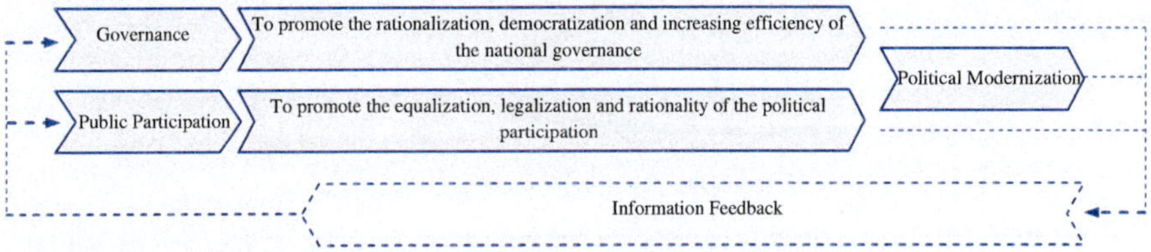

Fig. 6.20 Two-wheel drive model of political modernization

Broadly speaking, innovation is the fundamental source of political modernization; electioneering is the incentive mechanism for political changes; adaptation is the political adjustment to the changes in external environments; conflict (including political crisis and revolution) is the inducing factor of political changes; power distribution is the driving factor of political development; and public participation is the influencing factor of political changes.

The driving models of political modernization include innovation drive (Fig. 6.19), two-wheel drive (Fig. 6.20), associative action, innovation diffusion, innovation spillover (Table 6.41), etc. Driving forces of political modernization differ at different levels, in different countries, and at different stages.

(5) Models of Political Modernization

There are three basic paths (Fig. 6.21) and many subdivided paths for political modernization in the twenty-first century. The three basic paths are second political modernization, first political modernization, and integrated political modernization, for each of which there are many subdivided paths. The sphere of politics embraces four subfields (political participation, national governance, international politics, and political environment), and each subfield or sector has its own modernization path; the three basic paths serve as their "envelope curve."

Since there are optional paths, political modernization has neither standard nor optimal paths, but only appropriate ones. The selection of appropriate paths is subject not only to political modernization theories but also to such objective factors as countries' traditional politics, basic conditions, and external environment,

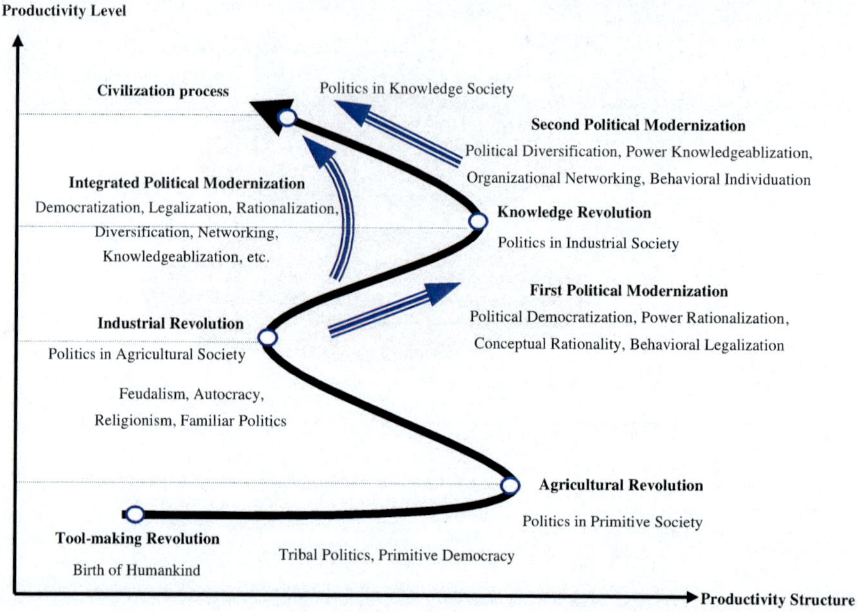

Fig. 6.21 Three basic paths of political modernization in the twenty-first century. Note: if affected by informatization and greening, the first political modernization will take on some new features in the twenty-first century

as well as international political interaction. The fact that paths are optional is relative and conditioned. Path choice has certain path dependency, is closely related to political modernization achievements, and involves rather high risk and opportunity cost. The risk can be effectively reduced by enhancing research on political modernization theories and policies.

There are a great variety of political modernization models. Different countries may, at different stages of political modernization, create different successful or unsuccessful models. Models of the second political modernization path include, among others, cyber democracy + diversification, consultative democracy + ecologicalization, etc. Models of the first political modernization path include democratization first and then industrialization, industrialization first and then democratization, coordinated development of democratization, industrialization, etc. Models of integrated political modernization path include democratization + industrialization + diversification, consultative democracy + industrialization + ecologicalization, etc. These models, of course, are not absolute but only have different focuses.

(6) Integrated Political Modernization

Integrated political modernization is a basic path for political modernization in broad sense in the twenty-first century, and it includes two political transitions in succession (from traditional to modern politics and from modern to postmodern politics) and the continuous transition toward knowledge politics. It requires the advancement of the first and second political modernization together as well as the simultaneous progressing of the democratization, rationalization, institutionalization, specialization, knowledgeablization, networking, diversification, greening, etc. It is an organic synthesis of the first and second political modernization, a new path of political modernization. Since different developing countries start and finish political modernization at different time, there is not just one path but a set of paths for integrated political modernization.

6.4 Cultural Modernization

Cultural modernization is the modernization of cultural sphere, and an expression of the modernization phenomenon in the cultural field. It includes the staged and stratified cultural modernization, and modernization of subfields and sectors of culture (Fig. 6.22). Culture has two properties: of nationality (cultural identity) and of commodity (cultural commodity). The cultural modernization is drove by both state interests and market demands.

6.4.1 Studies

Cultural modernization study, a part of the modernization study, refers to the modernization study of cultural sphere. Starting from the early years of eighteenth century, cultural modernization study can be analyzed from the perspectives of the historical process, the present and the future.

There are no agreed definitions about the culture and the cultural sphere. Generally, culture refers to the complex of knowledge, institution, and ideas that can impact and explain human lifestyles; and its extension includes pure culture, cultural industries, cultural facility, and other cultures (Fig. 6.23). The cultural

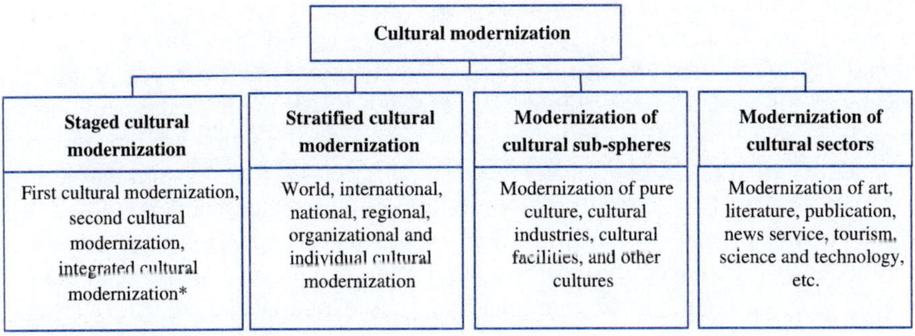

Fig. 6.22 Objects of cultural modernization study. Note: (*Asterisk*) Integrated cultural modernization means a coordinated development of twice cultural modernizations, which is a basic path of cultural modernization in developing countries

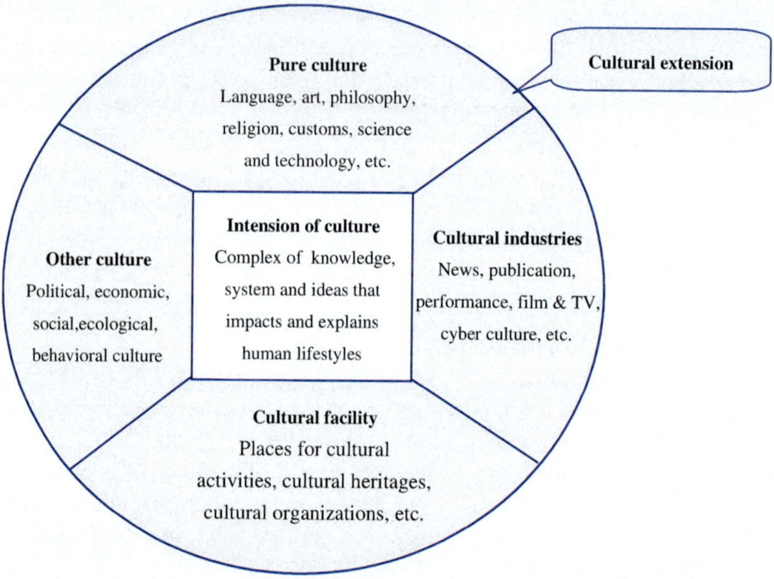

Fig. 6.23 Operational definitions of cultural intension and extension

sphere includes fields related to the creation, production, dissemination, distribution, provision, conservation, and consumption of cultures. Cultural modernization is a short form of the modernization of cultural field and has many overlapping aspects with the modernization of economy, society, politics, ecology, and individual.

6.4.1.1 Research Paradigm

The objects of cultural modernization study are the modernization of cultural field, including the modernization of pure culture, cultural industries, cultural facilities, and other cultures, and modernization of the world, national, regional, organizational, and individual cultures. The research contents include the modernization of cultural behavior, structure, institution, and ideas, as well as the process, result, dynamics, and model of the cultural modernization. All these factors can form a matrix (Table 6.50). This study also covers the staged cultural modernization, the modernization of cultural sectors, etc.

As an aspect of the modernization study, cultural modernization study can follow the methodology of modernization study. Analysis approaches are diverse, such as time-series analysis, cross-sectional analysis, process analysis, cultural investigation, case study, and coordinate analysis. Cultural modernization study can involve the whole process or a specific stage in terms of time span, and also can involve the world, a country, or region, in terms of the research scope.

Table 6.50 Matrix of cultural modernization study

Content		Object		
		Cultural sphere	Pure culture, cultural industries, cultural facility, and other cultures	Culture at six levels including the world level
		Cultural modernization	Modernization of four cultural subspheres	Cultural modernization at six levels
Element	Behavior	Modernization of cultural behavior, structure, institution, and ideas	Modernization of cultural behavior, structure, institution, and ideas in the four cultural subspheres	Modernization of cultural behavior, structure, institution, and ideas at the six levels
	Structure			
	Institution			
	Idea			
Aspect	Process	Process, result, dynamics, and model of the cultural modernization	Process, result, dynamics, and model of cultural modernization in the four cultural subspheres	Process, result, dynamics, and model of cultural modernization at the six levels
	Result			
	Dynamics			
	Model			

Note: Pure culture covers language, art, philosophy, region, law, ethics, customs, science and technology, etc.; cultural industries include news, publication, performance, radio and TV, film, design, advertising, entertainment, tourism, works of art, conference and exhibition, sports, cyber-culture, cultural goods, cultural trade, etc.; cultural facilities include places for cultural activities, cultural heritages, cultural organizations, etc.; other cultures refer to overlapping aspects between the cultural sphere and other sphere, including culture of economy, society, politics, environment, and individual behavior. The six levels refer to global, international, national, regional, organizational, and individual level. Besides, the cultural modernization research also involves in staged cultural modernization, modernization of cultural sectors, frontal analysis, analysis of cultural trends, elements of cultural modernization, interaction between different fields, etc.
Source: RGCMS (2009)

6.4.1.2 Historical Facts

As a form of cultural transformation, cultural modernization started in the eighteenth century. Generally, it is closely linked to economic and social modernization. The economic and social circles have undergone two stages of modernization and six waves, so has the cultural community (Table 6.51). *China Modernization Report 2009: Cultural Modernization Study* (RGCMS 2009) has made systematical analysis about the process, facts, experience, and inspiration of the cultural modernization as follows.

(1) Process Analysis

The first wave of cultural modernization came during the First Industrial Revolution (1763–1870), mainly in European and American countries. It focused on freeing people's mind, eradicating superstition, spreading scientific knowledge and advocating humanistic spirit, and realizing the independence of the cultural domain. It has made significant progress in the following aspects: first, promoting the scientific revolution and spreading knowledge, such as three major discoveries in natural science, namely, the cell theory, law of conservation and conversion of energy, and Darwin's theory of evolution, France's *Encyclopedia* (1751–1772);

Table 6.51 Two stages and six waves during the cultural modernization

Wave	Approx. time	Content	Annotation
First	1763–1870	The Enlightenment, cultural specialization, newspaper	*First cultural modernization* Specialization, secularization, rationalization, being scientific, commercialization, modern culture, industrial culture
Second	1870–1945	Industrial cultural, commercialization of culture, movie	
Third	1946–1970	Mass media, consumer culture, color TV	
Fourth	1970–2020	Cyberculture, ecological culture, digital multimedia	*Second cultural modernization* Industrialization, ecologization, diversification, humanization, globalization, postmodern culture, cyberculture
Fifth	2020–2050	Bionic culture, natural culture, democratization of culture	
Sixth	2050–2100	Global culture, universal culture	

Note: The fifth and sixth waves are just "scientific hypotheses"
Source: RGCMS (2009)

second, mind emancipation and institutional innovation, such as the *Declaration of Independence* (1776), *Declaration of the Rights of Man and of the Citizen* (1789), *France's Civil Code* (1804), and the patent institution; third, the prosperity of literature and art, including the development of classical music, romantic music, Rococo architectures, romantic literatures, and critical realism; fourth, freedom of faith and the prosperity of philosophy, represented by a large number of great ideologists, such as Voltaire, Rousseau, Adam Smith, Kant, and Marx; fifth, the independence of culture and vigorous development of press, publication, and performance; and sixth, the rising of urban culture.

The second wave occurred during the Second Industrial Revolution (1870–1913) and the two World Wars (1914–1945) and has made remarkable achievements in the following aspects: first, the technological revolution, such as electromagnetic theory, quantum mechanics, the theory of relativity, bicycle, electric generator, automobile, and air plane; second, the innovation in communications and cultural facilities, such as telephone, camera, gramophone, radio, radio receiver, recorder, movie, and TV; third, the development of modern literature and art, for example, realistic literature, modernist literature, modern fine arts, music, and dance; fourth, the development of modern philosophy, including philosophy of science and humanism philosophy, such as analytic philosophy, logical positivism, voluntarism, life philosophy, phenomenology, existentialism, psychological analytic, and Western Marxism; fifth, the commercialization of culture and the commercial production of film and pop music; and sixth, the booming of leisure culture and increasing popularity of sports and vacation tourism (Stearns et al. 1992).

The third wave was during the Third Industrial Revolution (1946–1970) and has made remarkable process, despite its short duration, including: first, technological revolution, such as atomic energy, automation, electronic technique, biological technology, satellite technology, and space technology; second, innovation of cultural facilities, such as transistor radio; third, development of modern literature and art, such as existentialism literature, absurd theater, black humor fictions, avant-garde music, and cinematographic art; fourth, the development of modern philosophy and ideology, such as modernism, structuralism, falsificationism, logical pragmatism, and scientific paradigm theory; fifth, the booming of mass media and consumer culture, embodied by the fact that a great deal of information was conveyed to the public through newspaper, radio, TV, and films, and TV, film, and pop music became the core of industrial culture; and sixth, the modern science and technology had increasing social influence and scientific culture developed rapidly.

The fourth wave occurred concurrently with the fourth wave of economic and social modernization (1970–2020) and was driven by the knowledge and information revolution. It has made achievements in about six aspects: first, high-tech revolution, such as information technology, biotechnology, materials technology, nanotechnology, and space technology; second, cultural innovation and cyberculture such as online games, cyber literature, online media, and cyber legalization, and eco-culture such as environmental protection campaign, ecological awareness and environmental law, and cultural diversification; third, postmodernist culture, such as postmodernist literature, art and architectures, postmodernism, feminism, ethics in cyberspace, and information philosophy; fourth, the rising of cultural industries and cultural trade and significantly increasing value added and much higher contribution to employment; fifth, the innovation in cultural systems and policies, diversification of cultural organizations and support, democratization of culture, cultural diversity, and protection of cultural heritages; and sixth, cultural has taken the dominant place, and cultural completion and consuming become a hot issue on the international arena.

The fifth wave of cultural modernization is expected to occur during 2020–2050, mainly featuring the bionic culture and natural culture. Thanks to the development of new biology and high technology; biology, information, and nanotechnology tend to be integrated, generating bioengineering technologies that can improve and manipulate life functions, enabling the controllability of the life span of living beings and the dominance of bioeconomy, and bringing radical changes to people's ideas. Information can be transmitted between human brains and computers through transcribers, free accessibility of knowledge and information become real, bionic men can be seen in both your houses and offices, and bionic culture and natural culture can be supportive to each other. To some degree, "bionic man" is the upgraded robot, featuring a humanized body (appearance of human being), humanized emotion (human being's emotion), and humanized capability (functions of human being). Its entry into people's families will trigger the fourth revolution in people's families. The first revolution of this kind is the appearance of small and nuclear families, the second is the mechanization and electrification of families, the third is the use of information and Internet in families, and the fourth is the entry of bionic men into and the diversification of families which will completely change the structure and function of the family.

The sixth wave is expected to emerge between 2050 and 2100, mainly featuring the global culture and universal culture. Based on the new revolution in physics and along with the development of high technologies and new energy, man's manufacturing and transportation technologies will undergo radical change, so will people's ideas about time and space; super-manufacturing systems will replace man's physical and manual work, super-transportation system will send people to wherever they want to go, and cultural activities and emotional experiences will play a dominant role in social economy; common view might be formed in the global culture, and the universal culture may become the way of life for some people.

(2) Cultural Modernization in Three Subfields

Cultural modernization involves pure culture, cultural facilities, and cultural industries (Table 6.52).

(3) Cultural Modernization and Evolution of Cultural Institutions

Cultural modernization includes the change of the cultural institution (Table 6.53). Generally, the basic cultural system is about the ownership, allocation, and distribution of cultural resources. In the primitive society, it is the primitive religious institution, and all cultural resources are owned and shared by all members of the society. In the agricultural society, it refers to the cultural control institution, under which the feudal court and religious organizations determine the production, allocation, and distribution of cultural resources and control folk culture. In the industrial society, it takes the form of cultural censorship, cultural market, and the intellectual property institution; and the production, allocation, and distribution of

Table 6.52 Three subfields of cultural modernization

Approx. time	Pure culture	Cultural facilities	Cultural industries
1763–1870	S&T revolution, the Enlightenment, emancipation of the mind, urban culture, etc.	Library, museum, theater, salon, etc.	Newspaper, books, periodicals, art, performance, etc.
1870–1945	S&T revolution, industrial culture, modern philosophy, leisure culture, etc.	Telephone, gramophone, radio receiver, camera, film, television, etc.	Press, publication, performance, broadcast, film, pop music, etc.
1946–1970	S&T revolution, modernism, consumer culture, scientific culture, etc.	Transistor radio, cultural heritage, etc.	Television industry, international tourism, cultural service, cultural trade, etc.
1970–2020	Cyberculture, ecological culture, postmodernist culture, cultural diversity, technical revolution, etc.	Internet, cell phone, digital cultural facilities, etc.	Online game, digital media, information revolution, etc.
2020–2050	Bionic culture, natural culture, S&T revolution, etc.	Transcriber between people and computer, etc.	E-emulation of people, etc.
2050–2100	Global culture, universal culture, S&T revolution, etc.	Spatial cultural facilities, etc.	Spatial experience, etc.

Note: S&T refers to the science and technology
Source: RGCMS (2009)

Table 6.53 Timing sequence change of basic cultural institution (specific features)

Stage	Primitive society	Agricultural society	Industrial society	Knowledge society
Historical time	Birth of mankind 3500 BC	3500 BC–AD 1763	About 1763–1970	About 1970–2100
Cultural type	Primitive culture	Agricultural culture	Industrial culture	Knowledge culture
Basic institution	Primitive religion	Cultural control	Cultural censorship and market	Internet-based and international
Language	Natural language	National and religious language	Official and nonofficial languages	Cyber language, protection of language
Literature	Oral literature	Religious literature, literature control	Publication censorship, specialization	Online literature, protection of literature
Art	Primitive art	Religious, court and folk art	Publication censorship, commercialization	Online art, protection of art
Religious	Primitive religion	Ethnical, national and folk religions	Differentiation and secularization of religion	Diversification and the folk style
Legal	Primitive customs	Ancient and classic laws	Legal institution, intellectual property	Law about the Internet and ecology
Morals	Primitive customs	Religious and feudal morals and rule by divine right	Industrial and market morals and privilege	Internet-based, diversified, human rights
Technological	Primitive tool	Individual behavior, technological organizations	Technological institution, specialization	Innovative institution, internationalization
Cultural facilities	Religious facilities	Governmental and nongovernmental cultural facilities	Cultural institution, specialization	Digital and international
Cultural industries	–	Governmental and nongovernmental cultural activities	Popular culture, market-based	Internet-based, globalization

Source: RGCMS (2009)

cultural resources are determined by both the government and the market. The knowledge society adopts an institution featuring networking (the wide use of Internet), ecologization, and internationalization, and its unique way of production, allocation, and distributing the cultural resource is taking shape.

(4) Facts of Cultural Modernization

The first is the facts in the field of pure culture. Since the eighteenth century, the language has undergone constant development from the classic to the modern then to the postmodern, with its types reducing; the adult literacy rates have increased and amounted to 100% in some countries, different schools of literature appeared in different periods, including classic, romantic, realistic, modernist, and postmodernist literature, so did the art (including classic, romantic, modernist, and postmodernist art) and philosophy (including classic, modernist, and postmodernist philosophy); religions have always been there and become diversified and tended to be secularized in some countries; science and technologies developed rapidly through several technological revolutions. Besides, green culture and Internet culture have prospered since the 1970s.

The second is the facts in the field of cultural facilities. Since the eighteenth century, places for cultural activities and cultural organizations become more diverse, and their numbers have increased. Since the nineteenth century, more diverse cultural facilities have been applied with the popularization rate being increased, and the information facilities were in the same case; the types of sports and entertainment facilities have been increased, and tourism, educational, and technological facilities have constantly developed. Since the twentieth century, the protection of natural and cultural heritages has been intensified.

The third is the facts related to the cultural industries. Since the eighteenth century, the circulation of newspaper of the world has increased, while that for developed countries has increased but then dropped. From the beginning of the nineteenth century, the amount of publications has grown at an annual approx. rate of 2%, the coverage of broadcast has been expanded, the quantity of movies produced has also risen, and leisure and entertainment industries have constantly developed. In the twentieth century, more people can spend more time watching TV, new media industry and online games have rapidly developed in the latter half of the century, and the value added and employment in the cultural industries and the cultural trade also have seen growth.

The fourth is the facts about political and economic culture. Since the eighteenth century, democratic culture and democratization have moved forward, and governments have made significant strides in being information-based in the latter half of the twentieth century. Since the nineteenth century, the working hours per week have been dropped while free time increased; the number and proportion of child labors have been both dropped; distribution in developed countries have become more fair, and the international difference in consumer culture has been obvious; the proportion of industrial labors in developed countries has been increased but then dropped; and the modern corporate culture is developing.

The fifth is the facts in social and individual culture. Since the start of the eighteenth century, the population growth rates in developed countries have increased but then dropped, the education enrollment and the proportion of people who received higher education have been increased, and the proportion of people receiving middle-level education in developed countries has been increased and then dropped. In the nineteenth century, the coverage of social insurance has been expanded with more expenditure on social welfare, families become smaller in some countries, and the total fertility rate was lower. In the twentieth century, more women tended to take measures on birth control, and the divorce rate increased while the marriage rate decreased; the smoking prevalence has increased but then dropped in some countries.

The sixth is about facts related to ecological and international culture. Since the nineteenth century, the number and proportion of coverage of national protection areas have been increased, and environmental protection has been better supported, and the recycling of wastes has been bettered in the twentieth century. The nineteenth century witnessed the increasing number of international organizations and conferences, more prosperous international tourism and more frequent sports exchanges, and the growing number of people studying abroad, while the twentieth century saw more translated books and immigrants.

The seventh is about the cultural policies. Since the eighteenth century, the cultural field has become more democratic, and intellectual property right has been better protected. In the nineteenth century, cultural investment became diverse, and some governments spent more on culture; scientific culture and human culture were separate, with the former playing a bigger role. In the twentieth century, more countries have ratified international cultural treaties, protection of the world's tangible and intangible cultural heritages and the international cultural cooperation have both been intensified; various cultural policies have been made to protect the cultural diversity, and cultural freedom has been respected more and more.

Finally are the comprehensive facts about cultural modernization. Cultural life and content have constantly changed, so have the cultural institution and ideas since the eighteenth century. Such changes are not linear, but in a diverse way and through various channels. Some traditional culture has been inherited. The cultural competitiveness and influence of specific countries varied since the nineteenth century. The proportions of the value added and employment in the cultural industries have surpassed those of the agriculture in particular countries at the end of the twentieth century (Table 6.54).

(5) Historical Experience

First of all, cultural modernization is both of a trend and a choice. Cultural modernization is historically inevitable to human culture and represents the dominant direction of human cultural development, as well as is a choice of different countries and nations. As the right to make cultural choices is a fundamental one for

Table 6.54 Cultural industries surpassing agriculture in size in some developed countries

Country	Proportion of value added of the cultural industries in GDP (%)	Proportion of employment in the cultural industries (%)	Proportion of value added of agriculture in GDP (%)	Proportion of employment in agriculture (%)
USA	6.6	4	1.2	2.5
Germany	3.4	–	1.0	2.5
UK	3.8	4.3	1.0	1.2
France	3.1	3.2	1.6	2.5
Canada	3.5	4.1	2.2	2.8
Australia	3.3	5.1	3.4	4.0

Note: Some data of this table are the data of available between 1999 and 2004, and the definitions and statistical standards for the cultural industries vary in different countries
Source: RGCMS (2009)

the mankind, all nations and countries enjoy such a right under the condition that their choices cannot affect others in a bad way. Those choice makers will make efforts to promote the cultural modernization, while those who do not make this choice otherwise will keep or stay in their original culture, traditional culture, or the stage of primitive culture, and thus, the cultural forefronts of different countries will vary more. All nations and countries shall be responsible for what they choose.

Second, cultural modernization involves the interest of the state and the market competition. Culture has two properties. (a) It has national identity and can represent the cultural rights of a nation or a country as its cultural identity. (b) It might be a commodity and can be produced and traded and make profits according to the market demand. The evolution of culture is affected by both national interest and the market demand. Such duality can undoubtedly cause the duality of cultural modernization that is manifested in the demands to maintain the state's cultural rights and creativity and to enhance the quality of cultural life and the cultural competitiveness. In most cases, these demands are consistent. The national interest and the market demand are also two driving forces in the process of cultural modernization. Different countries deal with the duality of cultural modernization in different ways, with some focusing on the countries' cultural rights while others stress the property of culture as a commodity.

Third, cultural modernization is highly diverse but is convergent as well. Its diversity is mainly manifested in (a) cultural modernization has different features in different countries and fields; (b) the international culture is diverse; (c) the national cultures of many countries, including some developed countries, are diverse; and (d) cultural activities are in various ways. Its convergence is reflected in (a) cultural facilities, cultural industries, science and technologies, economic culture, and ecological culture of different countries are convergent to some degree; (b) the quality of cultural life is constringent or convergent to some degree; (c) international culture and international institutions are convergent; and (d) industrial culture, urban culture, and Internet culture tend to have something in common to some degree. Despite such diversity, cultural modernization observes the general law.

Fourth, cultural modernization plays a guiding role in some content. (a) The cultural modernization started earlier than the modernization of the world. Generally, it can be dated back to the Renaissance, religious reform, scientific revolution, and the Enlightenment. The Enlightenment marked the start of the cultural modernization and was the prelude of the modernization of Europe and even the world, while the world' s modernization started with the industrial revolution that broke out in Britain. (b) According to the experience of developed countries, mind emancipation was prior to modernization. For example, scientific revolution and the Enlightenment were antecedent to Britain's industrial revolution and the revolution in America and France. (c) In developing countries, economic development and social progress can advance the cultural modernization.

Fifth, cultural innovation is the essential driving force for the cultural modernization. In human cultural frontier, cultural modernization is more a process of natural evolution; however, this process is not the same as the autorotation of celestial bodies but is driven by innovation and the spread of the innovation. Every revolutionary step forward in the cultural modernization results from major innovation and the spread of such innovation.

Sixth, cultural modernization is diverse, rather than in a single form. It can be rapid or, comparatively, slow; it may proceed through revolutionary changes or in a progressive way; or it can be quiet or a dynamic and influence social movement. The Great French Revolution breaking out in the eighteenth century and the cultural campaign triggered by the student movement in Europe and America in the 1960s were revolutionary; the change of environmental cultural caused by the environmental campaign in the 1970s was more like a social movement; and the emerge of cyberculture initiated by the information revolution in the 1980s–1990s is also revolutionary, although it is not in a violent form, but a peaceful and explosive informatization.

Seventh, the linear way of thinking is not suitable for the research of cultural modernization, as the cultural modernization is multidimensional and complicated, and has different features in different fields. Some changes are nonlinear, such as the change of cultural institutions and ideas, including the transition from traditional to modern culture and then from modern to postmodern culture, and the transformation of material to ecological culture; while some others are linear instead, such as the development of science and technology, knowledge, cultural facilities, and culture industry. Cultural modernization can be reversible under specific conditions, so unidirectional and rigid way of thinking is not advisable for the progress of cultural modernization.

Eighth, cultural modernization cannot be advanced in a blind way, as it is not isolated, but an international cultural interaction, including international cooperation, exchange, completion, and conflicts in the cultural field. There is no such a nation who learns nothing from other countries in its cultural modernization, and not such a national either who refuses international cultural exchange and cooperation. The cultural competitiveness and influence of different countries vary, with developed countries being more advantageous in competitions.

Ninth, there is no best model for the cultural modernization, but successful experience can be drawn as reference; instead, there are only rational choice and path dependence. Cultural modernization in different countries and fields is the same essentially and diverse in forms; its objectives are identical but may be realized in different ways; the requirements for cultural modernization are the same, but may be in various patterns. Given the difference in the languages, art, philosophies, religions, laws, cultural systems, and cultural traditions of different countries, their cultural policies and choices to be made differ a lot and should not be copied blindly. Later-coming ones can learn a lot of good experience from the early birds.

Tenth, simple comparison of the degree of cultural modernization is not reasonable between different countries and between different historical stages. The international comparison in this regard can only be confined in a specific scope, such as cultural activities, cultural facilities, and the cultural industries. Cultural modernization includes the changes of language, art, literature, philosophy, and religion, and it is not easy to make the transnational or historical comparison for the identification of their development level.

Eleventh, cultural modernization does not mean to completely deny and reject the traditional culture, to cut off the connections between traditional and modern, or an indiscriminate development of traditional culture; instead, it means to inherit and carry forward the "good part" of the traditional culture, deny and transform the "bad part," and also properly protect and effectively use the traditional culture. During the course of cultural modernization, traditional culture always remains and plays a role. For example, classic science, philosophy, art and literature, religion, language as well as the world cultural heritages are still significant contents in the textbooks of schools at various levels; and classic art and literature and common cultural heritage and intangible cultural heritage are also important resources for the cultural industries.

Twelfth, cultural modernization is to properly protect and use cultural heritages, rather than damage them. During the course of cultural modernization, people become increasingly aware about the role of cultural heritages. They are important as significant element in the cultural identity of a nation, source for cultural innovation and cultural industries, integral part of cultural diversity, and element of the cultural competitiveness and influence. The cultural globalization is not to weaken the role of cultural heritages, but to highlight their international significance. The proper protection and effective utilization of cultural heritages make an organic and irreplaceable part of the cultural modernization.

Thirteenth, cultural modernization may change in five ways: (a) Cultural centralization refers to the phenomenon that the central status of advantageous culture has been consolidated and strengthened, allowing the cultural diversity at the same time. (b) Cultural marginalization means the social status, and international influence of some cultures is declining. (c) Some parts of the culture are protected as cultural heritages due to the loss of social functions. (d) Some parts of culture disappear since they are not inherited, recorded, or protected. (e) Cultural commercialization indicates phenomena that cultural carriers and elements are commercially developed and operated. These five changes lead to the restructuring of the world's cultural system and the variation of international competitiveness and influence of specific cultures.

Fourteenth, the cultural competitiveness has gradually become a nation's core competitiveness. Generally, cultural modernization has two stages, namely, differentiation and dedifferentiation. The former means that culture is separated from the whole of the society and becomes an independent field like politics and economy. Its independence and autonomy is mainly manifested in cultural specialization and professionalization. The latter indicates high combination between culture and society and between culture and economy. Culture wins its independence through differentiation, and its influence penetrates into all aspects of the society by dedifferentiation. From this point of view, cultural competitiveness has become a core competitiveness of a country.

(6) Key Enlightenments

First, cultural modernization is an objective phenomenon. Despite dispute, cultural modernization is as real as we can see. In the history of modern culture, there is cultural inheritance, progress, adaptation, transformation, and interaction, and also innovation, communication, choice, loss, and planning. All these are closely related to modernization and are modernization phenomena in the cultural field.

Second, cultural modernization is partially predictable. According to Inglehart and Welzel, *the direction of modernization is predictable rather than determined. Modernization can be affected by many factors including economic and social ones. Economic development and social progress can make people more secular, tolerant and credible and pay more attention to self expression, participation and the quality of their life* (Inglehart and Welzel 2005). All these ideas are applicable to cultural modernization. For example, major scientific discoveries and new technologies can undoubtedly cause cultural change, so can the economic and social progress, international cultural cooperation and exchange, as well as the popularization of education and the development of information technology.

Third, cultural modernization is nonlinear, according to Inglehart and Welzel. *Industrialization leads to bureaucratization and secularization in the cultural change; postindustrialization pushed the cultural change into a new direction: to intensify individual autonomy and stress the value of self-expression, rather than be completely rational, centralized and bureaucratic. Industrialization leads to the transformation from traditional value to more secular and rational one; while postindustrialization leads the transformation from the value of survival to the value of self expression, the later of which stresses people's choice, autonomy and creativity* (Inglehart and Welzel 2005). The cultural modernization of developed countries has made two turns. The first turn is from traditional (feudal, autocratic, and religious) to modern culture (civic, democratic, and secular), and the second is from modern (productive, economic, and rational) to postmodern culture (service-oriented, ecologically friendly, and people-centered) (Fig. 6.24).

Fourth, cultural modernization is partially reversible, according to Inglehart and Welzel. *Social and economic development and economic collapse which failed to be recovered in a short term may reverse the cultural modernization. For example, many countries founded after the disintegration of Soviet Union in 1990 suffered from cultural reversion* (Inglehart and Welzel 2005).

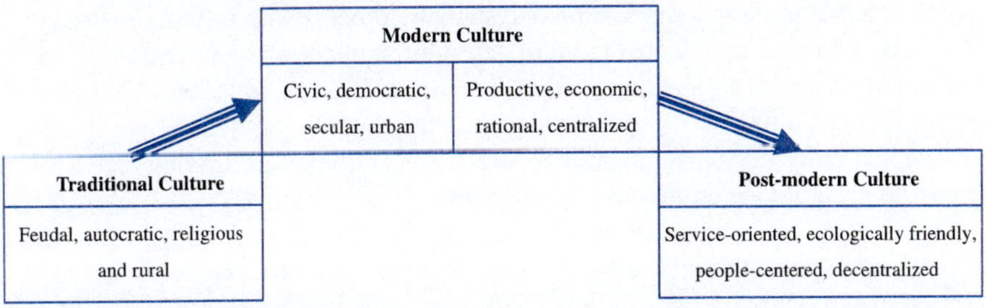

Fig. 6.24 Two turns of cultural modernization in developed countries. Source: RGCMS (2009)

Fifth, according to Inglehart and Welzel, cultural modernization is of path dependency. *Countries observing Protestantism, Catholics, Islam and Confucianism have totally different cultural value systems, and all of them are dynamic and vigorous.* ***Although significantly driven by modernization, value systems of different*** *countries develop in the same direction, they will by no means become the same* (Inglehart and Welzel 2005). Cultural modernization is affected by their traditional culture.

Sixth, cultural modernization enjoys diverse channels. Modernization occurs in pure culture, cultural facilities, cultural industries, and other cultures, as well as subfields of culture; and also takes place at different levels, such as world, international, national, regional, organizational, and individual levels. Obviously, cultural change differs in different fields and subfields and has different features at specific levels. Therefore, cultural modernization is through diverse channels, rather than a single one.

Seventh, the pluralism of cultural modernization is determined by the cultural diversity and the multipaths of cultural modernization. Culture diversity does exist not only worldwide but also in specific countries or regions, even in some transitional organizations, such as multinationals. At present, there are at least over 5,000 languages and more than 5,000 cultures. Diverse countries, regions, organizations, and individuals will by all means have diverse cultural modernization.

Eighth, cultural modernization is a complicated process. During the modernization, traditional culture keeps playing a role, rather than simply vanishes; and global cultures do not become totally the same (Inglehart and Welzel 2005). That means cultural modernization is a composite process during which traditional culture plays its role, modern culture keeps developing, cultural exchanges occur in the international arena, etc. Cultural modernization can also cause social tension, cultural conflicts, and psychological stress, so it is a risky and complex process.

Ninth, cultural modernization is a global trend and campaign. In the past three decades, it first took place in Europe, then spread to most countries and regions in the world. In the century to come, it will sweep the whole globe.

Tenth, cultural modernization will take long time, as it is a kind of cultural evolution rather than a cultural revolution, although it may cause revolutionary change; and even cultural revolution do occur, it does not last long, for example, the Great French Revolution. Generally, cultural modernization cannot be accomplished in an action.

Eleventh, cultural modernization is a systematic process with or without design. It includes the modernization of cultural activities, content, system, and ideas and the modernization of pure culture, cultural facilities, cultural industries, and other aspects of the culture. It is not isolated but international and interactive. The international cultural exchange and cooperation is an important driving force and channel to promote the cultural modernization.

Twelfth, cultural modernization advances through stages. During the 400 years between the eighteenth and the twenty-first centuries, the process can be divided into two major stages and six waves. The first stage features rationality, commercialization, secularization, and cultural differentiation, and the second one has such characteristics as being Internet-based and ecologically friendly as well as industrialization and cultural dedifferentiation at present.

6.4.2 Theories

Cultural modernization theory deals with phenomena of cultural modernization and is a branch of the modernization theory. It generally includes four categories of theories: classic cultural modernization theory, cultural modernization theory in the broad sense, theories on diverse modernity, and other modernization theories. This part focuses on the first two categories, and other categories are discussed in Chap. 4.

6.4.2.1 Classic Cultural Modernization Theories

Classic cultural modernization theory is an important part of the classic modernization theory. Up to date, academic literatures about cultural modernization are quite abundant, but systematic and agreed general theoretical elaboration about classic cultural modernization theory is lacked. Generally, classic cultural modernization theory has two sources: researches and explanations of cultural modernization by experts on culture, and those by modernization scholars in noncultural fields (such as history and sociology). Through combination of their research subjects and relevant ideas, the structure (Table 6.55) and general theory (Table 6.56) of classic cultural modernization theory can be established.

(1) Definition

There is no uniform definition about the classic cultural modernization. Generally, it refers to the transition from traditional to modern culture, from agricultural to industrial culture, and from religious to secular culture in the course of classic modernization.

Lash (1990), a British scholar, holds that *if modernization is regarded as a process of cultural differentiation, postmodernization is a process of dedifferentiation. The cultural modernization has undergone three stages: the primitive stage,*

Table 6.55 Structure of classic cultural modernization theory

Category	Theory	Main content
General theory	Core theory	Definition, process, result, dynamics, and model of classic cultural modernization
Branch theories	Cultural modernity theory	Definition and model of cultural modernity
	Modernization of cultural sectors	Technological modernization, publication modernization, leisure modernization, etc.
Related theories	Culture theories	Cultural study, contemporary culture study, culture change, cultural transformation, evolution and anthropology, etc.
	Relevant theories	Classic modernization theory, multiple modernities theory, second modernization theory, etc.

Note: Cultural modernization research includes studies on its concepts, empirical studies, and policy studies, and its findings have enriched the cultural modernization theories
Source: RGCMS (2009)

Table 6.56 General theory of classic cultural modernization

Aspect	Basic content
Definition	Classic cultural modernization refers the culture change in the course of classic modernization, and the transition from traditional to modern culture, from agricultural to industrial culture
Process	Classic cultural modernization is a historical process including cultural differentiation, rationalization, secularization, individualization, globalization, etc.
Outcome	The formation and spread of classic cultural modernity, and its features are generalized as classic cultural modernity, including democracy, differentiation, professionalism, secularization, rationality, popularity, etc.
Dynamics	Classic cultural modernization is affected by many factors, such as economy, society, politics, science and technology, international relations, etc.
Model	Classic cultural modernization proceeds through diverse ways and under various models, features path dependence and can be affected by historical factors and objective conditions

Source: RGCMS (2009)

religious and metaphysical stage and the modern stage. In the primitive society, culture and society did not separate from each other, and religion and religious rites made parts of the society. In the second stage, culture was separated from society; during the renaissance, secular culture became independent from religious culture; and in the eighteenth century, divides among theory, ethics and esthetics went further. Cultural differentiation and autonomy leads to the booming of realism of art and epistemology. In the modern stage, further differentiation and autonomy generates cultural modernity, and theories, ethics and esthetics in each cultural field are highly autonomic. The postmodern stage is a process of cultural dedifferentiation.

According to Nielsen (1993), a Danish scholar, *cultural modernization is a process and a process of individualization in nature; and it is also a new cultural structural state, featuring the breakup of limitations in traditional culture; differentiation of social practices into different autonomous fields, rationalization of behaviors and freedom of individuals.*

In the idea of Irrgang (2007), a German scholar, *modernization has three dimensions. The first is the modern times and art modernization, which is about the way and significance of art, and is progressive and leads to postmodern discussion. Second, the modernization of art is different from that in other fields. The modern times are a period of enlightenment, during which philosophy and religion was separated. This dimension is about the ideology of modernization. The third is from the perspective of technology, referring to industrialization or technicalization.*

Li (2001), a Chinese scholar, holds that *cultural modernization is a process to carry forward, criticize and innovate the traditional culture and a process of cultural innovation (such as knowledge innovation, ideological innovation, etc.). Cultural innovation, in a broader sense, has become the foundation and driving force for mankind's survival and development. It is not only an important task of modernization, but also a way to create advanced culture. It is the modernization of people's knowledge, and the survival and development conditions of human being; and it is also a process of constantly updating and reconstructing the people's value system. Cultural innovation and cultural modernization purports to realize the across-the-board development of human beings.*

(2) Process

Desai, an Indian scholar, has summarized four features of cultural modernization (Black 1976).

First, main elements of the cultural system become increasingly divided; the literacy rate is enhancing and secular education popularizing; and knowledge and institutional system based on knowledge training and aiming at producing and training professionals is established.

Second, a new view of culture appeared, which stresses progress and improvement, efficiency, happiness, free rein of capabilities, natural expression of emotions and feelings and development of personal features.

Third, a new trend appears, that is to adapt to increasingly broad social features with higher capability, enjoy individual flexibility, expand the range of interests, pay more attention to others and the environment, make efforts to develop self capabilities of development and change, respect others, have faith in science and technology, and agree to get paid according to one's own contribution.

Fourth, our society is capable to develop an institutional structure to deal with constantly changing problems and requirements.

Gerhards and Hackenbroch (2000) from Germany analyze the data of names (the first name) of newborn babies in Germany between 1894 and 1994, to explore the trend and reason of cultural modernization. They find out that the cultural modernization includes secularization, the change of family traditions and individualization and globalization, etc.

American scholars Divale and Seda (2000, 2001) analyze the cultural evolution in the course of modernization on the basis of data about 136 countries and regions. They find out that the modernization has undergone four stages: the change of government, trade, and education in the first stage; the change of health, technology, and transportation in the third stage; the change of family structure, region, and personal health; and the change of behaviors in the fourth stage.

(3) Outcome

Classic cultural modernization mainly results in the formation and spread of classic cultural modernity.

Cultural modernity is an abstract induction of the results of cultural modernization. If culture is embracive, cultural modernity and modernity is roughly identical, but if culture is regarded as an aspect of human being's civilization, cultural modernity is only one side of the modernity and a theoretical abstraction of results of cultural modernization. In some literatures, cultural modernity and cultural modernization as well as cultural modernity and modernity is not clearly distinguished.

Baudelaire (1821–1867), a French poet, holds that *part of the esthetics is eternal and never changes, but it is hard to define how much it is. The other part is relevant and temporary; and it can be the times, fashion, ethics, lust, one of them or several of them. Modernity is the transitory, temporary, incidental and artistic part, and the other half is eternality which never changes* (Habermas 1987). Some scholars regard this concept as the source of cultural modernity or esthetical modernity.

Habermas from Germany agrees with Webber, a German sociologist, *about the feature of cultural modernity which means the essential rationality manifested in the religious and metaphysical world outlook is divided into three autonomic fields, namely, science, ethics and art. Scientific language, ethical theories and law, and the production and criticism of art have been gradually institutionalized. Special cultural fields have corresponding professions to deal with problems these fields. Such professionalization reflects the inner structure of each of the three levels of culture, that is cognition—instrumental rational structure, ethics—practical rational structure and esthetics—expressive rational structure* (Habermas 1987).

According to Ginger, a Spanish scholar (2007), *cultural modernity is usually regarded as the stress on the way of expression. It holds that art is neither the imitation of the outside world nor the reflection of the life of artists themselves. French cultural modernity appeared approximately in the nineteenth century, but the multiple modernities about art and culture mentioned a lot recently are obviously different from the old model.*

Chuanqi He (2003) insists that the new culture features of six characters: new knowledge based on science; new education referring to the popularization of modern education and science; new ideas meaning the rationalization of ideas, secularization of religions, the central position of people and society, faith in science and technology, modernism, economism, and nationalism; new spirit of science, democracy, liberty, equality, and philanthropy; new pursuit for progress, wealth, change and self-expression, and the development of personal value and capability; and new world outlook featuring efficiency, flexibility, adaptability, awareness to open and participate, trust, responsibility, achievement and just.

(4) Dynamics

Cultural modernization is affected by many factors, such as economy, society, politics, science and technology, and international relations. Karl Marx holds that the superstructure is determined by the economic base; on this basis, we can say economic development can drive the cultural modernization forward. Max Webber expounds in his book *The Protestant Ethic and the Spirit of Capitalism* the upbeat Protestant culture, rationalization, bureaucratization, and other issues and regards the Protestant culture as the root of capitalism and modernization of Europe.

(5) Model

Classic cultural modernization features diversity of its paths and models. Instead of following a settled way, cultural modernization in developed and developing countries has different characteristics.

6.4.2.2 Cultural Modernization Theory in the Broad Sense

Cultural modernization theory in the broad sense is a theoretical explanation of cultural modernization phenomena between the eighteenth and the twenty-first centuries. Proposed by a Chinese scholar Chuanqi He, it is the application of second

Table 6.57 Structure of the cultural modernization theory in the broad sense

Type	Theory	Major content
General theory	Core theory	Definition, process, result, dynamics, and model of cultural modernization
Branch theories	Stage theory	First, second, or integrated cultural modernization
	Stratified study	Modernization of the world, international, national, regional, organizational, and individual cultures
	Subfields study	Modernization of pure culture, cultural facilities, cultural industries, cultural life, structure, institution, ideas, etc.
	Sector theory	Modernization of languages, art and literature, philosophy, religion, science and technology, entertainment, publication, sports, tourism, etc.
Related theories	Other modernization theories	Classic modernization theory, postmodernization theory, multiple modernities theory, the second modernization theory, etc.
	Culture theories	Cultural evolution theory, cultural anthropology, cultural sociology, cultural economics, contemporary cultural study, etc.
	Other relevant theories	Experience economy, creative industry, copyright industry, modernism, postmodernism, etc.

Source: RGCMS (2009)

modernization theory in the field of culture. It includes the general theory, branch theory, and relevant theory (Table 6.57). This part deals with its general theory (Table 6.58), which includes the definition, process, result, dynamics, and model of the cultural modernization. Currently, people have quite limited knowledge about the second cultural modernization and integrated cultural modernization, so the cultural modernization theory in the broad sense has a large room of development.

(1) Definition

Cultural modernization is a manifestation of modernization in the field of culture.

Generally, culture is a complex of knowledge, institution, and ideas that can influence and explain people's way of life, and embodies mankind's pursuit of the true, the good, and the beautiful. In this organic whole, knowledge is its basis, institution serves as its core, and ideas is its soul. Of course, these roles may change in some cases. Culture domain is one of the six fields of human civilization study and involves the creation, production, spread, distribution, service, reservation, and consumption of culture.

The intension: cultural modernization is a frontier change and international competition in the culture field since the Enlightenment in eighteenth century. It includes the formation, development, transformation, and international interaction of modern culture, and creation, selection, spread, and withdrawal of cultural elements, and also involves the international stratification and competition to catch up, reach, and maintain the leading position of the cultural change in the world.

The extension: cultural modernization covers the modernization of cultural behaviors, structure, institution, and ideas, and the modernization of pure culture,

Table 6.58 General theory of cultural modernization in the broad sense

Aspect	Basic content
Definition	Cultural modernization refers to the modernization of the cultural sphere. It is both a form of the cultural change and international completion which have emerged since the Enlightenment in the eighteenth century; a process of formation, development, transformation, and international interaction of modern culture; and a composite course of innovation, selection, spread, and withdrawal of cultural elements, and involves the international stratification and competition to catch up, reach, and maintain the leading position in the cultural change
Process	Cultural modernization is a historical process, including cultural development, cultural transformation, international cultural competition, and change of status in the global cultural arena; including change of cultural life, structure, institution, and ideas; including the world frontier of cultural change and the process of reaching the world frontier, and so on. Between the eighteenth and twenty-first centuries, the frontier track of cultural modernization can be divided into two stages. The first cultural modernization refers to the profound change and transformation from agricultural to industrial culture and from feudal to civic culture, featuring rationalization, professionalization, being scientific, commercialization, etc.; and the second cultural modernization involves the profound change and transformation from industrial to knowledge culture and from material to ecological culture, currently featuring the cultural industrialization, networking (wide use of Internet), diversification, globalization, etc. Integrated cultural modernization means the coordinate development of the two stages. New changes will occur in the twenty-second century. It follows the ten basic principles of modernization (Table 2.15)
Result	The formation of cultural modernity, particularity, and diversity and side effect; enhancement of quality of cultural life and cultural competitiveness in the international arena; development of cultural facilities and the cultural industries; self-emancipation and across-the-board development of human being; remaining and still effective traditional value, etc. The first cultural modernization results in the forming of the first cultural modernity, particularity, and diversity, and its side effect includes indifference between people, etc.; the second stage leads to the second cultural modernity, particularity, and diversity, and its side effect includes the Internet dependence, etc.
Dynamics	Driving forces for cultural modernization include innovation, exchange, competition, adaptation, national interests, market demand, etc. The impetus models include innovation drive, two-wheel drive, joint effect, four-step super circulation, composite interaction, spread of innovation, spillover of innovation, competition drive (Table 2.20), etc. The driving forces vary in different countries and stages and in developed and developing countries
Model	Cultural modernization advances through diverse path and models, features starting point dependence and path dependence, and is affected by historical tradition, development level of the specific country, and the international system. The basic paths for the twenty-first century include paths of the first cultural modernization, the second cultural modernization, and the integrated cultural modernization. And each of these basic paths has many subpaths and development models

Note: There is not uniform definition about modern culture. Generally, modern culture includes the cultures of the industries society (primary modern culture) and of the knowledge society (hypermodern culture), and the latter is sometimes called the postmodern culture
Source: RGCMS (2009, 2010)

cultural industries, cultural facilities, and other aspects of culture, the modernization of cultural activities, content, form, system, and cultural management, the modernization in specific stages, at different levels and in each sector of culture, and the interaction between culture and modernization in other aspects, as well as the change of modernization distribution in different times and spaces.

Generally, cultural modernization refers to the world frontiers of cultural change and the process and action to reach these frontiers and includes the transformation from traditional to modern culture and the transformation from modern to post-modern culture, enhancement of cultural creativity, and improvement of the quality of cultural life; the development of cultural facilities and cultural industries, and self-emancipation and full development of mankind.

It is the intersection between cultural change and modernization (Fig. 6.25). There are three criteria for judging the cultural modernization: whether it can help the emancipation and development of the productivity without damaging the natural environment, can promote the justice and progress of the society without impeding the economic growth, and can promote the liberation and full development of peoples while maintaining social harmony. Cultural change can be regarded as cultural modernization only when it meets these criteria.

Cultural modernization has three sources: first, the worthy part of traditional culture to be inherited and carried forward, such as language, art, literature, and science and technology; second, partly denial and reversion of the traditional culture, such as developing the good part of cultural institution and ideas while discarding or reversing the improper part; and third, cultural innovation and cultural exchange, including knowledge innovation, institutional innovation, creation of new ideas, cultural spread, etc.

Cultural modernization of different types has different features and different requirements in different stages. For example, the basic requirements of the first cultural modernization include the professionalization, rationalization, and commercialization of culture and the driving the economic development, etc.; those of the second cultural modernization include industrialization, diversification, democratization, and the full development of people (Table 6.59).

The conceptual model of cultural modernization (Table 6.60) includes as follows: first, cultural development refers to cultural advance, positive adaptation, and the intersection between the two; second, cultural modernization is the

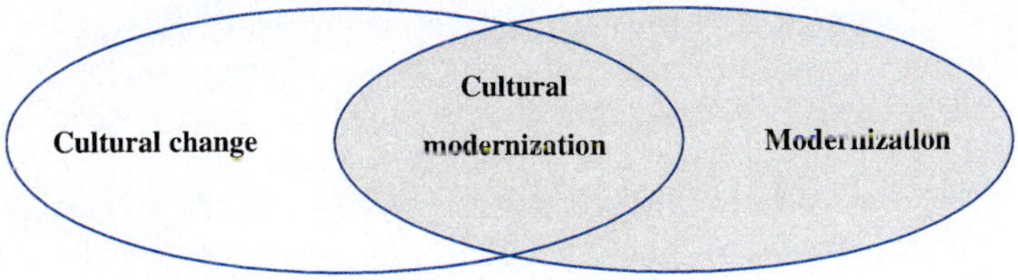

Fig. 6.25 Cultural modernization is the intersection of cultural change and modernization. Source: RGCMS (2009)

Table 6.59 Basic requirements of cultural modernization

First cultural modernization	Second cultural modernization
Professionalization: differentiation, specialization, and autonomy of culture	Industrialization: development of cultural commodities and service, cultural production and trade
Rationalization: secularization of culture, development of science, and self-discipline	Diversification: protection of cultural heritages, cultural diversity, and ecological culture
Commercialization: commercialization of cultural production and spread	Democratization: the central position of people, networking (wide use of Internet), and cultural liberty
Promoting economic development: help to liberate and enhance the productivity	All-round development of people: improvement of citizens' quality and more choices available for individuals

Source: RGCMS (2009)

Table 6.60 Conceptual model of cultural modernization

Item	Main content
Hypothesis 1	Cultural advance means the cultural change that can help the enhancement of the productivity, social progress, and the full development of people
Hypothesis 2	Positive adaptation of culture refers to cultural adjustment that can help the enhancement of the forces of production, social progress, and the full development of people
Hypothesis 3	Cultural transformation indicates the transition from agricultural to industrial culture and the transition from industrial to knowledge culture
Hypothesis 4	The change of international cultural status means that the position of a specific country's cultural creativity and quality of its cultural life varies in the global arena
Inference 1	Cultural development = cultural advance + positive adaptation of culture + cultural advance × positive adaptation of culture
Inference 3	Cultural modernization = cultural development × cultural transformation × international cultural competition and the change of international cultural status

Source: RGCMS (2009)

intersection of cultural development, cultural transformation, and international cultural competition and status change.

(2) Process

Cultural modernization is a complete, diverse, and long-lasting historical process. The process of cultural modernization can be divided into two types: frontier process and catch-up process with both common and different features. Between the eighteenth and twenty-first centuries, its frontier process can be divided into two stages (Table 6.61) with different connotations (Fig. 6.26).

The first cultural modernization refers to the transformation from agricultural to industrial culture, including the transition from authoritarian to democratic culture, feudal to civil culture, superstitious to scientific culture, dependent to professional culture, familial to welfare culture, and rural to urban culture.

Table 6.61 Periodic table of cultural modernization—change of cultural forms

Stage (approx. starting year)	Cultural change and forms (by examples)	Cultural modernization
Age of knowledge culture	*Culture of knowledge society (knowledge culture)*	
Transition stage (2050)	Global, universal culture, and experience culture	*The second cultural modernization*
Mature stage (2020)	Bionic, natural culture, and cultural humanization	Industrialization, networking, globalization, postmodern culture, knowledge, and ecological culture
Developing stage (1992)	Cyberculture, cultural industrialization, diversification	
Start stage (1970)	High technology, ecological, postmodern culture	
Age of industrial culture	*Culture of industrial society (industrial culture)*	
Transition stage (1946)	Modern culture, scientific philosophy, S&T revolution	***The first culture modernization*** Professionalization, rationalization, popularization, modern culture, industrial and material culture
Mature stage (1914)	Modern literature and art, leisure culture, commercialization	
Developing stage (1870)	Technological revolution, modern philosophy, rationalization	
Start stage (1763)	The Enlightenment, the French Revolution, professionalization	
Age of agricultural culture	*Culture of agricultural society (agricultural culture)*	
Transition stage (AD 1500)	The Renaissance, religious reform, scientific revolution	(Agricultural revolution, agricultural culture)
Mature stage (AD 618)	Autocratic, religious culture, art and literature, education	
Developing stage (500 BC)	Feudal culture, religion, philosophy, art, and science	
Start stage (3500 BC)	Slavery, written language, city, country, knowledge	
Age of primitive culture	*Culture of primitive society (primitive culture)*	
Transition stage (10,000 years ago)	Horticulture and pasturage, handicraft, religion, and patriarchy	(Primitive agricultural revolution, slash-and-burn)
Mature stage (40,000 years ago)	Tool making, art, witchcraft, and matriarchy	
Developing stage (200,000 years ago)	Processing of stone tools, division of labor, gens by blood	(Tool-making revolution, primitive culture)
Start stage (2,500,000 years ago)	Invention of stone tools, use of fire, bands, primitive knowledge	

Note: The time of chronology and the features were based on the frontier track of the change of world culture
Source: RGCMS (2009)

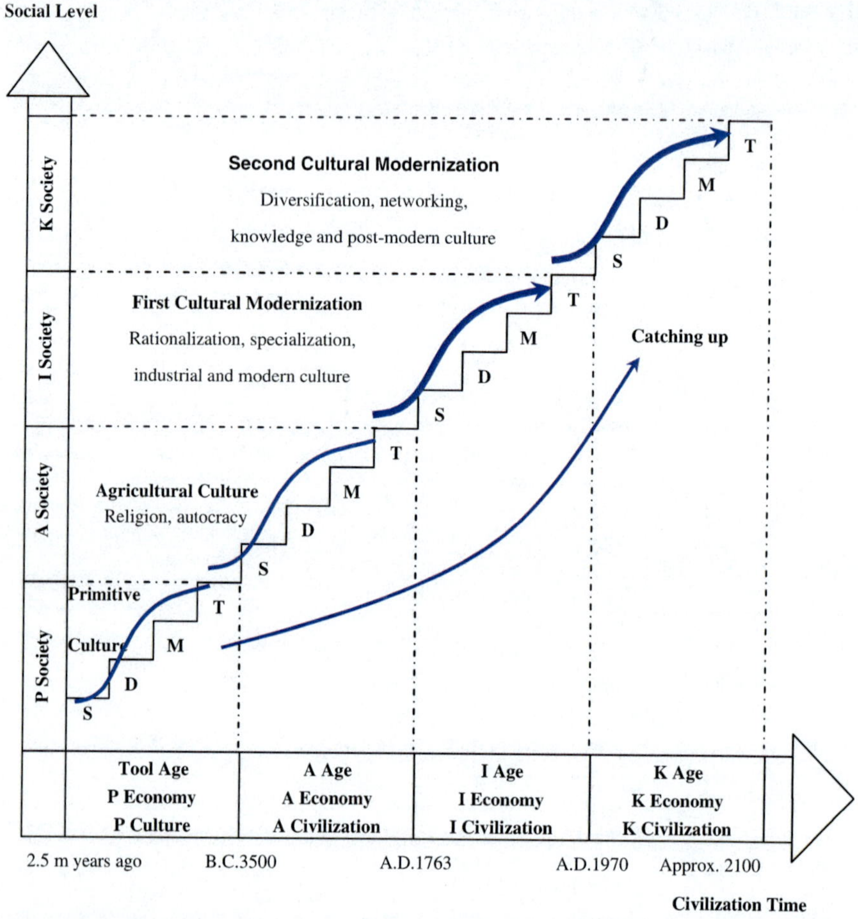

Fig. 6.26 Coordinates of cultural modernization. Note: P, A, I, and K refer to primitive, agricultural, industrial, and knowledge, respectively. S, D, M, and T refer to the start, developing, mature, and transition phase, respectively. The civilization time was the time based on the track of the forerunner of the civilization. Source: RGCMS (2009)

The second cultural modernization refers to the transformation from industrial to knowledge culture, including the transition from material to ecological culture, real physical to digital cyberculture, authoritative to civil culture, machine to humane culture, national to global culture, cultural convergence to cultural diversity, etc.

The two stages have different features (Table 6.62). If the first stage is a process of cultural differentiation, including the separation of culture from the whole society and the division insider culture, the second stage is a combination process with cultural integrating with and penetrating into economy and society and the cultural industries becoming a pillar industry.

Table 6.62 Features of the two stages

First cultural modernization	Second cultural modernization
Cultural differentiation, rationalization, secularization, specialization, professionalization, commoditization, individualization, popularization, systematization, concentration, bureaucratization, humanism, the development of scientific culture, etc.	Cultural dedifferentiation, industrialization, diversification, networking, digitalization, decentralization, ecologicalization, globalization, humanization, democratization, green and environmental friendly, intellectualization, and more new features will pop up

Source: RGCMS (2009)

If the first cultural modernization is the preliminary cultural modernization and a transition from traditional to primary modern culture, the second cultural modernization is the advanced cultural modernization and a transition from primary modern to the hypermodern culture. Integrated cultural modernization is the coordinate development of the twice cultural modernization. Cultural modernization will undergo new changes in the twenty-second century.

Cultural modernization has 12 features: being partially predictable, nonlinear, partially reversible, path dependence, multipaths, diverse, unbalanced, asynchronous, nonisolated, systematic, staged, and global.

Cultural modernization follows ten general principles of modernization (Table 2.15).

(3) Result

The outcomes of cultural modernization include the forming of cultural modernity, particularity, diversity, and side effect (Table 6.58).

The first cultural modernization results in forming of the first cultural modernity, particularity, and diversity and is the formation and spread of industrial and the modern culture, including cultural differentiation, democratic, scientific, popular, urban, welfare, and professional culture. Its side effect includes the indifference between people.

The second cultural modernization leads to the forming of the second cultural modernity, particularity, and diversity and is the forming and spread of knowledge and postmodern culture, including cultural dedifferentiation, cultural industrialization, cultural diversity, cyberculture, ecological culture, cultural innovation, individualized and global culture, etc., at present. Its side effect includes the excessive dependence on Internet. This stage will keep developing in the future.

From the perspective of cultural policies, the cultural modernization causes profound changes in six aspects: the completion of two cultural transformations; enhancement of cultural creativity and better quality of cultural life; change of cultural content and structure, different in cultural institution and ideas; liberation and full development of people; the change in international cultural system and the fact that cultural industries have become a pillar industry of the world economy, and so on. All these changes take place in pure culture, cultural facilities, cultural industries, and other aspects of the culture.

Theoretically, cultural modernization has three goals: to finish the first cultural modernization, to complete the second cultural modernization, and to catch up with, reach, and maintain the world frontier of the cultural change. Among them, the third one is dynamic and is applicable to limited subjects. For example, there is a world-leading level for cultural facilities, cultural industries, science and technology, information, sports, and tourism, but no for language, art, and religion.

From the perspective of policymaking, the cultural modernization also has three objectives, that is, to safeguard the cultural rights of a country or a nation, improve the quality of citizens' cultural activities and life, and enhance cultural creativity, cultural competitiveness, and cultural influence.

It is the ultimate goal of modernization and the key objective of the cultural and individual modernization to liberate and fully develop the human being. According to UNDP, human development is one of the people, by the people, and for the people (UNDP 2000).

Since the 1950s, the correlation between the results and objectives of cultural modernization has been gradually intensified both in the developed and developing countries.

(4) Dynamics

The dynamic factors and mechanism of cultural modernization are different (Table 6.58).

Generally, innovation is the fundamental source for cultural modernization, competition is the incentive for cultural change, adaptation is the adjustment made to deal with the change of the external environment, exchange can promote the cultural modernization, national interests direct the cultural development, and the market demands determine the development of the cultural industry. Innovation plays a bigger role in developed countries, while in developing countries, economic development and exchange is more important.

The impetus models of cultural modernization include innovation drive, two-wheel drive (Fig. 6.27), associative action (Fig. 6.28), and the spread and spillover of innovation. The driving forces for cultural modernization vary at different stages, in different countries, and during different stages.

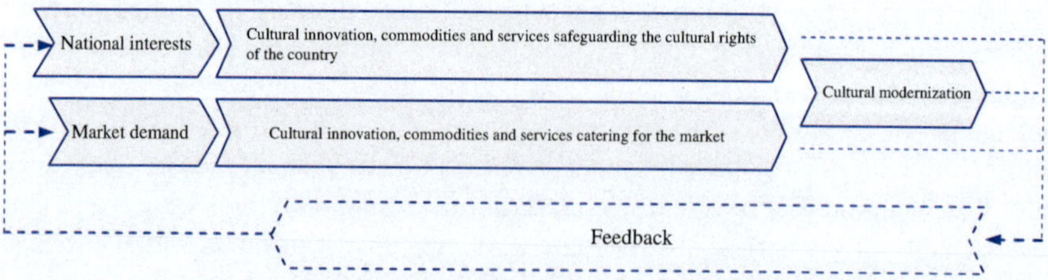

Fig. 6.27 Two-wheel drive model of cultural modernization. Source: RGCMS (2009)

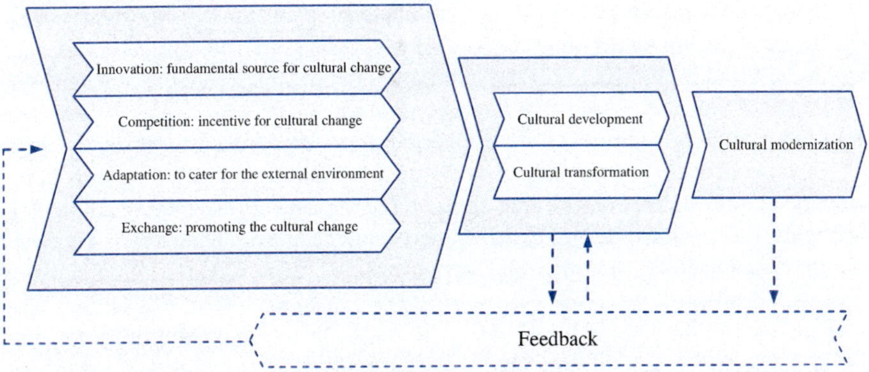

Fig. 6.28 Associative action model of cultural modernization. Source: RGCMS (2009)

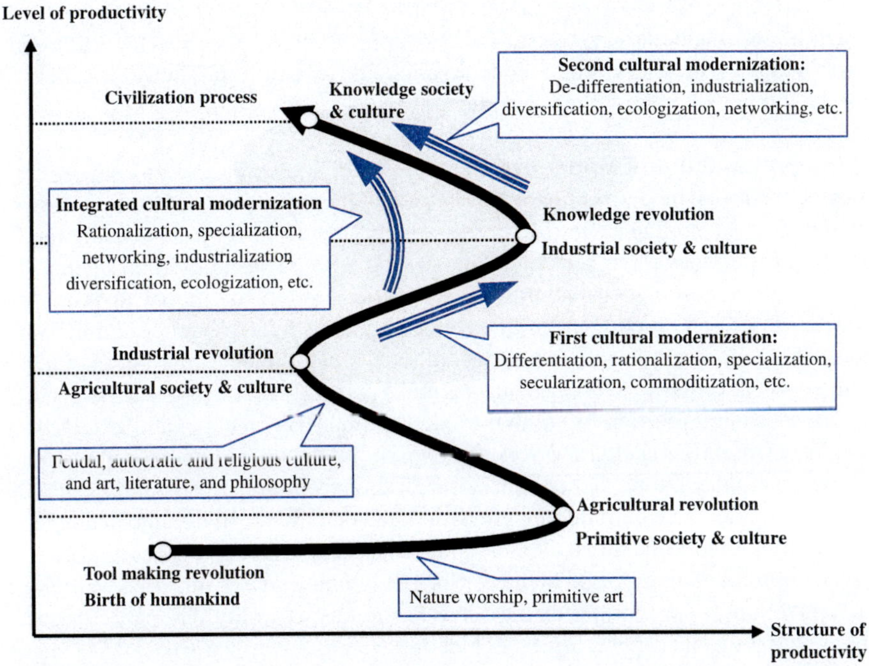

Fig. 6.29 Three paths of cultural modernization in twenty-first century. Note: affected by the networking and ecologization, the first cultural modernization in the twenty-first century may present some new features. The horizontal coordinate represents the labor structure of productivity and is the same as in Fig. 6.12. Source: RGCMS (2009)

(5) Model

There is no one-size-fits all best path for cultural modernization; instead, the cultural modernization follows three basic paths in the twenty-first century (Fig. 6.29).

There is no standard model but only rational selection for cultural modernization. Both successful and failing models may be created in different countries and regions and in different stages of the cultural modernization. These models can be researched, learned, and used as a reference later.

In the past three centuries, the models of cultural modernization differ a lot in developed countries. For example, French model of cultural modernization is both romantic and revolutionary, German model is rational and critical, American model highlights the practical use and the spirit of science, British model is of both commercialism and classic spirit, and Japanese model features both commercialism and Confucianism.

Generally, cultural modernization has different contents and features in specific stages and sectors and at different levels. Theories about the cultural modernization are applicable to the world and national levels but should be adjusted at the regional level.

China Modernization Report 2009: Cultural Modernization Study discusses the principle and methodology of cultural modernization and theories for different stages including the first cultural modernization, the second cultural modernization, and the integrated cultural modernization.

(6) Integrated Cultural Modernization

Integrated cultural modernization is a basic path of the cultural modernization and is suitable for developing countries in the twenty-first century. It is a compound process of the innovation, selection, spread, and withdrawal of cultural elements and the interaction of two cultural transformations (from traditional to primary modern culture and then from primary modern to the hypermodern culture) and constant development to the knowledge culture. It also involves the international competition in which developing countries make painstaking efforts to catch up with the world-leading position of cultural modernization. Its contents include the cultural industrialization, cultural diversity and plurality, Internet culture, professional culture, scientific culture, democratic culture, rational culture, green culture, etc.

Through integrated cultural modernization, the cultural creativity, the quality of cultural life, cultural facilities, and cultural industries shall reach the cutting-edge level of cultural modernization in the world. The ultimate goal of integrated cultural modernization is the forming of the second cultural modernity and particularity. The principles of its driving forces include innovation drive, two-wheel drive, and associative action; besides, the national goal, cultural globalization, and the international cultural exchange also impose great influence on the comprehensive cultural modernization.

The integrated modernization, as a new path, shall coordinate two transformations, namely, from agricultural to industrial culture, and then finally to the knowledge culture (Fig. 6.30).

If we see this planet as a physical homeland, culture is a spiritual one for the humankind, and cultural life is people's mental life; and if economic modernization is the modernization of people's material life, then cultural modernization is that of people's mental life and that of people's spiritual homeland. As the materials are

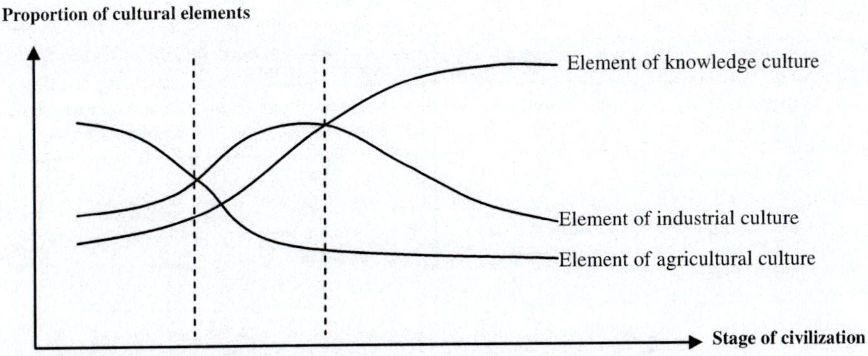

Fig. 6.30 Diagram of integrated cultural modernization. Source: RGCMS (2009)

becoming dramatically abundant, the importance of mental life is increasingly highlighted. In the twenty-first century, cultural innovation, industries, and modernization will play a bigger and bigger role.

6.5 Ecological Modernization

Humans have been living in the natural environment since their birth, which supports men's existence and provides men material and cultural services (MEA 2005). Ecological modernization is one kind of the interaction between modernization and natural environment and the ecological transformation of modernization. It includes staged and stratified ecological modernization, and that of different ecological subfields and sectors (Fig. 6.31).

6.5.1 Studies

The ecological modernization study is part of modernization study related to natural environment. It can start with the early twentieth century and be conducted from the three perspectives of the past, the present, and the future.

6.5.1.1 Research Paradigm

The objects of ecological modernization research refer to the interaction between modernization and natural environment and ecological transformation, including the formation and development of ecological civilization, the modernization in six fields such as ecological effect, and ecological modernization at six levels such as the world. The content of the research includes the modernization of ecological behavior, structure, institution, and ideas, as well as the process, result, dynamics, and model of ecological modernization, which together form the structural matrix as follows (Table 6.63). The research objects also cover the ecological modernization at different stages and of different sectors.

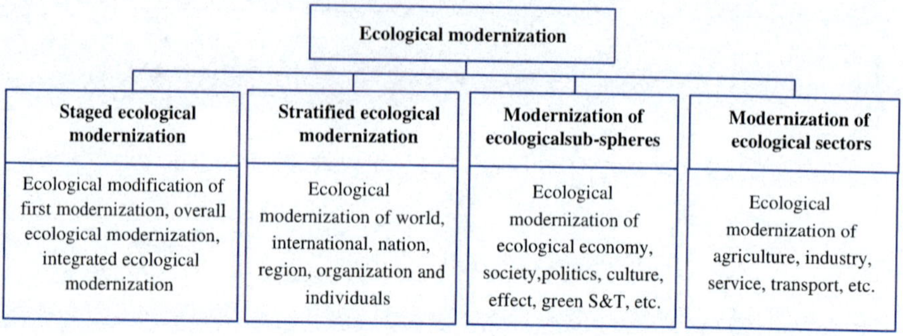

Fig. 6.31 Objects of ecological modernization study. Note: overall ecological modernization refers to that occurring in the process of second modernization, while integrated ecological modernization occurs in the process of integrated modernization, which is also a basic path of ecological modernization for developing countries. Green S&T plays a role in scientific and technological modernization and is the result of the ecological modernization in the S&T sector. Considering its importance in the process of ecological modernization, we can upgrade it as a subdomain of ecological modernization

Ecological modernization is the beneficial coupling of modernization and natural environment and the ecological interaction and transformation of modernization. Ecological interaction refers to the interaction between modernization and natural environment, which might be beneficial to both parties, favorable to only one party or detrimental to both, while ecological transformation refers to that of modernization and civilization, where the mode of modernization and civilization transforms from neglecting and controlling natural environment to valuing and protecting natural environment, including the environment-friendly changes of human behavior, structure, institution, and ideas caused by the modern ecology and environmental awareness.

Ecological modernization research is a subdomain of modernization research, the methods of which can be applied here too. It covers the whole process or a certain stage, the whole world, countries, or regions.

There are abundant methods applicable to ecological modernization research, such as modeling, case study, statistical analysis, quantitative evaluation, qualitative analysis, comparative analysis, social survey, experimental observation and measurement, time-series analysis, cross-sectional analysis, process analysis, coordinate analysis, etc. The relatively influential research methods are the pressure-state-response (PSR) model (Fig. 6.32), the analysis of social metabolism and material flow, ecological footprints, index of real progress, industrial ecology, ecological system evaluation and the coordinate analysis of ecological modernization, etc.

In the PSR model, pressure refers to the environmental pressure imposed by human activities, state refers to the state of environment and resources, and response refers to that of governments, enterprises, and individuals to the environmental state, the three of which form a feedback adjustment cycle. The environment and the economy, the environment and the society, and the economy and the society interact with each other in all human activities. The analysis of material flow

Table 6.63 Matrix of ecological modernization study

Content		Object		
		Ecological civilization	Ecological effect, economy, society, politics, culture, green S&T	The ecological transition of world, nation, region, organization, and individuals
		Ecological modernization	Ecological modernization in the six subspheres	Ecological modernization at the six levels
Element	Behavior Structure Institution Idea	Modernization of ecological behavior, structure, institution, and ideas	Modernization of ecological behavior, structure, institution, and ideas in the six subspheres	Modernization of ecological behavior, structure, institution, and ideas at six levels
Aspect	Process Result Dynamics Model	Process, result, dynamics, and model of the ecological modernization	Process, result, dynamics, and model of ecological modernization in the six subspheres	Process, result, dynamics, and model of ecological modernization at six levels

Note: Ecological civilization refers to a green civilization which is environment-friendly and ecological reasonable. It is part of or a representation of knowledge civilization. Ecological effect refers to the changes of natural environment, resources, and ecological system caused by modernization. Ecological economy refers to a green economy which is environment-friendly and ecological reasonable, including ecological agriculture, industries, and green services. Ecological society refers to a green society which is environment-friendly and ecological reasonable, including ecological cities and rural areas, green energies, and transportation and ecological safety. Ecological politics refers to green politics which is environment-friendly and ecological reasonable, including environmental legislation, taxation, and politics. Ecological culture is a green culture which is environment-friendly and ecological reasonable, including ecological and environmental awareness, etc. Green S&T is one which is environment-friendly and ecological reasonable, including green techniques, manufacture, process, clean production, etc. The ecological behavior, structure, institution, and ideas mentioned in the theory of ecological modernization refer to those related to ecological interaction and transformation in the process of modernization. The content of ecological modernization research also includes the ecological modernization at different stages and of different sectors (industries), frontier analysis, trend analysis, frontier process analysis, catch-up process analysis, and the interaction between elements of ecological modernization and different fields

Source: RGCMS (2007)

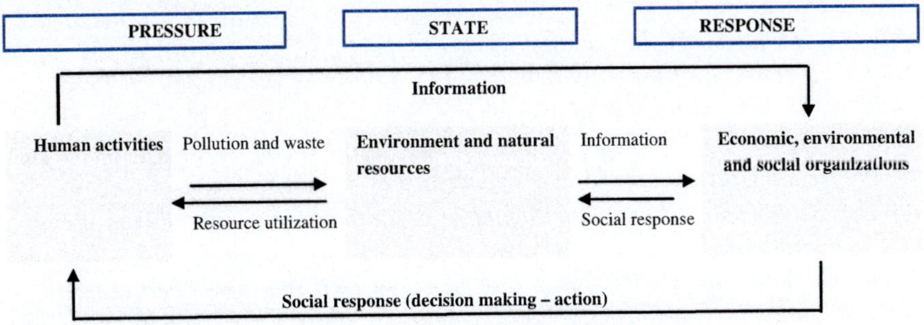

Fig. 6.32 The simplification of the PSR model of OECD. Note: it is the short representation of the PSR model of OECD (2003)

includes that of total material flow as well as that of material life cycle in the process of economy.

6.5.1.2 Brief History of Ecological Modernization Study

A number of schools studying the relationship between resources, environment, ecology, economy, and the society have emerged since the 1970s, with a huge amount of literature accumulated. Among all the theories, the ecological modernization theory (Huber 1982, 1985) proposed by a German scholar in the 1980s has become a major theory in the environmental sociology in developed countries (Mol and Sonnenfeld 2000). Ecological modernization research focuses on the interaction between and the changes of science and technology, economy, society, and natural environment in the process of modernization, instead of evolution of natural environment, ecological system, or ecology.

(1) Origin

Ecological modernization research is originated from environmental movements and reforms. Essentially, ecological modernization is an efficiency-oriented solution to environmental problems (Hajer 1995) and a reconstruction of the environmental agenda. In the 1970s, environmental movements exerted huge influence upon the society, and environmental protection was considered the burden of enterprises and governments. It was difficult for them to choose between environmental protection and employment and growth. In the late 1980s and the 1990s, the concept of ecological modernization was introduced in the policy agenda of developed industrial countries as a new option. According to the concept, under the guidance of ecological principles, the coordinated development of environmental management and economic growth is possible (Young 2000).

(2) Stages

According to the Dutch scholar Arthur P. J. Mol, ecological modernization research can be divided into three stages as the follows (Mol and Sonnenfeld 2000; Mol 2001):

Stage I (Early 1980s). (1) Emphasizing the role of technological innovation, especially that in industrial production in environmental reform; (2) criticizing the bureaucracy and low efficiency; (3) supporting the role and impetus of the market in environmental reform; (4) systematic view on social organizations and social conflicts; (5) analysis at the national level.

Stage II (Late 1980s to mid 1990s). (1) Relatively weakening the role of technological innovation; (2) placing more emphasis upon the balance between the government and the market; (3) placing more emphasis upon the role of system and culture and the role of social organizations in environment-caused social transformation; (4) focusing on the comparative studies of the industrial production in OECD countries.

Stage III (Since mid 1990s). Extending the research theoretically and geographically, including the transformation of consumption, study of non-OECD countries, and global process of ecological modernization. It is called ecological modernization age by some people. The research priorities in this stage include: (1) challenges imposed by environmental problems upon the society, technology and economic reform; (2) the transformation of core social systems of modernity, such as those of science and technology, production and consumption, politics and governance and market, at various levels such as regional, national and global; (3) locating in the field of science, differentiating from antiproductivity, anti-industrialization, postmodernism, strong social structuralism and a number of schools of new radicalism.

(3) Disputes

Disputes over ecological modernization have never ceased to exist since the theory came into being (Mol and Sonnenfeld 2000).

First of all, disputes over modernizations. In the 1970s, there was a powerful thought in the environmental movements and among the sociologists in western Europe, known as the theory of antimodernization, anti-industrialization, and antiproductivity, according to which, pollution and damages to resources were the result of industrialization and environmental and ecological degeneration was the evidence of dying modernization process. However, according to ecological modernization theory, some fundamental transformation of modernization models is necessary, the aim of which is to repair its structural defects. It is these defects that cause serious environmental damages. But by doing so, it does not mean to abandon modern social systems. Modernization is not outdated, but structural transformation is required.

Secondly, disputes over postmodernism. Some postmodernists place much emphasis upon postmaterial value and are against or critical toward modernization. However, according to the ecological modernization theory, we cannot weaken the material power of the society and must continue modernization, problems caused by modernization can be solved by the deepening of modernization, and likewise, problems of industrialization can be solved by superindustrialization.

Thirdly, disputes over radical ecologicalism. According to ecologicalism, modern value or modern production and consumption models need essential changes and real green value, green movements and politics are also needed. Some hold that ecological modernization is the reconciled product of environmental reform, which does not place environmental goals as its priority, but place them with economic goals as important factors the government has to consider in the process of policymaking. Some other people hold that the theory of ecological modernization is a sort of excuse for the government's conservative environmental policies.

Fourthly, disputes over ecological equality. It is thought that ecological reform and eco-friendly housing, vehicles, food, and services are all prepared for the rich, while the poor have to face the problems such as the environmental tax of food, energies, and water, which widens the social gap. The theory of ecological modernization focuses on the environmental reform and ecological transformation in developed countries, the latter of which also contributes to the widening inequality of international community. The deep ecology requires equal treatment of animals. The environment-related social inequality has become the hotspot of disputes.

6.5.1.3 Facts and Experience About Ecological Modernization

Ecological modernization, starting from the 1970s, is a representation form of modernization. Since the industrial revolution and political revolution in the eighteenth century, there have been four waves of modernization in the frontier. Ecological modernization is part of the fourth wave of modernization and also an ecological transformation of modernization. Facts of and experience gained from ecological modernization have been systematically analyzed in *China Modernization Report 2007: Ecological Modernization Study* (RGCMS 2007) as follows.

(1) Facts

The four aspects of the historical facts of ecological modernization will be discussed here.

First, basic facts in the field of ecological effects. Since the eighteenth century, the size and density of population have been increasing, so are the fossil energy production and ecological footprints; the cultivated land, grassland, and freshwater resource per capita have been decreasing, so are the forest resource per capita and biological diversity; the iron and steel production per capita has dropped down after a period of growing, so has the air pollution per capita and BOD (biochemical oxygen demand) of industrial wastewater per capita; mineral production per capita varies in different regions; the green gas emission is increasing generally but decreasing in some countries. Since the nineteenth century, the number of nature reserves has been increasing. In 1998, an article was published in the journal *Science* describing the influence of human activities upon the Earth: *about one third to half of the land has been changed by human activities; since the industrial revolution, the volume fraction (amount) of carbon dioxide in the atmosphere has increased by 30%; the total of artificial nitrogen fixation has surpassed that of natural nitrogen fixation; the fresh water on the land surface utilized by human beings has reached more than 50% of the total that can be utilized; in the past nearly 2,000 years, about one fourth of the bird species on the Earth have disappeared and about two thirds of the fishery resources in the oceans have been over exploited or used up* (Lubchenco 1998).

Secondly, basic facts in the field of ecological economy. Since the eighteenth century, the efficiency of material production and land production has increased, while the proportion of material economy has dropped down; the material output value per capita, grain yield per unit, and modern organic agriculture have increased. Since the twentieth century, the utilization of fertilizers per hectare in agriculture has first increased and then decreased, so have the economic energies density, resource density, and the carbon dioxide emission per unit of GDP; the waste recycling rate has climbed up, the consumption proportion of natural resources varies from place to place, and the phenomena of Environmental Kuznets Curve (EKC) have also increased. EKC refers to the inverted U-shaped curve illustrating the relationship between environmental degeneration and per capita income.

Thirdly, basic facts in the field of ecological society. Since the eighteenth century, the proportion of material labor has declined. Since the nineteenth century, per capita service income has risen, so has the proportion of population living a long life and the number of safe drinking water and sanitation facilities in urban and rural areas. Since the twentieth century, the urban wastewater treatment rate has ascended, so has the per capita urban waste; the urban air pollution has first increased and then decreased, while the energy utilization efficiency has first decreased and then increased; the environmental risks vary from place to place.

Fourthly, comprehensive facts in the field of ecological modernization. Since the twentieth century, ecological efficiency and structure have undergone continuous change, so has ecological system and ideas; ecological transformation is highly imbalanced and asynchronized; international environmental agreements and international pollution transfer have global influence; economic development is not obviously related to many per capita natural resources; the production and the consumption models of natural resources vary from variety to variety and from place to place. In the past over 20 years, developed countries have witnessed continuous economic growth and substantially improved environment, and the decoupling rate between national economic to environmental indicators has reached 52% in organization of economic cooperation development (OECD 2002).

(2) Technical Path

The efficiency and effect of human economic activities are closely related to techniques applied. Scientific and technological development is an ever evolving process. In different historical stages throughout the human civilization, there are different dominating techniques with different impacts upon the environment. Due to the technical progress of human beings, there is a technical path in the historical evolvement of ecological modernization. Since the development of the world does not synchronize with each other, we can find the coexistence of different techniques in a certain historical section, which leads to the diversified sectional features of technological influence and staged time-series features of ecological modernization.

For instance, in the agricultural civilization age, agricultural techniques including irrigation agriculture and water conservancy techniques, as well as handicraft and mining techniques, dominated the human society. The major consequence caused by then economic activities to the environment was land degradation in general. Mechanization and electrification in the industrial age led to the large-scale industrial production, whose influence upon the environment was extended to include air pollution and river pollution, etc. In the knowledge age, economic globalization and the development of information technology and biotechnology contribute to environmental management and climate change becoming a global issue.

(3) Ecological Modernization and Ecological Institution

It was in the industrial revolution period when environmental problems drew social attention; it was not until the 1970s when they drew global attention. Legislation and systems on environment can be traced back to the period of industrial revolution. For instance, Britain, the pioneer of industrial revolution, began environmental legislation as early as in the early nineteenth century. Since the nineteenth century, there have been four stages of the development of ecological and environmental systems. Particularly in the past over 20 years, there have appeared two trends of the world environmental legal systems: one is the drastic increase of the number of environmental legislation and international environmental agreements; the other is the growth of environmentalist nongovernmental organizations (NGOs) which have become the actual force of international environmental protection (Allenby 1999).

(4) Experience

Ecological modernization has a history of over three decades starting from the first United Nations Conference on Human Environment in 1972. It has been progressing on the way paved by disputes and conflicts. Its progress is substantial especially in developed countries such as some countries in the west and north Europe. The experience of ecological modernization in the past is of instructive significance.

First of all, ecological modernization is a historical necessity. With the increase of global population density, the material demands and waste emission of the human beings will approach the limit of natural environment. Though technological advance can ease part of the environmental pressure, it is not enough. The ecological transformation of the models of human lifestyle and modernization is a necessity. With the globalization and the development of ecological modernization in developed countries, it is inevitable for developing countries to avoid the international and domestic pressure of ecological modernization. Therefore, it has gradually become an irreversible trend of the world.

Secondly, the process of ecological modernization will not go smoothly. It requires the rational dealing of the relationship between economy and environment. People's notions change as the economy fluctuates and the environment changes. Environmental awareness will be challenged in economic downturn, while economic growth will be questioned in environmental crisis. Under different circumstances, people have different options choosing between vehicles and blue sky. Of course, it is best to have both vehicles and blue sky. Ecological modernization has been moving forward in disputes.

Thirdly, ecological modernization requires innovation and learning. It requires eco-friendly technological and system innovation and reasonable structural and model transformation. The key to this process is the change of people's notions. Innovation and idea change is the essence of pioneering countries of ecological modernization, while in those countries lagging behind, learning and idea change is the priority and regional innovation is a necessity too. Therefore, innovation and learning are the two levers to drive ecological modernization.

Fourthly, ecological modernization needs domestic cooperation. As an ecological revolution, it involves the ecologically reasonable transformation of economy, society, politics, culture, environmental management and individual behavior. Governments, enterprises, societies, and environmental protection organizations are all affected by this revolution. They are the subject and the object of the revolution; they need to change not only others but also themselves. Therefore, conflicts and cooperation are inevitable. In the 1960s and 1970s, conflicts and confrontation marked the distinct features of environmental movements. Since the 1980s, though the fight for environmental protection has been going on, cooperation for environment protection has become the mainstream. Cooperation between all people of and democratic participation in the environment agenda has become one of the typical features of ecological modernization.

Fifthly, ecological modernization needs international cooperation. There is only one Earth in the entire solar system, on which all the human beings live. The circulation of atmosphere, water, and carbon and the flow of materials and energies are carried out worldwide, which transcend national borders and different peoples. The concerted cooperation of all the citizens in the world is needed to deal with global climate change, damaged ozone layer, extending air pollution, waste pollution transfer, protection of biodiversity, and the reasonable development and utilization of natural resources and energies. Air is without boundaries. Though global equality and cooperation is more than a slogan than a reality, yet international cooperation in many fields has been carried out.

Sixthly, there is no best model for ecological modernization, which can be classified into the following three categories worldwide.

The first is the European model with idealism as its feature. Most European countries, with relatively small territories, are vulnerable to the impact of international environment. Thanks to the academic tradition of western European countries, they became the first to bring forward the theory of ecological modernization to promote the environmental cooperation in the Europe Union and actively spread it to other parts of the world.

The second is the North American model with pragmatism as its feature. Countries in the North America enjoy large territories and are endowed with abundant natural resources. They were the creator of industrial ecology, promoting environmental legislation and treatment, caring for the protection of biodiversity, and valuing the environmental quality and economic growth, yet with only a few theoretical innovations in this domain.

The third is the model of developing countries with realism as its feature. In developing countries, the promotion of ecological modernization is selectively done according to their respective national conditions, and the government and scientific communities play a larger role in their counterparts in developed countries. Among them, some choose integrated ecological modernization, while some prefer ecological modification of classical modernization.

Since the 1990s, international environmental trade and diplomacy have been very active with the economic growth and environmental improvement in developed countries and the double pressure caused by economic development and environmental protection facing developing countries. In this context, some scholars lay emphasis upon the bearing capacity of resource environment and ecological transformation of world modernization, while some apply double standards, requiring developing countries to protect the environment and save resources on the one hand while allowing developed countries to maintain a relatively high level of resource consumption and per capita ecological footprint.

6.5.1.4 Present State and Prospect of Ecological Modernization

(1) Present State

First of all, general level: by 2004, 58 countries in five continents of the world including Switzerland had entered ecological modernization. Among them, ten countries including Germany were in the developing stage, accounting for 8% of the sample countries, while 48 countries including the United States were in the beginning stage, accounting for 41% of the sample countries.

Secondly, the world frontier: the top ten countries with the highest ecological modernization index in the world in 2004 were ranked as follows: Switzerland, Sweden, Austria, Denmark, Germany, France, Finland, Britain, the Netherlands, and Italy.

Thirdly, progress: by the 1970s, 7 countries including the Netherlands had entered ecological modernization, by the 1980s, 11 countries including Italy, and 40 countries including South Korea by the 1990s.

(2) Prospect

First, the world's advanced level: given the yearly growth rate from 1980 to 2004, the ecological modernization index of developed countries in 2050 will be two times that in 2004 and that in 2100 will be two times that in 2050.

Secondly, the world average level: the average world level is about 50 years behind the average level of developed countries. By 2050, it will be equivalent to the average level of developed countries in 2004.

Thirdly, national distribution: by 2050, there will be over 70 countries entering ecological modernization, and by the end of twenty-first century, most countries in the world will enter ecological modernization, with some completing it and realizing the win–win coexistence of man and nature.

6.5.2 Theories

The ecological modernization theory is a field theory of modernization, covering ecological interaction and transformation in the process of modernization. So far, it consists of two schools: European theory of ecological modernization and ecological modernization theory in broad sense.

6.5.2.1 European Theory of Ecological Modernization

The theory of ecological modernization was generated in Europe in the early 1980s. Over the past more than 20 years, it has developed into a major theory in environmental sociology. It is mainly based on European experience with its researchers mainly from European countries. That is why it is known as European theory of ecological modernization. It is thought that German scholar Huber is the proposer of this theory (Mol 2001).

Since the 1970s, environmental reform and ecological transformation have generally occurred to the social systems and production models in industrial countries. And the theory of ecological modernization proposed in the 1980s was trying to explain and describe the nature, meaning, and impetus of this transformation process (Mol 2001). This school is very active and constantly progress, without unified theoretical definition and statement yet.

(1) Definition

There is no unified definition about ecological modernization yet (Table 6.64). Generally, ecological modernization is used to describe a new model seeking for the economically efficient, social just and eco-friendly development. It is a win–win

Table 6.64 Definitions of ecological modernization

No.	Definitions or explanations	References
1	Ecological modernization is not only an extensive social process of ecological transformation of industrial models of production and consumption but also an inevitable stage of industrial social development, that is, the third stage starting from 1980	Huber (1982), Murphy (2000), Andersen (2002)
2	Ecological modernization is an inevitable process of social transformation from industrial modernity to ecological modernity and industrial society to ecological society	Janicke (1985), Simonis (1988), Cohen (2000), Pataki (2005)
3	Ecological modernization refers to the restructure of macroeconomy and technical structure, advance of eco-friendly technologies, and the transformation of ecological structure, that is, the ecological transformation of production and consumption models	Janicke (1985), Simonis (1989a), Murphy (2000)
4	Ecological modernization is a solution of modernism and technology to environmental problems, which requires the combination of technology and system to solve environmental problems, and realize the win–win game of economy and environment	Hajer (1995)
5	Ecological modernization is often regarded as the synonym of strategic environmental management, industrial ecology, and ecological reconstruction. Ecological reconstruction is a continuous process of transformation and reform of core systems in modern society inspired by ecology and caused by environment	Buttel (2000), Mol (2001)
6	Ecological modernization has three levels of meaning: First, it is an environment-related sociology theory; secondly, it is a new paradigm used to analyze environmental politics and policy change; and thirdly, it truly reveals the actual progress industrial democratic countries have made concerning ecological problems and economic policies	Mol (1995)
7	The theory of ecological modernization describes the process of practical transformation of social practice and systems caused by the environment in industrial societies, including the characteristics, content, and impetus of the process	Mol (2001)

Source: RGCMS (2007)

model for economy and environment and allows the coordination between economic growth and environmental protection and delinking the connection of economic and material flow, and economic growth with environmental pressure.

The core of ecological modernization is prevention, innovation, and structural transformation, with the following six major points:

First, to foster ecological modernity, modern industrial society needs continuous ecological reconstruction, which is caused by ecological and environmental awareness, including social practice, and transformation and reform of systems. Though the present ecological transformation process is not linear or irreversible, yet to some extent, it will last forever and is hard to regress (Mol 2001).

Secondly, modern science and technology and market economy shall play an integrated role in ecological reconstruction. Modern science and technology is the core mechanism in ecological reform. Meanwhile, the importance of economy and market impetus in ecological reform shall be stressed. Industrial innovation encouraged by market economy and promoted by the government can facilitate environmental protection.

Thirdly, deal with environmental challenges correctly. We should regard environmental challenges not only as a crisis but also an opportunity, pollution reduction as a tool to strengthen economic competitiveness instead of an end-user processing technique requiring additional expensive maintenance costs, and ecological modernization as an opportunity for environment-sensitive technology (Christoff 1996).

Fourthly, establish a new environment agenda. To form an environment agenda alliance transcending all kinds of conflicts and interests, managing natural resources and environmental risks, and resolve regular conflicts between economic growth and corresponding environmental management.

Fifthly, formulate forward-looking and preventive environmental policies. Under the guidance of prevention principle, long-term structural change of macroeconomic structure, production and consumption model, technical structure and environmental policies shall be promoted, so is environmental reform.

Sixthly, apply the principle of industrial ecology and establish participatory strategic environmental management (Huber 2000).

(2) Basic Content

According to the Dutch scholar Hajer (1995), there are six changes of ecological modernization.

First of all, the technological change of environmental policies. The model changes from emergency response and treatment to forecast and prevention. Many new technologies are introduced to enable enterprises to integrate environmental awareness into their own cost and risk analysis. New environmental policy tools include the "polluter pays" policy, cost–benefit analysis, risk analysis, the prevention principle, tradable pollution right, pollution tax, resource tax, emission tax, etc.

Secondly, the new role of science in environmental policymaking. Ecology, especially systematic ecology, plays an increasingly important role. Scientists need to study the multiple pressures and critical loads of nature to determine the pollution level that nature is capable of bearing.

Thirdly, the change of microeconomy. The economic notion is changed from merely increasing cost to protect the environment to pollution prevention payment, which promotes the development of low or zero waste techniques and multivalue auditing (success is not measured merely by economic benefits but also by energy and resource utilization). As a result, preventive investment gradually replaces the end treatment technique.

Fourthly, the change of macroeconomy. According to ecological modernism, nature is public goods or resource. In traditional notions, nature was basically regarded as free goods and could be used as the receiver. It emphasizes the protection and management of rare natural resources and encourages ecological pricing, cycling, and technological innovation.

Fifthly, the change of environmental politics and legislation process. Nature is no long regarded as a receiver, and more and more enterprises support pollution prevention. Environmental statistics and relevant analysis lay the foundation for policymaking.

Sixthly, the participatory system of environmental policymaking. Environmental policymaking is an open, participatory process, involving environmental nongovernmental organizations, local residents, environmental evaluation organizations, consultancy organizations, and government organizations to form an environmental agenda alliance. For a new policy agenda, it is often the case that one core concept is brought forward after research, and then other departments make their opinions about it and propose changes to be made in relevant fields.

(3) Basic Features

According to the Dutch scholar Mol (1995, 2001), there are five features of ecological modernization.

First, the change of the role of science and technology in environmental degradation and reform. (1) Science and technology is not only the cause of environmental problems but also the potential and practical tool to deal with and prevent them. (2) Traditional treatment and recovery means will be replaced by more preventive social and technological means, which integrate environmental awareness in the design stage of technological and organizational innovation. (3) The increasing uncertainty of scientific and expert knowledge on the definition and reasons of and solutions to environmental problems will not weaken the role of science and technology in environmental reform.

Secondly, increasing importance of economy, market impetus, and economic organizations. Producers, clients, consumers, financial organizations, insurance companies, application departments, and business associations have increasingly become the social carrier of ecological reconstruction, innovation, and reform, which, together with governmental organizations and new social movements, change the relationship between the government and the market in environmental reform.

Thirdly, multiple changes of the traditional core position of the government in environmental reform. (1) The decentralizing, flexible, and consultation-based governmental management has become a trend, with less top-to-bottom command and control. (2) Nongovernmental organizations participate in and replace the government's traditional tasks to a larger extent. (3) Supranational and international organizations have to some extent weakened the traditional role of the national government in environmental reform.

Fourthly, the position, role, and notion modification of social movements in the process of ecological transformation. Environmentalists' position which was based on antimodernism principle, existed in the margin of core policymaking system or was even excluded from the policymaking system, has been changed; they have participated in the policymaking process of the government and the market to a larger extent. Hence, the bipolar or dual strategy of cooperation and conflict is formed.

Fifthly, the change of unorganized practice and the appearance of new principles in political and social agenda. Both those against economic and environmental interests and those neglecting the importance of environmental awareness are thought legal. It seems that the intergenerational solidarity based on the protection of food has become an undisputable common core principle.

(4) Basic Principles

British scholar Cohen and others have summarized six basic principles of ecological modernization (Cohen 1997, 1998; Picou 1999).

First, the principle of superindustrialization. It is applied in ecological modernization to improve the design program of industrial technologies. It includes the clean, low resource intensive technology and production process, reduces the demands for expensive, additional end techniques, and greatly lessens the relevance between economic development and environmental degradation, to bring modern industry onto a new track.

Secondly, the principle of governmental management. It is noticed in ecological modernization that enterprises' self-management of pollution used to be ineffective, and thus, more strict governmental environmental management is required. Such management will enlarge the first-mover advantage and promote economical and practical green products and innovative production system.

Thirdly, integrated management of pollution. According to ecological modernization, the development of integrated pollution management strategy can prevent the transfer of pollution in the biological environment. This strategy is part of the redesign of the production process and management.

Fourthly, the principle of prevention. According to ecological modernization, industrial departments shall set up prevention plans to deal with hazards to human health and environment more promptly and extensively.

Fifthly, the environmental responsibility system. It is required in ecological modernization process that all the organizations shall establish internal environmental responsibilities. All the public and private departments shall pay attention to environmental quality and include environmental problems into their agenda.

Sixthly, the network of policymaking. It is required in ecological modernization process that extensive organizational network shall be established for policymaking to deal with the ecological confrontation and conflicts of environmental policies. The industrial sector, the government, nongovernmental organizations, and the public shall establish a constructive relationship, to lay a foundation of trust and free information exchange for policymaking.

(5) Major Models

First, technological innovation and the superindustrialization. In the early 1980s, Huber (1982, 1984, 1985) published three articles on addressing environmental problems through superindustrialization. In the third article, he proposes ecological modernization as the solution to environmental problems. According to superindustrialization, the transformation of industrial production can be realized by developing and applying better techniques. According to Huber, the governmental interference is limited, so is the impact of environmental movements upon environmental transformation; what is the most important for the transformation required by ecological modernization is the economic sector and entrepreneurs; ecological economy and economic ecology shall be promoted at the same time.

Secondly, social transformation. According to Huber, ecological modernization is an inevitable stage of in the development of industrial society. There are totally three stages: the sprouting of industrial society (1789–1848), the formation of industrial society (1848–1980), and the transformation of industrial society (since 1980). These three stages were all driven by economy and technology. However, the development in the third stage is also driven by the need for coordination between environment and human activities.

According to Janicke (1985) and Simonis (1988), ecological modernization is an inevitable social transformation process. The development of human society can be divided into three stages: the agriculture-based premodern stage, the industrial production-based modernity stage, and the stage of ecological modernity. The third stage is superindustrialization stage, and the closed manufacturing system and advanced environment techniques will repair the design-defect of modern society (Cohen 2000).

Thirdly, the transition of economic structure and ecologicalization of structure. This is the early point suggested by Janicke (1985), Simonis (1989a, b), etc. Structural transformation of national economy, including technological reconstruction and departmental restructure, and ecological transformation of macroeconomic structure, is the core of ecological modernization. Ecological modernization seeks for structural transformation of macroeconomy, high-level economic development, and industrial sector with low-level environmental impact, and particularly the transformation of macroeconomy from energy and resource intensive industry to service and knowledge intensive industry.

Fourthly, the environmental strategy. Ecological modernization is the change of environmental politics, strategies, and polices (Janicke 1985; Hajer 1995). The changed environmental politics is sometimes called political modernization, including the decentralizing, flexible, and consultation-based governmental management model, with less top-to-bottom command and control; environmental strategies change from remedy strategies to prevention ones; and environmental problems change from the burden of government to major policy topics, with environmental goals integrated into all the governmental policies.

Fifthly, reflexive reconstruction of systems. Ecological modernization is a reflexive reconstruction of system by the modern industrial society to combat ecological crisis (Mol 1995). Such transformation happens in governments and enterprises, with the major aim to combat environmental crisis. Economic systems such as the commodities and labor market, and management systems such as the national government system and the scientific and technological system need ecological transformation, which is the ecological institutionalization of social practices of production and consumption.

Sixthly, the environmental agenda. Ecological modernization is an open, participatory environmental agenda, which means the production, reproduction, discussion, understanding, and acceptance of an environmental thought or notion, which is later turned into a social practice (Hajer 1995).

Seventhly, the model of national capacity (Janicke and Weidner 1997; Andersen 2002). National capacity in ecological modernization, related to national systems and the ability to solve technological problems, depends upon four basic variables: the pressure caused by environmental problems, the ability of consultancy, the ability of innovation, and the effectiveness of strategies.

Eighthly, the model of two categories. Hajer divides ecological modernization into two categories: technology-community ecological modernization and reflexive ecological modernization. The former regards ecological reform as a pure technological and managerial issue, while the latter regards ecological reform as the practice of social learning, cultural politics, and the arrangement of new systems and a democratic process involving the participation of common people.

(6) Actual Effects

Ecological modernization is a theory of environmental sociology which truly reveals the actual progress developed industrial countries have made in environmental reform. So far, developed countries have achieved huge progress in ecological modernization (Pataki 2005).

First, the macroeconomic structure has changed from resource and pollution intensive economic sectors to information and knowledge intensive sectors. It tends to decoupling the connection with energy and material application and move toward a more clean development direction.

Secondly, the government's environmental policies have changed from the model of emergency response, command, and control to one which is participatory and market-oriented.

Thirdly, the environmental awareness of consumers is growing. Their demands affect the operational mode of enterprises.

Fourthly, many environmental nongovernmental organizations change strategies, cooperate with each other to deal with environmental problems, and accept the strategy of reform.

(7) Limits

First of all, European theory of ecological modernization is basically the theoretical description of the environmental reform in Europe, and its international application still needs proof. For example, we should take into consideration factors such as the imperfect democratic system and ecological pressure of agriculture in developing countries which distinguish them from European countries. Secondly, without unified theoretical definition and systematic theoretical presentation, it is not standard or systematic enough. Thirdly, it is still not a mature modernization theory (Seippel 2000); with little connotation in terms of theoretical meaning of modernization, it needs to develop more types, explain more precisely historical phenomena reflected by various kinds of types, and develop more types at the middle level. Fourthly, ecological modernization is only one form of modern social transformation, not all of it.

6.5.2.2 Ecological Modernization Theory in Broad Sense

The ecological modernization theory in broad sense, brought forward by Chinese scholar Chuanqi He, is the extension and application of European theory of ecological modernization in the world and in the modernization sense, and also the application of the second modernization theory in the field of environment. *China Modernization Report 2007: Ecological Modernization Study* (RGCMS 2007) analyzes ecological transformation in the history of human civilization, particularly the period after industrialization, and discusses ecological modernization in Europe and the ecological modernization theory in broad sense. The ecological modernization theory in broad sense includes the general theory, branch theories, and relevant theories (Table 6.65), the first including five aspects such as the definition, process, result, dynamics, and model of ecological modernization (Table 6.66).

(1) Definition

Ecological modernization is the manifestation and ecological interaction and transformation of modernization.

The connotation: ecological modernization is a kind of ecological transformation and international competition of human civilization since the 1970s, including the formation, development, and international interaction of ecological civilization; the innovation, selection, spread, and withdraw of ecological civilization elements; as well as the international competition and stratification to catch up with, reach, and maintain the world's advanced level of development.

The denotation: ecological modernization includes the modernization of ecological behavior, structure, institution, and ideas, includes the modernization of ecological economy, society, politics, culture, effects, and green science and technology, and includes the ecological modernization in different stages, at different levels, and in different fields, subfields, and sectors. It also covers the temporal–spatial distribution change of ecological modernization.

Generally, ecological modernization is the world frontiers of ecological civilization and the process to reach these frontiers and includes the transformation from

Table 6.65 Structure of ecological modernization theory in broad sense

Category	Theory	Main content
General theory	Core theory	Definition, process, result, dynamics, and model of ecological modernization
Branch theories	Stage theory	Ecological modification of first modernization, overall ecological modernization, or integrated ecological modernization
	Stratified study	Ecological modernization at the world, transnational, national, regional, organizational, and individual level
	Subfield study	Ecological modernization in subfields of ecological economy, society, politics, culture, etc.
	Sector study	Ecological modernization in sectors of agriculture, industry, service, transport and energies, etc.
Related theories	Other modernization theories	Reflexive modernization theory, second modernization theory, etc.
	Ecology-related theories	Macroecology, human ecology, environmental science, ecological economy, ecological culture, ecological society, etc.
	Other relevant theories	Organic agriculture, clean production, green energy, green chemistry, green technology, green manufacture, etc.

Note: The theory of overall ecological modernization is an extension of European theory of ecological modernization
Source: RGCMS (2007)

material to ecological civilization, material to ecological economy, material to ecological society, material to ecological politics, and material to ecological culture. It also includes the improvement of ecological quality and effectiveness and the change of ecological structure, system, and ideas, as well as relevant international status.

Modernization and natural environment have always been interacting with each other. In the first modernization process, the interaction is favorable to only one party, with the positive correlation between economic development and environmental degradation, while in the second modernization process, the interaction is mutually beneficial, realizing the win–win result for both economic development and environmental protection.

Ecological modernization consists of four levels of meaning: a historical process, an ecological revolution, an ecological transformation, and international competition. The combination of these meanings may produce multiple operational definitions (Table 6.67).

The basic requirements of ecological modernization are dematerialization, greenization, ecologization, and the gradual decoupling of the connection between economy and environment, or specifically speaking, the dematerialization and greenization of production and consumption, ecologization of economy and society, and the disconnect between modernization and environmental degradation (Table 6.68).

Table 6.66 General theory of ecological modernization in broad sense

Aspect	Basic content
Definition	Ecological modernization refers to the interaction between modernization and natural environment and ecological transformation of modernization; the frontier process of the formation, development, and international interaction of ecological civilization; the process of innovation, selection, spread, and withdrawal of ecological civilization elements; and the international stratification and competition to catch up with, reach, and maintain the world's advanced level of development, etc.
Process	Ecological modernization is a historical process transforming from material to ecological civilization, including the transformation from material to ecological economy, material to ecological society, material to ecological politics, and material to ecological culture, including ecological interaction and transformation, international competition and stratification, as well as the ecological progress and ecologization of economy, society, politics, and culture. It also covers the change of ecological behavior, structure, system, and ideas, as well as the world frontier of ecological civilization and the process of reach world frontier, etc. From the 1970s to the end of twenty-first century, ecological modernization can be divided into the following four stages with 15 major features and ten principles: relatively dematerialization and greening, highly dematerialization and ecologization, a win–win situation for economy and environment, and mutually beneficial coexistence of man and nature
Result	The formation of ecological modernity, particularity, and diversity of ecological modernization. So far, the ecological modernity is featured with the following characteristics: dematerialization, greening, ecologization, the complete decoupling of modernization and environmental degradation, and the mutual coexistence (mutualism) and mutual evolution (coevolution) of man and nature. The basic requirement is the complete delinking of economic growth and environmental degradation and the sound interaction between modernization and natural environment, including profound changes in six aspects
Dynamics	The impetus factors of ecological modernization include quality of life (postmaterial value), ecological safety, knowledge innovation, ecological awareness, movements (civil society) and politics, corporate environmental responsibility, green technological and system innovation, structural dematerialization, internalization of environmental costs, international environmental politics and trade, etc. The drive force mechanism includes innovation drive, three-innovation driving, associative action, complex interaction, innovation spread, innovation spillover, competition drive (Table 2.20), etc.
Model	There are various paths and models for ecological modernization, which depends upon the starting point and path and is affected by the history, geographical conditions, and development level. There are three basic paths in the twenty-first century: overall ecological modernization, integrated ecological modernization, and the ecological modification of classical modernization. Basic models include environmental agenda, industrial ecology, green production and consumption, ecological gardens and zones, green industrialization, green urbanization, etc. Generally, European ecological modernization is more idealistic, North American ecological modernization is more pragmatic, and that of developing countries is more realistic

Source: RGCMS (2007, 2010)

(2) Process

Ecological modernization started from the 1970s, and its frontier track can be divided into four stages (Table 6.69). During the period from the eighteenth to

Table 6.67 Operational definition of general ecological modernization

No.	Definition of general ecological modernization	Characteristics
1.	Ecological modernization is the ecological transformation of modernization, a transition from material to ecological civilization, economy, society, politics, and culture, as well as the change of relevant international status	Emphasis on the process
2.	Ecological modernization is a kind of ecological interaction, and the mutually beneficial interaction and coupling of modernization and natural environment	Emphasis on the interaction
3.	Ecological modernization is an ecological revolution of modernization, including the ecologically reasonable transformation of economy, society, politics, culture, environment, and individual behavior models caused by the overall penetration and wide application of ecology principles	Emphasis on the change
4.	Ecological modernization is a development model, featured with dematerialization, greenization, ecologization, and the win–win situation of economy and environment	Popular definition
5.	Ecological modernization is a historical process where the connection between economic development and environmental degradation is gradually decoupling, and the international competition to catch up with, reach, and maintain the world's advanced level of development	Popular definition

Note: Dematerialization refers to the process of reducing the material and energy density of human activities, such as the dematerialization of production and consumption, etc. Greenization refers to the process of reducing and eliminating the hazards to the environment and human health, to be environmentally acceptable or friendly. Ecologization refers to promoting the ecologically reasonable transformation process of modernization model by adopting the principles of prevention and innovation
Source: RGCMS (2007)

twenty-first century, the frontier process of modernization can be divided into the first and the second modernization, and the latter of which is in accordance with the frontier process of ecological modernization (Table 6.70). However, the ecological effects of these two modernizations are different (Fig. 6.33). The frontier process and catch-up process of ecological modernization process have both common and different features.

Main features of ecological modernization are relatively predictable, global, long-term, complex, progressive, transitional, systematic, gradual, imbalanced, and irreversible world trend, dematerialization, greenization, ecologization, a win–win game for economy and environment, mutualism of man and nature, etc.

Ecological modernization is a part of modernization and follows the ten principles of modernization (Table 2.15). Ecological modernization is relatively independent, with its own basic principles (Table 6.71).

Generally, analysis methods of ecological modernization can be divided into four groups (Table 6.72). First, conceptualization: establishing models of some key concepts in ecological modernization research; second, ecological decision making: relevant models of decision making for ecological modernization; third, systematic adjustment: relevant models of systematic adjustment in ecological

Table 6.68 Basic requirements of ecological modernization

Requirements	Specific content
Dematerialization	High efficiency: improving the productivity of material, resource, energy and land, etc.
	Low cost: lowering economic and social consumption of material, resource, energy and carbon energy, etc.
	High quality: increasing the proportion of service, culture, information, and knowledge in the economy and improving the quality of economy and livelihood
	Low density: lowering economic and social density of material, resource, energy, carbon energy, etc.
Greenization	Toxic free: reducing the production and emission of toxic materials and waste to the environment and human health, detoxification, low-emission and pollution treatment, etc.
	Harmless: reducing the production and emission of harmful materials and waste to the environment and human health, on being harmless, low-emission and environmental treatment, etc.
	Clean: developing environment-friendly technology, clean production, green products, clean energies, green transportation and green lifestyle, lowering emission, etc.
	Healthy: raising the proportion of green elements which are of high quality, eco-friendly, harmless to human body, safe in economy and society, etc.
Ecologization	Prevention principle: developing ecological agriculture, industry, tourism, city and township, and protecting nature and biological resources, etc.
	Innovation principle: eco-friendly knowledge, technological and system innovation, improving ecological effectiveness and ecological culture, etc.
	Recycling economy: raising the rate of recycling, reutilizing, remanufacturing of waste and waste treatment rate, etc.
	Win–win principle: strengthening ecological reconstruction while developing the economy, reducing ecological degradation, the win–win situation for economy and environment, etc.
Decoupling between economy and environment	Decoupling between economy and material: delinking between economic development and the growth of material demands
	Decoupling between economy and resource: delinking between economic development and increasing natural resource consumption
	Decoupling between economy and energies: delinking between economic development and increasing energy consumption
	Decoupling between economy and pollution: delinking between economic development and worsening environmental pollution
	Decoupling between economy and ecological degradation: delinking between economic development and ecological degradation
	Mutually coupling of economy and environment: beneficial coupling of economic development and environmental improvement

Source: RGCMS (2007)

Table 6.69 Four stages of ecological modernization process

Stage	Approx. time	Basic characteristics
Stage I	1970–1990	Pollution treatment, environmental protection, awareness and movement, and relative decoupling between economic development and environmental degradation
Stage II	1990–2020	Relative dematerialization, greenization, ecologization, ecological awareness, and absolute decoupling between economic development and environmental degradation
Stage III	2020–2050	High-level dematerialization, greenization, ecologization, and mutually coupling of economy and environment
Stage IV	2050–2100	A win–win result of modernization and environment, and mutualism and coevolution of man and nature

Source: RGCMS (2007)

modernization process; and fourth, comprehensive evaluation: progress evaluation and supervision evaluation of ecological modernization, etc.

The master equation for environmental pressure is as follows (Tao 2003):

$$\begin{aligned} I &= P \times A \times T \\ &= \text{Population} \times (\text{GDP/Population}) \times (\text{Environmental Pressure/GDP}). \end{aligned}$$

I stands for environmental pressure, P refers to population, A refers to per capita GDP, and T refers to the environmental pressure per unit of GDP.

In the ecological modernization process, green technological innovation, green system innovation, and ecological transition of structure can help ease environmental pressure:

$$I_{\text{ecological modernization}} = I - I_{\text{technological innovation}} - I_{\text{system innovation}} - I_{\text{ecological structure}}.$$

Therefore, we can draw the environmental pressure curve in ecological modernization process as follows (Fig. 6.34).

Ecological modernization requires decoupling between economic growth and environmental pressure, including relative and absolute decoupling.

It is calculated as follows (OECD 2002):

$$\text{DR} = (\text{EP/DF})_{\text{end of the stage}}/(\text{EP/DF})_{\text{beginning of the stage LL}} \quad \text{DI} = 1 - \text{DR}.$$

DR stands for the decoupling rate, EP refers to environmental pressure indicator, DF refers to the factor of impetus (economic factors), and DI refers to decoupling index.

If DR is smaller than 1, economic growth is decoupled from environmental pressure; if DR is larger than or equal to 1, they are not disconnected.

The economy–environment decoupling index has some limits. For example, it cannot distinguish absolute decoupling from relative decoupling. Given negative growth of national economy, we need to carefully examine the meaning of

Table 6.70 Periodic table of ecological modernization: relationship between civilization and environment

Stage (approx. starting year)	Environmental features of civilization process	Environmental change and modernization process
Age of knowledge civilization	*Knowledge and ecological civilization and society*	
Transition stage (2050)	Mutualism and coevolution of man and nature	Second modernization and knowledge revolution. Ecological modernization and revolution; dematerialization, greenization, ecologization, etc.
Mature stage (2020)	High-level dematerialization, greenization, and ecologization	
Developing stage (1992)	Moderate dematerialization, greenization, and ecologization	
Start stage (1970)	Relative dematerialization, greenization, and ecologization	
Age of industrial civilization	*Industrial and material civilization and society*	
Transition stage (1946)	Environmental and resources degradation, pollution treatment	First modernization: industrial revolution. Ecological effects: ecological, environmental and resource degradation, infections, etc.
Mature stage (1914)	Industrial pollution, urban pollution, and domestic pollution	
Developing stage (1870)	Industrial pollution, urban pollution, and deforestation	
Start stage (1763)	Industrial pollution, urban pollution, and deforestation	
Age of agricultural civilization	*Agricultural and material civilization and society*	
Transition stage (AD 1500)	Deforestation, land degradation, and local pollution	Agriculturalization: agricultural revolution. Deforestation and land degradation
Mature stage (AD 618)	Deforestation, land degradation, and local pollution	
Developing stage (500 BC)	Deforestation, land degradation, and local pollution	
Start stage (3500 BC)	Deforestation, land degradation, and natural hazards	
Age of primitive culture	*Primitive culture and society, hunting–gathering society*	
Transition stage (10,000 years ago)	Horticulture, animal husbandry, slash-and-burn cultivation	Primitive agricultural revolution Socialization The birth of human beings: tool-making revolution
Mature stage (40,000 years ago)	Hunting–gathering and the impact of using fire	
Developing stage (200,000 years ago)	Hunting–gathering and the impact of using fire	
Start stage (2,500,000 years ago)	Hunting–gathering, etc.	

Note: Ecological revolution refers to profound changes of modernization caused by overall penetration and wide application of ecological principles
Source: RGCMS (2007)

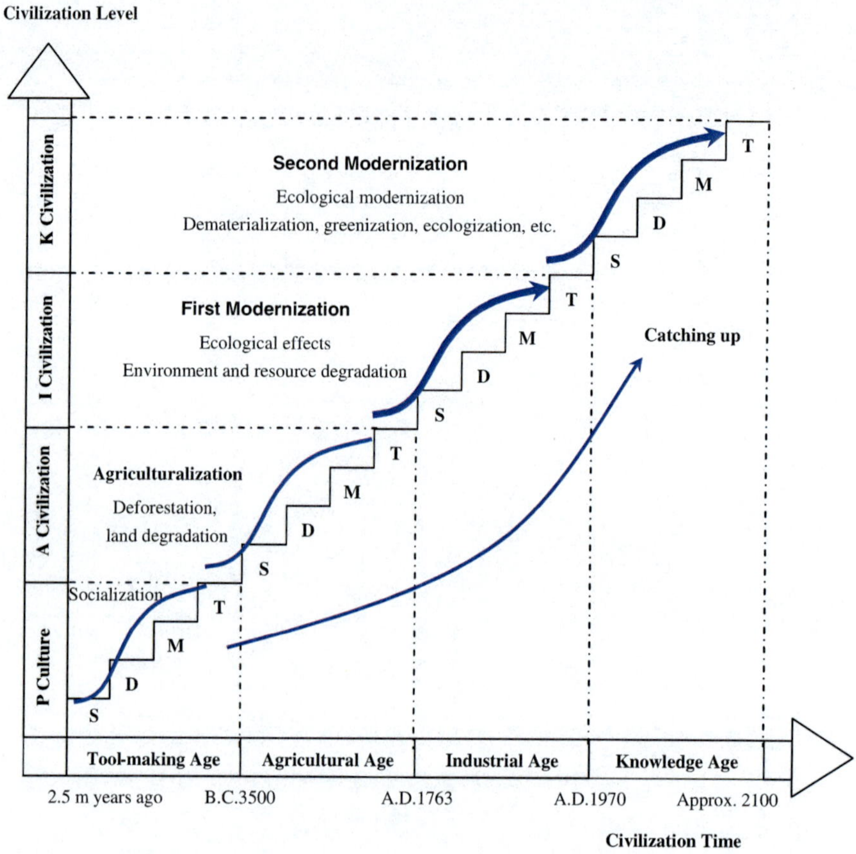

Fig. 6.33 Coordinates of ecological modernization. Note: P, A, I, and K refer to primitive, agricultural, industrial, and knowledge, respectively. S, D, M, and T refer to the start, developing, mature, and transition phase, respectively. The civilization time was the time based on the track of the forerunner of the civilization. Source: RGCMS (2007)

decoupling index. It might be caused by the fact that the influence of resource prices is not reflected, or international trade and environmental pressure transfer, etc. The relationship between economy and environment is more complicated than what the decoupling index shows.

Generally, ecological system is capable of self-adjusting (the ability to recover by adapting itself) which can ease part of the environmental pressure. Ecological construction and environmental protection by human beings can also help ease environmental pressure:

$$I_{\mathrm{ELM}} = P \times I_{\mathrm{P}} - E_{\mathrm{R}} - E_{\mathrm{P}}.$$

Table 6.71 Ten principles of ecological modernization

Principles	Basic content
Prevention	Environmental governance combined treatment with prevention and giving priority to prevention
Innovation	Knowledge, technological, and system innovation form the core mechanism to environmental problems
Efficiency	Improving resource and energy utilization efficiency and ecological efficiency are an important approach to solve environmental problems
Unequivalence	Given the same environment, resource, and economic element, their value and meaning vary in different countries and different periods
Dematerialization	Lowering the material and energy consumption and density in economy and society, improving the efficiency and quality of economy and livelihood
Greenization	Detoxification and innocuity of models and structures of production and consumption, economic and social behaviors, reducing waste emission, and applying clean environmental protection
Ecologization	Ecological transformation of models, structures, and systems of production and consumption, economic and social behaviors (prevention, innovation, circulation, and win–win situation)
Democratic participation	Scientific, social, and democratic environmental policymaking
Polluter pays	Internalizing environmental costs, adopting economic means to prevent and control environmental pollution
Win–win situation for economy and environment	Disconnecting economic development and environmental degradation, synchronizing and coordinating economic development and environmental improvement, etc.

Source: RGCMS (2007)

$I_{\mathbf{ELM}}$ stands for the environmental pressure of ecological modernization, P refers to population, $I_{\mathbf{P}}$ refers to per capita environmental pressure, $E_{\mathbf{R}}$ refers to the environmental pressure offset by the self-recovery of ecological system, and $E_{\mathbf{P}}$ refers to the environmental pressure mitigated by artificial environmental protection and ecological construction.

Decoupling between modernization and environmental pressure: the increased value of environmental pressure is or smaller than zero:

$$\Delta I_{\mathrm{ELM}} = 0 \text{ or } \Delta I_{\mathrm{ELM}} < 0.$$

Mutually beneficial coupling of modernization and natural environment: environmental pressure is or approaches to zero:

$$I_{\mathrm{ELM}} = 0 \text{ or } I_{\mathrm{ELM}} \to 0.$$

Table 6.72 Analysis methods of ecological modernization

Groups of methods	Content explanation
Group I: Conceptualization	
EM1. Technological classification	Green and white technology, environment friendly, acceptable, harmless technology, etc.
EM2. Product classification	Green and white products, standard products, organic food, etc.
EM3. Consumption classification	Green and white consumption, resource, energy and knowledge intensive consumption, etc.
EM4. Material economic growth model	Three sources of material economic growth: knowledge innovation, application, and ecological awareness
EM5. Ecological value model	The value related to environmental quality in the market demands for better life is ecological value
Group II: Ecological decision making	
EM6. Game model of four sides	Game between green and white producers, green and white consumers for interests
EM7. Game model of two sides	Choice difference of and interests games between poor countries and rich ones
EM8. Production decision-making model	Nine combinations of environmental protection and economic growth
EM9. Consumption decision-making model	Multiple combinations of consumption, income, and environmental protection
EM10. Environmental decision-making model	Decision-making model for environmental protection, design for environment (DfE), Life Cycle Assessment (LCA), etc.
Group III: Systematic adjustment	
EM11. System adjustment model	State identification and feedback adjustment of human ecological system
EM12. Model of EKC and environmental pressure	Model indicating the relationship between EKC, per capita income, and environmental pressure
EM13. Model of material flow analysis	Social metabolism and material flow analysis (including the material flow analysis on toxic and harmful materials) (WRI 2000)
EM14. Environmental management system	Environmental information, organization, individuals, strategies, and operation systems (Huber 2000)
EM15. Structural change model	The change of the proportion of green elements (green production, consumption, and system) and green index
Group IV: Comprehensive evaluation	
EM16. Ecological system evaluation	Ecological system service and state and ecological effectiveness evaluation (MEA 2005)
EM17. Environmental management evaluation	Environmental performance, indicators, policies, and cost–benefit analysis (OECD 2003)
EM18. Index of the decoupling between economy and environment	The change of the ratio of environmental pressure and economic indicators (OECD 2002)
EM19. Model of ecological modernization progress	16 combinations of economic growth and environmental change
EM20. Model of ecological modernization goal	Target function of ecological modernization

Source: RGCMS (2007)

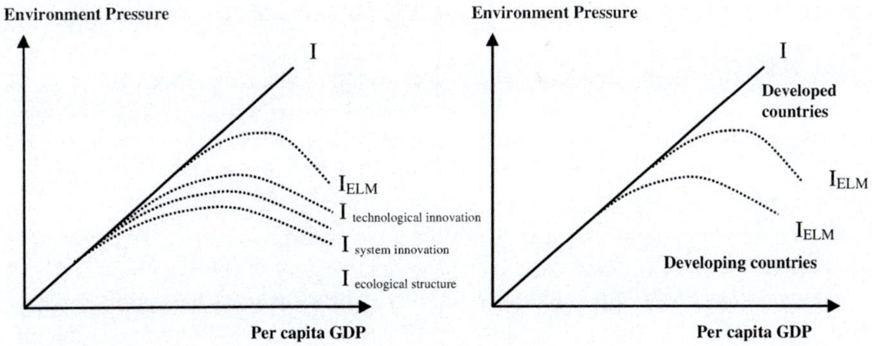

Fig. 6.34 Environmental pressure model of ecological modernization. Note: I stands for the environmental pressure of modernization, $I_{\mathbf{ELM}}$ refers to environmental pressure of ecological modernization ($I_{\text{ecological modernization}}$). $I_{\text{technological innovation}}$ refers to the change of environmental pressure caused by technological innovation, $I_{\text{system innovation}}$ refers to the change of environmental pressure caused by system innovation, and $I_{\text{ecological structure}}$ refers to the change of environmental pressure caused by ecological transition of structure. Source: RGCMS (2007)

Equation for the ecological balance of ecological modernization:

$$f(I_{\mathrm{P}}, E_{\mathrm{R}}, E_{\mathrm{P}}) = 0.$$

f stands for function, $I_{\mathbf{P}}$ refers to per capita environmental pressure, $E_{\mathbf{R}}$ refers to self-recovery of ecological system, and $E_{\mathbf{P}}$ refers to artificial environmental protection and ecological construction.

(3) Result

Firstly, the result shows profound changes in the following six aspects: (a) the completion of ecological transformation and the mutualism of man and nature; (b) the improvement of natural environment, minimization of environmental pressure, and environmental friendliness; (c) the improvement of ecological, resource, and energy efficiency; (d) ecological structure and system upgrading to the advanced level; (e) the popularization of ecological concepts; and (f) the change of international status of ecological transformation.

Secondly, the formation of the ecological modernity, particularity, and diversity. So far, ecological modernity is mainly characterized by dematerialization, greenization, ecologization, decoupling between modernization and environmental degradation, a win–win game for economy and environment, and mutually beneficial coexistence between human civilization and natural environment. As ecological modernization advances, it will show more new characteristics.

Thirdly, the goal of ecological modernization includes the complete delinking between modernization and environmental degradation, the realization of a win–win result for economy and environment, and catching up with, reaching, and maintaining the world's advanced level of development, etc.

Since the 1980s, the result of ecological modernization has been closer and closer to its goal.

(4) Dynamics

Ecological modernization is under the influence of various factors. The factor and the mechanism of drive force can be discussed separately (Table 6.69).

Factors of impetus with relatively important role include the quality of life (postmaterial value), green innovation, ecological awareness, internalization of environmental costs, international environmental politics, international environmental trade, etc.

The mechanism of impetus includes innovation drive (Table 2.20), three-innovation driving (Fig. 6.35), innovation spread (Table 6.69), etc.

(5) Model

There are various paths and models for ecological modernization. There are three basic paths for ecological modernization in the twenty-first century: overall ecological modernization, integrated ecological modernization, and ecological modification of first modernization (Fig. 6.36).

Basic models for ecological modernization in the twenty-first century include the model combining dematerialization, greening, and ecologization; the model combining green industrialization, green urbanization, and ecological transition of structure; and the model combining industrialization, urbanization, environmental management, etc. Models such as environmental agenda, industrial ecology, ecological gardens and green production and consumption can be widely applied.

Generally, European ecological modernization is more idealistic, North American ecological modernization is more pragmatic, and that of developing countries is more realistic.

Branch theories and methods of ecological modernization are discussed in *China Modernization Report 2007: Ecological Modernization Study*.

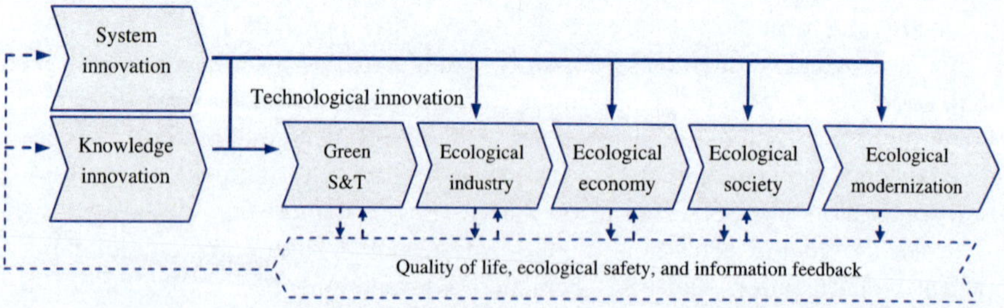

Fig. 6.35 Three-innovation driving model of ecological modernization. Source: RGCMS (2007)

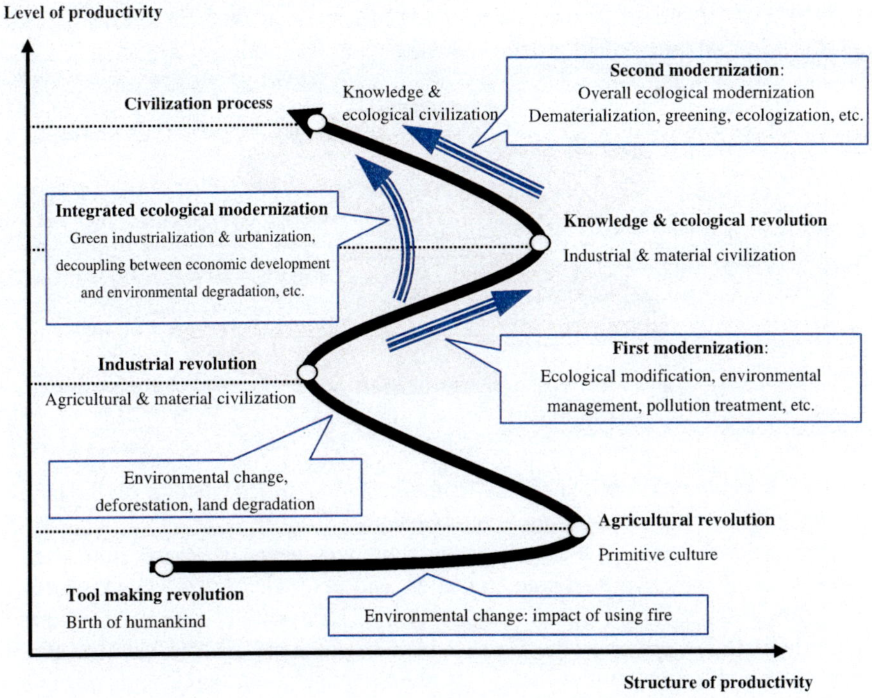

Fig. 6.36 Basic paths of ecological modernization in the twenty-first century. Source: RGCMS (2007)

(6) Integrated Ecological Modernization

Integrated ecological modernization is an option for developing countries and a combination of integrated modernization and ecological modernization. It requires to handle appropriately the relationship between economic development and environmental protection; promote the ecological transformation of modernization while maintaining economic growth; push forward green industrialization, green urbanization, and the ecological transition of structure; ease the environmental pollution and ecological damage caused by agriculture, delinking economic growth from environmental degradation; and catch up with the world's advanced level of ecological modernization.

The fulfillment of integrated ecological modernization requires three transitions (Fig. 6.37). First, the transition from agricultural to industrial civilization, as required by the first modernization; second, from industrial to knowledge civilization, as required by the second modernization; and third, from material to ecological civilization, as required by ecological modernization. These three turns are required by integrated ecological modernization. Ecological civilization is not only a way of manifesting knowledge civilization but also an important part of it.

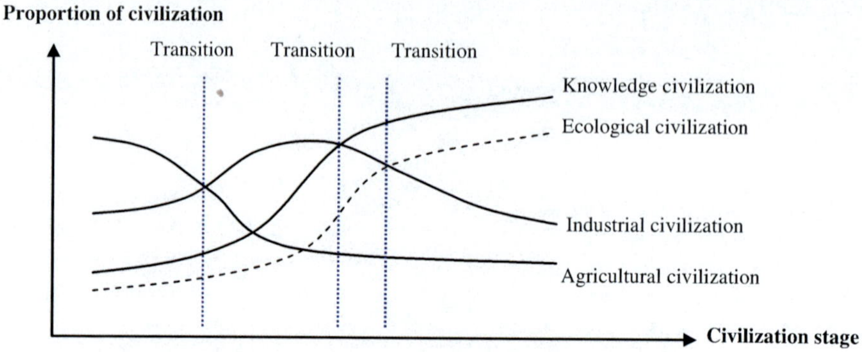

Fig. 6.37 Diagram of integrated ecological modernization (change of civilization structure)

In a sense, ecological civilization is a manifestation of knowledge civilization in terms of civilization–environment relationship.

There are two major challenges for integrated ecological modernization. One is the coupling of integrated modernization and ecological modernization; the reasonable degree of ecological modernization varies in different places and circumstances. The other is the conflict between national and global interests; international environmental politics and environmental trade have both positive and negative effects. In addition, since developed countries did not begin ecological modernization until the completion of first modernization, or the undergoing second modernization, they have less economic pressure but more environmental pressure. However, developing countries which have not completed the first modernization have more pressures on economic development and environmental protection. Therefore, relatively, it is more difficult to realize integrated ecological modernization than overall ecological modernization in developed countries. This is a challenge we have to deal with, which will become more difficult as globalization and international competition intensifies.

6.6 Human Modernization

Human modernization mainly refers to the individual changes of human beings during the modernization process and is one of the manifestations of modernization phenomena. It involves staged and stratified human modernization, human modernization of different type men and sectors, etc. (Fig. 6.38). Men are both the actor and final beneficiary of modernization and are both the object and researcher of modernization study. Human modernization has overlaps with modernization in other fields or levels, especially cultural modernization and individual modernization.

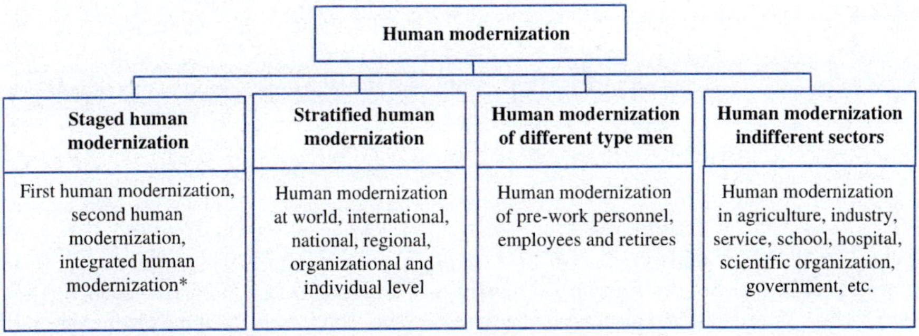

Fig. 6.38 Objects of human modernization study. Note: (*Asterisk*) integrated human modernization, the coordinated development of the first and second human modernizations, is a basic path to human modernization for developing countries

6.6.1 Studies

Human modernization study is part of modernization study concerned with individual behaviors and civic institutions of human beings in the modernization process. It can be dated back to the early eighteenth century and analyzed from the three aspects of the past, the present, and the future.

6.6.1.1 Research Paradigm

The human modernization research mainly targets at the individual and civic systemic changes of the humankind during the modernization process, including modernization of prework personnel, employees (workers engaged in material production, providing service, and knowledge workers), and retirees and individual modernization at six levels; the research contents include modernization of human behaviors, qualities, systems and ideas, the process, result, dynamics, and models of human modernization. They constitute a structure matrix (Table 6.73). Its research objects also include staged and sector-related human modernization.

Human modernization study, one kind of modernization study, could adopt the methodologies of modernization study. It has a variety of analysis methods, such as time-series analysis, cross-sectional analysis, process analysis, social survey, case study, coordinate analysis, etc. The research can span the whole process of human modernization or part of the period. The scope of research could be the world, a country, or a region.

(1) Historical Facts

Human modernization includes the changes of human behavior, qualities, institutions, and ideas in the process of modernization. Generally, changes of human behavior and qualities are individual changes, while institutional changes are social changes, the changes of the institutions concerning human behavior and development; changes of ideas are both individual and social changes.

Table 6.73 Matrix of human modernization study

Content		Object		
		Human being	Prework personnel, material product workers, service workers, knowledge workers, and retirees	World, international, nation, region, organization, and individuals
		Human modernization	Human modernization of five types of people	Human modernization at six levels
Element	Behavior	Modernization of human behavior, quality, institution, and ideas	Modernization of behavior, quality, institution, and ideas of five types of people	Modernization of human behavior, quality, institution, and ideas at six levels
	Quality			
	Institution			
	Idea			
Aspect	Process	Process, result, dynamics, and model of the human modernization	Process, result, dynamics, and model of modernization of five types of people	Process, result, dynamics, and model of human modernization at six levels
	Result			
	Dynamics			
	Model			

Note: Human qualities refer to the overall qualities of men, including physical qualities, psychological qualities, scientific literacy, cultural literacy, labor and life skills, etc. Human institutions refer to a variety of institutions concerning human behavior and development, such as the institution of civil rights and obligations. Based on the natures and characteristics of different jobs, the employees could be divided into three categories: material product workers refer to the employees mainly engaged in physical labor sectors such as agriculture and industry, service workers are those engaged in traditional service sector, and knowledge workers are those engaged in knowledge production and services (He 2000a). The research contents of human modernization also include staged human modernization, sector-related human modernization, frontier analysis, trend analysis, frontier process analysis, and the interaction between elements of human modernization and different fields, etc.

Between the eighteenth and the twenty-first centuries, the frontier track of modernization could be divided into two stages and six waves of development. The intension and characteristics of modernization vary a lot in different stages and waves of development, so do its influence and demands on people. In different stages and waves of development, human modernization is provided with varied intension and characteristics (Table 6.74). Though the cut-off points for the two stages and six waves of development are not definite, it is acceptable to use them as the analysis framework in this study.

(2) Process Analysis

First of all, the first wave of human modernization. Paralleled with the first industrial revolution, it took place in European countries and essentially involved emancipating the mind, advocating freedom, equality, humane and commercial spirit, participating in political activities, and developing citizens' legal and political rights, etc., as demonstrated by the *Declaration of the Rights of Man and Citizen* (1789) in France, religious secularization and freedom of belief, etc.

Secondly, the second wave of human modernization. It took place during the second industrial revolution and the World War I and World War II and extended to

Table 6.74 Two stages and six waves of human modernization

Wave	Approx. time	Main content	Annotation
First	1763–1870	Primary education, citizenship, secularization, legal rights, political rights	*First human modernization* Citizenship, professionalization, secularization, equalization, democratization, etc.
Second	1870–1945	Compulsory education, professionalization, liberalization, political rights, social rights	
Third	1946–1970	Secondary education, equalization, democratization, social rights, participation rights	
Fourth	1970–2020	Higher education, networking, internationalization, ecological awareness, participation rights	*Second human modernization* Networking, ecologization, knowledgization, individualization, internationalization, etc.
Fifth	2020–2050	Lifelong learning, individualization, innovation, longevity, nature awareness	
Sixth	2050–2100	Knowledge sharing, experience, transcendentalization, diversity, universe awareness	

Note: Different stages and waves of development of human modernization have overlaps in the contents. The fifth and sixth waves of modernization are a forecast

broader areas—Europe, America, and Asia. It is mainly characterized by professionalization, rationalization, liberalization, democratization, class differentiation, politicalization, economization, mechanization, compulsory education, industrialism, the development of political and social rights of citizens, and so on.

Thirdly, the third wave of human modernization. It roughly occurred in the third industrial revolution, including human modernization in industrialized countries and developing countries. Human modernization in industrialized countries was the heart of the third wave. The major contents include equalization, democratization, electrification, socialization, television, secondary education, the development of social and participation rights of citizens, and so on.

Fourthly, the fourth wave of human modernization. Propelled by information and ecological revolution, it generally parallels with the fourth wave of modernization and covers most regions around the world. Its contents mainly include networking, knowledge, internationalization, ecologization, individualization, higher education, civil rights and obligations, participation rights, and all-round development of mankind.

Fifthly, the fifth wave of human modernization. As forecasted, it will be set in a bioeconomic society and mainly characterized by lifelong learning, leisure, innovation, longevity, and nature awareness.

Sixthly, the sixth wave of human modernization. As forecasted, it will be set in a cultural economic society and mainly characterized by knowledge sharing, experience, transcendentalization, diversity, universe awareness, and so on.

(3) Human Modernization and Civil Rights

Civil rights serve as the institutional basis for human modernization. The development of civil rights is a substantial facet of human modernization. Janoski (1998) believes that, *the history of civil rights' development during the past hundreds of years could be divided into three periods: 1200–1815 for legal and political rights; 1789–1980 for legal and political rights; 1883–1990 for social and participation rights; it does not mean that any of these rights does not evolve in other periods, but respectively, they mostly grow in one of the periods* (Janoski 1998).

Generally, civil rights and obligations should be well balanced (Table 6.75). The civil rights and obligations in different countries and stages bear varied intensions. *Liberalism countries follow the order of legal, political and social rights successively. Legal and political rights have been developed from an early age but social* ***and participation rights are generally lagged behind. Democratic countries firstly*** *develop legal rights, then political and social rights concurrently, and participation rights lastly. In traditional countries, social rights are developed very early, but legal and political rights fall far behind* (Janoski 1998).

In the latter half of the twentieth century, civil rights drew much attention from the international community, and both international conventions and contracting states were on the rise (Table 6.76).

(4) Human Modernization and Human Development

Freedom, liberation, and all-round development of humankind are examples of the key goals of human modernization. UNDP had published *Human Development*

Table 6.75 Civil rights and obligations

Legal rights	Political rights	Social rights	Participation rights
Personal safety and rights	Individual political rights	Capacity promotion rights	Labor market intervention
Judicial and procedural rights	Organization rights	Opportunity rights	Suggestion/ decision-making rights
Expression and selection rights	Membership rights	Distribution rights	Capital supervision
Property and services rights	Objection rights	Compensation rights	
Legal obligations	Political obligations	Social obligations	Participation obligations
Interpersonal obligations: respecting human rights, etc.	Interpersonal obligations: respecting democracy, etc.	Obligations on health and disease prevention	Obligations of the labor market
Organization obligations: respecting laws, etc.	Organization obligations: observing the regulations and laws, etc.	Obligations on opportunity creation	Obligations of enterprises/ administrative organs
Compulsory obligations: paying taxes, etc.	Compulsory obligations: military services, etc.	Economic obligations: job-hunting, etc.	Obligations on capital participation

Source: Janoski (1998), Isin and Turner (2002)

Table 6.76 Conventions concerning culture, labor, and civil rights by international organizations

Name	Time	Contracting states	Name	Time	Contracting states
International Convention on the *Elimination of All Forms of Racial Discrimination*	1965	161	Convention concerning Freedom of Association and Protection of the Right to Organize**	1948	139
International Covenant on Civil and Political Rights	1966	148	Right to Organize and Collective Bargaining Convention**	1949	151
International Covenant on *Economic, Social, and Cultural Rights*	1966	145	*Convention concerning Forced or Compulsory Labor***	1930	160
Convention on the Elimination of All Forms of Discrimination Against Women	1979	168	Abolition of *Forced Labor Convention***	1957	155
UN Convention Against Torture	1984	128	Convention concerning Equal Remuneration for Men and Women Workers for Work of Equal Value**	1951	156
UN Convention on the Rights of the Child	1989	191	Convention concerning Discrimination in Respect of Employment and Occupation**	1958	154
Convention on the Prevention and Punishment of the Crime of Genocide	1948	118	Minimum Age Convention**	1973	138
Convention relating to the Status of Refugees	1951	112	Convention on the Worst Forms of Child Labor**	1999	116
Convention against Discrimination in Education*	1960	79	*Indigenous and Tribal Peoples Convention***	1989	9
Convention concerning the Protection of the World Cultural and Natural Heritage*	1972	154	Convention on the Means of Prohibiting and Preventing the Illicit Import, Export and Transfer of Ownership of Cultural Property*	1970	94

Note: Those marked with "*" are international conventions of UNESCO; the number of contracting states is calculated up to the year 2000. Those marked with "**" are international conventions of International Labor Organization. Others are UN's human rights conventions; the number of contracting states is calculated up to the year 2002
Source: UNDP (2002), UNESCO (2000)

Report since 1990, which analyzed issues on human development from different perspectives and proposes measurement methods—such as indicators of human development (UNDP 2000, 2001).

UNDP believes: *human development refers to the process of deepening the degree and enlarging the extent of development so as to enlarging people's choices.* ***Therefore, human development also reflects the achievements people have made in*** *terms of full development and extent of development. It is both a process and a goal. The three most basic requirements for human development are: health and longevity, being knowledgeable, and the access to resources needed for a decent life* (UNDP 2000).

UNDP has successively developed human development index (HDI), gender-related development index (GDI), and human poverty index (HPI), etc., to measure the achievements of human development. HDI is the measure of the average accomplishments in the three basic aspects of human development: health and longevity, knowledge acquired, and a decent life. GDI is the measure of gender differences in human development in a country and the indication of the progress in gender parity. HPI is the measure of the poverty in human development and the indication of the distribution of human development progress. UNDP also brought forward the world table of Human Development, which analyzes the worldwide progress and distribution of human development, including democracy and participation, economic equality, health and education, peace, and individual safety (UNDP 2002).

Inglehart and Welzel (2005) believe that *contemporary social change is part of human development process, leading to the development of humanistic societies, which highlight freedom and self-expression. Human development could be divided into three dimensions: socio-economic dimension, cultural dimension and institutional dimension. The core of human development result is the increase of choices and autonomy for mankind. The spread of self-expression values brings about the transition from modernization process to human development process, and displays humanistic transition of modernity.*

In *China Modernization Report 2010: World Modernization Outline 1700–2100*, Chinese scholar Chuanqi He proposes new human development indexes (HDI_N). He believes that the emergence of information and ecological revolution and knowledge economy has changed and will continue to change the lifestyle and basic concepts of people. HDI suggested by UNDP does not involve indicators on information and environment, and its knowledge indicator does not show the highlights.

HDI_N measures the average achievements in five basic aspects of human development of a country: (1) long and healthy life, indicated by life expectancy at birth; (2) universal higher education, indicated by the enrollment rate of universities and colleges; (3) information sharing, indicated by Internet penetration rate; (4) environmental improvement, indicated by sanitary wastewater treatment rate; and (5) wealthy life (or high-quality life), indicated by purchasing power per capita [*GDP per capita* calculated based on PPP (*Purchasing Power* Parity)]. Achievements in every aspect are shown by the figures between 0 and 100; the HDI_N is the average of the indexes in the five aspects (Table 6.77).

Table 6.77 Human development indexes and new human development indexes of four groups of countries in 2005

Country	HDI	HDI_N	Life	Education	Information	Country	HDI	HDI_N	Life	Education	Information
AC						PC					
USA	0.96	74	78	82	70	Philippines	0.74	29	71	28	5
Japan	0.96	65	82	55	67	South Africa	0.68	22	51	15	8
Germany	0.94	68	79	50	65	China	0.76	29	73	20	9
France	0.96	63	80	56	43	Morocco	0.64	27	71	11	15
UK	0.96	71	79	59	65	Egypt	0.78	29	70	35	12
MC						UC					
Argentina	0.86	46	75	64	18	India	0.60	18	64	11	4
Uruguay	0.86	42	76	42	20	Kenya	0.53	12	53	3	3
Czech	0.89	52	76	48	32	Nigeria	0.50	14	47	10	4
Poland	0.87	50	75	64	35	Nepal	0.54	14	63	6	1
Chile	0.87	44	78	48	22	Burundi	0.38	8	49	2	0

Note: HDI stands for human development index and HDI_N new human development index. Life refers to the average life expectancy at birth, education refers to the enrollment rate of higher education, and information refers to the penetration rate of Internet. AC refers to advanced countries, MC moderately developed countries, PC preliminarily developed countries, and UC underdeveloped countries

Source: RGCMS (2010)

6.6.2 Theories

Human modernization theory, concerned with human modernization phenomena, is a field theory of modernization science. It is generally comprised of two sets of theories: the classic human modernization and the human modernization theory in broad sense. It has overlaps with cultural modernization theory, social modernization theory, and individual modernization theory as well as behavioral psychology.

6.6.2.1 Classic Human Modernization Theory

Classic human modernization theory is an important part of classic modernization theory formed in 1960–1980. It is sometimes called behavioral psychology school of classic modernization theory. The publication of American scholars, *The achieving society* (McClelland 1961), *Becoming Modern: Individual Change in Six Developing Countries* (Inkeles and Smith 1974), and *Exploring Individual Modernity* (Inkeles 1983), marked the birth of the classic human modernization theory. Up to now, it is only the mixture of different academic thoughts, without any systematic, agreed general theoretic elaborations.

(1) Definition

Uniform definition on human modernization has not been provided. Generally, human modernization refers to the transition from traditional men to modern men, including the modernization of personality, psychology, individual behaviors, values, etc.

American scholars Inkeles and Smith (1974) believe that *in any society and at any age, man is the most basic element of modernization process. Only when the citizens make psychological and behavioral transitions to form their modern personalities, the employees in political, economic, scientific and technological, educational and cultural institutions could develop modernity in their personalities, and the society would be thus called a modern society. If the people of a country lack wide-ranging and modern psychological elements to equip the advanced institutions with vitality, and if the people who dominate and operate the advanced institutions have not achieved transition to modernity in their psychology, thoughts, attitudes and behaviors, then failure and deformed development will be inevitable.*

(2) Outcome

The formation and diffusion of human modernity is the major outcome of human modernization.

Professor Inkeles (1966) concludes nine psychological features of a modern man. *First, readiness for new experiences and openness to innovation and change; second, active-minded, forming and expressing opinions over a wide range of issues in surrounding environment; third, present or future-oriented rather than indulging in the past; fourth, confident in man's capabilities to control the environment and fulfill his goals; fifth, managing affairs in a planned and organized way; sixth, trusting in the society and other people; seventh, distribution equality; one's reward should have positive correlation with one's skills and contribution to the organization; eighth, ambitious, willing to receive formal education and learn scientific knowledge; ninth, aware of and respecting the dignity of others.*

Inkeles and Smith (1974) believe that, *modern personality mainly consists of four traits: participatory and well-informed; efficient; displaying a strong sense of independence and autonomy under the influence of traditions, especially while making decisions on personal affairs; open-minded, ready to take in new experiences and concepts and cognitive flexible.*

Kahl (1968) has researched and found out the seven core factors of modernity, namely, activism, low integration with relatives, preference to urban life, individualism, low community stratification, and low stratification of life chances. According to Black (1976), compared with the past, modern people are more open and tolerant, care more about the domination on the environment, and do not rest on their laurels.

(3) Human Modernity and Economic Development

According to McClelland (1961), *that economic development is closely related with the "need for achievement" which in turn is closely related to values, faith and ideology. In western industrialized countries, the themes on ambition and desire for achievement frequent the reading materials and fairy tales for children and primary school students, but relatively fewer in developing countries. A boy's need for achievement would be influenced by three factors: parents' high achievement standards, warmth and encouragement, and an unauthoritarian father. The society with higher achievement need would produce more energetic entrepreneurs, who will push forward the economic development more rapidly.*

6.6.2.2 Human Modernization Theory in Broad Sense

The human modernization theory in broad sense is developed for interpreting the human modernization during the eighteenth to the twenty-first centuries. Proposed by Chinese scholar Chuanqi He, it is the application of the second modernization theory in the field of individual behaviors. It consists of general theory, branch theories, relevant theories, etc. (Table 6.78). Here we highlight its general theory (Table 6.79), including the definition, process, result, dynamics, and model of human modernization.

(1) Definition

Human modernization is one of the manifestations of modernization and refers to the frontier changes of human development and relevant factors during the process of modernization.

The intension: human modernization refers to a frontier change and international competition in the field of human development since the eighteenth century, including the formation, development, transformation, and interaction of modern people; innovation, selection, diffusion, and withdrawal of individual elements and civil systems; and the international competition, differentiation, and stratification to catch up with, reach, and maintain the world's advanced level of human development.

Table 6.78 Structure of human modernization theory in broad sense

Category	Theory	Main contents
General theory	Core theory	Definition, process, result, dynamics, and model of human modernization
Branch theories	Stage theory	First, second, and integrated human modernization
	Stratified study	World, international, national, regional, organizational, and individual human modernizations
	Field-related study	Human modernization in the fields of economy, society, politics, culture, and environment
	Sector study	Human modernization in the sectors of agriculture, industry, education, science and technology, national defense and transport, etc.
	Type-related study	Modernization of knowledge workers, service workers, and material products workers
Related theories	Other modernization theories	Classic modernization theory, ecological modernization theory, and the second modernization theory
	Relevant theories of praxiology	Individual ethology, behavioral psychology, developmental psychology, the achievement motivation theory, and the need-hierarchy theory
	Other relevant theories	Modernism, postmodernism, sociology, economics, politics, culturology, etc.

The extension: human modernization includes modernization of human behaviors, qualities, institutions, and ideas; modernization of personality and psychology; modernization of prework personnel, employees, retirees, and male and female citizens; modernization of material products workers, service workers, and knowledge workers; staged, stratified, and sector-related human modernization; the interplay between human modernization and modernization in other fields; and changes in spatial and temporal distribution of human modernization, etc.

Generally, human modernization refers to the self-liberation and all-round development of human beings, and the world frontiers of human development and the process to reach these frontiers, and includes the transition from traditional to modern men and from modern men to postmodern men, improvement in citizens' qualities and capacities, development of civil rights and obligations, changes in human lifestyles, behavioral models and values, etc.

Throughout the history of human civilization, there have been three self-liberations of mankind (Table 6.80). The first human modernization is the liberation from religion and feudal autocracy; the second human modernization is the liberation from the control by organization and machine.

Human modernization is the intersection of individual changes and modernization. Human modernization refers not only to the personal changes of people but also to the changes of the institutions and environment where they live. Without modernization of institutions and environment, human modernization would be hard to achieve. During the process of modernization, the three elements—human, institution, and environment—could promote or restrain each other.

Table 6.79 General theory of human modernization in broad sense

Item	Main content
Definition	Human modernization refers to a frontier change and international competition in the field of human development since the industrial revolution in the eighteenth century; the frontier process of the formation, development, transformation, and interaction of modern people; the complex and alternate process of innovation, selection, diffusion, and withdrawal of individual elements, civil systems, and ideas; and the international stratification and competition to catch up with, reach, and maintain the world's advanced level of human development
Process	Human modernization is a long-term process and involves the development, transformation, interaction of humans, and the change in international status, including economization, socialization, politicalization, individualization, diversification, and all-round development of humankind, the world frontiers of human development and the process and action to reach these frontiers. The human modernization during the first modernization is named the first human modernization for short. It refers to the transition from traditional to modern men, which is mainly characterized by citizenship, professionalism, rationalization, equalization, economization, and socialization; the gradual formation of individual behaviors, qualities, capacities, institutions, and ideas that fit in with industrial civilization. The human modernization during the second modernization is called the second human modernization for short. It refers to the transition from industrial to knowledge men. It is characterized by the networking, ecologization, diversification, individualization, innovation, and intellectualization; the gradual formation of individual behaviors, qualities, capacities, institutions, and ideas that fit in with knowledge and ecological civilization. The coordinated development of first and second human modernizations leads to integrated human modernization
Result	Human modernity, particularity, diversity, self-liberation, and all-round development of human beings. The outcome of the first human modernization is the formation of the first human modernity, particularity, and diversity; the first human modernity is mainly characterized by citizenship, professionalism, equalization, discipline, responsibility, and individual values, etc., with human indifference as its side effect. The outcome of the second human modernization is the formation of the second human modernity, particularity, and diversity; the second human modernity is mainly characterized by networking, ecologization, autonomy, internationality, sense of happiness, and self-realization, with the increase of risks as its side effect
Dynamic	The impetus at the microlevel includes innovation, competition, adaptation, exchange, individual benefits, personal interests, etc.; impetus at the macrolevel involves national and regional modernization, informatization and globalization, etc. The dynamic models consist of innovation drive, dual-wheel motivation, associative action, diffusion of innovation, spillover of innovation (Table 2.15), etc. Different types of people at different ages in different stages have varied impetus for modernization
Model	Human modernization has no standard paths or models, relies on the starting point and the paths, and is influenced by history and traditions, cultural concepts, public opinions, educational level, national strength, and international situation. Three paths are available in the twenty-first century: the first human modernization, the second human modernization, and the integrated human modernization

Source: RGCMS (2010)

The conceptual model for human modernization (Table 6.81). First of all, human development is the intersection of individual progress, institutional development, and environmental improvement. Secondly, human modernization is the intersection of human development, transition, and interaction.

Table 6.80 Three self-liberations of mankind

Item	First	Second	Third
Time	3500 BC–AD 1763	Approx. 1763–1970	Approx. 1970–2100
Content	Liberation from natural food dependence	Liberation from religion and feudal autocracy	Liberation from the control by organization and machine
Outcome	Became food producer and got rid of the dependence upon nature	Became citizens with independence, freedom, and equality	Become world citizens with individuality and independence
New control	Religion and feudal autocracy	Control by organization and machine	Earth's check upon mankind
Note	Birth of civilization	First human modernization	Second human modernization

Table 6.81 Conceptual model for human modernization

Item	Main contents
Hypothesis I	Individual progress refers to the enhancement of individual qualities and capacities and the gradual conformity of individual behaviors and ideas with the needs of modernization
Hypothesis II	Institutional development refers to the rationalization and modernization of the relevant systems on civil rights and obligations
Hypothesis III	Environmental improvement refers to the modernization in economy, society, politics, and cultural environment for individual life
Hypothesis IV	Human transformation refers to the transition from traditional to modern men and from modern men to postmodern men
Hypothesis V	Human interaction refers to the interpersonal interaction and the interplay between man and nature as well as international competition
Inference I	Human development = individual progress × institutional development × environmental improvement
Inference III	Human modernization = human development × human transition × human interaction and change of status

(2) Process

Human modernization is a long-term process. The process of human modernization can be divided into two types: frontier process and catch-up process with both common and different features. During the eighteenth to the twenty-first centuries, its frontier process could be divided into two stages: first modernization and second modernization (Table 6.82), which have different intensions (Fig. 6.39).

The first human modernization is the transition from traditional to modern men, from agricultural to industrial men, from men of ethics to men of covenant, from familial to social men, from stratified to equal men, from *monarch–subject relationship to state citizens, from rural people to urban residents*, etc.

The second human modernization refers to the transition from modern to postmodern men, from industrial to knowledge men, from economic to ecological men, from material to cultural men, from men under organization to men with autonomy, from men of nationality to men of the world, etc.

Table 6.82 Periodic table of human modernization—frontier track of individual changes

Stage (approx. starting year)	Form and features of human changes (key points)	Human modernization
Knowledge age	*Men in the knowledge society (knowledge men and netizen)*	
Transition stage (2050)	Knowledge men: experience, diversification, knowledge sharing	*Second human modernization* Networking, knowledgization, individualization; men of culture, men of the world, postmodern men
Mature stage (2020)	Knowledge men: leisure, innovation, lifelong learning	
Developing stage (1992)	Netizen: Internet, internationalization, intellectualization	
Start stage (1970)	Ecological men: ecologization, individualization, higher education	
Industrial age	*Men in the industrial society (industrial and modern men)*	
Transition stage (1946)	Modern men: equalization, socialization, secondary education	*First human modernization* Citizenship, professionalism, equalization; rational men, social men, modern men
Mature stage (1914)	Modern men: politicalization, democratization, compulsory education	
Developing stage (1870)	Industrial men: professionalism, class differentiation, rationalization	
Start stage (1763)	Economic men: citizenship, secularization, liberalization	
Agricultural age	*Men in agricultural society (agricultural and traditional men)*	
Transition stage (AD 1500)	Traditional men: familial, predestinate, rural	(Men of a nationality, men of social ranks, men of ethics) (Agricultural revolution, stratification of men)
Mature stage (AD 618)	Traditional men: religious, hierarchical, conservative	
Developing stage (500 BC)	Men of agriculture: monks and priests, aristocrat, the commons, warrior	
Start stage (3500 BC)	Men of a family: slave owner, slave, the commons, warrior	
Primitive age (tool age)	*Men of the primitive society (primitive men, tribal men)*	
Transition stage (10,000 years ago)	Primitive men: patriarchal tribes	(Primitive agricultural revolution, stratification of men)
Mature stage (40,000 years ago)	Primitive men: maternal tribes	
Developing stage (200,000 years ago)	Primitive men: clans	(Tool-making revolution, birth of mankind)
Start stage (2,500,000 years ago)	Primitive men: migration	

Note: The time of chronology and the features were based on the frontier track of the human development

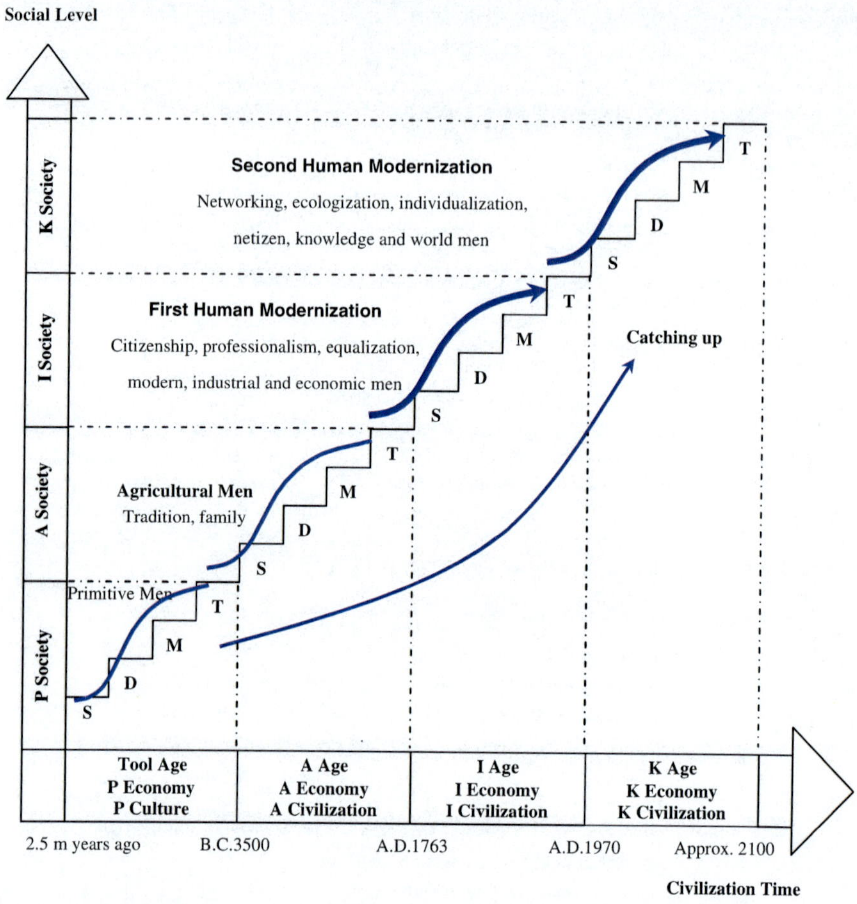

Fig. 6.39 Coordinates of human modernization. Note: P, A, I, and K refer to primitive, agricultural, industrial, and knowledge, respectively. S, D, M, and T refer to the start, developing, mature, and transition phase, respectively. The civilization time was the time based on the track of the forerunner of the civilization

Table 6.83 Staged features of human modernization

Characteristics of the first human modernization	Characteristics of the second human modernization
Stratification, citizenship, professionalism, rationalization, class differentiation, secularization, equalization, economization, politicalization, socialization, etc.	Networking, ecologization, internationalization, diversification, autonomation, individualization, leisurization, innovation, knowledgization (new characteristics will continue to emerge in the future)

The first and second human modernizations have different characteristics (Table 6.83); the characteristics of the second human modernization are still evolving.

There are ten general characteristics of human modernization: partly predictable, nonlinear, reversible, path dependent, multipath, polynary, unbalanced, asynchronous, staged, and global.

Human modernization, one of the manifestations of modernization, follows the ten principles of modernization (Table 2.15).

(3) Result

The outcomes of human modernization include human modernity, particularity, diversity, and side effect (Table 6.82). Theoretically speaking, it involves profound changes in six aspects: the completion of two human transitions, the improvement of individual qualities and capacities, the changes of individual values, the development of civil institutions, freedom and liberation and all-round development of mankind, changes in the distribution of human modernization, and so on.

The outcomes of the first human modernization refer to the first human modernity, particularity, and diversity, and it is mainly characterized by professionalism, citizenship, rationality, equality, class nature, democracy, organization, efficiency, openness, independence, participation, planning, actuality, equity, initiative, mobility, science, discipline, sense of responsibility, trust, achievement, individual values, etc., and the side effects such as indifference and the popular materialism.

The outcomes of the second human modernization refer to the formation of the second human modernity, particularity, and diversity, and it is mainly characterized by knowledge, networking, ecology, autonomy, diversity, interest, internationality, sense of happiness, lifelong learning, self-realization, and all-round development at present, and the side effects such as expedited aging of knowledge and skills, and the increase of risks in jobs and families, etc.

From the individual perspective, human modernization mainly has three goals: the completion of the first human modernization and the second human modernization and to catch up, reach, and maintain the world's advanced level in citizen qualities and human development.

From the perspective of policy, human modernization has three goals: to fully enhance citizen qualities and the all-round development of mankind, develop and improve the institution on civil rights and obligations, and boost the creativity of the citizens and the international competitive edge, etc.

Since the 1960s, the relevance between the outcome and the goal of human modernization has been gradually formed and enhanced while modernization study moves forward.

(4) Dynamics

Drive forces of human modernization include macro- and microfactors. Innovation is the fundamental source of institutional progress; competition, the motivation mechanism of individual progress; adaptation, individual and institutional adjustment to changes of external environment; exchange, a motivator of human development; and individual benefits and interests, a factor influencing individual development. In developed countries, innovation and competition play a more prominent role, while in developing countries, exchange and adaptation are more

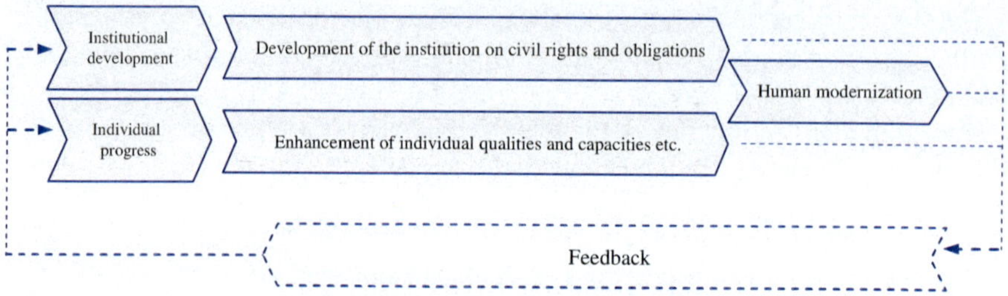

Fig. 6.40 Dual-wheel motivation model of human modernization

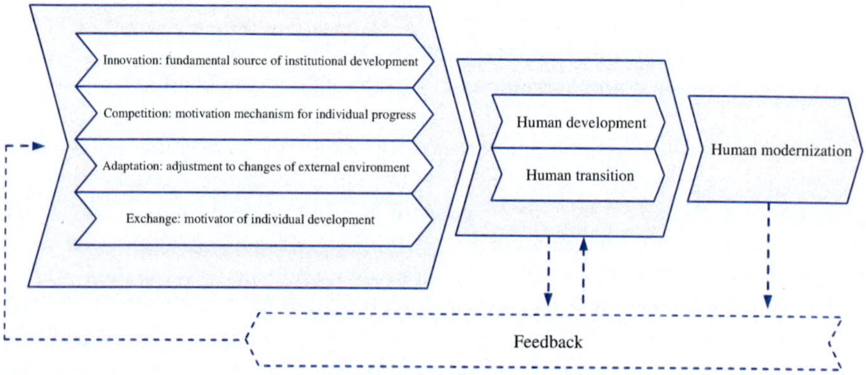

Fig. 6.41 Associative action model of human modernization

significant. Models of impetus include dual-wheel motivation (Fig. 6.40), associative action (Fig. 6.41), etc.

(5) Model

There is no best path universally applied to human modernization in the world. There are basically three paths for human modernization in the twenty-first century (Fig. 6.42).

If the first human modernization is the primary human modernization, then the second human modernization is the advanced human modernization; the co-ordinated development of the two human modernizations and the continued transitions to man of knowledge, cybercitizen and man of ecology would result in the integrated human modernization.

There is no standard model for human modernization, which is under the influence of traditional culture, occupation, and objective conditions.

Generally, the contents and models differ in different stages, fields, and sectors of human modernization.

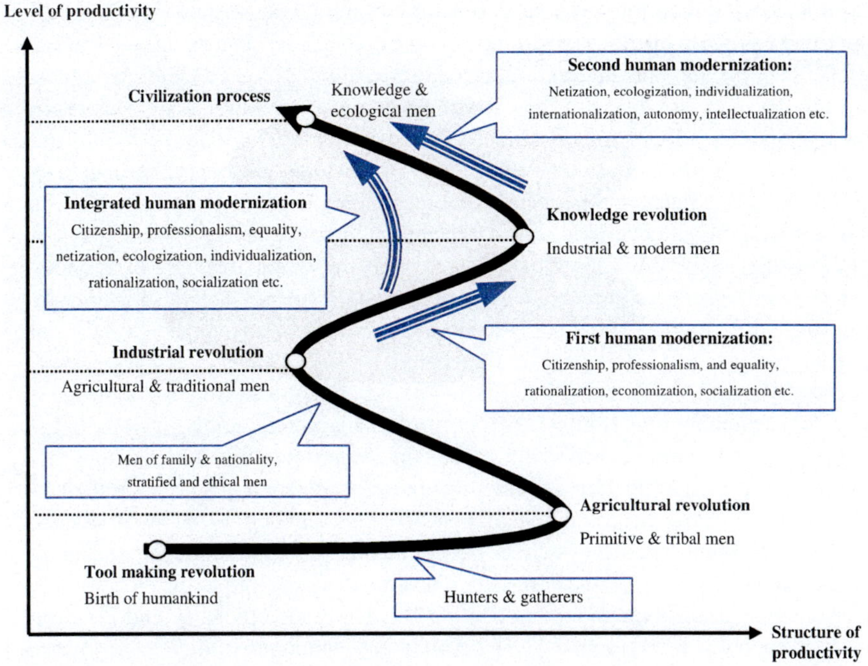

Fig. 6.42 Three paths of human modernization in twenty-first century. Note: under the influence of Internet, ecologization, etc., the first human modernization in the twenty-first century will develop new characteristics

Summary

Modernization occurs in all spheres of human civilization, such as the spheres of economy, society, politics, culture, ecology, and human development. Modernization in different spheres has both commonality and difference. Country is the basic unit for modernization, and modernization of each sphere is closely related with modernization of a country as a whole.

Economic Modernization

Economic modernization means the modernization of the economic sphere. Economic modernization theories include classic economic modernization theory and broad-sense economic modernization theory. The former is a branch of classic modernization theory, and the latter is an application of the second modernization theory in the economic sphere.

The economic modernization theory in broad sense holds that economic modernization is a sort of economic change and international competition since the industrial revolution in the eighteenth century; a frontier process of the formation, development, transformation, and international interaction of modern economy; a compound process of the innovation, selection, diffusion, and withdrawal of economic factors; and the international economic competition, differentiation, and stratification to catch up with, reach, and maintain the world's advanced level of the economic development. It includes the transition from agricultural to industrial economy and the transition from industrial to knowledge economy, the increasing of economic efficiency and per capita income, and the change of economic welfare and equity, national economic status, and international economy system.

Generally, economic modernization refers to the world frontiers of economic change and the process to reach the frontiers. During the eighteenth to twenty-first centuries, the frontier process of economic modernization can be divided into two stages.

First economic modernization refers to the transitions from agricultural to industrial economy and from self-supporting to market economy, etc. Its unique features included industrialization, mechanization, electrification, automation, standardization, scale operation, marketization, centralization, deagriculturalization, etc. Its results were the formation of first economic modernity, particularity, and diversity and the side effects such as environmental pollution and cyclic economic crises. The main marks for the completion of first economic modernization were the finish of industrialization and marketization and economic efficiency and per capita income reaching the advanced level of industrial economy (the average level of industrial countries in the 1960s).

The second economic modernization is the transitions from industrial to knowledge economy and from material to ecological economy, etc. Currently, its unique features include intellectualization, informatization, servicization, intelligentization, ecologization, globalization, greenization, dematerialization, decentralization, deindustrialization, etc. Its results are the formation of the second economic modernity, particularity, and diversity and the side effects such as network crimes and international economic risks. The main marks for the completion of second economic modernization are the realization of intellectualization and ecologization, and the level of productivity and per capita national income reaching the advanced level of knowledge economy (at some points in the future).

Integrated economic modernization is a basic path for developing countries in the twenty-first century. It comprises the coordinated development of the twice economic modernizations and the continuous movement toward knowledge economy and the coordinated development of the industrialization, deindustrialization, intellectualization, informatization, greenization, and globalization of national economy and the continuous movement toward intellectualization and greenization.

In the twenty-first century, economic modernization has roughly three basic paths. The path of the first economic modernization corresponds to the model of industrialization; the path of the second economic modernization corresponds to the model of information economy, ecological economy, biological economy, experience economy, etc.; and the path of integrated economic modernization corresponds to the model of new industrialization, including the coordinated development of industrialization, de-industrialization, intellectualization, informatization, and ecologization. Different models have many submodels.

Social Modernization

Social modernization means modernization of the social sphere. Social modernization theory includes classic social modernization theory and social modernization theory in broad sense. The former is a branch of classic modernization theory, while the latter is an application of the second modernization theory in the social sphere.

The social modernization theory in the broad sense believes that social modernization is a sort of social change and international competition since the industrial revolution in the eighteenth century. It is the frontier process of the formation, development, transformation, and international interaction of modern society; a compound process of the innovation, selection, diffusion, and withdrawal of social factors; and also the international social competition, differentiation, and stratification to catch up with, reach, and maintain the world's advanced level of social development. It comprises the transition from agricultural to industrial society and from industrial to knowledge society, the improvement of social effectiveness and quality of life, the change of lifestyle and living ideas, the enhancement of civic quality of culture and health, and the change of social welfare, equity, and international social status.

Generally, social modernization refers to the world frontiers of social change and the process to reach the frontiers. During the eighteenth to twenty-first centuries, the frontier process of social modernization can be divided into two stages.

The first social modernization is a transition from agricultural to industrial society and from familial to welfare society, etc., and its features include urbanization, welfarism, mobility, specialization, rationalization, electrification, technologization, equity, social differentiation and integration, universal primary education, and so on. Its result was the formation of the first social modernity, particularity, and diversity, and its side effects include the widening gap between the rich and the poor, etc. The completion of the first social modernization was mainly marked by the competition of urbanization, welfarism and social efficiency, and life standard reaching the advanced level of industrial society (the average level of industrial countries in the 1960s).

The second social modernization is a transition from industrial to knowledge society and from material to ecological society, etc. Currently, its features include intellectualization, informatization, suburbanization, urban–rural balance, greenization, ecologization, naturalization, innovation, internationalization, diversification, individualization, leisure, rights of women and children, universal higher education, lifetime learning, and so on. Its results are the formation of the second social modernity, particularity, and diversity, and its side effects include the information divide, etc. The completion of the second social modernization is mainly marked by the completion of intellectualization, greenization, and social effectiveness and quality of life reaching the world's advanced level of knowledge society (at some points in the future).

Integrated social modernization is a basic path for developing countries in the twenty-first century. It comprises the coordinated development of the twice social modernizations and the continuous transition to knowledge society and the coordinated development of urbanization, suburbanization, welfarism, intellectualization, informatization, and greenization and the continuous transition to intellectualization and greenization, etc.

Social modernization has roughly three basic paths in the twenty-first century. The path for the first social modernization corresponds to the model of urbanization and welfarism, the path for the second social modernization corresponds to the model of intellectualization and greenization, etc., and the path for integrated social modernization corresponds to the model of new urbanization, including the coordinated development of urbanization, suburbanization, welfarism, intellectualization, informatization, greenization, etc.

Political Modernization

Political modernization refers to modernization in the political sphere. The theory of political modernization includes classic political modernization theory and political modernization theory in broad sense. The former is a branch of classic modernization theory, while the latter is the application of the second modernization theory in the political sphere.

According to the political modernization theory in the broad sense, political modernization refers to a sort of political change and international competition since the industrial revolution in the eighteenth century; the frontier process of the formation, development, transformation, and international interaction of modern politics; the complex process of the innovation, selection, diffusion, and withdrawal of political factors; and the international political competition and stratification for catching up with, reaching, and maintaining the world's advanced level of political development. It includes the transition from traditional to modern politics and from modern to postmodern politics. It also involves the rational and democratic political power, legislative and equal political participation, institutional and professional political system, and rational and efficient political behaviors.

Generally, political modernization refers to the world frontiers of political change and the process to reach the frontiers. From the eighteenth century to twenty-first century, the frontier process of political modernization can be divided into two major stages.

The first political modernization refers to the transition from agricultural to industrial politics, from authoritarian to democratic politics, from familial to civil politics, etc. Its features include democratization, rationalization, secularization, systematization, rule of law, bureaucratization, professionalization, class-stratified, concentration, etc. Its result is the formation of first political modernity, particularity, and diversity, with the side effect of political corruption. The major indicator of the completion of the first political modernization is the formation of democratic, free, equal, and efficient modern politics.

The second political modernization refers to the transition from industrial to knowledge politics, power-oriented to service-oriented politics, material to ecological politics, etc. Currently, it is featured with networking, knowledgeablization, service-based, greenization, diversification, internationalization, topic-related and opening politics, individualized and scattered politics, etc. Its result is the formation of the second political modernity, particularity, and diversity, with the side effect of decreasing political credit. So far, the second political modernization has not been fully rolled out.

Integrated political modernization is a basic path for the developing countries in the twenty-first century, including the coordinated development of the twice political modernizations and the shift toward knowledge-based politics. It requires the simultaneous promotion of the two political modernizations, including democratization, rationalization, systematization, professionalization, knowledge-based, networking, diverse and green politics, etc.

In the twenty-first century, there are three basic paths and several specific subpaths for political modernization. The basic paths include the path of the second political modernization, the first political modernization, and the integrated political modernization, with several subpaths under each. There are four subfields in the political sphere (political participation, national governance, international politics, and political environment), each of which follows a specific path of modernization, with the three basic paths being their envelope.

Cultural Modernization

Cultural modernization refers to the modernization in the cultural sphere. The theory of cultural modernization includes classic cultural modernization theory and cultural modernization theory in broad sense. The former is a branch of classic modernization theory, while the latter is the application of the second modernization theory in the cultural sphere.

According to the cultural modernization theory in broad sense, cultural modernization refers to a sort of cultural change and international competition since the Enlightenment in the eighteenth century; the frontier process of the formation, development, transformation, and international interaction of modern culture; the complex process of the innovation, selection, diffusion, and withdrawal of cultural factors; and the international cultural competition and stratification for catching up with, reaching, and maintaining the world frontier status of cultural change. It includes the transformation from traditional to modern culture and from modern to postmodern culture, the improvement of cultural creativity and the quality of cultural life, the development of cultural facilities and cultural industries, the self-emancipation and all-round development of mankind, etc.

Generally, cultural modernization refers to the world frontiers of cultural change and the process to reach the frontiers. During the period from the eighteenth century to the twenty-first century, the frontier process of cultural modernization can be divided into two major stages.

The first cultural modernization refers to the transition from agricultural to industrial culture, including the transition from authoritarian to democratic culture, from feudal to civic culture, from superstitious to scientific culture, from dependent to professional culture, from familial to welfare culture, from rural to urban culture, and so on. Its features include cultural differentiation, specialization, professionalization, rationalization, secularization, commercialization, scientific and personalized culture, etc. Its result is the formation of the first cultural modernity, particularity, and diversity, with the side effect of weakening humanity. The major indicator of the completion of the first cultural modernization is the formation of modern industrial and democratic culture.

The second cultural modernization refers to the transition from industrial to knowledge culture, including the transition from material to ecological culture, from entity to cyber (virtual) culture, from authoritative to civil culture, from machine to humane culture, from national to global culture, from cultural convergence to diversity, and so on. Currently, it is featured with the dedifferentiation of culture, cultural industrialization, networking, digitalization, ecologization, democratization, humanity, plurality, diversification, globalization, etc. Its result is the formation of the second cultural modernity, particularity, and diversity, with the side effect of Internet dependency, etc. The second cultural modernization is the world frontier of cultural modernization which has not been accomplished yet.

Integrated cultural modernization is a basic path for the developing countries. It is the process of the coordinated development of the twice cultural modernizations and the continuous shift toward knowledge culture. Its contents include the cultural industrialization, cultural diversity, networking, professional and scientific culture, democratic, rational and green culture, and so on.

There are three basic paths for cultural modernization in the twenty-first century: the first cultural modernization, the second cultural modernization, and the integrated cultural modernization. There is no standard model for cultural modernization. We have to choose the model rationally. There might be different models of success or failure in different countries or regions and in different stages of cultural modernization, which latecomers can study and learn from.

Ecological Modernization

Ecological modernization refers to the ecological interaction and transformation of modernization since 1970. The theory of ecological modernization includes European ecological modernization theory and ecological modernization theory in broad sense. The former, a theory of environmental sociology, was generated in the 1980s, while the latter was the application of the second modernization theory in the field of natural environment.

According to ecological modernization theory in broad sense, ecological modernization is the interaction and mutual coupling of modernization and natural environment and refers to the ecological transformation and international competition of modernization; the frontier process of the formation, development, and international interaction of ecological civilization; the complex process of innovation, selection, diffusion, and withdrawal of factors of ecological civilization; and the international competition and stratification for catching up with, reaching, and maintaining the world's advanced level of ecological civilization. It includes the transition from material to ecological civilization, economy, society, politics, and culture, and also the improved ecological quality and efficiency, and the change of ecological structure, institution, and ideas, as well as relevant international status. Ecological modernization is the intersection of ecological improvement, ecological economy, ecological society, international competition, and the change of relevant international status.

From the 1970s to the end of the twenty-first century, the process of ecological modernization can be divided into four stages: dematerialization and greening, hyperdematerialization and ecologization, win–win game for economy and environment, and the mutualism and coevolution of men and nature.

Ecological modernization follows the following ten principles: prevention, innovation, efficiency, unequivalence, dematerialization, greenization, ecologization, democratic participation, polluter pays (internalization of environmental cost), and the win–win game for economy and environment.

The result of ecological modernization is the formation of ecological modernity, particularity, and diversity. Currently, the features of ecological modernity include dematerialization, greening, ecologization, and the absolute decoupling between modernization and environmental degradation, and the mutual coexistence and coevolution of men and nature. The basic requirements are the absolute delinking between economic growth and environmental degradation and beneficial interaction between modernization and natural environment.

The result of ecological modernization is demonstrated by the profound changes in the following six aspects: first, the completion of ecological transformation and the mutualism of man and nature; second, the improvement of natural environment, the minimization of environmental pressure, and environmental friendliness; third, the increasing of ecological efficiency and the decreasing of resource and energy density; fourth, the upgrading of ecological structure and system; fifth, the popularization of ecological consideration; and sixth, the change of the international status of ecological transformation.

There are three basic paths for ecological modernization in the twenty-first century: comprehensive ecological modernization, integrated ecological modernization, and the ecological modification of the first modernization. The basic models of the ecological modernization in the twenty-first century include the model combining dematerialization, greenization, and ecologization; the model combining green industrialization and urbanization and ecological transition of structure; and the model combining industrialization, urbanization, and environmental management. Models which can be widely applied include environmental agenda, industrial ecology, ecological garden, green production and consumption, etc.

Human Modernization

Human modernization refers to the human changes during the modernization process, including individual progress, institutional development, environmental improvement, and so on. The theory of human modernization includes classic human modernization theory and human modernization theory in broad sense. The former is a branch of the classic modernization theory, while the latter is the application of the second modernization theory in the field of human behaviors.

According to the human modernization theory in broad sense, human modernization refers to the frontier change and international competition in the field of human development since the eighteenth century; the frontier process of the formation, development, transformation, and interaction of modern men; the complex process of the innovation, selection, diffusion, and withdrawal of human factors and civil systems; and the international competition differentiation and stratification for catching up with, reaching, and maintaining the world's advanced level of human development.

Generally, human modernization refers to the self-emancipation and all-round development of mankind and the intersection of individual progress, institutional development, and environmental improvement. It includes the transition from traditional mankind to modern mankind and from modern mankind to postmodern mankind, the improved quality and capabilities of citizens, the development of the rights and obligations of citizens, and the change of individual lifestyle, behavior model and values.

Human modernization includes the world frontiers of human development and the process to reach the frontiers in general. From the eighteenth century to the twenty-first century, the frontier process of human modernization can be divided into two major stages.

The human modernization in the first modernization process is known as the first human modernization for short, including the transition from traditional to modern men. It is mainly characterized by citizenship, professionalization, rationalization, equalization, economization, socialization, politicalization, the emphasis upon accomplishment and individual values, and the gradual adaption of individual behavior, qualities, capabilities, systems, and ideas to the industrial civilization. Its result is the formation of the first human modernity, particularity, and diversity, with the side effect of indifference between people, etc.

The human modernization in the second modernization process is known as the second human modernization for short. Currently, it is characterized by the networking, ecologization, diversification, personalization, internationalization, innovation, knowledgization, the emphasis upon happiness and self-realization, and the gradual adaption of individual behavior, qualities, capabilities, systems, and ideas to knowledge and ecological civilization. Its result is the formation of the second human modernity, particularity, and diversity, with the side effect of increasing risks, etc.

There are three paths in the twenty-first century: the first human modernization, the second human modernization, and integrated human modernization.

Further Reading

Eisenstadt SN (1966) Modernization, protest and change. Prentice-Hall, Englewood Cliffs, NJ

Harrison D (1988) The sociology of modernization and development. Unwin Hyman, London

Huntington SP (1968) Political order in changing societies. Yale University Press, New Haven, CT

Inglehart R, Welzel C (2005) Modernization, cultural change, and democracy: the human development sequence. Cambridge University Press, New York

Inkeles A, Smith DH (1974) Becoming modern: individual change in six developing countries. Harvard University Press, Cambridge

Levy MJ (1966) Modernization and the structure of societies. Princeton University Press, Princeton, NJ

Mol APJ, Sonnenfeld DA (eds) (2000) Ecological modernization around the world: perspectives and critical debates. Frank Cass, London

Peters MA, Besley AC (2006) Building knowledge cultures: education and development in the age of knowledge capitalism. Rowman & Littlefield, Lanham, MD

Research Group for China Modernization Strategies (2002) China modernization report 2002. Peking University Press, Beijing

RGCMS (Research Group for China Modernization Strategies et al) (2005) China modernization report 2005: economic modernization study. Peking University Press, Beijing

RGCMS (Research Group for China Modernization Strategies et al) (2006) China modernization report 2006: social modernization study. Peking University Press, Beijing

RGCMS (Research Group for China Modernization Strategies et al) (2007) China modernization report 2007: ecological modernization study. Peking University Press, Beijing

RGCMS (Research Group for China Modernization Strategies et al) (2009) China modernization report 2009: cultural modernization research. Peking University Press, Beijing

RGCMS (Research Group for China Modernization Strategies et al) (2010) China modernization report 2010: world modernization outline 1700-2100. Peking University Press, Beijing

Rostow WW (1960) The stages of economic growth: a non-communist manifesto. Cambridge University Press, Cambridge (Trans. Guo Xibao, Wang Songmao (2001) China Social Sciences Press, Beijing)

Schelkle W et al (eds) (2000) Paradigms of social change: modernization, development, transformation, evolution. St. Martin's Press, Campus Verlag, Frankfurt, New York

Steward JH (1955) Theory of culture change: the methodology of multilinear evolution. University of Illinois Press, Urbana, IL

Ward SC (2003) Modernizing the mind: psychological knowledge and the remaking of society. Praeger, Westport, CT

Yan J (2006) Political development: concepts and theories. Peking University Press, Beijing

Sector-Specific Modernization 7

Experience is the best teacher (American proverb), *experience is the mother of wisdom* (English proverb). Modernization occurs in all sectors of human civilization, and the study on which generally falls into the category of applied research in modernization science. This chapter provides a brief discussion on this issue by taking the agricultural, educational, and scientific and technological (S&T) sectors as examples.

Modernization takes place in all sectors, and sector-specific modernization is an important part of the modernization science (Fig. 7.1), and intersects with field-related, stratified, and staged modernization. Generally, modernization in different sectors has not only similarities but also differences, and the core theory of general modernization applies to different sectors in different ways; countries are the basic units of modernization, and modernization in each sector is closely related to national modernization.

7.1 Agricultural Modernization

Agricultural modernization is the modernization of the agricultural system, which is a manifestation of the modernization phenomenon. It embraces staged and stratified agricultural modernization, modernization of agricultural subsystems and subsectors (Fig. 7.2). The agricultural sector is fundamental for the national economy, and agricultural modernization is an integral part of economic modernization. Agriculture has the duality of nonsubstitution of food supply and market competition of agricultural goods. There are two drive forces of national profit and market needs for agricultural modernization in general.

7.1.1 Studies

Agricultural modernization research, whose object is the agricultural system, is an integral part of modernization research. The agricultural modernization study may

C. He, *Modernization Science*,
DOI 10.1007/978-3-642-25459-8_7,

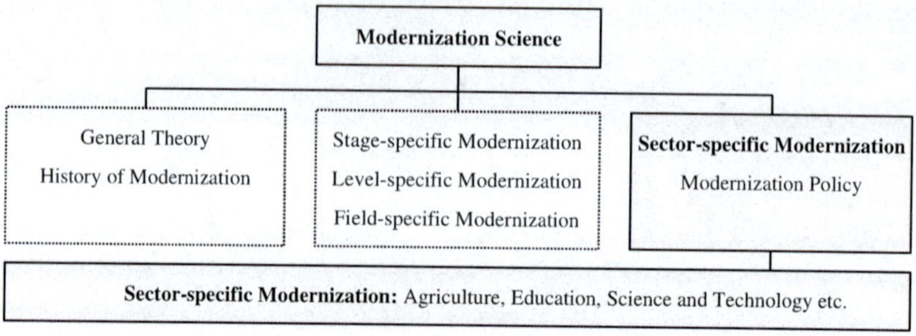

Fig. 7.1 Positioning and structure of sector-specific modernization

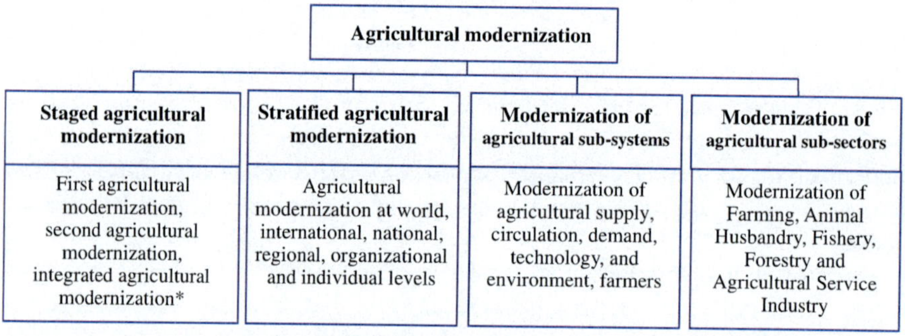

Fig. 7.2 Objects of agricultural modernization study. Note: As short words, "agriculture" here refers to the primary industry, including crop production (farming), animal husbandry, fishery, and forestry; the agricultural service industry refers to the industry directly serving agriculture. Agriculture is associated directly with farmers and rural areas, and agricultural modernization is related directly to farmers' and rural modernization. Farmers' modernization falls into the category of human modernization, and rural modernization is within the range of regional modernization; rural modernization needs to be specially treated, while farmers' modernization can be included into agricultural modernization; in advanced countries, most rural residents are not farmers, while most rural residents are farmers in developing countries. (*Asterisk*) Integrated agricultural modernization is the coordinated development of the first and second agricultural modernization, and it is a basic path of agricultural modernization in developing countries

start with the eighteenth century and may be analyzed from three dimensions including its historical process, objective reality, and future prospects.

7.1.1.1 Research Paradigm

The object of agricultural modernization research is modernization of the agricultural system, including modernization of agricultural supply, circulation, demand, technology, and environment as well as agricultural modernization at world, national, and regional levels. Research contents include modernization of agricultural behavior, structure, institutions, and concepts, as well as the process, outcomes, driving forces, and models of agricultural modernization, which together constitute a research matrix (Table 7.1). Other objects include stage-specific

Table 7.1 Matrix of agricultural modernization study

Content		Object		
		Agricultural system	Agricultural supply, circulation, demand, technology, environment, and farmers	World, national, and regional agriculture
		Agricultural modernization	Modernization of six agricultural subsystems	Agricultural modernization at the three levels
Element	Behavior Structure Institution Idea	Modernization of agricultural behavior, structure, institution, and ideas	Modernization of behavior, structure, institution, ideas in the six agricultural subsystems	Modernization of agricultural behavior, structure, institution, ideas at the three levels
Aspect	Process Result Dynamics Model	Process, result, dynamics, model of the agricultural modernization	Process, result, dynamics, model of modernization in the six agricultural subsystems	Process, result, dynamics, model of agricultural modernization at the three levels

Note: Agricultural supply involves enterprises, input, cost, efficiency, technologies, and systems. Agricultural circulation involves markets, trade, logistics, and finance. Agricultural demand involves consumption, investment, service, net export, etc. Agricultural technology involves agronomy, forestry, biology, agronomics, agroecology, etc. Agricultural environment includes domestic environment (economic, social, political, cultural, and ecological environment) and the international agricultural environment. Other contents of agricultural modernization research include, for example, stage-specific agricultural modernization, modernization in agricultural subsectors, agricultural frontier analysis, agricultural trend analysis, agricultural frontier process analysis, agricultural catch-up process analysis, international competition analysis, analysis of international agricultural gaps, and the interaction between the elements of agricultural modernization and various fields

agricultural modernization, modernization in agricultural subsectors, and the interaction between agriculture and modernization.

The agricultural modernization study is a part of modernization research where the methodology of the latter can be adopted. There are a wide variety of analysis methods to choose, such as time series analysis, cross-sectional analysis, process analysis, case study, qualitative analysis, statistical analysis, quantitative assessment, and coordinates analysis. The research may target the whole process or a particular stage of the process, or the world, a country, or a region, and is done mainly for the application of research findings, including the facts, characteristics, principles, and methods of agricultural modernization.

Agriculture is fundamental for national economy. It provides the food and materials people need to survive, and the food need is indispensable to human survival and social stability. Generally, food can only be preserved for a limited period of time. Ensuring the balance of food supply and demand is a basic requirement of agricultural modernization. Agricultural modernization concerns national interests, international competition, farmers' interests and social stability, immediate- and long-term food safety, etc. The research into agricultural modernization should be done systematically from multiple perspectives and at multiple levels.

7.1.1.2 Historical Facts

Broadly speaking, agricultural modernization is a sort of profound change in the agricultural system in the process of modernization—and it is a historical process in which agricultural efficiency is improved and the percentage of agriculture declines—and a process of transition toward agricultural marketization and mass production. Over the past 300 years, agricultural modernization has been an important part of economic modernization; it has finished the transition from traditional to modern agriculture in the first four waves of economic modernization and is now experiencing the transition from modern agriculture to knowledge-based agriculture, a new type of agriculture that is knowledge intensive and satisfies the needs of knowledge societies. It is predicted that in the twenty-first century, there will be two new waves of economic modernization and, at the same time, agricultural modernization will also see two new waves. The six waves of agricultural modernization have different features each (Table 7.2).

(1) Process Analysis

First, the first wave of agricultural modernization (about 1763–1870). It refers mainly to the agricultural revolution in Europe during the First Industrial Revolution, including in content: becoming scientific in agricultural production (by introducing new varieties and "farming in scientific ways"), commercialization of

Table 7.2 Two major stages and six waves of agricultural modernization

Wave	Approx. time	Economic modernization	Agricultural modernization	Annotation
First	1763–1870	First Industrial Revolution	Commercialization, marketization, and mechanization	*First agricultural modernization* Marketization, mechanization, use of chemicals, systematic; declining agricultural percentage
Second	1870–1945	Second Industrial Revolution	Application of chemicals, electrification, and specialization	
Third	1946–1970	Third Industrial Revolution	Intensification, systematic, and scientific	
Fourth	1970–2020	Knowledge revolution	Ecologicalization, informatization, and diversification	*Second agricultural modernization* Knowledgeablization, informatization, ecologicalization, diversify, plant-based, and internationalization
Fifth	2020–2050	New biological revolution	Internationalization, precision agriculture, and intellectualization	
Sixth	2050–2100	New physical revolution	Plant-based, order-based, and natural	

Note: Both a prediction, the fifth and sixth waves will depend on the future development of science and technology and population agricultural products, marketization of agricultural economy, mechanization of agricultural technologies, centralization of agricultural land, specialization of agricultural labor, the rise of modern agricultural organizational forms such as agricultural cooperatives and incorporated farms, improved literacy of farmers, and declined percentages of agricultural labor and value added.

Second, the second wave of agricultural modernization (about 1870–1945). It refers mainly to the frontier change of world agriculture during the Second Industrial Revolution and during the two World Wars, including in content: mechanization and electrification of agricultural technologies, commercialization and marketization of agricultural economy, specialization and large scale of agricultural production, institutionalization of agricultural management as enterprises, the use of fertilizers and pesticides, development of water conservancy, development of quality varieties and agricultural technology, improved qualities of farmers, and continually declined percentages of agricultural labor and value added. In the meanwhile, soil erosion sharpened, agricultural pollution arose, cyclical agricultural crises happened, and agriculture was still severely subject to natural disasters.

Third, the third wave of agricultural modernization (about 1946–1970). It included, among other things, the influence of the Third Industrial Revolution on world agriculture and green revolutions in agricultural countries. Frontier changes of world agriculture included the mechanization, electrification, and automation of agricultural technologies; the specialization, standardization, and large scale of agricultural production; the marketization and specialization of agricultural services; continued development of agriculture intensification, fine varieties, water conservancy, and the use of fertilizers; systematization of national agricultural policy and economy; continued development of modern agricultural technology; greatly improved qualities of farmers, continued decline of the percentages of agricultural labor and value added; increased international agricultural trade; and world attention drawn to pollution by fertilizers and pesticides. In the meanwhile, advanced countries completed in succession the first agricultural modernization featuring marketization, mechanization, systematization, and the intensive use of chemicals and established highly efficient and scientific economic, technological, and policy systems for modern agriculture.

Green revolutions were the technological revolutions happening in developing countries in the 1960s, featuring the wide use of improved crop varieties and the great improvement of modern agricultural technologies and grain yields. International agricultural research institutions successfully developed high-yield dwarf and semidwarf new varieties of wheat and rice, which were extended to developing countries and increased 11 developing countries' rice yield per unit by about 60%.

Fourth, the fourth wave of agricultural modernization (about 1970–2020). Affected by the high-tech information and ecological revolutions, profound changes have happened to the frontier of world agriculture. First, the information revolution gave rise to the wave of informatization in agriculture. Second, the ecological revolution caused the rise of ecological agriculture, sustainable agriculture, organic agriculture, green agriculture, etc. Third, the high-tech revolution, including development of high technologies such as biological technology, enriched the options of agricultural technologies and broadened the development prospects of agriculture. Fourth, the rise of knowledge economy and knowledge society fueled the knowledge and ecological transition of agricultural economy, leading to the rapid development of knowledge-based agriculture. Current features of knowledge-based agriculture include knowledgeablization, informatization, ecologicalization, diversification, intelligentization, precise and plant-type agriculture, and continued decline in the percentage of agriculture.

Fifth, the fifth wave of agricultural modernization, expected to come in 2020–2050, is based on a new biological revolution, including the application in agriculture of and the change in bioengineering, nanoengineering, information engineering, and new energy technologies. The downward trend in the percentage of agriculture is likely to reverse in advanced countries, and the percentages of knowledge-based agricultural labor and value added are likely to rise.

Sixth, the sixth wave of agricultural modernization, expected to come in 2050–2100, is based on a new physical revolution, including the application in agriculture of and the change in space technology, bioengineering, super manufacture, and transportation. Knowledge-based agriculture will be highly developed, with such basic features as plant- and order-based and natural agricultural production.

(2) Basic Facts

First, facts about agricultural supply. Since the eighteenth century, we saw the growth of agricultural labor and land productivity, agricultural investments and costs, the intensification of agricultural land, and the percentage of irrigated farming, as well as improved varieties and crops yields. From the nineteenth century onward, agricultural financial subsidies continued to grow, and the use of power, fertilizer, and pesticide continued to increase. Since the 1970s, the percentages of agricultural informatization, ecological agriculture, organic agriculture, and green agriculture have been on the rise.

Second, facts about agricultural circulation. Since the eighteenth century, we saw the increasing commercialization of agricultural products and marketization of agricultural factors of production, and the nineteenth century started to see the continued development of agricultural finance and international agricultural trade. Since the twentieth century, agriculture has become internationalized, tariffs on agricultural products have been on the decline, and conflicts in international agricultural trade have continued.

Third, facts about agricultural demand. From the eighteenth century on, the demand for the consumption of agricultural products and of protein and fat food rose continuously. The nineteenth century began to witness the continuous growth of the demand for agricultural machinery, fertilizer, and pesticide. Since the twentieth century, agricultural services have been socialized and marketized, and the intensiveness of agricultural capital has increased.

Fourth, facts about agricultural technologies. Since the eighteenth century, we saw the constant development of agricultural machinery and varieties, as well as farming and cultivation technologies, and the nineteenth century began to see the continuous development of fertilizer, pesticide, and agricultural technologies as well as the establishment of agricultural colleges, universities, research institutes, and institutions for promoting agricultural technologies. Since the twentieth century, high technologies have produced a considerable influence on agricultural technology, and the influence of bioengineering, information engineering, and green technologies has been expanding.

Fifth, facts about agricultural economy. From the eighteenth century onward, the percentage of agricultural value added in GDP and the percentage of agricultural labor in the total labor force declined continuously, and agricultural labor productivity was in inverse proportion to the percentage of agriculture (Table 7.3). The nineteenth century began to see the expanding government support of and international trade in agriculture. Since the twentieth century, there have been debates over agricultural protection and liberalization.

Sixth, facts about farmers. Since the eighteenth century, farmers' literacy has improved continuously. From the nineteenth century onward, primary education was popularized among farmers. Since the twentieth century, secondary education and higher education have been widely promoted among farmers, leading to a considerable increase in farmers' qualities. The ratio of farmers in the population decreased continually.

Over the past 300 years, agricultural behavior, structure, institutions, and concepts have been in constant flux: the form of agriculture has changed from subsistence to market-based and then to knowledge-based agriculture, the agricultural economy from small-scaled peasant economy to commodity economy and then to global agricultural economy, and the agricultural technology from natural cultivation to the increasing use of machinery and chemicals and then to informatization and ecologicalization. Agricultural changes have been highly unbalanced and asynchronous (Table 7.4).

Table 7.3 Percentages of the agricultural sector and per capita national income in the United States

Indicator	1900	1910	1920	1930	1940	1950	1960	1970	1980	1990	2000
Percentage of agricultural value added (%)	16.7	17.7	12.2	8.7	7.5	7.0	4.0	2.9	2.4	1.9	1.4
Percentage of agricultural labor (%)	37.6	31.6	27.4	9.4	6.8	4.8	3.3	1.9	1.9	1.6	1.7
Per capita national income (USD)	246	384	866	747	770	1,950	2,935	5,100	12,432	23,329	34,910

Source: RGCMS (2004)

Table 7.4 World agriculture in 2000

Item	Percentage of agricultural value added (%)	Percentage of agricultural labor (%)	Agricultural labor productivity (USD)	Agricultural mechanization (‰)	Crop yield per hectare (kg)
High-income countries	2	4	23,317	851	4,246
Middle-income countries	10	38	664	11	2,357
Low-income countries	26	62	355	5	1,309
World	4	42	859	20	2,143

Note: Agricultural mechanization refers to the number of tractors that per 1,000 agricultural laborers own. The data comes from World Bank (2008)

7.1.2 Theories

Agricultural modernization theory is a sector-specific modernization theory about the phenomenon of agricultural modernization. Currently, there are mainly three theories such as classical agricultural modernization theory, first and second agricultural modernization theory, and agricultural modernization theory in broad sense.

7.1.2.1 Classical Agricultural Modernization Theory

The history of classical agricultural modernization theory can be traced back to the 1960s. In his 1964 book, *Transforming Traditional Agriculture*, American economist Schultz proposed the transition from traditional to modern agriculture. A spate of works on agricultural modernization were published in the 1970s and 1980s, for example, *A Guide to Agricultural Modernization* (Malone et al. 1970), *Agricultural Modernization and Income Distribution* (Harrison 1973), and *Modernization of Agriculture in Developing Countries* (Arnon 1981). Since the 1960s, there has been substantial researches and works on agricultural modernization by Chinese scholars. But there are no universally recognized systematic theoretical expositions on classical political modernization. The theory is currently only a collection of academic thoughts about agricultural modernization (Table 7.5).

7.1.2.2 Twice Agricultural Modernization Theory

According to Huang and Deng (2008), *agricultural development can be divided into three stages: traditional agriculture, conventional modern agriculture and modern sustainable agriculture; the transition from traditional to conventional modern agriculture is the first agricultural modernization, and mainly characterized by mechanization, chemicalization, electrification, adequate irrigation, commercialization and socialization etc.; the transition from conventional*

Table 7.5 Main views of classical agricultural modernization theory

Aspect	Basic contents
Definition	Agricultural modernization is a process of transition from traditional to modern agriculture and the profound changes therein. It includes agricultural mechanization, electrification, adequate irrigation, chemicalization (use of chemicals), extensive use of improved varieties, labor and capital, standardization, scientific operation, socialization, specialization, commercialization, and marketization
Process	The process of agricultural modernization is a historical process, including agricultural commercialization and marketization, advancement of modern agricultural technology, introduction of modern factors of production and optimal allocation of factors, innovation and improvement of agricultural institutions, increased qualities and income of farmers, etc. There are multiple methods for defining the stages of the agricultural modernization process, for example, three stages, i.e., traditional agriculture and low-capital and low-technology agriculture, as well as high-capital and high-technology agriculture (Mellor 1966); two stages, i.e., subsistence farming and market-based agriculture which consists of three stages: diverse agriculture, specialized agriculture, and automated agriculture (Weitz 1971); or three stages, i.e., semimechanization, mechanization, and automation. The division of stages may vary from country to country
Outcomes	The transition from agricultural to modern agriculture includes considerable increase in agricultural labor productivity, land productivity, contribution by agricultural technological advances, and farmers' income; the establishment of a modern agricultural economy system, socialized service system, and agricultural technology system; the completion of mechanization, electrification, chemicalization, commercialization, and marketization; and the achievement of modernization in agricultural infrastructure, production technologies, and farmers' qualities
Driving forces	Views are different as to driving forces of agricultural modernization, for example, the four-element theory: agricultural market, agricultural technology, socialized agricultural service system in the main form of agricultural cooperatives, and government's macroeconomic control over agriculture (Xuan and Wang 1998); the theory of technological change: technological change is an endogenous variable, which drives agricultural development together with resource endowment, cultural condition, and institutional innovation (Hayami and Ruttan 1985)
Models	The models of agricultural modernization vary from country to country. Countries with low density of population, such as the USA, adopt the models of large-scale, mechanized, and labor-saving agricultural production; countries with high density of population, such as Japan, adopt the models of capita- and technology-intensive and land-saving agricultural production; countries with very limited per capita farmland, such as France, adopt the models of intensification, mechanization, and specialization

Source: Weitz (1971), Huang and Lin (2003), Liu (2006), Wang and Gao (2007), Wan and Zheng (2008), Jiang and Xin (2009)

modern to modern sustainable agriculture is the second agricultural modernization, and mainly characterized by standardization, informatization, knowledgeablization, specialization, the extensive use of biological technologies and facilities, farming management modernization, and the coordinated development of economy, society and ecological benefits.

In the opinion of Zhang and Huang (2002), *agricultural modernization can be divided into two levels: the first level of modernization is to improve land and labor productivity and meet people's growing needs for agricultural products; and the second level is to improve agricultural production efficiency, sustain the rapid growth of agriculture and meet people's needs for better and more varieties of products. In China, the first level of agricultural modernization was the change from natural production to semicommodity production and from natural to material economy; the second level of agricultural modernization was the shift from semicommodity to commodity production, and from material to knowledge economy. The technological development at the first level of agricultural modernization mainly featured agricultural mechanization, electrification, chemicalization and adequate irrigation, a process called the first agricultural modernization; the technological development at the second level of agricultural modernization mainly featured agricultural standardization, informatization, the extensive use of biological technologies and agricultural facilities, and the corresponding management modernization, a process called the second agricultural modernization.*

7.1.2.3 Agricultural Modernization Theory in Broad Sense

Raised by Chinese scholar Chuanqi He, the agricultural modernization theory in broad sense refers to the theoretical explanations about the phenomenon of agricultural modernization between the eighteenth and the twenty-first centuries, and it is the application of the second modernization theory in the agricultural system. It includes the general theory, branch theories, and relevant theories (Table 7.6). Below is a discussion of its general theory (Table 7.7), including five aspects of agricultural modernization: definition, process, result, dynamics, and models. Currently, the knowledge of the second agricultural modernization and integrated agricultural modernization is very limited.

Table 7.6 Structure of agricultural modernization theory in broad sense

Classification	Theories	Main contents
General theory	Core theory	The definition, process, result, dynamics, and models of agricultural modernization
Branch theories	Stage theory	First and second agricultural modernization and integrated agricultural modernization
	Stratified study	Agricultural modernization at world, national, regional, etc., levels
	Subsystem study	Modernization of agricultural supply, circulation, demand, environment, agricultural science and technology, and farmers
	Subsector study	Modernization of farming, animal husbandry, fishery, forestry, and agricultural service industry
Relevant theories	Other modernization theories	Classical agricultural modernization theory, twice agricultural modernization theory, second modernization theory, etc.
	Other relevant theories	Agricultural development theory, agricultural economics, agronomy, biology, ecology, etc.

Table 7.7 General theory of agricultural modernization theory in broad sense

Aspect	Basic contents
Definition	Agricultural modernization is modernization of the agricultural system in general. It is the agricultural change and international competition since the Industrial Revolution of the eighteenth century; the frontier process of the formation, development, transition, and international interaction of modern agriculture; and the composite process of the alternate innovation, selection, diffusion, and withdrawal of agricultural elements, as well as the international competition for and international differentiation as a result of catching up with, reaching, and maintaining the world's advanced level
Process	Agricultural modernization is a complex process, including, among other things, agricultural development, transition, international agricultural competition, international agricultural differentiation, and national agricultural stratification; the change of agricultural behavior, structure, institutions, and concepts; and the world frontier of agricultural change as well as the process of reaching the world frontier. In the eighteenth to twenty-first centuries, the frontier trajectory of agricultural modernization could be divided into two major stages: first agricultural modernization, the transition and profound change from traditional to primary modern agriculture and from subsistence to market-based agriculture, characterized mainly by marketization, intensification, mechanization, chemicalization, specialization, and decline in the percentage of agriculture; second agricultural modernization, the transition from primary modern to advanced modern agriculture and from market-based to knowledge-based and ecological agriculture, currently characterized mainly by knowledgeablization, informatization, ecologicalization, plant-based operation, internationalization, diversification, and improved international competition; the coordinated development of the first and second agricultural modernization is the integrated agriculture modernization. New changes will occur in agricultural modernization in the twenty-second century. Agricultural modernization follows the ten basic principles of modernization (Table 2.15)
Result	Formation of agricultural modernity, particularity, diversity, and side effects, including the increase of agricultural efficiency and farmers' income, the dynamic equilibrium between agricultural supply and demand, the improvement of farmers' welfare and agricultural environment, the development of agricultural technology and institutions, the decline in the percentage of agriculture, and the change in national agricultural level, international agricultural status, and international agricultural system. The outcome of the first agricultural modernization is the formation of the first agricultural modernity, particularity, and diversity, with side effects including agricultural environmental pollution and soil erosion; the completion of the first agricultural modernization is marked by agricultural marketization, mechanization, and systematization, as well as the agricultural efficiency, agricultural percentage, and farmers' income reaching the advanced level of market-based agriculture (the world's advanced level in the 1960s). The outcome of the second agricultural modernization is the formation of the second agricultural modernity, particularity, and diversity, with side effects including agricultural trade conflict and food risk; the completion of the second agricultural modernization is marked by knowledgeablization and ecologicalization, as well as the comprehensive agricultural benefits and farmers' qualities reaching the advanced level of knowledge-based agriculture (sometime in the future). The basic criterion of accomplishing agricultural modernization is that agricultural efficiency, farmers' income, agricultural percentage, and institutions reach the world's advanced level from the policy perspective

(continued)

Table 7.7 (continued)

Aspect	Basic contents
Dynamics	Driving factors of agricultural modernization include innovation, exchange, competition, adaptation, national interests, and market demand; economic growth, change of demand, industrialization, informatization, globalization, and rational anticipation; and natural resource endowments, technological advancement, institutional progress, and the change of agricultural structure, environment, and policies. The driving models include innovation drive, triple drive, two-wheel drive, associative action, four-step hypercycle, composite agricultural interaction, innovation diffusion, innovation spillover, competition drive, and agricultural productivity function (Table 2.20). The driving forces of agricultural modernization vary from country to country and from stage to stage
Models	Agricultural modernization has a diversity of paths and models, which are of path dependency and are subject to the influences of population, land, culture, and international environment. There are three basic paths in the twenty-first century: first agricultural modernization, second agricultural modernization, and integrated agricultural modernization. Models of agricultural modernization are diverse and depend on objective conditions; countries and regions with different objective conditions may create or choose different models, and different models may be chosen for different development stages

Note: There has been no standard definition of modern agriculture. Generally, modern agriculture includes primary modern agriculture and advanced modern agriculture. Primary modern agriculture refers to market-based agriculture featuring commercialization, specialization, and mechanization, represented by the market-based agriculture of industrialized countries in the 1960s. Advanced modern agriculture refers to knowledge-based agriculture featuring knowledgeablization, ecologicalization, and internationalization; currently, it is represented by the knowledge-based agriculture of advanced countries and is still developing
Source: RGCMS (2010)

(1) Definition

Agricultural modernization, modernization of the agricultural system, is a part of economic modernization and a manifestation of modernization.

In connotative terms, agricultural modernization is a sort of frontier change and international competition in the agricultural system beginning from the Industrial Revolution of the eighteenth century; it includes the formation, development, transition, and international interaction of modern agriculture; the innovation, selection, diffusion, and withdrawal of agricultural elements; and the international agricultural competition for and the international differentiation and national stratification as a result of catching up with, reaching, and maintaining the world's advanced level of agricultural development and transformation.

In denotative terms, agricultural modernization includes agricultural modernization at world, national, and regional levels; modernization of agricultural behavior, structure, institutions, and concepts; modernization of agricultural supply, circulation, demand, environment, technology, and farmers; modernization of agricultural production mode, operation mode, infrastructure, and management; modernization of farming, animal husbandry, fishery, forestry, and agricultural service industry; and the change in the temporal and spatial distribution of agricultural modernization.

Generally, agricultural modernization refers to the world frontier and the process to reach these frontier of agricultural change and includes the transition from traditional agriculture (subsistence agriculture) to primary modern agriculture (market-based agriculture) and from primary modern agriculture to advanced modern agriculture (knowledge-based agriculture), the continued increase of agricultural efficiency and farmers' income, the continued improvement of farmers' welfare and quality of life, and the change of agriculture's status in national economy and the international agricultural system. Countries are the basic units of research into and the practice of agricultural modernization, which is an integral part of national modernization and economic modernization.

Agricultural modernization is a type of change in the agricultural system. Obviously, not all changes in agriculture can be defined as a part of agricultural modernization. Broadly speaking, only agricultural changes conductive to productivity improvement, social progress, and farmers' development serve as components of agricultural modernization.

In general, agricultural development includes agricultural growth and progress; agricultural modernization is an intersection of agricultural development, agricultural transition, agricultural international competition, and the change of the international status (Table 7.8).

(2) Process

Agricultural modernization is a complex, long-standing, and global process, including changes in production modes, core technologies, infrastructure, farmers' qualities, and agricultural system. The process of agricultural modernization can be divided into two types: frontier process and catch-up process with both common and different features. In the eighteenth to twenty-first centuries, its frontier process can be divided into two stages: first and second agricultural modernization (Table 7.9), both of which include four stages—start, developing, mature, and transition (Fig. 7.3). According to their technological and economic features, the first agricultural modernization includes three waves, and the second agricultural

Table 7.8 Conceptual model of agricultural modernization

Item	Contents
Hypothesis 1	Agricultural growth refers to the growth of agricultural yield and output value
Hypothesis 2	Agricultural progress refers to the increase of agricultural efficiency and benefits, the advancement in agricultural technologies and institutions, and the improvement of farmers' welfare and quality of life
Hypothesis 3	Agricultural transition refers to the change and alternation of old agricultural patterns (including two agricultural transitions)
Hypothesis 4	Change of international agricultural status refers to the change of international status by agricultural economic level and agricultural competitiveness
Inference 1	Agricultural development = agricultural growth + agricultural progress + agricultural growth × agricultural advancement
Inference 2	Agricultural modernization = agricultural development × agricultural transition × international agricultural competition and status change

Table 7.9 Two stages of agricultural modernization in broad sense

Item	First agricultural modernization	Second agricultural modernization
Time	Approx. 1763–1970	Approx. 1970–2100
Content	Transition from subsistence to market-based agriculture	Transition from market-based to knowledge-based agriculture
Technology	Mechanization, chemicalization, electrification, automation, etc.	Intellectualization, informatization, intelligentization, greening, biological technology, etc.
Production	Specialized, standardized, scientific, and large-scale production	Precision, green, high quality, plant- and order-based production
Economy	Marketization, commercialization, industrialization, decline in the percentage of agriculture	Knowledgeablization, ecologicalization, internationalization, high efficiency, high competitiveness
Institutions	Agricultural cooperative, agricultural technological extension, policy support, etc.	Environmental protection, agricultural subsidy, low tariff, etc.
Concepts	Efficiency, yield, income, technology, etc.	Effectiveness, quality, innovation, environmental awareness, etc.
Farmers	Improved literacy and extended primary education	Improved competitiveness and extended higher education
Driving forces	Technology, institutions, capital, population, industrialization, etc.	Knowledge, information, innovation, ecological awareness, international competition, etc.
Goal	Balance of supply and demand of agricultural products, improvement of agricultural efficiency, etc.	Improvement of agricultural effectiveness and international competitiveness, assurance of food safety, etc.
Modernity	First agricultural modernity: primary modern agriculture, market-based agriculture, mechanized agriculture, high-efficiency agriculture, etc.	Second agricultural modernity: advanced modern agriculture, knowledge-based agriculture, ecological agriculture, organic agriculture, information-based agriculture, high-effectiveness agriculture, etc.
Side Effects	Agricultural environmental pollution, soil erosion, etc.	Agricultural trade conflict, food risk, etc.

modernization will also include three waves (Table 7.2). The first and the second agricultural modernization have different connotations and features.

The first agricultural modernization is the transformation from traditional to primary modern agriculture and from subsistence to market-based industrial agriculture. It includes the transitions from manual to mechanized agriculture, from natural to chemical agriculture, from extensive to intensive agriculture, from individual to industrialized agriculture, from household-based to socialized agriculture, from subsistence to specialized agriculture, from seasonal to artificial agriculture, from small-scaled peasant economy to commodity economy, from agricultural taxation to agricultural subsidization, and from boorish culture to market culture. Its features include marketization, commercialization, intensification, high efficiency, specialization, mechanization, electrification, automation, chemicalization,

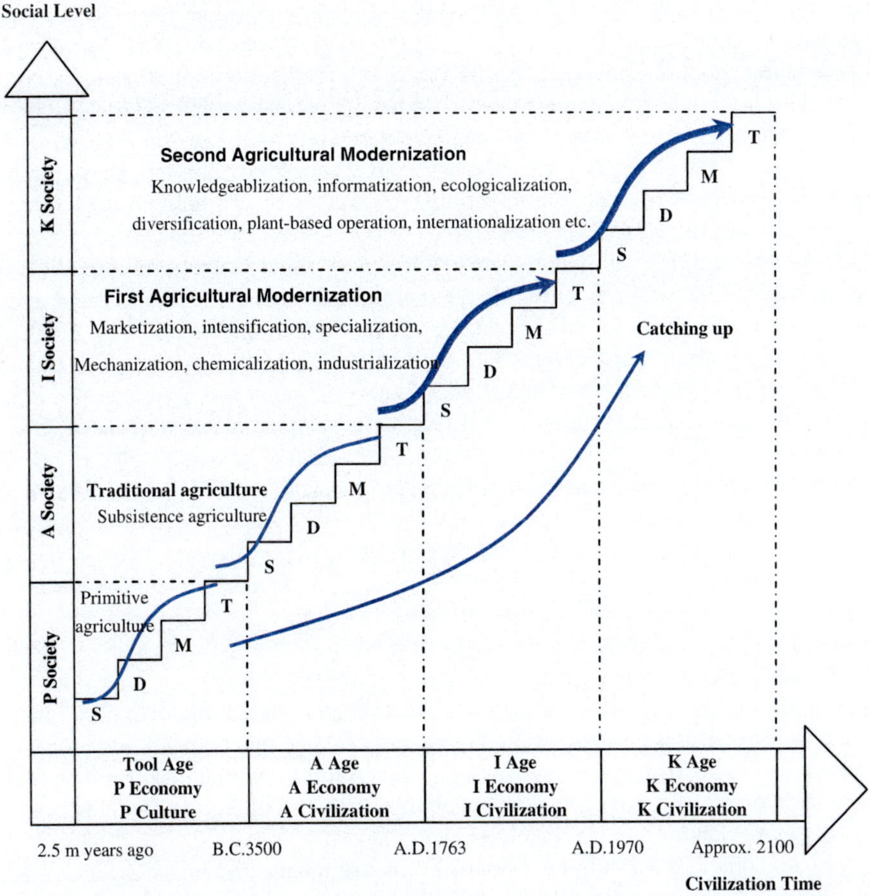

Fig. 7.3 *Coordinates of agricultural modernization.* Note: P, A, I, and K refer to primitive, agricultural, industrial, and knowledge, respectively. S, D, M, and T refer to the start, developing, mature, and transition phases, respectively. The civilization time was the time based on the track of the forerunner of the civilization

extensive use of improved varieties and irrigation facilities, large-scale operation, socialization, standardization, institutionalization, systematization, and increasing application of technologies; the improvement of agricultural labor productivity, land productivity, and farmers' living standards; and the declining percentages of agricultural labor in total employee and value added in GDP.

The second agricultural modernization is the transformation from primary modern agriculture to advanced modern agriculture and from market-based to knowledge-based, ecological, and sustainable agriculture. It includes the transitions from efficiency-focused to ecological agriculture, from chemical to organic agriculture, from mechanized to information-based agriculture, from open-air to plant-based agriculture, from supplier- to order-based agriculture, from standard to precision agriculture, from investment-intensive to economical agriculture, from national to international agriculture, and from specialized to diversified agriculture. Currently, its features include knowledgeablization, informatization, intelligentization, precision, high quality, ecologicalization, greening, naturalization, diversification, order- and plant-based production, and internationalization; the improvement of agricultural comprehensive effectiveness, international competitiveness, and farmers' quality of life; and the declining percentages of agricultural labor in all employees and value added in GDP.

If the first agricultural modernization is taken as primary agricultural modernization, i.e., the transition from traditional to primary modern agriculture, the second agricultural modernization is advanced agricultural modernization, i.e., the transition from primary to advanced modern agriculture. The coordinated development of the first and second agricultural modernization is integrated agricultural modernization. New changes will occur in the agricultural modernization in the twenty-second century.

The process of agricultural modernization is long standing, complex, systematic, global, progressive, risky, nonlinear, diverse, differentiated in agricultural efficiency, and convergent in agricultural percentages.

Agricultural modernization is a manifestation of modernization and follows the ten basic principles of modernization (Table 2.15).

(3) Result

Outcomes of agricultural modernization include the formation of agricultural modernity, particularity, diversity, and side effects. The outcomes of agricultural modernization in different countries not only share some common features but also have differences; the first agricultural modernization has different outcomes from the second agricultural modernization (Table 7.7).

The outcomes of agricultural modernization are manifested in six aspects: the completion of the two agricultural transitions, the improvement of agricultural efficiency and farmers' income, the improvement of farmers' welfare and quality of life, the decline of agricultural percentages, the development of agricultural technologies and institutions, and the change of the international agricultural system and national agricultural status.

In the process of agricultural modernization, a portion of countries reach and maintain the world's advanced level of agricultural development and transformation and become agriculturally advanced countries, and other countries become agriculturally developing ones; there is mobility between the two types of countries. Broadly speaking, agriculturally advanced countries account for less than 20% of all countries throughout the world, and agriculturally developing countries account for more than 80%; the two types of countries are in dynamic equilibrium.

The goals of national agricultural modernization include: completing the first agricultural modernization, achieving the transition from traditional to primary modern market-based agriculture; completing the second agricultural modernization, achieving the transition from primary to advanced modern agriculture; catching up with, reaching, and maintaining the world's agricultural advanced level;

becoming agriculturally advanced countries; or narrowing down international agricultural gaps; and ensuring food security.

According to the second modernization theory, the criteria of completing the first agricultural modernization include that the percentage of agricultural value added in GDP is below 15%, the percentage of agricultural labor in the total labor is below 30%, and the agricultural labor productivity stands at the world's advanced level in the 1960s (approximately $6,000 as prices in 2000); the criteria of entering the second agricultural modernization include that the percentage of agricultural value added in GDP is below 5%, the percentage of agricultural labor in the total labor is below 10%, and organic or ecological agriculture is underway.

(4) Dynamics

Driving forces of agricultural modernization are different at different levels, in different countries, and in different stages.

The driving forces of agricultural modernization include driving factors and mechanisms. The driving mechanisms of agricultural modernization include industrialization drive, innovation drive, triple drive, two-wheel drive (Fig. 7.4), and competition drive.

Agricultural productivity is one of the key indicators of agricultural modernization. The agricultural productivity function, which includes the driving factors of agricultural modernization, may be used to quantitatively analyze the driving forces of agricultural modernization.

Agricultural productivity function: Agricultural productivity is in direct proportion to agricultural technologies as well as the per capita capital and skills of agricultural labor.

$$P_{\mathrm{a}} = A \times C^{a} \times S^{1-a},$$

where "P_{a}" stands for agricultural productivity (per capita output of agricultural labor), "A" for multiplier of technological advancement, "C" for per capita capital of agricultural labor, "S" for per capita skills of agricultural labor, "a" for the share of output from agricultural capital, and $(1 - a)$ for the share of output from agricultural labor.

The multiplier of technological advancement reflects the effects of agricultural technological advancement, optimal allocation of resources, and economy of scale.

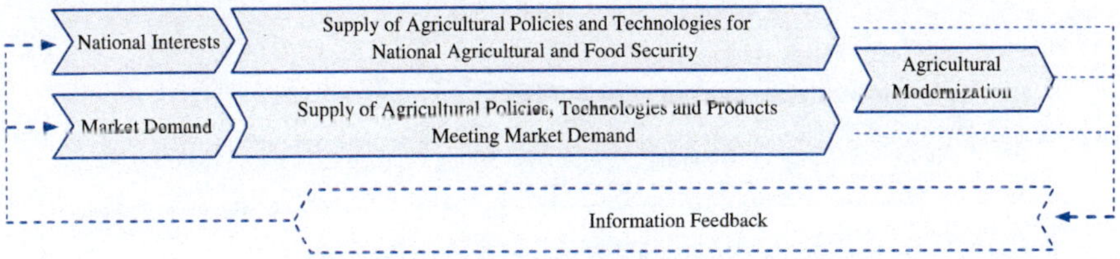

Fig. 7.4 Two-wheel drive model of agricultural modernization

(5) Models

There are roughly three basic paths of agricultural modernization in the twenty-first century (Fig. 7.5). Different countries and regions may choose different paths.

Generally, there are a variety of agricultural modernization models, and different countries and regions may choose or create different models.

There are no standard models of agricultural modernization, and the selection of a model is subject to the influences of objective conditions and international environment.

Choosing a model for the first agricultural modernization is more dependent on a country's actual conditions (Table 7.5), and that for the second agricultural modernization, more on its technological level and the international environment. Knowledge-based agriculture has multiple models (Table 7.10), such as integrated agriculture, information-based agriculture, plant-based agriculture, sustainable agriculture, and ecological agriculture.

(6) Integrated Agricultural Modernization

Integrated agricultural modernization, a basic path of agricultural modernization in the twenty-first century, includes two successive agricultural transitions (from subsistence to market-based agriculture and from market-based to knowledge-based and ecological agriculture) and the continued transition toward knowledge-based agriculture; the coordinated development of agricultural marketization,

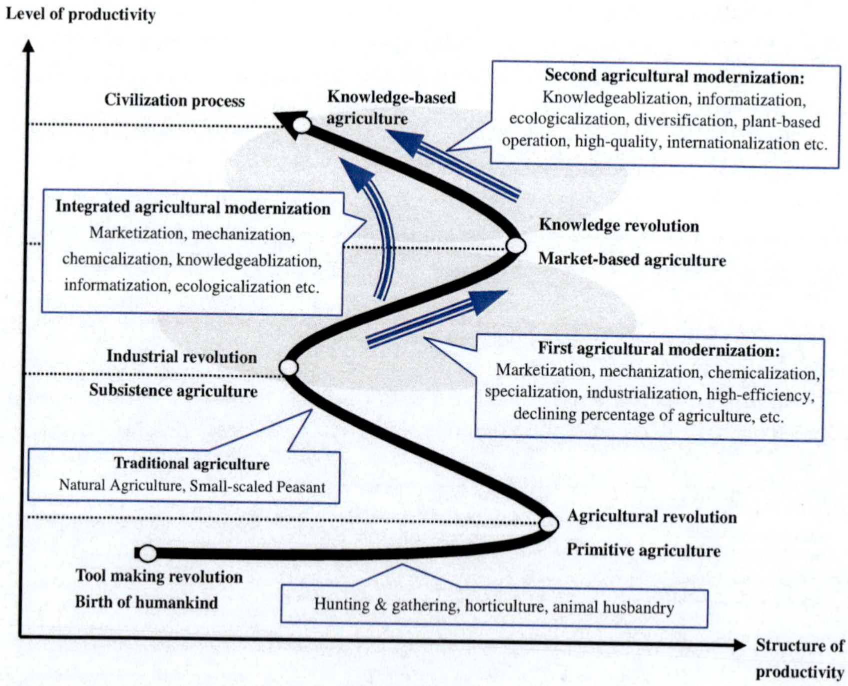

Fig. 7.5 Three paths of agricultural modernization in twenty-first century

Table 7.10 Main types of knowledge-based agriculture

Type	Features
Integrated agriculture	Knowledge-intensive, high-tech, integrated agriculture based on the organic combination of production, processing, warehousing, transportation, sales, and services. There may be a wide variety of forms of organization, for example, joint-stock agricultural cooperatives built on free will, equality, mutual benefit and democratic management, contractual production associations under leadership of distribution companies or product processing ones, regional farms, and large modern agricultural enterprises consisting of processing and service companies
Information-based agriculture	Information-based and intellectual agriculture, in which an "agricultural expertise system" provides farmers with appropriate information services and decision-making suggestions. Connected to the global positioning system and e-commerce system, this system monitors in real-time fashion the situations of global farm produce markets and enables located observation of farm crops and damage to plant by diseases and pests. Kept informed of market situations and farm crops; farmers will be able to take measures in time. Examples include precision agriculture
Plant-based agriculture	Employ soilless culture technologies, plant-based production technologies for agricultural products, and artificial food synthesis technologies to realize the plant-based production of food and other agricultural products. Design and produce food according to market needs. Examples include facility agriculture
Sustainable agriculture	Both the theory and practice of sustainable agriculture are in development. The purpose is, by using a particular way that enables the utilization and protection of natural resources and by practicing technological and institutional innovations, to ensure the needs of people of the time, and future generations can be satisfied on a continued basis. It requires the application of new knowledge and high technologies, improved literacy of farmers, and achievement of harmony between economy, society, ecology, man, and nature
Ecological agriculture	Ecological agriculture will be built on breakthroughs in ecology, cultural values, and biological technologies. Biological technologies are employed to design various high-quality, high-yield, disease-resistant, stress-tolerant, and characteristic new varieties with extensive use of water manure, and ecological friendly cropping technologies are used to produce agricultural products that meet the needs of users of different cultural values. New products are culturally meaningful and visually pleasing. Examples include organic agriculture, green agriculture, and pollution-free agriculture
Natural agriculture	Produce natural products by designing and planting crops according to local natural conditions; by taking such technical measures as natural farming, rotation method, and ecological leisure method; and by reducing or applying no fertilizer, pesticide, and artificial products. The new natural agriculture differs from the traditional natural agriculture
Sightseeing agriculture	Scenic areas will develop tourist agriculture, giving consideration to both tourism and food production. The crop structure, food processing, town development, road construction, natural landscape, and tourist facilities will be planned overall so that agriculture and tourism can benefit each other. Part of sightseeing agriculture will develop into culture-based agriculture that spreads culture, knowledge, and tradition

(continued)

Table 7.10 (continued)

Type	Features
Leisure agriculture	Farmers living around cities lend their land to urban residents, where they plant crops, raise animals, and produce their favorite agricultural products themselves at leisure time, and thus enjoy labor, nature, and leisure

Note: There is no standard classification of knowledge-based agriculture. Different classifications have different emphases, and some intersect with each other to a certain degree
Source: He (1999)

mechanization, informatization, greening, and internationalization; and the increase of agricultural efficiency and farmers' income, the improvement of farmers' welfare and quality of life, the decline in the percentage of agriculture, and the improvement of international agricultural competitiveness and status.

Integrated agricultural modernization is a historical process of the coordinated development of the first and second agricultural modernization and of the continued transition toward the second agricultural modernization. It includes the change in production modes, key technologies, agricultural structure, agricultural institutions and concepts, and the international competition for catching up with and reaching the world's agricultural advanced level. The completion of the integrated agricultural modernization is marked by the fact that agricultural efficiency, agricultural benefits, farmers' welfare and quality of life, agricultural institutions, and technologies all reach the world's advanced level then.

7.2 Modernization of Education

Educational modernization is the modernization of the education system. It is a manifestation of the modernization phenomenon, including stage-specific and level-specific educational modernization, modernization in educational subsectors and subsystems (Fig. 7.6). The educational sector is part of the social sphere, and educational modernization is a constituent part of social modernization. Educational modernization is closely related to human and cultural modernization. Education has the duality of not only for public welfare but also as a commodity. Educational modernization is driven by both national interest and market demand.

7.2.1 Studies

Educational modernization research, whose object is the educational system, is an integral part of modernization research. Educational modernization research may start with the eighteenth century and may be analyzed from three aspects—historical process, objective reality, and future prospects.

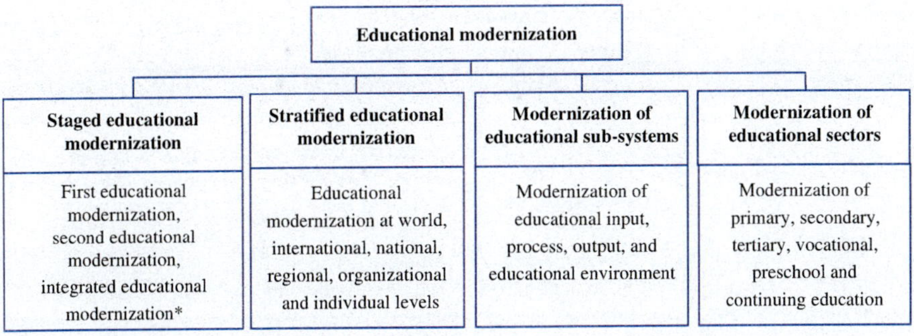

Fig. 7.6 Objects of educational modernization study. Note: (*Asterisk*) Integrated educational modernization means the coordinated development of twice educational modernizations and is a basic path for social modernization in developing countries

7.2.1.1 Research Paradigm

The object of educational modernization research is the modernization of the educational system, including the modernization of educational input, process, output, and environment as well as educational modernization at world, national, and regional levels. Research contents include the modernization of educational behavior, structure, institutions, and concepts as well as the process, outcomes, driving forces, and models of educational modernization. They may constitute a research matrix (Table 7.11). Other research objects include stage-specific educational modernization and modernization in educational subsectors.

Educational modernization research, an integral part of modernization research, may use the methodologies of modernization research, such as time series analysis, cross-sectional analysis, process analysis, cast study, qualitative analysis, and coordinates analysis. It may target the entire process or a particular stage of educational modernization within the range of the world or a particular country or region.

Educational modernization is a complex systematic process, involving educators and the students, public services and market competition, social fairness and social harmony, state interest and family interest, national interest and international competition, and present and future demands. Educational modernization research should be done from multiple perspectives, at multiple levels, and in a systematic way.

7.2.1.2 Historical Facts

Educational modernization, which started in around the eighteenth century, is a form of educational change. It is an integral part of social modernization closely related to economic modernization. The frontier trajectory of economic and social modernization includes two stages and six waves, and that of educational modernization is divided accordingly into two stages and six waves (Table 7.12).

Table 7.11 Matrix of educational modernization study

Content Element		Object		
		Educational system	Educational input, process, output, and environment	Education at world, national, and regional levels
		Educational modernization	Modernization of four educational subsystems	Educational modernization at three levels
	Behavior Structure Institution Idea	Modernization of educational behavior, structure, institution, and ideas	Modernization of behavior, structure, institution, ideas in the four educational subsystems	Modernization of educational behavior, structure, institution, ideas at the three levels
Aspect	Process Result Dynamics Model	Process, result, dynamics, model of the educational modernization	Process, result, dynamics, model of modernization in the four educational subsystems	Process, result, dynamics, model of educational modernization at the three levels

Note: Educational input includes educational funding, teachers, and educational facilities that include schools and other public and private educational facilities. The educational process involves educational participation, contents, methods, educational management, etc. Educational output involves educational achievements, efficiency, and educational returns that include personal and social returns (educational contributions to economic and social advances). Educational environments involve domestic educational environments (economy, society, politics, culture, etc.) and international educational environments. Research contents also include stage-specific modernization, modernization of educational subsectors, educational frontier analysis, educational trend analysis, analysis of the educational frontier and catch-up processes, and the interaction between educational modernization elements and different fields.

(1) Process Analysis

First, the first wave of educational modernization happened during the First Industrial Revolution, mainly in European and American countries, with such countries as Germany and France keeping ahead. In the beginning of the eighteenth century, Germany (Prussia) began introducing compulsory education, establishing practical and normal schools; in early nineteenth century, it founded the University of Berlin, which had autonomy over its management, advocated academic freedom and the unity of teaching and research, and emphasized teaching and learning freedom, and later on established a group of colleges and universities for engineering and applied sciences. In 1762, French thinker Rousseau published *Émile* in which he raised the thought of nature education. In 1763, French La Chalotais published his *Essay on National Education* in which he proposed educational secularization. During the French Revolution, France launched a number of educational reform programs, which stressed education as a public enterprise, and required that the state-run secular schools impose supervision and management on national education and establish relevant educational administrative institutions. In 1802, France enacted the *Fundamental Law on Public Education* and, afterward, established the national educational system and administered national education in a centralized manner; at

Table 7.12 Two major stages and six waves of educational modernization

Wave	Approx. time	Content	Annotation
First	1763–1870	Secularization, providing education in scientific and practical ways; popularization, developing compulsory education	*First educational modernization* Specialization, becoming scientific, standardization, institutionalization, spreading compulsory education
Second	1870–1945	Rule of law, standardization, popularizing compulsory primary education, developing secondary education	
Third	1946–1970	Democratization, electrification, popularizing secondary education, developing higher education	
Fourth	1970–2020	Informatization, individuation, internationalization, quality of education, popularizing higher education	*Second educational modernization* Informatization, individuation, internationalization, spreading higher education, lifelong learning
Fifth	2020–2050	Lifelong learning, information converter, unobstructed access to knowledge and information	
Sixth	2050–2100	Learning will become an experience; schools and education will change drastically in patterns	

Note: The fifth and sixth waves are just forecasts

the same time, mission schools were preserved, public and private schools coexisted, and emphasis was laid on secondary and higher education.

Second, the second wave of educational modernization happened during the Second Industrial Revolution and the two World Wars and spanned Europe, America, and Asia. It mainly embraced the popularizing of compulsory primary education and the development of secondary education, vocational education, and preschool education. In 1872, Germany enacted the *Common School Law*, prescribing that the 8-year primary education for children from the age of 6 to 14 was compulsory and requiring that on-the-job young people below 18 receive vocational education. Briton promulgated the *Elementary Education Act* in 1970, initiated free elementary education in 1891, enforced the state management of education in combination with local autonomy in 1902, and in 1918, required the vigorous development of secondary education throughout the nation and set the goal of popularizing secondary education. In 1882, France enacted its elementary education law—*Jules Ferry Law*, which prescribed the nonreligion educational principle and the compulsory education system; in 1883, it prescribed the setting of departments according to subjects at colleges and universities and afterward carried out an educational reform in the principle of developing "impartial, compulsory, and free" education; in 1933, it decided to provide free secondary education. The United States established a great variety of vocational middle schools after 1880; in 1918, compulsory elementary education was spread countrywide; in

Table 7.13 Educational modernization processes of five countries

Country	Gross enrollment rate of elementary education (%)			Gross enrollment rate of secondary education (%)			Gross enrollment rate of tertiary education (%)		
	1870	1900	1950	1900	1950	1970	1950	1970	2000
USA	100	100	100	6	49	84	18	47	71
Germany	–	100	100	–	17	–	3	–	49
France	100	100	100	3	24	73	4	19	54
UK	46	100	100	3	54	73	2	14	59
Japan	–	79	100	2	70	87	6	18	48

Note: Gross enrollment rates takes the value of 100% when above 100%; the same below. The data comes from World Bank (2008)

1862 and 1890, the federal government financed the states' establishment of agricultural and mechanical colleges; in 1940, the country had a total number of 1,800 colleges and universities for 1.5 million students. Between 1900 and 1950, many industrialized countries popularized elementary education countrywide and started the process of spreading secondary education and developing higher education (Table 7.13).

Third, the third wave of educational modernization mainly included the popularization of secondary education and the development of higher education. Compulsory education was extended to 9 years and, in some countries such as France, to 12 years. Governments all set up their special educational management bodies, but the management styles were different. The management of schools including elementary and secondary schools and universities mainly took the form of president's responsibility system; the board of education had the supreme authority over schools, whose members came from various circles including students and teachers, and practiced democratic management.

Fourth, the fourth wave of educational modernization mainly included informatization, individuation, internationalization, and the popularization of higher education, with the aim of improving the quality of education and advocating lifelong learning. Driven by technological and information revolutions, knowledge innovation and renewal gained speed, leading knowledge economies and societies to have greater demands for knowledge workers, and when people found that the knowledge they acquired at school could not meet their working and living needs, voluntary learning gradually became a fashion; at the same time, profound changes happened in educational, learning, and life concepts.

Fifth, the fifth and sixth waves of educational modernization are both forecasts. Information converters will realize the conversion of information between human brains and computers, knowledge and information can be obtained in an unobstructed way, learning will become an experience, and drastic changes will happen to the forms of school and education.

(2) Basic Facts

First, facts about educational input. Over the past 300 years, public education input has been increasing, leading to the improved quality and treatment of teachers and the continued development of educational facilities. From the twentieth century onward, public education and per capita educational spending grew, per capita funding for students increased, the teacher–student ratios at elementary and secondary schools declined, and in some countries such as France and Germany, elementary and secondary school teachers were treated as civil servants.

Second, facts about the educational process. Over the past 300 years, education has become increasingly scientific, standard, democratic, and law abiding in terms of its contents, methods, and management. In the nineteenth century, some countries extended compulsory primary education, and in the twentieth century, secondary education was spread and the years of compulsory education prolonged. In the late twentieth century, some countries basically popularized higher education and increased the application of information technology to education.

Third, facts about educational output. In the eighteenth century, adult literacy began to increase. From the nineteenth century onward, adults' average and expected years of education was prolonged. From the twentieth century onward, rates of graduation from elementary and secondary schools increased, rates of dropouts declined, and educational efficiency rose. In the twentieth century, education's economic, social, and individual returns were fully recognized.

Over the past 300 years, the educational behavior, structure, institutions, and concepts have changed continuously: the form of education changed from traditional to degree-giving to lifelong education; educational management changed from nonstandard to standardized education to diversified education; the way of teaching changed from using blackboard to electrified facilities to information equipment. Educational changes were highly unbalanced and asynchronous (Table 7.14).

Table 7.14 World education in 2000

Item	Public education input/GDP/(%)	Gross enrollment rate of elementary education/%	Gross enrollment rate of secondary education/%	Gross enrollment rate of tertiary education/%	Adult literacy/(%)	Average years of education
High-income countries	5.3	100	100	62	99	10.0
Middle-income countries	4.3	100	70	17	90	6.3
Low-income countries	3.2	95	44	8	58	4.4
World	4.1	100	67	22	79	6.5

Note: The data comes from World Bank (2008)

7.2.2 Theories

Educational modernization theory is a sector-specific modernization, theory about the phenomenon of educational modernization. Currently, there are mainly three theories such as classical educational modernization theory, twice educational modernization theory, and educational modernization theory in broad sense.

7.2.2.1 Classical Educational Modernization Theory

Modern educational thoughts may date back to the seventeenth and eighteenth centuries, and the classical educational modernization theory may be traced back to the 1970s. The 1970s and 1980s saw the publishing of a group of works on educational modernization, for example, *Educational Modernization in South Asia* (Kirpal 1971), *Educational Modernization in Japan* (Hiratsuka 1978), and *Modernization of Muslim Education in Egypt, Pakistan and Turkey* (Saqib 1983). Since the 1990s, there have been substantial researches and works on educational modernization by Chinese scholars. But there have been no universally recognized systematic theoretical expositions on educational modernization. The theory is currently only a collection of academic thoughts about educational modernization (Table 7.15).

Table 7.15 Main views of classical educational modernization theory

Aspects	Basic contents
Definition	Educational modernization is the transition and profound change from traditional to modern education. As a part of social modernization, it includes the secularization, rationalization, nationalization, specialization, democratization, becoming scientific, rule of law, and popularization of education
Process	Educational modernization is a historical process beginning from the Industrial Revolution of the eighteenth century, including changes at material, institutional, and value levels; modernization of educational facilities and teachers; modernization of educational methods and techniques; modernization of educational contents and management; and modernization of educational institutions, thoughts, and concepts. Educational modernization includes three waves, happening from the 1760s to the end of nineteenth century, from the end of the nineteenth century to the end of the two World Wars, and from the 1950s onward, respectively
Outcomes	Completion of the transition from traditional to modern education. Modern education is characterized by classical educational modernity, including equality, openness, democracy, being increasingly scientific, speciality, sociality, public welfare, and popularization of compulsory elementary education
Driving Forces	Classical educational modernization involves a great many influencing factors, such as national policy, economy, society, politics, culture, science and technology
Models	Classical educational modernization has a variety of models. Educational modernization has different features in advanced and developing countries

Source: Gu (1998), Chu (2000), Yu and Yan (2008), Yin (2009)

7.2.2.2 Twice Educational Modernization Theory

Broadly speaking, educational modernization is a sort of educational change in the process of modernization. In the eighteenth to twenty-first centuries, the process of modernization can be divided into two stages, first modernization and second modernization (He 1998a, b), and educational modernization can also be divided into first and second educational modernization alike. The first educational modernization is the transition from the education of agricultural society to that of industrial society, and the second education modernization is the transition from the education of industrial society to that of knowledge society.

Gu and Xue (1998) hold that *the development of education experienced three basic stages: education in agricultural society, in industrial society and in information society, respectively, each having different features in terms of personnel, property, structure and information; the process of educational modernization is about acquiring and deepening modernity. When the basic features of industrial society's education are shown, modernity is acquired; when the basic features of information society's education are shown, the deepness of modernity is completed. The two processes are not restricted by space, but only take place successively. The development of education in different countries takes on different features, which, however, are realistic and specific manifestations of the two processes.*

Liu and Xiong (2007) think that *since the eighteenth century education modernization has experienced two stages: the first was the transition from agricultural-age to industrial-age education, and the second one from industrial-age to knowledge-age education.*

Hu (2007) believes that *the second educational modernization has the following major features (1) stressing the development of human resources and giving top priority to the development of education; (2) stressing the training of innovative talents and the role of education in the national innovation system; (3) stressing the notion of lifelong learning and building platforms for a learning society; (4) information technology is widely applied in school management and teaching, giving rise to revolutionary changes in teaching contents, forms of educational organization and teacher–student relations; and (5) we will be confronted with the challenges of educational internationalization and cross-border trade in educational services. Educational resources are shared by schools across the world.*

According to Zhang and You, *educational modernization is to establish a new educational system that meets the development needs of modern society, economy, science and technology and aims to train innovative talents; the main features include educational popularization, lifelong orientation, individuation, internationalization and informatization; it can be divided into the first and second educational modernization, the latter being a type of educational development consistent with the second modernization* (Zhou et al. 2009).

7.2.2.3 Educational Modernization Theory in Broad Sense

Raised by Chinese scholar Chuanqi He, the educational modernization theory in broad sense refers to the theoretical explanations about the phenomenon of educational modernization between the eighteenth and the twenty-first centuries, and it is

Table 7.16 Structure of educational modernization theory in broad sense

Classification	Theories	Main contents
General theory	Core theory	The definition, process, result, dynamics, models, etc., of educational modernization
Branch theories	Stage theories	First and second educational modernization and integrated educational modernization
	Level-specific study	Educational modernization at world, national, regional, etc., levels
	Subsystems study	Modernization of educational input, process, output, and environment
	Subject-specific study	Modernization of schools, teachers, teaching materials, curriculum, teaching methods, educational system, educational management, etc.
	Subsectors study	Modernization of elementary education, secondary education, higher education, preschool education, vocational, and continuing education
Relevant theories	Other modernization theories	Classical modernization theory, postmodernization theory, reflexive modernization theory, second modernization theory, etc.
	Other relevant theories	Pedagogy, psychology, ecological pedagogy, modernism, postmodernity, etc.

the application of the second modernization theory in the sphere of education. It includes the general theory, branch theories, and relevant theories (Table 7.16). Below is a discussion of its general theory, including five aspects of educational modernization: definition, process, result, dynamics, and models (Table 7.17). Currently, the knowledge on the second educational modernization and integrated agricultural modernization is very limited, so the educational modernization theory in broad sense is yet to develop.

(1) Definition

Educational modernization is a manifestation of modernization; it is the modernization of the educational system.

In connotative terms, educational modernization is a sort of frontier change and international competition in the educational system beginning from the Industrial Revolution of the eighteenth century; it includes the formation, development, transition, and international interaction of modern education; the innovation, selection, diffusion, and withdrawal of educational elements; and the international competition for and the international differentiation and national stratification as a result of catching up with, reaching, and maintaining the world's educational advanced level.

In denotative terms, educational modernization includes the modernization of educational behavior, structure, institutions, thoughts, and concepts; the modernization of educational input, process, output, and environment; the modernization of schools, teachers, and educational facilities; the modernization of educational participation, contents, methods, and means; the modernization of teaching materials and curriculum; the modernization of educational achievements,

Table 7.17 General theory of educational modernization theory in broad sense

Aspect	Basic contents
Definition	Educational modernization is the modernization of the educational system. It is the educational change and international competition since the Industrial Revolution of the eighteenth century; the frontier process of the formation, development, transition, and international interaction of modern education; and the composite process of the alternate innovation, selection, diffusion, and withdrawal of educational elements, as well as the international competition for and international differentiation as a result of catching up with, reaching, and maintaining the world's educational advanced level
Process	Educational modernization is a historical process, including, among other things, educational development, educational transition, international educational competition, international educational differentiation, and national educational stratification; the change of educational behavior, structure, institutions, and ideas; and the world frontier of educational change as well as the process of reaching the world frontier. In the eighteenth to twenty-first centuries, the frontier trajectory of educational modernization could be divided into two major stages: first educational modernization, the transition and profound change from traditional to primary modern education and from feudal to public education, characterized mainly by specialization, becoming scientific, democratization, institutionalization, standardization, and popularization of compulsory elementary education; and second education modernization, the transition from primary modern to advanced modern education and from degree-giving education to lifelong learning, currently characterized mainly by informatization, diversification, individuation, internationalization, popularizing higher education, and lifelong learning. The coordinated development of the first and second education modernization is the integrated educational modernization. New changes will occur in educational modernization in the twenty-second century. Educational modernization follows the ten basic principles of modernization (Table 2.15)
Results	Formation of educational modernity, particularity, diversity, and side effects, including the improvement of educational efficiency and quality, the improvement of educational justice and civic qualities, and the change of educational system and international educational status. The outcome of the first educational modernization is the formation of the first educational modernity, particularity, and diversity, with side effects including suppression of students' personality; the completion of the first educational modernization is marked by the completion of the spreading of compulsory elementary education as well as the educational input, participation, and efficiency reaching the advanced level of industrial societies (the average level of industrialized countries in the 1960s). The outcome of the second educational modernization is the formation of the second educational modernity, particularity, and diversity, with side effects including information divide; the completion of the second educational modernization is marked by the completion of universal higher education as well as the educational input, educational quality, and students' literacy reaching the advanced level of knowledge society (at a particular future time). The basic criterion of accomplishing educational modernization is that the educational input, participation, efficiency, and quality, as well as students' literacy, reach the world's advanced level from the policy perspective
Dynamics	Driving factors of educational modernization include innovation, exchange, competition, adaptation, national interest, and social demand, as well as economic growth, social progress, political development, cultural change, scientific and technological advances, and globalization. Driving models include innovation drive, triple drive, associative action, four-step hypercycle, composite educational interaction, innovation diffusion, innovation spillover, and competition drive (Table 2.20). The driving forces of educational modernization vary from country to country

(continued)

Table 7.17 (continued)

Aspect	Basic contents
Models	Educational modernization has a diversity of paths and models and is subject to the influences of economic development, historical traditions, and cultural factors. There are three basic paths in the twenty-first century: first educational modernization, second educational modernization, and integrated educational modernization

Note: There has been no standard definition of modern education. Broadly speaking, modern education includes education in industrial society (primary modern education) and that in knowledge society (advanced modern education), sometimes known as postmodern education

efficiency, and returns; the modernization of elementary education, secondary education, higher education, and preschool education, as well as vocational and continuing education; the modernization of educational system, statutes, and management; the stage- and level-specific educational modernization; the educational environment modernization; and the change in the temporal and spatial distribution of educational modernization.

Generally, educational modernization refers to the world frontier of educational change and the process to reach the frontier and includes the transition from traditional to modern education and from degree-giving education to lifelong learning, the improvement of educational efficiency and quality, the change of educational thoughts and concepts, the improvement of educational popularity and national qualities, and the change of educational justice, student literacy, and international educational status.

Educational modernization is a type of change in the educational system. Obviously, not all changes in education system constitute a part of educational modernization. Broadly speaking, only educational changes conductive to the popularization of education, social progress, and human development can be taken as components of educational modernization.

Educational development includes educational growth and progress, and educational modernization includes educational development, educational transition and international educational competition, and the change of international status (Table 7.18). International educational status refers to a country's status in the world education circle. The change of international educational status includes maintaining the world's educational advanced level and the narrowing, unchanging, or expanding of the gaps to that level.

Generally, educational modernization is a type of educational change in the process of modernization, and it is a constituent part of social modernization. It is not only a constituent part of but also a contributing factor to modernization. Educational modernization is the important foundation for human modernization.

(2) Process

Educational modernization is a complex, global process. The process of educational modernization can be divided into two types: frontier process and catch-up process with both common and different features. In the eighteenth to twenty-first centuries,

Table 7.18 Conceptual model of educational modernization

Item	Contents
Hypothesis 1	Educational growth refers to the expansion of educational scale and the increase of educational participation
Hypothesis 2	Educational progress refers to the improvement of educational efficiency and quality as well as educational justice and students' literacy
Hypothesis 3	Educational transition refers to the transition from traditional to modern education and from degree-giving education to lifelong learning
Hypothesis 4	The change of international educational status refers to the change in international status of a country's educational input, participation, and output
Inference 1	Educational development = educational growth + educational progress + educational growth × educational progress
Inference 2	Educational modernization = educational development × educational transition × international educational competition and the change of international educational status

Table 7.19 Two stages of educational modernization in broad sense

Item	First educational modernization	Second educational modernization
Time	Approx. 1763–1970	Approx. 1970–2100
Content	Transition from feudal to public education	Transition from degree-giving education to lifelong learning
Input	Public running of schools, socialization, centralization, rule of law, standardization, electrification, specialization, etc.	Informatization, networking, ecologicalization, diversification, internationalization, mobilization, etc.
Process	Popularization, equalization, secularization, rationalization, becoming practical and scientific, democratization, systematization, etc.	Becoming lifelong, flexible, individualized, open, innovative, experiencing, dynamic, justice, etc.
Output	High efficiency, qualified citizens of industrial society	High quality, high-quality citizens of knowledge society
Modernity	First educational modernity: public education, scientific education, regular education, universal compulsory elementary education, etc.	Second educational modernity: lifelong education, lifelong learning, Internet-based education, open education, universal higher education, etc.
Side effects	Suppression of students' personality, etc.	Information divide, etc.

its frontier process can be divided into two stages: first and second educational modernization (Table 7.19), both of which include four stages—start, developing, mature, and transition (Fig. 7.7). The first educational modernization came in three waves, and the second educational modernization will also include three waves (Table 7.12).

The first educational modernization is the transition and profound change from the education of agricultural society to that of industrial society, from traditional to primary modern education, and from feudal to public education. It includes the transition from irregular to regular education, from scattered to concentrated

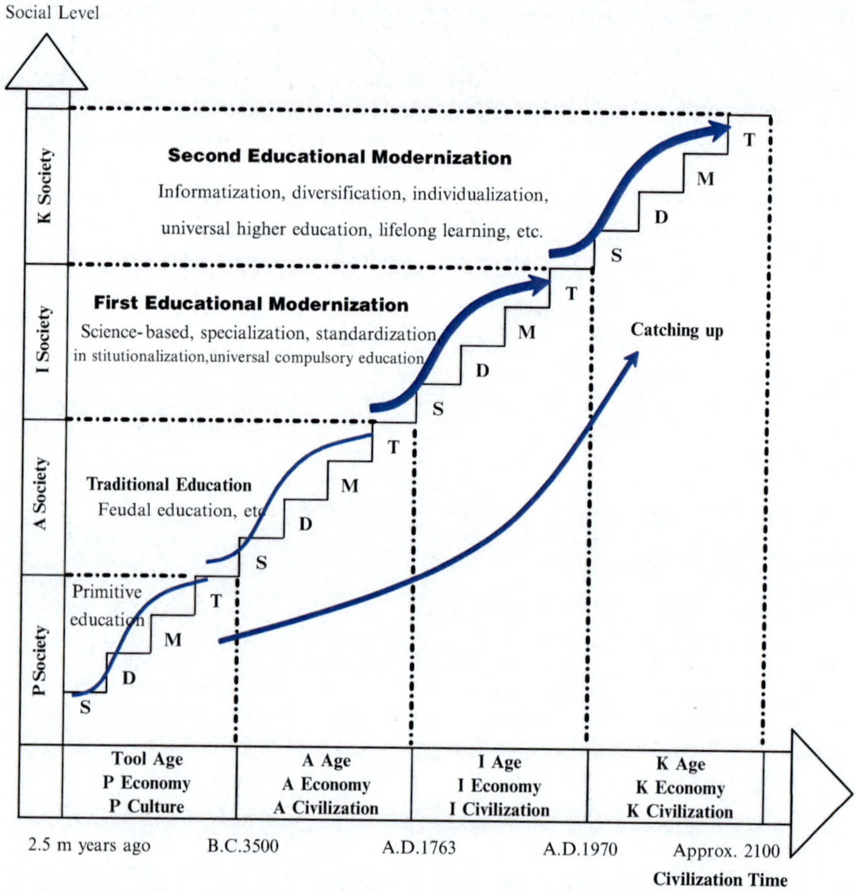

Fig. 7.7 Coordinates of educational modernization. Note: P, A, I, and K refer to primitive, agricultural, industrial, and knowledge, respectively. S, D, M, and T refer to the start, developing, mature, and transition phases, respectively. The civilization time was the time based on the track of the forerunner of the civilization

education, from unequal to equal education, and from autocratic to democratic education. Its features include specialization, rationalization, becoming scientific, electrification, democratization, institutionalization, and universal compulsory elementary education.

The second educational modernization is the transition and profound change from the education of industrial society to that of knowledge society, from primary modern to advanced modern education, and from degree-giving education to lifelong learning. It includes the transition from industrialized to information-based education, from school to lifelong education, from classroom to open education, from rigid to flexible education, from passive to active learning, and from standardized to individualized education. Currently, its features include informatization, individuation, opening, internationalization, innovation, high quality, universal higher education, and lifelong learning. New changes will take place in the future.

If the first educational modernization is taken as primary educational modernization, i.e., the transition from traditional to primary modern education, the second educational modernization should be taken as advanced educational modernization, i.e., the transition from primary to advanced modern education. The coordinated development of the first and second educational modernization is integrated educational modernization. There still will be new changes in the educational modernization in the twenty-second century.

The process of educational modernization is long standing, complex, systematic, global, progressive, risky, nonlinear, diverse, and convergent in structure.

Educational modernization is a manifestation of modernization and follows the ten basic principles of modernization (Table 2.15).

(3) Results

Outcomes of educational modernization include the formation of educational modernity, particularity, diversity, and side effects. The outcomes of educational modernization in different countries not only share some common features but also have differences, and the first educational modernization is different from the second one in terms of outcomes (Table 7.17). Generally, the first educational modernity is characterized by public welfare, being scientific, specialty, standard, democracy, equality, sociality, rule of law, and universal compulsory elementary education; the second educational modernity is currently characterized by lifelong learning, networking, ecology, diversity, openness, internationalism, duality (public and commercial), and universal higher education.

The outcomes of educational modernization are manifested in six aspects: the completion of two educational transitions, the improvement of education popularization, the increase of educational efficiency and quality, the change of national educational system, the development of educational institutions and concepts, and the change of international educational system and national educational status.

In the process of educational modernization, a portion of countries reach and maintain the world's educational advanced level and become educationally advanced countries, and other countries remain educationally developing ones; there is mobility between the two types of countries. Broadly speaking, educationally advanced countries account for about 20% of all countries throughout the world, and educationally developing countries account for about 80%.

The goals of national educational modernization include completing the first educational modernization, achieving the transition from traditional to primary modern education; completing the second educational modernization, achieving the transition from primary modern to advanced modern education; catching up with, reaching, and maintaining the world's advanced level of educational development; becoming educationally advanced countries or narrowing the gaps to international education.

According to the second modernization theory, the criteria of completing the first educational modernization include the popularization of compulsory elementary education and the educational input, participation, and efficiency reaching the world advanced level in the 1960s; the criteria of entering the second educational modernization include that the popularity of secondary education is above 80%, that of higher education is above 40%, and information-based education is underway.

(4) Dynamics

Driving forces of educational modernization are different at different levels, in different countries, and in different stages.

The driving forces of educational modernization include driving factors and mechanisms. Driving mechanisms of educational modernization include innovation drive, triple drive, two-wheel drive (Fig. 7.8), and competition drive (Table 2.20).

(5) Models

There are roughly three basic paths of educational modernization in the twenty-first century (Fig. 7.9). There is no standard model for educational modernization, and different countries may adopt different models in different stages; what model to choose depends on the historical traditions and objective conditions of the countries.

(6) Second Educational Modernization

The second educational modernization is a manifestation of educational modernization, and it is a frontier change in the educational system beginning in the 1970s, including the transition from industrialized to information-based education and from degree-giving education to lifelong learning, as well as the increase of educational quality and students' literacy, the improvement of educational justice, and the change in international educational differentiation and international educational system.

(7) Integrated Educational Modernization

The integrated educational modernization is a basic path of educational modernization in broad sense in the twenty-first century. It includes the coordinated development of the first and second educational modernization and the continued transition toward lifelong learning; the coordinated development of scientific

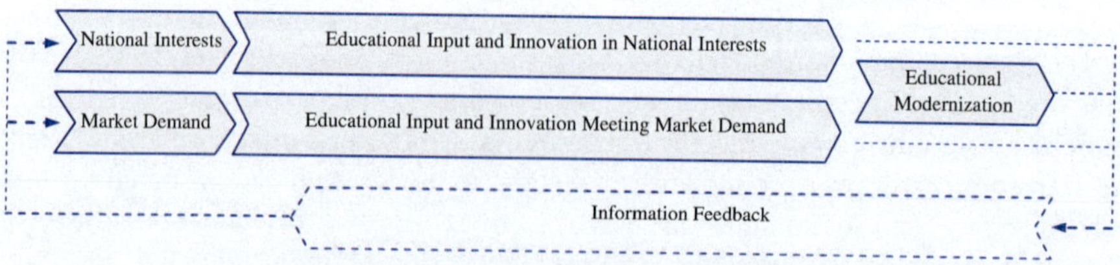

Fig. 7.8 Two-wheel drive model of educational modernization

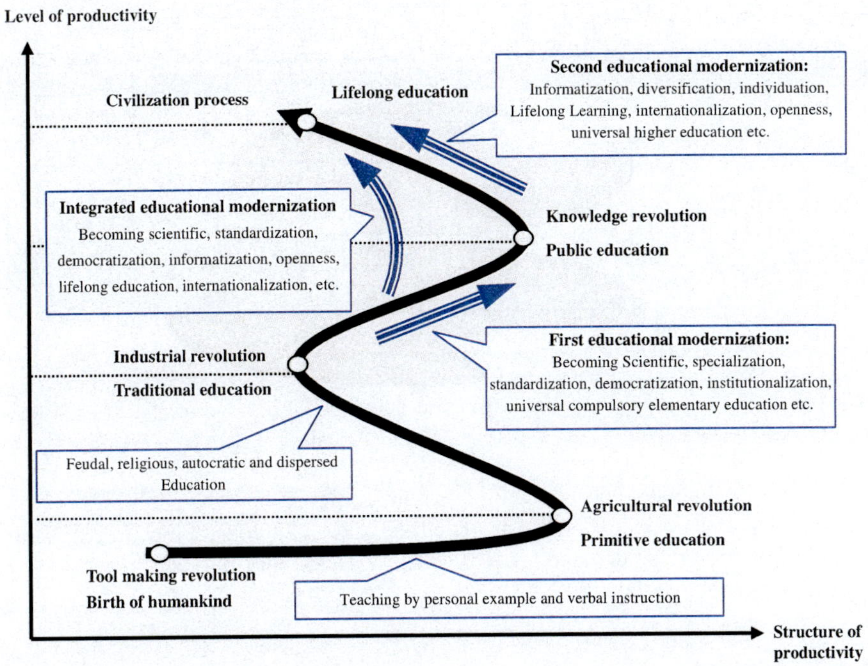

Fig. 7.9 Three paths of educational modernization in twenty-first century

education and educational standardization, democratization, informatization, opening and internationalization, and the transition toward information-based and lifelong education; the increase of educational efficiency and quality; the improvement of educational justice and national qualities; and the change in international educational competition and international educational status.

The integrated educational modernization is a path appropriate for developing countries, including the change in educational behavior, contents, structure, institutions, and concepts, and international competition for catching up and reaching the world's advanced level of educational development. The completion of integrated educational modernization is marked by the fact that educational input, efficiency, quality, and justice all reach the world's advanced level then.

7.3 Modernization of Science and Technology

Modernization of science and technology is the modernization of the system of science and technology. It is a manifestation of modernization phenomenon, including stage-specific and level-specific scientific and technological modernization, modernization of the subsectors, and subsystems of scientific and technological system (Fig. 7.10). Scientific and technological modernization is a constituent part of cultural modernization and overlaps with economic and social modernization.

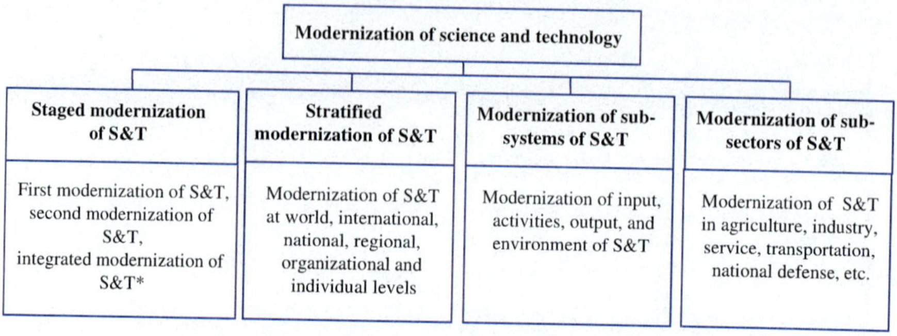

Fig. 7.10 Objects of Study on Modernization of Science and Technology (S&T). Note: (*Asterisk*) Integrated modernization of S&T is a basic path of scientific and technological modernization for developing countries and is the coordinated development of the first and second scientific and technological modernization

Science and technology has the duality of commodities and public welfare and gives rise to both progress and side effects. Scientific and technological modernization is driven triply by market demand, national interest, and human curiosity.

7.3.1 Studies

Study on modernization of science and technology, whose object is the scientific and technological system, is an integral part of modernization research. These studies may start with the eighteenth century and may be analyzed from three aspects—historical process, objective reality, and future prospects.

7.3.1.1 Research Paradigm

The object of modernization study on science and technology is modernization of the scientific and technological system, including the modernization of input, activities, output, and environment of science and technology as well as scientific and technological modernization at world, national, and regional levels. Research contents include the modernization of behavior, structure, institutions, and concepts of science and technology as well as the process, outcomes, driving forces, and models of scientific and technological modernization. They may constitute a structural matrix (Table 7.20). Other research objects include stage-specific scientific and technological modernization and modernization in scientific and technological subsectors.

Study on the modernization of science and technology, an integral part of modernization research, may use the methodologies for modernization research, such as time series analysis, cross-sectional analysis, process analysis, cast study, qualitative analysis, and coordinates analysis. It may target the entire process or a particular stage of scientific and technological modernization within the range of the world or a particular country or region.

Table 7.20 Matrix of modernization study on science and technology (S&T)

Content		Object		
Element		S&T system	Input, activities, output, and environment of S&T	World, national, and regional S&T
		Modernization of S&T	Modernization of four subsystems of S&T	Modernization of S&T at the three levels
	Behavior	Modernization of behavior, structure, institution, and ideas of S&T	Modernization of behavior, structure, institution, and ideas of four subsystems of S&T	Modernization of behavior, structure, institution, and ideas of S&T at the three levels
	Structure			
	Institution			
	Idea			
Aspect	Process	Process, result, dynamics, model of modernization of S&T	Process, result, dynamics, model of modernization of four subsystems of S&T	Process, result, dynamics, model of modernization of S&T at the three levels
	Result			
	Dynamics			
	Model			

Note: Scientific and technological input includes scientific and technological funding, personnel, and facilities. Scientific and technological activities include scientific research, technological development, technological transfer, spreading of scientific knowledge, and scientific and technological management. Scientific and technological output involves scientific and technological achievements, scientific and technological efficiency, active technologies, and scientific and technological returns. Scientific and technological environment involves domestic scientific and technological environment (economy, society, politics, culture, etc.) and international scientific and technological environment. Research contents also include stage-specific modernization, modernization of scientific and technological subsectors, scientific and technological frontier analysis, scientific and technological trend analysis, and interaction between scientific and technological modernization elements and different fields

Scientific discoveries and technological inventions are fundamental. There is no border in the circle of science, which is the source of human development, but technology concerns interest and serves as the foundation for national advancement. Scientific and technological modernization concerns human civilization and national interest, personal returns, and public interest. Scientific and technological modernization research should be done from multiple perspectives.

7.3.1.2 Historical Facts

Scientific and technological modernization, which started about in the eighteenth century, is a form of scientific and technological changes and a constituent part of cultural modernization. Generally, the frontier trajectory of economic, social, and cultural modernization is divided into two major stages and six waves. The frontier trajectory of scientific and technological modernization can also be divided roughly into two major stages and six waves (Table 7.21).

(1) Process Analysis

Scientific and technological modernization is not only the powerhouse but also an integral part of modernization. If the first technological revolution of the eighteenth century is taken as the start of scientific and technological modernization, then the first scientific revolution in the sixteenth and the seventeenth centuries is its

Table 7.21 Two major stages and six waves of scientific and technological modernization

Wave	Approx. time	Content	Annotation
First	1763–1870	Steam engine and mechanical revolution, specialization, research-related universities	*First educational modernization* Specialization, systematization, institutionalization, division of subjects, modern technology, intellectual property, and scientific and technological system
Second	1870–1945	Electrical, chemical, and transport revolution, enterprise laboratories	
Third	1946–1970	Electronic technology revolution; automation; national scientific and technological system	
Fourth	1970–2020	Information revolution, high technology, national innovation system	*Second educational modernization* High technology, big science, highly interdisciplinary, greening, internationalization, duality, and national innovation system
Fifth	2020–2050	New biology revolution, fusion of life, and information technology	
Sixth	2050–2100	New physics revolution, new energy and transport technology	

Note: Both the fifth and sixth waves are just forecasts, or "scientific conjectures"

foundation. Between the sixteenth and the twenty-first centuries, there were approximately three (or four) scientific revolutions, six technological revolutions, and six industrial revolutions, and the world center of science changed at least four times (Table 7.22). The process of scientific and technological modernization encompasses scientific and technological revolutions as well as the industrial revolutions thereof.

First, the first wave of scientific and technological modernization. It happened mainly in European countries during the First Industrial Revolution, including (1) development of modern sciences, such as chemistry, electromagnetism, astronomy, and biology; (2) the first technological revolution, encompassing the invention and application of steam engines and mechanical technologies; (3) systematization of scientific research, reflected by the independent status given to scientific research and the following founding of the Royal Society (1662), French Academy of Sciences (1666), and German Academy of Sciences at Berlin (1700); (4) development of patent systems, for example, the UK's establishment of its patent system in the seventeenth century, and the enactment of patent acts in the eighteenth century in the USA and France; (5) the establishment of research universities, for example, the tutorial system established in 1824 at the Giessen University, under which students researched under professors' guidance; and (6) the diffusion of scientific knowledge, for example, the publishing of *Encyclopédie* in France. During this period, science and production were not directly related, and science played a very limited role in the first technological revolution and the first industrial revolution.

Second, the second wave of scientific and technological modernization. It happened during the second industrial revolution and the two World Wars. Science began influencing the development of technology and industry, and more and more technologies and emerging industries were built on new scientific knowledge.

Table 7.22 Scientific and technological revolutions, industrial revolutions, and world science centers

Time	Scientific revolution	Technological revolution	Industrial revolution	World science center
Sixteenth century	First scientific revolution: birth of modern physics	–	–	Italy
Seventeenth century				UK
Eighteenth century	Overall development of modern sciences	First technological revolution: steam machine and mechanical revolution	First industrial revolution: mechanization	France
Nineteenth century		Second technological revolution: electric power, chemistry, and transport	Second industrial revolution: electrification	Germany
First half of the twentieth century	Second scientific revolution: scientific revolution initiated by the relativity and quantum theories	Third technological revolution: electronics and automation	Third industrial revolution: automation	USA
Second half of the twentieth century		Fourth technological revolution: high-technology and information revolution	Fourth industrial revolution: informatization	
First half of the twenty-first century	*Third scientific revolution: new biology revolution*	*Fifth technological revolution: fusion of biology and technology*	*Fifth industrial revolution: life engineering*	
Second half of the twenty-first century	*Fourth scientific revolution: new physics revolution*	*Sixth technological revolution: new energy and new transport*	*Sixth industrial revolution: transport engineering*	–

Note: The first and second scientific revolutions are historical facts; the third and fourth revolutions are the forecasts and likely to happen before and after the mid-twenty-first century separately. The first, second, third, and fourth technological revolutions are historical facts, while the fifth and sixth ones are forecasts. The fourth technological revolution is a high-technology and information revolution lasting from the 1970s to the 2020s; the fifth one, likely to happen in the 2020s–2050s, includes the fusion of biological technology, information technology, and nanotechnology; the sixth one will probably happen around the 2050s, including an energy and transport revolution as a result of the revolution in new physics. The first industrial revolution was the mechanization revolution from the 1760s to the 1860s, the second one was the electrification revolution from the 1860s to the 1940s, the third one was the automation revolution from the 1940s to 1970s, and the fourth one is the high-technology and information revolution from the 1970s to the 2020s; both the fifth and sixth industrial revolutions are forecasts, which correspond to the fifth and sixth technological revolutions and third and fourth scientific revolutions

It mainly encompassed five aspects (1) the second scientific revolution; the physics revolution at the turn of the century changed people's views about classical mechanics, and the ensuing momentous discoveries in the fields of astronomy, geology, and biology fundamentally changed human knowledge of universe and life; (2) the second technological revolution, including revolutions in electrical power, chemistry, and transport, as well as electrification; (3) establishment of industrial laboratories; in the second half of the nineteenth century, German chemical companies established their own laboratories for scientific research and for the development of new products; (4) development of military technologies; in 1919, Americans invented the rocket, and in 1943, Germans invented the missile, etc.; and (5) increased government support for scientific research; in the USA, beginning with the establishment of state colleges of agriculture in the nineteenth century, government-supported scientific research developed continuously; expanded rapidly during World Wars in such fields as aircrafts, military, agriculture, and medicine; and by 1946, there had been 2,303 research institutions, which employed 118,000 people; the success of the US Manhattan Project not only led to the birth of the first atomic bomb but also ushered in the age of big science.

Third, the third wave of scientific and technological modernization. It happened roughly during the third industrial revolution, mainly including five aspects (1) the third technological revolution, encompassing electronic technology, automation technology, atomic energy technology, satellite technology, and aerospace technology; the development of information technology, particularly, ultimately gave rise to an information revolution; (2) new development of modern sciences; remarkable achievements were made in physics, astronomy, biology, geoscience, and some interdisciplines; (3) revolution in scientific and technological systems; during World War II, some industrial countries and some agricultural ones began attempting to establish national research institutions and build national scientific and technological systems; in 1945, the USA published a report titled *Science: The Endless Frontier*, articulating that the government had the irreplaceable responsibility to support fundamental research and national security research; governments around the world established or restored government-run research institutions one after another, leading to the establishment of distinctive national scientific and technological systems and policy systems; (4) considerably increased national investments in science and technology and education, with the percentage of spending on research and development in GDP rising rapidly to more than 2% from approximately 1%; and (5) enhanced interaction between S&T and economy and the rapid development of scientific culture.

Fourth, the fourth wave of scientific and technological modernization. Corresponding to the fourth waves of economic, social, and cultural modernization, it mainly includes the following six aspects (1) the fourth technological revolution, which encompasses high-technology and information revolutions; the high-technology revolution includes the development of high technologies—knowledge-intensive sophisticated technologies which are produced based on modern scientific theories or latest scientific breakthroughs, are highly diffusible and value-added, or have strategic significance and high-tech industries—scientifically and technologically intensive enterprises in high-tech fields; the information revolution includes the development and application of modern information and communication technologies, for example, the widespread use of personal computers and the Internet; (2) widespread attention to big science, development of green technologies, and enhanced international cooperation in science and technology; (3) cooperation between production, educational, and research institutions, for example, in the form of scientific and technological parks, scientific parks, and high-tech parks, which shorten the period of translating science into technology and then into products; (4) enhanced intellectual property protection, development of international trade in technologies, etc.; (5) weakened roles governments play in scientific research as more and more enterprises plunge into scientific research and development, gradually becoming the main players of scientific and technological investment and scientific research behavior; and (6) wide attention paid to the national innovation system, an open network system comprising of innovation-related institutions and organizations, whose function is to improve national innovation capacity and promote socioeconomic development; the scientific and technological funding and staffing in the national innovation system differs from country to country: in the leading advanced countries, enterprises account for about 70%, universities about 20%, and research institutions about 10%. In addition, attention has been drawn to the duality of science and technology, i.e., science and technology can promote human development and also produce side effects such as environmental pollution.

Fifth, the fifth wave of scientific and technological modernization. It is expected to come in between 2020 and 2050, including the third scientific revolution and the fifth technological revolution, as well as a new biology revolution, and the fusion of biological, information, and nanotechnologies.

Sixth, the sixth wave of scientific and technological modernization. It is expected to come in between 2050 and 2100, including the fourth scientific revolution and the sixth technological revolution, as well as a new physics revolution, and new energy, hypertransport, and hypermanufacture.

(2) Objective Facts

First, facts about scientific and technological input. In the eighteenth and nineteenth centuries, science and technology funding and staffing was very limited. Since the twentieth century, in advanced countries, both governments and enterprises have increased investments in science and technology, with the former outperforming the latter for a time; in the late twentieth century, enterprises surpassed governments in scientific and technological investments, becoming the main players of scientific and technological investments. In the later 40 years of twentieth century, in major advanced countries, the percentage of scientific and technological input in GDP fluctuated between 2% and 3% for a long period of time (Table 7.23).

Second, facts about scientific and technological activities. In the eighteenth and nineteenth centuries, scientific and technological activities were carried out on a very small scale. In the nineteenth century, scientific and technological activities were concentrated in a minority of universities, enterprise laboratories, and government-run research institutions, and patent systems were established. The twentieth century witnessed the gradual establishment of national scientific and technological systems, the rapid development of sciences and technologies for national defense, the growth of technological development by enterprises,

Table 7.23 Percentages of R&D funds in GDP in five countries (%)

Country	1960	1970	1980	1990	2000	2005
USA	2.6	2.6	2.3	2.6	2.7	2.7
UK	2.3 (1964)	1.8	2.3	2.2	1.9	1.9
France	–	1.9	1.8	2.4	2.2	2.2
Germany	–	2.1	2.4	2.8	2.5	2.5
Japan	–	1.8	2.2	2.9	3.0	3.1

Note: The data comes from World Bank (2008)

Table 7.24 World S&T and economic output in 2000 (%)

Item	Scientific and technological treatise	Patent for invention	Income from technological export	Spending on technological import	High-technology export	GNP
High-income countries	85.4	92.4	98.5	88.8	83.8	81.0
Middle-income countries	12.7	7.5	1.4	10.7	16.0	16.3
Low-income countries	1.9	0.1	0.1	0.5	0.2	2.7
World	100	100	100	100	100	100

Note: Patents for invention refer to those obtained by domestic citizens, and income from technological export refers to income from international transfer of technology, accounting based on the data of *World Development Indicators 2008* (World Bank 2008)

recognized roles of universities and national scientific research institutions, attention paid to the popularization of scientific knowledge, and the continued development of international trade in technology. In the late twentieth century, high technologies and high-tech industries, innovation policies, and national innovation systems were given great importance.

Third, facts about scientific and technological output. Starting from the eighteenth century, both S&T treatises and patents for invention grew in number. From the nineteenth century onward, scientific and technological contribution to economic growth began to increase. Since the twentieth century, enterprises have gradually become the main players of technological innovation, universities have played an important role in fundamental sciences and technology transfer, and state-run research institutions have worked for the development of sciences and technologies for public application and national defense. In 2000, advanced countries' scientific and technological treatises, patents for invention, technological export, and high-technology transport accounted for 85%, 92%, 99%, and 84%, respectively, of the world's total (Table 7.24), and these countries were responsible for 80% of the world's scientific and technological output.

Fourth, general facts about scientific and technological modernization. From the eighteenth century on, scientific and technological behavior, structure, institutions, and concepts were in a state of constant flux. The close relation between scientific and technological modernization and national modernization, in the eighteenth and nineteenth centuries, emerged mainly in a few European and American countries, which spread in the twentieth century into other advanced countries and emerging industrialized countries. The percentage of scientific and technological input was generally low in the early and middle stages of industrialization and rose in the late stage of industrialization; throughout the period of informatization, the percentage witnessed no obvious growth; since the twentieth century, it has been manifested as an S-shaped curve—first rising and then fluctuating—in leading advanced countries.

7.3.2 Theories

The scientific and technological modernization theory is about the phenomenon of scientific and technological modernization. So far, there have been no universally recognized systematic theoretical expositions on scientific and technological modernization. The theory is currently only a collection of academic thoughts about scientific and technological modernization.

7.3.2.1 Science and Technology and Modernization

The modern scientific revolution occurred in the sixteenth to seventeenth centuries. The first technological revolution of the eighteenth century gave rise to the first industrial revolution, the start of world modernization. Since the eighteenth century, every industrial revolution has been driven by a technological revolution. Since the nineteenth century, every technological revolution has been closely related to scientific breakthroughs. Without modern sciences and technologies, there would be no modernization.

There are mainly four topics in the discussions about science and technology and modernization (1) science and modernity (Lelas 2000), (2) technology and modernity (Misa et al. 2003), (3) scientific and technological changes in the process of modernization (Russell 1983), and (4) the role of science and technology in the process of modernization (Wilson 1979; Suttmeier 1980; Christensen 1993).

7.3.2.2 Scientific and Technological Modernization

In 1964, the Chinese government raised "Four Modernizations," including agricultural modernization, industrial modernization, and the modernization of national defense, as well as scientific and technological modernization. In the 1980s, China's "Four Modernizations" drew the attention of Western scholars (Baum 1980; Wilson Center 1982).

As Li et al. (2002) hold, *scientific and technological modernization refers to the process that a country or region uses various scientific and technological resources, and its advantages and characteristics to the full, to scramble for the frontier fields of scientific and technological competition whereby to improve the level and leading position of future scientific and technological development, to accelerate sustainable economic and social development and to lead the country or region into the world frontier of modernization. Scientific and technological modernization encompasses three layers of connotation (1) on objective or orientation, the overall level of scientific and technological development goes up to the world's advanced level; (2) on function, scientific and technological development makes decisive contributions to modern economic and social development; and (3) on approaches, there is the need to continuously improve modern systems and operation mechanisms for scientific and technological development.*

7.3.2.3 Modernization Theory on Science and Technology in Broad Sense

The scientific and technological modernization theory in broad sense, raised by Chinese scholar Chuanqi He, refers to the theoretical explanations about the phenomenon of scientific and technological modernization between the eighteenth and twenty-first centuries, and it is the application of the second modernization theory in the system of science and technology. It includes the general theory, branch theories, and relevant theories (Table 7.25). Below is a discussion of its general theory, including five aspects of scientific and technological modernization: definition, process, result, dynamics, and models (Table 7.26). Currently, the knowledge on the second scientific and technological modernization and integrated scientific and technological modernization is very limited, so the scientific and technological modernization theory in broad sense is yet to develop.

Table 7.25 Structure of scientific and technological modernization theory in broad sense

Classification	Theories	Main contents
General theory	Core theory	The definition, process, result, dynamics, models, etc., of scientific and technological modernization
Branch theories	Stage theories	First and second scientific and technological modernization and integrated scientific and technological modernization
	Level-specific study	Scientific and technological modernization at world, international, national, regional, organizational, and individual levels
	Subsystems study	Modernization of scientific and technological input, activities, output, and environment
	Subsectors study	Scientific and technological modernization of agriculture, industry, service sector, national defense, and transport
Relevant theories	Other modernization theories	Postmodernization theory, ecological modernization theory, second modernization theory, etc.
	Other relevant theories	Science of science, scientific and technological management, history of science and technology, etc.

Table 7.26 General theory of scientific and technological modernization theory in broad sense

Aspect	Basic contents
Definition	Scientific and technological modernization is modernization in the system of science and technology. It is the scientific and technological change and international competition beginning from the eighteenth century; the frontier process of the formation, development, transition, and international interaction of the modern scientific and technological system; the composite process of the alternate innovation, selection, diffusion, and withdrawal of scientific and technological elements, as well as the international competition for and international differentiation as a result of catching up with, reaching, and maintaining the world's advanced level of science and technology
Process	Scientific and technological modernization is a historical process, including, among other things, scientific and technological development, scientific and technological transition, international scientific and technological competition, and the change of international scientific and technological status; the change of scientific and technological behavior, structure, institutions, and concepts; and the world frontier of scientific and technological change as well as the process of reaching the world frontier. In the eighteenth to twenty-first centuries, scientific and technological modernization could be divided into two major stages: first scientific and technological modernization, the transition and profound change from traditional to modern science and technology, characterized mainly by specialization, institutionalization, and systematization; second scientific and technological modernization, the transition and profound change from the modern scientific and technological system to the national innovation system, currently characterized mainly by high technology, big science, and internationalization. The coordinated development of the first and second scientific and technological modernization is the integrated scientific and technological modernization. Scientific and technological modernization follows the ten basic principles of modernization (Table 2.15)
Result	The formation of scientific and technological modernity, particularity, diversity, and side effects; the improvement of technological levels in enterprises, national scientific and technological efficiency, and international scientific and technological competitiveness, and the increase of scientific and technological contribution to economic growth, etc. The outcome of the first scientific and technological modernization is the formation of the first scientific and technological modernity, particularity, and diversity, with side effects including environmental pollution and technical unemployment. The outcome of the second scientific and technological modernization is the formation of the second scientific and technological modernity, particularity, and diversity, with side effects including international technical risk
Dynamics	Driving factors of scientific and technological modernization include innovation, exchange, competition, adaptation, national interest, market demand, curiosity, etc. Driving models include innovation drive, triple drive, associative action, four-step hypercycle, composite interaction, innovation diffusion, innovation spillover, and competition drive (Table 2.20). The driving forces of scientific and technological modernization vary from country to country and from stage to stage, and advanced countries differ from developing ones in driving forces. The drive factors and mechanism of the modernization of science and technology are different

(continued)

Table 7.26 (continued)

Aspect	Basic contents
Models	Scientific and technological modernization has a diversity of paths and models and is subject to historical tradition, economic level, and international system. Basic paths in the twenty-first century include first scientific and technological modernization, second scientific and technological modernization, and integrated scientific and technological modernization, each with many divided paths and development models, for example, national technological innovation system, national innovation system, and national knowledge innovation system. The models of the modernization of science and technology are different

(1) Definition

Scientific and technological modernization is a manifestation of modernization; it is the modernization of the scientific and technological system.

The scientific and technological system is an open system. It can be divided in multiple ways into several subsystems. From the perspective of knowledge and information flow, it can be divided into three subsystems (Fig. 7.11): scientific and technological production system (research and development), scientific and technological diffusion system (technology transfer and science popularization), and scientific and technological application system (active technologies and scientific literacy). Such division is, of course, relative; for example, enterprises are members of not only the scientific and technological production system but also the scientific and technological application system. From the perspective of the content, it can be divided into the science system and technology system with different characteristics.

In connotative terms, scientific and technological modernization is a sort of frontier change and international competition in the scientific and technological system beginning from the eighteenth century; it includes the formation, development, transition, and international interaction of modern scientific and

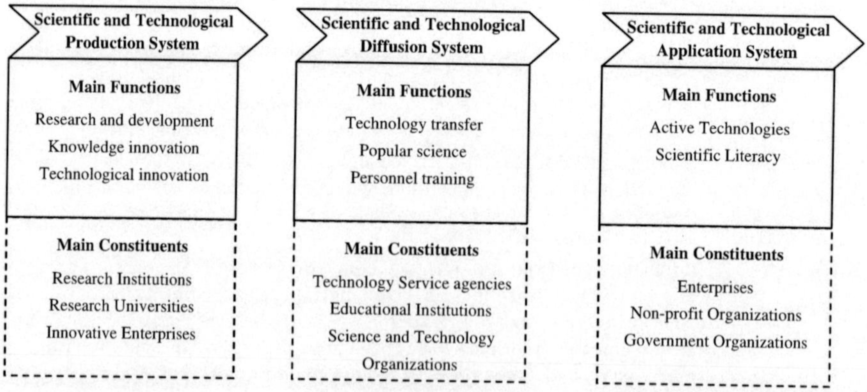

Fig. 7.11 Subsystems of scientific and technological system (from the perspective of knowledge and information flow)

technological system; the innovation, selection, diffusion, and withdrawal of scientific and technological elements; and the international competition for and the international differentiation and national stratification as a result of catching up with, reaching, and maintaining the world's advanced level of science and technology.

In denotative terms, scientific and technological modernization includes the modernization of scientific and technological behavior, structure, institutions, and concepts; the modernization of the scientific and technological production system, diffusion system, and application system; the modernization of corporate active technology, research and development (R&D), and national scientific literacy; the modernization of scientific and technological input, activities, output, and environment; the modernization of scientific and technological facilities, organizations, and personnel; the modernization of scientific research, technological development, technology transfer, science popularization, and scientific and technological management; the modernization of scientific and technological efficiency and returns (scientific and technological contribution to economic growth); the modernization of science system and technology system; the stage- and level-specific scientific and technological modernization; the scientific and technological modernization of such sectors as agriculture, etc.; and the interaction between science and technology and other modernization, as well as the change in the temporal and spatial distribution of scientific and technological modernization.

Broadly speaking, scientific and technological modernization refers to the world frontier of scientific and technological changes and the process to reach this frontier and includes the transition from traditional to modern scientific and technological system and from modern scientific and technological system to national innovation system; technological advances in enterprises; the improvement of international competitiveness; the improvement of national innovation capacity and scientific literacy; the increase of scientific and technological contribution to economic growth; and the change in the world scientific and technological system and international scientific and technological status.

In general, scientific and technological development includes technological advances in enterprises and enhanced national innovation capacity and scientific literacy; scientific and technological modernization is the intersection of scientific and technological development, scientific and technological transitions, international scientific and technological competition, and change of scientific and technological status (Table 7.27).

Scientific and technological modernization is a type of scientific and technological change in the process of modernization, and it is a constituent part of cultural modernization. It is not only a constituent part of but also a contributing factor to modernization. Scientific and technological modernization is an important foundation for economic and social modernization.

(2) Process

Scientific and technological modernization is a complex, global process. The process of scientific and technological modernization can be divided into two

Table 7.27 Conceptual model of scientific and technological modernization

Item	Main contents
Hypothesis 1	Technological advances of enterprises refer to the improved levels and international competitiveness of active technologies in enterprises
Hypothesis 2	National innovation capacity includes the capacity and efficiency of national knowledge innovation, technological innovation, and technology transfer
Hypothesis 3	Scientific and technological transition refers to the transition from traditional science and technology to the modern scientific and technological system and from the latter to the national innovation system
Hypothesis 4	The change of international scientific and technological status refers to the change of international status in national innovation capacity, innovation efficiency, and scientific and technological achievements
Inference 1	Scientific and technological development = technological advances in enterprises + improved national innovation capacity + improved national scientific literacy
Inference 2	Scientific and technological modernization = scientific and technological development × scientific and technological transition × international scientific and technological competition and the change of international scientific and technological status

Table 7.28 Two stages of scientific and technological modernization in broad sense

Item	First scientific and technological modernization	Second scientific and technological modernization
Time	Approx. 1760–1970	Approx. 1970–2100
Content	Transition from traditional science and technology to the modern scientific and technological system	Transition from the modern scientific and technological system to the national innovation system
Input	Institutionalization, professionalization, standardization, etc.	Diversification, internationalization, risk investment, etc.
Activities	Organization-based, specialization, systematization, autonomy, etc.	Greening, internationalization, informatization, networking, clustering
Output	Disciplinary division, modern technology, intellectual property, etc.	Interdisciplines, high technologies, big science, duality, commercialization, etc.
Modernity	First scientific and technological modernity: disciplinary division, modern technologies, systematization, specialty, normative, self-discipline, etc.	Second scientific and technological modernity: high technologies, big science, intersection, innovation, globality, diversity, etc.
Side effects	Environmental pollution, technical unemployment, etc.	International technological risk, ethic dispute, etc.

types: frontier process and catch-up process with both common and different features. In the eighteenth to twenty-first centuries, its frontier process can be divided into two stages, the first and the second scientific and technological modernization (Table 7.28), both of which include four stages—start, developing, mature, and transition (Fig. 7.12). The first scientific and technological modernization came in three waves, and the second one will also include three waves (Table 7.21).

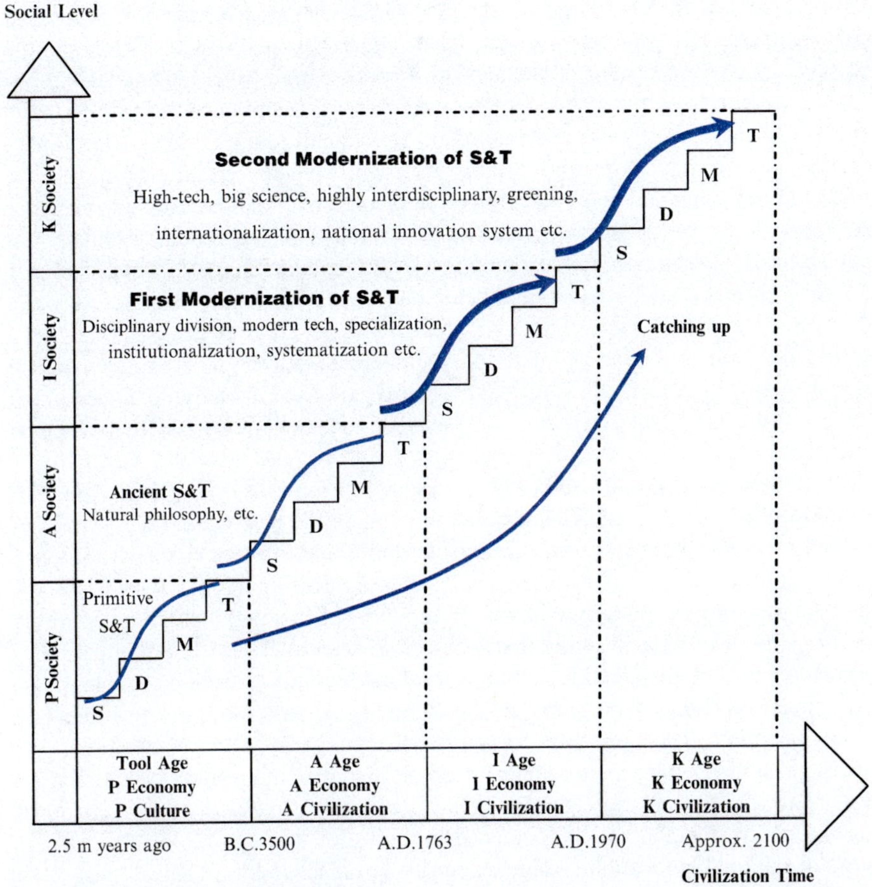

Fig. 7.12 Coordinates of modernization of science and technology. Note: P, A, I, and K refer to primitive, agricultural, industrial, and knowledge, respectively. S, D, M, and T refer to the start, developing, mature, and transition phases, respectively. The civilization time was the time based on the track of the forerunner of the civilization

The first modernization of science and technology is the transition and profound change from traditional science and technology to the modern scientific and technological system. It includes the transition from ancient to modern science and technology and from dispersed science and technology to scientific and technological system; the change in scientific research activities from out of personal interests to professionalization and from dependence to independence, as well as technological advances in enterprises; the improvement of productive efficiency; and the establishment and development of modern science and technology and national scientific and technological systems. The main features include professionalization, specialization, systematization, standardization, and institutionalization.

The second modernization of science and technology is the transition and profound change from the modern scientific and technological system to the national innovation system. It includes the transition from scientific and technological system to the national innovation system, from disciplinary division to intersection, from simple to green technologies, from small to big science, from low to high technologies, and from national to international science and technology; the institutionalization and diversification of innovation cooperation; the improvement of innovation capacity and efficiency; the shortening of technological innovation cycles and the acceleration of technology transfer; and the improvement of national scientific literacy and international scientific and technological competitiveness. Currently, the main features include high technologies, big science, internationalization, diversification, industrialization, commercialization, greening, networking, and clustering (e.g., scientific and technological parks and industrial parks), and the duality (advances and side effects) of science and technology has drawn social attention.

If modern science and technology is divided into two stages, primary modern and advanced modern science and technology, then the first scientific and technological modernization is the transition from traditional to primary modern science and technology, the second scientific and technological modernization is the transition from primary modern to advanced modern science and technology, and the coordinated development of the first and second scientific and technological modernization and the sustained transition toward the second scientific and technological modernization represent the integrated scientific and technological modernization.

The establishment and development of the national innovation system can be divided roughly into three stages: national technological innovation system, national innovation system, and national knowledge innovation system (Table 7.29). Generally, the national innovation system encompasses six subsystems (Table 7.30).

The national innovation system encompasses four key elements: innovation efficiency and capacities of innovators, rationality and effectiveness of innovation

Table 7.29 Three stages in the evolution of national innovation system

Item	National technological innovation system	National innovation system	National knowledge innovation system
Time	Age of industrial economy: 1940s–1980s	The period of transition from industrial to knowledge economy: since the 1990s	The age of knowledge economy: twenty-first century
Main features	Technological innovation, technological flow, interaction, and policy innovation	Technological innovation, knowledge creation, knowledge diffusion and application, and flow of personnel	Knowledge innovation and high-efficiency application of new knowledge
Relevant theories	Technological innovation and advancement	Human capital and new growth theory	Knowledge innovation theory and knowledge economy

Source: Zhang and He (1999), He and Zhang (2001)

Table 7.30 Structure and function of national innovation system (knowledge and technological innovation equally valued)

Subsystem	Central parts	Related parts	Main functions
Knowledge innovation system	Scientific research institutions and research universities	Other colleges and universities, scientific research institutes of enterprises, governments, scientific and technological infrastructure, international scientific environment, etc.	The production, diffusion, and transfer of new knowledge
Technological innovation system	Innovative enterprises and the applied research institutes	Scientific research institutes, colleges, and universities; technical service organizations; governments; international technological environment, etc.	The development, introduction, development and diffusion of new technologies
Knowledge diffusion system	Educational institutes and technical service organizations	Governments, scientific research institutes, academic societies, enterprises, knowledge and information infrastructure, international educational environment, etc.	Diffusion of new knowledge and talent training
Knowledge application system	Enterprises and organizations not directly engaged in R&D activities	Governments, industrial parks, international trade in technology, etc.	The storage, diffusion, and actual application of new knowledge and technologies
Industrial innovation system	Industrial scientific research institutes, universities, innovative enterprises, and technical service institutes	Related industrial scientific research institutes, universities, and innovative enterprises, international scientific and technological environment, etc.	The production, diffusion and application of industrial knowledge and technologies
Regional innovation system	Regional scientific research institutions, universities, innovative enterprises, and technical service institutions	National scientific research institutions, universities, and innovative enterprises, international technological environment, etc.	The production, diffusion, and application of regional knowledge and technologies

Source: Zhang and He (1999), He and Zhang (2001)

network and policies, diffusion and transfer efficiency of new knowledge and technologies, and the overall efficiency of the innovation system.

Scientific and technological modernization generally has 12 features: partially predictable, openness, systematic, autonomous, cooperative, global, commercial, patentable, conducive to public welfare, stage-specific, unbalanced, and asynchronous.

In the process of scientific and technological modernization, changes in science and technology have not only general features but also differences. For example, from the perspective of intellectual property, science and technology are unique, while from the perspective of market competition, technology is optional.

Scientific and technological modernization is a manifestation of modernization and follows the ten basic principles of modernization (Table 2.20).

(3) Result

Outcomes of scientific and technological modernization include, among other things, the formation of scientific and technological modernity, particularity, diversity, and side effects (Table 7.28).

The outcome of the first scientific and technological modernization is the formation of the first scientific and technological modernity, particularity, and diversity, including the formation of the modern scientific and technological system, the extensive application of modern science and technology, and technological advancement of enterprises. Features of the first scientific and technological modernity include disciplinary division, modern technology, systematicness, specialty, self-discipline, and progressiveness, with side effects including technical unemployment and pollution.

The outcome of the second scientific and technological modernization is the formation of the second scientific and technological modernity, particularity, and diversity, including the formation and development of national innovation system, the improvement of national innovation capacity and efficiency, and the improvement of national scientific literacy and international scientific and technological competitiveness. Currently, the features of the second scientific and technological modernity include high technology, big science, intersection, globality, innovation, cooperation among industries, universities and research institutes, and environmental friendliness, with side effects including international technological risk. There still will be new development in the future.

From the policy perspective, the main outcomes of scientific and technological modernization are profound changes in six aspects: the completion of the two scientific and technological transitions, the improvement of scientific and technological creativity and competitiveness, the change in scientific and technological content and structure, the change in scientific and technological institutions and concepts, technological advances of enterprises and the improvement of national innovation capacity, and the change in the international scientific and technological system and national scientific and technological status.

From the theoretical perspective, scientific and technological modernization has three main goals: completing the first scientific and technological modernization, forming the national scientific and technological system, and improving the technological levels of enterprises; completing the second scientific and technological modernization, forming the national innovation system, and improving national innovation capacity and international competitiveness; and catching up with, reaching, and maintaining the world's advanced level of science and technology, becoming scientifically and technologically advanced countries.

The criteria of completing the first scientific and technological modernization include that the national scientific and technological system is basically formed and the national scientific and technological investment, efficiency, enterprises' technological level, and production efficiency reach the world's advanced level in the 1960s (average level of industrialized countries).

The criteria of entering the second scientific and technological modernization include that the national innovation system is basically formed and the national innovation investment and efficiency, enterprises' innovation capacity and efficiency, enterprises' technological level, and production efficiency reach or surpass the world's advanced level in the 1980s.

From the policy perspective, scientific and technological modernization has three main goals, i.e., improving enterprises' technological level and international competitiveness, improving national innovation capacity and efficiency, and improving national scientific literacy and international scientific and technological status.

(4) Dynamics

Driving factors and mechanisms of scientific and technological modernization are different (Table 7.26).

Generally, innovation is the fundamental source of scientific and technological modernization, competition is the incentive for scientific and technological advancement, adaptation is the scientific and technological adjustment to the changes in external environment, exchange is a contributing factor to scientific and technological advancement, national interest is the leading factor of scientific and technological advancement, market demand is an external driving force of scientific and technological advancement, and curiosity is the inherent driving force of scientific and technological advancement. Economic development and S&T advancement promote each other. Advanced countries give more prominence to innovation, while developing ones highlight more the role of economic development and exchange.

Driving models of scientific and technological modernization include innovation drive, triple drive, three-wheel drive (Fig. 7.13), innovation diffusion, and innovation spillover (Table 2.20). Driving forces of scientific and technological modernization are different at different levels, in different countries, and in different stages.

(5) Models

There is no universal, optimal path of scientific and technological modernization. In the twenty-first century, there are three basic paths of scientific and technological modernization (Fig. 7.14).

There is no standard but rational model for scientific and technological modernization. Generally, in the twenty-first century, developing countries may choose the model of national technological innovation system, advanced ones may adopt the

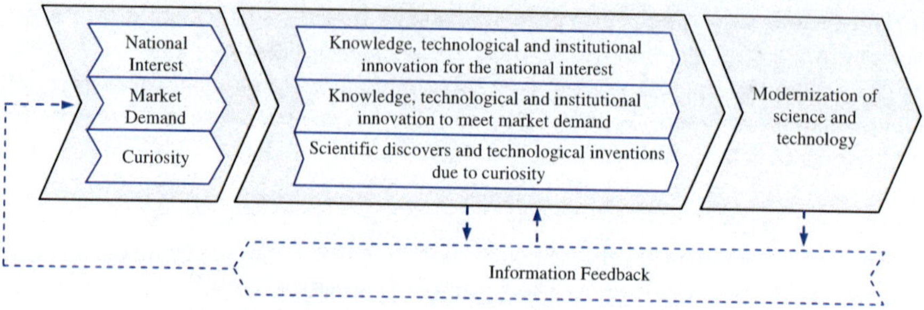

Fig. 7.13 Three-wheel drive model of scientific and technological modernization

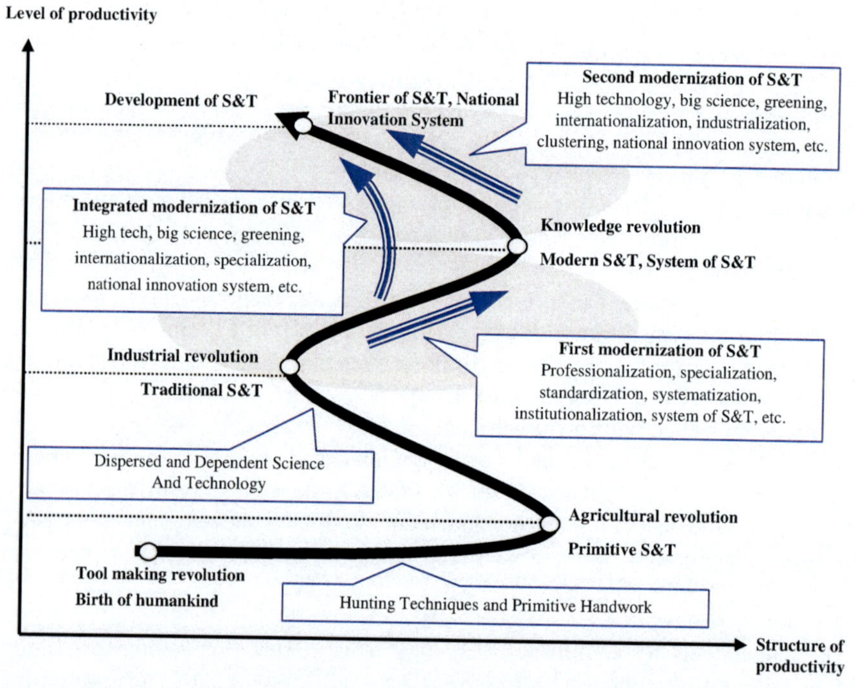

Fig. 7.14 Three paths of modernization of science and technology (S&T) in twenty-first century

model of national knowledge innovation system, and developing countries that choose the path of integrated scientific and technological modernization may adopt the model of national innovation system that gives equal importance to knowledge innovation, technological innovation, and knowledge application (Table 7.30).

(6) Integrated Modernization of Science and Technology

Integrated scientific and technological modernization is a basic path of scientific and technological modernization, and it is appropriate for developing countries in the twenty-first century. It is a composite process of alternate innovation, selection, diffusion, and withdrawal of scientific and technological elements; the combined interaction between the first and second scientific and technological modernization and the continued transition toward the second scientific and technological modernization; and the international competition whereby developing countries catch up with the world's advanced level of scientific and technological modernization.

The outcome of the integrated scientific and technological modernization is the achievement of the world's advanced level of scientific and technological modernization in such aspects as enterprises' innovation capacity and efficiency, national innovation capacity and efficiency, national scientific and technological input, achievements and returns, and national scientific literacy, with the final goal of forming the second scientific and technological modernity. Its driving mechanisms include innovation drive, triple drive, three-wheel drive, and associative action; national goals, scientific and technological globalization, and international scientific and technological interaction have a considerable influence on the integrated scientific and technological modernization.

Summary

Modernization happens in all sectors of human civilization, such as agriculture, industry, education, science and technology, and national defense. Modernization in different sectors has not only similarities but also differences. Countries are the basic units of modernization, and modernization in each sector is closely related to national modernization. Research on sector-specific modernization belongs to applied research in general. This chapter has dealt with sector-specific modernization, taking agricultural, educational, and scientific and technological modernization as examples.

Agricultural Modernization

Agricultural modernization is the modernization of the agricultural system. Agricultural modernization theories include the classical modernization theory, twice agricultural modernization theory, and agricultural modernization theory in broad sense, which is the application of the second modernization theory in the agricultural system.

According to the agricultural modernization theory in broad sense, agricultural modernization is a sort of agricultural change and international competition beginning from the Industrial Revolution in the eighteenth century; it is the frontier process of the formation, development, transition, and international interaction of modern agriculture; the composite process of alternate innovation, selection diffusion, and withdrawal of agricultural elements; and the international competition for and international differentiation and national stratification as a result of catching up with, reaching, and maintaining the world's agricultural advanced level; it includes the transition from subsistence to market-oriented agriculture and from market-oriented to knowledge-based and ecological agriculture, the continued increase of agricultural efficiency and farmers' income, the continued improvement of farmers' welfare and quality of life, decreasing of the percentage of agriculture, maintaining the balance of supply and demand of agricultural products as well as national food security, and the change of national agricultural status and international agricultural system.

Generally, agricultural modernization is an intersection of agricultural development, agricultural transition, international agricultural competition, and change of international status and is both the world frontier of agricultural change and the process and action to reach this frontier.

The process of agricultural modernization can be divided into two types: frontier process and catch-up process, and its frontier process in the eighteenth to twenty-first centuries can be divided into two major stages.

The first agricultural modernization is the transition from traditional to primary modern agriculture and from subsistence to market-oriented agriculture. Its features include marketization, commercialization, intensification, high efficiency, specialization, mechanization, chemicalization, extensive use of improved varieties and irrigation works, operation on large scale, and standardization, as well as the increase of agricultural labor productivity, land productivity, and farmers' living standards and the decline of the percentages of agricultural labor force in all labors and agricultural value added in GDP. Its outcome is the formation of the first agricultural modernity, particularity, and diversity, with side effects including agricultural environment pollution and soil erosion. The criteria of completing the first agricultural modernization include that the percentage of agricultural value added in GDP is below 15%, the percentage of agricultural labor force in the total labor force is below 30%, and the agricultural labor productivity reaches the world's advanced level in the 1960s (about $6,000 on the basis of prices in 2000).

The second agricultural modernization is the transition from primary modern to advanced modern agriculture and from market-oriented to knowledge-intensive, ecological, and sustainable agriculture. Currently, its features include knowledgeablization, informatization, intelligentization, precision, high quality, ecologicalization, greening, diversification, order- and plant-based operation, and internationalization, as well as the increase of comprehensive agricultural benefits, international competitiveness, and farmers' quality of living and the decline of the percentages of agricultural labor force in all labor and agricultural value added in GDP. Its outcome is the formation of the second agricultural modernity, particularity, and diversity, with side effects including agricultural trade conflict and food risk. The criteria of entering the second agricultural modernization include that the percentage of agricultural value added in GDP is below 5%, the percentage of agricultural labor force in the total labor force is below 10%, and organic or ecological agriculture has emerged.

The integrated agricultural modernization is a basic path of agricultural modernization in the twenty-first century. It includes the two successive agricultural transitions (from subsistence to market-oriented agriculture and from market-oriented to knowledge-intensive and ecological agriculture) and the continued transition toward knowledge-based agriculture; the coordinated development of agricultural marketization, mechanization, informatization, greening, and internationalization; increased agricultural efficiency and farmers' income; improved farmers' welfare and quality of life; reduced percentage of agriculture; and improved the quality of agricultural supply, international agricultural competitiveness, and international agricultural status.

There are mainly three basic paths of agricultural modernization in the twenty-first century: first agricultural modernization, second agricultural modernization, and integrated agricultural modernization. Different paths have different models, and different countries may choose different paths and models.

Modernization of Education

Educational modernization is the modernization of the educational system. Educational modernization theories include the classical educational modernization theory, twice educational modernization theory, and educational modernization theory in broad sense, which is the application of the second modernization theory in the educational system.

According to the educational modernization theory in broad sense, educational modernization is a sort of educational change and international competition beginning from the eighteenth century; it is the frontier process of the formation, development, transition, and international interaction of modern education; the complex process of alternate innovation, selection, diffusion, and withdrawal of educational elements; the international competition for and international differentiation and national stratification as a result of catching up with, reaching, and maintaining the world's educational advanced level; the transition from traditional to modern education and from degree-giving education to lifelong learning; the improvement of educational efficiency and quality; the change of educational thoughts and concepts; the improvement of educational dissemination and national literacy; and the change in educational justice, students' literacy, and international educational status.

Generally, educational modernization is an intersection of educational development, educational transition, international educational competition, and change of international status and is both the world frontier of educational change and the process and action to reach this frontier.

The process of educational modernization can be divided into two types: frontier process and catch-up process, and its frontier process in the eighteenth to twenty-first centuries can be divided into two major stages.

The first educational modernization is the transition and profound change from the education of agricultural society to that of industrial society, from traditional to primary modern education, and from feudal to public education. Its features include specialization, rationalization, becoming scientific, electrification, democratization, institutionalization, standardization, and universal compulsory elementary education. Its outcome is the formation of the first educational modernity, particularity, and diversity, with side effects including suppression of students' personalities. The criteria of completing the first educational modernization include that compulsory elementary education is popularized and that educational input, participation, and efficiency reach the world's advanced level in the 1960s.

The second educational modernization is the transition and profound change from the education of industrial society to that of knowledge society, from primary modern to advanced modern education, and from degree-giving education to lifelong learning. Currently, its features include informatization, individuation, openness, internationalization, innovation, high quality, universal higher education, and lifelong learning; there will be new changes in the future. Its outcome is the formation of the second educational modernity, particularity, and diversity, with side effects including information divide. The criteria of entering the second educational modernization include that the popularity of middle education exceeds 80%, that of higher education exceeds 40%, and information-based education has emerged.

The integrated educational modernization is a basic path of educational modernization in broad sense in the twenty-first century; it includes the coordinated development of the first and second educational modernization and the continued transition toward lifelong learning; the coordinated development of becoming scientific, standardization, democratization, informatization, openness, and internationalization and the continued transition toward information-based education and lifelong learning; the improvement of educational efficiency and quality; the improvement of educational justice and national literacy; and the change in international educational competition and international educational status.

There are roughly three basic paths of educational modernization in the twenty-first century: first educational modernization, second educational modernization, and integrated educational modernization. Different countries may choose different paths and models.

Modernization of Science and Technology

Scientific and technological modernization is the modernization of the system of science and technology. So far, there have been no universally recognized theoretical expositions about scientific and technological modernization. The scientific and technological modernization theory in broad sense is the application of the second modernization theory in the scientific and technological system.

According to modernization theory on science and technology in broad sense, scientific and technological modernization is the scientific and technological change and international competition beginning from the eighteenth century; the frontier process of the formation, development, transition, and international interaction of the modern scientific and technological system; the composite process of the alternate innovation, selection, diffusion, and withdrawal of scientific and technological elements; and the international competition for and national stratification as a result of catching up with, reaching, and maintaining the world's advanced level of science and technology. It includes the transition from traditional science and technology to the modern scientific and technological system and from the modern scientific and technological system to the national innovation system; the enterprises' technological advancement; the improvement of international competitiveness; the improvement of national innovation capacity and national scientific literacy; the increase of scientific and technological contribution to economic growth; and the change of the world scientific and technological system and international scientific and technological status.

Broadly speaking, scientific and technological modernization is an intersection of scientific and technological development, scientific and technological transition, international scientific and technological competition, and the change of international status, is both the world frontier of scientific and technological change and the process and action to reach this frontier.

The process of modernization of science and technology can be divided into two types: frontier process and catch-up process, and its frontier process in the eighteenth to twenty-first centuries can be divided into two major stages.

The first scientific and technological modernization is the transition and profound change from traditional science and technology to the modern scientific and technological system, including enterprises' technological advancement and improvement of production efficiency, and the establishment and development of modern S&T and national scientific and technological systems. Its main features include professionalization, specialization, systematization, standardization, and institutionalization. The outcome is the formation of the first scientific and technological modernity, particularity, and diversity, with side effects including environmental pollution and technical unemployment. The criteria of completing the first scientific and technological modernization include that the national scientific and technological system is basically put in place and that the national scientific and technological input and efficiency and enterprises' technological levels and production efficiency reach the world's advanced level in the 1960s (average level of industrialized countries).

The second scientific and technological modernization is the transition and profound change from the modern scientific and technological system to the national innovation system, including the institutionalization and diversification of innovation cooperation, the improvement of innovation capacity and efficiency, the shortening of technological innovation cycles, the acceleration of technology transfer, and the improvement of national scientific literacy and international scientific and technological competitiveness. At present, its features include high technology, big science, internationalization, diversification, industrialization, commercialization, greening, networking, and clustering (e.g., scientific and technological parks and industrial parks), and the duality of science and technology (advances and side effects) has drawn social attention. The outcome is the formation of the second scientific and technological modernity, particularity, and diversity, with side effects including international technological risk. The criteria of entering the second scientific and technological modernization include that the national innovation system is basically put in place and that national innovation input and efficiency, enterprises' innovation capacity and efficiency, and their technological levels and production efficiency reach or surpass the world's advanced level in the 1980s.

The integrated modernization of science and technology, a basic path of scientific and technological modernization, is a path appropriate for developing countries. It is the interaction of the first and second scientific and technological modernization and the continued transition toward the second scientific and technological modernization and the international competition whereby developing countries catch up with the world's advanced level of scientific and technological modernization.

There are three basic paths of scientific and technological modernization in the twenty-first century: first scientific and technological modernization, second scientific and technological modernization, and integrated scientific and technological modernization. Different countries may choose different paths and models.

Further Reading

Arnon I (1981) Modernization of agriculture in developing countries: resources, potentials, and problems. Wiley, New York

Christensen DC (ed) (1993) European historiography of technology: technology's role in the modernization process. University Press of Southern Denmark, Gylling

Gu M (2007) Basic characteristics and strategies of educational modernization. People's Educ 13–14:8–11

He C, Zhang F (2001) Knowledge innovation – new focus of competition: front of the second modernization. Economic Management, Beijing

Hiratsuka M (1978) Modernization of education in Japan. National Institute for Educational Research, Tokyo

Huang Z, Lin J, Zhang D (2003) Theory, process and path of agricultural modernization. China Agriculture Press, Beijing

Lelas S (2000) Science and modernity: toward an integral theory of science. Kluwer Academic, Dordrecht

Li J et al (2002) Report on the progress of Shanghai's scientific and technological modernization. Sci Sci Manage S&T 9:65–69

Misa TJ, Brey P, Feenberg A (2003) Modernity and technology. MIT Press, Cambridge, MA

Russell CA (1983) Science and social change 1700–1900. MacMillan, London

Wilson Center (1982) China's scientific and technological modernization: domestic and international implications. East Asia Program, Wilson Center, Washington, DC

Zhang F, He C (1999) National innovation system: an engine of the second modernization. Higher Education, Beijing

Modernization Policy

8

First comes, first gains (German proverb). *No way is impossible to courage* (American proverb). The main purpose of the policy study in the modernization science is to explore and find out the right or suitable way of the level-specific, field-related, and sector-relative modernization in the required time.

Generally, the issue of modernization is a strategic one, and the science of modernization is a one about strategies in some content. Modernization policies reflect not only the application of modernization theories in practice but also an integral part of the modernization science. The research on modernization policies covers modernization evaluation, modernization strategy and measures (Fig. 8.1), etc. Advanced and developing countries differ greatly in modernization policies. Modernization policies are not only to change the world but also to create a new world in which everyone has the equal access to all-round development.

8.1 Modernization Evaluation

An ancient Chinese said: *know yourself and your enemy, victory is assured.* Modernization is just like an international marathon of national civilization's competition (Fig. 1.1). Countries running ahead become developed ones, while the rest become developing ones; there is mobility between the two types of status. An objective evaluation of the modernization process makes it possible to monitor dynamically the level of a country's development and transformation and the change of its international status during this process. Modernization evaluation is an important basis for modernization-related decision making.

8.1.1 Principles of Evaluation

Modernization evaluation is one of the comprehensive process and outcome of modernization. It is a common method in modernization research and also a crucial part of modernization policy research. There are several types of modernization

C. He, *Modernization Science*,
DOI 10.1007/978-3-642-25459-8_8, © Springer-Verlag Berlin Heidelberg 2012

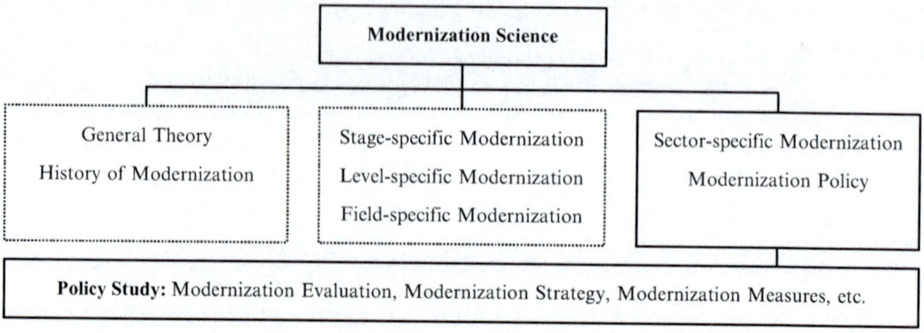

Fig. 8.1 Policy research of modernization science

Table 8.1 Main types of modernization evaluation (examples)

Type	Purpose	Features
Level evaluation	Relative level of modernization	International comparability, theoretical consistency, and continuity
Stage evaluation	Development stage of modernization	
Innovation capacity evaluation	Driving forces of modernization	International comparability, regional comparability, and relativity
Competitiveness evaluation	Competitive advantage of modernization	
Performance evaluation	Performance and progress of modernization	Policy applicability, pertinence, practicability, and timeliness
Diagnosis evaluation	Gains and losses in the process of modernization and causes thereof	
Theoretical evaluation	Examining if the theoretical hypotheses about modernization are scientific	Exploratory, varying as per research needs

evaluation (Table 8.1), each with different principles and methods. Below is a discussion of general principles and methods for modernization evaluation.

8.1.1.1 Theoretical Basis

The theoretical basis for modernization evaluation includes modernization theories, systems science, evaluation theories, etc.

(1) Modernization Theory

The modernization theory is not a single theory but a cluster of theories including general theory, stage-specific theory, level-specific theory, field-specific theory, sector-specific theory, and theories on special subjects. Here, the focus is on the evaluation based on the Second Modernization Theory.

According to the Second Modernization Theory, modernization involves the development and transformation of civilization, international competition, and the change in international status; between the eighteenth century and the twenty-first century, the frontier trajectory of modernization process could be divided into two stages: first and second modernization, and integrated modernization is the coordinated development of twice modernization; modernization is nonlinear, and its driving forces include innovation, competition, exchange, and adaptation.

Generally, the level of modernization and the development of civilization are closely related to international status, while the stage of modernization is to the transition of civilization, and modernization performance is to innovation and competition. Modernization at different stages has different connotations and characteristics, so it is necessary to do separate evaluations.

(2) Systems Science

The systems theory holds that human society is a large open system that can be controlled and evaluated. The social system comprises a number of subsystems, and each of them has its unique functions and features which need and can be evaluated separately.

(3) Evaluation Theory

Comprehensive evaluation is a commonly used evaluation approach. The basic idea is that the object to be evaluated is a complex system, so it is not enough to use just a single indicator. It is necessary to translate multiple indicators into a comprehensive index for evaluation. After statistical analysis, indicators can be converted into standard indexes which, through weighting and calculation, can be translated into a comprehensive index.

8.1.1.2 General Requirements

Generally, modernization evaluation should respect the laws governing modernization and evaluation rules. The following issues should be noted in doing the evaluation:

First, limited objective. The process of modernization is a nonlinear, complex historical process, and the system of modernization is a large, open, dynamic system, so it is impossible to cover every aspect in modernization evaluation. There should be priorities.

Second, rational evaluation indicators. Usually, typical, critical, comparable, and continuous statistical indicators are chosen.

Third, scientific evaluation method. Evaluation methods include qualitative evaluation, quantitative evaluation, and comprehensive evaluation.

Fourth, quality of the data for evaluation. Usually, statistics of international and official statistical agencies are adopted.

Fifth, relativity of evaluation results. Statistical methods and indicators may differ from country to country; some countries may have incomplete data for some years; there may be no statistics on some important new phenomena. All these may affect the evaluation results to some degree.

Sixth, objectivity and comparability of evaluation results. The influence of human factors should be minimized, for example, by using computers. Generally, the results of modernization evaluation should be of both historical and international comparability.

8.1.1.3 Basic Contents

Comprehensive evaluation generally includes six parts (1) defining the purpose and requirement of evaluation; (2) identifying the features of and laws governing the evaluation object; (3) identifying the theoretical basis and basic principles of evaluation; (4) choosing evaluation indicators to form a system of indicators; (5) choosing an evaluation method and establishing an evaluation model; and (6) gathering data, conducting evaluation, and reporting results.

Choosing evaluation indicators is a key component of modernization evaluation. Generally, when choosing evaluation indicators, the evaluation purpose should be considered and the laws governing modernization should be respected. There are also about six principles to follow (Table 8.2), and attention should be paid to the following three factors:

First, choosing evaluation indicators from two dimensions (Fig. 8.2). The first dimension is process, i.e., choosing indicators from the input, process, output, and

Table 8.2 Principles of choosing modernization evaluation indicators

No.	Principle	Annotation
1	Choosing indicators which reflect typical characteristics and are representative	Ascending variables, descending variables, transition variables, regional variables
2	Choosing indicators which reflect the level of development and are of international comparability	Per capita indicators, structural indicators, efficiency indicators, performance indicators
3	Choosing indicators which are easy to understand, acceptable, and have policy significance	Indicators which scholars frequently use and the public are concerned about
4	Choosing indicators that generate continuous data	Statistical indicators, social survey indicators, monitoring indicators, etc.
5	Choosing a proper number of evaluation indicators	Usually about 10–30 indicators
6	Noting the systematic relations and balance between the chosen indicators	Appropriate proportions of inert indicators and active indicators

Note: Generally, total amount indicators, saturation variables, fluctuating variables, random variables, and regional variables are not appropriate to be used as evaluation indicators

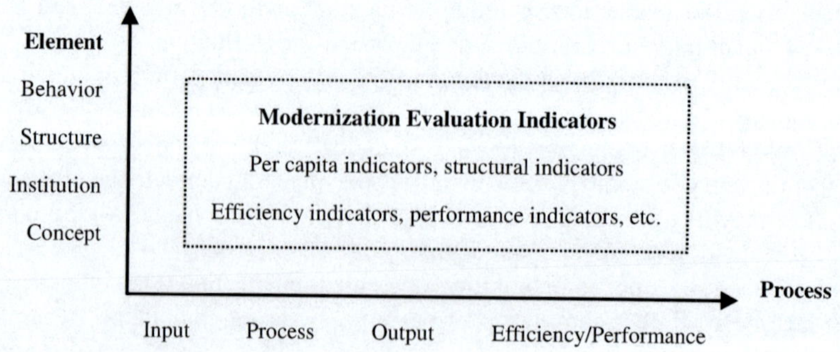

Fig. 8.2 Two dimensions for choosing evaluation indicators

efficiency (performance) of modernization; the second dimension is element, i.e., choosing indicators from four elements including modernization behavior (life), structure (content), institution, and concept.

Second, the number of evaluation indicators should be neither too big nor too small. Too many indicators will make it difficult to do the evaluation and understand, while too few indicators may lead to evaluation instability and distortion. For example, some 30 environmental indicators are enough to reflect about 90% of the demand for environmental policies (Jesinghaus 1999).

Third, the evaluation indicators should be systematic and rational. Modernization is not a synchronous process which means that in a particular period, different indicators may have different sensitivity (elasticity). Some indicators are relatively inert (changing slowly), while others are relatively active (changing fast). In the evaluation indicator system, if inert indicators outnumber active ones, the evaluation index is likely to be insensitive; if the latter outnumber the former, the evaluation index is likely to be unstable. When establishing the evaluation indicator system, attention should be paid to the balance between inert and active indicators.

8.1.1.4 Matters to be Noted

First, coordination between evaluation needs and evaluation rules. An effective evaluation involves not too many evaluation indicators. Researchers and policymakers may focus on many different issues and indicators, so it is necessary to strike a balance between them.

Second, coordination between importance and feasibility. Some modernization indicators are very important, but the acquisition of data, especially on developing countries, is rather difficult. Incomplete data will affect evaluation results.

Third, paying serious attention to nonlinear indicators. Some indicators are nonlinear or are not desirably relevant to other indicators. If involved in evaluation, they will affect evaluation results; if not, the evaluation would be questioned by experts.

Fourth, paying serious attention to new phenomena and new indicators. Some new phenomena and new indicators are quite important as they reflect the new trends of modernization. But there is no statistical data, or no worldwide, continuous statistical data, about them yet.

Fifth, paying serious attention to the weight of indicators. How much weight is given to indicators has a direct bearing on the evaluation results.

Sixth, paying serious attention to evaluation results. Overexplanation of the evaluation results from policy perspective should be avoided.

8.1.2 International Evaluation

An international evaluation targets worldwide modernization phenomena. The evaluation object may be a group of or all countries, and the evaluation results highlight international comparability. An international evaluation of modernization usually includes level evaluation, stage evaluation, and process evaluation. A process evaluation includes the evaluation of innovation capacity, competitiveness, influence, etc.

8.1.2.1 Evaluation of Modernization Level

An evaluation of modernization level is a qualitative one of the object's actual modernization progress and its relative level in the world. The qualitative evaluation of modernization level, which dates back to the 1960s, roughly includes the qualitative evaluation of national modernization level, field-specific (or sector-specific) modernization level, and regional modernization level (Table 8.3).

China Modernization Report, published each year since 2001, used the Second Modernization Theory as its theoretical basis and gave a qualitative evaluation of the modernization levels of 131 countries between 1950 and 2007. Each of the country had a population of more than one million in 2000. The evaluation covered the levels

Table 8.3 Examples of modernization level evaluation

Evaluation purpose	Evaluation object	Evaluation indicators	Evaluation time	References
National modernization	14 countries	11 variables	1960s	Cantril (1965)
	115 countries and regions	10 indicators	1960	Buck (1969)
	112 countries and regions	40 indicators	1950–1965	Harbison et al. (1970a, b)
	120 countries	10 indicators	1998	Zhu and Wu (2001)
	133 countries	16 indicators	1995	He (1999)
	131 countries	20 indicators	1970–1998	China Modernization Report (2001)
Field-specific modernization				
Economic modernization	131 countries	18 indicators	1950–2002	RGCMS (2005)
Social modernization	131 countries	24 indicators	1950–2003	RGCMS (2006)
Cultural modernization	131 countries	24 indicators	1990–2005	RGCMS (2009)
Ecological modernization	131 countries	30 indicators	1970–2004	RGCMS (2007)
Human modernization	Brazil and Mexico	14 variables	1960s	Kahl (1968)
Index of social progress (ISP)	124 countries and regions	36 indicators	Since 1970	Estes (1984, 1988)
Human development index (HDI)	175 countries and regions	4 indicators	Since 1975	UNDP (1990, 2003)
Index of human progress	128 countries and regions	10 indicators	1975–1999	Emes and Hahn (2001)
Regional modernization	48 US states	33 variables	1960	Crittenden (1967)
	50 US states	33 variables	1960–1990	Morgan and Kickham (1997)
	34 regions in China	20 indicators	1970–1998	China Modernization Report (2001)
	205 regions in 18 countries	20 indicators	1980–2000	RGCMS (2004)

Source: RGCMS (2008)

of national, regional, economic, social, ecological, and cultural modernization. Three evaluation models were adopted including the models for the first modernization, the second modernization, and integrated modernization (Example 8.1).

Example 8.1 Three Modernization Evaluation Models

The evaluation of the first modernization included ten evaluation indicators, and the reference values used for the evaluation were the mean values of the indicators of 19 industrial countries in 1960.

Evaluation indicators and model for the first modernization

Item	Evaluation indicator	Evaluation standard	Type of indicator	Evaluation model
FMI	First modernization index	100		$FMI = \sum S_i/10$
Economy	1. Per capita national income, US$	Calculated year on year[a]	Direct indicator	$S_i = 100 \times I_{actual\ value}/I_{standard\ value}$ (Direct indicator, $S_i \leq 100$) $S_i = 100 \times I_{standard\ value}/I_{actual\ value}$ (Reverse indicator, $S_i \leq 100$)
	2. Percentage of agricultural labor force (%)	≤30%	Reverse indicator	
	3. Percentage of value added of agriculture (%)	≤15%	Reverse indicator	
	4. Percentage of value added of service sector (%)	≥45%	Direct indicator	
Society	5. Percentage of urban population (%)	≥50%	Direct indicator	
	6. Rate of doctors, doctors per 1,000 people	≥1‰	Direct indicator	
	7. Infant mortality (‰)	≤30‰	Reverse indicator	
	8. Average life expectancy, years	≥70 years	Direct indicator	
Knowledge	9. Adult literacy (%)	≥80%	Direct indicator	
	10. Gross enrollment rate of tertiary education (%)	≥15%	Direct indicator	

Note: It is designed with reference to the evaluation indicators raised by Professor Alex Inkles (Sun 1988)

Source: RGCMS (2010)

[a]The mean value of per capita national income of 19 industrial countries in 1960 was used as the reference value, and each year afterward, the standard value was calculated based on the inflation rate of US dollar. For example, the standard value in 1960 was 1,280 US$ and 6,399 US$ in 2000. S_i refers to the degree of No. *i* indicator reaching the standard and is less than or equal to 100 in value. The *i* is the serial number of an evaluation indicator. The $i_{actual\ value}$ stands for the actual value of No. *i* indicator, and $i_{standard\ value}$ stands for the standard value of No. *i* indicator. Reverse indicator means the bigger figure, the less developed.

(continued)

The evaluation of the second modernization included 16 evaluation indicators in four categories and used the mean values of high-income countries as reference values for evaluation.

Evaluation indicators and model for the second modernization

Item	Evaluation indicator	Unit and type	Evaluation model
SMI	Second modernization index		SMI = (KII + KTI + LQI + EQI)/4
Knowledge innovation	1. Financial input into knowledge innovation	R&D/GDP (%)	*Knowledge innovation index:* KII = $\sum D_i/3$ *Direct indicator evaluation:* $D_i \leq 120$ $D_i = 100 \times i_{\text{actual value}}/i_{\text{reference value}}$
	2. Manpower input into knowledge innovation	Researchers per 10,000 people	
	3. Patent output from knowledge innovation	Patents per 10,000 people	
Knowledge diffusion	4. Middle school popularization	%	*Knowledge transmission index:* KTI = $\sum D_i/4$ *Direct indicator evaluation: same as above*
	5. University popularization	%	
	6. TV popularization	%	
	7. Internet popularization	%	
Quality of life	8. Percentage of urban population	%	*Life quality index:* LQI = $\sum D_i/5$ *Direct indicator evaluation: same as above* *Reverse indicator evaluation:* $D_i \leq 120$ $D_i = 100 \times i_{\text{reference value}}/i_{\text{actual value}}$
	9. Rate of doctors	Doctors per 1,000 people	
	10. Infant mortality	‰, reverse indicator	
	11. Average life expectancy	Years	
	12. Energy consumption per capita	Kg of oil equivalent	
Economic quality	13. Per capita GNI	US$	Economic quality index: EQI = $\sum D_i/4$ Direct indicator evaluation: same as above Reverse indicator evaluation: same as above
	14. Per capita purchasing power	International dollar	
	15. Percentage of value added of material industry	%, reverse indicator	
	16. Percentage of labor force in material industry	%, reverse indicator	

Note: Middle school popularization refers to gross enrollment of middle education. University popularization refers to gross enrollment of tertiary education. TV popularization refers to TV set per 100 household. Per capita purchasing power is GNI per capital (PPP). Material industry includes agriculture and industry. The *i* stands for the serial number of an indicator. D_i means the development index of No. *i* indicator and is less than or equal to 120 in value. Reference value was the mean value of high-income countries of the year
Source: RGCMS (2010)

The evaluation of integrated modernization included 12 evaluation indicators in three categories and used the mean values of the year's indicators of high-income countries as reference values for evaluation.

Evaluation indicators and model for integrated modernization

Item	Evaluation indicator	Unit	Evaluation model
IMI	Integrated modernization index		IMI = (EI + SI + KI)/3
Economic indicators	1. Per capita national income	US$	*Economic development index:* EI = $\sum D_i/4$ *Indicator evaluation:* $D_i \leq 100$ $D_i = 100 \times i_{\text{actual value}}/i_{\text{reference value}}$
	2. Per capita purchasing power	International dollar	
	3. Percentage of value added of service sector	%	
	4. Percentage of labor force in service sector	%	
Social indicators	5. Percentage of urban population	%	*Social development index:* SI = $\sum D_i/4$ *Indicator evaluation: same as above*
	6. Rate of doctors	Doctors per 1,000 people	
	7. Average life expectancy	Years	
	8. Eco-efficiency	US$/kg of standard oil	
Knowledge indicators	9. Financial input into knowledge innovation	R&D/GDP (%)	*Knowledge development index:* KI = $\sum D_i/4$ *Indicator evaluation: same as above*
	10. Output of patents from knowledge innovation	Patents per 10,000 people	
	11. Gross enrollment rate of tertiary education	%	
	12. Internet popularization	%	

Note: Per capita purchasing power is GNI per capita (PPP). Eco-efficiency is per capita GDP/energy consumption per capita. *i* stands for the serial number of an indicator. D_i means the development index of No. *i* indicator and is less than or equal to 100 in value. Reference value is the average value of high-income countries of the year

Source: RGCMS (2010)

8.1.2.2 Evaluation of Innovation Capacity and Competitiveness

From the 1980s onward, the competitiveness evaluation began drawing attention, and since the 1990s, the innovation capacity evaluation has been thought highly of (Table 8.4).

Competition is a major driving force of modernization. Competitiveness evaluation is an important part of modernization research. There has been no uniform definition of competitiveness so far. Competitiveness evaluation is roughly conducted at four levels: national competitiveness, regional competitiveness, sectoral competitiveness, and corporate competitiveness.

Table 8.4 Evaluation of innovation capacity and competitiveness

Item	Evaluation object	Number of indicators	Evaluation time	References
Innovation index	17 countries	12	1973–1995	Porter and Stern (1999)
National innovation capacity index	73 countries and regions	12	2001–2002	WEF (2003)
Innovation capacity index	117 countries and regions	6	1995–2001	UNCTAD (2005)
World competitiveness index[a]	55 countries and regions	323	1980 until now	IMD (2007)
Global competitiveness index[a]	125 countries and regions	90	1980 until now	WEF (2003)
Objective competitiveness index	131 countries	18	1990–2004	RGCMS (2008)
Per capita competitiveness index	131 countries	18	1990–2004	RGCMS (2008)

[a]From 1980 onward, IMD and WEF began copublishing competitiveness reports until 1996 when they split
Source: RGCMS (2008)

Innovation is also a major driving force of modernization. Innovation capacity evaluation is an important part of modernization research and is roughly conducted at four levels: national innovation capacity, regional innovation capacity, sectoral innovation capacity, and organizational innovation capacity.

8.1.3 Assessment for Policy Making

An assessment of modernization from the policy perspective generally includes performance evaluation, diagnosis evaluation, and policy effectiveness evaluation. Such evaluation is generally a practical goal-oriented evaluation, highlighting policy orientation, pertinence, and operability.

8.1.3.1 Performance Evaluation

A modernization performance evaluation is conducted to assess the outcome and effectiveness of the process of modernization.

First, evaluation purpose. The purposes of performance evaluation may be put into three categories: to find out the actual progress of modernization, to monitor the achievement of modernization goals, and to predict the goals of modernization strategies (Table 8.5). They have different functions and roles to play.

Second, evaluation objects. Objects of performance evaluation include level-specific modernization (national, regional, etc.), field-specific modernization (economic, social, etc.), sector-specific modernization (agricultural, industrial, etc.), and subject-specific modernization (urban, rural).

Third, evaluation indicators. Indicators used for performance evaluation may be chosen according to evaluation purpose and requirement and may include

Table 8.5 Types of modernization performance evaluation

Type of evaluation	Evaluation purpose and content	Function
Actual progress evaluation	Progress in modernization in a particular period	Strategy consulting, campaign consulting, diagnosis evaluation
Goal monitoring evaluation	Degree to which modernization goals are achieved	Goal management, policy consulting, diagnosis evaluation
Goal prediction evaluation	International comparison and goal prediction of modernization level	Setting strategic goals, campaign consulting, modernization planning

Table 8.6 Criteria for modernization performance evaluation

Country	Evaluation criteria	Function
Developed countries	World's top level, average level of developed countries, anticipated goals	Campaign consulting, policy consulting
Moderately developed countries	Average level of developed countries, anticipated goals	Goal management, policy consulting, modernization planning
Other developing countries	Average level of developed countries, world average level, anticipated goals	Goal management, policy consulting, modernization planning

behavioral, structural, institutional, and concept indicators of modernization, as well as modernization input, output, efficiency, and effectiveness indicators.

Fourth, weight of indicators. The weight of indicators may be determined according to policy needs and the laws governing modernization.

Fifth, evaluation criteria. Different criteria may be adopted for developed and developing countries (Table 8.6).

Six, evaluation model. Appropriate evaluation methods and models should be chosen as per evaluation needs and comprehensive evaluation methods.

8.1.3.2 Diagnosis Evaluation

Modernization diagnosis evaluation is conducted to assess the gains and losses in the process of modernization so as to find the causes of failure and come up with the countermeasures.

First, performance evaluation. It is the fundamental work of diagnosis evaluation, including actual progress evaluation and goal achievement evaluation.

Second, strength analysis. It is about analyzing the major achievements and advantages of modernization as well as the reasons behind them.

Third, weakness analysis. It is about analyzing the major mistakes and weaknesses of modernization as well as the causes thereof.

Fourth, countermeasure analysis. It is about making policy recommendations about maintaining and strengthening advantages and overcoming or improving weaknesses.

8.1.3.3 Strategy Evaluation

Modernization strategy evaluation is conducted to assess rationality and effectiveness of modernization strategies, which is applicable to strategy management.

First, performance evaluation. It is the fundamental work of strategy evaluation, including goal monitoring evaluation and goal prediction evaluation.

Second, strategic goal evaluation. It is about analyzing the guidance, rationality, feasibility, costs, etc., of strategic goals.

Third, strategy planning evaluation. It is about analyzing the consistency between strategic goals and measures, coordination between subsystems, etc.

Fourth, strategy implementation evaluation. It is about analyzing the experience and lessons from strategy implementation, the timeliness and applicability of strategic adjustment, etc.

Fifth, strategy advantage evaluation. It is about analyzing the comparative advantage and competitive advantage of the strategy and making suggestions for improving the competitive advantage, etc.

8.2 Modernization Strategy

Strategies are means to achieve goals. Likewise, modernization strategies are the means to attain modernization goals. The modernization goal of advanced countries is to maintain the world's leading or advanced level of development and transformation, while that of developing countries is to catch up with and reaching the world's advanced level. Advanced countries differ considerably from developing ones in modernization strategies. A bridge between modernization theories and practices, modernization strategies represent an integral part of the modernization science and a critical component of modernization policies.

Generally, modernization strategies and tactics are based on modernization theories, and development strategies and tactics are based on development theories. The former apply to all countries, while the latter are commonly seen in developing countries. Modernization includes the development of civilization, the transition of civilization, international competition, and the change of international status. Therefore, modernization strategies are related to yet different from development strategies (Table 8.7).

8.2.1 Modernization Goals

A modernization goal is what is expected to be achieved through modernization in a future period of time. There are many types of goals such as strategic and planned goals, long-term and immediate goals, dynamic and fixed goals, theoretical and policy goals, national and regional goals, field-specific goals, and sector-specific goals. To set modernization goals, one country has to follow the laws governing modernization, figure out the world's trends, and have a clear understanding of its status in the international system and national conditions. In this section, modernization goals in the twenty-first century are to be addressed.

Table 8.7 Comparison between modernization strategies and development strategies

Item	Modernization strategies	Development strategies
Goal	Objective goals: set according to the level of modernization	Subjective goals: set based on the anticipations of researchers
	Advanced countries: the world's top or advanced level	Advanced countries: set based on national needs
	Developing countries: the world's advanced or average level	Developing countries: set based on national anticipations
Path	Objective paths: three basic paths of modernization	Subjective paths: paths pictured by researchers
	Advanced countries: second modernization path	Advanced countries: varied
	Developing countries: catch-up modernization or integrated modernization path	Developing countries: different ideas raised by researchers
Emphasis	Advanced countries: law-driven, frontier innovation, competition analysis	Advanced countries: problem-driven, policy innovation
	Developing countries: law-driven, model innovation, competition analysis	Developing countries: problem-driven, follow-up imitation, policy analysis
Features	Scientific thinking: law—comparison—countermeasure	Practical logic: trend—status quo—countermeasure
	Advanced countries: modernization theory—maintaining advanced level—countermeasure	Advanced countries: development trend—national status quo—countermeasure
	Developing countries: modernization theory—modernization gap—countermeasure	Developing countries: development trend—national status quo—countermeasure
Basis	Modernization theories, science of strategy, etc.	Development theories, science of strategy, etc.

8.2.1.1 Theoretical Basis

Modernization goals are established based on modernization theories and relative national level. According to the Second Modernization Theory, the outcomes of modernization include the formation of modernity, particularity and diversity, international differentiation, national stratification, and side effects, as well as the changes in world frontier, international system, and national state; the first modernization, the second modernization, and the integrated modernization bring about different outcomes; the theoretical goal of national modernization is to complete the first modernization, the transition from agricultural to industrial civilization, and the second modernization, the transition from industrial to knowledge civilization, and catch up with, reach, and maintain the world's advanced level; the policy goal of national modernization is to improve productivity and quality of life, promote social equity and progress, the all-round development of people, and the

Table 8.8 Theoretical basis of modernization goals

Modernization theory	Content and features	Policy application
Outcome of modernization		
Modernity	First modernity, second modernity, and modernity in different fields and sectors	General goal of modernization
Particularity and diversity	Particularity, competitive advantage, etc., of national and regional modernization	Individual goal of modernization
Side effects	First modernization, second modernization, and modernization in different fields differ in side effects	Avoid and reduce side effects
Modernization goal		
Theoretical goal	Complete first and second modernization, catch up with, reach, and maintain the world's advanced level	Dynamic goal, fixed goal
Policy goal	(1) Internal goals: improve productivity and quality of life, promote social equity and progress, promote all-round development of people, and promote the mutualism between man and nature; (2) international goals: that of advanced countries is to maintain the world's advanced level, and that of developing country is to catch up with and reach the world's advanced level	Long-term goal, immediate goal, goal of advanced countries, goal of developing countries

mutualism between man and nature; the policy goal of advanced countries is to maintain the world's advanced level, while that of developing countries is to catch up with and reach the world's advanced level (Example 8.2). Modernization theories provide the theoretical basis for modernization goals (Table 8.8).

Example 8.2 Modernization Goals of Advanced and Developing Countries

In 1994, the US government released a science policy report, *Science in the National Interest*, putting forward five policy goals for the development of science and technology in the USA (1) maintain leadership across the frontiers of scientific knowledge; (2) enhance connections between fundamental research and national goals; (3) stimulate partnerships that promote investments in fundamental science and engineering and effective use of material, human, and financial resources; (4) produce the most outstanding scientists and engineers for the twenty-first century; and (5) raise science and technology literacy of all Americans (Clinton and Gore 1994).

In 1987, Deng Xiaoping launched the "three-step" development strategy for China, which was expected to lead the country to reach the world's moderately developed level and basically realize modernization by the middle of the twenty-first century (Deng 1993). *China Modernization Report 2010* predicts that China is likely to exceed the world's average level by around 2040, attaining the following six policy goals (1) Economic modernization goal: national income per capita exceeds US$ 20,000, and key economic indicators are ranked among the world's top 40; (2) social modernization goal: the coverage rate of both pension and medical insurance is 100%, the rate of both urbanization and informatization exceeds 80%, and absolute poverty is eliminated; (3) political modernization goal: establishing a democratic, free, fair, and efficient political civilization, and the international competitiveness is ranked among the world's top 10; (4) cultural modernization goal: the cultural life exceeds the world's average, and key indicators of cultural innovation capacity are ranked among the world's top 20; (5) human modernization goal: the gross enrollment rate of high education exceeds 80%, average life expectancy exceeds 80 years, and the human development index is ranked among the world's top 20; and (6) ecological modernization goal: economic growth is completely disconnected with environmental degradation, and the quality of living environment basically reaches the level of major advanced countries. China is predicted to reach the world's advanced level in the end of the twenty-first century (RGCMS 2010).

Generally, national modernization goals comprise three types of goals: general goal, individual goal, and the reduction of side effects. The general goal refers to completing the first and second modernization, catching up with, reaching, and maintaining the world's advanced level. The individual goal refers to developing, maintaining, and expanding unique characteristics and enhancing competitive advantages. The demand for reducing side effects may differ from country to country and from period to period.

Fixed goal: complete the first modernization, form the first modernity, and reduce side effects of the first modernization. Advanced countries (industrial countries) completed their first modernization in the 1960s, and their average level of development during the period can be used as the reference standard of completing the first modernization (Example 8.1).

Dynamic goal: complete the second modernization; catch up with, reach, and maintain the world's advanced level; and reduce side effects. No country has completed the second modernization so far. It is predicted that advanced countries can complete their second modernization in the late twenty-first century. By then, their second modernization level can be used as the reference standard of completing the second modernization.

Table 8.9 Methods of setting modernization goals

Type of goal	Content and features	Method
General goal	First modernity, second modernity, catching up with, reaching, or maintaining the world's advanced level of development	Benchmark method, modernization level evaluation, modernization stage evaluation, actual progress evaluation, goal prediction evaluation, etc.
Individual goal	Develop, maintain, and expand unique characteristics and enhance competitive advantage	International comparative analysis, competitive advantage analysis, etc.
Avoid side effects	Reduce side effects of the first and second modernization	Case analysis
Fixed goal	Complete the first modernization	Benchmark method, modernization level evaluation, and modernization stage evaluation
Dynamic goal	Complete the second modernization, catching up with, reaching, or maintaining the world's advanced level	Benchmark method, goal prediction evaluation, etc.
Long-term goal	Strategic goal, which may span over 10 years	Benchmark method, goal prediction evaluation, competitive edge analysis, etc.
Immediate goal	Policy goal, which generally spans 5 years or shorter	Benchmark method, goal prediction evaluation, competitive edge analysis, etc.

8.2.1.2 Goal Setting

There are different types of modernization goals with their respective features, and the methods to set them are also different (Table 8.9). Generally, the reference standard of fixed goals are established, so relevant policy goals can be set by using the benchmark method, modernization level evaluation, and modernization stage evaluation. The reference standard of dynamic goals is the world's advanced level, so relevant strategic and policy goals can be set by using the benchmark method and goal prediction evaluation.

(1) General Procedure

Generally, setting a strategic goal roughly includes three steps: strategic positioning, strategic analysis, and goal integration. Strategic positioning refers to the precise judgment about modernization level, stage, and international status. Strategic analysis refers to the analysis of international environment, objective conditions, competitive edge, etc. Goal integration refers to the integration of three types of goals (general goals, individual goals, and the reduction of side effects).

First, strategic positioning. It includes the evaluation of modernization stage and level, and the identification of modernization stage, level, and international status.

Second, strategic analysis. It includes analysis on world trends, world frontier, international environment, objective conditions, and competitive edge.

Third, choosing general goals by using such methods as benchmarking, actual progress evaluation, and goal prediction evaluation.

Fourth, choosing individual goals by using such methods as international comparative analysis and competitive advantage analysis.

Fifth, the goal of reducing side effects, which requires case analysis.

Sixth, setting integrated policy goals, including general goals, individual goals, and reduction of side effects.

(2) Major Methods

First, goal prediction. Policy goal prediction is conducted based on the actual progress evaluation or goal prediction evaluation. There are many goal prediction methods, for example, linear extrapolation, nonlinear prediction, and goal approximation.

Second, benchmarking. A particular level is chosen as the reference benchmark for setting policy goals. Generally, the policy benchmark value for advanced countries is the world's maximum or the mean value of advanced countries, and that for developing countries is the mean value of advanced countries, the lowest level (threshold value) of advanced countries, the world's average value, or the reference standard of the first modernization (Example 8.1).

Third, competitive advantage analysis. The outcome of modernization includes particularity and diversity. On the basis of following modernization laws, analyze national competitive advantage and weakness, choose advantages that can be maintained and expanded, develop and form new and characteristic advantages, and raise individual goals.

8.2.1.3 Matters to be Noted

In setting modernization goals, the following matters should be noted:

First, respecting laws. A policy goal should accord with modernization principles and the world's great trends.

Second, considering national conditions. A policy goal cannot be divorced from reality, and national condition and international environment must be considered.

Third, be moderately proactive. The time span of a strategic goal may be longer, while that of a policy goal is generally no longer than 5 years.

Fourth, feasibility. A goal should be such that it can only be achieved through endeavor, accepted by society, and supported by national strength.

Fifth, particularity. Policy goals for different regions may be used as reference to each other but should in no sense be the excuse for them to compete with each other.

Sixth, openness. Keep abreast of new trends, new engines of growth, and new technologies so as to ensure the elasticity of goals.

Generally, different types of modernization goals need to be set and managed separately. Policy goals for the first modernization, the second modernization, and integrated modernization of advanced and developing countries, for advanced and developing regions, and for different fields and industries all have their own features and requirements, so they should be set and achieved in different ways.

8.2.2 Modernization Planning

A modernization plan is a blueprint for modernization in a future period and is intended to achieve modernization goals. It is the operational approach of modernization strategies. There are a great variety of modernization plans, for example, strategic and implementation plans, national and regional plans, field-specific plans, sector-specific plans, and special plans. In developing modernization plans, the laws governing modernization should be followed; objective conditions and the international environment should be taken into account. In this section, modernization plans of the twenty-first century are to be discussed.

8.2.2.1 Theoretical Basis

Modernization plans are developed based on modernization theories and strategies. According to the Second Modernization Theory, the process of modernization comprises two stages, first and second modernization, each with different connotations, features, driving forces, and models, and that the coordinated development of both is integrated modernization. By 2005, all advanced countries and a few developing countries had entered the second modernization, the majority of developing countries were in their first modernization, and some adopted the path of integrated modernization. Modernization theories provide the theoretical basis for modernization plans (Table 8.10).

8.2.2.2 Planning

A modernization plan comprises a great many basic contents, for example, basic tasks, stage-specific goals and tasks, path choice, model choice, priority choices, policy, and measure choices (Table 8.11). Generally, the planning is a goal-oriented open process, in which goal analysis, task analysis, and diverse choices are made alternately.

First, goal analysis. It is about analyzing strategic goals, defining basic tasks, and setting stage-specific and yearly goals.

Second, path choice. It is about choosing a basic path as well as the subpaths to achieve the three types of goals.

Third, model choice. It is about choosing appropriate models for achieving three types of goals or making model innovation.

Fourth, priority choices. It is about defining priorities in the three types of goals and allocating resources accordingly.

Fifth, policy choice, including policy analysis and innovation, and choice of policy and measures.

Sixth, developing a complete plan, including goals, path, model, priorities, policy, and performance evaluation.

A strategic plan of modernization generally includes strategic goals, tasks, principles, overall arrangement, priorities, and measures.

An implementation plan of modernization should include yearly goals, tasks, priorities, and measures.

Table 8.10 Theoretical basis of modernization planning

Modernization theory	Content and features	Policy application
Two stages	The first modernization is the foundation of the second modernization. The second modernization is the continuity and development, or "reversion" or turning, of the first modernization in some aspects; in other aspects, it is innovation. The coordinated development of both is integrated modernization	Make it clear what stage modernization is in, understand relations and differences between the two stages, and priority choice
Stage features	The first modernization is featured by industrialization, urbanization, democratization, etc., and the second modernization by knowledgeablization, informatization, greening, etc. They both have different features in different fields	Priority choice
Basic principles	Process asynchronization, unbalanced distribution, structural stability, status changeability, behavioral predictability, optional paths, incremental demand, diminishing utility, no state repeat, and axis transition	General principles
Driving forces	Innovation, competition, adaptation, exchange, national interest, market demand, etc.	Policy choice
Dynamics	Innovation drive, three-innovation drive, two-wheel drive, associative action, composite interaction of three types of civilization, innovation diffusion, innovation spillovers, competition drive, productivity function, etc.	Policy choice
Basic paths	Path dependence; three basic paths, with many subdivided paths	Path choice
Basic models	A great diversity of models as a result of combining over 50 factors; different paths have different models	Model choice

8.2.2.3 Matters to be Considered

First, one priority. The way of achieving general goals is the key to the success of a modernization plan. The aim is to improve the level of modernization, to catch up with, reach, and maintain the world's advanced level. Advanced countries differ from developing ones in this regard.

Second, four choices. The path, model, policy, and priority should be chosen with discretion.

Table 8.11 Methods of modernization planning

Content	Features	Methods
Strategic goals	Long-term goals	See Table 8.9
Basic tasks	Tasks to be completed for achieving long-term goals	Task analysis
Stage-specific goals and tasks	Stage-specific goals, yearly goals and tasks	Decomposition of goals and tasks
Achievement of general goals	Ways and methods of improving the level of modernization	Make measures according to principles and methods of national advancement
Achievement of individual goals	Ways and methods of enhancing characteristic and competitive advantages	Make measures to enhance characteristic and competitive advantages through monographic study
Avoidance of side effects	Ways and methods of reducing side effects of modernization	Make measures to solve or curb side effects through special study
Path choice	Choice from three basic paths; subdivision of path	Raise specific indicators, path analysis, and innovation
Model choice	Model choice for different paths; subdivision of model	Model analysis, innovation, and choice
Priority choice	Make clear the key points of achieving strategic goals	Comparative analysis, principal component analysis, etc.
Policy choice	Policy innovation and choice on the basis of theories and goals	Policy analysis and innovation; choice of policy and measures
Cost–benefit analysis	Investment budgeting, output estimate, and performance analysis	Performance evaluation

Note: Both strategic goals and stage-specific goals include three parts: general goals, individual goals, and the avoidance of side effects. Basic tasks and stage-specific tasks refer to tasks necessary to achieve strategic goals and stage-specific goals, respectively

Third, stage-specific plans. Strategic plans for the first modernization, the second modernization, and integrated modernization are different.

Fourth, plans by category. Strategic plans of advanced and developing countries, national and regional plans, and field- and sector-specific plans are different.

Fifth, national plans. Particular attention should be paid to the ways for a country to get advanced and to prioritization of the six fields.

Six, regional plans. Particular attention should be paid to regional modernization levels, characteristics, competitive advantage, etc.

Generally, on modernization plans, advanced countries may pay more attention to per capita innovation value, efficient labor, advanced technology, skills, and investment efficiency, while developing countries may pay more attention to per capita capital, skills, efficient labor, useful labor, efficient investment, advanced assets, and technical progress.

8.2.3 Strategy Management

The management of modernization strategies includes the management of the entire process from strategy formulation, strategy implementation, to strategy evaluation

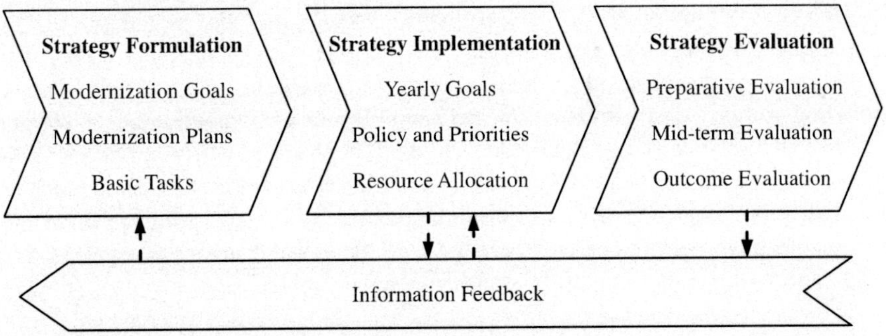

Fig. 8.3 Management of modernization strategies

(Fig. 8.3). It requires full cooperation between strategy makers and implementers, as well as good information communication between them in the whole process.

8.2.3.1 Strategy Formulation

The formulation of a strategy roughly includes three parts: goal setting, plan making, and the preliminary evaluation of the strategy.

First, at the core of modernization, goal setting is to identify long-term goals and basic tasks.

Second, at the core of modernization, plan making is to produce stage-specific and implementation plans.

Third, the preparative evaluation of the strategy is conducted to evaluate various strategic schemes, choose the best ones, and offer suggestions for improvement.

The cycle of a strategy refers to the period of time from the formulation to the implementation and conclusion of the strategy.

Strategy formulation is usually needed during tenure of office, election campaign, project cycle, or on an irregular basis.

8.2.3.2 Strategy Implementation

The implementation of a strategy roughly includes three parts: initiation, execution, and regular adjustment.

First, strategy initiation. It is about announcing the strategy and implementation plan for it, making clear the priorities and measures, and allocating resources.

Second, strategy execution. It is about carrying out the implementation, inspection, evaluation, etc., of yearly plans.

Third, strategy adjustment. It is about making necessary adjustments to the strategy according to external changes and internal progress.

8.2.3.3 Strategy Evaluation

The evaluation of a strategy roughly includes preparative evaluation, midterm evaluation, and outcome evaluation.

First, preparative evaluation, which takes place during the formulation of the strategy, including goal evaluation.

Second, interim evaluation, which takes place during the execution of the strategy, for offering adjustment suggestions.

Third, outcome evaluation, which takes place at the conclusion of the strategy, including comprehensive evaluation such as performance evaluation.

From the perspective of policy and national level in the world, modernization refers to the world's advanced level at present and the process and action to reach or maintain this advanced level, while modernization strategies should provide the approaches to identify, catch up, reach, or keep the world's advanced level continually. This is also the core aim of strategy management.

8.3 Modernization Measures

As the English proverbs *where there is a will, there is a way; well begun is half done*. The outstanding features of a modernization measure are its pertinence and timeliness. Different countries may select appropriate, innovative policies and measures according to their own conditions. Generally, policy innovation and measure selection should follow modernization laws and comply with the basic national conditions and international environment. The first modernization, the second modernization, and the integrated modernization differ from each other in policies and measures.

The modernization science includes core theory of general modernization, and stage-specific, level-specific, field-specific, sector-specific, and subject-specific modernization theory. Different theories have different policy implications. They provide the theoretical basis for modernization policies and measures. In this section, policy innovation and measure choice of the twenty-first century are to be addressed.

8.3.1 Innovation and Selection

Policy innovation and measure selection in the process of modernization represent an integral part of modernization strategies and plans.

8.3.1.1 Sources of Policies and Measures

Generally, there are mainly three sources of policies and measures: theories, international experience, and policy innovation.

First, theories. Every member in the big family of modernization theories has its unique policy implications.

Second, international experience. Abundant successful experience has been accumulated worldwide based on the modernization practices in the past 300 years.

Third, policy innovation. Policy innovation is a manifestation of institutional innovation.

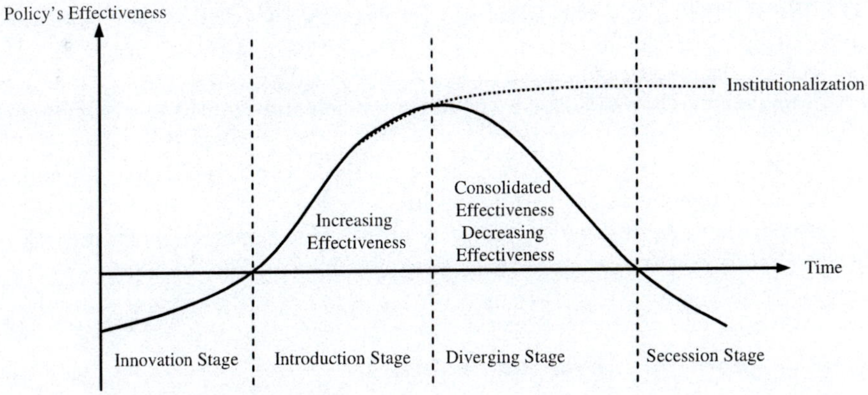

Fig. 8.4 Life cycle of policy innovation. Note: In the innovation stage, policies have no effectiveness, and negative effectiveness means the negative effect of institutional absence. The effectiveness of policies increases in the introduction stage. In the diverging stage, it is saturated; some policies change into institutions that function for a long period of time, with effectiveness being consolidated; some policies begin seeing decrease in effectiveness. In the secession stage, some policies finish their historical missions, lose their effectiveness, and secede automatically; some policies, if they do not secede, are likely to produce negative effects. Some policies function to the full as soon as introduced and then see decrease in or consolidation of effectiveness

8.3.1.2 Cycle of Innovation and Choice

Modernization includes the innovation, selection, diffusion, and secession of policies. There is a cycle of policy from its innovation to secession (Fig. 8.4).

It is a natural process of evolution for the effectiveness of a policy to experience increase, saturation, consolidation (institutionalization), decrease, loss, and then the shift to negative effects.

Generally, in the late stage of decreasing effectiveness, measures should be taken to facilitate the secession of policies so as to avoid negative effects.

8.3.1.3 Priority of Innovation and Selection

On policy innovation and measure selection, priorities should be made according to the principles and methods of national advancement (Table 2.35). Advanced and developing countries can and should have different priorities (Table 2.36). Generally, it will be considered on three layers.

First of all, choice of prior fields. One or more fields can be selected as the priority from the six fields which include economy, society, politics, culture, ecology, and humans in some periods.

Second, choice of prior sectors. One or more sectors can be selected as the priority from the different fields and all sectors in some stages.

Third, choice of prior issues. There are different key issues in different fields and sectors in different stages.

8.3.1.4 Principles of Innovation and Selection

Five principles are usually followed in policy innovation and measure selection.

First, it should be conducive to the emancipation and improvement of productivity.

Second, it should be conducive to social equity and progress.

Third, it should be conducive to the liberation and all-round development of the people.

Fourth, it should be conducive to the harmonious coexistence of man and nature and to both economic and environmental improvement.

Fifth, it should be conducive to technological advancement, cultural prosperity, and the improvement of international competitiveness.

8.3.2 Options for Advanced Countries

In the twenty-first century, advanced countries may adopt the second modernization path. Modernization policies are closely connected with second modernization paths and models. A modernization model is the stage-specific characteristic of a modernization path and is a type of modernization element mix.

8.3.2.1 Model Options of the Second Modernization Path

The second modernization path is a composite one, a mixture of national modernization paths in six fields.

(1) Cross Field Models of Element Mix

First, there are three models of the knowledgeablization–informatization mix, i.e., knowledgeablization first, informatization first, and the coordinated development of the two.

Second, there are three models of the knowledgeablization–ecologicalization mix, i.e., knowledgeablization first, ecologicalization first, and the coordinated development of the two.

Third, there are three models of the informatization–ecologicalization mix, i.e., informatization first, ecologicalization first, and the coordinated development of the two.

Fourth, three combination models of economy and society: economy first; society first; coordinated development of both.

Fifth, there are three models of the economy–ecology mix, i.e., economy first, ecology first, and the coordinated development of the two.

Sixth, there are three models of the society–ecology mix, i.e., society first, ecology first, and the coordinated development of the two.

Seventh, another model is the coordinated development of economy, society, and ecology.

(2) Models of Element Mix Within the Six Fields

First, different fields have different models of element mix. For example, in the field of international environment, there are three models of international interaction:

high trade and high investment, moderate trade and moderate investment, as well as low trade and low investment.

Second, the number of element mix models in different fields can be estimated. For example, 12 elements and variables of economic modernization may produce as many as 4,095 mixes, though not every mix is justifiable.

8.3.2.2 Policy Options at National Level

The policy priorities of the second modernization path should be adjusted timely. Currently, there are about ten priorities (Table 8.12). Both advanced and developing countries that adopted the second modernization path could select the policy priorities from seven aspects such as advanced productivity, social progress, human development, value, labor, capital, and technology, although there should be some difference between their choices (Table 2.36).

Table 8.12 Policy options of the second modernization path

No.	Main contents
1	Improve national innovation capacity and increase the percentage of innovation value. Build an innovation network, optimize the policy on innovation, foster an innovation culture, enhance knowledge innovation, technical innovation, institutional innovation, and concept innovation, and improve national knowledge infrastructure
2	Promote knowledgeablization. Develop knowledge industries, including knowledge production, knowledge and information dissemination, knowledge service industries, and high-tech industries, popularize higher education, accelerate industrial transfer and upgrading, and increase the knowledge content and labor productivity of economy
3	Accelerate informatization and networking. Build information infrastructure, develop the information technology industry, and build a network-based, learning society
4	Implement ecological modernization strategies. Coordinate economic growth and environmental protection and divorce economic development from environmental degradation to help improve both economy and environment
5	Improve cultural creativity and competitiveness, vigorously develop cultural industries, and improve the quality of cultural life
6	Promote suburbanization and urban upgrading as well as balanced urban–rural development
7	Economic globalization. Global operation, e-commerce, economy without boundaries, free trade zone, etc.
8	Distribution according to his contribution, adjustment as needed, and participation by knowledge capital and investment capital in net income distribution
9	Individualized democracy. Advocate tolerable, dialog-based, consultative, and direct democracy and respect individualized choice
10	Risk management. It is necessary to establish mechanisms used to control risks in science and technology, rationality, and decisions

Source: He (2003)

8.3.3 Options for Developing Countries

In the twenty-first century, developing countries may have three options: the catch-up modernization path, the integrated modernization path, and the second modernization path. The three paths have different connotations and features, and different policies can and need to be taken for them. The discussions here focus on the first two paths.

8.3.3.1 Policy Options of the Catch-Up Modernization Path

The catch-up modernization path is to follow the modernization path of advanced countries, completing the first modernization and then pursuing the second modernization. The policies and measures described in the classical modernization theory are appropriate for the first stage of the catch-up modernization path. The catch-up modernization path is a composite one, a mixture of national modernization paths in six fields also.

(1) Cross Field Models of Element Mix

First, there are three models of the industrialization–democratization mix, i.e., industrialization first, democratization first, and the coordinated development of both.

Second, there are three models of the industrialization–urbanization mix, i.e., industrialization first, urbanization first, and the coordinated development of both.

Third, there are three models of the economy–education mix, i.e., economy first, education first, and the coordinated development of both.

Fourth, there are three models of the economy–society mix, i.e., economy first, society first, and the coordinated development of both.

(2) Models of Element Mix Within the Six Fields

Modernization in every field involves many elements, such as behavior, structure, institution and concept, subfields, relevant departments, and the change of international status. Such elements may produce a great many mix models such as models of the economy–international interaction mix.

First, there are three models of the planning–market mix, i.e., planned economy, market economy, and mixed economy.

Second, there are three models of catch-up industrialization, i.e., import substitution, export orientation, and the coordinated development of both.

Third, there are three models of international interaction, i.e., national industry protection, free trade, and dependent development.

(3) Policy Priorities at National Level

The policy priorities of the catch-up modernization path should be adjusted timely. Currently, there are about ten priorities (Table 8.13). Developing countries that adopted the catch-up modernization path could also select the policy priorities from seven aspects such as advanced productivity, social progress, human development, value, labor, capital, and technology (Table 2.36).

Table 8.13 Policy options of the catch-up modernization path

No.	Main contents
1	Accelerate industrialization. Accelerate the transfer from agriculture to industry and service, increase effective labor and investment, actively bring in technology and capital, etc.
2	Advance urbanization. Speed up the migration of rural population into cities, strengthen the building of urban infrastructure, etc.
3	Promote democratization. Establish and perfect systems about democratic election, democratic legislation, and democratic supervision
4	Increase social welfare. Build a welfare society, achieve the social goal of having each person and family enjoy insurance and welfare, etc.
5	Vigorously promote education development. Popularize compulsory education and secondary education, develop vocational education and higher education, etc.
6	Moderately develop science and technology, improve technological innovation capacity, do away with feudal and autocratic culture, etc.
7	Promote ecological modernization. While accelerating economic growth, protect the natural environment as well as the rational utilization of resources, achieve sustainable development, etc.
8	Promote informatization. Strengthen the building of information infrastructure, provide extensive information services, develop the information technology industry, etc.
9	Participate in globalization. Participate in international market competition, support multinational enterprises, develop e-commerce, establish free trade zones, etc.
10	Enhance regional economic cooperation, promote the sharing of regional knowledge and experience, etc.

Source: He (2003)

8.3.3.2 Policy Options of the Integrated Modernization Path

Integrated modernization refers to the process in which the first and second modernization develops in a coordinated manner and the trend is still the transition to the second modernization. The integrated modernization path is a strategic choice for developing countries in the twenty-first century. It involves modernization in six fields and features starting-point dependence and model diversity.

(1) Cross Field Models of Element Mix

First, there are three models of the industrialization–knowledgeablization mix, i.e., industrialization first, knowledgeablization first, and the coordinated development of both.

Second, there are three models of the industrialization–informatization mix, i.e., industrialization first, informatization first, and the coordinated development of both.

Third, there are three models of the industrialization–ecologicalization mix, i.e., industrialization first, ecologicalization first, and the coordinated development of both.

Fourth, there are three models of the industrialization–democratization mix, i.e., industrialization first, democratization first, and the coordinated development of both.

Fifth, there are three models of the industrialization–urbanization mix, i.e., industrialization first, urbanization first, and the coordinated development of both.

Sixth, there are three models of the economy–society mix, i.e., economy first, society first, and the coordinated development of both.

Seventh, there are three models of the economy–ecology mix, i.e., economy first, ecology first, and the coordinated development of both.

Eighth, there are three models of the society–ecology mix, i.e., society first, ecology first, and the coordinated development of both.

Ninth, another model is the coordinated development of economy, society, and ecology.

(2) Models of Element Mix Within the Six Fields

First, different fields have different models of element mix. For example, in the field of international environment, there are three models of international interaction: high trade and high investment, moderate trade and moderate investment, as well as low trade and low investment.

Second, the number of element mix models in different fields can be estimated. For example, 12 elements and variables of economic modernization may produce as many as 4,095 mixes, though not every mix is justifiable.

(3) Policy Options at National Level

The policy priorities of the integrated modernization path should be adjusted timely. Currently, there are about ten priorities (Table 8.14). Developing countries that adopted the integrated modernization path could also select the policy priorities

Table 8.14 Policy options of the integrated modernization path

No.	Main contents
1	New industrialization. Develop industrialization, informatization, greening, globalization, and industry transfer in a coordinated way, increase investment and labor efficiency, etc.
2	New urbanization. Develop urbanization, informatization, greening, internationalization, and suburbanization in a coordinated way, build a society of balanced urban–rural development, etc.
3	Promote democratization. Perfect the democratic system, increase government efficiency and policy transparency, respect individualized choice, etc.
4	Accelerate informatization. Develop the information technology industry, promote the integration of telecom, radio and TV, and the Internet, etc.
5	Promote knowledgeablization. Develop scientific and technological industries, knowledge dissemination, and knowledge service industries
6	Economic globalization. Promote international trade, lower tariffs, promote the development of international economic cooperative zones and free trade zones, etc.
7	Build a learning society. Popularize compulsory education and secondary education, develop vocational education, distance education and higher education, etc.
8	Build an innovative country. Build innovation networks, optimize innovation policies, foster an innovation culture, improve enterprise innovation capacity, etc.
9	Build an environmentally friendly society. Implement ecological modernization strategies, promote the disconnection of economic growth from environmental degradation, etc.
10	Distribution according to his contribution, adjustment as needed, and participation by knowledge capital and investment capital in net income distribution

Source: He (2003)

from seven aspects such as advanced productivity, social progress, human development, value, labor, capital, and technology (Table 2.36).

Modernization refers to the frontier change and international competition of human civilizations since the eighteenth century. In this process, some countries have achieved enormous success, maintained the world's advanced level for a long period, and become advanced countries; other countries, despite their progress, have failed to reach the world's advanced level and thus have become developing countries. Some countries have ascended to advanced countries from developing ones, while some have degraded to developing countries from advanced ones. Stories of success and failure emerge one after another. The modernization science is an emerging science which deals with modernization phenomena and national advancement. It is much more than a science, while it represents a hope, a dream, and a future.

Summary

The modernization science is not only an interdisciplinary science but also a science of strategy. The issue of modernization is a strategic one, and modernization strategies are grand strategies. Modernization policies, the application of modernization theories, represent an important part of the modernization science. The goal of modernization policies is not to change the world but create a new world in which all the people are equal and enjoy all-round development.

Modernization Evaluation

Modernization is just like an international marathon figuratively: Countries running ahead become advanced or developed countries, while the rest become developing ones; there is mobility between the two types of status. An objective evaluation of the modernization process makes it possible to monitor the process of modernization dynamically.

A modernization evaluation is a comprehensive evaluation of the process and outcomes of modernization. The basic idea is that the object to be evaluated is a complex system, so it is not enough to use just a single indicator. It is necessary to translate multiple indicators into a comprehensive index for evaluation. After statistical analysis, indicators can be converted into standard indexes which, through weighting and calculation, can be translated into a comprehensive index.

There are many types of modernization evaluation, and different principles and methods are employed.

An international evaluation targets worldwide modernization phenomena, the results of which highlight international comparability. An international evaluation of modernization usually includes level evaluation, stage evaluation, and process evaluation. A process evaluation includes the evaluation of innovation capacity, competitiveness, influence, etc.

An evaluation of modernization from the policy perspective usually includes performance evaluation, diagnosis evaluation, and policy effectiveness evaluation. Such evaluation is generally a practical goal-oriented one, highlighting policy orientation, pertinence, and operability.

Modernization Strategies

Modernization strategies are the means to achieve modernization goals. From the perspective of policy and national level, modernization refers to the world's advanced level at present and the process to reach or keep this advanced level, while modernization strategies should provide the approaches to identify, catch up, reach, or keep the world's advanced level continually.

Generally, modernization strategies are based on modernization theories, the development strategies are based on development theories. The former apply to all countries, while the latter are commonly seen in developing countries. Modernization strategies are related to yet different from development strategies.

A modernization goal is what is expected to be achieved through modernization in a future period of time. There are many types of goals such as strategic and planned goals, long-term and immediate goals, and dynamic and fixed goals. To set modernization goals, one country has to follow the laws governing modernization, figure out the world's trends, and have a clear understanding of its level of modernization and national conditions.

A modernization plan is a blueprint for modernization in a future period and is intended to achieve modernization goals. It is the operational approach of modernization strategies. There are a great variety of modernization plans, for example, strategic and implementation plans, national and regional plans, field-specific plans, sector-specific plans, and special plans. In developing modernization plans, the laws governing modernization should be followed; objective conditions and the international environment should be taken into account.

The management of modernization strategies includes the management of the entire process from strategy formulation, strategy implementation, to strategy evaluation. It requires full cooperation between strategy makers and implementers as well as good information communication between them in the whole process.

Modernization Measures

The outstanding features of a modernization measure are its pertinence and timeliness. Different countries may select appropriate, innovative policies and measures according to their own conditions. Policy innovation and measure selection should follow modernization laws and comply with the basic national conditions and international environment. The first modernization, the second modernization, and the integrated modernization path differ from each other in policies and measures.

There are mainly three sources of policies and measures: theories, international experience, and policy innovation.

The life cycle of modernization policy has four stages: innovation stage, introduction stage, diverging stage, and secession stage.

There are five principles of innovation and selection: productivity, social progress, human development, environment friendliness, and competitiveness.

According to principles and ways of modernization and national advance, policy innovation and measure selection may have different priorities in different countries, regions, fields, and sectors in different stages. Generally, the focus should be on four aspects: everyone doing his best and fair competition, distribution according to contribution and adjustment as needed, promotion according to performance and selection according to public opinion, as well as making money perfectly, equality, and mutual benefit.

The option for advanced countries in the twenty-first century is the second modernization path which has multiple models and policy priorities.

Options for developing countries in the twenty-first century are the catch-up modernization path, the integrated modernization path, and the second modernization path, each having its unique models and policy priorities.

The ultimate goal of modernization science is to create a happier and better life with greater prosperity.

To change and to change for the better are two different things (German proverb).

The world is a ladder for some to go up and others to go down, and *not to advance is to go back* (English proverb).

Further Reading

Clinton WJ, Gore A Jr (1994) Science in the national interest. Executive Office of the President. Office of Science and Technology Policy, Washington, DC

David FR (1997) Concepts of strategic management, 6th edn. Prentice Hall, Englewood Cliffs, NJ

Harbison FH, Maruhnic J, Resnick JR (1970) Quantitative analyses of modernization and development. Princeton University, Princeton, NJ

He C (2003) Oriental renaissance: three roads to the modernization. Commercial, Beijing

Jesinghaus J (1999) *A European system of environmental pressure indices.* First volume of the environmental pressure indices handbook: the indicators. European Commission, Joint Research Centre. http://esl.jrc.it/envind/theory/handb_.htm. Accessed Oct 2009

RGCMS (Research Group for China Modernization Strategies et al) (2010) China modernization report 2010: World modernization outline 1700–2100. Peking University Press, Beijing

References

Adelman I (2000) Fifty years of economic development: what have we learned? World Bank Working Paper No. 28737. World Bank, Washington, DC

Adorno TW, Horkheimer M (1979) Dialectic of enlightenment. Verso, London

Adriaanse A (1997) Resource flows: the material basis of industrial economies. World resource institute research report [R/OL]. http://materials.wri.org/resourceflows-pub-2742.html. Accessed Oct 2009

Aguilar CT (ed) (2000) The interface of the social sciences and science and technology in development and modernization. International Federation of Social Science Organizations, Manila

Alexander JC (1995a) Modern, anti, post, neo, new. Left Rev 210(Mar–Apr):63–101

Alexander JC (1995b) Fin de Siècle social theory: relativism, reduction, and the problem of reason. Verso, London

Alexander JC, Colomy P (eds) (1990) Differentiation theory and social change. Columbia University Press, New York

Alford RR, Friedland R (1985) Powers of theory: capitalism, the state, and democracy. Cambridge University press, Cambridge

Alitto GS (1991) The trend of thought of anti-modernization in the world. Guizhou People's Press, Guizhou

Allenby BR (1999) Industrial ecology: policy framework and implementation. Prentice-Hall, Englewood Cliffs, NJ

Almond GA, Coleman JS (eds) (1960) The politics of the developing areas. Princeton University Press, Princeton, NJ

Amin S (1976) Unequal development. Harvester, London

Anand S, Sen A (2000) Human development and economic sustainability. World Dev 28 (12):2029–2049

Andersen MS (2002) Ecological modernization or subversion? The effects of Europeanization on Eastern Europe. Am Behav Sci 45(9):1394–1416

Andersen MA, Massa I (2000) Ecological modernisation: origins, dilemmas and future directions. J Environ Policy Plan 2(4):337–345

Anderson P (1998) The origin of postmodernity. Verso, London

Apter DE (1965) The politics of modernization. Chicago University Press, Chicago

Aristotle (1981) The politics (Trans. T. A. Sinclair). Penguin Books, New York

Armer M, Schnaiberg A (1972) Measuring individual modernity: a near myth. Am Sociol Rev 37:301–316

Arnon I (1981) Modernization of agriculture in developing countries: resources, potentials, and problems. Wiley, New York

Atkinson T (2002) Social indicators: the EU and social inclusion. Oxford University Press, Oxford

C. He, *Modernization Science*,
DOI 10.1007/978-3-642-25459-8, © Springer-Verlag Berlin Heidelberg 2012

Axinn GH, Thorat S (1972) Modernizing world agriculture: a comparative study of agricultural extension education. Praeger, New York
Babbie E (1999) The basics of social research. Wadsworth, Belmont, CA
Bairoch P, Levy-Leboyer M (eds) (1981) Disparities in economic development since the industrial revolution. Macmillan, London
Baran P (1957) The political economy of growth. Monthly Review, New York
Barber B (1952) Science and social order. Free, Glencoe, IL
Barro RJ (1997) Determinants of economic growth: a cross-country empirical study. MIT Press, Cambridge, MA
Barzun J (2000) From dawn to decadence 500 years of western cultural life 1500 to the present. Harper Collins, New York
Basile R et al (2001) Regional inequalities and cohesion policies in the European Union. ISAE, Rome
Baum RC (1974) Beyond convergence: toward theoretical relevance in quantitative modernization research. Sociol Inquiry 44(4):225–240
Baum R (ed) (1980) China's four modernizations: the new technological revolution. Westview, Boulder, CO
Beck U (1992) [1986] Risk society: toward a new modernity. Sage, London
Beck N, Katz JN (1995) What to do (and not to do) with time-series cross-section data. Am Polit Sci Rev 89:634–647
Beck U, Willms J (2000) Freiheit oder Kapitalismus. Ulrich Beck im Gespräch mit Johannes Willms. Suhrkamp, Frankfurt am Main
Beck U, Giddens A, Lash S (1994) Reflexive modernization: politics, tradition and aesthetics in the modern social order. Stanford University Press, Stanford, California
Bell D (1973) The coming of post-industrial society. Basic Books, New York
Bendix R (1964) Nation-building and citizenship. Wiley, New York
Bendix R (1967) Tradition and modernity reconsidered. Comp Stud Soc Hist IX 3:292–346
Bennett RJ (ed) (1990) Decentralisation, local governments and markets. Clarendon, Oxford
Berger P, Berger B, Kellner H (1974) The homeless mind. Penguin, Harmondsworth
Bernard JD (1939) The social function of science. Routledge, London
Bernstein H (1971) Modernization theory and the sociological studies of development. J Dev Stud 7(2):141–160
Bevir M, Rhodes R (2002) Interpretative theory. In: Marsh D, Stoker G (eds) Theory and methods in political science, 2nd edn. Palgrave Macmillan, New York, pp 131–152
Bird A (1998) Philosophy of science. Routledge, London
Black CE (1966) The dynamics of modernization: a study in comparative history. Harper & Row, New York
Black CE (ed) (1976) Comparative modernization: a reader. Free, New York
Bock K (1979) Theories of progress, development, evolution. In: Bottomore TB, Nisbet A (eds) A history of sociological analysis. Heinemann, London, pp 39–79
Bohman J, Rehg W (1997) Deliberative democracy: essays on reason and politics. MIT Press, Cambridge, MA
Bonnell VE, Hunt L (1999) Beyond the cultural turn: new directions in the study of society and culture. University of California Press, Berkeley
Borrego J (1995) Models of integration, models of development in the pacific. J World Syst Res 1(11):1–142
Braudel F (1967) Civilisation Matérielle et Capitalisme (XVe- XVIIIe siècle). Armand Colin, Paris
Braudel F (1973) Capitalism and material life 1400–1800. Harper Colophon Books, New York
Braudel F (1995) A history of civilizations (Trans. R. Mayne). Penguin, New York
Brooks AC (2008) Gross national happiness: why happiness matters for America and how we can get more of it. Basic Books, New York
Brown DE (1991) Human universals. McGraw-Hill, New York

Brulle R (2000) Agency, democracy, and nature: the US environmental movement from a critical theory perspective. MIT Press, Cambridge, MA
Buck G (1969) A quantitative analysis of modernization. Texas University at El Paso, El Paso
Buckley PJ, Pass CL, Prescott K (1988) Measure of international competitiveness: a critical survey. J Market Manage 4(2):175–200
Burns T, Stalker GM (1966) The management of innovation. Tavistock, London
Burns EM et al (1955) World civilizations, 6th edn. W.W. Norton, New York
Burns EM et al (1986) World civilizations, 7th edn. W. W. Norton, New York
Buttel FH (2000) Ecological modernization as social theory. Geoforum 31:57–65
Buzan B, Little R (2000) International system in world history -remaking the study of international relations. Oxford University Press, London
Cantril H (1965) The patterns of human concerns. Rutgers University Press, New Brunswick
Cardoso FH, Faletto E (1979) Dependency and development in Latin American. University of California Press, Berkeley
Carleheden M, Jacobsen MH (eds) (2002) The transformation of modernity: aspects of the past, present and future of an era. Ashgate, Burlington, VT
Carnoy M (1984) The stated and political theory. Princeton University press, Princeton, NJ
Castells M (1996–98) The information age: economy, society and culture, 3 vols. Blackwell, Oxford
Chalmers AF (1990) Science and its fabrication. Open University Press, Milton Keynes
Chaney D (1994) The cultural turn: scene-setting essays of contemporary cultural history. Routledge, London
Chen Z (1994) Income distribution of economic development. Shanghai Joint Publishing, Shanghai People's Publishing House, Shanghai
Chen J, Huang Q (2009) Research on China's industrialization and industrial modernization. Economic Management, Beijing
Chen J et al (2004) Research on China's industrial modernization. China Social Sciences, Beijing
Chenery HB, Syrquin M (1975) Patterns of development, 1950–1970. Oxford University Press, London
Chenery H, Robinson S, Syrquin M (1986) Industrialization and growth: a comparative study. Oxford University Press, New York
Christensen J (1983) Rural Denmark 1750 1980. Central Co-operative Committee of Denmark, Copenhagen
Christensen DC (ed) (1993) European historiography of technology: technology's role in the modernization process. University Press of Southern Denmark, Gylling
Christoff P (1996) Ecological modernisation, ecological modernities. Environ Polit 5(3):476–500
Chu H (2000) Paths of educational modernization. Education Science, Beijing
Clark G, Feenstra R (2001) Technology in the great divergence. NBER Working Paper No. 8596 [R/OL]. http://www.nber.org/papers/w8596. Accessed Oct 2005
Clinton WJ, Gore A Jr (1994) Science in the national interest. Executive Office of the President, Office of Science and Technology Policy, Washington, DC
Coetzee JK et al (eds) (2001) Development: theory, policy, and practice. Oxford University Press, Oxford
Cohen MJ (1997) Risk society and ecological modernisation: alternative visions for post-industrial nations. Futures 29(2):105–119
Cohen MJ (1998) Science and the environment: cultural capacity for ecological modernization. Public Understand Sci 7(2):149–167
Cohen MJ (2000) Ecological modernization, environmental knowledge, and national character: a preliminary analysis of the Netherlands. Environ Polit 9(1):77–106
Cohen MJ (2006) Ecological modernization and its discontents: the American environmental movement's resistance to an innovation-driven future. Futures 38:528–547
Coleman JS (1968) Modernization: political aspects. In: Sills DL (ed) International encyclopedia of the social sciences, vol 10. Macmillan, New York, pp 395–402

Collier P (2002) Globalization, growth, and poverty: building an inclusive world economy. World Bank, Washington, DC

Comte A (2003) [1830–1842] Course of positive philosophy (Cours de philosophie positive, 1830–42; Trans. H. Martineau). Kessinger, Whitefish, MT

Condorcet M (1955) [1795] Sketch for a historical picture of the progress of the human mind. Weidenfield and Nicolson, London

Coughenour CM, Stephenson JB (1972) Measures of individual modernity: review and commentary. Int J Comp Sociol 13(2):81–98

Crittenden J (1967) Dimensions of modernization in the American states. Am Polit Sci Rev 61 (12):989–1001

Crook S, Pakulski J, Waters M (1992) Post-modernization: change in advanced society. Sage, London

Cuadrado-Roura JR (2001) Regional convergence in the European Union: from hypothesis to the actual trends. Ann Reg Sci 35:333–356

Cutright P (1963) National political development: measurement and analysis. Am Sociol Rev 28 (2):253–264

Dahl R (1998) On democracy. Yale University Press, New Haven, CO

Dahrendorf R (1988) The modern social conflict. Weidenfeld & Nicholson, London

Darwin CR (2003) [1859] The ORIGIN OF SPECIES. New American Library, a division of Penguin Group (USA), New York

David FR (1997) Concepts of strategic management, 6th edn. Prentice Hall, Englewood Cliffs, NJ

Deng XP (1993) Selected works of Deng Xiaoping, vol III. People's Publishing House, Beijing

Deutsch K (1961) Social mobilization and political development. Am Polit Sci Rev 55:493–514

Diamond L (1992) Economic development and democracy reconsidered. Am Behav Sci 35:450–499

Diamond M (2005) Collapse: how societies choose to fail or succeed. Viking Books, New York

Ding J (ed) (1999) Modernization path of developed countries: a study from the perspective of historical sociology. Peking University Press, Beijing

Ding W (2000) Research on the models of economic modernization. Economic Science, Beijing

Divale W, Seda A (2000) Cross-cultural codes of modernization. World Cultures 11(2):152–170

Divale W, Seda A (2001) Modernization as changes in cultural complexity: new cross-cultural measurements. Cross-Cultural Res 35(2):127–153

Dodd N (1999) Social theory and modernity. Polity, Blackwell, Malden, MA

Dogan M, Pelassy D (1984) How to compare nations: strategies in comparative politics. Chatham House, Chatham

Dong J (2009a) Research on Brazil's modernization path: development under the military regime between 1964 and 1985. World Publishing Corporation Beijing, Beijing

Dong Z (2009b) Fifteen interpretations of the world modernization process. Peking University Press, Beijing

Dos Santos T (1970) The structure of dependence. Am Econ Rev 60(2):231–236

Du Y (ed) (2001) Agricultural modernization and sustainable development. China Agriculture Press, Beijing

Dube SC (1998) Modernization and development: in search for alternative paradigms. Zed Books, London

Duijn JJV (1983) The long wave in economic life. Allen & Unwin, London

Durkheim E (1964) [1893] The division of labour in society. Free, New York

Easton D (1953) The political system: an inquiry into the state of political science. Alfred A. Knopf, New York

Easton D (1965) A systems analysis of political life. John Wiley, New York

Eisenstadt SN (1957) Comparative analysis of processes of agricultural development and modernization: final report. Agricultural Research Service, European Regional Research Office, Davis, CA

Eisenstadt SN (1966) Modernization, protest and change. Prentice-Hall, Englewood Cliffs, NJ

Eisenstadt SN (1971) Social differentiation and stratification. Scott, Foresman, Glenview, IL

Eisenstadt SN (1998) Multiple and changing modernities in settings of globalization. Paper given at the 34th world congress of the international of sociology, Tel Aviv, 11–15 July 1998

Eisenstadt SN (2000) Multiple modernities. Deadalu 129(1):1–29

Eisenstadt SN (2001) The civilization dimension of modernity. Modernity as a distinct civilization. Int Sociol 16(3):320–340

Eisenstadt SN (2003) Comparative civilizations and multiple modernities. Brill, Leiden

Eisenstadt SN (2009) Contemporary globalization, new intercivilizational visions and hegemonies: transformation of nation-states. Proto Sociol 26:7–18

Elias N (2000) [1939] The civilizing process: sociogenetic and psychogenetic investigations, 2nd edn. Wiley-Blackwell, Oxford

Ember CR (1978) Myths about hunter-gatherers. Ethnology 17:439–448

Ember CR, Ember M (1996) Cultural anthropology. Prentice-Hall, London

Emes J, Hahn T (2001) Measuring development: an index of human progress [R/OL]. Public Policy Sources 36. http://canstats.org/admin/books/files/MeasuringDevelopmentIHP.pdf. Accessed Oct 2007

Engerman DC, Gilman N, Haefele MH (eds) (2003) Staging growth: modernization, development, and the global cold war. University of Massachusetts Press, Amherst

Estes RJ (1984) The social progress of nation. Praeger, New York

Estes RJ (1988) Trends in world social development. Praeger, New York

Evans PB (1979) Dependent development: the alliance of multinational, state, and local capital in Brazil. Princeton University Press, Princeton, NJ

Evans PB, Rueschemeyer D, Stephens J (1985) States versus markets in the world system. Sage, London

Flannery KV (1972) The cultural evolution of civilization. Annu Rev Ecol Syst 3:39–426

Florida R (2002) The rise of the creative class. Basic Books, New York

Förster M, Pearson M (2002) Income distribution and poverty in the OECD area: trends and driving forces. OECD Economic Studies No. 34. OECD, Paris

Foucault M (1966) The order of things: an archeology of human sciences. Tavistock, London

Frank AG (1966) The development of underdevelopment. Month Rev 18:17–30

Frank AG (1967) Capitalism and underdevelopment in Latin America. Monthly Review, New York

Freeman C, Louca F (2001) As time goes by from the industrial revolutions to the information revolution. Oxford University Press, Oxford

Gendzier SJ (1967) Denis Diderot's encyclopedia: selections. Harper and Row, New York

Gerhards J (2005) The name game: cultural modernization & first names. Transaction, New Brunswick, NJ

Gerhards J, Hackenbroch R (2000) Trends and causes of cultural modernization: an empirical study of first names. Int Sociol 15(3):501–531

Germani G (1981) The sociology of modernization. Transaction Books, New Brunswick, NJ

Gerschenkron A (1962) Economic backwardness in historical perspective—a book of essays. Harvard University Press, Cambridge

Gibbons DS et al (1980) Agricultural modernization, poverty and inequality: distributional impact of the green revolution in regions of Malaysia and Indonesia. Gower, Farnborough

Giddens A (1990) The consequences of modernity. Stanford University Press, Stanford

Gilman N (2007) Mandarins of the future: modernization theory in cold war America. The Johns Hopkins University Press, Baltimore

Gilpin R (1987) The political economy of international relations. Princeton University Press, Princeton, NJ

Ginger A (2007) Cultural modernity and Atlantic perspectives: Estanislao Del Campo's Fausto (1866) and its French contemporaries. Atlantic Stud 4(1):27–36

Glaeser EL, Kahn ME (2001) Decentralized employment and the transformation of the America City. NBER Working Paper No. 8117. National Bureau of Economic Research, Cambridge, MA

Gobble FG (1970) The third force: the psychology of Abraham Maslow. Grossman, New York
Graedel TE, Allenby BR (2003) Industrial ecology, 2nd edn. Prentice-Hall, Upper Saddle River, NJ
Grasso J, Cornin J, Kort M (2009) Modernization and revolution in China: from the opium wars to the Olympics, 4 Revisedth edn. M.E. Sharpe, New York
Gu M (1998) Educational modernization and ability-oriented education. J Chin Educ 3:3–5
Gu M (2007) Basic characteristics and strategies of educational modernization. People's Educ 13–14:8–11
Gu M, Xue L (1998) Introduction to comparative education: education and national development. People's Education, Beijing
Gu H, Zhang C (eds) (1998) Research on China's agricultural modernization. China Agricultural Science and Technology, Beijing
Ha Q (2006) Modernization of middle Eastern countries. People's Publishing House, Beijing
Habakkuk HJ, Postan MM (eds) (1965) The Cambridge economic of Europe, vol VI. The industrial revolutions and after: incomes, population and technological change. Cambridge University Press, London
Habermas J (1971) Toward a rational society. Heinemann, London
Habermas J (1972) Knowledge and human interests. Heinemann, London
Habermas J (1981) Modernity versus postmodernity. New German Critique 22:3–14
Habermas J (1987) The philosophical discourse of modernity. Polity, Cambridge
Hagen EE (1962) On the theory of social change: how economic growth begins. Dorsey, Homewood, IL
Hague R, Harrop M (2001) Comparative government and politics: an introduction. Palgrave Macmillan, New York
Hajer M (1995) The politics of environmental discourse: ecological modernization and the policy process. Oxford University Press, New York
Harbison FH, Maruhnic J, Resnick JR (1970a) Quantitative analyses of modernization and development. Princeton University, Princeton, NJ
Harbison FH et al (1970b) Quantitative analysis of modernization and development. Princeton University, Princeton
Harrison IQ (1973) Agricultural modernization and income distribution: an economic analysis of the impact of new seed varieties on the crop production of large and small farms in India. UMI, Ann Arbor, MI
Harrison D (1988) The sociology of modernization and development. Unwin Hyman, London
Harvey D (1989) The condition of post-modernity. Blackwell, London
Hassan I (1987) The postmodern turn: essays in postmodern theory and culture. Ohio State University Press, Columbus
Hayami Y, Ruttan VW (1985) Agricultural development: an international perspective. The John Hopkins University Press, Baltimore
Hayek F (1983) Knowledge, evolution and society. Adam Smith Institute, London
He C (1998a) Knowledge economy and China's modernization. Guangming Daily 7 Apr 1998
He C (1998b) Knowledge economy and the second modernization. Sci Technol Rev 6:3–4
He C (1999) The second modernization: inspiration of human civilization process. Higher Education, Beijing
He C (2000a) Modernization of citizenship: the second modernization agenda for action. China Economic Publishing House, Beijing
He C (2000b) K-management: modernization of business management: the second modernization agenda for action. China Economic Publishing House, Beijing
He C (2001) Distribution revolution–distribution according to contribution: front of the second modernization. Economic Management Press, Beijing
He C (2003) Oriental renaissance: three roads to the modernization. Commercial, Beijing
He C (2009) Three models of the modernization of China's mountainous areas. Bull Chin Acad Sci 24(3):256–264

He C (ed) (2010a) China modernization report outlook (2001–2010). Peking University Press, Beijing

He C (2010b) Modernization science: the principles of national advance. Science, Beijing

He C (ed) (2011) China modernization report 2011: an introduction to modernization science. Peking University Press, Beijing

He C, Zhang F (2001) Knowledge innovation–new focus of competition: front of the second modernization. Economic Management, Beijing

Held J (1980) The modernization of agriculture: rural transformation in Hungary, 1848–1975. Columbia University Press, New York

Held D (1996) Models of democracy. Polity, Cambridge

Herd D et al (1999) Global transformations: politics, economics and culture. Polity, Cambridge

Hiratsuka M (1978) Modernization of education in Japan. National Institute for Educational Research, Tokyo

Hobbs F, Stoops N (2002) U.S. Census Bureau, Census 2000 Special Reports, Series CENSR-4, Demographic trends in the 20th century. U.S. Government Printing Office, Washington, DC

Hopkins TK, Wallerstein I (1996) The age of transition trajectory of the world-system: 1945–2025. Zed, London

Horowitz IL (1972) Three worlds of development: the theory and practice of international stratification, 2nd edn. Oxford University Press, London

Hoselitz B (ed) (1952) The progress of underdeveloped areas. University of Chicago Press, Chicago, IL

Hu F (1994) Historical process of China's modernization. Anhui People's Publishing House, Hefei

Hu W (2007) Privately-run schools in Shanghai faced with opportunities and challenges. Explor Educ Dev 12:30–35

Hu W, Tang X (2010) Research on the process of China's educational modernization. Educational Science Publishing House, Beijing

Huang Z, Deng Q (2008) From the first modernization to the second modernization: theory and policies on efficient modern eco-agriculture and its influence on farmers. In: Huang Z, Zhang D, Pan W (eds) Exploring the path of agricultural modernization with Chinese characteristics. Zhejiang University Press, Hangzhou, pp 18–29

Huang Z, Lin ZD (2003) Agricultural modernization: theory, process and path. China Agriculture, Beijing

Huber J (1982) Die Verlorene Unschuld der Okologie: Neue Technologien und Superindustrielle Entwicklung (The lost innocence of ecology: new technologies and superindustrialized development). Fisher Verlag, Frankfurt am Main

Huber J (1984) Die Zwei Gesichter der Arbeit: Ungenutzte Moglichkeiten der Dualwirtschaft (The two faces of labour: unused possibilities of the dual economy). Fisher Verlag, Frankfurt am Main

Huber J (1985) Die Regenbogengesellschaft: Okologie und Sozialpolitik (The rainbow society: ecology and social politics). Fisher Verlag, Frankfurt am Main

Huber J (2000) Towards industrial ecology: sustainable development as a concept of ecological modernization. J Environ Policy Plan 2:269–285

Huntington SP (1968) Political order in changing societies. Yale University Press, New Haven, CT

Huntington SP (1971) The change to change: modernization, development, and politics. Comp Polit 3(3):283–322

Huntington SP (1991) The third wave: democratization in the late twentieth century. University of Oklahoma Press, Norman

Huntington SP (1996) The clash of civilizations and the remaking of the world order. Simon & Schuster, New York

IMD (2007) The IMD world competitiveness yearbook 2007 [R/OL]. http://www.imd.ch/research/publications/wcy/index.cfm. Accessed Oct 2008

Inglehart R (1977) The silent revolution: change values and political style among Western publics. Princeton University Press, Princeton, NJ

Inglehart R (1997) Modernization and post-modernization: cultural, economic and political change in 43 societies. Princeton University Press, Princeton, NJ

Inglehart R, Baker WE (2000) Modernization, cultural change and the persistence of traditional values. Am Sociol Rev 65(February):19–51

Inglehart R, Welzel C (2005) Modernization, cultural change, and democracy: the human development sequence. Cambridge University Press, New York

Inkeles A (1966) The modernization of man. In: Weiner M (ed) Modernization: the dynamics of growth. Basic Books, New York

Inkeles A (1983) Exploring individual modernity. Columbia University Press, New York

Inkeles A, Smith DH (1974) Becoming modern: individual change in six developing countries. Harvard University Press, Cambridge

Iowa State University Center for Agricultural Economic (1965) Economic development of agriculture: the modernization of farming. Iowa State University Press, De O'Heady, Iowa

Irrgang B (2007) Technology transfer and modernization: what can philosophers of technology contribute? ACM Ubiquity 8(48):3–10

ISEI (International Society for Education Information) (1986) The modernization of Japanese education. International Society for Education Information, Tokyo

Isin EF, Turner B (eds) (2002) Handbook of citizenship studies. Sage, London

Janicke M (1985) Preventive environmental policy as ecological modernisation and structural policy, discussion paper. Berlin Science Center, Berlin

Janicke M, Weidner H (eds) (1997) National environmental policies: a comparative study of capacity-building. Springer, New York

Janicke M et al (1989) Economic structure and environmental impacts: east west comparisons. Environmentalist 9(3):171–183

Janoski T (1998) Citizenship and civil society. Cambridge University Press, New York

Jesinghaus J (1999) A European system of environmental pressure indices. First volume of the environmental pressure indices handbook: the indicators. European Commission, Joint Research Centre [R/OL]. http://esl.jrc.it/envind/theory/handb_.htm. Accessed Oct 2009

Jiang H, Xin L (2009) Developing modern agriculture in China: thinking and practice. China Agriculture, Beijing

Jin Y (1979) [1966] From tradition to modernity. China Times, Taipei

Kahl LA (1968) The measurement of modernism: a study of values in Brazil and Mexico. University of Texas Press, Austin

Kavolis V (2006) Modernization, globality, and nationalism as cultural endeavours [R/OL]. http://www.eurozine.com/articles/2006-05-26-kavolis-en.html. Accessed Oct 2008

Kennedy P (1987) The rise and fall of the great powers: economic change and military conflict from 1500 to 2000. Vintage Books, New York

Kenwood AG, Lougheed AL (1990) The growth of the international economy, 1820–1990: an introductory text. Routledge, London

Keohane RO, Nye JS (2000) Introduction. In: Nye JS, Donahue JD (eds) Governance in a globalizing world. Brookings Institution Press, Washington, DC, pp 1–44

Kim S, Margo RA (2003) Historical perspectives on U.S. economic geography. NBER Working Paper No. 9594.

Kirpal P (1971) Modernization of education in South Asia: the search for quality. Int Rev Educ 17 (2):138–150

Koslowski P (1987) Die Postmodeme Kultur: GesellschaftHch-kulturelle Konsequenzen der technischen Entwicklung. CH Beck, München

Kuhn T (1962) The structure of scientific revolutions. University of Chicago Press, Chicago, Ill

Kuznets S (1955) Economic growth and income inequality. Am Econ Rev 45(1):1–28

Kuznets S (1971) Economic growth of nations. Harvard University Press, Cambridge, MA

Landes DS (1998) Wealth and poverty of nations: why some are rich and some so poor. W.W. Norton, New York

Lash S (1990) Sociology of postmodernism. Routledge, London

Latham ME (2000) Modernization as ideology: American social science and "nation building" in the Kennedy era. The University of North Carolina Press, Chapel Hill
Leakey R (1994) The origin of humankind. Basic Books, New York, NY
Lee RB (2004) The Cambridge encyclopedia of hunters and gatherers. Cambridge University Press, Cambridge, MA
Lelas S (2000) Science and modernity: toward an integral theory of science. Kluwer Academic, Dordrecht
Lerner D (1958) The passing of traditional society: modernizing the Middle East. Free, New York
Levy MJ (1966) Modernization and the structure of societies. Princeton University Press, Princeton, NJ
Lewis WA (1955) The theory of economic growth. George Allen & Unwin, London
Li Y (2001) Cultural modernization: a path of all-round human development. Teach Res 6:13–15
Li D (2005) On the three waves of China's science and technology modernization. Tribune Stud 21 (11):35–38
Li J et al (2002) Report on the progress of Shanghai's science and technology modernization. Sci Sci Manage S&T 9:65–69
Lijphart A (1999) Patterns of democracy: government forms and performance in thirty-six countries. Yale University Press, New Haven, CT
Lin C (2001) The road of India modernization. Peking University Press, Beijing
Lipset SM (1960) Political man: the social bases of politics. Doubleday, New York
Liu Y (1997) China's cultural modernization. Hebei University Press, Baoding
Liu X (1998) Theory of modernity society. Shanghai Joint Publishing, Shanghai
Liu Z (2006) Path of agricultural modernization. China Agriculture Press, Beijing
Liu H, Xiong M (2007) Establishing the indicator system of urban educational modernization. Stud Educ Dev 17:33–36
Locke J (1988) [1690] In: Laslett P (ed) Two treatises of government. Cambridge University Press, Cambridge
Lubchenco J (1998) Entering the century of the environment. Science 279(5350):491–497
Luhmann N (1987) Modern systems theory and the theory of society. In: Meja V, Misgeld D, Stehr N (eds) Modern German sociology. Columbia University Press, New York, pp 173–186
Luo R (1990) From "westernization" to modernization. Peking University Press, Beijing
Luo R (1993) New approach on modernization. Peking University Press, Beijing
Luo R, Dong Z (1997) Modernization of East Asia: new model and new experience. Peking University Press, Beijing
Luo R, Niu D (1992) Exploring the process of China's modernization. Peking University Press, Beijing
Lyotard J-F (1984) The postmodern condition: a report on knowledge. Manchester University Press, Manchester
Maddison A (1995) Monitoring the world economy 1820–1992. OECD, Paris
Maddison A (2001) The world economy: a millennial perspective. OECD, Paris
Malone CC, Shastry BD, Francis TS (1970) A guide to agricultural modernization. Ford Foundation, New Delhi
Mansell R, When U (1998) Knowledge societies: information technology for sustainable development. United States, Oxford University Press, New York
Marsh D, Stocker G (eds) (2002) Theory and methods in political science. Palgrave Macmillan, Basingstoke
Martinelli A (2005) Global modernization: rethinking the project of modernity. Sage, London
Marx K (1967) [1867] Capital. International, New York
Marx K, Engels F (1967) [1848] The Communist manifesto. Penguin, Harmondsworth
Marx K, Engels F (1968) [1846] The German ideology. Progress, Moscow
McClelland DC (1961) The achieving society. Van Nostrand, Princeton, NJ
MEA (Millennium Ecosystem Assessment) (2005) Our human planet: summary for decision-makers. The Millennium Ecosystem Assessment series, vol 5. Island, Washington

Meadows DH, Randers J, Meadows DL (1972) Limits to growth: a report for the club of Rome's project on the predicament of mankind. Universe Books, New York

Melchior A et al (2000) Globalisation and inequality: world income distribution and living standards, 1960–1998. Report 6B: 2000. Studies on foreign policy issues. Royal Norwegian Ministry of Foreign Affair, Oslo

Mellor JW (1966) Economics of agricultural development. Cornell University Press, Ithaca, NY

Merriam-Webster Online Dictionary (2009a) Merriam-Webster online dictionary [DB/OL]. http://www.merriam-webster.com/dictionary/modern. Accessed Oct 2010

Merriam-Webster Online Dictionary (2009b) Merriam-Webster online dictionary [DB/OL]. http://www.merriam-webster.com/dictionary/modernize. Accessed Oct 2010

Merriam-Webster Online Dictionary (2009c) Merriam-Webster online dictionary [DB/OL]. http://www.merriam-webster.com/dictionary/modernization. Accessed Oct 2010

Merriam-Webster Online Dictionary (2009d) Merriam-Webster online dictionary [DB/OL]. http://www.merriam-webster.com/dictionary/science. Accessed Oct 2010

Merriam-Webster Online Dictionary (2009e) Merriam-Webster online dictionary [DB/OL]. http://www.merriam-webster.com/dictionary/knowledge. Accessed Oct 2010

Merriam-Webster Online Dictionary (2009f) Merriam-Webster online dictionary [DB/OL]. http://www.merriam-webster.com/dictionary/history. Accessed Oct 2010

Merriam-Webster Online Dictionary (2009g) Merriam-Webster online dictionary [DB/OL]. http://www.merriam-webster.com/dictionary/economics. Accessed Oct 2010

Merriam-Webster Online Dictionary (2009h) Merriam-Webster online dictionary [DB/OL]. http://www.merriam-webster.com/dictionary/development. Accessed Oct 2010

Merton RK (1968) Social theory and social structure. Free, New York

Misa TJ, Brey P, Feenberg A (2003) Modernity and technology. MIT Press, Cambridge, MA

Mitchell BR (1993) International historical statistics: the Americas, 1750–1988. Stockton, New York

Mitchell BR (1995) International historical statistics: Africa, Asia & Oceania, 1750–1988. Stockton, New York

Mitchell BR (1998) International historical statistics: Europe, 1750–1993. Macmillan Reference, Stockton, London, New York

Mol APJ (1995) The refinement of production: ecological modernization theory and the chemical industry. Van Arkel, Utrecht

Mol APJ (1996) Ecological modernisation and institutional reflexivity: environmental reform in the late modern age. Environ Polit 5(2):302–323

Mol APJ (2001) Globalization and environmental reform: the ecological modernization of the global economy. MIT Press, Cambridge

Mol APJ, Sonnenfeld DA (eds) (2000) Ecological modernization around the world: perspectives and critical debates. Frank Cass, London

Mol APJ, Sonnenfeld DA, Spaargaren G (eds) (2009) The ecological modernisation reader: environmental reform in theory and practice. Routledge, London

Montesquieu C (1989) [1748] The spirit of the laws (A. Cohler, B. Miller, H. Stone, trans. and eds.). Cambridge University Press, Cambridge

Moor W (1979) World modernization: the limit of convergence. Elsevier, New York

Moore B (1966) The social origins of democracy and dictatorship: lord and peasant in the making of the modern world. Beacon, Boston

Morgan LH (1964) [1877] In: White LA (ed) Ancient society. Harvard University Press, Cambridge, MA

Morgan DR, Kickham K (1997) Modernization among the U.S. States: change and continuity from 1960 to 1990. J Federal 27(3):23–40

Morrissy ID (1974) Agricultural modernization through production contracting, the role of the fruit and vegetable processor in Mexico and Central America. Praeger, New York

Morse EL (1976) Modernization and the transformation of international relations. Free, New York

Mouzelis N (1999) Modernity: a Non-European conceptualization. Br J Sociol 50:141–159

Murphy J (2000) Ecological modernisation – editorial. Geoforum 31(1):1–8
Murphy J, Gouldson A (2000) Environmental policy and industrial innovation: integrating environment and economy through ecological modernisation. Geoforum 31(1):33–44
Nardo M et al (2005) Handbook on constructing composite indicators: methodology and user guide. OECD Statistics Working Paper. STD/DOC(2005)3 [R/OL]. http://www.oecd.org/std/research. Accessed Oct 2007
Neumayer E (2003) Beyond income: convergence in living standards, big time. Struct Change Econ Dyn 14:275–296
Nielsen HK (1993) Youth culture and the completion of cultural modernization. Young 1:16–26
Nisbet R (1969) Social change and history: aspects of the Western theory of development. Oxford University Press, New York
Nolan P, Lenski G (1999) Human societies: an introduction to macrosociology, 8th edn. McGraw-Hill, New York
North DC (1981) Structure and change in economic history. W.W. Norton, New York
O'Donnell GA (1972) Modernization and bureaucratic-authoritarianism: studies in South American politics. University of California Press, Berkeley, CA
O'Rourke KH (2001) Globalization and inequality: historical trends. NBER Working Paper No.8339 [R/OL]. http://www.nber.org/papers/w8339. Accessed Sept 2004
OECD (1976) Measuring social well-being: a progress report on the development of social indicators. OECD, Paris
OECD (1996) Science, technology and industry outlook. OECD, Paris
OECD (2001) OECD environmental outlook. OECD, Paris
OECD (2002) Indicators to measure decoupling of environmental pressure from economic growth. OECD, Paris
OECD (2003) OECD environmental indicators, development, measurement and use, reference paper. OECD, Paris
OECD (2005) Society at a glance 2005: OECD social indicators. OECD, Paris
ONS (Office for National Statistics) (2003) Social trends 30–33 [DB/OL]. http://www.statistics.gov.uk. Accessed June 2005
Oqionwo W (1969) Agricultural modernization: the adoption of agricultural innovations among cocoa, oilpalm [sic]. Rice and rubber farmers in Southern Nigeria. Sociologiska Institutionen, Stockholm
Palmer RR, Colton J, Kramer L (2002) A history of the modern world, 9th edn. McGraw-Hill, New York
Palmqvist R (2006) Having fun in the second modernization. J Drug Educ 36:1–14
Pandey R (1988) Modernisation and social change. Criterion, New Delhi
Parkin S (1989) Green party: an international guide. Heretic, London
Parsons T (1937) Structure of social action. McGraw-Hill, New York
Parsons T (1951) The social system. Free, Glencoe, IL
Parsons T (1971) The system of modern society. Prentice-Hall, Englewood Cliffs, NJ
Parsons T, Shils E (eds) (1962) Towards a general theory of action. Harper & Row, New York
Parsons T, Smelser NJ (1956) Economy and society. Free, New York
Pataki G (2005). Ecological modernization and its contradictions: corporate greening in Hungary in the 1990s. In: Ketola T (ed) Environmental economy: what research on environmentally economical business activities can give to business know-how. Publications of the Turku School of Economics and Business Administration, Series Research and Reports, KR-4: 2005, Turku, pp 101–132
Pattnayak SR (1996) Modernization, dependency, and the stage in Asia, Africa, and Latin America. Int J Comp Sociol 37(3–4):274–289
Pearson FS, Payaslian S (1999) International political economy conflict and cooperation in the global system. McGraw-Hill, New York
Peet JR, Hartwick E (2009) Theories of development: contentions, arguments, alternatives, 2nd edn. Guilford, New York

Perroux F (1983) A new concept of development: basic tenets. Croom Helm, London
Persson J (1997) Convergence across the Swedish counties, 1911–1993. Eur Econ Rev 41:1835–1852
Peters MA, Besley AC (2006) Building knowledge cultures: education and development in the age of knowledge capitalism. Rowman & Littlefield, Lanham, MD
Picou JS (1999) Theoretical trends in environmental sociology: implications for resource management in the modern world. In: The social and economic planning conference, Minerals Management Service, Park City, UT, USA, 24–26 Aug 1999
Pieterse JN (2009) Development theory, 2nd edn. Sage, London
Piketty T, Saez E (2001) Income inequality in the United States 1913–1998. NBER Working Paper No. 8467
Plato (1968) The republic of Plato (Trans. A. Bloom). Basic Books, New York
Poggi G (1978) The development of the modern state: a sociological introduction. Hutchinson, London
Popenoe D (2000) Sociology, 11th edn. Prentice Hall, Upper Saddle River, NJ
Porat MU (1977) The information economy. DOC, GPO, Washington, DC
Porter ME (1990) Competitive advantage of nations. Free, New York
Porter ME, Stern S (1999) The new challenge to America's prosperity: findings from the innovation index. Council on Competitiveness, Washington, DC
Postiglione GA (1990) Education and the modernization of science and technology. Chin Educ 23 (3):1–96
Prebisch R (1950) The economic development of Latin American and its principal problems. United Nations, New York
Przeworski A, Limongi F (1997) Modernization: theories and facts. World Polit 49:155–183
Pye LW (ed) (1963) Communications and political development. Princeton University Press, Princeton, NJ
Pye LW, Verba S (eds) (1963) Political culture and political development. Princeton University Press, Princeton, NJ
Qian C (1988) The first industrialized society. Sichuan People's Publishing House, Chengdu
Qian C, Chen X (1987) The road to a modern country. Sichuan People's Publishing House, Chengdu
Qian C, Liu J (1999) Global perspective: lost in modernization. Zhejiang People's Publishing House, Hangzhou
Qian C, Yang Y, Chen X (1997) World modernization process. Nanjing University Press, Nanjing
Qiu Y (1980) Agricultural modernization in West Germany. China Agriculture Press, Beijing
Quigley C (1961) The evolution of civilization: an introduction to historical analysis. Harper, New York
Radcliffe-Brown AR (1952) Structure and function in primitive society: essays and addresses. Cohen and West, London
Ralph PL et al (1991) World civilizations: their history and their culture. W. W. Norton, New York
Research Group for China Modernization Report (2001) China Modernization Report 2001: modernization and evaluation. Peking University Press, Beijing
Research Group for China Modernization Strategies (2002) China Modernization Report 2002: knowledge economy and modernization. Peking University Press, Beijing
RGCMS (Research Group for China Modernization Strategies et al) (2003) China Modernization Report 2003: theory and prospects. Peking University Press, Beijing
RGCMS (Research Group for China Modernization Strategies et al) (2004) China Modernization Report 2004: regional modernization study. Peking University Press, Beijing
RGCMS (Research Group for China Modernization Strategies et al) (2005) China Modernization Report 2005: economic modernization study. Peking University Press, Beijing
RGCMS (Research Group for China Modernization Strategies et al) (2006) China Modernization Report 2006: social modernization study. Peking University Press, Beijing
RGCMS (Research Group for China Modernization Strategies et al) (2007) China Modernization Report 2007: ecological modernization study. Peking University Press, Beijing

RGCMS (Research Group for China Modernization Strategies et al) (2008) China Modernization Report 2008: international modernization study. Peking University Press, Beijing
RGCMS (Research Group for China Modernization Strategies et al) (2009) China Modernization Report 2009: cultural modernization study. Peking University Press, Beijing
RGCMS (Research Group for China Modernization Strategies et al) (2010) China Modernization Report 2010: world modernization outline 1700–2100. Peking University Press, Beijing
Ricardo D (1821) [1817] On the principles of political economy and taxation. John Murray, London
Ritzer G, Goodman DJ (2004) Modern sociology theory. McGraw-Hill, New York
Roberts J (2001) The failure of modernization: globalization and culture [R/OL]. http://www.apexart.org/conference/Roberts.htm. Accessed Oct 2008
Roberts JT, Hite A (2000) From modernization to globalization. Blackwell, Malden, MA
Rose MA (1991) The post-modern and post-industrial: a critical analysis. Cambridge University Press, Cambridge
Rosenau PM (1992) Post-modernism and the social sciences: insights, inroads, and intrusions. Princeton University Press, Princeton, NJ
Rostow WW (1960) The stages of economic growth: a non-communist manifesto. Cambridge University Press, Cambridge
Rousseau J-J (1968) [1762] Social contract, or principles of political right. Penguin Books, London
Rubinson R (1981) Dynamics of world development. Sage, Beverly Hills, CA
Rugman A (2000) The end of globalization: a new and radical analysis of globalization and what it means for business. Random House, Amacom-McGraw Hill, London, New York
Russell CA (1983) Science and social change 1700-1900. MacMillan, London
Rustow DA (1967) A world of nation: problems of political modernization. Brookings Institution, Washington, DC
Samuelson PA, Nordhaus WD (1992) Economics, 14th edn. McGraw-Hill, New York
Saqib GN (1983) Modernization of Muslim education in Egypt, Pakistan and Turkey: a comparative study. Islamic Book Service, Lahore
Sarton GAL (1936) The history of science and the new humanism. Harvard University Press, Cambridge
Sarton GAL (1957) The study of the history of science. Dover, New York
Sayer A (1992) Method in social science: a realist approach. Routledge, London
Schelkle W et al (eds) (2000) Paradigms of social change: modernization, development, transformation, evolution. Campus Verlag, St. Martin's Press, Frankfurt, New York
Schultz TW (1964) Transforming traditional agriculture. Yale University Press, New Haven
Schumpeter JA (1934) [1912] Theory of economic development: an inquiry into profits, capital, credit, interest, and the business cycle. Harvard University Press, Cambridge, MA
Schweitzer A (1980) [1923] The philosophy of civilization (Trans. C.T. Campion). Prometheus Books, Buffalo, New York
Schweitzer PP et al (eds) (2000) Hunters and gatherers in the modern world. Berghahn Books, New York
Seers D (1977) The new meaning of development. Int Dev Rev 19(3):2–7
Seers D (ed) (1981) Dependency theory: a critical reassessment. Pinter, London
Seippel Ø (2000) Ecological modernisation as a theoretical device: strengths and weaknesses. J Environ Policy Plan 2(4):287–302
Sen A (2001) Development as freedom. Alfred Knopf, New York
Servaes N, Carpentier J (2006) Towards a sustainable information society. ECCR Book Series, Intellect, Bristol
Service E (1962) Origins of the state and civilization. W.W. Norton, New York
Shah H (2011) The production of modernization: Daniel Lerner, mass media, and the passing of traditional society. Temple University Press, Publisher
Shi M (2006) Agricultural modernization: an international comparison on development. Ethnic Publishing House, Beijing

Shils E (1966) Political development in the new states. Mouton, The Hague
Sieben I, Graaf PM (2001) Testing the modernization hypothesis and the socialist ideology hypothesis: a comparative sibling analysis of educational attainment and occupational status. Br J Sociol 52(3):441–467
Simon A (1982) Models of bounded rationality: behavioral economics and business organization, vol 1 and 2. MIT Press, Cambridge, MA
Simonis U (1988) Beyond growth: elements of sustainable development. Edition Sigma, Berlin
Simonis U (1989a) Industrial restructuring for sustainable development: three points of departure. Working Paper FS II 89–401, Internationales Institut Fur Umwelt und Gesellschaft, Wissenschaftszentrum Berlin für Sozialforschung (WZB)
Simonis U (1989b) Ecological modernization of industrial society: three strategic elements. Int Social Sci J 121:347–361
Smelser NJ (1959) Social change in the industrial revolution. Routledge and Kegan Paul, London
Smelser NJ (1964) Toward a theory of modernization. In: Etzioni A, Etzioni E (eds) Social change. Basic Books, New York, pp 268–284
Smith A (1977) [1776] In: Cannan E (ed) Inquiry into the nature and causes of the wealth of nations. University Of Chicago Press, Chicago
So AY (1990) Social change and development. Sage, Newbury Park
Sorokin PA (1941) Social and cultural dynamics. American Books, New York
Spencer H (1954) [1850] Social statics. Robert Schalkenbach Foundation, New York
Spengler O (1965) [1918] The decline of the West. Modern Library, New York
Sraffa P, Dobb MH (2005) The works and correspondence of David Ricardo, vol 1. Principles of political economy and taxation. Liberty Fund, Indianapolis
Stavrianos LS (1970) The world to 1500: a global history. Prentice-Hall, Englewood Cliffs, NJ
Stavrianos LS (1982) The world since 1500: a global history. Prentice-Hall, Englewood Cliffs, NJ
Stavrianos LS (1998) A global history from prehistory to the 21st century, 7th edn. Prentice Hall, Englewood Cliffs, NJ
Stearns PN et al (1992) World civilizations: the global experience. Harper Collins, New York
Stehr N (1994) Knowledge societies. Sage, London
Steward JH (1955) Theory of culture change: the methodology of multilinear evolution. University of Illinois Press, Urbana
Storey J (1993) An introductory guide to cultural theory and popular culture. University of Georgia Press, Athens, GA
Su Z (2006) Research on the modernization processes of Latin American countries. Social Sciences Academic Press, Beijing
Sun L (1988) Social modernization. Hauxia Publishing House, Beijing
Suttmeier RP (1980) Science, technology, and China's drive for modernization. Hoover Institution Press, Stanford, CA
Sutton F (1963) Social theory and comparative politics. In: Eckstein H, Apter D (eds) Comparative politics: a reader. Free Press of Glencoe, New York, pp 67–81
Tan C (ed) (2001) Development economics. Shanxi Economic Publishing House, Taiyuan
Tao Z (2003) Ecological burden and ecological footprint. Economic Science Press, Beijing
Taylor JG (1979) From modernization to modes of production: a critique of the sociologies of development and underdevelopment. Humanities, Atlantic Highlands, NJ
Thorndike L (1926) A short history of civilization. F. S. Crofts, New York
Tilley C et al (eds) (2006) Handbook of material culture. Sage, London
Tilly C (2003) Contention and democracy in Europe 1650–2000. Cambridge University Press, Cambridge
Tipps D (1973) Modernization theory and the comparative studies of societies: a critical perspective. Comp Stud Soc Hist 5:199–226
Tiryakian E (1991) Modernization: Exhumetur in pace (rethinking macrosociology in the 1990s'). Int Sociol 6(2):165–180

Toffler A (1980) The third wave. Bantam Books, New York, NY

Tönnies F (1965) [1887] Community and society (Gemeinschaft und gesellschaft). Harper & Row, New York

Toynbee AJ (1987) [1934–1961] A study of history: abridgement of volumes I–VI. Abridged by Somervell DC. Oxford University Press, New York

Turner BS (ed) (1990) Theories of modernity and postmodernity. Sage, London

Tylor E (1871) Primitive culture. John Murray, London

UN (United Nations) (2004) World Population to 2300. United Nations, New York

UN (United Nations) (2008) World urbanization prospects, the 2007 revision. United Nations, New York

UN (United Nations) (2009) World population prospects: the 2008 revision. United Nations, New York

UNCTAD (2005) Developing countries in international trade 2005: trade and development index. United Nations, New York, Geneva

UNDP (United Nations Development Programme) (various years) Human development report. Oxford University Press, New York

UNDP (United Nations Development Programme), UNEP (United Nations Environment Programme), World Bank and WRI (World Resources Institute) (2000) World resources 2000–2001: people and ecosystem-the fraying web of life. WRI, Washington, DC

UNESCO (1973) Modernization of education, teaching media and technology. SNTL, Prague

UNESCO (2000) World culture report 2000: cultural diversity, conflict and pluralism. UNESCO, Paris

UNESCO (2003) Measuring and monitoring the information and knowledge societies: a statistical challenge. UNESCO, Paris

UNESCO (2005) Towards knowledge societies: UNESCO world report. UNESCO, Paris

USCB (U.S. Census Bureau) (2002) Income inequality [R/OL]. http://www.census.gov. Accessed Oct 2009

Vago S (1999) Social change, 4th edn. Prentice Hall, Upper Saddle River, NJ

Valenzuela JS, Valenzuela A (1978) Modernization and dependency: alternative perspectives in the study of Latin American underdevelopment. Comp Polit 10(4):535–557

Venetoulis J, Cobb C (2004) The genuine progress indicator 1950–2002 (2004 Update) [DB/OL]. http://www.rprogress.org/projects/gpi/. Accessed Sept 2006

Vico G (1968) [1725] The new science (Trans. T. G. Bergin, M. H. Fisch). Cornell University Press, Ithaca, NY

Voltaire (1963) [1756] Essai sur les moeurs et l'esprit des nations [Essay on the Mores and the spirit of nations]. Garnier Freres, Paris

Wallerstein IM (1974) The modern world-system I: capitalist agriculture and the origins of the European world-economy in the sixteenth century. Academic, New York

Wallerstein I (1976) Modernization: Requiescat in pace. In: Coser LA, Larse ON (eds) The uses of controversy in sociology. Free, New York, pp 131–135

Wallerstein IM (1980) The modern world system II. Mercantilism and the consolidation of the European world-economy, 1600–1750. Academic, New York

Wallerstein IM (1988) The modern world-system III: the second era of great expansion of the capitalist world-economy, 1730s–1840s. Academic, New York

Wan Z, Zheng Y (eds) (2008) Agricultural modernization: theory and practice of Guangdong. China Agricultural Science and Technology, Beijing

Wang X (2002) Political system and economic modernization: re-exploring the "Japanese Model". Social Sciences Academic, Beijing

Wang Z (2006) World system and the rise and fall of nations. Peking University Press, Beijing

Wang X, Gao F (2007) Interaction between agricultural internationalization and modernization: an empirical analysis based on the development pattern of northern Shandong. People's Publishing House, Beijing

Ward SC (2003) Modernizing the mind: psychological knowledge and the remaking of society. Praeger, Westport, CT

Ward RE, Rustow DA (1964) Political modernization in Japan and Turkey. Princeton University Press, Princeton, NJ

WCED (World Commission on Environment and Development) (1987) Our common future: the world commission on environment and development. Oxford University Press, Oxford

Weber M (1949) The methodology of social sciences. Free, New York

Weber M (1958) [1904] The protestant ethic and the spirit of capitalism (Trans. T. Parsons). Charles Scribner's, New York

WEF (World Economic Forum) (2003) The global competitiveness report 2002–2003 [R/OL]. http://www.weforum.org/en/initiatives/gcp/Global%20Competitiveness%20Report/index.htm. Accessed June 2008

Weiner M (ed) (1966) Modernization: the dynamics of growth. Basic Books, New York

Weitz R (1971) From peasant to farmer: a revolutionary strategy for development. Columbia University Press, New York

Welzel C, Inglehart R, Klingemann H-D (2003) The theory of human development: a cross-cultural analysis. Eur J Polit Res 42:341–379

Wernic IK et al (1997) Materialization and dematerialization: measures and trends. Daedalus 125 (3):171–198

Williams R (1958) Culture and society 1780–1950. Harper & Row, New York

Williamson J (1964) Regional inequality and the process of national development: a description of the patterns. Econ Dev Cultural Change 13:3–45

Wilson TW (1979) Science technology and development: politics of modernization. Foreign Policy Association, New York

Wilson Center (1982) China's scientific and technological modernization: domestic and international implications. East Asia Program, Wilson Center, Washington, DC

World Bank (2002) Constructing knowledge societies: new challenges for tertiary education. World Bank, Washington, DC

World Bank (various years) World development indicators (2002–2010). World Bank, Washington, DC

World Bank (various years) World development report (1978–2010). World Bank, Oxford University Press, Washington, DC, New York

World Bank (2008) World development indicators 2008 CD-RUM. World Bank, Washington, DC

Wu S (1948) Chinese culture and modernization. Observation Society, Shanghai

Wu C (2001a) China's modernization: market and society. SDX Joint Publishing, Beijing

Wu H (2001b) A perspective on Brazil's modernization process: history and reality. Current Affairs, Beijing

Wu Y, Qi S et al (1994) World history, ancient history series. Higher Education, Beijing

Xin W (2007) On new democracy and the modernization of Chinese culture. Central Compilation and Translation, Beijing

Xu Z (2007) Political and cultural dimensions of modernization. People's Publishing House, Beijing

Xu F (2009) Modernization: the embarrassment of history and the thinking on embarrassment. Harbin Institute of Technology Press, Harbin

Xu J, Chen D (1995) History of Chinese modernization. Shanghai Joint Publishing, Shanghai

Xuan X, Wang C (1998) A perspective on the agricultural modernization of western countries. Shanghai Far East Publishers of China, Shanghai

Yan J (2006) The development politics: concepts and theories of political development research. Peking University Press, Beijing

Yang W, Xu X (2001) Assessment of agricultural modernization. Social Sciences Academic, Beijing

Ye N (1998) Modernization of Chinese people. Nanjing Publishing House, Nanjing

Yin B (1999) Common problems of modernization–experiences and lessons of over 20 countries and regions. Tianjin People's Publishing House, Tianjin
Yin B (2001) Modernization: exploring the concept and paradigm. People's Publishing House, Beijing
Yin Z (2009) On the basic characteristics of China's educational modernization. J Nanjing Normal Univ (Social Sci Ed) 6:80–86
Young S (ed) (2000) The emergence of ecological modernization: integrating the environment and the economy? Routledge, New York
Yu H (ed) (2002) China's modernization process. Jiangsu People's Publishing House, Nanjing
Yu D, Yan D (2008) On the modernization of education. J Jiangsu Inst Educ (Nat Sci Ed) 25 (4):93–95
Zapf W (ed) (1991) Die Modernisierung Moderner Gesellschaften. Verhandlungen des 25. Deutschen Soziologentages. Campus Verlag, Frankfurt, New York
Zapf W (1999) Modernisierung, Wohlfahrtsentwicklung und Transformation. Sigma, Berlin
Zeng Z (1996) Political stability and modernization–a historical survey of mexico's political model. Eastern, Beijing
Zeng Z (2000) Modernization strategy options and international relations–research on the experience of Latin America. Social Sciences Academic, Beijing
Zhang Z (1992) Ups and downs: China's modernization process and forecasts on its medium and long term development. China Social Sciences, Beijing
Zhang S (1996) Two paths of United States' early modernization. Peking University Press, Beijing
Zhang Y (ed) (2001) A perspective on Asia modernization. Social Sciences Academic, Beijing
Zhang F, He C (1999) National innovation system–an engine of the second modernization. Higher Education, Beijing
Zhang D, Huang Z (2002) A perspective on the relations between agricultural modernization process and agricultural science and technology. Chin Rural Econ 11:48–53
Zhang K, Luo F (1993) A comparative perspective: research on China's early modernization. People's Publishing House, Beijing
Zheng F (2003) Modernization and qualities of the people. Guangzhou People's Publishing House, Guangzhou
Zhou J (1996) Research on China's early modernization. Higher Education, Beijing
Zhou J et al (2009) Educational modernization: description of a specific historical period. Education Science Publishing House, Beijing
Zhu S (1998) Theory and practice of agricultural modernization. Shanghai University of Finance and Economics, Shanghai
Zhu T (2002) Urban modernization research. Red Flag, Beijing
Zhu Q, Wu H (2001) Social indicators system. China Social Sciences, Beijing
Ziehe T (2000) Engagement and abstention: youth and the school in the second modernization. Eur Educ 31:6–22

Author Index

C. He, *Modernization Science*,
DOI 10.1007/978-3-642-25459-8, © Springer-Verlag Berlin Heidelberg 2012

Subject Index

C. He, *Modernization Science*,
DOI 10.1007/978-3-642-25459-8, © Springer-Verlag Berlin Heidelberg 2012

B

C

E

G

H

I

J

K

T

U

Studies in Systems, Decision and Control

Volume 485

Series Editor

Janusz Kacprzyk, Systems Research Institute, Polish Academy of Sciences,
Warsaw, Poland

The series "Studies in Systems, Decision and Control" (SSDC) covers both new developments and advances, as well as the state of the art, in the various areas of broadly perceived systems, decision making and control–quickly, up to date and with a high quality. The intent is to cover the theory, applications, and perspectives on the state of the art and future developments relevant to systems, decision making, control, complex processes and related areas, as embedded in the fields of engineering, computer science, physics, economics, social and life sciences, as well as the paradigms and methodologies behind them. The series contains monographs, textbooks, lecture notes and edited volumes in systems, decision making and control spanning the areas of Cyber-Physical Systems, Autonomous Systems, Sensor Networks, Control Systems, Energy Systems, Automotive Systems, Biological Systems, Vehicular Networking and Connected Vehicles, Aerospace Systems, Automation, Manufacturing, Smart Grids, Nonlinear Systems, Power Systems, Robotics, Social Systems, Economic Systems and other. Of particular value to both the contributors and the readership are the short publication timeframe and the worldwide distribution and exposure which enable both a wide and rapid dissemination of research output.

Indexed by SCOPUS, DBLP, WTI Frankfurt eG, zbMATH, SCImago.

All books published in the series are submitted for consideration in Web of Science.

Imhade P. Okokpujie · Lagouge K. Tartibu

Modern Optimization Techniques for Advanced Machining

Heuristic and Metaheuristic Techniques

Springer

Imhade P. Okokpujie
Department of Mechanical and Industrial Engineering Technology
University of Johannesburg Doornfontein Campus
Johannesburg, South Africa

Department of Mechanical Engineering
Afe Babalola University
Ado-Ekiti, Ekiti State, Nigeria

Lagouge K. Tartibu
Department of Mechanical and Industrial Engineering Technology
University of Johannesburg Doornfontein Campus
Johannesburg, South Africa

ISSN 2198-4182 ISSN 2198-4190 (electronic)
Studies in Systems, Decision and Control
ISBN 978-3-031-35454-0 ISBN 978-3-031-35455-7 (eBook)
https://doi.org/10.1007/978-3-031-35455-7

This Springer imprint is published by the registered company Springer Nature Switzerland AG
The registered company address is: Gewerbestrasse 11, 6330 Cham, Switzerland

Preface

Advanced manufacturing via computer numerical machining is the art of producing mechanical components employed in aerospace, automobile and industrial applications where a high level of accuracy is needed. This book focuses on the machining of some selected alloys and its optimization. The application of aluminium alloy and titanium alloys in the manufacturing industry has increased tremendously due to its lightweight-to-high strength ratio and high-level resistance to corrosion. However, aluminium alloy and titanium alloys have some challenges during the machining and manufacturing stage such as material adhesion and titanium alloy is very difficult to cut, in order to solve real-life manufacturing challenges in advanced machining operation for sustainable production processes. There is a need for the implementation of a general algebraic modelling system (GAMS) and other heuristic and metaheuristic techniques for problem-solving and to effectively develop mathematical models for high accuracy prediction and optimization under nano-lubrication machining conditions. This book will discuss majorly on the three responses in machining such as surface roughness, cutting force and material removal rate, which will give an excellent guide to undergraduate and postgraduate students, senior research fellows in academia, operational and strategic staff in manufacturing industries, the theoretical and practical skills for implementing a sustainable and biodegradable nano-lubricant in machining processes. The structure of this book is as follows: Chap. 1: "Overview of Advanced Machining Process" that cut across the major four advanced machining process such as computer numerical control machining (CNCM), wire electro-discharge machining (WEDM), abrasive water jet machining (AWJM) and electro-discharge machining (EDM) and discusses their working principles, advantages and disadvantages. Chapter 2: "Cutting Fluid and Its Application with Different Delivering Machining Techniques" is presented in this chapter cut across the cryogenic cooling, flood cooling, solid lubrication, compressed air vapour gas as coolant, high-pressure lubrication and MQL. Chapter 3: "Development and Application of Nano-lubricant in Machining: A Review". Chapter 4: "Global Machining Prediction and Optimization"—This chapter discusses the Importance of prediction and optimization in machining via heuristic and metaheuristic techniques such as artificial neural network (ANN), adaptive neuro-fuzzy inference system, particle swarm optimization, genetic algorithm, whale optimization algorithm (WOA), ant lion optimization algorithm, grasshopper optimization algorithm. Chapter 5: "Multi-objective Grey Wolf Optimizer for Improved Machining Performance". Chapter 6: "Multi-objective Ant Lion Optimizer for Improved Machining Performance". Chapter 7: "Multi-objective Grasshopper Optimizer for Improved Machining Performance". Chapter 8: "A Multi-objective Optimization Approach for Improving Machining Performance Using the General Algebraic Modelling System (GAMS)". Chapter 9: "ANN and QRCCD Prediction of Surface Roughness Under Biodegradable Nano-lubricant". Chapter 10: "Cutting Force Optimization Under ANN and QRCCD". Chapter 11: "Material Removal Rate Optimization Under ANN and QRCCD". Chapter 12: "Application of Hybrid ANN and PSO for Prediction of Surface Roughness Under Biodegradable Nano-lubricant". Chapter 13: "Adaptive Neuro-Fuzzy Inference System for Prediction of Surface Roughness Under Biodegradable Nano-lubricant".

Johannesburg, South Africa and
Ado-Ekiti, Ekiti State, Nigeria
June 2023

Dr. Imhade P. Okokpujie
Prof. Lagouge K. Tartibu

Contents

About the Authors

Engr. Dr. Imhade P. Okokpujie MNSE, NIMechE is Senior Lecturer/Researcher at Afe Babalola University, Ado-Ekiti. She obtained her Doctor of Philosophy (Ph.D.), from Covenant University in 2020. Her Ph.D. research focus is on nano-lubricant in end-milling machining process for advance manufacturing. She has authored over one-hundred and fifty (150) scholarly scientific papers. She is formally the Chief Editor of *Covenant Journal of Engineering Technology (CJET)* and has served as a reviewer to many international journals and conferences. She is one of the top-rated researchers in her institution and has won numerous awards for her scholarly sagacity, which include Covenant University Chancellor's Exceptional Researcher of the Year (won twice, 2018 and 2019 successively). Her research areas are design and production, advanced manufacturing such as machining, tool wear, vibration, nano-lubricant, energy systems, modelling, optimization, mechatronics and a multi-disciplinary research. Recently, she was awarded the Global Excellence Stature Fellowship Grant Industry 4.0 2021 for advanced research in University of Johannesburg. She is a registered Engineer with the Council for the Regulation of Engineering in Nigeria (COREN), a Corporate Member of the Nigeria Society of Engineers (MNSE). She is very passionate about the Girl Child's Education, committed to women development initiative and offers quality mentorship to Young Researchers and Engineers'.

Prof. Lagouge K. Tartibu is Full Professor in the department of mechanical engineering at the University of Johannesburg. He received a doctorate degree in mechanical engineering focusing on engineering optimization and thermo-acoustic technology and a master's degree in mechanical engineering focusing on mechanical vibration from Cape Peninsula University of Technology. He holds a bachelor's degree in Electromechanical engineering from the University of Lubumbashi. His primary research areas are engineering optimization, applied thermal engineering, electricity generation and refrigeration using thermo-acoustic technology, artificial intelligence and mechanical vibration.

Chapter 1
Overview of Advanced Machining Process

Abstract Sustainable development depends on the dynamics of the manufacturing process. This chapter discusses an overview of the advanced machining processes that are currently in use in the manufacturing industry. In order to study the heuristic and metaheuristic techniques for advanced nanolubricant machining optimization. The need for an overview of modern techniques in machining was carried out, which cut across the application, working principle, advantages, and disadvantages of computer numerical control machining (CNCM), wire electro-discharge machining (WEDM), abrasive water jet machining (AWJM), and electro-discharge machining (EDM). From the study, CNCM is one of the best techniques until now in the machining industry, so the different aspects of CNCM such as the lathe, drilling, grinding, and milling processes were discussed. This will help researchers, students, and manufacturers understand the sustainable aspects of advanced machining processes. Also, from the study, it is seen that the application of cutting fluid is a significant aspect of all machining processes, so this study will recommend that manufacturers employ eco-friendly cutting fluid for sustainable machining. Therefore, chapter two of this book will be on the study of cutting fluid and its applications via different delivery techniques, abrasive water jet machining.

Keywords Machining · Computer numerical control · Wire electro-discharge machining · Milling process · Lathe

1.1 Introduction of Overview of the Advanced Machining Process

Non-conventional machining techniques are another name for modern machining techniques. These procedures comprise a collection of techniques that use mechanical, electrical, chemical, thermal, or a mix of these energy to remove extra material [1, 2]. The significance of this type of machining process is on the application in the monolithic metals, such as metals and alloys, can be machined using a method that is

I. P. Okokpujie and L. K. Tartibu, *Modern Optimization Techniques for Advanced Machining*, Studies in Systems, Decision and Control 485,
https://doi.org/10.1007/978-3-031-35455-7_1

well-known and widely used in a variety such as aerospace, biomedical, and automotive industries [3–6]. However, due to the disparity between the chemical and physical properties of the metal matrix and the hard reinforcement, metal matrix composites (MMCs) provide a unique set of difficulties [7]. The current metalworking sector has a number of difficulties, including cost management, product quality enhancement, a shorter preparation time from design to manufacturing, and product finishing [8]. A useful tool for processing sophisticated materials like MMC is non-conventional machining (NCM) [9], Modern machining process cut across Computer Numerical Control Machining, Wire Electro Discharge Machining (WEDM), Abrasive Water Jet Machining (AWJM), Electro Discharge Machining (EDM), Electro Discharge Machining (EDM). This chapter one will give brief over view of this method under types of modern machining operations. The types of advanced machining operations are analysed in the subsections.

1.2 Computer Numerical Control Machining

The automated use of a computer to manage machining equipment is known as numerical control. Without a manual intervention directly overseeing the milling cutter [10]. A computer numerical control CNC machine follows coded, programmed commands to process a piece of material in accordance with standards of the manufacturer [11–13]. This Sect. 1.2.1 discusses the working principles of CNC, advantages and disadvantages. Also, types of CNC operation such as milling, lathe, drilling and grinding.

1.2.1 Working Principle of CNC Machining Operations

All-automatic CNC machines are available nowadays. They only need digital data with details on the tools and cutting trajectories. Numerous tools are required for design or machining procedures to produce a certain product. Digital tool libraries that are connected to the machine itself can be made by machinists [14].

(a) The first stage of CNC manufacturing is the component design using CAD software. The 3D model is used to establish the required size and attributes for the finished product.
(b) Since some of these programs are a part of CAD-CAM packages, the flow can continue in the same programs. Otherwise, CAD models are employed with CAM software.
(c) If the CAD and CAM systems are integrated into the same item, file conversion is not necessary.The model is ready for the entire production process thanks to CAM (computer-aided manufacturing) software. It first looks for mistakes in the model. The physical portion is then created using a CNC software.

(d) The program is primarily a set of directives that controls the cutting head during the production process.
(e) The third stage involves choosing the suitable parameters. These include parameters like voltage, RPMs, and cutting speed. The configuration is influenced by the part's geometry as well as the equipment and tooling that are available.
(f) The software ultimately determines the nesting. The term "nesting" describes how parts are arranged and oriented in relation to raw materials. The objective is to make the most of the resources.
(g) From all of this data, M-code and G-code are formed, which the machinery can understand.M-Code versus G-Code is a language used to instruct a machine on how to move is referred to as G-code. It is essentially the geometric code. Cutting head motion and speed are controlled via G-code.
(h) An industrial computer known as a machine controller is provided the instructions. This then determines how the motors should operate. The path that will be taken is, of course, decided by the motors.
(i) On the other side, the M-code provides all the information that the G-code omits. It is referred to as machine code or miscellaneous code for this reason.

The instructions in M-code cover topics like changing tools, using coolant, stopping programs, and more. Therefore, while not identical, both are equally vital [15].

1.2.2 Advantages and Disadvantage of CNC

Table 1.1 shows the advantages and disadvantages of CNC machining operation. It clearly shown that CNC machining is viable and sufficients in manufacturing component.

There are several operating procedures of the CNC during manufacturing process such as, milling, lathe, drilling, grinding and shaping machining process. These processes are the manufacturing powerhouses because they can switch tooling automatically based on the digital instructions.

1.2.3 Milling Machining

With the use of a spinning cutter that revolves at a very high speed for effective metal removal, milling machines are used to remove metal pieces. Cutting edges on a rotating cutter aid in material cutting. Milling machines have the capacity to accommodate one or more cutters at once. On milling machines, operations can be carried out with a very high degree of accuracy [16]. Milling machines remove metal at a high rate as compared to other metal-removal equipment [1–18]. They are known

Table 1.1 Advantages and disadvantage of CNC machining processes

S/No.	Advantages of CNC machining	Disadvantage of CNC machining
1	The precision and accuracy of machining are very high	Despite costs gradually declining, Machineries are costlier than manually controlled equipment
2	It takes extremely little time to complete a task	The CNC machine operator just needs rudimentary training and abilities, which are sufficient to oversee multiple machines. The loss of many traditional talents is indicated by this
3	Operational safety and there is a reduction in the number of operators needed to operate a machine	CNC machines require minimal operators comparing to machinery that is operated manually. Investment in CNC machines could lead to employment loss
4	There is no chance for human error	In many countries, students and children are not taught how to operate manually controlled lathes and other machinery any more
5	Reliable Even extremely complicated designs can be created	The complex skills required by engineers in the past are no longer acquired by students or teachers. Engineering and math expertise are a couple of these
6	Minimum maintenance is necessary	

for their superior precision and superior surface finishing, milling machines can be applied with four different milling techniques, they are:

(a) Plain milling: This milling procedure, often referred to as surface milling, uses a cutting tool to remove material from the workpiece's surface. The rotation axis in plain milling is perpendicular to the workpiece.
(b) Face milling: makes use of a rotary axis that is parallel to the surface of the material. To remove material, the cutting or grinding tool is pressed firmly on the workpiece surface.
(c) Peripheral milling: a machining technique known as peripheral milling involves aligning the milling cutter parallel to the workpiece. To put it another way, the milling cutter is set up so that its sides grind away at the top of the workpiece.
(d) End milling: A cylindrical cutter used in the end milling process contains several cutting blades on both its periphery and its tip, allowing for both end and peripheral cutting. To lessen the impact that occurs when each flute engages the workpiece, these cutting edges or flutes are typically designed with helical spirals.

In milling machining process there are four major parameters involves in the operation that are very significant, such as spindle speed, radial depth of cut, feed rate and axial depth of cut [19]. These parameters are presented in Fig. 1.1.

This machining parameters can be calculated theatrically using the formula from Eqs. (1.1)–(1.4) for milling process

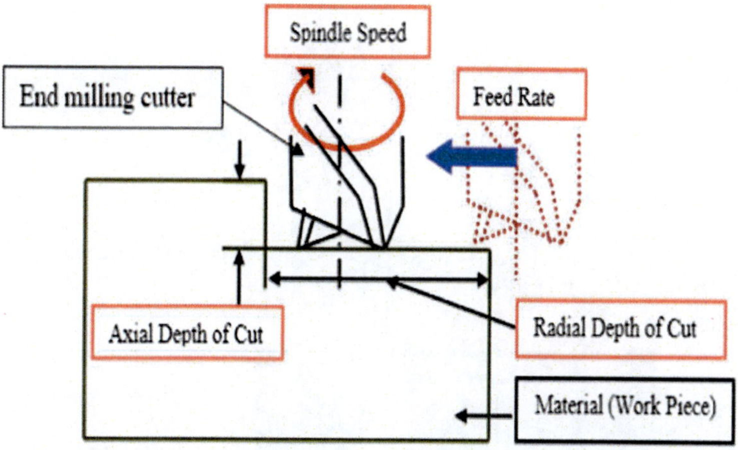

Fig. 1.1 The four most influential parameters and cutting tools in milling machining

$$Cutting\ speed\ (Cs) = \frac{\pi \times D \times n}{1000} \tag{1.1}$$

$$Spindle\ speed\ (Ss) = Cs \div \pi \div D \times 1000 \tag{1.2}$$

$$Feed\ rate\ (Fr) = Ss \times f \times Z \tag{1.3}$$

$$Depth\ of\ cut\ (DOC) = \frac{d_1 - d_2}{2} \tag{1.4}$$

where Cs is cutting speed in m/min, Ss is spindle speed in min^{-1}, D is diameter in mm, π is 3.14 in radius, z is number of flutes, ft is feed per tooth in mm/tooth, and Fr is feed rate in mm/min. Also, the d_1 is the workpiece diameter before machining and d_2 is the surface diameter of the machined worpiece.

Due to its extreme versatility, CNC milling machines can be utilized for a wide range of cuts and machining processes. In order to remove material and actualize the design. The cutting tool often moves and rotates while the workpiece generally stays still [20]. Different spindle configurations on CNC milling machines retain and move the workpiece in various ways.

- Vertical milling: To remove material from a still workpiece, a vertically oriented spindle drives a spinning cutting tool up and down. The spindle and table of the turret-style milling machine can move both perpendicularly and parallel to the axis.
- Horizontal milling: When pressing on the workpiece, a spindle with a mounted cutting tool is horizontally orientated. Use of larger and shorter cutting tools allows for deeper, heavier cuts during horizontal milling.

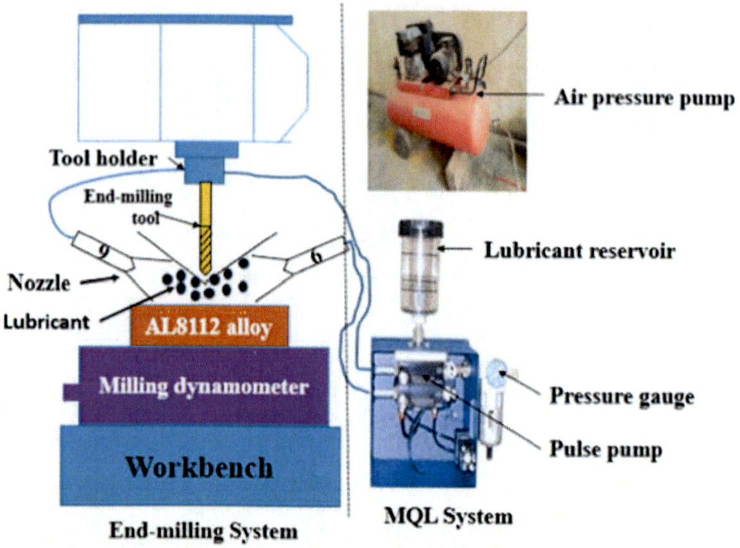

Fig. 1.2 Schematic illustration milling machining and MQL system [21]

- Multi-axis milling: CNC mills with 4 and 5 axes enable intricate or difficult machine operations. In addition to rotating on the A and B axes, multi-axis milling machines can also move along the X, Y, and Z axes. This makes it possible to approach the workpiece from any angle, frequently allowing numerous processes at once [21].

A typical illustration of a milling machining process with the minimum quantity lubricant process is presented in Fig. 1.2.

1.2.4 Lathes Machining

A lathe machine removes undesired material from a rotating workpiece in the form of chips by using a tool that may be fed deeply into the work and is traversed through it [22]. One of the most versatile and widely used machine tools in the world. Numerous objects, including nuts, bolts, piston, ram, pump parts, electric motor sleeves, airframe components, rifle barrels, candlesticks, railway spikes, cue sticks, wooden bowls, baseball bats, and crankshafts, can be produced using the lathe machine. There are various types of CNC lathe machining. Different types of CNC lathes can be identified based on the quantity of movement axes [23], and these are:

(i) 2-axis—can be used for drilling, tapping, facing, and machining of the outer and inner diameters. Adds a live tool system for milling, boring, etc.
(ii) 3-axis—A second tool carrier or turret is frequently added in a 4-axis machine.

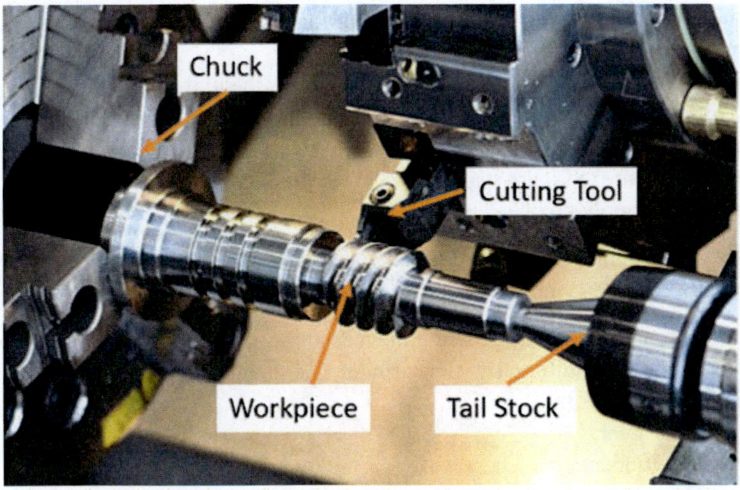

Fig. 1.3 Illustration of lathe machining process

(iii) 5 and 6-axis—adds an extra Y axis and, on occasion, a B axis to one or both tool carriers.
(iv) Multi-Spindle Machines—often known as specialized CNC lathes with more than six axes, are also offered with cutting-edge capabilities and versatility.

Furthermore, there are several methods for lathe machining, but the turning process is the most commonly used method in most industrial manufacturing. The most frequent machining operation on a lathe is turning as shown in Fig. 1.3. During the turning process, a cutting tool removes material from the outside diameter of a spinning object. The main objective of turning is to reduce the workpiece's diameter to a suitable size. There are two categories for turning operations: rough and finish [24].

1.2.5 Grinding Machining

A grinding wheel is employed in the machining process of grinding to remove material from a workpiece. The workpiece is chopped off by the grinding wheel as it rotates, producing a smooth surface characteristic [25]. In a nutshell, the grinding machine works by feeding the workpiece against a rotating abrasive wheel. The material is removed as a result of the friction that is created between the wok price and the tool. The following step can be followed to achieved a sustainable grinding process.

- Start by using a fresh brush to clean the machine.

- In the worktable, the workpiece is fixed. The grinding wheel tool is likewise placed in the portion with the tool holders.
- As the machine has not yet begun, we now adjust the tool and workpiece with the aid of the traversing wheel, bring them into contact, and check that there is only a small gap.
- After all, be sure to fill the space between the tool and the workpiece by inspecting the coolant supply nozzle.

Grinding machining has various types for manufacturing mechanical component. The various types of grinding machines [26] are as follows:

- The bench grinder. These grinding devices are mounted to a table or workbench.
- Hand chopper. Additionally, this grinder is mounted to a workbench or table Grinder on a platform
- Pedestal Grinder,
- Compact Grinder,
- Adjustable Grinder,
- Precision Grinder

These are a few examples of the different types of grinding machines, Fig. 1.4 illustrate grinding machining process.

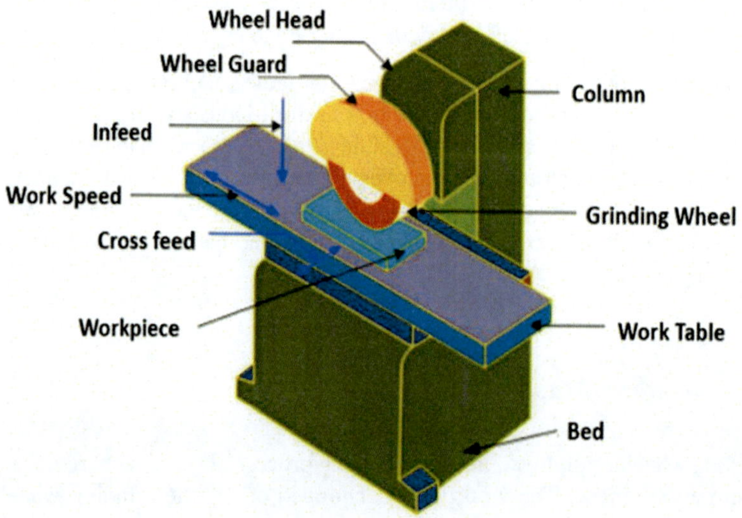

Fig. 1.4 Illustration of grinding machining process

1.2.6 Drilling Machining

The drilling machine, commonly referred to as the drill press, is a cutting procedure that creates circular holes in solid materials such as metal, plastic, wood, rocks, etc. by using drill bits of various diameters. The multi-point drill bit spins with the cutting tool [27]. The drill is firmly pressed on the workpiece as it turns at speeds between hundreds and thousands of revolutions per minute and illustration of drilling machining process is presented in Fig. 1.5. The cutting edge removes chips from the workpiece by cutting them off with the given force. Small hand-held power drills, bench-mounted models, and lastly floor-mounted models are all distinct sizes and types of drilling machines. They are used to do tasks including tapping both large and tiny holes as well as countersinking, counter boring, reaming, and spot facing. The principles and drill bits used to accomplish the activities vary greatly since drilling machines are capable of performing them. To accomplish different hole sizes on the tasks outlined above, drilling machines are utilized in conjunction with drill bits that have sharp cutting edges. To get a good hole, the operator needs to know how to set up the work, adjust speed and feed, as well as coolant.

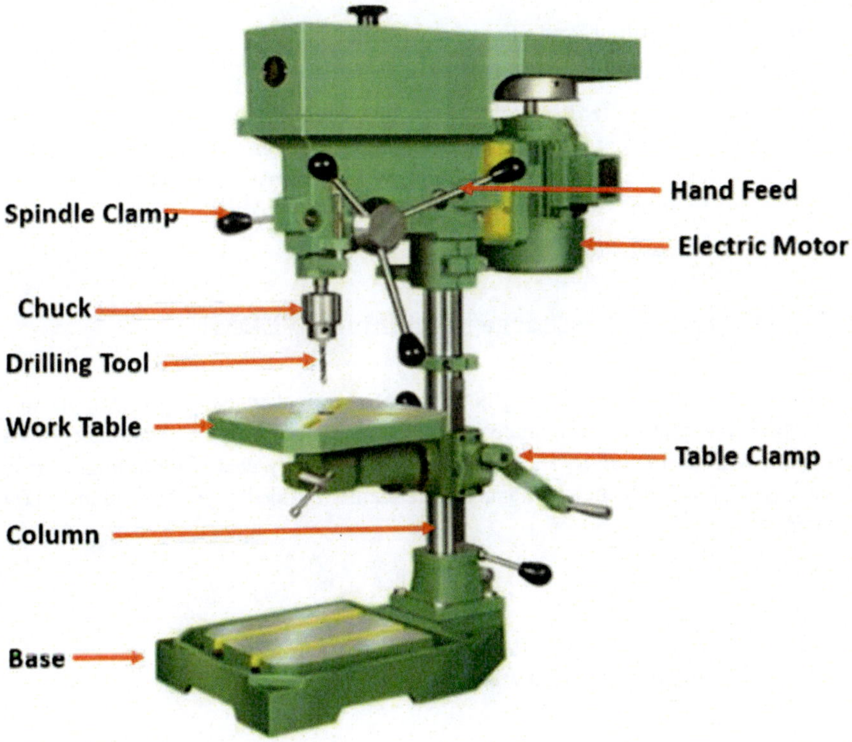

Fig. 1.5 Illustration of drilling machining process

Maintenance and Safety drilling process is very important in machining process. The following can be applied to maintain and provide safety are:

(a) Lubricating the interface between the drill bit and the workpiece as it is being used is one of the essential maintenance procedures for a drilling machine. By doing so, the temperature and friction produced by the moving parts are reduced. Some manufacturers include instructions for the appropriate cleaning and lubrication techniques [28, 29].
(b) To prevent damage to the moving parts, it is expected that the drilling machine will be cleaned up after each usage and cleared of chips.
(c) To prevent harming the precision fit, make sure the spindles and sleeves are free of grit. Oil should be sparingly covered on the surfaces of the machine parts, particularly the bed, to avoid rust.

There are various drilling machines used in manufacturing include the following:

- Portable Drilling
- Sensitive Drilling
- Standing Drilling
- Radial Drilling
- Gang Drilling
- Multi-Spindle Drilling Equipment
- Machine for Deep Mole Drilling.

In summary of the different machining method of CNC lies in the way and method of the machine and the component spin is the primary. For example, milling machines entail revolving a multi-bladed or tipped cutting tool against a fixed workpiece, while lathes involve rotating a workpiece against a single-bladed cutting tool.

1.3 Wire Electro Discharge Machining (WEDM)

Wire electro discharge machining is an unconventional machining technique that is frequently applied to hard materials. This technique is well-liked since EDM can work with all materials, regardless of how hard they are. Modern engineering materials used in harsh environments are frequently molded or created via the EDM technique [30].

1.3.1 Working Principle of Wire Electro Discharge Machining Operations

(a) The EDM wire-cut machine is a type of electro discharge machining in which an electrode is made of a thin electrically conducting wire, typically brass.

(b) The workpiece and the wire (electrode) in the EDM-wire cut machine are both connected to the terminals of the DC pulse generator, and they are both submerged in a dielectric fluid and separated by a little gap (spark-gap). The EDM-wire cut machine's dielectric fluid is deionized water.
(c) The metallic wire used in the EDM-wire cut machine moves slowly and has a variable speed. The top and bottom diamond wire guides allow the metallic wire to move continuously from the top spool (roller) to the bottom spool. Additionally, a tensioner is included to guarantee proper tension in the moving wire.
(d) The deionized water becomes conductive (ionized) as the EDM wire is moved along the specified path towards the workpiece, enabling spark discharge to happen at a specific spark gap and discharge voltage between the wire and the workpiece surface.
(e) The DC pulse current is briefly disrupted, and continuously flowing deionized water from the EDM-wire cut machine flushes away the small chips, cools the workpiece, and fills the spark-gap area with new deionized water.
(f) The material from the surface of the workpiece is melted and an-nihilated into tiny chips due to the intense electro-thermal heat produced by the spark discharge.
(g) The EDM-wire cut machine cuts material between the moving wire and the workpiece surface using continuous spark discharges. The sparks have a square wave, and the CNC controls the spark-on and spark-off periods.
(h) Since the wire weakens after spark discharge, the wire (electrode) in the EDM-wire cut machine is only used once. The used wire is then spooled at the bottom and cut into little pieces for scrap.
(i) Any complex profile or shape can be programmed and cut using the EDM-wire cut machine, and the profile can run the entire thickness of the workpiece. The movement of the wire is controlled by the CNC program. And annot machine blind cavities with an EDM-wire cut machine; it is only used to cut through cavities.
(j) The EDM-wire cut machine's top and bottom wire guides are crucial for correct wire movement and, consequently, accurate wire cutting;
(k) The wire must be threaded through the through-hole on the workpiece of the EDM-wire cut machine before cutting can begin. Threading is the act of placing the wire through the hole from the top guide to the bottom guide. Either an automatic threading system is available on the EDM-wire cut machine, or threading must be done manually [31].
(l) During the EDM-wire cut procedure, a sensor will be used to detect wire breakage or running out of wire (Fig. 1.6).

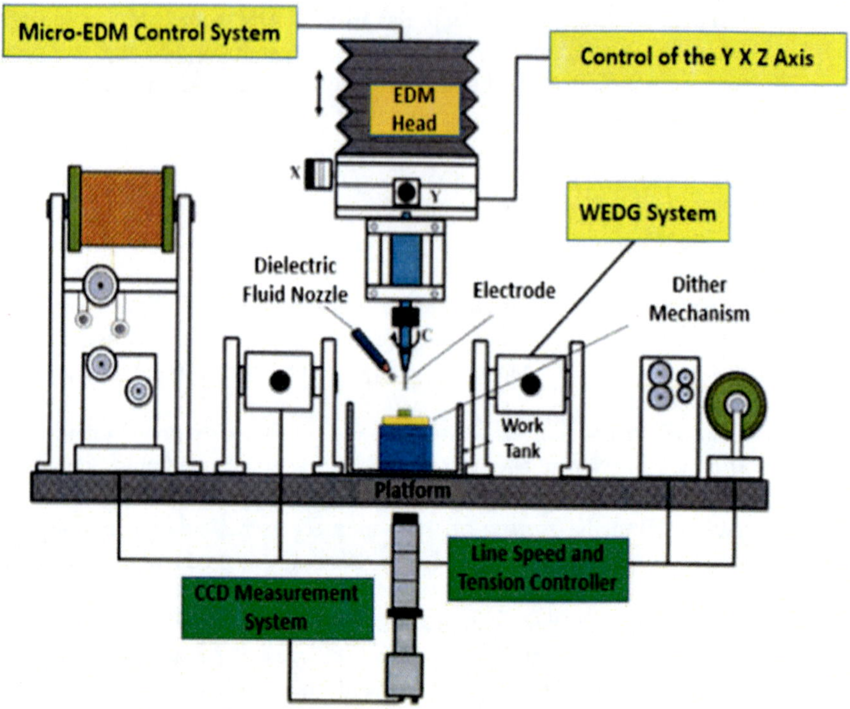

Fig. 1.6 Shows the setup for a method that combines coax cable grinding and micro-electrical discharge machining

1.3.2 Advantages and Disadvantage of WEDM

Table 1.2 depict the several advantages and disadvantages of the AWJM, this tabulated analysis is to give a clear picture of the benefit and limitation of the wire electro discharge machining operations.

Table 1.2 Advantages and disadvantages of WEDM machining operations

S/No.	Advantages of WEDM machining	Disadvantage of WEDM machining
1	Even on small workpieces, wire EDM can be used to cut challenging profiles with precise tolerances, which is not achievable with traditional machining methods	Only materials that are electrically conductive can be cut using EDM-wire cutting

(continued)

Table 1.2 (continued)

S/ No.	Advantages of WEDM machining	Disadvantage of WEDM machining
2	The wire EDM machine works equally well to cut brittle materials like graphite, strong materials like carbide and Inconel, and soft metals like brass and copper	EDM-wire cutting's low cutting speed or material removal rate makes it uneconomical; as a result, its employment is restricted to the machining of extremely hard materials or challenging profiles that cannot be achieved with conventional machines
3	Sharp corners can be cut with a wire cut machine (with negligible radius). And EDM wire cutting has a problem with wire breaking, which results in some time loss and a small amount of wire material	Since the wire (electrode) in EDM-wire cutting can only be used once, the cost is increased
4	Burrs and tool marks are not left after an EDM-wire cut operation	EDM-wire cutting may leave a recast layer on the surface of the workpiece that requires a follow-up procedure like polishing to remove
5	Since the electrode in the EDM-wire cut machine is only a simple wire, the tool's cost is extremely low because it doesn't need to be manufactured	

1.4 Laser Beam Machining (LBM)

The machining procedure known as "laser beam machining" removes material from the surface of the workpiece by heating it up with a laser. It is a specific kind of non-traditional machining method. The laser used in laser beam machining is created by a ruby crystal [32]. When the surface of the workpiece is exposed to the laser. The material surface is then melted and turned to vapor by the heat energy this laser produces. Use of laser beam machining. Currently, it has been determined that the laser machining process is only appropriate in extraordinary circumstances, such as when creating extremely small holes and cutting intricate features in thin, hard materials like ceramics. In partial cutting or engraving, it is also utilized. Other uses include resistor trimming, blanking, and steel metal trimming. Despite the fact that LBM is not a mass material removal technique, it can be used to produce microparts in large quantities.

1.4.1 The Operation of Laser Beam Machining

Let's assume that the atoms in a material are in their ground state, like those in a rod of ruby crystal. The atoms in this medium absorb radiation when a quantum of energy from a light source is made to fall on them [33]. As a result, an electron from one of the medium's atoms jumps to a higher energy level. The following procedure are employed:

(a) The workpiece that has to be cut is placed on the metal work table during operation (which is resistant to being cut by laser beam).
(b) While manually adjusting the control panel, the operator moves the laser head over the workpiece and visually examines the cut.
(c) The associated machine, which was built to duplicate the master drawing or actual profile and was set up on a nearby bench, provided the actual profile.
(d) The power output of the laser in brief bursts is almost 10 kW/cm of the beam cross-section.
(e) A laser beam can be focused in a brief burst to a power density of 100,000 kW/cm and energy of several joules lasting for a minute by focusing on a point that is 1/100 of a square mm in size.
(f) A laser beam can be focused in a brief flash to a power density of 100,000 kW/cm and energy of many joules lasting for a minute fraction of a second by focusing it on a point that is 1/100 of a square mm in size.
(g) Short pulses with, let's say, 100 J of energy are needed for machining.
(h) Therefore, the laser may generate enough heat to melt and evaporate any known substance (Fig. 1.7).

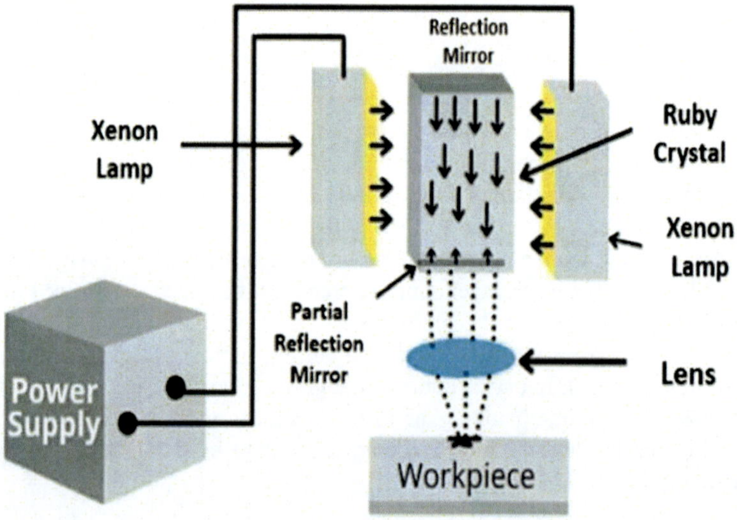

Fig. 1.7 Illustration of the setup of the laser beam machining process

1.4.2 Advantages and Disadvantage of Laser Beam Manufacturing

The following are some of the main benefits and limitation of laser beam machining: The laser's inability to cut metals with high heat conductivity or high reflectivity, such as aluminum, copper, and their alloys, is one of its fundamental drawbacks [34]. The procedure also has the following drawbacks presented in Table 1.3.

1.5 Abrasive Water Jet Machining (AWJM)

A high-velocity water jet powered by water is utilized in the unconventional machining method known as "water jet machining" (WJM) to cut the material. Abrasive Water Jet Machining (AWJM) is the name of the technique in which abrasive particles are added to a rising water jet to enhance trimming and machining [35]. High air velocity (between 180 and 200 m per second) propels the particulate. Because the surface fracture occurs more quickly when an abrasive jet strikes brittle materials like glass and ceramic, the impact of waterjet is more noticeable when cutting those materials. It is additionally more effective when cutting and machining components like tungsten and tungsten-carbide, which are challenging to machine using conventional techniques. There are two categories of water jets are involved kind and type suspended, the working principle during machining operation is presented in Fig. 1.8.

Table 1.3 Advantages and disadvantage of LBM machining operations

S/No.	Advantages of laser beam machining	Disadvantage of laser beam machining
1	The tool and the workpiece are in close proximity	Its overall effectiveness (10–15%) is rather modest
2	Any material, including nonmetals, can be machined	It has a remarkably low rate of material removal
3	There is a possibility of drilling and cutting in inaccessible locations	The technique is just for thin sheets
4	Because of the collimated beam, the heat-affected zone is quite tiny	Not all of the machined holes are square and straight
5	No tool wear exists	The short lifespan of the lash lamp makes the laser system rather ineffective
6	It is possible to machine very tiny holes and soft materials like rubber and plastic	It is expensive

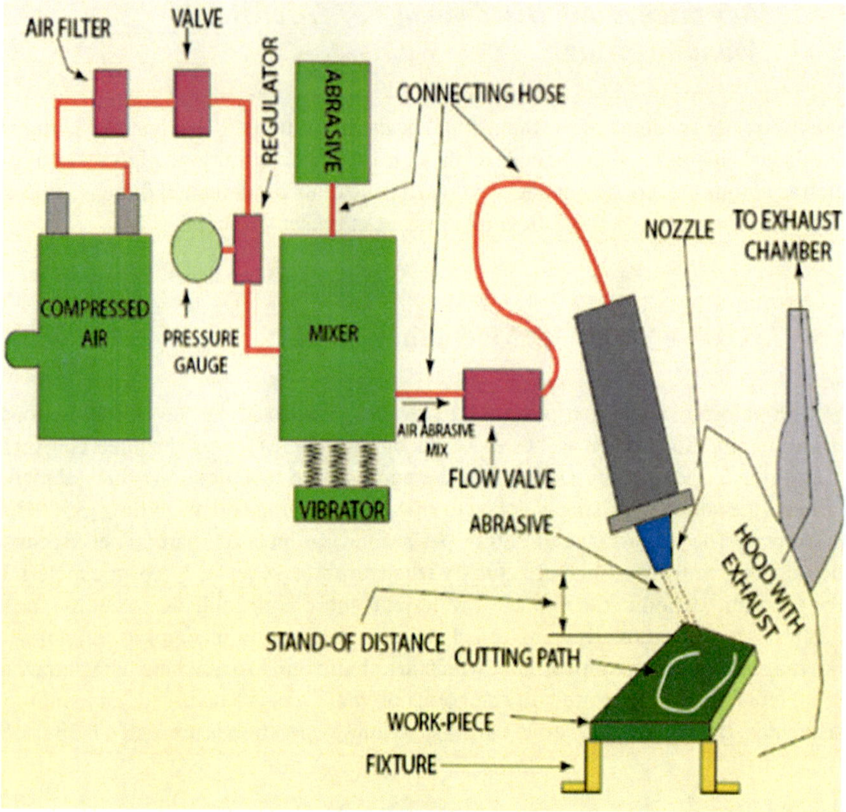

Fig. 1.8 Illustration of the abrasive jet machining in operations

1.5.1 Working Principle of Abrasive Jet Machining Operations

(a) The Water Jet Machine (WJM) employs a high-pressure water stream that has been transformed into a high-velocity water jet as a cutting tool to machine and cut the materials; the water jet leaves the nozzle at an extremely high velocity and impacts the point of cutting on the work-piece.
(b) The high-velocity water jet from the WJM strikes the workpiece and causes a crack in the material, which causes material failure and material particles to break off from the workpiece surface. In the WJM, the metal continues to fail, crack, and separate from the workpiece while being cut to the appropriate profile.
(c) The WJM process involves high pressure water that enters the nozzle and high velocity water that exits the nozzle aperture (0.2–0.5 mm) at 800–1000 m per

second. This is the recommended approach for cutting hard, brittle, and rubber-like materials. The WJM process can machine and cut any material, from rubber to metals.

(d) A water mist may be formed around the cutting region, and the tools in this area need to be covered. The water jet of the WJM removes the metal particles (chips) and sends them out through the drain system for further filtering and recycling.

(e) Abrasive water jet (AWJ) cutting is the technique of adding particulate to a rising water spray to increase the cutting efficiency of the WJM process is called AWJM [36].

1.5.2 Advantages and Disadvantage of AWJM

The benefits of the WJM and AWJM processes are listed in Table 1.4.

Table 1.4 Advantages and disadvantage of AWJM machining operations

S/No.	Advantages of AWJM machining	Disadvantage of AWJM machining
1	The WJM or AWJM technique can safely cut materials like tool steels where the extra heat produced during the cutting modifies the material's properties	Materials that are damaged or deteriorate when exposed to water cannot be cut with AWJM or WJM
2	A heat-affected zone is not created by WJM or AWJM (HAZ).and Materials cut with a WJM or AWJM typically don't need extra steps like deburring	Surface finish suffers when cutting at higher speeds
3	Reduced material waste as a result of narrower cutting (kerf)	As they cut the material, AWJM and WJM cause cracks to form and spread (due to the impact of a high-velocity jet of water and abrasive)
4	Since there is no tool wear, there is no need to re-sharpen the tool	The AWJM/WJM equipment has a higher initial cost, therefore the operators must carefully consider its utility and returns before making a choice
5	Cutting forces produced by the WJM and AWJM processes are minimal and the amount of tooling needed is minimal. Ra (surface finish) values between 150 and 250 microns are achievable	Brittle materials should be cut with particular care and attention since the cracks may extend beyond the cutting path
6	AWJM and WJM can cut brittle and hard materials like porcelain as well as soft materials like rubber and metals	Given that it cuts taper; the waterjet method is inaccurate for cutting thicker materials. Because of this, waterjet cutters are often only able to cut materials and sheet metals up to a 4-inch thickness

(continued)

Table 1.4 (continued)

S/ No.	Advantages of AWJM machining	Disadvantage of AWJM machining
7	For cutting reflective metals like copper and aluminum, which are challenging for lasers, the AWJM technique is perfect	The WJM/use AWJM's of high pressure and high velocity water raises safety issues as well as the noise level

1.6 Electro Discharge Machining (EDM)

EDM is a non-traditional machining method that is specifically intended to cut metals that cannot be cut using standard techniques. Only materials that are electrically conductive can be used for EDM. Electrical Discharge Machining, also known as EDM, can be used to create delicate holes and complicated curves that are challenging to make with a grinder or other tools [37]. EDM cutting tools can be manufactured of titanium carbide, Inconel, toughened too metal, or kovar. Another name for EDM is "Spark Machining." This name was given because the metal is removed using a quick succession of recurrent electrical discharges. These electrical discharges use the work piece and an electrode as their conducting paths. A fluid that is always flowing is used to flush away the minimal amount of removed material. The workpiece is given the desired shape through repeated discharge. Ram EDM and Wire EDM are the two main EDM techniques. The electrodes are where these two methods differ most from one another. Graphite electrodes are utilized in ram EDM. Traditional techniques are used to mill these electrodes, and a unique shape is created that connects to the power supply. Additionally, a ram is linked to the electrodes. The electrodes are introduced into the workpiece once all the setups are complete. The entire procedure is carried out in a fluid bath that is submerged. The electrode in wire electrode manufacturing is a thin wire. Brass wires that have undergone special processing are utilized to feed the substance. The workpiece is sliced using electrical discharges to achieve the required shape. Typically, wire EDM is carried out in a water bath. Figure 1.9 present a schematic illustration of an EDM.

Principle: The fundamental tenet of electrical discharge machining is the removal of metal via spark erosion. EDM spark erosion is the same as an electric spark, both of which leave a small hole in the metal they impact [38]. As a result of the spark created by this action, heat is created, which erodes and evaporates metal. Both the work piece and the tool used in this machining technique must be made of conductive material.

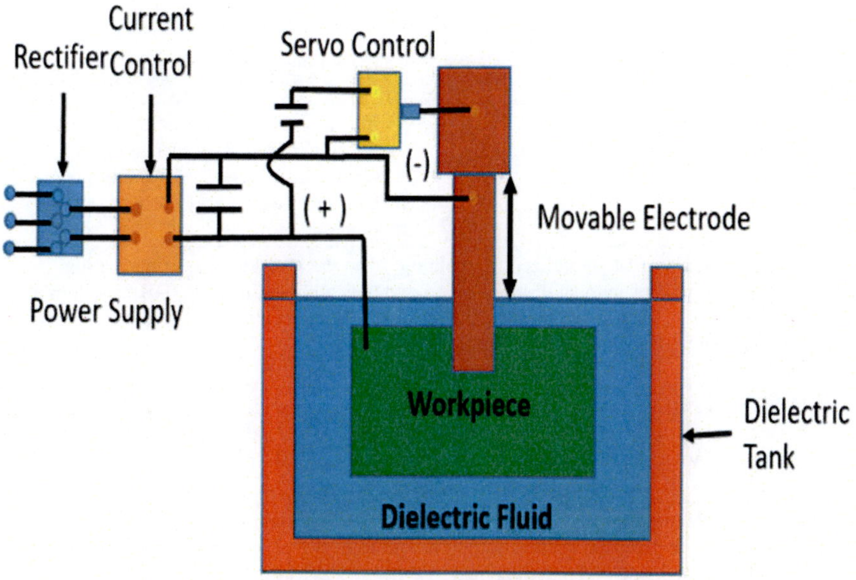

Fig. 1.9 Schematic illustration of an EDM during operation

1.6.1 Working Principles of Electrical Discharge Machining

The work piece in this procedure needs to have good electrical conductivity. This technique can only be used to machine electric conductive materials. The following is how EDM functions.

(a) First, dielectric fluid is applied to both the work piece and the tool. The dielectric fluid aids in arc discharge management. Additionally, this clears the work cavity of any dangling tools and material from the work piece.
(b) The work piece and the tool are separated by a very small distance thanks to a servomechanism. In order for an arc to form properly, this spacing is ideal. It is comparable to the width of a human hair.
(c) The tool is made to resemble the work piece's opposite shape.
(d) A spark is created between the tool and work piece by a high frequency current applied to an electrode. This spark produces a lot of energy in the work cavity.
(e) Due to erosion and evaporate ion, the metal was taken out of the work piece.
(f) To avoid them forming a bridge that would create a short circuit, the chips or suspended particles between the tool and work piece should be removed. Dielectric fluid is continuously supplied to accomplish this.
(g) Due to overcut, the EDM creates a cavity that is slightly larger than the electrode [39].

Table 1.5 Advantages and disadvantage of EDM machining operations

S/ No.	Advantages of EDM	Disadvantage of EDM
1	Hardened dies can be machined and Replicating intricate shapes is possible	In comparison to conventional machining, the power needed for machining is significantly higher. (120 J/mm^2) that is it consume more energy during machining process
2	Harder materials that are utilized for molding and other non-conventional machining techniques like forging and press tools, like steel alloys or tungsten carbides, can be replicated	The steel workpieces, a thin coating typically ranging from 0.01 to 0.10 mm thick and containing 4% carbon may be deposited
3	Workpieces created using EDM feature micro-craters that may efficiently hold lubricants, wear-resistant surfaces can be created	Surface cracking is a possibility when materials fragile at room temperature
4	It is possible to accurately drill very small holes and tThe precision is quite high. It is possible to attain a 0.005 mm tolerance	The Material Removal Rate (MRR) is just 75 mm^3/sec, which is quite low
5	The tool and workpiece avoid making physical touch with one another. Other than blasting pressure, no cutting force is applied	When the microstructures are deformed, etching often follows
6	Therefore, delicate tasks and cylinders can be machined without suffering any harm Compared to the standard machining method, harder metals can be processed relatively quickly	In EDM, sharp corners are challenging to reproduce

1.6.2 Advantages and Disadvantage of EDM

The EDM techniques has been discuses extensively in this chapter, therefore, the advantages and disadvantages of this techniques are depicted in Table 1.5.

1.7 Conclusion

Advanced machining processes such as computer numerical control machining (CNCM), wire electro discharge machining (WEDM), abrasive water jet machining (AWJM), electro-discharge machining (EDM), and electro-discharge machining (EDM) are introduced in chapter one of this book. The chapters discuss their working principles, advantages, and disadvantages as they relate to machining operations. From the analysis carried out on the different advanced machining processes, it can be seen that CNCM is viable for the production of different mechanical components and is one of the major processes currently employed by manufacturing companies. Therefore, this book is primarily focused on the computer numerical control optimization process. The chapter discusses the different types of CNC machining processes, such as lathe, milling, drilling, and grinding; however, from the application of these methods, milling machining processes have wider operation techniques.

From the working principles of the various types of advanced machining, it is stated that there is significance in the application of cutting fluid for the safety of the machining process. Therefore, Chap. 2 of this book will discuss the implementation of cutting fluid and the different techniques of lubrication delivery systems.

References

1. Khan, M.Y., Rao, P.S.: Electrical discharge machining: vital to manufacturing industries. Int. J. Inno. Technol. Explor. Eng. **8**(11), 1696–1701 (2019)
2. Hasan, M., Zhao, J., Jiang, Z.: A review of modern advancements in micro drilling techniques. J. Manuf. Process. **29**, 343–375 (2017)
3. Blakey-Milner, B., Gradl, P., Snedden, G., Brooks, M., Pitot, J., Lopez, E., Leary, M., Berto, F., du Plessis, A.: Metal additive manufacturing in aerospace: a review. Mater. Des. **209**, 110008 (2021)
4. Hasanov, S., Alkunte, S., Rajeshirke, M., Gupta, A., Huseynov, O., Fidan, I., Alifui-Segbaya, F., Rennie, A.: Review on additive manufacturing of multi-material parts: progress and challenges. J. Manuf. Mater. Process. **6**(1), 4 (2021)
5. Fereiduni, E., Ghasemi, A., Elbestawi, M.: Selective laser melting of aluminum and titanium matrix composites: recent progress and potential applications in the aerospace industry. Aerospace **7**(6), 77 (2020)
6. Okokpujie, I.P., Bolu, C.A., Ohunakin, O.S., Akinlabi, E.T., Adelekan, D.S.: A review of recent application of machining techniques, based on the phenomena of CNC machining operations. Procedia Manuf. **35**, 1054–1060 (2019)
7. Ramanathan, A., Krishnan, P.K., Muraliraja, R.: A review on the production of metal matrix composites through stir casting–furnace design, properties, challenges, and research opportunities. J. Manuf. Process. **42**, 213–245 (2019)
8. Singh, P., Singh, L., Singh, S.: A review on magnetically assisted abrasive flow machining and abrasive material type. Proc. Inst. Mech. Eng. Part E: J. Process Mech. Eng., p. 09544089221097356 (2022)
9. Bhowmik, S., Ray, A.: Abrasive water jet machining of composite materials. In: Advanced Manufacturing Technologies, pp. 77–97. Springer, Cham (2017)
10. Gibson, I., Rosen, D.W., Stucker, B., Khorasani, M., Rosen, D., Stucker, B., Khorasani, M.: Additive Manufacturing Technologies, vol. 17. Springer, Cham, Switzerland (2021)
11. Lynn, R., Helu, M., Sati, M., Tucker, T., Kurfess, T.: The state of integrated computer-aided manufacturing/computer numerical control: prior development and the path toward a smarter computer numerical controller. Smart Sustain. Manuf. Syst. **4**(2) (2020)
12. Gonçalves, M.A., Lorini, F.J., Benetti, C., Eckhardt, M., Scheuer, C.J.: Universal parameter language for the programming of numerical controlled machines. Int. J. Adv. Manuf. Technol. **110**(9), 2713–2725 (2020)
13. Papapaschos, V., Bontarenko, E., Krimpenis, A.A.: HydraX, a 3D printed robotic arm for hybrid manufacturing. part ii: control calibration & programming. Procedia Manuf. **51**, 109–115 (2020)
14. Fountas, N.A., Vaxevanidis, N.M., Stergiou, C.I., Benhadj-Djilali, R.: Globally optimal tool paths for sculptured surfaces with emphasis to machining error and cutting posture smoothness. Int. J. Prod. Res. **57**(17), 5478–5498 (2019)

15. Shin, S.J., Woo, J., Kim, D.B., Kumaraguru, S., Rachuri, S.: Developing a virtual machining model to generate MTConnect machine-monitoring data from STEP-NC. Int. J. Prod. Res. **54**(15), 4487–4505 (2016)
16. Jain, A., Bajpai, V.: Introduction to high-speed machining (HSM). In: High Speed Machining, pp. 1–25. Academic Press (2020)
17. Okokpujie, I.P., Ikumapayi, O.M., Okonkwo, U.C., Salawu, E.Y., Afolalu, S.A., Dirisu, J.O., Nwoke, O.N., Ajayi, O.O.: Experimental and mathematical modeling for prediction of tool wear on the machining of aluminium 6061 alloy by high speed steel tools. Open Eng. **7**(1), 461–469 (2017)
18. Singh, P.K., Saini, P., Kumar, D.: Multi response optimization of CNC end milling of AISI H11 alloy steel for rough and finish machining using TGRA. Mater. Today: Proc. **26**, 2564–2573 (2020)
19. Okokpujie, I.P., Ajayi, O.O., Afolalu, S.A., Abioye, A.A., Salawu, E.Y., Udo, M., Okonkwo, U.C., Orodu, K.B., Ikumapayi, O.M.: Modeling and optimization of surface roughness in end milling of aluminium using least square approximation method and response surface methodology. Int. J. Mech. Eng. Technol. (IJMET) **9**(1), 587–600 (2018)
20. Wang, W., Guo, Q., Yang, Z., Jiang, Y., Xu, J.: A state-of-the-art review on robotic milling of complex parts with high efficiency and precision. Robot. Comp. Integr. Manuf. **79**, 102436 (2023)
21. Okokpujie, I.P., Ohunakin, O.S., Bolu, C.A.: Multi-objective optimization of machining factors on surface roughness, material removal rate and cutting force on end-milling using MWCNTs nano-lubricant. Progr. Addit. Manuf. **6**(1), 155–178 (2021)
22. Sentyakov, K., Peterka, J., Smirnov, V., Bozek, P., Sviatskii, V.: Modeling of boring mandrel working process with vibration damper. Materials **13**(8), 1931 (2020)
23. Joch, R., Šajgalík, M., Czán, A., Holubják, J., Cedzo, M., Čep, R.: Effects of process cutting parameters on the Ti-6Al-4V turning with monolithic driven rotary tool. Materials **15**(15), 5181 (2022)
24. Zubair, A.F., Mansor, M.S.A.: Embedding firefly algorithm in optimization of CAPP turning machining parameters for cutting tool selections. Comput. Ind. Eng. **135**, 317–325 (2019)
25. Zhang, Y., Kang, R., Gao, S., Huang, J., Zhu, X.: A new model of grit cutting depth in wafer rotational grinding considering the effect of the grinding wheel, workpiece characteristics, and grinding parameters. Precis. Eng. **72**, 461–468 (2021)
26. Lopes, J.C., Garcia, M.V., Volpato, R.S., de Mello, H.J., Ribeiro, F.S.F., de Angelo Sanchez, L.E., de Oliveira Rocha, K., Neto, L.D., Aguiar, P.R., Bianchi, E.C.: Application of MQL technique using TiO_2 nanoparticles compared to MQL simultaneous to the grinding wheel cleaning jet. Int. J. Adv. Manuf. Technol. **106**(5), 2205–2218 (2020)
27. Hay, R.A., Galimberti, J.M.: Cutting and wear applications. In: Handbook of Industrial Diamonds and Diamond Films, pp. 1135–1147. CRC Press (2018)
28. Xu, J., Ji, M., Davim, J.P., Chen, M., El Mansori, M., Krishnaraj, V.: Comparative study of minimum quantity lubrication and dry drilling of CFRP/titanium stacks using TiAlN and diamond coated drills. Compos. Struct. **234**, 111727 (2020)
29. Okokpujie, I.P., Sinebe, J.E., Tartibu, L.K., Adeoye, A.O.M., Kelechi, S.E., Akinlabi, E.T.: Ratio study of high-pressure lubrication and cutting parameters effects on machining operations and its effect towards sustainable machining: a review. J. Eur. des Systemes Automatises **55**(2), 197–205 (2022)
30. Conde, A., Arriandiaga, A., Sanchez, J.A., Portillo, E., Plaza, S., Cabanes, I.: High-accuracy wire electrical discharge machining using artificial neural networks and optimization techniques. Robot. Comp. Integr. Manuf. **49**, 24–38 (2018)
31. Vembathurajesh, A., Selvakumar, S., Ramakrishnan, T., Sundaram, M.: Graphene applications in unconventional machining processes–a review. Mater. Today: Proc. **52**, 1326–1330 (2022)
32. Agrawal, R., Wang, C.: Laser beam machining. In: Encyclopedia of Nanotechnology, 2nd ed., pp.1739–1753. Springer, Netherlands (2016)
33. Fisher, J.C.: Basic laser physics and interaction of laser light with soft tissue. In: Endoscopic Laser Surgery Handbook, pp. 1–130. CRC Press (2020)

34. Ullah, S., Li, X., Guo, G., Rodríguez, A.R., Li, D., Du, J., Cui, L., Wei, L., Liu, X.: Influence of the fiber laser cutting parameters on the mechanical properties and cut−edge microfeatures of a AA2B06−T4 aluminum alloy. Opt. Laser Technol. **156**, 108395 (2022)
35. Chakraborty, S., Mitra, A.: Parametric optimization of abrasive water-jet machining processes using grey wolf optimizer. Mater. Manuf. Process. **33**(13), 1471–1482 (2018)
36. Karkalos, N.E., Karmiris-Obratański, P., Kudelski, R., Markopoulos, A.P.: Experimental study on the sustainability assessment of AWJ machining of Ti-6Al-4V using glass beads abrasive particles. Sustainability **13**(16), 8917 (2021)
37. Prasad, K., Chakraborty, S.: A decision guidance framework for non-traditional machining processes selection. Ain Shams Eng. J. **9**(2), 203–214 (2018)
38. Klocke, F., Klink, A., Veselovac, D., Aspinwall, D.K., Soo, S.L., Schmidt, M., Schilp, J., Levy, G., Kruth, J.P.: Turbomachinery component manufacture by application of electrochemical, electro-physical and photonic processes. CIRP Ann. **63**(2), 703–726 (2014)
39. Rashid, A., Jahan, M.P.: Microfabrication by electrical discharge machining-based hybrid processes. In: Micro Electro-fabrication, pp. 33–62. Elsevier (2021)

Chapter 2
Cutting Fluid and Its Application with Different Delivering Machining Techniques

Abstract Cutting fluid is a major aspect of the machining process when machining metals with material adhesion challenges, as the fluid assists in the flushing of the chips from the cutting region and reduces the temperature generation and friction during the process. This chapter focuses on the cutting fluid and its application with various delivery mechanisms for machining. Because the quality of the cutting fluid applied at the cutting region is what drives the current trend in sustainable machining processes, the classifications of cutting fluid—straight machining oils, soluble oils, semi-synthetic cutting fluids, and synthetic fluids—are covered in this chapter. Also, the chapter analyzed the six various machining lubrication supply methods, including the solid lubrication process, flood cooling (a traditional process), cryogenic cooling, high pressure cooling, and compressed air vapour gas (CAVG) as coolant. The advantages and disadvantages of the lubricant delivery systems were carried out to further bring out the sustainability factors of the techniques in the manufacturing process. The findings show that the MQL is a sustainable and efficient process for machining, and the study recommended that the trend of producing a hybrid delivery system that can cryogenically MQL-deliver with high pressure continue.

Keywords Cutting fluid · Cryogenic cooling · CAVG · Machining · MQL · Machining optimization

2.1 Introduction

A cutting lubricant is one of the essential parameters used in the manufacturing industry; the method has been in use for decades [1–3]. The primary reasons for adopting cutting oil in machining operations are to enhance the performance of the machining operations, reduce thermal deformations of working materials, help flush the chips away from the cutting region, and help reduce surface roughness, which in return will minimize the wear rate of the materials, protect and enhance the cutting tool life, reduce cutting force, friction, and vibration, and increase the rate

I. P. Okokpujie and L. K. Tartibu, *Modern Optimization Techniques for Advanced Machining*, Studies in Systems, Decision and Control 485,
https://doi.org/10.1007/978-3-031-35455-7_2

of material removal [4–6]. Cutting lubricants employed in machining have different classifications, including straight machining oils, soluble oils, semi-synthetic cutting fluids, and synthetic fluids [6].

(i) **Straight machining oils** are non-emulsifiable and are used in machining processes without dilution with water or any other solvent. The machinist applied straight oil in its original state without mixing the oil with any chemical substance. Manufacturers obtain straight oils from animal fat, vegetable, petroleum, or mineral sources and typically include high-pressure additives such as sulphur and chlorine [8]. They have the advantages of excellent lubricity, good resistance to corrosion, and good constancy. Straight-machining oil helps in reducing cutting force and friction during the machining operation. The primary issue with straight-machining oil is its insufficient cooling property coupled with its inability to function during the machining process without producing smoke. Straight oil cannot dissipate heat efficiently in the cutting region during machining [9].

(ii) **Soluble oils** are types of cutting fluids widely used in machining operations. They have little or no odor and are designed as lubricants and coolants for metal cutting processes. Industries develop soluble oils from hydro-treated mineral oils containing a mixture of inhibitors and emulsifiers [10]. From the literature, soluble oils have been established as machining lubricants with excellent cooling effects. Therefore, soluble oil is a suitable replacement for straight oil during a machining operation. It can be applied to metals with differing compositions. It is friendly to the environment, reduces thermal failure, accommodates water rigidity, and sustains pH stability between 9 and 10. It is worthy of note that including water in the mixture will increase the corrosion rate of the cutting fluid on the metal during machining and after machining [11].

(iii) **Synthetic fluids** are man-made cutting fluids that are extracted from metallic and non-metallic compounds. Manufacturers produce this lubricant from crude oil and synthetic raw materials. Synthetic cutting fluid is a replacement for refined petroleum cutting oil [12]. The advantages of synthetic cutting fluid are enormous. They have excellent cooling effects, good lubricating properties, high corrosion resistance, safe handling, hard water stability, neatness, ease of maintenance, and are effective in high-temperature machining operations. The major disadvantages are that they are relatively costly, toxic, and easily polluted by external lubricants [13].

(iv) **Semi-synthetic cutting fluids** are a combination of synthetic metal cutting liquid and soluble oil. The fat content in cutting solutions and synthetic liquids is minimal, at around 30% [14]. Semi-synthetic fluids combine the physical and chemical lubricity, cleanliness, and cooling characteristics of soluble oil and synthetic fluid, and they form a translucent liquid when mixed with water. They have excellent stability as lubricants and have cooling properties. The major disadvantage is that semi-synthetic oil has a high water content, which will aid in corrosion because of surface interactions [15].

The primary purpose of cutting fluids includes the following aspects: flushing of the chips, cooling, lubrication, and corrosion protection. The cooling effect of cutting fluids is to remove the excessive heat generated during the machining operation. Much heat is generated during the metal-to-metal machining process due to deformation and frictional sliding. This high heat generated can shorten the cutting tool life, affect production time, increase friction, increase vibrations, and cause unattractive surface quality [14].

Lubricants are employed in machining operations to reduce the friction generated by the contact between metal to metal during cutting or shaping operations. Oils also reduce the cutting force, moving unwanted chips from the cutting zone. A suitable lubricant should possess a useful viscosity index, excellent thermal stability, high boiling point, and low freezing point for the fluid to withstand high temperature [16]. An adequate cutting fluid provides excellent corrosion protection for the cutting tool and the workpieces. It also reduces rust during operation, minimises wear rate, and improves the life span of the cutting tool and workpiece alongside other machining parameters, during its application at the machining region [17]. Also, the flushing of the chips from the machining region needs the implementation of cutting fluids during machining without damaging the surface of the workpiece. This removal of the chips from the cutting region assists in prevents the occurrence of chips discontinuity that can lead to high vibration and reduce the cutting tool life [18]. The characteristics of cutting liquids include: good thermal conductivity for heat reduction, high-quality lubrication, high flash point to avoid fire threat, oxidation stability, high corrosion resistance, the cutting fluid must not be quickly rancid, cutting fluid must be free from unpleasant odour during machining operations, should be environmentally friendly to both the working materials and the operators, suitable viscosity and the ability to reduce friction, must be able to reduce heat generation at the cutting zone, the ability to recycle and should be economically viable, to lengthen the lifespan of the cutting tool, reduce workpiece thermal deformation and to enhance surface finishing.

Cutting fluid and machining parameter characteristics are the essential aspect of machining operation that either strengthen the mechanical component or cause it to fail during the process [19–21]. According to Joshua et al. [22], there is a need to develop and optimise a biodegradable cutting fluid for the machining process, to enable the manufacturers to produce quality mechanical components with a good quality machined surface. This biodegradable cutting fluid will assist in reducing the energy consumption, wear rate, and corrosion on the cutting tool and the workpiece material during operation. Osama et al. [23] in their review work, recommended the use of corrosion-free cutting fluid in machining operations. Phuoc et al. [24] studied the viscosity and thermal conductivity of nano-lubricant, and the result shows that nanoparticles have good thermal conductivity. The authors concluded and recommended that nano-lubricants should be efficiently-utilised in machining operation. Pervaiz et al. [25] affirm that cutting fluid is one of the parameters that can lead to good quality machining.

Sani et al. [26] concluded that the thermo-mechanical loads in machining operations have significant effects on the surface finish of the material and the cutting tool.

The result proved that the thermo-mechanical load leads to high surface roughness and breakage of the cutting tool during the machining. The authors also recommended that the use of vegetable oil is highly needed. This is due to the significant effects vegetable oil have on the microstructural characteristics of the metals after machining. Furthermore, when vegetable oil is disposed of, it is eco-friendly without causing any environmental pollutions. The authors carried out an experimental study on Jatropha-based cutting fluid and the synthetic Esther-based MQL machining fluid. The result shows that this vegetable oil-based machining fluid performs excellently in reducing friction between the cutting tool and the working materials during operations. Finally, the authors also recommended that the additions of nanoparticles in the base vegetable oil should be utilised to improve the thermal resistance of the vegetable oil in machining operations. According to Okonkwo et al. [27], the study of machining parameters in end milling, turning, and grinding cannot be overemphasised. These machining parameters, if not adequately studied before any experimental analysis, can lead to vibrations and friction that can damage the workpiece. Nwoke et al. [28] carried out a study on vibration analysis and discovered that the machining parameters have much influence on CNC machining. Onoroh et al. [29] studied the effects of machining parameters on the cutting tool. From the conclusion of the study, the authors stated that machining parameters could easily damage or reduce the tool life during the machining process. The authors also recommended that subsequent machining operations should involve an eco-friendly lubricant to minimise the vibration occurrences during machining. However, apart eco-friendly lubricant, the method of lubrication delivery still has significant effects in the manufacturing process, which is needed to be discussed in the Sect. 2.2 delivery techniques of machining process.

2.2 Lubricant Delivery Techniques for Machining Operations

The movement of globalization has made it possible for most nations to produce things. As a result of increased rivalry among manufacturing firms, the quality of the items produced has varied [30]. Therefore, each manufacturing industry want to produce quality product at low cost, reduce material waist, and increase machining accuracy. In order to achieve this desire and to overcome the challenges of vibration, friction, rough surface, high cutting force that led to high energy consumption have led to the development of different techniques of fluid delivery in machining operations [31]. This section of the chapter two discusses the application of different delivery system of fluid in machining process such as minimum quality lubrication, CAVG cooling, high pressure cooling, Compressed Air Vapour Gas as Coolant (CAVG), Flood cooling (Conventional process), cryogenic cooling, and solid lubrication process. These different machining techniques are thus adopted to obtain good quality products at a low cost as illustrated in Fig. 2.1.

Fig. 2.1 Lubricant delivery techniques in manufacturing

2.2.1 Flood Cooling Techniques Machining Operations

Various techniques can administer the lubrication process, and the most well-known type is flood cooling. This strategy provides a continuous lubricant flow to the tool work area. It requires a few apparatuses in the framework, primarily filters, a recirculation setup, nozzles, pipes, and the lubricant reservoir [7].

Flood cooling, which is best represented as a continuous stream of a controlled amount of coolant, evacuates chips through a blushing activity [32]. This technique is more often than not a yardstick for various experiments because of its extensive use in regular machining operations. Unfortunately, it is inadequate in a couple of instances. Flood cooling does not depend on the precise amount; it is applied straight to the cutting region. In some extraordinary cases, where titanium alloy is used, the chip blocks the coolant or lubricant from being administered to the area between the cutting tool and the workpiece. Figure 2.2 shows the typical flood cooling process in machining. Along these lines, the cutting edge encounters a substantial thermal load, resulting in reduced tool life [33].

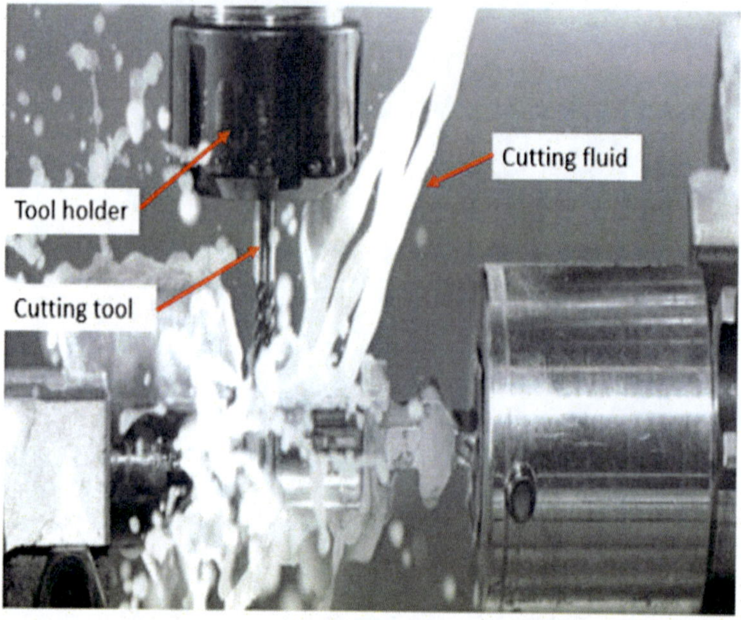

Fig. 2.2 Illustration of flood cooling process during machining operations

2.2.2 *Solid Coolants/Lubricants Operation*

Solid lubricants and coolants are elements in the solid state, for example, graphite, carbon nanotubes, diamond, molybdenum disulfide, and tungsten disulfide. They have uniform heat distribution, high conductivity, and perform better than conventional cutting liquids. In milling or lathe machining that works unevenly under high pressure and high machining speed, solid coolants or lubricants should be implemented for better performance [34].

Solid lubricants are free of the history of pathogens and don't provide any health risks to workers as a result. They are also easily accessible. A few illustrations are given to support the use of solid lubricants in machining. When grinding moderate and hard materials, lubricating like graphite and calcium fluoride (CaF_2) are used in a variety of ways. Use techniques include supplying fine powder at the grinding zone, blending it with paraffin, and supplying it there in paste form [35].

2.2.3 *Cryogenic Cooling in Machining Operation*

Cryogenic machining (using either CO_2 snow or LN_2, at 85 °C and 195.8 °C, respectively) is considered lethal-free and ecologically friendly when contrasted to traditional metalworking liquids [36]. Additionally, it has been demonstrated

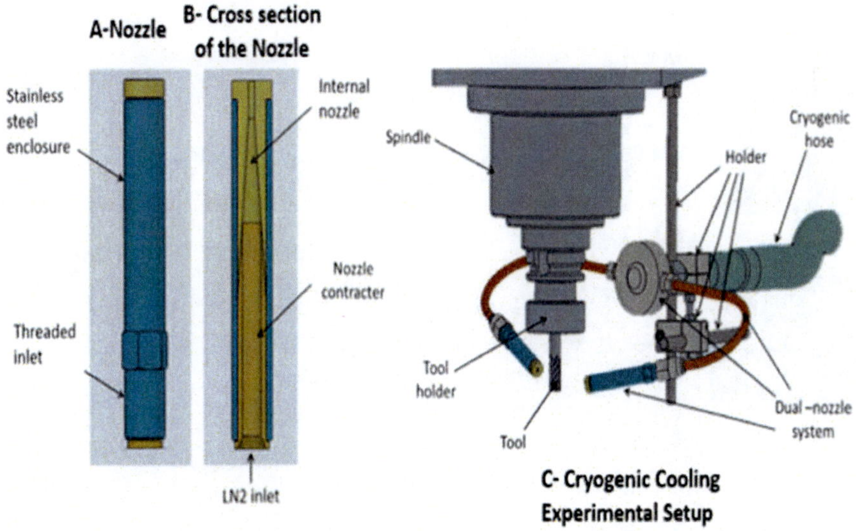

Fig. 2.3 Cryogenic cooling method for machining

that cryogenic chilling with LN_2 increases tool life and creates exceptional surface finish characteristics, such as residual compressive stresses, extremely hard nano-crystalline outer layer, and increased rust resistance [37]. Figure 2.3 illustrates cryogenic machining setup operations. The advantages of machining under a cryogenic condition when contrasted with customary cutting fluid, according to Aggarwal et al. [38], are as follows: Cryogenic cooling is a nature-friendly and clean innovation compared with traditional coolants; it is harmless and stable; it increases tool life and decreases tool wear primarily because of the decrease in tooltip temperature; Cryogenic cooling also has innovative advantage in terms of enlightening the product quality, reducing power consumption, and cutting force. However, the disadvantages of the application of cryogenic cooling are that the process incurs a high cost during the machining process.

2.2.4 MQL Machining Operations

Minimum quantity lubrication (MQL) is a technique developed in recent times whereby a minimal amount of cutting liquid, in aerosol form, is splashed into the cutting zone. The use of MQL minimizes the dangers related to job-related wellbeing and security [39]. A few investigations on MQL notice the constructive outcomes of the strategy on occupational well-being and safety [40]. MQL is administered in the form of micron-sized beads and droplets. The system can be balanced so that the drops are consumed and dried up by the heat generated during the machining. Any surplus quantity could be cleaned or flushed off as soon as the machining is done [41].

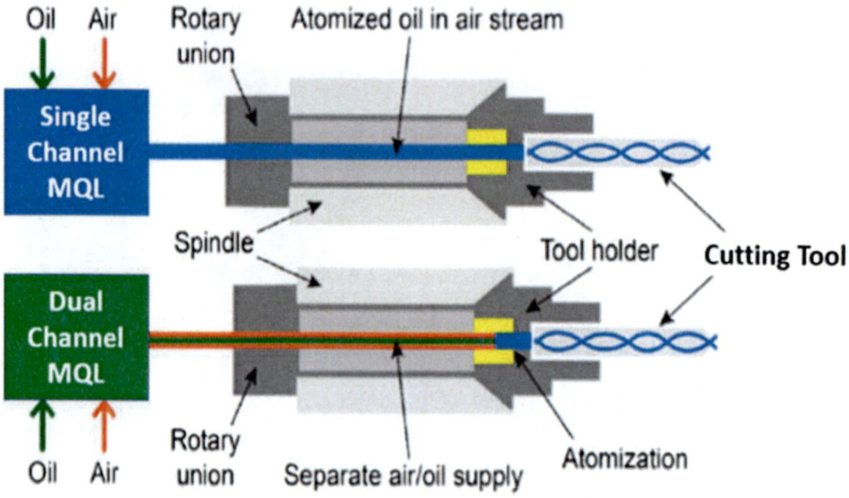

Fig. 2.4 MQL delivery procedure for both single and dual channel

Traditional methods of applying cutting fluids, such as wet and dry machining, have given rise to several environmental problems as well as safety and health hazards in the machining sector. Hence, numerous studies of the MQL fluid distribution method have been conducted over the years to ensure that cutting fluids are supplied optimally during machining in order to significantly lower production costs and increase machinability [42]. The MQL cutting fluid delivery technology, also known as microlubrications or near-dry lubrications, utilizes compressed air as the supply medium to significantly minimize the amount of lubricant or coolant that is applied from the spray nozzle to the cutting region, as presented in Fig. 2.4.

Superior lubrication, corrosion prevention, high spark and boiling temperatures, are frequent use [43], non-natural ester (usually vegetable oil), is frequently utilized. However, in contrast to the synthetic ester, fatty alcohols perform better in terms of heat transmission and produce less waste when they evaporate. When lubrication is a crucial requirement for the machining operation, the synthetic ester is used in certain operations. Fatty alcohol lubricant is also used in situations that call for cutting fluid to facilitate heat transmission throughout machining.

2.2.5 Compressed Air Vapour Gas as Coolant

Another attractive green method to make cooling and lubrication available during machining depends on the use of ice air as a coolant. The use of chilled, compressed air for cooling purposes is environmentally friendly, and it gives better tool life preservation than conventional cooling. However, various literature reveals that surface completion is delicate if chilled packed air cooling occurs [44]. The delicate surface finishing operation is linked to the interaction of the thermo-mechanics of distortion, which adjusts the microstructure of the developed surface produced by the machining tool. The application of the conventional cooling process and the MQL on the machined surface is superior to the ice air-cooling strategy. Although machining industries developed mist lubrication using vegetable oil and cryogenics to replace mineral oil-based flooding, its insufficient lubrication and cooling property at high speeds prompted a search for a new hybrid (compressed air vapour gas as coolant) solution that provides appropriate cooling and lubrication (C/L), according to Ross et al. [45]. Furthermore, there is currently no information available on the impacts of hybrid cooling on the milling of Nimonic-80A. To assess the viability of using cryogenics with a hybrid cooling strategy, the machining of Nimonic-80A under hybrid C/L was compared to various cooling approaches (flood, cryogenic and MQL). The best cutting circumstances were chosen using the Complex Proportional Assessment (COPRAS) technique to obtain the perfect surface trait. Along with enhancing surface superiority, the hybrid state is regarded as a pioneer in line with the most recent worldwide movement toward viable means of manufacturing. The optimization result showed that the best value, which regulates the energy consumption, is produced by machining with a feed rate of 0.04 mm/rev and a cutting speed of 60 m/min while using a hybrid cooling method. To develop the sustainability assessment among the various cooling settings, the Pugh matrix approach has been used. The study's conclusion demonstrates the viability of the hybrid cooling technique and outlines how turning green works. Besides that, there is a need to investigate the capability of this strategy for cutting hard-to-cut workpieces under a consistent machining approach.

2.2.6 High-Pressure Lubrication in Machining Operations

High-pressure lubrication techniques emerged during the 1980s and 1990s. The research account describes accurately adjusted coolant jets with exceptionally high pressures (100–1000 bar) as a part of the cutting parameter [46]. The preparation of hard-to-machine materials (for example, titanium) ran smoothly. Under this cooling technique, the coolant is injected under high pressure precisely in the cutting region between the workpiece and the rake of the cutting tool. As long as the parameters are in line with the machining process, there will be successful cooling and a decrease in the tool wear rate when compared with conventional cooling techniques. The cutting rate and thrust force will increase productivity. The high-pressure system will prolong the cutting tool in operation with a much lower load demand during the cooling process when contrasted with the conventional cooling method [47].

The important goal of HPC machining is to fundamentally reduce the temperature produced at the machining region between the cutting tool and the workpiece. Furthermore, when machining at a higher cutting speed with the HPC assist at tool-chip interfaces, the chip discontinuity at the machining region is reduced [48]. This is accomplished by applying coolant with high pressure at the cutting zone interface [49]. This procedure can likewise achieve high chip brittleness and control the expulsion rate of the chips with compressive pressure. Flood cooling at the machining region can reduce the machining temperature while machining at a lower speed. The coolant additionally acts as a lubricant in this manner, limiting friction and reducing the cutting forces and, subsequently, tool wear [50]. Kramar and Kopac [51] carried out a study on the use of high-pressure cooling when performing turning operations on materials that are difficult to cut during machining operations. In the experiments, the lubrication pressure was adjusted while the cutting feed, breadth of cut, and cutting speeds remained unchanged. It was found that the breakability of the chips increased with increased lubricant pressure, which had a major impact on washing out the chips at the cutting region throughout operations.

2.3 Advantages and Disadvantages of the Lubricant Delivery Techniques

The advantages and disadvantages of the six techniques of lubricant delivery in machining operations discussed in this chapter are presented in the following sections.

2.3.1 Advantages of Lubrication Delivery System

(i) When applied during delivery, the lubricant in the cutting region enhances the tribological procedures that take place at the tool-workpiece contact to increase the machinability of metals.
(ii) eliminate adverse effects on the environment and lessen some issues relating to the employees' well-being and safety.
(iii) Improve the machining surface of the product.
(iv) Reduce vibration and friction by using high pressure to flush out the chips at the cutting region.
(v) Reduce the contact between the cutting tool and the workpiece in operation by converting the sliding friction into a rolling mechanism.

The advantages are generally analyzed over flood cooling and dry machining processes. It is worthy of note that, from the literature, MQL, known as the minimum quantity lubrication process, is viable and highly efficient. All the experiments and the experimental data employed for the modeling, prediction, and optimization discussed in this book are under the MQL machining operations.

2.3.2 *Disadvantages of Lubrication Delivery System*

(i) The delivery system is very expensive, and as a result, only large industry companies can afford it.
(ii) High-quality and knowledgeable operators are required.
(iii) Heavy lubricant mixtures, extremely cold temperatures, and extremely long supply line runs between the pump and nozzles are not ideal for it.

However, with the use of lubricant delivery systems in machining operations, manufacturers are still faced with the challenge of producing a high-quality product at a low cost. This is due to other factors like the machining parameters during the cutting process, types of lubricants, measurement of lubricant, and having an idea of the precise surface finishing of the product. This challenge leads to the study of prediction and optimization in machining processes, which will be briefly discussed in Sect. 2.4. Also, this is what this book is all about: the application of heuristic and metaheuristic techniques for advanced nano-lubricant machining optimization.

2.4 Machining Optimization

The machining optimization techniques are powerful statistical instruments employed for obtaining the optimal parameters for a sustainable manufacturing process. This book discusses the design of experimental optimization techniques in Chap. 3 and also the heuristic and metaheuristic techniques for advanced nano-lubricant machining optimization in the other chapters. The current trend in manufacturing lies in the ability to optimize the machining process, which has led to the study of machining optimizations. Davoudinejad et al. [52] developed a mathematical model to predict the performance of the machining parameters in end-milling machining with the finite element method. In the experiment, three machining parameters with three levels were considered to study the surface roughness of the material. The authors discovered that there are lots of machining parameters that lead to low performance in manufacturing mechanical components using computerized numerical control (CNC) machines. Furthermore, they recommended that more research be done on machining parameters to study the influential parameters. Okokpujie et al. [53] also developed a model with response surface methodology to predict the surface roughness under four-factor, five-level experiments. From the result, the model was able to predict the surface roughness with 96% accuracy. The authors recommend the need to develop more mathematical models using different numerical tools, increasing the factors and levels, to study the potential influence of the machining parameters. Masmiati et al. [54] worked on the optimization of machining parameters during end-milling machining. The study confirmed that for proper optimization to be done, there is a need for mathematical models to be developed.

2.5 Conclusion

This chapter focuses on the cutting fluid and its application with different delivery machining techniques. Due to the fact that the current trend in sustainable machining processes lies in the quality of the application of cutting fluid at the cutting region, this chapter discusses the classifications of cutting fluid, which are straight machining oils, soluble oils, semi-synthetic cutting fluids, and synthetic fluids. Furthermore, the study looked into six different machining lubrication delivery techniques: MQL, high pressure cooling, compressed air vapour gas as coolant (CAVG), flood cooling (a traditional process), cryogenic cooling, and the solid lubrication process. These various techniques have their uniqueness as well as their disadvantages. This chapter's conclusion and recommendation are as follows:

(i) MQL delivery techniques are highly efficient in the machining process as well as the cryogenic cooling process. However, a current trend delivery system that can be cryogenic and deliver a minimum amount of lubricant at high pressure is required.
(ii) The manufacturing industry should consider studying the optimization of the MQL cryogenic machining process with precise amounts of lubricants at a specific time during the cutting process.

However, even with the application of MQL in machining operation there are still changelings due to the lack of cooling properties of the cutting fluid, which has led to the study of Nanolubricant in machining operations by several researchers. Therefore, chapter three of this book will discuss the development and application of nano-lubricant in machining.

References

1. Sen, B., Mia, M., Krolczyk, G.M., Mandal, U.K., Mondal, S.P.: Eco-friendly cutting fluids in minimum quantity lubrication assisted machining: a review on the perception of sustainable manufacturing. Int. J. Precis. Eng. Manuf. Green Technol. **8**(1), 249–280 (2021)
2. Xu, W., Li, C.H., Zhang, Y., Ali, H.M., Sharma, S., Li, R., Yang, M., Gao, T., Liu, M., Wang, X., Said, Z.: Electrostatic atomization minimum quantity lubrication machining: from mechanism to application. Int. J. Extreme Manuf. **4**(4) (2022)
3. Sarikaya, M., Gupta, M.K., Tomaz, I., Danish, M., Mia, M., Rubaiee, S., Jamil, M., Pimenov, D.Y., Khanna, N.: Cooling techniques to improve the machinability and sustainability of light-weight alloys: a state-of-the-art review. J. Manuf. Process. **62**, 179–201 (2021)
4. Okonkwo, U.C., Okokpujie, I.P., Sinebe, J.E., Ezugwu, C.A.: Comparative analysis of aluminium surface roughness in end-milling under dry and minimum quantity lubrication (MQL) conditions. Manuf. Rev. **2**, 30 (2015)
5. Bashir, M.A., Mia, M., Dhar, N.R.: Investigations on surface milling of hardened AISI 4140 steel with pulse jet MQL applicator. J. Inst. Eng. (India): Ser. C, **99**(3), 301–314 (2018)
6. Okokpujie, I.P., Ikumapayi, O.M., Okonkwo, U.C., Salawu, E.Y., Afolalu, S.A., Dirisu, J.O., Nwoke, O.N., Ajayi, O.O.: Experimental and mathematical modeling for prediction of tool wear on the machining of aluminium 6061 alloy by high speed steel tools. Open Eng. **7**(1), 461–469 (2017)

7. Benedicto, E., Carou, D., Rubio, E.M.: Technical, economic, and environmental review of the lubrication/cooling systems used in machining processes. Procedia Eng. **184**, 99–116 (2017)
8. Sankaranarayanan, R., Krolczyk, G.M.: A comprehensive review on research developments of vegetable-oil based cutting fluids for sustainable machining challenges. J. Manuf. Process. **67**, 286–313 (2021)
9. Pinheiro, C.T.: Characterization of lubricant oils and regeneration studies by green solvent extraction. Doctoral dissertation, 00500: Universidad de Coimbra (2018)
10. Shokoohi, Y., Khosrojerdi, E., Shiadhi, B.R.: Machining and ecological effects of a new developed cutting fluid in combination with different cooling techniques on turning operation. J. Clean. Prod. **94**, 330–339 (2015)
11. Brito, P.P., Diniz, A.S.A., Kazmerski, L.L.: Materials design and discovery: potential for application to soiling mitigation in photovoltaic systems. Sol. Energy **183**, 791–804 (2019)
12. Ahmed, Z.A.M.: Study of physical and chemical characteristics for Hibiscus sabdariffa L using different techniques. Doctoral dissertation, Sudan University of Science and Technology (2019)
13. Arnault, J.C. (ed).: Nanodiamonds: advanced material analysis, properties and applications. William Andrew (2017)
14. Kumar, A., Singh, G., Singh, I., Bhardwaj, K.: An approach to green manufacturing during machining of AISI-202 stainless steel using minimum quantity lubrication. In: 3rd National Conference, p. 164 (2016)
15. Liew, P.J., Shaaroni, A., Sidik, N.A.C., Yan, J.: An overview of the current status of cutting fluids and cooling techniques of turning hard steel. Int. J. Heat Mass Transf. **114**, 380–394 (2017)
16. Stephenson, D.A., Agapiou, J.S.: Metal cutting theory and practice. CRC Press is an imprint of Taylor & Francis Group (2016)
17. Gupta, K., Laubscher, R.F.: Sustainable machining of titanium alloys: a critical review. Proc. Inst. Mech. Eng. Part B: J. Eng. Manuf. **231**(14), 2543–2560 (2017)
18. Markopoulos, A.P., Pressas, I.S., Papantoniou, I.G., Karkalos, N.E., Davim, J.P.: Machining and machining modeling of metal matrix composites—a review. In: Modern Manufacturing Engineering, pp. 99–141. Springer, Cham. (2015)
19. Ogundimu, O., Lawal, S.A., Okokpujie, I.P.: Experimental study and analysis of variance of material removal rate in high speed turning of AISI 304L alloy steel. IOP Conf. Ser.: Mater. Sci. Eng. **413**, 1–9 (2018)
20. Poornima, S.: Optimisation of machining parameters in CNC turning of martensitic stainless steel using RSM and GA. Int. J. Modern Eng. Res. **2**(2), 539–542 (2012)
21. Yan, P., Rong, Y., Wang, G.: The effect of cutting fluids applied in the metal cutting process. Proc. Inst. Mech. Eng. Part B: J. Eng. Manuf. **230**(1), 19–37 (2016)
22. Joshua, O.S., David, M.O., Sikiru, I.O.: Experimental investigation of cutting parameters on surface roughness prediction during end milling of aluminum 6061 under MQL (minimum quantity lubrication). J. Mech. Eng. Autom. **5**(1), 1–13 (2015)
23. Osama, M., Singh, A., Walvekar, R., Khalid, M., Gupta, T.C.S.M., Yin, W.W.: Recent developments and performance review of metalworking fluids. Tribol. Int. **114**, 389–401 (2017)
24. Phuoc, T.X., Massoudi, M., Chen, R.H.: Viscosity and thermal conductivity of nanofluids containing multi-walled carbon nanotubes stabilized by chitosan. Int. J. Therm. Sci. **50**(1), 12–18 (2011)
25. Pervaiz, S., Kannan, S., Kishawy, H.: An extensive review of the water consumption and cutting fluid-based sustainability concerns in the metal cutting sector. J. Clean. Prod. **197**, 134–153 (2018)
26. Sani, A.S.A., Rahim, E.A., Sharif, S., Sasahara, H.: Machining performance of vegetable oil with phosphonium-and ammonium-based ionic liquids via MQL technique. J. Clean. Prod. **209**, 947–964 (2019)
27. Okonkwo Ugochukwu, C., Nwoke Obinna, N., Okokpujie Imhade, P.: Comparative analysis of chatter vibration frequency in CNC turning of AISI 4340 alloy steel with different boundary conditions. J. Covenant Eng. Technol. (CJET) **1**(1), 13–30 (2018)

28. Nwoke, O.N., Okonkwo, U.C., Okafor, C.E., Okokpujie, I.P.: Evaluation of chatter vibration frequency in CNC turning of 4340 alloy steel material. Int. J. Sci. Eng. Res. **8**(2), 487–495 (2017)
29. Onoroh, F., Ogbonnaya, M., Echeta, C.B.: Experimental investigation of cutting parameters on a turning tool flank wear (industrial and production engineering). Covenant J. Eng. Technol. (Special Edition) **1**(1), 55–72 (2018)
30. Okokpujie, I.P., Bolu, C.A., Ohunakin, O.S., Akinlabi, E.T., Adelekan, D.S.: A review of recent application of machining techniques, based on the phenomena of CNC machining operations. Procedia Manuf. **35**, 1054–1060 (2019)
31. Okokpujie, I.P., Tartibu, L.K.: A mini-review of the behaviour characteristic of machining processes of aluminium alloys. Mater. Today: Proc. **62**, 4526–4532 (2022). https://doi.org/10.1016/j.matpr.2022.05.006
32. Byers, J.P.: Metalworking Fluids, Third edition, pp. 1–48. CRC Press (2017)
33. Prins, C., Treurnicht, N.F.: An overview of advanced cooling techniques for titanium alloy machining in aerospace. SAIIE25 Proceed **657**, 1–15 (2013)
34. Dipeshkumar, B.T.: Machining of difficult-to-cut superalloys: a review. Int. J. Adv. Eng. Res. Dev. **4**(10), 2348–4470 (2017)
35. Krishna, P.V., Rao, D.N.: Performance evaluation of solid lubricants in terms of machining parameters in turning. Int. J. Mach. Tools Manuf **48**(10), 1131–1137 (2008)
36. Busch, K., Hochmuth, C., Pause, B., Stoll, A., Wertheim, R.: Investigation of cooling and lubrication strategies for machining high-temperature alloys. Procedia CIRP **41**, 835–840 (2016)
37. Schoop, J., Sales, W.F., Jawahir, I.S.: High-speed cryogenic finish machining of Ti 6Al4V with polycrystalline diamond tools. J. Mater. Process. Technol. **250**, 1–8 (2017)
38. Aggarwal, A., Singh, H., Kumar, P., Singh, M.: Optimisation of multiple quality characteristics for CNC turning under cryogenic cutting environment using desirability function. J. Mater. Process. Technol. **205**(1–3), 42–50 (2008)
39. Narayanan, S.V., Benjamin, D.M., Keshav, R., Raj, D.S.: A combined numerical and experimental investigation of minimum quantity lubrication applied to end milling of Ti6Al4V alloy. Mach. Sci. Technol. **25**(2), 209–236 (2020)
40. Sarıkaya, M., Yılmaz, V., Güllü, A.: Analysis of cutting parameters and cooling/lubrication methods for sustainable machining in turning of Haynes 25 superalloy. J. Clean. Prod. **133**, 172–181 (2016)
41. Khan, A., Maity, K.: Influence of cutting speed and cooling method on the machinability of commercially pure titanium (CP-Ti) grade II. J. Manuf. Process. **31**, 650–661 (2018)
42. Kui, G.W.A., Islam, S., Reddy, M.M., Khandoker, N., Chen, V.L.C.: Recent progress and evolution of coolant usages in conventional machining methods: a comprehensive review. Int. J. Adv. Manuf. Technol., 1–38 (2021)
43. Banerjee, N., Sharma, A.: A comprehensive assessment of minimum quantity lubrication machining from a quality, production, and sustainability perspectives. Sustain. Mater. Technol. **17**, 70–84 (2018)
44. Canders, W.R., Hoffmann, J., Henke, M.: Cooling technologies for high power density electrical machines for aviation applications. Energies **12**(23), 4579 (2019)
45. Ross, N.S., Mia, M., Anwar, S., Manimaran, G., Saleh, M., Ahmad, S.: A hybrid approach of cooling lubrication for sustainable and optimized machining of Ni-based industrial alloy. J. Clean. Prod. **321**, 128987 (2021)
46. Klocke, F., Soo, S.L., Karpuschewski, B., Webster, J.A., Novovic, D., Elfizy, A., Axinte, D.A., Tönissen, S.: Abrasive machining of advanced aerospace alloys and composites. CIRP Ann. **64**(2), 581–604 (2015)
47. Anton, S., Andreas, S., Friedrich, B.: Heat dissipation in turning operations by means of internal cooling. Procedia Eng. **100**, 1116–1123 (2015)
48. Naves, V.T.G., Da Silva, M.B., Da Silva, F.J.: Evaluation of the effect of application of cutting fluid at high pressure on tool wear during turning operation of AISI 316 austenitic stainless steel. Wear **302**(1–2), 1201–1208 (2013)

49. Chinchanikar, S., Choudhury, S.K.: Machining of hardened steel—experimental investigations, performance modeling, and cooling techniques: a review. Int. J. Mach. Tools Manuf **89**, 95–109 (2015)
50. Patel, M.T., Deshpande, V.A.: Experimental investigation of effect of process parameters on MRR and surface roughness in turning operation on conventional lathe machine for aluminum 6082 grade material using Taguchi method. J. Eng. Res. Appl. **4**(1), 177–185 (2014)
51. Kramar, D., Kopac, J.: High-pressure cooling in the machining of hard-to-machine materials. J. Mech. Eng. **55**(11), 685–694 (2009)
52. Davoudinejad, A., Li, D., Zhang, Y., Tosello, G.: Optimisation of corner micro end milling by finite element modeling for machining thin features. Procedia CIRP **82**, 362–367 (2019)
53. Okokpujie, I.P., Ajayi, O.O., Afolalu, S.A., Abioye, A.A., Salawu, E.Y., Udo, M., Okonkwo, U.C., Orodu, K.B., Ikumapayi, O.M.: Modeling and optimization of surface roughness in end milling of aluminium using least square approximation method and response surface methodology. Int. J. Mech. Eng. Technol. (IJMET) **9**(1), 587–600 (2018)
54. Masmiati, N., Sarhan, A.A., Hassan, M.A.N., Hamdi, M.: Optimisation of cutting conditions for minimum residual stress, cutting force, and surface roughness in end milling of S50C medium carbon steel. Measurement **86**, 253–265 (2016)

Chapter 3
Development and Application of Nano-lubricant in Machining: A Review

Abstract The development and the implementation of nano-lubricants together with the use of numerical approach for prediction and optimization in the machining process is state of the art in the manufacturing of engineering and structural component. This study has reviewed the application of the development of nano lubricants, and the implementation of various optimization techniques for advanced manufacturing systems. Numeral approaches in machining process is a viable process that manufacturers use to produce different parts employed to develop machines. However, the challenge of the CNC system is cutting fluid application due to excess heat generation during the cutting process. Therefore, the review of various nano lubricants development and implementation in the milling, turning, and grinding processes were studied in this chapter. Also, the chapter discusses the modern optimization techniques via design experts such as response surface methodology, Taguchi method, Full Factorial design and Plackett–Burman Design.

Keywords Machining · Nano-Lubricant · Cutting fluid classification · Modern Multi-Objective Optimization · Response surface methodology

3.1 Introduction

Nano-lubricants are state of the art in manufacturing mechanical components for sustainable development. Since the inception of the application of nano-lubricant, there has been a sustainable improvement in the manufacturing sector via numerical approaches applied to the machining process. The implementation of nanoparticles in the base fluid to form Nano-lubricant for the machining process improved the efficiency of the manufacturer output of the CNC machining process [1]. The global CNC machine market was projected to grow from $83.99 billion in 2021 to $128.41 billion in 2028 at a Compound annual growth rate (CAGR) of 6.3% due to the high efficiency growing demand for precision products [2].

Machining with nano-lubricants is mainly formed with a base fluid called lubricant, oil, and water before the application during the cutting operation. Figure 3.1

I. P. Okokpujie and L. K. Tartibu, *Modern Optimization Techniques for Advanced Machining*, Studies in Systems, Decision and Control 485,
https://doi.org/10.1007/978-3-031-35455-7_3

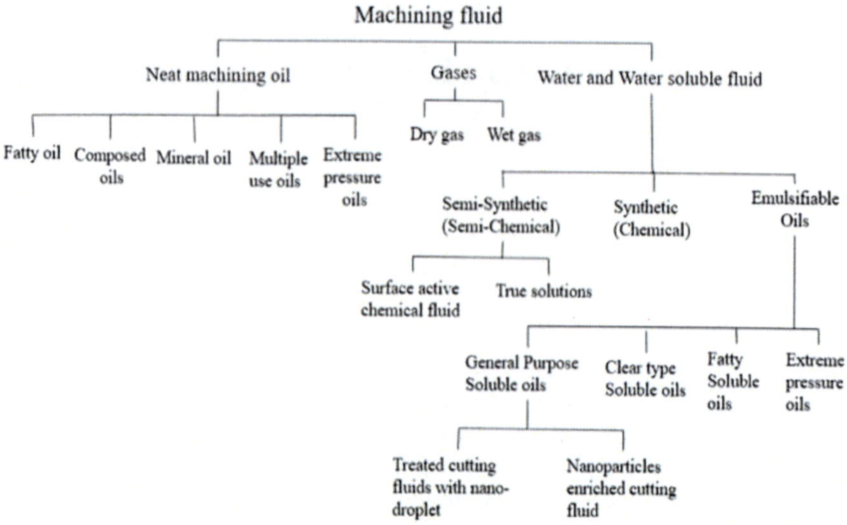

Fig. 3.1 Machining fluid classification during the manufacturing process

shows the various machining lubricants that can be applied in the turning, milling, and grinding operations. These cutting fluids are classified according to their function in the manufacturing process. Nano-lubricant is implemented in different ways to improve cutting fluid performance. Cutting fluids, Spreaders, and Nanoparticles are combined to make nano lubricants. Thermal destruction to work units and tools happens because of the vital forces of friction. The machining costs rely directly on the rate at which metals are removed. Including nano-particulate matter in the lubricants increases structural stability, lubrication properties, and how effective it is in transmitting heat. The NFMQL technique is being developed, in comparison with other lubrication techniques, to significantly increase machining performance, minimize tool wear, and boost the quality of surfaces [3].

The application of current optimization techniques for machining is highly needed to protect the sustainability of the manufacturing process globally. Researchers have critically carried out machining various metals and non-metals with various optimization techniques from the experiment design. Including the response surface methodology (which entails Central Composite Design, Box-Behnken Design, and 3-Level Factorial Design), Taguchi method, full factorial, and Two-Level Factorial Design. However, this chapter focuses on the review process of the development of nano-lubrication and its application in machining operations. This chapter further discusses some selected optimization techniques used for machining.

3.2 Different Methods of Nano-lubricant Preparations

A nano-cutting fluid is developed by immersing a distinctive size of 0–100 nm of organic or non-organic nano-element in base oil [4]. The preparation of nano-liquid is a significant step to enhance the thermal conductivity of the fluids. There are two significant ways of preparing nano lubricants: single-step and dual-step techniques [5]. Nanoparticles (the additives of nano-lubricant) play a significant part in varying the thermal transfer properties of nano-liquids. Recently, different types of nanoparticles, such as organic and non-organic nanoparticles, have been employed in nano-liquid development. The nanoparticles are put into base oil by applying a stirring device and ultrasonic vibration cleaning machine to break down the aggregation of the nanoparticles. The addition of dispersants to regulate the pH value of the mixture will ensure that the re-aggregation of nano-elements is avoided, thereby leading to stable nano-liquid [6].

The dual-step techniques are commonly used to prepare nanotubes, nanofibers, nano-lubricants with various nanomaterials. The process starts by developing the nanoparticles in dry powder form through physical and chemical processes. The characterization of the powder is to identify the percentage of purity and determine the specific side of the nanoparticles. The nanoparticles are dispersed into the base fluid [7]. The mixtures of the base fluid and the nanoparticles are stirred using a rigorous magnetic force with a mechanical stirrer. After that, the ultrasonic vibrator is used to homogenize the nano-lubricant.

This dual-step technique is the most economical process for developing nano-lubricant at low cost and in large quantities. The nanoparticle synthesis method was established at the nano-industrial manufacturing level. As a result, there is a high tendency that the nanoparticle will aggregate with high surface area activity. The required method to improve the stability of nanopowder in the base fluid is the implementation of surfactants. However, the surfactants have some challenges in operating in an environment of high-temperature applications [8].

The one-step technique involves the preparation and suspension of the nanopowder mixed with the base oil; in this case, both the base oil and the nanopowder are produced simultaneously. In the one-step method, the drying of the nanoparticles, storing, transportation, and dispersion of the nanoparticles into the base oil is prevented from eliminating or reducing particle agglomeration. Many techniques are used in this one-step method, such as vapor deposition, pulsed wire evaporation (PWE), Laser Ablation Method, and Submerged Arc Method [9].

The most employed method is the vapour deposition technique which is a process where a tinny film is produced due to the rotating disc acting creating a centrifugal force at the boundary of the vessel. The mixture of the base oil and the nanoparticles are heated and evaporated in the vessel containing inert gas at low pressure. The nano-lubricant is formed at the interaction of the tinny film with the raw materials due to condensation. The nanoparticles are mixed with the base oil. The different methods of nano-lubricant preparation and characterization are presented in Fig. 3.2.

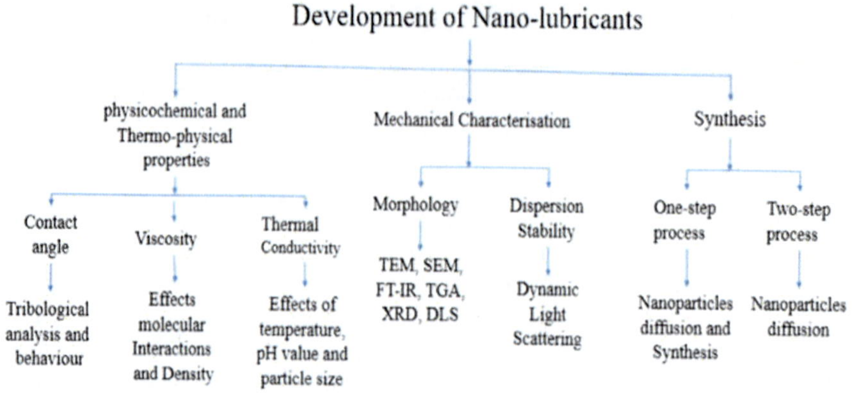

Fig. 3.2 Flow chart for nano-lubricant development, characterization and physiochemical properties

Also, Table 3.1 summarizes the nano-lubricant preparation technique used by several researchers [10].

3.3 Application of Nano-lubricant in Milling Machining

Nano-ointments are the recent trend of lubricant for machining that have been found to improve rheological and tribological properties during the machining process widely [24]. Scientists have, as of late, used nanoparticles in regular oil because of the noticed change in thermo-physical and temperature trade capacities. To diminish the coefficient of crushing and wear sway, work on the usefulness and constancy of mechanical devices.

Different nanoparticles have been widely used to study machining performance in milling machines, such as fullerene, diamond, silicon dioxide, graphite, etc. Due to the outstanding lubricity performance, molybdenum disulphide (MoS_2) is generally used in lubrication. A combination of two different materials and oil [25]. Wang et al. [26] the nano-size of molybdenum disulphide (MoS_2) exhibits excellent tribological properties when compared with the bulksize. MoS_2 and graphite are found among the conventional lubricants because of their morphology and crystalline structure. They are available in the market in a wide variety of sizes. Rahmati et al. [27] studied the effects of different concentrations between 0.5 and 1 wt% of MoS_2 mixed in ECOCUT HSG 905S as a base oil on the surface morphology of AL6061-T6. The study applied the MQL system to minimize lubricant consumption while delivering the nano-lubricant to the cutting region. The result shows that the MoS_2 during the machining operations generally has better surface roughness. At 0.5 wt% concentration of the MoS_2, the minimum surface roughness of 0.223 μm was achieved.

Table 3.1 Summary of different preparation techniques of nano-lubricant employed in the manufacturing industry

Researchers	Nano-liquid	Mixing apparatus
[11]	TiO_2 and MWCNTs + Copra oil	The mixture was stirred for 2 h at room temperature and ultra-sonicated for 5 h before implementation
[12]	Nitric acid–MWCNT	The solution was ultra-sonicated in an ultrasonic water bath for 4 h at 60 °C
[13]	MWNTs + H_2O	Magnetic stirrer for about 3 h and ultrasonic tub for 60 min
[14]	MWNTs + H_2O	The magnetic stirrer was used for 20 min and 10 min. Ultrasonic vibration continues for 1 h
[15]	The mixture of MWNTs + H_2O – ethylene glycol	Magnetic stirrer for 30 and 90 min ultra-sonication
[16]	Carbon + H_2O	Mixed for 30 min with Magnetic stirrer and ultrasonic liquid processor for 30 min (repeated five times)
[17]	Cu + R113 (refrigerant-based)	1 h ultra sonication workstation
[18]	MWCNTs + H_2O	30 min ultrasonication vibration process
[19]	Al_2O_3 + H_2O – Egg mixture	The mixtures were stirred for five (5) h with a magnetic stirrer and also Ultrasonic for four (4) h for the proper mix of the lubricant
[20]	CuO + H_2O	Homogenizer with an ultrasonic cleaner for a 1 h
[21]	Al_2O_3 and TiO_2 + H_2O – EG mixture	The magnetic stirrer was employed for 2 h, homogenizer for 30 min, and ultrasonic liquid processor for 30 min
[22]	Cu + H_2O	An ultrasonic bath was employed to sonicate for about 10 h
[23]	Al_2O_3 + H_2O	An ultrasonic disruptor was employed for 30 min to sonicate the mixture

Sayuti et al. [28] applied silicon dioxide (SiO_2) nano-lubricant in the machining of AL6061-T6 to study the surface morphology of the material. The authors discovered that during machining of the said workpiece using conventional oil, the function of the oil is negligible at high pressure and temperature. Because the oil evaporates at high temperatures and pressure when applied to the machining region between the cutting tool and the workpiece. However, introducing SiO_2 nanoparticles mixed with the base oil could withstand several conditions, such as flushing chips from the cutting region. Also, it reduced cutting force and prolonged the cutting tool life from quick damage. The nano-lubricant applied in this work was prepared by mixing the ECOCUT SSN 322 as base oil with 40.2 CST at 40 °C from FUCHS with SiO_2 and then homogenizing the solution for 48 h. With nanoparticles sizes of 5–15 nm with different concentrations such as 0, 0.2, 0.5, and 1 wt%. The lubricant is free from chlorine, phenol, or any other additive. The grease was delivered to the cutting zone with the help of a developed thin jet pulsed nozzle having a 1 mm diameter with a delivering rate of 2 ml/min. The result shows thin protective films formed in the cutting region between the cutting tool and the workpiece containing a large SiO_2. During the machining process, which helps reduce friction and cutting tool deformation, the surface roughness of the workpiece is reduced.

Ooi et al. [29] developed a model for the nano-lubricant delivery system to predict the machine's performance on the workpiece during milling operation under SiO_2 nano-lubrication conditions. The parameters considered as the input parameters are the concentration of the nano-lubrication, air pressure, and nozzle location, with the responses, such as surface roughness, cutting force, and cutting temperature. However, huge amounts of SiO_2 would lead to a poor machining environment due to crashes and impedance within the elements and asperities of the material. The fuzzy mathematical model displayed the accuracy of predicting the cutting force with about 95.39%, surface finish with 93.78%, and cutting temperature with 98.27%. Also, Paturi et al. [30] worked on the artificial neural network and Taguchi L27 (3^{13}) experimental design to develop a scientific model for predicting surface roughness during the machining of AISI 52100 under three experimental factors. ANOVA and MATLAB toolbox was employed to check the effect of the machining factors on the surface finishing result. The findings show that the Taguchi L27 (3^{13}) and the ANN models are in good agreement with the experimental results when compared.

Singh et al. [31] studied the effects of graphene nano additive found in olive, canola, and sunflower oils on grinding planes of titanium at a grade of 23 compared to the conventional cutting fluid. The research has its limitations in terms of how rough the plane surfaces were (Rz, Ra), the amount of force needed to grind (Fn, Ft), the friction coefficient, and the exact energy needed to grind (U). Low tocopherol levels have been used to improve oxidation stability in vegetable oils in additives. In order to have an equal graphene-nanoplatelet dispersion in oils, nanofluids were put under sonication for probing, using a stirrer for an hour and thirty minutes at 20 kHz followed by an ultrasonication at the same time but 40 kHz. In order to make further enhancements, an addition of a surfactant known as Sodium Laurel Sulphate was used by adding a ten percent graphene weight concentration. Using a technique that has proven to show a stable development experimentally, by comparing, was analyzed in the study. Tests were carried out repeatedly, and the averaged values were considered. A grinding process that is technologically sustainable and benign to the surroundings was proposed. Canola, olive, and sunflower oils with graphene were researched using the Minimum Quantity Lubrication method. Comparing and measuring how effectively they worked with these inclusive and exclusive prerequisites, testing the grind using the standard method of flooding water-soluble synthetic fluids at a twenty-to-one ratio was done. The results obtained using this method were used as a standard throughout the research.

Setti et al. [32] studied nano-lubricants impact during MQL machining of solidified AISI 52100 steel. The result shows that nanofluid with higher complex nanoparticles reduces granulating power, crushing temperature, and surface unpleasantness. The authors also found that the utilization of nanoparticles with a bigger width disintegrated the surface wrap-up. Molybdenum disulphide (MoS_2) nanoparticle has been utilized as a heavy grease in metal cutting for a long time. MoS_2 is one of the suitable grease materials that reduce the coefficient of harshness up to 0.05 with the end goal to enhance the execution of ointment and decrease warm bending. Sridharan and Malkin [33] included CNT and MoS_2 nanopowder to ester grease for the MQL environment. Zhang et al. [34] also carried out an experimental study on the grinding operation of hard-to-cut Ni-based amalgam. The result affirmed that the MoS_2-CNT nano-cutting fluid employed in the cutting process enhanced the materials' cutting accuracy and surface nature.

Diamonds (precious stones) have sizes under 1 ml with paramount consideration due to their incredible automated physical possessions. It has proper surface zones, an excellent composition area, and low cytotoxicity. Nano-diamonds have risen as a standout amongst the most encouraging carbon nanoparticles devoid of health hazards during the machining operation [35, 36]. To justify nanofluid utilization, Sharma et al. [37] spread nano-diamond particles with distance across 30 nm, separately in petroleum jelly and vegetable lubricants, for a smaller-scale penetrating procedure of aluminum 6061 alloys. The result shows that the paraffin mixed with vegetable oils nanofluid decreases penetrating torques and increases the number of boring gaps.

Furthermore, the authors confirmed that the paraffin nanofluid was more viable than the vegetable nanofluid. Lee et al. [38] furthered the examination by testing nano-diamond particles in a based fluid known as paraffin oil for the micro-grinding process. The authors discovered the nano-diamond with paraffin performed better than the base oil. In Abbasi et al. [39] the utilization of nano-diamond particles as nanofluid was not viable for boring with massive width. Similar findings were confirmed in the work of Kim et al. [40] for small-scale end-processing of titanium composite (Ti–6AL–4 V) that is diamond-nano-fluid performed better in end milling machining.

3.4 Turning Operations

The base oil or water mixture with non-metallic or metallic nanoparticles is called a nano-lubricant (NL). Sharma et al. [41] carried out a study on TiO_2 nano-lubricant thermal conductivity, viscosity, and the performance during turning of AISI1040 steel. The nano-lubricant was developed by mixing 5% volume of vegetable oil containing water with different volume percentages of TiO_2 from 0 to 3% in the mixture to achieve the nano lubricants stability. The solution was kept for 6 h on the ultrasonic vibrator. The MQL technique was used to deliver the lubricant to the machining zone. This process was also compared with the wet/MQL and dry machining. The result shows that the nano-lubricant improved the efficiency of the machining process by decreasing the cutting tool wear, cutting force, and surface roughness.

Mahadi et al. [42] carried out research that employed boric acid as a nanoparticle mixed with palm kernel oil to form a machining cutting fluid for turning operations of AISI 431 steel under MQL operations to study surface roughness. A full factorial experimental design of 2^4 factorials was applied with three factors, two experiment levels, which amount to 16 experimental runs. The factors considered are depth of cut varying from 0.5 to 1 mm, feed rate of 0.16 to 0.24 mm/rev, and cutting speed of 150 to 200 m/min. From the comparison result, the palm kernel oil mixed with the boric acid performed better than the flood cooling process, and feed rate was the most significant parameter of the surface roughness. The nano-lubricant developed with the boric acid has a performance difference with a surface roughness of about 7.21%. The developed model predicted the experimental result with 99.15% from the ANOVA analysis.

Rapeti et al. [43] experimented using L27 Taguchi's orthogonal array with four-factor three-level experiment consideration parameters. In the study, various cutting fluids such as coconut oil, canola oil, and sesame oil were mixed with molybdenum disulphide (MoS_2) of 0.25%, 0.5%, and 1% during lathe machining of AISI 1040 steel. The multi unbiased optimization was carried out with the Taguchi grey relational-based analysis, which was employed to determine the best machining environment. The authors discovered that 0.5% MoS_2-coconut oil with the machining parameters of spindle speed of 40 m/min and 0.14 mm/rev reduces the heat generated, surface finish, cutting force, and wear rate of the cutting tool. The authors performed the cost analysis to determine the economic advantage of the MQL when compared with the conventional way of fluid supply to the machining zone. The study revealed that there were cost savings of up to 22,422 INR.

Gutnichenko et al. [44] developed a nano-lubricant using graphene nanoparticles and rapeseed oil. The rapeseed oil was obtained from Accu-Svenska AB in Sweden. The graphene nanoparticles formed from the thermally expanded graphite (TEG). In 1 g of 10% (vol.) alcohol media and was ultra-sonicated for 24 h, the ultra-sonication machine operates with 350 W power. The nanoparticle size was 1 μm and had a thickness of 50 nm. The authors dispensed a 0.2% volume of graphene nanoparticles in rapeseed oil obtained from vegetables. They studied the effects of the nano-lubricant in the lathe machining of tempered ~60 HRC alloy steel with cemented carbide cutting tool under the cooling technics of MQL and dry turning operations. The surface roughness was determined using a portable roughness tester of Mahr MarSurf PS10. It was measured 5 times after each machining operation, and the average is taken as the surface roughness result. The investigation concluded that the implementation of GnP in the rapeseed oil helped reduce the friction during the turning operation. This led to an improvement in the cutting tool life and reduced the surface roughness. The dry turning process had a high adhesiveness in the machining region, which led to excess heat generation and increased surface roughness.

Sharma et al. [45] studied the effects of Al_2O_3 on different conventional cooling fluids employed during the turning operation of AISI 1040 steel. The materials considered are AISI 1040 of 70 mm long and having a diameter of 300 mm, uncoated cemented carbide insert, Al_2O_3 nanoparticles (1 and 5%) mixed with water, Olympus BX51M microscope. In order to analyze the surface roughness, the Mitutoyo Surftest SJ-210 were employed to measure the surface roughness of the machined face after turning operations The parameters are cutting feed of 0.1 mm/rev, depth of cut of

1 mm, and a spindle speed of 96.7 m/min. The nano-lubricant was ministers with a 50 ml/min flow rate with a pressure of 4 bar. The researchers experimented with dry turning, MQL, and wet machining processes. However, the result shows that nano-lubricant significantly lessens the cutting force than dry and wet turning operations with about 59.1% and 29.2%. Also, it reduces the wear rate and the surface roughness by about 47.8% and 29.1%, respectively. Finally, it was concluded that the increase of the nanoparticles on the base lubricant enhances the viscosity of the base fluid's grease, density, and thermal conductivity. Also, the specific heat analysis shows that the increase of the Al_2O_3 nanoparticles will decrease the specific heat capacity.

3.5 Grinding Operations

The role of lubricants in grinding operations is very significant because of their need for environmental protection. To prevent the increase of health risks in the operators' lives, the issue of traditional cutting fluid is progressively fading away. Nano-lubricant has the potential to serve as a green lubricant because of the effects of the nanoparticles in the grease. Various researchers have discovered that nano-lubricant in grinding operation enhanced the heat transfer ability and the lubricant properties. During grinding operation, friction between the abrasive grains and the work materials can rightly impact the wear rate of the grinding wheel, the quality of the material's surface, and the grinding force. Therefore, using nano-lubricant will help improve the grinding performance [46].

Wang et al. [47] carried out a study on the tribological performance of Al_2O_3 during grinding operations. The authors developed a Nano-cutting fluid, using palm oil as the base fluid and 0.5 to 4% volume concentration of Al_2O_3 as the additives, during the grinding operations of Ni-base alloy, under the MQL method. The study was carried out on the macro factors (G-ratio, force ratio, and specific energy) and micro factors (surface superiority, the microstructure of coarse grains and grinding fragments, viscosity, and angle contact). Results show that the nano-cutting fluid runs through the grinding wheel, work material at the grinding zone, and developed a lubricating oil film that significantly decreases friction. The best concentration of nano-lubricant was obtained. At the 1.5% volume concentration, the minimum grinding force ratio of 0.281 was achieved. In contrast, the minimum coarseness of 0.301 mm, tiny grinding fragments, and maximum drop moistening zone was obtained at the volume concentration of 2.0%.

Huang et al. [48] study the effects of multi-wall carbon nanotubes (MWCNTs) nano cutting fluid, using ultrasonic-assisted MQL, and dry in grinding NAK80 mold steel. The oscillator agitation ultrasonic MQL is to maintain the nano-lubricant stability during the grinding process. The three grinding environments were conducted experimentally, and the grinding performance analysis was determined. The result shows that MWCNT's nano-lubricant using the MQL could reduce the temperature generated at the grinding zone, the surface finish, and the cutting force compared with dry machining. This is credited to the ultrasonic oscillator applied to the MQL techniques, which reduced the particle agglomeration to the minimum lubricant. According to Zhang et al. [49] the sustainability of manufacturing quality products during the application of computer numerical control (CNC) in the grinding process depends strongly on the employment of lubricant delivery systems. The authors employed three lubrication techniques in their research work: the nano-lubricant MQL, nano-lubricant cryogenic air minimum quantity lubrication (CNMQL), and cryogenic air with Al_2O_3 as the nano-lubricant during the grinding operation of Ti–6Al–4V. In order to study the specific energy consumption and the coefficient of friction during the machining process. The study shows that the minimum specific energy and the resistance ratio were achieved at 51.96 J/mm^3 and 0.60, respectively, in the grinding environment of CNMQL. From the comparative analysis, it is seen that the CNMQL is superior. Its performance was better than the CA and the NMQL in terms of energy-saving, economic efficiency, use of low carbon, outstanding cooling, and lubrication influences on the grinding process.

3.6 Current Modern Optimization Techniques for Advanced Machining Processes

The current modern optimization techniques in the advanced machining process are borne out of experiment design, such as response surface methodology, Central Composite Design, Box-Behnken Design, Taguchi method, full factorial, and Two-Level Factorial Design employed for machining optimizations [50]. This section will discuss this method in other to introduce a new research method for machining optimization. Most of the multi-optimization techniques are classified under the experiment design, which enables the study of input parameters interaction as it affects the responses during the machining.

3.6.1 Response Surface Methodology

Response surface technique (R. S. M) is an assortment of numerical and measurable strategies for planning, creating, improving, and streamlining item plans. The numerous variables affect the characteristics of the products [51]. First, the estimation function is generated among the output and then input. A first-order model is in place [52]. The following illustrates the most accessible model based upon a first-order polynomial that can be used for RSM in Eqs. (3.1) and (3.2).

$$y = \beta_0 + \sum_{i}^{k} \beta_i x_i + \varepsilon \tag{3.1}$$

In comparison, a polynomial in Eq. (3.1) can be expressed in the following manner.

$$y = \beta_0 + \sum_{i=1}^{k} \beta_i x_i + \sum_{i=1}^{k} \sum_{j \geq i}^{k} \beta_{ij} x_i x_j + \varepsilon \tag{3.2}$$

i: linear-coefficient, **j**: quadratic-coefficient **k**: factor quantity.

$\mathbf{x_i}$ and $\mathbf{x_j}$: independent variables **y**: expected response.

$\boldsymbol{\beta_0}$: constant, $\boldsymbol{\beta_i}$: linear-coefficient constant $\boldsymbol{\beta_{ij}}$: interactive-coefficient constant $\boldsymbol{\varepsilon}$: noise error.

3.6.2 Box-Behnken Design

A three-level fragmentary factorial arrangement created by Box and Behnken [53] is the Box-Behnken technique for the plan. For each block factorial plan, numerous variables are obtained through all mixes. At the same time, various components are retained at the focal levels. Some focal plans are normally included in contrast to the central composite layout. It has fewer composite design factor levels and does not have exceptionally high or insufficient levels. For example, Singh et al. [54] employed Box-Behnken design to developed a model that predict the performance of the material removal rate and optimised the machining factors during the computer numerical machining process of AL6061. The factors employed are feed rate, the cutting tool speed, depth of cut at three levels. The results show that the Box-Behnken design was capable to predict the response MRR and the optimised factor achieved was cutting speed of 1800 rpm, feed rate of 0.15 mm/rev and depth of cut 1.5 mm.

3.6.3 Central Composite Design

Olawoye [55] states that the Central Composite design and Box-Behnken design are the two classifications of surface response theory. A focal Composite design is a response surface design with a hub or star point separated from the 3 level variables. The hub or star point, usually signified as (α), expands the number of levels to 5 levels, giving the trial design adaptability. Its points of interest over Box-Behnken are that it permits the exploratory designer to realize what impact the variables had on response. The test designer goes past or beneath the picked factors. Notwithstanding, in Central Composite Design, the base number of elements it can oblige is two (i.e., mathematical or consistent components). The recipe gives the quantity tentatively acquired at each number of elements in Eq. (3.3):

$$N = 2^n + 2n + n_c \tag{3.3}$$

N is the number of runs, n is the number of factors, n_c is the number of center points the designer desires.

3.6.4 Taguchi Method

This is a factual technique, additionally called vigorous plan strategies, created by Genichi Taguchi to work on the nature of produced products. More recently, this statistical method has found application in the engineering discipline [56].

Taguchi identified three situations seen in Eqs. (3.4)–(3.10):

(i) Larger the better (e.g., agricultural yield);

$$\frac{S}{N} = -10 * \log\left(\frac{\sum\left(\frac{1}{Y^2}\right)}{N}\right) \tag{3.4}$$

Y = reactions for the element level blend; n = the number of reactions in the variable level mix.

(ii) Smaller the better (e.g., carbon dioxide emissions) Eq. (3.5);

$$\frac{S}{N} = -10 * \log\left(\frac{\sum\left(Y^2\right)}{N}\right) \tag{3.5}$$

(iii) Nominal is best.

(a) Nominal is best (i):

$$\frac{S}{N} = 10 * \log\left(s^2\right) \tag{3.6}$$

(b) Nominal is best (ii):

$$\frac{S}{N} = 10 * \log\left(\frac{\sum\left(\overline{Y}^2 - \frac{s^2}{n}\right)}{N}\right) \tag{3.7}$$

$\overline{Y}$ = mean of responses for the given factor level combination.

For dynamic designs, the Signal-to-noise ratio can be calculated using Eqs. (3.8)–(3.10):

$$\frac{S}{N} = 10 * \log\left(\frac{\sum \text{slope}^2}{\text{MSE}}\right) \tag{3.8}$$

Or

$$\frac{S}{N} = 10 * \log\left(\frac{\sum \text{slope}^2}{\text{MSE}} - \left(\frac{1}{r}\right)\right) \tag{3.9}$$

MSE = Mean square error

$$r = \sum (\text{signal} - \text{reference signal or mean signal})^2 \tag{3.10}$$

This process involves three stages:

- System design: This is design at the conceptual level
- Boundary (measure) plan: The different aspects and configuration boundaries' qualities should be set when the idea has been perceived. The selection of boundaries limits the consequences for execution brought about by variety in the assembling, climate, and aggregate harm, additionally called robustification.
- Resilience plan: The boundary plans are credited, the different boundaries' impact on execution is perceived. The assets can be placed into limiting and directing variety in the primary few aspects.

Khare et al. [57] used titanium (grade 5) as a work material with a copper electrode for conducting experiments to minimize surface roughness. L-9 Taguchi array was employed in carrying out this experiment. Kumar and Kulkarni [58] Obtained optimum surface roughness and tool wear by using the Taguchi L-9 orthogonal array for analysing the results from the turning operations of Ti–6Al–4V titanium alloy with carbide insert tools. Cetin et al. [59] in an assessment of vegetable-based cutting fluid (VBCF) in the turning of AISI 304L, employed the use of Taguchi's lower-the better quality characteristic of S/N ratio. For the analysis of surface roughness, cutting force, and feed force. The S/N ratio was calculated with the Eq. (3.11):

$$\frac{S}{N} = -10\log\left[\frac{1}{n}\left(\sum_{i=1}^{n} {y_i}^2\right)\right] \tag{3.11}$$

where n represents the number of measurements in a row, and y_i is the measured value in a run.

The Taguchi method for experimental design is anything but difficult to apply to many design issues as it permits the investigation of numerous boundaries without a high measure of experimentation. It distinguishes essential boundaries that influence the performance, and the boundaries that have a negligible impact are disregarded. Taguchi's strategy makes a standard symmetrical cluster to assess the impacts of design boundaries on the response esteem in an impartial way. The utilization of symmetrical clusters limits the quantity of all-out exploratory runs. Little-scope tests' results are legitimate over a whole exploratory locale traversed by the control factors and their settings [60]. In this way, Azadeh et al. [61] detailed that the Taguchi strategy has developed into a setup approach for breaking down cooperation impacts when positioning and screening different controllable components. Also, this strategy applies to tackle different issues, including consistent, discrete, and subjective design factors. The Taguchi technique for test design has been generally used to locate the fundamental factors in accomplishing practical assembling measures.

Also, Rajesh et al. [62] announced that Taguchi's method utilizes a remarkable symmetrical exhibit to look at the quality attributes through a base number of analyses. The trial results dependent on the symmetrical cluster are then changed into S/N proportions to assess the exhibition qualities. Taguchi's Design of examinations is utilized to design the symmetrical exhibit for three boundaries shifted through three levels. Examinations have been completed utilizing Taguchi's L9 Orthogonal Array, comprising eight blends of cutting side rake point, back rake point, and nose sweep. As indicated by Taguchi's design inventory, three-cycle boundaries (without association) are to have fluctuated in three limited levels.

The Taguchi L9 symmetrical exhibit boundary design and response improvement approach were used by Venkatesan et al. [63]. The Taguchi signal-to-noise ratio chart and the 3D surface graph showed that a 0.14 mm/fi feed rate and cutting speed of 60 mm/min are accountable for minimum surface hardness. And the device wears with the greatness of 0.58 and 158 μm at 0.25% (device wear) and 1.00% (surface unpleasantness). For cutting power, 169 N is seen at 0.14 mm/fire up, 100 m/min, next to 0.25%. From the effects of Signal-to-response and ANOVA, it is more likely that cutting pace takes care of rate emphasis to restrict deliberate responses. The developers effectively recognized the ideal environment for prevailing machining performance using the research model Taguchi.

3.6.5 The Grey-Taguchi Multi-objective Optimization Method

The conflicting nature of objective functions makes the use of mono-objective formulation unsuitable. Therefore, it is advised to use multi-objective optimization [64]. A renowned scientist Prakash et al. [65] developed a grey system that can solve problems with multiple quality characteristics of a re-enforce aluminium metal composite. These equations and procedures prove instrumental in optimizing multiple responses, and optimum input factors can be determined [66]. Optimization is divided into 'Maximization,' 'Minimization,' and 'Reach a Target.'

3.6.6 Factorial Design

Factorial design can be used at different levels (two or more to analyze the effects of factors on the response parameters. Compared to the one-factor-at-a-time design, experimentation demonstrates interactions between factors that combine different factors and makes it more effective in handling more factors. There are two (2) categories of factorial design: full-factorial design and fractional factorial design.

Table 3.2 Design for a 2^2 factorial design of experiment [67]

	A	B	AB
− 1	− 1	− 1	+ 1
A	+ 1	− 1	− 1
B	− 1	+ 1	− 1
AB	+ 1	+ 1	+ 1

3.6.7 Full Factorial Design

Complete factorial design is effective for a smaller number of factors that assume resources are available. Two 2^2 and three 2^3 factors and 2k factorial design explain the theoretical method about the design of experiment (DOE), where k signifies different factors. At the same time, the number of levels is characterized by the number 2. Factor designation is used for upper case letters, and lowercase letters are treatments. Each combination is called treatment and is marked with a small letter [67]. The design matrix is provided in Table 3.2 for a 2^2 factorial design.

Arif et al. [68] carried out experiments using a full-factorial design, and wear losses were discovered from the experiments. It was specified that ANOVA is a statistical means that displays percentage contributions used to distinguish the control of independent variables. Also, their respective percentage contributions to the results from experiments of the wear loss for this situation was analysed. Minitab was used to perform calculations, as shown in Table 3.2.

The analysis was taken for a 5% significance level. ANOVA calculates the F-ratio, which gives each independent variable the significance level by considering the variance of all terms discovered from the error term at the ideal significance level.

Although factorial DoEs have attractive highlights, they have a few drawbacks, including (i) they are appropriate for creating observational models or direct relapse but do not take into account the structure of main nonlinear models; (ii) the research does not take into account the earlier boundary data proportionately when planning new investigations; (iii) they require a fixed number of exploratory runs.

3.6.8 Fractional Factorial Design

The expectations of this method are at the stage at which the number of runs is moderately high for a complete factorial schedule. The experiment may use the fractional factorial method to streamline the ideal data, also referred to as a fractional factorial plan, to distinguish it from the complete factorial plan [69]. The fractional factorial approach offers an optional method where the number of runs for a complete factorial plan is too high ever to be feasible. Certain variables' impacts on a reaction can be concentrated with a fractional factorial design under a reasonable and efficient condition.

3.6.9 *Plackett–Burman Design*

A two-tier fractional factorial system is the Plackett–Burman model developed by Plackett and Burman. It has been commonly used for screening basic components for further study. Karlapudi et al. [70] express that Plackett–Burman's design is commonly used and is now valuable in considering during machining of mechanical parts. It is a two-factorial design (i.e., − 1 and + 1) that finds distinct variables as "n + 1" tests. All elements picked in the analysis were tried at these two levels depending on the Plackett–Burman network plan. The principle impact was determined to distinguish between every factor's normal estimations at a significant level (+ 1) and a low level (− 1). This planning technique is a basic apparatus for screening the impacts of cycle factors on yield and can reduce the number of redundant trials directed in a further streamlining study utilizing a reaction surface system [71–76].

3.7 Conclusion

The development and application of nano-lubricant in machining is the current trend in the manufacturing process. This is one of the unique contribution of this book because this chapter has reviewed the various methods of developing nano-lubricants with a base oil. The application of the lubricants in milling, turning, and grinding operations in advanced machining processes. Also, it discusses the existing method of optimization. Knowing the existing method used for machining optimization via experimental design techniques. From the review of various articles on the application of Nano-lubricant this study will have the following conclusion:

(i) The nano-lubricants significantly improve the machining process during the milling, turning, and grinding operations.
(ii) It has been justified that the development of nanoparticles with base oil is majorly prepared in two ways techniques.
(iii) Optimization study is the most significant aspect of the machining process.

This will lead the authors to introduce global optimization techniques to improve the machining and manufacturing process for the sustainable development of engineering components in Chap. 4.

References

1. Ali, M.A.M., Azmi, A.I., Murad, M.N., Zain, M.Z.M., Khalil, A.N.M., Shuaib, N.A.: Roles of new bio-based nanolubricants towards eco-friendly and improved machinability of Inconel 718 alloys. Tribol. Int. **144**, 106106 (2020)
2. Yang, H., Wang, Z., Zhang, T., Du, F.: A review on vibration analysis and control of machine tool feed drive systems. Int. J. Adv. Manuf. Technol. **107**(1), 503–525 (2020)

3. Okokpujie, I.P., Ohunakin, O.S., Bolu, C.A.: Multi-objective optimization of machining factors on surface roughness, material removal rate and cutting force on end-milling using MWCNTs nano-lubricant. Progr. Addit. Manuf. **6**(1), 155–178 (2021)
4. Azwadi, C.N., Adamu, I., Jamil, M.: Preparation methods and thermal performance of hybrid nanofluids. J. Adv. Rev. Sci. Res. **24**(1), 13–23 (2016)
5. Li, Y., Tung, S., Schneider, E., Xi, S.: A review on the development of nanofluid preparation and characterization. Powder Technol. **196**(2), 89–101 (2009)
6. Abubakar, S., Azwadi, C.N., Ahmad, A.: The use of Fe3O4-H2O4 nanofluid for heat transfer enhancement in rectangular microchannel heatsink. J. Adv. Res. Mater. Sci. **23**, 15–24 (2016)
7. Okokpujie, I.P., Tartibu, L.K.: Performance investigation of the effects of nano-additive-lubricants with cutting parameters on material removal rate of AL8112 alloy for advanced manufacturing application. Sustainability **13**(15), 8406 (2021)
8. Yu, W., Xie, H.: A review on nanofluids: preparation, stability mechanisms, and applications. J. Nanomater., 1–17 (2012)
9. Ali, H., Babar, H., Shah, T., Sajid, M., Qasim, M., Javed, S.: Preparation techniques of TiO_2 nanofluids and challenges: a review. Appl. Sci. **8**(4), 587–616 (2018)
10. Yuvarajan, D., Babu, M.D., BeemKumar, N., Kishore, P.A.: Experimental investigation on the influence of titanium dioxide nanofluid on emission pattern of biodiesel in a diesel engine. Atmos. Pollut. Res. **9**(1), 47–52 (2018)
11. Okokpujie, I.P., Bolu, C.A., Ohunakin, O.S.: Comparative performance evaluation of TiO_2, and MWCNTs nano-lubricant effects on surface roughness of AA8112 alloy during end-milling machining for sustainable manufacturing process. Int. J. Adv. Manuf. Technol. **108**(5), 1473–1497 (2020)
12. Abbasi, F.M., Hayat, T., Alsaedi, A.: Peristaltic transport of magneto-nanoparticles submerged in water: model for drug delivery system. Physica E **68**, 123–132 (2015)
13. Lotfi, R., Rashidi, A.M., Amrollahi, A.: Experimental study on the heat transfer enhancement of MWNT-water nanofluid in a shell and tube heat exchanger. Int. Commun. Heat Mass Transfer **39**(1), 108–111 (2012)
14. Phuoc, T.X., Massoudi, M., Chen, R.H.: Viscosity and thermal conductivity of nanofluids containing multiwalled carbon nanotubes stabilized by chitosan. Int. J. Therm. Sci. **50**(1), 12–18 (2011)
15. Kumaresan, V., Velraj, R., Das, S.K.: The effect of carbon nanotubes in enhancing the thermal transport properties of PCM during solidification. Heat Mass Transf. **48**(8), 1345–1355 (2012)
16. Teng, T.P., Yu, C.C.: Heat dissipation performance of MWCNTs nano-coolant for vehicle. Exp. Thermal Fluid Sci. **49**, 22–30 (2013)
17. Peng, H., Ding, G., Hu, H.: Effect of surfactant additives on nucleate pool boiling heat transfer of refrigerant-based nanofluid. Exp. Thermal Fluid Sci. **35**(6), 960–970 (2011)
18. Yousefi, T., Shojaeizadeh, E., Veysi, F., Zinadini, S.: An experimental investigation on the effect of pH variation of MWCNT–H_2O nanofluid on the efficiency of a flat-plate solar collector. Sol. Energy **86**(2), 771–779 (2012)
19. Raveshi, M.R., Keshavarz, A., Mojarrad, M.S., Amiri, S.: Experimental investigation of pool boiling heat transfer enhancement of alumina–water–ethylene glycol nanofluids. Exp. Thermal Fluid Sci. **44**, 805–814 (2013)
20. Li, H., Li, C., Han, L., Li, C., Zhang, S.: Photocatalytic reduction of CO_2 with H_2O on CuO/ TiO_2 catalysts. Energy Sources, Part A: Recov Util Environ Effects **38**(3), 420–426 (2016)
21. Nieh, H.M., Teng, T.P., Yu, C.C.: Enhanced heat dissipation of a radiator using oxide nano-coolant. Int. J. Therm. Sci. **77**, 252–261 (2014)
22. Kathiravan, R., Kumar, R., Gupta, A., Chandra, R.: Preparation and pool boiling characteristics of silver nanofluids over a flat plate heater. Heat Transfer Eng. **33**(2), 69–78 (2012)
23. Yousefi, T., Veysi, F., Shojaeizadeh, E., Zinadini, S.: An experimental investigation on the effect of Al_2O_3–H_2O nanofluid on the efficiency of flat-plate solar collectors. Renew. Energy **39**(1), 293–298 (2012)

24. Okokpujie, I.P., Tartibu, L.K., Sinebe, J.E., Adeoye, A.O., Akinlabi, E.T.: Comparative study of rheological effects of vegetable oil-lubricant, TiO_2, MWCNTs nano-lubricants, and machining parameters' influence on cutting force for sustainable metal cutting process. Lubricants **10**(4), 54 (2022)
25. Sayuti, M., Karim, A.: Application of nano base lubricants in machining process for performance improvements. Doctoral dissertation, University of Malaya (2013)
26. Wang, P., Tian, J., Hu, J., Zhou, X., Li, C.: Supernormal conversion anode consisting of high-density MoS_2 bubbles wrapped in thin carbon network by self-sulfuration of polyoxometalate complex. ACS Nano **11**(7), 7390–7400 (2017)
27. Rahmati, B., Sarhan, A.A., Sayuti, M.: Morphology of surface generated by end milling AL6061-T6 using molybdenum disulfide (MoS2) nanolubrication in end milling machining. J. Clean. Prod. **66**, 685–691 (2014)
28. Sayuti, M., Sarhan, A.A., Salem, F.: Novel uses of SiO_2 nano-lubrication system in hard turning process of hardened steel AISI4140 for less tool wear, surface roughness and oil consumption. J. Clean. Prod. **67**, 265–276 (2014)
29. Ooi, M.E., Sayuti, M., Sarhan, A.A.: Fuzzy logic-based approach to investigate the novel uses of nano suspended lubrication in precise machining of aerospace AL tempered grade 6061. J. Clean. Prod. **89**, 286–295 (2015)
30. Paturi, U.M.R., Devarasetti, H., Narala, S.K.R.: Application of regression and artificial neural network analysis in modelling of surface roughness in hard turning of AISI 52100 steel. Mater. Today: Proc. **5**(2), 4766–4777 (2018)
31. Singh, H., Sharma, V.S., Dogra, M.: Exploration of graphene assisted vegetables oil based minimum quantity lubrication for surface grinding of TI-6AL-4V-ELI. Tribol. Int. **144**, 106113 (2020)
32. Setti, D., Ghosh, S., Rao, P.V.: Application of nano cutting fluid under minimum quantity lubrication (MQL) technique to improve grinding of Ti–6Al–4V alloy. In: Proceedings of World Academy of Science, Engineering and Technology, vol. 70, pp. 512–516 (2012)
33. Sridharan, U., Malkin, S.: Effect of minimum quantity lubrication (MQL) with nanofluid on grinding behavior and thermal distortion. Trans. NAMRI/SME **37**, 629–636 (2009)
34. Zhang, Y., Li, C., Jia, D., Li, B., Wang, Y., Yang, M., Zhang, X.: Experimental study on the effect of nanoparticle concentration on the lubricating property of nanofluids for MQL grinding of Ni-based alloy. J. Mater. Process. Technol. **232**, 100–115 (2016)
35. Hayat, T., Qayyum, S., Imtiaz, M., Alsaedi, A.: Comparative study of silver and copper water nanofluids with mixed convection and nonlinear thermal radiation. Int. J. Heat Mass Transf. **102**, 723–732 (2016)
36. Ghasemi, S.E., Vatani, M., Hatami, M., Ganji, D.D.: Analytical and numerical investigation of nanoparticle effect on peristaltic fluid flow in drug delivery systems. J. Mol. Liq. **215**, 88–97 (2016)
37. Sharma, A.K., Tiwari, A.K., Dixit, A.R.: Mechanism of nanoparticles functioning and effects in machining processes: a review. Mater. Today: Proc. **2**(4–5), 3539–3544 (2015)
38. Lee, P.H., Nam, J.S., Li, C., Lee, S.W.: An experimental study on the micro-grinding process with nanofluid minimum quantity lubrication (MQL). Int. J. Precis. Eng. Manuf. **13**(3), 331–338 (2012)
39. Abbasi, S., Zebarjad, S.M., Baghban, S.N., Youssefi, A.: Synthesis of TiO_2 nanoparticles and decorated multiwalled carbon nanotubes with various content of rutile titania. Synth. React. Inorg., Met.-Org., Nano-Met. Chem. **45**(10), 1539–1548 (2015)
40. Kim, D.H., Lee, P.H., Kim, J.S., Moon, H., Lee, S.W.: Experimental study on the micro end-milling process of Ti-6AL-4V using nanofluid minimum quantity lubrication (MQL). In: ASME 2014 International Manufacturing Science and Engineering Conference collocated with the JSME 2014 International Conference on Materials and Processing and the 42nd North American Manufacturing Research Conference, 15–22 (2014)
41. Sharma, A.K., Singh, R.K., Dixit, A.R., Tiwari, A.K.: Characterization and experimental investigation of Al_2O_3 nanoparticle-based cutting fluid in turning of AISI 1040 steel under minimum quantity lubrication (MQL). Mater. Today: Proc. **3**(6), 1899–1906 (2016)

42. Mahadi, M.A., Choudhury, I.A., Azuddin, M., Nukman, Y.: Use of boric acid powder aided vegetable oil lubricant in turning AISI 431 steel. Procedia Eng. **184**, 128–136 (2017)
43. Rapeti, P., Pasam, V.K., Gurram, K.M.R., Revuru, R.S.: Performance evaluation of vegetable oil-based nano cutting fluids in machining using grey relational analysis-a step towards sustainable manufacturing. J. Clean. Prod. **172**, 2862–2875 (2018)
44. Gutnichenko, O., Bushlya, V., Bihagen, S., Ståhl, J.E.: Influence of GnP additive to vegetable oil on machining performance when MQL-assisted turning Alloy 718. Procedia Manuf. **25**, 330–337 (2018)
45. Sharma, A.K., Tiwari, A.K., Singh, R.K., Dixit, A.R.: Tribological investigation of TiO_2 nanoparticle-based cutting fluid in machining under minimum quantity lubrication (MQL). Mater. Today: Proc. **3**(6), 2155–2162 (2016)
46. Naves, V.T.G., Da Silva, M.B., Da Silva, F.J.: Evaluation of the effect of application of cutting fluid at high pressure on tool wear during turning operation of AISI 316 austenitic stainless steel. Wear **302**(1–2), 1201–1208 (2013)
47. Wang, B., Liu, Z.: Investigations on deformation and fracture behaviour of workpiece material during high-speed machining of 7050–T7451 aluminum alloy. CIRP J. Manuf. Sci. Technol. **14**, 43–54 (2016)
48. Huang, W.T., Liu, W.S.: Investigations into lubrication in grinding processes using MWCNTs nanofluids with ultrasonic-assisted dispersion. J. Clean. Prod. **137**, 1553–1559 (2016)
49. Zhang, J., Li, C., Zhang, Y., Yang, M., Jia, D., Liu, G., … Cao, H.: Experimental assessment of an environmentally friendly grinding process using nanofluid minimum quantity lubrication with cryogenic air. J. Clean. Prod. **193**, 236–248 (2018)
50. Okokpujie, I.P., Tartibu, L.K.: Experimental analysis of cutting force during machining difficult to cut materials under dry, mineral oil, and TiO_2 nano-lubricant. J. Meas. Eng. **9**(4), 218–230 (2021)
51. Riswanto, O.F., Rohman, A., Pramono, S., Martono, S.: Application of response surface methodology as mathematical and statistical tools in natural product research. J. Appl. Pharm. Sci., 125–133 (2019)
52. Kiran, B., Pathak, K., Kumar, R., Deshmukh, D.: Statistical optimization using Central composite design for biomass and lipid productivity of microalga: a step towards enhanced biodesel production. Ecol. Eng., 73–81 (2016)
53. Box, G.E.P., Behnken, D.W.: Some new three-level designs for the study of quantitative variables. Technometrics **2**, 455–475 (1960)
54. Singh, P., Singh, L., Singh, S.: A box Behnken design approach for parametric optimization in processing of aluminum 6061 tubes. Mater. Manuf. Process., 1–12 (2021). https://doi.org/10.1088/1757-899X/1057/1/012058
55. Olawoye, B.: A comprehensive handout ON central composite design (CCD). In: *NIST/SEMATECH e-Handbook of Statistical Methods* (2016)
56. Rosa, J.L., Robin, A., Silva, M.B., Baldan, C.A., Peres, M.P.: Electrodeposition of copper on titanium wires: Taguchi experimental design approach. J. Mater. Process. Technol., 1181–1188 (2009)
57. Khare, S.K., Phull, G.S., Agarwal, S.: Optimization the machining parameters of surface roughness during micro-EDM by Taguchi method. Mater. Today: Proc. **27**, 475–479 (2020)
58. Kumar, S.R., Kulkarni, S.K.: Analysis of hard machining of titanium alloy by Taguchi method. Mater. Today: Proc. **4**(10), 10729–10738 (2017)
59. Cetin, M.H., Ozcelik, B., Kuram, E., Demirbas, E.: Evaluation of vegetable based cutting fluids with extreme pressure and cutting parameters in turning of AISI 304L by Taguchi method. J. Clean. Prod., 2049–2056 (2011)
60. Mitra, A.C., Jawarkar, M., Soni, T., Kiranchand, G.R.: Implementation of Taguchi method for robust suspension design. Procedia Eng. **144**, 77–84 (2016)
61. Azadeh, A., Miri-Nargesi, S.S., Goldansaz, S.M., Zoraghi, N.: Design and implementation of an integrated Taguchi method for continuous assessment and improvement of manufacturing systems. Int. J. Adv. Manuf. Technol. **59**(9–12), 1073–1089 (2012)

62. Rajesh, R., Lilly Mercy, J., Ravikumar, S., Singh, A.: Design and analysis of tool wear characteristics during turning using deform 3D. ARPN J. Eng. Appl. Sci. **12**(17), 4940–4952 (2017)
63. Venkatesan, K., Mathew, A.T., Devendiran, S., Ghazaly, N.M., Sanjith, S., Raghul, R.: Machinability study and multi-response optimization of cutting force, surface roughness, and tool wear on CNC turned Inconel 617 superalloy using Al_2O_3 Nanofluids in Coconut oil. Procedia Manuf. **30**, 396–403 (2019)
64. Mia, M., Rifat, A., Tanvir, M.F., Gupta, M.K., Hossain, M.J., Goswami, A.: Multi-objective optimization of chip-tool interaction parameters using Grey-Taguchi method in MQL-assisted turning. Measurement, 156–166 (2018)
65. Prakash, K.S., Gopal, P.M., Karthik, S.: Multi-objective optimization using Taguchi based grey relational analysis in turning of Rock dust reinforced Aluminum MMC. Measurement **157**, 107664 (2020). https://doi.org/10.1016/j.measurement.2020.107664
66. Mia, M., Bashir, M., Khan, M., Dhar, N.: Optimization of MQL flow rate for minimum cutting force and surface roughness in end milling of hardened steel (HRC 40). Int. J. Adv. Manuf. Technol., 675–690 (2017)
67. Durakovic, B.: Design of experiments application, concepts, examples: state of the art. Period. Eng. Nat. Sci. **5**(3), 421–439 (2015). https://doi.org/10.21533/pen.v5i3.145
68. Arif, S., Jamil, B., Shaikh, M.B.N., Aziz, T., Ansari, A.H., Khan, M.: Characterization of surface morphology, wear performance, and modelling of graphite-reinforced aluminium hybrid composites. Eng. Sci. Technol. Int. J. **23**(3), 674–690 (2020)
69. Kauffman, K.J., Dorkin, J.R., Yang, J.H., Heartlein, M.W., DeRosa, F., Mir, F.F., …, Anderson, D.G.: Optimization of lipid nanoparticle formulations for mRNA delivery in vivo with fractional factorial and definitive screening designs. Nano Lett. **15**(11), 7300–7306 (2015)
70. Karlapudi, A.P., Krupanidhi, S., Reddy, R., Indira, M., Md, N.B., Venkateswarulu, T.C.: Plackett-Burman design for screening of process components and their effects on production of lactase by newly isolated Bacillus sp. VUVD101 strain from Dairy effluent. Beni-Suef Univ. J. Basic Appl. Sci. **7**(4):543–546 (2018)
71. Li, M., Yu, T., Yang, L., Li, H., Zhang, R., Wang, W.: Parameter optimization during minimum quantity lubrication milling of TC4 alloy with graphene-dispersed vegetable-oil-based cutting fluid. J. Clean. Prod. **209**, 1508–1522 (2019)
72. Okokpujie, I.P., Bolu, C.A., Ohunakin, O.S., Akinlabi, E.T., Adelekan, D.S.: A review of recent application of machining techniques, based on the phenomena of CNC machining operations. Procedia Manuf. **35**, 1054–1060 (2019)
73. Aboubakar, X., Goudoum, A., Bébé, Y., Mbofung, C.M.F.: Optimization of Jatropha curcas pure vegetable oil production parameters for cooking energy. S. Afr. J. Chem. Eng. **24**, 196–212 (2017)
74. Agrawal, S.M., Patil, N.G.: Experimental study of non-edible vegetable oil as a cutting fluid in machining of M2 Steel using MQL. Procedia Manuf. **20**, 207–212 (2018)
75. Benedicto, E., Carou, D., Rubio, E.M.: Technical, economic, and environmental review of the lubrication/cooling systems used in machining processes. Procedia Eng. **184**, 99–116 (2017)
76. Okokpujie, I.P., Tartibu, L.K.: A mini-review of the behaviour characteristic of machining processes of aluminium alloys. Mater. Today: Proc. **62**, 4526–4532 (2022). https://doi.org/10.1016/j.matpr.2022.05.006

Chapter 4
Global Machining Prediction and Optimization

Abstract Optimization in the manufacturing process enhances the quality and productivity of the industry. This chapter is aimed at discussing and reviewing global optimization and prediction techniques in the machining process. This study covered the review of heuristic and metaheuristic techniques for advanced manufacturing optimization, such as the artificial neural network, adaptive neuro-fuzzy inference system, particle swarm optimization (PSO), genetic algorithm (GA), whale optimization algorithm (WOA), ant lion optimization algorithm (ALOA), and grasshopper optimization algorithm (GOA). The various procedures and steps for implementing these techniques were also covered. Also, a review of related literature on optimization techniques in the machining process was carried out to enable a concrete study to significantly improve the machining process. According to the findings, global optimization techniques are viable, sustainable, and can be used to optimize machining parameters and responses during the manufacturing process. However, several studies have implemented the techniques for only multi-objective optimization; therefore, this study will recommend that studies of multi-response-objective optimization be carried out.

Keywords Global optimization and prediction · ANN · ANFIS · ALOA · GOA · Machining

4.1 Introduction to Optimization in Machining

Optimization is the process of finding solutions that maximize or decrease certain research criteria, such as minimizing expenses associated with producing a thing or service, maximizing profits, minimizing the amount of raw materials needed to make a good, or maximizing output, optimization techniques are often used [1]. Optimization techniques has been applied in various field of engineering application such as Program optimization, coding, or software optimization are all terms used to describe the process of changing a software system such that some component of it operates more effectively or consumes less resources [2]. Global optimization techniques are

I. P. Okokpujie and L. K. Tartibu, *Modern Optimization Techniques for Advanced Machining*, Studies in Systems, Decision and Control 485,
https://doi.org/10.1007/978-3-031-35455-7_4

applied in machining process to optimized parameters values employed during the manufacturing process of mechanical component [3]. In order to reduced energy consumption, surface roughness, tool wear, cutting force and increases the material removal rate in machining process sustainable production of quality products these techniques are employed. There are several optimization and prediction techniques that has been employed in different area of research [4–7]. However, the current trend is the hybrid formulation and application which this book will be applying. Figure 4.1 depict a flow chart of global optimization tool and prediction techniques in the modelling world. The Conventional prediction and optimization techniques has been discussed in Chap. 3 of this book under the Sect. 3.6 current modern optimization techniques for advanced machining processes. The Non-conventional and the global prediction techniques will be discussed in this chapter in subsections.

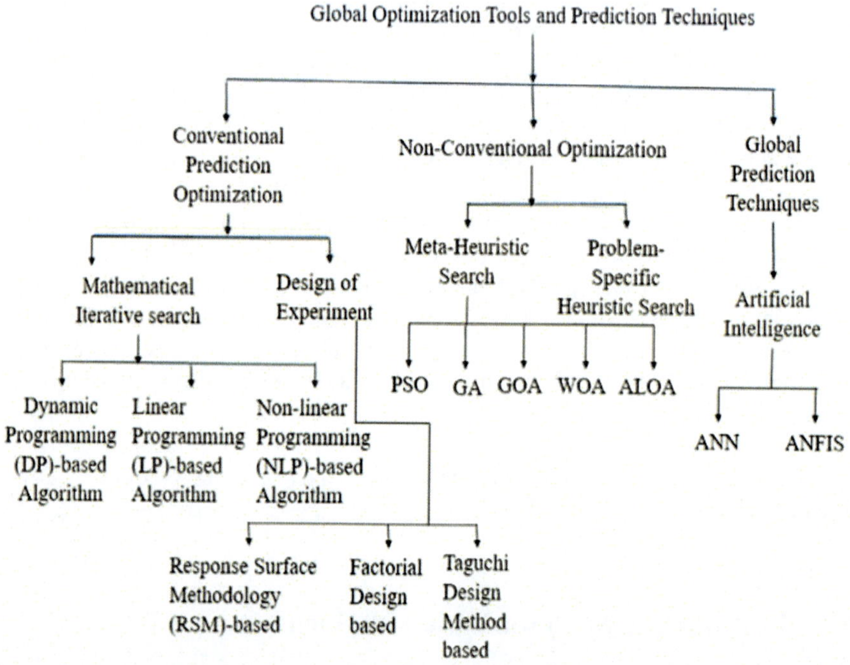

Fig. 4.1 Global optimization tool and prediction techniques

4.2 Artificial Neural Network (ANN) as a Global Prediction Technique

Artificial neural network (ANN) is a nonlinear computational based model that comprises artificial neurons likened to brain cells. This neural system can learn to execute tasks such as classification, visualisation, decision making, and prediction [8–10]. The neurons have three interconnected layers, namely input, hidden, and output layers. The input layer sends the information to the hidden layer; at the hidden layer, inputs interact with the assigned weight of each hidden layer, and this weighted inputs produce the activated signal and sent it to the transfer function. This activated signal interacts with the transfer function to define the output from the neuron [11]. There are seven major types of ANN used for prediction analysis they are as follows:

(i) Radial basis function Neural Network,
(ii) Recurrent Neural Network (RNN),
(iii) Convolutional Neural Network,
(iv) Kohonen Self Organizing Neural Network,
(v) Long/Short Term Memory,
(vi) Modular Neural Networks,
(vii) Feedforward Neural Network—Artificial Neuron.

There are seven step to train a model via ANN they as follows.

- Model an approximate solution.
- Set up the data.
- Decide on a network architecture.
- Neural network training.
- Boost generalization abilities.
- Test outcomes.
- Create a model.

Also, there are different ways of determining the percentage error of the neurons. The one considered in this study is the backpropagation feed-forward method. The backpropagation feed-forward method is a supervised learning technique used in the domain of artificial neural networks for multilayer feed-forward networks [11–13]. The information processing of one or more neurons, also known as neural cells, serves as the model for feed-forward neural networks. Artificial neural network (ANN) is a novel method used in building scientific models to predict and improve engineering systems [14]. Asiltürk and Çunkaş [15] developed an experimental model to predict the turning operation of AISI 1040 steel using an artificial neural network (ANN) and the full factorial design of the experiment. The three-factor applied as input data are: cutting velocity, machining rate, and width of cut, with a response known as surface finishing. The result showed that the ANN back-propagation training algorithms used to train the system could predict the experimental outcome with 98.9% certainty. From the analysis, the feed rate has more influence on cutting when compared to the other factors (Fig. 4.2).

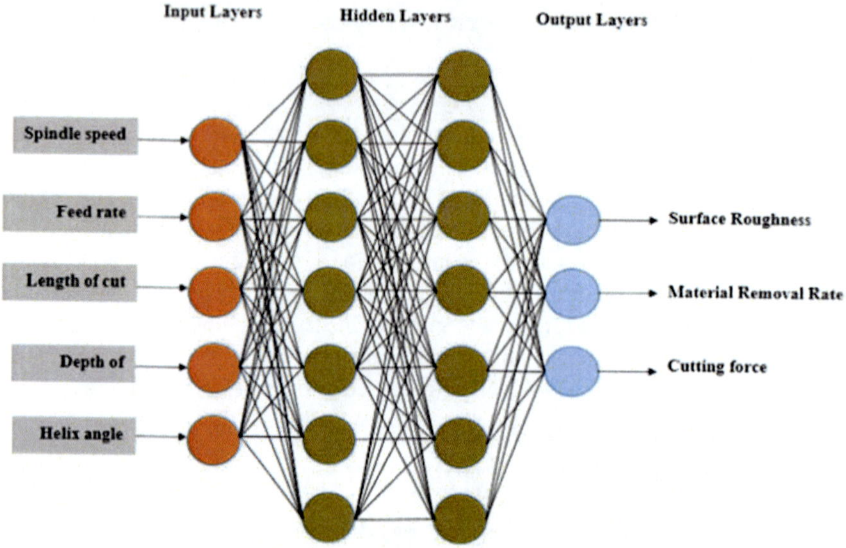

Fig. 4.2 The standard ANN structure for modelling and prediction analysis

Input, hidden, and output are the three layers that make up the network. The hidden layer provides the link between the input and output layers using various numbers of neurons, and the input and output layers are defined as nodes or neurons [16]. The output layer's neurons get the processed data from the hidden layer's processing neurons via the input layer's neurons. The generic form, for instance, can be used to describe the input data to the neurons in the hidden layer as seen in Eqs. (4.1) and (4.2).

$$x_{hidden,j} = \sum_{i=1}^{n} w_{ij}u_i + \theta_j \tag{4.1}$$

$$f(x) = \frac{e^{2x} - 1}{e^{2x} + 1} \tag{4.2}$$

where u_i is the value of the input, W_{ij} is the weight coefficient between the input neurons and hidden neurons, and j stands for the biases of the hidden neurons. Neural network models' performance depends on a number of factors, including network architecture, activation functions, and training procedures. In this study, the Broyden-Fletcher-Goldfarb-Shanno (BFGS) method, conjugate gradient, and the steepest descent training algorithm were all used to train the MLP network.

Additionally, during learning, testing, and validation, the error function was employed to identify discrepancies between actual values and computed values, which is defined as in Eq. (4.3):

$$Errors\ analysis = \sum_{i=1}^{n} (y_i - t_i)^2 \tag{4.3}$$

The root mean square error (RMSE), determination coefficient (R), and mean absolute percentage error (MAPE) were used to assess the efficacy of the regression models and selected neural networks (MAPE) [17], as presented in Eqs. (4.4) to (4.6).

$$RMSE = \left(\left(\frac{1}{N}\right)\left(\sum_{I=1}^{N} |t_i - y_i|^2\right)\right)^{1/2} \tag{4.4}$$

$$R^2 = 1 - \left(\frac{\sum_{I=1}^{N} |t_i - y_i|^2}{\sum_1^N (y_i)^2}\right) \tag{4.5}$$

$$MAPE = \frac{\sum_{I=1}^{N}((t_i - y_i)/t_i) \times 100)}{N} \tag{4.6}$$

where N is the number of samples used in the analysis, y is the predicted value, and t is the target value.

4.3 Adaptive Neuro-fuzzy Inference System

The Adaptive Neuro-Fuzzy Inference System (ANFIS) combines the benefits of Fuzzy Logic (FL) and Artificial Neural Networks (ANNs) into a single framework. In order to model complicated patterns and comprehend nonlinear interactions [18]. It offers rapid learning capacity and adaptive interpretation skills. System for Adaptive Neuro-Fuzzy Inference. The Takagi–Sugeno Fuzzy System, also known as adaptive neuro-fuzzy inference systems, was created in 1993 by J. S. Roger Jang and is commonly recognized as a universal estimator. The Takagi–Sugeno Fuzzy Model is a Type 3 Fuzzy Inference System, where the final output is the weighted average of the outputs of all the rules, and the rule outputs are a linear combination of the input variables and a constant [19].

IF–THEN the rules for 3-input Takagi–Sugeno System are described as follows:

(i) Rule 1: IF $X = A_1$, $Y = B_1$, $Z = C_1$, THEN

$$f_1 = P_1X + q_1y + r_1Z + S_1$$

(ii) Rule 2: IF $X = A_2$, $Y = B_2$, $Z = C_2$, THEN

$$f_1 = P_2X + q_2y + r_2Z + S_2$$

(iii) Rule 2: IF X = A_3, Y = B_3, Z = C_3, THEN

$$f_1 = P_3X + q_3y + r_3Z + S_3$$

where the inputs in the crisp set are x, y, and z; the linguistic labels are A_i, B_i, and C_i; the consequent parameters are p_i, q_i, and r_i; and the output fuzzy membership functions are f_1, f_2, and f_3. The five layers of interconnected neurons of the typical ANFIS architecture, shown in Fig. 4.3, provide evidence of artificial neural networks with similar functionality. The following is a basic explanation of the architecture.

Layer 1: Each neuron in this layer is an adaptive node that stores the fuzzy value of the crisp inputs.

The formula for calculating the node output is given in Eq. (4.7):

$$O_i^1 = \begin{cases} \mu_{A_i(x)}, & \forall_i = 1, 2, \\ \mu_{B_{i-2}(x)}, & \forall_i = 3, 4, \\ \mu_{C_{i-4}(x)}, & \forall_i = 5, 6, \end{cases} \tag{4.7}$$

where the fuzzy sets A_i, B_i, and C_i membership function is.

There are many membership functions, including Gaussian, Trapezoidal, Triangular, and others. In ANFIS, we favour a bell-shaped function. As a result, the

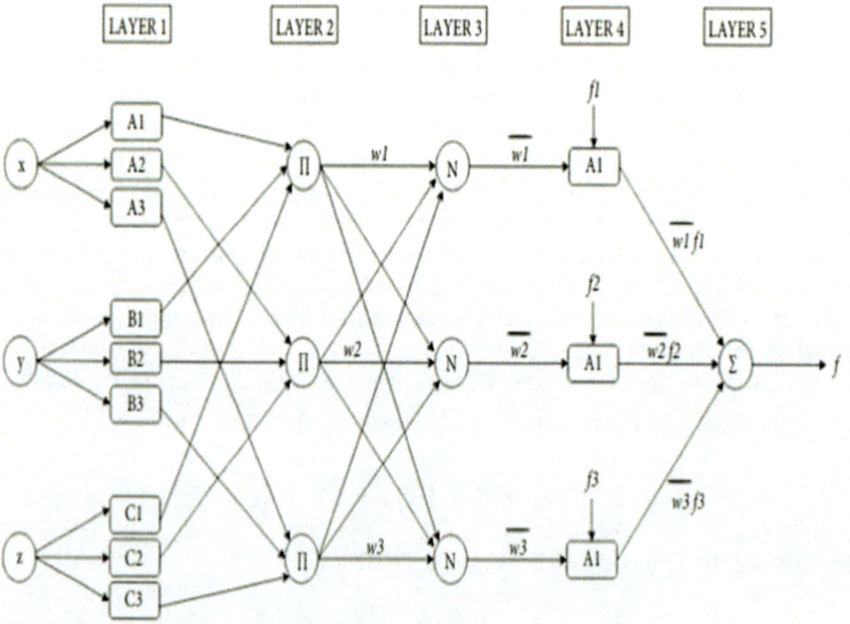

Fig. 4.3 The ANFIS standard structure for modelling and prediction analysis

Gaussian function is the best option. The Gaussian function's formula expressed in Eq. (4.8).

$$f(x) = a.\exp\left\{\frac{(x-b^2)}{(2C^2)}\right\} \tag{4.8}$$

Fuzzification Layer 2: This is an Implication Layer where the weight of the premise parameters is stored in the neurons as the product of the inputs. The formula for calculating the node output expressed in Eq. (4.9):

$$O_i^2 = w_i = \mu_{Ai}(x) * \mu_{Bi}(x) * \mu_{Ci}(x), \quad \forall i = 1, 2, 3 \tag{4.9}$$

where w_i is the neuron's weight

Layer 3: The neurons in the normalizing layer are fixed and are normalized using the weights of all the neurons in this layer. The formula for determining the node output is:

$$O_i^3 = \overline{w_i}\ f_i = \frac{w_i}{\sum w_i} \quad \forall i = 1, 2, 3 \tag{4.10}$$

where $\overline{w_i}$ is the normalized weight of the neuron

Layer 4: In the defuzzification layer, each neuron serves as an adaptable node and stores the architecture's ensuing parameters. This is how the node output is determined as shown in Eqs. (4.10) to (4.11):

$$O_i^4 = \overline{w_i}\ f_i = \overline{w_i} * (p_i x + q_i y + r_i z + s_i) \quad \forall i = 1, 2, 3 \tag{4.11}$$

Layer 5: There is only one neuron in the output layer, which is the sum of all the input layers. The formula for calculating the node output expressed in Eq. (4.12):

$$O_i^5 = \overline{w_i}\ f_i = f(x, y, z) = \sum_i \overline{w_i}\ f_i = \frac{\sum_i \overline{w_i} f_i}{\sum_i \overline{w_i}} \quad \forall i = 1, 2, 3 \tag{4.12}$$

The hybrid learning method, where parameters are updated over two passes and use two separate optimization algorithms, is preferred by traditional ANFIS. This five layers are employed for the modelling and prediction analysis of ANFIS [20].

4.4 Particle Swarm Optimization (PSO)

One of the bio-inspired algorithms, particle swarm optimization (PSO), is straightforward in its search for the best solution in the problem area. It differs from other optimization techniques in that it does not depend on the gradient or any differential form of the objective and simply requires the objective function. There are also not many hyperparameters [21]. PSO can be applied in various area of engineering process such as energy storage, renewable energy system, machining process optimisation such electrochemical, Micro-EDM optimization [22]. In order to maximize the measures of process performance, it is crucial to choose the ideal values for key electrochemical machining process parameters such the tool feed rate, electrolyte flow velocity, and applied voltage. Dimensional accuracy, tool life, material removal rate, and machining cost are examples of these performance indicators. For the purpose of determining the ideal set of process parameters for an electrochemical machining process, a particle swarm optimization approach is proposed in this research. Dimensional accuracy, tool life, and material removal rate are the goals taken into account. These goals are subject to temperature, choking, and passivity restrictions [23]. Aspects of both single- and multi-objective optimization are taken into account. The suggested algorithm's outcomes are contrasted with those of existing optimization methods that have already been published.

In the current study of Quarto et al. [24] a methodology for choosing the ideal process parameters for the EDM process was established up using an artificial neural network (ANN) and a heuristic algorithm known as particle swarm optimization (PSO). The created methodology has a dual direction feature that adapts to various industry needs. Typically, in an industrial setting, the operators are constrained by the requirements of the project or by the time constraints. Because of this, a methodology that has only been tried on a single type of workpiece material, has a small number of input variables, or was created to optimize a single performance is constrained. The created 2-step model gives operators the freedom to decide which criteria to include in the optimization and helps them to determine the optimum production option.

4.5 Genetic Algorithm (GA)

The genetic algorithm, which is based on natural selection, the mechanism that propels biological evolution, is a metaheuristic algorithm technique for resolving both limited and unconstrained optimization issues [25]. A search-based technique known as a genetic algorithm is used to address optimization issues in machine learning. This method is crucial because it resolves challenging issues that would require a lot of time to resolve. Data centers, electronic circuit design, code-breaking, picture processing, and artificial creativity are just a few of the real-world uses for it. The Generational GA (GGA), Steady-State (SSGA), Steady-Generational (SGGA), and (+)-GA are the four different forms of Genetic Algorithms (GA) that are described

[26]. Each crossover method for each type of GA is split into its comparable classes based on 30 runs of the top 12 EC variants. A heuristic search algorithm called a genetic algorithm (GA) is used to tackle search and optimization issues. A subset of evolutionary algorithms, which are utilized in computation, includes this algorithm. Genetic algorithms employ the concept of genetics and natural selection to provide solutions to problems.

These algorithms are more intelligent than random search algorithms because they direct the search to the best performing area of the solution space using historical data [27]. GAs are also based on chromosomal behavior and genetic structure. Every chromosome plays a part in offering a potential answer. The fitness function assists in supplying the traits of each person inside the population [7]. The solution is better the larger the function. In the 1960s and 1970s, Holland [76] developed the concept of GA, which he adapted from natural genetics and evolution. To get the best solution, randomly combined solutions are examined and their information is shared. GA can be used by functions with one or more objectives. By maximizing radial rake angle, speed, and feed rate throughout the end milling machining process, a single-objective function minimizes SR for Ti–6Al4V [28].

A process for optimizing genetic algorithms is as follows:

1. Select a coding scheme, a crossover operator, a mutation operator, and a selection operator to describe the problem parameters. Select the n-fold crossover probability, pc, and the p-fold mutation probability. Create a random population of strings with a length of l. Select the tmax generation number as the most permitted. Set $t = 0$.
2. Assess each string in the sample.
3. Terminate if t tmax or other termination requirements are met.
4. Encourage population reproduction.
5. Use probability PC to do a crossover on a pair of strings.
6. Apply PM probability to string mutations.
7. Assess the new population's strings. Go to Step 3 after setting $* = t + 1$.

4.6 Whale Optimization Algorithm

Whale optimization algorithm (WOA) is a meta-heuristic optimization algorithm inspired by nature that imitates the behavior of humpback whales when hunting. The bubble-net searching tactic served as the basis for the algorithm. Bubble-net feeding is the term used to describe the humpback whales' foraging activity [29]. An optimization algorithm is a methodical process used to find the highest or minimum value of an objective function [30]. Engineering applications are increasingly using meta-heuristic optimization techniques because they:

(i) rely on relatively simple ideas and are straightforward to put into practice.
(ii) They do not need gradient information to avoid local optima and
(iii) can be used to a wide range of issues from many academic fields.

Fig. 4.4 How humpback whales feed while using bubble-nets

Bubble-net feeding is the term used to describe the humpback whales' foraging activity. Hunting krill or small fish in schools near the surface is preferred by humpback whales [31]. This foraging has been seen to involve the formation of characteristic bubbles along a circular or '9'-shaped path, as depicted in Fig. 4.4. Only humpback whales have been documented to engage in bubble-net feeding, which is a distinctive behavior. The spiral bubble-net feeding movement is mathematically described in the whale optimization algorithm (WOA) in order to accomplish optimization.

- WOA mimicked hunting behavior by using the best search agent or a random search agent to pursue the prey.
- To mimic humpback whales' bubble-net attacking technique, WOA employs a spiral.

In the machining industrial sector, choosing the right cutting parameters is crucial for enhancing product quality. The use of optimization techniques in metal cutting operations is therefore essential for a high-quality end result [32, 33]. Because multiple conflicting objectives must be optimized at once due to the complexity of the machining operations, single objective optimization techniques have drawbacks [34]. In order to resolve this conundrum, the multi-objective optimization method is introduced [35]. Tanvir et al. [36] this paper's primary goal is to create a multi-objective optimization method using a hybrid version of the Whale Optimization Algorithm (WOA). The WOA algorithm incorporates grey analysis to complete the multi-objective optimization. This study examines the impact of machining parameters such as cutting speed, feed rate, and depth of cut on surface roughness, cutting forces, power, peak tool temperature, material removal rate, and heat rate when turning stainless steel 304. Through a number of simulations and experiments, the output parameters are acquired. Then, by taking into account unit cost and production quality, the hybrid optimization algorithm achieves the best machining conditions for a turning operation. It is also discovered that the ideal cutting condition changes when the output parameter weight varies. The effects of various cutting parameters on surface roughness and power consumption are also examined. This study has shown that the application of Whale optimization algorithm is a viable tool for machining process to optimized the machining parameters during production process.

4.7 Ant Lion Optimization Algorithm (ALOA)

A more recent meta-heuristic, the Ant Lion Optimizer (sometimes called Antlion Optimizer), describes mathematically how ants and antlions interact in the natural world [37]. In order to resolve optimization issues with ant random walks, trap building, ant entrapment in traps, prey capture, and trap re-building are applied, an optimization algorithm has been created to address engineering. The ALO algorithm imitates the way ant lions hunt, that is, how the ant lions engage with their prey (ant) [38]. The several processes that outline the interaction between antlions and ants are shown in Fig. 4.5.

The mathematical models are shown in the sections and Eqs. (4.13)–(4.14) [39]:

$$X(t) = [0, cumsum(2r(t_1) - 1), cumsum(2r(t_2) - 1), \ldots, cumsum(2r(t_n) - 1] \tag{4.13}$$

$$r(t) = \begin{cases} 1\, rand > 0.5 \\ 0\, rand \leq 0.5 \end{cases} \tag{4.14}$$

where r(t) is a stochastic function, rand is a random integer generated with uniform distribution in the range [0, 1], cumsum calculates the cumulative sum, n is the maximum number of iterations, t shows the step of the random walk (iteration in this research), and r(t) is a stochastic function.

The five primary phases of the ant lions' hunting strategy are described in the following steps.

4.7.1 *Random Walks of Ants*

Ants adjust their placements according to a random walk search at each stage of optimization as presented in Eq. (4.13) [40]. The ant positions are normalized using the following expression to make sure that all of them fall inside the search space's perimeter as given in Eq. (4.15):

$$X_i^t = \frac{(X_i^t - a_i)x(d_i - c_i^t)}{(d_i^t - a_i)} + c_i \tag{4.15}$$

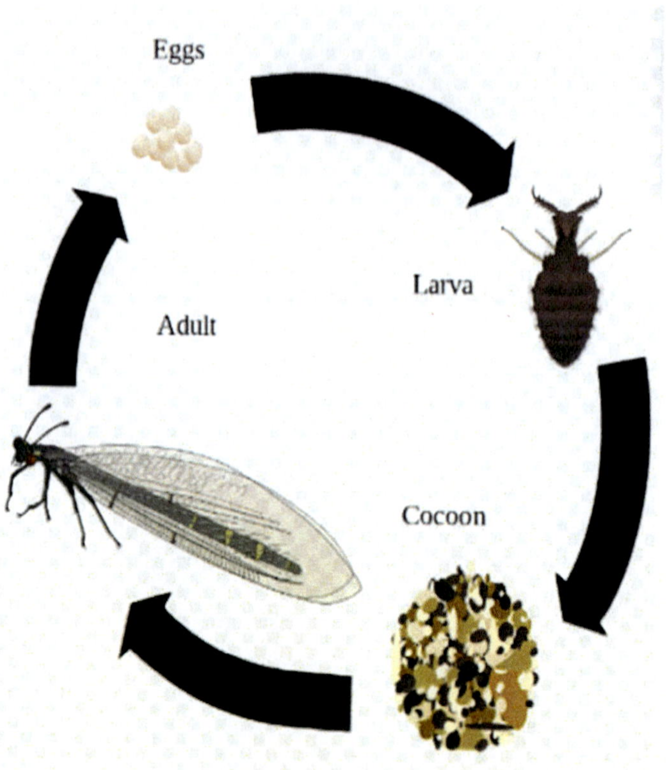

Fig. 4.5 The structural formulation of the interaction between antlions and ants

where display style a_i presents the minimum random walk in the i-th variable, displaystyle b_i represents the maximum random walk in the i-th variable, displaystyle c_i^t it represents the minimum of the i-th variable at the t-th iteration, and displaystyle d_i^t it represents the maximum of the i-th variable at the t-th iteration.

4.7.2 *Trapping in the Pits of Antlions*

According to a model, antlions have the following effects on ant movement as presented in Eqs. (4.16) and (4.17):

$$c_i^t = Antlion_j^t + c^t \tag{4.16}$$

$$d_i^t = Antlion_j^t + d^t \tag{4.17}$$

where display style c^t represents the minimum value for all variables at iteration t and display style d^t is the vector containing the maximum value for all variables at iteration t. The i-th ant's minimum set of variables is View the MathML code. The sum of all the variables for the i-th ant is View the MathML code, and The position of the chosen j-th antlion at the t-th iteration can be seen by viewing the MathML source.

4.7.3 Building Traps

Using a roulette wheel, traps are constructed. During optimization, the operator of the roulette wheel chooses the lions based on their fitness. The fitter antlions have a greater probability of catching ants thanks to this technique.

4.7.4 Ants Sliding Toward the Antlion

The aforementioned methods explain how antlions can build traps in proportion to their fitness and how ants travel toward the center of the pit [41]. Equations (4.18) and (4.19) is the mathematical representation of this step of the hut. The hyper-radius sphere's for ants' random movements is reduced, as can be seen in the equation.

$$adaptive.C^t = \frac{C^t}{I} \tag{4.18}$$

$$d^t = \frac{d^t}{I} \tag{4.19}$$

Knowing I is a ratio, c^t is the minimum value for all variables at iteration t, and d^t denotes the vector containing its maximum value for all variables.

4.7.5 Re-building the Pit and Catching Prey

When ants become more physically fit (dives deeper into the sand than their linked antlion), they can grab prey in ALO [42]. In order to increase its chances of snagging fresh prey, an antlion must then adjust its position to match the most recent location of the chased ant. This behavior is simulated by the Eq. (4.20):

$$Antlion_j^t = Ant_i^t \quad iff\left(Ant_i^t\right) > f(Antlin_j^t) \tag{4.20}$$

where the present iteration is shown by t, the placement of the chosen j-th antlion at the t-th iteration can be seen in the MathML source. The position of the i-th ant at the t-th iteration is shown in the MathML source.

4.7.6 Elitism

The ability of evolutionary algorithms to keep the best solution(s) found at any step of the optimization process is known as elitism [43]. The top antlion from each iteration is preserved and treated as an elite in this study. Since the elite is the strongest antlion, it ought to be able to have an impact on how the ants move over iterations. As a result, it is supposed that each ant simultaneously moves around an antlion chosen by the elite and the roulette wheel this expression is shown in Eq. (4.21):

$$Ant_i^t = \frac{R_A^t + R_E^t}{2} \tag{4.21}$$

where Ant_i^t denotes the position of the i-th ant at the t-th iteration and Rt A denotes the random walk around the antlion chosen by the roulette wheel at the t-th iteration. Ant Lion Optimizer can be applied as a single (ALO), Binary ALO (*BALO), and Multi-objective ALO (MOALO) in all world applications [44]. However, since the study of optimization in machining operation is very complex, due to several responses (cutting force, materials removal rate, surface roughness, temperature distribution, friction, and vibration). Machining parameters (cutting speed, depth of cut, feed rate, and length of cut), and environment of the cutting such as nanolubricants and vegetable oil, a multi-objective ALO is preferable. According to Kalita et al. [45] the multi-objective antlion optimization (MOALO) and the multi-objective dragonfly algorithm (MODA) are two nature-inspired optimization algorithms that are used in this research to optimize a variety of process parameters during the machining of MMCs. An ensemble strategy merging MOALO and MODA techniques is proposed here to reduce uncertainty in the global optimality of the anticipated Pareto optimal fronts resulting from the stochastic character of the metaheuristics. Two case studies are used to show how the MOALO-MODA ensemble is significantly better than its separate equivalents and may be used to create solid and trustworthy Pareto optimum fronts. Therefore, this book applied the MOALO in optimizing the cutting force and surface roughness in Chap. 7.

4.8 Grasshopper Optimization Algorithm (GOA)

Saremi, Mirjalili, and Lewis introduced the Grasshopper Optimization Algorithm (GOA) as an optimization method in 2017. It comprises both the attraction of the most desirable individual and social interaction between common agents (grasshoppers). In the course of our research, these intriguing exploratory skills of the GOA will be further studied, as evidenced by the authors' initial tests [46]. The objective of this contribution is to assess the machining response, optimizing the machining parameters, using the GOA as the optimization strategy. Figure 4.6 depicts how grasshoppers behave. Some search agents locally fly the search space during implementation. While this is happening, these relationships are driving a dramatic change in the other phase. Equation (4.22) describes the swarming behavior of grasshoppers using X_i as the position of the i-th insect:

$$X_i = r_1 S_i + r_2 G_i + r_3 A_i \tag{4.22}$$

While S_i represents a social connection, G_i stands for gravity, and A_i represents wind advection. Additionally, the random values for r_1, r_2, and r_3 range from 0 to 1 [34, 47] provide additional mathematical details concerning the approach.

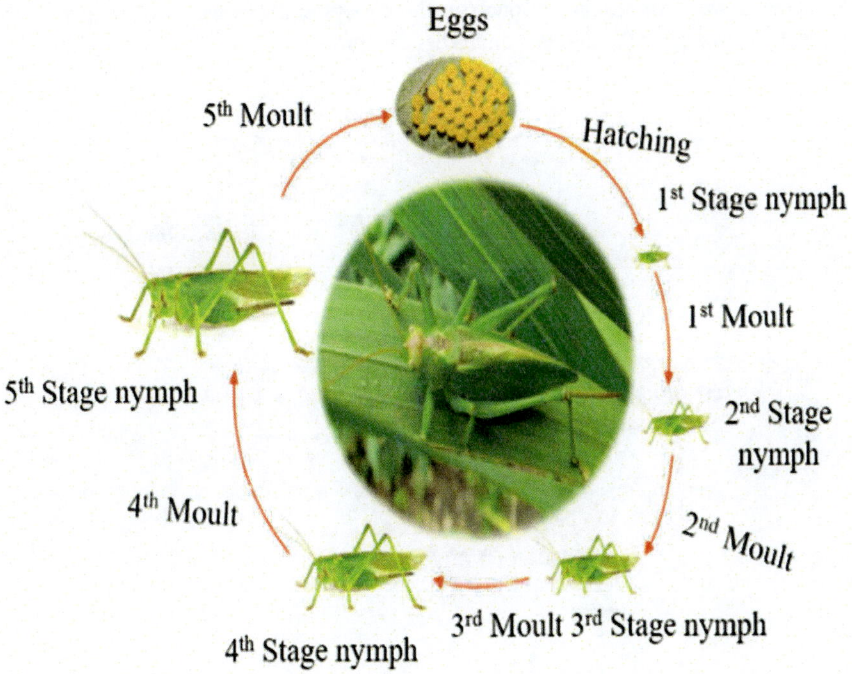

Fig. 4.6 The implementation of grasshopper optimization algorithm life cycle for machining operations

One of the most frequently referenced case cases in the literature is this structural design issue [48], which lead to the formulation of the measures for GOA as presented in the following steps of implementation:

(i) Initialization
(ii) first population and assessment
(iii) The entire beat solution is assigned
(iv) updating the parameter for the decreasing coefficient
(v) measuring grasshopper distances
(vi) updating the answer
(vii) Limitations of the solution
(viii) visiting all of the population's solutions
(ix) assessments of solutions
(x) Termination standards
(xi) delivering the top response

Figure 4.7 show the different step of the GOA flowchart for performance evaluation. The following are the Benefits of the application of GOA in manufacturing process:

(a) Even though grasshoppers can seriously harm a farmer's crops, the ecology wouldn't be the same without them [49].
(b) They have a significant impact on the ecosystem, enhancing its capacity to support the growth of plants and other creatures.

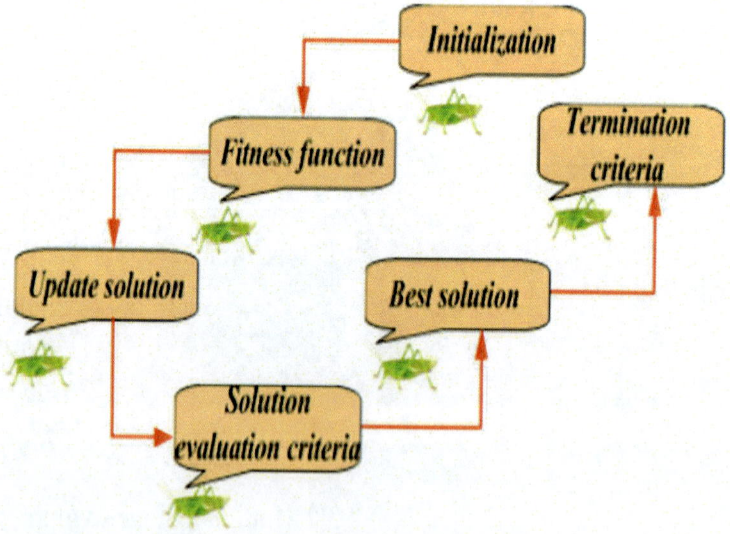

Fig. 4.7 GOA analysis flowchart for implementation

(c) The grasshopper facilitates plant decay and regrowth, maintaining a balance between the varieties of plants that survive, which helps people and the ecosystem as a whole.
(d) The ability of the grasshopper to dramatically alter the kinds of plants that flourish in his surroundings is proof that he benefits the ecology by promoting plant growth [50].
(e) Because the waste is smaller, bacteria can break it down more quickly and fertilize the soil more quickly.
(f) The grasshopper may not be aware of this particular function he performs in the ecosystem, but in the wild, he serves as a crucial source of food for predators.
(g) The insect's appetite can generally cause havoc on farm crops, but it also helps the ecosystem by ensuring that plant development is kept at its ideal levels [51].

Adapa et al. [52] in this study, the milling capabilities of polymer nanocomposite materials modified with glass fiber and multiwall carbon nanotube are examined (MWCNT). Spindle speed (S), Feed rate (F), Depth of Cut (D), and weight% MWCNT (wt.%), which are among the variables taken into consideration, have successfully controlled to obtain the desired value. Planning for the experiment used the Taguchi L9 Orthogonal array (OA). Using the Technique for Order of Preference by Similarity to Ideal Solution, the responses Material removal rate (MRR), cutting force (Fc), and surface roughness (Ra) were combined (TOPSIS). The Grasshopper optimization algorithm achieves the ideal combination of machining constraints (GOA). To choose the optimal target among the many possible solutions, GOA mitigates the bionic-inspired concepts. The larval phase of the GOA is characterized by the grasshopper's sluggish movement and little movements.

4.9 Review of Related Literature of the Optimization Techniques in Machining Process

This section gives details of research's that as implemented the global optimization tool and prediction techniques for machining process via various machining environment (Table 4.1).

According to Jawade et al. [68] the optimization of processing variables for the surface roughness of AISI316 austenitic stainless steel is discussed in this paper. Experimental parameters such feed rate (fd), speed (vc), and depth of cut (DoC) were utilized to examine the effects on the workpiece's surface roughness (Ra). The experiment was conducted on a computer numerical control (CNC) lathe utilizing the design of experiments (DOE). Following the turning process, the surface roughness is evaluated under three different conditions: dry, wet, and cryogenic. With a set of experiments planned, samples are step turned on a CNC lathe for each of the three circumstances. For all three scenarios, the response surface methodology is used, and mathematical models are created. It is best to use the algorithm that was inspired by nature to the optimal values for the machining parameters. In

Table 4.1 Summary of selected optimization techniques and their analysis in machining operations

Authors details	Optimization tools	Factors	Responses	Machining types	Findings
Han et al. [53]	Particle swarm algorithm in milling	Spindle speed (rpm), width of cutting (mm), feed rate (mm/min), and depth of cutting (mm)	Material removal rate (MRR) and cutting power (P)	Milling	The optimization model and technique given here address the trade-off issue involving P and MRR The findings show that the compared to not, the weighting optimization is more thorough just improving the empirical cutting power P and MRR not only guaranteeing the minimum P and the highest MRR. Research demonstrates the process and results. It is legitimate and practical to optimize objectively
Osorio-Pinzon et al. [54]	Multi-objective particle swarm optimization (PSO) algorithm	Rake angle (α), velocity (V), and cutting feed (f)	Reduce cutting force, improve microstructure, and increase material removal rate (MRR)	Turning of Al-6063	Through the incorporation of the multi-objective PSO (MOPSO) algorithm during the machining of Aluminum 6063, the optimization models may be able to help meet the intended objectives for optimizing the cutting force and materials removal rate

(continued)

Table 4.1 (continued)

Authors details	Optimization tools	Factors	Responses	Machining types	Findings
Kahya et al. [55]	Reconfigured particle swarm optimization algorithm	Depth of cut, Stepover, feed per tooth, and cutting velocity	Specific cutting energy, material removal rate, and surface roughness	Ball-end milling	PSO was a successful and simple to use multi-objective optimization technique. It was successful in producing a 3D Pareto front of the three-objective finish ball-end milling process. It was possible to recommend and validate three different machining scenarios based on a company's strategies in an industrial context using the created Pareto front

(continued)

Table 4.1 (continued)

Authors details	Optimization tools	Factors	Responses	Machining types	Findings
Das et al. [56]	Particle Swarm optimisation technique, and Taguchi technique	Depth of cut, d (mm), Cutting speed, V (m/min), and Feed, f (mm/rev)	Average surface roughness (Ra), cutting tool temperature (T), and tool flank wear	Turning operation of reinforced Al 7075 matrix composite	Compared to the outcomes of the traditional Taguchi technique, the multi-objective PSO produced better results for the answers. It successfully produced a set of non-dominated answers. For T, Ra, and VBc, Pareto optimum fronts were assembled and plotted; these could be chosen based on production needs. When comparing the experimental and PSO results, the confirmation experiments revealed errors of 2.12%, 2.76%, and 3% for T, Ra, and VBc, respectively. These findings suggested that this strategy was incredibly realistic and can be thought of as a workable substitute for resolving various objective optimisation issues

(continued)

Table 4.1 (continued)

Authors details	Optimization tools	Factors	Responses	Machining types	Findings
Balonji et al. [57]	Particles swarm optimisation (PSO) and artificial neural network (ANN)	Rotational speed, feed rate, radial depth cut, and axial depth cut of the tool	Surface roughness (SR)	End milling of Al6061 alloy	With respect to this investigation, the highest trained regression value (R 2) was reported to be 0.9938, and the lowest mean square error was reported to be 0.00044. These values correspond to nine (9) neurons, a 200-person swarm, and acceleration factors of 1.5 and 2.25. This work demonstrates the hybrid ANN-potential PSO's for surface roughness prediction, which may improve aluminum machining
Imani et al. [58]	Hybrid ANN and GA	Cutting depth, feed rate, coolant, and speed of cutting	Cutting force and surface roughness	Turning of Inconel 738	For both wet and dry milling of Inconel 738, the optimal artificial network developed in this study is beneficial for predicting the machining force and surface roughness of milling based on the values of cutting speed, feed rate, and axial depth of cutting

(continued)

Table 4.1 (continued)

Authors details	Optimization tools	Factors	Responses	Machining types	Findings
Karthikeyan et al. [59]	Genetic algorithm and feed forward artificial neural network	Voltage, input power, pulse on and off, and pulse	Material removal rate (MRR) and surface roughness (SR)	Wire cut electric discharge machining (WCEDM)	An artificial neural network was used to build the model between the process factors and output values. While the root mean square error for the MRR model was found to be as low as 0.0059386 and the determination coefficient to be 1, the root mean square error for the SR model was found to be as low as 0.0033068 and the determination coefficient to be 0.99991. The evolutionary computational methods of genetic algorithms for optimization were properly combined with the model developed by ANN

(continued)

Table 4.1 (continued)

Authors details	Optimization tools	Factors	Responses	Machining types	Findings
Nguyen et al. [60]	Genetic algorithms	Feed rate, cutting speed, cutting depth	Surface roughness and the maximum value of the material removal rate	Grinding process of 9CrSi alloy	To obtain the least amount of surface roughness and the highest amount of material removal rate, the genetic algorithms (GAs) were used to calculate the ideal values of external cylindrical grinding conditions
Santhosh et al. [61]	RSM and ANN-genetic algorithms using a face-centered CCD method	Depth of cut, rotating speed, and feed rate	*Surface roughness*	Turning operation for AISI 4340 alloy steel	To find the best machining process parameters and get a satisfactory output response in real-world settings, a combination of artificial neural network and genetic algorithm technique is advised
Sahoo et al. [62]	Taguchi-Whale optimization algorithm	Feed rate, spindle speed and tool condition	Surface roughness, maximizing power and torque	CNC-drilling of Inconel 718	To decrease surface roughness and maximize torque and thrust force during drilling operations, the process parameters are optimized using the Whale optimization method

(continued)

Table 4.1 (continued)

Authors details	Optimization tools	Factors	Responses	Machining types	Findings
Tanvir et al. [36]	Hybrid Whale optimization algorithm	Cutting speed, feed rate and depth of cut	Cutting pressures, power, maximum tool temperature, rate of material removal, and heat rate	Turning stainless steel 304	Numerous simulations and tests are used to acquire the output parameters. The best machining conditions for turning operations are therefore attained by employing this hybrid optimization technique while taking unit cost and production quality into account. Additionally, it has been discovered that the ideal cutting condition changes when the weight of the output parameter changes
Joshi et al. [63]	The multi-objective ant lion optimization (MOALO), non-dominated sorting genetic algorithm II (NSGA-II), and multi-objective dragonfly optimization (MODA)	Cutting depth (D), feed rate (f), and cutting speed (N)	Material removal rate (MRR) and surface roughness (SR)	Micro-machining processes	According to a comparison of the metaheuristics for multi-objective optimization, MOALO is faster at solving these kinds of problems than MODA or NSGA-II. Additionally, it is discovered that MOALO and MODA have considerably superior Pareto front recognition and generating skills than NSGA-II. Both of the COPRAS solutions for MODA performed significantly better than NSGA-II, with MOALO being only slightly superior to COPRAS

(continued)

Table 4.1 (continued)

Authors details	Optimization tools	Factors	Responses	Machining types	Findings
Laouissi et al. [64]	ANN-MOALO	Cutting depth, feed rate and cutting speed	Surface roughness	Turning of EN-GJL-250 cast iron	Future industrial applications for accurately predicting part quality and power consumption as well as optimizing cutting parameters to obtain the greatest production control have been discovered to benefit from the ANN-MOALO technique
Sinha et al. [65]	Multi-objective grasshopper optimization	Servo voltage, peak current, spark-on time, spark-off time	Material remcval rate (MRR) and Surface Roughness (SR)	Wire electro discharge machining (WEDM) of Inconel 625	Multiple objective particle swarm optimization (MOPSO) and non-dominated sorting genetic algorithm II (NSGA-II) were compared with MOGOA, and MOGOA was determined to be superior to both
Kumarand Verma [66]	Grasshopper-inspired optimization algorithm (GOA)	Feed rate (F), depth of cut (D), weight percentage of MWCNT (wt.%), and spindle speed (S)	Cutting force (Fc), material removal rate (MRR), and surface roughness (Ra)	Milling of polymer nanocomposite	The Grasshopper optimization algorithm achieves the ideal combination of machining constraints (GOA). To choose the optimal target among the many possible solutions, GOA mitigates the bionic-inspired concepts
Nagarajan et al. [67]	Grey wolf optimizer (GWO)	Applied voltage, flow rate, and electrolyte concentration	Material removal rate (MRR)	Electrochemical machining	This proves that the GWO metaheuristic algorithms are more suited for determining the ideal process variables for milling Monel 400 alloys using ECM

Table 4.2 Present the grasshopper optimization algorithm's optimal settings for the machining parameters

Surface roughness	Cutting speed (Vc)	Feed rate (fd)	Depth of cut (D.O.C.)	Optimal values
Ra (dry)	160	0.3	1.01	0.4535
Ra (wet)	200	0.3	0.5	0.7916
Ra (cryogenic)	165.58	0.1	1.5	0.3895

order to get the best parameter values for the problem being presented in the study, which involves minimizing surface roughness under all predetermined conditions, naturalistic methodologies are applied. The approach that works well for practical applications is the Grasshopper optimization algorithm (GOA). In this study, GOA is employed to obtain the best surface roughness (Ra) values under dry, wet, and cryogenic circumstances as shown in Table 4.2. Finally, findings are contrasted, and it is found that GOA values have the lowest surface roughness values.

However, it can be seen from the optimal results from Table 4.1 that for each machining environments there are different optimal machining values. This is the challenge and limitation of most studies done in the area of optimization with modern optimization tools. This study book will address this challenges in the different chapters employing the multi-optimization tools such as multi-objective grasshopper optimizer, multi-objective grey wolf optimizer and multi-objective ant lion optimizer.

4.10 Conclusion

This chapter has successfully discussed Global optimization tool and prediction techniques as it pertained to machining process. The optimization and prediction tools discussed in this chapter cut across the Artificial Neural Network (ANN), Adaptive Neuro-Fuzzy Inference System, particle swarm optimization, genetic algorithm, Whale optimization algorithm, Ant Lion Optimization Algorithm (ALOA), and Grasshopper Optimization Algorithm (GOA). From the results obtained from the review and discussion of the various techniques this chapter has the following conclusion such as:

(i) It has been proven that the GOA and ALOA is a viable optimization tools for machining operations.
(ii) The global prediction tool employed such as Artificial Neural Network (ANN), Adaptive Neuro-Fuzzy Inference System has also proven viable, which assist the predictions of the future works in the response surface parameters during machining.

(iii) Due to the complexity in studying the optimizations parameters of the factors and the responses in machining, single optimization tool will not be satisfactory, however, it can give optimal value but not as sustainable as the multi-optimization tools.

Therefore, the application of Multi-Heuristic and Metaheuristic Techniques for Advanced Machining Optimization is high needed to improve the manufacturing production system. Chapter 5 of this book discusses the multi-objective Grey Wolf Optimizer for improved machinability performance employing various factors and studying various responses.

References

1. Farid, M., Latip, R., Hussin, M., Abdul Hamid, N.A.W.: A survey on QoS requirements based on particle swarm optimization scheduling techniques for workflow scheduling in cloud computing. Symmetry **12**(4), 551 (2020)
2. Abualigah, L.: Multi-verse optimizer algorithm: a comprehensive survey of its results, variants, and applications. Neural Comput. Appl. **32**(16), 12381–12401 (2020)
3. Lee, W.J., Mendis, G.P., Sutherland, J.W.: Development of an intelligent tool condition monitoring system to identify manufacturing tradeoffs and optimal machining conditions. Procedia Manuf. **33**, 256–263 (2019)
4. Koopialipoor, M., Ghaleini, E.N., Haghighi, M., Kanagarajan, S., Maarefvand, P., Mohamad, E.T.: Overbreak prediction and optimization in tunnel using neural network and bee colony techniques. Eng. Comput. **35**(4), 1191–1202 (2019)
5. Gupta, M.K., Sood, P.K., Sharma, V.S.: Machining parameters optimization of titanium alloy using response surface methodology and particle swarm optimization under minimum-quantity lubrication environment. Mater. Manuf. Process. **31**(13), 1671–1682 (2016)
6. Mohd, M.R.H., Sarkheyli, A., Mohd, A., Haron, H.: Fuzzy logic for modeling machining process: a review. Artif. Intell. Rev. **43**(3), 345–379 (2015)
7. Zolpakar, N.A., Yasak, M.F., Pathak, S.: A review: use of evolutionary algorithm for optimisation of machining parameters. Int. J. Adv. Manuf. Technol. **115**(1), 31–47 (2021)
8. Li, D., Du, Y.: Artificial intelligence with uncertainty. CRC Press (2017). https://doi.org/10.1201/9781315366951
9. Shanmuganathan, S.: Artificial neural network modelling: an introduction. In: Artificial Neural Network Modelling, pp. 1–14. Springer, Cham (2016)
10. Güven, İ, Şimşir, F.: Demand forecasting with color parameter in retail apparel industry using artificial neural networks (ANN) and support vector machines (SVM) methods. Comput. Ind. Eng. **147**, 106678 (2020)
11. Almási, A.D., Woźniak, S., Cristea, V., Leblebici, Y., Engbersen, T.: Review of advances in neural networks: neural design technology stack. Neurocomputing **174**, 31–41 (2016)
12. Milosevic, S., Bezdan, T., Zivkovic, M., Bacanin, N., Strumberger, I., Tuba, M.: Feed-forward neural network training by hybrid bat algorithm. In: International Conference on Modelling and Development of Intelligent Systems, pp. 52–66. Springer, Cham (2021)
13. Correia, S.D., Tomic, S., Beko, M.: A feed-forward neural network approach for energy-based acoustic source localization. J. Sens. Actuator Netw. **10**(2), 29 (2021)
14. Asfaram, A., Ghaedi, M., Azqhandi, M.A., Goudarzi, A., Dastkhoon, M.J.R.A.: Statistical experimental design, least squares-support vector machine (LS-SVM) and artificial neural network (ANN) methods for modeling the facilitated adsorption of methylene blue dye. RSC Adv. **6**(46), 40502–40516 (2016)

15. Asiltürk, I., Çunkaş, M.: Modeling and prediction of surface roughness in turning operations using artificial neural network and multiple regression method. Expert Syst. Appl. **38**(5), 5826–5832 (2011)
16. Lin, Y.C., Wu, K.D., Shih, W.C., Hsu, P.K., Hung, J.P.: Prediction of surface roughness based on cutting parameters and machining vibration in end milling using regression method and artificial neural network. Appl. Sci. **10**(11), 3941 (2020)
17. Chicco, D., Warrens, M.J., Jurman, G.: The coefficient of determination R-squared is more informative than SMAPE, MAE, MAPE, MSE and RMSE in regression analysis evaluation. Peer J. Comput. Sci. **7**, e623 (2021)
18. Pezeshki, Z., Mazinani, S.M.: Comparison of artificial neural networks, fuzzy logic and neuro fuzzy for predicting optimization of building thermal consumption: a survey. Artif. Intell. Rev. **52**(1), 495–525 (2019)
19. Chopra, S., Dhiman, G., Sharma, A., Shabaz, M., Shukla, P., Arora, M.: Taxonomy of adaptive neuro-fuzzy inference system in modern engineering sciences. In: Computational Intelligence and Neuroscience, 2021 (2021)
20. Shahnazar, A., Nikafshan, H., Hasanipanah, M., Tahir, M.M., Jahed, D., Ghoroqi, M.: A new developed approach for the prediction of ground vibration using a hybrid PSO-optimized ANFIS-based model. Environ. Earth Sci. **76**, 1–17 (2017)
21. Igiri, C.P., Singh, Y., Poonia, R.C.: A review study of modified swarm intelligence: particle swarm optimization, firefly, bat and gray wolf optimizer algorithms. Recent Adv. Comput. Sci. Commun. (Formerly: Recent Patents on Computer Science) **13**(1), 5–12 (2020)
22. Faisal, N., Kumar, K., Verma, R.K.: Optimization of machine process parameters in EDM for EN 31 using evolutionary optimization techniques. Technologies **6**(2), 54 (2018)
23. Kapoor, P., Costall, A.W., Sakellaridis, N., Lammers, R., Buonpane, A., Guilain, S.: Multi-objective optimization of turbocharger turbines for low carbon vehicles using meanline and neural network models. Energy Conver. Manag. X **15**, 100261 (2022)
24. Quarto, M., D'Urso, G., Giardini, C.: Micro-EDM optimization through particle swarm algorithm and artificial neural network. Precis. Eng. **73**, 63–70 (2022)
25. Singh, S., Mittal, N., Thakur, D., Singh, H., Oliva, D., Demin, A.: Nature and biologically inspired image segmentation techniques. Arch. Computat. Methods Eng. 1–28 (2021)
26. Jenkins, A., Gupta, V., Myrick, A., Lenoir, M.: Variations of Genetic Algorithms (2019). arXiv preprint arXiv:1911.00490
27. Bouktif, S., Fiaz, A., Ouni, A., Serhani, M.A.: Optimal deep learning lstm model for electric load forecasting using feature selection and genetic algorithm: Comparison with machine learning approaches. Energies **11**(7), 1636 (2018)
28. Ganesan, H., Mohankumar, G.: Optimization of machining techniques in CNC turning centre using genetic algorithm. Arab. J. Sci. Eng. **38**, 1529–1538 (2013)
29. Mirjalili, S., Lewis, A.: The whale optimization algorithm. Adv. Eng. Softw. **95**, 51–67 (2016)
30. Abualigah, L.: Group search optimizer: a nature-inspired meta-heuristic optimization algorithm with its results, variants, and applications. Neural Comput. Appl. **33**(7), 2949–2972 (2021)
31. Nedjah, N., Mourelle, L.D.M., Morais, R.G.: Inspiration-wise swarm intelligence meta-heuristics for continuous optimisation: a survey-part ii. Int. J. Bio-Inspired Computat. **16**(4), 195–212 (2020)
32. Okokpujie, I.P., Ikumapayi, O.M., Okonkwo, U.C., Salawu, E.Y., Afolalu, S.A., Dirisu, J.O., Nwoke, O.N., Ajayi, O.O.: Experimental and mathematical modeling for prediction of tool wear on the machining of aluminium 6061 alloy by high speed steel tools. Open Eng. **7**(1), 461–469 (2017)
33. Okokpujie, I.P., Akujieze, C.T., Sinebe, J.E., Tartibu, L.K., Adeoye, A., Kelechi, S.E., Akinlabi, E.: Experimental study and finite element analysis of temperature reduction and distribution during machining of Al-Si-Mg composite using deform 3D. J. Adv. Res. Fluid Mech. Therm. Sci. **97**(2), 8–25 (2022)
34. Mirjalili, S.Z., Mirjalili, S., Saremi, S., Faris, H., Aljarah, I.: Grasshopper optimization algorithm for multi-objective optimization problems. Appl. Intell. **48**, 805–820 (2018)

35. He, Y., Liao, N., Lin, K.: Can China's industrial sector achieve energy conservation and emission reduction goals dominated by energy efficiency enhancement? A multi-objective optimization approach. Energy Policy **149**, 112108 (2021)
36. Tanvir, M.H., Hussain, A., Rahman, M.T., Ishraq, S., Zishan, K., Rahul, S.T.T., Habib, M.A.: Multi-objective optimization of turning operation of stainless steel using a hybrid whale optimization algorithm. Journal of manufacturing and materials processing **4**(3), 64 (2020)
37. Sharma, R., Saha, A.: Ant Lion optimizer for state based object oriented testing. J. Inf. Optim. Sci. **40**(2), 219–232 (2019)
38. Heidari, A.A., Faris, H., Mirjalili, S., Aljarah, I., Mafarja, M.: Ant lion optimizer: theory, literature review, and application in multi-layer perceptron neural networks. *Nature-Inspired Optimizers: Theories, Literature Reviews and Applications*, pp. 23–46 (2020)
39. Mouassa, S., Bouktir, T., Salhi, A.: Ant lion optimizer for solving optimal reactive power dispatch problem in power systems. Eng. Sci. Technol. Int. J. **20**(3), 885–895 (2017)
40. George, T., Youssef, A.R., Ebeed, M., Kamel, S.: Ant lion optimization technique for optimal capacitor placement based on total cost and power loss minimization. In: 2018 International Conference on Innovative Trends in Computer Engineering (ITCE), pp. 350–356. IEEE (2018)
41. Zhang, H., Gao, Z., Zhang, J., Liu, J., Nie, Z., Zhang, J.: Hybridizing extended ant lion optimizer with sine cosine algorithm approach for abrupt motion tracking. EURASIP J. Image Video Process. **2020**(1), 1–18 (2020)
42. Sharifi, M.R., Akbarifard, S., Madadi, M.R., Qaderi, K., Akbarifard, H.: Optimization of hydropower energy generation by 14 robust evolutionary algorithms. Sci. Rep. **12**(1), 7739 (2022)
43. Alperen, Y., Sertac, C.: Multi objective optimization of a micro-channel heat sink through genetic algorithm. Int. J. Heat Mass Transf. **146**, 118847 (2020)
44. Pathak, V.K., Gangwar, S., Singh, R., Srivastava, A.K., Dikshit, M.: A comprehensive survey on the ant lion optimiser, variants and applications. J. Exp. Theor. Artif. Intell. 1–52 (2022)
45. Kalita, K., Kumar, V., Chakraborty, S.: A novel MOALO-MODA ensemble approach for multi-objective optimization of machining parameters for metal matrix composites. Multiscale Multi. Model. Exp. Des. 1–19 (2023)
46. Moayedi, H., Nguyen, H., Kok, L.: Nonlinear evolutionary swarm intelligence of grasshopper optimization algorithm and gray wolf optimization for weight adjustment of neural network. Eng. Comput. **37**, 1265–1275 (2021)
47. Aljarah, I., Al-, A.M., Faris, H., Hassonah, M.A., Mirjalili, S., Saadeh, H.: Simultaneous feature selection and support vector machine optimization using the grasshopper optimization algorithm. Cogn. Comput. **10**, 478–495 (2018)
48. Wang, Z., Sobey, A.: A comparative review between Genetic Algorithm use in composite optimisation and the state-of-the-art in evolutionary computation. Compos. Struct. **233**, 111739 (2020)
49. Bhadoria, A., Kamboj, V.K.: Optimal generation scheduling and dispatch of thermal generating units considering impact of wind penetration using hGWO-RES algorithm. Appl. Intell. **49**, 1517–1547 (2019)
50. Legha, M.M., Javaheri, H., Legha, M.M.: Optimal conductor selection in radial distribution systems for productivity improvement using genetic algorithm. Iraqi J. Electr. Electron. Eng. **9**(1) (2013)
51. Nosratabadi, S.M., Bornapour, M., Gharaei, M.A.: Grasshopper optimization algorithm for optimal load frequency control considering predictive functional modified PID controller in restructured multi-resource multi-area power system with redox flow battery units. Control. Eng. Pract. **89**, 204–227 (2019)
52. Adapa, S.K., Yanda, S., Raju, S.S.: Optimization of AWJM process on processing of lite bamboo reinforced polymer composite by using grasshopper algorithm. In: Advances in Manufacturing Engineering: Select Proceedings of ICFAMMT 2022, pp. 55–64. Springer Nature, Singapore (2022)
53. Han, F., Li, L., Cai, W., Li, C., Deng, X., Sutherland, J.W.: Parameters optimization considering the trade-off between cutting power and MRR based on linear decreasing particle swarm algorithm in milling. J. Clean. Prod. **262**, 121388 (2020)

54. Osorio-Pinzon, J.C., Abolghasem, S., Maranon, A., Casas-Rodriguez, J.P.: Cutting parameter optimization of Al-6063 using numerical simulations and particle swarm optimization. Int. J. Adv. Manuf. Technol. **111**, 2507–2532 (2020)
55. Kahya, M., Ozbayoglu, M., Unver, H.O.: Precision and energy-efficient ball-end milling of Ti6Al4V turbine blades using particle swarm optimization. Int. J. Comput. Integr. Manuf. **34**(2), 110–133 (2021)
56. Das, D., Chakraborty, V., Nayak, B.B., Satpathy, M.P., Samal, C.: Machining of aluminium-based metal matrix composite-a particle swarm optimisation approach. Int. J. Mach. Mach. Mater. **22**(1), 79–97 (2020)
57. Balonji, S., Okokpujie, I.P., Tartibu, L.K.: Parametric analysis of the process performance of surface roughness data of machined aluminium using PSO-ANN. In: 2021 International Conference on Artificial Intelligence, Big Data, Computing and Data Communication Systems (icABCD), pp. 1–6. IEEE (2021)
58. Imani, L., Rahmani, A., Hamzeloo, R., Davoodi, B.: Modeling and optimizing of cutting force and surface roughness in milling process of Inconel 738 using hybrid ANN and GA. Proc. Inst. Mech. Eng. Part B J. Eng. Manuf. **234**(5), 920–932 (2020)
59. Karthikeyan, R., Senthil, V., Punitha, A., Chavan, U.M.: An integrated ANN-GA approach to maximize the material removal rate and to minimize the surface roughness of wire cut EDM on Titanium alloy. Adv. Mater. Process. Technol. **8**(1), 22–32 (2022)
60. Nguyen, T.L., Nguyen, N.T., Hoang, L.: Multi-objective optimization using the genetic algorithms for external cylindrical grinding process of 9CrSi alloy. Int. J. Modern Phys. B **34**(22n24), 2040161 (2020)
61. Santhosh, A.J., Tura, A.D., Jiregna, I.T., Gemechu, W.F., Ashok, N., Ponnusamy, M.: Optimization of CNC turning parameters using face centred CCD approach in RSM and ANN-genetic algorithm for AISI 4340 alloy steel. Results Eng. **11**, 100251 (2021)
62. Sahoo, A.K., Jeet, S., Bagal, D.K., Barua, A., Pattanaik, A.K., Behera, N.: Parametric optimization of CNC-drilling of Inconel 718 with cryogenically treated drill-bit using Taguchi-Whale optimization algorithm. Mater. Today Proc. **50**, 1591–1598 (2022)
63. Joshi, M., Ghadai, R.K., Madhu, S., Kalita, K., Gao, X.Z.: Comparison of NSGA-II, MOALO and MODA for multi-objective optimization of micro-machining processes. Materials **14**(17), 5109 (2021)
64. Laouissi, A., Nouioua, M., Yallese, M.A., Abderazek, H., Maouche, H., Bouhalais, M.L.: Machinability study and ANN-MOALO-based multi-response optimization during Eco-Friendly machining of EN-GJL-250 cast iron. Int. J. Adv. Manuf. Technol. **117**(3–4), 1179–1192 (2021)
65. Sinha, A., Majumder, A., Gupta, K.: A RSM based MOGOA for process optimization during WEDM of Inconel 625. Proc. Inst. Mech. Eng. Part E J. Process Mech. Eng. **236**(5), 1824–1832 (2022)
66. Kumar, K., Verma, R.K.: Nature-inspired grasshopper optimization algorithm (GOA) for predictive modeling and machinability evaluation of laminated polymer nanocomposites. Multiscale Multi. Model. Exp. Des. 1–19 (2022)
67. Nagarajan, V., Solaiyappan, A., Mahalingam, S.K., Nagarajan, L., Salunkhe, S., Nasr, E.A., Shanmugam, R., Hussein, H.M.A.M.: Meta-heuristic technique-based parametric optimization for electrochemical machining of Monel 400 alloys to investigate the material removal rate and the sludge. Appl. Sci. **12**(6), 2793 (2022)
68. Jawade, S., Kulkarni, O.K., Kakandikar, G.M.: Parameter optimization of AISI 316 austenitic stainless steel for surface roughness by Grasshopper optimization algorithm. J. Mech. Eng. Autom. Control Syst. **2**(2), 87–97 (2021)

Chapter 5
Multi-objective Grey Wolf Optimizer for Improved Machining Performance

Abstract Real engineering difficulties come in a variety of forms, each requiring a unique set of tools to solve. Multi-objectivity is one of the key elements of real situations that makes them difficult to solve. In this section, the machinability performance problem is studied using two indicators namely the cutting force and the surface roughness. The speed of cutting, the feed rate and the depth of cut are the parameters, describing the setting of the CNC lathe machine, to optimize. In this study, titanium alloy (Ti–6Al–4V) was chosen as the turning work material. Quadratic equations of the cutting force and the surface roughness were extracted from an existing study to illustrate the approach. A single objective optimization problem was developed to optimize the cutting force and the surface roughness separately using the grey wolf optimizer. Details showing the formulation of the problem and the results have been disclosed. The Multi-objective grey wolf optimizer (MOGWO) was the metaheuristic-based approach proposed for the formulation of the problem and the computation of the non-dominated or Pareto optimal solutions. The best compromise was obtained by optimizing these two objectives simultaneously. The optimal settings corresponding to the optimal values of cutting force and surface roughness were computed and reported in this section.

Keywords Grey Wolf Optimizer · Multi-objective optimisation · Machining · Cutting force · Surface roughness

5.1 Introduction

One of the earliest and most common techniques for cutting metal has been turning operations utilizing single-point cutting tools. With shorter lead times, it has even taken the position of grinding in some applications without sacrificing surface quality. Cutting forces and workpiece surface roughness are two significant factors that are

I. P. Okokpujie and L. K. Tartibu, *Modern Optimization Techniques for Advanced Machining*, Studies in Systems, Decision and Control 485,
https://doi.org/10.1007/978-3-031-35455-7_5

extensively researched in turning operations [1, 2]. When examining the process capabilities of any machining operation, process parameter optimization is quite important. In order to understand cutting forces in turning operations, Shaw and Cookson [3] have underlined their significance. Surface precision, tool wear, tool breakage, cutting temperature, self-excited and forced vibrations, etc. are only a few of the aspects that are influenced by cutting forces. Özel and Karpat [4] among other studies, discovered that the surface quality of machined components is directly influenced by the cutting parameters (Feed rate, Cutting Speed, Depth of Cut, Tool Geometry, and Material Properties of Tool). The cutting force, thrust, and feed forces all have different effects on power consumption, however only the cutting force is taken into account as an endogenous element in this study.

Another crucial parameter is surface roughness, which can affect the wear resistance, fatigue strength, or creep life of machined components. A better surface finish (low surface roughness) is crucial for turned components as it can minimize or even totally eliminate the need for additional machining [2]. Many researchers have discovered that surface roughness affects a variety of factors, including heat transmission, lubricant retention, surface friction, wearing, etc. The machining process does not have perfect control over the surface finish obtained, despite the fact that surface roughness plays a significant role in the usefulness and lifespan of a machined component due to its dependence on several process parameters and numerous uncontrollable factors. Therefore, the ongoing process of adjusting process parameters to create the optimal surface finish involves a variety of material-to-tool combinations and machining circumstances [5].

Because turning is crucial for metal cutting, there is a wealth of literature on the subject. Speed, feed, and cut depth are the three key process variables in this study. To create a prediction model for surface roughness and cutting force, Lin et al. [6] used an abdicative network. This network can forecast the surface roughness and cutting force given the process parameters namely the cutting speed, the feed rate, and the depth of cut. It is essential to design the components in a way that can boost productivity, lengthen tool life, and lower overall machining costs. The machining process is optimized to increase productivity and product quality in order to reach the aim. The selection of variable parameters is regarded as a crucial task in machining optimization since it aids in assessing the effectiveness of the machining process. Typically, human (machinist) judgment and experience are used to determine the machining parameters. The optimum machining procedure, however, might not have been produced by the given parameters. In order to increase the efficiency of the machining process, optimization must be used [7].

As shown in Fig. 5.1, there are two main groups of optimization tools and techniques: traditional approaches and advanced methods. The majority of traditional optimization methods are gradient search based. Depending on the level of nonlinearity in the objective function and the initial assumption about the starting point, the standard optimisation technique has the potential to converge in a local optimum. Thus, the global optimum promised by the traditional optimisation technique was not achieved. In recent years, researchers have had a tendency to optimize machining operations using new techniques. Unlike the traditional approach, the advanced

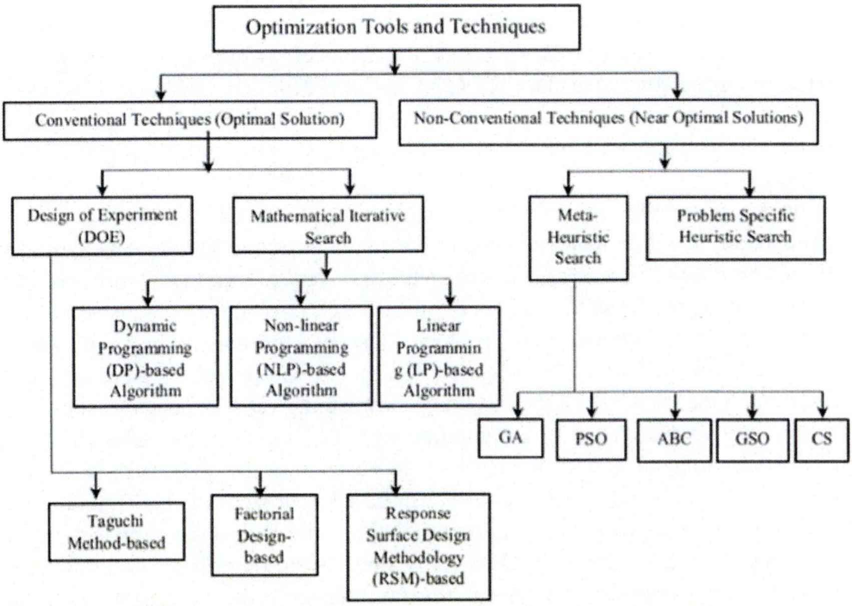

Fig. 5.1 Typical optimisation tools and techniques in the machining process [7]

approach, particularly metaheuristic search, is based on an evolutionary algorithm (EA) [such as genetic algorithm (GA), particle swarm optimisation (PSO), artificial bee colony (ABC), simulated annealing (SA), cuckoo search algorithm (CSA), firefly algorithm (FA), and glow worm swarm (GWS)] that imitates biological processes like natural selection, recombination, and mutation to identify the best design possible given a set of constraints. These evolutionary algorithms (EA) can be implemented to optimize machining parameters. An illustration of the formulation and the implementation of some evolutionary algorithms to solve classical mathematical problems is provided in the study of Okwu and Tartibu [8].

The foundation of bio-inspired algorithms (BIA) is the concept of the orderly, natural movement of organisms and a phenomenon that is frequently seen in various animal species. Amazing examples of self-organized coordination are flocks of birds and schools of fish. Particle Swarm Optimization (PSO), for instance, mimics the social behavior of birds. The system begins with a population of randomly distributed particles, or "swarm," and it continuously iterates through new generations in order to find the best value. Each particle in the swarm makes an effort to find a potential solution, and the group then makes an effort to achieve its overall goal based on feedback from the other members. Swarm intelligence-based algorithms (SIA) take advantage of the notion that a swarm's aggregate intelligence exceeds the sum of its constituent parts. The swarm's agents are all thought to be less than intelligent, but because they adhere to a few simple principles, the swarm as a whole can exhibit self-organizing behavior and act as though it had some form of collective intelligence.

These algorithms were developed by first studying the common habits of several animal species, such as wolves. This work aims to develop a new approach to optimize the machining performance of a CNC lathe machine. This approach seeks to optimize the cutting force and the surface roughness which are a function of the speed of cutting, the feed rate and the depth of cut using the grey wolf optimizer (GWO) algorithm.

The processing of a single objective function in optimization is known as a single objective, and the simultaneous handling of many objective functions is known as multi-objective optimization [9]. Through the discovery of a group of workable solutions known as non-dominated or Pareto optimal solutions, multi-objective optimization attempts to optimize a specific problem. The need for more effective methods is growing as a result of the abundance of multi-objective optimization issues in various study areas. One study has suggested using and adapting various metaheuristic-based approaches in research fields like engineering [10]. Based on the behavior of the method searching, the metaheuristic-based approaches are divided into three primary classes: trajectory, evolutionary, and swarm-based approaches [11]. The ability of the swarm-based approaches to approximate the entire Pareto front made them the most effective at addressing multi-objective optimization problems. To address the multi-objective optimization problem, several multi-objective optimization swarm-based techniques have been developed. This includes multi-objective optimization salp swarm optimizer [12]. MO moth-flame optimization [13], multi-objective optimization ant lion optimizer [14] and multi-objective optimization grey wolf optimizer (MOGWO) [15].

The Multi-objective grey wolf optimizer (MOGWO) draws inspiration from grey wolves and their natural habitat (such as their leadership hierarchy and hunting mechanism) and has been effectively used to address a variety of issues [11]. Due to the fact that the grey wolf optimizer (GWO) is gradually being implemented in many engineering fields, there are no studies about the use of this method for the optimization of problems involving the cutting force and the surface roughness in order to enhance machinability performance.

5.2 Grey Wolf Optimization (GWO) Background

The grey wolves typically coexist in packs of between 5 and 12 individuals. These wolves are divided into four groups based on their prevailing strategies: alpha (α), beta (β), delta (δ), and omega (ω) wolves. α wolves are the most dominating, and the dominance progressively declines to ω wolves. Important decisions are made by the α wolves regarding hunting, sleeping arrangements, and walking schedules. The group is informed of these choices. α wolves may also choose to follow other wolves in the pack, creating a democratic system. Despite not always being the group's strongest member, the α wolves serve as its leader [16]. The second degree of authority in the pack is represented by the β wolves, who aid α wolves in decision-making and other activities. In the event that α wolves pass away or get very old, they are nominated to replace those α wolves. The β wolves serve as the remainder of the pack's leaders and counselors. The group's lowest dominance is the ω wolves. These wolves are permitted to eat last. They could give birth to group members. The δ wolves rule over the ω wolves and provide information to the α and β wolves. There are three primary steps in the grey wolf hunt, which are as follows [17]:

1 Looking for, pursuing, and getting close to the prey.
2 Surrounding and agitating the prey until it stops moving (Fig. 5.2).
3 Taking the prey by force.

The following can be used to model the GWO algorithm:

(a) Social Strategy

The fittest solution in the GWO algorithm is referred to as α wolf. Consequently, the β and δ wolves are referred to as the second and third best options. The remaining potential solutions are the ω wolves. In general, the optimization process is guided by α, β, and δ wolves which are followed by ω wolves.

(b) Surrounding the prey

The following equations describe how grey wolves circle their prey:

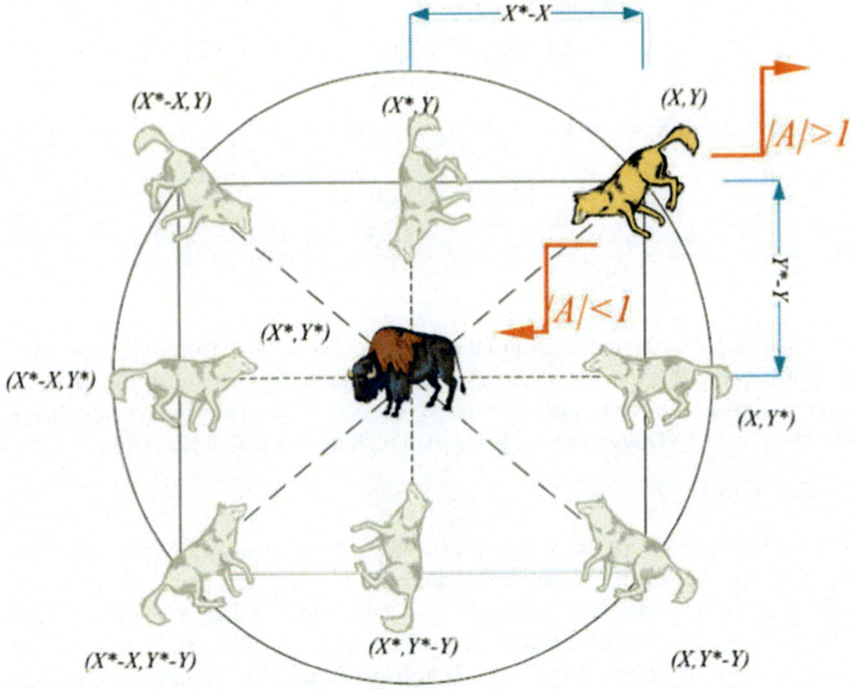

Fig. 5.2 Illustration of grey wolves surrounding a prey

$$D = |C.X_p(t) - X(t)| \tag{5.1}$$

$$X(t+1) = X_p(t) - A.D \tag{5.2}$$

where $X_p(t)$ represents the position vector of the prey, D is the problem dimension, A and C are the coefficient vectors given as follows:

$$A = 2a.r_1 - a \tag{5.3}$$

$$C = 2.r_2 \tag{5.4}$$

With each iteration, the components of the vector a linearly drop from 2 to 0; r_1 and r_2 are random vectors [0, 1].

(c) Hunting

It is assumed that α (best candidate solution), β and δ wolves have adequate knowledge of the prey position to replicate the hunting behavior of the grey wolves. In order to update their positions based on the positions of the top search agents, the first three best solutions are saved. The hunting behavior is described by the following equations:

$$D_\alpha = |C_1.X_\alpha - X|,\ D_\beta = |C_2.X_\beta - X|,\ D_\delta = |C_3.X_\delta - X| \tag{5.5}$$

$$X_1 = X_\alpha - A_1.D_\alpha,\ X_2 = X_\beta - A_2.D_\beta,\ X_3 = X_\delta - A_3.D_\delta \tag{5.6}$$

$$X(t+1) = \frac{X_1 + X_2 + X_3}{3} \tag{5.7}$$

(d) Attacking the prey

When the target stops moving, an attack is launched to end the hunting process. Mathematically, this can be accomplished by repeatedly decreasing the value of vector a from 2 to 0. It has been discovered that $|A| < 1$ can make the wolves charge their prey. The GWO algorithm is being exploited by this malicious action.

(e) Searching for the prey

The grey wolves look for the prey based on where the three other α, β, and δ wolves are. They split off from one another to look for the prey and then come together to attack it. It has been noted that $|A| > 1$ can compel wolves to look for more advantageous prey. This divergence behavior relates to the GWO algorithm's global search. Figure 5.3 shows a thorough flowchart of the GWO algorithm. The best candidate solution (X_α) is reached at the end of the suggested process, which begins with a random population of grey wolves.

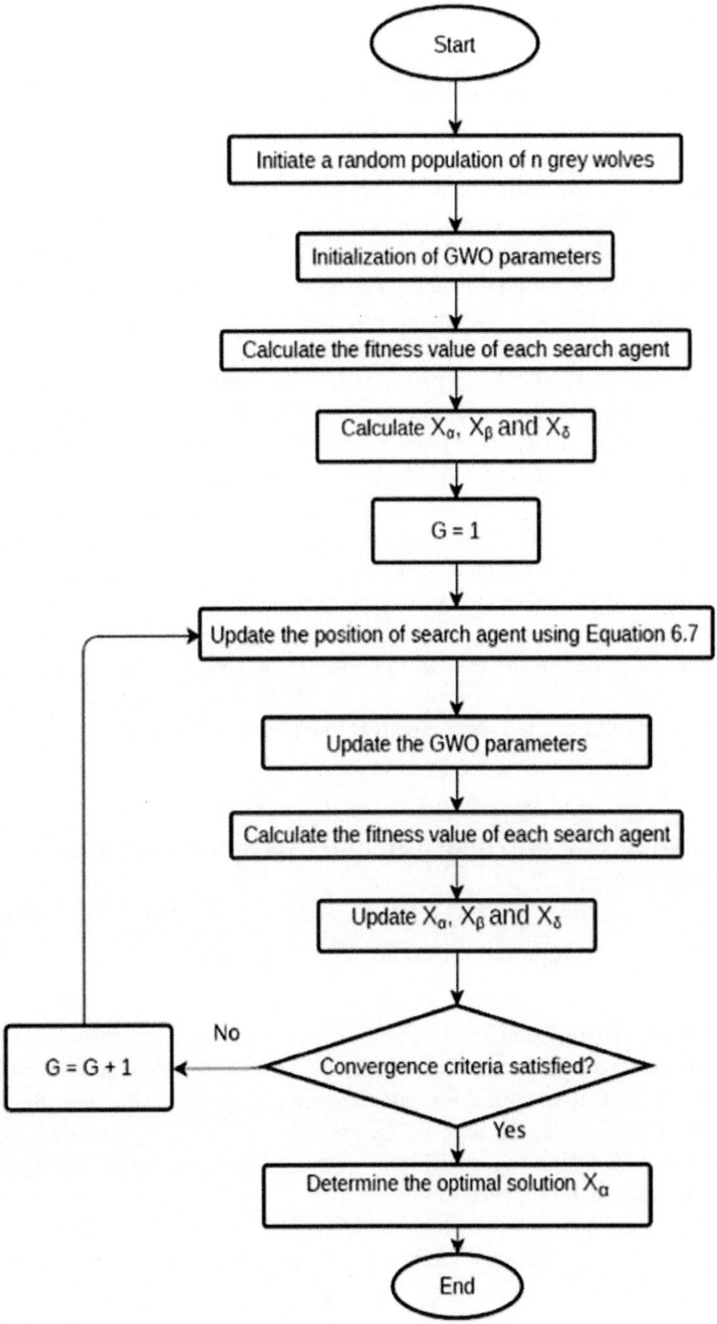

Fig. 5.3 Flowchart of the GWO algorithm

5.3 Brief Description of Data Extraction and Processing

In order to illustrate the approach proposed in this study, quadratic equations were extracted from the study conducted by Sahu and Andhare [18]. In the reported study, titanium alloy (Ti–6Al–4V) was chosen as the turning work material. The bar size for turning was determined to be 32 mm in diameter, 100 mm in length, and 35 mm in length cut. The turning operations were carried out on a CNC lathe machine with a 5.5 kW power capacity. The machine's controller provided fine motion and spindle speed control with 0.005 mm position precision and 0.004 mm repeatability during cutting. During turning operations, the cutting force was measured using a dynamometer that was interfaced with a control unit.

The design of experiment was performed with a central composite design (CCD) based on Response Surface Methodology (RSM). The speed of cutting, the feed rate and the depth of cut were the input factors. The regression coefficient and subsequently the quadratic equation of the cutting force were generated based on the experimental design and the response measured. The model adequacy was checked using the analysis of variance (ANOVA) and non-significant parameters were discarded. A similar approach was adopted to develop the quadratic equation describing the surface roughness [19]. The roughness of the machined surface and the force of cutting were the two responses. In the formulation of the multi-objective optimization models described in the following sections, the speed of cutting, the feed rate and the depth of cut are the variables to be optimized while the surface roughness and the cutting force are the two objective functions to minimize.

5.4 Formulation of Quadratic Equations and Mathematical Formulation

5.4.1 Design Variables and Objectives Functions

Three different variables namely the cutting speed (S), the feed rate (F) and the depth of cut (D) have been considered. These three variables are closely related to the setting of the CNC lathe machine used for data extraction and processing described in the previous section. The lowest and the highest level of cutting parameters used for central composite design reported in the study of [18] were taken into account to illustrate the approach proposed in this study.

$$\begin{aligned} S_{min} &= 69.9 < S < S_{max} = 150 \\ F_{min} &= 55.6 < F < F_{max} = 120.6 \\ D_{min} &= 0.66 < D < D_{max} = 2 \end{aligned} \tag{5.8}$$

S, F and D $\in \Re^+$.

In this study, the machinability of Ti–6Al–4V alloy is measured with the cutting force (CF) and the surface roughness (SR). The two objective functions in the formulation of the mathematical programming problem are these indicators. They are given by the following quadratic Equations:

$$\begin{aligned} CF = {} & 513.915 - 0.2466 \times S + 5.3773 \times F + 64.92 \\ & \times D - 2.594e - 4 \times S^2 - 0.055 \times F^2 + 0.0052 \times S \times F \end{aligned} \tag{5.9}$$

$$\begin{aligned} SR = {} & 1.27686 - 0.000897964 \times S + 0.0008937 \\ & \times F + 0.036303 \times D + 1.69203e - 7 \times S^2 \end{aligned} \tag{5.10}$$

These equations suggest that the three variables (S, F and D) have a significant effect on the cutting force and the surface roughness of Ti–6Al–4V alloy. The optimum values of the parameters describing the setting of the CNC lathe machine can be obtained by solving Eqs. 5.9 and 5.10.

5.4.2 *Multi-objective Optimization*

The following Equation is a formulation of the general multi-objective optimization problem with equality and inequality constraints [20]:

$$\begin{aligned} & \text{Minimize} \left\{\overrightarrow{F_i(x)}\right\}, \forall_i \in N_{oj}, \\ & \text{Subject to:} \begin{cases} \overrightarrow{g_m(x)}, \forall_m \in N_{EQ} \\ \overrightarrow{h_k(x)}, \forall_k \in N_{INQ} \end{cases} \end{aligned} \tag{5.11}$$

where F_i is the ith objective function, $g_m(x)$ and $h_k(x)$ are the constraints, N_{EQ} and N_{INQ} are respectively the numbers of equality and inequality constraints, and N_{oj} is the number of objective functions.

If the following criteria are met, the solution $\overrightarrow{x_1}$ prevails over $\overrightarrow{x_2}$ in the multi-objective minimization problem:

$$F_i(\overrightarrow{x_1}) \le F_i(\overrightarrow{x_2}), \quad \forall_i \in N_{oj} \tag{5.12}$$

Pareto optimum solutions are the prevailing options across the whole search space.

A fuzzy membership function μ_i can be used to represent the ith objective function F_i as follows:

$$\mu_i = \frac{F_i - F_i^{min}}{F_i^{max} - F_i^{min}} \tag{5.13}$$

where the parameters F_i^{min} and F_i^{max} are respectively the minimum and the maximum values of the ith objective function among all Pareto solutions.

The normalized membership function μ^k is calculated as follows for each Pareto solution:

$$\mu^k = \frac{\sum_{i=1}^{N_{oj}} \mu_i^k}{\sum_{k=1}^{M} \sum_{i=1}^{N_{oj}} \mu_i^k}, \quad \forall k \in M \tag{5.14}$$

The minimal value of μ^k is the best compromise option. M is the number of Pareto solutions.

5.5 Results and Discussion

The optimization of the CNC lathe machine problem to improve machining performance is solved in this section using the GWO algorithms. The proposed algorithm is applied to solve the single-objective optimization problem described by the objective function 1 (OF1) corresponding to Eq. 5.9. The proposed approach was implemented in a MATLAB environment. Details of the mathematical programming model are provided in Appendix B. Additional details of the formulation of the single objective optimization using the GWO algorithm are provided in the work of Okwu and Tartibu [8]. The simulation results are carried out using an 11th Gen Intel(R) Core (TM) i5-1135G7 @ 2.40 GHz Processor, 8 GB RAM, 64-bit operating system, PC. Table 5.1 provides details showing how the parameters of the suggested algorithm are configured.

The optimal solutions that minimise the cutting force (CF) are shown in Fig. 5.4 and presented graphically in Fig. 5.5. These results suggest that the cutting force can be optimised by setting the cutting speed to a minimum of 69.9, setting the feed rate to a maximum of 120.6 and ensuring that the depth of cut is set to a minimum of 0.66. The corresponding value of the minimum cutting force is 430.6557.

The optimal solutions that minimise the surface roughness (SR) are shown in Fig. 5.6 and presented graphically in Fig. 5.7. These results suggest that the surface roughness can be optimised by setting the cutting speed to a maximum of 150, setting the feed rate to a minimum of 55.6 and ensuring that the depth of cut is a minimum of 0.66.

Table 5.1 GWO parameters

Number of wolves: 100
Maximum iteration: 1000
Grid inflation parameter α: 0.1
Number of grids per each dimension: 10
Leader selection pressure parameter β: 4

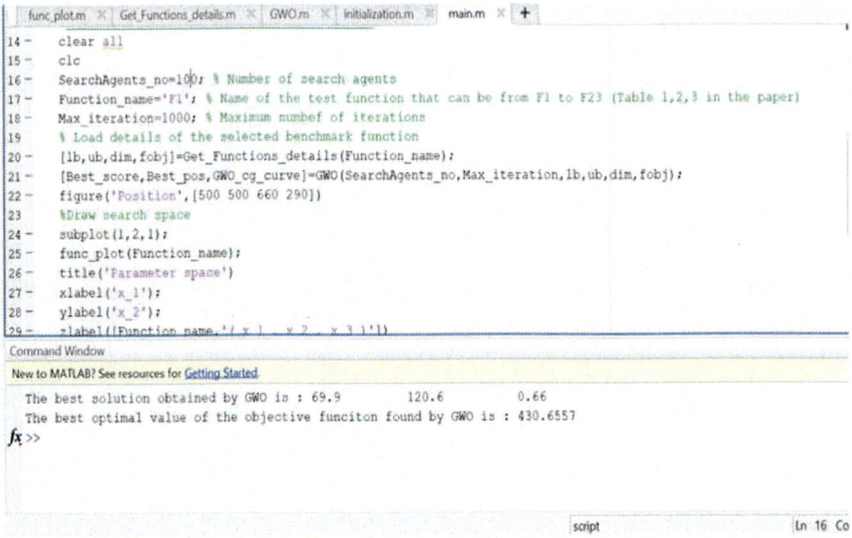

Fig. 5.4 Screenshot of MATLAB main code and corresponding results considering minimization of the cutting force

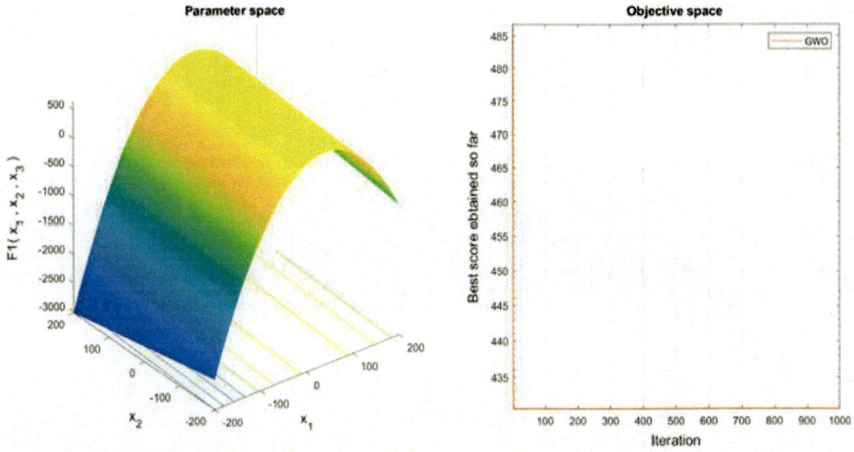

Fig. 5.5 Graphical representation of the parameter space and objective space considering the minimization of the cutting force

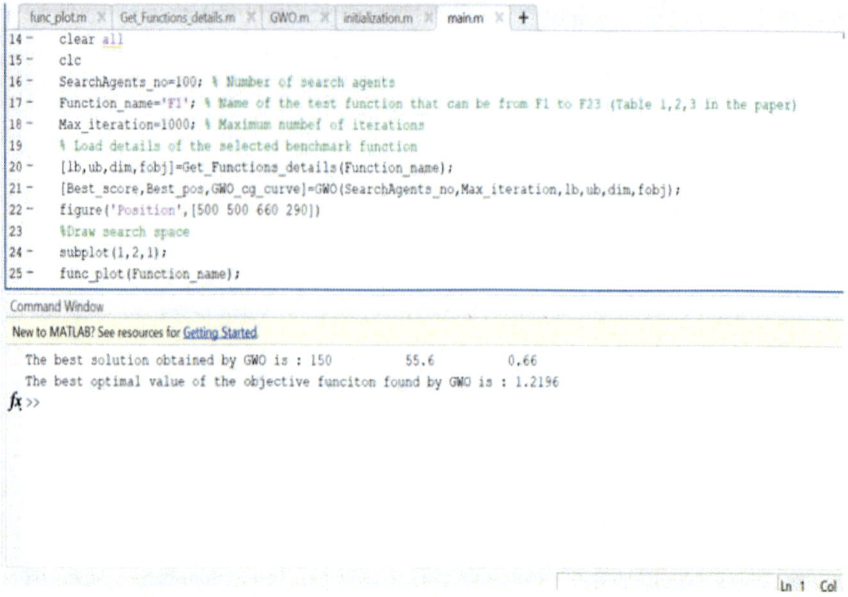

Fig. 5.6 Screenshot of MATLAB main code and corresponding results considering minimization of the surface roughness

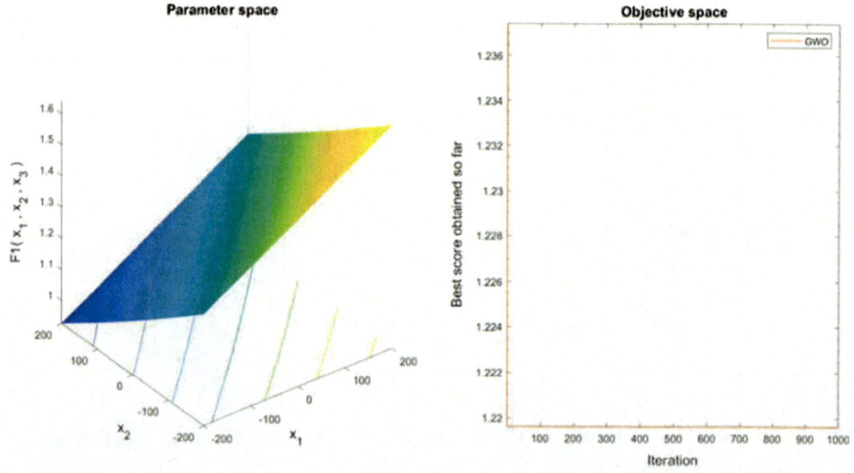

Fig. 5.7 Graphical representation of the parameter space and objective space considering minimization of the surface roughness

The proposed algorithm is applied to solve the multi-objective problem described by the objective function 1 (OF1) and objective function 2 (OF2) corresponding to Eqs. 5.9 and 5.10 respectively. As described in the previous sections, the cutting force and the surface roughness are conflicting in nature. Therefore, the best compromise was obtained by optimizing these two objectives simultaneously. The optimal settings corresponding to the optimal values of cutting force and surface roughness are described in Table 5.2 by values of OF1 and OF2 respectively. Figure 5.8 shows two-dimensional Pareto optimal solutions that achieved the best compromise solution. Details of the main MATLAB code are provided in Appendix C.

Table 5.2 Pareto optimal solutions

Index	OF1	OF2	Index	OF1	OF2
1	635.7987	1.247029	51	516.6977	1.270052
2	441.5449	1.318489	52	643.3	1.244936
3	518.6081	1.2693	53	666.8548	1.238423
4	438.7592	1.325797	54	657.0877	1.2412
5	439.8855	1.322851	55	659.9708	1.239524
6	537.2843	1.266471	56	586.3027	1.258123
7	437.6217	1.328761	57	445.5637	1.307814
8	432.4052	1.342203	58	443.6822	1.312832
9	597.33	1.25601	59	442.3123	1.316463
10	499.6039	1.272167	60	654.1663	1.241704
11	490.027	1.273971	61	455.9888	1.279327
12	514.4365	1.270059	62	442.5006	1.315965
13	448.4277	1.300106	63	596.7871	1.256329
14	445.6978	1.307455	64	441.4369	1.320452
15	682.7093	1.227418	65	441.3214	1.321388
16	684.1928	1.22613	66	684.6534	1.22532
17	686.3116	1.22199	67	657.4318	1.24075
18	663.5179	1.238618	68	595.0838	1.256944
19	454.3478	1.285381	69	613.6401	1.252846
20	455.2681	1.281336	70	618.3204	1.251461
21	475.3236	1.275596	71	648.755	1.243432
22	455.6825	1.280181	72	606.3711	1.254722
23	452.3699	1.289851	73	610.4124	1.253348
24	652.3743	1.242647	74	614.7563	1.252182
25	595.875	1.256442	75	612.8183	1.253072
26	554.7898	1.263973	76	440.6746	1.321644

(continued)

Table 5.2 (continued)

Index	OF1	OF2	Index	OF1	OF2
27	673.7655	1.23343	77	447.8408	1.301954
28	675.2952	1.232579	78	612.8872	1.252889
29	531.4623	1.267371	79	585.3317	1.258493
30	670.7082	1.234988	80	583.7969	1.258533
31	557.1943	1.263251	81	585.4353	1.258223
32	677.2935	1.231497	82	587.7068	1.257806
33	644.8196	1.244673	83	589.0514	1.257628
34	538.176	1.266331	84	637.3647	1.246963
35	562.5508	1.262373	85	445.265	1.309514
36	544.9744	1.265254	86	448.894	1.299503
37	547.3097	1.264878	87	448.1362	1.3019
38	541.7005	1.265776	88	587.1483	1.258068
39	546.6957	1.264978	89	659.0943	1.239881
40	540.1496	1.266021	90	535.8299	1.266923
41	528.1256	1.267898	91	443.2242	1.314084
42	608.7939	1.25398	92	439.4763	1.323923
43	497.5352	1.27286	93	613.6645	1.252653
44	527.4849	1.267976	94	530.8407	1.267668
45	673.5649	1.233872	95	439.4374	1.324792
46	676.9673	1.2322	96	444.2782	1.311246
47	621.3261	1.251199	97	587.4205	1.258062
48	533.7528	1.267019	98	614.2238	1.252414
49	521.5029	1.268872	99	448.3293	1.300372
50	447.6523	1.304206	100	446.9346	1.304298

5.6 Conclusion

In this section, a Multi-Objective Grey Wolf Optimizer (MOGWO) is proposed to enhance the machining performance during the turning of a titanium alloy. This advanced approach has been described in detail to demonstrate the applicability of metaheuristic optimization methods in manufacturing. The cutting force and the surface roughness were the two objective functions to optimize. This study reveals that setting the cutting speed to the minimum, setting the feed rate to the maximum and ensuring that the depth of cut is set to a minimum would minimise the cutting force. However, setting the cutting speed to the maximum, setting the feed rate to the minimum and ensuring that the depth of cut is minimum would minimise the surface roughness. The proposed Multi-Objective Grey Wolf Optimizer (MOGWO) was applied to solve the multi-objective problem and the best compromise between

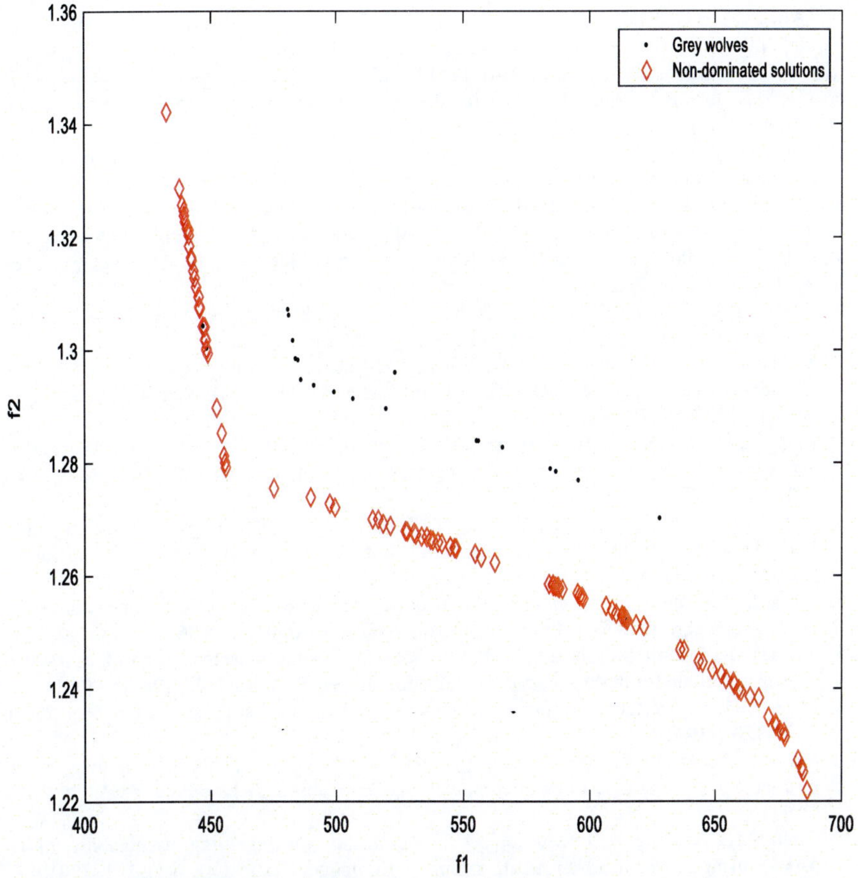

Fig. 5.8 Graphical representation of the Pareto optimal solutions

the two objective functions was computed to assist the decision-maker in the selection of the best setting that could potentially improve machinability performance.

References

1. Lalwani, D.I., Mehta, N.K., Jain, P.K.: Experimental investigations of cutting parameters influence on cutting forces and surface roughness in finish hard turning of MDN250 steel. J. Mater. Process. Technol. **206**(1–3), 167–179 (2008)
2. Rao, C.J., Rao, D.N., Srihari, P.: Influence of cutting parameters on cutting force and surface finish in turning operation. Proc. Eng. **64**, 1405–1415 (2013)
3. Shaw, M.C., Cookson, J.O.: Metal Cutting Principles, vol. 2, no. 3. Oxford University Press, New York (2005)
4. Özel, T., Karpat, Y.: Predictive modeling of surface roughness and tool wear in hard turning using regression and neural networks. Int. J. Mach. Tools Manuf **45**(4–5), 467–479 (2005)

5. Okonkwo, U.C., Okokpujie, I.P., Sinebe, J.E., Ezugwu, C.A.: Comparative analysis of aluminium surface roughness in end-milling under dry and minimum quantity lubrication (MQL) conditions. Manuf. Rev. **2**(30), 1–11 (2015)
6. Lin, W.S., Lee, B.Y., Wu, C.L.: Modeling the surface roughness and cutting force for turning. J. Mater. Process. Technol. **108**(3), 286–293 (2001)
7. Zolpakar, N.A., Yasak, M.F., Pathak, S.: A review: use of evolutionary algorithm for optimisation of machining parameters. Int. J. Adv. Manuf. Technol. **115**, 31–47 (2021)
8. Okwu, M.O., Tartibu, L.K.: Metaheuristic Optimization: Nature-Inspired Algorithms Swarm and Computational Intelligence, Theory And Applications, vol. 927. Springer Nature (2020)
9. Deb, K., Sindhya, K., Hakanen, J.: Multi-objective optimization. In: Decision Sciences, pp. 161–200. CRC Press (2016)
10. Starke, A.R., Cardemil, J.M., Escobar, R., Colle, S.: Multi-objective optimization of hybrid CSP+PV system using genetic algorithm. Energy **147**, 490–503 (2018)
11. Makhadmeh, S.N., Alomari, O.A., Mirjalili, S., Al-Betar, M.A., Elnagar, A.: Recent advances in multi-objective grey wolf optimizer, its versions and applications. Neural Comput. Appl. **34**(22), 19723–19749 (2022)
12. Mirjalili, S., Gandomi, A.H., Mirjalili, S.Z., Saremi, S., Faris, H., Mirjalili, S.M.: Salp swarm algorithm: a bio-inspired optimizer for engineering design problems. Adv. Eng. Softw. **114**, 163–191 (2017)
13. Zhang, Z., Qin, H., Yao, L., Liu, Y., Jiang, Z., Feng, Z., Ouyang, S.: Improved multi-objective moth-flame optimization algorithm based on R-domination for cascade reservoirs operation. J. Hydrol. **581**, 124431 (2020)
14. Mirjalili, S., Jangir, P., Saremi, S.: Multi-objective ant lion optimizer: a multi-objective optimization algorithm for solving engineering problems. Appl. Intell. **46**, 79–95 (2017)
15. Mirjalili, S., Saremi, S., Mirjalili, S.M., Coelho, L.D.S.: Multi-objective grey wolf optimizer: a novel algorithm for multi-criterion optimization. Expert Syst. Appl. **47**, 106–119 (2016)
16. Mech, L.D.: Alpha status, dominance, and division of labor in wolf packs. Can. J. Zool. **77**(8), 1196–1203 (1999)
17. Muro, C., Escobedo, R., Spector, L., Coppinger, R.P.: Wolf-pack (Canis lupus) hunting strategies emerge from simple rules in computational simulations. Behav. Proc. **88**(3), 192–197 (2011)
18. Sahu, N.K., Andhare, A.B.: Multiobjective optimization for improving machinability of Ti-6Al-4V using RSM and advanced algorithms. J. Computat. Design Eng. **6**(1), 1–12 (2019)
19. Sahu, N.K., Andhare, A.B.: Optimization of surface roughness in turning of Ti-6Al-4V using response surface methodology and TLBO. In: International Design Engineering Technical Conferences and Computers and Information in Engineering Conference, vol. 57113, p. V004T05A020. American Society of Mechanical Engineers (2015)
20. Santana-Quintero, L.V., Coello, C.A.C.: An algorithm based on differential evolution for multi-objective problems. Int. J. Comput. Intell. Res. **1**(1), 151–169 (2005)

Chapter 6
Multi-objective Ant Lion Optimizer for Improved Machining Performance

Abstract Titanium alloys are challenging to cut due to low thermal conductivity and excessive tool wear. This work seeks to address poor machinability through optimization. In this section, titanium alloy (Ti–6Al–4V) was chosen as the turning work material. The cutting force and the surface roughness were considered indicators of the machining performance. The speed of cutting, the feed rate and the depth of cut are the variables to optimize. Quadratic equations of the cutting force and the surface roughness were extracted from an existing study to illustrate the approach. A single objective optimization problem was developed to optimize the cutting force and the surface roughness separately using the Antlion optimizer. Details showing the formulation of the problem and the results have been disclosed. The Multi-objective antlion optimizer (MALO) was the metaheuristic-based approach proposed for the formulation of the problem and the computation of the non-dominated or Pareto optimal solutions. The best compromise was obtained by optimizing these two objectives simultaneously. The optimal settings corresponding to the optimal values of cutting force and surface roughness were computed and reported in this section.

Keywords Ant lion optimization · Machining · Titanium alloy · Metaheuristic techniques

6.1 Introduction

Due to its desirable and advantageous mechanical qualities, titanium alloys are a fantastic substitute for materials used in marine, biomedical, and aerospace applications. enhanced corrosion resistance, high strength-to-weight ratio, and superior longevity. The fracture toughness of titanium alloys is one of their attractive qualities. Although having beneficial properties, titanium alloys are challenging to cut due to low thermal conductivity and excessive tool wear. Because they result in poor machinability, high cutting temperatures are a major issue that requires rapid treatment [1]. One of the most important industrial processes is turning, which involves rotating a cylindrical workpiece while a single-point cutting tool removes material

I. P. Okokpujie and L. K. Tartibu, *Modern Optimization Techniques for Advanced Machining*, Studies in Systems, Decision and Control 485,
https://doi.org/10.1007/978-3-031-35455-7_6

from it. Three cutting forces are generated while turning: a thrust force acting in the cutting speed's direction, a feed force operating in the feed direction, and a radial force acting in the direction perpendicular to the cutting speed. Many parameters' effects on cutting power have been studied [2]. Several researchers have worked to increase the machinability of titanium alloys by enhancing process variables. The impact of cutting parameters on titanium alloys and surface roughness were studied in relation to the effects of cutting settings [3]. The outcomes showed that surface roughness is significantly influenced by feed rate and cutting speed. The tool nose radius has an impact on the product's surface quality as well [4]. Cutting temperature has been discovered to be more affected by cutting speed and feed [5]. A multi-objective optimization approach was proposed by Shah et al. [6] to optimize the cutting force, the cutting temperature and the surface roughness using a genetic algorithm. This study demonstrates the potential of the proposed approach to achieve a desirable combination of machining performance.

One of the finest methods to enhance the machining of titanium alloys is the use of optimization techniques. The primary flaw of conventional optimization methods, local optima stagnation, has led to their general depreciation [7]. Stochastic optimization techniques are the primary possibilities for designers. These methods approximate the ideal designs while treating difficulties as black boxes. They begin the optimization process by refining a set of arbitrary potential solutions to a particular problem over a predetermined number of iterations. Notwithstanding these methods' benefits, real-world optimization requires dealing with several challenges, including numerous objectives [8, 9], limitations [10], uncertainties [11], local solutions [12], deceptive global solutions [13], etc. Different operators should be included in optimization techniques to overcome these problems [14].

Finding solutions for issues with many objectives is the major goal of this effort, which is multi-objective optimization. Due to the nature of such problems, there are multiple solutions for a multi-objective problem [15]. A single-objective issue, however, only has one global optimum. The major issue in multi-objective optimization is addressing numerous objectives, which are frequently at odds with one another. A stochastic multi-objective optimization algorithm's job is to identify the set of best trade-offs among the objectives, or the Pareto optimal set.

In the research on multi-objective optimization employing stochastic optimization techniques, a posteriori versus a priori are the two basic approaches [16]. Using a priori methods, aggregating the objectives reduces a multi-objective optimization problem to a single-objective problem. An expert in the problem domain typically provides a set of weights that describe the importance of the objectives. A single-objective optimization approach can quickly resolve the issue following the objective aggregation. The primary flaw with these approaches is that in order to find the Pareto optimal set, an algorithm needs to be performed numerous times. Moreover, seeking professional advice is necessary, and using this method makes it impossible to find some particular Pareto optimal fronts [17]. The advantages of posterior techniques include keeping the multiobjective formulation of the problem and locating the Pareto optimal set in a single run. Another benefit is that these techniques can be used to find any type of Pareto front. Yet, they cost more to compute and must simultaneously handle several goals. According to the literature, these techniques have been successfully applied to real-world issues ever since they were created [18].

This study proposes the antlion technique to improve machining performance namely minimising the cutting force and the surface roughness. Therefore, it is critical to determine the optimal parameters corresponding to the setting of the CNC machine. In this study, the machining parameters are made of the cutting speed, the feed rate and the depth of cut. This issue can be resolved using the ant lion optimization technique with a global minimum convergence outcome [18]. The uniqueness and contribution of this research is the ability to appropriately enhance the machining performance during the turning of a titanium alloy using a relatively recent MALO technique. Due to the following benefits, the optimization results generated with MALO can result in a worldwide optimal solution for optimization issues.

- In machining optimization, the MALO technique is a population-based approach that increases the possibility of reaching global minima and prevents local minima.
- Due to the random selection of ants and ant pathways and the adaptively reducing border of the ant lion trap, convergence may be assured when exploring the search space.
- The MALO technique uses a small number of gradient-free parameters, which facilitates convergence and results in less computational work.

6.2 Ant Lion Optimization (ALO) Background

The Multiobjective Ant Lion Optimization (MALO) method belongs to a group of artificial intelligence-based methods. Mirjalili was the one who first suggested this method [18]. The Multiobjective Ant Lion Optimization approach takes its cues from a common occurrence in nature: ant lion creatures seek food by hunting prey [19]. Ant lions hunt prey by setting up traps to grab ants that cross a path, catching captured ants, and then setting up new traps to catch more ants. Ant lions go through two stages of development: the 35-week-long larval stage and the 3-year-long adult stage. Similar to butterflies, ant lions go through a transformation known as a cocoon in order to mature and reach adulthood. During the larval stages, hunting for food takes place. Additionally, the cocoons go through reproductive procedures during the adult stage.

The ant lions use their powerful jaws to dig holes in sandy soil to trap their food. A cone-shaped crater is created by the hole that was dug in the sandy soil. As seen in Fig. 6.1, the ant lion successfully makes a cone-shaped crater and then conceals itself by exactly descending into the center of the cone's tip. The ant lion's position is concealed by the sand covering it, but its powerful jaw is facing upward in readiness to receive the small ant prey that landed. Such a crater's design allows for the trapping of little ants, which then fall to the cavity's bottom where the ant lion can easily capture them. During the adult cocoons' growth period, this technique is repeated until there is enough food available [18].

Fig. 6.1 Illustration of an ant lion's method of trapping prey

To describe the interaction of ants with their predators, it is assumed that the ants move in a search space since the ants that become victims to the ant lion travel randomly in quest of food. The following equation explains the random walk model as ant movement in this situation, where ants move stochastically in search of food.

$$V(s) = [0, cs(2w(s_1) - 1), cs(2w(s_2) - 1), \ldots, cs(2w(s_n) - 1)] \tag{6.1}$$

The symbols in Eq. (6.1) have the following meanings. The cumulative counter operator (cs) is used in addition operations. The greatest number of times this method can be repeated is n. The s is a random ant step; in the ant lion approach, iteration is compared to the ant step. In this instance, the w(s) is a stochastic function. The following definition applies to the stochastic function w(s).

$$w(s) = \begin{cases} 0 \text{ if gen} < 0.5 \\ 1 \text{ if gen} > 0.5 \end{cases} \tag{6.2}$$

where gen is a random number created at a predetermined interval of [0, 1] and s is a random ant step, which is similar to the iteration process.

The ants' positions are updated with each action they take to complete the optimization. Since each ant food search space for the optimization step has a changeable range, updating the ant's role directly using an equation is not possible (6.2). The min–max normalization equation must therefore be used to normalize in order to retain random pathways in the search space.

$$W_i^s = \frac{(W_i^s - a_i) \times (d_i^s - c_i^s)}{(b_i - a_i)} \quad (6.3)$$

Here is an explanation of the notation used in Eq. (6.3). The notation a_i represents the random ant's minimum step for the i-th variable, b_i represents its top step, c_i^s represents its minimum value in the s-th iteration, and d_i^s represents its maximum value in the s-th iteration. The construction of an optimization matrix based on the ant's position is represented by Eq. (6.4) as follows.

$$T_{ant} = \begin{bmatrix} T_{1.1} & \cdots & T_{1,d} \\ \vdots & \ddots & \vdots \\ T_{n.1} & \cdots & T_{n.d} \end{bmatrix} \quad (6.4)$$

Based on Eq. (6.4), T_{ant} is a matrix that states the location of each ant. $T_{i.j}$ is the value of the variable, where j is the j-th order of variables and i is the i-th order of ants. Notation of n is the total number of ants, and d is the real variable. Let us consider other AI-based optimization methods. The ants in the ant lion method are similar to individuals in the genetic algorithm or particles in the PSO method [20]. In the antlion method, the ant position states the parameters used to represent the variables in a particular solution. Matrix T_{ant} was made to fit all possible ant places that may be saved after optimization. By analyzing each ant stored in the following matrix, objective functions are also used in the optimization process.

$$T_{Oant} = \begin{bmatrix} f([T_{1,1} & \cdots & T_{1,d} \\ \vdots & \ddots & \vdots \\ f([T_{n,1} & \cdots & T_{n,d} \end{bmatrix} \quad (6.5)$$

It is clear from Eq. (6.5) that T_{Oant} is a matrix that is utilized to store each ant's fitness. The i-th ants in the j-th dimension are represented in the matrix T^{Oant} by the elements of the matrix $T_{i,j}$. The cost function is represented by the letter f, whereas n stands for the overall number of ants.

The ant lion technique makes the assumption that ants can use the search space to conceal themselves. The positions and fitness values of the ants are also stored in a matrix, as illustrated in the following section.

$$T_{AL} = \begin{bmatrix} TL_{1,1} & \cdots & TL_{1,d} \\ \vdots & \ddots & \vdots \\ TL_{n,1} & \cdots & TL_{n,d} \end{bmatrix} \quad (6.6)$$

According to Eq. (6.6), T_{AL} is the matrix that is utilized to store each ant lion's position. The elements of the $Tl_{i,j}$ matrix are stated by the matrix T_{AL}, which consists of the i-th ant lion with the j-th dimension value. The notation n represents the overall number of ant lions, and d represents all dimensions taken into account in a case.

$$T_{OAL} = \begin{bmatrix} f([TL_{1,1} & \cdots & TL_{1,d} \\ \vdots & \ddots & \vdots \\ f([TL_{n,1} & \cdots & TL_{n,d} \end{bmatrix} \tag{6.7}$$

Equation (6.7) indicates that T_{OAL} is the fitness-storing matrix. The elements of the $Tl_{i,j}$ matrix are stated in the matrix T_{OAL}, which consists of the i-th ant lion with the j-th dimension value. The cost function is denoted by the letter f, and n is the total number of ant lions.

As shown in Fig. 6.2, the ant lion's capacity for hunting can be replicated using a roulette wheel to further explain how the ant lion approach operates. One ant lion was thought to contain all of the ants in the roulette wheel area. The selection of ant lions based on fitness was done using a roulette wheel operator.

The following two equations are used to model this process.

$$c_j^s = AL_j^s + c^s \tag{6.8}$$

$$d_j^s = AL_j^s + d^s \tag{6.9}$$

This section provides an explanation of the notations used in Eqs. (6.8) and (6.9). The variables AL_j^s represents the position of the j-th ant lion at the s-th iteration, c^s represents the smallest value of the s-th iteration variable, c_j^s represents the smallest

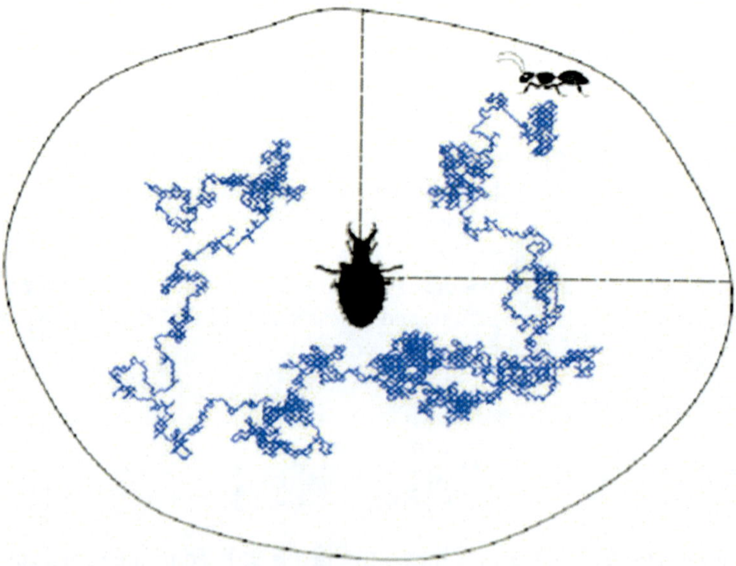

Fig. 6.2 Search space boundary of antlion

value of the j-th ant, d^s represents the vector containing the maximum values of the s-th iteration variable, and d_j^s represents the maximum value of the j-th ant.

The reaction of the ant when it discovers it has been caught in the ant lion's trap is another mechanism of this strategy. The ant typically doesn't become aware that there is an ant lion waiting to pounce at the bottom of the sandpit until after it has entered the cone-shaped sand device and has sunk to the bottom. The ants attempt to flee under the supposition that they are in excellent condition by sprinkling sand around the hole in order to diminish the radius of the hole that forms their trail. The following two mathematical equations can be used to model this mechanism.

$$c^s = \frac{c^s}{R} \tag{6.10}$$

$$d^s = \frac{d^s}{R} \tag{6.11}$$

Equations (6.10) and (6.11)'s notations can be understood using the following information. The ratio factor is R. The variable with the smallest value in the s-th iteration is called c^s, while the vector with the highest value in the s-th iteration is called d^s.

The ant lion technique's final mechanism is elitism. The best ant lion is stored at each iteration to be regarded as an elite; elitism is the most potent ant lion in the computational process. The mathematical representation of elitism is shown in the following equation.

$$\mathrm{Ant}_i^s = \frac{R_{AL}^s + R_{Elite}^s}{2} \tag{6.12}$$

In Eq. (6.12), R_{AL}^s is a random walk around the ant lion, and Ant_i^s is the position of the i-th ant at the s-th iteration. The choice was made using a roulette wheel. A random walk-around elite at the s-th iteration is known as R_{Elite}^s. The optimization process of ant lion algorithm is summarized in Fig. 6.3.

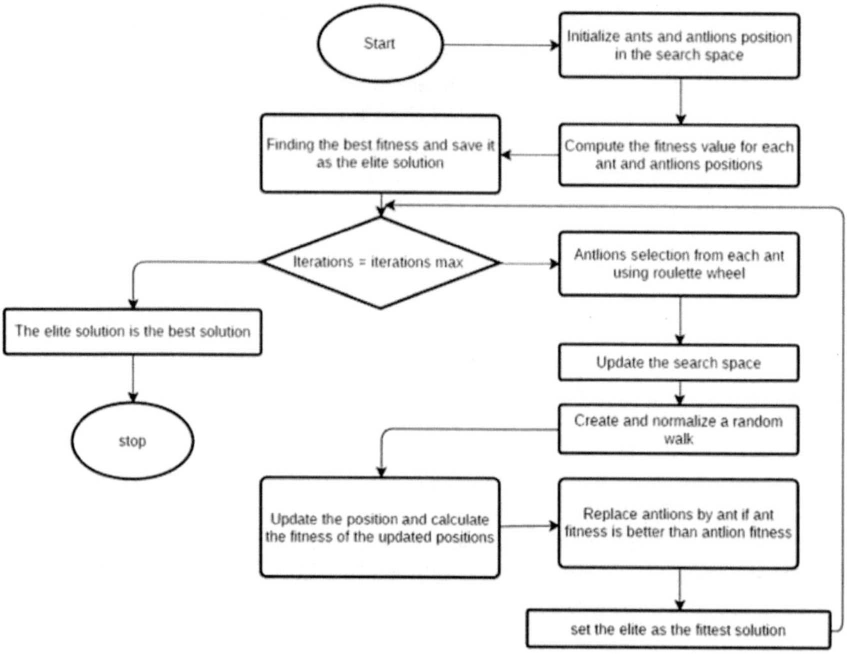

Fig. 6.3 Flowchart of ant lion optimizer

6.3 Brief Description of Data Extraction and Processing

In order to illustrate the approach proposed in this study, quadratic equations were extracted from the study conducted by Sahu and Andhare [21]. In the reported study, titanium alloy (Ti–6Al–4 V) was chosen as the turning work material. The bar size for turning was determined to be 32 mm in diameter, 100 mm in length, and 35 mm in length cut. The turning operations were carried out on a CNC lathe machine with a 5.5 kW power capacity. The machine's controller provided fine motion and spindle speed control with 0.005 mm position precision and 0.004 mm repeatability during cutting. During turning operations, the cutting force was measured using a dynamometer that was interfaced with a control unit.

The design of experiment was performed with a central composite design (CCD) based on Response Surface Methodology (RSM). The speed of cutting, the feed rate and the depth of cut were the input factors. The regression coefficient and subsequently the quadratic equation of the cutting force were generated based on the experimental design and the response measured. The model adequacy was checked using the analysis of variance (ANOVA) and non-significant parameters were discarded. A similar approach was adopted to develop the quadratic equation describing the surface roughness [22]. The roughness of the machined surface and the force of cutting were the two responses. In the formulation of the multi-objective optimization models described in the following sections, the speed of cutting, the feed rate and the depth of cut are the variables to be optimized while the surface roughness and the cutting force are the two objective functions to minimize.

6.4 Formulation of Quadratic Equations and Mathematical Formulation

6.4.1 Design Variables and Objectives Functions

Three different variables namely the cutting speed (S), the feed rate (F) and the depth of cut (D) have been considered. These three variables are closely related to the setting of the CNC lathe machine used for data extraction and processing described in the previous section. The lowest and the highest level of cutting parameters used for central composite design reported in the study of Sahu and Andhare [21] were taken into account to illustrate the approach proposed in this study.

$$\begin{aligned} S_{min} &= 69.9 < S < S_{max} = 150 \\ F_{min} &= 55.6 < F < F_{max} = 120.6 \\ D_{min} &= 0.66 < D < D_{max} = 2 \end{aligned} \tag{6.13}$$

S, F and D $\in \Re^+$

In this study, the machinability of Ti–6Al–4V alloy is measured with the cutting force (CF) and the surface roughness (SR). The two objective functions in the formulation of the mathematical programming problem are these indicators. They are given by the following quadratic Equations [21].

$$\begin{aligned} CF = {} & 513.915 - 0.2466 \times S + 5.3773 \times F + 64.92 \\ & \times D - 2.594e - 4 \times S^2 - 0.055 \times F^2 + 0.0052 \times S \times F \end{aligned} \tag{6.14}$$

$$\begin{aligned} SR = {} & 1.27686 - 0.000897964 \times S + 0.0008937 \\ & \times F + 0.036303 \times D + 1.69203e - 7 \times S^2 \end{aligned} \tag{6.15}$$

These equations suggest that the three variables (S, F and D) have a significant effect on the cutting force and the surface roughness of Ti–6Al–4V alloy. The optimum values of the parameters describing the setting of the CNC lathe machine can be obtained by solving Eqs. 6.13 and 6.14.

6.4.2 Multi-objective Optimization

The following Equation is a formulation of the general multi-objective optimization problem with equality and inequality constraints [23];

$$\begin{aligned} &\text{Minimize}\left\{\overrightarrow{F_i(x)}\right\}, \forall_i \in N_{oj}, \\ &\text{Subject to: } \begin{cases} \overrightarrow{g_m(x)}, \forall_m \in N_{EQ} \\ \overrightarrow{h_k(x)}, \forall_k \in N_{INQ} \end{cases} \end{aligned} \tag{6.16}$$

where F_i is the ith objective function, $g_m(x)$ and $h_k(x)$ are the constraints, N_{EQ} and N_{INQ} are respectively the numbers of equality and inequality constraints, and N_{oj} is the number of objective functions.

If the following criteria are met, the solution $\overrightarrow{x_1}$ prevails over $\overrightarrow{x_2}$ in the multi-objective minimization problem:

$$F_i(\overrightarrow{x_1}) \le F_i(\overrightarrow{x_2}), \quad \forall_i \in N_{oj} \tag{6.17}$$

Pareto optimum solutions are the prevailing options across the whole search space.

A fuzzy membership function μ_i can be used to represent the ith objective function F_i as follows:

$$\mu_i = \frac{F_i - F_i^{min}}{F_i^{max} - F_i^{min}} \tag{6.18}$$

where the parameters F_i^{min} and F_i^{max} are respectively the minimum and the maximum values of the ith objective function among all Pareto solutions.

The normalized membership function μ^k is calculated as follows for each Pareto solution:

$$\mu^k = \frac{\sum_{i=1}^{N_{oj}} \mu_i^k}{\sum_{k=1}^{M} \sum_{i=1}^{N_{oj}} \mu_i^k}, \quad \forall k \in M \tag{6.19}$$

The minimal value of μ^k is the best compromise option. M is the number of Pareto solutions.

6.5 Results and Discussion

The optimization of the CNC lathe machine problem to improve machining performance is solved in this section using the ALO algorithms. The proposed algorithm is applied to solve the single-objective optimization problem described by the objective

Table 6.1 ALO parameters

Number of antlions: 40
Maximum iteration: 500

Table 6.2 Optimal solutions considering an emphasis on CF

S*	F*	D*	SR*
69.9	120.6	0.66	430.6557

Table 6.3 Optimal solutions considering an emphasis on SR

S*	F*	D*	SR*
150	55.6	0.66	1.2196

function 1 (OF1) corresponding to Eq. 6.2. The proposed approach was implemented in a MATLAB environment. Details of the mathematical programming model are provided in Appendix D. Additional details of the formulation of the single objective optimization using the GWO algorithm are provided in the work of Okwu and Tartibu [20]. The simulation results are carried out using an 11th Gen Intel(R) Core(TM) i5-1135G7 @ 2.40 GHz Processor, 8 GB RAM, 64-bit operating system, PC. Table 6.1 provides details showing how the parameters of the suggested algorithm are configured.

The optimal solutions that minimise the cutting force (CF) are shown in Table 6.2. These results suggest that the cutting force can be optimised by setting the cutting speed to a minimum of 69.9, setting the feed rate to a maximum of 120.6 and ensuring that the depth of cut is set to a minimum of 0.66. The corresponding value of the minimum cutting force is 430.6557.

The optimal solutions that minimise the surface roughness (SR) are shown in Table 6.3. These results suggest that the surface roughness can be optimised by setting the cutting speed to a maximum of 150, setting the feed rate to a minimum of 55.6 and ensuring that the depth of cut is a minimum of 0.66.

The proposed algorithm is applied to solve the multi-objective problem described by the objective function 1 (OF1) and objective function 2 (OF2) corresponding to Eqs. 6.2 and 6.3 respectively. As described in the previous sections, the cutting force and the surface roughness are conflicting in nature. Therefore, the best compromise was obtained by optimizing these two objectives simultaneously. The optimal settings corresponding to the optimal values of cutting force and surface roughness are described in Table 6.4 by values of OF1 and OF2 respectively. Figure 6.4 shows two-dimensional Pareto optimal solutions that achieved the best compromise solution. Details of the main MATLAB code are provided in Appendix D and E.

Table 6.4 Pareto optimal solutions

Index	OF1	OF2	Index	OF1	OF2
1	682.8249	1.227025	51	561.6548	1.262498
2	456.1512	1.278873	52	561.6222	1.262505
3	683.2253	1.226601	53	561.6537	1.262499
4	479.2329	1.274789	54	561.6421	1.262499
5	684.9679	1.224297	55	561.6842	1.262492
6	662.807	1.239083	56	561.673	1.262494
7	451.2938	1.292305	57	561.628	1.262505
8	451.0648	1.292932	58	561.6786	1.262493
9	618.3685	1.251486	59	600.6687	1.255215
10	455.4038	1.280958	60	600.7076	1.255206
11	495.3195	1.27263	61	600.6885	1.25521
12	526.4183	1.268333	62	600.7352	1.2552
13	572.7151	1.260565	63	600.7027	1.255208
14	575.7213	1.260076	64	600.697	1.255209
15	578.1053	1.259711	65	600.6641	1.255222
16	448.2942	1.300467	66	600.6725	1.255214
17	512.3523	1.270764	67	660.7904	1.239255
18	473.8894	1.275492	68	666.5354	1.236884
19	460.9717	1.278422	69	666.5325	1.236886
20	435.4067	1.334498	70	666.5336	1.236885
21	442.0974	1.317031	71	666.5344	1.236885
22	438.7703	1.325768	72	666.5337	1.236885
23	445.8303	1.311738	73	666.5347	1.236884
24	434.9602	1.335649	74	666.5331	1.236885
25	434.994	1.335581	75	666.5341	1.236885
26	434.9437	1.335692	76	666.5332	1.236885
27	444.0201	1.311933	77	643.9034	1.24476
28	444.0086	1.311964	78	643.8996	1.244762
29	441.437	1.318774	79	643.9011	1.244761
30	441.4609	1.318711	80	643.9008	1.244761
31	441.4964	1.318641	81	643.8988	1.244762
32	431.0774	1.345587	82	643.9006	1.244761
33	431.0779	1.345586	83	643.9005	1.244761
34	431.0738	1.345597	84	684.0245	1.225661
35	431.0768	1.345589	85	684.0245	1.225661
36	431.0779	1.345586	86	684.0245	1.225661

(continued)

Table 6.4 (continued)

Index	OF1	OF2	Index	OF1	OF2
37	431.0765	1.34559	87	684.0245	1.225661
38	641.1141	1.245565	88	684.0245	1.225661
39	641.1149	1.245563	89	684.0245	1.225661
40	593.0178	1.2572	90	684.0245	1.225661
41	593.0378	1.257194	91	684.0246	1.225661
42	593.0974	1.257185	92	684.0245	1.225661
43	665.1326	1.237478	93	684.0245	1.225661
44	665.1654	1.237465	94	684.0246	1.225661
45	665.121	1.23748	95	684.0245	1.225661
46	665.1495	1.237469	96	613.6276	1.253991
47	665.1408	1.237472	97	613.6278	1.253991
48	636.8775	1.246738	98	613.6277	1.253991
49	636.8951	1.246733	99	613.6279	1.253991
50	561.7064	1.262489	100	613.6276	1.253991

6.6 Conclusion

In this section, a Multi-objective Ant Lion Optimizer (MALO) is proposed to enhance the machining performance during the turning of a titanium alloy. This advanced approach has been described in detail to demonstrate the applicability of meta-heuristic optimization methods in manufacturing. The cutting force and the surface roughness were the two objective functions to optimize. This study reveals that setting the cutting speed to the minimum, setting the feed rate to the maximum and ensuring that the depth of cut is set to a minimum would minimise the cutting force. However, setting the cutting speed to the maximum, setting the feed rate to the minimum and ensuring that the depth of cut is minimum would minimise the surface roughness. The proposed Multi-objective Ant Lion Optimizer (MALO) was applied to solve the multi-objective problem and the best compromise between the two objective functions was computed to assist the decision-maker in the selection of the best setting that could potentially improve machinability performance.

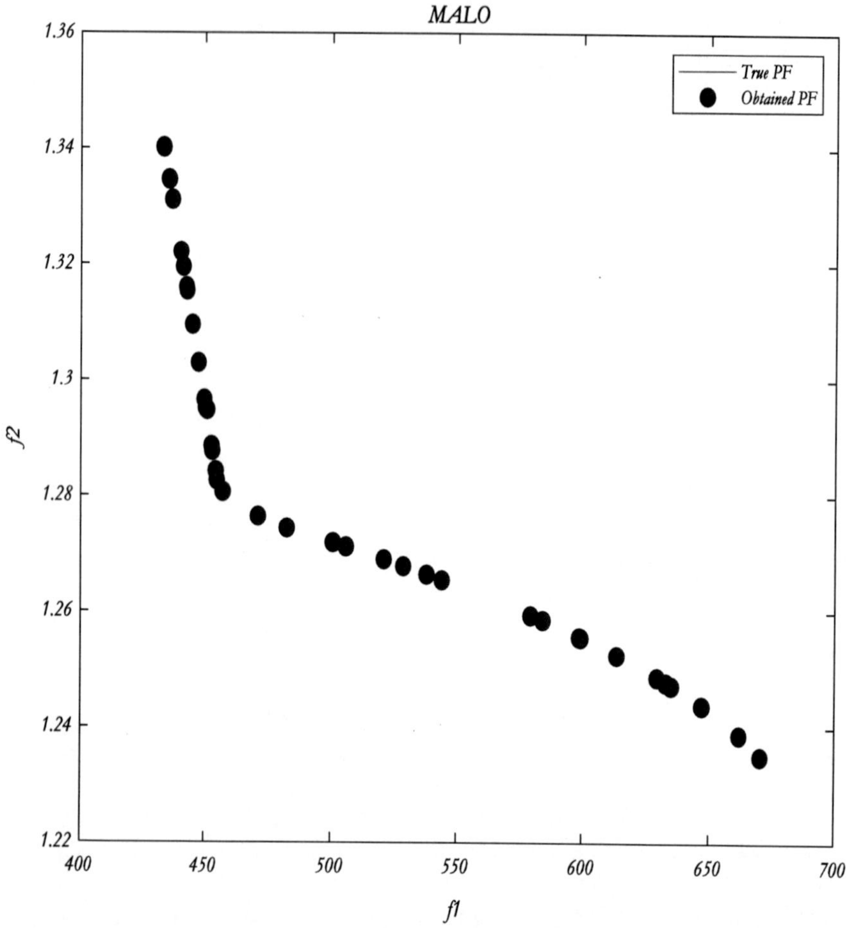

Fig. 6.4 Graphical representation of the Pareto optimal solutions

References

1. Pramanik, A.: Problems and solutions in machining of titanium alloys. Int. J. Adv. Manuf. Technol. **70**, 919–928 (2014)
2. Valera, H.Y., Bhavsar, S.N.: Experimental investigation of surface roughness and power consumption in turning operation of EN 31 alloy steel. Proc. Technol. **14**, 528–534 (2014)
3. Sulaiman, M.A., Che Haron, C.H., Ghani, J.A., Kasim, M.S.: Optimization of turning parameters for titanium alloy Ti-6Al-4V ELI using the response surface method (RSM). J. Adv. Manuf. Technol. (JAMT) **7**(2) (2013)
4. Yildiz, T., Irez, A.B., Sur, G.: Effect of cementite carbide tool coating type and tool radius on cutting performance. In: 2016 7th International Conference on Mechanical and Aerospace Engineering (ICMAE), pp. 78–82. IEEE (2016)
5. Nath, C., Kapoor, S.G., Srivastava, A.K.: Finish turning of Ti-6Al-4V with the atomization-based cutting fluid (ACF) spray system. J. Manuf. Process. **28**, 464–471 (2017)

6. Shah, D.R., Pancholi, N., Gajera, H., Patel, B.: Investigation of cutting temperature, cutting force and surface roughness using multi-objective optimization for turning of Ti-6Al-4 V (ELI). Mater. Today Proc. **50**, 1379–1388 (2022)
7. Kelley, C.T.: Detection and remediation of stagnation in the Nelder-Mead algorithm using a sufficient decrease condition. SIAM J. Optim. **10**(1), 43–55 (1999)
8. Tartibu, L.K., Sun, B., Kaunda, M.A.E.: Multi-objective optimization of the stack of a thermoacoustic engine using GAMS. Appl. Soft Comput. **28**, 30–43 (2015)
9. Tartibu Kwanda, L.: Multi-objective optimization of a rectangular micro-channel heat sink using the augmented ε-constraint method. Eng. Optim. **52**(1), 22–36 (2020)
10. Coello, C.A.C.: Theoretical and numerical constraint-handling techniques used with evolutionary algorithms: a survey of the state of the art. Comput. Methods Appl. Mech. Eng. **191**(11–12), 1245–1287 (2002)
11. Beyer, H.G., Sendhoff, B.: Robust optimization–a comprehensive survey. Comput. Methods Appl. Mech. Eng. **196**(33–34), 3190–3218 (2007)
12. Knowles, J.D., Watson, R.A., Corne, D.W.: Reducing local optima in single-objective problems by multi-objectivization. In: Evolutionary Multi-criterion Optimization: First International Conference, EMO 2001 Zurich, Switzerland, March 7–9, 2001 Proceedings 1, pp. 269–283. Springer, Berlin (2001)
13. Deb, K., Goldberg, D.E.: Analyzing deception in trap functions. In: Foundations of Genetic Algorithms, vol. 2, pp. 93–108. Elsevier (1993)
14. Mirjalili, S., Jangir, P., Saremi, S.: Multi-objective ant lion optimizer: a multi-objective optimization algorithm for solving engineering problems. Appl. Intell. **46**, 79–95 (2017)
15. Coello, C.A.C., Lamont, G.B., Van Veldhuizen, D.A.: Evolutionary Algorithms for Solving Multi-objective Problems, vol. 5, pp. 79–104. New York: Springer (2007)
16. Marler, R.T., Arora, J.S.: Survey of multi-objective optimization methods for engineering. Struct. Multidiscip. Optim. **26**, 369–395 (2004)
17. Zink, F., Waterer, H., Archer, R., Schaefer, L.: Geometric optimization of a thermoacoustic regenerator. Int. J. Therm. Sci. **48**(12), 2309–2322 (2009)
18. Mirjalili, S.: The ant lion optimizer. Adv. Eng. Softw. **83**, 80–98 (2015)
19. Soesanti, I., Syahputra, R.: Multiobjective ant lion optimization for performance improvement of modern distribution network. IEEE Access **10**, 12753–12773 (2022)
20. Okwu, M.O., Tartibu, L.K.: Metaheuristic Optimization: Nature-Inspired Algorithms Swarm and Computational Intelligence, Theory And Applications, vol. 927. Springer Nature (2020)
21. Sahu, N.K., Andhare, A.B.: Multiobjective optimization for improving machinability of Ti-6Al-4V using RSM and advanced algorithms. J. Computat. Des. Eng. **6**(1), 1–12 (2019)
22. Sahu, N.K., Andhare, A.B.: Optimization of surface roughness in turning of Ti-6Al-4V using response surface methodology and TLBO. In: International Design Engineering Technical Conferences and Computers and Information in Engineering Conference, vol. 57113, p. V004T05A020. American Society of Mechanical Engineers (2015)
23. Santana-Quintero, L.V., Coello, C.A.C.: An algorithm based on differential evolution for multi-objective problems. Int. J. Comput. Intell. Res. **1**(1), 151–169 (2005)

Chapter 7
Multi-objective Grasshopper Optimizer for Improved Machining Performance

Abstract One of the most popular meta-heuristic optimization algorithms today is the grasshopper algorithm. Several industries, including engineering design, wireless networking, machine learning and control of power systems have effectively used it to solve a variety of optimization challenges. Despite its potential for optimization, grasshopper optimizer algorithm has not been used for machining performance. Therefore, the present work is the first study that utilized grasshopper algorithm to optimize the cutting force and the surface roughness simultaneously in a multi-objective approach. In order to illustrate the approach proposed in this study, quadratic equations were extracted from an existing study. The speed of cutting, the feed rate and the depth of cut were the input factors. Details showing the formulation of the problem and the results have been disclosed. The Multi-objective grasshopper optimizer (MOGOA) was the metaheuristic-based approach proposed for the formulation of the problem and the computation of the non-dominated or Pareto optimal solutions. The best compromise was obtained by optimizing these two objectives simultaneously. The optimal settings corresponding to the optimal values of cutting force and surface roughness were computed and reported in this section.

Keywords Multi-objective optimisation · Grasshopper optimizer · Machining · Cutting force · Surface roughness

7.1 Introduction

In the aerospace industry, high-speed turning is becoming a crucial industrial technology. High-speed turning is typically done at a pace that is five to ten times faster than usual cutting. It has several benefits, including decreased cutting forces and temperatures, low power usage, improved surface polish, low-stress components, burr-free surfaces, improved dimensional accuracy, and higher part quality. Higher tool life results from reduced temperature effects on the workpiece and the tool [1].

I. P. Okokpujie and L. K. Tartibu, *Modern Optimization Techniques for Advanced Machining*, Studies in Systems, Decision and Control 485,
https://doi.org/10.1007/978-3-031-35455-7_7

The process, workpiece, and tool-related factors used while machining has a significant impact on the efficiency and quality of the completed component in high-speed turning.

Turning characteristics including cutting speed, feed rate, depth of cut, and edge geometry have a big impact on performance indicators like surface roughness and cutting forces [2]. Typically, the manufacturers' recommendations or their experience are used to choose the machining parameters. The quality of the surface produced and the optimal and economical usage of the machines are not the results of this selection process. Scientific techniques based on Taguchi orthogonal arrays are occasionally employed [3]. A given set of independent parameters and a response variable can be analyzed using this method, and the best parameters can be provided. The methodology offers a different set of optimum operating conditions for each response variable if there are numerous response variables for a given set of independent factors. For instance, in machining, the ideal conditions for decreasing surface roughness and cutting forces need not be the same. Under these circumstances, it may be required to find a solution that provides the finest surface finish at the least amount of cutting force. The Taguchi approach may not offer a suitable answer in such cases [4].

In many different fields, including data mining, engineering applications, machine learning, energy, networks, economics, text mining, medicine, and others, a variety of optimization approaches have been used to solve diverse complicated problems. In order to fully solve the underlying problem, it is mostly used to achieve the optimal solution by obtaining numerous optimal values (decisions). In order to make better decisions, meta-heuristic optimization algorithms often run based on taking into account the optimal value by minimizing or maximizing the objective function. Finding the best selection from a variety of accessible possibilities is the primary goal of decision-making. Finding the best choice value from all provided alternatives as a single unit is the ultimate goal of optimization processes (solution). A sufficiently obtained solution that is the best alternative so far to address the underlying issue is referred to as the best expression. Also, the best solution that was found through several development cycles is regarded as a satisfactory solution [5].

Many research problems in the optimization fields are still interesting today. Due to their nature and reality, they require positive results (i.e., mathematical problems, industrial-type problems, real-world problems, and other problems). Hard optimization problems, or NP-hard problems, are what these issues fall under [6]. By optimizing (minimizing or maximizing) a problem's objective function or fitness function, the main goal of using the various optimization techniques is to obtain optimal decisions (problem solutions). Many optimization issues can be broken down into four broad groups: the first group examines limited and unconstrained issues, while the second group examines continuous and discrete issues. There are either single- or multi-objective tasks in the third class. Problems that are static or dynamic are covered in class 4.

Lately, several biological or naturalistic-inspired algorithms have been developed to locate nearly optimal solutions to several types of challenging optimization problems. These techniques have been successfully utilized to resolve similar optimization issues in practical situations. They are superior to other approaches

Fig. 7.1 Optimization algorithms

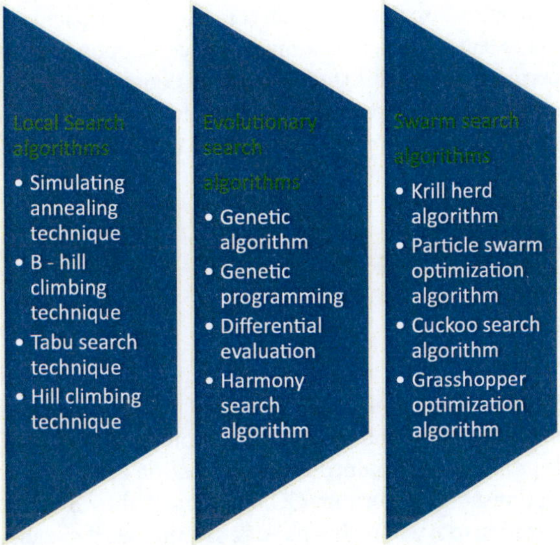

due to their excellent searchability and ability to handle high-dimensional instances (such as calculus-based methods). Optimization algorithms typically examine natural phenomena, such as animal foraging behaviour [7]. The most common varieties of these optimization methods can be broken down into local, evolutionary, and swarm search algorithms (Fig. 7.1).

- Local Search algorithms: Simulated tabu search [8], annealing [9], B-hill climbing, and hill-climbing [10] are examples of local search algorithms that operate with a single solution and enhance it (raise its fitness function) over a predetermined number of rounds.
- Evolutionary search Algorithms: These algorithms include the genetic algorithm [11], genetic programming [12], salp swarm algorithm [13], firefly algorithm [11], harmony search algorithm [14], and ant colony optimization which operate with a population design (a set of initial solutions) that will be improved iteratively through a specific number of iterations in order to get the best solution.
- Swarm search, the third class of algorithms, eventually uses a population mechanism for each iteration. These algorithms are created using data on the past evolution of several potential solutions. Particle swarm optimization method [15], biogeographical-based optimization algorithm [16], artificial bee colony algorithm [17], krill herd algorithm, bacterial foraging algorithm [18], flower pollination algorithm [19], and more related algorithms can be found in Abualigah and Diabat [5].

Despite its potential for optimization, the grasshopper optimizer algorithm has not been used for machining performance. Therefore, the present work is the first study that utilized the grasshopper algorithm to optimize the cutting force and the surface roughness simultaneously in a multi-objective approach. This study aims to assess the extent to which this multi-objective optimizer could be applied to machining performance. In this study, quadratic equations extracted from an existing work were used to illustrate how the grasshopper optimization algorithm could be employed for multi objective-optimization related to machining performance.

7.2 Grasshopper Optimisation Algorithm (GOA) Background

The foundation of mathematical optimization techniques is the gradient search. Local Optima is one of the disadvantages of these techniques. Stochastic approaches make use of random operators to avoid local optima. The nature-inspired stochastic approaches have gained the most traction during the past few decades. Grasshopper Optimisation Algorithm GOA was created by Saremi et al. [20]. It is a potent optimization tool that makes use of a swarm-based metaheuristic optimization algorithm that takes inspiration from nature.

GOA imitates grasshopper swarms' organic behaviours. Millions of these insects jump and move around the crops in a manner similar to rolling cylinders. The search procedure is logically divided into two sections by algorithms with natural inspiration namely exploration and exploitation. During the exploration stage, the search agents of the optimization algorithm move quickly. However, they frequently stay put during the exploitation phase. The following mathematical equations combine the natural behaviour of grasshoppers with the logic of optimization search [20].

$$X_i = r_1 S_i + r_2 G_i + r_3 A_i \tag{7.1}$$

The social interaction, gravitational pull, and wind advection of the ith grasshopper, respectively, define X_i, S_i, G_i, and A_i, which determine the ith grasshopper's position. The [0, 1] range of random numbers makes up the r parameters. The social interaction (attraction and repulsion of grasshoppers) is calculated by the following equation and illustrated in Fig. 7.2 [20]:

$$S_i = \sum_{\substack{j=1 \\ j \neq i}}^{N} s(d_{ij})\widehat{d_{ij}} \tag{7.2}$$

Thus, f stands for the intensity of attraction, l for the attractive length scale, and s is the function that represents the strength of social forces. N is the grasshoppers' total number. $\widehat{d_{ij}}$ $\left(\widehat{d_{ij}} = \frac{(x_j - x_i)}{d_{ij}}\right)$ is a vector between two grasshoppers and d_{ij} $(d_{ij} = |x_j - x_i|)$ represents the distance between the ith and jth grasshopper. S

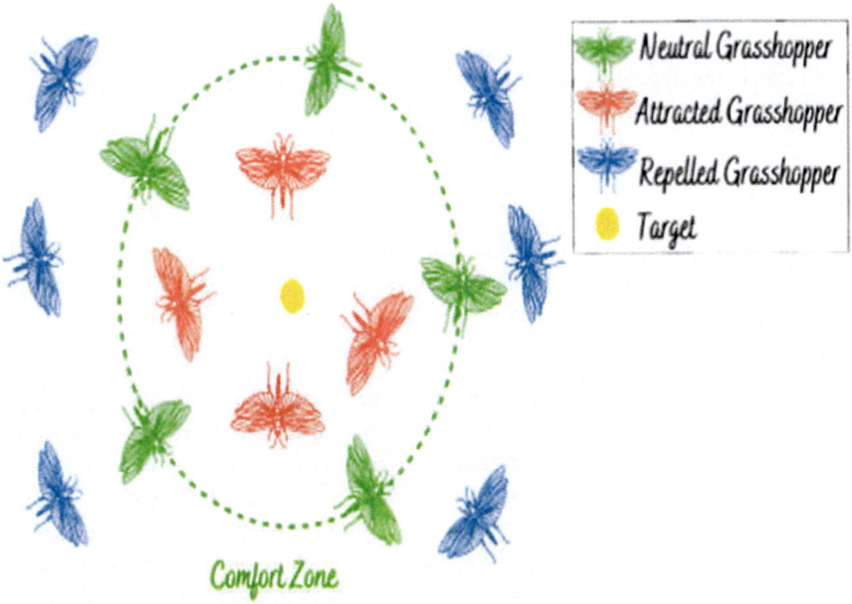

Fig. 7.2 Grasshoppers' social interactions

function affects the social behaviour (attraction and repulsion) of artificial grasshoppers. Three parts are created using this function to divide the space between two grasshoppers (repulsion region, comfort zone, and attraction region). Saremi et al. [20] investigated distances from 0 to 15 and found out that the repulsion happened between [0, 2.079]. They suggested defining the comfort distance as the separation of two artificial grasshoppers at a distance of 2.079 units (there is no attraction or repulsion in this comfort zone). The l and f settings modify this comfort zone. Unfortunately, the s function resets to zero when the distance exceeds 10. Hence, large forces cannot be applied between grasshoppers across great distances using this function. G_i, also known as the gravitational force on the ith grasshopper, is a part of X_i that may be determined using Eq. (7.3).

$$G_i = -g\widehat{e_g} \tag{7.3}$$

g stands for the gravitational constant, while $\widehat{e_g}$ is a unit vector pointing at the earth's center. The component A_i is given by the following Equation:

$$A_i = u\widehat{e_w} \tag{7.4}$$

where $\widehat{e_w}$ is a unit vector pointing in the direction of the wind and u is a continuous drift. In conventional swarm-based algorithms, the swarm is modelled as searching and taking advantage of the search space surrounding a solution. The swarm's mathematical model, the grasshopper algorithm, is in free space. As a result, the X_i model mimics the behaviour of a swarm of grasshoppers. Equation (7.5) replicates grasshopper behaviour in two-dimensional, three-dimensional, and hyperdimensional areas. It is an enlarged version of Eq. (7.1).

$$X_i^d = c\left(\sum_{\substack{j=1 \\ j \neq i}}^{N} c\frac{ub_d - lb_d}{2} s\left(\left|x_j^d - x_i^d\right|\right)\frac{x_j - x_i}{d_{ij}}\right) + \widehat{T_d} \tag{7.5}$$

In the Dth dimension sr, the upper (ub) and lower bounds (lb) are represented by ub_d and lb_d, respectively. The third component, c, is a decreasing coefficient that causes the comfort, repellency, and attraction zones to contract. $\widehat{T_d}$ is the target value (optimal solution). Each search agent only has one location vector, according to GOA. To determine each search agent's subsequent position in GOA, all search agents are used. The first term of Eq. (7.5) (the summation) simulates grasshopper interaction in nature by taking into consideration the positions of other grasshoppers. The second term $\widehat{T_d}$ simulates their propensity to travel in the direction of the sources of food. Last but not least, Eq. 7.6 uses parameter c to implement the slowdown of grasshoppers approaching the food source.

$$c = c_{max} - l\frac{c_{max} - c_{min}}{L} \tag{7.6}$$

where l denotes the current iteration and L is the maximum number of iterations, and c_{max} and c_{min} stand for the highest and lowest values, respectively. In this section, values of $c_{max} = 1$ and $c_{min} = 0.00001$ were used as recommended by Saremi et al. [20]. In summary, the swarm gradually moves towards a stationary target by reducing its comfort zone by the c parameter. Also, the swarm correctly pursues a moving object by $\widehat{T_d}$. Throughout iterations, the grasshoppers will flock together toward the objective. The optimization process of ant lion algorithm is summarized in Fig. 7.3.

7.3 Brief Description of Data Extraction and Processing

In order to illustrate the approach proposed in this study, quadratic equations were extracted from the study conducted by Sahu and Andhare [21]. In the reported study, titanium alloy (Ti–6Al–4V) was chosen as the turning work material. The bar size for turning was determined to be 32 mm in diameter, 100 mm in length, and 35 mm in length cut. The turning operations were carried out on a CNC lathe machine with a 5.5 kW power capacity. The machine's controller provided fine motion and spindle speed control with 0.005 mm position precision and 0.004 mm repeatability

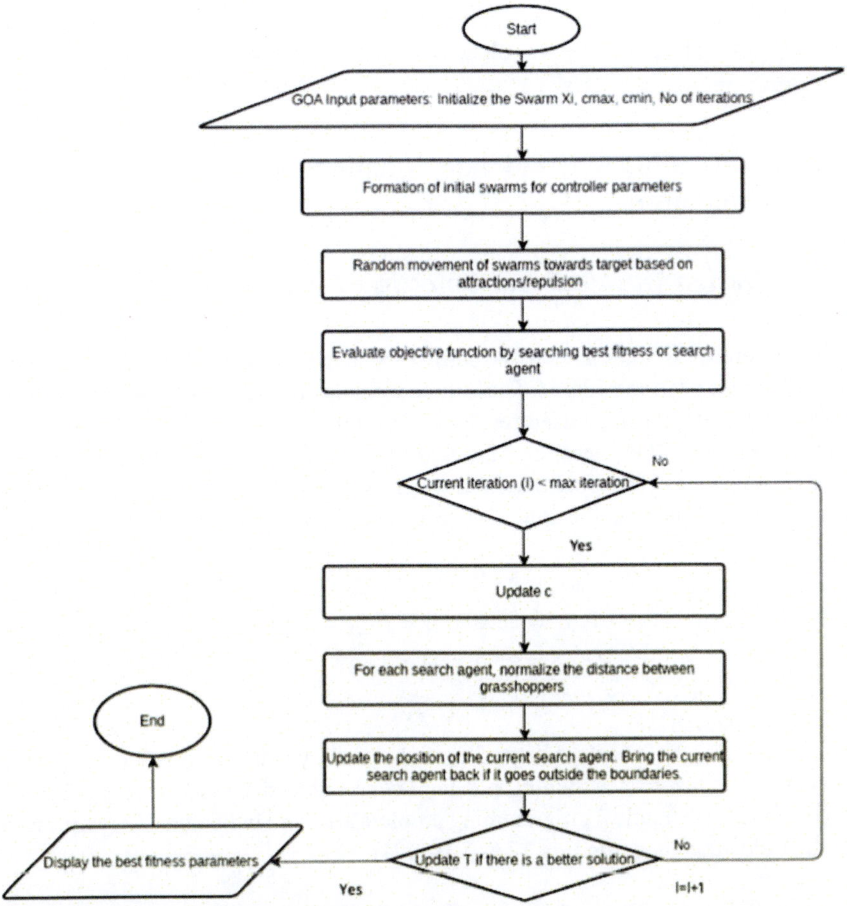

Fig. 7.3 Flowchart of grasshopper optimizer algorithm

during cutting. During turning operations, the cutting force was measured using a dynamometer that was interfaced with a control unit.

The design of experiment was performed with a central composite design (CCD) based on Response Surface Methodology (RSM). The speed of cutting, the feed rate and the depth of cut were the input factors. The regression coefficient and subsequently the quadratic equation of the cutting force were generated based on the experimental design and the response measured. The model adequacy was checked using the analysis of variance (ANOVA) and non-significant parameters were discarded. A similar approach was adopted to develop the quadratic equation describing the surface roughness [22]. The roughness of the machined surface and the force of cutting were the two responses. In the formulation of the multi-objective optimization models described in the following sections, the speed of cutting, the feed rate and the depth of cut are the variables to be optimized while the surface roughness and the cutting force are the two objective functions to minimize.

7.4 Formulation of Quadratic Equations and Mathematical Formulation

7.4.1 Design Variables and Objectives Functions

Three different variables namely the cutting speed (S), the feed rate (F) and the depth of cut (D) have been considered. These three variables are closely related to the setting of the CNC lathe machine used for data extraction and processing described in the previous section. The lowest and the highest level of cutting parameters used for central composite design reported in the study of Sahu and Andhare [21] were taken into account to illustrate the approach proposed in this study.

$$\begin{aligned} S_{min} &= 69.9 < S < S_{max} = 150 \\ F_{min} &= 55.6 < F < F_{max} = 120.6 \\ D_{min} &= 0.66 < D < D_{max} = 2 \end{aligned} \tag{7.7}$$

S, F and D $\in \Re^+$

In this study, the machinability of Ti–6Al–4V alloy is measured with the cutting force (CF) and the surface roughness (SR). The two objective functions in the formulation of the mathematical programming problem are these indicators. They are given by the following quadratic Eqs. (7.8–7.10) [21]:

$$\begin{aligned} CF = {} & 513.915 - 0.2466 \times S + 5.3773 \times F + 64.92 \\ & \times D - 2.594e - 4 \times S^2 - 0.055 \times F^2 + 0.0052 \times S \times F \end{aligned} \tag{7.8}$$

$$\begin{aligned} SR = {} & 1.27686 - 0.000897964 \times S + 0.0008937 \\ & \times F + 0.036303 \times D + 1.69203e - 7 \times S^2 \end{aligned} \tag{7.9}$$

These equations suggest that the three variables (S, F and D) have a significant effect on the cutting force and the surface roughness of Ti–6Al–4V alloy. The optimum values of the parameters describing the setting of the CNC lathe machine can be obtained by solving Eqs. 7.7 and 7.9.

7.4.2 Multi-objective Optimization

The following Equation is a formulation of the general multi-objective optimization problem with equality and inequality constraints [23]:

$$\text{Minimize}\left\{\overrightarrow{F_i(x)}\right\}, \quad \forall_i \in N_{oj},$$
$$\text{Subject to: } \begin{cases} \overrightarrow{g_m(x)}, \forall_m \in N_{EQ} \\ \overrightarrow{h_k(x)}, \forall_k \in N_{INQ} \end{cases} \tag{7.10}$$

where F_i is the ith objective function, $g_m(x)$ and $h_k(x)$ are the constraints, N_{EQ} and N_{INQ} are respectively the numbers of equality and inequality constraints, and N_{oj} is the number of objective functions.

If the following criteria are met, the solution $\overrightarrow{x_1}$ prevails over $\overrightarrow{x_2}$ in the multi-objective minimization problem:

$$F_i\left(\overrightarrow{x_1}\right) \le F_i\left(\overrightarrow{x_2}\right), \quad \forall_i \in N_{oj} \tag{7.11}$$

Pareto optimum solutions are the prevailing options across the whole search space.

A fuzzy membership function μ_i can be used to represent the ith objective function F_i as follows:

$$\mu_i = \frac{F_i - F_i^{min}}{F_i^{max} - F_i^{min}} \tag{7.12}$$

where the parameters F_i^{min} and F_i^{max} are respectively the minimum and the maximum values of the ith objective function among all Pareto solutions.

The normalized membership function μ^k is calculated as follows for each Pareto solution:

$$\mu^k = \frac{\sum_{i=1}^{N_{oj}} \mu_i^k}{\sum_{k=1}^{M} \sum_{i=1}^{N_{oj}} \mu_i^k}, \quad \forall k \in M \tag{7.13}$$

The minimal value of μ^k is the best compromise option. M is the number of Pareto solutions.

7.5 Results and Discussion

The optimization of the CNC lathe machine problem to improve machining performance is solved in this section using the ALO algorithms. The proposed algorithm is applied to solve the multi-objective optimization problem described by the objective

Table 7.1 MOGOA parameters

Number of Grasshoppers: 200
Maximum iteration: 100
cMax = 1
cMin = 0.00004

functions 1 OF1 and OF2 corresponding to Eqs. 7.7 and 7.9. The proposed approach was implemented in a MATLAB environment. Details of the mathematical programming model are provided in Appendix F. The simulation results are carried out using an 11th Gen Intel(R) Core (TM) i5-1135G7 @ 2.40 GHz Processor, 8 GB RAM, 64-bit operating system, PC. Table 7.1 provides details showing how the parameters of the suggested algorithm are configured.

The proposed algorithm is applied to solve the multi-objective problem described by the objective function 1 (OF1) and objective function 2 (OF2) corresponding to Eqs. 7.2 and 8.3 respectively. As described in the previous sections, the cutting force and the surface roughness are conflicting in nature. Therefore, the best compromise was obtained by optimizing these two objectives simultaneously. The optimal

Table 7.2 Pareto optimal solutions

Index	OF1	OF2	Index	OF1	OF2
1	513.9150	1.2769	51	513.7916	1.2764
2	513.9125	1.2769	52	513.7892	1.2764
3	513.9101	1.2768	53	513.7867	1.2764
4	513.9076	1.2768	54	513.7842	1.2764
5	513.9051	1.2768	55	513.7818	1.2764
6	513.9027	1.2768	56	513.7793	1.2764
7	513.9002	1.2768	57	513.7768	1.2764
8	513.8977	1.2768	58	513.7744	1.2763
9	513.8953	1.2768	59	513.7719	1.2763
10	513.8928	1.2768	60	513.7694	1.2763
11	513.8903	1.2768	61	513.7669	1.2763
12	513.8879	1.2768	62	513.7645	1.2763
13	513.8854	1.2768	63	513.7620	1.2763
14	513.8829	1.2767	64	513.7595	1.2763
15	513.8805	1.2767	65	513.7571	1.2763
16	513.8780	1.2767	66	513.7546	1.2763
17	513.8755	1.2767	67	513.7521	1.2763
18	513.8731	1.2767	68	513.7497	1.2763
19	513.8706	1.2767	69	513.7472	1.2762

(continued)

Table 7.2 (continued)

Index	OF1	OF2	Index	OF1	OF2
20	513.8681	1.2767	70	513.7447	1.2762
21	513.8657	1.2767	71	513.7423	1.2762
22	513.8632	1.2767	72	513.7398	1.2762
23	513.8607	1.2767	73	513.7373	1.2762
24	513.8583	1.2767	74	513.7348	1.2762
25	513.8558	1.2766	75	513.7324	1.2762
26	513.8533	1.2766	76	513.7299	1.2762
27	513.8509	1.2766	77	513.7274	1.2762
28	513.8484	1.2766	78	513.7250	1.2762
29	513.8459	1.2766	79	513.7225	1.2762
30	513.8435	1.2766	80	513.7200	1.2762
31	513.8410	1.2766	81	513.7176	1.2761
32	513.8385	1.2766	82	513.7151	1.2761
33	513.8361	1.2766	83	513.7126	1.2761
34	513.8336	1.2766	84	513.7101	1.2761
35	513.8311	1.2766	85	513.7077	1.2761
36	513.8287	1.2765	86	513.7052	1.2761
37	513.8262	1.2765	87	513.7027	1.2761
38	513.8237	1.2765	88	513.7003	1.2761
39	513.8213	1.2765	89	513.6978	1.2761
40	513.8188	1.2765	90	513.6953	1.2761
41	513.8163	1.2765	91	513.6928	1.2761
42	513.8139	1.2765	92	513.6904	1.2760
43	513.8114	1.2765	93	513.6879	1.2760
44	513.8089	1.2765	94	513.6854	1.2760
45	513.8064	1.2765	95	513.6830	1.2760
46	513.8040	1.2765	96	513.6805	1.2760
47	513.8015	1.2764	97	513.6780	1.2760
48	513.7990	1.2764	98	513.6756	1.2760
49	513.7966	1.2764	99	513.6731	1.2760
50	513.7941	1.2764	100	513.6706	1.2760

settings corresponding to the optimal values of cutting force and surface roughness are described in Table 7.2 by values of OF1 and OF2 respectively. Figure 7.4 shows two-dimensional Pareto optimal solutions that achieved the best compromise solution. Details of the main MATLAB codes are provided in Appendices F and G.

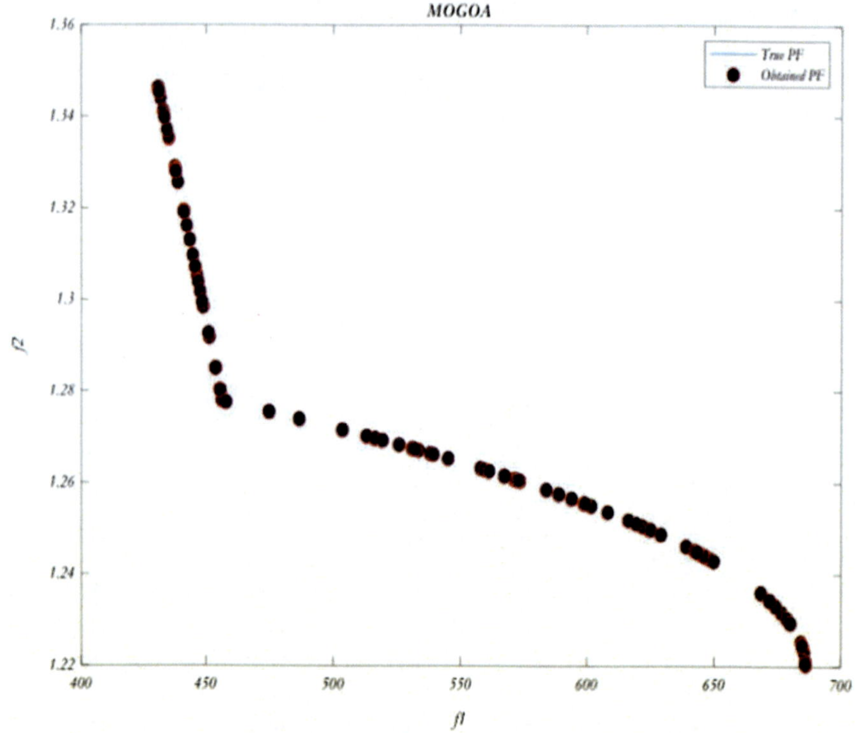

Fig. 7.4 Graphical representation of the Pareto optimal solutions

7.6 Conclusion

In this section, a Multi-objective Grasshopper Optimizer (MOGOA) is proposed to enhance the machining performance during the turning of a titanium alloy. This advanced approach has been described in detail to demonstrate the applicability of metaheuristic optimization methods in manufacturing. The cutting force and the surface roughness were the two objective functions to optimize. Details describing the proposed optimization approach are provided. The approach was implemented in software MATLAB. The proposed Multi-objective Grasshopper Optimizer (MOGOA) was applied to solve the multi-objective problem and the best compromise between the two objective functions was computed to assist the decision-maker in the selection of the best setting that could potentially improve machinability performance.

References

1. Rahman, M., Wang, Z.G., Wong, Y.S.: A review on high-speed machining of titanium alloys. JSME Int J. Ser. C **49**(1), 11–20 (2006)
2. Pawade, R.S., Joshi, S.S., Brahmankar, P.K., Rahman, M.: An investigation of cutting forces and surface damage in high-speed turning of Inconel 718. J. Mater. Process. Technol. **192**, 139–146 (2007)
3. Pawade, R.S., Joshi, S.S.: Multi-objective optimization of surface roughness and cutting forces in high-speed turning of Inconel 718 using Taguchi grey relational analysis (TGRA). Int. J. Adv. Manuf. Technol. **56**(1), 47 (2011)
4. Lin, J.L., Lin, C.L.: The use of the orthogonal array with grey relational analysis to optimize the electrical discharge machining process with multiple performance characteristics. Int. J. Mach. Tools Manuf **42**(2), 237–244 (2002)
5. Abualigah, L., Diabat, A.: A comprehensive survey of the Grasshopper optimization algorithm: results, variants, and applications. Neural Comput. Appl. **32**(19), 15533–15556 (2020)
6. Arora, S.: Approximation schemes for NP-hard geometric optimization problems: a survey. Math. Program. **97**(1), 43–69 (2003)
7. Abualigah, L., Shehab, M., Alshinwan, M., Alabool, H.: Salp swarm algorithm: a comprehensive survey. Neural Comput. Appl. **32**, 11195–11215 (2020)
8. Glover, F.: Tabu search—part I. ORSA J. Comput. **1**(3), 190–206 (1989)
9. Kirkpatrick, S.: Optimization by simulated annealing: quantitative studies. J. Stat. Phys. **34**, 975–986 (1984)
10. Tsamardinos, I., Brown, L.E., Aliferis, C.F.: The max-min hill-climbing Bayesian network structure learning algorithm. Mach. Learn. **65**, 31–78 (2006)
11. Okwu, M.O., Tartibu, L.K.: Metaheuristic optimization: nature-inspired algorithms swarm and computational intelligence, theory and applications, vol. 927. Springer Nature (2020)
12. Koza, J.R.: Evolution of subsumption using genetic programming. In: Proceedings of the First European Conference on Artificial Life, pp. 110–119. MIT Press, Cambridge, MA, USA (1992)
13. Abualigah, L.M., Khader, A.T., Hanandeh, E.S.: Modified krill herd algorithm for global numerical optimization problems. Advances in Nature-Inspired Computing and Applications, pp. 205–221 (2019)
14. Geem, Z.W., Kim, J.H., Loganathan, G.V.: A new heuristic optimization algorithm: harmony search. Simulation **76**(2), 60–68 (2001)
15. Okwu, M.O., Tartibu, L.K.: Particle swarm optimisation. Metaheuristic Optimization: Nature-Inspired Algorithms Swarm and Computational Intelligence, Theory and Applications, pp. 5–13 (2021a)
16. Simon, D.: Biogeography-based optimization. IEEE Trans. Evol. Comput. **12**(6), 702–713 (2008)
17. Okwu, M.O., Tartibu, L.K.: Artificial bee colony algorithm. Metaheuristic Optimization: Nature-Inspired Algorithms Swarm and Computational Intelligence, Theory and Applications, pp. 15–31 (2021b)
18. Niu, B., Wang, H.: Bacterial colony optimization. Discrete Dynamics in Nature and Society (2012)
19. Yang, X.S.: Flower pollination algorithm for global optimization. In: Unconventional Computation and Natural Computation: 11th International Conference, UCNC 2012, Orléan, France, September 3–7, 2012. Proceedings 11, pp. 240–249. Springer, Berlin (2012)
20. Saremi, S., Mirjalili, S., Lewis, A.: Grasshopper optimisation algorithm: theory and application. Adv. Eng. Softw. **105**, 30–47 (2017)
21. Sahu, N.K., Andhare, A.B.: Multiobjective optimization for improving machinability of Ti-6Al-4V using RSM and advanced algorithms. J. Computat. Des. Eng. **6**(1), 1–12 (2019)

22. Sahu, N.K., Andhare, A.B.: Optimization of surface roughness in turning of Ti-6Al-4V using response surface methodology and TLBO. In: International Design Engineering Technical Conferences and Computers and Information in Engineering Conference, vol. 57113, p. V004T05A020. American Society of Mechanical Engineers (2015)
23. Santana-Quintero, L.V., Coello, C.A.C.: An algorithm based on differential evolution for multi-objective problems. Int. J. Comput. Intell. Res. **1**(1), 151–169 (2005)

Chapter 8
A Multi-objective Optimization Approach for Improving Machining Performance Using the General Algebraic Modelling System (GAMS)

Check for updates

Abstract Machining performance can be assessed through indicators such as cutting force and surface roughness. These indicators can be predicted and optimized by adjusting parameters such as the cutting speed, the feed rate and the depth of cut. Several studies have pointed out the conflicting nature of cutting force and surface roughness when attempting to optimize them simultaneously. Unlike previous studies, the machinability performance is analysed in this work using an improved version of the augmented ε-constraint approach that takes cutting force and surface roughness into account as objective functions. In order to illustrate the approach proposed in this study, quadratic equations were extracted from an existing study related to a CNC lathe machine. These equations relate variables such as cutting speed, the feed rate and the depth of cut to the cutting force and surface roughness considered as objective functions in the mathematical programming formulation. The General Algebraic Modeling System (or GAMS) was used to construct and implement the Non-Linear Problem. The proposed new multi-objective approach provides accurate Pareto sets that correspond to the optimal setting of the CNC lathe machine. In addition, this study provide clarity on the implication of an adjustment of machining parameters to optimize machining performance.

Keywords General algebraic modeling system · Machining · Cutting force and surface roughness · Optimization

8.1 Introduction

Due to the exceptional qualities indicated in the literature, titanium alloys are widely used in the aviation and biomedical industries [1, 2]. However, the literature also reports challenges in machining titanium alloys [2–4]. Cutting force and surface roughness, which serve as indicators of surface integrity, are frequently utilized as response parameters for assessing machining performance [5]. This is due to the explanations provided in the paragraphs that follow.

I. P. Okokpujie and L. K. Tartibu, *Modern Optimization Techniques for Advanced Machining*, Studies in Systems, Decision and Control 485,
https://doi.org/10.1007/978-3-031-35455-7_8

After machining, surface integrity is a crucial indicator of reliability, as are fatigue life and end-part quality [6, 7]. A widely used technique for determining the integrity of a machined surface is to quantify the surface roughness [8]. In past studies, traditional machining was used to determine the influence of machining input parameters on the roughness of machined surfaces in operations like turning and milling [9, 10]. According to Sahu and Andhare [11], although cutting speed and feed rate are important elements for turning and facing operations, feed rate and radial depth of cut are key factors for surface roughness for milling operations. In the past, researchers have conducted experiments to create empirical models with variables like cutting parameters to identify the ideal circumstances for minimal surface roughness [12–14].

As it relates to the power needed for machining, cutting force is a crucial machinability evaluation criterion. Because cutting pressures rise with tool wear, surface quality depends on cutting force. In order to find the best cutting parameters for machining a challenging titanium alloy under minimal quantity lubrication (MQL) conditions, Liu et al. [15] suggested a new approach referring to coupling response surface methodology (CRSM). As a result, cutting forces were minimized when the feed rate and depth of cut were set to the lowest levels while the cutting speed was set to the greatest levels. From the previous studies, it appears that, while cutting Ti–6Al–4V, cutting force reduces with increasing cutting speed for constant feed rate, depth of cut, and given rake angle [16]. According to the literature, it is possible to create models that predict and optimize cutting forces and surface roughness based on cutting parameters.

Rao and Kalyankar [17] propose the use of a multi-objective optimization approach to determine the variables that optimize multiple objectives while taking restrictions into account. Many studies discuss the theory of optimization for single- and multi-objective optimizations [18, 19]. Advanced optimization algorithms, such as the Particle Swarm Optimization (PSO), Genetic Algorithm (GA), Artificial Bee Colony (ABC), Ant Colony Optimization (ACO) etc. are described by Okwu and Tartibu [20] to illustrate how optimization problems could be formulated and resolved. Although most of these algorithms yield robust solutions, improper tuning of algorithm-specific parameters either increases the computational effort or yields a locally optimal solution. In addition to the tuning of algorithm-specific parameters, the common control parameters also need to be tuned which further enhances the effort. There is no universal rule for the choice of these parameters. Improper selection of these parameters leads to a local optimum solution. The repeatability of results obtained with the same design variables and initial conditions is not guaranteed with these non-traditional optimization techniques.

Sahu and Andhare [16] proposed the use of Teaching Learning Based Optimization (TLBO), "JAYA," and Genetic Algorithm (GA) to show how the turning of titanium alloys (Ti–6Al–4V) can be optimized to reduce surface roughness and the resulting cutting forces. The results show that when cutting Ti–6Al–4V, a greater cutting speed combined with a lower feed rate can result in better surface roughness and less cutting force. Unlike previous studies, the machinability performance is analysed in this work using an improved version of the augmented ε-constraint approach

(AUGMENCON2) that takes cutting force and surface roughness into account as objective functions. Mavrotas and Florios [21] created the proposed AUGMENCON2 technique. A high-level modeling system for mathematical programming and optimization called the General Algebraic Modeling System (or GAMS) is used to construct and implement Non-Linear Problems. With a fair level of precision and quick computation times, this new multi-objective approach aims to provide accurate Pareto sets that correspond to the optimal setting of the CNC lathe machine.

8.2 Modelling with GAMS

GAMS stands for General Algebraic Modeling System. It is an optimization and programming modeling. This chapter illustrates how problems related to machining processing could be formulated in GAMS in order to compute optimal solutions. The GAMS technology is made to make it easier for modelers to build mathematical representations of the world around us. It frees modelers from having to create model algorithms in addition to developing models. Consequently, creating algorithms for mathematical models is the primary functional goal of GAMS.

Though the acronym of GAMS incorporates the word "Algebraic", this does not imply that this system is limited to algebraic equation-based mathematical models. Those who are familiar with the techniques for solving partial differential equations know that they are always converted to a system of algebraic equations. An iteration approach is used to solve these algebraic equations. That is to say, GAMS has a considerably larger range of applications.

Each GAMS model is composed mostly of the following components [22]:

- Sets: The indices in the algebraic representations of models are defined by sets.
- Data: Each GAMS model's input data are expressed as parameters, tables, or scalars.
- Variables: Prior to solving the model, the variables are uncertain decision sets.
- Equations: The relationships between the variables and data are described by the equations.
- Model and Solve Statements: An objective function-containing set of equations is referred to as the model. GAMS is commanded to solve the model in the solve sentence.
- Output: The results of the solved model can be seen in a variety of ways, including by displaying them or saving them in an XLS file.

Figure 8.1 depicts the general GAMS code structure and its components.

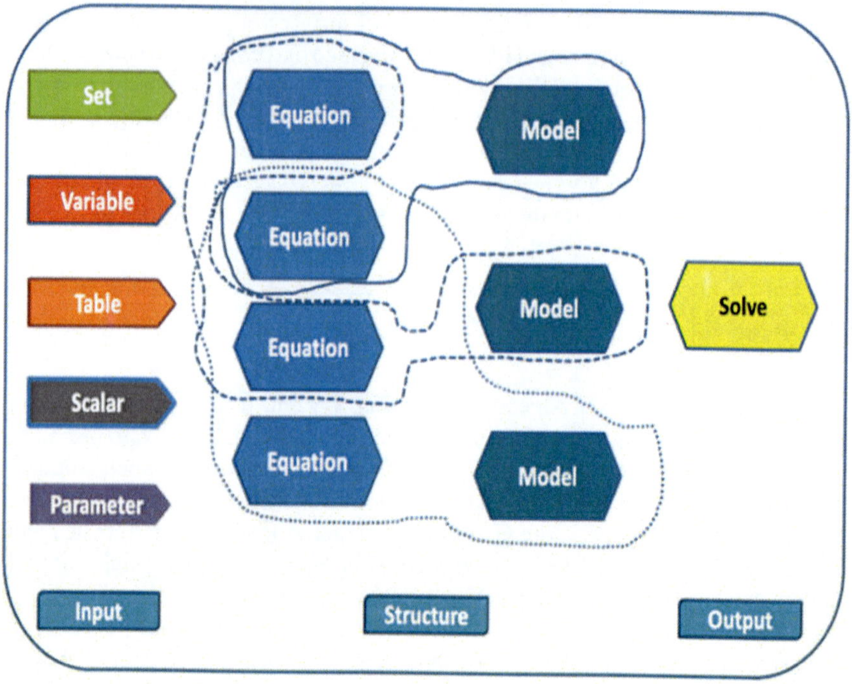

Fig. 8.1 GAMS code structure and its components

8.3 Brief Description of Data Extraction and Processing

In order to illustrate the approach proposed in this study, quadratic equations were extracted from the study conducted by Sahu and Andhare [16]. In the reported study, titanium alloy (Ti–6Al–4V) was chosen as the turning work material. The bar size for turning was determined to be 32 mm in diameter, 100 mm in length, and 35 mm in length cut. The turning operations were carried out on a CNC lathe machine with a 5.5 kW power capacity. The machine's controller provided fine motion and spindle speed control with 0.005 mm position precision and 0.004 mm repeatability during cutting. During turning operations, the cutting force was measured using a dynamometer that was interfaced with a control unit.

The design of experiment was performed with a central composite design (CCD) based on Response Surface Methodology (RSM). The speed of cutting, the feed rate and the depth of cut were the input factors [23]. The regression coefficient and subsequently the quadratic equation of the cutting force were generated based on the experimental design and the response measured. The model adequacy was checked using the analysis of variance (ANOVA) and non-significant parameters were discarded. A similar approach was adopted to develop the quadratic equation describing the surface roughness [11]. The roughness of the machined surface and the force of cutting were the two responses. In the formulation of the multi-objective optimization models described in the following sections, the speed of cutting, the feed rate and the depth of cut are the variables to be optimized while the surface roughness and the cutting force are the two objective functions to minimize.

8.4 Formulation of Quadratic Equations and Mathematical Programming Models

8.4.1 *Design Variables and Objectives Functions*

Three different variables namely the cutting speed (S), the feed rate (F) and the depth of cut (D) have been considered. These three variables are closely related to the setting of the CNC lathe machine used for data extraction and processing described in the previous section. The lowest and the highest level of cutting parameters used for central composite design reported in the study of Sahu and Andhare [16] were taken into account to illustrate the approach proposed in this study.

$$\begin{aligned} &S_{min} = 69.9 < S < S_{max} = 150 \\ &F_{min} = 55.6 < F < F_{max} = 120.6 \\ &D_{min} = 0.66 < D < D_{max} = 2 \\ &S, F \text{ and } D \in \Re^{+} \end{aligned} \tag{8.1}$$

In this study, the machinability of Ti–6Al–4V alloy is measured with the cutting force (CF) and the surface roughness (SR). The two objective functions in the formulation of the mathematical programming problem are these indicators. They are given by the following quadratic Eqs. (8.1–8.6):

$$\begin{aligned} CF = {} & 513.915 - 0.2466 \times S + 5.3773 \times F + 64.92 \times D \\ & - 2.594e - 4 \times S^2 - 0.055 \times F^2 + 0.0052 \times S \times F \end{aligned} \tag{8.2}$$

$$\begin{aligned} SR = {} & 1.27686 - 0.000897964 \times D + 0.0008937 \times F \\ & + 0.036303 \times D + 1.69203e - 7 \times S^2 \end{aligned} \tag{8.3}$$

These equations suggest that the three variables (S, F and D) have a significant effect on the cutting force and the surface roughness of Ti–6Al–4V alloy. The optimum values of the parameters describing the setting of the CNC lathe machine can be obtained by solving Eqs. 8.2 and 8.3.

8.4.2 *Single Objective Optimization*

In the preceding section, descriptions of each phrase used in the Mathematical Problem Formulation (MPF) are provided. They are the basis of the Non-Linear Programming Problem (NLP) that is represented by the following equation:

$$\text{(MPF)} \min_{S,F,D} \xi = w_1(CF) + w_2(SR) \tag{8.4}$$

This mathematical model captures the main elements that describe the machinability of Ti–6Al–4V alloy. The analysis of restricted cases of objectives and the identification of geometric parameter trends with respect to each objective function are covered in the discussion that follows.

8.4.2.1 Emphasising Cutting Force

All proposed NLPs developed in this study were solved by GAMS 23.8 on a personal computer Intel Core i5, 2.4 GHz with 8 GB RAM. Although there are several optimization solvers incorporated in GAMS, the solver LINDOGLOBAL was adopted for this study (Fig. 8.2). This is because LINDOGLOBAL identifies solutions that are guaranteed to be globally optimal for nonlinear problems involving continuous and/or discrete variables [24]. This study includes information on the input file and the GAMS compilation models used for the analysis and optimization of machining processes, with the GAMS process shown in Fig. 8.3.

In order to emphasise the cutting force, the objective function weight $w_2 = 0$. Hence, the problem would be reduced to Eq. 8.2 and the variable restrictions described in Eq. 8.1. The objective function (Eq. 8.4) becomes:

$$\text{(MPF)} \min_{S,F,D} \xi_{CF} = CF \tag{8.5}$$

A screenshot showing the mathematical programming model and the compilation process is shown in Fig. 8.4. Details of the GAMS code are provided in Fig. 8.4.

The optimal solutions that minimise ξ_{CF} are represented in a tabulated format with letters subscripted with an asterisk (Table 8.1). Practically, this optimal solution suggests that the cutting force can be optimised by:

- Setting the cutting speed to the minimum.
- Setting the feed rate to the maximum.
- Ensuring that the depth of cut is minimum.

The minimum and the maximum cutting force are respectively 430.656 and 774.451.

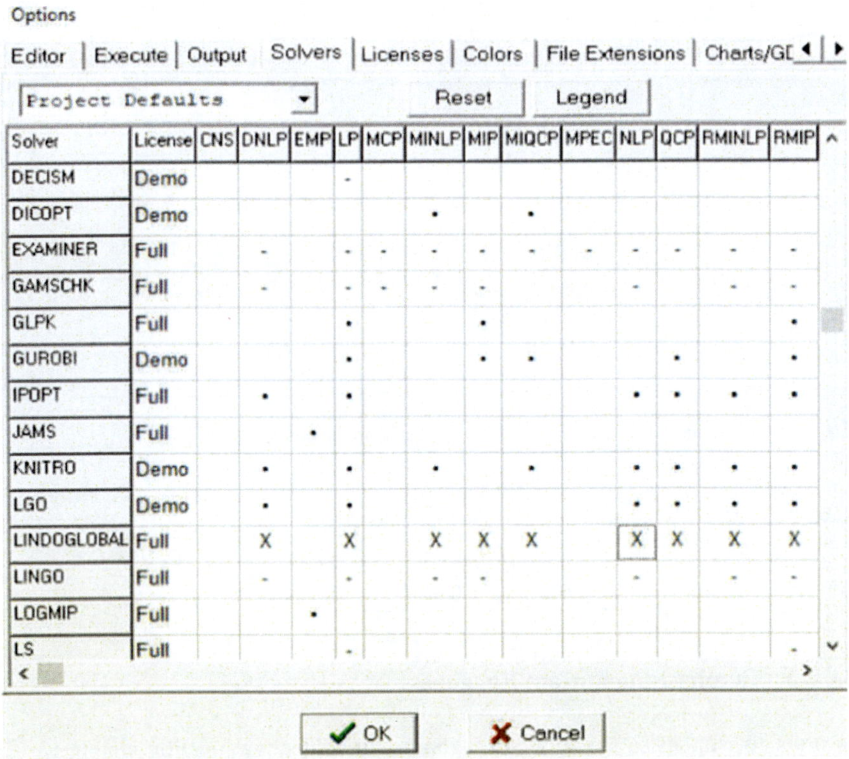

Solver	License	CNS	DNLP	EMP	LP	MCP	MINLP	MIP	MIQCP	MPEC	NLP	QCP	RMINLP	RMIP
DECISM	Demo				-									
DICOPT	Demo						•		•					
EXAMINER	Full		-		-	-	-	-	-	-	-	-	-	-
GAMSCHK	Full		-		-	-	-	-			-		-	-
GLPK	Full				•			•						•
GUROBI	Demo				•			•	•			•		•
IPOPT	Full		•		•						•	•	•	•
JAMS	Full			•										
KNITRO	Demo		•		•		•		•		•	•	•	•
LGO	Demo		•		•						•	•	•	•
LINDOGLOBAL	Full		X		X		X	X	X		X	X	X	X
LINGO	Full		-		-		-	-			-		-	-
LOGMIP	Full			•										
LS	Full				-									-

Fig. 8.2 GAMS solvers

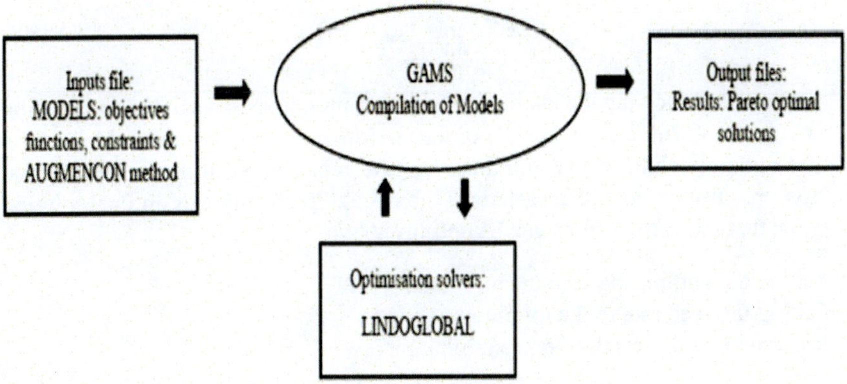

Fig. 8.3 Process illustration using GAMS

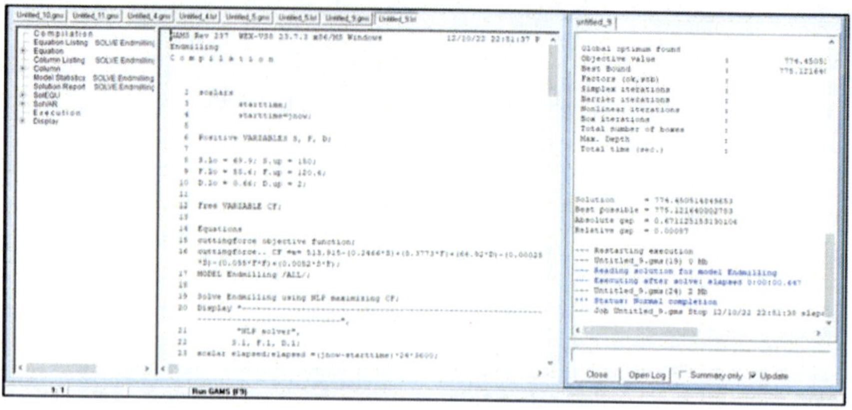

Fig. 8.4 GAMS model formulation with an emphasis on the cutting force

Table 8.1 Optimal solutions minimising the cutting force

	S*	F*	D*	ξ^*_{CF}	CPU time (s)
x*	69.900	120.600	0.660	430.656	0.616

8.4.2.2 Emphasising Surface Roughness

In order to emphasise the surface roughness, the objective function weight $w_1 = 0$. Hence, the problem would be reduced to Eq. 8.3 and the variable restrictions described in Eq. 8.1. The objective function (Eq. 8.4) becomes:

$$(\text{MPF}) \min_{S,F,D} \xi_{SR} = SR \tag{8.6}$$

A screenshot showing the mathematical programming model and the compilation process is shown in Fig. 8.5. Details of the GAMS code are provided in Fig. 8.5.

The optimal solutions that minimise ξ_{SR} are represented in a tabulated format with letters subscripted with an asterisk (Table 8.2). Practically, this optimal solution suggests that the cutting force can be optimised by:

- Setting the cutting speed to the minimum.
- Setting the feed rate to the minimum.
- Ensuring that the depth of cut is minimum.

The minimum surface roughness is 1.289.

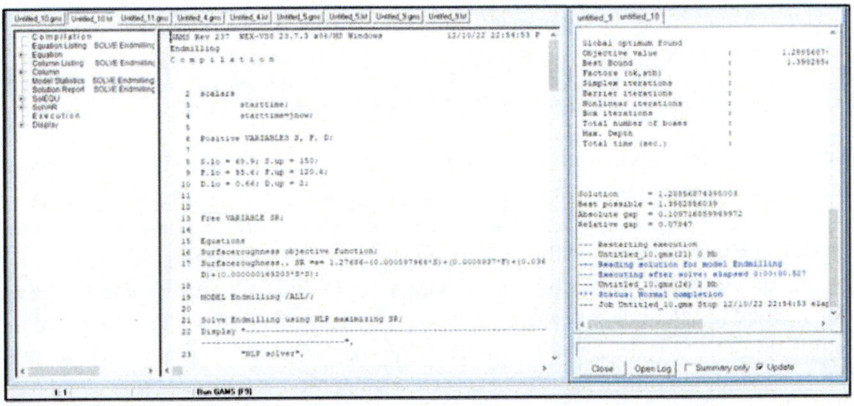

Fig. 8.5 GAMS model formulation with an emphasis on the surface roughness

Table 8.2 Optimal solutions minimising surface roughness

	S*	F*	D*	ξ_{SR}^{*}	CPU time (s)
x*	69.900	55.600	0.660	1.289	1.929

Table 8.3 Tendencies of parameters considering an individual objective function

	CF	SR
S	↓	↓
F	↑	↓ ≠
D	↓	↓

8.4.2.3 Single Objective Optima: Variable Analysis

Table 8.3 summarises the results of the two previous sections, highlighting the trends of parameters. In this analysis, ↑ indicates an increasing tendency, ↓ indicates a decreasing tendency and ≠ indicates conflicting tension between parameters.

The conflicting nature of objective functions is observed when considering the trends of the feed rate in Table 8.3. Therefore, the use of adoption of a multi-objective optimization approach would be suitable to compute the optimal solutions that would optimize the two objective functions simultaneously.

8.4.3 Emphasising All Objective Components

An enhanced version of the augmented ε-constraint approach is suggested in this study. As a result, a summary of the original augmented ε-constraint approach is given. Mavrotas [25] provide information on how the ε-constraint technique is implemented as compared to the augmented ε-constraint approach.

(a) Augmented ε-constraint method (AUGMENCON)

Numerous studies on thermal systems by Tartibu et al. [26] and [27] have successfully used the original augmented ε-constraint approach (AUGMENCON), which was proposed by Mavrotas [25]. The AUGMENCON is a modification of the conventional ε-constraint approach that addresses many of its shortcomings. (1) Unlike the traditional ε-constraint method, the AUGMENCON uses a lexicographic optimization method to calculate the ranges of the objective functions; (2) the efficiency of the returned solutions is demonstrated, and (3) the AUGMENCON significantly reduces the computational time by utilizing several acceleration techniques. It is possible to formulate the increased ε-constraint approach as follows:

$$\max\left(f_1(x) + eps \times \left(\frac{s_2}{r_2} + \frac{s_3}{r_3} + \cdots + \frac{s_p}{r_p}\right)\right) \tag{8.7}$$

Subject to

$$f_2(x) - s_2 = \varepsilon_2;\ f_3(x) - s_3 = \varepsilon_3, \ldots;\ f_p(x) - s_p = \varepsilon_p$$
$$x \in s \text{ and } s_i \in \Re^+$$

where $\varepsilon_2, \varepsilon_3, \ldots, \varepsilon_p$ are the right-hand side parameters corresponding to the objective functions 2, 3, ..., p. The ranges are denoted with $r_2, r_3, \ldots, r_p$, the surplus variables are described as $s_2, s_3, \ldots, s_p$ while eps represent a small number whose value is in-between 10^{-3} and 10^{-6} [25]. Figure 8.6 shows the flowchart of the AUGMENCON method for optimizing several objective functions.

(b) Improved version of the augmented ε-constraint method (AUGMENCON2)

According to Mavrotas and Florios [21], the enhanced version of the ε-constraint approach (AUGMENCON2) is used in the following ways:

- To locate any additional optima (unlike AUGMENCON), the lexicographic optimization is applied to the primary objective and the remaining objective functions.
- The payout table is used to compute the objective function range.
- Ranges are divided into equidistant grid points.

The Mathematical Formulation Problem (MPF) established by Eq. 8.7 is somewhat altered in AUGMENCON2 as follows:

$$\max\left(f_1(x) + eps \times \left(\frac{s_2}{r_2} + 10^{-1}\frac{s_3}{r_3} + \cdots + 10^{-(p-2)}\frac{s_p}{r_p}\right)\right) \tag{8.8}$$

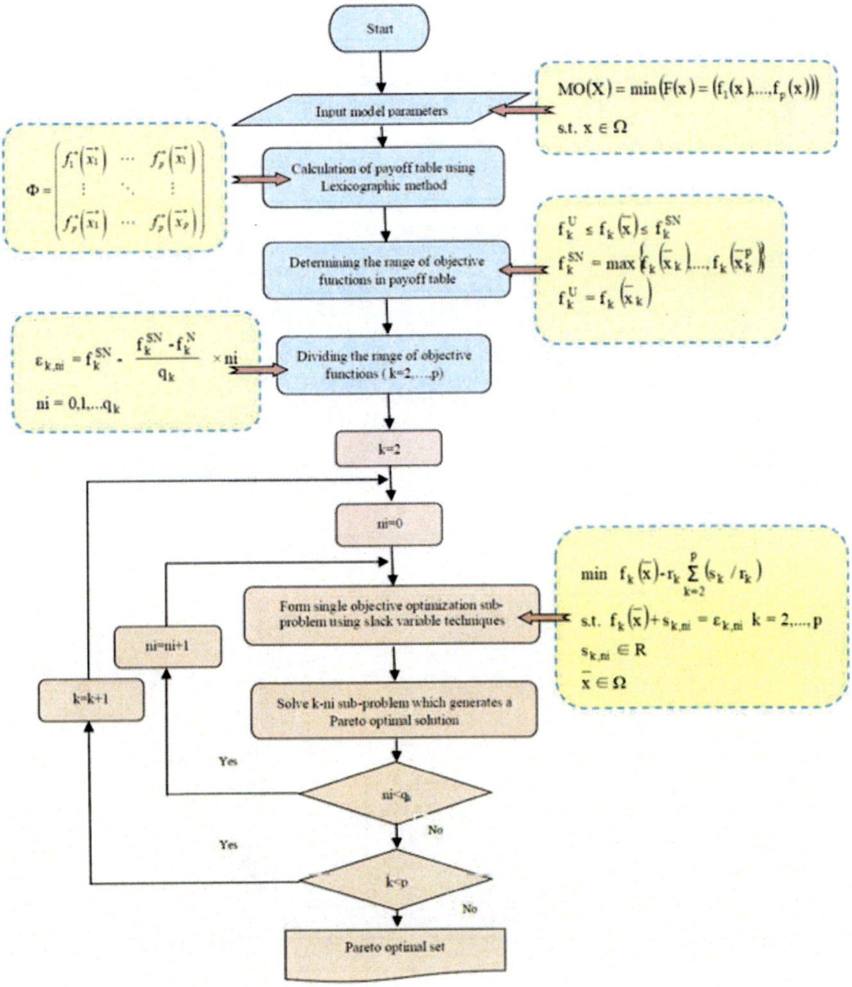

Fig. 8.6 Flowchart of AUGMENCON method. Adapted from Tartibu et al. [19]

This change is made to do lexicographic optimization on all objective functions, not just the main one, in order to find any potential alternate optima. Therefore, in contrast to the preceding formulation, the solver is compelled to carry out the sequential optimization of the restricted objectives and discover sequentially their optimum. The potential improvement of this approach was demonstrated in the two studies related to a microchannel heat sink [28, 29]. Figure 8.7 gives a flowchart of AUGMENCON 2.

(c) GAMS Model implementation

The two objective components (cutting force and surface roughness) are taken into account simultaneously in this section. The previous section provided descriptions

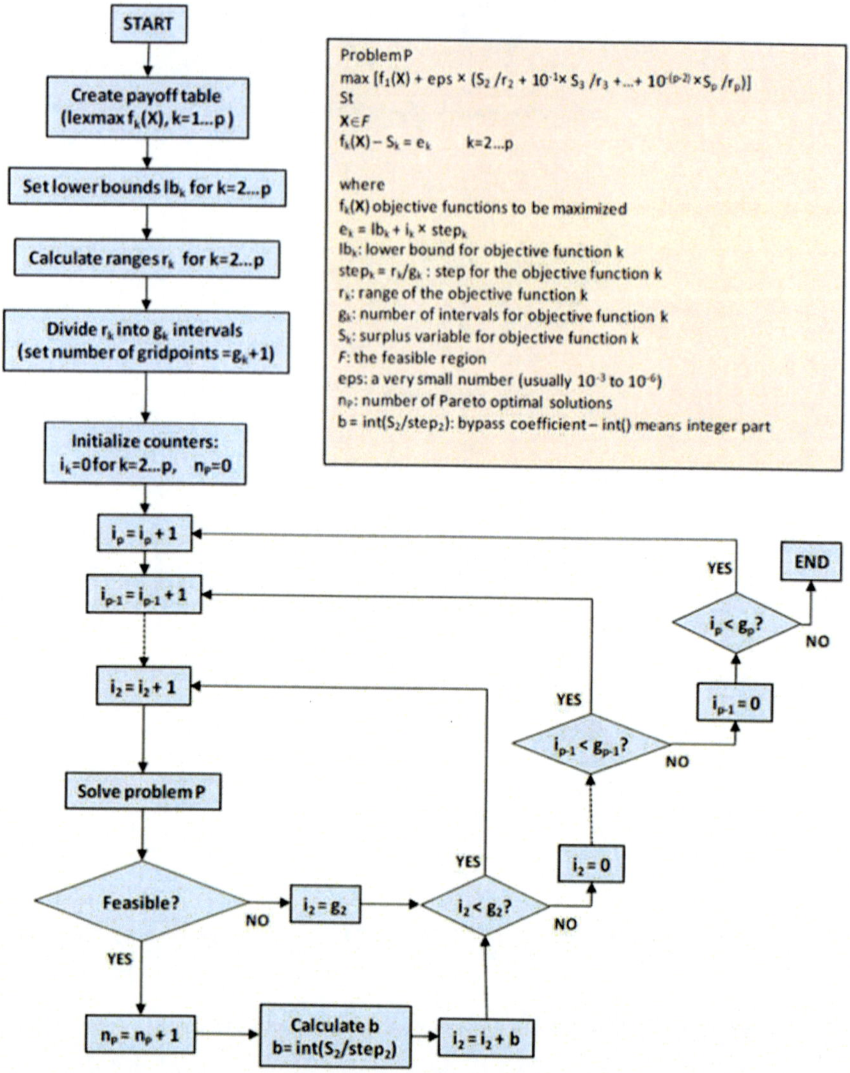

Fig. 8.7 Flowchart of AUGMENCON2 method. Adapted from Mavrotas and Florios [21]

of the majority of the equations used in the formulation of the Multi-objective mathematical Programming Formulation (MPF). The two-criteria NLP used to formulate the optimization problem minimizes both the cutting force (CF) and the surface roughness (SR).

$$(\text{MPF}) \min_{\text{S,F,D}} \xi = \{\text{CF}_{\text{S,F,D}}; \text{SR}_{\text{S,F,D}}\} \tag{8.9}$$

Subject to bound limits detailed in Eq. 8.1.

In the formulation (Eq. 8.9), S, F, and D denote the parameters describing the setting of the CNC lathe machine. The two objective functions cannot be optimized simultaneously by a single optimal solution. However, in these circumstances, the decision-makers look for the "most favoured" solutions. The improved augmented ε-constraint method (AUGMENCON2) is used to locate these solutions. The GAMS code for the AUGMENCON2 technique has been developed. The GAMS library includes an example that uses a multi-objective integer programming problem to demonstrate the method and adapt it to diverse optimization problems (https://www.gams.com/latest/gamslib_ml/libhtml/gamslib_epscmmip.html). The portion of the code that deals with the example (specific objective functions, constraints, and variables) has been altered to take into account the machining processes problem, even though the parts of the code that perform the calculation of the payoff table with lexicographic optimization and the generation of Pareto optimal solutions are fully parameterized and almost ready to use.

Only Pareto optimum solutions are produced when the payoff table for the MPF is constructed using the lexicographic optimization for each objective function [30]. Weakly efficient solutions are avoided. The model can be solved using the enhanced ε-constraint technique (Eq. 8.10), which can be written as follows:

$$\min\left(\mathrm{CF}_{\mathrm{S,F,D}} + \mathrm{eps} \times \left(\frac{s_2}{r_2}\right)\right) \tag{8.10}$$

Subject to

$$\mathrm{SR}_{\mathrm{S,F,D}} - s_2 = \varepsilon_2$$

and variable restrictions described by Eq. 8.1.

$$s_i \in \Re^+$$

where eps, s_2, r_2 and ε_2 represents, respectively a small number (between 10^{-3} and 10^{-6}), the surplus variables of the respective constraints, the range of objective function $\mathrm{SR}_{\mathrm{S,F,D}}$, and the parameters of the right-hand side of $\mathrm{CF}_{\mathrm{S,F,D}}$. Equation 8.10 is known as the "augmented ε-constraint approach" because the second term augments the objective function $\mathrm{CF}_{\mathrm{S,F,D}}$. With this approach, each objective function is subjected to lexicographic optimization in order to find any other optima and steer clear of any suboptimal Pareto solutions. A screenshot showing the mathematical programming model and the compilation process is shown in Fig. 8.8. Details of the GAMS code are provided in Appendix H. The maximum CPU time taken to compute the results was 68.734 s.

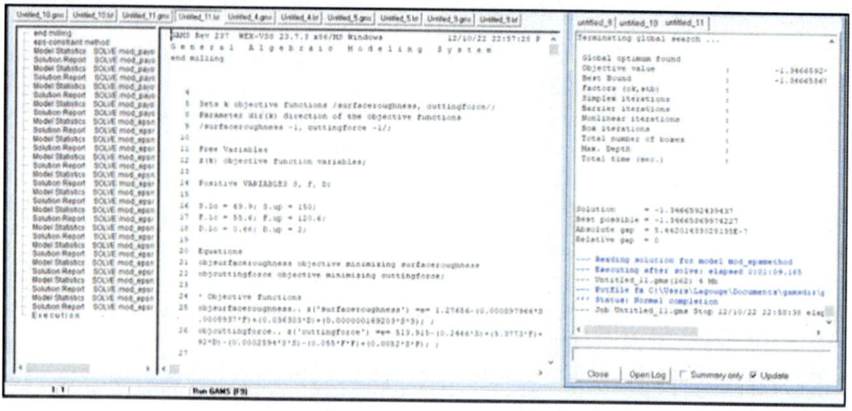

Fig. 8.8 GAMS model formulation with an emphasis on all objective functions

8.5 Results and Discussion

8.5.1 Pareto Optimal Solutions

The objective function optimization is carried out using the AUGMENCON2 algorithm. To analyze the trade-off between cutting force and surface roughness, the Pareto optimal solutions were calculated, and the Pareto optimal front was built. Table 8.4 provides the details of the 11 Pareto optimal solutions obtained by considering the optimization of the surface roughness and the cutting force simultaneously. As indicated in the previous section, there is no unique solution that optimizes the problem. The first two columns give the magnitude of the surface roughness and the cutting force. The third column provides details of the three variables namely the cutting speed (S.L), the feed rate (F.L) and the depth of cut (D.L). These results suggest that to improve the machinability of Ti–6Al–4V alloy, multiple settings yield the best performance with respect to the surface roughness and the cutting force. A decision maker would be able to get an insight into the implication of his decision and set the CNC lathe machine accordingly.

Figure 8.9 shows the magnitude of the optimal objective functions plotted against one another. This graph shows that the relation between the two objective functions is nonlinear. However, each set of results would potentially enhance the machinability of the Ti–6Al–4V alloy. There are trade-offs to consider depending on the preference of a decision maker which could include a strong emphasis on the reduction of the cutting force or the surface roughness.

Figure 8.10 shows a graphical representation of the Pareto optimal solutions corresponding to the three variables. The graph shows higher machinability performance could be achieved through adjustment of the setting of the CNC lathe machine. It points out that several settings could be determined using the proposed AUGMENCON2 method. It appears that the three variables considered namely the

Table 8.4 Optimal objective functions and variables

	Surface roughness	Cutting force	Pareto optimal solutions
1	1.22	686.26	Variable S.L: 150.000 Variable F.L: 55.600 Variable D.L: 0.660
2	1.24	660.70	Variable S.L: 150.000 Variable F.L: 77.536 Variable D.L: 0.660
3	1.25	635.14	Variable S.L: 150.000 Variable F.L: 86.465 Variable D.L: 0.660
4	1.25	609.58	Variable S.L: 150.000 Variable F.L: 93.316 Variable D.L: 0.660
5	1.26	584.02	Variable S.L: 150.000 Variable F.L: 99.092 Variable D.L: 0.660
6	1.27	558.46	Variable S.L: 150.000 Variable F.L:: 104.181 Variable D.L: 0.660
7	1.27	532.90	Variable S.L:: 150.000 Variable F.L: 108.782 Variable D.L: 0.660

(continued)

Table 8.4 (continued)

	Surface roughness	Cutting force	Pareto optimal solutions
8	1.27	507.34	Variable S.L: 150.000 Variable F.L: 113.013 Variable D.L: 0.660
9	1.27	481.78	Variable S.L: 150.000 Variable F.L: 116.951 Variable D.L: 0.660
10	1.28	456.22	Variable S.L: 148.843 Variable F.L: 120.600 Variable D.L: 0.660
11	1.35	430.66	Variable S.L: 69.900 Variable F.L: 120.600 Variable D.L: 0.660

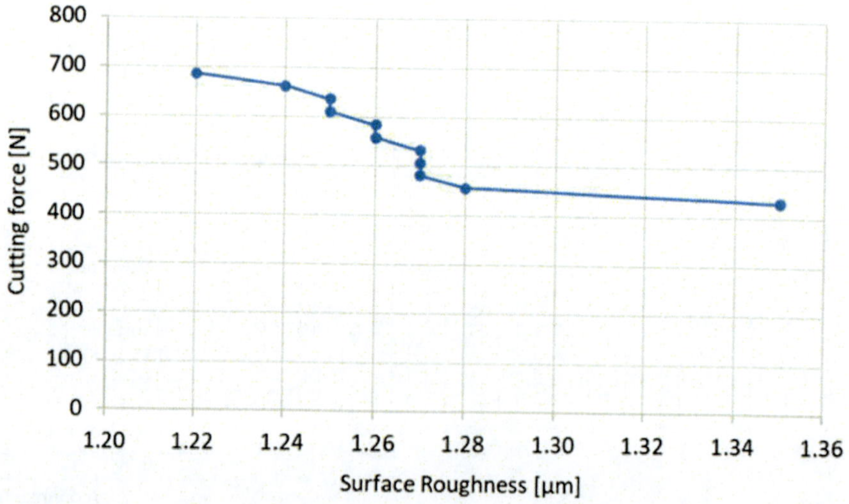

Fig. 8.9 Global optimal Pareto solutions showing the two objective functions

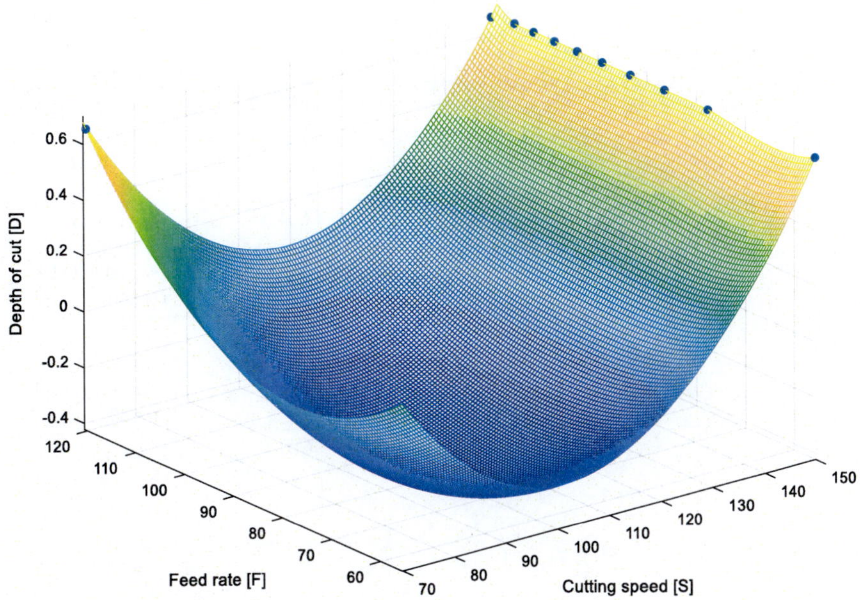

Fig. 8.10 Plot showing the profile of Pareto optimal solutions

cutting speed, the feed rate and the depth of cut are interdependent meaning that there is a specific cutting speed corresponding to a specific feed rate and depth of cut to improve the machinability of Ti–6Al–4V alloy.

8.5.2 Parametric Analysis of the Solutions

(a) Analysis of the cutting speed [S]

The impact of the variation of each variable, corresponding to the setting of the lathe machine, has been examined in order to gain a further understanding of the Pareto optimal solutions. Tables 8.5, 8.6 and 8.7 shows the optimal objective function and variables corresponding to a cutting speed of 70, 110 and 150 respectively. This study shows that an adjustment of the cutting speed would affect the surface roughness and the cutting speed. It was interesting to note that the lowest surface roughness is achieved with the highest cutting speed (Table 8.7). Conversely, the lowest cutting force is achieved at a lower cutting speed (Table 8.5).

The results reported in Tables 8.5, 8.6 and 8.7 have been summarised graphically in Fig. 8.11. It is interesting to note how an increase in the cutting speed results in a relative decrease in surface roughness in general. This finding is similar to the result reported by Sahu and Andhare [16].

Table 8.5 Optimal objective functions and variables [S = 70]

	Surface roughness	Cutting force	Pareto optimal solutions
1	1.29	687.42	Variable F.L: 55.600 Variable D.L: 0.660
2	1.3	661.75	Variable F.L: 74.066 Variable D.L: 0.660
3	1.31	636.07	Variable F.L: 82.937 Variable D.L: 0.660
4	1.32	610.4	Variable F.L: 89.770 Variable D.L: 0.660
5	1.32	584.73	Variable F.L: 95.538 Variable D.L: 0.660
6	1.33	559.06	Variable F.L: 100.624 Variable D.L: 0.660
7	1.33	533.38	Variable F.L: 105.225 Variable D.L: 0.660
8	1.34	507.71	Variable F.L: 109.457 Variable D.L: 0.660
9	1.34	482.04	Variable F.L: 113.397 Variable D.L: 0.660
10	1.34	456.36	Variable F.L: 117.099 Variable D.L: 0.660
11	1.35	430.69	Variable F.L: 120.600 Variable D.L: 0.660

Table 8.6 Optimal objective functions and variables [S = 110]

	Surface roughness	Cutting force	Pareto optimal solutions
1	1.25	687.25	Variable F.L: 55.600 Variable D.L: 0.660
2	1.27	662.93	Variable F.L: 75.168 Variable D.L: 0.660
3	1.28	638.61	Variable F.L: 83.862 Variable D.L: 0.660
4	1.29	614.29	Variable F.L: 90.539 Variable D.L: 0.660
5	1.29	589.97	Variable F.L: 96.169 Variable D.L: 0.660
6	1.29	565.65	Variable F.L: 101.130 Variable D.L: 0.660
7	1.3	541.33	Variable F.L: 105.616 Variable D.L: 0.660
8	1.3	517.01	Variable F.L: 109.742 Variable D.L: 0.660
9	1.31	492.69	Variable F.L: 113.582 Variable D.L: 0.660
10	1.31	468.36	Variable F.L: 117.188 Variable D.L: 0.660
11	1.31	444.04	Variable F.L: 120.600 Variable D.L: 0.660

Table 8.7 Optimal objective functions and variables [S = 150]

	Surface roughness	Cutting force	Pareto optimal solutions
1	1.22	686.26	Variable F.L: 55.600 Variable D.L: 0.660
2	1.24	663.29	Variable F.L: 76.415 Variable D.L: 0.660
3	1.25	640.32	Variable F.L: 84.878 Variable D.L: 0.660
4	1.25	617.35	Variable F.L: 91.373 Variable D.L: 0.660
5	1.26	594.38	Variable F.L: 96.849 Variable D.L: 0.660
6	1.26	571.41	Variable F.L: 101.673 Variable D.L: 0.660
7	1.26	548.44	Variable F.L: 106.034 Variable D.L: 0.660
8	1.27	525.47	Variable F.L: 110.045 Variable D.L: 0.660
9	1.27	502.5	Variable F.L: 113.778 Variable D.L: 0.660
10	1.27	479.54	Variable F.L: 117.284 Variable D.L: 0.660
11	1.28	456.57	Variable F.L: 120.600 Variable D.L: 0.660

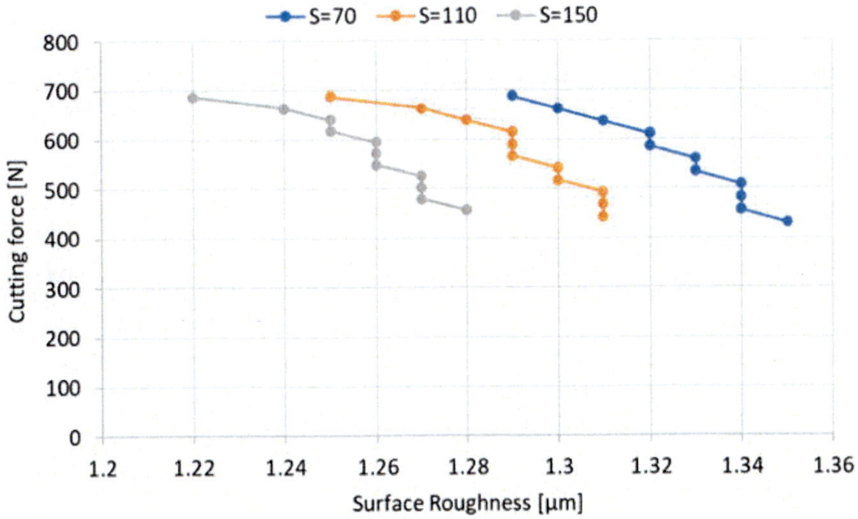

Fig. 8.11 Effect of the cutting speed [S]

(b) Analysis of the feed rate [F]

Tables 8.8, 8.9 and 8.10 shows the optimal objective function and variables corresponding to feed rates of 60, 88 and 120 respectively. This study shows that an adjustment of the feed rate would affect the surface roughness and the cutting speed. It was interesting to note that the lowest surface roughness would be achieved at a lower feed rate (Table 8.8). Conversely, the lowest cutting force is achieved at a relatively higher feed rate (Table 8.10).

The results reported in Tables 8.8, 8.9 and 8.10 have been summarised graphically in Fig. 8.12. It is interesting to note that a lower feed rate improves surface roughness. This finding is similar to the result reported by Sahu and Andhare [16]. It appears that a relatively higher feed rate results in a decrease in the cutting force.

(c) Analysis of the depth of cut [D]

Tables 8.11, 8.12 and 8.13 show the optimal objective function and variables corresponding to the depth of cut of 0.8, 1.4 and 2 respectively. This study shows that an adjustment of the depth of cut affects the surface roughness and the cutting speed. It was interesting to note that the lowest surface roughness would be achieved at a lower depth of cut (Table 8.11). Similarly, the lowest cutting force is achieved at a relatively lower depth of cut as well (Table 8.11).

The results reported in Tables 8.11, 8.12 and 8.13 have been summarised graphically in Fig. 8.13. It is interesting to note that a relatively lower feed rate improves the surface roughness and the cutting force.

Table 8.8 Optimal objective functions and variables [F = 60]

	Surface roughness	Cutting force	Pareto optimal solutions
1	1.22	685.37	Variable S.L: 150.000 Variable D.L: 0.660
2	1.27	685.31	Variable S.L: 97.230 Variable D.L: 0.660
3	1.27	685.24	Variable S.L: 93.056 Variable D.L: 0.660
4	1.28	685.17	Variable S.L: 89.354 Variable D.L: 0.660
5	1.28	685.11	Variable S.L: 85.992 Variable D.L: 0.660
6	1.28	685.04	Variable S.L: 82.891 Variable D.L: 0.660
7	1.28	684.97	Variable S.L: 79.999 Variable D.L: 0.660
8	1.29	684.91	Variable S.L: 77.278 Variable D.L: 0.660
9	1.29	684.84	Variable S.L: 74.701 Variable D.L: 0.660
10	1.29	684.77	Variable S.L: 72.247 Variable D.L: 0.660
11	1.29	684.7	Variable S.L: 69.900 Variable D.L: 0.660

Table 8.9 Optimal objective functions and variables [F = 88]

	Surface roughness	Cutting force	Pareto optimal solutions
1	1.25	629.86	Variable S.L: 150.000 Variable D.L: 0.660
2	1.26	628.62	Variable S.L: 140.902 Variable D.L: 0.660
3	1.26	627.39	Variable S.L: 132.104 Variable D.L: 0.660
4	1.27	626.16	Variable S.L: 123.580 Variable D.L: 0.660
5	1.28	624.93	Variable S.L: 115.306 Variable D.L: 0.660
6	1.29	623.69	Variable S.L: 107.260 Variable D.L: 0.660
7	1.29	622.46	Variable S.L: 99.424 Variable D.L: 0.660
8	1.3	621.23	Variable S.L: 91.784 Variable D.L: 0.660
9	1.3	619.99	Variable S.L: 84.324 Variable D.L: 0.660
10	1.31	618.76	Variable S.L: 77.033 Variable D.L: 0.660
11	1.32	617.53	Variable S.L: 69.900 Variable D.L: 0.660

Table 8.10 Optimal objective functions and variables [F = 120]

	Surface roughness	Cutting force	Pareto optimal solutions
1	1.28	460.81	Variable S.L: 150.000 Variable D.L: 0.660
2	1.28	458.25	Variable S.L: 141.497 Variable D.L: 0.660
3	1.29	455.68	Variable S.L: 133.116 Variable D.L: 0.660
4	1.3	453.11	Variable S.L: 124.851 Variable D.L: 0.660
5	1.31	450.55	Variable S.L: 116.698 Variable D.L: 0.660
6	1.31	447.98	Variable S.L: 108.653 Variable D.L: 0.660
7	1.32	445.42	Variable S.L: 100.710 Variable D.L: 0.660
8	1.33	442.85	Variable S.L: 92.867 Variable D.L: 0.660
9	1.33	440.28	Variable S.L: 85.120 Variable D.L: 0.660
10	1.34	437.72	Variable S.L: 77.466 Variable D.L: 0.660
11	1.35	435.15	Variable S.L: 69.900 Variable D.L: 0.660

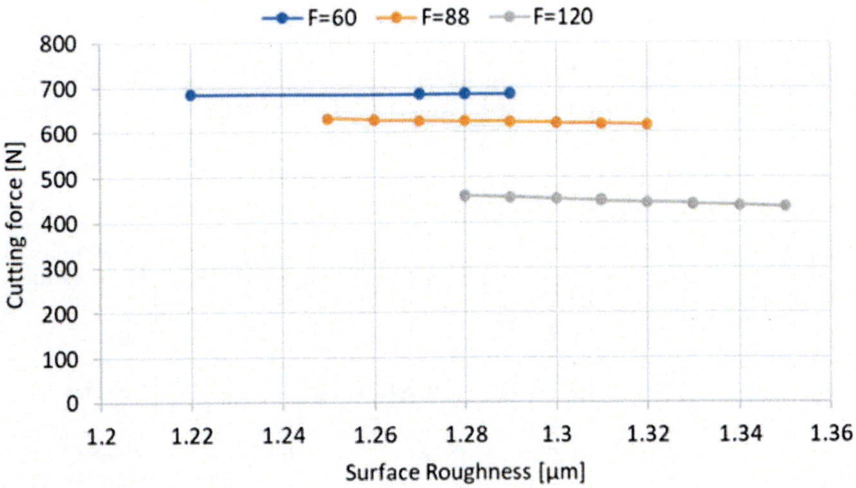

Fig. 8.12 Effect of the feed rate [F]

Table 8.11 Optimal objective functions and variables [D = 0.8]

S/N	Surface roughness	Cutting force	Pareto optimal solutions
1	1.22	695.35	Variable S.L: 150.000 Variable F.L: 55.600
2	1.24	669.79	Variable S.L: 150.000 Variable F.L: 77.536
3	1.25	644.23	Variable S.L: 150.000 Variable F.L: 86.465
4	1.26	618.67	Variable S.L: 150.000 Variable F.L: 93.316
5	1.26	593.11	Variable S.L: 150.000 Variable F.L: 99.092
6	1.27	567.55	Variable S.L: 150.000 Variable F.L: 104.181

(continued)

Table 8.11 (continued)

S/N	Surface roughness	Cutting force	Pareto optimal solutions
7	1.27	541.98	Variable S.L: 150.000 Variable F.L: 108.782
8	1.28	516.42	Variable S.L: 150.000 Variable F.L: 113.013
9	1.28	490.86	Variable S.L: 150.000 Variable F.L: 116.951
10	1.28	465.3	Variable S.L: 148.843 Variable F.L: 120.600
11	1.35	439.74	Variable S.L: 69.900 Variable F.L: 120.600

Table 8.12 Optimal objective functions and variables [D = 1.4]

	Surface roughness	Cutting force	Pareto optimal solutions
1	1.25	734.3	Variable S.L: 150.000 Variable F.L: 55.600
2	1.27	708.74	Variable S.L: 150.000 Variable F.L: 77.536
3	1.27	683.18	Variable S.L: 150.000 Variable F.L: 86.465
4	1.28	657.62	Variable S.L: 150.000 Variable F.L: 93.316
5	1.29	632.06	Variable S.L: 150.000 Variable F.L: 99.092

(continued)

Table 8.12 (continued)

	Surface roughness	Cutting force	Pareto optimal solutions
6	1.29	606.5	Variable S.L: 150.000 Variable F.L: 104.181
7	1.29	580.94	Variable S.L: 150.000 Variable F.L: 108.782
8	1.3	555.38	Variable S.L: 150.000 Variable F.L: 113.013
9	1.3	529.82	Variable S.L: 150.000 Variable F.L: 116.951
10	1.31	504.26	Variable S.L: 148.843 Variable F.L: 120.600
11	1.37	478.7	Variable S.L: 69.900 Variable F.L: 120.600

Table 8.13 Optimal objective functions and variables [D = 2]

	Surface roughness	Cutting force	Pareto optimal solutions
1	1.27	773.25	Variable S.L: 150.000 Variable F.L: 55.600
2	1.29	747.69	Variable S.L: 150.000 Variable F.L: 77.536
3	1.3	722.13	Variable S.L: 150.000 Variable F.L: 86.465
4	1.3	696.57	Variable S.L: 150.000 Variable F.L: 93.316
5	1.31	671.01	Variable S.L: 150.000 Variable F.L: 99.092
6	1.31	645.45	Variable S.L: 150.000 Variable F.L: 104.181
7	1.32	619.89	Variable S.L: 150.000 Variable F.L: 108.782

(continued)

Table 8.13 (continued)

	Surface roughness	Cutting force	Pareto optimal solutions
8	1.32	594.33	Variable S.L: 150.000 Variable F.L: 113.013
9	1.32	568.77	Variable S.L: 150.000 Variable F.L: 116.951
10	1.33	543.21	Variable S.L: 148.843 Variable F.L: 120.600
11	1.4	517.65	Variable S.L: 69.900 Variable F.L: 120.600

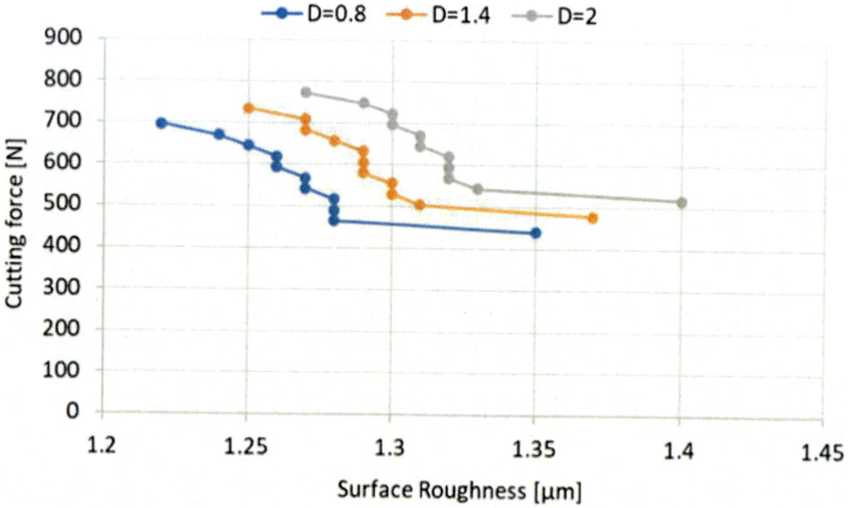

Fig. 8.13 Effect of the depth of cut [D]

8.6 Conclusion

Many existing studies point out the possibility to create models that predict and optimize cutting forces and surface roughness based on cutting parameters. In this chapter, the machinability performance of a titanium alloy is analysed using an improved version of the augmented ε-constraint approach (AUGMENCON2) that takes cutting force and surface roughness into account as objective functions. Unlike many existing multi-objective optimization approach, the augmented ε-constraint approach (AUGMENCON2) yield Pareto optimum solutions only and avoid weakly efficient solutions. The problem was formulated in implemented in the software GAMS. In order to illustrate the approach proposed in this study, quadratic equations were taken from an existing study. The speed of cutting, the feed rate and the depth of cut were the variables to optimize. The quadratic equations of the cutting force and surface roughness were the two objective functions to optimize. The conflicting nature of these objective functions was demonstrated through the tendencies of variables after performing single objective optimization. Details of the modelling development and implementations have been provided. The graph shows higher machinability performance could be achieved through adjustment of the setting of the CNC lathe machine. It points out that several settings could be determined using the proposed AUGMENCON2 method. This study reveals that the three variables considered namely the cutting speed, the feed rate and the depth of cut are interdependent meaning that there is a specific cutting speed corresponding to a specific feed rate and depth of cut to improve the machinability of Ti–6Al–4V alloy. The results show that an increase in the cutting speed results in a relative decrease in surface roughness in general. A lower feed rate could potentially improve surface roughness but a relatively higher feed rate results in a decrease in the cutting force. A relatively lower feed rate improves the surface roughness and the cutting force. The comprehensive machining optimization proposed in this study provides clarity about the handling of conflicting criteria involved in setting a CNC lathe machine and improves the understanding of the relative sensitivity of variables affecting the outcome. This contribution would potentially help decision makers to handle CNC lathe machines and improve the machinability performance taking several design constraints into account.

References

1. Çelik, Y.H., Yildiz, H., Özek, C.: Effect of cutting parameters on workpiece and tool properties during drilling of Ti–6Al–4V. Mater. Test. **58**(6), 519–525 (2016)
2. Denkena, B., Dittrich, M.A., Jacob, S.: Energy efficiency in machining of aircraft components. Procedia CIRP **48**, 479–482 (2016)
3. Arrazola, P.J., Garay, A., Iriarte, L.M., Armendia, M., Marya, S., Le Maître, F.: Machinability of titanium alloys (Ti6Al4V and Ti555. 3). J. Mater. Process. Technol. **209**(5), 2223–2230 (2009)
4. Pramanik, A.: Problems and solutions in machining of titanium alloys. Int. J. Adv. Manuf. Technol. **70**(5), 919–928 (2014)
5. Okokpujie, I.P., Tartibu, L.K., Sinebe, J.E., Adeoye, A.O., Akinlabi, E.T.: Comparative study of rheological effects of vegetable oil-lubricant, TiO_2, MWCNTs nano-lubricants, and machining parameters' influence on cutting force for sustainable metal cutting process. Lubricants **10**(4), 54 (2022)
6. Ulutan, D., Ozel, T.: Machining induced surface integrity in titanium and nickel alloys: a review. Int. J. Mach. Tools Manuf. **51**(3), 250–280 (2011)
7. Ginting, A., Nouari, M.: Surface integrity of dry machined titanium alloys. Int. J. Mach. Tools Manuf. **49**(3–4), 325–332 (2009)
8. Upadhyay, V., Jain, P.K., Mehta, N.K.: In-process prediction of surface roughness in turning of Ti–6Al–4V alloy using cutting parameters and vibration signals. Measurement **46**(1), 154–160 (2013)
9. Rao, B., Dandekar, C.R., Shin, Y.C.: An experimental and numerical study on the face milling of Ti–6Al–4V alloy: tool performance and surface integrity. J. Mater. Process. Technol. **211**(2), 294–304 (2011)

10. Amin, A.N., Ismail, A.F., Khairusshima, M.N.: Effectiveness of uncoated WC–Co and PCD inserts in end milling of titanium alloy—Ti–6Al–4V. J. Mater. Process. Technol. **192**, 147–158 (2007)
11. Sahu, N.K., Andhare, A.B.: Optimization of surface roughness in turning of Ti–6Al–4V using response surface methodology and TLBO. In: International Design Engineering Technical Conferences and Computers and Information in Engineering Conference, vol. 57113, p. V004T05A020. American Society of Mechanical Engineers (2015)
12. Sharif, S., Mohruni, A.S., Noordin, M., Venkatesh, V.C.: Optimization of surface roughness prediction model in end milling Titanium Alloy (Ti-6Al–4V). In: Proceedings of ICOMAST2006 International Conference on Manufacturing Science and Technology August 28–30, 2006, Melaka, Malaysia, pp. 55–58. Faculty of Engineering and Technology, Multimedia University, Melaka, Malaysia (2006)
13. Davoodi, B., Hosseini Tazehkandi, A.: Cutting forces and surface roughness in wet machining of Inconel alloy 738 with coated carbide tool. Proc. Inst. Mech. Eng. Part B: J. Eng. Manuf. **230**(2), 215–226 (2016)
14. Okokpujie, I.P., Ohunakin, O.S., Bolu, C.A.: Multi-objective optimization of machining factors on surface roughness, material removal rate and cutting force on end-milling using MWCNTs nano-lubricant. Prog. Addi. Manuf. **6**(1), 155–178 (2021)
15. Liu, Z., Xu, J., Han, S., Chen, M.: A coupling method of response surfaces (CRSM) for cutting parameters optimization in machining titanium alloy under minimum quantity lubrication (MQL) condition. Int. J. Precis. Eng. Manuf. **14**(5), 693–702 (2013)
16. Sahu, N.K., Andhare, A.B.: Multiobjective optimization for improving machinability of Ti–6Al–4V using RSM and advanced algorithms. J. Comput. Des. Eng. **6**(1), 1–12 (2019)
17. Rao Venkata, R., Kalyankar, V.D.: Parameter optimization of machining processes using a new optimization algorithm. Mater. Manuf. Processes **27**(9), 978–985 (2012)
18. Gupta, M.K., Sood, P.K., Sharma, V.S.: Machining parameters optimization of titanium alloy using response surface methodology and particle swarm optimization under minimum-quantity lubrication environment. Mater. Manuf. Processes **31**(13), 1671–1682 (2016)
19. Tartibu, L.K., Sun, B., Kaunda, M.A.E.: Multi-objective optimization of the stack of a thermoacoustic engine using GAMS. Appl. Soft Comput. **28**, 30–43 (2015)
20. Okwu, M.O., Tartibu, L.K.: Metaheuristic optimization: nature-inspired algorithms swarm and computational intelligence, theory and applications, vol. 927. Springer Nature (2020)
21. Mavrotas, G., Florios, K.: An improved version of the augmented ε-constraint method (AUGMECON2) for finding the exact Pareto set in multi-objective integer programming problems. Appl. Math. Comput. **219**(18), 9652–9669 (2013)
22. Soroudi, A.: Power System Optimization Modeling in GAMS, vol. 78. Springer, Switzerland (2017)
23. Okokpujie, I.P., Bolu, C.A., Ohunakin, O.S.: Comparative performance evaluation of TiO_2, and MWCNTs nano-lubricant effects on surface roughness of AA8112 alloy during end-milling machining for sustainable manufacturing process. Int. J. Adv. Manuf. Technol. **108**(5), 1473–1497 (2020)
24. McCarl, B.A., Meeraus, A., van der Eijk, P., Bussieck, M., Dirkse, S., Steacy, P., Nelissen, F.: McCarl GAMS User Guide. GAMS Development Corporation (2014)
25. Mavrotas, G.: Effective implementation of the ε-constraint method in multi-objective mathematical programming problems. Appl. Math. Comput. **213**(2), 455–465 (2009)
26. Tartibu, L.K., Sun, B., Kaunda, M.A.E.: Lexicographic multi-objective optimization of thermoacoustic refrigerator's stack. Heat Mass Transf. **51**(5), 649–660 (2015)
27. Tartibu, L.K., Sun, B., Kaunda, M.A.E.: Optimal design of a standing wave thermoacoustic refrigerator using GAMS. Procedia Comput. Sci. **62**, 611–618 (2015)

28. Tartibu Kwanda, L.: Multi-objective optimization of a rectangular micro-channel heat sink using the augmented ε-constraint method. Eng. Optim. **52**(1), 22–36 (2020)
29. Tartibu, L.K.: Numerical analysis on thermal performance of a trapezoidal micro-channel heat sink using an improved version of the augmented ε-constraint method. Int. J. Math. Model. Numer. Optimisation **10**(1), 49–67 (2020)
30. Tartibu, K., Sun, B., Kaunda, M.A.E.: Geometric optimization of micro-thermoacoustic cooler for heat management in electronics. In: 2013 IEEE International Conference on Industrial Technology (ICIT), pp. 527–532. IEEE (2013)

Chapter 9
ANN and QRCCD Prediction of Surface Roughness Under Biodegradable Nano-lubricant

Abstract Sustainable manufacturing of machine parts lies in predicting and optimizing the machining parameters for the machining operations. The optimized parameters will produce sustainable products with reduced corrosion and fatigue problems because the roughness of the surface of the product will lead to the failure of the component or part during the production process. This investigation focuses on the prediction and optimization of the **experimental data** of surface roughness of AA8112 alloys obtained during the end-milling process with a biodegradable nano-lubricant. The study employed vegetable oil as the base cutting fluid (copra oil) and MWCNTs nanoparticles as an additive. This study prediction analysis was carried out with an artificial neural network (ANN) and quadratic rotatable central composite design (QRCCD). The results show that the ANN and QRCCD predicted the **experimental data** with 95.50% and 99.50%, respectively. Both prediction analyses' error percentages are 5.5% from the ANN and 0.5% from the QRCCD. The QRCCD optimized parameters for the minimum surface roughness are spindle speed of 3366 rpm, 101 mm/min feed rate, 1 mm depth of cut, 20 mm length-of-cut, and 39.6° helix angle. These parameters achieved the minimum surface roughness of 1.16 μm, which is closely related to the optimized value from the **experimental data**. Therefore, the study in this chapter will recommend manufacturers employ the optimized machining parameters for product production.

Keywords ANN · QRCCD · Surface roughness · Biodegradable nano-lubricant · Machining

9.1 Introduction

The application of intelligent systems during the manufacturing process is a significant way to follow when advanced manufacturing of mass production of mechanical or parts via computer numerical control (CNC) with good quality [1]. Many

I. P. Okokpujie and L. K. Tartibu, *Modern Optimization Techniques for Advanced Machining*, Studies in Systems, Decision and Control 485,
https://doi.org/10.1007/978-3-031-35455-7_9

researchers have employed several intelligent methods in prediction and optimization during the machining process [2]. However, there is a great need to look into the manufacturing process with multiple prediction techniques to predict surface roughness end-milling machining, which will be considered in this Chap. 10 of this book. A nanoparticle material's ability to produce Nano-lubricant for manufacturing creates progress in developing mechanical parts utilizing machining, which can't be overemphasized [3, 4]. At the same time, creating mechanical parts for aviation, car, and underlying application through the end-processing aluminum alloy composites. Notwithstanding, end-milling creates intensity and grating because of the machining boundary that starts the contact between the cutting instrument and the workpiece. This overabundance of heat prompts high surface harshness, low material evacuation rate, and high cutting power. Okokpujie et al. [5] study meant to determine the machining boundaries and the material bond via a trial assessment with multi-objective streamlining of the machining factors on end-processing of AL8112 combination utilizing copra oil-based multi-walled carbon nanotube as a nano-ointment. The nano-ointment arrangement was finished utilizing the two-venture technique, and nano-greases were carried out through the base amount oil strategy with the five machining factors.

Moreover, the multi-objective streamlining and expectation study was accomplished utilizing the incline and allure bar plot for the three reactions, i.e., surface roughness, MRR, and cutting force under the quadratic rotatable focal composite plan. The multi-objective enhancement result shows that the surface roughness of 1.2 μm, the highest material removal rate of 52 mm 3/min, and the least cutting force of 34 N were acquired at the improved machining factors. Besides, the models anticipated the exploratory outcomes precisely. Overall, the multi-objective advancement with copra oil-based MWCNT'S-nano-grease improved machine parts' creation for practical added substance production.

Dubey et al. [6] The cutting liquid is improved with alumina nanoparticles of two standard molecule sizes of 30 and 40 nm. The info boundaries picked for examination are cutting velocity, the profundity of cut, feed rate, and nanoparticle fixation. The reaction surface methodology is utilized in the plan of the trial. To assess the surface harshness at the trial worth to the anticipated qualities, AI-based models, including direct relapse, irregular backwoods, and backing vector machine, are likewise used. The motivation behind assessing the precision of the anticipated qualities is the coefficient of assurance, mean outright rate blunder, and mean square error. Irregular backwoods outflanked the other two models in both the molecule sizes of 30 and 40 nm, with an R-squared of 0.818 and 0.723, individually.

Consequently, this study gives an original methodology in foreseeing the surface unpleasantness by differing the molecule size in the cutting liquid utilizing AI, which can save time and wastage of material and energy [7]. However, this study considered only three factors at three levels, limiting the experimental runs 27. There is a need for a good number of experimental runs to have a reasonable prediction rate using artificial intelligence. Alharthi et al. [8] The authors carried out surface roughness prediction analysis under ANN and regression analysis. The study developed Five models of neural networks best fit with investigational results with six neurons in the hidden layer. Also, the study used regression analysis to build a precise model on behalf of the surface roughness as a meaning of the process parameters. The coefficient of prediction originated at 95 and 94% for the perfect ANN prediction and regression investigation, respectively. The evaluation of the models with 13 experimental authentication test optical microscopy was directed on the workpiece surfaces with two unique upsides of feed rates while keeping up with the axle speed and profundity of cut at similar qualities. Analyzing the surface geography and surface harshness profile for the two surfaces uncovered that a higher feed rate generally brings about thick harshness markings that are remotely dispersed. While low upsides of feed rate bring about slim surface unpleasantness markings firmly separated, giving better surface completion.

However, this chapter considered the prediction and optimization of surface roughness under the multi-walled carbon nano-lubricant machining operation via ANN and QRCCD with five factors five-level experimental analysis. The machining factors considered are helix angle, depth of cut, cutting length, feed rate, and spindle speed.

9.2 Methodology

In this study, the authors conducted an empirical examination to study the effect of the nano-lubricants and machining factors on surface roughness. Furthermore, mathematical models were developed to predict surface roughness by an end milling operation. SIEG 3/10/0016 CNC machine with high-speed-steel-cutting-tool inserts was used for the experimental study of the machining process with machining cutting conditions via MWCNTs-nano-lubricant. The authors created the part programs code G and M to instruct each of the experimental coordinates to mill the AL8112 alloy workpiece used for this study. The M42-high-speed-steel cutting tool of 13 mm diameter was employed in this study, having molybdenum of 9.5%, Cobalt of 8.25%, Chromium of 3.9%, Carbon of 1.1%, Tungsten of 1.6%, and Vanadium 1.2%. With explicit orders, the CNC part programs were created for the machining activity. The various lengths of cut, feed rate, cutting depth, helix angle, and cutting speed were carried out with reference to the Y-hub and Z-hub. This reference of the Y and Z-hub is finished for every 50 examples. Figure 9.1 represents the exploratory arrangement of the end-processing of the AL8112 combination.

After each trial, the surface roughness of the workpiece was additionally estimated utilizing the Mitutoyo surface analyzer. The workpiece is permitted to dry correctly, and afterward, the surface roughness analyzer is locked in to gauge the outer layer of the workpiece. The test is put on the AL8112 composite with an estimating range: Ra, Rq: 0.05 ~ 10.00 μm/1.000 ~ 400.0, Rz, Rt: 0.020 ~ 100.0 μm/0.780 ~ 4000 unit in inch. The roughness is estimated in three distinct places of the workpiece. And its normal was recorded as the surface unpleasantness of the workpiece. Figure 9.2 shows the trial arrangement of the SRT-6210S surface severity analyzer utilized for this evaluation (Table 9.1).

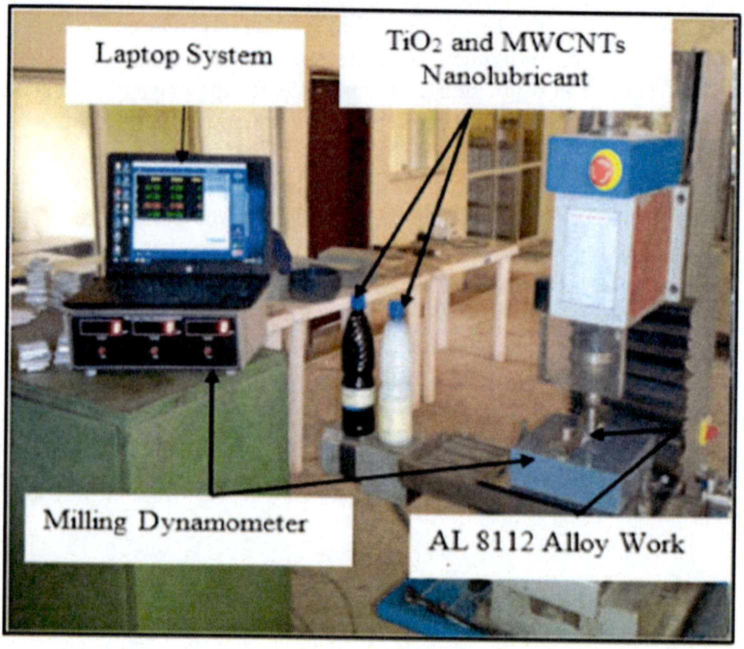

Fig. 9.1 The CNC milling experimental setup

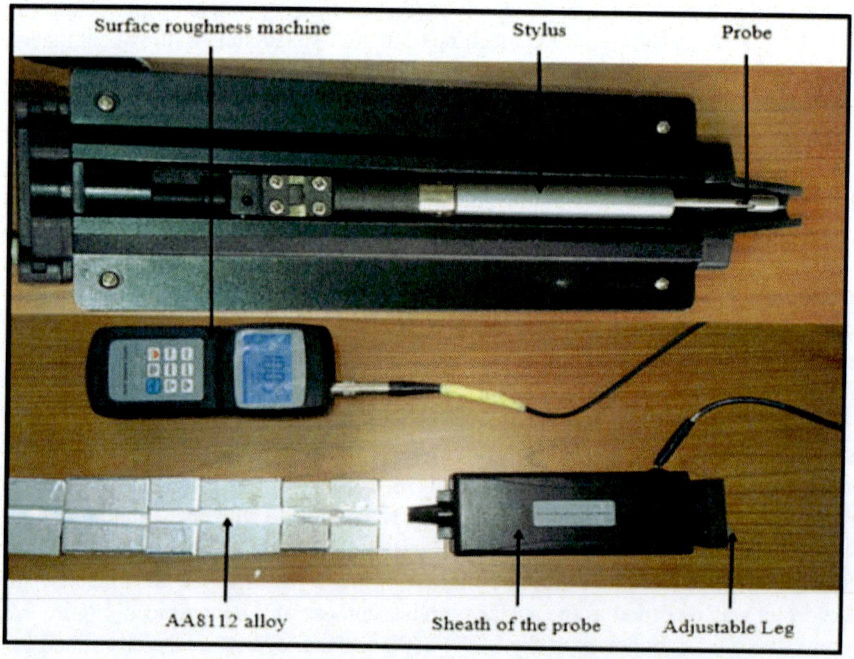

Fig. 9.2 Experimental setup of the Mitutoyo surface roughness tester and the AA8112 alloy

Table 9.1 Machining conditions for the study of the surface roughness using MWCNTs nano-lubricant

Name	Units	Low	High	– alpha	+ alpha
Spindle speed	rpm	2000	4000	621.586	5378.41
Feed rate	mm/min	100	300	– 37.8414	437.841
Length of cut	mm	20	60	– 7.56828	87.5683
Depth of cut	mm	1	3	– 0.378414	4.37841
Helix angle	o	0	60	– 41.3524	101.352

9.2.1 *Experimental Procedures for the Preparation of the Nano-lubricant and Machining Process*

Multi-walled carbon nano-lubricants are synthesized using the two-step techniques. It is the most inexpensive technique used in current times to develop nano-lubricant in large amounts. In this Chapter, the nanoparticles (MWCNTs) were in a dry powder form using the chemical methods by Sigma-Aldrich Corporation. The SEM and EDS of the nanoparticles are shown in Fig. 9.3. The proportion concentration of 0.6 g of MWCNTs nanoparticles was mixed with a liter of copra oil made from the local production process. Furthermore, the authors used the Stuart magnetic stirrer for 2 h to stir the particles and the based fluid with a speed of 1400 rpm and also employed the Branson 2800 ultrasonic cleaner machine for 5 h to homogenize the nanoparticles with the copra oil, as shown in the experimental setup in Fig. 9.4.

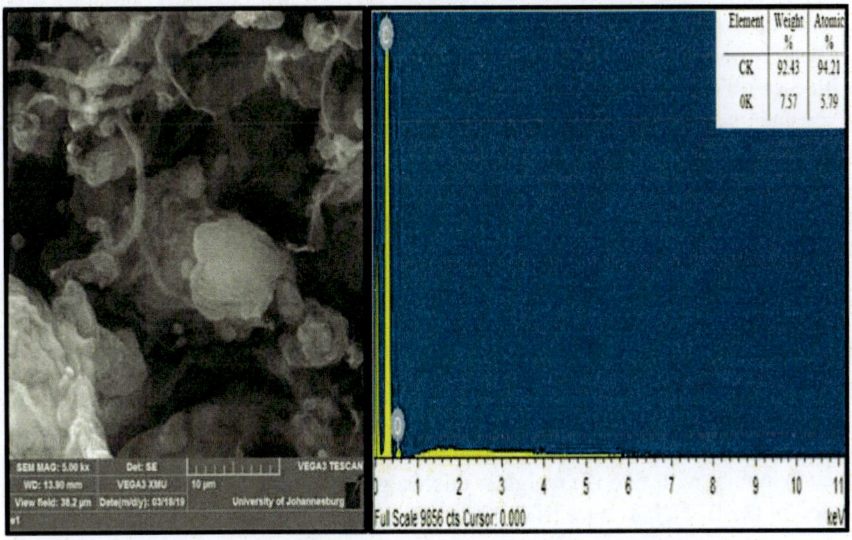

Fig. 9.3 The SEM of MWCNTs nanoparticles used in preparing the nano-lubricant

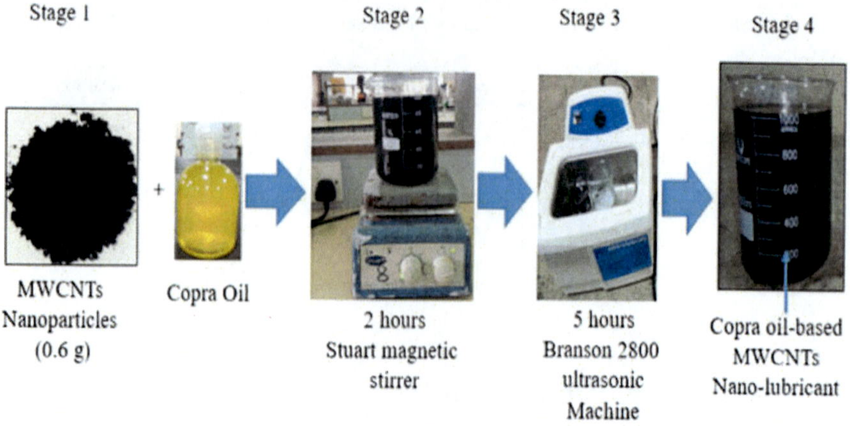

Fig. 9.4 Stages 1–5 shows the different processes used to synthesise the nano-lubricant

9.2.2 Mathematical Modelling Using Artificial Neural Network

Artificial Neural Network (ANN) is a data handling procedure that emulates the natural nervous system using workstations. ANN comprises the number of basic units known as a neuron that uses a precise model with simple workstations that receive one or more input variables and process them to produce the correct output. These neurons are a group of data for information processing using connected links. Every neuron has an associated load based on the strength of the input variables used to determine the output responses.

A layer is a group of neurons arranged in parallel without having any interaction with each other. The workstation consists of three processes: the input layer, hidden layer, and output layer. Variables are presented to the workstation via the input layer and transferred to hidden layers where the work is done through a weight connections process; the hidden layers determine the output responses layer. After the experiment has been carried out, the values of the responses are recorded. The neuron has a bias Ø, which is added with the weighted sum W_n and input variables (U_n) to determine the total net input (T_n), as presented in Eq. (9.1) [9].

$$T_n = \sum_{i=1}^{n} (W_n * U_n) + \emptyset \tag{9.1}$$

The neuron for this Back Propagation feed-forward Neural Network (BPNN) has five (5) inputs, with five (5) weights; this weight is randomized during the training period of the BPNN. The transformation process is carried out through the sigmoid non-linear transfer function (Z), which is given in Eq. (9.2).

$$Z = U_1 * W_1 + U_2 * W_2 + \cdots + U_n * W_n + \emptyset * 1 \tag{9.2}$$

where the total net input (T_n), is transposed as given in Eq. (9.3)

$$\hat{T} = Y_{out} = \text{sigmoid}(Z) \tag{9.3}$$

The sigmoid transfer function (Z_i) is given in Eq. (9.4) as:

$$\text{Sigmoid}(Z_i) = \frac{1}{1 + e^{-Z_i}} \tag{9.4}$$

The output (Y_{out}) is determined by multiplying the activated transfer function with the weight W_{ni} between the inner last layer of the hidden neuron and the output layer, which becomes Eq. (9.5).

$$Y_{out} = W_{ni} * Z_i \tag{9.5}$$

The error is e_i, and is obtained by subtracting the experimental values from the predicted values. The equation is given in Eq. (9.6), and the total error (SSE) is computed using Eq. (9.7).

$$e_i = SR_e - SR_p \tag{9.6}$$

$$SSE = \frac{1}{2} \sum_{I=1}^{n} e_1^2 \tag{9.7}$$

Depending on the problem to be solved, ANN has numerous techniques for training a neural system. In this work, the BPNN was adopted to build and train the system for the prediction of output parameters. The structure of the ANN employed for this study is presented in Fig. 9.5. The inputs (U_n) correspond to feed rate, spindle speed, length of cut, helix angle, and depth of cut. The signal (Ø) is the interior threshold of a neuron, i.e., the bias, and Z_i is the nonlinear transfer function. The neuron is trained with 70% input data, 15% of the input data for testing, while the remaining 15% input data is used for the validation process.

9.2.3 Mathematical Modelling Using Quadratic Rotatable Central Composite Design

Quadratic rotatable central composite design (QRCCD) is a design tool employed to analyze engineering problems. QRCCD is one of the packages in response surface methodology in Design expert software, mainly used for factors above four and five-level to study the relationship's effects on the response parameters. QRCCD is

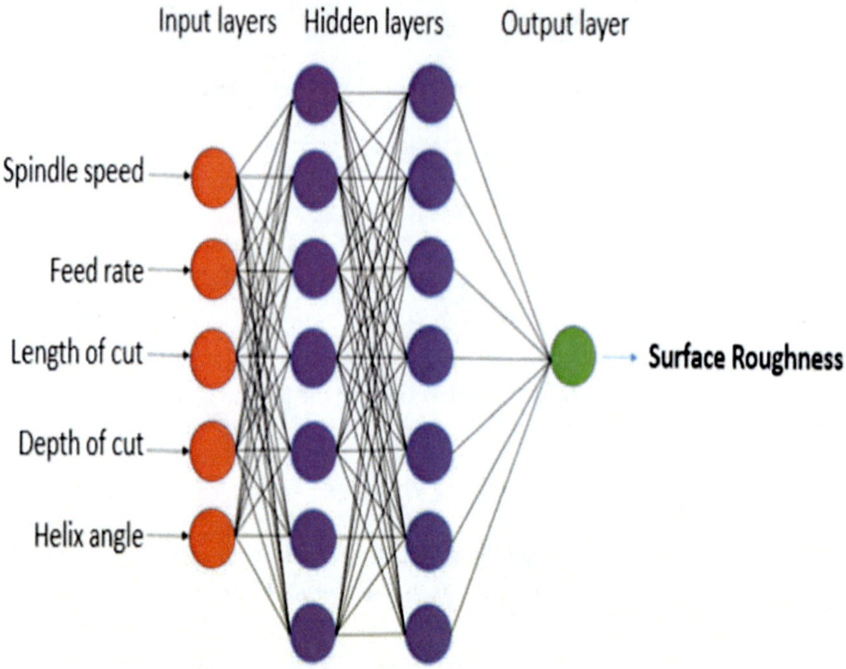

Fig. 9.5 The surface roughness system structure for the ANN

suitable for prediction, optimization, and model developments in the manufacturing of mechanical components. In this study, the relationship between surface roughness (the response parameters) and the cutting parameters under multi-walled carbon nano-lubricant cutting conditions is given in Eq. (9.8) [10–12].

$$\mathrm{Y_i} = \theta(S_s, \mathrm{F}_r, L_c, D_c, \alpha) \tag{9.8}$$

The desired machinability feature is $\mathrm{Y_i}$ and the response function is θ. However, the evaluation $\mathrm{Y_i}$ They are projected using a nonlinear scientific model, which is suitable for evaluating the effects of cutting parameters interface on machinability features. The interactions become Eq. (9.9).

$$\mathrm{Y_i} = \theta\left(S_s^{X_x}, F_r^{Y_y}, L_c^{Z_z}, D_c^{\mathrm{zr}}, \alpha^{\mathrm{zi}}\right) \tag{9.9}$$

$$\begin{aligned}\log(\mathrm{Y_i}) = \log(\theta) + X_x.\log(S_s) + Y_y.\log(F_r) + Z_z.\log(L_c)\\ + Z_r.\log(D_c) + Z_i.\log(\alpha)\end{aligned} \tag{9.10}$$

where,

$$Y_i = \log(Y_i)\ \beta_0 = \log(\theta)\ x_1 = \log(S_s)\ x_2 = \log(F_r)$$
$$x_3 = \log(L_c)\ x_4 = \log(D_c)\ x_5 = \log(\alpha)$$

and

$$x = \beta_1, y = \beta_2, z = \beta_3, zr = \beta_4, zi = \beta_5.$$

The overview of a replacement gets the following expression in Eq. (9.10), where the constant and exponents θ, X_x, Y_y, Z_z, Z_r, and Z_i are determined by the least-squares regression procedure. This research work, the Quadratic rotatable central composite design-based regression model second-order, is implemented and given in Eq. (9.11) as:

$$Y_i = \beta_0 + \sum \beta_i x_i + \sum \beta_{ii} {x_i}^2 + \sum \beta_{ij} x_i x_j + e \quad (9.11)$$

The regression constant is β_0, and the coefficients are β_1 to β_5, and the logarithmic alteration of parameters are $x_1, x_2, x_3, x_4,$ and x_5. i.e., S_s, F_r, L_c, D_c, α, and e represent the spindle speed, feed rate, length-of-cut, depth-of-cut, helix angle, and the error term, respectively. The input variables and levels were undoubtedly within the interludes recommended by the computer numerical control manufacturer. Equation (9.11) is the regression model employed to develop the prediction model from the response surface method from the design experts. The flow chart of the research method is presented in Fig. 9.6.

9.2.4 Validation of the Surface Roughness Results

In order to ascertain the accuracy of the developed model from the **experimental data**, both the percentage deviation φ_i, and the average deviation $\overline{\varphi}$ was used. After the prediction of the surface roughness, the percentage deviation was utilized to validate the rate of prediction of the surface roughness. The general equation to determine the validation accuracy is presented in Eq. (9.12) [13].

$$\varphi_i = \left(\frac{R_{(m)} - R_{(e)}}{R_{(e)}}\right) \times 100\% \quad (9.12)$$

where, φ_i: percentage deviation of single variables, R(m) measure results, R(e) experimental results.

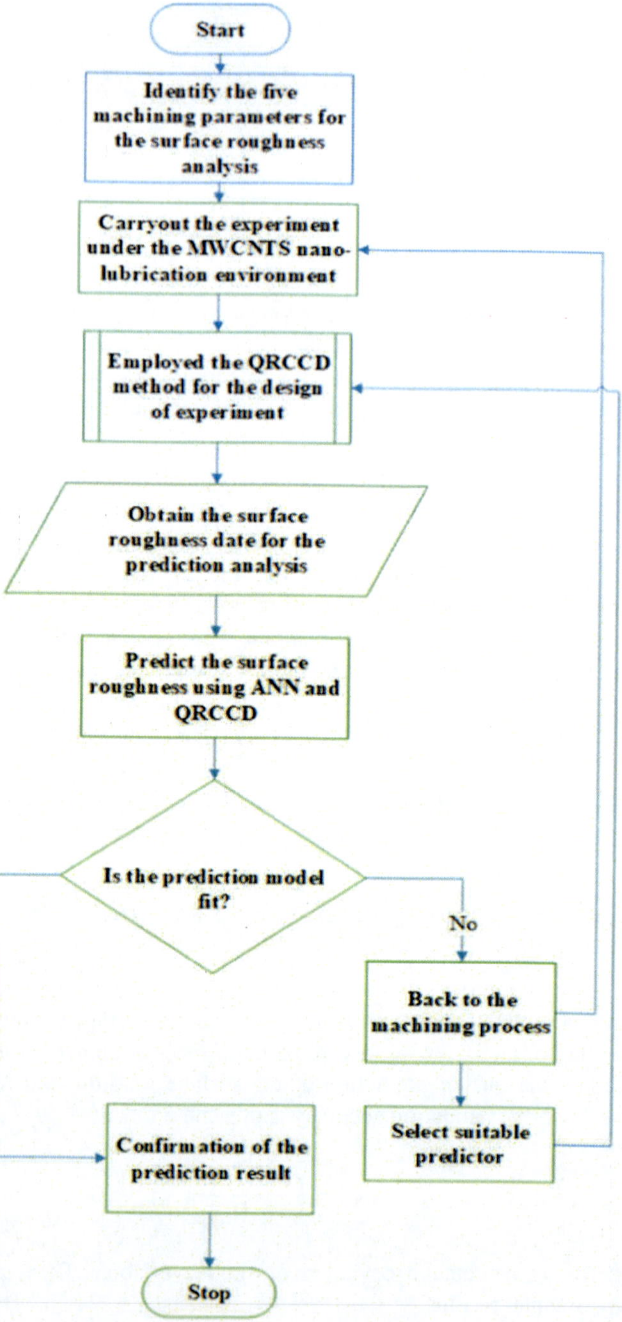

Fig. 9.6 The flow chart showing the research design employed in this study

9.3 The Experimental Data and Mathematical Model for Surface Roughness

This section explains the nano-lubrication machining environments, i.e., multi-walled carbon nanolubricant. The experiment is carried out to study the effects of the machining parameters on the end-milling machining surface of AA8112 alloy and to develop predictive models using ANN and QRCCD for sustainable manufacturing processes.

9.3.1 The Results of Surface Roughness Obtained in Machining Operation

The investigation of surface roughness (SR) was analyzed using a five-factor, five-level experiment during the end-milling of AA8112 alloy in machining environments under multi-walled carbon nano-lubricant. Table 9.2 presents the evaluation of the multi-walled carbon nano-lubricant used in the end-milling machining of AA8112 alloy, this data is used for the prediction analysis using ANN and QRCCD.

9.3.2 The QRCCD Model and the Prediction of the Surface Roughness

This section explains the process of development of the quadratic model and the importance of individual machining parameters involved in the end-milling machining of AA8112 alloy.

The response surface methodology used QRCCD, it was observed that the model developed was significant, having a 52.64 F-value, entailing that the alteration of sound (error) rate is 0.01%. The important factors were gotten using the *P*-value. The factors with a $P\text{-value} < 0.05$ demonstrate that it is substantial in the predictive prototypical. However, factors with $P\text{-value} > 0.1\%$ are not important in the generated model. Hence, the important factors for surface roughness with the biodegradable nano-lubricant (MWCNTs) as presented in Table 9.3. The lack-of-fit of 0.46 designates is not significant when associated with the error value. Table 9.4 **shows that an acceptable adequate precision** value of 39.188 was obtained during this analysis. It entails that the signal-to-noise ratio has a good correlation, and the model can be engaged to direct the design universe.

The estimation of the ANOVA coefficient is a significant aspect of this analysis. It represents the expected transformation of the surface roughness per unit alteration of each value of machining factors. However, the intercept of the orthogonal plan for the average surface roughness experiment and coefficients are used to adjust the settings of the machining factors. The value of variance inflation factors (VIFs) is used to determine the existence between the predictor model and the variable factors used for

Table 9.2 Surface roughness experimental data

Runs	Spindle speed (rpm)	Feed rate (mm/min)	Length of cut (mm)	Depth of cut (mm)	Helix angle (α) (o)	SR (MWCNTs) (μm)
1	2500	150	30	2.5	45	2.04
2	2500	250	50	2.5	15	2.06
3	2500	250	30	1.5	15	1.98
4	3500	250	50	1.5	45	1.46
5	2500	250	30	1.5	45	1.75
6	2500	150	50	1.5	45	1.68
7	3000	200	40	2	30	1.53
8	3500	250	30	2.5	45	1.51
9	2500	150	50	2.5	45	1.66
10	3500	150	30	1.5	15	1.44
11	2500	250	50	2.5	45	1.69
12	3000	200	40	2	30	1.54
13	2500	150	30	2.5	15	1.71
14	3500	150	50	2.5	45	1.52
15	3500	150	30	2.5	15	1.65
16	2500	250	30	2.5	15	1.76
17	2500	250	50	1.5	45	1.74
18	3000	200	40	2	60	1.59
19	3000	200	40	2	30	1.58
20	4000	200	40	2	30	1.16
21	3000	200	40	2	30	1.58
22	3000	300	40	2	30	2.51
23	3500	150	50	1.5	45	1.49
24	3000	200	60	2	30	1.61
25	3000	200	40	1	30	1.56
26	3500	150	30	1.5	45	1.36
27	3500	250	30	1.5	45	1.51
28	3500	250	50	2.5	45	1.61
29	3500	150	30	2.5	45	1.59
30	2500	150	50	1.5	15	1.92
31	2500	250	50	1.5	15	2
32	3000	200	40	2	30	1.66
33	3500	250	50	2.5	15	1.52
34	3000	200	40	3	30	2.2
35	3500	150	50	1.5	15	1.54

(continued)

Table 9.2 (continued)

Runs	Spindle speed (rpm)	Feed rate (mm/min)	Length of cut (mm)	Depth of cut (mm)	Helix angle (α) (o)	SR (MWCNTs) (μm)
36	3000	200	40	2	30	1.61
37	3500	150	50	2.5	15	1.52
38	3000	100	40	2	30	1.21
39	3500	250	50	1.5	15	1.5
40	2000	200	40	2	30	2.3
41	3000	200	20	2	30	1.51
42	3500	250	30	2.5	15	1.49
43	2500	150	30	1.5	45	1.74
44	3500	250	30	1.5	15	1.45
45	3000	200	40	2	0	1.61
46	2500	150	50	2.5	15	1.76
47	2500	250	30	2.5	45	1.77
48	3000	200	40	2	30	1.61
49	3000	200	40	2	30	1.61
50	2500	150	30	1.5	15	1.77

the prediction. The VIFs pace of one (1) implies the elements are symmetrical, while a worth higher than one (1) suggests multi-collinearity of the variables, as displayed in Table 9.5. The more noteworthy the VIFs, the more the multi-collinearity of the machining elements.

The developed mathematical model for the surface roughness analysis under the machining environment with multi-walled carbon nano-lubricant using QRCCD is presented in two forms as coded and actual. Equation (9.13) gives the model in the coded form and Fig. 9.7 shows the predicted analysis of the QRCCD.

$$\begin{aligned}
SR_{\text{coded}} = {} & +1.59 - 0.5700S_c + 0.6500F_c - 0.0042L_c - 0.0625D_c \\
& - 0.0100\alpha_c - 0.0663SF_c + 0.0212SL_c + 0.0988SD_c \\
& + 0.1037S\alpha_c + 0.0712FL_c - 0.0612FD_c - 0.0613F\alpha_c \\
& - 0.0637LD_c - 0.1238L\alpha_c + 0.0988D\alpha_c + 0.1400S_c^2 \\
& + 0.2700F_c^2 - 0.0300L_c^2 + 0.2900D_c^2 + 0.0100\alpha_c^2 \\
& - 0.0925SFL_c + 0.0025SFD_c + 0.2825SF\alpha_c \\
& - 0.0225SLD_c + 0.2775SL\alpha_c - 0.1175SD\alpha_c \\
& + 0.2975FLD_c + 0.0275FL\alpha_c - 0.0875FD\alpha_c \\
& - 0.0925LD\alpha_c - 2.50S^2F_c - 0.1975S^2\alpha_c + 1.06SF_c^2 \\
& + 0.0542L_c^3 + 0.3825D_c^3 - 0.1750SFL\alpha_c \\
& + 0.1950SFD\alpha_c + 0.3850SLD\alpha_c - 1.57S^2F_c^2
\end{aligned} \tag{9.13}$$

Table 9.3 ANOVA of surface roughness under QRCCD

Source	Sum of squares	Degree of freedom	Mean square	F-value	*p*-value	% Concentration	
Model	3.05	39	0.078	52.64	< 0.0001	99.52	Significant
S_s-(spindle speed)	0.649	1	0.649	438.04	< 0.0001	21.24	
F_r-(feed rate)	0.845	1	0.845	569.62	< 0.0001	27.61	
L_c-(length of cut)	0.0001	1	0.0001	0.0421	0.8415	0.003	
D_c-(depth of cut)	0.0141	1	0.0141	9.48	0.0117	0.461	
α-(helix angle)	0.0002	1	0.0002	0.1348	0.7211	0.007	
S_sF_r	0.0088	1	0.0088	5.92	0.0353	0.288	
S_sL_c	0.0009	1	0.0009	0.6088	0.4533	0.029	
S_sD_c	0.0195	1	0.0195	13.15	0.0046	0.637	
$S_s\alpha$	0.0215	1	0.0215	14.51	0.0034	0.703	
F_rL_c	0.0102	1	0.0102	6.84	0.0258	0.333	
F_rD_c	0.0075	1	0.0075	5.06	0.0483	0.245	
$F_r\alpha$	0.0075	1	0.0075	5.06	0.0483	0.245	
L_cD_c	0.0081	1	0.0081	5.48	0.0413	0.265	
$L_c\alpha$	0.0306	1	0.0306	20.65	0.0011	1	
$D_c\alpha$	0.0195	1	0.0195	13.15	0.0046	0.637	
S_s^2	0.0314	1	0.0314	21.14	0.001	1.026	
F_r^2	0.1166	1	0.1166	78.63	< 0.0001	3.81	
L_c^2	0.0014	1	0.0014	0.9707	0.3477	0.046	
D_c^2	0.1346	1	0.1346	90.71	< 0.0001	4.399	
α^2	0.0002	1	0.0002	0.1079	0.7494	0.007	
SFL	0.0043	1	0.0043	2.88	0.1203	0.141	
SFD	3.13E−06	1	3.13E−06	0.0021	0.9643	0	
SFα	0.0399	1	0.0399	26.9	0.0004	1.304	
SLD	0.0003	1	0.0003	0.1706	0.6883	0.009	
SLα	0.0385	1	0.0385	25.96	0.0005	1.258	
SDα	0.0069	1	0.0069	4.65	0.0564	0.225	
FLD	0.0443	1	0.0443	29.83	0.0003	1.448	
FLα	0.0004	1	0.0004	0.2549	0.6246	0.013	
FDα	0.0038	1	0.0038	2.58	0.1393	0.124	
LDα	0.0043	1	0.0043	2.88	0.1203	0.141	
S^2F	0.6238	1	0.6238	420.48	< 0.0001	20.386	

(continued)

Table 9.3 (continued)

Source	Sum of squares	Degree of freedom	Mean square	F-value	*p*-value	% Concentration	
S^2L	0.0039	1	0.0039	2.63	0.136	0.127	
SF^2	0.1129	1	0.1129	76.1	< 0.0001	3.689	
L^3	0.0026	1	0.0026	1.78	0.2117	0.085	
D^3	0.1317	1	0.1317	88.76	< 0.0001	4.304	
SFLα	0.0038	1	0.0038	2.58	0.1393	0.124	
SFDα	0.0048	1	0.0048	3.2	0.1037	0.157	
SLDα	0.0185	1	0.0185	12.49	0.0054	0.605	
S^2F^2	0.049	1	0.049	33.02	0.0002	1.601	
Residual	0.015	10	0.002			0.484	
Lack-of-fit	0.002	3	0.001	0.458	0.7201	0.078	Not significant
Pure error	0.012	7				0.41	
Corrected total	3.06	49				100	

Table 9.4 The ANOVA statistics justification of the **experimental data** of surface roughness

Standard deviation	0.0385		R^2	0.9952
Mean	1.66		Adjusted R^2	0.9762
Coefficient of variation (C.V.) %	2.32		Adequate. Precision	39.1881

In Eq. (9.13), the model is in the state of coded form for proper identification of the comparative effect of the machining factors or parameters when comparing the coefficients. The equation developed for the prediction of surface roughness in the coded parameters can be employed to validate the model with a given level of the original unit of the machining parameters, to predict the response. However, this model should not be employed to study the interactions of the machining parameters because the estimated coefficient of the parameters is embedded to accommodate each parameter. It should be known that the intercept is not at the midpoint of the design space. The actual parameters model can be employed to predict the response in a given level of controlled parameters. The actual factors of the model are presented in Eq. (9.14).

$$\begin{aligned} SR_{actual} = & -18.29 + 0.008S + 0.477F + 0.037L + 0.100D - 0.158\alpha \\ & - 0.0003SF + 0.00002SL + 0.0014SD + 0.00067S\alpha \\ & - 0.0004FL + 0.00009FD - 0.0002F\alpha + 0.033LD \\ & + 0.001L\alpha + 0.143D\alpha - 9.275E - 07S^2 - 0.002F^2 \\ & - 0.001L^2 - 2.005D^2 + 0.00001\alpha^2 + 4.125E - 08SF \\ & - 1.925E - 06SFD + 8.083E - 08SF\alpha - 0.00002SLD \end{aligned}$$

Table 9.5 ANOVA coefficients of surface roughness for the QRCCD

Factor	Coefficient estimate	Df	Standard error	95% CI low	95% CI high	VIF
Intercept	1.59	1	0.0136	1.56	1.62	
S_s-(spindle speed)	– 0.5700	1	0.0272	– 0.6307	– 0.5093	5.00
F_r-(feed rate)	0.6500	1	0.0272	0.5893	0.7107	5.00
L_C-(length of cut)	– 0.0042	1	0.0203	– 0.0494	0.0411	2.78
D_C-(depth of cut)	– 0.0625	1	0.0203	– 0.1077	– 0.0173	2.78
α-(helix angle)	– 0.0100	1	0.0272	– 0.0707	0.0507	5.00
SF	– 0.0663	1	0.0272	– 0.1269	– 0.0056	1.0000
SL	0.0212	1	0.0272	– 0.0394	0.0819	1.0000
SD	0.0988	1	0.0272	0.0381	0.1594	1.0000
Sα	0.1037	1	0.0272	0.0431	0.1644	1.0000
FL	0.0712	1	0.0272	0.0106	0.1319	1.0000
FD	– 0.0612	1	0.0272	– 0.1219	– 0.0006	1.0000
Fα	– 0.0613	1	0.0272	– 0.1219	– 0.0006	1.0000
LD	– 0.0637	1	0.0272	– 0.1244	– 0.0031	1.0000
Lα	– 0.1238	1	0.0272	– 0.1844	– 0.0631	1.0000
Dα	0.0988	1	0.0272	0.0381	0.1594	1.0000
S^2	0.1400	1	0.0304	0.0722	0.2078	1.25
F^2	0.2700	1	0.0304	0.2022	0.3378	1.25
L^2	– 0.0300	1	0.0304	– 0.0978	0.0378	1.25
D^2	0.2900	1	0.0304	0.2222	0.3578	1.25
α^2	0.0100	1	0.0304	– 0.0578	0.0778	1.25
SFL	– 0.0925	1	0.0545	– 0.2139	0.0289	1.0000
SFD	0.0025	1	0.0545	– 0.1189	0.1239	1.0000
SFα	0.2825	1	0.0545	0.1611	0.4039	1.0000
SLD	– 0.0225	1	0.0545	– 0.1439	0.0989	1.0000
SLα	0.2775	1	0.0545	0.1561	0.3989	1.0000
SDα	– 0.1175	1	0.0545	– 0.2389	0.0039	1.0000
FLD	0.2975	1	0.0545	0.1761	0.4189	1.0000
FLα	0.0275	1	0.0545	– 0.0939	0.1489	1.0000
FDα	– 0.0875	1	0.0545	– 0.2089	0.0339	1.0000
LDα	– 0.0925	1	0.0545	– 0.2139	0.0289	1.0000
S^2F	– 2.50	1	0.1218	– 2.77	– 2.23	5.00

(continued)

Table 9.5 (continued)

Factor	Coefficient estimate	Df	Standard error	95% CI low	95% CI high	VIF
S^2L	– 0.1975	1	0.1218	– 0.4689	0.0739	5.00
SF^2	1.06	1	0.1218	0.7911	1.33	5.00
L^3	0.0542	1	0.0406	– 0.0363	0.1446	2.78
D^3	0.3825	1	0.0406	0.2920	0.4730	2.78
$SFL\alpha$	– 0.1750	1	0.1089	– 0.4177	0.0677	1.0000
$SFD\alpha$	0.1950	1	0.1089	– 0.0477	0.4377	1.0000
$SLD\alpha$	0.3850	1	0.1089	0.1423	0.6277	1.0000
S^2F^2	– 1.57	1	0.2723	– 2.17	– 0.9582	2.25

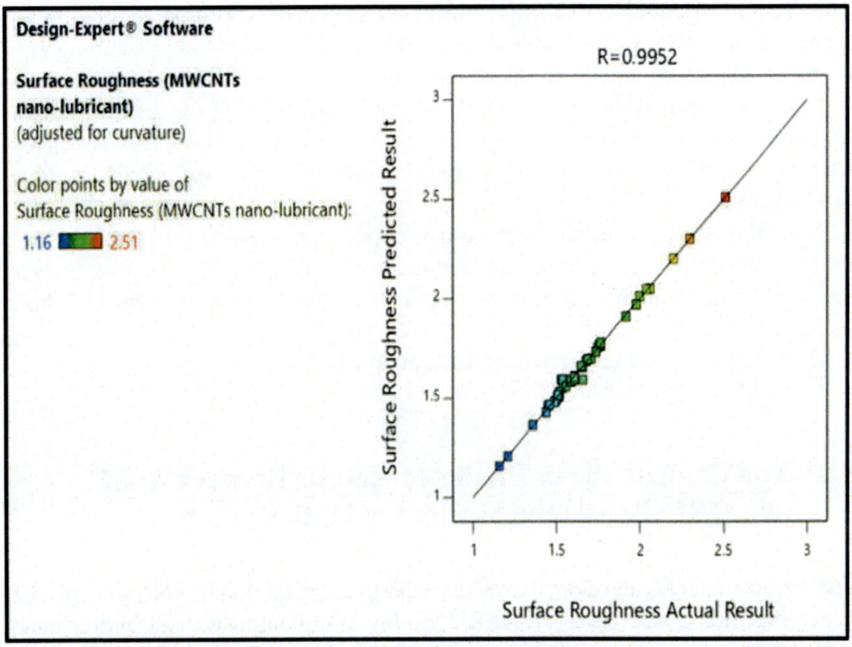

Fig. 9.7 Experimental data and predicted data of surface roughness

$$
\begin{aligned}
&- 2.375E - 07SL\alpha - 0.00004SD\alpha + 0.0002FLD \\
&+ 9.208E - 06FL\alpha - 0.002FD\alpha - 0.002LD\alpha + 3.763E \\
&- 08S^2F - 6.583E - 09S^2F + 1.045E - 06SF^2 \\
&+ 6.771E - 06L^3 + 0.383D^3 - 2.916E - 09SFL\alpha \\
&+ 6.500E - 08SFD\alpha + 6.4167E - 07SLD\alpha - 1.565E \\
&- 10S^2F^2
\end{aligned}
\tag{9.14}
$$

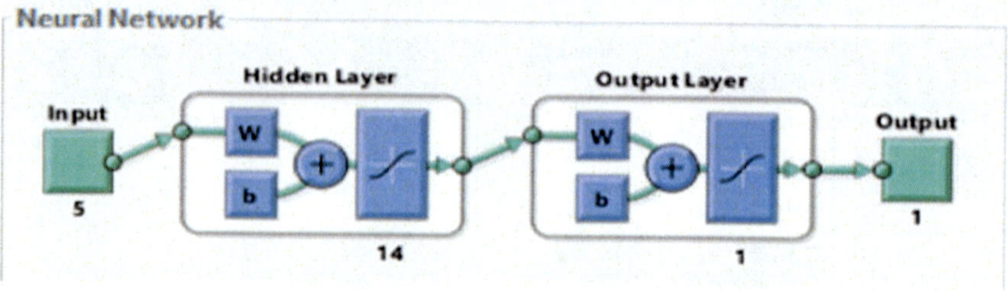

Fig. 9.8 The ANN model used for the prediction analysis of the surface roughness

9.3.3 The Prediction of Surface Roughness Using ANN

This section presents the ANN prediction of surface roughness during the end-milling operation of AA8112 alloy under the MWCNT's nano-lubricant machining environment. Figure 9.8 shows the performance of the ANN model under the multi-walled carbon nano-lubricant. From the analysis, the R-value for the data training set, data validation, and data testing is 0.90919, 0.95479, and 0.98872, respectively. The overall performance of the training, validation and testing is 0.91959, as shown in Fig. 9.9a–b.

From the ANN model, the best validation performance is 0.10917 as measured using the SSE; this occurs at epoch 0 and iteration 6 (Fig. 9.10). From the analysis, the SSE gradually increased from zero epoch to the peak point. Figure 9.11 shows the gradient constant of 0.15668, Marquardt unit parameter (Mu) of 1e−09, total validation checks, and the iterations value at epoch 6.

9.4 The Comparison of Predicted Results Between ANN and QRCCD and the Machining Optimization

The predicted models developed from the experimental data using ANN and QRCCD under machining operation of AA8112 alloy using multi-walled carbon nano-lubricant machining environment, the experimental data predicted result for ANN, and QRCCD is depicted in Fig. 9.12. The ANN and QRCCD models predicted the experimental data of surface roughness by 95% and 99%, respectively. Hence, both the ANN and the QRCCD are useful innovative design tools for the prediction process [14–17].

Figures 9.13, 9.14 and 9.15 shows the factors of objective optimization of the machining parameters obtained from the quadratic rotatable central composite design (QRCCD). The result shows that the spindle speed of 3366 rpm, 101 mm/min feed rate, 1 mm depth of cut, 20 mm length of cut, and 39.6° helix angle achieved the minimum surface roughness of 1.16 μm with the desirability of 0.926. This result is closely related to the experimental data from the machining operations, this result

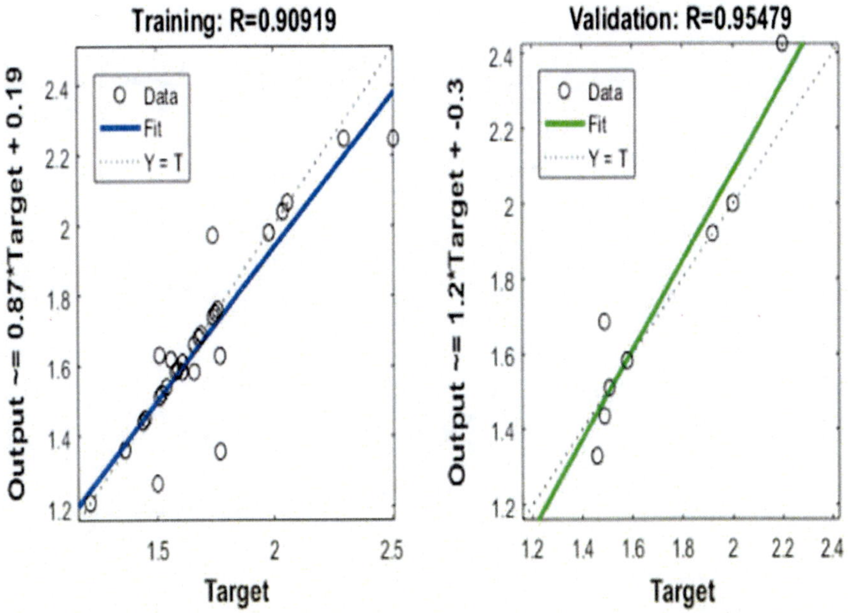

(a)

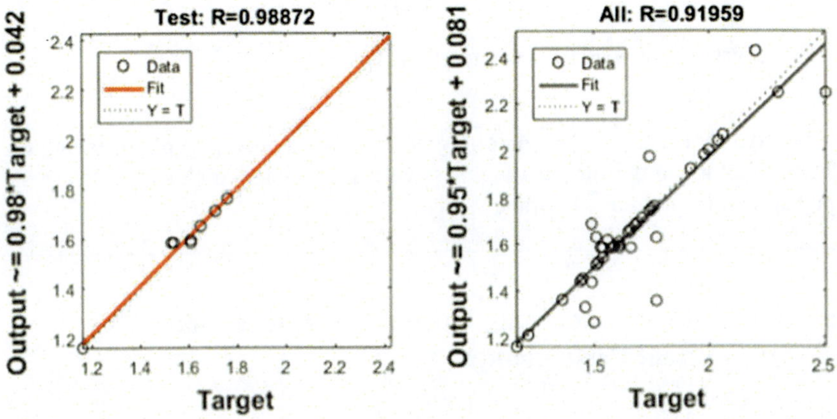

(b)

Fig. 9.9 **a** The ANN regression plot for surface roughness. **b** The ANN regression plot for surface roughness

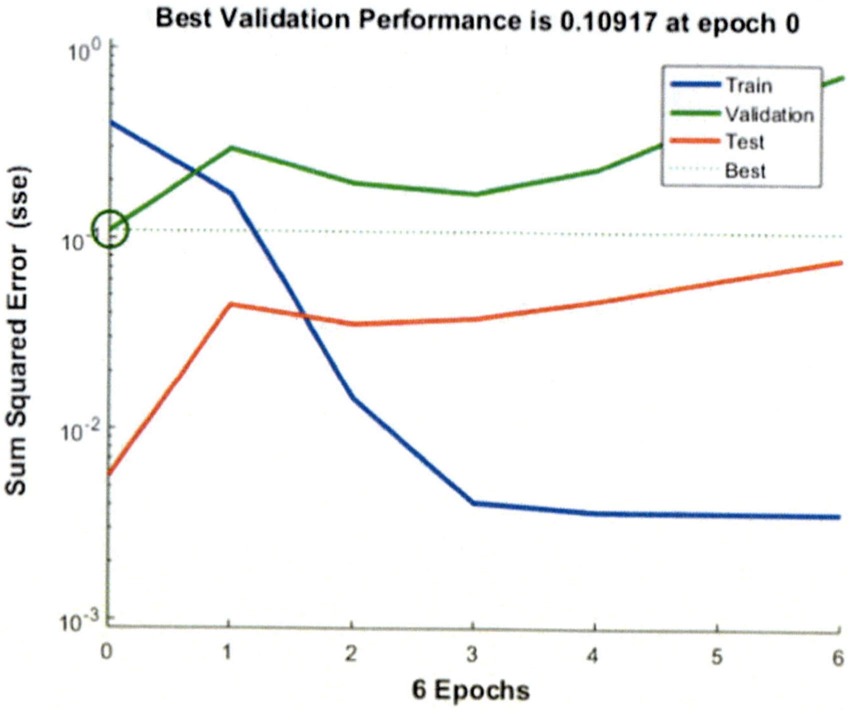

Fig. 9.10 ANN validation plot for surface roughness

is supported by Refs. [18, 19]. Also, Fig. 9.16 depict the overlay plot showing the influence factors on the surface roughness values at low and high surface areas are depicted with the colour variations.

9.5 Study of the Machining Parameters Interaction for Optimal Performance

Interaction study of machining parameters during machining process leads to high performance operation with quality product. As the optimal interactions parameters assist to improve the surface finishing of the workpiece. Surface roughness is a significant response in machining operations, because it prolongs the work life of the product, reduces the rate of corrosion activity of the workpiece during operations [20]. Therefore, the five machining parameters in this study is analyses using QRCCD to study the interactions between them. From Figs. 9.17, 9.18, 9.19, 9.20, 9.21, 9.22, 9.23, 9.24, 9.25 and 9.26 present the interactions plots. Figure 9.17 shows that the depth of cut and the helix angle has good interactions, however, the two parameters when increased it increases the surface roughness. Figure 9.18 depict the relation

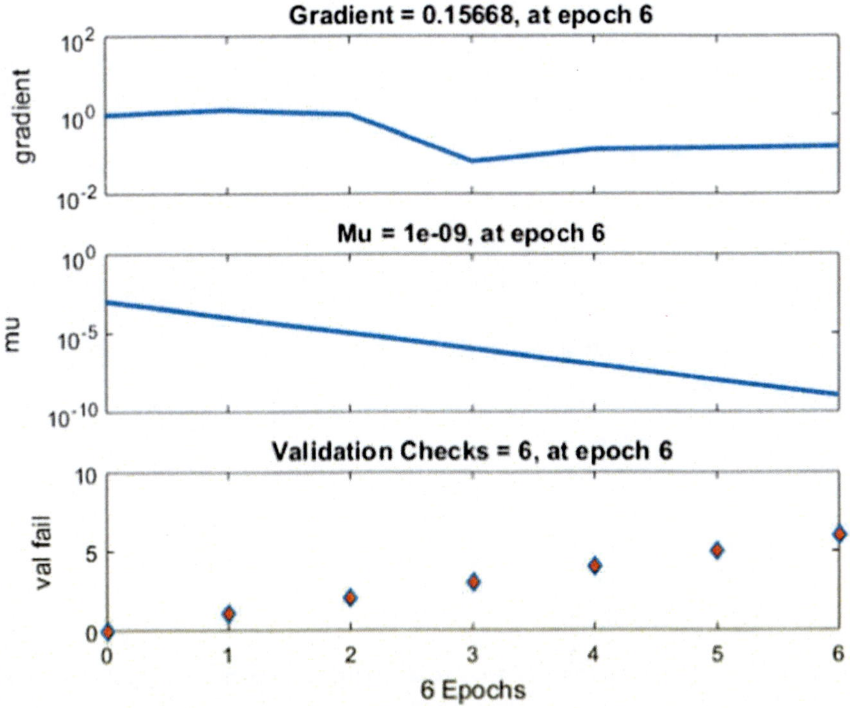

Fig. 9.11 ANN performance training state for surface roughness

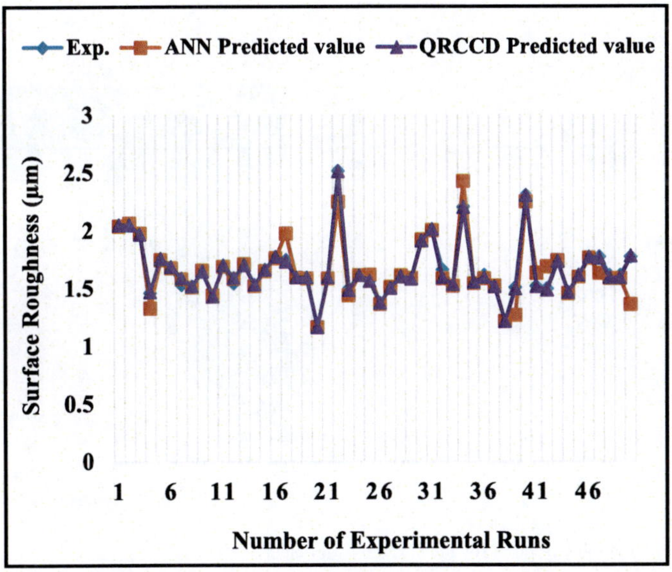

Fig. 9.12 Experimental data, ANN, and QRCCD predictions of the surface roughness

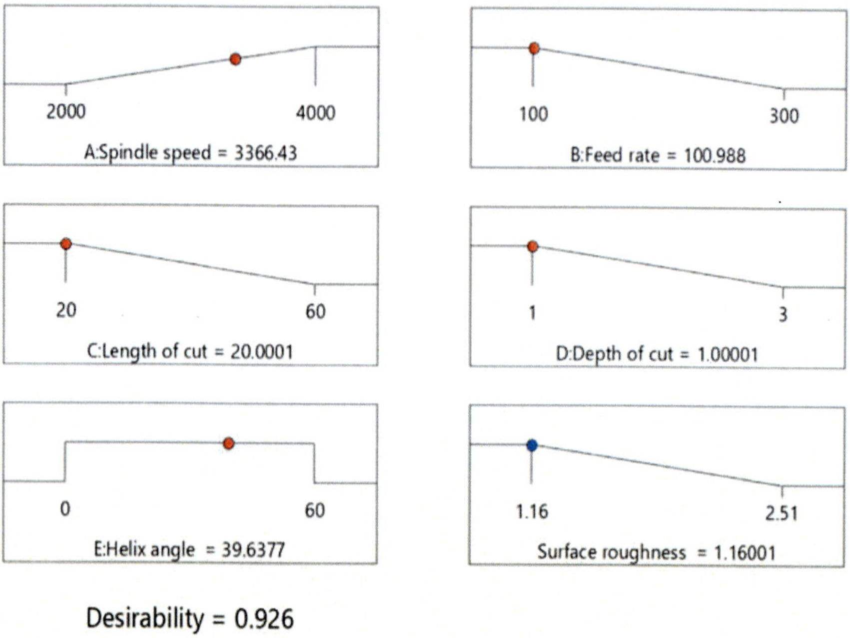

Fig. 9.13 The ramps plots for the objective five factors five levels of optimization of the surface roughness

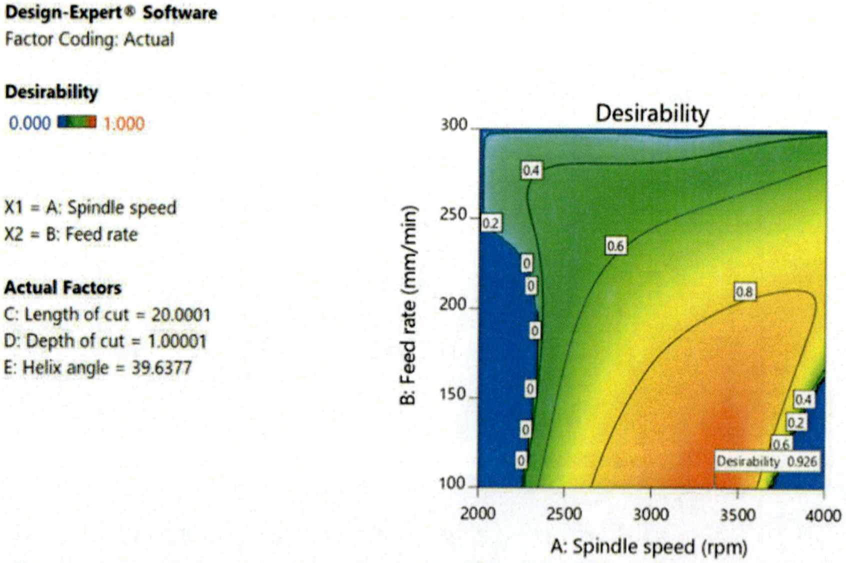

Fig. 9.14 The desirability plots for the surface roughness

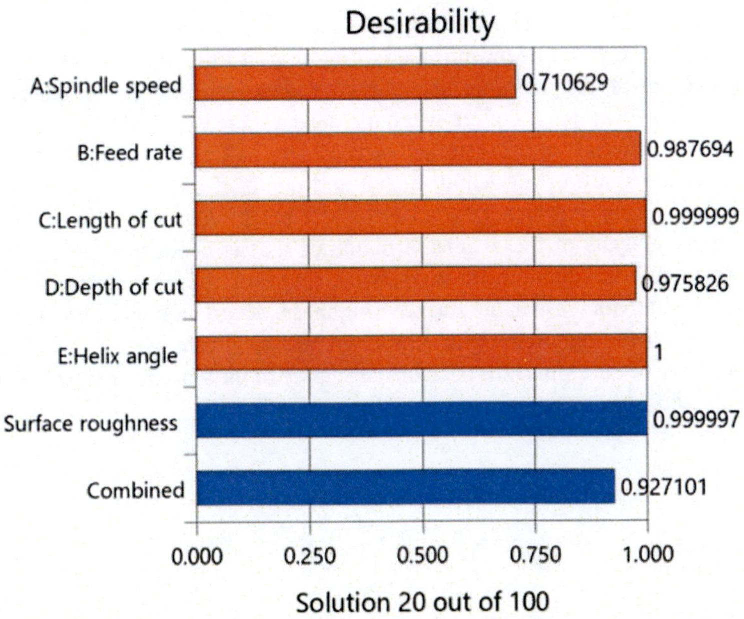

Fig. 9.15 The desirability bar plots for the multi-objective optimization parameters and the combine function

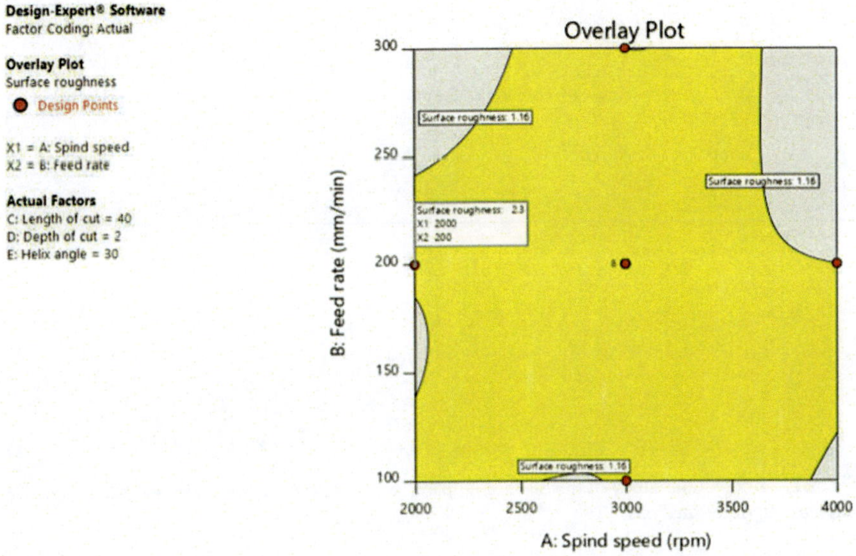

Fig. 9.16 The overlay plots showing the different surface area concentration for the multi-objective optimization parameters

between the helix angle and the length of cut, the helix angle when increased it allows the intake of lubricant into the cutting region to reduce the heat generated during operations, sot therefore, it relatively reduces the surface roughness when increased. However, length of cut when increase it increases the surface roughness, increases the material removal rate, and increases the cutting force. Figure 9.19 shows the interaction study of the length of cut and depth of cut, these two machining parameters is very significant because for any machining process to occur there must be an analysis of the estimated materials that is needed to be removed for the manufacturer to obtain the desired shape. However, these two parameters when increase, it led to increase in the surface roughness, due to high vibration occurrence during the machining. Also, when the chips are been relatively removal in high volume, some of the chip's falls back on the surface of the workpiece which increases material adhesion.

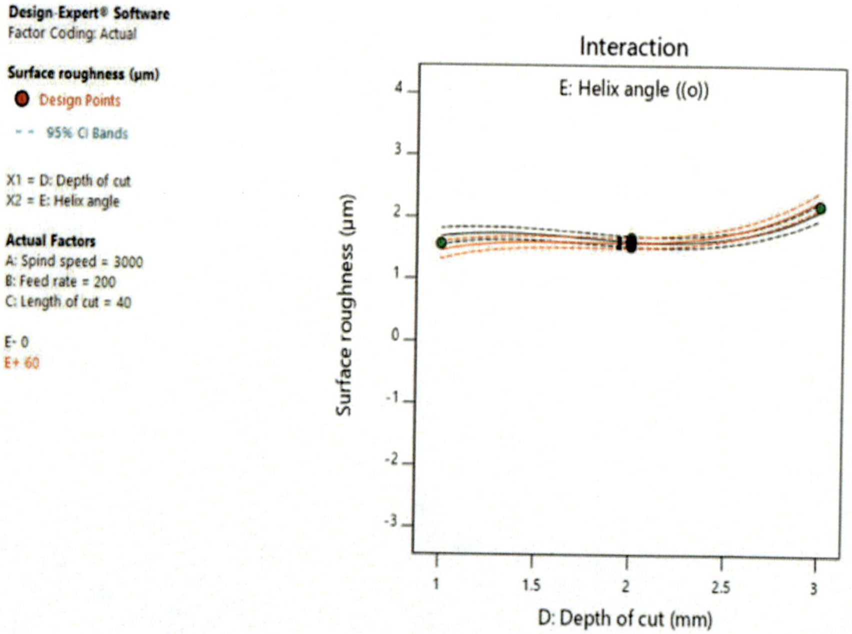

Fig. 9.17 Interactions study of the machining parameters between depth of cut and helix angle for surface roughness analysis

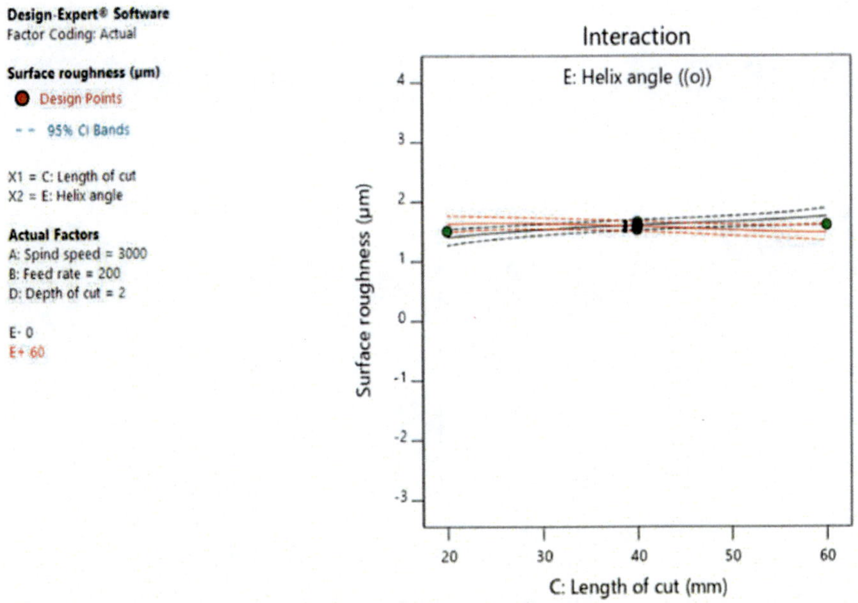

Fig. 9.18 Interactions study of the machining parameters between length of cut and helix angle for surface roughness analysis

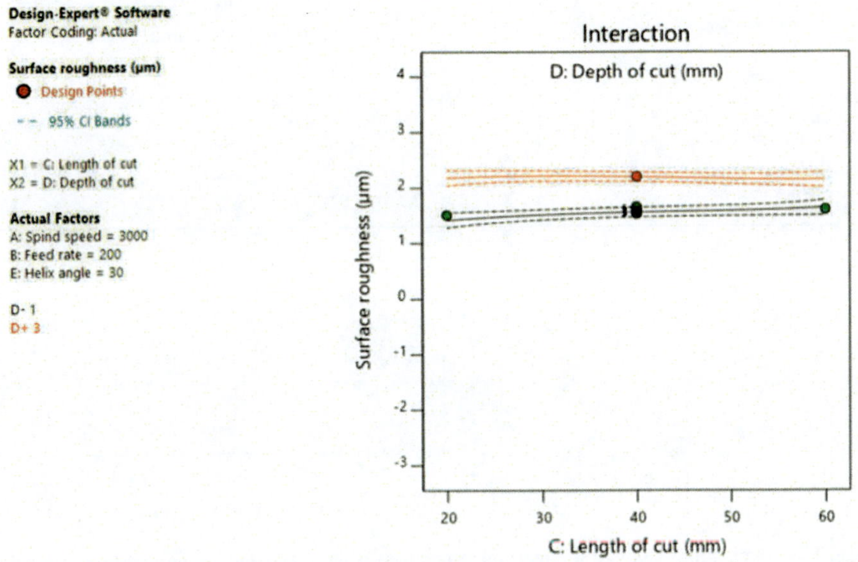

Fig. 9.19 Interactions study of the machining parameters between length of cut and depth of cut for surface roughness analysis

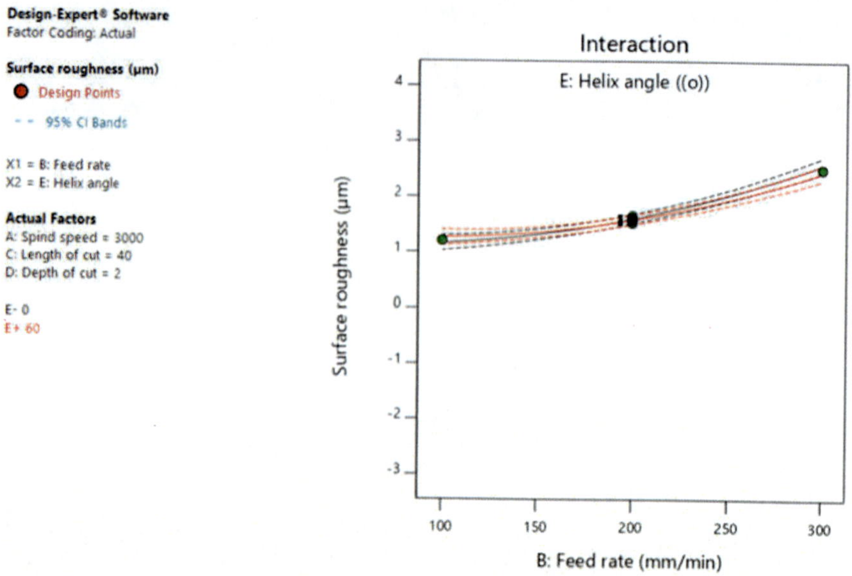

Fig. 9.20 Interactions study of the machining parameters between feed rate and helix angle for surface roughness analysis

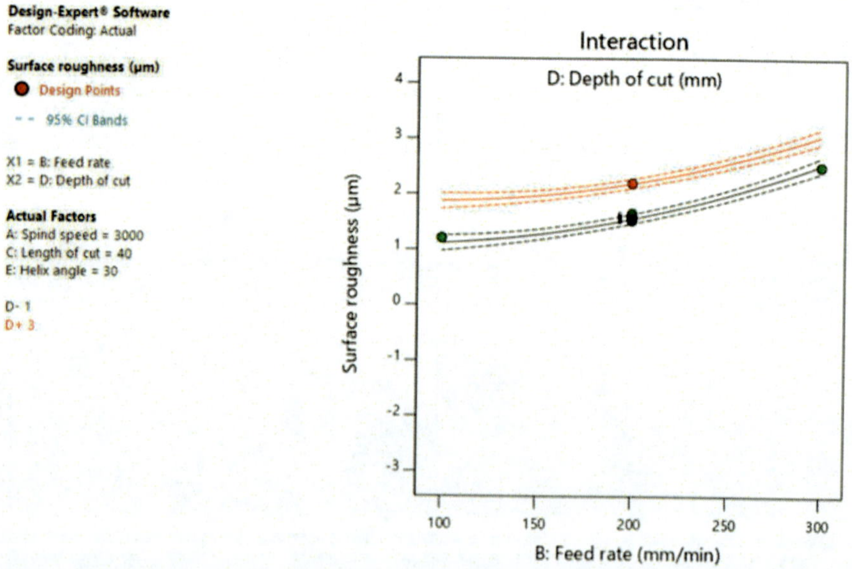

Fig. 9.21 Interactions study of the machining parameters between depth of cut and feed rate for surface roughness analysis

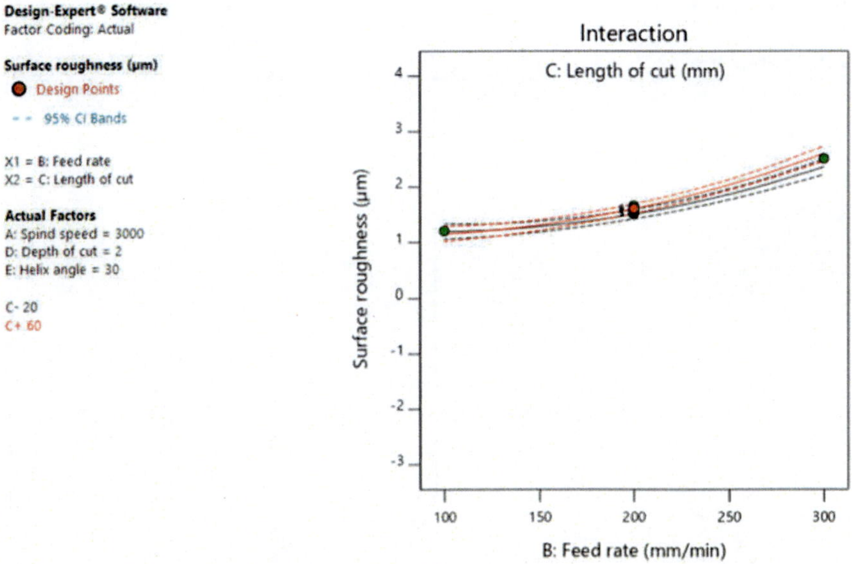

Fig. 9.22 Interactions study of the machining parameters between feed rate and length of cut for surface roughness analysis

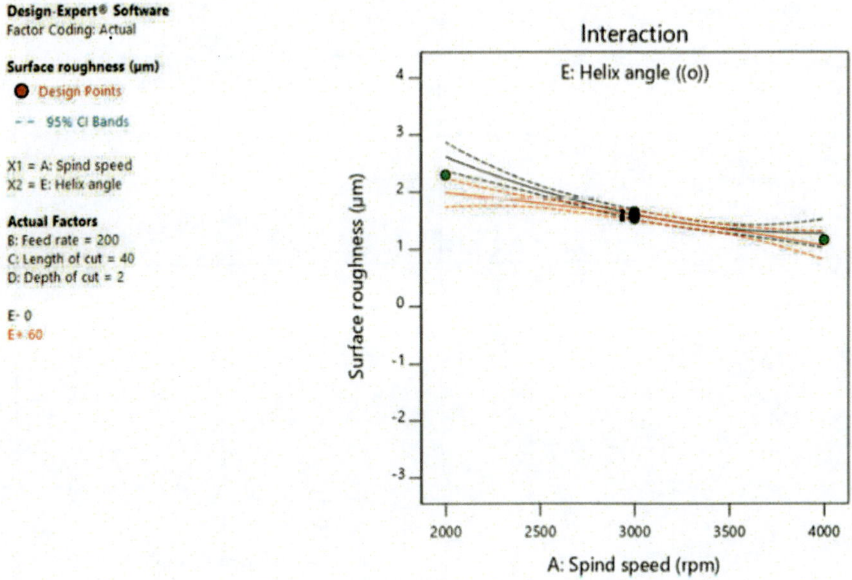

Fig. 9.23 Interactions study of the machining parameters between spindle speed and helix angle for surface roughness analysis

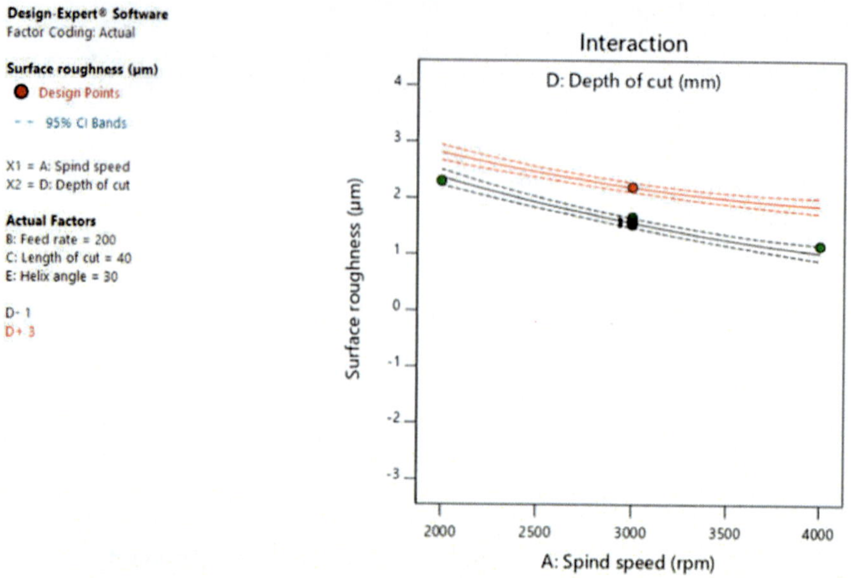

Fig. 9.24 Interactions study of the machining parameters between spindle speed and depth of cut for surface roughness analysis

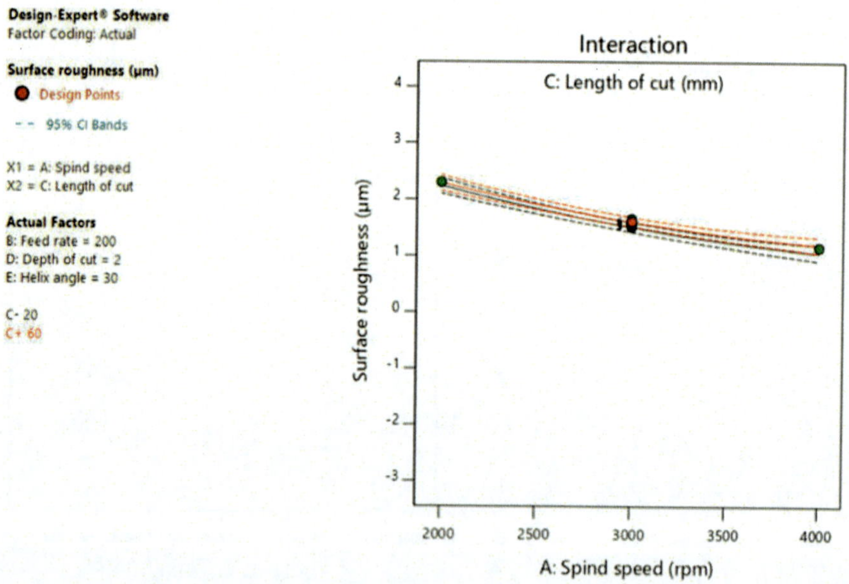

Fig. 9.25 Interactions study of the machining parameters between spindle speed and length of cut for surface roughness analysis

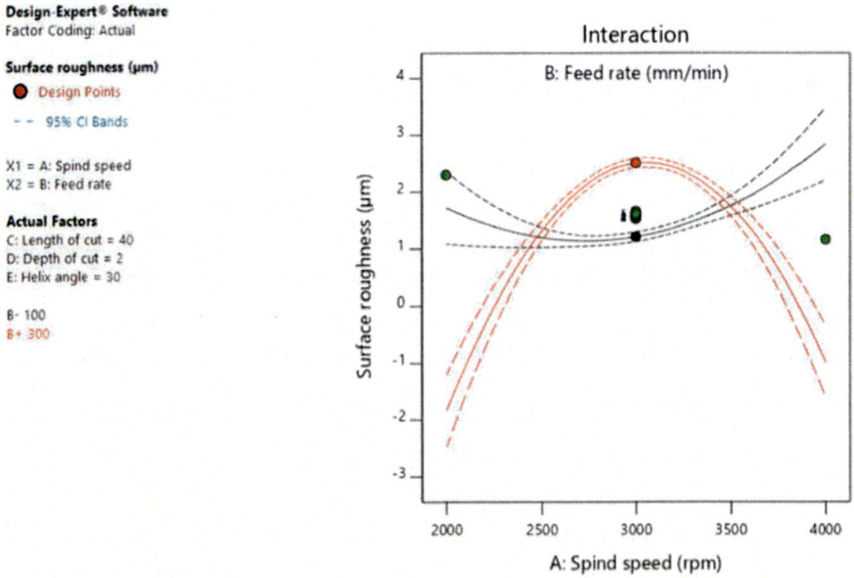

Fig. 9.26 Interactions study of the machining parameters between spindle speed and feed rate for surface roughness analysis

9.6 Conclusion

In this chapter, the conclusion drawn from the surface roughness prediction analysis using ANN and QRCCD with five-factors five-levels of cutting parameters. The machining parameters considered are spindle speed (S_s), feed rate (F_r), cutting length (L_c), cutting depth (D_c) and helix angle (α) as the following conclusion:

(i) Feed rate F_r was found to have the most significant effects on the surface roughness. The percentage contribution shows that F_r contributed 27.13% and 27.60%, followed by S_s with 23.70% and 21.24%, respectively.
(ii) From the experimental data, the optimized machining parameter for the five-factor, five-level experiment for the surface roughness was achieved at a S_s of 4000 rpm, a F_r of 200 mm/min, L_c of 40 mm, Dc of 2 mm, and helix angle of 30° to attain a minimum surface roughness values of 1.16 µm. However, the QRCCD optimized parameters for the minimum surface roughness are S_s of 3366 rpm, 101 mm/min F_r, 1 mm D_c, 20 mm L_c, and 39.6° helix angle achieved the lowest surface roughness of 1.16 µm.
(iii) The models developed using ANN and QRCCD predicted the experimental data with predicted values are 95.50% and 99.50%, respectively.

From the results of this research, the prediction and optimization of surface roughness under biodegradable Nano-lubricant via ANN and QRCCD is a sustainable tool to increase manufacturing processes.

References

1. Kim, H., Jung, W.K., Choi, I.G., Ahn, S.H.: A low-cost vision-based monitoring of computer numerical control (CNC) machine tools for small and medium-sized enterprises (SMEs). Sensors **19**(20), 4506 (2019)
2. Moradzadeh, A., Mansour-Saatloo, A., Mohammadi-Ivatloo, B., Anvari-Moghaddam, A.: Performance evaluation of two machine learning techniques in heating and cooling loads forecasting of residential buildings. Appl. Sci. **10**(11), 3829 (2020)
3. Wang, H., Liu, Y., Zhou, B., Li, C., Cao, G., Voropai, N., Barakhtenko, E.: Taxonomy research of artificial intelligence for deterministic solar power forecasting. Energy Convers. Manage. **214**, 112909 (2020)
4. Bui, X.N., Nguyen, H., Le, H.A., Bui, H.B., Do, N.H.: Prediction of blast-induced air overpressure in open-pit mine: assessment of different artificial intelligence techniques. Nat. Resour. Res. **29**(2), 571–591 (2020)
5. Okokpujie, I.P., Ohunakin, O.S., Bolu, C.A.: Multi-objective optimization of machining factors on surface roughness, material removal rate and cutting force on end-milling using MWCNTs nano-lubricant. Prog. Addit. Manufact. **6**(1), 155–178 (2021)
6. Dubey, V., Sharma, A.K., Pimenov, D.Y.: Prediction of surface roughness using machine learning approach in MQL turning of AISI 304 steel by varying nanoparticle size in the cutting fluid. Lubricants **10**(5), 81 (2022)
7. Ramesh, P., Mani, K.: Prediction of surface roughness using machine learning approach for abrasive waterjet milling of alumina ceramic. Int. J. Adv. Manufact. Technol. **119**(1), 503–516 (2022)
8. Alharthi, N.H., Bingol, S., Abbas, A.T., Ragab, A.E., El-Danaf, E.A., Alharbi, H.F.: Optimizing cutting conditions and prediction of surface roughness in face milling of AZ61 using regression analysis and artificial neural network. Adv. Mater. Sci. Eng. **2017** (2017)
9. Baranitharan, P., Ramesh, K., Sakthivel, R.: Measurement of performance and emission distinctiveness of Aegle marmelos seed cake pyrolysis oil/diesel/TBHQ opus powered in a DI diesel engine using ANN and RSM. Measurement **144**, 366–380 (2019)
10. Tyagi, L., Butola, R., Kem, L., Singari, R.M.: Comparative analysis of response surface methodology and artificial neural network on the wear properties of surface composite fabricated by friction stir processing. J. Bio- Tribo-Corros. **7**(2), 1–14 (2021)
11. Paturi, U.M.R., Devarasetti, H., Narala, S.K.R.: Application of regression and artificial neural network analysis in modelling of surface roughness in hard turning of AISI 52100 steel. Mater. Today: Proc. **5**(2), 4766–4777 (2018)
12. Okokpujie, I.P., Bolu, C.A., Ohunakin, O.S.: Comparative performance evaluation of TiO_2, and MWCNTs nano-lubricant effects on surface roughness of AA8112 alloy during end-milling machining for sustainable manufacturing process. Int. J. Adv. Manufact. Technol. **108**(5), 1473–1497 (2020)
13. Okonkwo, U.C., Okokpujie, I.P., Sinebe, J.E., Ezugwu, C.A.: Comparative analysis of aluminium surface roughness in end-milling under dry and minimum quantity lubrication (MQL) conditions. Manuf. Rev. **2**, 30 (2015)
14. Sizemore, N.E., Nogueira, M.L., Greis, N.P., Davies, M.A.: Application of machine learning to the prediction of surface roughness in diamond machining. Procedia Manufact. **48**, 1029–1040 (2020)
15. Yeganefar, A., Niknam, S.A., Asadi, R.: The use of support vector machine, neural network, and regression analysis to predict and optimize surface roughness and cutting forces in milling. Int. J. Adv. Manufact. Technol. **105**(1), 951–965 (2019)
16. Quarto, M., D'Urso, G., Giardini, C., Maccarini, G., Carminati, M.: A comparison between finite element model (FEM) simulation and an integrated artificial neural network (ANN)-particle swarm optimization (PSO) approach to forecast performances of micro electro discharge machining (micro-EDM) drilling. Micromachines **12**(6), 667 (2021)

17. Balonji, S., Okokpujie, I.P., Tartibu, L.K.: August. parametric analysis of the process performance of surface roughness data of machined aluminium using PSO-ANN. In: International Conference on Artificial Intelligence, Big Data, Computing and Data Communication Systems (icABCD), pp. 1–6. IEEE (2021)
18. Lalwani, V., Sharma, P., Pruncu, C.I., Unune, D.R.: Response surface methodology and artificial neural network-based models for predicting performance of wire electrical discharge machining of inconel 718 alloy. J. Manufact. Mater. Process. **4**(2), 44 (2020)
19. Okokpujie, I.P., Tartibu, L.K.: Performance investigation of the effects of nano-additive-lubricants with cutting parameters on material removal rate of AL8112 alloy for advanced manufacturing application. Sustainability **13**(15), 8406 (2021)
20. Safiei, W., Rahman, M.M., Yusoff, A.R., Arifin, M.N., Tasnim, W.: Effects of SiO_2-Al_2O_3-ZrO_2 tri-hybrid nanofluids on surface roughness and cutting temperature in end milling process of aluminum alloy 6061–T6 using uncoated and coated cutting inserts with minimal quantity lubricant method. Arab. J. Sci. Eng. **46**, 7699–7718 (2021)

Chapter 10
Cutting Force Optimization Under ANN and QRCCD

Abstract The prediction analysis of cutting force in the cutting process is very significant in the manufacturing of products for industrial use. Cutting force is one of the responses in machining operations that affect energy consumption via computer numerical control of the manufacturing process. The focus of this chapter is to employ artificial neural network (ANN) and quadratic rotatable central composite design (QRCCD) to carry out prediction and optimisation to study the cutting force to minimised the energy consumption. The data employed in this study is obtained from experimental machining operation of AA 8012 alloy under vegetable oil TiO_2 biodegradable nano-lubricant for sustainable machining process. The result obtained showed that the minimum cutting force occurs at the optimal machining parameter of spindle speed of 2351 rpm, 101 mm/min feed rate, 1 mm depth of cut, 20 mm length of cut, and 60° helix angle and the minimum cutting force of 31 N with the desirability of 0.968. Also, the generated models developed for the cutting force using ANN and QRCCD predicted the experimental results with 97.5% and 95.56% accuracy under the biodegradable TiO_2 nano-lubricant. This result has proven that the implementation of Heuristic and Metaheuristic Techniques for Advanced Nano-lubricant Machining Optimization is a sustainable manufacturing process.

Keywords Cutting force · Artificial neural network · QRCCD · Nano-lubricant

10.1 Introduction

A high rate of energy consumption affects the economical aspect of the production of goods products of mechanical parts. This challenge of most mechanical processes use consume high energy during production as a result of the contact of the materials and the machining parameters, as lead to implementation of nano-lubrication system and optimisation techniques for sustainable production process with less energy consumption. Yeganefar et al. [1] the study predicted the cutting force of aluminium 7075-T6 alloy using artificial neural network (ANN), regression analysis

I. P. Okokpujie and L. K. Tartibu, *Modern Optimization Techniques for Advanced Machining*, Studies in Systems, Decision and Control 485,
https://doi.org/10.1007/978-3-031-35455-7_10

(RA) and support vector regression (SVR). Also the authors carried out optimisation of the cutting factors such as tool types, cutting depth, feed per tool and the machining speed via desirability and ANOVA. In order to validate the predictive models the Grid search and cross-validation approaches were employed to find the best fit of the ANN and SVR models. The analysis of this researcher was trained using Levenberg–Marquardt and RMSprop algorithms for the cutting force. The findings show that Hyper-parameter tuning is totally urgent to choose legitimate ANN and SVR models. Since ANN models own numerous hyperparameters, tuning is tedious, yet all at once the significance of this undertaking can't be overemphasized. Also, the RMSprop could anticipate Fz all the more definitively interestingly, with LMA. Hence, preparing calculations with versatile learning rate might prompt better reaction expectation.

Imani et al. [2] the current review uses man-made brainpower as a successful technique for anticipating processing powers and surface unpleasantness in view of exploratory outcomes. To examine the way of behaving of this combination, four levels for the two previous info boundaries and two levels for the two other, absolutely 64 trials, were satisfied and considered. In view of the trial results, the impact of information boundaries on the results, or at least, cutting power and surface unpleasantness, was researched, and afterward, brain network for displaying and anticipating and hereditary calculation for the streamlining of the results have been used. The improved counterfeit organization, which was gotten in this exploration, is helpful for expectation of machining power and surface unpleasantness of processing in view of the benefits of cutting pace, feed rate, and the hub profundity of cutting, for wet and dry processing of Inconel 738.

Wang et al. [3] as of late, the developing prominence of counterfeit brain networks has encouraged an ever increasing number of scientists to attempt acquaint these techniques with the machining field, with some of them really delivering great outcomes. The obtaining of reducing information frequently implies higher expense and time, restricting the use of brain network in the machining area, somewhat. In this paper, for the errand of cutting power expectation, a "move organization" was laid out, in light of information got by reproduction, joined with the hypothesis and strategy in the field of move learning. Contrasted with "common organization", that is, conventional back-engendering brain network in light of exploratory examples alone, move network shows clear execution benefits. On one hand, this intends that, utilizing similar exploratory examples, the expectation blunder of move organization will be controlled; while then again, when a similar forecast mistake is accomplished, the quantity of trial tests expected by the exchange organization will be less.

Daniel et al. [4] this study plans to enhance the info boundaries, for example, mass portion and molecule size of SiC alongside profundity of cut, feed and cutting pace in the processing of Al5059/SiC/MoS2. The cross breed metal network composites are by and large created by building up of various sizes (10, 20 and 40 mm) of SiC with aluminum at an alternate level (5, 10 and 15%) though the MoS2 expansion is fixed as 2%. The impact of each control factor on reaction factors are examined through Taguchi S/N proportion technique. Likewise, the main technique for expectation of reaction boundaries is fulfilled by ANN model than the relapse model. Examination of difference (ANOVA) results conceive that mass part of SiC, feed rate is the most oppressive component on reaction variable.

Kilickap et al. [5] in this paper, an exploratory review was led to decide the impact of various cutting boundaries, for example, cutting speed, feed rate, and profundity of cut on cutting power, surface harshness, and device wear in the processing of Ti-6242S combination utilizing the established carbide (WC) end factories with a 10 mm measurement. Test results were described using both Response Surface Methodology and Artificial Neural Networks (ANN). Utilizing Levenberg–Marquardt (LM), ANN prepared a network and loads. On the other hand, the Box Behnken plan was used to create the numerical models in RSM. Values obtained from the ANN and RSM were thought to be quite close to the knowledge obtained through trial research. High cutting velocities, low feed rates, and deep cuts produced the least cutting power and surface discomfort. Low cutting velocity, feed rate, and cut depth resulted in the base instrument wear. The difficulty with this study is that it did not take into account the helix angle and length of cut, which are important factors in the cutting process. However, this chapter has address this and as created a sustainable optimisation. Several studies have been done to predict cutting force, but the implementation of Heuristic and Metaheuristic Techniques for Advanced Nano-lubricant Machining Optimization for cutting force has not been done. The novelty of this chapter is the prediction and optimisation of cutting force during machining operations via ANN and QRCCD.

10.2 Materials and Method

The procedure for conducting an experimental examination of the effects of milling settings on the cutting force for alloys AA 8112 is described in this section. The experiment was done using a CNC milling SIEG 3/10/0016 and an HSS cutting tool. Tables 10.1 and 10.2 provide a detailed breakdown of the chemical composition of the tool and the alloy made of aluminum 8112. Table 10.3 also includes the levels and cutting settings.

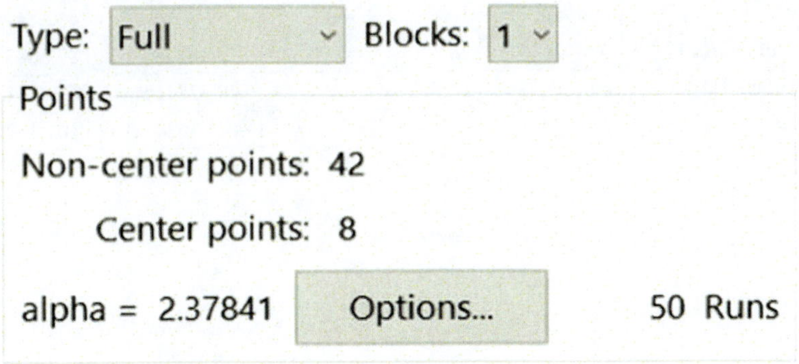

Table 10.1 Machining factors and response parameters

Exp. runs	Workpiece	Machining tool	Variable parameters	Response parameters
1–50	AA8112 alloy	Coated high-speed steel (the M42-high-speed-steel cutting tool of 13 mm diameter was employed in this study, having molybdenum of 9.5%, cobalt of 8.25%, chromium of 3.9%, carbon of 1.1%, tungsten of 1.6%, and vanadium 1.2%)	Spindle speed, feed rate, length of cut, depth of cut, helix angle	Cutting force

Table 10.2 Chemical properties of AA8112 alloy

Elemental composition	Weight %
Aluminium (AL)	94.7
Magnesium (Mg)	0.8
Silicon (Si)	1.2
Iron (Fe)	1.2
Copper (Cu)	0.45
Chromium (Cr)	0.25
Zinc (Zn)	0.3
Manganese (Mn)	0.6
Titanium (Ti)	0.3
Others	0.05
Residuals	0.15

Table 10.3 Variables and their levels in the experiment

Name	Units	Low	High	– alpha	+ alpha
Spindle speed (S_s)	rpm	2000	4000	621.586	5378.41
Feed rate (F_r)	mm/min	100	300	– 37.8414	437.841
Length of cut (L_c)	mm	20	60	– 7.56828	87.5683
Depth of cut (D_c)	mm	1	3	– 0.378414	4.37841
Helix angle (α)	0	0	60	– 41.3524	101.352

A 4 arms strain gauge dynamometer having bridge resistance of 350 Ω, 5 V' maximum with a wide range of 0–300 KGF was employed in the machining process to measure the cutting force. The three (3) phases dynamometer measures the x-axis, y-axis, and z-axis during the cutting operations and the Eq. (10.1) shows the formulae used to calculate the final cutting force [6, 7].

$$C_f = \sqrt{C_{fx}^2 + C_{fy}^2 + C_{fz}^2} \quad (10.1)$$

where C_f is the consequential force, C_{fx}, C_{fy} and C_{fz} are the machining cutting forces along the x-axis, y-axis, and z-axis, respectively as shown in the experimental setup in Fig. 10.1.

The scanning electron microscopy (SEM) and energy dispersive spectroscopy (EDS) analysis of the TiO_2 nano-powder used in preparing the nano-lubricant are shown in Figs. 10.2. The EDS analysis confirmed that the chemical composition of the nano-powders is 99.7% titanium-oxide (TiO_2). The morphology of the TiO_2 on the SEM analysis is stable, with a specific area of 240 m/g and particle size of 15 nm. The stability of the nanoparticle size is very significant for the development of the nano-lubricant because the homogenisation process of nano-particles and the base oil needs uniform nanoparticle sizes.

Fig. 10.1 The experimental setup of the CNC milling machine

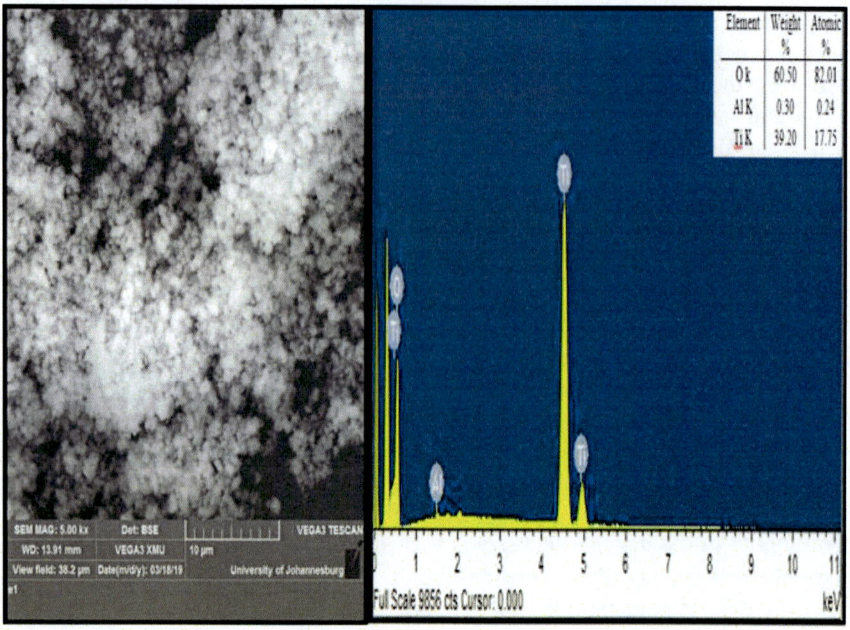

Fig. 10.2 The SEM and EDS micrograph of TiO_2 nano-powder used for the study

The Nanolubricant were developed with five different stages, the first stage is the weighing of the nanoparticles and the base oil. The second stage is the application of magnetic stirrer via mechanical process of mixing the nanopowder and the copra oil which is the cutting fluid for 2 h. The third stage is the used of ultrasonic machine to homogenised the Nanolubricant for 5 h, after the 5 h process the nanolubricant is then formed as shown in Fig. 10.3. After developing the Nanolubricant the results show an excellent crystalline structure of the copra oil. This characteristic is in line with findings in the work of [8, 9] on the effects of coconut oil lubricant on the carbide cutting tool during turning operations. The EDS analysis shows the percentage chemical composition of the copra oil, by weight. The copra oil contains seven elements with a reasonable amount of carbon, oxygen, and silicon. The procedure followed during the experiment and the optimisation of the cutting force is presented in Fig. 10.4.

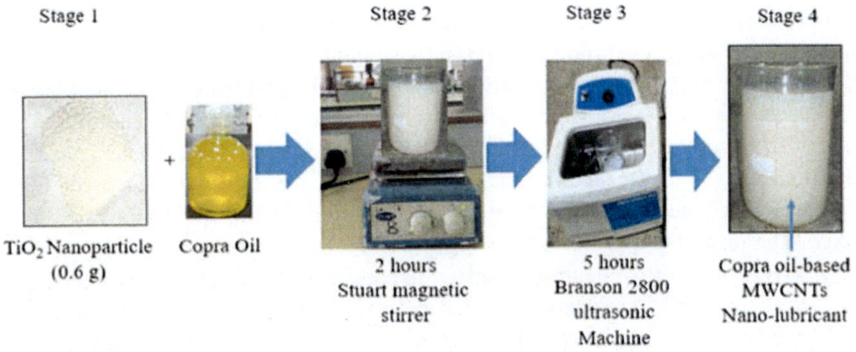

Fig. 10.3 Experimental set-up for the preparation of the nano-lubricant used for the study

Fig. 10.4 Procedure of the research design

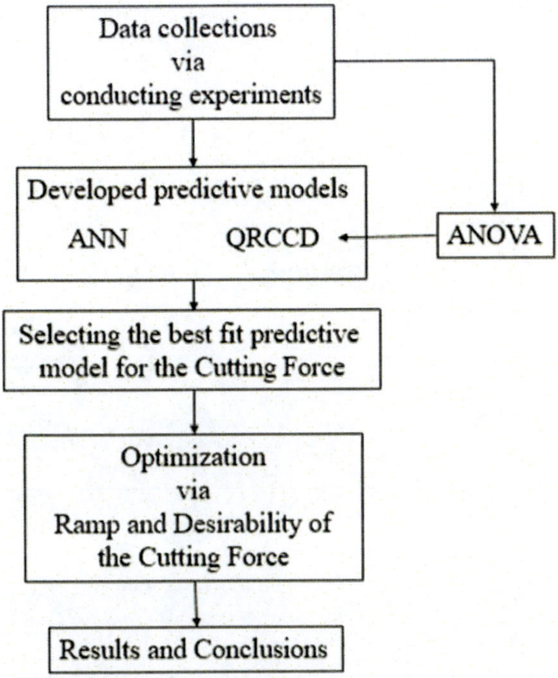

10.2.1 Mathematical Modelling Using Artificial Neural Network

The design of ANN is roused by the natural brain organization to copy the mind execution to settle complex issues. The fake neurons are associated with one another to build the ANN. Every neuron's information vector is boosted by the weight vector, which is combined with a predisposition term to include the contribution of an initiation capacity. A neuron's output is the consequence of the enactment capability.

One of the most well-known networks for capability estimate is the feedforward brain network (Fig. 10.5), which includes one or more secret layers in addition to the information and result layers. The information layer does not handle data; instead, it has the ability to locate the information's noteworthy features. Layer by layer, input signal is distributed across the organization's neurons. While the synaptic loads are fixed. The result layer presents the measures of reaction factors.

A layer is a group of neurons arranged in parallel without having any interaction with each other. The workstation consists of three processes that are: the input layer, hidden layer, and output layer. Variables are presented to the workstation via the input layer and transferred to hidden layers where the actual work is done through a weight connections process; the hidden layers determine the output responses layer. After the experiment has been carried out, the values of the responses are recorded. The neuron has a bias Ø, which is added with the weighted sum W_n and input variables (U_n) to determine the total net input (T_n), as presented in Eq. (10.2) [10].

$$T_n = \sum_{i=1}^{n} (W_n * U_n) + Ø \tag{10.2}$$

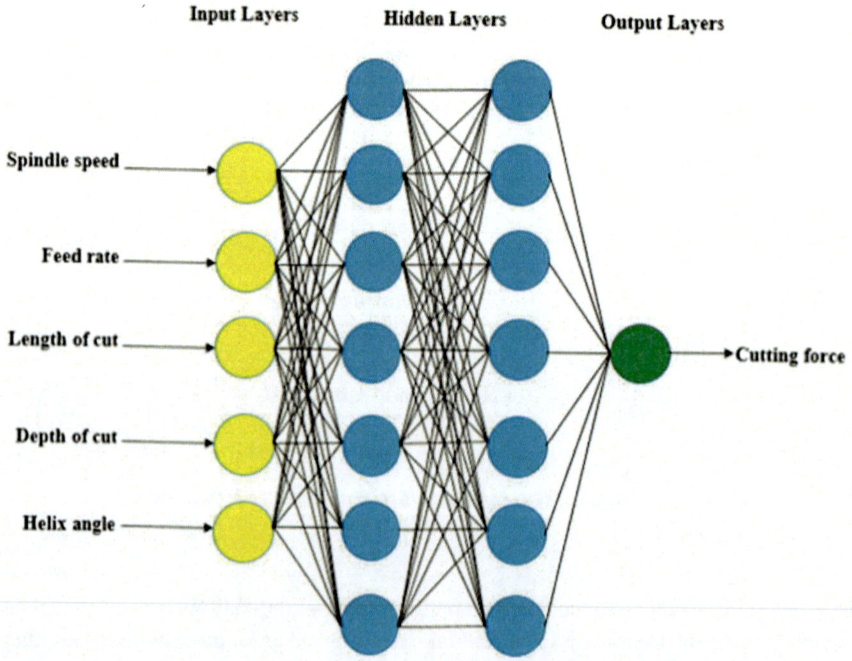

Fig. 10.5 The neural network system for the end-milling operation of AA8112 alloy

The neuron for this Back Propagation feed-forward Neural Network (BPNN) has five (5) inputs, with five (5) weights; this weight is randomised during the training period of the BPNN. The transformation process is carried out through the sigmoid non-linear transfer function (Z), which is given in Eq. (10.3).

$$Z = U_1 * W_1 + U_2 * W_2 + \cdots + U_n * W_n + \emptyset * 1 \tag{10.3}$$

where the total net input (T_n), is transposed as given in Eq. (10.4)

$$\hat{T} = Y_{out} = \text{sigmoid}\ (Z) \tag{10.4}$$

The sigmoid transfer function (Z_i) is given in Eq. (10.5) as:

$$\text{Sigmoid}\ (Z_i) = \frac{1}{1 + e^{-Z_i}} \tag{10.5}$$

The output (Y_{out}) is determined by multiplying the activated transfer function with the weight W_{ni} between the inner last layer of the hidden neuron and the output layer, becomes Eq. (10.6).

$$Y_{out} = W_{ni} * Z_i \tag{10.6}$$

The error is e_i, and is obtained by subtracting the experimental values from the predicted values. The equation is given in Eq. (10.7), and the total error (SSE) is computed using Eq. (10.8).

$$e_i = SR_e - SR_p \tag{10.7}$$

$$SSE = \frac{1}{2} \sum_{I=1}^{n} e_1^2 \tag{10.8}$$

Depending on the problem to be solved, ANN has numerous techniques for training a neural system. In this work, the BPNN was adopted to build and train the system for the prediction of output parameters. The structure of the ANN employed for this study is presented in Fig. 10.5. The inputs (U_n) correspond to feed rate, spindle speed, length of cut, helix angle, and depth of cut are built in the ANN structure. The signal (Ø) is the interior threshold of a neuron, i.e., the bias, and Z_i is the nonlinear transfer function. The neuron is trained with 70% input data, 15% of the input data for testing, while the remaining 15% input data is used for the validation process.

10.2.2 Mathematical Modelling Using Quadratic Rotatable Central Composite Design

Quadratic rotatable central composite design (QRCCD) is a design tool employed to analyze engineering problems. QRCCD is one of the packages in response surface methodology in Design expert software, mainly used for factors above four and five-level to study the relationship's effects on the response parameters. QRCCD is suitable for prediction, optimization, and model developments in the manufacturing of mechanical components. In this study, the relationship between surface roughness (the response parameters) and the cutting parameters under multi-walled carbon nano-lubricant cutting conditions is given in Eq. (10.9) [11–13].

$$C_f = \theta(S_s, \mathrm{F}_r, L_c, D_c, \alpha) \tag{10.9}$$

The desired machinability feature is C_f and the response function is θ. However, the evaluation C_f They are projected using a s scientific model, which is suitable for evaluating the effects of cutting parameters interface on machinability features. The interactions become Eq. (10.10–10.11).

$$C_f = \theta\left(S_s^{X_x}, F_r^{Y_y}, L_c^{Z_z}, D_c^{\mathrm{zr}}, \alpha^{\mathrm{zi}}\right) \tag{10.10}$$

$$\log(C_f) = \log(\theta) + X_x.\log(S_s) + Y_y.\log(F_r) + Z_z.\log(L_c) + Z_r.\log(D_c) + Z_i.\log(\alpha) \tag{10.11}$$

where,

$$C_f = \log(\mathrm{Y_i})\beta_0 = \log(\theta)\mathrm{x}_1 = \log(S_s)\mathrm{x}_2 = \log(F_r)$$
$$\mathrm{x}_3 = \log(L_c)\mathrm{x}_4 = \log(D_c)\mathrm{x}_5 = \log(\alpha)$$

and

$$\mathrm{x} = \beta_1, \mathrm{y} = \beta_2, \mathrm{z} = \beta_3, \mathrm{zr} = \beta_4, \mathrm{zi} = \beta_5.$$

The overview of a replacement gets the following expression in Eq. (10.10), where the constant and exponents θ, X_x, Y_y, Z_z, Z_r, and Z_i are determined by the least-squares regression procedure. This research work, the Quadratic rotatable central composite design-based regression model second-order, is implemented and given in Eq. (10.12) as:

$$\mathrm{Y_i} = \beta_0 + \sum \beta_i \mathrm{x_i} + \sum \beta_{ii} \mathrm{x_i^2} + \sum \beta_{ij} \mathrm{x_i x_j} + \mathrm{e} \tag{10.12}$$

The regression constant is β_0, and the coefficients are β_1 to β_5, and the logarithmic alteration of parameters are x_1, x_2, x_3, x_4, and x_5. i.e., S_s, F_r, L_c, D_c, α, and e represent the spindle speed, feed rate, length-of-cut, depth-of-cut, helix angle, and the error term, respectively. The input variables and levels were undoubtedly within the interludes recommended by the computer numerical control manufacturer. Equation (10.12) is the regression model employed to develop the prediction model from the response surface method from the design experts.

10.2.3 *Validation of the Surface Roughness Results*

In order to ascertain the accuracy of the developed model from the **experimental data**, both the percentage deviation φ_i, and the average deviation $\overline{\varphi}$ was used. After the prediction of the surface roughness, the percentage deviation was utilized to validate the rate of prediction of the surface roughness. The general equation to determine the validation accuracy is presented in Eq. (10.13) [14].

$$\varphi_i = \left(\frac{C_{f(m)} - C_{f(e)}}{C_{f(e)}}\right) \times 100\% \tag{10.13}$$

where, φ_i : percentage deviation of single variables, C_f (m) measure results, C_f (e) experimental results.

10.3 Results and Discussion

The result used in the ANN and QRCCD prediction analysis was obtained from the experimental results from the study of cutting force during the end-milling machining of AA8112 alloy with a biodegradable TiO_2-nano-lubricants. This data is applied for the development of the mathematical models. The total experimental number of fifty (50) is derived from the trial runs, which is based on the quadratic rotatable central composite design (QRCCD) for five factors-five levels of machining parameters. The results gotten from the experiment is presented in Table 10.4.

Table 10.4 Data for the cutting force prediction and optimization

		Factor 1	Factor 2	Factor 3	Factor 4	Factor 5	Response 1
Std	Run	A: spindle speed (Ss)	B: feed rate (Fr)	C: length of cut (Lc)	D: depth of cut (Dc)	E: helix angle (α)	Cutting force (Cf)
		rpm	mm/min	mm	mm	0	N
27	1	2500	150	30	2.5	45	74.34
6	2	2500	250	50	2.5	15	102.62
44	3	2500	250	30	1.5	15	99.62
42	4	3500	250	50	1.5	45	84.29
20	5	2500	250	30	1.5	45	88.24
37	6	2500	150	50	1.5	45	86.27
14	7	3000	200	40	2	30	89.39
12	8	3500	250	30	2.5	45	94.68
30	9	2500	150	50	2.5	45	93.58
16	10	3500	150	30	1.5	15	78.76
38	11	2500	250	50	2.5	45	94.23
1	12	3000	200	40	2	30	59.78
22	13	2500	150	30	2.5	15	68.67
10	14	3500	150	50	2.5	45	59.23
23	15	3500	150	30	2.5	15	58.52
19	16	2500	250	30	2.5	15	86.11
28	17	2500	250	50	1.5	45	67.11
24	18	3000	200	40	2	60	55.67
25	19	3000	200	40	2	30	59.29
48	20	4000	200	40	2	30	32.56
40	21	3000	200	40	2	30	59.47
13	22	3000	300	40	2	30	105.11
5	23	3500	150	50	1.5	45	98.51
26	24	3000	200	60	2	30	102.53
41	25	3000	200	40	1	30	50.24
8	26	3500	150	30	1.5	45	78.59
15	27	3500	250	30	1.5	45	91.34
2	28	3500	250	50	2.5	45	89.56
35	29	3500	150	30	2.5	45	60.57
36	30	2500	150	50	1.5	15	61.12
49	31	2500	250	50	1.5	15	68.45
21	32	3000	200	40	2	30	59.46
11	33	3500	250	50	2.5	15	85.56

(continued)

Table 10.4 (continued)

		Factor 1	Factor 2	Factor 3	Factor 4	Factor 5	Response 1
Std	Run	A: spindle speed (Ss)	B: feed rate (Fr)	C: length of cut (Lc)	D: depth of cut (Dc)	E: helix angle (α)	Cutting force (Cf)
4	34	3000	200	40	3	30	110.23
46	35	3500	150	50	1.5	15	76.86
33	36	3000	200	40	2	30	59.48
50	37	3500	150	50	2.5	15	65.12
47	38	3000	100	40	2	30	33.59
34	39	3500	250	50	1.5	15	58.58
45	40	2000	200	40	2	30	108.56
17	41	3000	200	20	2	30	59.55
29	42	3500	250	30	2.5	15	59.11
18	43	2500	150	30	1.5	45	64.15
39	44	3500	250	30	1.5	15	65.11
32	45	3000	200	40	2	0	60.23
31	46	2500	150	50	2.5	15	52.55
43	47	2500	250	30	2.5	45	63.12
7	48	3000	200	40	2	30	59.25
3	49	3000	200	40	2	30	59.25
9	50	2500	150	30	1.5	15	54.53

10.3.1 The Cutting Force Models Prediction via QRCCD

The model uses factor coding. A partial Type III sum is the square sum. The Model F-value of 4.20 suggests that the model is significant. Only 1.89% of the time could noise account for an F-value this high. When the *P*-value is less 0.0500, model terms are deemed significant. Important model terms in this case include A, B, C, D, ABE, BCD, A2B, A2D, and AB2. If the value is higher than 0.1000, model terms are not significant. If your model has a lot of extraneous terms, model reduction may improve it. When compared to the pure error at 0.05, the F-value for the lack of fit suggests that it is not significant. A "Lack of Fit F-value" this significant has an 82.22% possibility of being caused by noise, per Table 10.5. We prefer a non-significant lack of fit since we want the model to fit. Adeq Precision measures the signal-to-noise ratio. The ideal ratio is at least 4. Your ratio of 8.517 indicates a suitable signal, according to Table 10.6. Use this model to navigate the design area.

The coefficient estimate displays the anticipated change in reaction per unit change in factor value when all other factors remain constant. In an orthogonal design, the intercept is the mean response over all runs. The coefficients alter the average in the vicinity of it depending on the factor values. When the factors are orthogonal, the

Table 10.5 ANOVA analysis of the cutting force

Source	Sum of squares	df	Mean square	F-value	*p*-value	
Model	17,038.81	41	415.58	4.20	0.0189	Significant
A-spindle speed (S_s)	2888.00	1	2888.00	29.17	0.0006	
B-feed rate (F_r)	2557.56	1	2557.56	25.84	0.0009	
C-length of cut (L_c)	923.64	1	923.64	9.33	0.0157	
D-depth of cut (Dc)	1799.40	1	1799.40	18.18	0.0027	
E-helix angle (α)	10.40	1	10.40	0.1050	0.7542	
AB	120.98	1	120.98	1.22	0.3011	
AC	0.4705	1	0.4705	0.0048	0.9467	
AD	347.29	1	347.29	3.51	0.0979	
AE	161.01	1	161.01	1.63	0.2380	
BC	84.63	1	84.63	0.8549	0.3822	
BD	438.52	1	438.52	4.43	0.0684	
BE	83.53	1	83.53	0.8438	0.3852	
CD	290.89	1	290.89	2.94	0.1248	
CE	102.67	1	102.67	1.04	0.3383	
DE	61.66	1	61.66	0.6229	0.4527	
A^2	87.35	1	87.35	0.8824	0.3750	
B^2	61.08	1	61.08	0.6170	0.4548	
C^2	510.87	1	510.87	5.16	0.0528	
D^2	465.87	1	465.87	4.71	0.0619	
E^2	43.62	1	43.62	0.4406	0.5255	
ABC	13.76	1	13.76	0.1389	0.7190	
ABD	444.62	1	444.62	4.49	0.0669	
ABE	1243.01	1	1243.01	12.56	0.0076	
ACD	85.09	1	85.09	0.8595	0.3810	
ACE	274.60	1	274.60	2.77	0.1344	
ADE	29.95	1	29.95	0.3026	0.5973	
BCD	937.23	1	937.23	9.47	0.0152	
BCE	162.99	1	162.99	1.65	0.2354	
BDE	9.72	1	9.72	0.0982	0.7620	
CDE	41.45	1	41.45	0.4187	0.5357	
A^2B	1029.21	1	1029.21	10.40	0.0122	
A^2C	510.01	1	510.01	5.15	0.0529	
A^2D	1524.48	1	1524.48	15.40	0.0044	

(continued)

Table 10.5 (continued)

Source	Sum of squares	df	Mean square	F-value	*p*-value	
A^2E	209.31	1	209.31	2.11	0.1840	
AB^2	2158.55	1	2158.55	21.81	0.0016	
ABCD	189.35	1	189.35	1.91	0.2040	
ABCE	12.15	1	12.15	0.1228	0.7351	
ABDE	59.24	1	59.24	0.5984	0.4614	
ACDE	226.85	1	226.85	2.29	0.1685	
BCDE	8.57	1	8.57	0.0866	0.7761	
A^2B^2	18.84	1	18.84	0.1904	0.6742	
Residual	791.95	8	98.99			
Lack of fit	6.11	1	6.11	0.0544	0.8222	Not significant
Pure error	785.84	7	112.26			
Cor Total	17,830.76	49				

Table 10.6 Fit statistics validation of cutting force

Std. Dev	9.95	R^2	0.9556
Mean	73.05	Adjusted R^2	0.7280
C.V. %	13.62	Adeq Precision	8.5175

VIFs are 1, multi-collinearity is indicated by VIFs more than 1, and Table 10.7 demonstrates that the higher the VIF, the more severe the correlation of the components is. VIFs under 10 are generally considered tolerable.

$$\begin{aligned} \textit{Cutting force}\ (Cf) = {} & +63.17 - 38.00\text{A} + 35.76\text{B} + 21.49\text{C} \\ & + 30.00\text{D} - 2.28\text{E} - 7.78\text{AB} + 0.4850\text{AC} \\ & - 13.18\text{AD} + 8.97\text{AE} - 6.50\text{BC} + 14.81\text{BD} \\ & - 6.46\text{BE} + 12.06\text{CD} + 7.17\text{CE} - 5.55\text{DE} \\ & + 7.39A^2 + 6.18B^2 + 17.87C^2 + 17.06C^2 \\ & + 17.06D^2 - 5.22E^2 + 5.24\text{ABC} + 29.82\text{ABD} \\ & + 49.86\text{ABE} - 13.05\text{ACD} - 23.44\text{ACE} \\ & - 7.74\text{ADE} + 43.29\text{BCD} - 18.06\text{BCE} \\ & - 4.41\text{BDE} - 9.11\text{CDE} - 101.45A^2B \\ & - 71.42A^2C - 123.47A^2D + 45.75A^2E \\ & + 146.92AB^2 \end{aligned} \tag{10.14}$$

Table 10.7 ANOVA coefficients of the cutting force under TiO_2 nano-lubricant

Factor	Coefficient estimate	df	Standard error	95% CI low	95% CI high	VIF
Intercept	63.17	1	3.52	55.06	71.28	
A-spindle speed (S_s)	– 38.00	1	7.04	– 54.22	– 21.78	5.00
B-Feed rate (F_r)	35.76	1	7.04	19.54	51.98	5.00
C-length of cut (L_c)	21.49	1	7.04	5.27	37.71	5.00
D-depth of cut (D_c)	30.00	1	7.04	13.77	46.22	5.00
E-helix angle (α)	– 2.28	1	7.04	– 18.50	13.94	5.00
AB	– 7.78	1	7.04	– 24.00	8.45	1.0000
AC	0.4850	1	7.04	– 15.74	16.71	1.0000
AD	– 13.18	1	7.04	– 29.40	3.05	1.0000
AE	8.97	1	7.04	– 7.25	25.20	1.0000
BC	– 6.50	1	7.04	– 22.73	9.72	1.0000
BD	14.81	1	7.04	– 1.42	31.03	1.0000
BE	– 6.46	1	7.04	– 22.69	9.76	1.0000
CD	12.06	1	7.04	– 4.16	28.28	1.0000
CE	7.17	1	7.04	– 9.06	23.39	1.0000
DE	– 5.55	1	7.04	– 21.78	10.67	1.0000
A^2	7.39	1	7.87	– 10.75	25.53	1.25
B^2	6.18	1	7.87	– 11.96	24.32	1.25
C^2	17.87	1	7.87	– 0.2698	36.01	1.25
D^2	17.06	1	7.87	– 1.07	35.20	1.25
E^2	– 5.22	1	7.87	– 23.36	12.92	1.25
ABC	5.24	1	14.07	– 27.20	37.69	1.0000
ABD	29.82	1	14.07	– 2.63	62.27	1.0000
ABE	49.86	1	14.07	17.41	82.31	1.0000
ACD	– 13.05	1	14.07	– 45.49	19.40	1.0000
ACE	– 23.44	1	14.07	– 55.88	9.01	1.0000
ADE	– 7.74	1	14.07	– 40.19	24.71	1.0000
BCD	43.29	1	14.07	10.85	75.74	1.0000
BCE	– 18.06	1	14.07	– 50.50	14.39	1.0000
BDE	– 4.41	1	14.07	– 36.86	28.04	1.0000
CDE	– 9.11	1	14.07	– 41.55	23.34	1.0000

(continued)

Table 10.7 (continued)

Factor	Coefficient estimate	df	Standard error	95% CI low	95% CI high	VIF
A^2B	– 101.45	1	31.46	– 174.00	– 28.90	5.00
A^2C	– 71.42	1	31.46	– 143.97	1.14	5.00
A^2D	– 123.47	1	31.46	– 196.02	– 50.92	5.00
A^2E	45.75	1	31.46	– 26.80	118.30	5.00
AB^2	146.92	1	31.46	74.37	219.47	5.00
ABCD	– 38.92	1	28.14	– 103.81	25.97	1.0000
ABCE	– 9.86	1	28.14	– 74.75	55.03	1.0000
ABDE	21.77	1	28.14	– 43.12	86.66	1.0000
ACDE	– 42.60	1	28.14	– 107.49	22.29	1.0000
BCDE	– 8.28	1	28.14	– 73.17	56.61	1.0000
A^2B^2	30.69	1	70.35	– 131.54	192.93	2.25

Using the equation stated in terms of coded factors, it is possible to predict the reaction for given concentrations of each element. The high values of the factors are by default recorded as + 1 and the low levels as – 1. The coded equation is helpful for determining the elements' relative importance. By comparing the factor coefficients given in Eq. (10.14). Figure 10.6 shows the prediction analysis of the cutting force graph done with QRCCD and also, Table 10.8 present the detail analysis of the predicted, actual, residual and influence on fitted value.

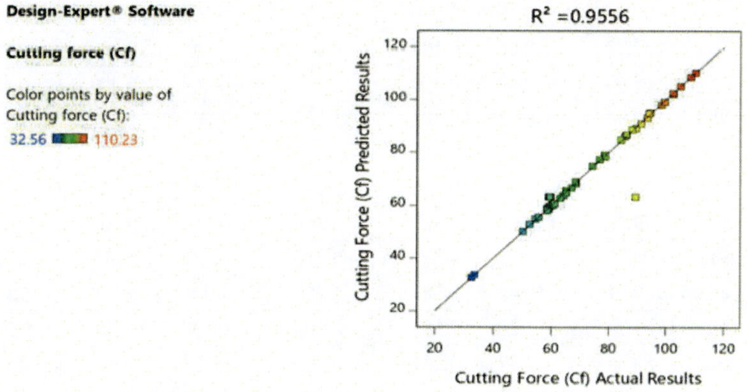

Fig. 10.6 The plot of the **Experimental data** and predicted data of cutting force

Table 10.8 The actual, predicted, internal and external residual analysis of the cutting force

Run Order	Actual value	Predicted value	Residual	Leverage	Internally studentized residuals	Externally studentized residuals	Cook's distance	Influence on fitted value DFFITS
1	74.34	75.55	– 1.21	0.581	– 0.202	– 0.198	0.002	– 0.233
2	102.62	96.83	5.79	0.581	0.973	0.971	0.049	1.144
3	99.62	100.48	– 0.8642	0.581	– 0.145	– 0.142	0.001	– 0.167
4	84.29	75.75	8.54	0.581	1.434	1.470	0.106	1.732
5	88.24	77.69	10.55	0.581	1.772	1.865	0.161	2.197
6	86.27	85.89	0.3817	0.581	0.064	0.063	0.000	0.074
7	89.39	62.13	27.26	0.100	3.122	4.022(1)	0.040	1.341
8	94.68	84.79	9.89	0.581	1.661	1.731	0.142	2.040
9	93.58	86.86	6.72	0.581	1.128	1.135	0.065	1.337
10	78.76	74.90	3.86	0.581	0.648	0.640	0.022	0.754
11	94.23	92.94	1.29	0.581	0.216	0.212	0.002	0.249
12	59.78	62.13	– 2.35	0.100	– 0.269	– 0.263	0.000	– 0.088
13	68.67	66.92	1.75	0.581	0.294	0.288	0.004	0.339
14	59.23	61.83	– 2.60	0.581	– 0.436	– 0.428	0.010	– 0.504
15	58.52	57.37	1.15	0.581	0.193	0.188	0.002	0.222
16	86.11	89.25	– 3.14	0.581	– 0.527	– 0.519	0.014	– 0.611
17	67.11	70.44	– 3.33	0.581	– 0.559	– 0.550	0.016	– 0.648
18	55.67	68.99	– 13.32	0.200	– 1.618	– 1.681	0.024	– 0.840
19	59.29	62.13	– 2.84	0.100	– 0.325	– 0.318	0.000	– 0.106
20	32.56	33.05	– 0.4875	0.900	– 0.167	– 0.164	0.009	– 0.492
21	59.47	62.13	– 2.66	0.100	– 0.304	– 0.298	0.000	– 0.099
22	105.11	105.60	– 0.4875	0.900	– 0.167	– 0.164	0.009	– 0.492
23	98.51	88.94	9.57	0.581	1.606	1.667	0.133	1.965
24	102.53	103.02	– 0.4875	0.900	– 0.167	– 0.164	0.009	– 0.492
25	50.24	50.73	– 0.4875	0.900	– 0.167	– 0.164	0.009	– 0.492
26	78.59	79.30	– 0.7095	0.581	– 0.119	– 0.117	0.001	– 0.137
27	91.34	94.26	– 2.92	0.581	– 0.490	– 0.482	0.012	– 0.568
28	89.56	100.01	– 10.45	0.581	– 1.755	– 1.844	0.158	– 2.173
29	60.57	61.77	– 1.20	0.581	– 0.202	– 0.198	0.002	– 0.233
30	61.12	58.35	2.77	0.581	0.465	0.457	0.011	0.538
31	68.45	74.32	– 5.87	0.581	– 0.986	– 0.985	0.050	– 1.161
32	59.46	62.13	– 2.67	0.100	– 0.305	– 0.299	0.000	– 0.100
33	85.56	81.70	3.86	0.581	0.648	0.640	0.022	0.754
34	110.23	110.72	– 0.4875	0.900	– 0.167	– 0.164	0.009	– 0.492

(continued)

Table 10.8 (continued)

Run Order	Actual value	Predicted value	Residual	Leverage	Internally studentized residuals	Externally studentized residuals	Cook's distance	Influence on fitted value DFFITS
35	76.86	89.09	− 12.23	0.581	− 2.054	− 2.223	0.217	− 2.619(2)
36	59.48	62.13	− 2.65	0.100	− 0.303	− 0.297	0.000	− 0.099
37	65.12	61.98	3.14	0.581	0.527	0.519	0.014	0.611
38	33.59	34.08	− 0.4875	0.900	− 0.167	− 0.164	0.009	− 0.492
39	58.58	57.43	1.15	0.581	0.193	0.188	0.002	0.222
40	108.56	109.05	− 0.4875	0.900	− 0.167	− 0.164	0.009	− 0.492
41	59.55	60.04	− 0.4875	0.900	− 0.167	− 0.164	0.009	− 0.492
42	59.11	61.92	− 2.81	0.581	− 0.472	− 0.464	0.011	− 0.546
43	64.15	64.98	− 0.8345	0.581	− 0.140	− 0.137	0.001	− 0.161
44	65.11	71.39	− 6.28	0.581	− 1.055	− 1.057	0.057	− 1.246
45	60.23	55.26	4.97	0.200	0.603	0.595	0.003	0.297
46	52.55	59.32	− 6.77	0.581	− 1.137	− 1.145	0.066	− 1.349
47	63.00	66.45	− 3.45	0.581	− 0.580	− 0.571	0.017	− 0.673
48	59.25	62.13	− 2.88	0.100	− 0.329	− 0.323	0.000	− 0.108
49	59.25	62.13	− 2.88	0.100	− 0.329	− 0.323	0.000	− 0.108
50	54.53	56.36	− 1.83	0.581	− 0.307	− 0.301	0.005	− 0.355

The superscript values 1 and 2, shows that there are wide varations between the actual and predicted value, which can because by several factors during machining

10.3.2 The Prediction of the Cutting Force Using ANN for TiO_2 Nano-lubricant

This section presents the result of the prediction of cutting force experimental results with the TiO_2 nano-lubricant during the end milling of AA8112 alloy using ANN. The Back Propagation feed-forward Neural Network (BPNN) was used to predict the experimental outcome and Levenberg–Marquardt (trainlm) to train the neuron for better performance. The BPNN employed the sigmoid non-linear transfer function (Z) and the total sum of squared error (SSE) to determine the error performance. The statistical formulation is presented in Eqs. (10.2)–(10.8). Figure 9.8 shows the neuron network used for the cutting force (that is the pattern for surface roughness prediction).

From the analysis, the R-value for the data training set, data validation, and data testing are 0.93394, 0.97481, and 0.93984, respectively. The overall performance of the training, validation, testing is 0.93751, as depicted in Fig. 10.7a–d. The solid line shows the level of performance of the regression model. While the dashed line is the perfect line of the regression, both lines help to show the relationship between the target and the predicted cutting force under TiO_2 nano-lubricant machining environment. From the ANN model, the best validation performance as measured applying the SSE occurs at epoch 0 and iteration 6, as presented in Fig. 10.7a–d. From the analysis, the SSE gradually decreased from the zero epoch to the peak point. Figure 10.8 shows the performance analysis of the ANN model for the TiO_2 nano-lubricant machining environment using SSE with the coefficient relationship (R-value) of the regression model. The R-value explains the nearness of the ANN model predicted output target (cutting force) with the experimental result obtained from the machining operation. Figure 10.9 shows the gradient constant of the Marquardt unit parameter (Mu), total validation checks, and the iterations value.

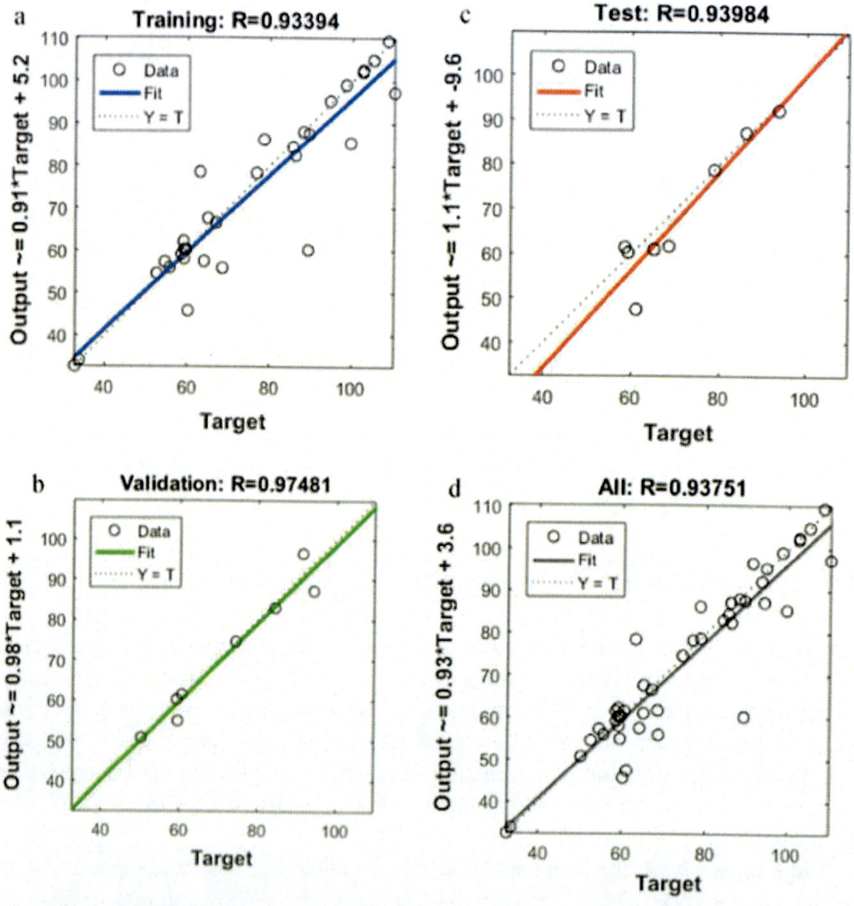

Fig. 10.7 The ANN regression plot for cutting force under TiO_2 nano-lubricant, **a** training, **b** validation analysis, **c** testing analysis and **d** all prediction

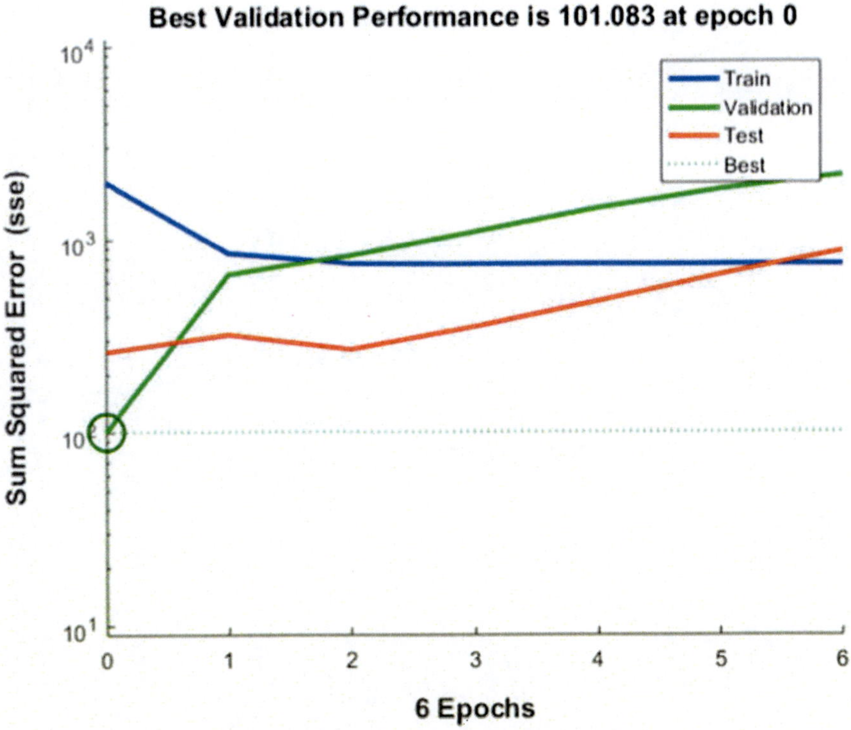

Fig. 10.8 ANN validation plot of the cutting force under the TiO_2 nano-lubricant

10.3.3 Validation and Comparison of the Predicted Result for Cutting Force from ANN and QRCCD Model

The predicted outcome from the developed models from ANN, QRCCD, and the experimental data under TiO_2 nano-lubricant machining of AA8112 alloy is shown in Fig. 10.10. Applying the percentage deviation method presented in Eq. (10.13) and the ANN and the QRCCD model predicted the cutting force experimental result with 97.5% and 89.1%, respectively. Figure 10.10 show that the ANN and QRCCD employed for the prediction of the cutting force have performed reasonably well with the standard of machining operations when compared with other related work from Chabbi et al. [15].

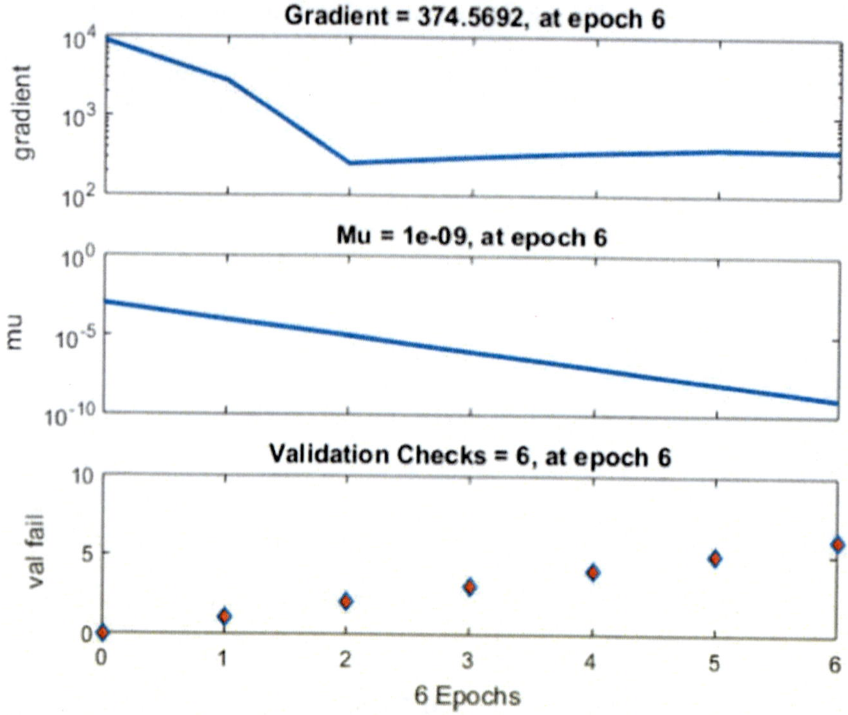

Fig. 10.9 ANN performance training state of the cutting force under the TiO_2 nano-lubricant

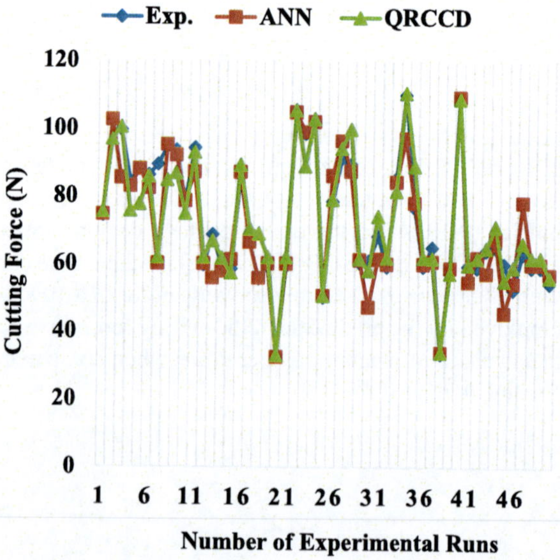

Fig. 10.10 Experimental result, predicted values of ANN, and QRCCD of the cutting force

Figures 10.11, 10.12 and 10.13 shows the factors of the cutting force objective optimization of the machining parameters obtained from the Quadratic rotatable central composite design (QRCCD). The result shows that the spindle speed of 2351 rpm, 101 mm/min feed rate, 1 mm depth of cut, 20 mm length of cut, and 60° helix angle achieved the minimum cutting force of 31 N with the desirability of 0.968. This result is closely related to the experimental data from the machining operations, this result is supported by Refs. [16, 17]. The desirability value of 0.968 shows that the prediction rate of the cutting force is satisfactory in the manufacturing industry. The ANN and QRCCD prediction of cutting force is significant when it comes to energy consumption during manufacturing via CNC. The prediction parameters is slightly different from the experimental result, this can be as a result of human error during the experimental analysis during the machining process [18–20].

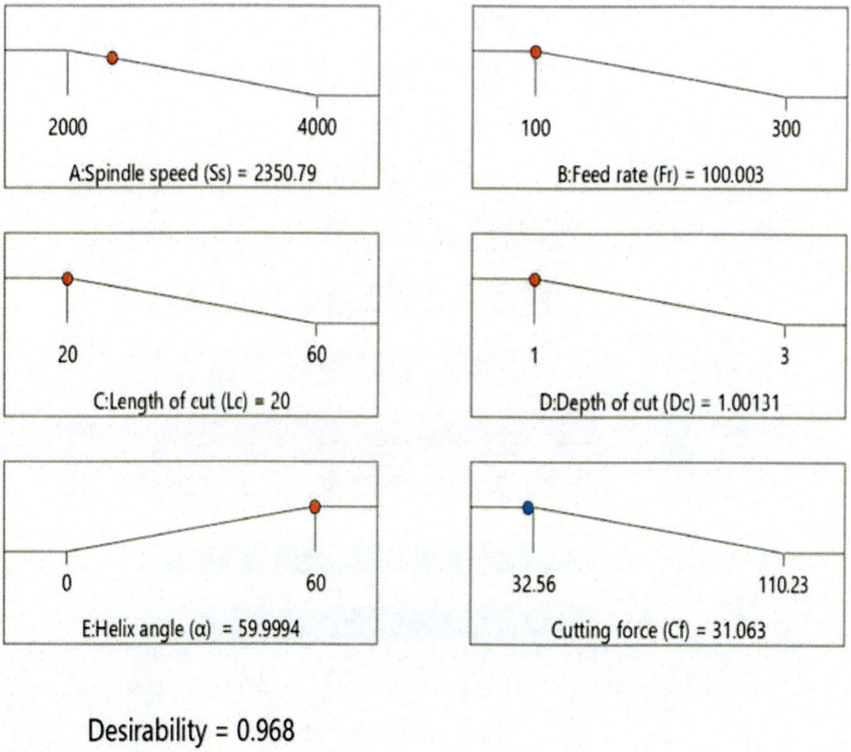

Fig. 10.11 The ramps plots for the objective five factors five levels of optimization of the cutting force

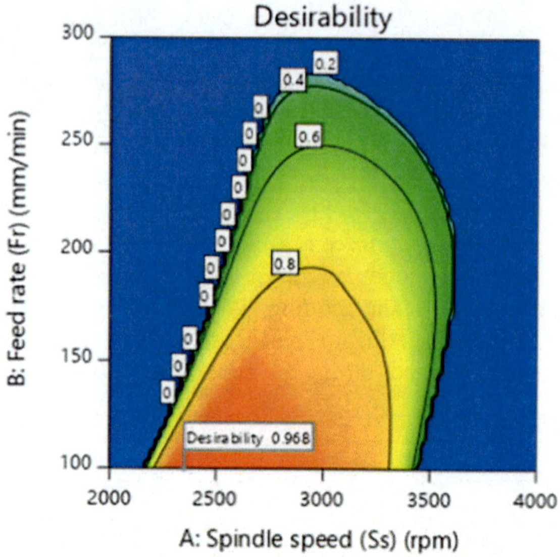

Fig. 10.12 The desirability plots for the cutting force

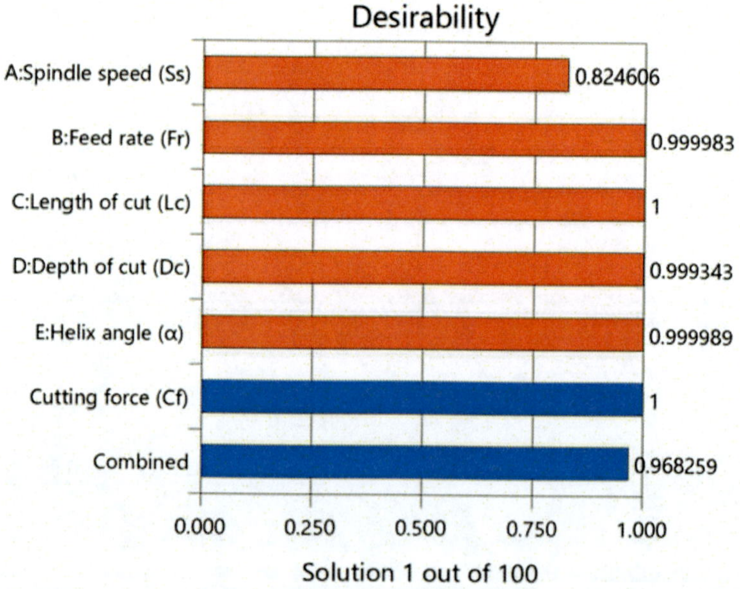

Fig. 10.13 The desirability bar plots for the multi-objective optimization parameters and the combine function for the cutting force

10.4 Parameters Interactions Study for Cutting Force

The study of the machining parameters for cutting force optimization during machining has been carried out with five (5) machining parameters such depth of cut, helix angle, feed rate, length of cut and spindle speed. Cutting force is a significant response parameter that affect the energy consumption during machining process. Therefore, to reduce the high amount of energy consumption during machining process the need to study the cutting force is needed. The major ways are to look into the parameters interaction to understand the formulation between to parameter to be able to predict the cutting force during manufacturing [21]. From Figs. 10.14, 10.15, 10.16, 10.17, 10.18, 10.19, 10.20, 10.21 and 10.22 shows the interaction study of the five machining parameters considered in this study. The most significant machining interactions parameters for the cutting force prediction and optimizations are spindle speed and length of cut as shown in Fig. 10.15. The analysis shows that the spindle speed was at 4000 rpm and the length of cut is 40 mm, why other parameters were held constant at depth of cut of 2 mm, feed rate of 200 mm/min, and helix angle of 30°, which produces a cutting force of 32.56 N. The second most interaction parameters are helix angle and length of cut. Furthermore, at the high spindle speed with a moderate length of cut, the machining process has a relatively low cutting force [22]. This has proven that the inclusion of helix angle can be implemented and still have a relatively low cutting force during machining operations, as presented in Fig. 10.17.

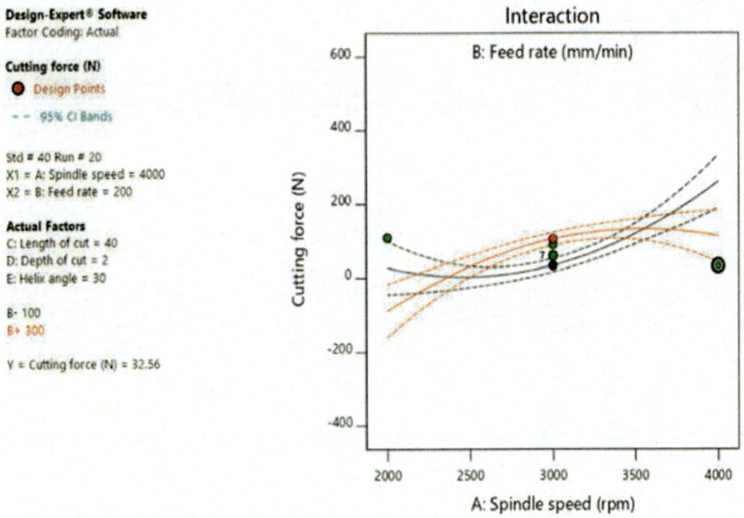

Fig. 10.14 Study of the parameters interactions between feed rate and spindle speed for cutting force optimization

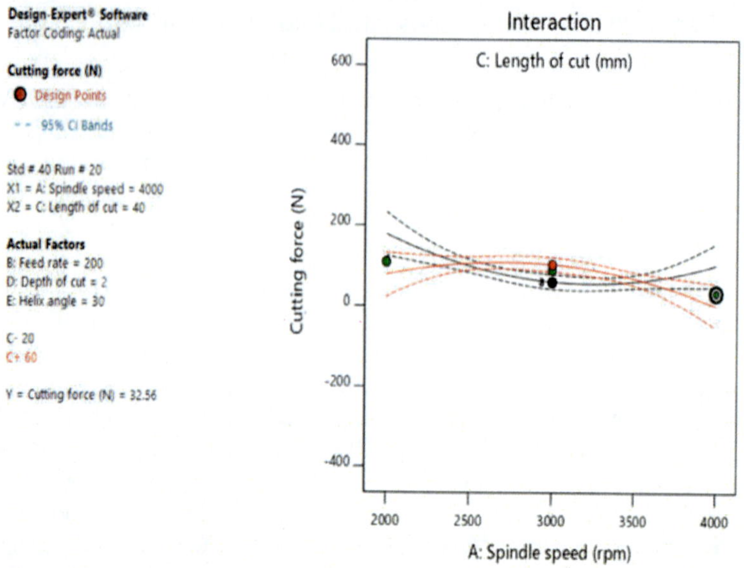

Fig. 10.15 Study of the parameters interactions between length of cut and spindle speed for cutting force optimization

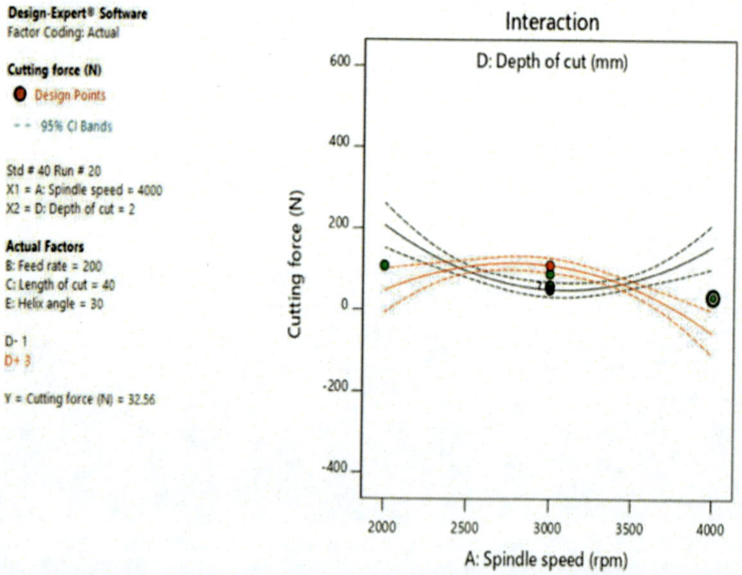

Fig. 10.16 Study of the parameters interactions between depth of cut and spindle speed for cutting force optimization

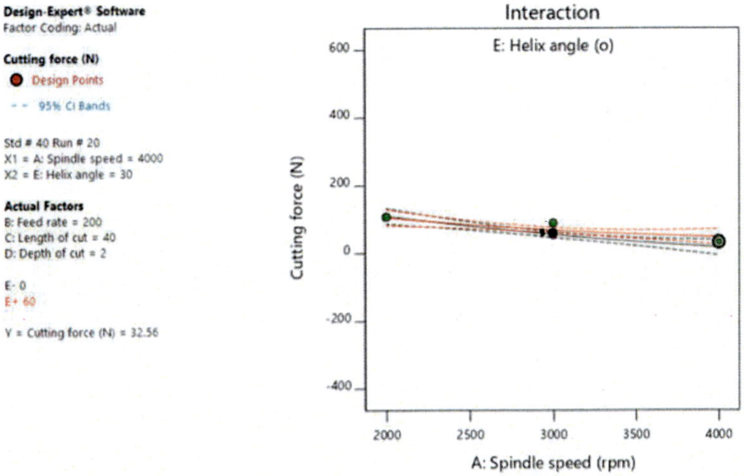

Fig. 10.17 Study of the parameter's interactions between spindle speed and helix angle for cutting force optimization

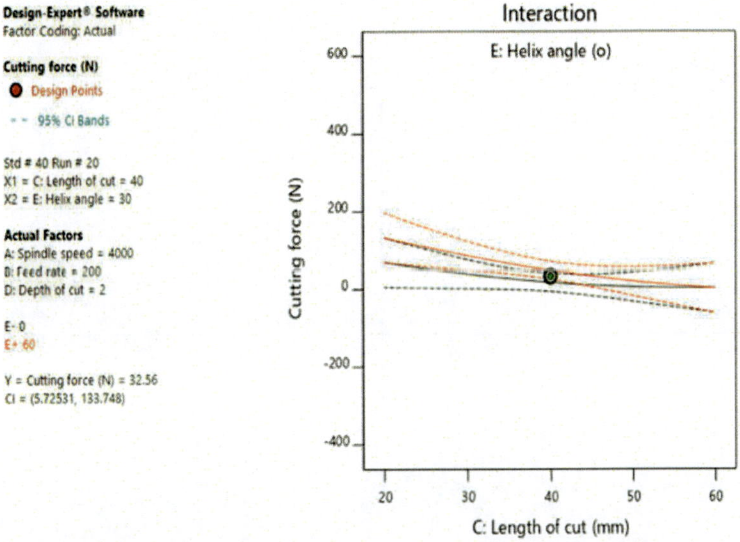

Fig. 10.18 Study of the parameter's interactions between helix angle and length of cut for cutting force optimization

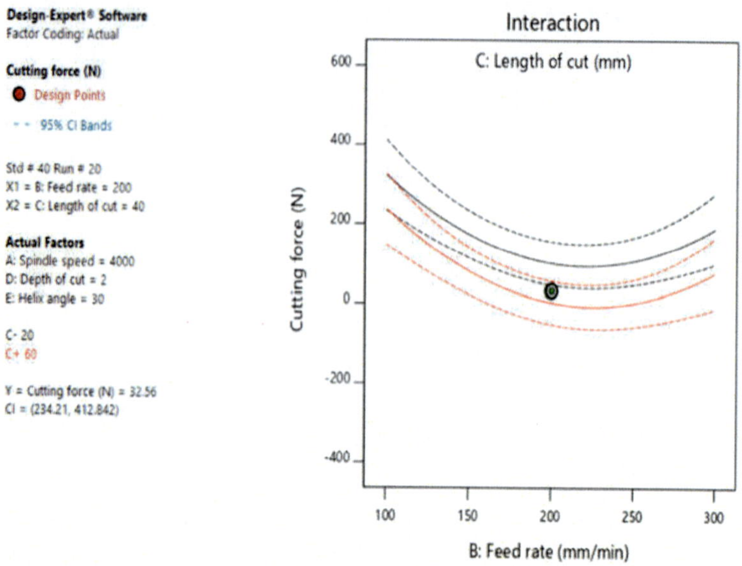

Fig. 10.19 Study of the parameters interactions between feed rate and length of cut for cutting force optimization

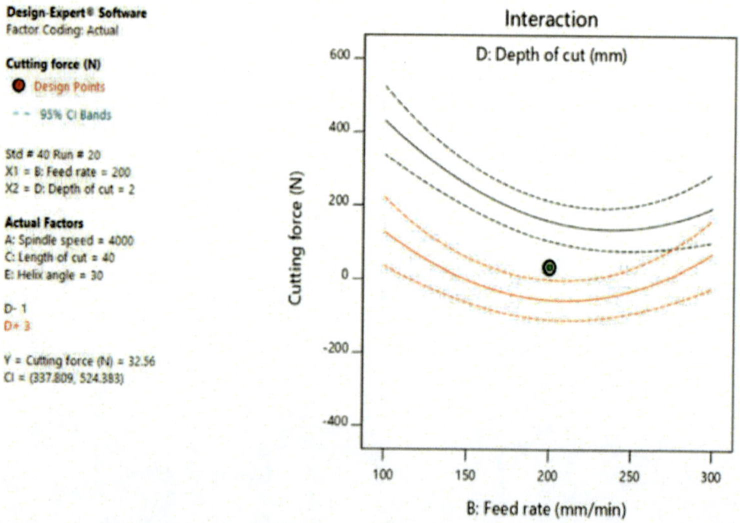

Fig. 10.20 Study of the parameters interactions between feed rate and depth of cut for cutting force optimization

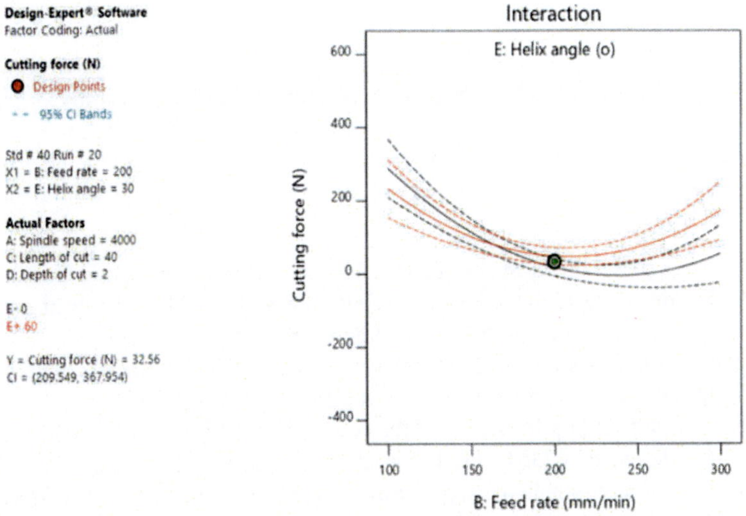

Fig. 10.21 Study of the parameters interactions between feed rate and helix angle for cutting force optimization

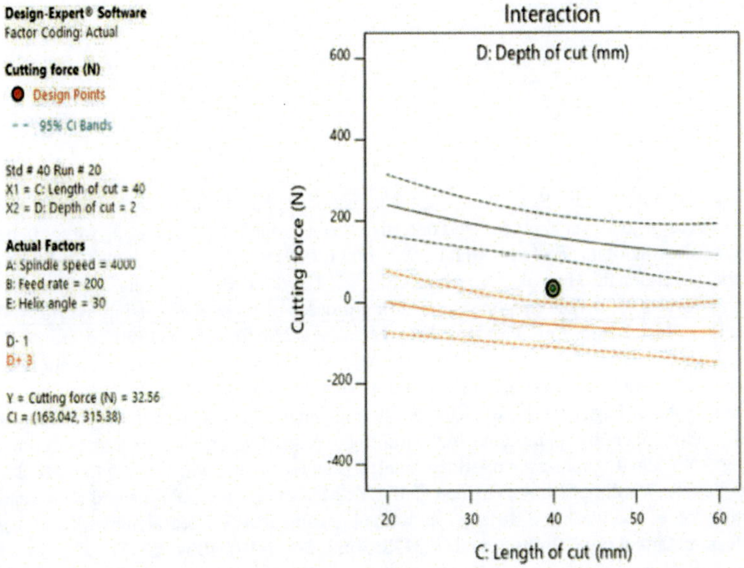

Fig. 10.22 Study of the parameters interactions between length of cut and depth of cut for cutting force optimization

10.5 Conclusion

This chapter entails the study of cutting force both in experimental study, prediction and optimization via ANN and QRCCD to achieve a sustainable machining process with less cutting force. The study employed the five machining parameters varies in five different stages such as cutting speed, helix angle, feed rate, cutting depth and length of cut.

- Spindle speed has the most significant effect on cutting force, having a percentage contribution of 16.19%, followed by feed rate with 14.34%, depth of cut with 10.09%, length of cut with 5.18%, and helix angle with 2.64%.
- The most significant interactions between the machining parameters are feed rate and depth of cut as it pertains to the cutting force analysis.
- The prediction and optimization of the cutting force at it minimum was achieved with spindle speed of 2351 rpm, 101 mm/min feed rate, 1 mm depth of cut, 20 mm length of cut, and 60° helix angle and the minimum cutting force of 31 N with the desirability of 0.968 was obtained.
- The models developed for the cutting force using ANN and QRCCD predicted the experimental results with 97.5 and 95.56% accuracy under the biodegradable TiO_2 nano-lubricant.

References

1. Yeganefar, A., Niknam, S.A., Asadi, R.: The use of support vector machine, neural network, and regression analysis to predict and optimize surface roughness and cutting forces in milling. Int. J. Adv. Manufact. Technol. **105**(1), 951–965 (2019)
2. Imani, L., Rahmani Henzaki, A., Hamzeloo, R., Davoodi, B.: Modeling and optimizing of cutting force and surface roughness in milling process of Inconel 738 using hybrid ANN and GA. Proc. Inst. Mech. Eng. Part B: J. Eng. Manufact. **234**(5), 920–932 (2020)
3. Wang, J., Zou, B., Liu, M., Li, Y., Ding, H., Xue, K.: Milling force prediction model based on transfer learning and neural network. J. Intell. Manuf. **32**(4), 947–956 (2021)
4. Daniel, S.A.A., Pugazhenthi, R., Kumar, R., Vijayananth, S.: Multi objective prediction and optimization of control parameters in the milling of aluminium hybrid metal matrix composites using ANN and Taguchi-grey relational analysis. Defence Technol. **15**(4), 545–556 (2019)
5. Kilickap, E., Yardimeden, A., Hışman Çelik, Y.: Mathematical modelling and optimization of cutting force, tool wear and surface roughness by using artificial neural network and response surface methodology in milling of Ti-6242S. Appl. Sci. **7**(10), 1064 (2017)
6. Agu, C.K., Lawal, S.A., Abolarin, M.S., Agboola, J.B., Abutu, J., Awode, E.I.: Multi-response optimisation of machining parameters in turning AISI 304L using different oil-based cutting fluids. Niger. J. Technol. **38**(2), 364–375 (2019)
7. Okokpujie, I.P., Tartibu, L.K., Sinebe, J.E., Adeoye, A.O., Akinlabi, E.T.: Comparative study of rheological effects of vegetable oil-lubricant, TiO_2, MWCNTs nano-lubricants, and machining parameters' influence on cutting force for sustainable metal cutting process. Lubricants **10**(4), 54 (2022)
8. Vardhaman, A., Amarnath, M., Jhodkar, D., Ramkumar, J., Chelladurai, H., Roy, M.K.: Influence of coconut oil on tribological behavior of carbide cutting tool insert during turning operation. J. Braz. Soc. Mech. Sci. Eng. **40**(9), 1–23 (2018)

9. Pandiselvam, R., Manikantan, M.R., Kothakota, A., Rajesh, G.K., Beegum, S., Ramesh, S.V., Niral, V., Hebbar, K.B.: Engineering properties of five varieties of coconuts (Cocos nucifera L.) for efficient husk separation. J. Nat. Fibers (2018)
10. Baranitharan, P., Ramesh, K., Sakthivel, R.: Measurement of performance and emission distinctiveness of Aegle marmelos seed cake pyrolysis oil/diesel/TBHQ opus powered in a DI diesel engine using ANN and RSM. Measurement **144**, 366–380 (2019)
11. Meena, S.L., Butola, R., Khan, M.A., Walia, R.S., Murtaza, Q.: Influence of process parameters in synergic MIG welding of 304L stainless steel using response surface methodology. Adv. Mater. Process. Technol. 1–10 (2022)
12. Paturi, U.M.R., Devarasetti, H., Narala, S.K.R.: Application of regression and artificial neural network analysis in modelling of surface roughness in hard turning of AISI 52100 steel. Mater. Today: Proc. **5**(2), 4766–4777 (2018)
13. Okokpujie, I.P., Bolu, C.A., Ohunakin, O.S.: Comparative performance evaluation of TiO_2, and MWCNTs nano-lubricant effects on surface roughness of AA8112 alloy during end-milling machining for sustainable manufacturing process. Int. J. Adv. Manufact. Technol. **108**(5), 1473–1497 (2020)
14. Sizemore, N.E., Nogueira, M.L., Greis, N.P., Davies, M.A.: Application of machine learning to the prediction of surface roughness in diamond machining. Procedia Manufact. **48**, 1029–1040 (2020)
15. Chabbi, A., Yallese, M.A., Meddour, I., Nouioua, M., Mabrouki, T., Girardin, F.: Predictive modeling and multi-response optimization of technological parameters in turning of Polyoxymethylene polymer (POM C) using RSM and desirability function. Measurement **95**, 99–115 (2017)
16. Lalwani, V., Sharma, P., Pruncu, C.I., Unune, D.R.: Response surface methodology and artificial neural network-based models for predicting performance of wire electrical discharge machining of inconel 718 alloy. J. Manufact. Mater. Process. **4**(2), 44 (2020)
17. Okokpujie, I.P., Tartibu, L.K.: Experimental analysis of cutting force during machining difficult to cut materials under dry, mineral oil, and TiO_2 nano-lubricant. J. Meas. Eng. **9**(4), 218–230 (2021)
18. Rodić, D., Sekulić, M., Gostimirović, M., Pucovsky, V., Kramar, D.: Fuzzy logic and subclustering approaches to predict main cutting force in high-pressure jet assisted turning. J. Intell. Manuf. **32**(1), 21–36 (2021)
19. Okokpujie, I.P., Ikumapayi, O.M., Okonkwo, U.C., Salawu, E.Y., Afolalu, S.A., Dirisu, J.O., Nwoke, O.N., Ajayi, O.O.: Experimental and mathematical modeling for prediction of tool wear on the machining of aluminium 6061 alloy by high speed steel tools. Open Eng. **7**(1), 461–469 (2017)
20. Slamani, M., Chatelain, J.F.: Kriging versus Bezier and regression methods for modeling and prediction of cutting force and surface roughness during high speed edge trimming of carbon fiber reinforced polymers. Measurement **152**, 107370 (2020)
21. Wu, D., Liu, H., Wang, C., Xu, X., Liu, X., Wang, Q.: The interaction effect of particle composition and matric suction on the shear strength parameters of unsaturated granite residual soil. Arab. J. Sci. Eng. **47**(10), 12453–12467 (2022)
22. Jiang, S., Buck, D., Tang, Q., Guan, J., Wu, Z., Guo, X., Zhu, Z., Wang, X.: Cutting force and surface roughness during straight-tooth milling of Walnut wood. Forests **13**(12), 2126 (2022)

Chapter 11
Material Removal Rate Optimization Under ANN and QRCCD

Abstract Numerical analysis is a significant aspect of the manufacturing process. This process is used to study the performance of lubricants and cutting parameters during machining operations. Material removal rate (MRR) is an important factor to consider to enhance the machining and production processes of manufacturing components. Using an artificial neural network (ANN) and a quadratic rotatable central composite design (QRCCD), this study focuses on the numerical analysis of the copra oil-based TiO_2 nano-lubricant performance with the machining parameters on the material removal rate during the end-milling machining operation. This study considered five machining parameters that are the control factors, such as spindle speed, feed rate, length-of-cut, cutting depth, and helix angle, on the response known as MRR under end-milling of AA8112 alloy. The measured experimental result from the end-milling machining operation is used to develop a model for the MRR to predict the performance of the nano-lubricant with the machining parameters. The ANN model developed could predict the surface roughness with 99.85% accuracy and the MRR with 98.7%. The results also show that increasing the spindle speed reduced surface roughness, which increased the material removal rate slightly during the machining process.

Keywords Material removal rate · Nano-lubricant · Copra oil · Artificial neural network · QRCCD

11.1 Introduction

An artificial neural network is a nonlinear computational based model that comprises artificial neurons derived from brain cells. This neuron can learn to execute tasks such as classification, visualization, decision making, and prediction [1]. It is a novel method used in building scientific models to predict and improve engineering systems [2]. Using ANN and the full factorial design of the experiment, Asiltürk and Unkaş [3] created an experimental model to predict the turning operation of AISI 1040 steel. The three factors applied as input data are: cutting velocity, machining rate,

I. P. Okokpujie and L. K. Tartibu, *Modern Optimization Techniques for Advanced Machining*, Studies in Systems, Decision and Control 485,
https://doi.org/10.1007/978-3-031-35455-7_11

and width of cut, with a response known as surface finishing. The result showed that the ANN back-propagation training algorithms used to train the system could predict the experimental outcome with 98.9% certainty. From the analysis, the feed rate has more influence on cutting when compared to the other factors. A quadratic rotatable central composite design from RSM is an essential tool used to study the effect of various parameters in machining operations. This process aids in the optimization and forecasting of the response function for optimal performance of the end milling system. Prajina [4] concentrated on a superficial level of completion and material removal rate (MRR) in processing machining utilizing second-request quadratic models. The model that was created was used to advance the machining boundaries. Also, Okokpujie and Okonkwo [5] created a model using RSM. The result shows that the RSM predicted the experimental date with 96% accuracy. Reddy et al. [6] applied RSM in their exploration to evaluate the exhibition of the machining boundaries on surface completion in the processing activities of pre-solidified steel (P20). In the examination, the RSM and the hereditary technique utilized achieved the ideal machining factor values to convey superb surface completion.

Cutting fluid and machining parameter characteristics are the essential aspect of machining operation that either strengthen the mechanical component or cause it to fail during the process [7–9]. According to Joshua et al. [10], there is a need to develop and optimize a biodegradable cutting fluid for the machining process, to enable the manufacturers to produce quality mechanical components with a good quality machined surface. This biodegradable cutting fluid will assist in reducing the energy consumption, wear rate, and corrosion on the cutting tool and the workpiece material during operation. Saini et al. [11] in their review work, recommended the use of corrosion-free cutting fluid in machining operations. Phuoc et al. [12] studied the viscosity and thermal conductivity of nano-lubricant, and the result shows that nanoparticles have good thermal conductivity. The authors concluded and recommended that nano-lubricants should be efficiently-utilised in machining operation. Pervaiz et al. [13] affirm that cutting fluid is one of the parameters that can lead to good quality machining.

Sani et al. [14] concluded that the thermo-mechanical loads in machining operations have significant effects on the surface finish of the material and the cutting tool. The result proved that the thermo-mechanical load leads to high surface roughness and breakage of the cutting tool during the machining. The authors also recommended that the use of vegetable oil is highly needed. This is due to the significant effects vegetable oil have on the microstructural characteristics of the metals after machining. Furthermore, when vegetable oil is disposed of, it is eco-friendly without causing any environmental pollutions. The authors carried out an experimental study on Jatropha-based cutting fluid and the synthetic Esther-based MQL machining fluid. The result shows that this vegetable oil-based machining fluid performs excellently in reducing friction between the cutting tool and the working materials during operations. Finally, the authors also recommended that the additions of nanoparticles in the base vegetable oil should be utilised to improve the thermal resistance of the vegetable oil in machining operations. According to Okonkwo et al. [15], the study of machining parameters in end milling, turning, and grinding cannot be overemphasized. These machining parameters, if not adequately studied before any experimental analysis, can lead to vibrations and friction that can damage the workpiece. Nwoke et al. [16] carried out a study on vibration analysis and discovered that the machining parameters have much influence on CNC machining. Onoroh et al. [17] studied the effects of machining parameters on the cutting tool. From the conclusion of the study, the authors stated that machining parameters could easily damage or reduce the tool life during the machining process. The authors also recommended that subsequent machining operations should involve an eco-friendly lubricant to minimize the vibration occurrences during machining.

Davoudinejad et al. [18] developed a mathematical model to predict the performance of the machining parameters in end-milling machining with the finite element method. In the experiment, three machining parameters with three-levels were considered to study the surface roughness of the material. The authors discovered that there are lots of machining parameters that lead to low performance in manufacturing mechanical components using computerized numerical control (CNC) machines. Furthermore, they recommended that more research work on machining parameters should be looked into to study the influential parameters. Masmiati et al. [19] worked on the optimization of machining parameters during end-milling machining. The study confirmed that for proper optimization to be done, there is a need for mathematical models to be developed.

However, this Chap. 12 has address this and as created a sustainable optimization. Several studies have been done to predict material removal rate, but the implementation of Heuristic and Metaheuristic Techniques for Advanced Nano-lubricant Machining Optimization for material removal rate has not been done. The novelty of this chapter is the prediction and optimization of material removal rate with five machining factors during machining operations via ANN and QRCCD.

11.2 Materials and Method

The study of the material removal rate (MRR) was carried out via SIEG 3/10/0016 CNC machine with high-speed steel-cutting-tool inserts. The workpiece was dimensions in different lengths of the cut with the specification to machining with other machining parameters as shown in Tables 11.1 and 11.2. Chapter 10 of this book in Sect. 10.2 entails the workpiece chemical composite and also the cutting tool. In this machining operation, TiO_2 copra-based nano-lubricant was employed as a sustainable lubrication process for this Chap. 12. Figure 11.1 shows the experimental set-up for the MRR study, the cutting speed, the helix angles, cutting depth, cutting length, and feed rate were varying during the machining process via the design template from the quadratic rotatable center composite design to enable the study to carry out prediction and optimization of the machining factors on the MRR. Figure 11.2

illustrate the procedure employed for the development of the TiO_2 copra-based nano-lubricant employed to study the MRR for sustainable removal of chips at the cutting region during the machining of aluminium alloys. Also, Fig. 11.3 shows the QRCCD method employed to carry out the optimization and prediction for this study.

Table 11.1 Details of materials, factors and responses parameters used for the experiment

Exp. runs	Workpiece	Machining tool	Variable parameters	Response parameters	Lubricant
1 to 50	AL 8112 alloy	Coated high-speed steel	Spindle speed	Material removal rate	TiO_2
			Feed rate		
			Length of cut		
			Depth of cut		
			Helix angle		

Table 11.2 Machining conditions for the study MRR

Name	Units	Low	High	− α	+ α
Spindle speed	rpm	2000	4000	621.586	5378.41
Feed rate	mm/min	100	300	− 37.8414	437.841
Length of cut	mm	20	60	− 7.56828	87.5683
Depth of cut	mm	1	3	− 0.378414	4.37841
Helix angle	o	0	60	− 41.3524	101.352

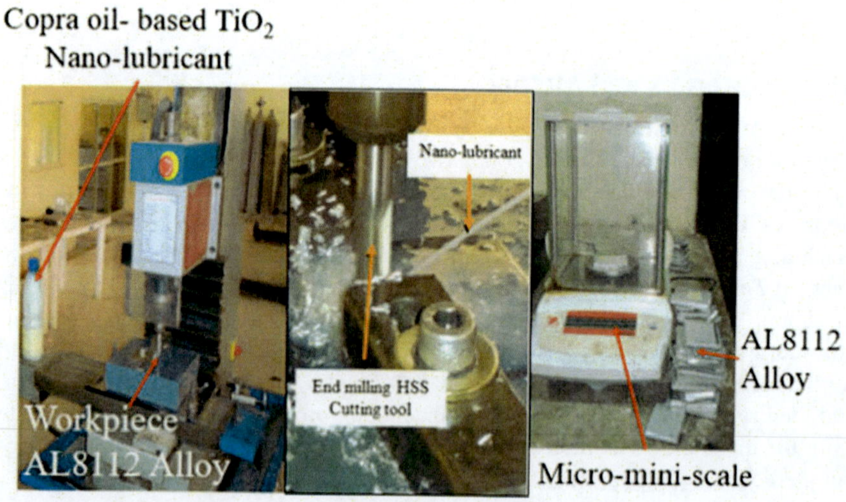

Fig. 11.1 Experimental set-up for the MRR

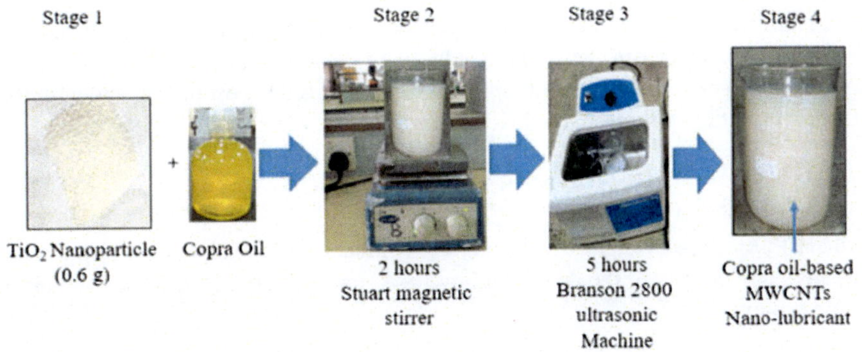

Fig. 11.2 Experimental set-up for the preparation of the nano-lubricant used for the study

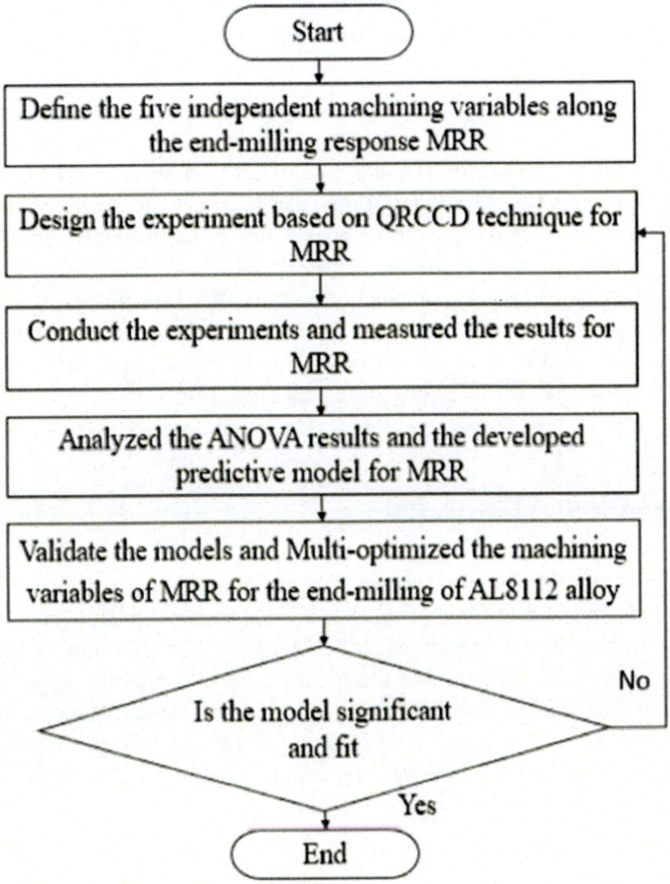

Fig. 11.3 The experimental flow chart design

A mini normal scaling machine was utilized to gauge every one of the cut examples when the end processing machining activity, to decide the first and the last weight of the workpiece. During machining, the machining time is estimated, and with the thickness of the workpiece, the MRR is figured utilizing Eq. (11.1) [19].

$$\mathrm{MRR} = (\mathrm{P}_1 - \mathrm{P}_2)/\rho * \mathrm{t} \tag{11.1}$$

where P_1 = initial weight (in grams), P_2 = final weight of the AL8112 alloy (in grams), ρ = density of the AL8112 alloy workpiece (in g/mm^3), and t = machining time (minutes).

11.2.1 *Artificial Neural Network (ANN) and Quadratic Rotatable Central Composite Design (QRCCD)*

ANN is a simple workstation that receives one or more input variables and process them to produce corrected output. These neurons are a group of data for information processing using connected links; every neuron has an associated load bases on the strength of the input variables that will be used to determine the output responses. The mathematical expression are presented in Chap. 10 of this book from Eqs. (10.1) to (10.7).

Quadratic rotatable central composite design (QRCCD) employed for the MRR is given in Eqs. (10.8)–(10.12). The study used it for the experimental design and also for the prediction analysis of the MRR due to its important in the prediction and optimization system in manufacturing industry (Fig. 11.4).

11.3 Results and Discussion

The investigate of material removal rate was carried out with five factors; five levels experiment during end milling of AL-8112 alloy under the TiO_2 nano-lubricant machining environment is presented in Table 11.3. Fifty (50) runs of the experiment were carried out according to the quartic rotatable central composite design (QRCCD) for five factors, five levels of machining parameters. The need to predict and optimized machining parameters in terms of MRR is significant because the rate at which the unwanted materials is removed determined the performance of the production of the mechanical components [20, 21].

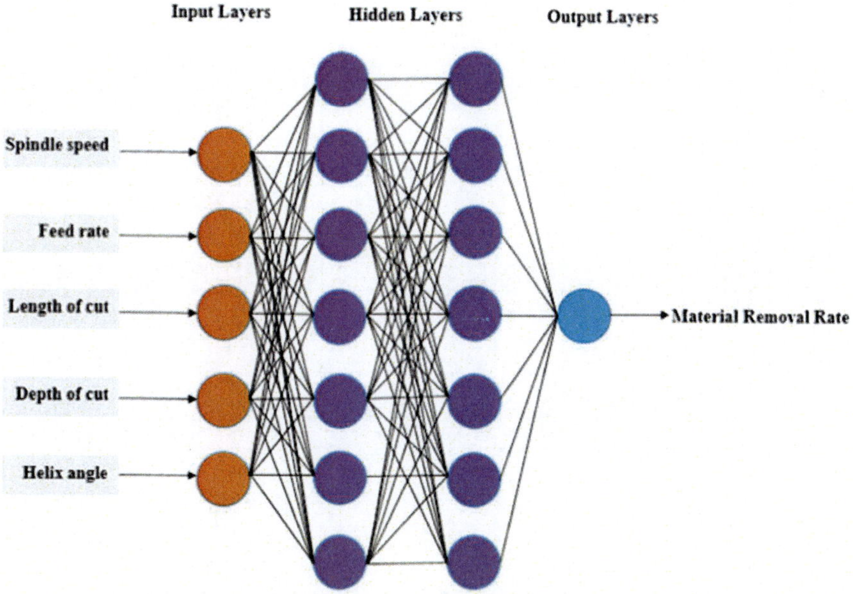

Fig. 11.4 The ANN mathematical structure employed for the prediction of the material removal rate (MRR)

11.3.1 The Models and Prediction Analysis for MRR Using QRCCD

The experimental result obtained from the study of MRR during the end-milling of AL8112 alloy under TiO_2-nano-lubricants was employed to develop a mathematical model to predict and ascertain the accuracy of the experiments. The experimental results were made up of 50 experimental runs, which is according to the quadratic rotatable central composite design (QRCCD) for five factors-five levels of machining parameters. This section explains the generated of the QRCCD model, and the significance of the individual machining parameters involve in studying the MRR in the end-milling of AL8112 alloy under the TiO_2 nano-lubricant machining environment. From the response surface methodology carried out for the MRR using QRCCD, the model developed was significant, having an F-value of 19.36, which implies that the change of noise (experimental error) occurrence is 0.01%. The significant parameters are determined using the P-value. Parameter having a P-value less than 0.05 shows that the parameter in the model is significant, why the parameters higher than 0.1 are not significant in the model. Furthermore, the significant parameters for the TiO_2 nano-lubricant machining environment are F, L, D, Sα, FD, as present in Table 11.4. The F-value of the lack of fit is 1.80 indicate that the lack of fit is not significant when compared with the error value.

Table 11.3 Material removal rate experimental results

Run	Spindle speed (rpm)	Feed rate (mm/min)	Length of cut (mm)	Depth of cut mm)	Helix angle (α) (°)	Time of cut TiO_2 (min)	Total weight (g)	Density g/ mm^3	TiO_2 MRR mm^3/ min
1	2500	150	30	2.5	45	0.33	2.56	0.275	27.98
2	2500	250	50	2.5	15	0.3	4.33	0.275	52.42
3	2500	250	30	1.5	15	0.2	1.43	0.275	25.96
4	3500	250	50	1.5	45	0.28	2.57	0.275	32.97
5	2500	250	30	1.5	45	0.18	1.54	0.275	30.68
6	2500	150	50	1.5	45	0.45	2.52	0.275	20.39
7	3000	200	40	2	30	0.3	3.25	0.275	39.36
8	3500	250	30	2.5	45	0.2	2.56	0.275	46.63
9	2500	150	50	2.5	45	0.47	4.32	0.275	33.6
10	3500	150	30	1.5	15	0.33	1.5	0.275	16.42
11	2500	250	50	2.5	45	0.3	4.24	0.275	51.41
12	3000	200	40	2	30	0.3	3.25	0.275	39.36
13	2500	150	30	2.5	15	0.35	2.5	0.275	26.01
14	3500	150	50	2.5	45	0.45	4.27	0.275	34.48
15	3500	150	30	2.5	15	0.35	2.96	0.275	30.74
16	2500	250	30	2.5	15	0.2	2.54	0.275	46.15
17	2500	250	50	1.5	45	0.27	2.6	0.275	35.41
18	3000	200	40	2	60	0.28	3.25	0.275	41.67
19	3000	200	40	2	30	0.3	3.25	0.275	39.36
20	4000	200	40	2	30	0.32	2.74	0.275	31.41
21	3000	200	40	2	30	0.3	3.25	0.275	39.36

(continued)

Table 11.3 (continued)

Run	Spindle speed (rpm)	Feed rate (mm/min)	Length of cut (mm)	Depth of cut mm)	Helix angle (α) (°)	Time of cut TiO_2 (min)	Total weight (g)	Density g/ mm^3	TiO_2 MRR mm^3/min
22	3000	300	40	2	30	0.22	2.87	0.275	48.18
23	3500	150	50	1.5	45	0.47	2.6	0.275	20.22
24	3000	200	60	2	30	0.42	4.13	0.275	36.06
25	3000	200	40	1	30	0.32	1.33	0.275	15.28
26	3500	150	30	1.5	45	0.33	1.5	0.275	16.38
27	3500	250	30	1.5	45	0.22	1.48	0.275	24.95
28	3500	250	50	2.5	45	0.3	4.21	0.275	51
29	3500	150	30	2.5	45	0.33	2.52	0.275	27.48
30	2500	150	50	1.5	15	0.45	2.54	0.275	20.56
31	2500	250	50	1.5	15	0.28	2.55	0.275	32.68
32	3000	200	40	2	30	0.3	2.71	0.275	32.82
33	3500	250	50	2.5	15	0.28	4.25	0.275	54.54
34	3000	200	40	3	30	0.32	4.29	0.275	49.19
35	3500	150	50	1.5	15	0.45	2.67	0.275	21.6
36	3000	200	40	2	30	0.3	2.79	0.275	33.79
37	3500	150	50	2.5	15	0.48	4.2	0.275	31.59
38	3000	100	40	2	30	0.6	2.81	0.275	17.05
39	3500	250	50	1.5	15	0.2	2.52	0.275	45.89
40	2000	200	40	2	30	0.32	2.81	0.275	32.27
41	3000	200	20	2	30	0.22	1.42	0.275	23.79
42	3500	250	30	2.5	15	0.17	1.72	0.275	37.62

(continued)

Table 11.3 (continued)

Run	Spindle speed (rpm)	Feed rate (mm/min)	Length of cut (mm)	Depth of cut mm)	Helix angle (α) (°)	Time of cut TiO_2 (min)	Total weight (g)	Density g/ mm^3	TiO_2 MRR mm^3/ min
43	2500	150	30	1.5	45	0.33	2.99	0.275	32.57
44	3500	250	30	1.5	15	0.2	1.86	0.275	33.89
45	3000	200	40	2	0	0.28	2.64	0.275	33.93
46	2500	150	50	2.5	15	0.43	3.64	0.275	30.56
47	2500	250	30	2.5	45	0.2	3	0.275	54.57
48	3000	200	40	2	30	0.28	2.59	0.275	33.31
49	3000	200	40	2	30	0.28	2.61	0.275	33.54
50	2500	150	30	1.5	15	0.33	1.73	0.275	18.94

Table 11.4 ANOVA analysis of the MRR

Source	Sum of squares	Df	Mean square	F-value	*p*-value	%C	
Model	4913.88	1	327.59	19.36	< 0.0001	89.52	Significant
S-(Spindle speed)	5.78	15	5.78	0.3418	0.5627	0.11	
F-(Feed rate)	2394.91	1	2394.91	141.52	< 0.0001	43.63	
L-(Length of cut)	234.69	1	234.69	13.87	0.0007	4.28	
D-(Depth of cut)	1891.86	1	1891.86	111.8	< 0.0001	34.46	
α-(Helix angle)	23.45	1	23.45	1.39	0.2473	0.43	
SF	3.07	1	3.07	0.1814	0.6729	0.06	
SL	60.53	1	60.53	3.58	0.0671	1.1	
SD	0.4395	1	0.4395	0.026	0.8729	0.01	
Sα	82.92	1	82.92	4.9	0.0337	1.51	
FL	48.49	1	48.49	2.87	0.0997	0.88	
FD	99.93	1	99.93	5.91	0.0205	1.82	
Fα	10.36	1	10.36	0.6124	0.4393	0.189	
LD	4.88	1	4.88	0.2881	0.5949	0.09	
Lα	40.21	1	40.21	2.38	0.1325	0.73	
Dα	12.36	1	12.36	0.7306	0.3987	0.23	
Residual	575.36	34	16.92			10.48	
Lack of fit	502.97	27	18.63	1.8	0.215	9.16	Not significant
Pure error	72.39	7	10.34			1.32	
Cor. total	5489.25	49				100	

Table 11.5 shows the adequate precision value of 16.909 measured during this analysis. With the value of 16.909, the adequate precision is satisfactory, which implies that the signal to noise ratio has a good relationship, and the model can be employed to predict the design space. Table 11.6 shows the ANOVA coefficient estimation, which is a significant aspect of the analysis that represents the expected transformation in the MRR per unit alteration of each machining factor value when other factor's values are kept constant. The intercept of the orthogonal plan is the whole MRR experimental runs. The coefficients are to adjust the machining factors settings. The variance inflation factors (VIFs) value is to determine the existence between the predictor model and the variable parameter factors used for the prediction.

Table 11.5 Statistical validation of the MRR

Standard deviation	4.11	$\mathbf{R^2}$	0.8952
Mean	33.72	**Adjusted** $\mathbf{R^2}$	0.8489
Coefficient of variation (C.V.)%	12.20	**Adequate precision**	16.9085

Table 11.6 ANOVA coefficients analysis of the MRR

Factor	Coefficient estimate	df	Standard error	95% CI low	95% CI high	VIF
Intercept	33.72	1	0.5818	32.54	34.90	
S-(Spindle speed)	– 0.7605	1	1.30	– 3.40	1.88	1.0000
F-(Feed rate)	15.48	1	1.30	12.83	18.12	1.0000
L-(Length of cut)	4.84	1	1.30	2.20	7.49	1.0000
D-(Depth of cut)	13.75	1	1.30	11.11	16.40	1.0000
α-(Helix angle)	1.53	1	1.30	– 1.11	4.18	1.0000
SF	1.24	1	2.91	– 4.67	7.15	1.0000
SL	5.50	1	2.91	– 0.4102	11.41	1.0000
SD	– 0.4687	1	2.91	– 6.38	5.44	1.0000
Sα	– 6.44	1	2.91	– 12.35	– 0.5273	1.0000
FL	4.92	1	2.91	– 0.9877	10.84	1.0000
FD	7.07	1	2.91	1.16	12.98	1.0000
Fα	– 2.28	1	2.91	– 8.19	3.64	1.0000
LD	1.56	1	2.91	– 4.35	7.47	1.0000
Lα	– 4.48	1	2.91	– 10.40	1.43	1.0000
Dα	2.49	1	2.91	– 3.43	8.40	1.0000

The VIFs value of one (1) means the factors are orthogonal, and the VIFs values greater than one (1) implies the factors are multi-collinearity [22]. The greater the VIFs, the higher the multi-collinearity of the connection of the factors. The model developed for the MRR analysis under the TiO_2 nano-lubricant machining environment from the quartic rotatable central composite design (QRCCD) of the experiment is presented in two forms the coded and actual form. Equation (11.2) gives the model in the coded form for the MRR.

$$\begin{aligned} \mathrm{MRR}_{\mathrm{coded}} = {} & +33.72 - 0.7605\mathrm{S}_c + 15.48\mathrm{F}_c + 4.84\mathrm{L}_c + 13.75\mathrm{D}_c + 1.53\alpha_c \\ & + 1.24\mathrm{SF}_c + 5.50\mathrm{SL}_c - 0.4687\mathrm{SD}_c - 6.44\mathrm{S}\alpha_c + 4.92\mathrm{FL}_c \\ & + 7.07\mathrm{FD}_c - 2.28\mathrm{F}\alpha_c + 1.56\mathrm{LD}_c - 4.48\mathrm{L}\alpha_c + 2.49\mathrm{D}\alpha_c \end{aligned} \quad (11.2)$$

The Eq. (11.2) is the model in the state of coded form for proper identification of the comparative effect of the machining factors or parameters when comparing the coefficients.

The model, in terms of the actual factors, is presented in Eq. (11.3).

$$\begin{aligned}MRR_{actual} = {} & +30.30 - 0.007S - 0.099F - 1.007L - 4.586D + 0.979\alpha \\ & + 0.00001SF + 0.0003SL - 0.0005SD - 0.0002S\alpha \\ & + 0.0025FL + 0.071FD - 0.0008F\alpha + 0.078063LD \\ & - 0.0075L\alpha - 0.0075L\alpha + 0.083D\alpha \end{aligned} \quad (11.3)$$

Therefore, the final model for prediction of the MRR for TiO_2 nano-lubricant end milling of AA8112 alloy machining environment given in Eq. (11.3), was used to predict the MRR under the TiO_2 nano-lubricant environment, and Fig. 11.5 shows the prediction plot and Table 11.7 present the prediction results, residual, leverage, externally and internal studentized residuals.

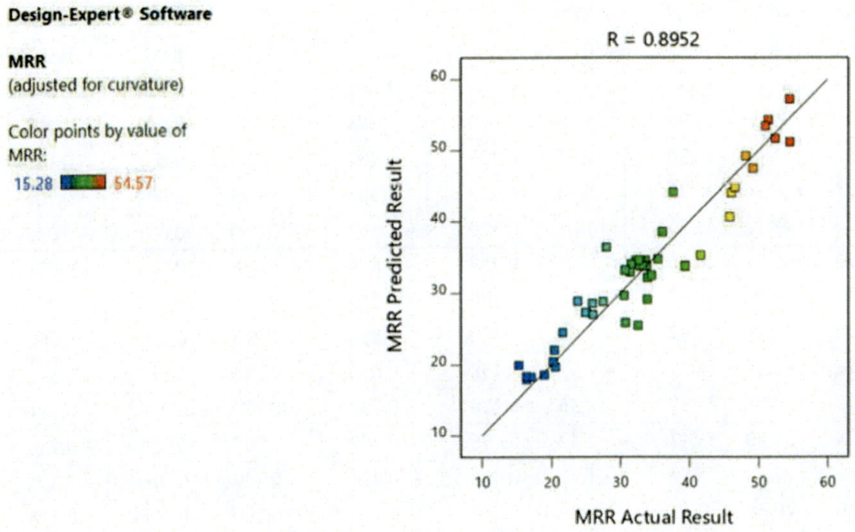

Fig. 11.5 The experimental result and predicted result of the MRR under TiO_2 nano-lubricant

Table 11.7 The analysis of the predicted values with the internal and external residual

Run order	Actual value	Predicted value	Residual	Leverage	Internally studentized residuals	Externally studentized residuals	Cook's distance	Influence on fitted value DFFITS
1	27.98	36.38	– 8.40	0.458	– 2.773	– 3.105	0.405	– 2.851
2	52.42	51.65	0.7685	0.458	0.254	0.250	0.003	0.230
3	25.96	28.57	– 2.61	0.458	– 0.863	– 0.859	0.039	– 0.789
4	32.97	34.34	– 1.37	0.458	– 0.453	– 0.448	0.011	– 0.411
5	30.68	33.19	– 2.51	0.458	– 0.827	– 0.823	0.036	– 0.756
6	20.39	22.07	– 1.68	0.458	– 0.555	– 0.550	0.016	– 0.505
7	39.36	33.72	5.64	0.020	1.385	1.405	0.002	0.201
8	46.63	44.83	1.80	0.458	0.596	0.590	0.019	0.542
9	33.60	34.55	– 0.9513	0.458	– 0.314	– 0.310	0.005	– 0.284
10	16.42	17.90	– 1.48	0.458	– 0.488	– 0.483	0.013	– 0.443
11	51.41	54.27	– 2.86	0.458	– 0.942	– 0.941	0.047	– 0.864
12	39.36	33.72	5.64	0.020	1.385	1.405	0.002	0.201
13	26.01	27.01	– 0.9965	0.458	– 0.329	– 0.325	0.006	– 0.298
14	34.48	32.47	2.01	0.458	0.664	0.658	0.023	0.605
15	30.74	25.86	4.88	0.458	1.610	1.651	0.137	1.516
16	46.15	44.07	2.08	0.458	0.685	0.680	0.025	0.624
17	35.41	34.72	0.6915	0.458	0.228	0.225	0.003	0.207
18	41.67	35.25	6.42	0.120	1.663	1.710	0.024	0.631
19	39.36	33.72	5.64	0.020	1.385	1.405	0.002	0.201
20	31.41	32.96	– 1.55	0.120	– 0.402	– 0.397	0.001	– 0.146
21	39.36	33.72	5.64	0.020	1.385	1.405	0.002	0.201
22	48.18	49.20	– 1.02	0.120	– 0.263	– 0.260	0.001	– 0.096
23	20.22	20.46	– 0.2388	0.458	– 0.079	– 0.078	0.000	– 0.071
24	36.06	38.56	– 2.50	0.120	– 0.649	– 0.643	0.004	– 0.238
25	15.28	19.97	– 4.69	0.120	– 1.214	– 1.223	0.013	– 0.452
26	16.38	18.35	– 1.97	0.458	– 0.650	– 0.644	0.022	– 0.591
27	24.95	27.31	– 2.36	0.458	– 0.778	– 0.774	0.032	– 0.711
28	51.00	53.42	– 2.42	0.458	– 0.799	– 0.795	0.034	– 0.730
29	27.48	28.80	– 1.32	0.458	– 0.434	– 0.429	0.010	– 0.394
30	20.56	19.67	0.8910	0.458	0.294	0.290	0.005	0.266
31	32.68	34.59	– 1.91	0.458	– 0.631	– 0.625	0.021	– 0.574
32	32.82	33.72	– 0.9004	0.020	– 0.221	– 0.218	0.000	– 0.031
33	54.54	57.25	– 2.71	0.458	– 0.893	– 0.890	0.042	– 0.818

(continued)

Table 11.7 (continued)

Run order	Actual value	Predicted value	Residual	Leverage	Internally studentized residuals	Externally studentized residuals	Cook's distance	Influence on fitted value DFFITS
34	49.19	47.47	1.72	0.120	0.444	0.439	0.002	0.162
35	21.60	24.49	− 2.89	0.458	− 0.955	− 0.954	0.048	− 0.876
36	33.79	33.72	0.0696	0.020	0.017	0.017	0.000	0.002
37	31.59	34.02	− 2.43	0.458	− 0.801	− 0.797	0.034	− 0.732
38	17.05	18.24	− 1.19	0.120	− 0.310	− 0.305	0.001	− 0.113
39	45.89	40.65	5.24	0.458	1.728	1.783	0.157	1.637
40	32.27	34.48	− 2.21	0.120	− 0.573	− 0.567	0.003	− 0.209
41	23.79	28.88	− 5.09	0.120	− 1.318	− 1.333	0.015	− 0.492
42	37.62	44.17	− 6.55	0.458	− 2.161	− 2.292	0.246	− 2.105
43	32.57	25.46	7.11	0.458	2.345	2.524	0.290	2.318
44	33.89	29.14	4.75	0.458	1.569	1.605	0.130	1.474
45	33.93	32.19	1.74	0.120	0.451	0.446	0.002	0.165
46	30.56	29.66	0.8990	0.458	0.297	0.293	0.005	0.269
47	54.57	51.17	3.40	0.458	1.122	1.126	0.066	1.034
48	33.31	33.72	− 0.4104	0.020	− 0.101	− 0.099	0.000	− 0.014
49	33.54	33.72	− 0.1804	0.020	− 0.044	− 0.044	0.000	− 0.006
50	18.94	18.58	0.3642	0.458	0.120	0.118	0.001	0.109

11.3.2 Material Removal Rate Prediction Using ANN

This section presents the predicting result of the MRR during the end-milling of AA8112 alloy under the TiO_2 nano-lubricant using ANN. The Back Propagation feed-forward Neural Network (BPNN) was used to predict the experimental result obtained from experimental data by employing Levenberg–Marquardt (trainlm) to train the neuron for better performance. Furthermore, the best validation performance is analysed by the sigmoid non-linear transfer function (Z) and the total sum of squared error (SSE). The statistical formulation is presented in Eqs. (3.7)–(3.13). Figure 11.6 shows the neuron network pattern used for the prediction of the MRR under the machining environment of the TiO_2 nano-lubricant.

Figure 11.7a, b shows the performance analysis of the ANN model for the TiO_2 nano-lubricant machining environment using SSE with the coefficient relationship (R-value) of the regression model. The R-value shows the nearness of the ANN model predicted output target (MRR) with the experimental result obtained from the machining operation. From the analysis, the R-value for the data training set and data validation, 0.9865, and 0.9926, respectively. The overall performance and testing are 0.94084 and 0.95872, as depicted in Fig. 11.8a, b.

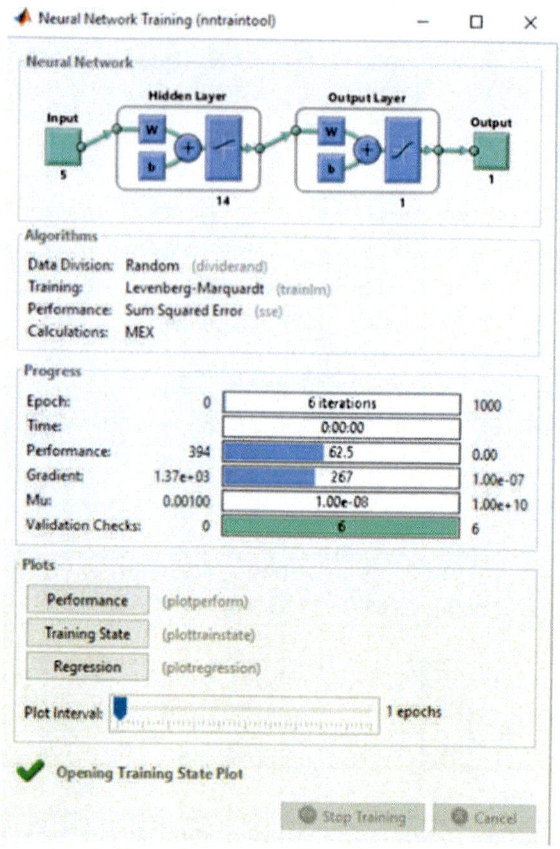

Fig. 11.6 The Model structure of the ANN for the MRR

The solid line shows the level of performance of the regression model. In contrast, the dashed line is the perfect line of the regression, and both lines help to show the relationship between the target and the predicted MRR under TiO_2 nano-lubricant machining environment. From the ANN model, the best validation performance, as measured by applying the SSE, occurs at epoch 0 and iteration 6, as presented in Fig. 11.9. The analysis depicts that the SSE decreased gradually from the zero epoch to the peak point. Figure 11.10 shows the gradient constant of the Marquardt unit parameter (Mu), total validation checks, and the iterations value.

Fig. 11.7 ANN regression plot of MRR under the TiO_2 nano-lubricant **a** Training process, and **b** the validation analysis

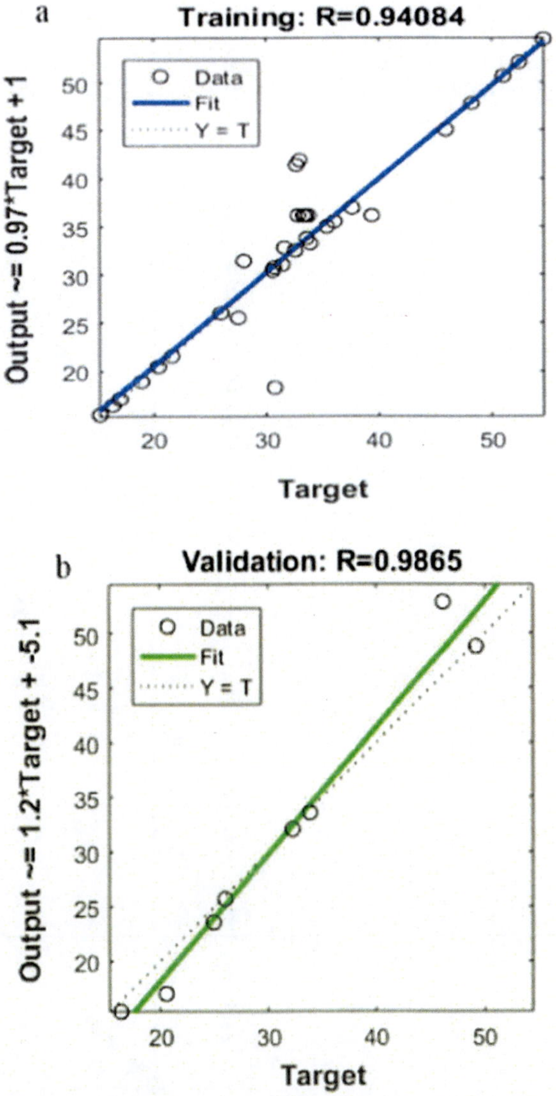

11.4 Comparative Analysis Between the ANN and QRCCD and Machining Optimization

The models developed used in training of the experimental data for the ANN and the RSM under TiO_2 nano-lubricant machining of AL 8112 alloy is depicted in Fig. 11.11. Applying the percentage deviation method presented and equation of the ANN and the QCCD model could predict the MRR experimental result with about 98.7% and 89.5%, respectively. Figure 11.11 it can be noted that the two

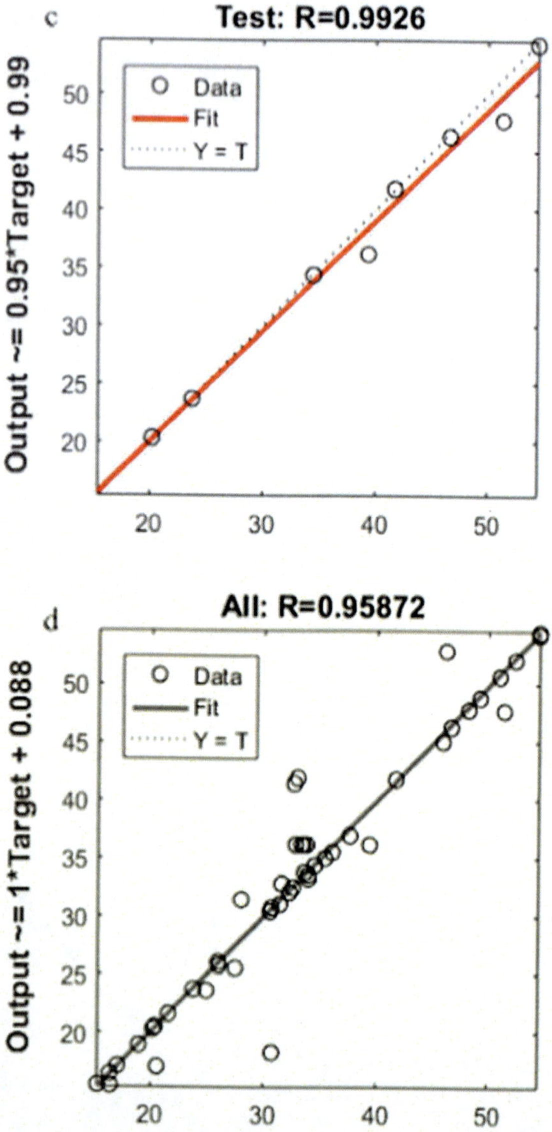

Fig. 11.8 ANN regression plot of MRR under the TiO_2 nano-lubricant **a** Testing process, and **d** overall prediction of the MRR

techniques employed for the prediction of the MRR for performance and productivity improvement have performed reasonably well within the standard of machining operations when compared with other previous work of Gjeldum et al. [23], Hadad and Ramezani [24], and Basar et al. [25]. The high rate of the model prediction has proven that the experiment carried out has a high level of accuracy and can be implemented in the manufacturing company.

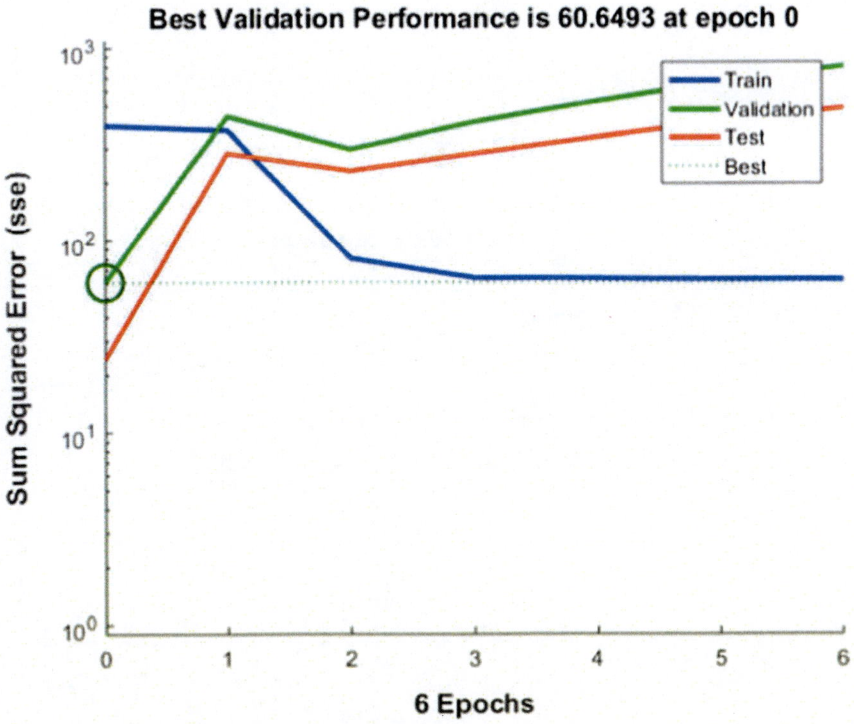

Fig. 11.9 ANN validation performance plot for MRR

Figures 11.12, 11.13, and 11.14 shows the factors of objective optimization of the machining parameters obtained from the Quadratic rotatable central composite design (QRCCD) for the MRR. The result shows that the spindle speed of 2000 rpm, a feed rate of 192 mm/min, length of cut of 59 mm, depth of cut of 2.99 mm, and helix angle of 60° to have the maximum MRR of 53.87 with the desirability of 0.895.

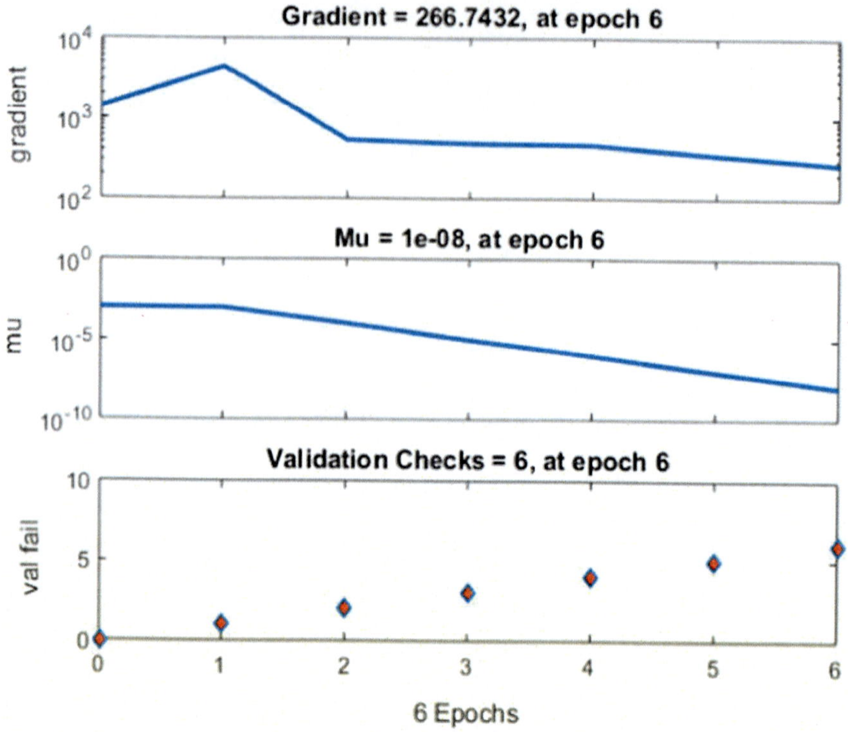

Fig. 11.10 ANN performance training state for the MRR

Fig. 11.11 Experimental result, predicted values (ANN) and predicted values (RSM) of the MRR under TiO_2 nano-lubricant machining environment

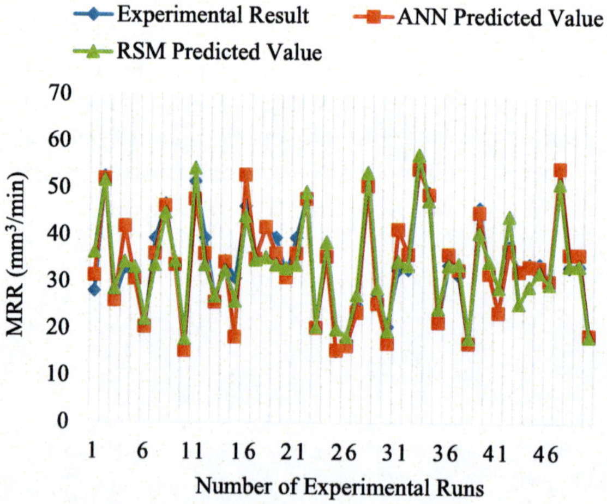

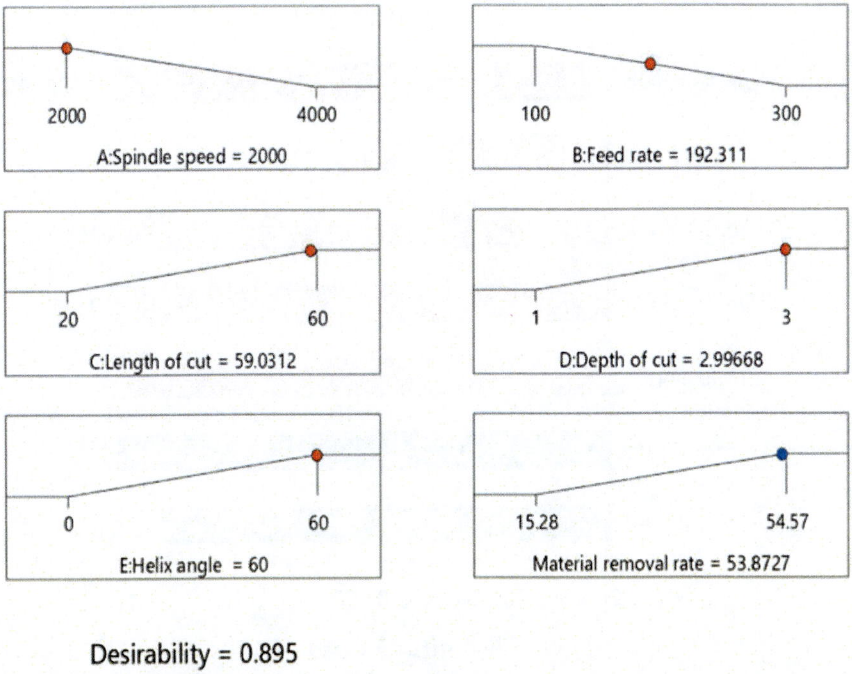

Fig. 11.12 The MRR ramps plots for the optimisation of the five factors five levels parameters

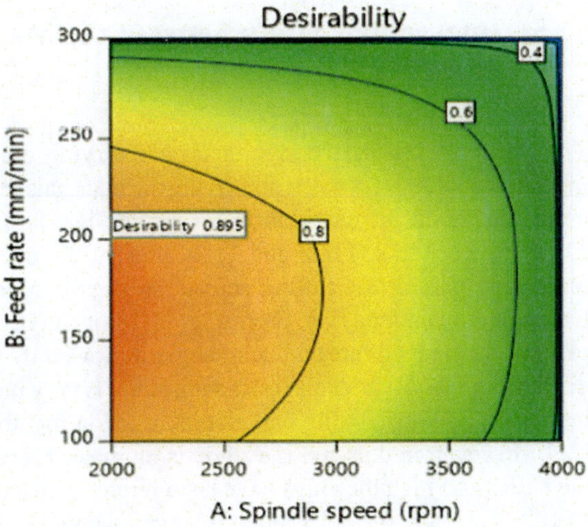

Fig. 11.13 The desirability plots for the MRR

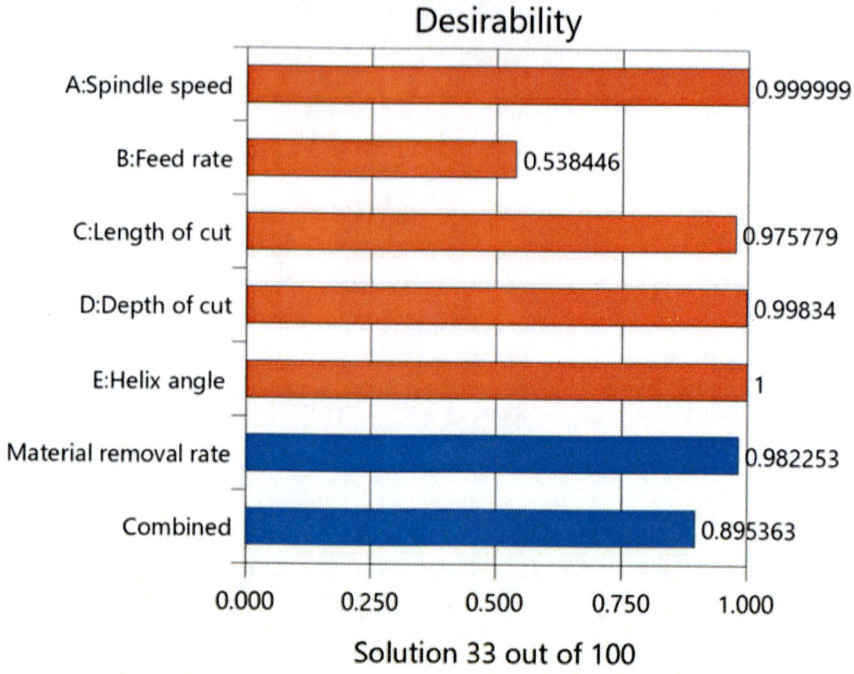

Fig. 11.14 The desirability bar plots for the multi-objective optimization parameters for MRR

11.5 Interactions Study Between the Machining Parameters for MRR

This section explains the significant of carrying out the interaction study of the machining parameters when discussing the materials removal rate during end-milling under biodegradable nano-lubricants. From Figs. 11.15, 11.16, 11.17, 11.18, 11.19, 11.20, 11.21, 11.22, 11.23 and 11.24 present the interaction study for the five (5) machining parameters cutting across the spindle speed, depth of cut, helix angle, length of cut and feed rate. From Fig. 11.18, it can be seen that the most interaction parameters are feed rate and helix angle, followed by spindle speed and helix angle depicted in Fig. 11.21. This interaction study is very important and it gives the correlations on how machining parameters function together during machining process [26]. However, in this case the study is on materials removal rate and in machining the easier and high the chips have been removed from the workpieces the better the MRR. Therefore, the helix angle interactions with the spindle speed, feed rate and length of cut is very significant because it assists to increase the MRR [27].

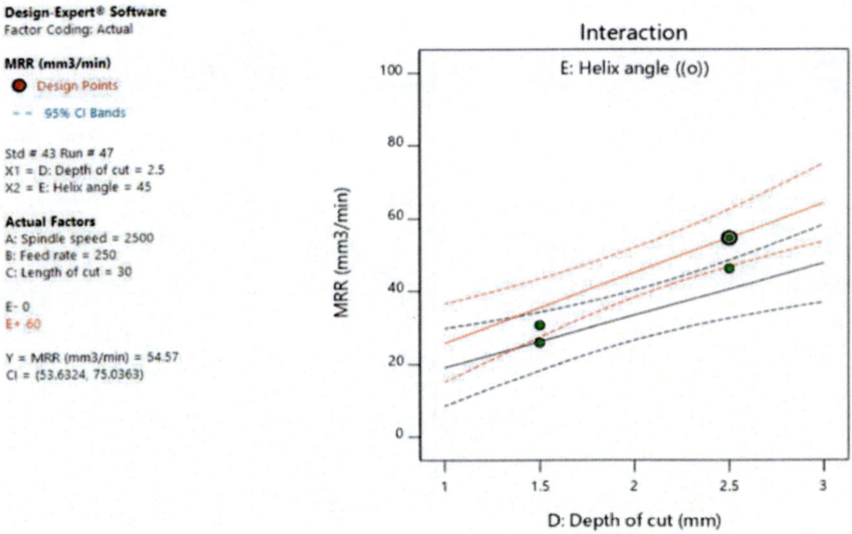

Fig. 11.15 MRR machining parameters interactions between depth of cut and helix angle

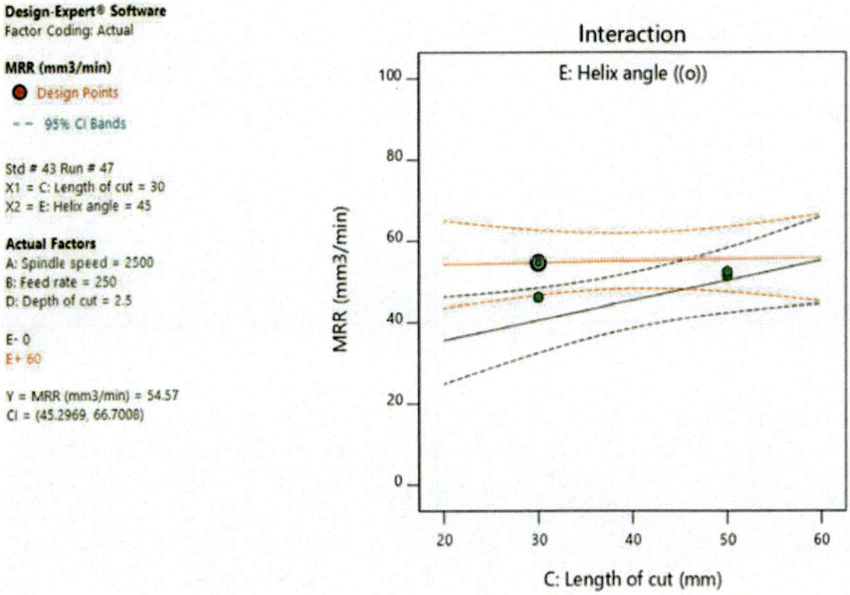

Fig. 11.16 MRR machining parameters interactions between length of cut and helix angle

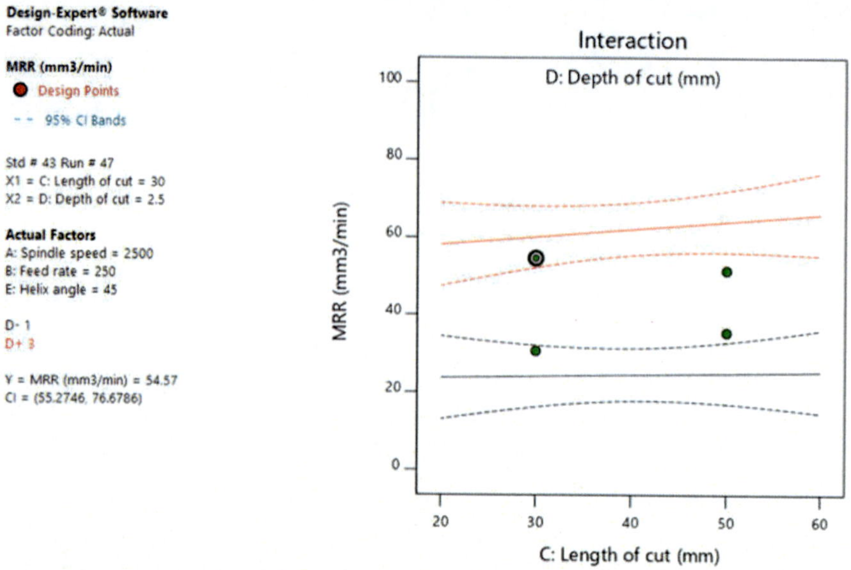

Fig. 11.17 MRR machining parameters interactions between length of cut and depth of cut

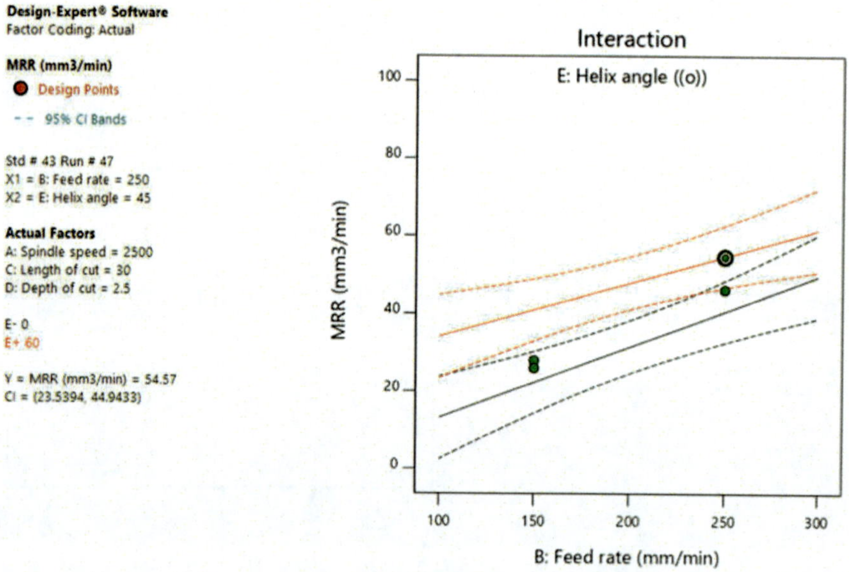

Fig. 11.18 MRR machining parameters interactions between feed rate and helix angle

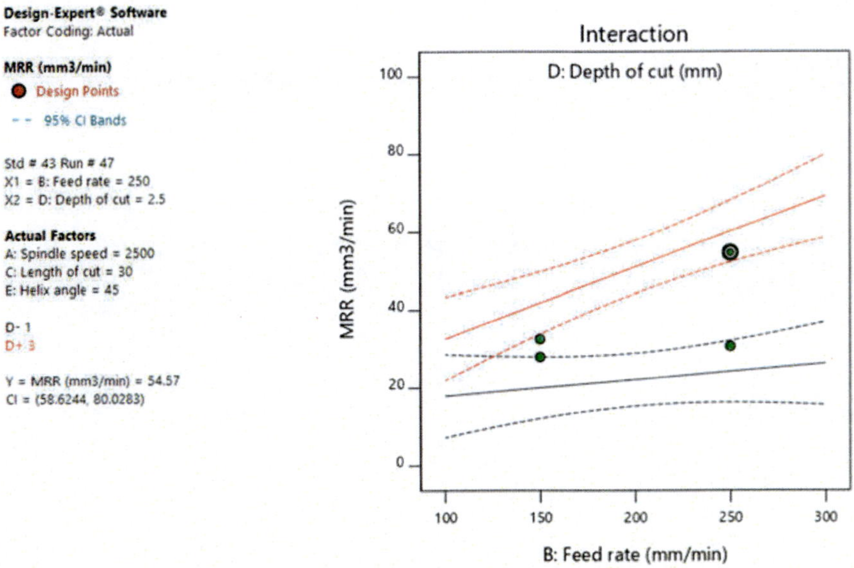

Fig. 11.19 MRR machining parameters interactions between feed rate and depth of cut

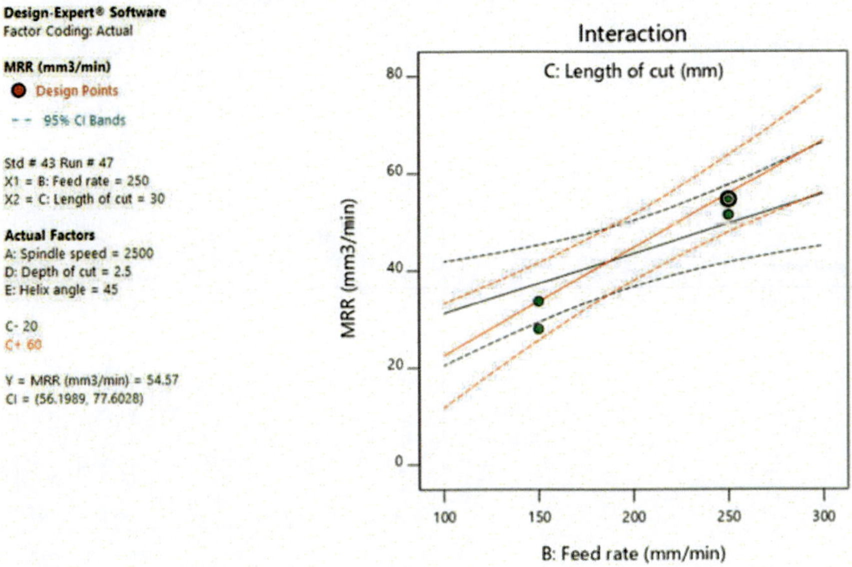

Fig. 11.20 MRR machining parameters interactions between feed rate and length of cut

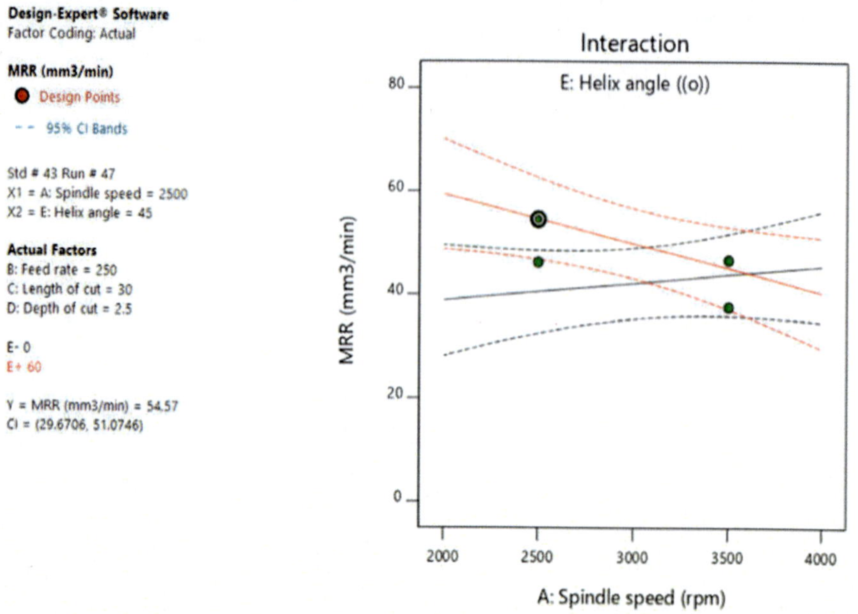

Fig. 11.21 MRR machining parameters interactions between spindle speed and helix angle

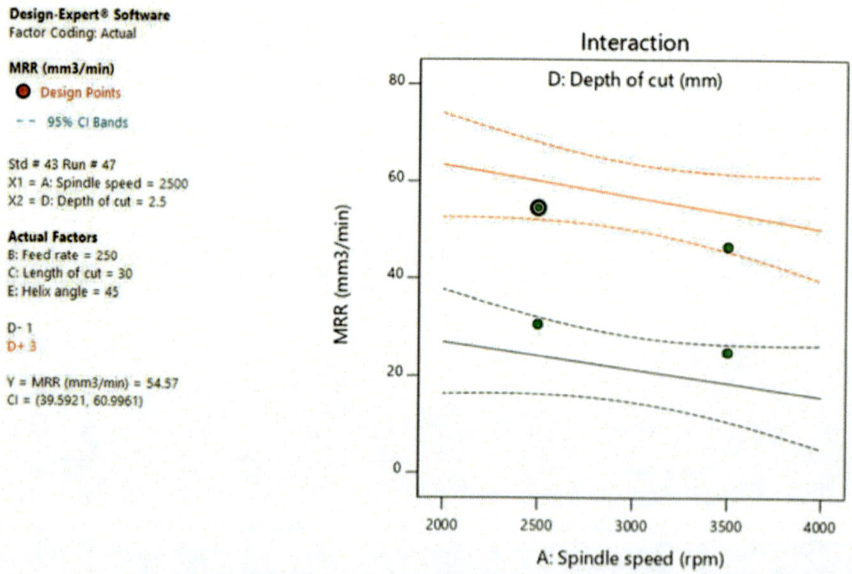

Fig. 11.22 MRR machining parameters interactions between spindle speed and depth of cut

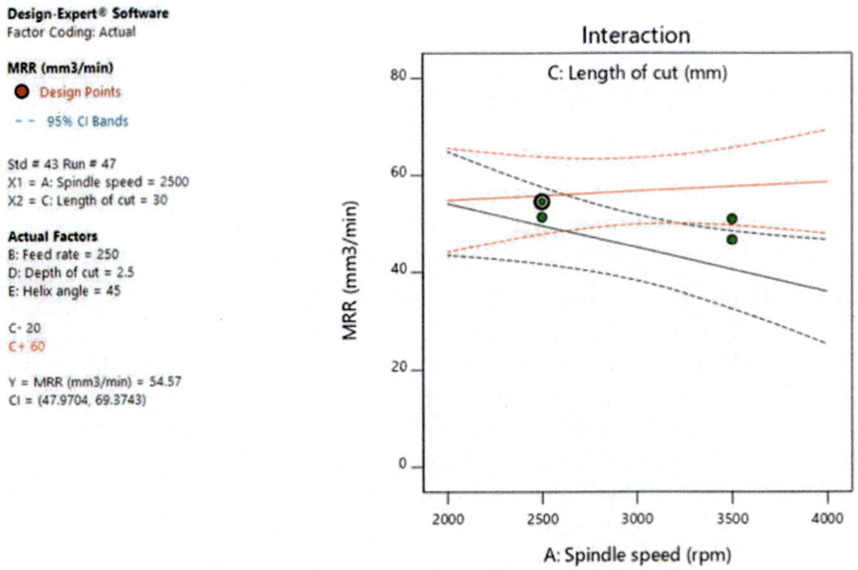

Fig. 11.23 MRR machining parameters interactions between length of cut and spindle speed

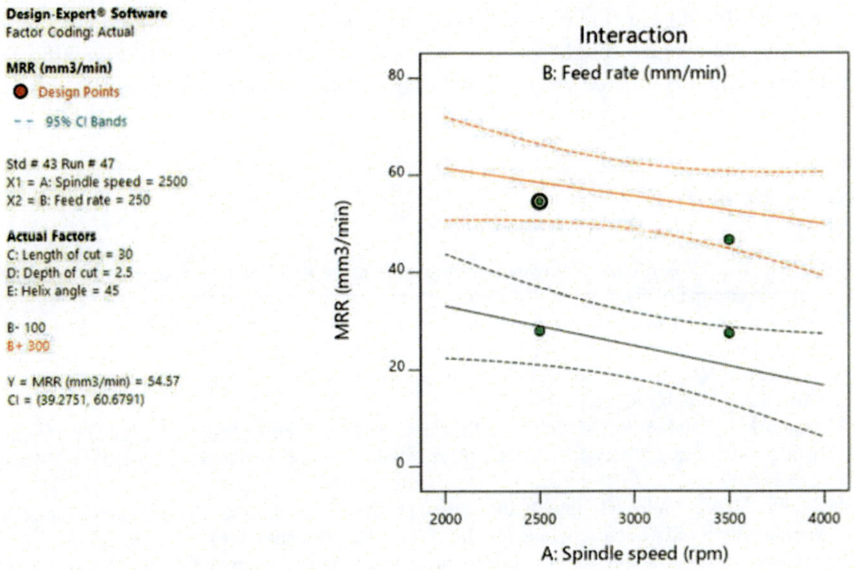

Fig. 11.24 MRR machining parameters interactions between spindle speed and feed rate

11.6 Conclusion

In this paper, a numerical analysis of the performance of copra oil-based TiO_2 nano-lubricant on end-milling of AL 8112 alloy using ANN and QCCD was carried out. The developed copra oil-based TiO_2 nano-lubricant was implemented to study the surface roughness and the material removal rate with the five-factors, five-levels (such as spindle speed, feed rate, length of cut, depth of cut and helix angle) of experiment. From the analysis, the following conclusion depicted as follows:

(i) Feed rate has the most significant effect on MRR because of its percentage contribution of 43.63%, followed by the depth of cut with 34.46%, length of cut with 4.28% under machining environment with TiO_2 nano-lubricant.
(ii) The feed rate and length of cut are the most interacted machining parameters, followed by the length of cut and helix angle in MRR analysis.
(iii) The optimised machining parameters from QRCCD are spindle speed of 2000 rpm, a feed rate of 192 mm/min, length of cut of 59 mm, depth of cut of 2.99 mm, and helix angle of 60° to have the maximum MRR of 53.87 with the desirability of 0.895.
(iv) The ANN and QRCCD models could predict the experimental results with 98.7% and 89.5% accuracy.

Finally, the most accurate model is the artificial neural network which were able to predict the surface roughness and the material removal rate with a significant difference when compared with and quadratic rotatable central composite design.

References

1. Li, D., Du, Y.: Artificial intelligence with uncertainty. CRC Press is an imprint of Taylor & Francis Group (2017)
2. Asfaram, A., Ghaedi, M., Azqhandi, M.A., Goudarzi, A., Dastkhoon, M.J.R.A.: Statistical experimental design, least squares-support vector machine (LS-SVM) and artificial neural network (ANN) methods for modeling the facilitated adsorption of methylene blue dye. RSC Adv. **6**(46), 40502–40516 (2016)
3. Asiltürk, I., Çunkaş, M.: Modeling and prediction of surface roughness in turning operations using artificial neural network and multiple regression method. Expert Syst. Appl. **38**(5), 5826–5832 (2011)
4. Prajina, N.V.: Multi response optimization of CNC end milling using response surface methodology and desirability function. Int. J. Eng. Res. Technol. **6**(6), 739–746 (2013)
5. Okokpujie, I.P., Okonkwo, U.C.: Effects of cutting parameters on surface roughness during end milling of aluminium under minimum quantity lubrication (MQL). Int. J. Sci. Res. **4**(5), 2937–2943 (2013)
6. Reddy, B.S., Kumar, J.S., Reddy, K.V.K.: Optimization of surface roughness in CNC end milling using response surface methodology and genetic algorithm. Int. J. Eng. Sci. Technol. **3**(8), 102–109 (2011)
7. Adler, D.P., Hii, W.S., Michalek, D.J., Sutherland, J.W.: Examining the role of cutting fluids in machining and efforts to address associated environmental/health concerns. Mach. Sci. Technol. **10**(1), 23–58 (2006)

8. Ogundimu, O., Lawal, S.A., Okokpujie, I.P.: Experimental study and analysis of variance of material removal rate in high speed turning of AISI 304L alloy steel. IOP Conf. Ser.: Mater. Sci. Eng. **413**(1), 012030 (2018)
9. Yan, P., Rong, Y., Wang, G.: The effect of cutting fluids applied in metal cutting process. Proc. Inst. Mech. Eng. Part B: J. Eng. Manuf. **230**(1), 19–37 (2016)
10. Joshua, O.S., David, M.O., Sikiru, I.O.: Experimental investigation of cutting parameters on surface roughness prediction during end milling of aluminium 6061 under MQL (Minimum Quantity Lubrication). J. Mech. Eng. Autom. **5**(1), 1–13 (2015)
11. Saini, V., Bijwe, J.: Polyaniline nanoparticles: a novel additive for augmenting thermal conductivity and tribo-properties of mineral oil and commercial engine oil. Lubricants **10**(11), 300 (2022)
12. Phuoc, T.X., Massoudi, M., Chen, R.H.: Viscosity and thermal conductivity of nanofluids containing multi-walled carbon nanotubes stabilized by chitosan. Int. J. Therm. Sci. **50**(1), 12–18 (2011)
13. Pervaiz, S., Kannan, S., Kishawy, H.A.: An extensive review of the water consumption and cutting fluid based sustainability concerns in the metal cutting sector. J. Clean. Prod. **197**, 134–153 (2018)
14. Sani, A.S.A., Abd Rahim, E., Sharif, S., Sasahara, H.: Machining performance of vegetable oil with phosphonium-and ammonium-based ionic liquids via MQL technique. J. Clean. Prod. **209**, 947–964 (2019)
15. Okonkwo, U.C., Nwoke, O.N., Okokpujie, I.P.: Comparative analysis of chatter vibration frequency in CNC turning of AISI 4340 alloy steel with different boundary conditions. J. Coven. Eng. Technol. (CJET) **1**(1), 13–30 (2018)
16. Nwoke, O.N., Okonkwo, U.C., Okafor, C.E., Okokpujie, I.P.: Evaluation of chatter vibration frequency in CNC turning of 4340 alloy steel material. Int. J. Sci. Eng. Res. **8**(2), 487–495 (2017)
17. Onoroh, F., Ogbonnaya, M., Echeta, C.B.: Experimental investigation of cutting parameters on a turning tool flank wear (Industrial and production engineering). Coven. J. Eng. Technol. (Special Edition) (2018)
18. Davoudinejad, A., Li, D., Zhang, Y., Tosello, G.: Optimization of corner micro end milling by finite element modelling for machining thin features. Procedia CIRP **82**, 362–367 (2019)
19. Masmiati, N., Sarhan, A.A., Hassan, M.A.N., Hamdi, M.: Optimization of cutting conditions for minimum residual stress, cutting force and surface roughness in end milling of S50C medium carbon steel. Measurement **86**, 253–265 (2016)
20. Ojolo, S.J., Adjaottor, A.A., Olatunji, R.S.: Experimental prediction and optimization of material removal rate during hard turning of austenitic 304l stainless steel. J. Sci. Technol. (Ghana) **36**(2), 34–49 (2016)
21. Okokpujie, I.P., Tartibu, L.K.: Performance investigation of the effects of nano-additive-lubricants with cutting parameters on material removal rate of AL8112 alloy for advanced manufacturing application. Sustainability **13**(15), 8406 (2021)
22. Okokpujie, I.P., Ohunakin, O.S., Bolu, C.A.: Multi-objective optimization of machining factors on surface roughness, material removal rate and cutting force on end-milling using MWCNTs nano-lubricant. Progr. Addit. Manuf. **6**(1), 155–178 (2021)
23. Gjeldum, N., Bilic, B., Veza, I.: Investigation and modelling of process parameters and work-piece dimensions influence on material removal rate in CWEDT process. Int. J. Comput. Integr. Manuf. **28**(7), 715–728 (2015)
24. Hadad, M., Ramezani, M.: Modeling and analysis of a novel approach in machining and structuring of flat surfaces using face milling process. Int. J. Mach. Tools Manuf **105**, 32–44 (2016)
25. Basar, G., Kirli Akin, H., Kahraman, F., Fedai, Y.: Modeling and optimization of face milling process parameters for AISI 4140 steel. Tehnički Glasnik **12**(1), 5–10 (2018)
26. Karmiris-Obratański, P., Papazoglou, E.L., Leszczyńska-Madej, B., Karkalos, N.E., Markopoulos, A.P.: An optimalization study on the surface texture and machining parameters of 60CrMoV18-5 steel by EDM. Materials **15**(10), 3559 (2022). https://doi.org/10.3390/ma15103559

27. Perumal, A., Kailasanathan, C., Stalin, B., Suresh Kumar, S., Rajkumar, P.R., Gangadharan, T., Venkatesan, G., Nagaprasad, N., Dhinakaran, V., Krishnaraj, R.: Multiresponse optimization of wire electrical discharge machining parameters for Ti-6Al-2Sn-4Zr-2Mo (α-β) alloy using Taguchi-grey relational approach. Adv. Mater. Sci. Eng. **2022**, 1–13 (2022). https://doi.org/10.1155/2022/6905239

Chapter 12
Application of Hybrid ANN and PSO for Prediction of Surface Roughness Under Biodegradable Nano-lubricant

Abstract Modelling of surface roughness is challenging because machining conditions cannot be well covered by theoretical models. In this section, 50 configurations corresponding to various spindle speed, feed rate, length of cut, depth of cut, helix angle were considered to predict the surface roughness of the end milling machining of an AA8112 alloy. In this study, an ANN-PSO approach has been considered for the development of a suitable prediction model for surface roughness. The sensitivity analysis of numerous Particle Swarm Optimization (PSO) parameters, including the population size of the swarm, the number of neurons in the hidden layer, and the magnitude of the acceleration factors, was carried out. This study reveals that the prediction performance metric is closely related to the model configuration or parameters. The best configurations of the ANN-PSO models were identified. This study shows that the hybrid ANN-PSO enhances the performance of ANN. The proposed approach would address time-consuming and expensive experiment required to identify a configuration that yield the minimum surface roughness.

Keywords ANN-PSO models · ANN · Particle swarm optimization · Surface roughness · Machining

12.1 Background

The surface roughness plays a major role in the performance of mechanical parts. It can affect their performance during operations [1]. Hence, several studies are focusing on minimizing surface roughness through the adjustment of machining parameters and the implementation of lubricant during manufacturing. Shivanna et al. [2] analyse the impacts of machining parameters on the surface roughness of machined surfaces. Surface roughness parameters were measured using a computer vision system. This study shows that surface quality depends on the speed, the feed, and the depth of cut in a CNC milling machine. A critical assessment of lubrication techniques in machining processes was performed by Lawal et al. [3]. This study points out that irrespective of the lubrification techniques, workpiece material,

I. P. Okokpujie and L. K. Tartibu, *Modern Optimization Techniques for Advanced Machining*, Studies in Systems, Decision and Control 485,
https://doi.org/10.1007/978-3-031-35455-7_12

tool material and machining conditions were vital to the performance of machining processes. Any modification to a process variable or the state of the cutting tool affects the surface geometry and texture.

Manufacturers have investigated several methods for applying cutting fluid during environmentally friendly machining operations. Minimum quantity lubrication (MQL) strategies are potentially more suitable to save manufacturing costs and environmental pollutants. The need for cleaner and greener machining cannot be met by using MQL for lubricants with low thermal conductivity [4]. Therefore, adding nanoparticles to the base oil (which is created) improves its rheological characteristics, thermal conductivity, and stability [5]. According to Lee et al. [6], adding graphite nanoparticles to conventional fluid improved its lubricating properties.

Because roughness is nonlinear, modelling it analytically is difficult. The wide range of machining conditions cannot be well covered by the proposed theoretical models, necessitating the development of additional novel techniques to identify the ideal machining settings and forecast the roughness of machined surfaces [7, 8]. Studies on the effects of the variables that could reduce surface roughness were done, but the findings were not very gratifying in light of the complex interactions of so many contributing variables. For instance, contrary to what was expected, a strong tendency for surface roughness to grow as the depth of the cut rose was not seen [9]. To tackle the challenges, researchers used artificial intelligence techniques like genetic algorithms (GAs) and artificial neural networks (ANNs).

The advantages of ANNs include input–output mapping, handling nonlinearity, managing incomplete data, processing data in parallel, and improving computing power [10, 11]. The optimization of the ANN design, however, is a problem with ANNs [12]. They also lack a warranty for application performance as result, which is a drawback [10]. The design of the ANN architecture frequently used the process of trial and error [12]. The determination of the number of layers and neurons in an ANN needed for an application lacks a general and ideal solution [13]. It was difficult to choose appropriate (but not necessarily optimal) process parameters like feed rate and depth of cut when any permissible surface roughness may be one of an ANN's inputs. Additionally, the competing goals of product quality, cost, and production rate present optimization issues [14].

In order to estimate the degree of roughness on sample surfaces turned using diamond and carbide tools, Zhong et al. [9] used neural networks with seven inputs. The activation function and network design were optimized for good prediction accuracy to produce the optimal network. Additionally, this study showed that the constructed ANN could accurately forecast the roughness of the sample surfaces turned on a different machine. Sofuoglu [15] showed that the ANN technique could simulate the roughness of the machined wood surfaces by predicting the surface roughness using an ANN. Additionally, Tiryaki et al. [16] revealed that they could forecast the roughness of their machined wood surfaces by utilizing ANNs.

Several studies suggest that ANN training parameters (bias and weight) could be enhanced using Particle Swarm Optimization (PSO). The Stirling engine performance was improved using a hybrid ANN-PSO in comparison with a typical ANN model in a study reported by Machesa et al. [17]. Seguini et al. [18] indicated that ANN combined with PSO was more accurate in the prediction of the crack in the pipeline. The prediction of the transverse vibration peak, the vertical vibration peak, and the longitudinal vibration peak, as a result of the blast, was improved using ANN-PSO compared to ANN in a study conducted by Tartibu et al. [19]. The clad characteristics in the laser metal deposition process were predicted by Pant and Chatterjee [20] using ANN and combined PSO-ANN algorithms. This study revealed that better-clad properties can be predicted by the combined PSO-ANN based supervised learning model. This is by no means all the existing works that indicate the enhancement of ANN parameters when combined with PSO but it justifies the rationale behind the selection of ANN-PSO as a potential modelling approach for the analysis of Surface Roughness.

Therefore, in this work, a readily available dataset was used to build ANN and ANN-PSO models. A parametric analysis was performed to analyse how parameters involved in the building of the ANN-PSO model affect its prediction accuracy.

12.2 Modelling Approaches

In this study, an ANN-PSO approach has been considered for the development of a suitable prediction model for surface roughness. Prior to the description of the proposed approach, ANN is described. This ANN model was used as a benchmark to analyse the performance indicators considered for the prediction of surface roughness. ANN is one of the most common intelligent systems created by imitating the human brain. ANN draws inspiration from the complex operation of human brains where hundreds of billions of linked neurons process information in parallel [21].

An artificial neural network, often known as a "neural network," is made up of three layers of neurons: an input layer of neurons (or nodes, units), one to three hidden layers of neurons, and a layer of output neurons as shown in Fig. 12.1. Backpropagation is a popular technique for neural network training [22]. Numerous data-intensive applications have seen success in implementing neural networks. The ANN strategy has been used in this study despite the fact that the ANN technique tends to become stuck in local minima, which is one potential drawback of this approach. Successful implementation of neural networks has been documented in various data-driven applications.

The equation describing the ANN backpropagation approach can be described as follows [23]:

$$f(net_k) = \frac{1}{1 + x^{-net_k}} \tag{12.1}$$

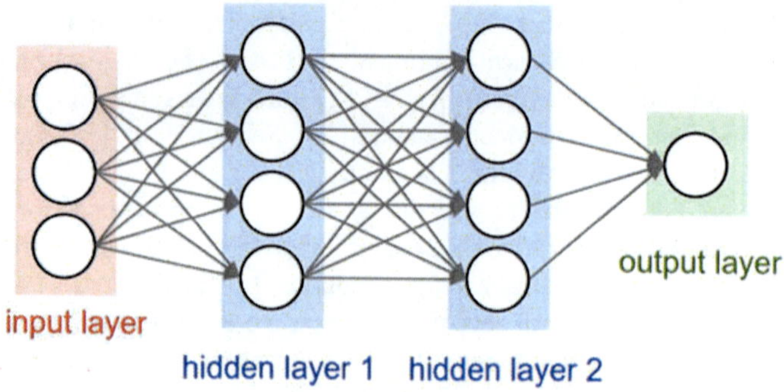

Fig. 12.1 Typical architecture of an ANN model

$$
\begin{aligned}
x_j &= normalizedX_d & 1 < d \le m \\
net_k &= \sum_{j=1}^{k-1} W_{kj}x_j + b_j & m+1 \le k \le N+n \\
x_k &= f(net_k) & m+1 \le k \le N+n \\
O_s &= x_{N+s} & 1 \le s \le n
\end{aligned}
$$

where,

m	The number of inputs to the network
n	Number of outputs of the ANN
X_d	The actual inputs of the ANN
$f(net_k)$	Log-sigmoid function
N	Number of intermediate neurons in the ANN
W	The weight matrix in each layer
W_{kj}	The elements of the matrix weight
x_j	The activation level of the neuron
O_s	The output from ANN.

One metaheuristic optimization technique, known as particle swarm optimization, is based on the social and cooperative cooperation of several species in a multidimensional search space. Numerous research has demonstrated that hybridizing ANN and PSO considerably enhances the network's performance [24]. Neurons are the building blocks of an ANN. Through weights and biases, these units are interconnected. To determine the network's ideal weights and biases, training using inputs and outputs that are known must be done after the ANN model has been created. Particle Swarm Optimization (PSO) was used in this paper even though there are other ways to obtain appropriate weights and biases. Once training is effective, ANN will be able to link complex input and output datasets.

The beginning position Pbest, the initial best particle position Gbest, and the particle's location in the search spaces serve as identifiers for each particle. To determine the Gbest and Pbest values and to update the optimized weights and biases of the ANN, each particle's fitness is evaluated throughout training. The flowchart in Fig. 12.2 provides an overview of this procedure. Eberhart and Kennedy [25] go into detail on how PSO was put into practice. Using Eqs. (12.2) and (12.3), the updating of particle position and velocity is condensed. In these Equations, c_1 and c_2 are the acceleration constants and r_1 and r_2 are referred to as random integers. The weight of inertia (Pbest), which includes x, v, P^t, and G^t.

$$V_{ij}^{t} = \chi\left[\omega v_{ij}^{t-1} + c_1 r_1\left(p_{ij}^{t-1} - x_{ij}^{t-1}\right) + c_2 r_2\left(G_{j}^{t-1} - x_{ij}^{t-1}\right)\right] \tag{12.2}$$

$$x_{ij}^{t} = x_{ij}^{t-1} + v_{ij}^{t} \tag{12.3}$$

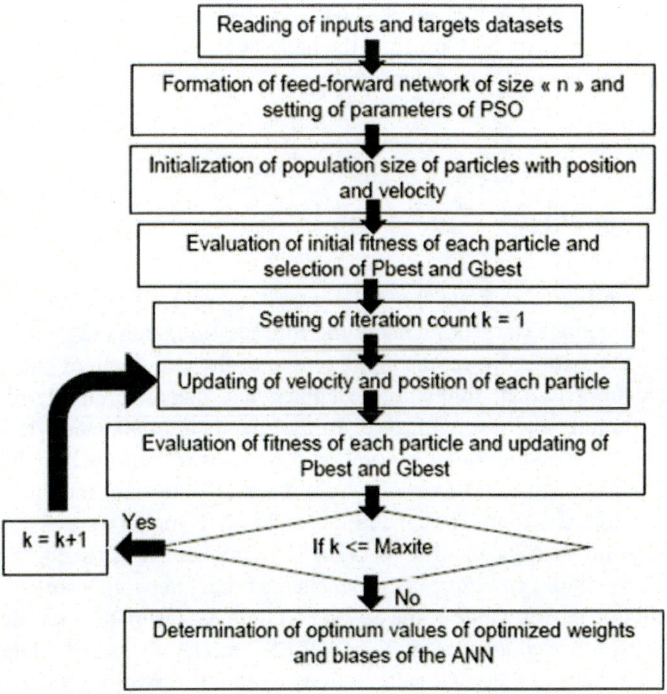

Fig. 12.2 Training flowchart describing the ANN-PSO approach (Adapted from [24])

12.3 Description of Dataset Extraction

In this study, the end milling machining of an AA8112 alloy was performed on a SIEG 3/10/0016 CNC machine. Details describing the experimental setup and the variables (spindle speed, feed rate, length of cut, depth of cut, helix angle) are available in Okokpujie et al. [26]. The machining parameters were derived using a quadratic rotatable central composite design. In order to develop nano-lubricant in large quantities, a two-step method was used. The first step consisted of synthesizing nanomaterials in dry powder. The second step consisted of dispersing them into base oil by mixing techniques.

Titanium dioxide (TiO_2) and multi-walled carbon nanotube (MWCNTs) nano-lubricants mixed with copra oil were used as the cutting fluid [27]. The rectangular plate of the AA8112 alloy was cut into 20, 30-, 40-, 50- and 60-mm lengths. The 150 pieces were divided equally namely 50 pieces of TiO_2, 50 pieces of MWCNTs and 50 pieces of copra oil. The CNC machine was programmed for the length of cut to be adjusted between 20 and 60 mm, the spindle speed was adjusted between 2000 to 4000 RPM, the feed rate was adjusted between 100 to 300 mm/min, the depth cut was adjusted between 1 and 3 mm, and the helix angle was adjusted between 0 and 60°. The 50 experimental runs considered as a dataset in this study are provided in Table 12.1.

12.4 Methodology

The dataset considered to build the ANN model is provided in Table 12.1. These data relate the outputs (targets), namely the Surface Roughness (SR) to the inputs described by the spindle speed, feed rate, length of the cut, depth of cut, and helix angle. The dataset is then split into the appropriate places to clearly distinguish between the training and testing phases. 80% of the data, or 40 data, were used for training the ANN model in order to forecast the values of Surface Roughness. The remaining 10% of the data (or five data) were utilized for testing, and the remaining 10% was used for validation. The capabilities of the ANN model were assessed using the validation and testing data. The MATLAB environment was used to implement this process (Appendix I). Figure 12.3 depicts the neural network's structure.

The prediction performance of the Surface Roughness taken into consideration in this study was examined using a hybrid ANN-PSO model. A total of 50 data points were divided in half; of these, 42 were utilized to train the hybrid ANN-PSO model and 8 were used to test it. The MATLAB environment was used to implement the model (Appendix J). The sensitivity analysis of numerous PSO parameters, including the population size of the swarm (N), the number of neurons in the hidden layer (n), and the magnitude of the acceleration factors (c_1 and c_2), must be carried out, according to Momeni et al. [28]. It is required to perform numerous runs and take into account various parameter combinations in order to construct a robust network.

Table 12.1 Dataset

Index	Spindle speed (rpm)	Feed rate (mm/min)	Length of cut (mm)	Depth of cut (mm)	Helix angle (α) (o)	SR (MWCNTs) (μm)
1	2500	150	30	2.5	45	2.04
2	2500	250	50	2.5	15	2.06
3	2500	250	30	1.5	15	1.98
4	3500	250	50	1.5	45	1.46
5	2500	150	50	1.5	45	1.68
6	3000	200	40	2	30	1.53
7	3500	250	30	2.5	45	1.51
8	2500	150	50	2.5	45	1.66
9	3000	200	40	2	30	1.54
10	3500	150	50	2.5	45	1.52
11	3500	150	30	2.5	15	1.65
12	2500	250	30	2.5	15	1.76
13	2500	250	50	1.5	45	1.74
14	3000	200	40	2	60	1.59
15	3000	200	40	2	30	1.58
16	4000	200	40	2	30	1.16
17	3000	300	40	2	30	2.51
18	3500	150	50	1.5	45	1.49
19	3000	200	60	2	30	1.61
20	3000	200	40	1	30	1.56
21	3500	150	30	1.5	45	1.36
22	3500	250	30	1.5	45	1.51
23	3500	250	50	2.5	45	1.61
24	3500	150	30	2.5	45	1.59
25	2500	150	50	1.5	15	1.92
26	2500	250	50	1.5	15	2
27	3000	200	40	2	30	1.66
28	3500	250	50	2.5	15	1.52
29	3000	200	40	3	30	2.2
30	3500	150	50	1.5	15	1.54
31	3000	200	40	2	30	1.61
32	3000	100	40	2	30	1.21
33	3500	250	50	1.5	15	1.5
34	2000	200	40	2	30	2.3
35	3000	200	20	2	30	1.51

(continued)

Table 12.1 (continued)

Index	Spindle speed (rpm)	Feed rate (mm/min)	Length of cut (mm)	Depth of cut (mm)	Helix angle (α) (o)	SR (MWCNTs) (μm)
36	2500	150	30	1.5	45	1.74
37	3500	250	30	1.5	15	1.45
38	3000	200	40	2	0	1.61
39	2500	150	50	2.5	15	1.76
40	2500	250	30	2.5	45	1.77
41	3000	200	40	2	30	1.61
42	3000	200	40	2	30	1.61
43	2500	250	30	1.5	45	1.75
44	3500	150	30	1.5	15	1.44
45	2500	250	50	2.5	45	1.69
46	2500	150	30	2.5	15	1.71
47	3000	200	40	2	30	1.58
48	3500	150	50	2.5	15	1.52
49	3500	250	30	2.5	15	1.49
50	2500	150	30	1.5	15	1.77

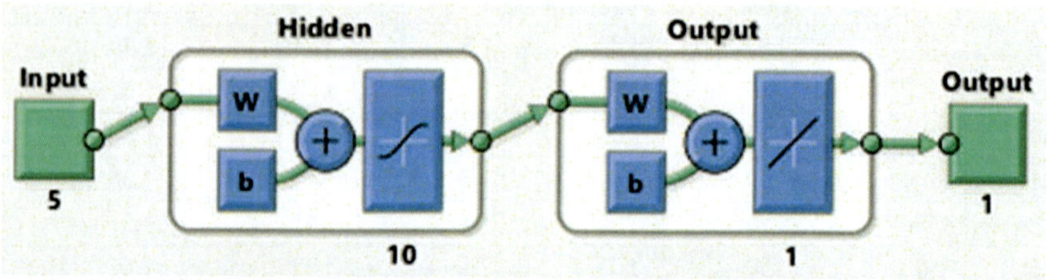

Fig. 12.3 Neural network's structure

According to Alam et al. [29], the present investigation took into account six different values of neurons (5–6–7–8–9–10), six different swarm size populations (10–20–50–100–200–400), and acceleration factors c_1 and c_2 that fell within the range of 1–2.5 and 2–3, respectively. One thousand iterations have been specified as the maximum. If after 100 iterations the improvement in the objective function did not surpass 10^{-8}, the run was stopped.

Assessment indices were used to examine the model's error rates and prediction accuracy. The Mean Square Error (MSE) and Coefficient of determination (R^2) are the statistical measurements utilized. The system of Eqs. 12.4 and 12.5 is used to compute the statistical measurements.

$$R^2 = 1 - \frac{\sum_k (y_k - \hat{y}_k)^2}{\sum_k (y_k - \overline{y}_k)^2} \tag{12.4}$$

$$MSE = \frac{1}{2}\sum_{k=1}^{n} (y_k - \hat{y}_k)^2 \tag{12.5}$$

where the details of y_k, $\hat{y}_k$, $\overline{y}_k$ n and k are given. The symbols y_k, $\hat{y}_k$ and $\overline{y}_k$ stand for the experimental data sample, the algorithm's projected values and the mean value of the experimental data samples, respectively. N stands for the number of data samples, and K stands for the set of all source points indexed by k.

12.5 Results and Discussions

12.5.1 ANN Results

Figure 12.4 allow an easy visual comparison between the predicted Surface Roughness against the actual values respectively. The regression value R^2 of 0.91272 suggests that the output tracks the targets effectively.

Figure 12.5 the ANN predictions versus the actual data of the Surface Roughness considering the 50 data. The anticipated outputs frequently match the desired values very nearly. The average percentage of the deviation was approximately 5.49%. A discrepancy exceeding 12% was observed for 5 data while most of the deviation of the predicted value was under 10%.

12.5.2 ANN-PSO Results

A parametric analysis was performed to identify the configuration of the ANN-PSO model that yields the highest performance metrics. It has been determined which acceleration factors (c_1 and c_2) are most effective given the population size and the number of neurons in the hidden layer. For the training and testing dataset, the Mean Squared Error (MSE) and R squared value (R^2) was used to assess the model's prediction accuracy. The best training outcome was obtained with 10 neurons, a 200-swarm population, and acceleration factors c1 and c2 of 1 and 2.75, respectively, according to Table 12.2. This corresponds to configuration 35. The training regression value R^2 and MSE were 0.99671 and 4.5886e−04 respectively. Conversely, the best result considering training and testing was obtained when the number of neurons is 8, swarm population size is 10, and acceleration factors c_1 and c_2 are 1 and 2.75. This corresponds to configuration 19. The training regression value R^2 and MSE

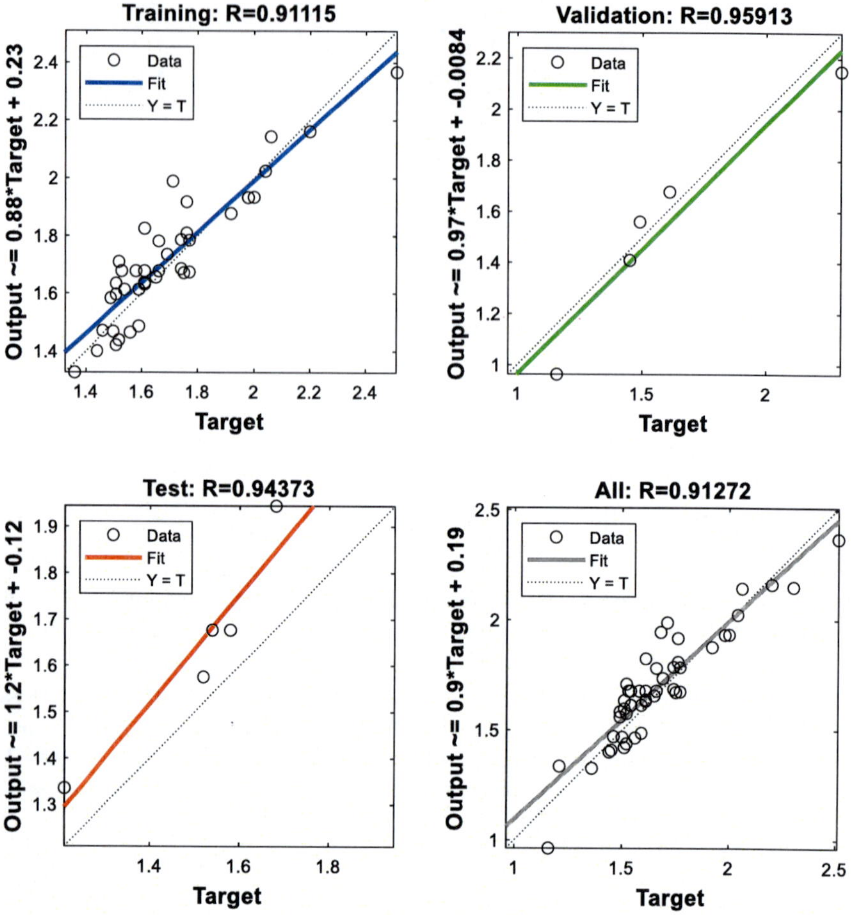

Fig. 12.4 Performance indicators of ANN models considering training, testing and validation

were 0.91641 and 0.0112 respectively. Interestingly, the best model configuration considering training performance only exhibits a poor testing performance of 0.1997 while the best model configuration considering training and testing yields 0.8567. Nevertheless, these results show that the ANN performance metric was enhanced from 0.91115 (Fig. 12.4) to 0.99671 (Fig. 12.6-configuration 35), using ANN-PSO.

The network's training responses of all the 36-configuration considered are shown in Fig. 12.6, and their testing responses are shown in Fig. 12.7.

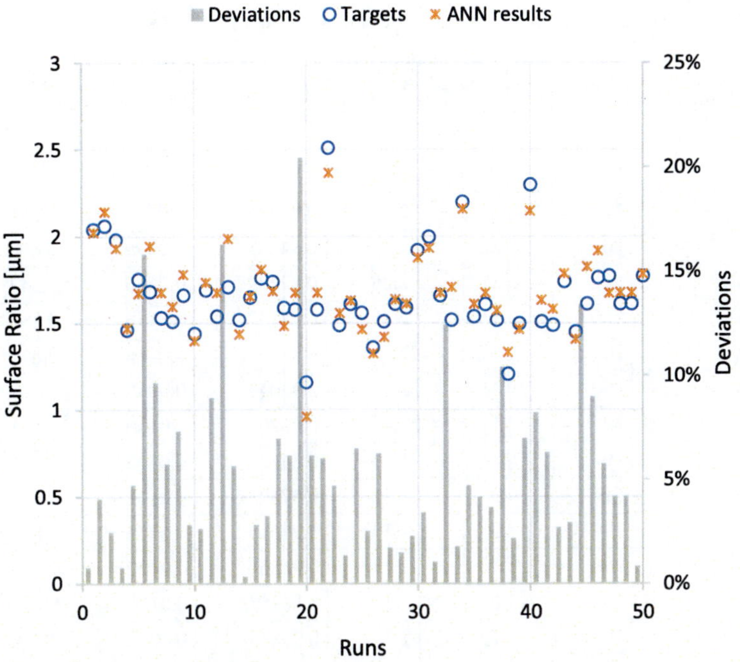

Fig. 12.5 Performance of ANN predictions

A crucial finding from the data is that the parameters of the PSO have an impact on performance prediction. Additionally, the outcomes of the finest testing and training were not the same. As a result, the most ideal network found was ANN-PSO 10-200-1-2.75 considering the training performance (configuration 35). However, considering training and testing performance, the best model configuration was ANN-PSO 8-10-1-2.75 (configuration 19). A comparison between these two best configurations was done. Figure 12.8 shows that the performance prediction of these two configurations was very close. The average deviations of the ANN-PSO 10-200-1-2.75 (configuration 35) and ANN-PSO 8-10-1-2.75 (configuration 19) were 15.14% and 14.06% respectively.

The ANN-PSO 8-10-1-2.75 model (configuration 19) was considered for further analysis. As mentioned in the previous part, the 50 data were divided into two groups: 42 data were used for the hybrid ANN-PSO model's training, and 8 data were utilized for the model's testing. The testing performance R^2 was 0.8567. Compared to the testing performance of 0.94373 exhibited by the ANN model, the proposed ANN-PSO model was less robust. Figure 12.9 shows clearly that most targets were hit (or were closer to) by ANN results. However, several reasons could justify these findings:

Table 12.2 Summarized training and testing performance for all ANN-PSO configurations

			Acceleration factors				
	Number of neurons	Swarm population size	c_1	c_2	Training R^2	MSE	Testing R^2
1	5	10	2.25	2	0.87886	0.0159	0.3411
2	5	20	2.25	2	0.84861	0.0195	0.6002
3	5	50	1.5	2.25	0.87277	0.0166	0.5472
4	5	100	1	2.75	0.88137	0.0156	0.2904
5	5	200	1.5	2	0.91317	0.0116	0.6768
6	5	400	1.5	2	0.96013	0.0055	0.6972
7	6	10	1	3	0.90203	0.0130	0.5419
8	6	20	2	2.25	0.84777	0.0196	0.5927
9	6	50	1	2.5	0.87693	0.0161	0.5835
10	6	100	1	2.5	0.94649	0.0073	0.0959
11	6	200	1	2.75	0.9086	0.0122	0.56
12	6	400	1	2.25	0.86753	0.0173	0.0336
13	7	10	1.5	2.5	0.95834	0.0057	0.5098
14	7	20	1	2.75	0.96653	0.0046	0.3564
15	7	50	1	2.5	0.96475	0.0048	0.2747
16	7	100	1	2.5	0.92512	0.0102	0.3592
17	7	200	1.5	2.25	0.96838	0.0044	0.6541
18	7	400	2	2	0.89297	0.0143	0.0339
19	8	10	1	2.75	0.91641	0.0112	0.8567
20	8	20	1	2.5	0.93957	0.0082	0.4328
21	8	50	1.5	2.25	0.89193	0.0143	0.3082
22	8	100	1	2.5	0.97414	0.0036	0.2846
23	8	200	1	2.75	0.86246	0.0179	0.8557
24	8	400	1	2.25	0.92936	0.0095	0.135
25	9	10	1	2.75	0.90869	0.0122	0.535
26	9	20	1	3	0.89998	0.0133	0.174
27	9	50	1.5	2.25	0.95093	0.0067	0.4457
28	9	100	2	2	0.96381	0.0050	0.6959
29	9	200	1.5	2.25	0.9754	0.0034	0.0744

(continued)

Table 12.2 (continued)

			Acceleration factors				
	Number of neurons	Swarm population size	c_1	c_2	Training R^2	MSE	Testing R^2
30	9	400	1	2.5	0.94264	0.0078	0.0439
31	10	10	1	2.75	0.9286	0.0096	0.3589
32	10	20	1.5	2.5	0.90495	0.0127	0.3903
33	10	50	1.5	2.5	0.92313	0.0103	0.7149
34	10	100	1	2.75	0.93147	0.0092	0.6535
35	10	200	1	2.75	0.99671	4.5886e-04	0.1997
36	10	400	1.5	2.5	0.98866	0.0016	0.3323

- The split of data: While building the ANN model, the split between training, testing and validation data is done within MATLAB. When retraining an ANN model, the testing data are reallocated to enhance the prediction performance. This is in contrast with the ANN-PSO model. In this latter approach, the testing data must be picked randomly within the parameter's domain.
- The performance of the ANN-PSO model: This performance depends on the values attributed to the number of neurons, the swarm population size and the acceleration factors. This study shows that an adjustment of these parameters could improve or deteriorates the prediction performance. Therefore, performing an optimization to identify the best configuration of the ANN-PSO model would potentially improve its prediction performance.
- The limitations of the data available: This study was based on 50 data. It is expected that performance could be enhanced with a larger dataset.

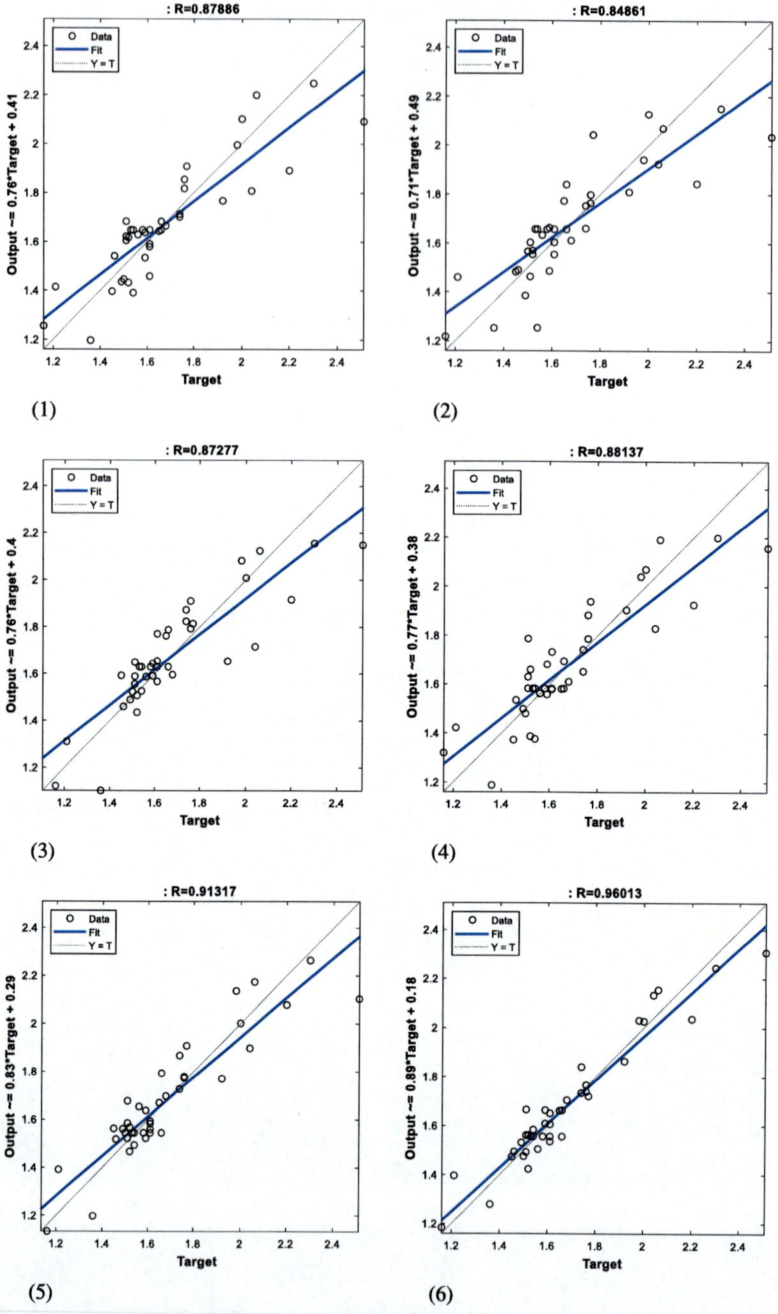

Fig. 12.6 ANN-PSO training results per configuration number (1–36)

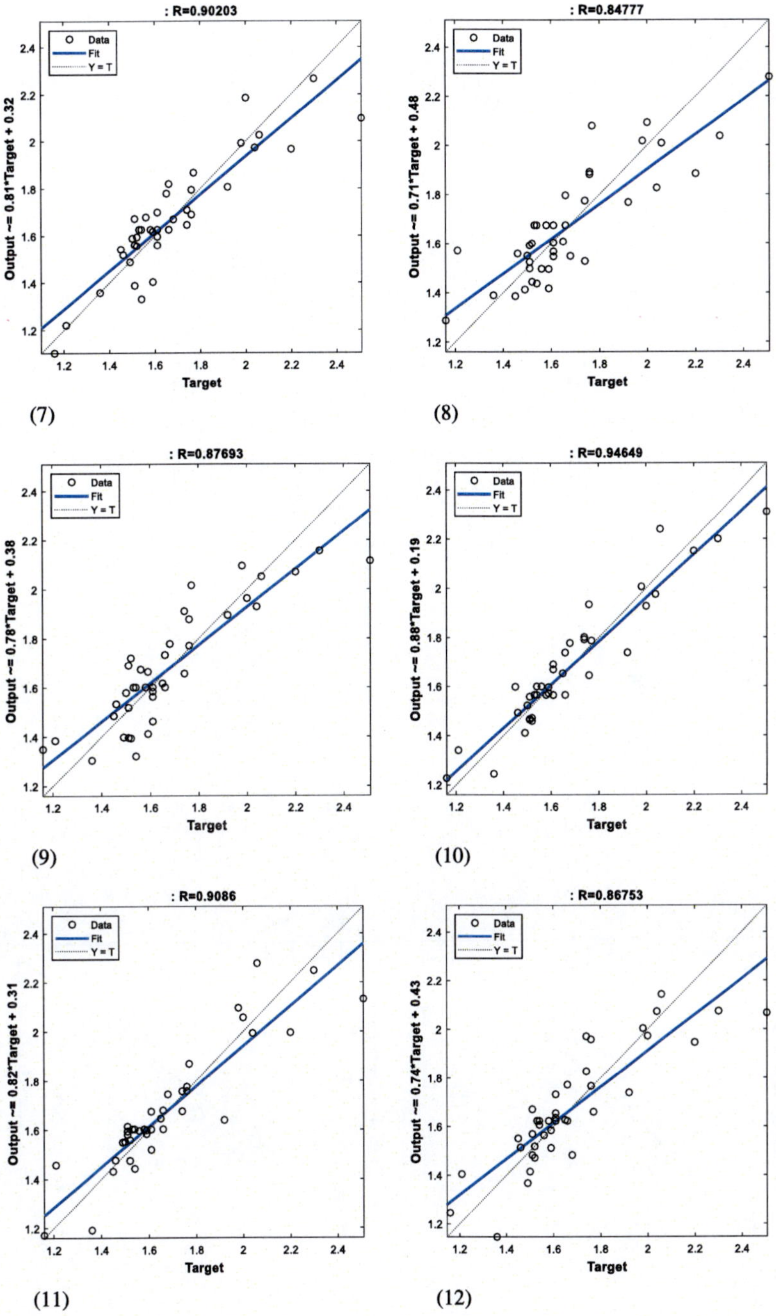

Fig. 12.6 (continued)

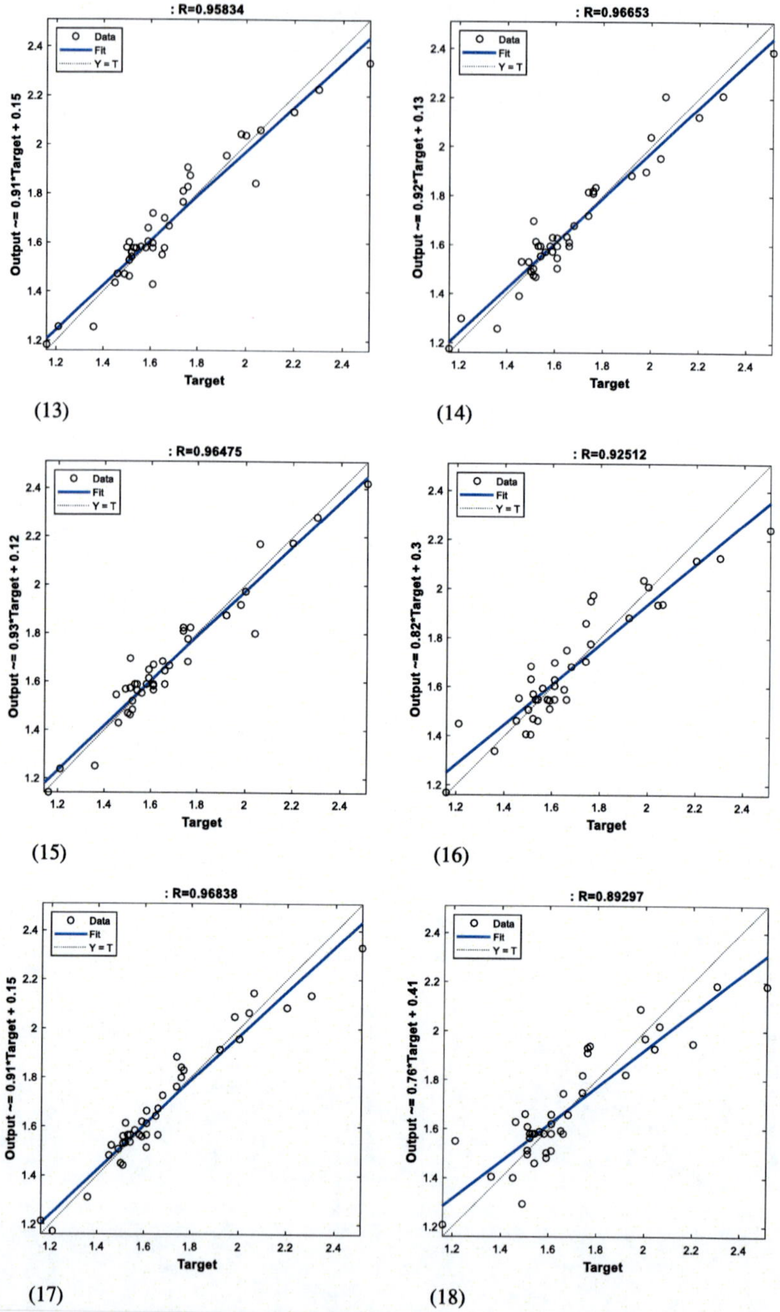

Fig. 12.6 (continued)

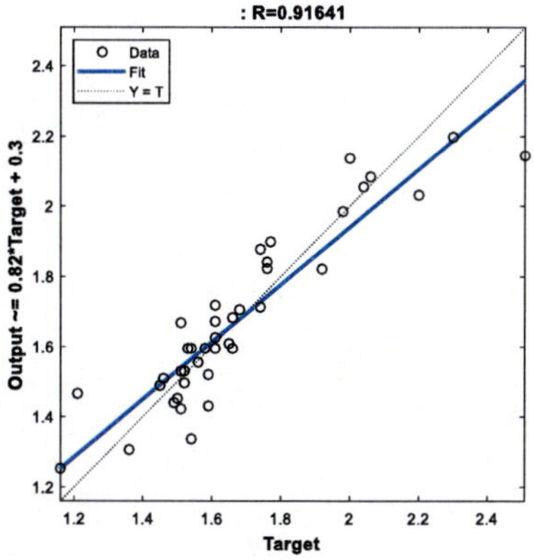

(19)

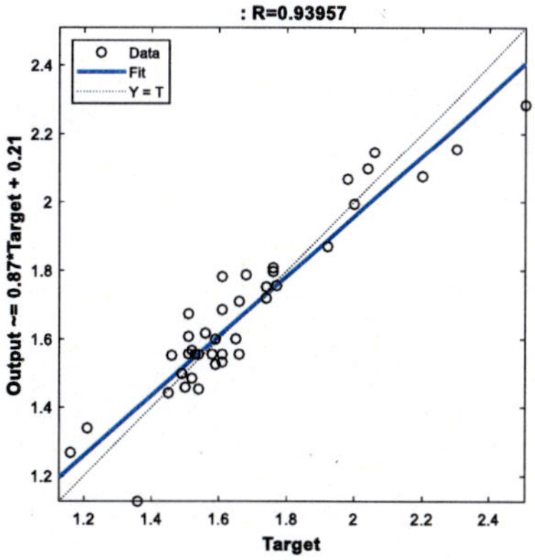

(20)

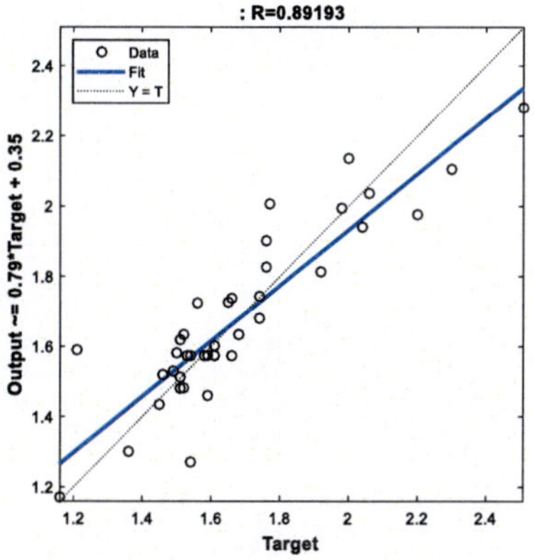

(21)

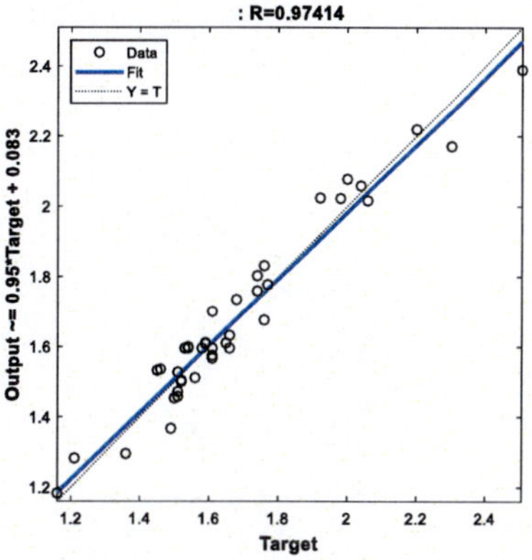

(22)

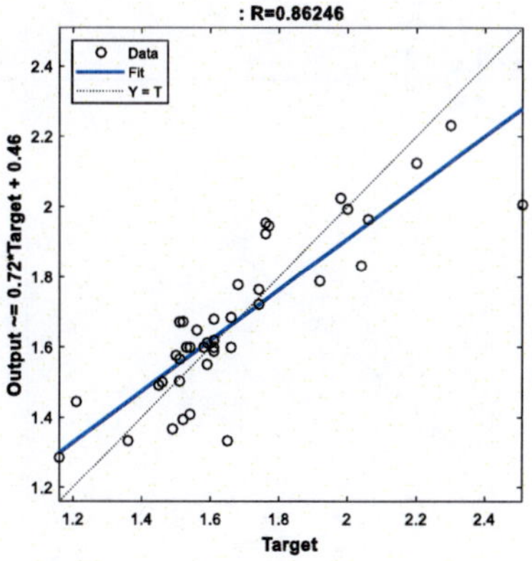

(23)

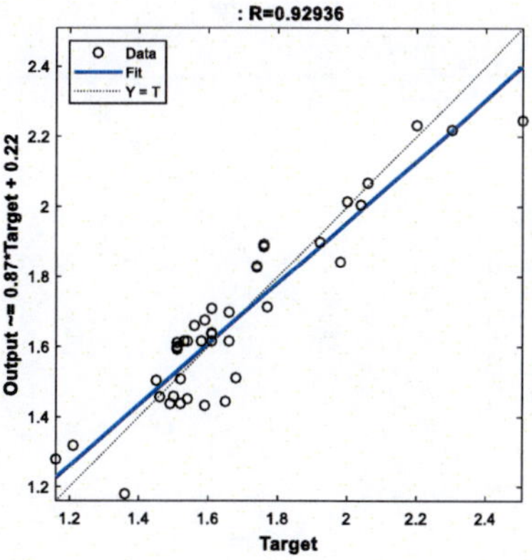

(24)

Fig. 12.6 (continued)

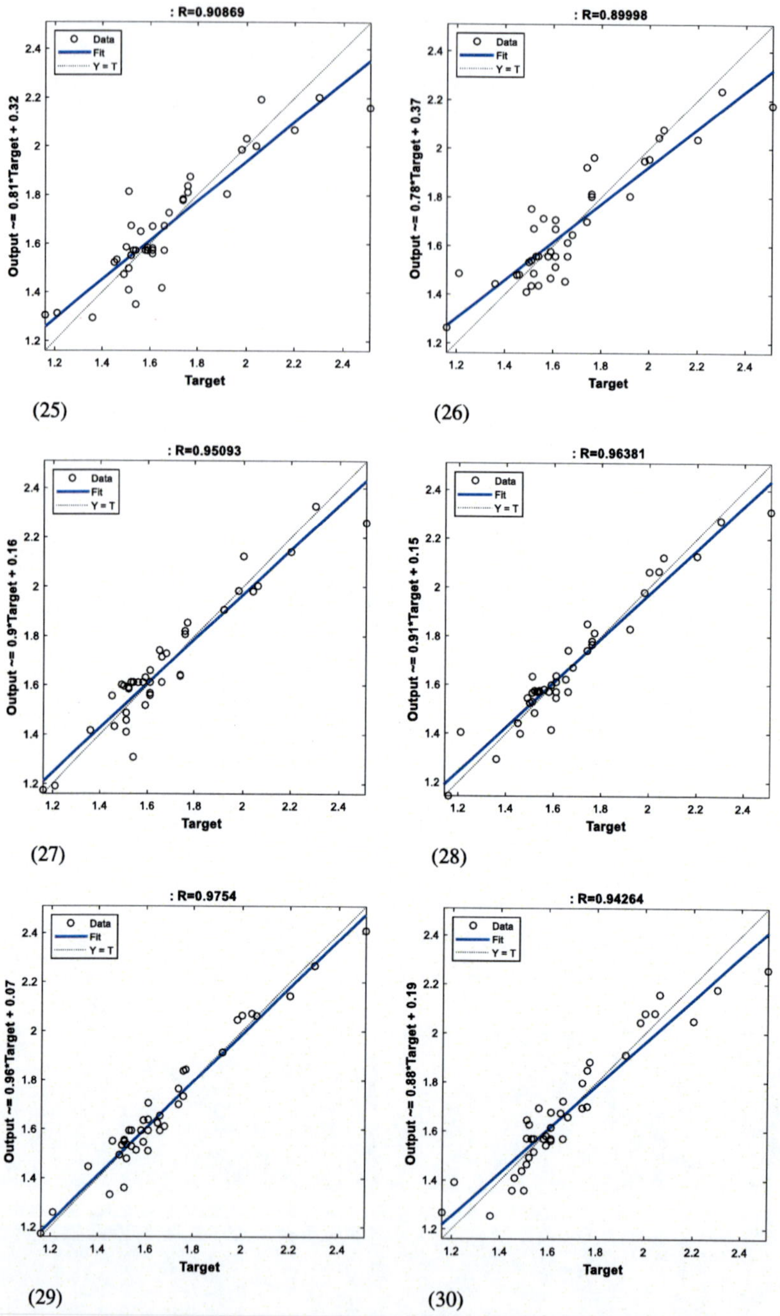

Fig. 12.6 (continued)

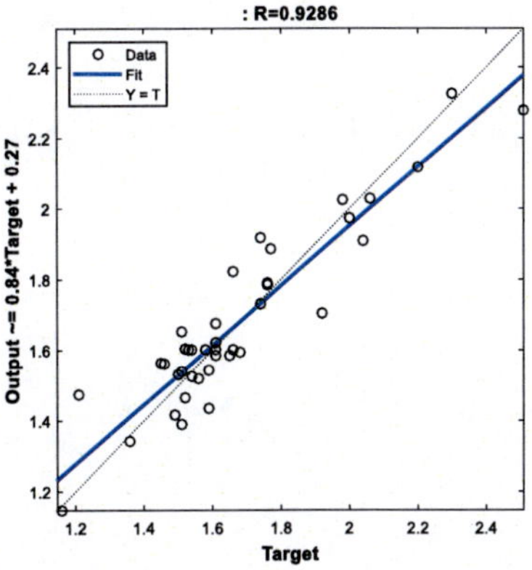

(31)

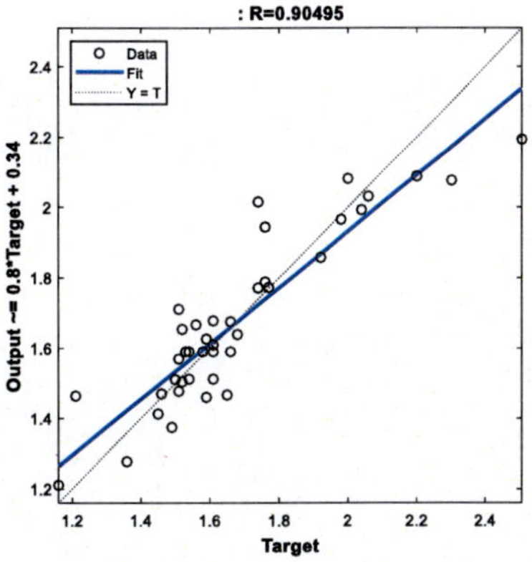

(32)

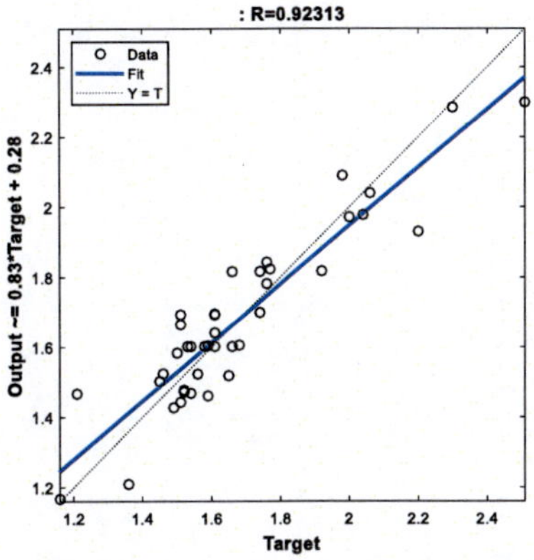

(33)

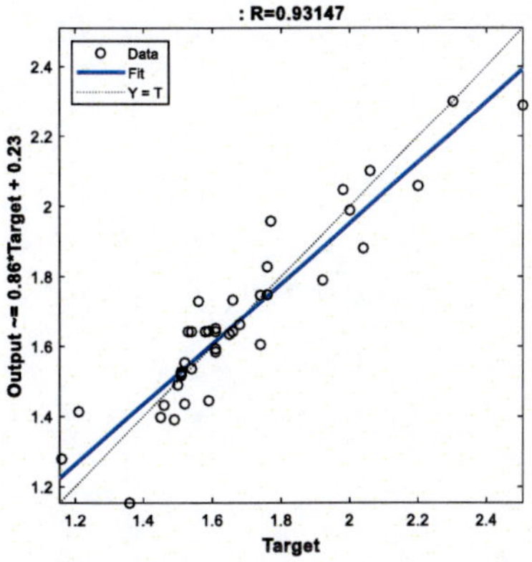

(34)

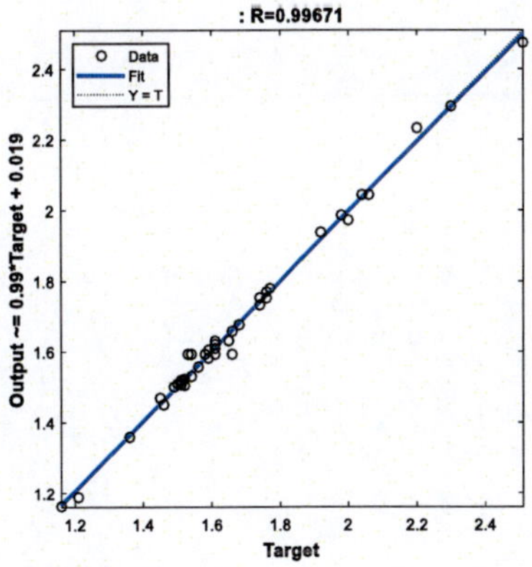

(35)

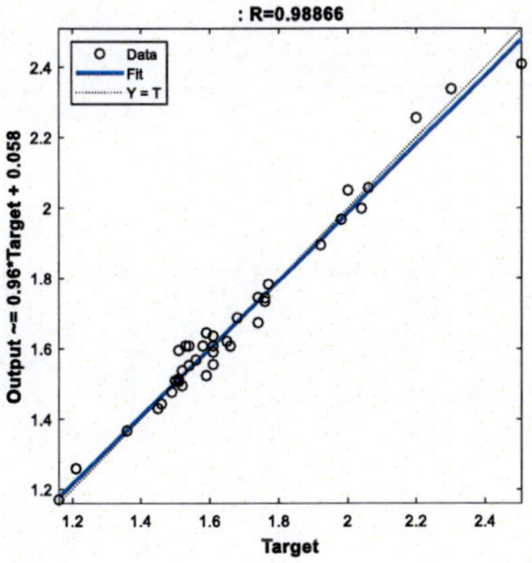

(36)

Fig. 12.6 (continued)

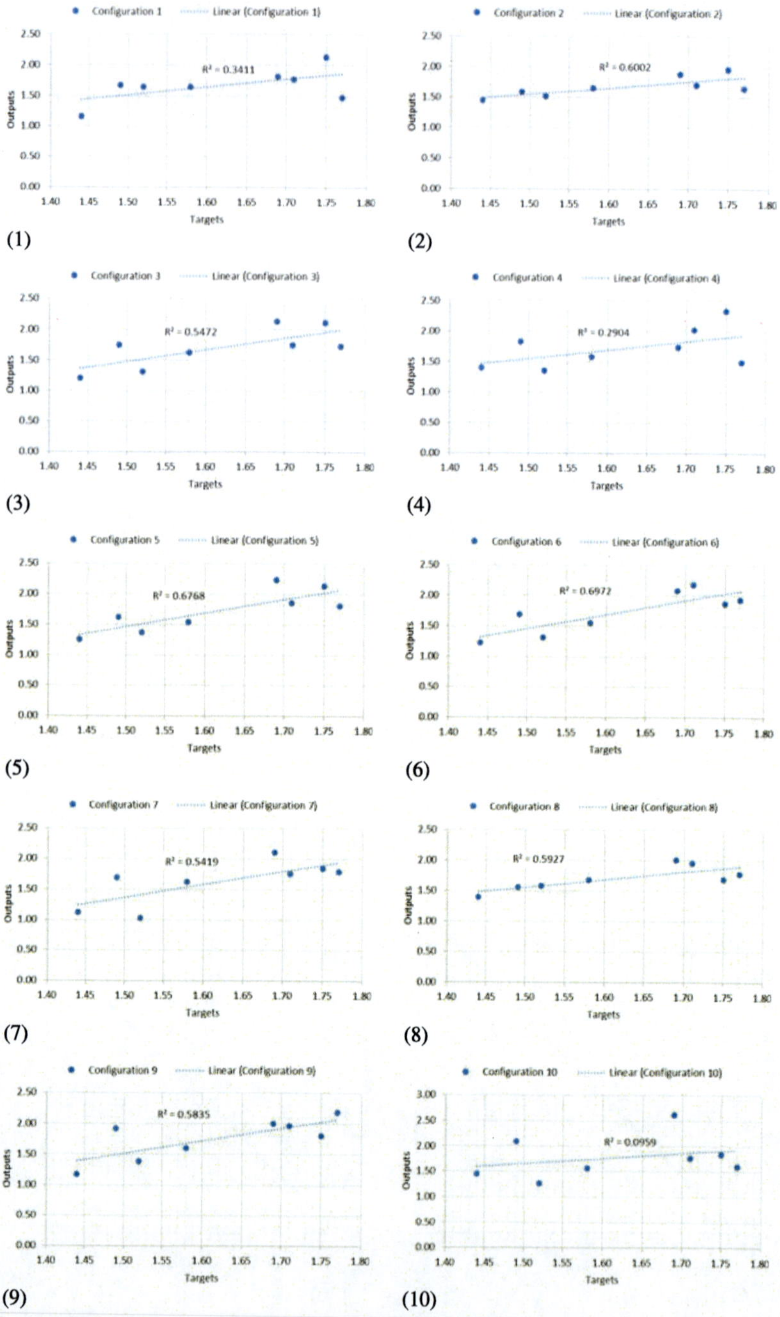

Fig. 12.7 ANN-PSO testing results per configuration number (1–36)

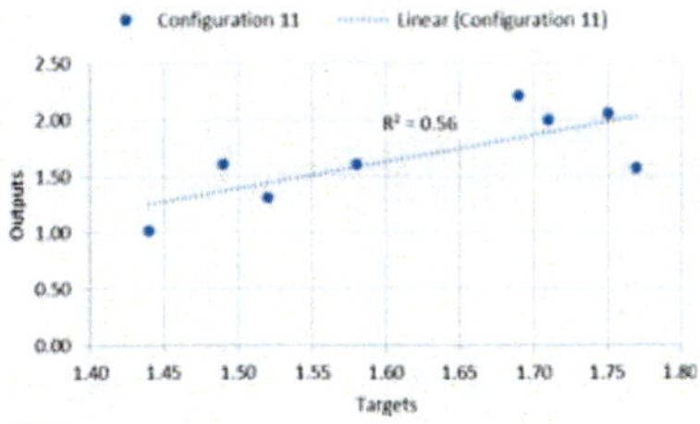

(11)

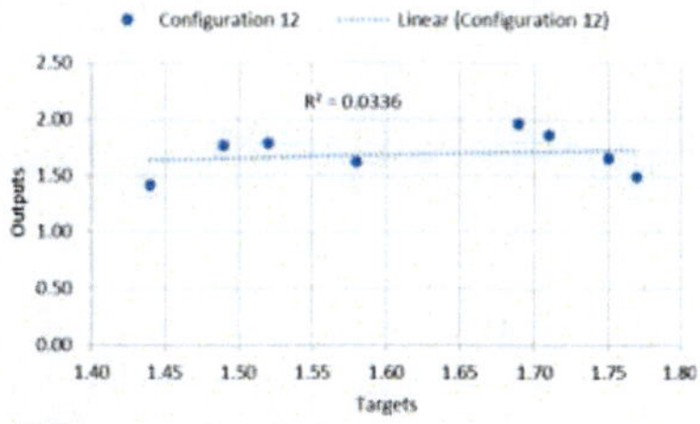

(12)

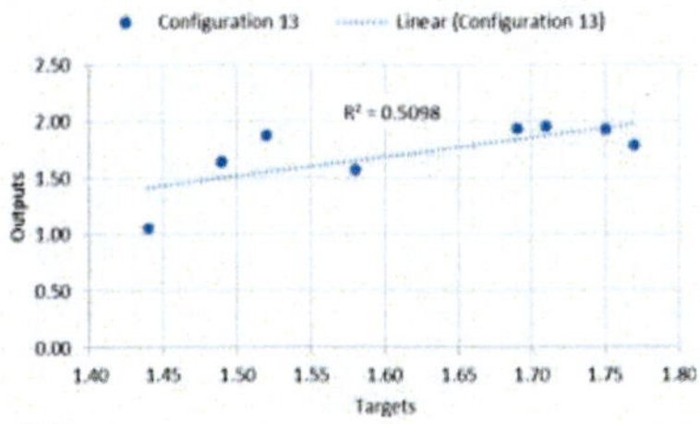

(13)

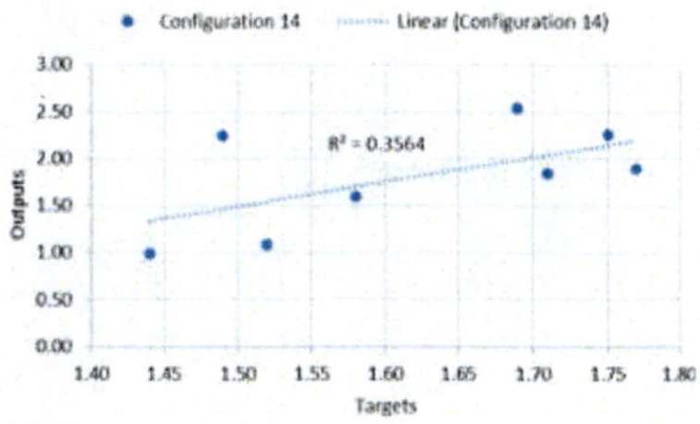

(14)

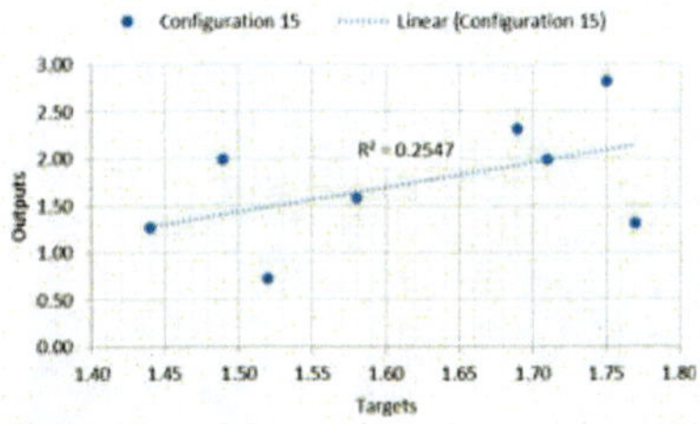

(15)

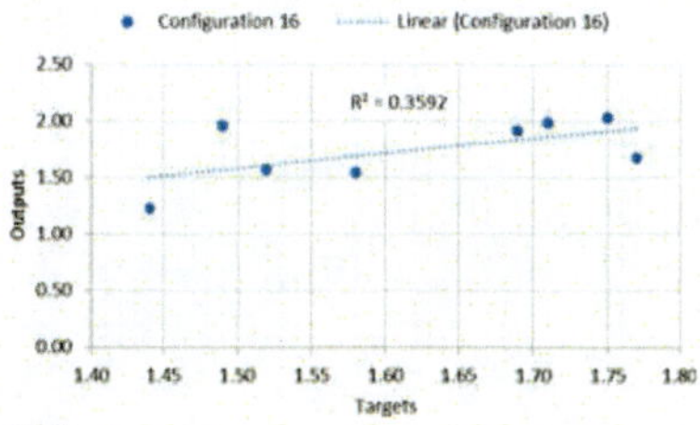

(16)

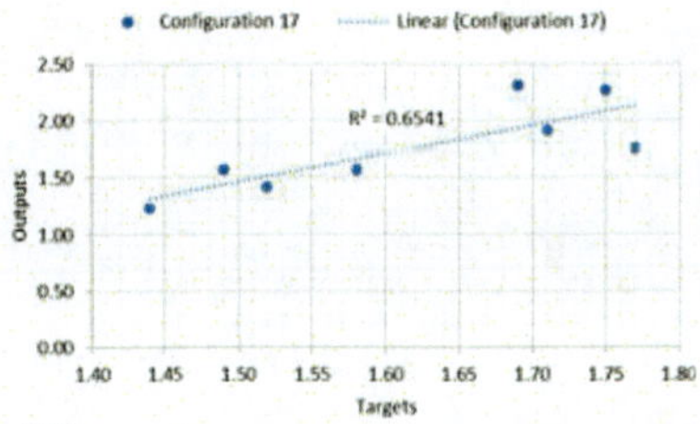

(17)

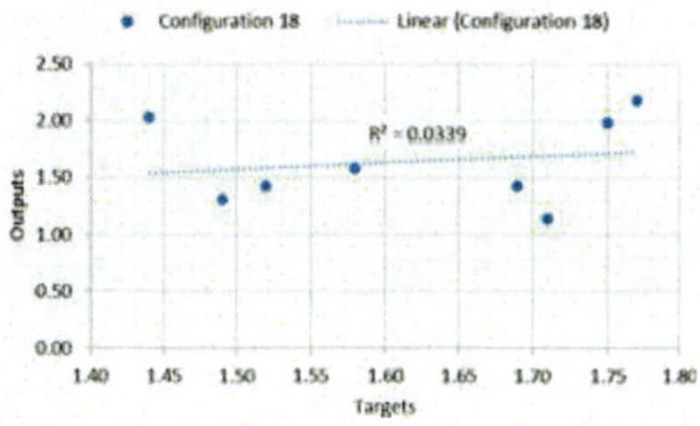

(18)

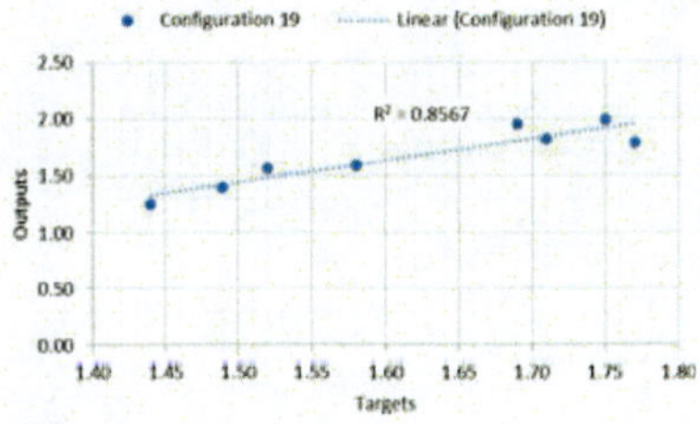

(19)

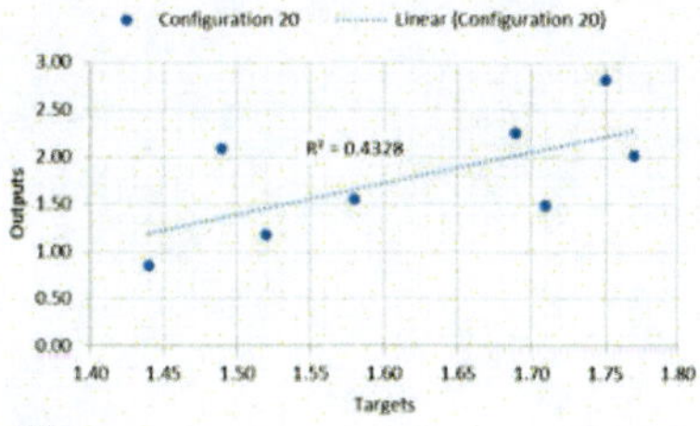

(20)

Fig. 12.7 (continued)

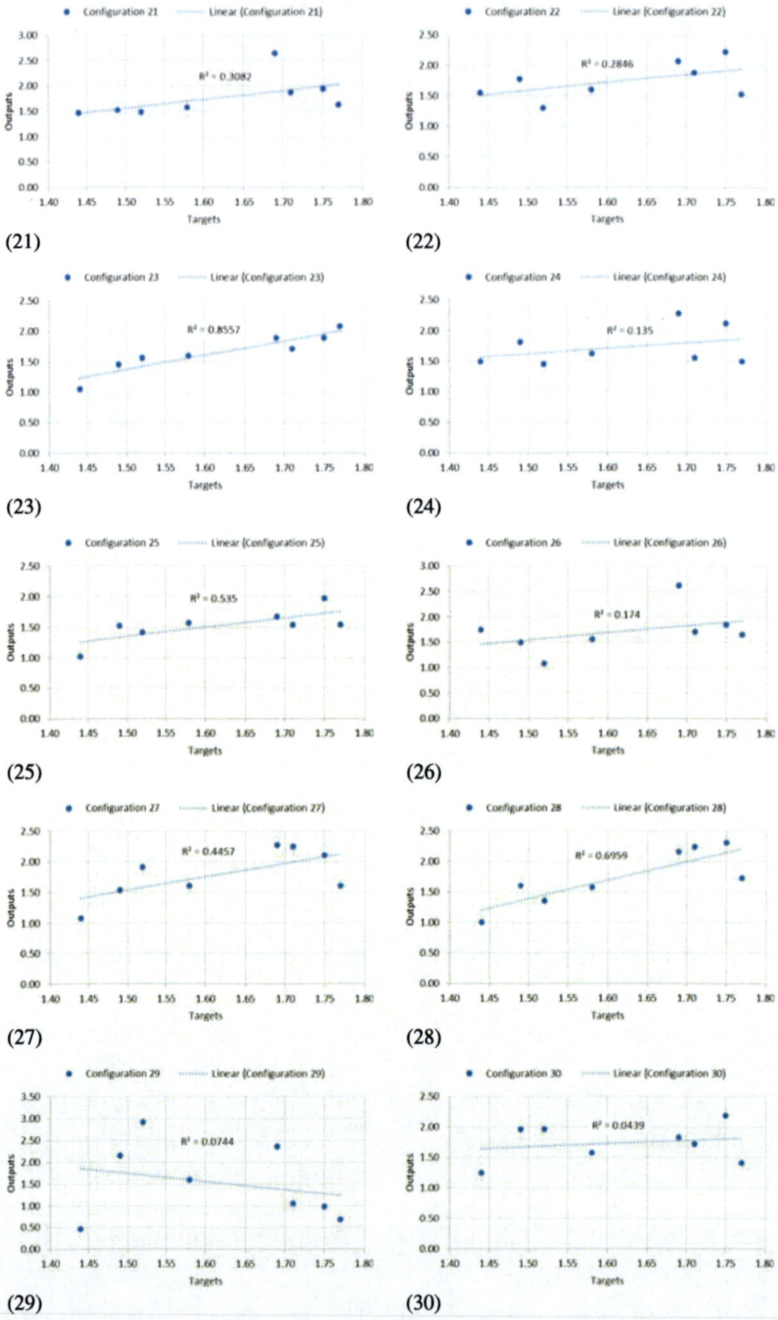

Fig. 12.7 (continued)

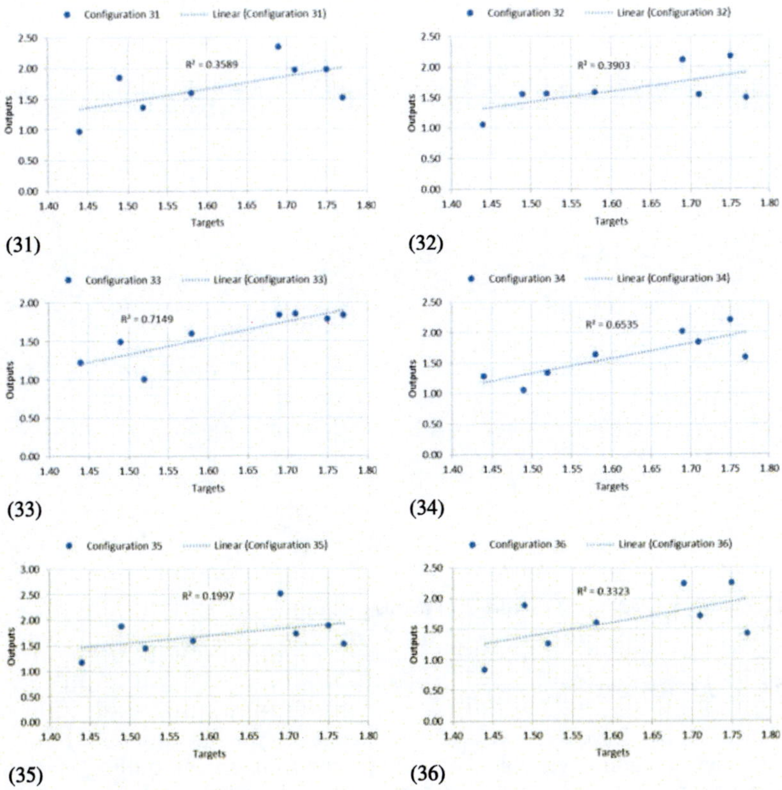

Fig. 12.7 (continued)

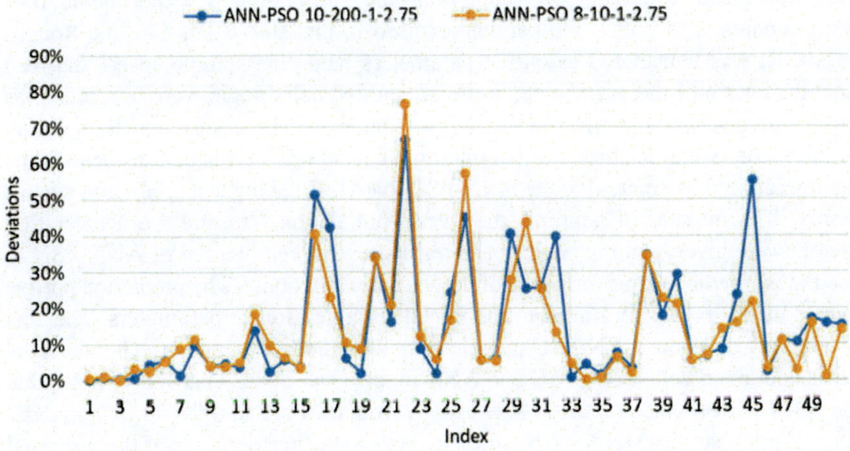

Fig. 12.8 Comparison of ANN-PSO results

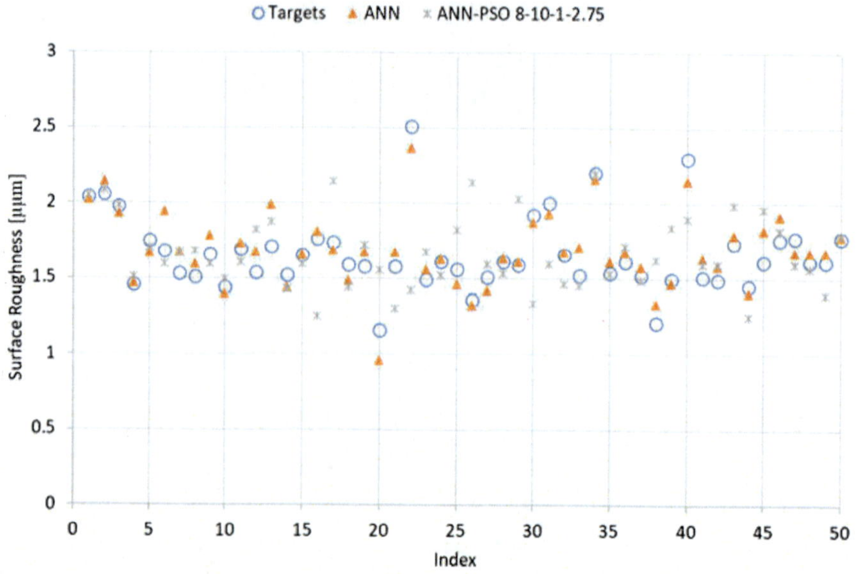

Fig. 12.9 ANN and ANN-PSO 8-10-1-2.75 results comparison

12.6 Conclusion

In this paper, a readily available dataset extracted from an end milling machining of an AA8112 alloy performed on a SIEG 3/10/0016 CNC machine was considered. Titanium dioxide (TiO_2) and multi-walled carbon nanotube (MWCNTs) nanolubricants mixed with copra oil were used as the cutting fluid. 50 experimental runs were conducted to obtain the parameters used in this study. The Surface Roughness (SR) was considered as output parameters while the spindle speed, the feed rate, the length of the cut, the depth of cut, and the helix angle were considered as input parameters. An ANN-PSO model was built. Details describing the building of the model were disclosed. A parametric analysis was performed to identify the configuration (parameters) of the ANN-PSO that yield the highest prediction performance. The number of neurons, the swarm population size and the acceleration factors were given random values. The results reveal the potential of ANN-PSO to accurately predict the performance of the Surface Roughness. The prediction performance metric is closely linked to the model configuration or parameters. The best configurations of the ANN-PSO models were identified. A comparison between the results obtained with ANN-PSO and ANN models was done. This study shows that the ANN performance metric was enhanced from 0.91115 to 0.99671 using ANN-PSO. Further studies would be required to analyse the performance of the proposed model with test data. The lower performance, with respect to test data reported in this study, can be attributed to the selection of test data, the limited number of data and the need to optimize the parameters of the ANN-PSO model. Nevertheless, this study gives an insight into possible strategies that will cut down on time-consuming and expensive experimentation and help decision-makers find the configuration that maximizes efficiency during machining operations.

References

1. Okokpujie, I.P., Bolu, C.A., Ohunakin, O.S., Akinlabi, E.T., Adelekan, D.S.: A review of recent application of machining techniques, based on the phenomena of CNC machining operations. Proc. Manuf. **35**, 1054–1060 (2019)
2. Shivanna, D.M., Kiran, M.B., Venkatesh, G.S., Kavitha, S.D.: Analyzing the effects of machining parameters on surface roughness of machined surfaces using vision system. Materials Today Proc. **47**, 4885–4890 (2021)
3. Lawal, S.A., Choudhury, I.A., Nukman, Y.: A critical assessment of lubrication techniques in machining processes: a case for minimum quantity lubrication using vegetable oil-based lubricant. J. Clean. Prod. **41**, 210–221 (2013)
4. Okokpujie, I.P., Ohunakin, O.S., Adelekan, D.S., Bolu, C.A., Gill, J., Atiba, O.E., Aghedo, O.A.: Experimental investigation of nano-lubricants effects on temperature distribution of mild steel machining. Proc. Manuf. **35**, 1061–1066 (2019)
5. Gugulothu, S., Pasam, V.K.: Testing and performance evaluation of vegetable-oil–based hybrid nano cutting fluids. J. Test. Eval. **48**(5), 3839–3854 (2018)
6. Lee, C.G., Hwang, Y.J., Choi, Y.M., Lee, J.K., Choi, C., Oh, J.M.: A study on the tribological characteristics of graphite nano lubricants. Int. J. Precis. Eng. Manuf. **10**(1), 85–90 (2009)
7. Ghosh, G., Mandal, P., Mondal, S.C.: Modeling and optimization of surface roughness in keyway milling using ANN, genetic algorithm, and particle swarm optimization. Int. J. Adv. Manuf. Technol. **100**(5), 1223–1242 (2019)
8. Okokpujie, I.P., Ajayi, O.O., Afolalu, S.A., Abioye, A.A., Salawu, E.Y., Udo, M., Okonkwo, U.C., Orodu, K.B., Ikumapayi, O.M.: Modeling and optimization of surface roughness in end milling of aluminium using least square approximation method and response surface methodology. Int. J. Mech. Eng. Technol. (IJMET) **9**(1), 587–600 (2018)
9. Zhong, Z.W., Khoo, L.P., Han, S.T.: Prediction of surface roughness of turned surfaces using neural networks. Int. J. Adv. Manuf. Technol. **28**(7), 688–693 (2006)
10. Jesuthanam, C.P., Kumanan, S., Asokan, P.: Surface roughness prediction using hybrid neural networks. Mach. Sci. Technol. **11**(2), 271–286 (2007)
11. Jenarthanan, M.P., Subramanian, A.A., Jeyapaul, R.: Comparative analysis of surface roughness prediction using DOE and ANN techniques during endmilling of glass fibre reinforced polymer (GFRP) composites. Pigm. Resin Technol. **45**(2), 126–139 (2016)
12. Pontes, F.J., De Paiva, A.P., Balestrassi, P.P., Ferreira, J.R., Da Silva, M.B.: Optimization of Radial Basis Function neural network employed for prediction of surface roughness in hard turning process using Taguchi's orthogonal arrays. Expert Syst. Appl. **39**(9), 7776–7787 (2012)
13. Zhong, Z.W., Khoo, L.P., Han, S.T.: Neural-network predicting of surface finish or cutting parameters for carbide and diamond turning processes. Mater. Manuf. Process. **23**(1), 92–97 (2007)
14. Horváth, R., Dregelyi-Kiss, A.: Analysis of surface roughness of aluminum alloys fine turned: united phenomenological models and multi-performance optimization. Measurement **65**, 181–192 (2015)

15. Sofuoglu SD. Using artificial neural networks to model the surface roughness of massive wooden edge-glued panels made of Scotch pine (Pinus sylvestris i.) In a machining process with computer numerical control. Bioresources **10** 6797–6808 (2015)
16. Tiryaki, S., Malkoçoğlu, A., Özşahin, Ş: Using artificial neural networks for modeling surface roughness of wood in machining process. Constr. Build. Mater. **66**, 329–335 (2014)
17. Machesa, M.G.K., Tartibu, L.K., Okwu, M.O.: Performance analysis of stirling engine using computational intelligence techniques (ANN & Fuzzy Mamdani Model) and hybrid algorithms (ANN-PSO & ANFIS). Neural Comput. Appl. 1–21 (2022)
18. Seguini, M., Khatir, S., Boutchicha, D., Nedjar, D., Abdel Wahab, M.: Crack prediction in pipeline using ANN-PSO based on numerical and experimental modal analysis. Smart Struct. Syst. **27**(3), 507–523 (2021)
19. Tartibu, L.K., Okwu, M.O., Ighawe, D.E., Mulaba–Bafubiandi, A.F.: Analysis of vibration prediction accuracy in underground mining operation based on monitored blast records. In: Proceedings of International Conference on Noise and Vibration Engineering (ISMA2020) & International Conference on Uncertainty in Structural Dynamics (USD2020). Leuven 7 to 9 September 2020, pp. 987–100 (2020)
20. Pant, P., Chatterjee, D.: Prediction of clad characteristics using ANN and combined PSO-ANN algorithms in laser metal deposition process. Surf. Interfaces **21**, 100699 (2020)
21. Wang, S.C.: Artificial neural network. In Interdisciplinary Computing in Java Programming, pp. 81–100. Springer, Boston, MA (2003)
22. Karnin, E.D.: A simple procedure for pruning back-propagation trained neural networks. IEEE Trans. Neural Netw. **1**(2), 239–242 (1990)
23. Okwu, M.O., Tartibu, L.K.: Metaheuristic optimization: Nature-inspired algorithms swarm and computational intelligence, theory and applications, vol. 927. Springer Nature (2020). https://doi.org/10.1007/978-3-030-61111-8_14
24. Rukhaiyar, S., Alam, M.N., Samadhiya, N.K.: A PSO-ANN hybrid model for predicting factor of safety of slope. Int. J. Geotech. Eng. **12**(6), 556–566 (2018)
25. Eberhart, R., Kennedy, J.: A new optimizer using particle swarm theory. In: MHS'95. Proceedings of the Sixth International Symposium on Micro Machine and Human Science, pp. 39–43. IEEE, Washington, DC, USA (1995)
26. Okokpujie, I.P., Bolu, C.A., Ohunakin, O.S.: Comparative performance evaluation of TiO_2, and MWCNTs nano-lubricant effects on surface roughness of AA8112 alloy during end-milling machining for sustainable manufacturing process. Int. J. Adv. Manuf. Technol. **108**(5), 1473–1497 (2020)
27. Okokpujie, I.P., Ohunakin, O.S., Bolu, C.A.: Multi-objective optimization of machining factors on surface roughness, material removal rate and cutting force on end-milling using MWCNTs nano-lubricant. Prog. Addit. Manuf. **6**(1), 155–178 (2021)
28. Momeni, E., Armaghani, D.J., Hajihassani, M., Amin, M.F.M.: Prediction of uniaxial compressive strength of rock samples using hybrid particle swarm optimization-based artificial neural networks. Measurement **60**, 50–63 (2015)
29. Alam, M.N., Das, B., Pant, V.: A comparative study of metaheuristic optimization approaches for directional overcurrent relays coordination. Electr. Power Syst. Res. **128**, 39–52 (2015)

Chapter 13
Adaptive Neuro-Fuzzy Inference System for Prediction of Surface Roughness Under Biodegradable Nano-lubricant

Abstract Machining processes involve many nonlinear parameters which make them complex. Setting of machines is generally relying on decision-making skills based on intuition and common sense learned through experience. In this work, five variables namely the spindle speed, the feed rate, the length of the cut, the depth of cut and the helix angle were considered to predict the surface roughness during the end-milling machining of AA8112 alloy. The adaptive neuro-fuzzy inference system (ANFIS) is proposed in this study. A dataset made of 50 data was used. Each data corresponds to a specific configuration of the end-milling machine and the corresponding surface roughness. In order to assess the prediction performance of ANFIS, various types of membership functions. This includes π-shaped (PIMF), generalized bell shape (GBELLMF), triangular shape (TRIMF), trapezoidal shape (TRAPMF), and Gaussian curve (GAUSSMF). This study shows that the various outputs track the targets effectively irrespective of the membership functions adopted the deviations between the predicted results and the targets were within 7%. This study demonstrates the potential of ANFIS models for the prediction of surface roughness.

Keywords Adaptive neuro-fuzzy inference system · Surface roughness · Nano-lubricant · Machining

13.1 Background

Surface roughness during manufacture is important because the surface of the element influences its performance throughout operations [1]. The product can be produced with the least amount of surface roughness by optimizing the machining settings and the lubricant used during the machining operations [2]. The lubricant's lubricity and cooling actions aid to lower the temperature and friction at the cutting region [3]. The thermal, rheological, and tribological properties of lubricants can be improved by new types of lubricants called nano-cutting fluids [4]. Because of the newly noticed change in thermo-physical and temperature exchange capacities, researchers have started utilizing nanoparticles in conventional oil [5]. Okokpujie et al. [6] proposed

I. P. Okokpujie and L. K. Tartibu, *Modern Optimization Techniques for Advanced Machining*, Studies in Systems, Decision and Control 485,
https://doi.org/10.1007/978-3-031-35455-7_13

the use of vegetable oil consisting of copra oil lubricant, titanium dioxide (TiO_2) and multi-walled carbon nanotube (MWCNTs) nano-lubricants during end-milling of AA8112 alloy. Their study reports an improvement in surface roughness.

Machining processes are generally complex. They involve many nonlinear parameters. In addition, the process takes place amid external disturbances. A proficient operator often completes a machining operation using decision-making skills based on intuition and common sense learned through experience. This method is not precise enough, and product flaws frequently occur. This is why intelligent machining—a dependable, automated machining system with cognitive functions—is required to achieve extremely productive and adaptable machining [7].

In an end milling operation, the cutting force is utilized to forecast surface quality during cutting. Milled surfaces benefit greatly from surface quality because it increases fatigue strength, corrosion resistance, and creep life. Additionally, the quality of a part's surface influences a number of its functional characteristics, including contact that results in surface friction, wear, light reflection, heat transmission, the capacity to distribute and hold lubricant, coating, and fatigue resistance [8].

The association between cutting force and surface roughness must be modelled in order to obtain greater levels of surface quality. Soft computing technologies enable modeling based on cutting force and surface roughness data [9]. Soft computing technologies enable modeling based on cutting force and surface roughness data [10]. When exact mathematical knowledge is unavailable, soft computing techniques can be helpful. These techniques differ from conventional computing in that they accommodate imprecision, uncertainty, approximation, and other heuristics [11]. One of the soft computing methods that are important in describing the relationship between the input–output matrix and the output is ANFIS. It is employed for defining the objective function and decision variables when expert advice and subjective knowledge are important. Because of the nonlinear nature of the machining process, ANFIS is the best tool for predicting surface roughness based on input data [12].

The adaptive neuro-fuzzy inference system (ANFIS) blends fuzzy logic theory and artificial neural networks, two well-known machine learning techniques [13]. Similar to an ANN, the ANFIS method can learn from training data and then map out the results onto a fuzzy inference system (FIS) [14]. As a result, a FIS in the ANFIS network precisely determines the hidden layers. By doing so, the ANN model's infamously difficult problem of identifying the hidden layer is solved, enhancing prediction accuracy overall [15]. As a result, ANFIS is taken into consideration since it can quickly and adaptively create the prediction model of surface roughness without requiring a complicated mathematical model. Previously, the ANFIS technique was used to estimate surface roughness and cutting zone temperature in dry turning processes of AISI304 stainless steel [16] and surface roughness in ball end milling processes [17].

In this study, ANFIS is proposed for the prediction of surface roughness using data collected during the end-milling machining of AA8112 alloy.

13.2 Modelling Approach

Classification jobs, rule-based process controls, pattern recognition issues, and function approximation issues have all benefited from the application of ANFIS [18]. The ideal distribution of membership functions is determined by the mapping relation between the input and output data in the ANFIS architecture, which combines fuzzy logic and artificial neural networks. It incorporates fuzzy logic (FL) theory and adaptive neural network (ANN) principles into adaptive network frameworks. The fuzzy interference system (FIS) application has been derived from FL theory, and by trial and error, the membership functions (MF) in FIS have been enhanced. In the ANFIS technique, the FIS model is developed using the ANN procedure, which also enables the learning of the neural network training data from the supplied data. The factors in the Sugeno category IF–THEN rule arrangement have simultaneously mapped the results.

Figure 13.1 depicts the overall architecture of the ANFIS framework. This inference system is fundamentally composed of five separate layers. They are the following: (i) layer fuzzy, (ii) product layer, (iii) normalized layer, (iv) de-fuzzy layer and, (v) total output layer. Each layer is made up of unique nodes, where the adaptive nodes are represented by squares and the factors could change. The fixed nodes, however, where the factors are fixed, are represented by circles.

The nodes in the preceding layers serve as the inputs for the current layers. For the sake of simplicity, it is assumed that this system has two inputs (a, b) and one output (S_i) in order to demonstrate the ANFIS operations [20]. Sugeno-type IF–THEN fuzzy rules are present in the ANFIS rule base. The two IF–THEN rules for a first-order

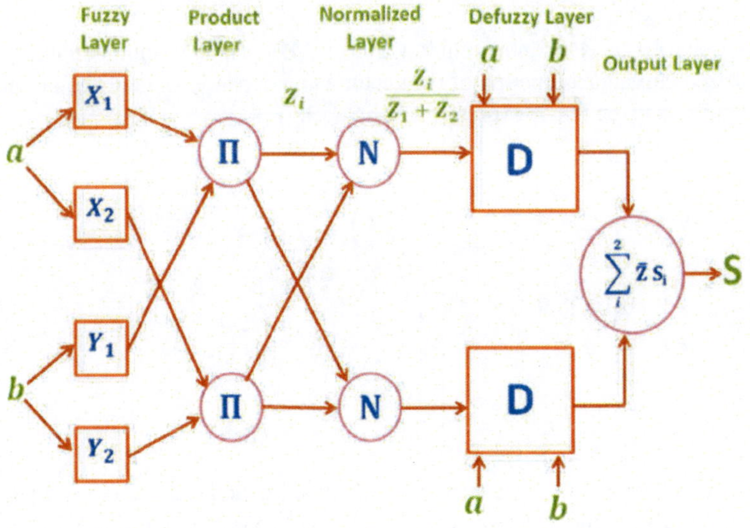

Fig. 13.1 Typical architecture of ANFIS [19]

Sugeno-fuzzy inference system (FIS) can be written as follows in Eqs. (13.1) and (13.2).

$$\text{Rule 1} \rightarrow \text{IF a is } X_1 \text{ and b is } Y_1; \text{ THEN c is } S_1(a, b) \tag{13.1}$$

$$\text{Rule 2} \rightarrow \text{IF a is } X_2 \text{ and b is } Y_2; \text{ THEN c is } S_2(a, b) \tag{13.2}$$

P_i and Q_i stand for fuzzy sets, where a and b are the ANFIS inputs. $S_i(a, b)$ is a Sugeno-FIS of first order.

(a) Fuzzy layer

The adaptive nodes with node functions make up the fuzzy layer. The inputs (a, b) are transformed into the linguistic labels (X_1, X_2, Y_1 and Y_2) that are utilized to divide the membership functions. Each node's output is governed by Eqs. (13.3) and (13.4) [19].

$$O_{1,i} = u_{X_i}(a) \quad \text{for} = 1, 2 \tag{13.3}$$

$$O_{1,i} = u_{Y_{i-2}}(b) \quad \text{for} = 3, 4 \tag{13.4}$$

where u_{X_i} and $u_{Y_{i-2}}$ are the membership functions, $O_{1,i}$ is the output function.

Typically, several membership functions are accessible, including the π-shaped membership function (PIMF), the generalized bell shape membership function (GBELLMF), the triangular shape membership function (TRIMF), the trapezoidal shape membership function (TRAPMF), and the Gaussian curve membership function (GAUSSMF).

The π-shaped curve membership function (PIMF), which is another name for the spline-based curve, is a function of the vector a and depends on the four parameters p, q, r, and s as given in the expression in Eq. (13.5) [21].

$$u_{X_i}(a, p, q, r, s) = \begin{bmatrix} 0, & a \le p \\ 2\left(\frac{a-p}{q-r}\right)^2, & p \le a \le \frac{p+q}{2} \\ 1 - 2\left(\frac{a-q}{q-p}\right)^2, & \frac{p+q}{2} \le a \le q \\ 1, & q \le a \le r \\ 1 - 2\left(\frac{a-r}{s-r}\right)^2, & r \le a \le \frac{r+s}{2} \\ 2\left(\frac{a-s}{s-r}\right)^2, & \frac{r+s}{2} \le a \le s \\ 0, & a \ge s \end{bmatrix} \tag{13.5}$$

The generalized bell-shaped curve in GBELLMF depends on three parameters p, q, and r, and is a function of a vector a. The Eq. (13.6) is presented as [21]:

$$u_{x_i}(a, p, q, r) = \frac{1}{1 + \left|\frac{a-r}{p}\right|^{2q}} \tag{13.6}$$

The generalized bell-shaped curve's foot, where the parameter q is often positive, are located by the parameters p and r. The center of the curve is represented by the parameter r.

The triangular curve in TRIMF depends on three scalar parameters, p, q, and r, and is a function of a vector, a. The Eq. (13.7) is given as follows.

$$u_{X_i}(a, p, q, r, s) = \begin{bmatrix} 0, & a \le p \\ \frac{a-p}{q-p}, & p \le a \le q \\ \frac{r-a}{r-q}, & q \le a \le r \\ 0, & r \le a \end{bmatrix} \tag{13.7}$$

The triangle's feet are located by the parameters p and r, while the peak is located by the parameter q.

As illustrated in the following expression in the Eq. (13.8), the trapezoidal curve in TRAPMF depends on four scalar parameters: p, q, r, and s.

$$u_{X_i}(a, p, q, r, s) = \begin{bmatrix} 0, & a \le p \\ \frac{a-p}{q-p}, & p \le a \le q \\ 1, & q \le a \le r \\ \frac{s-a}{s-r}, & r \le a \le s \\ 0, & s \le a \end{bmatrix} \tag{13.8}$$

The trapezoid's feet are located by the parameters p and s, while its shoulders are located by the parameters q and r.

As shown in Eq. (13.9), curves in GAUSSMF are a function of a vector a and depend on two parameters σ and r [22].

$$u_{X_i}(a; \sigma, c) = e^{\frac{(a-c)^2}{2\sigma^2}} \tag{13.9}$$

(b) Product layer

This layer, denoted by a circle and the letter P, employs fixed nodes. Each node's output is the sum of all the signals it has received from the layer before. The output of this layer is shown in the following Eq. (13.10).

$$O_{2,i} = Z_i = u_{x_i}(a).u_{y_i}(b) \quad \text{for } I = 1, 2 \tag{13.10}$$

The firing strength of a rule is shown by the output Z_i of each node.

(c) Normalized layer

A fixed node with a circle and the letter N are used to symbolize each node in a normalized layer. It is defined as the ratio of the firing power of the ith node (Z_i) to the total firing power of the rules, as given in Eq. (13.11) [22].

$$O_{3,i} = \overline{Z} = \frac{Z_i}{Z_1 + Z_2} \quad \text{for } i = 1, 2 \tag{13.11}$$

where $O_{3,i}$ and Z stand for the normalized layer's and firing strength's respective outputs. Only within a range of 0 to 1 are the output of the normalized layer and normalized firing strength acceptable.

(d) Defuzzy layer

The defuzzification layer, which is the fourth layer and is identified by the square and the letter D, is made up of adaptive nature nodes. It calculates the multiplication of the first-order polynomial and the normalized firing strength. Consequently, the following Eq. (13.12) defines this defuzzy layer's output [23].

$$O_{4,i} = \overline{Z}.S_i = \overline{Z}(e_i a + f_i b + g_i) \quad \text{for } i = 1, 2 \tag{13.12}$$

where the ensuing parameters are e_i, f_i, and g_i.

(e) Output layer

The output layer, which is the fifth layer, contains one fixed node and is identified by a circle. Here, the node function must calculate the overall output according to the Eq. (13.13) below [23].

$$O_{5,i} = \sum_i^2 \overline{Z}.S_i = \sum_i^2 \overline{Z}(e_i a + f_i b + g_i) = \text{Overall output for } i = 1, 2 \tag{13.13}$$

To increase the convergence rate, an algorithm used for this present work is a hybrid learning algorithm. This algorithm is used to integrate the least square and gradient descent methods in order to update the premise parameters. The least square method is utilized to optimize the consequent parameters. The gradient descent approach is used to regulate the premise parameters optimally after obtaining the best consequent parameters. Indirect parameters are used to determine ANFIS' output. The following Eq. (13.14) provides the entire output

$$\begin{aligned}\text{Total output} &= \overline{Z}S_1 + \overline{Z}S_2 = \frac{Z_1}{Z_1 + Z_2}S_1 + \frac{Z_2}{Z_1 + Z_2}S_2 \\ &= \frac{Z_1}{Z_1 + Z_2}(e_1F_1 + f_1F_2 + g_1) + \frac{Z_2}{Z_1 + Z_2}(e_2F_1 + f_2F_2 + g_2)\end{aligned} \tag{13.14}$$

13.3 Description of Dataset Extraction

The end-milling machining of AA8112 was done in this investigation using the SIEG 3/10/0016 CNC machine [24]. Three (3) planes x, y, and z planes make up the CNC milling machine. Five variables (namely the spindle speed, the feed rate, the length of the cut, the depth of cut and the helix angle) and five levels of the experiment make up the end-milling process, and the cutting fluid is a nano-lubricant made of multi-walled carbon Nanotube (MWCNTs) and titanium dioxide (T_iO_2) combined with copra oil. This section is broken down into several steps. The experimental inquiry used the following techniques:

- Aluminum 8112 alloy rectangular plate was divided into several lengths, including 20, 30, 40, 50, and 60 mm, respectively. 150 pieces overall, 50 pieces for T_iO_2, 50 pieces for MWCNTs nano-lubrications, and 50 pieces for copra oil machining were considered in a cut-off machine environment.
- T_iO_2 and MWCNTs nano-lubricants are set up for end-milling machining while the vertical CNC milling machine is being cleaned.
- The spindle head of the end-milling tool was mounted with a 13 mm diameter High-Speed Steel (HSS) cutting tool.
- Mounting the AA8112 alloy and dynamometer on the machine's table bed and securing them with a vibration-reducing device.
- The Y-axis and Z-axis were used as references while developing the CNC part programming, which included particular commands for implementing various cut lengths, feed rates, axial depths of cuts, helix angles, and spindle speeds.
- After each sample has been machined, the surface roughness of the workpiece is measured using the SRT-6210S surface roughness tester.
- Following all of the experimental analyses, Okokpujie et al. [24] investigated the surface interaction between the nano lubricant and the AA8112 alloy using the linear polarization resistance method.

The 50 experimental runs considered as a dataset in this study are provided in Table 13.1.

13.4 Methodology

The dataset considered to build the ANN model is provided in Table 13.1. These data relate the outputs (targets), namely the Surface Roughness (SR) to the inputs described by the spindle speed, feed rate, length of the cut, depth of cut, and helix angle. The dataset is then split into the appropriate places to clearly distinguish between the training and testing phases. 80% of the data, or 40 data, were used for training the ANN model in order to forecast the values of Surface Roughness. The remaining 10% of the data (or five data) were utilized for testing, and the remaining 10% was used for validation. The capabilities of the ANN model were assessed using

Table 13.1 Dataset

Index	Spindle speed (rpm)	Feed rate (mm/min)	Length of cut (mm)	Depth of cut (mm)	Helix angle (α) (o)	SR (MWCNTs) (μm)
1	2500	150	30	2.5	45	2.04
2	2500	250	50	2.5	15	2.06
3	2500	250	30	1.5	15	1.98
4	3500	250	50	1.5	45	1.46
5	2500	150	50	1.5	45	1.68
6	3000	200	40	2	30	1.53
7	3500	250	30	2.5	45	1.51
8	2500	150	50	2.5	45	1.66
9	3000	200	40	2	30	1.54
10	3500	150	50	2.5	45	1.52
11	3500	150	30	2.5	15	1.65
12	2500	250	30	2.5	15	1.76
13	2500	250	50	1.5	45	1.74
14	3000	200	40	2	60	1.59
15	3000	200	40	2	30	1.58
16	4000	200	40	2	30	1.16
17	3000	300	40	2	30	2.51
18	3500	150	50	1.5	45	1.49
19	3000	200	60	2	30	1.61
20	3000	200	40	1	30	1.56
21	3500	150	30	1.5	45	1.36
22	3500	250	30	1.5	45	1.51
23	3500	250	50	2.5	45	1.61
24	3500	150	30	2.5	45	1.59
25	2500	150	50	1.5	15	1.92
26	2500	250	50	1.5	15	2
27	3000	200	40	2	30	1.66
28	3500	250	50	2.5	15	1.52
29	3000	200	40	3	30	2.2
30	3500	150	50	1.5	15	1.54
31	3000	200	40	2	30	1.61
32	3000	100	40	2	30	1.21
33	3500	250	50	1.5	15	1.5
34	2000	200	40	2	30	2.3
35	3000	200	20	2	30	1.51

(continued)

Table 13.1 (continued)

Index	Spindle speed (rpm)	Feed rate (mm/min)	Length of cut (mm)	Depth of cut (mm)	Helix angle (α) (o)	SR (MWCNTs) (μm)
36	2500	150	30	1.5	45	1.74
37	3500	250	30	1.5	15	1.45
38	3000	200	40	2	0	1.61
39	2500	150	50	2.5	15	1.76
40	2500	250	30	2.5	45	1.77
41	3000	200	40	2	30	1.61
42	3000	200	40	2	30	1.61
43	2500	250	30	1.5	45	1.75
44	3500	150	30	1.5	15	1.44
45	2500	250	50	2.5	45	1.69
46	2500	150	30	2.5	15	1.71
47	3000	200	40	2	30	1.58
48	3500	150	50	2.5	15	1.52
49	3500	250	30	2.5	15	1.49
50	2500	150	30	1.5	15	1.77

the validation and testing data. The MATLAB environment was used to implement this process (Appendix J). Figure 13.2 depicts the neural network's structure.

The prediction performance of the Surface Roughness taken into consideration in this study was examined using a hybrid ANFIS model. A total of 50 data points were divided in half; of these, 42 were utilized to train the hybrid ANFIS model and 8 were used to test it. This study used the ANFIS structure and network model to forecast the Surface Roughness, as seen in Figs. 13.3 and 13.4. It carries out Sugeno-type FIS systems, and the membership function is used to carry out the training process. In this study, the FIS takes into account five machining inputs, including spindle speed (X1), feed rate (X2), length of the cut (X3), depth of cut (X4), and helix angle (X5). The Surface Roughness (Y) is the only output.

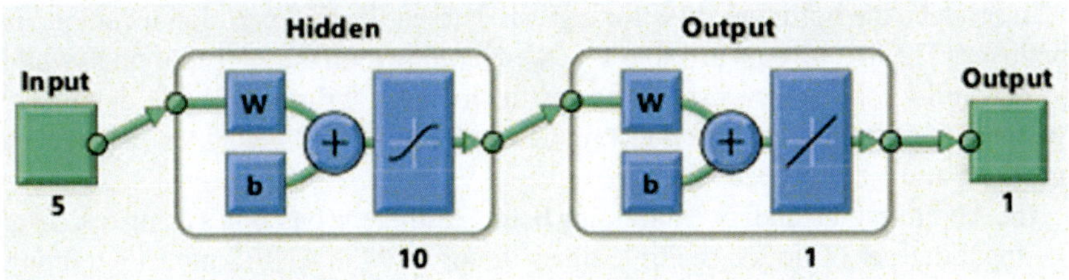

Fig. 13.2 Neural network's structure

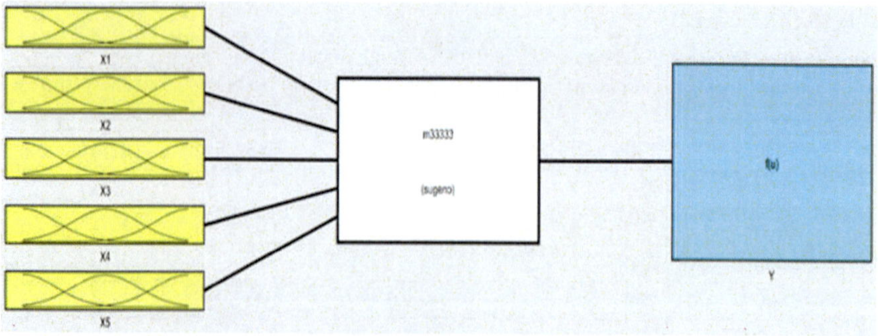

Fig. 13.3 ANFIS structure

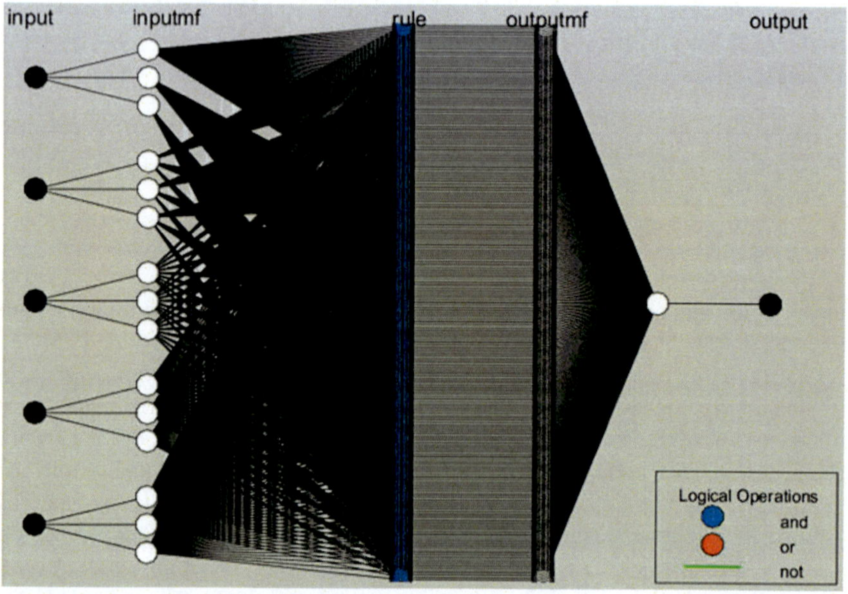

Fig. 13.4 Neural network model for surface roughness

To produce the optimum rules for a given dataset, the grid partition technique is employed. The first 42 data in Table 13.1 were used to train the ANFIS model, while the remaining 8 data were used to assess the model's ability to predict outcomes. The loading of training data and testing data into the ANFIS model are depicted in Figs. 13.5 and 13.6 respectively.

The ANFIS model underwent training before testing the outcomes using test data. The input dataset is plotted multiple times throughout the ANFIS model's training to lower the prediction error. Epochs are the units used to express the number of iterations necessary for mapping. It can be seen from Figs. 13.5 and 13.6 that the

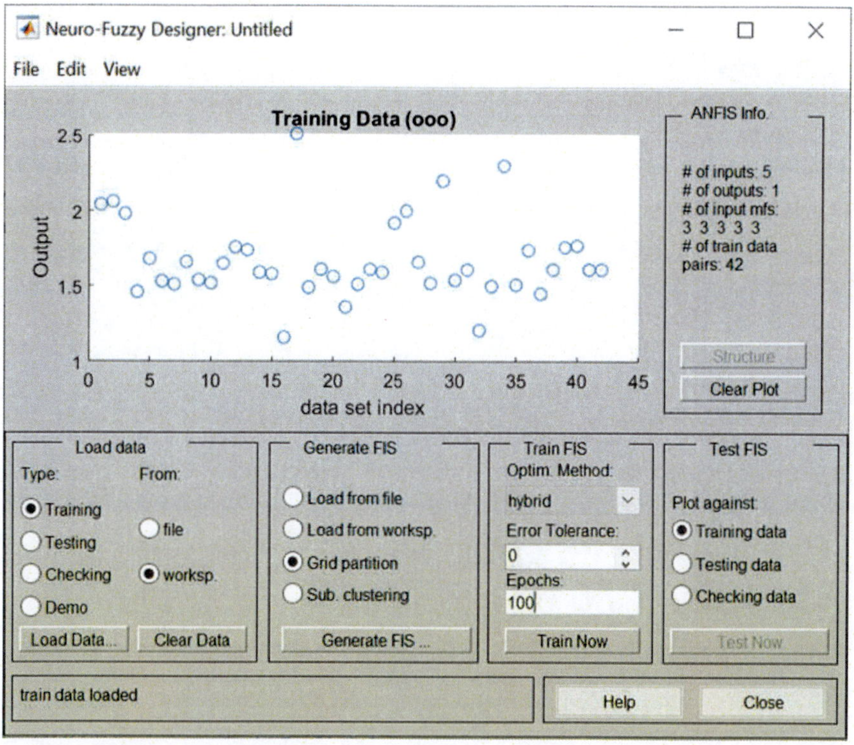

Fig. 13.5 Loading of training data

100 epochs (number of iterations) are necessary to complete the training process on 42 data.

Assessment indices were used to examine the model's error rates and prediction accuracy. The Coefficient of determination (R^2) is the statistical measurement utilized. Equation 13.15 is used to compute the statistical measurements.

$$R^2 = 1 - \frac{\sum_k \left(y_k - \hat{y}_k\right)^2}{\sum_k \left(y_k - \overline{y}_k\right)^2}. \tag{13.15}$$

where the details of y_k, $\hat{y}_k$, $\overline{y}_k$ n and k are given. The symbols y_k, $\hat{y}_k$ and $\overline{y}_k$ stand for the experimental data sample, the algorithm's projected values and the mean value of the experimental data samples, respectively. N stands for the number of data samples, and K stands for the set of all source points indexed by k.

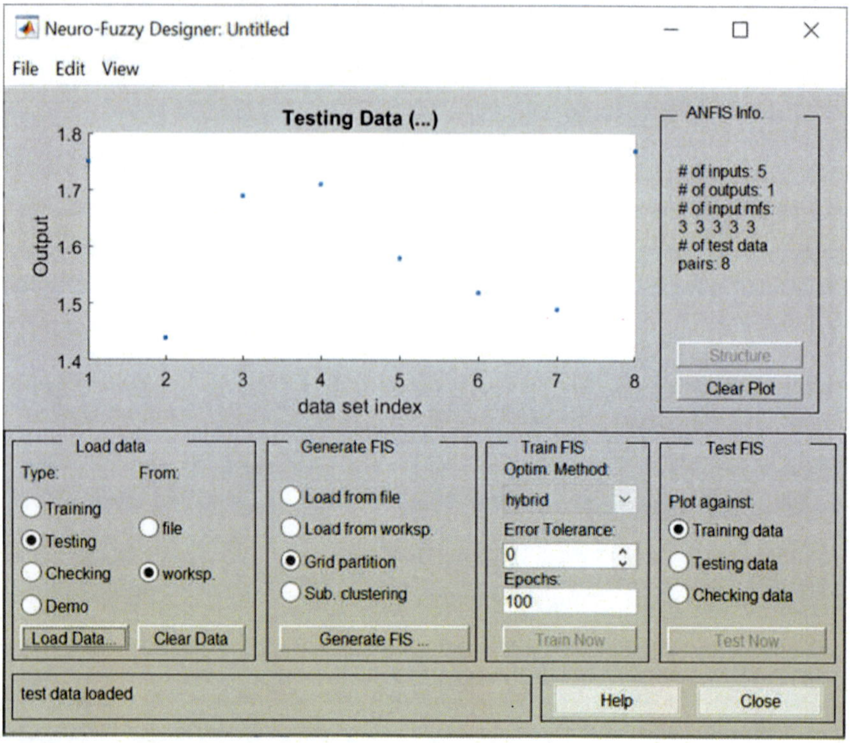

Fig. 13.6 Loading of testing data

13.5 Results and Discussions

The outcomes of the ANFIS model's training and testing process were assessed using various types of membership functions described in Sect. 13.2. Considering a Triangular membership function (TRIMF), Fig. 13.7a, b allow easy visual comparison between the predicted Surface Roughness against the actual values. The training and testing regression value R^2 of 0.9958 and 0.8921, respectively, suggests that the output tracks the targets effectively. Figure 13.7 (c) shows the surface plot of Surface Roughness (Y) of sample values at the different spindle speeds (X1) and feed rates (X2). This Figure shows that when the spindle speed is decreased from 4000 to 2000 rpm and the feed rate is set to 100 or 300 mm/min, the Surface Roughness will be relatively high, resulting in a lower surface quality finishing.

Considering a Trapezoidal membership function (TRAPMF), Fig. 13.8a, b allow easy visual comparison between the predicted Surface Roughness against the actual values. The training and testing regression value R^2 of 0.9958 and 0.8921, respectively, suggests that the output tracks the targets effectively. Interestingly, these results suggest that the adoption of a trapezoidal membership function doesn't affect the results. The surface plot of Surface Roughness (Y) of samples values at the different

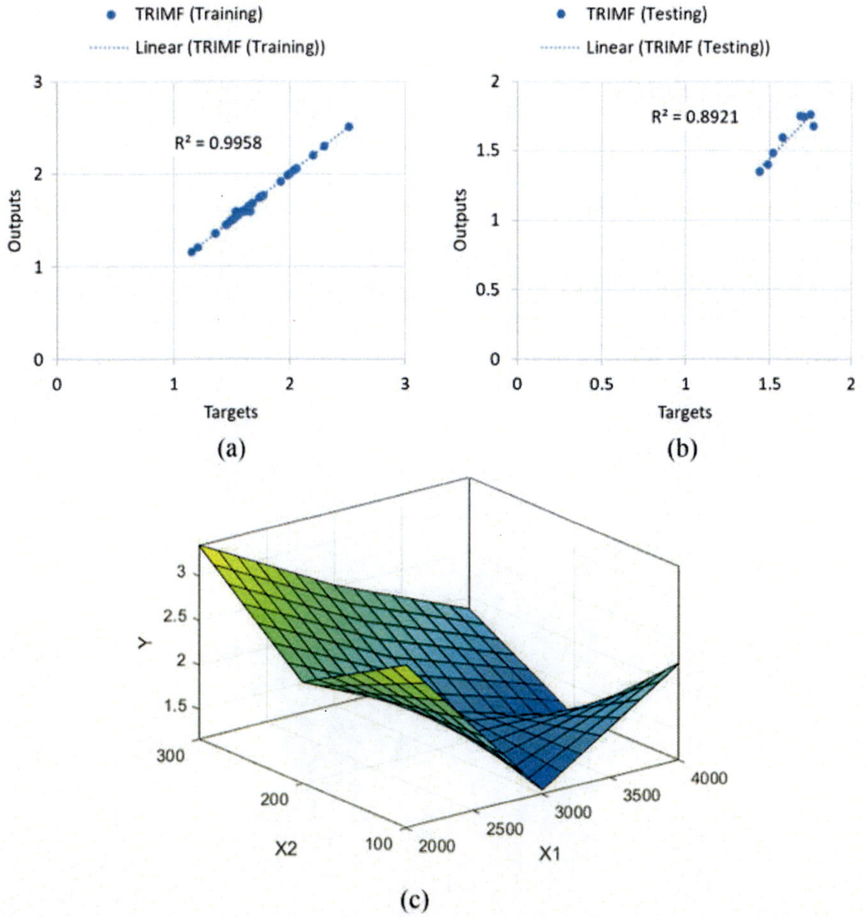

Fig. 13.7 TRIMF results

spindle speeds (X1) and feed rate (X2) is shown in Fig. 13.8c. This Figure shows that when the spindle speed is decreased from 4000 to 2000 rpm and the feed rate is set to 100 or 300 mm/min, the Surface Roughness will be relatively high, similar to the conclusion reported previously.

Considering a generalized bell-shaped curve membership function (GBELLMF), Fig. 13.9a, b allow easy visual comparison between the predicted Surface Roughness against the actual values. The training and testing regression value R^2 of 0.9958 and 0.8959, respectively, suggests that the output tracks the targets effectively. These results suggest that the adoption of a generalized bell-shaped curve membership function improves the prediction slightly. The surface plot of Surface Roughness (Y) of samples values at the different spindle speeds (X1) and feed rates (X2) is shown in Fig. 13.9c. This Figure shows that when the spindle speed is decreased from 4000

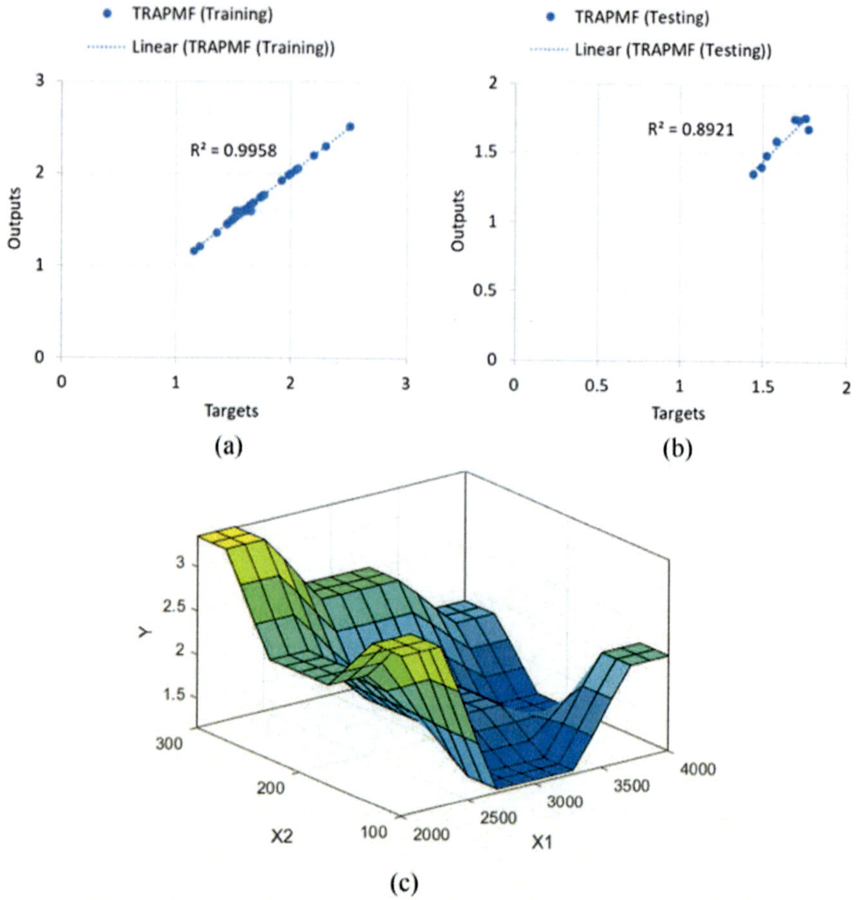

Fig. 13.8 TRAPMF results

to 2000 rpm and the feed rate is set to 100 or 300 mm/min, the Surface Roughness will be relatively high, similar to the conclusion reported previously.

Considering a Gaussian curve membership function (GAUSSMF), Fig. 13.10a, b allow easy visual comparison between the predicted Surface Roughness against the actual values. The training and testing regression value R^2 of 0.9958 and 0.847, respectively, suggests that the output tracks the targets effectively. However, the testing regression value was poorer. These results suggest that the adoption of a Gaussian curve membership function results in a poorer prediction. The surface plot of Surface Roughness (Y) of samples values at the different spindle speeds (X1) and feed rates (X2) is shown in Fig. 13.10c. This Figure shows that when the spindle speed is decreased from 4000 to 2000 rpm and the feed rate is set to 100 or 300 mm/min, the Surface Roughness will be relatively high, similar to the conclusion reported previously.

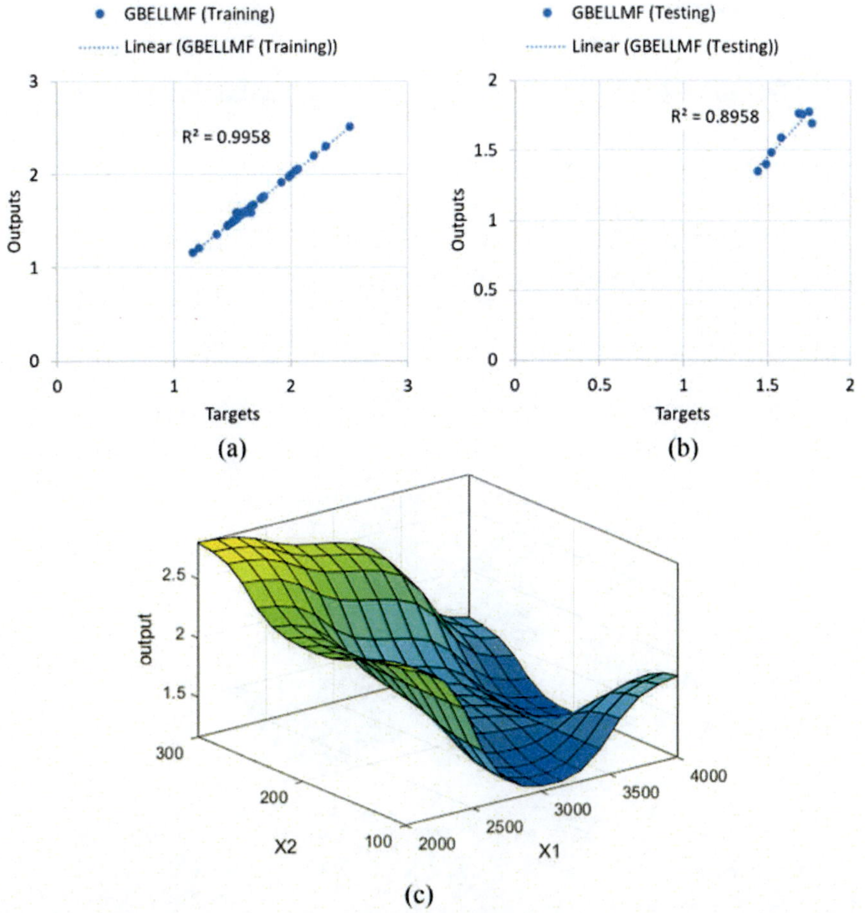

Fig. 13.9 GBELLMF results

Considering a π-shaped curve membership function (PIMF), Fig. 13.11a, b allow easy visual comparison between the predicted Surface Roughness against the actual values. The training and testing regression value R^2 of 0.9958 and 0.8921, respectively, suggests that the output tracks the targets effectively. These results suggest that the adoption of a generalized bell-shaped curve membership function improves the prediction slightly. The surface plot of Surface Roughness (Y) of samples values at the different spindle speeds (X1) and feed rates (X2) is shown in Fig. 13.11c. This Figure shows that when the spindle speed is decreased from 4000 to 2000 rpm and the feed rate is set to 100 or 300 mm/min, the Surface Roughness will be relatively high, similar to the conclusion reported previously.

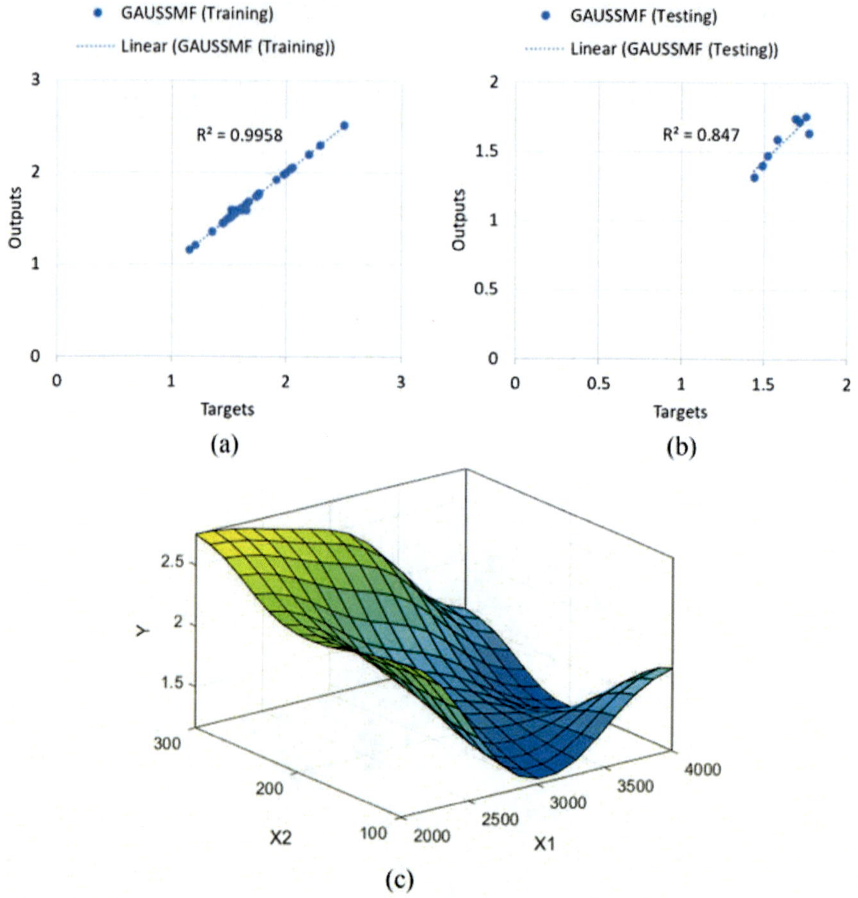

Fig. 13.10 GAUSSMF results

A comparison between the results reported in the previous section was made. The performance metrics of the various membership function is presented in a tabulated format (Table 13.2). The results reported suggest that the training of the ANFIS model is not affected by the selection of the membership function. However, the highest testing performance was achieved with a generalized bell-shaped curve membership function (GBELLMF) while the lowest performance was obtained with a Gaussian curve membership function (GAUSSMF).

The predicted results were compared to the experimental results to assess visually how the predictions match the targets. Considering a Triangular membership function (TRIMF), the anticipated outputs and target values match in more than 50% of cases. The average deviations between results were approximately 3.47%. All deviations were under 10% as shown in Fig. 13.12.

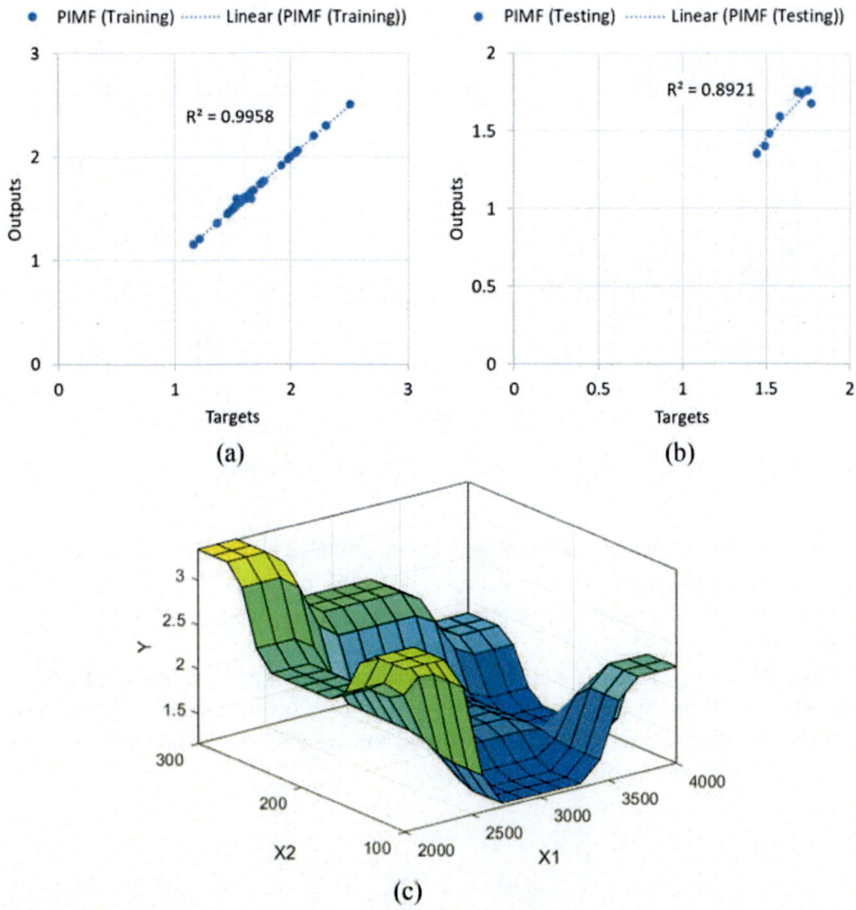

Fig. 13.11 PIMF results

Table 13.2 Comparison of the result of different membership functions

	Number of membership function	Function type	Output function	R^2 training	R^2 testing
1	33,333	TRIMF	Constant	0.9958	0.8921
2	33,333	TRAPMF	Constant	0.9958	0.8921
3	33,333	GBELLMF	Constant	0.9958	0.8958
4	33,333	GAUSSMF	Constant	0.9958	0.847
5	33,333	PIMF	Constant	0.9958	0.8921

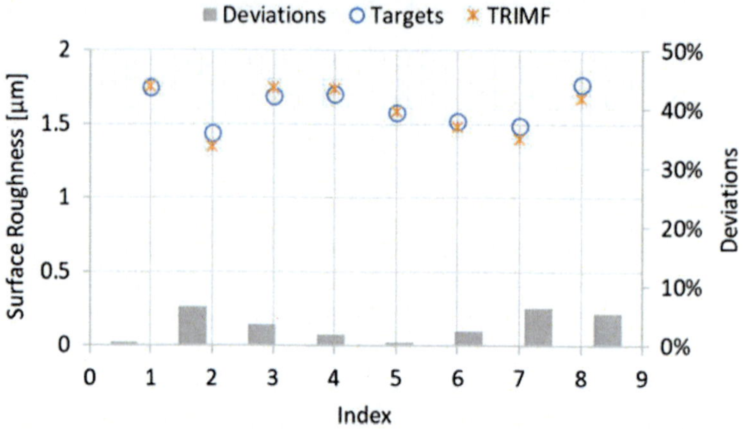

Fig. 13.12 Comparison between the "targets" and "outputs" → TRIMF

Considering a Triangular membership function (TRAPMF), the anticipated outputs and target values match in more than 50% of cases. The average deviations between results were approximately 3.47%. All deviations were under 10% as shown in Fig. 13.13.

Considering a generalized bell-shaped curve membership function (GBELLMF), the anticipated outputs and target values match in more than 50% of cases. The average deviations between results were approximately 3.62%. All deviations were under 10% as shown in Fig. 13.14.

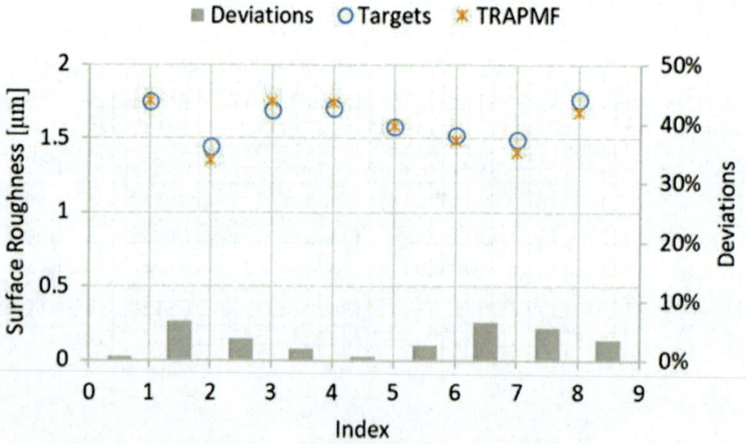

Fig. 13.13 Comparison between the "targets" and "outputs" → TRAPMF

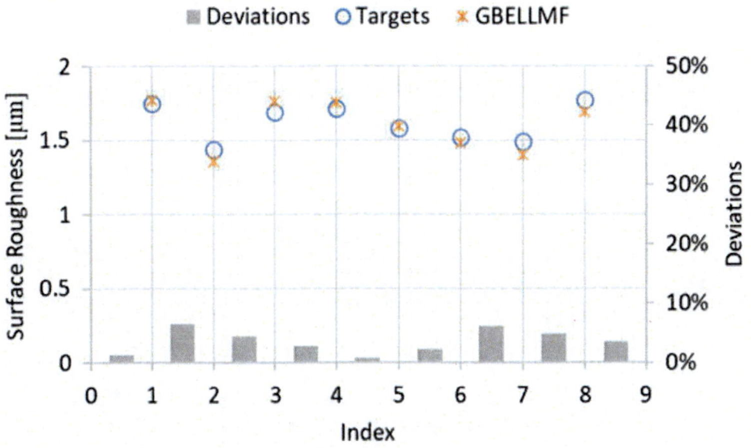

Fig. 13.14 Comparison between the "targets" and "outputs" → GBELLMF

Considering a Gaussian curve membership function (GAUSSMF), the anticipated outputs and target values match in more than 50% of cases. The average deviations between results were approximately 3.88%. All deviations were under 10% as shown in Fig. 13.15.

Considering the π-shaped curve membership function (PIMF), the anticipated outputs and target values match in more than 50% of cases. The average deviations between results were approximately 3.47%. All deviations were under 10% as shown in Fig. 13.16.

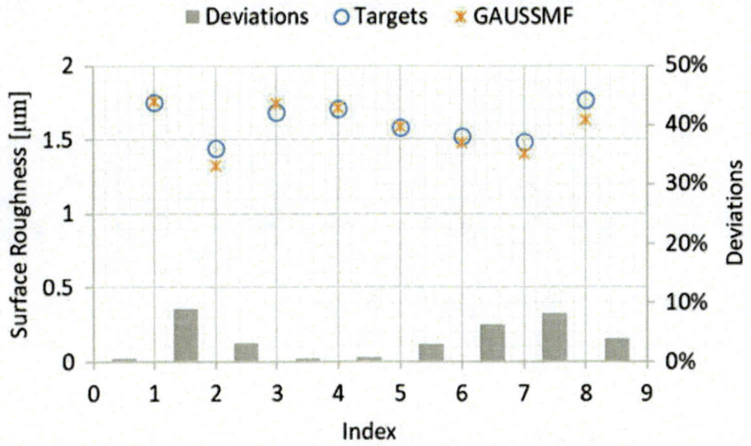

Fig. 13.15 Comparison between the "targets" and "outputs" → GAUSSMF

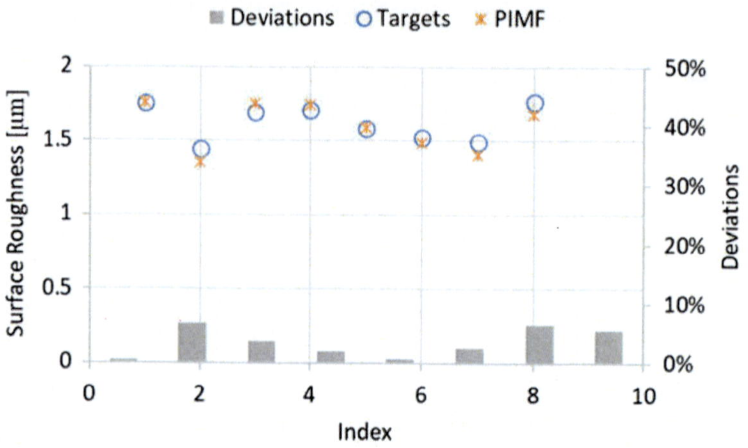

Fig. 13.16 Comparison between the "targets" and "outputs" → PIMF

In this section, the results obtained with ANFIS were compared to those obtained using ANN models. Figure 13.17 shows the various predictions against the targets. The graph clearly shows the superiority of ANFIS models in comparison to the ANN model. While the highest deviations of ANN models were beyond 12%, all ANFIS deviations were under 7%.

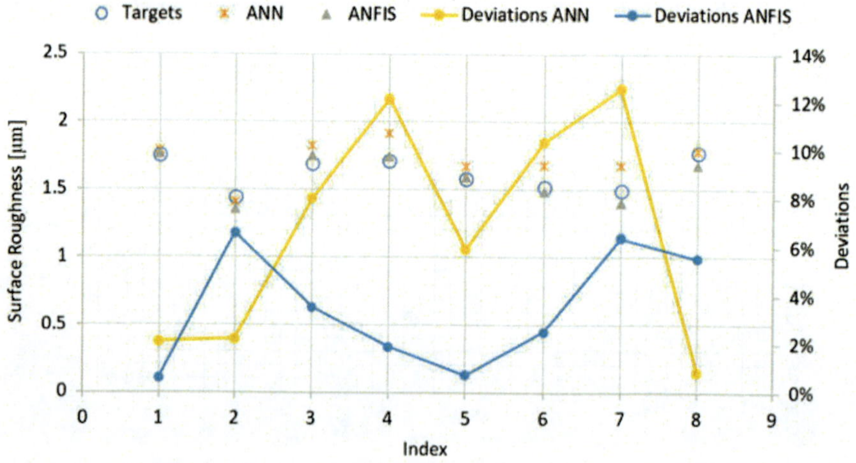

Fig. 13.17 Comparison between ANN and ANFIS model

13.6 Conclusion

In this section, an Adaptive Neuro-Fuzzy Inference System is proposed for the Prediction of Surface Roughness Under Biodegradable Nano-Lubricant. Fifty data were extracted experimentally from the end-milling machining of AA8112. Five machining input parameters including the spindle speed, the feed rate, the length of the cut, the depth of cut, and the helix angle were adjusted to extract the configurations that made up the data. The Surface Roughness was the only output. The outcomes of the ANFIS model's training and testing process were assessed using various types of membership functions. The study is limited to the following membership functions: π-shaped (PIMF), generalized bell shape (GBELLMF), triangular shape (TRIMF), trapezoidal shape (TRAPMF), and Gaussian curve (GAUSSMF). Through this parametric analysis, this study shows that the various outputs track the targets effectively irrespective of the membership functions adopted. In general, the training and the testing performance indicators were relatively higher. This demonstrates that ANFIS models are suitable for the modelling and the prediction of Surface Roughness. However, the highest testing performance was achieved with a generalized bell-shaped curve membership function (GBELLMF) while the lowest performance was obtained with a Gaussian curve membership function (GAUSSMF). The results obtained with ANFIS were compared to those obtained using ANN models. While the highest deviations of ANN models were beyond 12%, all ANFIS deviations were under 7%. These results demonstrate that ANFIS models would be more suitable for the predictions and the analysis of surface roughness in order to make adjustments to the machining parameters and improve surface finishing.

References

1. Okokpujie, I.P., Bolu, C.A., Ohunakin, O.S., Akinlabi, E.T., Adelekan, D.S.: A review of recent application of machining techniques, based on the phenomena of CNC machining operations. Procedia Manuf. **35**, 1054–1060 (2019)
2. Li, M., Yu, T., Yang, L., Li, H., Zhang, R., Wang, W.: Parameter optimization during minimum quantity lubrication milling of TC4 alloy with graphene-dispersed vegetable-oil-based cutting fluid. J. Clean. Prod. **209**, 1508–1522 (2019)
3. Pervaiz, S., Kannan, S., Kishawy, H.A.: An extensive review of the water consumption and cutting fluid based sustainability concerns in the metal cutting sector. J. Clean. Prod. **197**, 134–153 (2018)
4. Okokpujie, I.P., Ajayi, O.O., Afolalu, S.A., Abioye, A.A., Salawu, E.Y., Udo, M., Okonkwo, U.C., Orodu, K.B., Ikumapayi, O.M.: Modeling and optimization of surface roughness in end milling of aluminium using least square approximation method and response surface methodology. Int. J. Mech. Eng. Technol. (IJMET) **9**(1), 587–600 (2018)
5. Prajina, N.V.: Multi response optimization of CNC end milling using response surface methodology and desirability function. Int. J. Eng. Res. Technol. **6**(6), 739–746 (2013)

6. Okokpujie, I.P., Bolu, C.A., Ohunakin, O.S.: Comparative performance evaluation of TiO_2, and MWCNTs nano-lubricant effects on surface roughness of AA8112 alloy during end-milling machining for sustainable manufacturing process. Int. J. Adv. Manuf. Technol. **108**(5), 1473–1497 (2020)
7. Ramesh, R., Ravi Kumar, K.S., Anil, G.: Automated intelligent manufacturing system for surface finish control in CNC milling using support vector machines. Int. J. Adv. Manuf. Technol. **42**(11), 1103–1117 (2009)
8. Soltan, I.M., Eltaib, M.E.H., El-Zahry, R.M.: Surface roughness prediction in end milling using multiple regression and adaptive neuro-fuzzy inference system. In: Proceedings of the Fourth International Conference on Mechanical Engineering Advanced Technology for Industrial Production (MEATIP4), Assiut, Egypt, pp. 12–14 (2006)
9. Abellan-Nebot, J.V., Romero Subirón, F.: A review of machining monitoring systems based on artificial intelligence process models. Int. J. Adv. Manuf. Technol. **47**(1), 237–257 (2010)
10. Özel, T., Karpat, Y.: Predictive modeling of surface roughness and tool wear in hard turning using regression and neural networks. Int. J. Mach. Tools Manuf **45**(4–5), 467–479 (2005)
11. Zalnezhad, E., Sarhan, A.A., Hamdi, M.: A fuzzy logic based model to predict surface hardness of thin film TiN coating on aerospace AL7075-T6 alloy. Int. J. Adv. Manuf. Technol. **68**(1), 415–423 (2013)
12. Maher, I., Eltaib, M.E.H., Sarhan, A.A., El-Zahry, R.M.: Investigation of the effect of machining parameters on the surface quality of machined brass (60/40) in CNC end milling—ANFIS modeling. Int. J. Adv. Manuf. Technol. **74**(1), 531–537 (2014)
13. Jang, J.S.: ANFIS: adaptive-network-based fuzzy inference system. IEEE Trans. Syst. Man Cybern. **23**(3), 665–685 (1993)
14. Samuel, O.D., Okwu, M.O., Tartibu, L.K., Giwa, S.O., Sharifpur, M., Jagun, Z.O.: Modelling of Nicotiana Tabacum L. Oil biodiesel production: comparison of ANN and ANFIS. Front. Energy Res. **8**, 612165 (2021)
15. Melin, P., Soto, J., Castillo, O., Soria, J.: A new approach for time series prediction using ensembles of ANFIS models. Expert Syst. Appl. **39**(3), 3494–3506 (2012)
16. Aydın, M., Karakuzu, C., Uçar, M., Cengiz, A., Çavuşlu, M.A.: Prediction of surface roughness and cutting zone temperature in dry turning processes of AISI304 stainless steel using ANFIS with PSO learning. Int. J. Adv. Manuf. Technol. **67**(1), 957–967 (2013)
17. Shahriar, J.H., Nafis, A.: Adaptive neuro-fuzzy inference system (ANFIS) based surface roughness prediction model for ball end milling operation. J. Mech. Eng. Res. **4**(3), 112–129 (2012)
18. Surajudeen-Bakinde, N.T., Faruk, N., Popoola, S.I., Salman, M.A., Oloyede, A.A., Olawoyin, L.A., Calafate, C.T.: Path loss predictions for multi-transmitter radio propagation in VHF bands using adaptive neuro-fuzzy inference system. Eng. Sci. Technol. Int. J. **21**(4), 679–691 (2018)
19. Mathur, N., Glesk, I., Buis, A.: Comparison of adaptive neuro-fuzzy inference system (ANFIS) and Gaussian processes for machine learning (GPML) algorithms for the prediction of skin temperature in lower limb prostheses. Med. Eng. Phys. **38**(10), 1083–1089 (2016)
20. Mishra, R.N., Mohanty, K.B.: Real time implementation of an ANFIS-based induction motor drive via feedback linearization for performance enhancement. Eng. Sci. Technol. Int. J. **19**(4), 1714–1730 (2016)
21. Kumar, R., Hynes, N.R.J.: Prediction and optimization of surface roughness in thermal drilling using integrated ANFIS and GA approach. Eng. Sci. Technol. Int. J. **23**(1), 30–41 (2020)
22. Natarajan, E., Kaviarasan, V., Lim, W.H., Ramesh, S., Palanikumar, K., Sekar, T., Mok, V.H.: Gorilla troops optimizer combined with ANFIS for wire cut EDM of aluminum alloy. Adv. Mater. Sci. Eng. (2022)

23. Katta, L.N., Pasupuleti, T., Natarajan, M., Reddy, N.S.R., Somsole, L.N.: Development of adaptive neuro fuzzy inference system model for CNC milling of AA5052 alloy with minimum quantity lubrication by natural cutting fluid (No. 2022-28-0511). SAE Technical Paper (2022)
24. Okokpujie, I.P., Ohunakin, O.S., Bolu, C.A.: Multi-objective optimization of machining factors on surface roughness, material removal rate and cutting force on end-milling using MWCNTs nano-lubricant. Progr. Addit. Manuf. **6**(1), 155–178 (2021)

Appendix A

The computer numerical control (CNC) programming language employed in the machining operation.

I. P. Okokpujie and L. K. Tartibu, *Modern Optimization Techniques for Advanced Machining*, Studies in Systems, Decision and Control 485,
https://doi.org/10.1007/978-3-031-35455-7

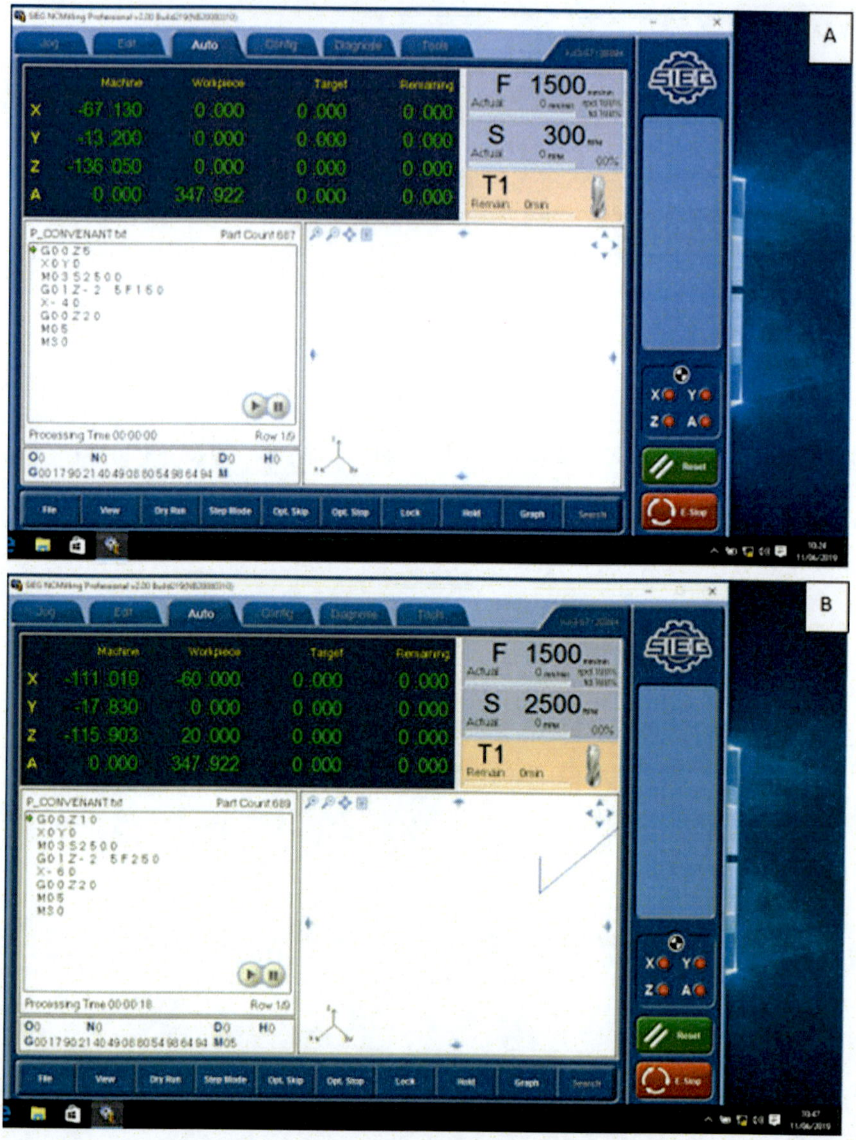
A
Jog
Edit
Auto
Config
Diagnose
Tools
Machine
Workpiece
Target
Remaining
X -67.130 0.000 0.000 0.000
Y -13.200 0.000 0.000 0.000
Z -136.050 0.000 0.000 0.000
A 0.000 347.922 0.000 0.000
F 1500
S 300
T1
P_CONVENANT.txt
Part Count 687
G00Z5
X0Y0
M03S2500
G01Z-2.5F150
X-40
G00Z20
M05
M30
Processing Time 00:00:00
Row 1/9
File
View
Dry Run
Step Mode
Opt. Skip
Opt. Stop
Lock
Hold
Graph
Search
Reset
E-Stop
B
Jog
Edit
Auto
Config
Diagnose
Tools
Machine
Workpiece
Target
Remaining
X -111.010 -60.000 0.000 0.000
Y -17.830 0.000 0.000 0.000
Z -115.903 20.000 0.000 0.000
A 0.000 347.922 0.000 0.000
F 1500
S 2500
T1
P_CONVENANT.txt
Part Count 689
G00Z10
X0Y0
M03S2500
G01Z-2.5F250
X-60
G00Z20
M05
M30
Processing Time 00:00:18
Row 1/9
File
View
Dry Run
Step Mode
Opt. Skip
Opt. Stop
Lock
Hold
Graph
Search
Reset
E-Stop

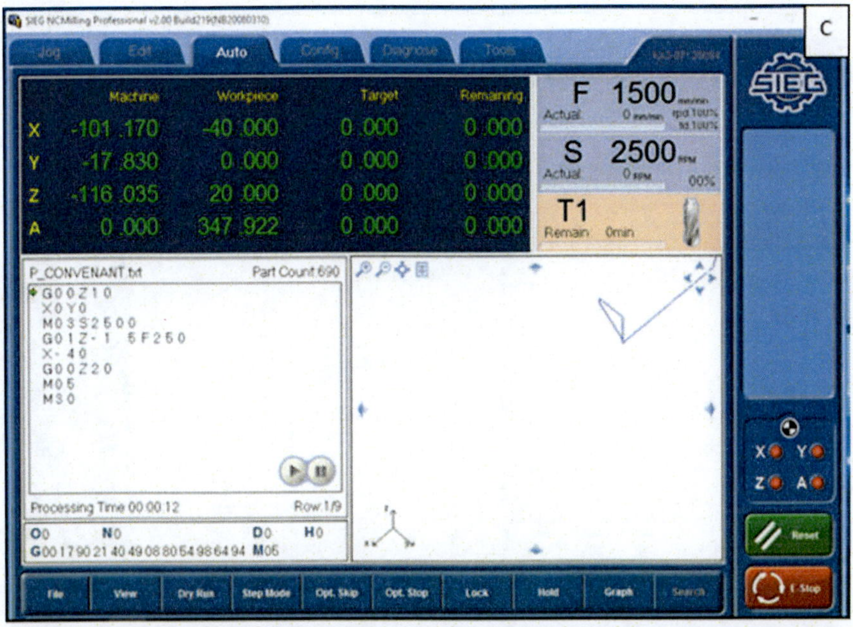
C
Auto
Machine
Workpiece
Target
Remaining
X -101.170 -40.000 0.000 0.000
Y -17.830 0.000 0.000 0.000
Z -116.035 20.000 0.000 0.000
A 0.000 347.922 0.000 0.000
F 1500
S 2500
T1
P_CONVENANT.txt
Part Count 690
G00Z10
X0Y0
M03S2500
G01Z-1.5F250
X-40
G00Z20
M05
M30
Processing Time 00:00:12
Row 1/9
File
View
Dry Run
Step Mode
Opt. Skip
Opt. Stop
Lock
Hold
Graph
Reset
E-Stop

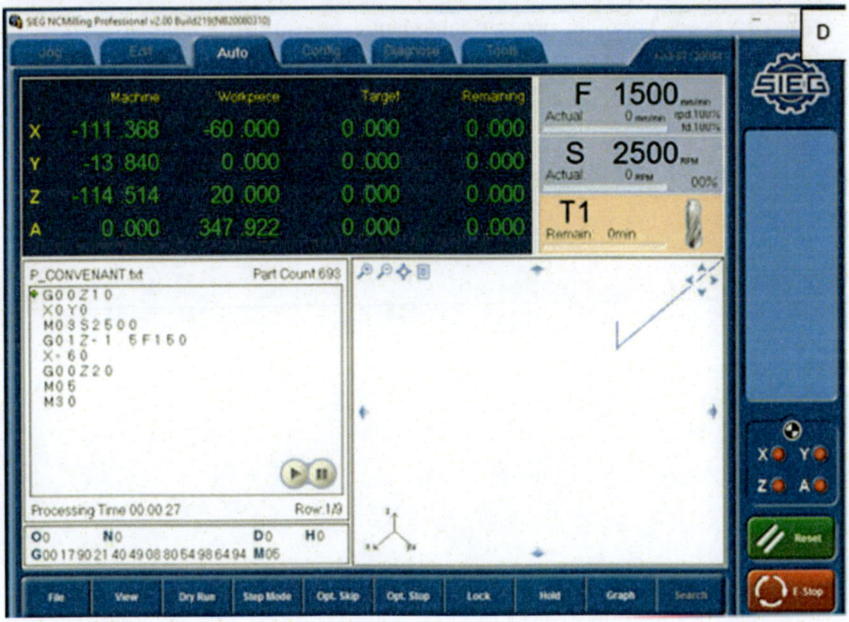
D
Auto
Machine
Workpiece
Target
Remaining
X -111.368 -60.000 0.000 0.000
Y -13.840 0.000 0.000 0.000
Z -114.514 20.000 0.000 0.000
A 0.000 347.922 0.000 0.000
F 1500
S 2500
T1
P_CONVENANT.txt
Part Count 693
G00Z10
X0Y0
M03S2500
G01Z-1.5F150
X-60
G00Z20
M05
M30
Processing Time 00:00:27
Row 1/9
File
View
Dry Run
Step Mode
Opt. Skip
Opt. Stop
Lock
Hold
Graph
Reset
E-Stop

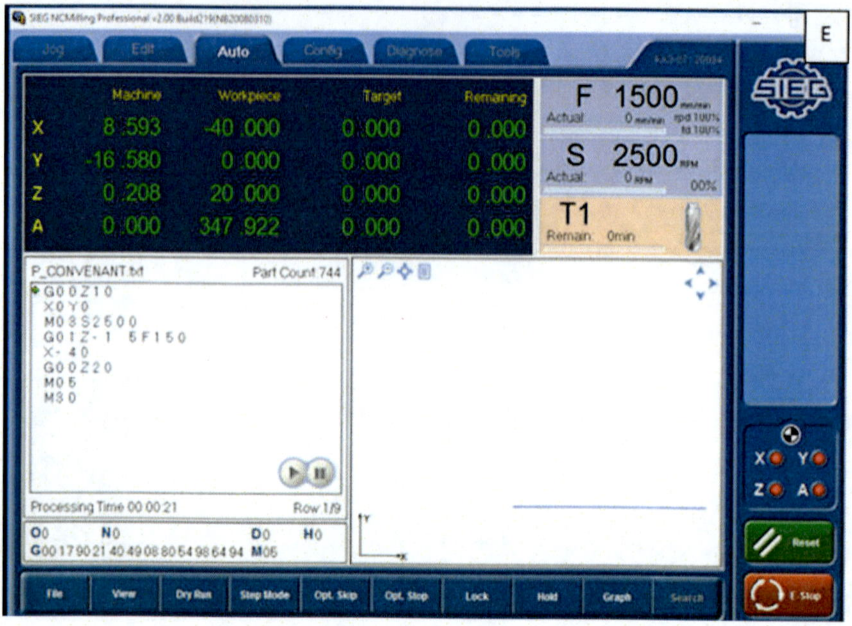

Appendix A–E: The CNC programming language software employed for various machining parameters during operations

Appendix B

MATLAB Codes Grey Wolf Optimizer

Supplementary codes can be found on the following link: https://es.mathworks.com/matlabcentral/fileexchange/44974-grey-wolf-optimizer-gwo

I. P. Okokpujie and L. K. Tartibu, *Modern Optimization Techniques for Advanced Machining*, Studies in Systems, Decision and Control 485,
https://doi.org/10.1007/978-3-031-35455-7

```
% Cutting force
function [lb,ub,dim,fobj] = Get_Functions_details(F)
switch F
   case 'F1'
       fobj = @F1;
       lb=[69.9 55.6 0.66];
       ub=[150 120.6 2];
       dim=3;
end
end
% F1
function o = F1(x)
o=513.915-(0.2466*x(1))+5.3773*x(2)+64.92*x(3)-0.0002594*(x(1)^2)-
0.055*(x(2)^2)+0.0052*x(1)*x(2);
end
```

```
% Surface roughness
function [lb,ub,dim,fobj] = Get_Functions_details(F)
switch F
   case 'F1'
       fobj = @F1;
       lb=[69.9 55.6 0.66];
       ub=[150 120.6 2];
       dim=3;
end
end
% F1
function o = F1(x)
o=1.27686-
0.000897964*x(1)+0.0008937*x(2)+0.036303*x(3)+0.000000169203*(x(1)^2);
end
```

```
% Grey Wolf Optimizer
function [Al-
pha_score,Alpha_pos,Convergence_curve]=GWO(SearchAgents_no,Max_iter,lb,
ub,dim,fobj)
% initialize alpha, beta, and delta_pos
Alpha_pos=zeros(1,dim);
Alpha_score=inf; %change this to -inf for maximization problems
```

```
Beta_pos=zeros(1,dim);
Beta_score=inf; %change this to -inf for maximization problems
Delta_pos=zeros(1,dim);
Delta_score=inf; %change this to -inf for maximization problems
%Initialize the positions of search agents
Positions=initialization(SearchAgents_no,dim,ub,lb);
Convergence_curve=zeros(1,Max_iter);
l=0;% Loop counter
% Main loop
while l<Max_iter
  for i=1:size(Positions,1)

     % Return back the search agents that go beyond the boundaries of the search
space
      Flag4ub=Positions(i,:)>ub;
      Flag4lb=Positions(i,:)<lb;
      Posi-
tions(i,:)=(Positions(i,:).*(~(Flag4ub+Flag4lb)))+ub.*Flag4ub+lb.*Flag4lb;

      % Calculate objective function for each search agent
      fitness=fobj(Positions(i,:));

      % Update Alpha, Beta, and Delta
      if fitness<Alpha_score
         Alpha_score=fitness; % Update alpha
         Alpha_pos=Positions(i,:);
      end

      if fitness>Alpha_score && fitness<Beta_score
         Beta_score=fitness; % Update beta
         Beta_pos=Positions(i,:);
      end

      if fitness>Alpha_score && fitness>Beta_score && fitness<Delta_score
         Delta_score=fitness; % Update delta
         Delta_pos=Positions(i,:);
      end
  end

  a=2-l*((2)/Max_iter); % a decreases linearly fron 2 to 0

  % Update the Position of search agents including omegas
  for i=1:size(Positions,1)
     for j=1:size(Positions,2)
```

```
            r1=rand(); % r1 is a random number in [0,1]
            r2=rand(); % r2 is a random number in [0,1]

            A1=2*a*r1-a;
            C1=2*r2;

            D_alpha=abs(C1*Alpha_pos(j)-Positions(i,j));
            X1=Alpha_pos(j)-A1*D_alpha;

            r1=rand();
            r2=rand();

            A2=2*a*r1-a;
            C2=2*r2;

            D_beta=abs(C2*Beta_pos(j)-Positions(i,j));
            X2=Beta_pos(j)-A2*D_beta;

            r1=rand();
            r2=rand();

            A3=2*a*r1-a;
            C3=2*r2;

            D_delta=abs(C3*Delta_pos(j)-Positions(i,j));
            X3=Delta_pos(j)-A3*D_delta;

            Positions(i,j)=(X1+X2+X3)/3;

        end
    end
    l=l+1;
    Convergence_curve(l)=Alpha_score;
end
```

Appendix C

MATLAB Codes Multi-Objective Grey Wolf Optimizer

Supplementary codes can be found on the following link: https://es.mathworks.com/matlabcentral/fileexchange/55979-multi-objective-grey-wolf-optimizer-mogwo

I. P. Okokpujie and L. K. Tartibu, *Modern Optimization Techniques for Advanced Machining*, Studies in Systems, Decision and Control 485,
https://doi.org/10.1007/978-3-031-35455-7

```
%% Objective functions
function fobj = cec09(name)
   switch name
      case 'UF1'
         fobj = @UF1;
   end
end
%% UF1
% x and y are columnwise, the input x must be inside the search space and
% it could be a matrix
function y = UF1(x)
y = [0, 0];
y(1) = 513.915-(0.2466*x(1))+5.3773*x(2)+64.92*x(3)-0.0002594*(x(1)^2)-
0.055*(x(2)^2)+0.0052*x(1)*x(2);
y(2) = 1.27686-
0.000897964*x(1)+0.0008937*x(2)+0.036303*x(3)+0.000000169203*(x(1)^2);
end
```

```
% MOGWO
clear all
clc
drawing_flag = 1;
TestProblem='UF1';
nVar=3;
fobj = cec09(TestProblem);
xrange = xboundary(TestProblem, nVar);
% Lower bound and upper bound
lb=[69.9 55.6 0.66];
ub=[150 120.6 2];
VarSize=[1 nVar];
GreyWolves_num=100;
MaxIt=1000;  % Maximum Number of Iterations
Archive_size=100;   % Repository Size
alpha=0.1;  % Grid Inflation Parameter
nGrid=10;   % Number of Grids per each Dimension
beta=4; %=4;    % Leader Selection Pressure Parameter
gamma=2;    % Extra (to be deleted) Repository Member Selection Pressure
% Initialization
```

```
GreyWolves=CreateEmptyParticle(GreyWolves_num);
for i=1:GreyWolves_num
  GreyWolves(i).Velocity=0;
  GreyWolves(i).Position=zeros(1,nVar);
  for j=1:nVar
    GreyWolves(i).Position(1,j)=unifrnd(lb(j),ub(j),1);
  end
  GreyWolves(i).Cost=fobj(GreyWolves(i).Position')';
  GreyWolves(i).Best.Position=GreyWolves(i).Position;
  GreyWolves(i).Best.Cost=GreyWolves(i).Cost;
end
GreyWolves=DetermineDomination(GreyWolves);
Archive=GetNonDominatedParticles(GreyWolves);
Archive_costs=GetCosts(Archive);
G=CreateHypercubes(Archive_costs,nGrid,alpha);
for i=1:numel(Archive)
  [Archive(i).GridIndex Archive(i).GridSubIndex]=GetGridIndex(Archive(i),G);
end
% MOGWO main loop
for it=1:MaxIt
  a=2-it*((2)/MaxIt);
  for i=1:GreyWolves_num

    clear rep2
    clear rep3

    % Choose the alpha, beta, and delta grey wolves
    Delta=SelectLeader(Archive,beta);
    Beta=SelectLeader(Archive,beta);
    Alpha=SelectLeader(Archive,beta);

    % If there are less than three solutions in the least crowded
    % hypercube, the second least crowded hypercube is also found
    % to choose other leaders from.
    if size(Archive,1)>1
      counter=0;
      for newi=1:size(Archive,1)
        if sum(Delta.Position~=Archive(newi).Position)~=0
          counter=counter+1;
          rep2(counter,1)=Archive(newi);
        end
      end
      Beta=SelectLeader(rep2,beta);
    end
```

```
    % This scenario is the same if the second least crowded hypercube
    % has one solution, so the delta leader should be chosen from the
    % third least crowded hypercube.
    if size(Archive,1)>2
      counter=0;
      for newi=1:size(rep2,1)
        if sum(Beta.Position~=rep2(newi).Position)~=0
          counter=counter+1;
          rep3(counter,1)=rep2(newi);
        end
      end
      Alpha=SelectLeader(rep3,beta);
    end

    c=2.*rand(1, nVar);

    D=abs(c.*Delta.Position-GreyWolves(i).Position);

    A=2.*a.*rand(1, nVar)-a;

    X1=Delta.Position-A.*abs(D);

    c=2.*rand(1, nVar);

    D=abs(c.*Beta.Position-GreyWolves(i).Position);

    A=2.*a.*rand()-a;

    X2=Beta.Position-A.*abs(D);

    c=2.*rand(1, nVar);

    D=abs(c.*Alpha.Position-GreyWolves(i).Position);

    A=2.*a.*rand()-a;

    X3=Alpha.Position-A.*abs(D);

    GreyWolves(i).Position=(X1+X2+X3)./3;
    % Boundary checking
    GreyWolves(i).Position=min(max(GreyWolves(i).Position,lb),ub);

    GreyWolves(i).Cost=fobj(GreyWolves(i).Position')';
  end
```

```
  GreyWolves=DetermineDomination(GreyWolves);
  non_dominated_wolves=GetNonDominatedParticles(GreyWolves);

  Archive=[Archive
    non_dominated_wolves];

  Archive=DetermineDomination(Archive);
  Archive=GetNonDominatedParticles(Archive);

  for i=1:numel(Archive)
    [Archive(i).GridIndex Ar-
chive(i).GridSubIndex]=GetGridIndex(Archive(i),G);
  end

  if numel(Archive)>Archive_size
    EXTRA=numel(Archive)-Archive_size;
    Archive=DeleteFromRep(Archive,EXTRA,gamma);

    Archive_costs=GetCosts(Archive);
    G=CreateHypercubes(Archive_costs,nGrid,alpha);

  end

  disp(['In iteration ' num2str(it) ': Number of solutions in the archive = '
num2str(numel(Archive))]);

  % Results

  costs=GetCosts(GreyWolves);
  Archive_costs=GetCosts(Archive);

  if drawing_flag==1
    hold off
    plot(costs(1,:),costs(2,:),'k.');
    hold on
    plot(Archive_costs(1,:),Archive_costs(2,:),'rd');
    legend('Grey wolves','Non-dominated solutions');
    drawnow
  end
end
```

Appendix D

MATLAB Codes Ant Lion Optimizer

Supplementary codes can be found on the following link: https://es.mathworks.com/matlabcentral/fileexchange/49920-ant-lion-optimizer-alo

I. P. Okokpujie and L. K. Tartibu, *Modern Optimization Techniques for Advanced Machining*, Studies in Systems, Decision and Control 485,
https://doi.org/10.1007/978-3-031-35455-7

```
% Cutting force
function [lb,ub,dim,fobj] = Get_Functions_details(F)
switch F
   case 'F1'
      fobj = @F1;
      lb=[69.9 55.6 0.66];
      ub=[150 120.6 2];
      dim=3;
end
end
% F1
function o = F1(x)
o=513.915-(0.2466*x(1))+5.3773*x(2)+64.92*x(3)-0.0002594*(x(1)^2)-
0.055*(x(2)^2)+0.0052*x(1)*x(2);
end
```

```
% Surface roughness

function [lb,ub,dim,fobj] = Get_Functions_details(F)
switch F
   case 'F1'
      fobj = @F1;
      lb=[69.9 55.6 0.66];
      ub=[150 120.6 2];
      dim=3;
end
end
% F1
function o = F1(x)
o=1.27686-
0.000897964*x(1)+0.0008937*x(2)+0.036303*x(3)+0.000000169203*(x(1)^2);
end
```

```
% Antlion optimizer
function
[Elite_antlion_fitness,Elite_antlion_position,Convergence_curve]=ALO(N,Max_it
er,lb,ub,dim,fobj)
% Initialize the positions of antlions and ants
```

```
antlion_position=initialization(N,dim,ub,lb);
ant_position=initialization(N,dim,ub,lb);
% Initialize variables to save the position of elite, sorted antlions,
% convergence curve, antlions fitness, and ants fitness
Sorted_antlions=zeros(N,dim);
Elite_antlion_position=zeros(1,dim);
Elite_antlion_fitness=inf;
Convergence_curve=zeros(1,Max_iter);
antlions_fitness=zeros(1,N);
ants_fitness=zeros(1,N);
% Calculate the fitness of initial antlions and sort them
for i=1:size(antlion_position,1)
   antlions_fitness(1,i)=fobj(antlion_position(i,:));
end
[sorted_antlion_fitness,sorted_indexes]=sort(antlions_fitness);

for newindex=1:N
    Sorted_antlions(newindex,:)=antlion_position(sorted_indexes(newindex),:);
end

Elite_antlion_position=Sorted_antlions(1,:);
Elite_antlion_fitness=sorted_antlion_fitness(1);
% Main loop start from the second iteration since the first iteration
% was dedicated to calculating the fitness of antlions
Current_iter=2;
while Current_iter<Max_iter+1

   % This for loop simulate random walks
   for i=1:size(ant_position,1)
      % Select ant lions based on their fitness (the better anlion the higher chance
of catching ant)
      Rolette_index=RouletteWheelSelection(1./sorted_antlion_fitness);
      if Rolette_index==-1
         Rolette_index=1;
      end

      % RA is the random walk around the selected antlion by rolette wheel
      RA=Random_walk_around_antlion(dim,Max_iter,lb,ub, Sort-
ed_antlions(Rolette_index,:),Current_iter);

      % RA is the random walk around the elite (best antlion so far)
      [RE]=Random_walk_around_antlion(dim,Max_iter,lb,ub,
Elite_antlion_position(1,:),Current_iter);

      ant_position(i,:)= (RA(Current_iter,:)+RE(Current_iter,:))/2;
```

```
    end
    for i=1:size(ant_position,1)

        % Boundary checking (bring back the antlions of ants inside search
        % space if they go beyoud the boundaries
        Flag4ub=ant_position(i,:)>ub;
        Flag4lb=ant_position(i,:)<lb;

ant_position(i,:)=(ant_position(i,:).*(~(Flag4ub+Flag4lb)))+ub.*Flag4ub+lb.*Flag
4lb;

        ants_fitness(1,i)=fobj(ant_position(i,:));
    end

    % Update antlion positions and fitnesses based of the ants (if an ant
    % becomes fitter than an antlion we assume it was cought by the antlion
    % and the antlion update goes to its position to build the trap)
    double_population=[Sorted_antlions;ant_position];
    double_fitness=[sorted_antlion_fitness ants_fitness];

    [double_fitness_sorted I]=sort(double_fitness);
    double_sorted_population=double_population(I,:);

    antlions_fitness=double_fitness_sorted(1:N);
    Sorted_antlions=double_sorted_population(1:N,:);

    % Update the position of elite if any antlinons becomes fitter than it
    if antlions_fitness(1)<Elite_antlion_fitness
        Elite_antlion_position=Sorted_antlions(1,:);
        Elite_antlion_fitness=antlions_fitness(1);
    end

    % Keep the elite in the population
    Sorted_antlions(1,:)=Elite_antlion_position;
    antlions_fitness(1)=Elite_antlion_fitness;

    % Update the convergence curve
    Convergence_curve(Current_iter)=Elite_antlion_fitness;
    % Display the iteration and best optimum obtained so far
    if mod(Current_iter,50)==0
        display(['At iteration ', num2str(Current_iter), ' the elite fitness is ',
num2str(Elite_antlion_fitness)]);
    end
        Current_iter=Current_iter+1;
    end
```

Appendix E

MATLAB Codes Multi-Objective Ant Lion Optimizer (MALO)

Supplementary codes can be found on the following link: https://es.mathworks.com/matlabcentral/fileexchange/58460-multi-objective-ant-lion-optimizer-moalo

I. P. Okokpujie and L. K. Tartibu, *Modern Optimization Techniques for Advanced Machining*, Studies in Systems, Decision and Control 485,
https://doi.org/10.1007/978-3-031-35455-7

```
% Objective functions to optimize
function o = ZDT1(x)
o = [0, 0];
o(1) = 513.915-(0.2466*x(1))+5.3773*x(2)+64.92*x(3)-0.0002594*(x(1)^2)-
0.055*(x(2)^2)+0.0052*x(1)*x(2);
o(2) = 1.27686-
0.000897964*x(1)+0.0008937*x(2)+0.036303*x(3)+0.000000169203*(x(1)^2);
```

```
% MALO
clc;
clear;
close all;
% Change these details with respect to your problem%%%%%%%%%%%%%%
ObjectiveFunction=@ZDT1;
dim=3;
lb=[69.9 55.6 0.66];
ub=[150 120.6 2];
obj_no=2;
if size(ub,2)==1
   ub=ones(1,dim)*ub;
   lb=ones(1,dim)*lb;
end
%%%%%%%%%%%%%%%%%%%%%%%%%%%%%%%%%%%%%%%%
%%%%%%%%%%%%%%%%%%%%%%%%%%%%
% Initial parameters of the MALO algorithm
max_iter=100;
N=100;
ArchiveMaxSize=100;
Archive_X=zeros(100,dim);
Archive_F=ones(100,obj_no)*inf;
Archive_member_no=0;
r=(ub-lb)/2;
V_max=(ub(1)-lb(1))/10;
Elite_fitness=inf*ones(1,obj_no);
Elite_position=zeros(dim,1);
Ant_Position=initialization(N,dim,ub,lb);
fitness=zeros(N,2);
V=initialization(N,dim,ub,lb);
```

```
iter=0;
position_history=zeros(N,max_iter,dim);
for iter=1:max_iter

   for i=1:N %Calculate all the objective values first
      Particles_F(i,:)=ObjectiveFunction(Ant_Position(:,i)');
      if dominates(Particles_F(i,:),Elite_fitness)
         Elite_fitness=Particles_F(i,:);
         Elite_position=Ant_Position(:,i);
      end
   end

   [Archive_X, Archive_F, Archive_member_no]=UpdateArchive(Archive_X,
Archive_F, Ant_Position, Particles_F, Archive_member_no);

   if Archive_member_no>ArchiveMaxSize
      Archive_mem_ranks=RankingProcess(Archive_F, ArchiveMaxSize,
obj_no);
      [Archive_X, Archive_F, Archive_mem_ranks, Ar-
chive_member_no]=HandleFullArchive(Archive_X, Archive_F, Ar-
chive_member_no, Archive_mem_ranks, ArchiveMaxSize);
   else
      Archive_mem_ranks=RankingProcess(Archive_F, ArchiveMaxSize,
obj_no);
   end

   Archive_mem_ranks=RankingProcess(Archive_F, ArchiveMaxSize, obj_no);

   % Chose the archive member in the least population area as arrtactor
   % to improve coverage
   index=RouletteWheelSelection(1./Archive_mem_ranks);
   if index==-1
      index=1;
   end
   Elite_fitness=Archive_F(index,:);
   Elite_position=Archive_X(index,:)';

   Random_antlion_fitness=Archive_F(1,:);
   Random_antlion_position=Archive_X(1,:)';

   for i=1:N

      index=0;
      neighbours_no=0;
```

```
    RA=Random_walk_around_antlion(dim,max_iter,lb,ub, Ran-
dom_antlion_position',iter);

    [RE]=Random_walk_around_antlion(dim,max_iter,lb,ub,
Elite_position',iter);

    Ant_Position(:,i)=(RE(iter,:)'+RA(iter,:)')/2;

    Flag4ub=Ant_Position(:,i)>ub';
    Flag4lb=Ant_Position(:,i)<lb';

Ant_Position(:,i)=(Ant_Position(:,i).*(~(Flag4ub+Flag4lb)))+ub'.*Flag4ub+lb'.*Fl
ag4lb;

  end
  display(['At the iteration ', num2str(iter), ' there are ',
num2str(Archive_member_no), ' non-dominated solutions in the archive']);
end
figure
Draw_ZDT1();
hold on
plot(Archive_F(:,1),Archive_F(:,2),'ko','MarkerSize',8,'markerfacecolor','k');
legend('True PF','Obtained PF');
title('MALO');
set(gcf, 'pos', [403   466   230   200])
```

Appendix F

MATLAB Codes Grasshopper Optimisation Algorithm (GOA)

Supplementary codes can be found on the following link: https://es.mathworks.com/matlabcentral/fileexchange/61421-grasshopper-optimisation-algorithm-goa

I. P. Okokpujie and L. K. Tartibu, *Modern Optimization Techniques for Advanced Machining*, Studies in Systems, Decision and Control 485,
https://doi.org/10.1007/978-3-031-35455-7

```
% Cutting force
function [lb,ub,dim,fobj] = Get_Functions_details(F)
switch F
   case 'F1'
      fobj = @F1;
      lb=[69.9 55.6 0.66];
      ub=[150 120.6 2];
      dim=3;
end
end
% F1
function o = F1(x)
o=513.915-(0.2466*x(1))+5.3773*x(2)+64.92*x(3)-0.0002594*(x(1)^2)-
0.055*(x(2)^2)+0.0052*x(1)*x(2);
end
```

```
% Surface roughness

function [lb,ub,dim,fobj] = Get_Functions_details(F)
switch F
   case 'F1'
      fobj = @F1;
      lb=[69.9 55.6 0.66];
      ub=[150 120.6 2];
      dim=3;
end
end
% F1
function o = F1(x)
o=1.27686-
0.000897964*x(1)+0.0008937*x(2)+0.036303*x(3)+0.000000169203*(x(1)^2);
end
```

```
% The Grasshopper Optimization Algorithm
function [TargetFit-
ness,TargetPosition,Convergence_curve,Trajectories,fitness_history, posi-
tion_history]=GOA(N, Max_iter, lb,ub, dim, fobj)
disp('GOA is now estimating the global optimum for your problem....')
```

```
flag=0;
if size(ub,1)==1
   ub=ones(dim,1)*ub;
   lb=ones(dim,1)*lb;
end
if (rem(dim,2)~=0) % this algorithm should be run with a even number of varia-
bles. This line is to handle odd number of variables

   ub = [150 120.6 2];
   lb = [69.9 55.6 0.66];
   flag=1;
end
%Initialize the population of grasshoppers
GrassHopperPositions=initialization(N,dim,ub,lb);
GrassHopperFitness = zeros(1,N);
fitness_history=zeros(N,Max_iter);
position_history=zeros(N,Max_iter,dim);
Convergence_curve=zeros(1,Max_iter);
Trajectories=zeros(N,Max_iter);
cMax=1;
cMin=0.00004;
%Calculate the fitness of initial grasshoppers
for i=1:size(GrassHopperPositions,1)
   if flag == 1
      GrassHopperFitness(1,i)=fobj(GrassHopperPositions(i,1:end-1));
   else
      GrassHopperFitness(1,i)=fobj(GrassHopperPositions(i,:));
   end
   fitness_history(i,1)=GrassHopperFitness(1,i);
   position_history(i,1,:)=GrassHopperPositions(i,:);
   Trajectories(:,1)=GrassHopperPositions(:,1);
end
[sorted_fitness,sorted_indexes]=sort(GrassHopperFitness);
% Find the best grasshopper (target) in the first population
for newindex=1:N
   Sort-
ed_grasshopper(newindex,:)=GrassHopperPositions(sorted_indexes(newindex),:);
end
TargetPosition=Sorted_grasshopper(1,:);
TargetFitness=sorted_fitness(1);
% Main loop
l=2; % Start from the second iteration since the first iteration was dedicated to cal-
culating the fitness of antlions
while l<Max_iter+1
```

```
c=cMax-l*((cMax-cMin)/Max_iter);

for i=1:size(GrassHopperPositions,1)
    temp= GrassHopperPositions';
    for k=1:2:dim
        S_i=zeros(2,1);
        for j=1:N
            if i~=j
                Dist=distance(temp(k:k+1,j), temp(k:k+1,i)); % Calculate the distance
between two grasshoppers

                r_ij_vec=(temp(k:k+1,j)-temp(k:k+1,i))/(Dist+eps);
                xj_xi=2+rem(Dist,2); % |xjd - xid| in Eq. (2.7)

                s_ij=((ub(k:k+1) - lb(k:k+1))*c/2)*S_func(xj_xi).*r_ij_vec;
                S_i=S_i+s_ij;
            end
        end
        S_i_total(k:k+1, :) = S_i;

    end

    X_new = c * S_i_total'+ (TargetPosition);
    GrassHopperPositions_temp(i,:)=X_new';
end
% GrassHopperPositions
GrassHopperPositions=GrassHopperPositions_temp;

for i=1:size(GrassHopperPositions,1)
    % Relocate grasshoppers that go outside the search space

Tp=GrassHopperPositions(i,:)>ub';Tm=GrassHopperPositions(i,:)<lb';GrassHopp
erPositions(i,:)=(GrassHopperPositions(i,:).*(~(Tp+Tm)))+ub'.*Tp+lb'.*Tm;

    % Calculating the objective values for all grasshoppers
    if flag == 1
        GrassHopperFitness(1,i)=fobj(GrassHopperPositions(i,1:end-1));
    else
        GrassHopperFitness(1,i)=fobj(GrassHopperPositions(i,:));
    end
    fitness_history(i,l)=GrassHopperFitness(1,i);
    position_history(i,l,:)=GrassHopperPositions(i,:);

    Trajectories(:,l)=GrassHopperPositions(:,1);
```

```
    % Update the target
    if GrassHopperFitness(1,i)<TargetFitness
      TargetPosition=GrassHopperPositions(i,:);
      TargetFitness=GrassHopperFitness(1,i);
    end
  end

  Convergence_curve(l)=TargetFitness;
  disp(['In iteration #', num2str(l), ' , target''s objective = ',
num2str(TargetFitness)])

  l = l + 1;
end
if (flag==1)
  TargetPosition = TargetPosition(1:dim-1);
end
```

Appendix G

MATLAB Codes Multi-Objective Grasshopper Optimization Algorithm (MOGOA)

Supplementary codes can be found on the following link: https://es.mathworks.com/matlabcentral/fileexchange/63786-mogoa-multi-objective-grasshopper-optimization-algorithm

I. P. Okokpujie and L. K. Tartibu, *Modern Optimization Techniques for Advanced Machining*, Studies in Systems, Decision and Control 485,
https://doi.org/10.1007/978-3-031-35455-7

```
% Objective functions to optimize
function o = ZDT1(x)
o = [0, 0];
o(1) = 513.915-(0.2466*x(1))+5.3773*x(2)+64.92*x(3)-0.0002594*(x(1)^2)-
0.055*(x(2)^2)+0.0052*x(1)*x(2);
o(2) = 1.27686-
0.000897964*x(1)+0.0008937*x(2)+0.036303*x(3)+0.000000169203*(x(1)^2);
```

```
% MOGOA
clc;
clear;
close all;
% Change these details with respect to your problem%%%%%%%%%%%%%%
ObjectiveFunction=@ZDT1;
dim=3;
lb=[69.9 55.6 0.66];
ub=[150 120.6 2];
obj_no=2;
if size(ub,2)==1
   ub=ones(1,dim)*ub;
   lb=ones(1,dim)*lb;
end
%%%%%%%%%%%%%%%%%%%%%%%%%%%%%%%%%%%%%%%%%%%
%%%%%%%%%%%%%%%%%%%%%%%%%%%%%
flag=0;
if (rem(dim,2)~=0)
   dim = dim+1;
   ub = [ub, 1];
   lb = [lb, 0];
   flag=1;
end
max_iter=100;
N=200;
ArchiveMaxSize=100;
Archive_X=zeros(100,dim);
Archive_F=ones(100,obj_no)*inf;
Archive_member_no=0;
%Initialize the positions of artificial whales
```

```
GrassHopperPositions=initialization(N,dim,ub,lb);
TargetPosition=zeros(dim,1);
TargetFitness=inf*ones(1,obj_no);
cMax=1;
cMin=0.00004;
%calculate the fitness of initial grasshoppers
for iter=1:max_iter
   for i=1:N

      Flag4ub=GrassHopperPositions(:,i)>ub';
      Flag4lb=GrassHopperPositions(:,i)<lb';
      GrassHopperPosi-
tions(:,i)=(GrassHopperPositions(:,i).*(~(Flag4ub+Flag4lb)))+ub'.*Flag4ub+lb'.*
Flag4lb;

      GrassHopperFitness(i,:)=ObjectiveFunction(GrassHopperPositions(:,i)');
      if dominates(GrassHopperFitness(i,:),TargetFitness)
         TargetFitness=GrassHopperFitness(i,:);
         TargetPosition=GrassHopperPositions(:,i);
      end

   end

   [Archive_X, Archive_F, Archive_member_no]=UpdateArchive(Archive_X,
Archive_F, GrassHopperPositions, GrassHopperFitness, Archive_member_no);

   if Archive_member_no>ArchiveMaxSize
      Archive_mem_ranks=RankingProcess(Archive_F, ArchiveMaxSize,
obj_no);
      [Archive_X, Archive_F, Archive_mem_ranks, Ar-
chive_member_no]=HandleFullArchive(Archive_X, Archive_F, Ar-
chive_member_no, Archive_mem_ranks, ArchiveMaxSize);
   else
      Archive_mem_ranks=RankingProcess(Archive_F, ArchiveMaxSize,
obj_no);
   end

   Archive_mem_ranks=RankingProcess(Archive_F, ArchiveMaxSize, obj_no);
   index=RouletteWheelSelection(1./Archive_mem_ranks);
   if index==-1
      index=1;
   end
   TargetFitness=Archive_F(index,:);
   TargetPosition=Archive_X(index,:)';
```

```
   c=cMax-iter*((cMax-cMin)/max_iter);

   for i=1:N

      temp= GrassHopperPositions;

      for k=1:2:dim
         S_i=zeros(2,1);
         for j=1:N
            if i~=j
               Dist=distance(temp(k:k+1,j), temp(k:k+1,i));
               r_ij_vec=(temp(k:k+1,j)-temp(k:k+1,i))/(Dist+eps);
               xj_xi=2+rem(Dist,2);

%%%%%%%%%%%%%%%%%%%%%%%%%%%%%%%%%%%%%%%%%%%%
%%
               s_ij=((ub(k:k+1)' - lb(k:k+1)') .*c/2)*S_func(xj_xi).*r_ij_vec;
               S_i=S_i+s_ij;

%%%%%%%%%%%%%%%%%%%%%%%%%%%%%%%%%%%%%%%%%%%%
%
            end
         end
         S_i_total(k:k+1, :) = S_i;

      end

      X_new=c*S_i_total'+(TargetPosition)';
      GrassHopperPositions_temp(i,:)=X_new';
   end
   % GrassHopperPositions
   GrassHopperPositions=GrassHopperPositions_temp';

   display(['At the iteration ', num2str(iter), ' there are ',
num2str(Archive_member_no), ' non-dominated solutions in the archive']);
end
if (flag==1)
   TargetPosition = TargetPosition(1:dim-1);
end
figure
Draw_ZDT1();
hold on
plot(Archive_F(:,1),Archive_F(:,2),'ro','MarkerSize',8,'markerfacecolor','k');
legend('True PF','Obtained PF');
title('MOGOA');
set(gcf, 'pos', [403   466   230   200])
```

Appendix H

GAMS Code: AUGMENCON2

```
$inlinecom [ ]
$eolcom //
$STitle end milling

Sets k objective functions /surfaceroughness, cutting-
force/;
$set min -1
$set max +1
Parameter dir(k) direction of the objective functions
/surfaceroughness %min%, cuttingforce %min%/;

Free Variables
z(k) objective function variables;

Positive VARIABLES S, F, D;

S.lo = 69.9; S.up = 150;
F.lo = 55.6; F.up = 120.6;
D.lo = 0.66; D.up = 2;
```


I. P. Okokpujie and L. K. Tartibu, *Modern Optimization Techniques for Advanced Machining*, Studies in Systems, Decision and Control 485,
https://doi.org/10.1007/978-3-031-35455-7

```
Equations
objsurfaceroughness objective minimizing surfacerough-
ness
objcuttingforce objective minimizing cuttingforce;

* Objective functions
objsurfaceroughness.. z('surfaceroughness') =e=
1.27686-
(0.000897964*S)+(0.0008937*F)+(0.036303*D)+(0.000000169
203*S*S); ;
objcuttingforce.. z('cuttingforce') =e= 513.915-
(0.2466*S)+(5.3773*F)+(64.92*D)-(0.0002594*S*S)-
(0.055*F*F)+(0.0052*S*F); ;


z.lo('surfaceroughness')=0; z.up('surfaceroughness')=
5;
z.lo('cuttingforce')=430.655;
z.up('cuttingforce')=774.45;
Model Endmilling / all /;

Endmilling.optfile =1;

$STitle eps-constraint method

Set k1(k) the first element of k,
km1(k) all but the first elements of k
kk(k) active objective function in constraint allobj;
k1(k)$(ord(k)=1) = yes; km1(k)=yes; km1(k1) = no;
```

```
Parameter
rhs(k) right hand side of the constrained obj functions
in epsconstraint
maxobj(k) maximum value from the payoff table
minobj(k) minimum value from the payoff table
numk(k) ordinal value of k starting with 1

Scalar
iter total number of iterations
infeas total number of infeasibilities
elapsed_time elapsed time for payoff and e-sonstraint
start start time
finish finish time

Variables
a_objval auxiliary variable for the objective function
obj auxiliary variable during the construction of the
payoff table
sl(k) slack or surplus variables for the eps-
constraints

Positive Variables sl

Equations
con_obj(k) constrained objective functions
augm_obj augmented objective function to avoid weakly
efficient
solutions
allobj all the objective functions in one expression;
con_obj(km1).. z(km1) - dir(km1)*sl(km1) =e= rhs(km1);
* We optimize the first objective function and put the
others as constraints
```

```
* the second term is for avoiding weakly efficient
points
augm_obj.. a_objval =e= sum(k1,dir(k1)*z(k1))
+ 1e-3*sum(km1,power(10,-(numk(km1)-
1))*sl(km1)/(maxobj(km1)-
minobj(km1)));
allobj.. sum(kk, dir(kk)*z(kk)) =e= obj;

Model mod_payoff / Endmilling, allobj / ;

Model mod_epsmethod / Endmilling, con_obj, augm_obj / ;

Parameter
payoff(k,k) payoff tables entries;
Alias(k,kp);

option optcr=0, limrow=0, limcol=0, solprint=off,
solvelink=%Solvelink.LoadLibrary%;
* Generate payoff table applying lexicographic optimi-
zation
loop(kp,
kk(kp)=yes;
repeat

solve mod_payoff using nlp maximizing obj;
payoff(kp,kk) = z.l(kk);
z.fx(kk) = z.l(kk); // freeze the value of the last ob-
jective optimized
kk(k++1) = kk(k); // cycle through the objective func-
tions
until kk(kp); kk(kp) = no;
* release the fixed values of the objective functions
for the new iteration
z.up(k) = inf; z.lo(k) =-inf;
);
if (mod_payoff.modelstat<>%ModelStat.Optimal% and
mod_payoff.modelstat<>%ModelStat.integer Solution%,
abort 'no optimal solution for mod_payoff');
file fx / 2kp50_augmecon2_results.txt /;
put fx ' PAYOFF TABLE'/ ;

loop (kp,
loop(k, put payoff(kp,k):12:2);
```

```
put /);
minobj(k)=smin(kp,payoff(kp,k));
maxobj(k)=smax(kp,payoff(kp,k));
* gridpoints are calculated as the range (difference
between max and min) of
* the 2nd objective function from the payoff table
$if not set gridpoints $set gridpoints 10
Set g grid points /g0*g%gridpoints%/
grid(k,g) grid

Parameter
gridrhs(k,g) rhs of eps-constraint at grid point
maxg(k) maximum point in grid for objective
posg(k) grid position of objective
firstOffMax, lastZero some counters
* numk(k) ordinal value of k starting with 1
numg(g) ordinal value of g starting with 0
step(k) step of grid points in objective functions
jump(k) jumps in the grid points traversing;
lastZero=1; loop(km1, numk(km1)=lastZero;
lastZero=lastZero+1); numg(g) =
ord(g)-1;
grid(km1,g) = yes; // Here we could define different
grid intervals for different objectives
maxg(km1) = smax(grid(km1,g), numg(g));
step(km1) = (maxobj(km1)- minobj(km1))/maxg(km1);
gridrhs(grid(km1,g))$(dir(km1)=-1) = maxobj(km1) -
numg(g)/maxg(km1)*(maxobj(km1)- minobj(km1));
gridrhs(grid(km1,g))$(dir(km1)= 1) = minobj(km1) +
numg(g)/maxg(km1)*(maxobj(km1)- minobj(km1));
put / ' Grid points' /;
loop (g,
loop(km1, put gridrhs(km1,g):12:2);
put /);
put / 'Efficient solutions' /;
* Walk the grid points and take shortcuts if the model
becomes infeasible or
* if the calculated slack variables are greater than
the step size
posg(km1) = 0; iter=0; infeas=0; start=jnow;
repeat
rhs(km1) = sum(grid(km1,g)$(numg(g)=posg(km1)),
gridrhs(km1,g));
```

```
solve mod_epsmethod maximizing a_objval using nlp;

Display "----------------------------------------------
-----------------------------------------------",
        "NLP solver",
       S.l, F.l, D.l;

iter=iter+1;
if (mod_epsmethod.modelstat<>%ModelStat.Optimal% and
mod_epsmethod.modelstat<>%ModelStat.integer Solution%,
infeas=infeas+1; // not optimal is in this case infea-
sible
put iter:5:0, ' infeasible' /;
lastZero = 0; loop(km1$(posg(km1)>0 and lastZero=0),
lastZero=numk(km1));
posg(km1)$(numk(km1)<=lastZero) = maxg(km1); // skip
all solves for more demanding values of rhs(km1)
else
put iter:5:0;
loop(k, put z.l(k):12:2);
jump(km1)=1;
* find the first off max (obj function that hasn't
reach the final grid point).
* If this obj.fun is k then assign jump for the 1..k-th
objective functions
* The jump is calculated for the innermost objective
function (km=1)
jump(km1)$(numk(km1)=1)=1+floor(sl.L(km1)/step(km1));
loop(km1$(jump(km1)>1), put ' jump');
put /;
);
* Proceed forward in the grid
firstOffMax = 0;
loop(km1$(posg(km1)<maxg(km1) and firstOffMax=0),
posg(km1)=min((posg(km1)+jump(km1)),maxg(km1));
firstOffMax=numk(km1));
posg(km1)$(numk(km1)<firstOffMax) = 0;
abort$(iter>1000) 'more than 1000 iterations, something
seems to go wrong'
until sum(km1$(posg(km1)=maxg(km1)),1)= card(km1) and
firstOffMax=0;
finish=jnow; elapsed_time=(finish-start)*60*60*24;
put /;
put 'Infeasibilities = ', infeas:5:0 /;
put 'Elapsed time: ',elapsed_time:10:2, ' seconds' / ;
```

Appendix I

ANN Model

```
% Solve an Input-Output Fitting problem with a Neural Network
% Script generated by Neural Fitting app
%
% This script assumes these variables are defined:
%
%   Inputs - input data.
%   Output - target data.

x = Inputs';
t = Output';

% Choose a Training Function
% For a list of all training functions type: help nntrain
% 'trainlm' is usually fastest.
% 'trainbr' takes longer but may be better for challenging problems.
% 'trainscg' uses less memory. Suitable in low memory situations.
trainFcn = 'trainlm';  % Levenberg-Marquardt backpropagation.

% Create a Fitting Network
hiddenLayerSize = 10;
net = fitnet(hiddenLayerSize,trainFcn);

% Choose Input and Output Pre/Post-Processing Functions
% For a list of all processing functions type: help nnprocess
net.input.processFcns = {'removeconstantrows','mapminmax'};
net.output.processFcns = {'removeconstantrows','mapminmax'};
```


I. P. Okokpujie and L. K. Tartibu, *Modern Optimization Techniques for Advanced Machining*, Studies in Systems, Decision and Control 485,
https://doi.org/10.1007/978-3-031-35455-7

```
% Setup Division of Data for Training, Validation, Testing
% For a list of all data division functions type: help nndivision
net.divideFcn = 'dividerand';  % Divide data randomly
net.divideMode = 'sample';  % Divide up every sample
net.divideParam.trainRatio = 80/100;
net.divideParam.valRatio = 10/100;
net.divideParam.testRatio = 10/100;

% Choose a Performance Function
% For a list of all performance functions type: help nnperformance
net.performFcn = 'mse';  % Mean Squared Error

% Choose Plot Functions
% For a list of all plot functions type: help nnplot
net.plotFcns = {'plotperform','plottrainstate','ploterrhist', ...
  'plotregression', 'plotfit'};
% Train the Network
[net,tr] = train(net,x,t);
% Test the Network
y = net(x);
e = gsubtract(t,y);
performance = perform(net,t,y)

% Recalculate Training, Validation and Test Performance
trainTargets = t .* tr.trainMask{1};
valTargets = t .* tr.valMask{1};
testTargets = t .* tr.testMask{1};
trainPerformance = perform(net,trainTargets,y)
valPerformance = perform(net,valTargets,y)
testPerformance = perform(net,testTargets,y)
```

```
% View the Network
view(net)

% Plots
% Uncomment these lines to enable various plots.
%figure, plotperform(tr)
%figure, plottrainstate(tr)
%figure, ploterrhist(e)
%figure, plotregression(t,y)
%figure, plotfit(net,x,t)

% Deployment
% Change the (false) values to (true) to enable the following code blocks.
% See the help for each generation function for more information.
if (false)
   % Generate MATLAB function for neural network for application
   % deployment in MATLAB scripts or with MATLAB Compiler and Builder
   % tools, or simply to examine the calculations your trained neural
   % network performs.
   genFunction(net,'myNeuralNetworkFunction');
   y = myNeuralNetworkFunction(x);
end
if (false)
   % Generate a matrix-only MATLAB function for neural network code
   % generation with MATLAB Coder tools.
   genFunction(net,'myNeuralNetworkFunction','MatrixOnly','yes');
   y = myNeuralNetworkFunction(x);
end
if (false)
   % Generate a Simulink diagram for simulation or deployment with.
   % Simulink Coder tools.
   gensim(net);
end
```

Appendix J

ANN-PSO Model

```
% myfunc.m
%The myfunc.m file and the nn_pso.m files must be put
in the same directory %as an excel spreadsheet contain-
ing the data (sheet 1: Inputs; sheet 2: %output)
%Run the code nn_pso
function [f] = myfunc(x,n,m,o,net,inputs,targets)
k=0;
for i=1:n
    for j=1:m
        k=k+1;
        xi(i,j)=x(k);
    end
end
for i=1:n
    k=k+1;
    xl(i)=x(k);
    xb1(i,1)=x(k+n);
end
for i=1:o
    k=k+1;
    xb2(i,1)=x(k);
end
net.iw{1,1}=xi;
net.lw{2,1}=xl;
net.b{1,1}=xb1;
net.b{2,1}=xb2;
f=sum((net(inputs)-targets).^2)/length(inputs);
```


I. P. Okokpujie and L. K. Tartibu, *Modern Optimization Techniques for Advanced Machining*, Studies in Systems, Decision and Control 485,
https://doi.org/10.1007/978-3-031-35455-7

```
% nn_pso.m
clc
tic
close all
clear all
rng default
filename = 'datafile.xlsx';
sheetname1 = 'Sheet1';
sheetname2 = 'Sheet2';
input = xlsread(filename,sheetname1,'A1:Z10000');
target = xlsread(filename,sheetname2,'A1:Z10000');
inputs=input';
targets=target';
m=length(inputs(:,1));
o=length(targets(:,1));
```

```
% Number of neurons
n=
net=feedforwardnet(n);
net=configure(net,inputs,targets);
kk=m*n+n+n+o;
for j=1:kk
    LB(1,j)=-1.5;
    UB(1,j)=1.5;
End
% Swarm population size
pop=10;
for i=1:pop
    for j=1:kk
        xx(i,j)=LB(1,j)+rand*(UB(1,j)-LB(1,j));
    end
end
maxrun=1;
for run=1:maxrun
    fun=@(x) myfunc(x,n,m,o,net,inputs,targets);
    x0=xx;
    % pso initialization-------------------------------
---------------start
    x=x0; % initial population
    v=0.1*x0; % initial velocity
    for i=1:pop
        f0(i,1)=fun(x0(i,:));
    end
    [fmin0,index0]=min(f0);
    pbest=x0; % initial pbest
    gbest=x0(index0,:); % initial gbest
    % pso initialization-------------------------------
-----------------end
    % pso algorithm------------------------------------
---------------start
% Acceleration factors
    c1=1; c2=2.75;
    ite=1; maxite=1000; tolerance=1;
    while ite<=maxite && tolerance>10^-8
        w=0.1+rand*0.4;
        % pso velocity updates
        for i=1:pop
            for j=1:kk
                v(i,j)=w*v(i,j)+c1*rand*(pbest(i,j)-
x(i,j))+c2*rand*(gbest(1,j)-x(i,j));
            end
        end
```

```
        % pso position update
        for i=1:pop
            for j=1:kk
                x(i,j)=x(i,j)+v(i,j);
            end
        end
        % handling boundary violations
        for i=1:pop
            for j=1:kk
                if x(i,j)<LB(j)
                    x(i,j)=LB(j);
                elseif x(i,j)>UB(j)
                    x(i,j)=UB(j);
                end
            end
        end
        % evaluating fitness
        for i=1:pop
            f(i,1)=fun(x(i,:));
        end
        % updating pbest and fitness
        for i=1:pop
            if f(i,1)<f0(i,1)
                pbest(i,:)=x(i,:);
                f0(i,1)=f(i,1);
            end
        end
        [fmin,index]=min(f0); % finding out the best
particle
        ffmin(ite,run)=fmin; % storing best fitness
        ffite(run)=ite; % storing iteration count
        % updating gbest and best fitness
        if fmin<fmin0
            gbest=pbest(index,:);
            fmin0=fmin;
        end
        % calculating tolerance
        if ite>100;
            tolerance=abs(ffmin(ite-100,run)-fmin0);
        end
        % displaying iterative results
        if ite==1
            disp(sprintf('Iteration Best particle Ob-
jective fun'));
        end
        disp(sprintf('%8g %8g %8.4f',ite,index,fmin0));
```

```
        ite=ite+1;
    end
    % pso algorithm------------------------------------
-----------------end
    xo=gbest;
    fval=fun(xo);
    xbest(run,:)=xo;
    ybest(run,1)=fun(xo);

disp(sprintf('*****************************************'
));
    disp(sprintf(' RUN fval ObFuVa'));
    disp(sprintf('%6g %6g %8.4f
%8.4f',run,fval,ybest(run,1)));
end
toc
% Final neural network model
disp('Final nn model is net_f')
net_f = feedforwardnet(n);
net_f=configure(net_f,inputs,targets);
[a b]=min(ybest);
xo=xbest(b,:);
k=0;
for i=1:n
    for j=1:m
        k=k+1;
        xi(i,j)=xo(k);
    end
end
for i=1:n
    k=k+1;
    xl(i)=xo(k);
    xb1(i,1)=xo(k+n);
end
for i=1:o
    k=k+1;
    xb2(i,1)=xo(k);
end
net_f.iw{1,1}=xi;
net_f.lw{2,1}=xl;
net_f.b{1,1}=xb1;
net_f.b{2,1}=xb2;
%Calculation of MSE
err=sum((net_f(inputs)-
targets).^2)/length(net_f(inputs))
%Regression plot
plotregression(targets,net_f(inputs))
disp('Trained ANN net_f is ready for the use');
%Trained ANN net_f is ready for the use
```